An Introduction to Accounting

Accountability in Organisations and Society

2e

Craig Deegan

An Introduction to Accounting

Accountability in Organisations and Society

2e

CENGAGE

An introduction to accounting: Accountability in organisations and society
2nd Edition
Craig Deegan

Portfolio manager: Fiona Hammond
Product manager: Rachael Pictor / Geoff Howard
Content developer: Eleanor Yeoell / Sarah Payne / Kylie Scott
Senior project editor: Nathan Katz
Cover designer: Cengage Creative Studio
Text designer: Cengage Creative Studio
Permissions/Photo researcher: Liz McShane
Editor: Sylvia Marson
Proofreader: James Anderson
Indexer: Julie King
Art direction: Danielle Maccarone
Cover: Courtesy Adobe Stock/Яна Шадурская (wind farm, parasailor, trees); Adobe Stock/Flash concept (food truck); Depositphotos/ iam-frukt (van)
Typeset by KnowledgeWorks Global Ltd.

This second edition published in 2023

For product information and technology assistance,
in Australia call **1300 790 853**;
in New Zealand call **0800 449 725**

For permission to use material from this text or product, please email
aust.permissions@cengage.com

National Library of Australia Cataloguing-in-Publication Data
ISBN: 9780170460194
A catalogue record for this book is available from the National Library of Australia.

Cengage Learning Australia
Level 7, 80 Dorcas Street
South Melbourne, Victoria Australia 3205

Cengage Learning New Zealand
Unit 4B Rosedale Office Park
331 Rosedale Road, Albany, North Shore 0632, NZ

For learning solutions, visit **cengage.com.au**

Printed in China by 1010
2 3 4 5 6 7 26 25 24 23

Brief Contents

Contents

Guide to the text

As you read this text you will find a number of features in every chapter to enhance your study of accounting and help you understand how the theory is applied in the real world.

CHAPTER OPENING FEATURES

Identify the key concepts you will engage with through the **Learning objectives** at the start of each chapter.

LEARNING OBJECTIVES

After completing this chapter readers should be able to:

- LO4.1 explain what a budget is, as well as describe the context and purpose of budgeting, and the relationship between an organisation's budget and its strategic plan
- LO4.2 identify who needs to prepare a budget
- LO4.3 identify the various benefits associated with budgeting
- LO4.4 explain the meaning of a 'master budget', and how the various components of this budget relate to each other
- LO4.5 explain the meaning of a 'budget variance' and identify when to investigate such variances
- LO4.6 understand the difference between static budgets and flexible budgets, and explain the need for flexible budgeting
- LO4.7 explain why budgeting can be undertaken for both financial and non-financial aspects of organisational performance, and illustrate social and environmental aspects of performance that can be addressed through the process of budgeting
- LO4.8 describe some behavioural implications of the budgetary process.

Check your understanding of accounting concepts with the **Opening questions**. Answers to these opening questions can be found at the end of the chapter so you can check how your understanding has changed.

OPENING QUESTIONS

Before reading this chapter, please consider how you would answer the following questions. We will return to these questions at the end of the chapter, where we suggest some answers.

1 Is it necessary for all organisations to prepare budgets?

2 What is a master budget? Which individual budget would typically be the first one prepared within a master budget, and why?

3 Can budgets be used as a means of motivating managers, and if so, how?

FEATURES WITHIN CHAPTERS

Why do I need to know ...? boxes provide context to complex subject matters to show how the topic relates to the real world.

Why do I need to know that there can be significant differences between the cash flows that an organisation generates, and its reported profits or losses?

NEW

For-profit organisations are expected to generate profits, and generally speaking, the bigger the profit, the better. However, just because an organisation has generated profits does not mean it will survive. Survival depends upon a number of factors and one very important factor is cash flows. Many profitable organisations have failed because of poor management of cash flows. Therefore, we need to understand the reasons for the difference between cash flows and profits, and we need to ensure that an organisation manages both properly.

Examine how theoretical accounting concepts can be used in practice through the **Learning exercise** boxes, many of which present important worked examples.

11.5 Learning Exercise

Determining the cash paid in relation to prepayments

Scenario: Clovelly Ltd pays for its insurance in advance of receiving the insurance service. It started the accounting period with prepaid insurance of \$5000. The insurance expense for the year was \$110 000 and the closing balance of prepaid insurance was \$12 000.

Issue: How much cash was actually paid for insurance in the accounting period?

Solution: If Clovelly Ltd started the year with prepaid insurance of \$5000, recognised insurance expenses of \$110 000 for the accounting period, and ended the accounting period with prepaid insurance of \$12 000, then \$117 000 must have been paid in relation to insurance; that is:

Cash payment for insurance = closing balance of prepaid insurance + insurance expense recognised during the accounting period – opening balance of prepaid insurance

= \$12 000 + \$110 000 – \$5000

= \$117 000

Revise critical accounting concepts with the **Key concept** boxes.

Key concept

There can be a significant difference between the cash flows that an organisation generates from its operating activities in a given accounting period and the profit or loss it reports for that same period.

Important **Key terms** are marked in bold in the text and **defined in the margin** when they are used for the first time.

informed decision
A decision based on reliable and relevant information

For somebody to make an informed decision in respect to an organisation, obviously, need information. The type of information someone needs will d decisions they want to make and the expectations they hold about what aspects they believe are important to enable them to make those decisions. Informatio and relevant, effectively provides us with the power to make informed decisions the issues of relevance and reliability in more detail later in this chapter, wher

END-OF-CHAPTER FEATURES

At the end of each chapter you will find several tools to help you to review, practise and extend your knowledge of the key learning objectives.

Review your understanding of the key chapter topics with the **Summary**.

STUDY TOOLS

SUMMARY

In this chapter, we have described the nature and purpose of management accounting and noted that it is predominantly unregulated, generates reports that cover a variety of time periods, covers financial and non-financial issues, and provides information about past and projected performance.

We have also provided a description of the activities undertaken by managers and stressed that accountants can, and should, contribute to all phases of management activities. We concentrated especially on the planning stage of running an organisation, emphasising the need for managers and accountants to consider the issue of sustainability, the need for long- and short-run considerations, and the need to focus on value creation. In discussing value creation, we also explored how value can be viewed in a different way by different stakeholders, and we provided insights into how different perspectives of value might be addressed by an accounting system.

We also considered the behaviour of costs, and how they can be considered as either variable or fixed costs (there can also be mixed costs). We discussed various assumptions that can be made about costs, including that variable costs per unit will remain constant and that fixed costs will remain unchanged within a relevant range of activities. We also discussed how to calculate contribution margin per unit, the break-even point, margin of safety, and how many units of a product or service need to be produced and sold to generate a desired level of profit. In doing so, we also addressed the issue of operating gearing.

END-OF-CHAPTER FEATURES

Refer to the **Answers to the opening questions** to assess how your understanding has developed as a result of reading the material provided within the chapter.

ANSWERS TO THE OPENING QUESTIONS

At the beginning of the chapter we asked the following three questions. As a result of reading this chapter, you should now be able to provide informed answers to these questions – ours are shown below.

1 What do we mean by 'cost behaviour', and why do managers need to know how costs 'behave'?

By cost behaviour, we are referring to how costs change as a result of changes in the level of activity of an organisation. Some costs change in total as activity or volume increases – these are called variable costs. Some costs remain unaltered as activity changes – these are called fixed costs. Some costs have fixed and variable components – these are called mixed costs. Managers need to know about cost behaviour so they can plan to have the necessary resources for particular levels of activity. Knowing about how costs should behave also provides managers with cost-related targets which then can be used to assess actual performance as part of the control function of managers.

2 What do we mean by 'break-even point', and how would we calculate how many units of a product or service an organisation needs to produce in order to break even?

The break-even point is the point at which the total costs incurred to produce and sell a particular good or service match the associated revenues; that is, the point at which there is neither a profit nor a loss. The break-even point is calculated by dividing total fixed costs by the contribution margin per unit. The contribution margin per unit is calculated as revenue per unit minus variable cost per unit.

Revise your knowledge with the multiple-choice **Self-test quiz**. Detailed answers are provided in the Appendix.

SELF-TEST QUIZ

Answers to this quiz appear in the Appendix of this book.

1 In relation to management accounting, which of the following statements is true?

a Management accounting is subject to limited regulation compared to financial accounting.

b The forms of management accounting employed within an organisation will be influenced by the organisation's mission statement.

c The information generated through management accounting will be of interest not only to managers but also to other categories of stakeholders.

d Some management accounting information generated within an organisation will not be disclosed publicly because of concerns that it might reduce an organisation's competitive advantage.

e All of these choices.

NEW

Each chapter's **Case study** box connects the chapter to the integrated and innovative case study. Ask your Instructor for access to the case study file.

ONLINE RESOURCES

Accompanying the book is an innovative online case study that follows an organisation initially established by two friends, which grows into a large and successful company. Acquire this chapter's case study from your instructor.

CASE STUDY

Armadillo Surf Designs: Don't do anything rash

Armadillo Surf Designs (ASD) are advertising for a part-time accountant. After a successful interview, you got the job. Congratulations! The team are also excited to be launching a special edition rash vest line, but meanwhile, there has been negative media attention relating to one of ASD's competitors and this has the ASD team questioning if, and how, they should respond.

Demonstrate that an accountant can 'add value' to ASD and use your knowledge of the surfing industry to apply Porter's Value Chain to ASD. Undertake break-even analysis on the new rash vest line and consider the costs and benefits of importing surfboards. Advise if, and how, ASD should report on the origins of their surfboards.

Test your knowledge and consolidate your learning through the **End-of-chapter questions**.

END-OF-CHAPTER QUESTIONS

3.1 Do you agree with the statement, 'Accountants should not be involved in the management of an organisation'?

3.2 What are some of the factors that managers might have to consider when deciding whether or not to publicly disclose information that was produced within the management accounting system?

3.3 What does critical thinking mean and why should accountants be expected to be critical thinkers?

3.4 What is information overload and how might the possibility of this be reduced?

3.5 Should cost-versus-benefits considerations be applied when deciding whether or not to collect particular information?

3.6 Provide a basic list of the activities that managers undertake.

3.7 Why might the existence of well-constructed organisational plans have the effect of enabling organisations to attract the necessary funding at lower costs?

3.8 What is the role of an organisation's mission statement?

3.9 What are positive and negative screening, and how are they relevant to planning organisational activities?

Extend your understanding with the list of **References** relevant to each chapter.

REFERENCES

A.P. Moller – Maersk A/S (2020). *Sustainability report 2020*. www.maersk.com/en/about/sustainability/reports

Audi (2018). *Life cycle assessment: Audi looks one step ahead*. https://www.audi.com/content/dam/gbp2/company/sustainability/downloads/documents-and-policies/umweltbilanzen/en/Audi_A6_LCA_English.pdf

Audi (2020). *Audi is pursuing the vision of a circular economy*. https://www.audi.com/en/company/sustainability/core-topics/products-and-services/circular-economy-vision.html

BHP (2017). *BHP annual report 2017*. https://www.bhp.com/-/media/documents/investors/annual-reports/2017/bhpannualreport2017.pdf

BHP (2018). *BHP annual report 2018*. https://www.bhp.com/-/media/documents/investors/annual-reports/2018/bhpannualreport2018.pdf

BHP (2021). *BHP annual report 2021*. https://www.bhp.com/investors/annual-reporting/annual-report-2021

Christ, K., & Burritt, R. (2015). Material flow cost accounting: A review and agenda for future research. *Journal of Cleaner Production*, 108, pp. 1378–89.

Guide to the online resources

FOR THE INSTRUCTOR

Cengage is pleased to provide you with a selection of resources that will help you to prepare your lectures and assessments when you choose this textbook for your course.
Log in or request an account to access instructor resources at au.cengage.com/instructor/account for Australia or nz.cengage.com/instructor/account for New Zealand.

MINDTAP

Premium online teaching and learning tools are available on the *MindTap* platform – the personalised eLearning solution.

MindTap is a flexible and easy-to-use platform that helps build student confidence and gives you a clear picture of their progress. We partner with you to ease the transition to digital – we're with you every step of the way.

The *Cengage Mobile App* puts your course directly into students' hands with course materials available on their smartphone or tablet. Students can read on the go, complete practice quizzes or participate in interactive real-time activities.

MindTap for Craig Deegan's *An Introduction to Accounting: Accountability in Organisations and Society* is full of innovative resources to support critical thinking, and help your students move from memorisation to mastery! Includes:

- Craig Deegan's *An Introduction to Accounting: Accountability in Organisations and Society* eBook
- Author videos
- Chapter case study
- Concept clips
- Revision quizzes, and more.

MindTap is a premium purchasable eLearning tool. Contact your Cengage learning consultant to find out how *MindTap* can transform your course.

Cengage MindTap

SOLUTIONS MANUAL

The **Solutions Manual** provides detailed solutions to every question in the text.

COGNERO® TEST BANK

A bank of questions has been developed in conjunction with the text for creating quizzes, tests and exams for your students. Create multiple test versions in an instant and deliver tests from your LMS, your classroom, or wherever you want using Cognero. Cognero test generator is a flexible online system that allows you to import, edit, and manipulate content from the text's test bank or elsewhere, including your own favourite test questions.

POWERPOINT™ PRESENTATIONS

Use the chapter-by-chapter **PowerPoint slides** to enhance your lecture presentations and handouts by reinforcing the key principles of your subject.

ARTWORK FROM THE TEXT

Add the digital files of figures, exhibits and flow charts into your learning management system, use them in student handouts, or copy them into your lecture presentations.

ARMADILLO CASE STUDY

The Armadillo Surf Company is a premium case study with an introductory video, developed specifically for delivery alongside each chapter of the book.

FOR THE STUDENT

MINDTAP

MindTap is the next-level online learning tool that helps you get better grades!

MindTap gives you the resources you need to study – all in one place and available when you need them. In the *MindTap Reader*, you can make notes, highlight text and even find a definition directly from the page.

If your instructor has chosen *MindTap* for your subject this semester, log in to *MindTap* to:

- Get better grades
- Save time and get organised
- Connect with your instructor and peers
- Study when and where you want, online and mobile
- Complete assessment tasks as set by your instructor.

When your instructor creates a course using *MindTap*, they will let you know your course link so you can access the content. Please purchase *MindTap* only when directed by your instructor. Course length is set by your instructor.

Cengage MindTap

Preface

About this book

The decision to write the first edition of this book was initiated as a result of a view held by the author, and other colleagues, that there is a need for an introductory accounting book that explores and explains the many roles that accounting plays within organisations and the broader society and which properly explains that accounting is both a technical and a social practice. With this in mind, the author of this book initiated a project within his previous university (RMIT University) to totally revamp how introductory accounting was being taught, particularly within larger 'common core' units. Subsequently, a new approach was trialled with several thousand students, and the overwhelming result was very positive, with students and staff being extremely supportive of the new approach taken. The material developed and tested across a number of semesters by the author then formed the foundation for the material included within this book.

Embracing a much broader view of accounting than is commonly accepted in other introductory books, this book provides insights into the meaning and role of accounting and of accountants in the larger context, and of a changing and interconnected world of people, organisations and the changing planet upon which we live. The concepts of sustainability and social responsibility are embedded across the chapters and – unlike most other accounting texts – not treated as a separate standalone component of organisational management and accountability.

This book identifies key ideas and concepts that students need to reflect upon and understand in order to appreciate the role of accounting in society – hence the book goes beyond the 'technical' aspects of accounting. Readers are provided with material to enable them to appreciate accounting's strong influence in organisations and society. Throughout the text many references/links are provided to 'real life' organisations to emphasise that the discussion throughout the chapters is directly relatable to the 'real world'.

This book instils a broad knowledge base that can be returned to throughout an accounting course/program. It provides a necessary foundation for various topics that are studied in an accounting program, including: auditing, financial accounting, external reporting, management accounting, business advising, strategic accounting, and governance and ethics.

In writing the book, the author drew on many years of his own research, and the research of others, which explores the roles and impacts of organisations within society, and the responsibilities and accountabilities organisations are perceived as having. The first edition of this book was a shortlisted finalist in the 2020 publishing awards convened by Educational Publishing Awards Australia. Pleasingly, within its first two years of publication the book has been prescribed for use within numerous universities within Australia, New Zealand and a number of other countries and the feedback from both academics and students has been highly positive. Based upon feedback received in relation to the first edition, further refinements have been made to this second edition.

The book's structure, content and learning activities provide readers with an understanding of accounting's pervasive and transformative role as a social practice and organisational driver. It will show that environments, ideas, values and so forth change; that the world is interconnected; that the planet is a key resource; and that people are affected/influenced by the information they receive and the way it is presented. It is emphasised that accounting and accountability are key aspects of every person's life and that the practice of accounting, whilst often being seen as very technical in nature, has many social implications. The book shows that rather than being a mundane number-crunching activity, accounting is actually very interesting, vital, thought provoking and, dare we say it ... exciting!

New to this edition

This book has been updated since the first edition to incorporate various new financial, social and environmental reporting requirements as well as updating reference materials. Reflecting the evolving nature of reporting, some of the new material includes new requirements relating to modern slavery reporting, climate change-related accountability, and the revised reporting standards or guidelines of various standard setters and organisations – such as the Global Reporting Initiative, the International Accounting Standards Board, the International Integrated Reporting Council, the Task Force on Climate Related Financial Disclosures, the International Sustainability Accounting Standards Board, and so forth.

New features of this second edition include the 'Why do I need to know ....?' boxes that now appear throughout every chapter, and which enhance 'real world relevance' of the material by pointing out the respective materials' likely relevance to readers' working lives post university. More 'key concepts' have been highlighted throughout each chapter, and each chapter also now comes with a self-test multiple choice quiz at the end of each chapter (see Appendix: Answers to Self-Test Quizzes) that help readers assess their comprehension of the material.

How is this book different to other books?

From the very start, we explore the relationship between organisational responsibilities and the relationship between these responsibilities and associated accountabilities. While the book does include necessary technical material, we do not initially launch into debits and credits, the regulation of accounting, or the definitions of the elements of accounting as is common in many introductory accounting texts. Accounting has a much richer context than this that students need to understand.

The book emphasises early on – particularly in Chapters 1 and 2 – the link between the responsibilities accepted by the managers of an organisation and how these responsibilities in turn influence the accepted accountability, which in turn affects the way the 'accounting' is undertaken (and therefore, the 'accounts' that are ultimately produced). Throughout the chapters we utilise an accountability model that emphasises four major issues for consideration/evaluation, these being:

- **Why** is the organisation providing a particular account – be it social, environmental or financial in nature?
- **Who** should that account be made available to – who are the targeted stakeholders?
- **What** information should be included within the account?
- **How** should that account be presented and distributed?

That is, we are adopting a conceptual approach to writing this book – one that is grounded in the notion of 'accountability'. The book encourages students to consider what 'accounts' they believe should be produced in given circumstances and encourages them to reflect upon why and how they would make such judgements.

Established frameworks for financial accounting, social and environmental accounting and management accounting are addressed, and their role in demonstrating organisational accountability explained and assessed.

The intent is to make the material interesting and conceptual in focus, and to show students that accounting is actually a very thought-provoking activity that can be utilised to foster greater accountability and to generate positive financial, social and environmental benefits for organisations and society. Nevertheless, instances are also highlighted where various accounting practices – possibly poorly conceived – have been linked ultimately to various negative outcomes for a variety of 'stakeholders' (that is, at times, particular accounting practices can be implicated in contributing to adverse social and environmental outcomes). By the end of the book students will understand the central role that 'accounting' plays in all of our lives. It is emphasised throughout the book that good quality accounting information provides 'power' to stakeholders to make informed choices from amongst competing alternatives.

Accompanying the book is an innovative online case study. The case study follows an organisation that is initially established by two friends, and which grows into a large company. As students finish reading each chapter, the case study will provide them with additional information about the organisation and will require them to undertake particular tasks that relate to the material covered within the respective chapter. By using one organisation, students will see how the 'accountability' and 'accounting' changes as the organisation itself changes and adapts to different environments with different stakeholder expectations and accountabilities. The case study is available from your instructor.

How to use this book

The expectation is that each chapter of this book could be studied within a traditional teaching term/semester of around 12 weeks. Further, this book has been written with an expectation that students study the chapters in the order in which they have been presented. As the 'Contents' pages show, we initially address (Chapters 1 and 2) fundamental concepts relating to organisational responsibilities, organisational accountabilities, 'accounting' and the role of 'accountants'. Having set this important foundation, the book then addresses issues necessarily considered in the formative stages of an organisation. Topics explored in Chapters 3 to 5 include an analysis of the roles of managers, the need to understand future 'costs', the use and behavioural implications of budgeting, value chain analysis, life cycle analysis and tools for planning capital investments.

The book then moves to exploring how to report the result/impacts of the operations. Chapter 6 explores various issues associated with reporting social and environmental performance, and Chapters 7 to 11 explore how to account for, and report, the financial performance and financial position of an organisation. Chapter 8 provides a detailed explanation of the use of the double-entry system (debits and credits). However, for those instructors who do not want to go into such detail, the balance of the book can be studied without prescribing Chapter 8.

Reflecting the logical flow of the book, the final chapter – Chapter 12 – provides various useful tools for analysing the reports (financial, social, environmental, sustainability) that organisations release to stakeholders.

About the author

Craig Deegan, BCom (University of NSW), MCom (Hons) (University of NSW), PhD (University of Queensland), FCA, is Professor of Accounting in the School of Accounting and Governance at the University of Tasmania. Craig has taught at both undergraduate and postgraduate level for many years and has supervised 25 PhDs to completion. Prior to working in the university sector, Craig worked as a chartered accountant. His research focuses on various social and environmental accountability and financial accounting issues, and has been published in a number of leading international accounting journals, including: *Accounting, Organizations and Society*; *Accounting and Business Research*; *Accounting, Accountability and Auditing Journal*; *Accounting and Finance*; *British Accounting Review*; *Critical Perspectives on Accounting*; *Journal of Business Ethics*; *Australian Accounting Review*; *Australian Journal of Management* and *The International Journal of Accounting*. According to Google Scholar, Craig's work has attracted approximately 30 000 citations making him one of the most highly cited researchers internationally within the accounting and/or finance literature. On 28 September 2018, and reflective of the extent to which Craig's research has been relied upon by many researchers and practitioners, the leading national newspaper, *The Australian* (within its annual feature on research), identified Craig as being *Australia's Research Field Leader* in the Field of Accounting and Taxation.

Craig has regularly provided consulting services to corporations, government and industry bodies on issues pertaining to financial accounting, stakeholder engagement and corporate social and environmental accountability. He was former Chairperson of the Triple Bottom Line Issues Group of the Institute of Chartered Accountants in Australia and for many years was involved in developing the CPA Program of CPA Australia, as well as being a judge on the *Australasian Sustainability Reporting Awards*. He is on the editorial board of a number of academic accounting journals and has been the recipient of various teaching and research awards, including teaching prizes sponsored by KPMG and the Institute of Chartered Accountants in Australia. He was the inaugural recipient of the *Peter Brownell Manuscript Award*, an annual research award presented by the Accounting and Finance Association of Australia and New Zealand. He was also awarded the *University of Southern Queensland Individual Award for Research Excellence*. Craig is currently a member of the United Nations sponsored organisation, Education for Sustainability (EfS), is a member of the University of Tasmania Sustainability Committee, and is a member of the Australian Accounting Standards Board (AASB) Academic Advisory Panel.

Craig is also the author of the leading corporate accounting textbook, *Financial Accounting*, now in its ninth edition (McGraw Hill), as well as being the author of the leading financial accounting theory textbook, *Financial Accounting Theory*, a fifth edition of which is being published by Cengage in 2023. Both books are widely used throughout Australia as well as in many other countries.

Above all, Craig has a passion for emphasising the role of accounting in providing information about how managers of organisations have, or have not, fulfilled their responsibilities, and accountabilities, to various stakeholder groups. This passion is very well reflected and encapsulated within the contents of this innovative book.

Acknowledgements

Throughout the process of preparing this book there were many people who provided valuable input. I would like to thank many colleagues at RMIT – where I worked for 18 years – for their input and for trialling my material across a number of semesters while I was developing content for this book. Particular thanks go to Dr Sonia Magdziarz and Dr Shannon Sidaway for generously and thoughtfully reading through each chapter and providing valuable critical commentary. Shannon also has prepared the innovative case study that accompanies this book, while Sonia prepared various test bank questions – all of which enhance the contribution of the project as an 'educational package'. Great colleagues! I would also like to thank the University of Tasmania – where I commenced work in 2020 – for also supporting my efforts to develop educational material that incorporates broader notions of accountability and 'accounting'.

Thanks go to the team at Cengage too. I would like to thank Geoff Howard who – while at Cengage – initiated this project and who was very excited by how different this book was to any other book on the market. Thanks also go to James Cole who provided some insightful advice when I was developing the first edition of this book. Appreciation is extended to Paul Petrulis, the managing director at Cengage Australia for supporting this project. In relation to this second edition, I would like to thank Rachael Pictor and Eleanor Yeoell for their constructive advice and guidance.

I would like to thank the very many colleagues at other universities (too many to specifically identify) with whom I have discussed this book and who have provided encouragement and advice. I am also appreciative of the many positive and constructive comments I have received from both academics and students since this book was first published.

Lastly, I would like to thank my daughter Cassie for supporting my various projects and for being the 'bestest' daughter imaginable.

In updating this book, we have benefited from the input of a wide range of talented people. We would like to thank all those people who helped us with this task:

- Meiting Lu, Macquarie University
- Jackie Liu, Southern Cross University
- Youngdeok Lim, UNSW Sydney
- Hajar Roudaki, University of Wollongong
- Pattarin Adithipyangkul, Curtin University
- Tracy-Anne De Silva, Lincoln University
- Terri Trireksani, Murdoch University.

MODULE 1

ORGANISATIONS, RESPONSIBILITIES, ACCOUNTABILITY AND ACCOUNTING

CHAPTER 1

WHAT IS ACCOUNTING?

LEARNING OBJECTIVES

After completing this chapter readers should be able to:

- **LO1.1** provide a definition of accounting and explain that the accounting process can provide information about the financial, social and environmental performance of an organisation
- **LO1.2** explain the meaning of accountability, as well as the relationship between accounting and accountability
- **LO1.3** identify the possible audiences of the accounts generated by accounting, and understand that accounting generates information for use by people both inside and outside an organisation
- **LO1.4** explain who does accounting and who might be considered to be an accountant
- **LO1.5** describe the qualitative characteristics that accounting information should possess if it is to be useful in allowing different stakeholders to make informed decisions
- **LO1.6** describe how we can use the accountability model introduced in this chapter to explain the practice of accounting within different organisations
- **LO1.7** explain the evolutionary nature of the accountant's role
- **LO1.8** explain why accounting can be considered both a technical and a social practice.

OPENING QUESTIONS

Below are a number of questions that we want you to consider before reading this chapter. We will ask these same questions again at the end of the chapter, in the 'Study tools' section. Each chapter is organised in this manner so that you can assess whether your views have changed, and therefore whether your knowledge has been advanced, as a result of reading the material provided within the chapter. Please spend some time now briefly answering these questions.

1 What aspects of an organisation's performance are measured by accounting?
2 What factors are likely to influence the types of accounts being presented by an organisation?
3 Who are the users of accounting reports?
4 Is accounting likely to be at all interesting?
5 Is accounting really that relevant to many people in society, other than perhaps shareholders (or the owners of an organisation) and managers?

Introduction

It is tempting to accept the narrow definition of accounting that appears in many textbooks. According to this definition, accounting is simply the process of identifying, measuring and then reporting economic information about an organisation, to enable informed decisions to be made by those individuals or groups with a financial stake in that organisation. But in reality, accounting is a much richer, more interesting and exciting process than this! It is a process that continues to evolve as expectations of organisations' responsibilities and, importantly, their accountabilities themselves change. At its most dynamic and influential, accounting generates highly useful information not just about the financial performance of an organisation, but its social and environmental performance as well.

As you read through this chapter, you'll learn about the key ideas that underpin accounting, and more broadly the role of accounting within society. We will emphasise how the various accounts that the managers of an organisation compile internally, and potentially also present to external stakeholders, are influenced by the responsibilities and associated accountabilities that managers believe they have. To help you understand the strong connection between accounting and accountability, as well as the various facets of the practice of accounting, we will introduce a four-stage accountability model, which we will continue to refer to throughout this book.

The practice of accounting is continually developing in response to the various changes occurring within the community, so much so that while accounting can at times be very technical in nature, the use of the various accounts being generated can have a multitude of social effects. Indeed, as you work your way through this book, you'll see that we embrace the perspective that accounting is both a technical and a social practice.

LO1.1 What does 'accounting' mean?

As this is a book about 'accounting', it probably makes sense to begin by being clear about what we mean by the term. At a very broad level, accounting can be defined as a process of collecting, summarising, analysing and communicating information to enable users of that information to make *informed decisions*. It involves the provision of information about aspects of the *performance* of an organisation to a particular group of people with an interest, or stake, in the organisation – we call these parties *stakeholders*.

The above definition makes reference to three key concepts that we shall now discuss:

- informed decisions
- performance
- stakeholders.

Informed decisions

informed decision
A decision based on reliable and relevant information

For somebody to make an **informed decision** in respect to an organisation, they, somewhat obviously, need information. The type of information someone needs will depend upon the decisions they want to make and the expectations they hold about what aspects of performance they believe are important to enable them to make those decisions. Information, if it is reliable and relevant, effectively provides us with the power to make informed decisions (we will consider the issues of relevance and reliability in more detail later in this chapter, when we discuss the qualitative characteristics of accounting information).

Accounting provides various people – inside and outside an organisation – with information to make decisions, and it is the role of the accountant to determine what information is most appropriate to enable those people to make informed decisions. Managers within an organisation, for example, might need information that helps them to understand the profitability of particular product lines, or whether certain products should be expanded or terminated. Or they might need information that enables them to determine whether they have the necessary cash available, or coming into the organisation, to repay additional borrowings. People outside an organisation might need information to determine whether they would want to invest in that organisation, work for it, supply goods to it, or purchase goods or services from it. In determining what information particular stakeholders want or need, the accountant will often engage with different stakeholder groups.

performance
The results, impacts, or accomplishments associated with completing a particular task or group of tasks

financial performance
A measure or assessment of an organisation's performance measured in financial terms, perhaps through the application of financial accounting standards

profit
The difference between the total income and total expenses of an organisation for a specified period of time

social performance
The impacts – both positive and negative – that an organisation's activities have on its stakeholders, including employees, customers and the wider community

Performance

In relation to **performance**, issues arise as to what aspects accounting should address. That is, for what aspects of performance should we produce an account in order to allow others to make informed decisions? Broadly speaking, we could categorise performance in three ways: financial performance, social performance and environmental performance (see **Figure 1.1**). Accounting can – and we will argue it should – address aspects of each of these broad performance categories.

Financial performance

Financial performance can take various forms. For example, an organisation's total sales revenue, total cost of goods sold, total expenses, and **profit** are all measures of financial performance which might indicate how well the organisation is being managed in financial terms.

Social performance

Social performance can also take various forms. For example, the amount and type of training provided to employees, the satisfaction of staff, the satisfaction of customers, initiatives put in place for employees with disabilities, the results of audits of worker health and safety

FIGURE 1.1 Categories of performance

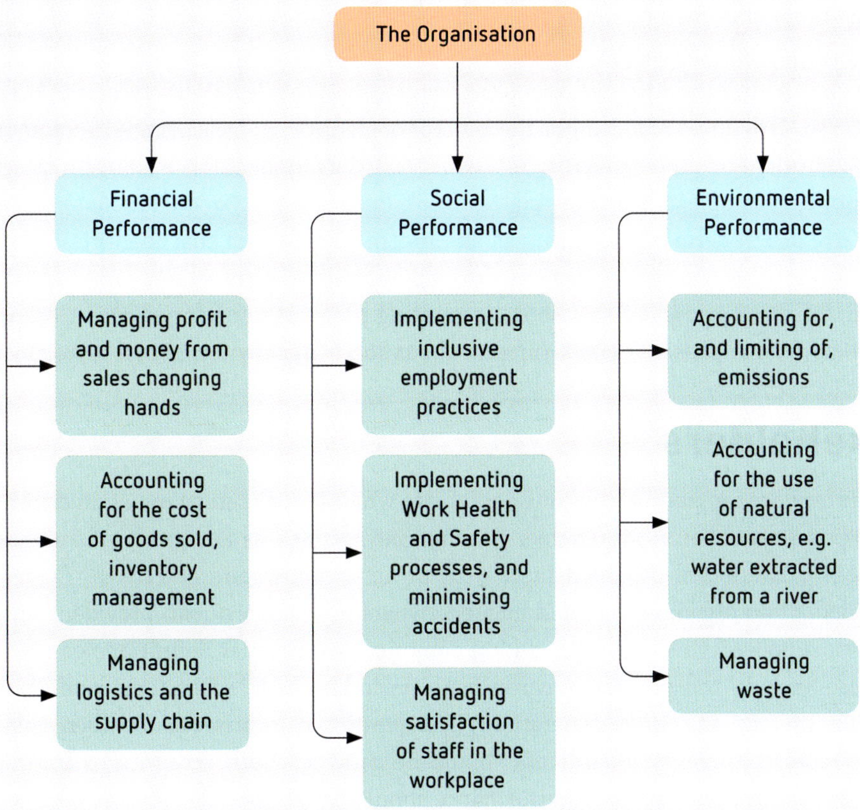

within supply chain factories and the number of accidents in the workplace are all measures, or indicators, of the social performance of an organisation. What should be apparent here is that we do not have to measure aspects of performance in financial terms for this to still be considered as 'accounting'. This is an important point. The number of accidents in a workplace is a significant indicator – or 'account' – of how seriously an organisation is taking its occupational health and safety obligations, but this does not need to be presented in financial terms for it to be considered an account, and therefore a product of the accounting process.

Environmental performance

Environmental performance similarly takes various forms. For example, the amount and type of waste being generated, the amount of water being consumed, instances of non-compliance with environmental legislation, the amount of greenhouse gases being generated, or the occurrence of chemical spills are all indicators of environmental performance. Again, it needs to be emphasised that these measures do not necessarily need to be measured in financial terms for them to be considered part of an accounting process.

environmental performance The impacts – positive and negative – that an organisation has on the physical and natural environments in which it operates

A broad perspective of accounting

This book regards accounting as a much broader process than just providing information about the financial (or economic) performance of an organisation, or simply presenting accounts in financial terms. Again, accounting systems can, and arguably should, be put in place to capture various aspects of an organisation's financial, social and environmental performance. So, from the outset, it needs to be appreciated that this book takes a much broader perspective on accounting than that adopted in many other introductory books on the topic, which tend to concentrate primarily on providing measures of financial performance.

For example, the introductory textbook *Accounting: Business Reporting for Decision Making* (Birt et al., 2018, p. 4) defines accounting as the 'process of identifying, measuring and communicating economic information about an entity to a variety of users for decision-making purposes'.

As another example, the accounting textbook *Principles of Financial Accounting* (Weygandt et al., 2018, p. 10) defines accounting as an 'information system that identifies, records and communicates the economic events of an entity to interested users'.

Again, for the purposes of this book, accounting provides information about economic (or financial) performance *as well as* information about social and environmental performance.

Stakeholders

stakeholder
Any group or individual who can affect, or is affected by, the achievement of an organisation's objectives

The other term we can now briefly consider (and to which we will return many times throughout this book) is **stakeholder**. A stakeholder is commonly defined as any group or individual who can affect, or is affected by, the achievement of an organisation's objectives. Therefore, the stakeholders of an organisation could include owners or investors, loan providers, employees, customers, suppliers, government and local communities. Broader definitions of stakeholders would also include the physical environment (including local ecosystems and the various inhabitants therein) and future generations. The question then arises as to which stakeholders (or their representatives or guardians) should be provided with accounts of organisational performance, and what aspects of performance should be reported in the 'accounts' that those stakeholders receive.

Please consider how you would answer the questions on this theme in **Learning exercise 1.1**. Note that, throughout this book, many learning exercises will be provided along with their associated solutions. To improve your learning experience, please take some time to consider how you might answer the exercises before reading the solutions that follow.

As evidenced by the examples given in **Learning exercise 1.1**, if there is regulation that specifically requires a certain group (or groups) of stakeholders to receive particular information, then that

1.1 Learning Exercise

Stakeholders and their information needs

Different stakeholders have different information needs, but who is entitled to what information, and why? Let's explore a few examples.

Should investors receive information about the financial performance of the organisation they have invested in?

Investors would expect to be provided with enough information to monitor their investment, and hence they have a reasonable right to know about an organisation's financial performance. Further, it might be difficult for an organisation to attract new investors if they are unwilling to provide enough information for those investors to determine if an investment would be worthwhile!

Regardless, in this case, managers and organisations – particularly larger ones – do not have a choice when it comes to providing information about financial performance. In most jurisdictions, there are laws requiring that information about an organisation's financial performance and position be provided to investors.

Should competitors receive information about the organisation's financial performance?

Most managers would probably prefer not to disclose financial information to a competitor because this could result in competitive disadvantage. As managers are not legally required to share this information with competitors, it's sensible to assume that this information would not be disclosed; of course, any information that an organisation publicly releases will be available to competitors.

Should local residents receive information about the chemicals being released into the air by an organisation operating within their community?

It is reasonable to suggest that local residents have a right to know about the chemicals being released by an organisation in their community. In the absence of regulations that require disclosure, whether or not management elects to provide this information will really be up to the managers' judgement. This will depend on whether they believe they have a responsibility to do so, or whether they believe there is a benefit to the organisation in doing so. Different managers will have different opinions about the responsibility and accountability to provide information about environmental performance to local residents.

Should employees be provided with information about how much money is being spent by their organisation on training?

It would also be reasonable to suggest that employees have a right to know about the extent to which their employer is supporting different training initiatives. Again, whether management elects to provide the information will depend upon whether they believe they have a responsibility and a related accountability to do so, or whether there are rules which require them to make such disclosures.

information will be expected to be disclosed. Matters which are not regulated are disclosed at a manager's discretion.

In the next section, on the relationship between accounting and accountability, we will reflect on when a manager might be expected to be responsible for disclosing information to a stakeholder.

The role of accounting

In respect to the role of accounting, we can now say this:

- Accounting provides information to guide decisions made by people both within (internal to) and outside (external to) the organisation.
- The information that is collected and reported will be influenced by what aspects of performance an organisation's management believes it needs to monitor, control and/or improve, as well as what aspects of performance it believes it needs to disclose to people outside the organisation.

- Accounting provides the mechanism by which organisations can inform the relevant stakeholders about the extent to which the actions for which an organisation is deemed to be responsible have actually been fulfilled.
- Reporting provides a vehicle for an organisation to be accountable to various stakeholders, and the accounts being reported do not all have to be prepared in financial terms.

We will now consider the relationship between judgements about an organisation's responsibilities and its accountabilities, and how this in turn has implications for the accounts that an organisation will ultimately prepare and present. What shall be explained is that a manager's perceptions of the extent and nature of organisational accountability will influence what aspects of performance are measured and reported.

LO1.2 The relationship between accounting and accountability

accounts
Records detailing an organisation's performance in relation to a specific aspect of performance

creditors
External parties to whom an organisation (or individual) owes a debt, often in relation to goods or services provided to the organisation on credit terms

The nature of the **accounts** (or reports) produced by an organisation, and the individuals or groups who will be given access to those accounts, will be influenced by judgements concerning an organisation's responsibilities and its associated accountabilities. For example, if we were to embrace the view that an organisation is only responsible for its financial performance, and that this responsibility is restricted to owners (shareholders) and loan providers (and other **creditors**), then organisations might decide to only produce financial accounts, and those accounts would only be distributed to owners and creditors. This would be considered a very restricted, or narrow, view of accountability.

By contrast, if an organisation's managers believe that they are also responsible for the organisation's social and environmental performance, and that this responsibility is extended to all affected stakeholders, then such an organisation will also produce various social and environmental accounts (as well as financial accounts) and will generally not restrict access to such accounts (for example, they might make the information available on their website). This would represent a broader view of accountability.

Source: Shutterstock.com/humphery

If a large multinational is buying some of its products from this factory, then should that multinational produce publicly available accounts about how the factory's employees are being treated?

Some clothing companies, for example, will collect and disclose detailed information about where their clothes are being sourced, and what actions are being taken to ensure that the factories supplying the garments are providing a safe and healthy environment for employees. This could be in the absence of any regulations that require them to provide such accounts. By contrast, other clothing companies might disclose very little information. The managers of the organisations disclosing the detailed information have likely embraced the view that it is their responsibility to be accountable for the health and safety of employees in their supply chain, whereas the managers of the other organisations might not have accepted such a responsibility and hence might disclose little information.

Source: Shutterstock.com/Milos Muller

Who is accountable for these emissions?

As another example, a decade or two ago it would have been very unusual for an organisation to collect and publicly disclose information about its emissions of greenhouse gases, which are known to contribute to climate change. However, as global concern about climate change has increased, it is now quite common for organisations – particularly large ones in carbon-intensive industries – to disclose information about their emissions, as well as the initiatives being undertaken to reduce them.

When it comes to the question of what accounts *should* be prepared, it really is a matter of opinion. Often, there is not one absolutely right answer. Nevertheless, there is a direct relationship between the responsibilities (or duties) that managers believe their organisation has, and the accepted accountabilities. The argument is that, if the managers of an organisation accept a responsibility to particular stakeholders for certain aspects of performance, then they also accept that those stakeholders have a right to information about those aspects of the organisation's performance. This is diagrammatically represented in Figure 1.2.

FIGURE 1.2 The relationship between responsibility, accountability and accounts

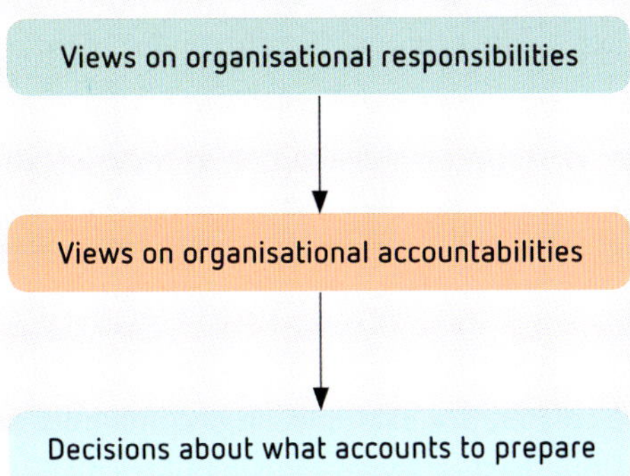

What do we mean by accountability?

A useful definition of **accountability** is provided by Gray, Adams and Owen (2014, p. 50): 'The duty to provide an account or reckoning of those actions for which one is held responsible'.

accountability
The duty to provide an account of those actions for which an organisation is deemed to be responsible. The accounts can take a variety of forms and would be provided to those stakeholders most affected by the activities of the organisation

Again, we can see from the above definition that there is a direct linkage between perceptions of responsibilities, or duties, and the provision of accounts. Gray, Adams and Owen (2014) also emphasise that accountability involves two key responsibilities or duties:

1. to undertake certain actions (or to refrain from taking actions) in accordance with the expectations of a group of stakeholders
2. to provide a reckoning, or account, of those actions to the stakeholders.

Consistent with what we have already covered in this chapter, Gray, Adams and Owen (2014) further explain that these accounts do not have to be presented in financial terms. So, for example, if a clothing company is acquiring its clothes from a supplier in a developing country, such as Bangladesh, and its managers accept responsibility for ensuring that the supplier is providing a safe and healthy environment for its employees, then the clothing company would provide accounts which would disclose such information about the supplier. These accounts might provide information about working hours and employee training in terms of health and safety, as well as information about checks, or audits, of the safety of the buildings being used by the suppliers.

We can also consider the following definitions of accountability:

> Accountability involves an obligation to answer for one's decisions and actions when authority to act on behalf of one party (the principal) is transferred to another (the agent) ... Accountability requires openness, transparency and the provision of information, and the acceptance of responsibility for one's actions.
>
> Source: Barton (2006), p. 257.

> Accountability is acknowledging, assuming responsibility for and being transparent about the impacts of your policies, decisions, actions, products and associated performance.
>
> Source: AccountAbility (2008), p. 6.

> [Accountability is] the obligation of an individual or organization to account for its activities, accept responsibility for them, and to disclose the results in a transparent manner.
>
> Source: BusinessDictionary (2017).

In essence, accountability is an obligation to present an account of, and answer for, the execution of responsibilities to those who entrusted those responsibilities (Grey and Jenkins, 1993, p. 55). As with the definition of accountability provided by Gray, Adams and Owen (2014), the above definitions also link an organisation's responsibilities to the obligation to provide information about the organisation's performance, and its adherence to the expectations of others.

Different people will have different views about the responsibilities and accountabilities of organisations, and this in turn will have implications for the accounts that they believe an organisation *should* produce. While the law imposes certain minimum requirements in terms of the accounts that must be created (for example, large companies are typically required by law to produce specific forms of financial statements using particular accounting standards/rules), organisations will typically provide many other accounts on a voluntary basis, and the nature of these accounts will be influenced by the responsibilities (and accountabilities) that the various managers believe, and accept, that they have. Again, if a manager believes they do not have a responsibility for certain actions, or outcomes, then, in the absence of any specific disclosure regulation, they might elect to provide no account of such actions or outcomes.

It is not an easy exercise to understand why some managers' perspectives of responsibilities and accountabilities are so different to others. These perspectives will likely have been influenced by a variety of factors, such as the managers' cultural backgrounds, the type of education they received and where they received it, their prior professional experience and workplaces, the social and sporting clubs and professional groups they are associated with, their families, their friends, and so forth. All of these factors are likely to impact a manager's views about their responsibilities within an organisation.

Learning exercise 1.2 explores some of the judgements that might be made when managers are deciding whether or not to disclose particular information.

1.2 Learning Exercise

Determining what accounts to produce

The major export industry of Bangladesh is clothing. Many multinational clothing companies are keen to buy their wares from suppliers in Bangladesh because the products can be both high in quality and very low in price. However, there have been many injuries and fatalities within supply factories in Bangladesh, most notably the Tazreem factory fire in November 2012 that killed 112 people and seriously injured over 300 others, and the collapse of the Rana Plaza in April 2013, which killed approximately 1200 factory workers and seriously injured many more. In more recent years, many other fatalities have been reported within the country's factories.

Given this information, let's explore a few questions about what accounts should be produced in this context.

If a multinational organisation buys clothes from a Bangladeshi supplier, should that multinational organisation provide an account of what it's doing to ensure the health and safety of the supplier's employees?

Whether or not the managers of a multinational organisation should provide an account of the health and safety of the employees of supply factories is a matter of opinion. This would depend on whether the managers are considered to have some responsibility for how workers in supply factories are treated.

As supply factories are not typically owned by the organisation that uses them, it could be argued that the organisation is not responsible for the welfare of the factory employees. People with such a view might therefore provide no accounts. However, evidence thankfully shows that the managers of many (though not all) large multinational companies are accepting responsibility for employees within the supply chain. They are showing a willingness to provide information about the health and safety policies they expect their suppliers to adhere to, and the implications for suppliers if they are found to have breached these expectations.

What should be included in an account of the health and safety of employees within a multinational's supply chain?

The types of disclosures that could be made include:

- whether accepted international safety codes have been adopted by supply factories and whether compliance with these codes has been assessed by independent third parties
- what policies exist in factories in relation to child labour and reasonable working hours, and how performance with respect to these policies has been monitored for compliance
- what training is being provided to employees in relation to health and safety
- how hazardous products and materials are being safeguarded within the factory
- what actions have recently been undertaken with regard to fire and building safety
- where problems are found to exist, what mechanisms are in place for swift corrective action.

Once prepared, to whom should these accounts be made available?

If the managers of an organisation believe they have a responsibility to certain stakeholders for particular aspects of performance, then the organisation should provide the stakeholders with an account of such performance. These accounts could be made available to stakeholders such as investors, customers, government, factory employees, and lenders.

Why do I need to know about the relationship between organisational responsibility, accountability and accounting?

Knowing about the relationship between organisational responsibility, accountability and accounting helps us to understand the context relating to why managers might have made some disclosures, but not others.

Generally speaking, in the absence of legal or other professional requirements, managers will elect to make particular disclosures (provide particular 'accounts') if they believe they have a responsibility, and an associated accountability, for a particular aspect of performance. Conversely, in the absence of particular accounts being released by an organisation, and applying the insights provided by this relationship, we might therefore be able to reasonably assume that the managers do not believe they have particular responsibilities and associated accountabilities in respect of those aspects of performance that go unreported/unaccounted.

When we see organisations voluntarily producing a wide range of various accounts, or reports, to a broad range of stakeholders then, with this relationship in mind, that will signal to us that this organisation is embracing a wider set of responsibilities in terms of what aspects of performance it is responsible for, and to whom it is responsible.

LO1.3 Internal and external accounts

While much of our discussion so far has focused on providing information to people outside (external to) the organisation, obviously people within (internal to) the organisation will require information about various aspects of performance. The information collected for internal management purposes will also be influenced by managers' views about their responsibilities and associated accountabilities. For example, if management believes it has a responsibility to minimise its water consumption, then for internal purposes the organisation might collect information, and generate **internal accounts**, concerning how much water is being used in particular processes. Such information can then be monitored and possible improvements made. Subsequent accounts of water use would then show whether previous actions were successful in reducing this use.

internal accounts Information about an organisation's position and performance intended for use by people within the organisation, such as managers

If, by contrast, managers do not consider that water consumption is important, then this particular information will not be collected and no accounts of water use will be compiled. This makes it very difficult to manage the related activities (which is why people often say, 'You cannot manage what you do not measure'). Similar decisions will be made in relation to different aspects of environmental, social and financial performance.

Key concept

Information collected for internal management purposes may or may not then be provided to people externally.

Continuing our water use example, if management believes it is accountable to various stakeholders for water use, then it might also decide to make its information publicly available, perhaps by way of disclosures on a website. The decision to make particular financial, social or environmental information publicly available through **external accounts** will be influenced by various factors, including whether there are laws that require public disclosure, as well as judgements made by managers about whether people outside the organisation have a 'right to know' about particular aspects of the organisation's operations.

external accounts Information about an organisation's position and performance intended for use by people outside the organisation, such as shareholders, NGOs, customers, local communities, news media and regulators

Learning exercise 1.3 considers managers' choices about what information to collect and to whom to disclose the information.

1.3 Learning Exercise

Choosing what information to collect and report

Imagine that you are the general manager of a company that produces paper, and that you're concerned about the social and environmental impacts of the company's operations. Given your concerns, you're trying to determine what sort of information you might want to collect about the organisation's operations, and whether you would be likely to share this information with people outside the organisation. Let's consider how to work through this process.

Why would you collect information?

Given that you are concerned about the social and environmental impacts of your organisation, you are more likely to collect and disclose information about these impacts than a manager who has no such concerns.

What information would be collected?

What information is collected will be linked to what aspects of the organisation's operations you believe the organisation is responsible for, and therefore also accountable for. This might require some prioritisation of the impacts in terms of which ones create the greatest negative, or positive, effects.

The information that might be collected in relation to social impacts might include:

- the training provided to employees
- employment diversity and inclusive hiring practices
- occupational health and safety policies, and details of any workplace injuries
- support for local community initiatives.

The information that might be collected in relation to environmental impacts could include:

- sources of the timber from which the paper is made, and whether it's from sustainable forests
- the amount of paper made from recycled paper
- the amount of energy being used, whether it is from renewable sources, and what efforts are being taken to reduce energy consumption
- the types of waste being generated, where it is being disposed, and the environmental consequences of this disposal
- how much water is being used in the various production processes, and efforts to reduce water consumption
- the total amount of transport being used, and what efforts are being taken to reduce the total kilometres travelled.

To whom would you disclose the information?

Collecting this information will allow the organisation to manage aspects of its social and environmental impacts internally, but then a manager needs to decide which specific items will be disclosed to people outside the organisation.

We would naturally prioritise the disclosure of information that is valuable to our stakeholders. We would make these accounts publicly available to any stakeholders we think have a right to know about those particular aspects of our performance.

In practice, many organisations do publicly disclose information of the type that we have identified above, and they typically do this in the absence of any laws that require them to do so. But because the disclosure of many items of information is voluntary – particularly in relation to social and environmental aspects of performance – some managers will tend to disclose information of a positive or favourable nature, rather than information of a negative nature. Therefore, stakeholders always need to consider whether voluntarily disclosed information is credible.

We will now consider who prepares the accounts that might be used internally by various managers, and those used externally by a variety of different stakeholders.

LO1.4 Who produces these accounts?

Because we are embracing a relatively broad perspective of accounting, we could say that any person who provides an account of some aspect of an organisation's financial, social or environmental performance is in effect performing an accounting function. Regarding the preparation of accounts, these could be reported in a variety of ways, such as in the form of a spreadsheet, a printed report/document, an annual report, a social media post, a disclosure made on a website, a department meeting presentation, a media release, and so forth. Effectively, anything that provides information in relation to an organisation's activities and/or performance could be considered to be an account. Therefore, in the workplace, it could be argued that most people could, at some stage, be deemed to be an accountant.

Indeed, in most jurisdictions throughout the world, anybody can call themselves an accountant, even if they lack qualifications in this area and despite how misleading this could be. However, they cannot give themselves a title such as CPA (certified practising/public accountant), chartered accountant, registered accountant or licensed accountant – not unless they actually have earned that designation, which would require certain levels of professional education beyond university, as well as ongoing compliant professional education.

Key concept

Any person who provides an account of some aspect of an organisation's performance is undertaking an accounting function.

The accounting function

accounting function Generation of accounts detailing organisational position and performance

For the purposes of this book, we will accept that many people within an organisation will generate accounts about various processes and hence perform an **accounting function**. This is the case even though they might not be known as accountants within their workplace. For example, somebody who is monitoring and recording the use of electricity, in an endeavour to try to determine the energy efficiency of particular machines, is performing an accounting function.

Whether somebody should be deemed an accountant or not isn't really something that we need to worry too much about right now. It is one of those arguments that could go either way. Within the community, somebody would generally be considered to be an accountant if they have done a reasonable amount of training in accounting (perhaps a degree or diploma) and they hold a position that has some designation referring to accounting.

To this point of the chapter, we have covered a number of issues in relation to the meaning of accounting; the relationship between accounting and accountability; the choice to collect information for use internally by managers and/or for use externally by various stakeholders; and perspectives about who performs various accounting functions. **Learning exercise 1.4** and **Learning exercise 1.5** further address some of these issues.

1.4 Learning Exercise

The relationship between responsibilities and accounts

To explore some of the above issues further, we now consider whether the managers of an organisation should collect and disclose information about:

- the organisation's carbon emissions
- its water use
- its employment of staff with physical or intellectual disabilities
- the workplace health and safety policies of companies that supply significant amounts of products or services to the organisation
- the use of renewable energy by the organisation.

Further, when you are considering the above questions, do you think other readers of this book, such as other people in your class, might have the same opinions as you, and if not, why do you think their opinions might be different?

In addressing the above points, something that needs to be emphasised is that the responsibilities and accountabilities we accept – and therefore the accounts that we will create and possibly make publicly available – will be influenced by our own views, such that different people have different opinions.

Given ongoing concerns about climate change and the focus of the community on efforts undertaken by organisations to reduce their contribution to the problem, then disclosures about carbon emissions and the use of renewable energy would seem very reasonable. Further, in some areas there is not an abundance of water. If this is the case in respect of an organisation's operations, then it would seem appropriate to make information available about water use, including the initiatives being embraced to reduce it.

Providing information about the workplace health and safety practices of companies within a supply chain, as well as the organisation's employment practices as they relate to people with disabilities, would also seem to be a reasonable expectation – but again, this is a matter of judgement. Many companies – particularly those with suppliers in developing countries – do provide information about various employee-related health and safety issues, but there are also many companies that do not.

It is likely that different people within your class will have different opinions about whether managers have a responsibility to disclose the above information, and this is why accounting can be a very interesting and challenging practice. People can disagree as to what accounts should be prepared because they hold different opinions about the responsibilities that organisations should accept. As we have already briefly explained, different perspectives about corporate responsibilities could be due to a variety of factors, such as the different social, cultural and educational backgrounds we all have.

1.5 Learning Exercise

The meaning of accounting, revisited

Earlier in this chapter, a commonly used (but narrow) definition of accounting was provided which said that accounting is the process of identifying, measuring and communicating economic information about an entity to a variety of users for decision-making purposes.

Do you agree with the above definition?

Whether or not you agree with this definition of accounting will depend upon the answers you give to questions about:

- why an entity should collect and report information
- to whom an entity should report information
- what aspects of performance should be reported.

If you believe that the only accountability of an organisation relates to its economic (or financial) performance, then you might accept the above definition of accounting. But if you embrace a broader view of organisational responsibilities and accountabilities that also encompasses social and environmental impacts, then you are likely to reject this narrow definition of accounting.

LO1.5 Qualitative characteristics of accounting information

Up until now, we have been emphasising the point that accounting information should be produced to allow various stakeholders to make informed decisions about how they will manage an organisation (in the case of managers) or whether they will support an organisation (external stakeholders) in terms of such activities as investment, employment, loaning funds, or consuming goods or services. In part, the decisions made by various stakeholders in relation to an organisation will be influenced by whether they believe they have been provided with accounts that enable them to assess whether the organisation has fulfilled particular responsibilities. As we have noted, good quality information provides the users of that information with the power to make informed decisions.

There are some generally accepted characteristics that information should possess – we can call these qualitative characteristics – if it is to be useful in enabling its internal or external users to make informed decisions. Some of these qualitative characteristics have been enunciated by organisations such as the International Accounting Standards Board (IASB; focuses on generating financial reporting standards for large business organisations), the Global Reporting Initiative (GRI; provides frameworks for economic, social and environmental reporting) and the Task Force on Climate-Related Financial Disclosures (TCFD develops frameworks for climate change-related financial disclosures, social and environmental reporting). We will consider the guidance generated by these three bodies in other chapters of this book. But what is interesting here is that, despite the differences in the focus of each of these bodies, there is general agreement on what qualitative characteristics information should possess if it is to be useful for decision making.

These characteristics relate to:

- relevance
- reliability (or faithful representation)
- comparability
- verifiability
- understandability
- timeliness.

Relevance

For information to be able to influence a decision, it needs to be **relevant** – information is relevant if it is capable of changing the decisions of those people receiving the information. Managers of organisations will often engage with different stakeholder groups to try to determine what information they need, or want, in order to enable them to make their respective decisions. Determining what information is relevant relies on a high degree of professional judgement. Relevance is often affected by the location of the organisation, as well as by time. For example, if an organisation is conducting operations on top of an important groundwater system that provides water to surrounding communities, then information about the release of various chemicals into the soil might be of much more relevance than if the organisation was operating thousands of kilometres away from anyone. In terms of time, what we consider as relevant might also change across the years. For example, a company's greenhouse gas emissions were not perceived as terribly relevant to the vast majority of people several decades ago, but as we have come to understand the science of climate change, the relevance of greenhouse gas emissions to many decisions made by a variety of stakeholders has increased dramatically.

relevant
In terms of information, information is relevant if it is capable of making a difference to the decisions made by the recipients of that information

Relevant information will have either *predictive value* or *confirmatory value*. Information has predictive value if it enables the prediction of future events (for example, next year's profits, or the likely consumption of energy by a particular machine), whereas it has confirmatory value if it allows us to confirm past events (for example, measuring last year's profits, or the last month's energy consumption of a particular machine).

reliable
In terms of information, information is reliable if it is free from error, complete, and free from bias

Reliability

If information is likely to be relevant, then it is also very important that the information is **reliable**. Reliability is also often termed *faithful representation*. For information to be reliable, it should be free from error, complete and balanced (neutral) – that is, free from bias. Managers of organisations will prepare much of the information that is released to different stakeholders, and it is always to be hoped that they have not introduced some form of bias into that information. Before information is released by an organisation, it is sometimes

Source: Alamy Stock Photo/Peter Jarvis

If an organisation conducts activity that may affect a local waterway, and it accurately and transparently informs the local community, this disclosure is likely to be both *relevant* and *reliable*.

subject to an independent review by an external party that is not related to the reporting organisation. For example, there is a legal requirement that the financial statements released by large companies be subject to an audit by an independent and qualified financial statement auditor before they are made available to shareholders. The audit enhances the reliability of the information.

However, while there is an expectation that accounting information be reliable and therefore free from error, this does not mean that the information should always be expected to be perfectly accurate, as in practice this is rarely possible. It simply means that care should be taken to make the information as reliable as possible.

Relevance and reliability are typically considered to be the most important, or fundamental, qualitative characteristics that information should possess, and all useful information would be both relevant and reliable. However, there are other qualitative characteristics that enhance the usefulness of information. We will consider these now.

Comparability

comparable
Information is comparable if it is selected, compiled and measured in a similar way so that reports from different periods (and different organisations) can be compared

Information should ideally be **comparable**, which means it should be selected, compiled, measured and reported in a similar way from period to period, to enable stakeholders to compare aspects of performance across different time periods. Further, the information should also allow, where possible, the performance of one organisation to be compared with the performance of similar organisations (this is often referred to as *benchmarking*). To assist with achieving comparability, it is useful for the preparers of the information to provide clear notes about the accounting methods or policies used to measure particular items. If it is clear that different methods have been used to measure a particular item (either across time within a certain organisation, or at the same time by different organisations), then we know that care must be taken when comparing the different measurements.

Verifiability

verifiable
Information is verifiable if different people who are knowledgeable and independent could reach agreement that it reliably depicts a particular item, phenomenon or event

Ideally, the information should also be **verifiable**, which means that if different people are provided with the same underlying data, they will derive the measures shown in the information being presented by the organisation. That is, there would be some level of consensus if different people prepared the same type of information for the same organisation.

Understandability

understandable
In terms of information, presented so that its meaning, and the basis of its compilation, are clear to the user

Another qualitative characteristic we can consider is **understandability**, which means that users understand what the information means and the basis on which it was prepared or measured. The knowledge of stakeholders has to be considered when providing them with information. For example, it would be meaningless to provide stakeholders with information about the release of particular chemicals if they did not understand the significance of such release to the relevant environments. When we look at the environmental disclosures made by many large organisations, this seems to be a common mistake. They often provide information on their websites or in publicly available sustainability reports about the release of various chemicals without explaining the significance of this information in terms of its potential impact on the environment. It appears at times that they assume all the readers have some form of advanced scientific knowledge. This would not be considered good accounting practice.

Timeliness

One other qualitative characteristic we can consider is **timeliness**. For the information to be considered timely, users should have access to it in time to make informed decisions. In general, the older the information is, the less useful it tends to be.

timeliness
Information should be provided to stakeholders in quick enough time to be able to influence their decisions. Generally, the older the information is the less useful it is

As we talk about accounting information throughout the remainder of this book, we need to remember that information needs to have certain qualitative characteristics – as just described – before it can be useful to the people receiving this information. That is, for it to be 'decision useful'. There is no point releasing a whole lot of useless information – that would just be stupid! Therefore, managers not only have a responsibility to ensure that they are providing information to show they are behaving responsibly, they also need to ensure that the information has the necessary attributes, or qualitative characteristics, to make it 'useful'.

Learning exercise 1.6 revisits the two fundamental (or most important) qualitative characteristics that information should possess: relevance and reliability. The qualitative characteristics of useful information are summarised in **Figure 1.3**.

1.6 Learning Exercise

Information needs to be useful: relevance and reliability

We will now reconsider the question of why it is necessary that the information released by an organisation be both relevant and reliable. Also, we will look again at the additional characteristics that information should possess for it to be relevant and reliable, and therefore useful for making decisions.

As a result of reading the material provided so far in this chapter, you should now understand that to be useful, information needs to be *relevant*; that is, it needs to be capable of changing the decisions being made by the people receiving the information. It also needs to be *reliable*, meaning that the information presented is complete, free from errors, and balanced (neutral).

Inappropriate and potentially costly decisions can be made if information is relevant but not reliable. And if information is never likely to be relevant, then it really does not matter how reliable it is since it is likely to be disregarded and not used for decision-making purposes. Therefore, it is essential that the information released by an organisation is both relevant and reliable, and this is why these are often referred to as the two fundamental characteristics of useful information.

To enhance the relevance of the information, it should also have the attributes of:

- *comparability*
- *understandability*
- *timeliness.*

To enhance the reliability of the information, it should also be *verifiable*, which means that it is relatively free of error and bias.

FIGURE 1.3 An overview of the qualitative characteristics of useful information

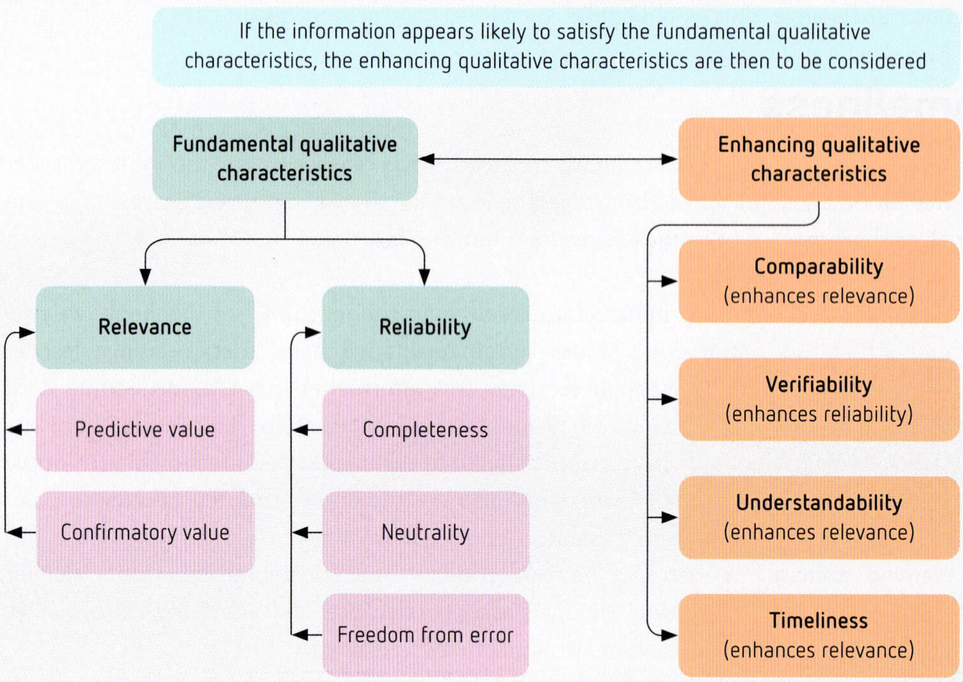

Why do I need to know about the qualitative characteristics of useful information?

In your professional career you will be required to provide information to others for their respective decision making. The more useful that information is for the decisions being made by those other people, or stakeholders, the more effective you will be in your role. Therefore, it makes good sense that you should know about what qualitative characteristics useful information possesses so that you can strive to ensure that the information you provide is as useful as possible.

As users of information, we will also need to consider whether particular information provided to us, or compiled by us, is really that useful for the decisions we individually need to make. Knowing about the different qualitative characteristics of useful information provides us with criteria to assess the potential usefulness of the information provided to us. If it does not seem to meet the criteria then we may be better placed to ignore the information.

LO1.6 An accountability model

To this point, we have mentioned the idea of accountability many times, explaining how it is influenced by managers' perceptions of an organisation's responsibilities. We will now turn our attention to various assessments, or decisions, that need to be made as part of the process of accounting for, and reporting aspects of, an organisation's performance. We will consider four issues throughout this book as we study various aspects of accounting:

- *Why* do the managers of an organisation decide to collect and disclose information (or accounts) about particular aspects of the organisation's performance?

- *Who* are the stakeholders to whom the disclosures (accounts) will be directed?
- *What* types of information will be collected, and what disclosures will be made to stakeholders outside the organisation (what are their information needs)?
- *How* should the information be disclosed (for example, what should the format and media of the disclosures/accounts be)?

Figure 1.4 reflects the sequential nature of our four-step accountability model, emphasising how each step then leads to the next; that is, the answer to one step (or question) informs the answer to the next step.

As we will show, these four issues are usefully addressed at various times throughout the process of accounting. We will now consider each of them in turn.

FIGURE 1.4 A diagrammatic representation of our four-step accountability model

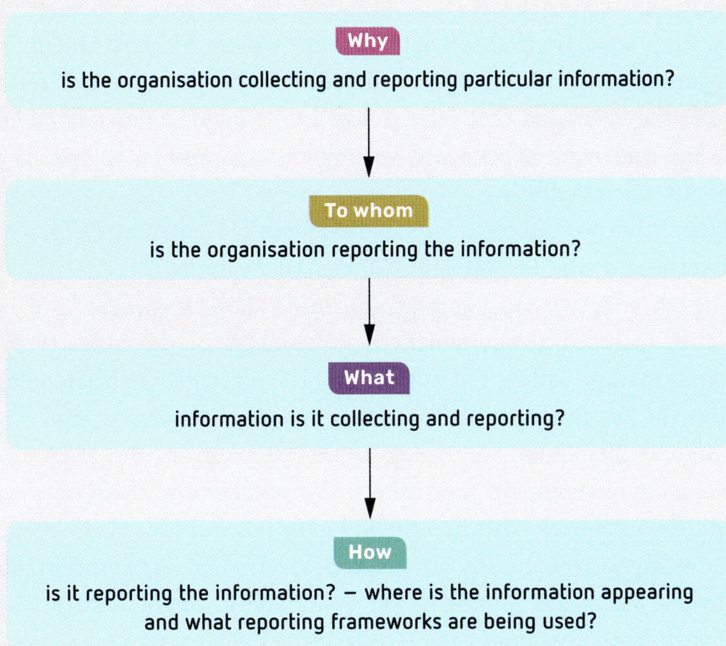

Why is an organisation collecting and disclosing particular information?

In deciding what information to collect and repost, various factors might be considered by managers, as outlined in the following sections.

Legal requirements

In many cases, managers will effectively have no choice about whether to collect and disclose particular information. Therefore, in terms of why they would report, they will simply be complying with legal requirements. For example, the disclosure of various items of information about an organisation's financial performance is required by law, particularly for larger organisations (although not *all* aspects of financial performance are required to be disclosed). Further, in many countries throughout the world there are legal requirements for larger organisations to make disclosures about such things as their greenhouse gas emissions, emissions of other toxic substances, workplace injuries, and the risks that 'modern slavery' might exist within their supply chains.

Forestalling the imposition of mandatory reporting requirements

Often, various interest groups within society, such as environmental groups or employee trade unions, will lobby government to put in place laws which require organisations to make particular disclosures. Evidence has shown that companies and industry bodies often understand that this lobbying might be happening, and might decide to collect and publicly disclose particular information in an effort to placate lobby groups, and potentially forestall more onerous disclosure/accounting regulations that might be put in place by government. The argument is that, if an organisation is making at least some disclosures in respect of certain aspects of performance, then the likelihood that related disclosures might be mandated by government will be reduced, and this might explain why the organisation decides to prepare the particular accounts and disclose them publicly.

As an example of this, we can consider some evidence presented by Deegan and Blomquist (2006). They investigated why the Minerals Council of Australia (MCA) – the industry body that works on behalf of Australian mining companies – developed a Code of Environmental Management which included a requirement that members of the industry provide certain environmental information within the annual reports presented to shareholders. This was introduced despite the fact there was no legal requirement for such reporting.

When Deegan and Blomquist interviewed senior people from the MCA about why they included this reporting requirement, they were told it was because there was a view by senior people in the minerals industry that, had the industry not introduced the requirement, then the government, acting in response to various non-government organisation lobbying efforts (for example, by the Australian Conservation Foundation), might have imposed reporting requirements that perhaps were not of the type that the industry wanted. One senior member of the minerals industry noted:

> I guess to be frank, it (the Code) was developed to try and stop somebody else developing it ... The Australian Conservation Foundation had specifically developed its own code and that had quite a bit of support from a number of non-government organisations and they were putting pressure on the Federal Government to do something ... so really I guess from that perspective it forced the Minerals Council's hand.
>
> Source: Deegan and Blomquist (2006, p. 360).

Managers' perceived responsibilities

As discussed earlier in this chapter, managers might want to ensure that their operations do not adversely impact others, and so they might voluntarily collect a variety of information about their organisation's social, economic and environmental performance. As an example, if managers are particularly concerned about saving water because the organisation is operating in a populated environment with low water levels, then they might put in place processes to measure the water used in various activities, with the intention of monitoring, controlling and reducing water usage. They might then disclose such information publicly because they believe that people outside the organisation have a right to know about how much water the organisation is using and what the organisation is doing to reduce future water use. By contrast, if managers in other organisations do not believe they have a responsibility to control their water use, then they might elect not to collect, or publicly disclose, information about this.

Source: Shutterstock.com/Mark Agnor

Do managers of a mining organisation have a responsibility and accountability for the various social and environmental impacts related to their operations?

Demands of powerful stakeholders

As we will emphasise in other chapters, organisations often collect and disclose information because certain powerful stakeholders want to know about particular aspects of their operations – disclosing information is a means of managing such stakeholders. For example, a company selling eggs might determine that customers (stakeholders upon whom the organisation depends for survival) actively favour eggs that come from producers who allow the hens to walk around outdoors (free-range farms), not those from farms that hold the hens in crowded cages under artificial light. As such, the organisation might choose to collect and report information about the processes in place within egg farms, to assure concerned people that the hens are treated properly, so as to maintain customer support. If powerful stakeholders – for example, the customers on which the egg producers depend – do not care about particular aspects of performance (in this case, the treatment of the hens laying the eggs in the supply chain), then the organisation might not choose to collect and disclose information about that aspect of performance.

Source: Shutterstock.com/Matee Nuserm

If consumers care about the welfare of hens, then egg sellers should provide an account of the average amount of space devoted to each laying hen.

While it is common for organisations to only report information because powerful stakeholders want it (if these stakeholders are not provided with the information they desire, they might withdraw valuable support from the organisation), ideally all stakeholders – regardless of their power – that are significantly impacted by the operations of an organisation will be provided with information to enable them to understand both these impacts and what initiatives are being implemented to reduce such impacts.

Increased profits

Related to the above point, at times it would appear that some managers elect to make disclosures primarily to enhance the financial position and performance of an organisation, rather than because they believe that people have a right to know about particular aspects of organisational performance. What this means is that some managers are simply reactionary and will effectively 'do the right thing' because it will generate higher profits, not because they believe they should be responsible, or accountable, for particular actions. Following on from our example above, perhaps some egg producers would provide better living conditions for their hens, and disclose information about such initiatives, not because they genuinely feel responsible for, or care about, the hens, but because they know that providing accounts of such actions will have direct business benefits.

Responding to a crisis

From time to time, there will be events which appear to adversely affect how the public perceives an organisation. For example, in 2011, a number of newspaper articles were published around the world about a Chinese factory, Sturdy Products, that supplied toys to Disney (see Chamberlain, 2011). The factory was subject to an undercover investigation by a human rights group: Students and Scholars against Corporate Misbehavior (SACOM). Among the findings were allegations of the use of child labour, forced overtime at levels three times in excess of that allowed by Chinese law, concerns about poisonous chemicals and poor ventilation, various forms of abuse, and an instance of employee suicide. Disney did react to these concerns and now has very strict policies in place regarding the human rights of employees within factories supplying products to the company. In addition, the company now provides extensive disclosures on its website about how it seeks to ensure that workers within its supply chains are treated with respect (see **https://thewaltdisneycompany.com/about/#corporate-citizenship**).

There is much available evidence that if the reputation or legitimacy of an organisation appears to be badly damaged, then the organisation in question (and perhaps even other organisations within the same industry) will produce public accounts of how seriously it is taking the matter, and what initiatives it has put in place to help ensure such events will not reoccur in the future. Such disclosures would be considered responsive, or reactive, rather than being driven by real concerns about the need to be accountable and responsible – otherwise, why would the organisation wait until the public raises its concerns before making disclosures?

Understanding motivations for disclosures

What the above discussion is seeking to demonstrate is that it is not always an easy exercise to try to understand why some organisations elect to make some disclosures, while others do not. Some disclosures will be made because managers believe they have an underlying responsibility to inform various people about particular aspects of performance, whereas other managers might make disclosures simply because they think there are business benefits in doing so. That is, the broad reasons driving any particular organisation to generate particular accounts for use by stakeholders external to the organisation can range from an ethically motivated desire to ensure that the organisation benefits society, or at least does not have a negative impact on society and the natural environment, through to an economically focused motive to use reporting to protect or enhance profits, and therefore owner/shareholder value.

Another point to be made here is that, before we read particular disclosures, it is useful to try to understand *why* the disclosures have been made in the first place. If a particular management team typically only makes disclosures when there are direct business benefits in doing so, then perhaps we would be right to question how much we should rely upon such disclosures. By contrast, if an organisation has always seemed to have respected the rights of people to be informed about the various impacts of the organisation, then we might be more inclined to rely upon the organisation's disclosures, particularly those made voluntarily.

The reason why an organisation has elected to provide particular accounts will have direct consequences for the next question about to whom those accounts are directed, as we will now discuss.

To whom is the information, or 'account', being directed?

Once it is determined *why* an entity decides to report, this decision will in turn inform the decision as *to whom* the information will be directed. If an organisation's reporting is motivated exclusively by managerial reasoning and strategising (for example, it is primarily focused on increasing the wealth of the owners and/or managers), the stakeholders to whom that organisation's reporting is directed might be narrowly defined as those who hold and exercise the greatest economic power, or influence, over the organisation.

Conversely, reporting motivated by ethical/moral reasoning will seek to address the information needs of a broader range of stakeholders. Specifically, a broader ethical approach to reporting would direct the reports towards those stakeholders most affected by the operations of the organisation, regardless of the economic or other power held by those stakeholders, and would focus on issues such as various stakeholders' 'right to know'.

What we're emphasising is that who the reports or accounts will target will ultimately depend on managers' views about organisational responsibilities and accountabilities, and hence upon views about the initial issue of *why* the organisation has decided to produce a report. That is, what motivated the organisation to make the disclosures in the first place? Again, views will vary from manager to manager. Ultimately, proper or *full* accountability requires that all stakeholders – including those with and without the power to influence the operations of an organisation – have the ability to hold more powerful people (such as the managers of large companies) to account for the impacts of their operations. Proper accountability requires managers to be responsive to the legitimate concerns held by those parties receiving accounts of organisational performance.

Different perceptions of organisational responsibilities

There are many views on the responsibilities of business. At one extreme are those of the famous economist Milton Friedman. In his widely cited book *Capitalism and Freedom*, Friedman (1962, p. 133) rejected the view that corporate managers have any moral obligations or responsibilities, noting that such a view

> shows a fundamental misconception of the character and nature of a free economy. In such an economy, there is one and only one social responsibility of business [and that is] to use its resources and engage in activities designed to increase its profits as long as it stays within the rules of the game, which is to say, engages in open and free competition, without deception or fraud.
>
> Source: Friedman (1962), p. 133.

Learning exercise 1.7 explores how the adoption of a narrow view of corporate responsibilities, such as that embraced by Friedman, influences the accountability that managers might adopt.

1.7 Learning Exercise

Friedman's perspective on corporate responsibilities

You might wonder if corporate managers tend to agree or disagree with Milton Friedman's perspective on accountability. Many managers do seem to agree with Friedman, given that they seem to prioritise financial performance and the rights of investors over and above other aspects of performance, and other stakeholders. But there are many managers who take a broader view of corporate responsibilities.

A broader view of corporate responsibility

Managers who agree with Friedman's narrow perspective on corporate responsibilities might not be in favour of collecting and disclosing information about social and environmental performance unless they felt that disclosure would ultimately lead to financial benefits that favour investors. Additionally, they would not be responsive to the concerns held by those stakeholders who do not have the power to influence the successful operations of an organisation.

Managers with a broader view of organisational responsibilities and accountabilities, however, believe that they should provide information to stakeholders who are significantly impacted by an organisation's operations, regardless of whether the respective stakeholders have any power. This perspective also requires managers to be responsive to the legitimate concerns of all stakeholders. These managers may more readily accept that if the evidence (as represented in various accounts) shows that an organisation has not performed in accordance with stakeholder expectations, then they have a responsibility to amend the organisation's behaviour accordingly.

At the other end of the responsibility spectrum are those people who believe that managers should manage an organisation for the benefit of all stakeholders, not just those with control over scarce resources. For example, in contrast to Friedman, Anita Roddick, founder of cosmetics company The Body Shop, made the following statement in the introduction to her book *Business as Unusual: The Journey of Anita Roddick and The Body Shop*:

> In terms of power and influence, you can forget the church, forget politics. There is no more powerful institution in society than business, which is why I believe it is now more important than ever before for business to assume a moral leadership. The business of business should not be about money, it should be about responsibility. It should be about public good, not private greed.
>
> Source: Roddick (2007).

Taking a broader perspective on the responsibilities of business, Freeman and Reed (1983, p. 91) defined an entity's stakeholders as 'any identifiable group or individual who can affect the achievement of an organisation's objectives, or is affected by the achievement of an organisation's objectives'. This is consistent with a definition we provided earlier in this chapter. If we accept that an organisation has a responsibility to its stakeholders, then the more broadly an organisation defines its stakeholders, the greater the responsibilities and associated accountabilities it will tend to accept, and the broader will be its accounting.

What information shall be reported?

Once an organisation has determined which stakeholders will be the target recipients of its accounts – that is, once it has addressed the *why report* and *to whom to report* questions – it can then take the next step of considering the information demands of the identified stakeholders. That is, it can address the *what to report* question in terms of what types of information will be disclosed and what issues the accounts should address.

Identifying which issues various stakeholders believe an entity should be held responsible and accountable for involves discussion between the organisation and its target stakeholders – this is often referred to as the process of *stakeholder engagement*. However, the issue about who to engage will depend upon managers' motivations for reporting.

If managers are simply disclosing information to keep powerful stakeholders happy (and therefore to help bolster the financial value of the organisation), then they might only concentrate on providing the information that is demanded by those powerful stakeholders – that is, those stakeholders who might impact the flow of resources into an organisation, such as investors, lenders and key customers. However, if they are more concerned about being accountable to those stakeholders most impacted by their operations, then they would consider the nature of their various economic, social and environmental impacts and provide information to the most affected people about them, perhaps including what is being done to address or mitigate negative impacts in the future.

In deciding what information to collect, and then subsequently disclose, another factor that would typically be considered is whether there is a demand for particular information from the identified stakeholders. For example, if local residents have been identified as key stakeholders of an organisation that uses dangerous chemicals in its production activities, and if those residents are concerned about the effects created by the various chemicals being released by the organisation, then disclosures are warranted.

Beyond considering whether there is a *demand* for information, we might also consider whether particular stakeholders have a *need* for information. If stakeholders are able or want to make informed choices, they need information. But they might not know if particular information is commonly available, and even if it is, how it could be used to make decisions. So sometimes some education is necessary.

Suppose the only tool you know about is a screwdriver; you do not know that shovels or spades also exist. You want to dig a hole and, in the absence of knowledge to the contrary, you ask for a screwdriver as you know it will at least enable you to soften the land you want to dig in. What you need is for somebody to show you that spades/shovels exist, at which point you will demand one of these if you are digging a hole. The point being made here is that, when asking stakeholders what information they want, you'll sometimes need to educate them about what information could be made available, and in turn, how that information might be used to make informed decisions. So just because stakeholders do not demand information does not necessarily mean they should not be supplied with it, or have a right to it. Again, we see that the decisions to be made by accountants are not always straightforward.

Key concept

Stakeholders might not know what they don't know, and what they don't know might be very important to them. Stakeholders might need education to know what information could be made available to them, and in turn, how that information might be used to make informed decisions.

Another point to consider here is that an organisation cannot disclose every conceivable type of information it has available about the various aspects of its performance, otherwise the reports it issues would be very long and too hard to comprehend. Some prioritisation and compromise between the information needs and demands of various stakeholders is inevitable. This can be a very subjective exercise. For example, assume that an organisation creates many social and environmental impacts. Rather than providing information about every different impact, the organisation might provide details of, say, the five most significant social and environmental effects, along with explanations of why these are considered the most important to monitor and control.

Because a manager's decisions about what to report can be rather subjective, it is becoming common for organisations to provide some form of explanation towards the front of their reports about why particular information is being disclosed within its reports. That is, managers will often provide the readers of the report with information about the processes the organisation applied to determine what information to disclose publicly. This is commonly referred to as providing information about the 'materiality determination process'. Information is 'material' if its presence, or absence, is likely to impact the decisions being made by the readers of that information. Determining whether information is likely to be material relies upon a great deal of professional judgement by those responsible for deciding whether to make disclosures.

As an example of the type of disclosures that organisations might make in relation to determining what information to disclose, we can refer to the following extract from the BHP Ltd website. This explanation from BHP relates to explaining why certain sustainability-related disclosures were included within the BHP 2021 Annual Report (**www.bhp.com**, accessed October 2021). Because such disclosures are being made voluntarily, disclosures such as these made by BHP allow readers of the report to understand the context, or logic, of particular disclosures.

> **Our material sustainability issues**
>
> Each year we identify the sustainability issues most material to our business and stakeholders. We also assess the economic, social, environmental and cultural impact of our activities.
>
> We review a wide variety of internal and external sources, such as our Group Risks, issues raised at our Annual General Meetings and through industry associations, non-government organisations and media areas of focus, and BHP's Our Requirements standards. We also consult with stakeholders, such as through the BHP Forum on Corporate Responsibility, via investor round tables and advisory groups and with internal and external stakeholders via surveys and focused discussions. Through these sources we aim to identify the issues of most concern to our stakeholders and critical to our business. The Board's Sustainability Committee and the BHP Forum on Corporate Responsibility review our approach.
>
> This assessment informs our sustainability strategies and helps to guide the depth of transparent coverage of key topics to be included in our Annual Report in line with the Global Reporting Initiative (GRI) Standards Reporting Principles.
>
> The following material sustainability issues formed part of our materiality assessment in FY2021:
>
> - Air quality and emissions
> - Anti-competitive behaviour
> - Automation
> - Biodiversity and land management
> - Climate change and greenhouse gas emissions
> - Community engagement and health and wellbeing
> - Community livelihoods and social investment
> - Compliance with laws and regulations

- Critical incident risk management
- Cybersecurity
- Dams and tailings management
- Economic contribution
- Employment practices
- Environmental impacts on our business
- Ethics and business conduct, anti-corruption
- Freedom of association and collective bargaining
- Governance and management of our joint venture operations and non-operate joint ventures
- Indigenous peoples (including cultural heritage)
- Pandemic preparedness and response
- Political contributions and influence
- Portfolio resilience to climate change
- Product stewardship
- Remuneration policies
- Respecting human rights
- Sustainability governance
- Taxes and royalties
- Training, skills and capacity
- Transparency
- Trust in institutions and corporations
- Value chain sustainability and responsible sourcing
- Waste management (excluding tailings and waste rock)
- Water stewardship
- Workforce inclusion and diversity
- Workforce health and wellbeing
- Workforce safety.

Of the issues listed above, the issues shown below were identified as the most material issues identified through our FY2021 materiality assessment. These issues are the areas of focus for our sustainability disclosures in our Annual Report 2021. Refer to the section reference in the below table for where our most material sustainability issues are covered in the Annual Report 2021.

EXHIBIT 1 Material sustainability issues

Employees	Environmental matters	Social matters and human rights	Anti-corruption and anti-bribery matters	Other
People and culture Refer to section 1.12 Workforce safety Refer to section 1.13.4 Workforce health Refer to section 1.13.5	Climate change Refer to section 1.13.7 Portfolio resilience to climate change Refer to section 1.13.7 Water Refer to section 1.13.13 Environment Refer to section 1.13.12 Land and biodiversity Refer to section 1.13.14	Indigenous peoples Refer to section 1.13.10 Human rights Refer to section 1.13.9 Local community engagement Refer to section 1.13.8 Community livelihoods and social investment Refer to section 1.13.11	Ethics and business conduct Refer to section 1.13.6 Our conduct Refer to section 2.1.15	Critical incident risk management Refer to sections 1.9 and 1.15 Tailings, tailings storage facilities (TSF) Refer to section 1.13.15 Compliance with laws and regulation Refer to sections 2.3.17 and 4.8.2 Sustainability governance Refer to section 2.1.11

Employees	Environmental matters	Social matters and human rights	Anti-corruption and anti-bribery matters	Other
Policies and standards available online[2]				
Our Code of Conduct *Our Requirements for Safety* standard *Our Requirements for Health* standard	*Our Requirements for Environment and Climate Change* standard Water Stewardship Position Statement Climate Change Position Statement	Our Requirements for Community Human Rights Policy Statement Indigenous Peoples Policy Statement Indigenous Peoples Strategy	*Our Code of Conduct* *Our Requirements for Supply (Minimum requirements for suppliers)* standard	*Our Charter* Sustainability Committee Terms of Reference Tailings Storage Facility Policy Statement
Principal risks that have key links to the matters mentioned above[3]				
Operational events Refer to section 1.16 Inadequate business resilience Refer to section 1.16	Significant social or environmental impacts Refer to section 1.16 Low-carbon transition Refer to section 1.16 Inadequate business resilience Refer to section 1.16	Significant social or environmental impacts Refer to section 1.16	Ethical misconduct Refer to section 1.16	Operational events Refer to section 1.16 Ethical misconduct Refer to section 1.16
Non-financial key performance indicators *Refer to section 1.13.3, for details of our key performance indicators. In addition, details of our sustainability performance metrics can be found in the sections referred to below.*				
People performance data Refer to section 4.8.1 Health and safety performance data Refer to section 4.8.2	Environment performance Refer to data section 4.8.4 Climate change performance data Refer to section 4.8.5 Water performance data Refer to section 4.8.6	Society performance data Refer to section 4.8.3	Ethics and business conduct Refer to section 1.13.6	Our sustainability performance: Non-financial KPIs Refer to section 1.13.3

[1] We comply with the Non-financial Reporting Directive requirements and therefore report sustainability matters from sections 414CA and 414CB of the UK *Companies Act 2006*. This table sets out where relevant information is located in this Annual Report.

[2] Although these standards are for internal use, we have made the HSEC-related elements of several of the Our Requirements standards and related documents publicly available at bhp.com.

[3] For further information on BHP's principal risks, refer to section 1.16.

Source: BHP Annual Report (2021), https://www.bhp.com/investors/annual-reporting/annual-report-2021, p. 33

One last issue we can raise is that the way in which a manager's considerations of *why* and *who* will influence *what* is disclosed will also be affected by whether the information being disclosed is fundamentally balanced (reliable), or whether it is merely information of a predominantly favourable or positive nature (and therefore biased). If the answer to *why* the information is being disclosed is that the choice is influenced by perceived business benefits, and *who* the information is to be reported to is restricted to powerful stakeholders, then when prioritising the information to be reported, managers might choose to report only those items of information which project the organisation in a favourable way. Such a strategy would result in the information not meeting the qualitative characteristic of reliability, as previously discussed. While qualitative characteristics such as reliability and relevance are those that accounting information should ideally attain, in practice, not all accounting information will meet these attributes.

How should the information be disclosed?

Once an organisation has identified *why* it is collecting and disclosing information (or accounts) about particular aspects of its performance, *who* are the stakeholders to whom the disclosures will be directed, and *what* types of information will be collected and disclosures made to stakeholders outside the organisation, it will then be in a position to answer the fourth question in our accountability model: *How* should the information be disclosed? For example, what should be the format and media of the disclosures/accounts?

To understand how information should be disclosed, we need to determine if an appropriate reporting framework exists, and where the related information should be disclosed.

Reporting frameworks

Various **reporting frameworks** and conventions are available that address different aspects of performance, such as an organisation's:

- financial performance
- environmental performance
- social performance.

reporting framework A standardised format for presenting accounting information

For example, if we are providing information about the financial performance of a large company, then we might elect to use the International Financial Reporting Standards issued by the IASB. Or if we are providing information about social or environmental performance, then we might use the framework provided by the GRI or the TCFD. If we are particularly concerned about providing information about carbon emissions, then we might use the framework developed by the Greenhouse Gas Protocol (GHGP). Alternatively, if we are concerned about providing information about our water use, then we might use the standards developed within Australia by the Water Accounting Standards Board (WASB). We will consider some of these reporting frameworks in other chapters of this book.

We could give many more examples of reporting frameworks, but what we are trying to emphasise here is that many reporting frameworks are available for reporting different aspects of organisational performance. We will also need to consider whether our targeted stakeholders will be able to actually understand the information being generated by the different reporting frameworks (remember, *understandability* was one of the qualitative characteristics of useful information discussed earlier). If not, or if we think the available frameworks are not meeting the demands or needs of the stakeholders, then we might devise our own reporting frameworks.

Where to disclose

Apart from considering which reporting frameworks might be appropriate, we also need to consider where the information should be disclosed. For example, should it be provided on corporate websites, or within reports mailed to stakeholders, or by way of posters put up within particular buildings? There are indeed many choices with regards to the best media to make information (or accounts) available to interested stakeholders.

As an example, if we are dealing with stakeholders with knowledge of and access to the Internet, then it is quite reasonable to supply the required accounting information on the organisation's website. However, if the stakeholders are, for example, employees working within factories in developing countries, then it might be more appropriate to provide the information by way of posters on factory walls or printed documents. You can see that in this fourth step of our accountability model, there are many judgements to be made.

Learning exercise 1.8 will now further consider how each of the four steps in our accountability model relate to each other.

1.8 Learning Exercise

The four-step accountability model

We have discussed the four steps within our accountability model, being:

- why report
- whom to report to
- what to report
- how to report.

Let us now consider how these four steps relate to each other, in particular how the response to each step impacts the response to the subsequent step, as evidenced in **Figure 1.4**.

Let us start with the first step in the model. If your response to the issue *why report* is that you believe you have a primary duty (responsibility) to your shareholders/investors to maximise their wealth, then perhaps the answer to *whom to report to* will be investors.

Once you have identified investors as the target of your reporting, then you can ask them *what* types of information they want. Based on who you are reporting to (investors in this case), it would more likely be information about various aspects of financial performance.

If it is determined that the investors only want information about financial performance, then in terms of *how* this information will be presented, would be by using a financial reporting framework which relies upon various accounting standards. Since investors would be expected to have access to the Internet, the financial reports would typically be made available on your organisation's website.

Real-world examples of our accountability model

Having explored our accountability model, with its four separate steps, we can now briefly consider some real-world examples of how large organisations have identified their stakeholders, the information requirements or demands of those stakeholders, and how these have been satisfied.

Previously (see **Exhibit 1**) we provided information about the processes BHP – the large global mining company – undertook to understand the expectations of stakeholders. This explanation from BHP explained why certain sustainability-related disclosures were included within the BHP 2021 Annual Report (**www.bhp.com**, accessed October 2021). Because such disclosures are being made voluntarily, disclosures such as these made by BHP allow the report readers to understand the context, or logic, of particular disclosures.

In terms of how the company identifies and communicates with its stakeholders, the following information is also provided by BHP in its 2021 Annual Report. What should be obvious from the following extract is that there is a variety of media that can be used to provide different accounts to different stakeholder groups.

> **Our stakeholders**
>
> As a global company, we interact with a range of stakeholders. Our methods, frequency of engaging with and approach to listening to stakeholders are diverse and we use a

range of formal and informal communication and engagement channels to understand the views of our stakeholders:

- Globally, we communicate and engage with external stakeholders via our Annual General Meetings, Group publications (including the Annual Report and other topic-specific reports), our website and our social media platforms, releases to the market and media, brand campaigns, analyst briefings, speeches and interviews with senior executives and investor round tables.
- At a regional and local level, each operated asset is required to plan, implement and document stakeholder engagement activities. This includes engagement via community forums, newsletters, reports, community perception surveys and consultation groups, implementing community complaint and grievance mechanisms, representation on specific industry association committees and initiatives, and engagement to develop social and environmental programs. We also engage on sustainability issues with a broader range of stakeholders, including local governments, non-government organisations (NGOs), schools and universities and others.
- Within our business, we engage with our people (employees and contractors) via tailored internal channels. These channels include our intranet, email and newsletters, town hall meetings and by inviting feedback and comment through Engagement and Perception Surveys. Key internal announcements and videos are made available in English and Spanish.

EXHIBIT 2 Sustainability – Stakeholders

Stakeholder	Interest	How we engage
Customers		
Broad customer base, geographically dispersed across multiple commodities.	Sales agreements; product quality; performance and price; environmental laws and regulations; sustainability metrics and performance; alignment with regional regulations.	Regular engagement according to commodity, sector and geography to understand our customers' needs and determine optimal product placement; participation in relevant industry associations and conferences; and establishing partnerships and collaboration in areas of mutual interest such as supply chain innovation and sustainability.
Employees		
Our global workforce of more than 80 000 employees and contractors.	Group financial and sustainability performance; health and safety; our work with communities; working conditions; mental health and wellbeing; inclusion and diversity; external factors such as COVID-19; development opportunities; proposed changes to our operated assets or practices.	Regular communication through tailored internal channels which include our intranet; email and newsletters; town hall meetings; toolbox talks; field leadership activities; ongoing dialogue between leaders and teams; HSEC Awards; and through our Engagement and Perception Surveys.
Host Governments		
National, regional or state level and local governments in the countries where we have a presence.	Fiscal and tax arrangements; global trade systems; labour relations and employment practices; supplier payment arrangements; environmental laws, regulations and project approvals; mineral and petroleum royalties; local infrastructure; and community wellbeing.	Direct Group engagement at all levels of government, as well as participation in industry associations where relevant to national (or international), regional / state or local issues.

Stakeholder	Interest	How we engage
Indigenous peoples		
A broad spectrum of Indigenous communities including Traditional Owner groups in Australia.	Environmental and social or cultural impacts associated with our operated assets; cultural heritage; opportunities for social investment; local employment, local suppliers and business creation; improved community engagement mechanisms; and environmental performance.	Community engagement and participation in BHP activities; consultation, negotiation and agreement-making processes; work and local supply opportunities; social investment; preserving cultural heritage; targeted communications, community perception surveys.
Industry peers and associations		
Commodity-specific associations, as well as sector-specific associations, at regional, national and international levels.	Diverse range of issues associated with the resources sector or specific commodities; issues include the environment; health and safety; communities; skills and training and economic policy.	Representation on specific committees and engagement on specific projects with industry associations, to develop guidelines, standards and programs, agree advocacy priorities and share best practices.
Investment community		
Debt and equity analysts, ESG analysts and corporate governance analysts.	Alignment of our performance with shareholder interests, including good financial returns; strong governance and expectations of strong performance; and consideration of financial and non-financial risk.	Regular communication through analyst briefings on key issues, exchange releases, sharing Group publications such as Annual Reports and Operational Reviews; participation in external benchmarking initiatives.
Labour unions		
Labour unions represented at many of our operated assets.	Workers' rights and interests; freedom of association and collective bargaining; health and safety; remuneration; working hours; roster arrangements; risk management.	Direct communication as required; respecting the right to freedom of association.
Local communities		
A broad spectrum of local communities with interests and concerns.	Environmental, economic and social impacts associated with our operated assets; opportunities for social investment; local employment, local suppliers and business creation; support for social infrastructure and programs; improved community engagement mechanisms; and environmental performance.	Community consultation, engagement and participation in BHP activities; work and local supply opportunities; social investment; targeted communications, community perception surveys.
Media		
Representatives from print, online, broadcast and social media.	Broad range of issues reflecting diverse stakeholder interests.	Media releases, briefings, presentations and interviews; publicly available information (Annual Report and other topic-specific reports, our website; linkedin.com/company/bhp; youtube.com/bhp; twitter.com/bhp).
Non-government organisations (NGOs) and civil society		
Environmental, social and human rights organisations at local, national and international levels.	Ethical, social and environmental performance of our operated assets, proposed operated assets, or closed operated assets; governance mechanisms, risk management; complaint and grievance mechanisms and remedy; transparency; practices to respect human rights; social investment; non-operated joint ventures; social and environmental impacts.	Local engagement through each operated asset's stakeholder engagement plan; regular engagement at the Group level with relevant national and international organisations, various multi-stakeholder initiatives and partnerships, and through the BHP Forum for Corporate Responsibility.

Stakeholder	Interest	How we engage
Shareholders		
A diverse group who have invested in our business, with significant representation in Australasia, UK, Europe, South Africa and North America.	Creation of long-term shareholder value through consistent financial returns and good governance. Ensuring high-quality governance and maintaining focus on continuous improvement and understanding shareholder concerns.	Annual General Meetings; publicly available information (Annual Report and other topic-specific reports, our website); regular meetings with institutional shareholders and investor representatives; investment and community presentations.
Society partners		
Public or private organisations we partner with on specific projects to benefit society, the communities where we operate or the environment.	Ethical, social and environmental performance of our operated assets, proposed operated assets, or closed operated assets; governance mechanisms, risk management.	Boards and operating committees; publicly available information (Annual Report and other topic-specific reports, our website); regular engagement at both the Group and local / regional levels.
Suppliers		
Businesses local to our operated assets (including local Indigenous suppliers), as well as national and multinational suppliers, including maritime vessel charterers.	Procurement, Inbound Marketing Procurement and charter party agreements, payments and minimum supplier requirements, safety standards.	Regular engagement throughout the supplier life cycle determined according to supplier segmentation and risk including with respect to health, safety environment and community; modern slavery; transparency; inclusion and diversity; and business conduct more broadly.

Source: BHP (2021), https://www.bhp.com/materialityassessment

We can also consider statements made by the global sportswear company Nike in its 2020 Nike Inc Impact Report. The following extract emphasises how important it is to engage stakeholders to help ensure that the information they want or need is actually being provided. Of course, not all such information needs can be met, meaning that the disclosure of some information must be prioritised over that of other information.

> This year, we refreshed the list of priority issues to be more inclusive of the evolving environmental and political landscape that we, and all companies, face. It was also driven by a moment of reflection for the company as we closed down one set of targets and established new five-year corporate targets. Updating the list allowed us to expand the scope of issues, but made it harder to track issue importance year-over-year. We learn, grow, and refresh our perspective by considering the global view of our internal and external stakeholders.
>
> As we did last year, we surveyed employees, NGOs, academics, suppliers, and corporate peers to determine the most relevant issues for our company and the impacts most directly linked to those issues. We combined this survey information with peer disclosure benchmarking, government regulations, and analysis of online news and social trends to create a more nuanced understanding of priority issues. We did this through Datamaran, a digital tool that uses real-time data and artificial intelligence to track issue relevance over time and integrate results into strategic discussions. The combination of stakeholder responses and Datamaran insights produced our FY20 list of 14 essential priority issues.
>
> 1 GHG emissions
> 2 Product design and circularity
> 3 Climate change adaptation
> 4 Labour rights in supply chain

5 Employee diversity, equity, and inclusion
6 Material waste
7 Materials sourcing
8 Supply chain management and transparency
9 Health and safety in the supply chain
10 Forced labour
11 Ethical and transparent business practices
12 Renewables and energy use
13 Employee health and safety
14 Air and water pollution

Source: FY20 NIKE, Inc. Impact Report, BREAKING BARRIERS, p. 101.

It is important to understand the reason why an organisation voluntarily elects to produce particular information. In the case of the organisations we have just considered (BHP and Nike), they have made it fairly clear that certain information has been produced because of specific demands from particular stakeholders. Also, the organisations would seem to have an objective of attending to, or managing, many issues that have been identified as being of concern to specific stakeholders, and to provide an account of the success of its management efforts.

The above extracts from the reports of BHP and Nike reinforce much of the discussion in this chapter. They support our argument that managers of organisations will seek, through various forms of engagement, to determine which stakeholders are impacted by their operations, the types of information such stakeholders would like to receive, and the format or media in which they would like to receive the information. This is a very important aspect of managing an organisation.

The influence of organisational objectives on accounting

organisational objectives An organisation's primary aims

It should be clear by now that an **organisation's objectives** will also influence how it does its accounting. If an organisation's primary objective is to maximise profits, then the accounting/reporting will tend to fixate on financial measures. If an organisation has the objective of reducing its greenhouse gas emissions, then the accounting/reporting will focus on improvements in emissions, targets, and so forth.

If a university has the goal of increasing its research publications, then this will impact what information is collected and what accounts are generated. Information about who is and who isn't generating publications will be gathered, as will publication rates by other universities as a means of comparison (benchmarking). The amounts being spent on initiatives to support publishing will also be collected. Relatedly, if the university has the goal of making sure its students like the lecturers' way of teaching, then it will collect information from students about their assessments of the lecturers. This is all considered accounting.

Many more examples could be provided here, but the point is that just as assessments of organisational responsibilities and accountabilities influence the practice of accounting, so will the objectives of an organisation influence the types of accounting being practised.

We imagine that there will also be some form of relationship between organisational objectives and the responsibilities and accountabilities the organisation accepts. For example, if a not-for-profit organisation is established to provide emergency housing for homeless people, then its objectives will tend to focus on helping disadvantaged people in the community and ensuring that the funds provided to the organisation are used as efficiently as possible to create the greatest benefit to the homeless, rather than simply being used to maximise profits. The main accounts would probably provide information about how quickly people are being housed, how many were housed, how many could not be housed, where they were housed, what negative impacts flowed to nearby residents, and so forth. The key responsibilities and accountabilities would seem to be to funding bodies, the homeless, and those interest groups which work for the benefit of the homeless. This example emphasises again that how we do accounting will be impacted by an organisation's objectives, as well as by the responsibilities and accountabilities that the managers within the organisation accept.

Source: Newspix/Mike Burton

A not-for-profit organisation's reports will likely seek to highlight measures of performance that relate to its objectives and mission, rather than its financial performance.

Why do I need to know the logic associated with the four-step accountability model?

Managers have a great deal of choice when it comes to producing reports and making them publicly available. While some reporting is legally required, many of the reports managers produce are voluntary.

The four-step accountability model helps to explain why the managers have chosen to produce particular accounts.

By applying the model to explain past or proposed reporting practices, we are able to understand that the question of 'why' management is reporting has implications for each of the next three steps (to whom, what, and how). The stakeholders to whom reports are directed are linked to the motivation that drove managers to report in the first place. The 'to whom to report' issue is very much linked to 'why' they decided to report.

The targeted audiences of the disclosures will also help us to place into context what has been disclosed by the managers. Our model explains the link between the issues of to whom to report, and what to report.

'How' we report can only be logically determined once we have considered to whom we are reporting, and what we are reporting. Depending on what we are reporting, we will need to use various reporting frameworks. For example, the managers of a particular organisation might be reporting (the 'why') because they believe they have an accountability to impacted stakeholders, including nearby communities (the 'who'), for their environmental impacts. Through stakeholder engagement it has been determined that the organisation's water usage (the 'what') is a key concern of nearby communities, and the organisation has decided to use a water reporting framework developed by a standard setter known as the Water Accounting Standards Board to measure and report water usage (the 'how').

In summary, our four-step accountability model hopefully allows us to make sense of what managers are reporting, or can also be used to guide us through the steps we need to consider when we are compiling reports.

LO1.7 The changing role of accountants

With time, the perspective on what an accountant does, or should do, has changed quite dramatically, and it will continue to change and evolve. Traditionally, an accountant was primarily considered to have the role of managing and reporting information about the financial performance and position of an organisation, but it is now much more than this.

As expectations of the role of organisations change, what the accountant does must also change. An accountant's job is very interesting and challenging and requires clear, innovative and creative thinking. For example, as different stakeholders have become more and more concerned about the social and environmental performance of an organisation, the accountant has needed to develop skills in this area, and the profession has needed to ensure this becomes part of their members' knowledge requirements. With growing concern about climate change, many organisations are now required to produce information about their carbon emissions, and particular accounting techniques have been developed to measure them. Years ago there was no such carbon accounting.

The drivers of change in accounting

In terms of the drivers of change for the accounting profession, the Association of Chartered Certified Accountants (ACCA) released an interesting report in June 2016 entitled *Professional accountants – the future: Drivers of change and future skills*, in which it noted the following:

- Professional accountants must be able to meet current needs and also anticipate emerging demands. Accountants need to be adaptive.
- The expert use of analytics will enable more, better, and closer-to-real-time reporting; increase predictive analysis; and highlight the interconnectedness of financial and non-financial performance.
- The continued globalisation of markets and organisations will present opportunities and challenges to those in and around the accounting profession.
- The adoption of *cloud computing* – where accounting-related software is held on remote servers which then process and return data to an organisation – will have a large impact on organisations, and therefore on accountants, in terms of the security of the data as well as how the data is processed.
- Different aspirations and expectations of coming generations will affect the practice and focus of accounting.
- There will be greater levels of outsourcing which will create further monitoring, reporting and governance requirements throughout supply chains.
- The emergence of a cashless society will create many issues for accountants.
- Integrated reporting – reports which combine information about financial, social and environmental performance – is expected to become mandatory throughout the world and thereby needs a response from accountants.
- The evolution of various forms of social media will impact accounting.

Accounting is expected to continually change as the expectations and values of society change, and as technology changes. Accounting – and accounting education – must necessarily continue to evolve.

Learning exercise 1.9 explores how the training of accountants has evolved across time as expectations held within society about the responsibility of organisations has also evolved.

1.9 Learning Exercise

Changing corporate accountability

Increasingly, the accounting programs being taught by universities delve into how organisations might account for the various social and environmental impacts caused by their operations. However, two decades ago it would have been extremely uncommon for an accounting program to consider, in any real detail, how to account for such impacts. So what has influenced this change?

Accounting is an ever-evolving process. As community expectations about how organisations should operate change, accounting and accounting education practices will also typically change.

Communities now seem to be very much more focused on the social and environmental impacts of organisations, and they expect organisations to be socially and environmentally responsible. The managers of organisations know that, as time goes by, organisations have to continually improve their social and environmental reporting practices, and universities have begun to respond to this change.

In terms of whether an accounting program should teach students how to do social and environmental accounting, this is a matter of opinion. If we accept that organisations should be accountable for their social and environmental performance, then accounting programs should arguably provide education and training in this area.

You might like to investigate the extent of social and environmental accounting included in the educational program that you are currently enrolled within.

LO1.8 Accounting as both a technical and social practice

Accounting can be a very technical practice, with quite detailed rules about how particular aspects of performance, or particular resources, are to be measured and reported. For example, large organisations are typically required to prepare financial statements that comply with various corporations law stipulations and accounting standards – some of which can be quite complicated. If the organisation is listed on a **securities exchange**, then it might have further accounting requirements that need to be addressed as part of the securities exchange listing. The rules embodied within various financial accounting requirements can be very detailed, and years of education are required to understand how to fully comprehend and prepare financial statements. Those students pursuing a degree specialising in accounting will learn many technical requirements in relation to how to record particular types of transactions and events.

securities exchange A specialised financial marketplace for the buying and selling of securities such as shares and bonds, which has specific rules for how share-trading organisations must maintain and report information

Other forms of accounting that address aspects of an organisation's social and environmental performance can also be very technical. In many countries, there are government bodies that have developed water accounting standards, which explain how to prepare and present reports involving the recognition, quantification, presentation and disclosure of particular items relating to water use. Many countries also require particular measurement practices to be used by large organisations regarding the greenhouse gas emissions that have been generated as a result of their operations. Approaches to accounting for occupational health and safety, which relate to a component of an organisation's social performance, can also be very technical in nature, with different forms of injury being defined and measured in specific ways.

Of course, while the processes involved in collecting and reporting various aspects of an organisation's performance – be it financial, environmental or social – can be very technical in nature, the way in which the readers of the various accounts use the data can ultimately generate various social impacts. Various people throughout society use accounting reports to make decisions. If this was not the case, then preparing the reports would fundamentally be a waste of time. And the decisions the account readers will make, such as whether they will continue to support an organisation, can have various social implications.

Key concept

Preparing reports is a *technical* practice with *social* implications, as stakeholders will use an organisation's reports to make decisions about whether to continue to support the organisation.

For example, users of financial statements will make various decisions on the basis of the information they contain. Investors or lenders might decide to provide more funding to an organisation if the financial accounts indicate it is performing well. Such funds will then be used by the firm in a variety of ways, which might lead to greater employment of people by the organisation or its suppliers, greater payments of taxes, and so forth – all of which provides positive benefits for various members of society. Conversely, if the financial accounts show that the firm is performing poorly, then the funds being advanced to it might decline, which could generate a variety of negative social impacts (for example, people losing their jobs because the organisation is perceived as no longer being able to pay wages).

The environmental accounts being generated by an organisation might show that an organisation is producing excessive amounts of greenhouse gases or other waste, or is using excessive amounts of water. This might cause various stakeholders, such as lenders or customers, to no longer want to support the organisation and could also lead to a loss of employment for various staff. However, if people decide to shift support away from the highly polluting organisation as a result of the information they have been provided with, then this could also have positive social and environmental effects, as a result of the reduction in pollution. By being provided with information, the account readers effectively are given the power to make informed choices which can in turn create social and environmental impacts.

Similarly, an organisation might produce accounts that show that many of its employees have suffered various forms of workplace accident, leading to reduced support for the organisation, which in turn could have a number of social and financial implications – some positive and some negative.

There can also be interactions between the various measures of performance. For example, a highly polluting company might be generating very high profits, as evidenced by the results presented in its financial accounts. Investors who prioritise financial performance above other aspects of performance might invest further funds in this company, thereby leading to even greater pollution and the adverse social and environmental implications with which that is associated. However, at the same time, this might create greater employment, which would create some positive social impacts.

While much of the discussion above refers to social impacts that might arise as a result of different stakeholders using the information prepared by an organisation, the very act of recording and reporting particular information can also affect the behaviour of the organisation, and this can have social impacts. For example, if an organisation knows that, in the near future, it will be required to report information about the treatment of the workers in its supply chain, then this may prompt the managers to switch suppliers and use a more ethical supply chain. Therefore, the social impacts can actually occur before the information is even reported. (For those readers who are interested, information about measurement and reporting modern slavery laws which will require disclosures about the treatment of employees within supply factories in developing countries can be found in a 2017 article by Christ, Burritt and Rao – see the 'References' section at the end of this chapter).

What is being emphasised here is that, while the preparation of various financial, social and environmental accounts might be a fairly technical activity, with a reliance on various frameworks which themselves can be quite complicated, the users/readers of those accounts will make various decisions which in turn could have a variety of social and environmental implications. Therefore, with this in mind, we will be emphasising throughout this book that accounting is both a technical *and* social practice.

Throughout society, many people make decisions on the basis of accounting reports, and these decisions in turn have many social (and environmental) implications. Because accountants provide information to allow others to make informed choices, and because these choices will have a variety of social and environmental impacts, accountants themselves can be considered to be very important, and indeed very powerful, members of society. Who knew?

Why do I need to know that accounting is both a technical and social practice?

In our professional careers we need to remember that good quality accounting information (which would therefore satisfy the qualitative characteristics of useful information as discussed earlier in this chapter) provides power to the readers of the reports to make informed choices. These choices will likely have subsequent impacts which can be social and/or environmental in nature.

Disclosure decisions should incorporate considerations of the costs and benefits that will likely flow from disclosures. When considering the costs and benefits of particular disclosures, we need to remember that accounting informs decisions, and these decisions will likely divert resources to particular activities which might in turn generate a myriad of social and environmental impacts which are hopefully positive.

Accounting plays a vital role in society and through making organisations accountable for their activities, accounting is central to moving us towards good social and environmental outcomes. Accounting, while often very technical in its application, is therefore very much a social practice. For example, accounting for greenhouse gas emissions is a very technical exercise particularly if the emissions are classified into Scope 1, Scope 2 and Scope 3 emissions (as is required by various governments). If this information is then used by stakeholders to enable them to choose less polluting organisations to buy from, then this conceivably can lead to a reduction in total pollution with various associated social benefits for current and future generations.

STUDY TOOLS

SUMMARY

This chapter has provided an introduction to accounting. In doing so, it has embraced a broad perspective in which accounting is described as a process linked to considerations of an organisation's responsibilities and accountabilities. We have learned that accounting information – which can be used by people both outside and inside an organisation – can relate to various aspects of an organisation's financial, social and environmental performance. The qualitative characteristics that useful accounting information will possess – which we described as relating to relevance and reliability, together with considerations of comparability, verifiability, timeliness, and understandability – were also identified and explained.

To explain the process of accounting, we introduced a four-step accountability model which highlighted the linkage between four key issues: Why should an organisation report? To whom should an organisation report? What should an organisation report? And how should an organisation report? We learned that there are various reasons as to why an organisation might elect to collect and report particular information, and that this in turn will impact to whom the organisation is reporting, what it is reporting, and how it is reporting.

We also learned that, as community expectations change in relation to the responsibilities of organisations, accounting will also evolve to reflect those changing expectations. Changes in the way markets are organised (for example, greater globalisation and greater outsourcing) and in how members of society interact (for example, evolving social media and an increasing reliance on cashless transactions) will also lead to changes in how accounting is undertaken.

The chapter concluded by emphasising that accounting is both a technical and social practice. Undertaking accounting requires knowledge of many measurement and reporting frameworks, a number of which are very technical in nature. And the ways in which the various accounts are used by different stakeholders, in terms of the decisions they make, in turn has a host of social and environmental implications. As such, accounting is correctly described as both a technical and social practice.

ANSWERS TO THE OPENING QUESTIONS

At the beginning of the chapter we asked the following five questions. As a result of reading this chapter, you should now be able to provide informed answers to these questions – ours are shown below.

1 What aspects of an organisation's performance are measured by accounting?

We can account for various aspects of an organisation's performance which can be financial, social and/or environmental in nature.

2 What factors are likely to influence the types of accounts being presented by an organisation?

The types of accounts being presented will be influenced by the perceptions of organisational responsibilities held by people within and external to the organisation. That is, if managers believe they have responsibility for particular actions or outcomes, then they are likely to provide related accounts. As stakeholder expectations change concerning corporate responsibilities, this can create pressure on organisations to change the way they account for particular aspects of performance. Legal requirements also influence what accounts are prepared.

3 Who are the users of accounting reports?

A multitude of stakeholders will have an interest in the operations of an organisation, and therefore the audience of accounting can potentially be very large and varied. For example, managers need reports to manage an organisation; owners need reports in order to assess whether the organisation is operating in the manner they expect; employees need reports to assess the security of their employment, as well as to monitor whether the organisation is performing in a manner consistent with their own values; local communities will want reports in order to assess the local impact of the organisation; government will need reports in order to determine tax payments; and so forth. There are many diverse groups throughout society that have an interest in how an organisation is operating.

4 Is accounting likely to be at all interesting?

This is obviously a matter of opinion, but hopefully as a result of reading this chapter, you will answer a resounding YES!! Please consider how your answer to this question might have changed due to you reading this chapter.

5 Is accounting really that relevant to many people in society, other than perhaps shareholders (or the owners of an organisation) and managers?

Accounting is relevant to everybody! All organisations provide some form of accounts of various aspects of their performance, and throughout our lifetimes we will make great use of a variety of these accounting reports. To make informed decisions about whether we will support particular organisations (working for them, investing in them, buying from them) requires information, and it is the role of accounting to provide it.

SELF-TEST QUIZ

Answers to this quiz appear in the Appendix of this book.

1 What is the order of sequence in our four-step accountability model?
   - a What to report, why report, how to report, when to report
   - b To whom to report, why report, what to report, how to report
   - c How to report, what to report, why to report, to whom to report
   - d Why report, to whom to report, what to report, how to report
   - e Why report, to whom to report, how to report, what to report

2 What are the most important, or fundamental, characteristics that useful information possesses?
   - a Information is reported in monetary terms, and is audited
   - b Relevance and reliability
   - c Timeliness and understandability
   - d Can predict future profits, is prepared by experts
   - e Understandability, timeliness, verifiability

3 To enhance the usefulness of information, apart from the two fundamental qualitative characteristics, there are also other important characteristics of useful information. These are:
   - a Monetary calculation, profit-related, future oriented
   - b Comparability, verifiability, understandability, timeliness
   - c Nice presentation, clear, concise
   - d Colourful, interesting, current
   - e Profits, assets, liabilities

4 Which of the following statements are true?
   a The broader the managers' views of organisational responsibilities, the broader the range of 'accounts' that will be prepared by the managers
   b Accounting can be described as both a technical practice and a social practice
   c As an accountant, we will use a variety of reporting frameworks
   d Accounting has evolved over the years as perceptions of organisational accountability have evolved
   e All of these choices

5 A stakeholder can best be defined as:
   a Somebody who has a financial investment in the organisation
   b Any group or individual who can affect the organisation, or is affected by the organisation
   c Somebody who acquires merchandise from the organisation
   d Future generations
   e The community

ONLINE RESOURCES

Accompanying the book is an innovative online case study that follows an organisation initially established by two friends, which grows into a large and successful company. Acquire this chapter's case study from your instructor.

CASE STUDY

Armadillo Surf Designs: An eventful start

The team at Armadillo Surf Designs (ASD) are busy as they begin to implement their marketing plan. As part of this plan, they are sponsoring their first promotional event, which is a beach 'clean-up' at some of the local surf beaches. They are also busy with human resources (HR) and logistics matters too. They have just employed their first staff member and are looking for a warehouse space to rent.

Identify ASD's stakeholders and consider the information that ASD might provide now and in the future. Discuss ways that ASD can ensure that the information reported in relation to the beach 'clean-up' meets the qualitative characteristics required of useful information.

END-OF-CHAPTER QUESTIONS

1.1 What is accounting?

1.2 What is the role of accounting?

1.3 Provide two examples of how the use of accounting reports might create social impacts.

1.4 Does accounting generate accounts that only provide information that is measured in financial terms?

1.5 Do you think that organisations should provide information about any significant environmental impacts caused by their operations? Who should be able to receive such information?

1.6 Have you been the recipient of an organisational account recently? What was the organisation, and what was the nature of the account?

1.7 What qualitative characteristics should information have for it to be useful for making informed decisions?

1.8 Is it more important for information to be relevant than it is for it to be reliable?

1.9 Why do you think that accountants can justifiably be described as very powerful members of society?

1.10 Who is a stakeholder of an organisation, and why might this be of relevance to the practice of accounting?

1.11 Identify five organisations in which you consider yourself to be a stakeholder.

1.12 Who would be the stakeholders of a public university?

1.13 Would all managers identify the same people as being stakeholders?

1.14 Should the 'environment' or 'future generations' be considered as stakeholders of an organisation?

1.15 Provide two examples of:

- a financial information an organisation might disclose
- b social information an organisation might disclose
- c environmental information an organisation might disclose.

1.16 Assuming that you are the general manager of a mining company, please provide answers to the following questions:

- a How would you determine who were the company's stakeholders?
- b How would you decide what information to collect and report?

1.17 What does the term 'accountability' mean?

1.18 Explain the relationship between an organisation's responsibilities, its accountabilities and its accounting.

1.19 How would you determine which stakeholders of an organisation should be provided with information about the organisation?

1.20 Would we expect all organisations within the same industry to produce the same accounts? Why?

1.21 Explain why accounting might be considered to be both a technical and social practice.

1.22 Some people say that 'information provides power'. What might this mean?

1.23 An organisation produces financial reports that show it has made significant losses and appears to be in a position where it might not be able to pay some of its debts when they become due for payment. What social consequences might arise following the public release of these reports?

1.24 We have noted in this chapter that different managers might have different perspectives on organisational responsibilities, and that this in turn will influence the types of accounts they might choose to present to stakeholders. Provide some possible reasons as to why different managers will have different views about organisational responsibilities.

1.25 If you were a senior manager within an organisation, what factors would you consider when determining what information to collect about your organisation's performance?

1.26 Why would we expect the practice of accounting to evolve and change across time?

1.27 What are some of the reasons why an organisation might produce particular accounts and how would these in turn impact:

- a who the organisation is reporting to
- b what the organisation is reporting
- c the selected media of the reporting?

1.28 If you were in charge of a university:

a To whom do you think you should provide accounts?

b What might those accounts disclose?

c Where would you make those accounts available?

1.29 If you were a shareholder of a bank:

a What information about the bank would you want?

b Do you think the bank would disclose your desired information? Why?

1.30 As social media has changed, do you think this has affected the types of information being disclosed by companies? Why?

1.31 If we were to embrace the same view of organisations' responsibilities as Milton Friedman, then in what circumstances would you disclose information about the social and environmental performance of an organisation?

1.32 Residents who live close to an airport are often believed to have been conditioned to the noise of aircraft. However, a BBC News report in 2016 revealed that one study that researched 3.6 million people who lived near London's Heathrow Airport found that these people had a 10–20 per cent higher than average risk of suffering heart disease, stroke and circulatory disease. Should Heathrow Airport provide a publicly available account of the noise being generated by the airport, the efforts being taken to reduce noise, and the health effects that could be associated with noise pollution? What is the basis of your argument?

REFERENCES

AccountAbility (2008). AA1000 AccountAbility Principles Standard. www.accountability.org/standards

Association of Chartered Certified Accountants (2016). *Professional accountants – the future: Drivers of change and future skills.* www.accaglobal.com/content/dam/members-beta/docs/ea-patfdrivers-of-change-and-future-skills.pdf

Barton, A. D. (2006). Public sector accountability and commercial-in-confidence outsourcing contracts. *Accounting, Auditing & Accountability Journal*, 19(2), pp. 256–71.

BHP (2021). Annual Report. https://www.bhp.com/investors/annual-reporting/annual-report-2021.

BHP (2021). Sustainability Approach. https://www.bhp.com/materialityassessment.

Birt, J., Chalmers, K., Maloney, B., Brooks, A., & Oliver, J. (2018). *Accounting: Business Reporting for Decision Making* (6th edition). Sydney: Wiley.

BusinessDictionary (2017). Accountability. www.businessdictionary.com/definition/accountability.html

Chamberlain, G. (2011). Disney factory faces probe into sweatshop suicide claims. *The Guardian*, 28 August. www.guardian.co.uk/law/2011/aug/27/disney-factory-sweatshop-suicide-claims

Christ, K., Burritt, R., & Rao, K. (2017). Modern slavery and how accountants can fight it. *Acuity Magazine*, 21 August. www.acuitymag.com/business/how-modern-slavery-impacts-big-brands-and-accountants

Deegan, C., & Blomquist, C. (2006). Stakeholder influence on corporate reporting: An exploration of the interaction between WWF-Australia and the Australian Minerals Industry. *Accounting, Organizations and Society*, 31, pp. 343–72.

Freeman, R. E., & Reed, D. L. (1983). Stockholders and stakeholders: A new perspective on corporate governance. *California Management Review*, 3.

Friedman, M. (1962). *Capitalism and Freedom*. Chicago: University of Chicago Press.

Gray, A., & Jenkins, B. (1993). Codes of accountability in the new public sector. *Accounting, Auditing and Accountability Journal*, 6(3), pp. 52–67.

Gray, R., Adams, C., & Owen, D. (2014). *Accountability, Social Responsibility and Sustainability*. Harlow, UK: Pearson.

Nike Impact Report (2020), https://purpose.nike.com/fy20-nike-impact-report, p. 101.

Roddick, A. (2007). *Business as Unusual: The Journey of Anita Roddick and The Body Shop*. London: Anita Roddick Books.

Weygandt, J., Mitrione, L., Rankin, M., Chalmers, K., Kieso, D., & Kimmel P. (2018). *Principles of Financial Accounting* (3rd edition). Sydney: Wiley.

CHAPTER 2

ORGANISATIONS AND THEIR REPORTING BOUNDARIES

LEARNING OBJECTIVES

After completing this chapter, readers should be able to:

- **LO2.1** explain the concept of reporting boundaries, and describe how reporting boundaries might expand as the managers of organisations accept broader responsibilities in respect of the impacts of their operations
- **LO2.2** identify the types of resources an organisation uses, and how the use of different resources might, or might not, be recognised and reported within an organisation's accounts
- **LO2.3** explain what we mean by the broad term 'costs', and how the costs generated by organisations might include those that can be measured in monetary terms as well as those that cannot
- **LO2.4** explain that organisations use various inputs and generate a variety of outputs (impacts), both planned and unplanned, and how these outputs (impacts) might be reported
- **LO2.5** explain why different aspects of an organisation's operations might require the use of different measurement and reporting frameworks
- **LO2.6** understand the meaning of the term 'supply chain', and explain some of the decisions that must be made to determine whether impacts created throughout a supply chain should be addressed by an organisation's accounting system
- **LO2.7** explain why accounting should not be considered a one-size-fits-all practice
- **LO2.8** explain the role of management accounting, and describe various factors that will influence the types of information that are collected in order to manage an organisation

LO2.9 demonstrate a broad understanding of some of the different reporting frameworks that could be used to generate the information to be used by external stakeholders

LO2.10 explain the difference between for-profit and not-for-profit organisations, and describe how this difference might influence the process of accounting

LO2.11 provide descriptions of a sole trader, partnership and company, and explain how the accounts produced for each will differ.

OPENING QUESTIONS

Before reading this chapter, please consider how you would answer the following two questions. We will return to these questions at the end of the chapter, where we suggest some answers.

1 What do we mean by 'reporting boundary', and why would managers of similar organisations potentially adopt different reporting boundaries?

2 Why would we argue that accounting is not a one-size-fits-all practice?

Introduction

Building upon the discussion in Chapter 1, this chapter explores the idea of reporting boundaries. It describes how the boundary of accounting will expand as the managers of an organisation broaden their consideration of the various impacts the organisation has on wider groups of affected stakeholders.

As the boundary of accounting is extended, a more diverse range of resources will be considered in terms of which are being used by the organisation (including financial, natural, human-based and social resources), and what are the costs, or impacts, associated with their use. Although some costs might not be easily measurable in monetary terms, that does not necessarily preclude them from being addressed by accounting.

Since the managers of an organisation often choose which impacts (financial, social or environmental) are reported, and which stakeholders will receive accounting-based information, this chapter emphasises that accounting should not be considered a one-size-fits-all practice. We also explain that a great deal of the information generated for managing an organisation might also be used for external reporting purposes. In doing so, our discussion provides a broad overview of a variety of external reporting frameworks.

The chapter will conclude with a description of three forms of organisations: sole traders, partnerships and companies. Differences in the accounting practices of these organisation forms will be broadly identified and explained.

LO2.1 What is the reporting boundary?

In Chapter 1, we considered the relationships between organisational responsibilities, accountability, and accounting. Specifically, we said that managers' beliefs about an organisation's responsibilities will influence the accountability they believe they should demonstrate (*to whom* and *for what*). In turn, this will affect the beliefs that managers have about the nature of the accounts that should be produced for both internal management purposes and external reporting. In Chapter 1 this was diagrammatically represented in **Figure 1.2** reproduced here.

FIGURE 1.2 The relationship between responsibility, accountability and accounts

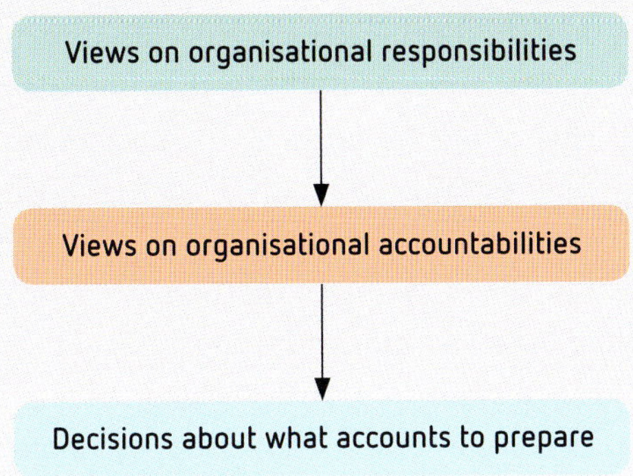

In Chapter 1, we also acknowledged that if we go beyond collecting and reporting information about financial performance – that is, we also collect and report information about the social and environmental impacts of an organisation – then we are effectively extending the reach of our accounting. If we choose to account for the social and environmental impacts of an organisation, then we are extending the boundary of accounting beyond the organisation itself.

We will now consider the issue of the **reporting boundary** – or the range of accounting – in more depth. Here, we are referring to the judgements that have been made by an organisation's managers in respect of how far the responsibilities of the organisation have been extended in terms of:

- *to whom* (to which stakeholders) the organisation is accountable
- *for what* aspects of performance it should be accountable.

reporting boundary
A reflection of how far the responsibilities of the organisation have been extended both in terms of to which stakeholders it owes an accountability, and for what aspects of performance it should be accountable

If we, as managers of an organisation, are just interested in collecting information about financial performance, together with information about the resources and obligations of the organisation as measured in financial terms, then the reporting boundary might be narrowly restricted to the confines of the organisation itself. We would have a restricted, or narrow, view of organisational responsibilities. However, if we are concerned about the social and environmental implications of our operations regarding societies and environments beyond our organisation (which we might consider to be external stakeholders), then we are, by consequence, extending the reporting boundary beyond the confines (or 'walls') of the organisation. Therefore, our reporting boundary is extended as we extend our beliefs about our organisation's responsibilities and associated accountabilities.

The reporting boundary in the context of financial reporting

For a particular organisation, it might also be possible that we have different boundaries of reporting depending on the type of reporting being undertaken, or the reporting frameworks being utilised. Organisations will report various types of information and will use a variety of frameworks. For example, with financial reporting, the frameworks that are typically used (we will consider the frameworks for financial reporting in much more depth in Chapters 7 to 11) embrace what is known as the **accounting entity concept**, in which the financial effects of transactions and events of the business are kept quite separate from the personal transactions of the owners.

accounting entity concept
The principle within financial accounting that an organisation should have its own dedicated accounting records separate from those of its owners or other people involved in its operations

Under financial reporting, the organisation is treated as a separate entity, and if a transaction or event does not affect the performance, resources or obligations of that organisation, as measured in financial terms, then these transactions or events are generally ignored despite their possible importance or impact. One outcome of this is that financial reporting typically ignores an organisation's social and environmental impacts on stakeholders outside the organisation (unless these impacts lead to fines or other cash outflows). It also ignores financial transactions that do not involve the organisation, as outlined in the following examples.

A casino is an organisation that may foster the behaviour of problem gamblers (people who are addicted to gambling) who patronise the organisation, and possibly suffer various social problems caused by the losses incurred. Such social problems, which can be linked to the operations of the casino, can be considered to be adverse social impacts and include issues such as depression and family-related problems. Nevertheless, when undertaking financial reporting, the casino would not recognise social costs when determining its own financial profits, as there are no direct financial implications for the business. This example emphasises that, just because an organisation might be making financial profits, it does not necessarily mean that the organisation is socially desirable. This is an issue we will return to in Chapter 6.

Source: Newspix/Cameron Richardson

The social costs of problem gambling are not accounted for by a casino's financial reporting.

As a further example of the separation of the organisation from outside parties, the personal assets of owners (or investors) are not considered resources of the organisation (the accounting entity). These assets are considered to be 'outside the entity' for financial reporting purposes. If an owner of an organisation buys a car for personal use out of their own personal funds, then this has nothing directly to do with the business. This transaction did not affect the accounting entity and therefore would be ignored by the organisation for financial reporting purposes. However, if the owner withdrew a vehicle from the business for personal use, then this would affect the accounting records of the organisation (it would be shown as a withdrawal by the owner which had the effect of reducing the resources controlled by the business).

The reporting boundary beyond an organisation

Consolidated financial statements and subsidiaries

While financial reporting frameworks typically focus on providing financial reports about an individual organisation, if one organisation controls another (for example, one company has a **subsidiary**), then the accounting entity might be comprised of both organisations consolidated together. In this case, the combined financial reports would be referred to as *consolidated financial statements*.

subsidiary
An organisation that is controlled by another organisation

It is common for the reporting boundary of financial reporting to include information about the financial performance, resources and obligations of subsidiaries (measured in financial terms) that are controlled by the central organisation (which might be referred to as the 'parent' organisation). For example, when we look at the financial reports of the Australia and New Zealand Banking Group (ANZ), we see that the consolidated financial statements include the results of the parent organisation plus over 100 of its subsidiaries, and that the financial results are combined into one larger accounting entity. A review of the website of the ANZ (www.anz.com) reveals that the bank's main financial statements – the balance sheet, statement of profit or loss and other comprehensive income, statement of cash flows, and statement of changes in equity, all of which we will explain in Chapters 7 to 11 – have two columns under each year (the current year and the previous year): one entitled 'The Company', which relates to the parent entity, and the other entitled 'Consolidated', which is the aggregation of the financial accounts of the parent entity and all the organisations it controls.

The preparation of consolidated financial statements is fairly complicated and is typically dealt with in the second or third year of an accounting program. It is not something that we will further explore within this book.

Sustainability reporting

In addition to financial reporting, if the managers of an organisation are also interested in undertaking some form of **sustainability reporting**, or *social responsibility reporting*, which takes into account the organisation's impacts on various communities and environments external to it, then the reporting boundaries would be required to extend beyond the organisation itself – and beyond its subsidiaries if consolidated financial statements are being produced. The reporting might include details of effects of the organisation's operations on climate change, on workers in supply factories, the discharge of waste into waterways, noise, and so forth.

sustainability reporting A form of reporting, both financial and non-financial, that takes into account an organisation's impacts on the communities and environments in which it operates, and which provides insights into how the organisation's operations are consistent with the idea of sustainable development

A hypothetical example relating to the reporting boundary is provided in Learning exercise 2.1.

2.1 Learning Exercise

A consideration of the reporting boundary at Brucester & Co.

Imagine that there is a large Australian organisation called Brucester & Co. that imports various surfing-related goods from companies located in Indonesia and Vietnam. It stores the imported products in its large warehouses in Torquay, Victoria, until the goods are transported to various retailers by a company that is a fully owned subsidiary of Brucester & Co.

Brucester & Co. employs approximately 100 people in Torquay. It has a policy of employing, where possible, people with various disabilities who might not easily gain employment elsewhere. The organisation also tries to contribute positively to local communities, and it currently sponsors a number of sporting clubs.

Surfing is, by nature, a relatively risky sport, and Brucester & Co. has also taken action to design surfing products to reduce the risks to customers.

The organisation has outsourced the manufacturing of its products to developing countries because it can get good-quality products at much lower costs. However, various issues have been raised about the treatment and health and safety of employees in these developing countries, which is of concern to the managers of Brucester & Co.

Setting an appropriate reporting boundary

The organisation necessarily needs to do some accounting, but it needs to consider its reporting boundary. Using the simple diagram in **Figure 2.1** that outlines how far Brucester & Co.'s reporting boundaries could be extended, we can consider if Brucester & Co. should only consider accounting for its own financial performance and position (the innermost circle), or whether it should extend its financial reporting to include its fully owned subsidiary (the two innermost circles). This would generally be the full extent of the reporting boundary for financial reporting purposes.

FIGURE 2.1 An illustration of possible reporting boundaries

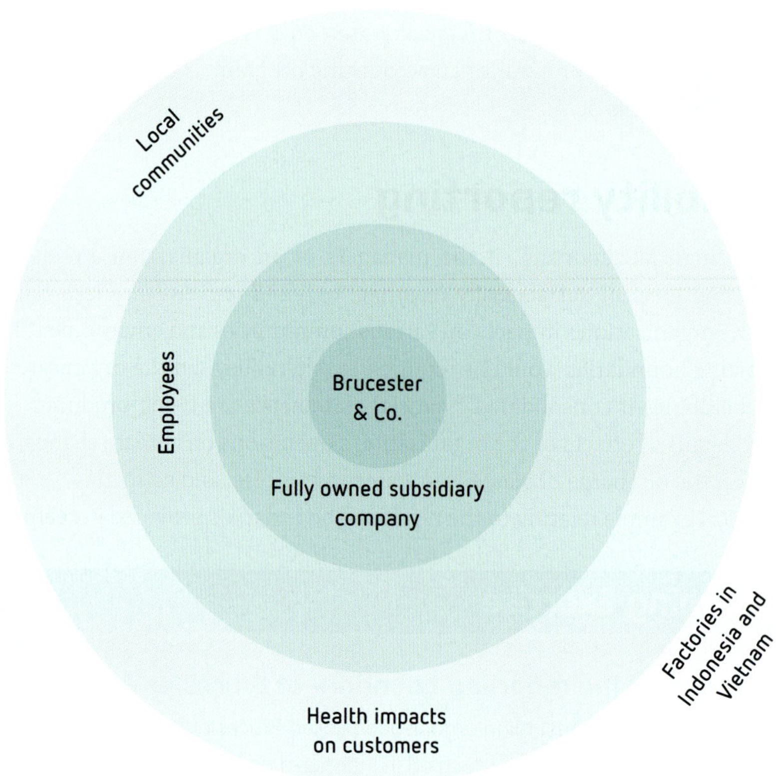

What if Brucester & Co. extends its reporting boundary to include information about how its employees in Torquay are prospering from the organisation's employment and training policies, or goes even further to gather and report information about the health impacts of products on customers, or the effects the organisation has had on the local communities in which it operates? Or should the company extend the reporting boundary even further, to include gathering and reporting information about how employees in supplier factories in Indonesia and Vietnam are treated (despite the fact that Brucester & Co. does not have any ownership of these factories)?

Determining where to set the reporting boundary is clearly not always a straightforward exercise. This decision will link back to the question about why an organisation is reporting. Think back to the accountability model we introduced in Chapter 1 and its four related phases:

- Why report?
- To whom to report?
- What to report?
- How to report?

If an organisation is only reporting because managers want to provide information to owners, and if these owners prioritise financial performance, then managers might restrict the reporting boundary to the first or second innermost circles and the reporting itself to financial reports.

However, if the reason that managers are collecting the information is because they want to monitor and improve the broader impacts of their operations on stakeholders across the supply chain, then the focus of the accounting might extend to the outer circles of **Figure 2.1**. What this means is that the more the managers of an organisation widen their responsibilities and accountabilities (for example, to local communities and perhaps to employees in overseas supply factories), the more information they will ultimately collect, analyse and report.

Because different organisations will have different purposes or goals, and different stakeholders (who – as we discussed in Chapter 1 – can be considered as those individuals or groups who are able to either *affect the organisation*, or *who are affected by* the operations of the organisation), this will result in them accepting different responsibilities. As we should now appreciate, different responsibilities mean different accountabilities, and therefore different demands of accounting. However, again, please keep in mind that organisations – for the purposes of their financial reporting – will generally be required to restrict their reporting boundary to the organisation itself (and its subsidiaries if they have any), but when we talk about other aspects of performance – such as social and environmental performance – then we can necessarily extend the reporting boundary.

In **Learning exercise 2.2**, we will consider how you might personally elect to extend the reporting boundary of an organisation.

2.2 Learning Exercise

Further consideration of the reporting boundary

How far would Brucester & Co. realistically extend the reporting boundary, and why?

Given what we know about Brucester & Co. and the company's inclusive policies, it's reasonable to believe that the managers of the organisation would accept responsibility for ensuring that their operations do not negatively impact the wellbeing of people throughout their supply chain (and hopefully, that their activities have positive impacts upon people). A business with these core philosophies would likely extend its reporting boundary to the outer circles. However, it needs to be accepted that, as the reporting boundary extends outwards, the costs associated with collecting, analysing and reporting information increase, constraining the extent of the reporting undertaken.

Would Brucester & Co.'s reporting boundary for reports that address social and environmental impacts be different to the reporting boundary for its financial reports?

Financial reporting typically does not address the impacts of an organisation's operation on stakeholders outside the organisation, including the impacts on owners. Financial reporting treats the organisation as an entity quite distinct from the stakeholders and environments with which it engages or affects, hence the reporting boundary does not extend far.

However, once we start considering the social and environmental impacts of an organisation, we are looking at stakeholders and environments beyond the organisation, and this necessarily requires the extension of the reporting boundary. The differences between the reporting boundaries of financial reporting and those of social and environmental reporting will become clearer as we work our way through this book.

In effect, the reporting boundary can be considered to have two dimensions. We can refer to the breadth of information about performance that is collected and reported (such as whether it will include a wide variety of social, environmental and financial performance information), as well as the breadth of the organisations and stakeholders that are the subjects of the collection and reporting (for example, the decision to include, or not, the social and environmental impacts of organisations within the supply chain).

It should also be remembered that however we extend the reporting boundary, we will still produce accounts which might reflect the whole operation or simply parts thereof. For example, within an organisation, we might produce disaggregated financial reports of particular divisions or processes, or perhaps we might produce reports about overall energy consumption as well as the energy consumption of individual machines.

Why do I need to know about the concept of the reporting boundary?

The reporting boundary is a useful concept to allow us to understand the reporting/accountability-related practices of organisations. It allows us to visualise how the stakeholders, and impacts that are considered by the organisations, extends further out and away from the organisation as the managers accept broader responsibilities in relation 'to whom' they are responsible, and 'for what' aspects of performance they are responsible.

If we are attempting to assess the range of accountabilities that an organisation is embracing, then we should try to obtain information about the organisation's reporting boundary. Arguably, an organisation with a very condensed or small reporting boundary is exposing itself to various risks relating to its potential inability to understand the various social and environmental impacts that exist throughout its supply chain. For example, if a clothing organisation that outsources its production decided that its responsibilities and accountabilities did not extend beyond its own country's borders, then perhaps it would not monitor, and be accountable for, the treatment of workers within factories in developing countries that were producing products for the organisation. This could then expose the organisation to the risk of being linked to unsafe or unethical work practices.

resource
Something that has value in the sense that it allows an organisation to undertake an activity so as to enable it to achieve a desired outcome

LO2.2 The resources of an organisation

Directly related to what we have been discussing is consideration of the various resources that an organisation uses to perform its operations. A **resource** can be broadly defined from an organisational perspective as something that has value in the sense that it allows an organisation to undertake an activity so as to enable it to achieve a desired outcome.

As we will learn in Chapters 7 to 11, for financial reporting purposes, an organisation will typically only report about those resources it uses as part of its business if it controls those resources. Resources are considered to be controlled when an organisation can deny, or regulate, the access of other people to the resources. Apart from control, another requirement that must exist before a resource is recognised for financial reporting purposes is that it is capable of being measured in financial terms. Examples of controlled resources that would be included in financial statements are:

- financial resources such as cash at bank or term deposits
- property, plant and equipment.

But organisations will also draw upon many other resources that they do not own or control in order to operate, such as:

- natural resources (for example, air, water)
- human-based resources (factory labour, managerial labour, intellectual capital)
- social or community-based resources/infrastructure (roads, waterways, universities, hospitals).

For example, an organisation might draw water from a local river (which is a natural resource) which it also uses for transporting its products, perhaps by barge. The organisation probably does not own or control the river. Also, the organisation will use local roads, draw in air for its furnaces, and release emissions back into the air. These can all be considered resources necessary to the organisation, but they would not be considered resources that are owned or controlled by the organisation. Therefore, they would not be shown (recognised) within the financial statements. If a particular resource is not shown in the financial statements as a resource of an organisation, the implication is that the use of, or negative impact upon, that resource would typically not be shown as an expense of that organisation when determining its financial profits.

Source: Shutterstock.com/Lamax

An organisation might use a barge to transport its products on a river. The river might be a valuable resource of the organisation, even though it will not appear within any financial statements.

Accounting for non-financial resources

At issue is whether we should *only* record and report information about the usage of, and potential damage to, resources *controlled* by the organisation, or if we should consider impacts on the resources not owned or controlled by the organisation; for example, upon the environment (these resources might also be referred to as *shared resources* or *public resources*).

In the absence of any regulation requiring disclosure, the decision to disclose particular social or environmental information is generally made by managers in consultation with their accounting teams. It would be hoped that, if an organisation is causing significant impacts to particular resources (including natural, human-based and social-based resources), then they would provide some account of such impacts. Again, if the managers think they have a responsibility for ensuring that particular resources are not adversely impacted by their operations, then they are accepting an accountability with respect to that resource. Consequently, they should generate various accounts to enable them to monitor, control and improve their performance with regards to the respective resources.

Key concept

If managers think they are responsible for ensuring that resources are not adversely impacted by their operations, then they are accepting accountability for that resource.

In relation to the use of a local river to transport products (see the example above), what if the transportation barge we are using regularly pollutes the river, thereby causing ongoing damage to local fish stocks and water vegetation? And what if, despite the damage to the river, no fines are ever imposed upon the organisation? Should we recognise this damage in the accounts? From a financial reporting perspective, the answer would typically be 'No'. Because there are no fines, there are no financial costs to be recognised and therefore no outflow of financial resources. But if we are providing information about our environmental performance – preparing environmental accounts – and thereby extending the reach of our accounting, then such damage *should* be reported.

As another example, if an oil company has a tanker that strikes a reef and spills all of its oil into the ocean, then what costs do you think it should record and report? Should it measure and record:

- the damage to the ship (owned by the company)
- the cost of the lost oil (owned by the company)
- the damage to the reef, local vegetation and sea life
- the lost earnings of local fishing people who can no longer fish within the polluted waters?

While all the above points represent costs that will arise as a result of the ship hitting the reef, whether we recognise these costs in the accounts of the organisation will depend on how far we want to extend our responsibilities, which in turn relates to how far we want to extend our accountability and therefore the boundary of our accounting.

Learning exercise 2.3 considers how a university might account for some of its resources.

2.3 Learning Exercise

Identifying and accounting for an organisation's resources

Universities typically seek to produce world-class graduates and world-class research. In this exercise, we will identify some of the resources of a typical university and consider if each one would be identified, measured and reported for accounting purposes, and if so, where?

What resources can we identify?

While this list is far from exhaustive, the resources of a university could include:

1 buildings
2 land
3 machinery
4 furniture and fittings
5 various books and other important collections

6 good staff
7 good students
8 local transport systems for students.

Which resources would be measured?

The first five items in our list would be recorded by the university in financial terms and included within its financial reports (which universities now typically make available on their websites). Any reductions in the value of these resources would generally be reflected by monetary measurements and recognised as expenses.

The last three items are resources used by a university, but they are not *controlled by the organisation* and hence would not be recorded by the organisation within its financial reports.

Nevertheless, various aspects pertaining to the students and staff would be expected to be collected and reported, such as:

- the satisfaction levels of staff and students
- demographics
- staff training
- employment diversity
- diversity of students

In the following chapters of this book, we will consider various approaches to measuring the use of different types of resources.

Why do I need to know that not all the resources used by an organisation will be recognised within the organisation's financial reports?

When we look at the balance sheet of an organisation it will show the various 'assets' of the organisation. From a financial accounting perspective, an asset is defined as a present economic resource controlled by the entity as a result of past events.

As we can see here, and as we have already discussed, 'control' is necessary before a resource can be recognised as an asset of the organisation. The organisation uses, or relies upon, many resources that are not controlled (such as the air, transport waterways, fresh water sources, roads and other community infrastructure), but these resources are typically not recognised by the organisation. They do not meet the financial accountants' definition of an 'asset'.

When an organisation recognises an expense, this recognition typically arises because an 'asset' of the organisation has declined in value (or a liability has increased in value). That is, if the assets of the organisation (which are the resources it controls) decline, then unless this decline in value was because it was transferred to an owner, then the reduction in value would be recognised as an expense.

By contrast, resources that are used by the organisation, but which are not controlled, are not recognised anywhere within the financial statements. Again, financial accounting does not allow uncontrolled resources to be recognised by an organisation. Because they are not initially recognised, any reduction in their value also will go unrecognised. This is a very important point to appreciate. It means that any damage an organisation does to non-controlled resources will in turn not be recognised as expenses of the organisation. Therefore, an organisation could be doing all sorts of environmental damage to resources it does not control, but unless some form of fines or taxes are imposed, then no expenses will be recognised. Profits, which represent the difference between income and expenses, could be very high at the same time the organisation is destroying the environment. As an example, a large manufacturing organisation might be using furnaces that emit large volumes of greenhouse gases into the air. If there are no carbon taxes or other payments levied on these emissions then, because the 'air' is not an 'asset' of the organisation, no expenses would be recognised for financial reporting purposes. Profits would not be negatively impacted by the emissions and reported profits would not reflect the environmental costs being imposed on current and future generations.

So, as students of accounting, we need to appreciate that just because an organisation is very profitable from a financial reporting perspective, this in itself does not necessarily mean that the organisation is socially desirable. We will return to this issue in later chapters of this book. Because financial reports do not reflect environmental and social costs, responsible organisations also release other reports – such as 'sustainability reports' – which provide information about social and environmental performance. We will study such reports in depth within Chapter 6.

LO2.3 What constitutes a cost?

costs
A measure, either expressed in financial or non-financial terms, of the value of resources consumed or impacted as a result of the operations of an organisation. Can include both 'private costs' and 'social and environmental costs' ('external costs')

externalities
Impacts that an entity has on parties external to the organisation, where such parties are not the buyers or sellers of the goods or services, or did not agree to, or take part in, the activities causing the externality

Please note that in our discussion we are embracing a broad view of **costs**. Often, costs are simply calculated as the amount of money that needs to be paid by an organisation to buy something or produce something or perhaps repair something. Such calculated costs are often referred to as *private costs*. But there are other costs that are not necessarily measurable in monetary terms which might also be significant, and which we might call *external costs*. External costs are often referred to as **externalities**, which can be defined as 'impacts that an entity has on parties external to the organisation, where such parties are not the buyers or sellers of particular goods or services, or did not agree to, or take part in, the activities causing the externality'.

For example, the damage to the reef caused by an oil tanker that we previously discussed would impact many people other than the buyers or sellers of the oil, and these impacts will not all be measurable in monetary terms – they would be considered external costs. When most manufacturers of goods produce something, they generally create some level of pollution that impacts people beyond either the producer or the customer – they create external costs. Because it is very problematic to try and attempt to place a monetary value on many external costs, they often are not reflected in the prices of particular goods or services. In a sense, this is a failing of many of our pricing systems – many externalities simply fail to be factored into the prices we pay. If we were to consider the full costs to society of particular products (often termed the *social cost*), then we would need to consider both the private costs and the external costs.

However, while external costs might be difficult to quantify in monetary terms, we can still provide a description of the costs that have arisen. That is, we can provide a description of the impacts an organisation's operations have had on particular environments and/or societies, even if we cannot place a monetary value on such costs.

Which costs could be recognised?

With the above discussion of costs in mind, in practice, the most common approach used would be to recognise as a cost, and in financial terms, the first two points in our oil tanker example above: the cost of repairing the damage to the ship, and the cost of the lost oil. These costs could be considered to represent private costs. Such costs would be reflected within the financial statements, representing financial expenses that relate to resources, or assets, that were controlled by the organisation and which were acquired at a particular monetary cost, thereby making measurement in monetary terms relatively easy. Typically, no financial costs would be attributed to the remaining two points (damage to the reef and sea life, and lost earnings of fishermen), other than those paid by the organisation to contribute to fixing the damage, and those associated with paying any related fines. The externalities, or social costs, associated with destroyed reefs, dead sea creatures and polluted waters that are now unable to sustain fishing would not directly find their way into an organisation's financial statements. However, that would not preclude the organisation – should it choose – from describing the damage created and providing descriptions, or accounts, of what is being done by the organisation to try to address the damage.

The ocean is a resource used by the oil organisation, but it is not controlled by that organisation, so it would not appear in the organisation's financial statements as prepared using generally accepted financial reporting frameworks. However, we should nevertheless expect the organisation to provide some form of account of the damage being inflicted upon the ocean if that damage is significant.

In terms of a real-life example of the use of natural resources, we can consider some results reported by the global mining company BHP in its 2021 Annual Report in relation to the use of water (available at **www.bhp.com**). This information, some of which is reproduced in **Exhibit 2.1**, details the amount of the resource (water) used (inputs), as well as the release of water from the organisation (outputs). This reflects BHP's acceptance of responsibility for its use of water, and further acceptance that it should provide a publicly available account of such use.

EXHIBIT 2.1 BHP's use of water

		2021	2020	2019
Water[5,8]				
Withdrawals[6]	ML	**438 660**	380 330	**352 950**
Water withdrawals by quality – Type 1	ML	54 310	51 610	58 850
Water withdrawals by quality – Type 2	ML	36 970	35 670	37 560
Water withdrawals by quality – Type 3	ML	347 390	293 060	256 550
Water withdrawals by source – Surface water[7]	ML	30 350	45 190	50 660
Water withdrawals by source – Groundwater	ML	100 700	123 660	140 020
Water withdrawals by source – Sea water	ML	284 700	211 510	162 260
Water withdrawals by source – Third-party water	ML	22 910		
Total water withdrawals (water stress areas)[9]	ML	233 190		
Discharges	ML	**203 450**	**147 850**	**119 250**
Water discharges by quality – Type 1	ML	**0**	0	**0**
Water discharges by quality – Type 2	ML	**2 390**	**3 470**	**3 060**
Water discharges by quality – Type 3	ML	**201 060**	**144 110**	**116 190**
Water discharges by destination – Surface water	ML	**2 250**	3 970	2 940
Water discharges by destination – Groundwater	ML	9 670	9 440	1 540
Water discharges by destination – Sea water	ML	190 660	134 120	114 460
Water discharges by destination – Third party	ML	660	310	320

		2021	2020	2019
Total water discharges (water stress areas)	ML	123 200		
Consumption	ML	**267 130**	259 070	**271 680**
Consumption – evaporation	ML	141 430	127 080	143 040
Consumption – entrainment	ML	107 270	109 550	107 270
Consumption – other	ML	18 450	22 440	21 370
Total consumption (water stress areas)	ML	106 950		
Recycled/reused	ML	262 430	250 090	246 420
Diversions	ML			
Diversions – withdrawals	ML	103 220	103 750	122 670
Diversions – discharges	ML	68 910	79 430	72 500
Waste				
Hazardous waste – Mineral total (including tailings)[10]	kilotonnes	20 420	15 000	13 500
Non-hazardous waste – Mineral tailings[10]	kilotonnes	178 000	175 000	167 000
Accidental discharges of water and tailings[11,12]	megalitres	0	0	0

(5) Data has been rounded to the nearest 10 megalitres to be consistent with asset/regional water information in this Annual Report. In some instances the sum of totals for quality, source and destination may differ due to rounding. All water performance data excludes Discontinued operations (Onshore US assets, divested in FY2019).

(6) Third-party water withdrawals have been reported as a distinct category in FY2021 to align with external reporting frameworks (e.g. GRI/SASB). These volumes were included under the originating source in prior years.

(7) Data includes rainfall and run-off volumes captured and used during the reporting year; rainfall and run-off volumes that have been captured and stored are excluded and will be reported in the future year of use.

(8) Data for water consumption metrics was collected for the first time in FY2019 across all operations.

(9) Based on the physical risk rating from the WWF Water Risk filter and the definition of water stress in the CEO Water Mandate's 'Corporate Water Disclosure Guidelines (2014)'.

(10) For tailings related minerals waste these figures represent the total deposited in the reporting year.

(11) Data reported for environmentally significant incidents.

(12) Does not include the dam failure at Samarco, our non-operated minerals joint venture.

(13) Data drawn from Australian NPI and US EPA Emission Factors and represent emissions over CY2021 for all assets except Olympic Dam and US Petroleum, which report emissions for FY2021.

Source: BHP (2021), p. 273.

What you should appreciate by now is that the contents of **Exhibit 2.1** are the outcome of an accounting process, even though no financial amounts are attributed to the use and release of water. Disclosures within **Exhibit 2.1** would not be considered to constitute part of a financial reporting process. Instead, the disclosures might be considered to be part of an organisation's environmental reporting, which in turn is part of its broader sustainability reporting practices.

There would be various stakeholders with an interest in, or a need for, the information in **Exhibit 2.1** (or else, arguably, the company should not bother reporting it). For example, residents in nearby communities might be particularly interested in how much water the company is using if water is relatively scarce in that location. They might also be interested in knowing where wastewater is being released and the impact this might be having on the local environment. Government might also have an interest in how much water the organisation is drawing from local water supplies, and how wastewater is being disposed of.

Another important point to be made here is that if there are various ways to measure the use and release of water (or any other resource), then it is important that an organisation identifies what specific accounting framework it has elected to use to make its measurements. Different frameworks can potentially generate different measurements. As **Exhibit 2.1** above shows, BHP has referred to various frameworks to guide its reporting practices.

Learning exercise 2.4 poses issues associated with how particular externalities might be accounted for by an organisation.

2.4 Learning Exercise

Accounting for the use of particular resources – the Deepwater Horizon case

The Deepwater Horizon oil spill, which involved a drilling rig belonging to the multinational oil company BP, occurred on 20 April 2010 in the Gulf of Mexico. It took approximately five months to seal the well after the rig exploded and sank, although there were reports that it continued to leak for some years after this. Eleven people were killed when the oil platform exploded.

Significant damage occurred to local marine and wildlife habitats, as well as the fishing and tourism industries, as a result of the spill (damage that might also be referred to as costs that have been imposed on the environment and society, remembering that costs do not necessarily have to be measured simply in financial terms). The impacts of the disaster were ongoing for a number of years. Dolphins and various types of fish continued to die in large numbers, and various forms of marine plant life over thousands of square kilometres were damaged or destroyed. It was a major environmental catastrophe.

In November 2012, BP and the United States Department of Justice settled federal charges, with BP pleading guilty to various offences. The company has since paid billions of dollars in fines.

What sort of information do you think BP should have publicly reported?

The information an organisation elects to report will depend on how far it extends its reporting boundary, and which impacted resources it believes it has responsibility for. Using our four-stage accountability model from Chapter 1, the answer to the first question of why an organisation should account/report will impact the subsequent questions of who to report to and what to report.

Let's say we believe that BP should provide an account of the oil leak because it has an accountability for the impacts of the catastrophe on the various stakeholders affected. The organisation might elect to provide a clear description of:

- what caused the leak and what was done to stop the leak
- what the financial costs associated with the oil leak have been
- what environmental damage has occurred in both the short and long term (being very clear about the various types of negative impacts)
- the actions being taken to reduce these negative impacts
- the actions taken to ensure this type of event will not happen again
- what it has learned from the catastrophe
- what operating procedures failed
- how its emergency response procedures worked or did not work.

How to account for the oil leak?

Given the impact the massive oil leak had on the environment, workers and various communities, and will potentially have upon future generations, BP necessarily seems to have a clear obligation, or responsibility, to report in a manner that is accessible to a wide range of stakeholders.

Various frameworks are available to measure environmental impacts, and the most appropriate should be selected. Decisions have to be made as to how to disseminate the accounts to the different stakeholders. Website disclosures would seem appropriate, as would disclosures made in the media.

When to account for this environmental catastrophe?

The best time to start providing an account of this leak is as soon as it happens, and the accounting should continue until it is clear that the matter has been resolved – however long this will take.

Arguably, before the incident occurred, BP should have been providing disclosures about the actions it was taking to help ensure such events do not occur. Details of its emergency response procedures in the event of such a disaster should also have been available, so that stakeholders could assess the risks to the environment from the ongoing activities of the organisation.

LO2.4 The inputs and outputs of an organisation

Just as an organisation will use various resources as part of its operations, it will also create various *outputs* (or impacts), some which are intended (such as its goods and services) and some which might not be intended (for example, various wastes, or oil spills, which might create external costs). The outputs of an organisation could include:

- goods and services for sale
- educated people (for example, universities)
- healthy people (hospitals)
- healthy environments (environmental groups)
- proposed regulations to create safe and healthy environments for workers (employee unions)
- waste material and other rubbish
- CO_2 emissions
- polluted water
- noise.

The *inputs* (resources being used) and outputs (and impacts) being generated can be diagrammatically represented as in **Figure 2.2**.

FIGURE 2.2 A simple input/output diagram

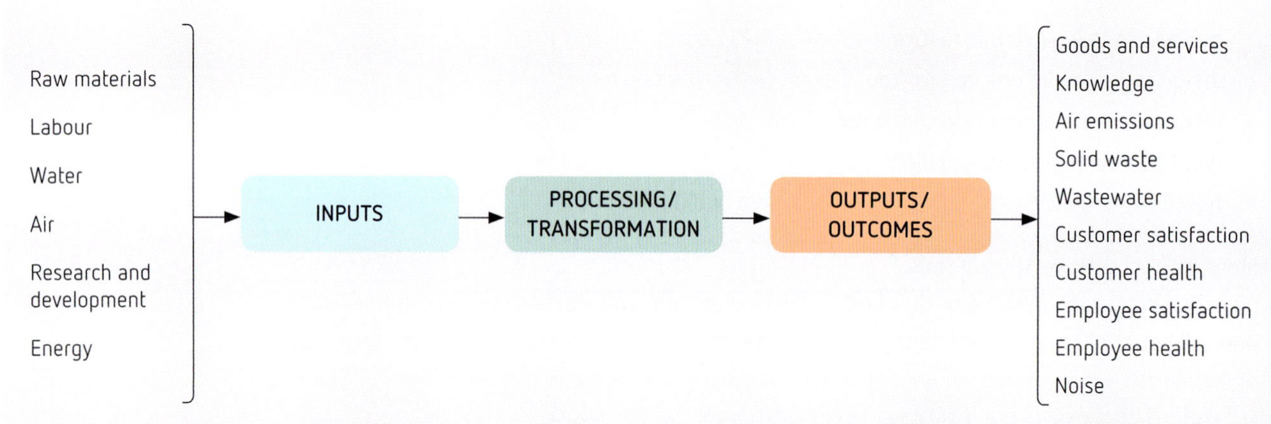

Deciding what to measure

The decision as to which inputs and outputs an organisation measures and reports really depends upon the underlying purpose of the organisation and the goals of the people managing it. That is, from an internal perspective, managers want to make informed decisions to achieve particular goals, and they need information in order to do this. For example, if they want to minimise noise from their factory (an external cost – or externality – imposed upon others), then they need to collect information about noise output. If they do not feel any responsibility for minimising noise, then they will not collect such information. As we have said before, *you cannot manage what you do not measure* (and conversely, you probably will not measure what you do not want to manage).

Key concept

You cannot manage what you do not measure, and you probably will not measure what you do not want to manage.

What an organisation measures and reports also depends upon the expectations of the stakeholders who are entitled to information. For example, from an external perspective, investors in a company will want to know about its profits, resources and **liabilities** so they can evaluate the security of their investment and the prospects for future **dividends** and capital growth. A bank might also want to know about the profits, resources and liabilities of a borrower so that it can assess the likelihood that a loan will be repaid. Other stakeholders will want other types of information, much of which might relate to external costs; for example:

liabilities
A present obligation of the entity to transfer an economic resource as a result of past events

dividends
Distributions of profits made to owners (shareholders) of a company

- Environmental groups will want to know about the impacts of an organisation on its local environment, and what the organisation is doing to reduce such impacts.
- Animal welfare groups will want to know if an organisation's operations use animals, or animal-related products, and how the organisation monitors and controls its activities to ensure the proper treatment of animals.
- Consumer groups will want to know how an organisation is monitoring the quality of its products, and how it is accounting for the health and safety aspects associated with using the organisation's products and services.
- Trade union groups will want information about such things as the training being provided to staff, the working conditions of staff, employment statistics concerning minorities, and information about workplace accidents.

Learning exercise 2.5 further considers the measurement and reporting of different outputs, or impacts, of an organisation.

2.5 Learning Exercise

Measuring and reporting externalities

Let's now consider measuring and reporting externalities in greater detail.

Are externalities typically measured and reported by an organisation?

Historically, most externalities created by organisations have been ignored, and that is why, at least in part, our natural environment is so degraded. For many years, the impacts of industry on waterways, natural habitats, the air and so forth have not been factored into the prices we pay for goods and services. Wrongly, they were treated as 'free goods'. This has meant that a great deal of damage occurred for years that was relatively unabated. But things are changing (although many people argue that the change is not occurring fast enough).

While most of our discussion so far has been about negative externalities (costs), externalities can also be viewed as positive (benefits). An example of a positive externality might be the benefits to the environment from a zoo releasing, into appropriate habitats, endangered animals that have been bred in captivity.

Should externalities be measured and reported by an organisation?

If the externalities are deemed to be significant, then they should be reported by an organisation, as stakeholders reasonably have a right to know about potentially significant impacts. Managers also need to collect the information in order to enable them to manage the impacts of the organisation.

For example, people impacted by the disaster at the Deepwater Horizon rig – these would include employees and their families, investors, local communities, fishing people, and environmental groups – all had a right to information.

How should externalities be reported?

This will not always be straightforward, as the full extent of impacts and the assignment of costs are complicated. It is not necessary to quantify the effects of externalities in monetary terms – describing the externalities in qualitative terms is sometimes the best and most appropriate approach. For example, in relation to a massive ocean oil spill, an organisation's account of this disaster might include information about the amount of oil spilled, a description of the actions being taken to minimise the impacts of the spill, details of the amount of money being spent on those actions, the actual and expected impacts on vegetation and wildlife, and the impacts upon local communities.

Is the disclosure of information about externalities part of the role of an accountant?

Absolutely! Coming up with appropriate disclosures about the impacts created – both positive and negative – by an organisation is not always a straightforward exercise, but this only helps make accounting a very interesting and important practice! If managers accept responsibility for the social and environmental impacts of their organisation, then any related information should be disclosed.

Externalities – the focus of **Learning exercise 2.5** – will be considered in more depth later in this book, in particular within Chapter 6, which focuses on social and environmental reporting. But by this point, you should appreciate how interesting accounting can be, and have some insights into the many judgements that accountants need to make about what information to collect and disclose.

Reflective of how far our analysis of the use of resources and the generation of externalities can be taken, have you ever thought about the costs associated with a common hamburger? What resources are actually consumed as part of making a hamburger? **Learning exercise 2.6** addresses this interesting issue.

2.6 Learning Exercise

The true profit of a hamburger

It has been reported (Harvey, 2015; see www.businessinsider.com.au/one-hamburger-environment-resources-2015-2?r=US&IR=T) that the creation of each McDonald's hamburger requires about 660 litres of water – this relates to the consumption of water by the cow, and the water used to grow the pasture. In addition, each burger requires 6 kilograms of animal feed, which relies upon the farming of 6 square metres of land. In all, one Quarter Pounder burger also has a carbon footprint of almost 2 kilograms. Yet we only pay a few dollars for the burger.

Let's consider whether these externalities are being accounted for.

Are the externalities being accounted for in terms of the price being charged for a hamburger?

The cost of feeding the cattle and looking after the land would be included in the price of the meat going into the hamburger – these would be considered the private costs that are captured within the price of the burger. But the externalities, specifically the water used, are not being fully accounted for, as most of the water is being treated as a free good. Methane emissions and the carbon footprint are also likely to be unaccounted for, as they do not constitute an immediate private cost either. However, as water scarcity increases in some areas, it is likely that the amount of water being used to generate the final product will tend to be accounted for more fully.

While the water use and methane emissions might not be accounted for in financial terms, an organisation can elect to provide information to interested stakeholders about these factors. Although perhaps if the consumers of hamburgers knew this information, then they might decide to consume fewer burgers.

Are these hamburgers generating a profit?

From a financial accounting perspective, McDonald's is generating a financial profit, given that the water being used is probably being sourced at no, or very little, cost. If McDonald's was to develop a more holistic notion of profit and treated the water as a real cost, as well as consider the impact of a hamburger's production on climate change, then it would become arguable as to whether McDonald's is generating a true profit at all.

LO2.5 The influence of accounting frameworks on reporting

If we were to adopt conventional financial accounting practices – which we will address in some detail in Chapters 7 to 11 – then only the consumption of resources controlled by an entity would be recorded and reported. The use of air, waterways and other natural resources – and therefore the creation of pollution and the contribution to climate change – would not be recorded, as they are not controlled. However, if we adopt alternative frameworks, such as that produced by the Global Reporting Initiative (GRI), which we will discuss later in this chapter and in more detail in Chapter 6, then various social and environmental impacts would also be recorded and reported (although not necessarily in monetary terms).

What needs to be appreciated is that an organisation will typically use a variety of different accounting/reporting frameworks to provide the various accounts that relate to different aspects of performance. For the generation of its financial reports, it will use generally accepted financial accounting practices which rely upon the use of various accounting standards issued by organisations such as the International Accounting Standards Board (IASB; see www.ifrs.org/groups/international-accounting-standards-board). If the organisation then elects to provide information about its social and environmental performance, it might decide to use the sustainability reporting frameworks provided by an organisation such as the GRI (see www.globalreporting.org). In doing so, it might also use various measurement frameworks provided by different organisations. For example, when measuring its use of water for inclusion in its sustainability report, it might use the accounting framework provided by the Minerals Council of Australia (MCA; see www.minerals.org.au), and when measuring its carbon emissions, it might use the framework provided by the Greenhouse Gas Protocol (GHGP; see www.ghgprotocol.org). These frameworks will be discussed in more detail in Chapter 6.

LO2.6 Supply chain considerations

supply chain
The network between an organisation and its suppliers and customers, as necessary to produce and distribute a specific good or service

A **supply chain** can be defined as the network between an organisation and its suppliers and customers, as necessary to produce and distribute a specific good or service. Organisations often outsource aspects of their operations to other, unrelated organisations – these are part of the supply chain. For example, sportswear companies might outsource the production of T-shirts to factories in developing countries such as Bangladesh, India, Pakistan or Indonesia, while car manufacturers might outsource the production of windscreens, tyres and wheels to other local businesses.

At issue is whether organisations should provide some form of account of, or report about, aspects of the operations of their supply factories – for example, in terms of the health and safety of workers, or the environmental impacts on local environments – even though those factories are not owned by the organisation buying the goods and services. Or should they just account for the direct financial costs (private costs) they pay for the products?

A diagrammatic representation of a supply chain for a multinational clothing company is provided in Figure 2.3. In terms of the terminology within the figure, Tier 1 suppliers could be the suppliers producing the finished goods, whereas Tier 2 suppliers might be the providers of fabric to Tier 1 suppliers, while Tier 3 suppliers might be the providers of cotton to the makers of the fabric.

While the clothing company might not own the suppliers but simply outsource production to them, should it consider providing accounts of the social and environmental impacts of these suppliers (water use, waste, employee accidents, and so forth) despite not actually paying for these impacts/costs? The answer to this question really depends upon your own views about how far an organisation's responsibilities and accountabilities extend.

Since these suppliers are making products to satisfy the demands of a company, then arguably the company does have some accountability for the aforementioned impacts. Whether managers and their accountants will agree with this will depend on their approach to the accountability model introduced in Chapter 1.

While Figure 2.3 depicts the supply chain as ending with customers and starting with Tier 3 suppliers, should we take our accounting even further and consider the entire life cycle of the products being used? For example, where did the raw materials used by the suppliers come from, and what were the social and environmental impacts there? Also, what happens to the products at the end of their lives, when customers no longer use them? Are there any environmental issues caused by their disposal?

FIGURE 2.3 Diagrammatic representation of a supply chain

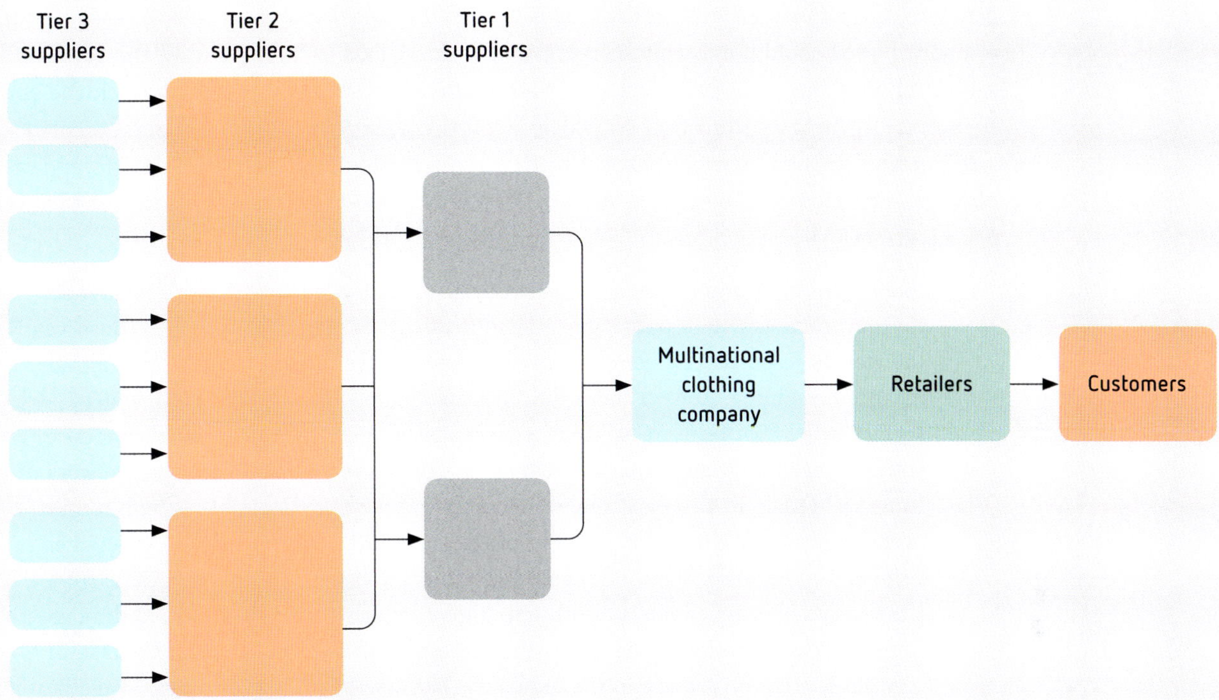

Of some relevance here are the recent movements worldwide to introduce Modern Slavery Acts. For example, within Australia, the *Modern Slavery Act 2018* was introduced in 2018 and became operative from 2020. This followed the introduction of similar acts in other countries, such as the Modern Slavery Act in the UK in 2015. 'Modern slavery' refers to forced/involuntary labour, debt bonded labour, human trafficking, traditional slavery, domestic servitude and child labour. It involves situations of exploitation that a person cannot refuse or leave because of threats, violence, coercion, deception, and/or abuse of power.

The Modern Slavery Act within Australia requires certain organisational types – for example, those large organisations with consolidated revenue of over $100 million – to report annually, by way of a 'Modern Slavery Statement', on the actions they are taking, across their supply chains, to address and monitor the risk that modern slavery is present within those supply chains. The statements – which are publicly available on a government-backed website – must also include information about actions taken by the organisation to address those risks. The Act does not apply any penalties to organisations for information uncovered and disclosed as a result of the audits of their supply chains. Rather, by making the information publicly available, the intention is to leave it to 'the market' and consumers to punish perceived poor behaviour.

We will discuss Modern Slavery Acts more fully in Chapter 6, but what such regulation does is to effectively require certain organisations to extend their reporting boundaries to include the workers employed throughout their supply chains. Of course, some organisations might have done this voluntarily in the absence of any such regulation.

Life cycle considerations

Let us briefly consider the mobile phone, a device that we all seem to have. Due to rapid technological change, and even planned technical obsolescence, many hundreds of millions of mobile phones eventually end up in landfills throughout the world, with their components potentially leaching into nearby groundwater systems. Further, if they are burned, they can generate dangerous toxic emissions. This is despite the fact that a great deal of the contents of a mobile phone could potentially be recycled. So an obvious issue is whether the producers of mobile phones should be responsible and accountable for phones when they reach the end of their lives? Again, if we think they should be accountable, and if the manufacturers accepted such a responsibility, then we would expect to find some form of account pertaining to end-of-life phones. In this regard, if we look at Apple's 2020 *Environmental progress report* (accessed at **www.apple.com/environment** in June 2022), we find the following statement:

> In 2017, we announced our goal to one day use only recycled and renewable materials for our products and packaging—demonstrating our commitment to conserve the world's resources. By using materials from recycled sources, we aim to end our reliance on mining. And we focus on renewable materials from biological sources—such as wood fiber from trees—that are responsibly managed to continually produce without depleting the earth's resources. As we switch to sources like these, we work to use materials in the most environmentally efficient way possible to reduce our overall demand. We're making steady progress toward our goal. Based on supplier reports, 10 percent of the total material we shipped in products in 2019 came from either recycled or renewable sources, one-third of which has been confirmed through third-party certifications. And because certain materials have a high percentage of recycled content on average in the industry—like steel—the actual amount could be much higher.
>
> Four products launched in 2019 were made of 17 percent or more recycled and renewable content, led by MacBook Air with Retina display with more than 40 percent recycled content. There is still much progress to be made, so we continue to responsibly source materials by conducting due diligence in our supply chain; considering the human rights impact on surrounding communities; and fostering the same opportunities as we do in other parts of Apple's supply chain.
>
> Source: Environmental Progress Report. Covering fiscal year 2019, Apple.com, p. 32.

Similarly, if we look at the *Samsung electronics sustainability report 2021* (see **samsung.com**, accessed June 2022), we find the following statement:

> We support the circular economy by promoting take-back and recycling of e-waste and run diverse recycling programs in 55 countries, including South Korea. Since we opened the Asan Recycling Center, South Korea's first comprehensive recycling center for e-waste, in 1998, we established e-waste take-back systems in regional logistics centers. Outside South Korea, we promote take back and e-waste recycling, taking into account regional characteristics when partnering with recycling associations and recycling companies.
>
> The collected e-waste is used as raw materials for metals, plastics, etc., through processes such as sorting, pre-treatment and crushing. Some of the raw materials, such as plastic, are used in manufacturing new products. We have also established guidance in Samsung Requirements for Waste Electrical and Electronic Equipment (WEEE) Managing, which includes matters concerning compliance with environmental, health and safety laws and regulations, satisfaction with requirements for suppliers and prohibition of illegal export of waste.
>
> From 2009 to 2020, we collected a total of 4.54 million tonnes of e-waste and the amount has increased continuously for the past three years. Our Asan Recycling Center

in South Korea, gathered 29,435 tonnes of valuable resources in 2019, including copper, aluminum, steel, and plastic. We reused some 3,366 tonnes of recycled plastics collected from e-waste in product manufacturing. Through these efforts, we have reduced the amount of plastic waste and the use of petrochemical raw materials needed to manufacture new products.

We are continuously improving the manufacturing and product design process to minimize waste. All our global worksites monitor the amount of waste generated and recycled every month. If a target is not fully met, we focus on improving the recycling rate by analyzing ways to process waste. In 2020, we achieved 95% of waste recycling rate. We will make continuous efforts to receive Zero-Waste to Landfill certification for all of our global manufacturing worksites.

Source: Samsung Electronics Sustainability Report 2021, p. 33.

The information presented above as produced by Apple and Samsung are accounts and therefore are an output of an accounting process. While we have only provided a brief discussion of life cycle considerations here, the interesting issue of life cycle analysis will be considered in greater depth in Chapter 5.

As a further example of life-cycle analysis, when ships reach the end of their useful life, they are often sold to other companies and ultimately turn up in developing countries, where they are broken up on beaches often without consideration given to the health and safety of the people dismantling the ships, or the environmental damage caused by the release of the various oils and chemicals. Many injuries and deaths have occurred in such processes. While we will discuss this later in Chapter 5, consider if original owners of the ships – such as cruise ship companies which have sold their vessels to ship-wrecking companies – should be accountable for these accidents and deaths?

Source: Getty Images/Majority World/UIG

Should shipping companies have a responsibility and accountability for what happens to ships at the end of their useful life?

LO2.7 Accounting: not a one-size-fits-all practice

There are many different forms of organisations (for example, sole traders, partnerships, companies, trusts and government departments) involved in different types of activities (which might or might not be aimed at making a financial profit), with different stakeholders and perceived responsibilities, and which use different resources and incur or create different costs. As you should now appreciate, this will all impact the accounts they produce both internally and externally. As such, we should not perceive accounting as a *one-size-fits-all* practice.

This is the case even though in reporting certain aspects of performance, such as financial performance, the existence of many rules and regulations means that large organisations tend to report the same types of financial accounting information to external stakeholders (that is, the financial statements are very similar in form). The external reporting of social and environmental information, however, tends to be quite varied, with some organisations producing little information while others produce a lot. Unlike financial reporting, there is very little regulation governing the reporting of social and environmental performance information, and therefore much of the accounting undertaken is at the option of the organisation.

People within an organisation need various types of information to enable them to manage the organisation. As explained in Chapter 1, what information they collect will depend upon a variety of factors, including what aspects of performance they feel responsible for and therefore want to manage. This, in turn, could be influenced by personal values, stakeholder pressure, the basis of their remuneration (that is, whether they receive bonuses linked to particular performance indicators), the scarcity and/or ecological importance of the resources they are using, their professional and educational background, and so forth. As with external reporting, the information collected for internal use could relate to financial and/or social and/or environmental performance.

LO2.8 A brief introduction to management accounting

Management accounting is the focus of Chapters 3 to 5. Nevertheless, it is appropriate to briefly discuss the term now as effectively we have been discussing it without defining it. According to the website of the Institute of Certified Management Accountants (ICMA; **www.cmawebline.org**):

> A management accountant applies his or her professional knowledge and skill in the preparation and presentation of financial and other decision oriented information in such a way as to assist management in the formulation of policies, and in the planning and control of the operation of the undertaking.
>
> Source: Institute of Certified Management Accountants (2022).

Again, what information is collected and used will depend on the objectives or mission of the organisation, the types of resources being used, the values/ethics of the managers, and so forth. It is not a one-size-fits-all approach.

management accounting The process of generating financial and non-financial information to be used by managers for planning, monitoring and controlling an organisation

The above quote refers to a 'management accountant'. Simply stated, accounting is often divided into two branches: management accounting and financial accounting. **Management accounting** is a broad term referring to information produced for internal decision making by managers; that is, information that is required for various decisions pertaining to aspects associated with planning, monitoring and control, including aspects of financial, social or environmental performance. The management accountant is somebody who collects, analyses and/or reports such information.

By comparison, *financial accounting* is typically understood as that branch of accounting that generates financial reports for use by people *outside* the organisation; for example, investors who want to monitor the performance of a company they have invested in. Financial accounting is very heavily regulated, whereas management accounting is basically unregulated. In an accounting degree, a student would typically undertake a number of separate units/subjects on financial accounting, as well as a number of separate subjects in the area of management accounting.

Traditionally, much of the accounting information collected for internal decision making (which as we now know would be referred to as management accounting information) focused upon the *maximisation of financial revenues* and the *minimisation of financial costs*. Further, much management accounting has focused upon the control of processes/activities, and compliance with predetermined policies and procedures. However, *competition* is now accepted as a key component of management accounting; for example, the strategies that need to be embraced to increase market share and/or achieve various social or environmental goals. To achieve a competitive advantage, most managers understand that they must also consider the social and environmental consequences/costs of their operation. The community expects it. Such expectations have changed relative to say 30 years ago. Therefore, accounting for internal decision making is much more than just a focus on financial costs or financial performance.

If managers want to reduce their use of various raw materials, including water, energy and air, and also reduce their levels of waste, CO_2 emissions, releases of polluted water and so forth, then they would undertake a careful analysis of all the inputs and outputs of their production process and concentrate on reducing the negative aspects of their operations. This is management 'accounting', yet it relies on various forms of measurement rather than measuring things only in monetary terms.

Information used by management can also form the basis of public reports

The information necessarily collected for internal management decision-making (management accounting information) could also form the basis for reports that are to be released publicly. For example, a large retail company might be concerned about the treatment of employees within its supply factories. As such, it might require that suppliers allow an independent third party to enter their factories and assess the health and safety of the employees. The related report, or account, could then be used by management to make decisions about such things as whether they will continue doing business with the supplier, or whether they will assist the supplier in making improvements that support the workers. The assessment of workplace conditions within the factories, while prepared for internal management purposes, might also form the basis of a report that is released to the public.

As a real-world example, leading sportswear companies like Nike now regularly have independent organisations visit the factories of suppliers to check on various aspects of worker employment, including:

- the use of child labour
- whether employees are allowed to freely join labour unions
- whether there are cases of physical, sexual or verbal abuse
- whether appropriate complaint mechanisms for employees exist
- whether work hours are excessive
- whether employees are paid fair wages
- whether the buildings appear safe
- whether the equipment being used is safe
- whether proper health and safety training is provided to employees.

Information – such as the above – is used for internal decisions, and hence can be considered as 'management accounting' information. However, it is often also reported in their publicly available reports. For example, see Nike's *Impact Report 2020* (available at **https://nike.com**) which provides information about how workers are treated within the company's supply factories.

Learning exercise 2.7 explores some of the social information that managers of an organisation might elect to make publicly available.

2.7 Learning Exercise

The decision to disclose social information

So why would an organisation like Nike make the results of its factory audits publicly available? While we can never be fully sure of management's motivations for particular actions, the likely answer is that the management of Nike believe that many people within the community – including consumers of Nike's products – think that organisations should take some responsibility for the working conditions of employees within their supply chain. As such, Nike might have felt it was their responsibility to initiate factory audits and to provide public accounts of the results. A failure to do so might have resulted in stakeholders – such as consumers – electing not to support the organisation, and this would ultimately have had implications for the financial performance of the organisation.

LO2.9 Some frameworks used to produce accounts for external stakeholders

As you should by now understand, we can broadly categorise external reporting into three types:

- financial reporting
- social reporting
- environmental reporting.

We will now consider, in more depth, the external reporting of financial, social and environmental performance information. At the same time, we will talk of *sustainability reporting*, which addresses all three aspects.

External reporting – financial

financial accounting
The identification, measurement, recording and communication of information about the financial performance and financial position of an organisation for external users

As we now know, financial reports or accounts are generated through the process of **financial accounting**. The purpose of financial accounting/reporting is generally to provide information about the financial performance and position of an organisation. The main audience for these reports is generally considered to be the managers and owners of the organisation, as well as others with a financial stake in it, such as those who are owed money by the organisation (for example, lenders and creditors). There will also be other groups with an interest in the financial performance of an organisation. For example, employees will want to know how well the organisation is being managed financially in order to understand how secure is their employment, or perhaps whether the organisation can afford to pay higher wages. Customers will be interested in the financial performance of an organisation in order to assess whether it will be able to continue supplying goods or services, or perhaps whether it appears that the organisation is too profitable and can therefore afford to reduce the selling prices of its goods and services.

With smaller organisations, where the owners are also the managers, there will typically be a lack of any regulations requiring them to publicly release financial statements of a particular form. However, as organisations get larger, the owners (who might be, for example, individual investors or superannuation funds) will typically not have anything to do with the management of the organisation and will therefore rely upon general-purpose financial reports to inform them about how the organisation is performing and how secure their investment seems to be. As such, and because of this dependence of owners (shareholders) upon the general-purpose financial reports released by large companies, the financial reporting undertaken by these organisations – where there is a high degree of separation between ownership and management – tends to be very highly regulated, as we will discuss in Chapters 7 to 11.

Most countries throughout the world (other than the United States, which has its own accounting standard setter: the Financial Accounting Standards Board or FASB) typically require larger organisations to apply the accounting standards produced by the IASB when producing their financial reports for owners, lenders, creditors and other parties with an interest in the financial performance and position of an organisation. These accounting standards, which are referred to as the International Financial Reporting Standards (IFRS), are also adopted by many government departments.

According to the IASB (2022), the objective of financial reporting is 'to provide financial information about the reporting entity that is useful to existing and potential investors, lenders and other creditors in making decisions about providing resources to the entity'. The accounting standards cover a multitude of financial reporting issues. For those who are interested, see the website of the IASB for an overview of the various accounting standards in place (www.ifrs.org).

External reporting – social

Social accounts are generated through the process of **social accounting**, which provides information about an organisation's interaction with, and associated impacts upon, particular societies. Social accounting can generate information about an organisation's:

- interaction with the local community
- level of support for community projects
- support for employees within the supply chain
- health and safety record.

social accounting
The identification, measurement, recording and communication of information about an organisation's impact on particular societies, or stakeholders

Social (and also environmental) performance is not generally addressed by the financial reporting standards released by the IASB. The GRI's Sustainability Reporting Standards, however, provide a number of indicators against which organisations can report, including various indicators relating to the following areas (the GRI guidelines can also be used to assist internal reporting):

- employment
- labour/management relations
- occupational health and safety
- training and education
- diversity and equal opportunity
- non-discrimination
- child labour
- Indigenous people's rights.

The Sustainability Reporting Standards of the GRI can be found at www.globalreporting.org/standards. They will be discussed in depth in Chapter 6.

environmental accounting
The identification, measurement, recording and communication of information about an organisation's impact on living and non-living natural systems (including land, air, water and ecosystems)

External reporting – environmental

Environmental accounts are generated through the process of **environmental accounting**, which can address an organisation's impact on living and non-living natural systems, including land, air, water and ecosystems. The GRI's Sustainability Reporting Standards provide a number of indicators against which organisations can report, relating to such broad classifications as:

- materials usage
- energy usage
- water usage
- impact on biodiversity
- emissions into the air
- effluent and waste release
- environmental compliance
- environmental assessments of suppliers.

LO2.10 For-profit and not-for-profit organisations

To this point of the book, it might have been inferred that we were predominantly focusing on organisations that seek to make a profit, for the ultimate purpose of making payments (dividend payments in the case of a company) to owners. These are known as *for-profit organisations*, as the generation of profits is their main objective in operating.

However, there are many organisations in society which are established to fulfil social and/or environmental goals, and which do not have profit making as their principal focus. For example, environmental groups such as Greenpeace, the World Wide Fund for Nature, Rainforest Action Network, Surfrider Foundation, and Friends of the Earth have as their main goal protecting the environment and do not focus on profits. These are called *not-for-profit organisations*. Not-for-profit entities can take various forms, even companies.

Apart from environmental protection, not-for-profit organisations are also often involved in:

- education
- religion
- promoting and supporting particular sports
- supporting particular community groups
- business and professional associations
- trade unions
- the government sector.

As you should now appreciate, whether an organisation is for-profit or not-for-profit will in turn influence the accounting being undertaken. Some information might be important to managers of a not-for-profit organisation but not be perceived as important by a for-profit organisation, and vice-versa.

Key concept

Whether an organisation is for-profit or not-for-profit will influence what information the managers consider to be important, and by extension influence the accounting that is undertaken.

Returning our attention to organisations that have been established to generate profits and provide financial returns to owners, these might also be subdivided into further general categories, such as:

- service businesses (for example, airlines) – these do not tend to provide physical products but instead can provide services (such as travel, medical treatment or entertainment) or repairs to products produced by other organisations
- merchandising businesses (for example, large retail operations) – these buy goods that are already fit for sale and then resell them at a profit
- manufacturing businesses (for example, car producers) – these produce goods that others sell or service.

Some organisations are a mixture of the above.

Learning exercise 2.8 considers what sort of information could be reported by a not-for-profit organisation that has the protection of animals as its key organisational focus.

2.8 Learning Exercise

The RSPCA – analysing a not-for-profit organisation and its reporting boundaries

If we look at the website of the Royal Society for the Prevention of Cruelty to Animals (RSPCA; www.rspca.org.au), we will find the following information about its mission, vision, and objectives. We can use this information to consider what kind of organisation is the RSPCA and how it might operate.

> Mission
>
> To prevent cruelty to animals by actively promoting their care and protection.
>
> Vision
>
> To be the leading authority in animal care and protection.
>
> Objectives
>
> The objectives of the RSPCA in Australia are:
>
> - To prevent cruelty to animals by ensuring the enforcement of existing laws at federal and state level.
> - To procure the passage of such amending or new legislation as is necessary for the protection of animals.
> - To develop and promote policies for the humane treatment of animals that reflect contemporary values and scientific knowledge.
> - To educate the community with regard to the humane treatment of animals.
> - To engage with relevant stakeholders to improve animal welfare.
> - To sustain an intelligent public opinion regarding animal welfare.
> - To operate facilities for the care and protection of animals.

Source: Royal Society for the Prevention of Cruelty to Animals (2022).

What types of performance-related information might RSPCA managers be particularly interested in collecting?

Given the above mission, vision and objectives, the RSPCA might be interested in collecting the following information in order to assist its managers to do their jobs:

- types and amounts of animals being cared for
- adoption rates for various types of animals

- numbers and types of animals being euthanised and why
- numbers of wildlife being cared for, and the outcomes of that care in terms of the numbers that were released or euthanised
- cruelty complaints investigated by the RSPCA and the outcomes of these complaints
- financial costs associated with the various activities
- sources of funds
- reserve of funds available for future endeavours.

After gathering this information, is the RSPCA likely to report it publicly?

Given the nature of the organisation (dedicated to animal care and protection) and its reliance on public donations, we might expect that the RSPCA would want to demonstrate a high level of public accountability. A look at the organisation's website confirms that the information identified above has been disclosed publicly.

Is the RSPCA interested in collecting information about particular aspects of its financial performance?

Even though the organisation is not-for-profit, it nevertheless needs to keep records of its costs and revenues to ensure that it is able to monitor and control them, so as to continue providing the necessary services. Without financial resources, it cannot achieve its objectives. All organisations need to carefully account for their finances.

Do you think the boundary of the reporting entity extends beyond the organisation itself?

Given the goals of the organisation, it makes sense that the RSPCA will want to know the reasons why various animals are being treated the way they are, or kept under certain conditions. It will want to know that its efforts are creating positive change beyond the organisation, and hence it will have an extended reporting boundary.

Who might be some of the stakeholders of the RSPCA?

The main stakeholders would be:

- the animals themselves
- the various interest groups that work to ensure the proper treatment of animals
- other organisations and people who work in the interests of animals.

Other stakeholders would include pet owners, government agencies (particularly those charged with prosecuting animal offenders), the RSPCA's employees and volunteers, and the providers of the necessary funds to allow the organisation to operate.

LO2.11 Some general forms of organisations

We have already discussed how organisations often have a choice as to how far they extend the boundary of their accounting and reporting. This will be the case regardless of whether the organisation is for-profit or not-for-profit. While we have been discussing organisations in a general sense, such organisations can actually take on various forms. They might, for example, be a:

- sole trader
- partnership
- company.

Sole traders

A **sole trader** – or, as it is also often called, a *sole proprietorship* – is considered to be in existence when one individual owns a business and is responsible for all of its debts. Sole traders, which are much more numerous than partnerships or companies, are generally established to generate a profit, but organisations that are sole traders might also have as their principal goals the achievement of various social or environmental outcomes. Relative to other forms of business, a sole trader is usually small in terms of total income, profits and the number of employees. Many small businesses – such as milk bars, restaurants, newsagents, landscapers, plumbers, painters and caterers – are sole traders.

sole trader
An organisation where one individual controls and manages a business, and is responsible for all of its debts

In a sole trader, the owner is also typically the manager. A sole trader is not a separate legal entity, so for legal purposes the business is not separate from the owner's non-business affairs. As such, the business is not separately taxed but rather the earnings are included in the owner's personal tax return.

Source: Alamy Stock Photo/Wiskerke

Many businesses that are owner-operated are sole traders.

A sole trader is not difficult to set up. Apart from having to comply with certain tax obligations, there are generally no specific accounting requirements that apply to sole traders. Sole traders do not have to apply the multitude of accounting standards issued by organisations such as the IASB, and they can be flexible with their reporting, but like all organisations they still need to do some forms of accounting.

The accounting reports that are produced for a sole trader will tend to focus on providing information about the financial performance and position of the business. In terms of financial performance, the sole trader will want details of the various costs being incurred, where revenues are being generated, and the overall profits. Such information will also be required by taxation authorities. Details of the cash flows being generated by the organisation will also be extremely important to the sole trader. For those sole traders that are not for-profit organisations, other accounts about social or environmental aspects of the organisation might also be generated. In any case, unlike for legal purposes, from an accounting perspective the owner is seen to be separate to the sole trader organisation.

In terms of its financial position, a sole trader will want to know about its various assets and liabilities, as well as the amounts owed to, and due from individual creditors (suppliers) and customers, respectively. In terms of stakeholders outside the organisation, if banks have provided funds to the sole trader, then they might demand various types of financial information in order to enable them to determine the ability of the sole trader to pay back the amounts due.

Since a sole trader is not considered to be a separate legal entity, if something goes wrong with the business being conducted, then the owner is considered to have **unlimited liability**. This results in no distinction being made between the personal wealth of the owner and the resources that have been contributed to the business. This means that if the business cannot pay its outstanding debts, then the owner's personal assets will be called upon to pay them. Therefore, while for financial accounting purposes we will distinguish between the business and the owner, for legal purposes no such distinction will be made for a sole trader. Because there is no separate identity for legal purposes, a sole trader's business will cease to exist on the death of the owner.

unlimited liability
Liability that extends beyond the assets of an organisation. In the case of a sole trader, if a business fails then the sole trader's personal assets may have to be used to repay debts

The features of a sole trader can be summarised as follows:

- The owner has unlimited liability, so they can potentially lose their home and other personal assets if their business cannot pay its debts.
- The business has no separate legal identity and ceases operation on the departure or death of the owner – it therefore has a limited life.
- As a sole trader has only one person, the business may have limited skills, time and access to financial resources.
- There is usually no separation between ownership and management.
- From an accounting perspective, the owner and the business are seen as separate entities.
- Taxes are paid by the owner on all their income (aggregated together), including that from the business.
- If there is a loss, then one person (the owner) incurs it.
- There is generally no regulation requiring the preparation of financial statements by sole traders.

Learning exercise 2.9 explores some accounting issues as they relate to a sole trader.

2.9 Learning Exercise

Understanding accounting and accountability for sole traders

Suzie Angles is a plumber working for herself. She is a sole trader.

For what purposes might Suzie need accounting?

Suzie will need accounting to inform her about:

- financial costs
- financial income
- profits.

She will need to know about the financial resources she has, as well as to whom she owes funds, and who owes her funds. She will also need to know whether she will be able to pay her debts as and when they become due, as well as how much cash can be withdrawn from the business without impacting its ability to keep operating.

To whom is a sole trader accountable?

Suzie is accountable to herself, as she needs to ensure that she is able to pay her own bills. To the extent that she has borrowed funds from external organisations, such as banks, she will also be accountable to these organisations. Because it is necessary to lodge tax returns, the business is also accountable to the tax authorities.

The focus of a sole trader is typically on financial aspects of performance (both past and projected performance) rather than on the social or environmental impacts of the business. As Suzie's organisation is relatively small (likely just herself), its social and environmental impacts will be similarly small. That is not to say that Suzie does not care about these factors, but it is unlikely that she will be expected to report upon them. However, she might choose to.

Accounting by sole traders

We can summarise the accounting generally undertaken by a sole trader in terms of the accountability model we introduced in Chapter 1. As represented in **Figure 2.4**, we can make the judgement that, for the majority of sole traders, the focus will be on financial measures of performance rather than on measures of social and/or environmental performance. In terms of these financial measures, the sole trader will want information about past performance as well as projections of what the future financial performance and financial position will be, based on current expectations and objectives, and knowledge of the business. We will consider how we do future projections, which we can refer to as *budgeting*, in Chapter 4. The reporting frameworks to be used will involve applying the financial accounting principles that are appropriate for a sole trader. As there will likely not be other parties who depend on reports from the sole trader – other than banks, perhaps, who might demand specific items of information as determined in the lending agreements – then there will be no expectation that the financial reports will be prepared in accordance with accounting standards, or that they will be subjected to an audit by an independent third party.

FIGURE 2.4 An overview of the accounting undertaken by a sole trader

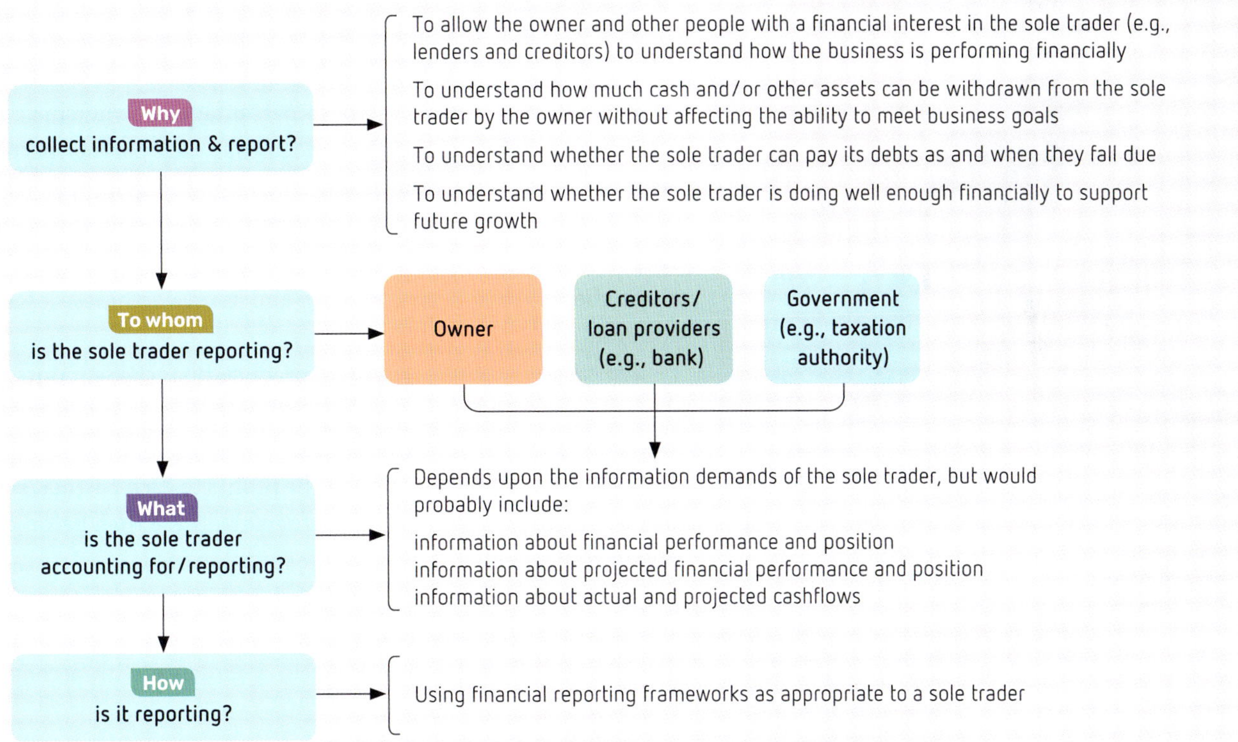

Partnerships

A **partnership** exists when two or more people come together with a common purpose, usually to make a profit. Like a sole trader, partnerships tend to be small businesses, although there can be exceptions; for example, some legal and accounting partnerships can be very large.

partnership
When two or more people establish an organisation for a common purpose, sharing its control and management, and being jointly responsible for all of its debts

Within a partnership, people with different skills and resources come together. The profit is generally shared according to a partnership agreement, although in many jurisdictions there is no legal requirement for such a formal arrangement to exist. That is, depending on the actions of individuals, a partnership can be considered to be in existence even in the absence of a formal partnership agreement. However, while a partnership agreement does not have to formally exist, it certainly helps if disputes or disagreements subsequently arise.

mutual agency
The idea that each partner becomes responsible for the actions undertaken by other partners, just as they would be if they had made particular decisions themselves

The partnership agreement will generally stipulate:

- the names of the partners
- the required contributions of cash and/or other assets
- working responsibilities – who does what
- the basis of sharing profits or losses
- what happens on termination of the partnership.

Source: Getty Images/Noel Hendrickson

Two friends who start a surf shop could operate as a partnership. One partner may be good at shaping surfboards, while the other may be good at running the business.

A partnership is considered for accounting purposes to be a separate entity; that is, an entity that is separate to the individual partners such that the individual assets and liabilities of the partners, which have not been contributed to the partnership, are not considered to be part of the assets and liabilities of the partnership. However, like a sole trader, for legal purposes the partnership is not a separate legal entity. As such, the partners have unlimited liability for the obligations of the partnership, meaning that if the resources of the partnership are insufficient to meet its debts, then the partners' individual assets can, by law, be seized to pay those debts (and the assets will not necessarily be seized on the basis of the partners' percentage of ownership). This is known as **mutual agency** – the idea that each partner becomes responsible for the actions undertaken by other partners, just as they would be if they had made particular decisions themselves. Therefore, it is essential that, before forming a partnership, one is satisfied with the competency and trustworthiness of their potential partners.

Typically, the partnership will produce financial accounts that show the contributions made by each partner; the amounts withdrawn by each partner; the income, expenses and profits of the partnership; and the allocation of the profits to each partner. When partners contribute assets to a partnership, these then become the partnership's assets.

Some of the features of a partnership are that:

- they are easy to set up
- they are not subject to a requirement to produce reports in accordance with accounting standards
- they allow for more skills and expertise relative to a sole trader
- each partner acts as an *agent* of the business (often referred to as *mutual agency*)
- like a sole trader, they are subject to unlimited liability, and all partners are liable for the debts incurred; that is, if there are not enough assets within the partnership to satisfy obligations, then the personal assets of each partner may be used to do so
- they typically cease to exist when a partner exits the partnership.

Learning exercise 2.10 considers some accounting issues as they relate to a partnership.

2.10 Learning Exercise

Understanding accounting and accountability in regards to partnerships

Bill and Ben form a partnership to provide gardening services to local households.

For what purposes would Bill and Ben need accounting?

As partnerships are usually relatively small in size – like a sole trader – the purposes of partnership accounting tend to be very similar to those of sole trader accounting. For a partnership, however, there will be a need for very detailed information about:

- the contributions made by each partner
- the profits distributed to each partner
- the drawings made by each partner.

Together, this information will provide details of the amounts of each partner's share of the partnership – their partnership account.

While not necessarily quantified in financial terms, because of the existence of mutual agency, it is also essential that each partner knows of the agreements entered into by every other partner.

To whom is a partnership accountable?

Like a sole trader, a partnership is accountable to the providers of funds – lenders and creditors – as well as to government departments such as the Australian Taxation Office. A partnership is accountable to each partner, and perhaps to any employees the partners have hired to work for the business (employees typically have an interest in knowing whether a partnership is profitable and can continue to offer them employment).

As partnerships are generally quite small, relative to organisations such as companies, their social and environmental impacts are also small, so there do not tend to be many stakeholders with an interest in reporting on the partnership's social and environmental performance.

Accounting by partnerships

The accounting undertaken by a partnership is summarised in **Figure 2.5**. We can make the judgement that, as with a sole trader, for the majority of partnerships the focus of the stakeholders is on financial measures of performance and position (actual and projected) and not also on measures of social and/or environmental performance. In terms of the financial measures, the partners will want information about past performance as well as projections of future performance. As with the sole trader, the reporting frameworks to be used are based on the application of financial accounting principles that are appropriate for a partnership. As there will not be other parties who depend on receiving reports from the partnership – other than banks, perhaps, who could demand specific items of information as determined in the lending agreements – there will be no expectations that the financial reports will be prepared in accordance with accounting standards, or that they will be subject to an audit by an independent third party. Further, because the social and environmental impacts of a partnership will be relatively minimal, there generally will not be various stakeholders with an interest in, or need for, information about the social and environmental impacts of a

FIGURE 2.5 An overview of the accounting undertaken by a partnership

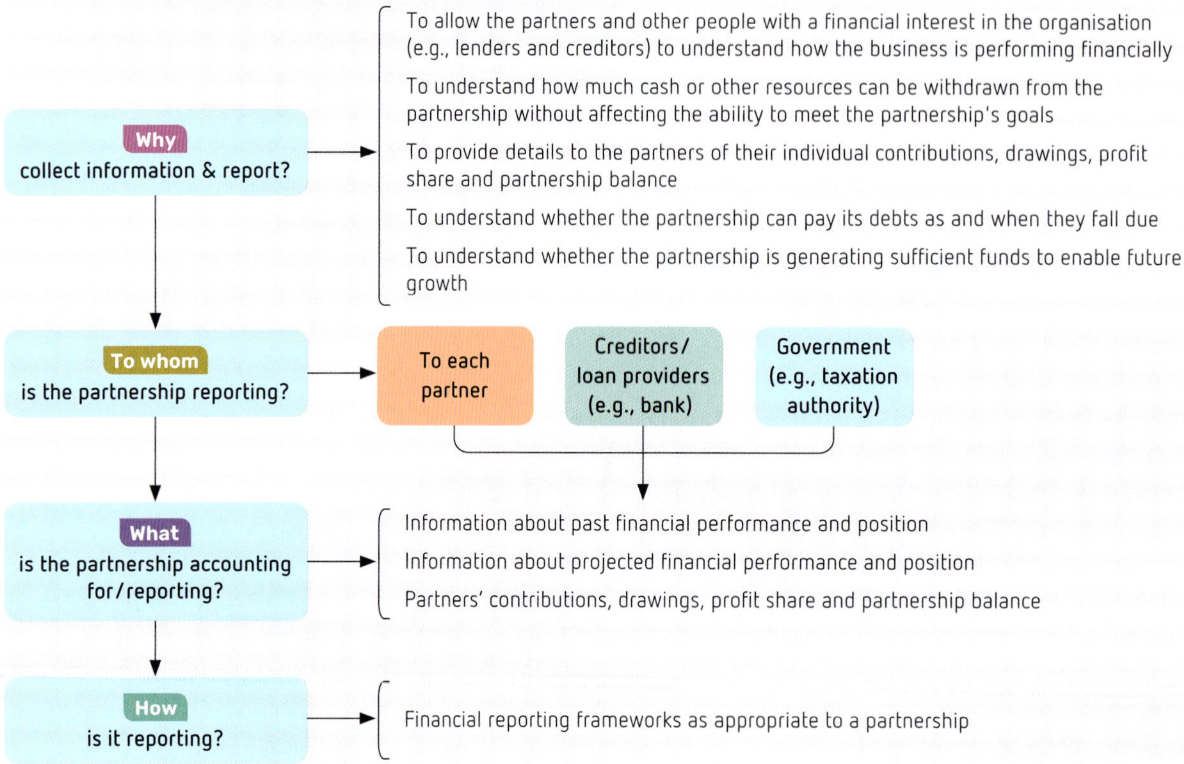

partnership business. (That said, for some partnerships, the partners might believe that they can competitively differentiate themselves from other organisations on the basis of their social and environmental performance. In this case, they might elect to produce publicly available social and environmental performance information.)

company
An organisation that has a separate legal personality from that of its owners (shareholders), meaning they are not personally responsible for its debts

limited liability
An ownership arrangement for companies whereby each owner pays a set amount for a number of shares in a company and has no responsibility for the company's debts beyond the cost of their shares

Companies

A **company** is an entity that has a separate legal identity from that of its owners. Each owner of a company owns shares in it and hence is considered to be a shareholder. Shareholders generally have no liability for debts other than if they still owe some amounts on the shares they have acquired. That is, the liability of a shareholder is generally limited to the amount they have agreed to pay for their shares. Hence, unlike sole traders and partnerships, companies are considered to be **limited liability** organisations. Limited liability encourages people to invest in a company even when they have very little, or nothing, to do with its ongoing management. That is, there is usually a separation of ownership and management, particularly in larger companies. The shares are transferable to others and might be traded on a securities exchange (stock exchange) if they relate to public companies, which are allowed to offer their shares for sale to the public.

Because there is generally a separation between the ownership and management of a company, the owners will often depend on receiving accounts from the company to inform them as to how the managers have used the shareholders' funds, as well as accounts about what the managers intend to do in the future. This can be contrasted with sole traders and partners in a partnership who, because they are usually involved in the ongoing management of the organisation, will not depend on some form of general-purpose financial statements being released by the organisation. Shareholders in large companies, however, will not have access to information particularly tailored to their own needs. Rather, they will receive general-purpose reports which generally meet the information needs of all shareholders.

As is the case with sole traders and partnerships, the owners of a company, from an accounting perspective, are considered separate entities from the organisation when accounting for that organisation. Additionally, because shareholders typically have nothing to do with the ongoing management of an organisation, and because their main source of information about the financial performance and position of a company is the financial reports (which are made available to all shareholders), the financial reporting of companies is heavily regulated. In most countries, corporations legislation exists which requires companies to lodge their financial accounts with corporate regulators as well as make them available to all shareholders. There will be a requirement that the company's financial statements – particularly the financial statements of larger companies – comply with the relevant accounting standards issued by bodies such as the IASB. The regulation of financial reporting will be considered more fully in Chapters 7 to 11.

Other than for small companies, there is also a legal requirement that the financial statements of a company be audited by an independent third party before they are made available to shareholders. This will increase the reliability of the information, which is one of the qualitative characteristics that information should possess if it is to be useful (as we discussed in Chapter 1).

Shareholders in companies generally receive returns from their investments from two sources, these being *dividends* and increases in the value of the shares. Dividends are the distribution of profits to shareholders. However, not all profits of a company will necessarily be paid out as dividends. Companies often retain profits (referred to as retained earnings or *retained profits*) in order to fund various initiatives, such as investing in more plant and machinery, or new businesses. By retaining some of its profits, a company will reduce its reliance on external borrowings, which will also have the effect of reducing some of the organisation's risk.

Some of the features of a company, therefore, are as follows:

- The owners of a company are known as its shareholders.
- A company is a separate legal entity, independent of the owners, and is taxed as such.
- It is also a separate entity for accounting purposes.
- It can enter into its own contracts.
- It can buy, own and sell assets.
- It can distribute profits to owners as dividends.
- Owners are not personally liable for a company's debts (other than amounts unpaid on shares acquired); that is, the shareholder's liability is limited (and that's why in many countries companies have 'Ltd' after their name).
- If a company fails and owes funds, then it will be the company that is sued (unless the directors knew that the company could not pay its debts as and when they were due but nevertheless kept trading, in which case the directors could become personally liable for the debts of the company).
- A company does not cease trading when a shareholder sells their shares.
- It is more difficult to form than a sole trader or partnership.

- It will have certain reporting obligations as detailed in the relevant corporations legislation.
- It is subject to the requirement that its financial accounts get audited by an independent external auditor (does not apply to small companies).
- Large companies will have to comply with accounting standards.

Let's now discuss two different types of companies: private and public.

Private (proprietary) companies

In many countries, private companies are denoted by 'Pty Ltd', which is an abbreviation of 'Proprietary Limited'. They might also have the designation 'Pte' (for private). Private companies are typically family owned and are often referred to as small- or medium-sized organisations. They are not permitted to offer shares to the public, and by law there are typically restrictions on the number of shareholders (for example, in Australia it is generally 50 shareholders).

For small private companies, there are very limited reporting requirements, and the accounting standards developed by bodies such as the IASB do not have to be followed.

Public companies

The most common form of public company is that which offers its shares to the public. As already noted, shares held in a public company are generally transferable to others and typically traded on a securities exchange. There is also a high level of separation between ownership and control.

Public companies have quite a significant number of reporting obligations and must produce financial reports – referred to as general purpose financial reports – that comply with accounting standards. These reports must be audited by a qualified financial statement auditor.

Because public companies are typically very large, they will create various economic, social and environmental impacts that will influence the lives of a vast array of stakeholders. As such, and because of the broader reach of the impacts of public companies relative to many other forms of organisations, they tend to report a variety of financial, social and environmental information to a large cross-section of stakeholders, and will use a variety of reporting frameworks.

Learning exercise 2.11 considers some accounting issues that might apply to a public company.

2.11 Learning Exercise

Information that might be demanded from a public company

Big Co Ltd is a public company involved in mining coal in Australia. Rob Adonis is a shareholder in Big Co Ltd, with a large amount of his wealth invested in the company.

What information might be available to Rob?

Although Rob, as a shareholder, owns some of the company, he likely has nothing to do with its management. Rob would probably depend on the company to provide him with information to enable him to determine how well it is operating, and how secure is his investment. That information will help Rob decide whether to buy more shares, sell his existing shares, or just hold on to the shares he currently owns.

What information about Big Co Ltd might Rob need or want?

In terms of the types of information Rob would want, this will depend on what facets of organisational performance he is concerned about. If he is focused on financial indicators, then he might just want financial reports that tell him about the various expenses, income and profits of the firm, as well as information about the total assets and liabilities of the organisation.

If Rob is also concerned about the organisation's social and environmental impacts – as many shareholders are – then he would also want information on this, together with information about how the organisation is trying to control such impacts. Because this company is involved in mining coal, and because of specific global concerns about how burning coal contributes to climate change, Rob might want to know how the company is responding to these concerns and how it might be transitioning to other forms of business.

As Big Co Ltd is a public company, one involved in mining, it would be typical for it to provide various types of accounts about social and environmental performance, which ideally should be available to Rob.

Other forms of companies

There are other forms of companies apart from public and private companies, which include the following:

- *Companies limited by guarantee* – Often not-for-profit organisations that might function as sporting clubs or charities. Within this form of company, owners agree to pay a certain amount – typically not very large – which is only enforced in the event of the company being discontinued (wound up).
- *Unlimited liability companies* – Not very common, these companies have no liability limit placed on the owners in terms of contributing to the debts of the company. They are used mainly by professional service organisations that operate in a manner similar to a partnership; for example, as with many legal and accounting firms.
- *No liability companies* – These are companies that do not have the power to demand the payment of amounts unpaid on partly paid shares. Such companies sometimes exist within the mining industry.

Groups of companies

As indicated earlier in this chapter, companies often acquire shares or ownership interests in other organisations in order to control them. These controlled organisations are referred to as subsidiaries, and the ultimate controlling organisation is the parent entity. For example, many of the companies listed on securities exchanges control over 100 subsidiaries.

These groups of organisations might be international in nature, with the parent company located in one country and the subsidiaries dispersed throughout many different countries. In practice, separate accounts are provided for the parent company, as well as one aggregated set of accounts for the entire group (the consolidated entity).

Accounting by companies

The accounting undertaken by a public company is summarised in **Figure 2.6**. Because a public company will be large, it will likely impact the lives of many different categories of stakeholders; for example, shareholders, creditors, lenders, employees, local communities, news media, non-government organisations that take responsibility for looking after the interests of other stakeholders, corporate regulators, the environment and so forth.

Accounting for the range of social, environmental and financial impacts it creates for a diverse group of stakeholders means that a public company would tend to have a broad reporting

FIGURE 2.6 An overview of the accounting undertaken by a public company

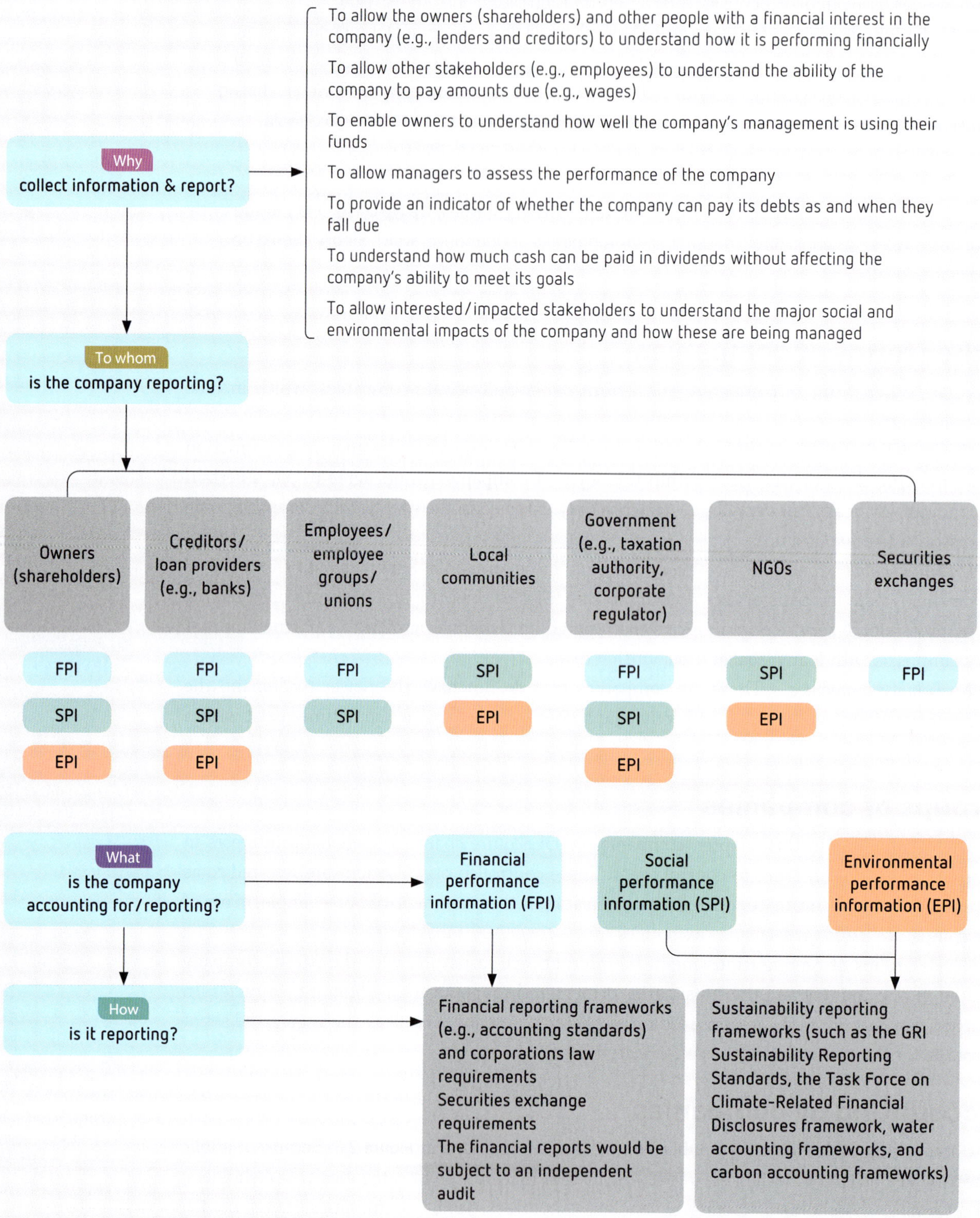

boundary. Various aspects of the company's performance would be relevant to people both within the organisation (who need to manage these aspects) as well as those outside the organisation.

The financial reporting frameworks that can be used by a public company are heavily regulated. A public company is required to comply with various financial accounting standards as well as other obligations imposed by corporations legislation and the relevant securities exchanges.

As **Figure 2.6** shows, different stakeholder groups have different information demands, and these tend to be satisfied by the company applying different reporting frameworks. That is, a public company would be expected to apply numerous measurement and reporting frameworks, and a number of the accounts would be subject to some form of audit from an independent third party.

What we have emphasised in the above sections is that the focus of accounting can take on many different forms, depending on the organisation, and have vastly different account users. In some cases, such as in public companies, there will be a separation of ownership and management (or ownership and control), while in other situations (for example, within a sole trader or partnership) there will be no such separation. Some organisations will focus on profits while others will not. All of this influences the accounting being undertaken – there is no one-size-fits-all approach when it comes to accounting!

A good overview of sole traders, partnerships and companies is also provided by an Australian Government video on these topics (use search terms 'Australian Government' and 'Business Structures').

Why do I need to know about different organisational types?

In your professional career you will be exposed to different forms of organisations. These different forms will have different responsibilities, legal obligations, or rules in relation to such matters as

- the difficulties or ease associated with establishment
- the maximum membership numbers and obligations
- requirements with respect to external reporting
- the extent of the owners' obligations in relation to the cessation of the organisation, or in the event of the organisation not being able to pay its debts as and when they fall due
- the extent of accountability expected, given the likely judgements about reporting boundaries and stakeholders' rights.

If you are in a position which requires you to deal with different forms of organisations, or to consider establishing an organisation, it is important that you understand the legal rights and obligations associated with the different organisational structures. It will be particularly important to understand the financial (and perhaps reputational and mental health) risk exposure created by being associated with different organisational forms which have different involvement expectations of owners. For example, if you decide to start a business and you are considering doing it through either a partnership or a small private company then you would need to understand that although it is easier to establish a partnership, the financial implications of being in a partnership could be higher if the organisation subsequently collapses. Also, the reporting burden of a private company would typically be greater.

STUDY TOOLS

SUMMARY

In providing a summary of this chapter, we will also reflect on where we are now in terms of the contents of Chapters 1 and 2.

As a result of reading the first two chapters of this book, you have been exposed to a different perspective on, or idea of, accounting than you might have anticipated. We have now extended the idea of accounting beyond what you might have previously considered constituted accounting. To this point, we have considered:

- the broad nature of accounting and its necessary relationship to perspectives on responsibility and accountability
- how the different perspectives of responsibility and accountability held by internal and external stakeholders will influence the form of accounting undertaken by an organisation
- how accounting is ever-evolving as community expectations about organisational responsibilities and accountabilities change
- how accounting can be undertaken in a way that either has a broad or a narrow reach; for example, we may or may not have an accounting system that has a relatively broad reporting boundary that considers the impacts an organisation's products have on the health and safety of consumers or those employees in the supply chain
- how organisations utilise various resources, which can be measured or described in a variety of ways (or in some organisations, ignored altogether)
- how organisations create a variety of impacts and outputs which can be measured (or not) in a variety of ways, depending on the reporting and measurement frameworks that might be used
- how reporting is influenced by a variety of factors, including legal issues, perspectives on accountability, the demands of powerful stakeholders, management strategies, the desire to look legitimate, and so forth
- how accounts generated for managing an organisation (management accounts) might also be released externally
- how reporting can address financial, social and environmental issues (or a combination thereof)
- how the organisations that generate accounts can take on a variety of forms and have a variety of aims, all of which influence what type of accounting is undertaken
- how organisations can take different forms, each with their own implications for accountability and reporting.

What will be emphasised throughout this book, and hopefully throughout your education, is that accounting is both a technical and social practice which has widespread importance to, and implications for, current and future generations and the environment. Accounting is both a necessary and exciting part of our everyday lives. (Yes … accounting is exciting!)

Having set the necessary foundation in relation to the role and potential boundaries of accounting, together with providing insights into the internal and external use of accounting information, the balance of this book will consider:

- *management accounting* – Chapters 3 to 5 will explore how different types of accounts are used by managers to manage an organisation
- *social and environmental accounting* – Chapter 6 will explore the practice of social and environmental (sustainability) accounting and consider various reporting and measurement frameworks

- *financial accounting* – Chapters 7 to 11 will explore the process of financial accounting, discussing how financial accounts are generated and used by stakeholders inside and outside an organisation.

Our final chapter, Chapter 12, will provide insights into how to analyse the financial, social and environmental accounts that have been produced for external stakeholders. In doing so, we will highlight the usefulness of various items of information, and emphasise areas where great caution needs to be used when reading reports publicly released by large organisations.

We hope that you have enjoyed the journey so far, and that you enjoy the rest of this book. Importantly, we hope you understand that much of what we shall be discussing will be of great use and value to you throughout your chosen career.

ANSWERS TO THE OPENING QUESTIONS

At the beginning of the chapter we asked the following two questions. As a result of reading this chapter, you should now be able to provide informed answers to these questions – ours are shown below.

1 What do we mean by 'reporting boundary', and why would managers of similar organisations potentially adopt different reporting boundaries?

When we are discussing the reporting boundary of an organisation, we are referring to the judgements that have been made by its managers in respect of how far the responsibilities of the organisation have been extended: both in terms of which stakeholders it owes accountability to, and for what aspects of performance it should be accountable. Because different managers will have different perceptions of organisational responsibilities, this means they will have different perceptions of which accountabilities an organisation should accept and the types of accounts it should prepare. So although two organisations might be very similar, the perspectives of their managers might be very different, and therefore the accounts the respective organisations decide to produce might be very different.

2 Why would we argue that accounting is not a one-size-fits-all practice?

We argue that accounting is not a one-size-fits-all practice because how we account for an organisation depends on factors such as:

- the various resources it uses, which can create different types of impacts for different stakeholders and therefore different accountabilities
- where its operations are being conducted, which may be in highly populated areas with many potentially affected stakeholders, or in areas of significant environmental or cultural importance
- the differing perceptions of managers on why they should be reporting, which in turn will influence to whom they have accountability, and to which aspects of performance the accounts should relate
- managers' perceptions of the information demands, or needs, of different stakeholder groups.

Because different managers will have different views about the above questions, they will tend to provide sets of accounts that are different to those provided by other managers.

SELF-TEST QUIZ

Answers to this quiz appear in the Appendix of this book.

1 In relation to the concept of an organisation's 'reporting boundary', which of the following statements are **true**?

a Smaller organisations, such as sole traders and partnerships, tend to have more restricted reporting boundaries relative to companies.

b The reporting boundary will be influenced by managers' views about 'to whom' the organisation has a responsibility, and 'for what' aspects of performance it has a responsibility.

c The reporting boundary applied through the application of generally accepted financial reporting practices tends to be more restricted relative to the reporting boundary applied when undertaking some form of sustainability-related reporting.

d The reporting boundaries accepted and implemented by managers will often extend well beyond the range of reporting required by law.

e All of these choices.

2 An organisation relies on various resources – both controlled and not controlled by the organisation – to allow it to achieve its objectives. In relation to these resources, which of the following statements is **false**?

a The accounts generated by all organisations will always identify all the resources used or consumed by the organisation.

b The reported profits of an organisation will not take account of all the resources used or consumed by an organisation.

c When recognising the expenses of an organisation for financial reporting purposes, generally there will be no recognition of expenses or costs associated with the use of resources that are not controlled by the organisation.

d To gain an insight into the impacts an organisation has on resources not controlled by an organisation, interested stakeholders should review other reports, if they are available, such as the organisation's sustainability reports.

e When an organisation provides information about the 'costs' it has created as a result of consuming particular resources, this information does not always need to be presented in monetary terms.

3 In relation to external reporting, which of the following statements is **false**?

a Larger organisations, such as public companies, are required by law to produce financial statements, such as balance sheets and income statements.

b Many larger organisations voluntarily produce information about their impacts upon particular societies and stakeholders.

c Many larger organisations voluntarily produce information about their impacts upon the environment.

d The form of reporting undertaken by not-for-profit organisations will tend to be different to that undertaken by for-profit organisations due to differences in managers' perceptions about organisational responsibilities and accountabilities.

e Organisations will not, and should not, publicly disclose information about their recycling initiatives or what happens to their manufactured products at the end of the life cycle.

4 In relation to partnerships, which of the following options are **true**?
   a The actions of one partner create legal responsibilities for the other partners.
   b Partners can have unlimited liabilities in relation to the debts incurred within the partnership.
   c Partnerships cease to exist when a partner leaves the partnership.
   d For accounting purposes, the partnership is generally considered to be a separate entity; however for legal purposes, the partnership is not separate to the owners.
   e All of these choices.

5 Depending upon their perceptions of organisational responsibilities and accountabilities, managers of organisations – particularly larger organisations – will often choose to publicly report information about:
   a the organisation's emissions of greenhouse gases.
   b the efforts taken (for example, through 'social audits') to ensure the health and safety of employees within their supply chains.
   c the profits and total assets and liabilities of their organisation.
   d the amount of water consumed and released by the organisation.
   e All of these choices.

ONLINE RESOURCES

Accompanying the book is an innovative online case study that follows an organisation initially established by two friends, which grows into a large and successful company. Acquire this chapter's case study from your instructor.

CASE STUDY

Armadillo Surf Designs: Drawing a line in the sand

Archer, Maddie and Dillon are having second thoughts in relation to Armadillo Surf Designs (ASD) being set up as a partnership and are now considering whether they should change the business structure to a company. Maddie is also keen to define ASD's reporting boundary, but the team are unsure at this stage how far they should extend this.

Provide the information needed to assist the ASD team with the decision of whether they should restructure. Consider the resources of ASD and distinguish those resources that are controlled by ASD from those that are not. Provide ASD with a range of possible reporting boundary options ranging from a very narrow, to a very broad, boundary.

END-OF-CHAPTER QUESTIONS

2.1 What do we mean when we refer to the reporting boundary of an organisation?

2.2 What is the difference between internal reporting and external reporting?

2.3 What is a resource of an organisation, and should an organisation measure all the resources it uses?

2.4 What is management accounting?

2.5 What is financial accounting?

2.6 Why would we say that accounting is not a one-size-fits-all practice?

2.7 What are the main features of a:
a sole trader b partnership c company.

2.8 If we were to look at the reports released publicly by two similar organisations in the same industry, we might find that they report very different types of information. Why might this happen?

2.9 For an accountant, why would it be useful to have a diagram clearly depicting the inputs and outputs of an organisation?

2.10 What is an externality? Would an organisation account for its externalities?

2.11 This chapter noted that this book embraces a broad view of costs. What does this mean?

2.12 Different organisational types have different accounting requirements. Discuss the following:
- a What might be some differences between the accounts produced by a sole trader as opposed to those created by a partnership?
- b What might be some of the differences in the information required by a sole trader compared with the information required by a shareholder in a large public company?

2.13 Should an organisation produce an account (for internal and/or external use) of:
- a its financial profit
- b the water it uses and the source(s) of that water
- c employee health and safety policies and the related performance of organisations within its supply chain
- d its own CO_2 emissions
- e the CO_2 emissions of its suppliers?

2.14 How would the accounts prepared by a public company and made publicly available be different to those prepared by a private company?

2.15 The Deepwater Horizon catastrophe caused extensive damage to the local environment and killed 11 people. What are some of the possible accounts that BP could have publicly provided following this disaster?

2.16 What are some of the outputs or impacts of a museum (both good and bad)? For each type of output or impact, do you think they would be identified, measured and reported for accounting purposes by the museum, and if so, where would they be reported?

2.17 You are a manager of T-shirt Tommy Ltd, a global seller of T-shirts. You are contemplating buying a large quantity of T-shirts from Dhaka Textiles, a supply company located in Bangladesh.
- a As part of the process of deciding to place an order, what information would you want in respect of the T-shirts to be produced by Dhaka Textiles?
- b Assuming you have committed to a long-term supply arrangement with Dhaka Textiles, what ongoing information would you collect (and monitor) in regards to the T-shirts being supplied from Bangladesh, and what is the purpose of collecting this information?
- c Would you call this internal (management) accounting or externally oriented accounting?
- d Would you release this information to the public?

2.18 Most university accounting degrees focus predominantly on the financial aspects of performance, with very little consideration given to social and environmental performance (perhaps a few weeks here and there). Why do you think this is the case?

2.19 The *KPMG survey of sustainability reporting 2020* (see https://home.kpmg.com) indicated that over 80 per cent of the largest 100 companies in 52 different countries such as Australia, South Africa, France, Japan, the United States, Singapore, India, Indonesia and Canada – 5200 companies in total (by market capitalisation) – produce a publicly available social responsibility, or sustainability, report. The survey also indicated that 96 per cent of the world's 250 largest companies also produce a publicly available sustainability report.

a Select a large multinational organisation (for example, a large mining organisation, airline, bank or clothing company) and review its website for details of its sustainability reports (they could be on a page titled something like 'sustainability' or 'community'). It will probably have a publicly available sustainability report.

b Identify the types of information it provides in relation to the social aspects of its performance.

c Identify the types of information it provides in relation to the environmental aspects of its performance.

REFERENCES

Apple (2020). *Environmental progress report.* https://www.apple.com.

BHP (2021). *Annual report 2021.* https://www.bhp.com/

Harvey, C. (2015). We are killing the environment one hamburger at a time. *Business Insider Australia*, 6 March. www.businessinsider.com.au/one-hamburger-environment-resources-2015-2?r=US&IR=T

Institute of Certified Management Accountants (2022). Background. www.cmawebline.org/about-icma/background.html

International Accounting Standards Board (2022), *IFRS Conceptual Framework: Conceptual Framework for Financial Reporting*, IASB, London.

KPMG (2020). The time has come: *The KPMG Survey of Sustainability Reporting 2020.* home.kpmg.sustainabilityreporting

Royal Society for the Prevention of Cruelty to Animals (2022). Mission. https://rspca.org.au/what-we-do/about-us/mission

Samsung (2020). *Samsung electronics sustainability report 2021.* www.samsung.com.

MODULE 2

ACCOUNTING AND ITS ROLE IN MANAGERIAL DECISION MAKING

CHAPTER 3

AN INTRODUCTION TO MANAGEMENT ACCOUNTING

LEARNING OBJECTIVES

After completing this chapter, readers should be able to:

- LO3.1 explain the role of management accounting using our accountability model
- LO3.2 provide a general description of the functions of managers
- LO3.3 explain why managers and accountants need to incorporate long- and short-term considerations into their organisational planning
- LO3.4 explain why managers and accountants need to incorporate considerations of sustainability into their organisational planning
- LO3.5 explain what is meant by the term 'adding value', and describe some of the ways in which accounting can add value to an organisation and for its stakeholders
- LO3.6 explain what is meant by the term 'cost behaviour', as well as what is meant by relevant costs, variable costs, fixed costs and mixed costs
- LO3.7 understand why and how to calculate the contribution margin, and use this in turn to calculate the break-even point, margin of safety, and the number of units of a good or service required to generate a target profit; and identify operating gearing
- LO3.8 explain how and why non-financial variable costs should be considered part of managers' decision making
- LO3.9 explain the need to maximise the returns that can be generated from factors of production that are in scarce supply
- LO3.10 explain the meaning of the term 'special order', and know how to manage and account for one
- LO3.11 understand the meaning of the term 'critical thinking', describing some key competencies, or skills, that accountants should possess if they are going to be critical thinkers and thereby add value to an organisation and for its stakeholders.

OPENING QUESTIONS

Before reading this chapter, please consider how you would answer the following three questions. We will return to these questions at the end of the chapter, where we suggest some answers.

1 What do we mean by 'cost behaviour', and why do managers need to know how costs 'behave'?
2 What do we mean by 'break-even point', and how would we calculate how many units of a product or service an organisation needs to produce in order to break even?
3 In undertaking a break-even analysis, what assumptions are made about fixed costs and variable costs?

Introduction

In this chapter we focus on an area of accounting that has traditionally been referred to as management accounting. In Chapter 2, we defined management accounting as a broad term that refers to the information produced by accountants to assist decision making by *internal* managers; that is, information required for various decisions pertaining to planning, monitoring and controlling the operations of an organisation. This information could relate to different aspects of financial, social and/or environmental performance. The information will be produced to cover various time periods – for example, daily, weekly, monthly, trimonthly, annually, or even longer time frames – and can relate to both past and projected performance. The management accounting system will typically become more sophisticated as the size of the organisation increases and as the number of products or services being produced/provided also increases.

All organisations need to apply components of management accounting – such as planning, budgeting, and mechanisms to compare actual performance against budgeted performance – if they are to succeed. Arguably, the more competitive the market in which an organisation is operating, the greater the need for various forms of management accounting. The management accountant is the person who provides such information.

By contrast, financial accounting was described in Chapter 2 as that branch of accounting that generates financial reports for use by people *outside* the organisation; for example, investors who want to monitor the financial performance of the organisations in which they have invested. We noted that financial reporting by large organisations is very regulated, whereas management accounting is basically unregulated. Financial accounting reports are typically prepared less frequently relative to management accounting reports, and they tend to be historical in focus, providing an account of what has been achieved rather than being forward looking like management accounting.

Some of the differences between management accounting and financial accounting as applied by larger organisations are summarised in Table 3.1.

TABLE 3.1 A summary of some of the differences between management accounting and financial accounting

	Management accounting	Financial accounting
Type of report	Special-purpose reports designed to satisfy specific information needs of managers	General-purpose reports designed to generally satisfy the information needs of existing and potential investors, lenders and other creditors
Main audience	Managers	Investors, potential investors, lenders and other creditors
Regulation	Basically unregulated, meaning there is much variation across organisations in the types and forms of management accounts they elect to produce	Regulated and standardised
Reporting frequency	As needed – could be daily, weekly, monthly, quarterly, annually or longer term	Annual or semiannual
Orientation	Focuses on projected and past performance, and highlights reasons for variances between projected and actual results	Focuses on past performance
Financial or non-financial	Focuses on aspects of performance prioritised by management – can be financial or non-financial, depending on what aspects of performance management wants to monitor, control and improve	Focuses on producing information about the financial position and performance of an organisation for people who might not be involved in its management but who depend on general-purpose financial reports for the information they need
Organisation level of reporting	As determined by management and typically disaggregated – can be at an individual level (e.g., use of energy by a particular machine), or that of process, product, segment or business	Tends to be at an aggregated level, although limited information is provided in respect of the performance of different operating segments

Apart from financial accounting and management accounting, there is also social and environmental accounting, which provides information for use by managers (and therefore forms part of management accounting), as well as by external stakeholders, about various aspects of an organisation's impacts upon the physical and social environments in which it operates. We will cover social and environmental accounting in detail in Chapter 6.

One of the key components of management accounting relates to planning; for example, determining what future activities the organisation will be involved in, and the likely implications of such activities for:

- future cash flows
- future financial position and performance
- future social and environmental impacts and implications
- stakeholder support and approval.

Much planning (and the related collection of information) through the process of management accounting occurs *before* you can subsequently report the results by means of financial accounting (financial accounting tends to report on an after-the-fact basis – that is, after the managers' plans have been completed and actions implemented). Hence, as management accounting utilises various forms of budgeting and cost predictions – and business planning in general – it would seem to make sense for us to discuss it before we discuss financial accounting (this will be the focus of Chapters 7 to 11).

Management accounting can, and should, address various aspects of social and environmental performance both in terms of setting targets (budgets) and measuring and assessing the actual performance. Managers often decide to make some of this information available to external stakeholders. Chapter 6 will explore the various frameworks that are used to externally report information about an organisation's social and environmental performance.

LO3.1 The role of management accounting

While the term 'management accounting' is generally used to refer to the process that generates information for use by people (managers) within an organisation, as we have indicated above, much of this information will also be of relevance to various stakeholders located outside the organisation. Therefore, it can be somewhat artificial to say that particular information is *only* relevant to internal stakeholders (for example, managers and their use of management accounting information) or *only* to external stakeholders (for example, shareholders and their use of financial accounting information). In effect, there will be a pool of information for managers and others to draw from, and which will be of interest (or not) to a variety of stakeholders both inside and outside an organisation. Many items of information will have multiple uses/purposes – the same item might appear in management accounting reports as well as financial accounting reports and/or social and environmental reports.

While many external stakeholders are interested in the information used internally, for proprietary or competitive advantage reasons, such information might not always be shared with external parties. The achievement of some of an organisation's goals – such as increasing its market share, or wanting to be known as producing superior-quality products relative to its competitors – might rely on keeping particular information away from competitors. However, moderating this disinclination to share information will be consideration of stakeholders' rights-to-know, and the regulative requirements for disclosure (for example, in many countries, the release or emission of certain chemicals or other substances must be disclosed despite the negative implications for an organisation's reputation). Also, certain powerful stakeholders will be able to access information not necessarily made available to other stakeholders because of their relationship with that organisation. For example, providers of finance – such as banks – might, as part of the lending agreement negotiated with the organisation, be able to demand that the organisation provides projections of future cash flows and financial performance, details of product costings, and so forth.

To further explore the role of management accounting, we will now apply the accountability model we introduced in Chapter 1. Specifically, we will address the *why*, *to whom*, *what* and *how* questions with which you should now be familiar.

Why produce management accounts?

Management accounts are produced to help managers achieve an organisation's mission and goals. A variety of management accounts will be generated within an organisation – some using financial measures, others not. The focus of the management accounts will be influenced by what aspects of performance the managers prioritise in terms of achieving the organisation's missions and goals. This, in turn, will be influenced by the managers' perspectives on their responsibilities pertaining to managing the organisation. As we know, the responsibilities managers accept could relate to various aspects of financial, social and environmental performance, and consequently, the responsibilities being accepted will relate to different stakeholders.

To whom are management accounts directed?

The primary audience of management accounting is, somewhat obviously, the managers of an organisation. While this is the case, the information an organisation collects will be influenced by consideration of *to whom* (which stakeholders), and *for what* aspects of performance, it believes it is ultimately responsible. As we have already emphasised, you cannot manage what you do not measure, so it is important to be clear about what aspects of performance any organisation seeks to manage.

If managers accept certain responsibilities, then ultimately their organisation needs to generate certain accounts to inform those managers about whether these responsibilities have been properly addressed. As we have already noted, the information collected for managing the various aspects of an organisation's operations might also be of interest, or relevance, to many other stakeholders outside the organisation. For example, in Chapter 2 we showed how the global mining company BHP collected information about its water use to assist it to be more water efficient. This information – used for internal management purposes – was also publicly disclosed within the company's annual report, probably because it was considered by management that many external stakeholders had a valid interest in the water being used, and released, by the organisation.

Information about the following, which could all be captured within a management accounting system, will be relevant to many different stakeholders:

- an organisation's actual and projected performance (financial, social and environmental, with the evaluation influenced by whether the organisation is for profit, not-for-profit, community-based and so forth)
- its control of resources
- its resource usage
- organisational impacts, which can include economic, social and environmental impacts
- compliance with organisational goals, regulations and/or particular stakeholder expectations
- the implications of future plans for various stakeholders, including the environment.

However, it needs to be remembered that the target audience of management accounts is ultimately managers. Whether they elect to release information from their management accounts to external stakeholders will be influenced by whether they believe they are accountable to such stakeholders regarding particular aspects of performance, or whether they believe that it is in the best interests of the organisation to disclose the information. Also, as previously indicated, considerations of competitive advantage will also influence the public disclosure of certain information.

What information is generated?

The management accounting system should produce information that helps enable managers to manage the organisation to achieve its goals and to operate consistently with its mission. The types of information to be collected, analysed and reported will partly depend on what aspects of financial and non-financial performance the organisation's managers believe they need to manage. This will be influenced by various factors, including:

- the responsibilities and associated accountabilities being embraced by the managers (as discussed in Chapter 1)
- the range of the reporting boundary, which will be influenced by the responsibilities and accountabilities accepted by managers (as discussed in Chapter 2, managers need to decide, for example, whether they will collect information about the social and environmental performance of suppliers within their supply chain)
- the type of products or services being offered by the organisation
- the types of resources being consumed, and the nature of the outputs/impacts being created and measured
- the location of the organisation's activities, and the impacts of the organisation's operations on local environments and societies
- the level of competition that the organisation encounters (for example, the extent of competition from other organisations will influence the degree to which information needs to be collected to control costs so as to potentially enable the prices of the organisation's goods and services to be lowered)
- whether the organisation is operating as a for-profit or not-for-profit organisation.

Costs versus benefits

Another factor that needs to be considered when collecting, analysing, and reporting information is whether the costs involved in doing so exceed the related benefits. Costs could include the wages paid to staff or outside experts to collect, analyse and possibly audit the necessary information. Benefits might arise because the information allows more informed decision making, resulting in better decisions – the better decisions might lead to a reduction in financial costs, and in the social and environmental impacts of the organisation.

All decisions need some form of costs-versus-benefits test to be applied, including those about what information to collect. While difficult to assess, particularly as some costs and benefits might be non-monetary in nature, a consideration of costs versus benefits will tend to limit the amount of information that is collected. If the relevant information is costly to collect and analyse, and if the benefit to decision making is perceived as minimal, then a rational decision would be to not collect the information.

While collecting too little information is bad for decision making, collecting and supplying vast amounts of information can also be detrimental to decision making. It can lead to what is known as *information overload*, which occurs when the amount of information being provided to an individual or organisation exceeds their ability to process that information. It is commonly accepted that individuals have a limit in relation to how much information they can meaningfully assimilate at any one time. There comes a point when too much information can actually lead to a reduction in the quality of the decisions being made. One role of the accountant is to determine the optimal amount of relevant information to provide to managers and other stakeholders. It is therefore important that those people involved in an accounting function restrict the available information to that which is both *relevant* to, and *understandable* by, the respective stakeholders.

It is also important that the information being presented to managers is reliable, although increasing the reliability of information can create costs that need to be considered; for example, an external expert might be employed to provide an opinion on the reliability of particular information.

Key concept

Information overload occurs when the amount of information being provided to an individual or organisation exceeds their ability to process that information.

Apart from being relevant, reliable and understandable, the other desired qualitative characteristics of accounting information (discussed in Chapter 1) also need to be considered. That is, for information to be useful, its comparability, verifiability and timeliness should also be addressed. However, for some types of management accounting information, it might be difficult to achieve some of these attributes. For example, if you are moving into a particularly new area of operations, then you might not be able to provide a sound basis of comparison, and hence it might be difficult to satisfy the qualitative characteristic of comparability. Nevertheless, when considering the issue of what information accountants should provide to managers (and to other stakeholders), you should always keep in mind the fundamental qualitative characteristics that the information should possess (being relevance and reliability), together with a consideration of the enhancing qualitative characteristics (these being understandability, comparability, verifiability, and timeliness).

Learning exercise 3.1 further considers the issue of costs versus benefits.

3.1 Learning Exercise

Collecting information – a consideration of costs and benefits

Scenario: An organisation is deciding whether to collect information about its use of, and release of, water. The organisation is contemplating whether collecting the information is worth the cost.

Issue: Should costs and benefits be considered when determining whether to collect the information?

Solution: Yes. Costs and benefits should be considered, but determining the costs and benefits associated with collecting and then using information is not necessarily an easy task. You need to ask yourself:

1. Is it possible to collect the information reliably?

   If there is no ability to collect reliable information, then there is no benefit to collecting it. Collecting unreliable information can lead to wrong decisions being made by those people using the information. There is little point in paying to collect information that is unreliable.

2. Is the information relevant to the organisation?

   Will collecting the information potentially change future decision making? If it is unlikely to change a decision – meaning it is not relevant to decision making – then there is little point in collecting the information. Only potentially relevant information should be collected.

3. Do other stakeholders have a justifiable right to know certain information?

   The managers of an organisation might collect information because they believe they are creating particular social or environmental impacts that some stakeholders have a right to know about. There will, of course, be limits as to how much information about impacts can be collected and disclosed, but if the organisation is creating significant social and environmental impacts, then information about these impacts should be collected and reported.

Let us now think about the organisation's water use and discharge. Specifically, is information about water use and discharge relevant to the organisation? In relation to water usage:

- Yes: If water is particularly scarce in this environment, such that consumption will impact a variety of stakeholders, then the organisation arguably has a responsibility, and an associated accountability, to collect information about water usage.
- No: If there is an abundance of water and the usage has little or no impact upon other stakeholders, including the environment, then we would question the wisdom in collecting the information and paying the assorted costs involved.

In relation to water discharge:

- What is of relevance is how polluted is the water being released, and what impact that will have on the environment in which it is being released.
- This information needs to be known by an organisation, and if the impact is significant, then the organisation has a responsibility and associated accountability to collect information about the release of water.
- The greater the potential impact of the released water on the receiving environment (and therefore the greater the potential benefit in controlling the discharge of water), the more the organisation should be prepared to pay to collect the information.

The other point to be appreciated here is that deciding to collect information about particular aspects of performance can actually help to identify otherwise unknown risks within the organisation as well as potential opportunities. This is because the information collected might highlight previously unknown or ignored aspects of performance.

How is management accounting information disclosed?

Management accounting information will be produced internally in various formats, and as requested by the various managers utilising the information. Because this information is tailored to meet the specific needs of different managers, and as all organisations will differ to some extent, then the management accounting being undertaken within organisations will vary, and the management accounts in different organisations are unlikely to be the same.

Various reporting frameworks will be used for different aspects of measurement and reporting. For example, if water usage and releases are being measured, then particular water measurement standards might be used; if CO_2 emissions are to be measured, then particular carbon measurement frameworks will be used; and if workplace health and safety is to be measured, then particular occupational health and safety measurement approaches will be used. Different reporting periods will also be used by different organisations.

The above discussion is summarised in Figure 3.1.

LO3.2 What does management do?

We have been discussing the activities of managers in general terms, but we will now be more specific. In order to understand the types of information that will be needed by an organisation's

FIGURE 3.1 An overview of management accounting using our accountability model

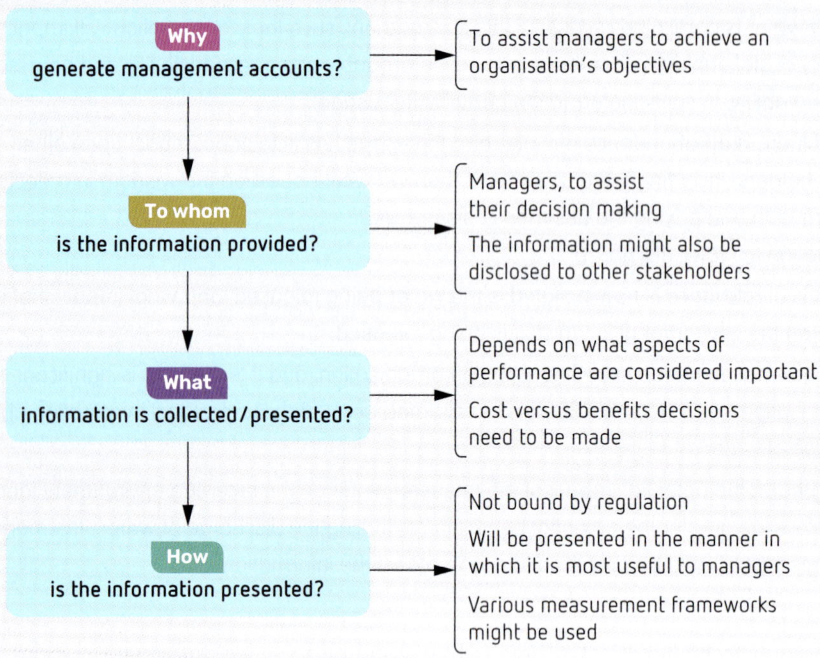

managers, it is useful to have a broad understanding of the role of managers in terms of what they do. Generally speaking, with the assistance of accountants, management:

1 identifies a problem
2 collects relevant information to potentially solve the problem
3 determines alternative courses of action and the consequences of each
4 evaluates alternative courses of action and identifies the best one(s) in terms of achieving the organisation's goals
5 makes a decision
6 implements an action
7 monitors and evaluates performance pertaining to the chosen actions
8 revises plans in light of performance/feedback (and the cycle continues).

The first five points above can be referred to as the planning stage. They require a degree of critical thinking whereby the implications of future possibilities are logically evaluated (we will discuss some attributes of critical thinking towards the end of this chapter). The above aspects of a manager's role are represented in Figure 3.2.

We will now consider the various phases of management as identified in Figure 3.2. We will start with the planning phase.

Planning

In this chapter we predominantly focus on planning, which is central to managing any organisation. Planning should be a continuous process that starts well before an organisation commences operations. The plan provides a benchmark against which future performance can be assessed. Once plans have been implemented and actual results compared with projected results (projected results will be documented within budgets, which are the focus of Chapter 4), then

FIGURE 3.2 A manager's role

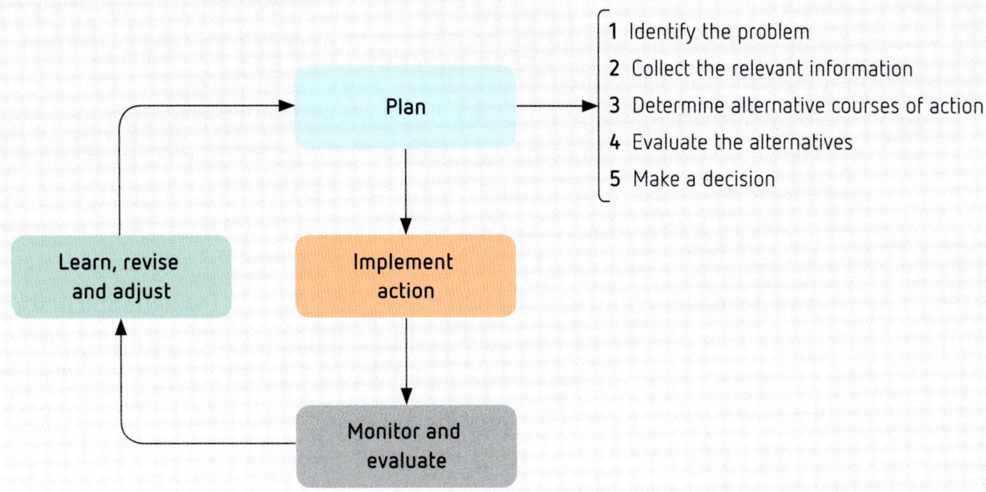

subsequent plans can be revised in light of what has just occurred, and what has been learned, and the process continues.

Comparing actual performance with plans, and determining the reason for any variance, is referred to as the *control phase* of operations. Plans also provide targets which can be used as a basis to motivate and reward people undertaking roles in relation to those plans.

Plans should be subjected to expert critical review, from people involved in the relevant processes within the organisation, and potentially also from experts outside the organisation. This will help ensure that important or critical factors have not been overlooked in the planning process.

Another valuable aspect of undertaking rigorous planning is that it sends an important message to key stakeholders, such as investors and lenders. Having clear and well-articulated plans, and sharing these plans with potential providers of funds, will act to reduce their uncertainty and the perceived risk, and this will likely enable the organisation to attract funds at a lower cost than might otherwise be possible. For example, lenders will charge lower interest rates because of the perceived lower levels of risk. Further, if the actual results compare favourably with the projected budgets, this suggests that the managers and accountants of the organisation understand the operating environment in which they are working, and this could further reduce the risks perceived by investors and lenders, thereby further reducing the costs of attracting funds. 'Sensible planning' is an indicator of the presence of 'sensible management'.

We will now consider the five individual components of the planning phase as identified in Figure 3.2.

Identifying the problem

The first phase of planning is to identify a problem that needs solving. This relates to what the organisation wants to achieve, the problem being how best to achieve that objective. These proposed achievements will not just relate to the financial aspects of operations. Planning must incorporate consideration of an organisation's vision and mission.

Organisations typically have a formally stated mission and also often a formally stated vision. Larger organisations will often document their vision and mission in writing and make this publicly available, such as on a corporate website.

An organisation's stated vision, if it has one that is formally stated, will provide an insight into where the organisation hopes to be in the future and reflects what the organisation aspires to achieve – it is therefore aspirational in nature. The organisation's vision will be influenced by the values and expectations held by the key stakeholders in the organisation. Very often, it is considered that the vision then informs the organisation's mission.

An organisation's mission reflects its core purpose and focus, and generally does not change that often; for example, it might stay unaltered for several years. The mission represents an organisation's guiding principle and should reflect the overall purpose of the organisation. The mission – if well written – acts to identify what aspects of performance are considered important, and it provides overall direction for the managers.

As a guiding principle, managers should review the mission regularly and make sure that their ongoing plans remain consistent with the organisation's mission. If they are not consistent then perhaps the plans need to be adjusted, or perhaps it is time to consider reviewing the mission.

The mission will then shape the goals and objectives of the organisation. Goals tend to be quite wide ranging and linked to the organisation's mission, whereas objectives focus on achievable outcomes which can then be linked to particular strategies. Strategies are operational plans for how the managers will achieve the organisation's objectives.

Figure 3.3 reflects the above discussion in terms of how an organisation's values (and these values are not necessarily documented) and vision influence an organisation's mission, and how the mission ultimately influences planning. This is just another way to consider the planning process in addition to how we described it in Figure 3.2. We accept that some people might arrange these steps in a different order (for example, some organisations or writers might place mission before vision).

FIGURE 3.3 How the mission of an organisation influences strategy.

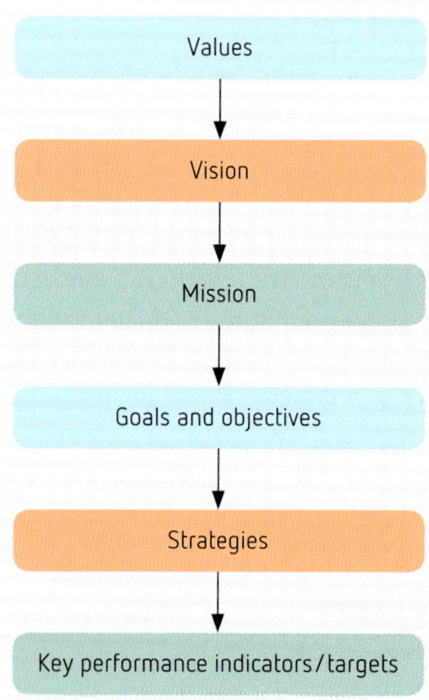

We will consider, as an example, the *mission statements* of three quite different organisations to see how each of them differs. These organisations are:

- The Walt Disney Company

- Greenpeace
- Harvard University.

Their respective mission statements are as follows.

Walt Disney mission statement

https://thewaltdisneycompany.com/about/

Our mission

The mission of The Walt Disney Company is to entertain, inform and inspire people around the globe through the power of unparalleled storytelling, reflecting the iconic brands, creative minds and innovative technologies that make ours the world's premier entertainment company.

Source: The Walt Disney Company (2022).

Greenpeace mission statement

www.greenpeace.org/international/en/about/our-core-values

Mission statement

Greenpeace is an independent campaigning organisation, which uses peaceful, creative confrontation to expose global environmental problems, and to develop solutions for a green and peaceful future.

Our goal is to ensure the ability of the earth to nurture life in all its diversity. That means we want to:

- protect biodiversity in all its forms
- prevent pollution and abuse of the earth's oceans, land, air and fresh water
- end all nuclear threats
- promote peace, global disarmament and non-violence.

Source: Greenpeace (2022).

Harvard University mission statement

https://college.harvard.edu/about/mission-and-vision

Mission

The mission of Harvard College is to educate the citizens and citizen-leaders for our society. We do this through our commitment to the transformative power of a liberal arts and sciences education. Beginning in the classroom with exposure to new ideas, new ways of understanding, and new ways of knowing, students embark on a journey of intellectual transformation. Through a diverse living environment, where students live with people who are studying different topics, who come from different walks of life and have evolving identities, intellectual transformation is deepened and conditions for social transformation are created. From this we hope that students will begin to fashion their lives by gaining a sense of what they want to do with their gifts and talents, assessing their values and interests, and learning how they can best serve the world.

Vision

Harvard College sets the standard for residential liberal arts and sciences education. We have committed to creating and sustaining the conditions that enable all Harvard College students to experience an unparalleled educational journey that is intellectually, socially and personally transformative.

Source: Harvard University (2022).

A review of the above mission statements highlights the core issues that subsequent planning should address. For example, when considering the sorts of problems Walt Disney wants to address, a key feature is profitability, and this will factor into the planning phase more than it would at Greenpeace or Harvard – albeit these organisations still need to ensure their resources are used efficiently so as to enable them to achieve their mission and objectives.

Identifying the problem for Walt Disney

We can see that the focus of Walt Disney is entertainment and the provision of information. Therefore, there would have to be a very good justification before planning operations in other areas, such as, for example, commercial construction. A great deal of the information collected by Walt Disney will relate to addressing the major problem of how to create content, services and products that are accepted by stakeholders as being creative and innovative (two key terms in the mission statement) while at the same time being profitable. This in turn might require various forms of research and planning, such as:

- the current and projected demands of consumers
- stakeholder perceptions of what aspects of the industry are reflective of creativity and innovation
- research to identify current and projected innovations and innovation opportunities in the intended areas of operation
- the apparent innovations being introduced by competitors.

As potential projects are identified, budgeting is undertaken to ensure that the intended actions appear likely to generate the desired level of profits.

Identifying the problem for Greenpeace

Turning our attention to Greenpeace, it is reasonably clear that the planning would not be expected to be about generating profits. Greenpeace is clearly a 'not-for-profit' organisation. Rather, the central problem relates to how to create the most positive environmental and social outcomes with the available funds. Issues to be addressed within planning might include:

- identifying areas of biodiversity that are currently or potentially at risk, and prioritising them in terms of importance
- identifying and prioritising important initiatives to reduce dangerous levels of pollution in vulnerable areas
- identifying and prioritising initiatives to reduce nuclear risk
- identifying and prioritising strategies to address global peace
- identifying and maintaining sources of funding to enable key initiatives to be undertaken.

If a manager within Greenpeace wanted to operate in an area not concerned with advancing the interests of particular habitats, species or people, then much justification would be required, as it would represent a departure from the organisation's mission. The mission statement of Greenpeace also emphasises that the organisation is independent, therefore planning (which flows from, or is 'informed by', the mission) must ensure that the organisation does not appear to depend on particular stakeholders; for example, particular providers of financial resources.

Identifying the problem for Harvard University

When it comes to Harvard, the mission again seems to have little to do with making profits or other financial gains. Rather, the problem seems to be about creating a place of education excellence which fashions future leaders, sets standards for other universities to follow, and transforms the lives of students intellectually, socially and personally. As with all organisations, to achieve its goals, Harvard will need to manage its resources efficiently and be clear about the plans it has for generating funding.

The above discussion of the mission statements of three organisations is rather brief. Nonetheless, the point we are making is that the problems managers set, which will then be addressed/solved through establishing the plans to be followed (and there can be many levels to these plans), will be influenced by the underlying mission of the organisation. As **Figure 3.3** showed, the mission can be considered to be a very-high-level direction which then will be broken down into manageable plans that are each consistent with achieving the mission.

Since organisations typically have multiple objectives (which then lead to the identification of various problems that need to be solved) that can be both financial and non-financial in nature, there is a need to accept some trade-offs. For example, if an organisation wants to maximise the returns to shareholders while also wanting to be environmentally responsible and employ disadvantaged individuals, then some trade-offs are inevitable. It is important that such trade-offs are acknowledged and debated within an organisation as part of the planning stage. For example, in the short run, a decision to recycle water might adversely impact profits – because, say, of the need to build an expensive recycling facility – and therefore dividends for shareholders, but in the longer run the organisation might be more sustainable – financially and environmentally – because of the initiative.

Learning exercise 3.2 further examines the trade-off between being profitable and socially responsible.

3.2 Learning Exercise

Profits versus social responsibility

Are the goals of maximising profits and being socially and environmentally responsible mutually exclusive?

The answer to this question really depends on whether managers are taking a long-term or short-term perspective on the operations of their organisation.

A short-term perspective

In the short run, focusing on maximising profits might mean that managers make decisions that have the lowest financial costs regardless of their social and environmental impacts. The short-term nature of the decisions may enable them to avoid scrutiny in relation to financial performance, but it might ultimately create scrutiny in relation to the apparent social and environmental impacts.

Examples include:

- dumping wastewater into local waterways, rather than paying to recycle or purify the water, if there are no financial costs in doing so
- using materials that are cheaper to acquire but have a more harmful effect on the environment when the product is ultimately scrapped
- forgoing costly workplace health and safety training for staff.

A long-term perspective

In the long run, however, if managers neglect issues to do with the social and environmental impacts of the organisation's operations, then stakeholders will ultimately become dissatisfied with the organisation. Inevitably, they will decide not to provide resources to the organisation (such as financial capital, raw materials or labour), and profitability may be adversely impacted in the following ways:

- customers might not buy the organisation's goods or services
- people might not want to work for it
- investors will not want to invest in it
- banks will not want to lend to it
- governments might seek to regulate against its activities.

Hence, organisations do need to demonstrate that they are socially and environmentally responsible if they want to be profitable in the longer run. That is, managers need to employ what is often referred to as 'systems thinking', meaning that managers need to understand that organisations do not operate in isolation, but are part of a broader economic, social and environmental system in which they depend for survival. Organisations both impact, and are impacted by, the systems in which they operate.

Why do I need to know about the role of an organisation's mission statement?

As we know, the mission statement represents an organisation's guiding principle and should reflect the overall purpose of the organisation. If you are wanting to understand the rationale behind an organisation's existence, it is wise to find and read their mission (hopefully it has been kept up-to-date).

Therefore, when you are working for an organisation, it is important that you understand the mission of the organisation so that what you are doing, or intending to do, in the workplace is consistent with the mission. If you find that what is happening in an organisation's workplace is not consistent with the mission, then you might suggest that perhaps the mission needs updating.

Collecting the relevant information

Once we have identified our problem(s), then, in the process of formulating plans to solve this problem/s, there is a need to know about a variety of factors, such as those outlined in Table 3.2. Managers need a variety of relevant and reliable information. The list in the table is far from exhaustive but it does give an indication of the sorts of background information that managers require as part of their planning process.

TABLE 3.2 Collecting the relevant information

Information required	Source and example information
Identification of key stakeholders and their current, and projected, expectations	• Customers: *What sorts of products or services do customers seek, and what are their expectations concerning issues such as pricing, service before and after sales, credit terms, and the social and environmental performance of organisations throughout the supply chain? How might customer preferences change in the future, and what threats or opportunities might this create?* • Finance providers: *Who are the potential providers of finance, their respective charges, their expectations about the timing of repayments, and their expectations about how borrowers shall conduct their business?* • Suppliers: *Where are potential suppliers located, and what are their respective pricing policies, credit terms, and past and likely future social and environmental performances?*

Information required	Source and example information
	• Relevant codes of behaviour/governance practices: *What generally accepted performance codes are there within the industry, and are the identified suppliers signatories to such codes?* • Government requirements: *What are the respective government requirements and taxes for the line of operations being conducted, including with respect to patents, trademarks and so forth?* • Special interest groups/non-government organisations: *What are the concerns of special interest groups/NGOs as they pertain to the likely operations of the organisation?* • Employees: *What is the availability of suitably qualified employees and what are their expectations with regards to the conditions offered by employers? What are the requirements of the relevant employment legislation?* • Competitors: *Who are the competitors and what are their key strengths and weaknesses?*
Required resources	• *What resources are needed to run the organisation?* • *What is their availability, and what are the alternatives?* • *What are the significant social and environmental implications of using particular resources?*
Currently available and projected technologies	• *What are the various production technologies available now, or will be available in the future, to produce the likely goods and services?* • *What are the advantages and disadvantages of the alternative technologies?*
Cost behaviour (see 'The behaviour of costs' in this chapter)	• *What types of costs are likely to be incurred/generated, and how will these costs vary with changes in the volume of activity?*
Other social and environmental impacts	• *What are the social and environmental impacts throughout the supply chain?* • *What happens to the products when they come to the end of their useful lives?*

Determining alternative courses of action

As Figure 3.2 shows, once we have collected the relevant information, we can then start identifying alternative courses of action that appear consistent with the overall goals of the organisation, and which help answer the problems that were identified. Some alternatives might be eliminated at this stage because of the consequences particular actions might have for certain stakeholders, or because the potential projects are not consistent with the organisation's overall missions and objectives.

In undertaking this phase of planning, some form of *screening* might be undertaken. There might be a strict rule that certain activities or products shall not be made, or acquired, because of concerns about their risks or impacts on particular parts of society, or on the environment. This would be referred to as **negative screening**. Alternatively, some form of **positive screening** might be used which requires that certain activities or products have certain attributes, such as utilising processes that are environmentally or socially responsible. Such screening might require a relatively complex analysis of factors such as product safety, pollution (which might include an analysis of what forms of power are being used in different processes along the supply chain, such as solar, hydro or wind power), the workplace health and safety practices of potential suppliers, and so forth.

negative screening
A strict rule that certain activities or products shall not be supported or acquired because of concerns about their risks or impacts on particular parts of society, or on the environment

positive screening
An organisational requirement that prior to their acceptance, support or acquisition, particular products or services shall have specific attributes, such as utilising processes that satisfy particular environmental or social standards

Evaluating the alternatives

Once some acceptable alternatives have been identified, there is a need to evaluate them in terms of the likely outcomes they will generate. To do so, some knowledge of how costs and associated cash flows fluctuate with activity (or volume) is necessary. As we explained in Chapter 1, these costs do not have to be restricted to monetary costs but could also include some form of recognition of the externalities being generated by the use of particular resources.

Producing budgets

To evaluate alternatives, various budgets will need to be produced. Budgets are reports that provide a description, or account, of what is likely to happen in the future as a result of implementing particular plans. Many budgets are expressed purely in financial terms, though that does not have to be the case. Budgets that might be prepared include the sales (service revenue) budget, operating expenses budget, purchases budget, advertising budget, capital acquisition budget, budgeted cash flow statement, budgeted statement of profit or loss, or budgeted balance sheet. From a non-financial perspective, budgets might also be prepared that pertain to projected social and environmental performance. For example, there could be budgets of projected water use, CO_2 emissions or electricity usage.

Budgets generally relate to shorter time periods, such as a year, or perhaps a month. They act to set short-term targets and to operationalise an organisation's strategic plan in terms of providing guidance for what needs to be achieved in the immediate future. Budgets act as a mechanism for control, as they enable managers to monitor how actual performance compares with budgeted performance (targets), and to explore reasons for any variances. The term 'control' is used here in the sense that it relates to those actions taken to help ensure plans are achieved; that is, control aims to ensure conformance with plans.

Exploring 'What if?' situations

When evaluating alternatives within the planning phase, it is also wise to do some 'What if?' analysis. This will adjust certain variables – such as the predicted demand for a product, or the expected prices of some raw materials – and then see how this might impact the overall projected results. For example, how sensitive are the results to slight variations in particular variables? With the use of various commonly available spreadsheet programs, the manipulation of variables as part of a 'What if?' analysis is not difficult to do. Lists of the advantages and disadvantages of each alternative can be produced to enable decision makers to better understand the respective implications.

Making a decision

Applying the sequence of events depicted in Figure 3.2, managers then need to decide which of the available options creates the greatest value for the organisation and its stakeholders, in terms of the objectives that the organisation is seeking to achieve. As we continue to emphasise, these objectives do not just have to be financial in nature but could be a mixture of financial, social and environmental considerations. Indeed, as we shall discuss shortly, to help ensure the longer-term survival of organisations, it is essential that managers consider not only the financial implications of their potential actions, but also the likely social and environmental impacts of their operations.

Managers might need to devise some form of weighting system for the various implications. Again, there might be some decision rules/screens that eliminate some alternatives as simply unacceptable. For example, it might come to light that a potential supplier uses child labour and is linked to other forms of modern slavery, and the organisation might have a strict policy of not buying products from such suppliers.

It is essential that, whatever options are chosen, they are economically viable and generate sufficient cash flows to enable the business to operate into the future. This will be identified through the production of various cash-flow budgets.

Implementing action

The next major step in **Figure 3.2** is to implement the chosen alternative. In doing so, it needs to be ensured that the policies and procedures in place to assist the organisation to meet its objectives – which we can refer to as its *governance policies* – are complied with once the planned operations commence. That is, when implementing an action, it is essential that the designated people charged with making various decisions throughout the process actually *do* make those decisions, and that the required accounts pertaining to inputs, outputs, impacts and so forth are collected in the manner that was planned.

While we will not pursue the area of corporate governance in great depth within this book – except to say that proper accounting, monitoring and reporting are components of a well-functioning governance system – it is nevertheless useful to provide a definition of the term. According to Standards Australia's *Good governance principles*, governance

> refers to the framework of rules, relationships, systems and processes by which an enterprise is directed, controlled and held to account and whereby authority within an organisation is exercised and maintained. It encompasses authority, accountability, stewardship and leadership, and direction and control exercised in any organisation.
>
> Source: Standards Australia (2003).

As you can see, accountability and accounting is a central element of good governance, and therefore of the proper functioning of an organisation.

Monitoring and evaluating

As **Figure 3.2** shows, once the planning has been done and the alternatives have been reviewed, selected and implemented, then monitoring and evaluation needs to take place. Monitoring involves measuring/assessing actual performance (actual outcomes) and comparing it with the planned (budgeted) performance/outcomes to identify variances – a *variance* being the difference between a particular planned outcome and the actual outcome – and these are then investigated. This is commonly regarded as part of the control phase. It is unlikely that actual performance will precisely match planned performance – the more uncertain the environment, the more likely this is. We can nearly always expect some form of variance between actual and planned outcomes.

There could be many reasons for variances. For example, some variances will be due to error – perhaps human or machine error/failure that can be relatively easily addressed. Some might simply be due to a random occurrence that could not be controlled. Some variances that are not random might also be beyond control; for example, changes in the political stability of particular countries, or unexpected severe storms that might have caused problems for an organisation. It is also possible that the variance could be the result of an unrealistic budget (target) initially being set, or a budget that was poorly constructed in the first place. Where variances are deemed to be significant, they need to be investigated, understood and, where possible, addressed, so as to prevent the same problems arising in the future.

It is appropriate to mention that evaluating actual outcomes against planned performance is probably easier when the performance targets are quantified, or numerical, in nature. When targets are not in the form of numbers – for example, the target might be that local residents shall not be 'concerned' about the noise being generated by a newly constructed factory – it is not always immediately obvious how to assess whether or not the target or goal has been successfully achieved. Regarding the example above, an instrument/survey to measure 'concern' might need to be developed, or perhaps it is stipulated that a certain number of complaints are the indicator of 'concern'. Again, if you are accepting accountability for issues like noise, then you need to somehow devise an accounting system to inform you about whether the accepted responsibility has been appropriately addressed by managers, and the associated accountability has been properly discharged.

Learning exercise 3.3 extends our discussion of the benefits of clear plans.

3.3 Learning Exercise

The benefits of clear plans

What are some of the benefits that might arise as a result of carefully planning future organisational activities? In answering this question, we can note that creating plans requires the managers of an organisation to think about the future in terms of:

- what the organisation might produce
- who it might sell it to
- where it will obtain its funding
- what other resources are needed
- what costs and impacts should arise
- what is the relevant legislation
- what are the expectations of various stakeholders
- what is the availability and expectations of employees?

This all means that the managers of an organisation need to gain an appreciation of what their organisation is doing and whether the plans are viable before they actually do anything. They need to understand the various economic, social and environmental systems in which they are operating. Establishing plans and related targets also enables managers to assess subsequent performance in terms of whether or not the targets have been achieved, and if not, why not. This control aspect will then facilitate learning and revisions to plans, and the cycle will continue. Good planning is part of a broader strategy of reducing risks as the planning phase can identify likely problems before they actually occur. By analogy, without planning, an organisation is effectively sailing along without a map, and at some stage it is likely to run onto rocks!

Learning, revising and adjusting

This is the last phase in the cycle represented in **Figure 3.2**. We are emphasising that once plans have been developed, they need to be implemented with the related activities (and costs) being monitored and controlled for compliance with the standards/goals that were established. Opportunities for improvement to processes also need to be continuously considered. In light of performance and experience, previous plans can be revised and new plans established. Much learning might occur and could include revising the understanding of how costs behave as the volume of activity changes. At this stage, further research might also introduce other opportunities to consider.

Feedback from interested stakeholders can also be used in terms of how they have responded to the actual process/outputs of an organisation. For example, the organisation should consider implementing stakeholder surveys, or social audits. Customers might, for instance, be surveyed to ask how satisfied they are with the products and services being provided. Or an organisation might employ an independent third party to enter a factory of the organisation, or of a supplier (with approval), to provide an account of the treatment of employees and the safety of the work environment (audits of workplaces are often referred to as an example of a social audit).

Key concept

Feedback from stakeholders can be used to determine how satisfied stakeholders are with an organisation, and can provide the accountant with information so they can revise and adjust processes.

Accountants are central to the successful operations of an organisation. As should now be clear, an accountant is much more than somebody who provides an account of the financial costs that have been incurred within a set period, or the income that has been earned in that period; that is, a good accountant is much more than simply a record keeper. Accountants should play a key role in planning activities, suggesting innovative ways of doing things, and putting in place (governance) policies that encourage an organisation to achieve its goals. This important role of accountants was reflected in a report released in 2019 by the International Federation of Accountants (IFAC) entitled *Future-fit Accountants*. In this report, IFAC identified seven key roles or attributes for finance and accounting professionals to retain relevance and to enhance their potential contribution to their respective organisations. The seven key attributes that are required of the accounting professional are outlined in **Figure 3.4.**

The above IFAC report was consistent with an earlier report (2011) released by IFAC, entitled *Competent and versatile: How professional accountants in business drive sustainable organisation success*. According to IFAC (2011, p. 6), professional accountants in all organisations have a significant role in:

- *framing business models* – that is, determining the appropriate way to run a business in terms of where it might earn its revenue, what costs it could and should incur, and how it should manage its risks together with considerations of when, throughout the process, decisions should be made and why
- *challenging conventional assumptions of doing business and redefining success in the context of achieving sustainable value creation* – that is, being innovative and prepared to do things differently in a way that creates ongoing value for a broad group of stakeholders. This periodically requires challenging 'business-as-usual' philosophies
- *encouraging and rewarding the right behaviours* – that is, when helping devise systems to monitor actual performance against plans, it is essential that the targets being set – and the associated rewards – are consistent with the overall mission of the organisation
- *ensuring that decisions are supported by the necessary information, analysis and insights* – that is, information that is both relevant to, and reliable for, planning and assessing organisational activities is collected and presented in a way that is clear and concise
- *ensuring that monitoring and reporting performance go beyond the traditional ways of thinking about economic success* – that is, the systems in place to collect and report information consider aspects of performance which also include social and environmental impacts and stakeholder satisfaction.

FIGURE 3.4 The seven key attributes required of the accounting professional

1. Leads strategically, facilitates change, and influences people and decisions. Is actively involved in all significant business decisions and major initiatives to drive change and growth.
2. Steers an organisation toward value creation and sustained profitability by providing decision relevant and actionable insights.
3. Protects an organisation and its reputation through stewardship of tangible and intangible assets and financial and non-financial performance.
4. Enlightens internal and external stakeholders on the organisation's narrative, how it creates value over time, and the opportunities and challenges it faces.
5. Enables a cognitive and data-driven business that utilises digitalisation, including automation, artificial intelligence and data, in ways that drive decisions and growth.
6. Ensures efficient and effective end-to-end processes and work flows within and across finance and the organisation.
7. Challenges the organisation, and themselves, when needed with professional objectivity.

Successful, innovative organisations will invariably have top-quality, innovative accountants!

LO3.3 Short-term and long-term planning: a balanced approach

A theme that has clearly emerged in our discussion is that planning needs to be both long term as well as short term in orientation, and with clear links between the two.

Long-term planning, which might have a time horizon of several years, relates to *strategic planning*. As **Figure 3.3** shows, it is also linked to organisational values, vision, mission, goals and objectives. Strategic planning is the responsibility of senior management, and relates to decisions such as moving into new product lines, new countries, new industries and so forth. Such strategic plans then require the implementation of shorter-term plans and related budgets which are the responsibility of middle-level managers. Day-to-day decision making is the responsibility of lower-level managers.

Decisions which incorporate a mixture of long-term and short-term considerations include investments in cleaner technologies. For example, an organisation might be concerned about the amount of waste or emissions being generated. To address these concerns, it might be necessary to invest in relatively expensive machinery that is more efficient. This could increase costs (and thereby decrease profits) in the short run, but in the long run this could be good for business – disposing of waste could become more costly over time, or fines or taxes might be introduced by government to discourage certain emissions. Another example is investments in plant and equipment which produce products with lower defect rates. Again, this might be costly at the time of implementation (new plant, new training and so forth), but in the long run this could create significant business benefits together with reducing waste.

Balancing planned long-term outcomes with short-term performance

Managers, and accountants, also need to consider the implications of existing and proposed remuneration plans in terms of encouraging longer- or shorter-term thinking by managers. People within organisations often receive bonuses linked to aspects of performance. For example, managers might be provided with a bonus calculated as a certain percentage of profits or sales, or it might be linked to measures such as return on assets, or the achievement of certain financial targets appearing in various budgets. Such metrics, or performance indicators, are generated by the financial accounting system and are typically based on the results for a time period of just one year (or less). Rewarding key employees/managers in terms of such indicators might motivate them to focus on short-term measures of performance rather than on longer-term priorities. This is something that organisations need to be careful about. A more sensible way of rewarding managers and other key employees is to provide them with a mixture of rewards based on shorter-term and longer-term performance measures.

Whilst managers should have a focus on both the long and short term, there will be various factors which can create pressures to focus more on the short-run. Managers need to be aware of these pressures and not take their focus away from longer-run objectives. This discussion is also consistent with the views of IFAC (2011, p. 9), which notes that the need for short-term results can distract managers from their long-term vision.

As IFAC (2011, p. 9) states:

> Although short-term needs cannot be ignored, governing bodies and professional accountants need to recognise that some short-term pressures can distract from the long-term vision.

For example, some factors that might bias a manager towards focusing on the shorter term (see **Learning exercise 3.4**) include short-term bonus plans (that provide a bonus based on, say, six monthly or yearly profit), which we have already discussed, as well as the related fact that organisations present financial statements on a yearly basis. Profit is a key figure in these financial statements, a performance indicator that attracts a great deal of news media attention, particularly for larger organisations. While profit is an important measure of performance, focusing on it too much for just one year could cause managers to shift their focus from longer-run performance. Short-term employment contracts, which are frequently used in some industries, might also act to reduce the inclination of managers to think in terms of the longer run.

3.4 Learning Exercise

The dysfunctional effects of some reward mechanisms

A manager who oversees research and development (R&D) at his company is approaching retirement. This manager has a significant role in determining which R&D projects will commence. Within the organisation, the average project is in the R&D phase for four years before it generates any income. During this time, the expenses associated with R&D reduce the profits of the company because a lot of the R&D costs are immediately treated as expenses of the financial period in which they are incurred, thereby reducing that period's profits. The manager receives a fixed annual salary of $250 000 plus an annual bonus of 2 per cent of the company's annual profit.

Based on this scenario, is it a good idea for the manager to continue receiving a bonus, particularly as they are approaching retirement?

Consider how managers are rewarded over the short term

The way in which a manager is rewarded for their efforts will affect the manager's decision making and can have negative implications for the longer-term success of the organisation. A few major points need to be made here:

- If a manager is being rewarded in terms of annual profits, then the horizon of their decision making might be biased towards the same period – that is, towards 12 months, as the manager's bonus is paid annually.
- If a manager is expected to be involved in R&D decisions that will not generate profits for four years, but which might generate costs early on regarding the R&D activities, then common sense tells us that such managers should not receive bonuses based on short-term results. This manager might not be inclined to start expensive but important projects because it would lower their bonus.
- The inclination for this particular manager to be focused on the short term is further compounded by their imminent retirement, which means they will not be in the organisation when the R&D projects they are planning are expected to ultimately generate profits – which in this case is four years.

How could this manager be more sensibly rewarded?

This manager should be taken off their annual bonus plan and provided with a bonus that is focused on the long term. Perhaps the bonus could even be deferred for a number of years and tied to the change in share price that occurs over the next four years. These related payments could be made to the manager some time after their retirement. This approach would encourage the manager to think in a longer-term way.

Why do I need to know that successful planning requires both a long-term and short-term focus?

Successful organisations need to plan for both the short term and the long term. In the short term, there will be needs for cash, various raw materials, labour, and so forth. If access to such resources cannot be satisfied in the near term, perhaps because of poor planning, then an organisation can easily go out of business. However, to succeed in the longer term needs longer-term planning. Such planning requires consideration of potential future changes in production technologies, labour supplies, raw materials supplies, costs, legislation, consumer preferences and so on. If you are to be a good manager you will plan for various time horizons, such as the next week, next month, six months, year, two years, five years and so forth. In principle, you will always need to consider the short run but if your view is predominantly short-run in focus (perhaps focusing on the profits of each year only), then it is likely that your organisation will not be sustainable in the longer term.

LO3.4 Planning for sustainable development

When managers consider the issues associated with sustainability, they are taking a longer-term view of the organisation's operations. As we have emphasised in this chapter, and in the previous two chapters of this book, when performing managerial duties, broader issues of sustainability need to be incorporated within the organisational strategy.

In using the term *sustainability*, we mean organisational activities that are consistent with the idea of *sustainable development*. One of the most recognisable definitions of sustainable development is the one that appeared in a book-length report initiated by the World Commission on Environment and Development (1987, p. 10) entitled *Our Common Future*. This definition is 'Development that meets the needs of the present world without compromising the ability of future generations to meet their own needs'.

This definition projects a perspective of intergenerational equity in terms of the view that globally we must ensure that our generation's activities (consumption patterns and so forth) do not negatively impact upon future generations' quality of life. Specifically, we should be in a position to say that the planet we leave for our children is in as good a shape as the planet we inherited – ideally, in better shape.

The definition of sustainable development provided above also incorporates the idea of intragenerational equity in noting that the needs of the 'present world' must be met if we are to have sustainable development globally. Given the great disparity in wealth that exists across the world, and within particular countries and communities, it is imperative for sustainable development that all people now have access to appropriate food and shelter. We cannot expect particular people and particular communities to care about the environment (and therefore future generations) if they are struggling to have enough food and shelter now. Such people will do what they need to do now to survive – regardless of the consequences for the environment (for example, they might cut down important areas of biodiversity as a source of heating or farming land if this is the most immediate and only way of accessing food and/or shelter). Sustainability therefore requires that organisations pay fair wages throughout the world so that all people everywhere have the opportunity to think longer term.

Incorporating considerations of sustainability into our planning processes necessarily means prioritising the longer-term performance of an organisation.

The need for sustainability

Sustainable business operations require an organisation to be economically responsible while at the same time considering the impacts on both the environment and the societies in which it operates. As noted above, a focus on sustainable operations is considered to represent a long-term view or perspective, as a failure to consider such issues might generate short-term economic benefits but arguably will be detrimental to the long-term operations, and therefore success, of the organisation.

Society has ever-increasing expectations with regards to the treatment of people and care for the environment, so failure to consider such factors will be bad for business in the longer run. Addressing issues to do with sustainability will also lower the risks associated with an organisation. Across time, legislation will become more demanding with respect to social and environmental performance. Markets and consumers will be more reactive to this performance, such that organisations that do not address these issues properly will inevitably be subject to some form of market-based or regulative discipline. Those organisations not embracing sustainability will be regarded as higher risk, which will increase the cost of attracting sources of finance: generally speaking, the higher the perceived risk, the higher the cost of finance.

The above discussion is consistent with the views of IFAC, which emphasises in the following points that accountants need to embrace sustainability when working within an organisation:

- Sustainable development and the sustainability of organizations have become mainstream issues for politicians, consumers, and business leaders.
- From an economic as well as an environmental and social perspective, sustainability issues are transforming the competitive landscape, forcing organizations to change the way they think about products and services, technologies, processes, and business models.
- Long-term sustainable value creation requires responsible organizations to direct their strategies and operations to achieving sustainable economic, environmental, and social performance. It also requires incorporating wider stakeholder perspectives and issues into decision-making.
- Ensuring that organizations pursue sustainable business models and development practices will require radical changes in the way they do business. Achieving a sustainable future is possible only if organizations recognize the role that they can and need to play.
- Effective action by the accountancy profession and professional accountants to better integrate and account for sustainability is an essential part of the response.
- Governing bodies and organizational governing bodies and organizational leaders should be focused on the long-term sustainability of their organization, and they should be confident that their business models will deliver this.

Source: International Federation of Accountants (2011), p. 6.

IFAC further emphasises that, when planning future activities and evaluating past performance, both financial and non-financial indicators need to be taken into account:

- A narrow focus on financial performance, such as short-term earnings and profits, at the expense of social or environmental performance can result in a loss of trust in an organization and damage overall performance, resulting in value destruction for all stakeholders, and, in some cases, losing its license to operate.
- Issues of human rights; corruption and bribery; non-compliance with labor and environmental standards and responsibility; and discrimination in respect to employment and occupation can be as important to the long-term prospects of larger, publicly owned organizations, as well as to smaller organizations.

Source: International Federation of Accountants (2011), p. 8.

As organisations embrace sustainability, they are effectively increasing the range of the stakeholders they accept responsibility for, and owe accountability to. In terms of the discussion in Chapter 2, organisations that embed sustainability considerations throughout their operations are extending the boundary of their accounting well beyond the confines of the organisation itself.

LO3.5 Planning to create value

Apart from the issues associated with sustainable business practices, and the various long- and short-term factors we have just addressed, there's another related factor that needs to be considered: the need for an organisation to add value throughout the various processes it undertakes. In this sense, adding value means that the organisation performs its operations in a way that is more efficient than its competitors, or that it combines its activities in a way that enables it to generate goods or services that are superior to those that are available elsewhere. Reducing costs in a particular process, for example, is a means of adding value. The cost reduction might relate to financial, social or environmental costs.

Value creation is achieved by utilising various resources in a way which leads to desirable outcomes. What is deemed 'desirable' will evolve and change across time as stakeholder expectations change. Different stakeholders will have different perspectives on what might be valuable, as we will shortly discuss. At its core, an organisation would be expected to create value for various stakeholders who might include shareholders (owners), employees, customers, local communities, suppliers and their employees, community-based groups, and the environment. And the value creation should occur in an ecologically and socially sustainable way.

Key concept

At its core, an organisation is expected to create value for its various stakeholders

Michael Porter (1985) described the sequence of activities undertaken by an organisation as a *value chain*. Although this term was introduced many years ago, it is still commonly referred to today as a key management tool. Well-performing organisations create relatively more value through the various steps involved in acquiring and transforming resources into final products and services. Central to Porter's reasoning is that:

- greater organisational efficiency creates greater value
- value creation requires clear vision, strategy and planning
- value creation relies upon well-functioning corporate governance (as we learned earlier in this chapter, 'corporate governance' refers to the processes, policies and systems in place to direct an organisation towards meeting its mission and related objectives).

Porter's five primary activities of organisations

The problem for managers, and accountants, is how to create the most value at each step of the organisation's processes. Products or services are seen as passing through a chain of activities (the value chain), in a particular order, and at each activity the product or service should gain some value. Porter (1985) identified five *primary activities* of organisations, which are accompanied by four supporting activities. The five primary activities in the 'value chain' described by Porter (1985) can be diagrammatically represented as shown in Figure 3.5.

FIGURE 3.5 Primary activities within Porter's value chain

These five primary activities, which occur in the order shown in Figure 3.5, can be ascribed to most organisations. Here is a summary of what occurs in each of these components of the value chain:

1. *Inbound logistics*: These are the activities involved in receiving, storing and distributing the raw materials used in the production or service process.
2. *Operations*: This is the stage where raw materials are converted into the final product or service.
3. *Outbound logistics*: These are the activities required to deliver the product or service to the end users.
4. *Marketing and sales*: This stage involves activities such as customer management, advertising, salesforce organisation, and the selection of distribution channels and pricing. Of increasing importance in many businesses is the use of social media, which is a low-cost way of promoting products and services, creating brand awareness and brand identity, and engaging with customers.
5. *Service*: This relates to the processes that are needed to create better customer experiences and to maintain the product's performance. These processes include installation, training, maintenance, repair, warranty and after-sales service.

The idea is that an organisation should attempt, through careful planning, to create competitive advantage in each primary activity. Each such activity requires a separate detailed analysis in its own right with respect to such things as identifying the costs and revenues (if any) that might be associated with them, together with considerations of the efficiency and potential improvements inherent within them. For example, with outbound logistics, it might be possible to find more efficient shipping options, which will lead to a reduction in costs (financial as well, perhaps, as a reduction in the carbon emissions associated with transportation), which in turn will lead to higher profits and/or better social and environmental outcomes.

Porter's four supporting activities for organisations

Facilitating the efficiency of these five primary activities are four *supporting activities*, which Porter (1985) identified as follows:

1. *Procurement*: These activities relate to how the raw materials are sourced, supplier management, and subcontracting. Of increasing importance to many stakeholders is that organisations should seek to ensure that supply chains only include suppliers that act in a socially and environmentally responsible manner.
2. *Technology development*: This relates to product and process design, product engineering, market testing, and research and development.
3. *Human resource management*: This refers to the processes involved in hiring and retaining the appropriate employees to help design, build and market an organisation's products and services.
4. *Firm infrastructure*: This refers to an organisation's structure and its management, planning, accounting, finance and quality-control mechanisms.

Each of these four supporting activities is expected to be efficient in their own right and work to create efficiencies, and value, in each of the five primary activities. Accounting, which is deemed to be part of firm infrastructure, is expected to be a value-adding process – a process which adds value to each of the primary activities.

Value chain analysis

Organisations conduct **value chain analysis** by reviewing each step required to create a product or service, and identifying ways of increasing the efficiency of each part of the value chain. Organisation-specific processes should be mapped and value-adding activities identified. If value cannot be added through particular activities within the organisation, then it should consider outsourcing the products or services. For example, if a car manufacturer cannot produce seats, windscreens, spark plugs and so forth as cost efficiently as some other organisations, then it should consider outsourcing those products to other organisations that have a competitive advantage in that area.

value chain analysis Reviewing each step required to create a product or service, and identifying ways of increasing the efficiency of each part of the value chain

The overall goal of value chain analysis is to generate the maximum value for the least possible cost, thereby creating a competitive advantage. The typical aim of value chain analysis is to increase profits and the incidence of positive social and environmental outcomes by creating greater value at each point across the entire process.

A successful organisation will generate the greatest value in the process of acquiring and transforming inputs into goods and services. Customers seek value, and they will support the good or service that provides them with the greatest value. Organisations create value by doing things differently and in ways that are better than those of their rivals.

The following video provides further insights into the value chain: www.youtube.com/watch?v=g8p2H7EvoGM

IFAC's view on value creation

The IFAC report *Competent and versatile* (2011) highlights how accountants are expected to play a central role in identifying opportunities for enhanced value creation throughout the organisation's various activities. The report notes that accountants should act as:

> - *creators of value*, by taking leadership roles in the design and implementation of strategies, policies, plans, structures, and governance measures that set the course for delivering sustainable value creation.
> - *enablers of value*, by informing and guiding managerial and operational decision making and implementation of strategy for achieving sustainable value creation, and the planning, monitoring, and improvement of supporting processes.
> - *preservers of value*, by ensuring the protection of a sustainable value creation strategy against strategic, operational, and financial risks, and ensuring compliance with regulations, standards, and good practices.
> - *reporters of value*, by enabling the transparent communication of the delivery of sustainable value to stakeholders.
>
> Source: International Federation of Accountants (2011), pp. 15–16.

Again, we see that accountants do more than just provide accounts of past financial performance. They are expected to add value to an organisation (see **Learning exercise 3.5**), and the better the accountant, the greater the value-add created by their actions.

3.5 Learning Exercise

Accountants assisting in adding value

Snappy Dresser Ltd outsources the production of shirts to a supplier in Indonesia. It believes that one way it can add value to what it does is to improve the health and safety of the employees in the Indonesian factory. Let's consider how an accountant might assist with this quest to add value.

Operationalising the goal

The goal of 'improving the health and safety of the employees in the Indonesian factory' needs to be operationalised; that is:

- some form of target needs to be aligned with this goal
- some form of account needs to be developed to allow managers to subsequently determine whether the goal has been achieved.

Devising an appropriate performance measure and adding value

The accountant might organise an independent third party with expertise in factory-based health and safety issues to do audits of the factory on a regular basis, and provide a description of what needs to be improved and what has been accomplished since the last site visit. There are many organisations globally that provide such services.

To encourage the supplier to take meaningful action, Snappy Dresser Ltd might stipulate that it is a requirement that third-party audits of the factory are done, before it is prepared to start purchasing a new product line of shirts from the factory.

The site audit reports represent an account of factory health and safety policies, and performance. The accountant will need to devise a system which allows the organisation to make a judgement as to whether the improvements since the last site visit are enough to represent the successful achievement of the project goal.

Why do I need to know about the need to maximise 'value'?

First, we need to understand that 'value' is a broad term, and not all 'values' can be quantified in monetary terms.

Organisations succeed to the extent they create value, and the more 'value' an organisation creates, the more support it will receive from different stakeholders and the more successful it will be. Organisations that create greater value from a stakeholder's perspective will tend to garner more support than other organisations.

In maximising value you will need to consider how different stakeholders determine 'value'. Knowing you need to maximise value at each step of the value chain, it should prompt you to consider which stakeholders have an interest in each activity within the value chain, and what aspects of the organisation's operations they value most highly. A successful manager will be one who is able to consider the expectations of the different stakeholder groups and to provide an overall maximisation of value creation. This will require some trade-offs between the expectations or needs of different stakeholder groups and an acceptance that not all 'values' can be measured in financial terms.

For example, if customers and local communities value products and operations that have lower environmental and social impacts, then this might require an organisation to invest in relatively costly new production technologies which reduce waste and emissions. This might be valued by these stakeholders even though some investors – who might be more interested in higher profits and higher dividends – might be displeased. It would be in the longer-run interests of the organisation to have processes that are socially and environmentally responsible.

IFAC's eight drivers of sustainable organisational success

Slightly different to the value-chain analysis introduced by Porter (1985) are the prescriptions provided by IFAC relating to the creation of value. According to IFAC (2011), and linking with areas to consider when attempting to maximise value creation, there are eight drivers of sustainable organisational success (see **Figure 3.6**) that accountants need to consider when seeking to help organisations achieve sustainable value creation:

1. *A customer and stakeholder focus* – successful organisations create value for their customers and this in turn creates value for investors and other providers of funding.
2. *Effective leadership and strategy* – the long-term implications of decisions need to be considered in terms of how they impact operations, key stakeholders and reputation.
3. *Integrated governance, risk and control* – the policies and procedures put in place to direct the organisation towards achieving its goals must incorporate mechanisms to reduce risk and address departures from agreed plans (see **Learning exercise 3.6**).
4. *Innovative and adaptive capability* – organisations need to be innovative and adaptive regarding changing circumstances throughout their various planning, implementation and review phases.
5. *Financial management* – strong financial management is essential to successful operations. Managers and accountants must think beyond the short term and provide confidence to stakeholders, inclusive of providers of funding, that the organisation is sustainable financially.
6. *People and talent management* – successful organisations need to attract and retain talented employees.
7. *Operational excellence* – choices made within the organisation during operations need to be consistent with the organisation's mission, strategic direction, goals and objectives.
8. *Effective and transparent communication* – successful organisations need to communicate with stakeholders in a way that is understandable and relevant.

These eight drivers of value identified by IFAC provide a general representation of the areas that organisations should concentrate on to be competitive and sustainable in the long run. The three components of sustainability (economic, social and environmental performance) are relevant to all of the factors.

In discussing value creation, we need to acknowledge that different stakeholders will likely have different views or perspectives on what represents value. While far from exhaustive, **Table 3.3** provides some possible perceptions of value that might be held by different stakeholders. The table also identifies how these perceptions of value might be addressed by an accounting system. (For a discussion of value creation by management, with the support of accountants, in the context of Table 3.3, see **Learning exercise 3.7**.)

FIGURE 3.6 Drivers of sustainable organisational success

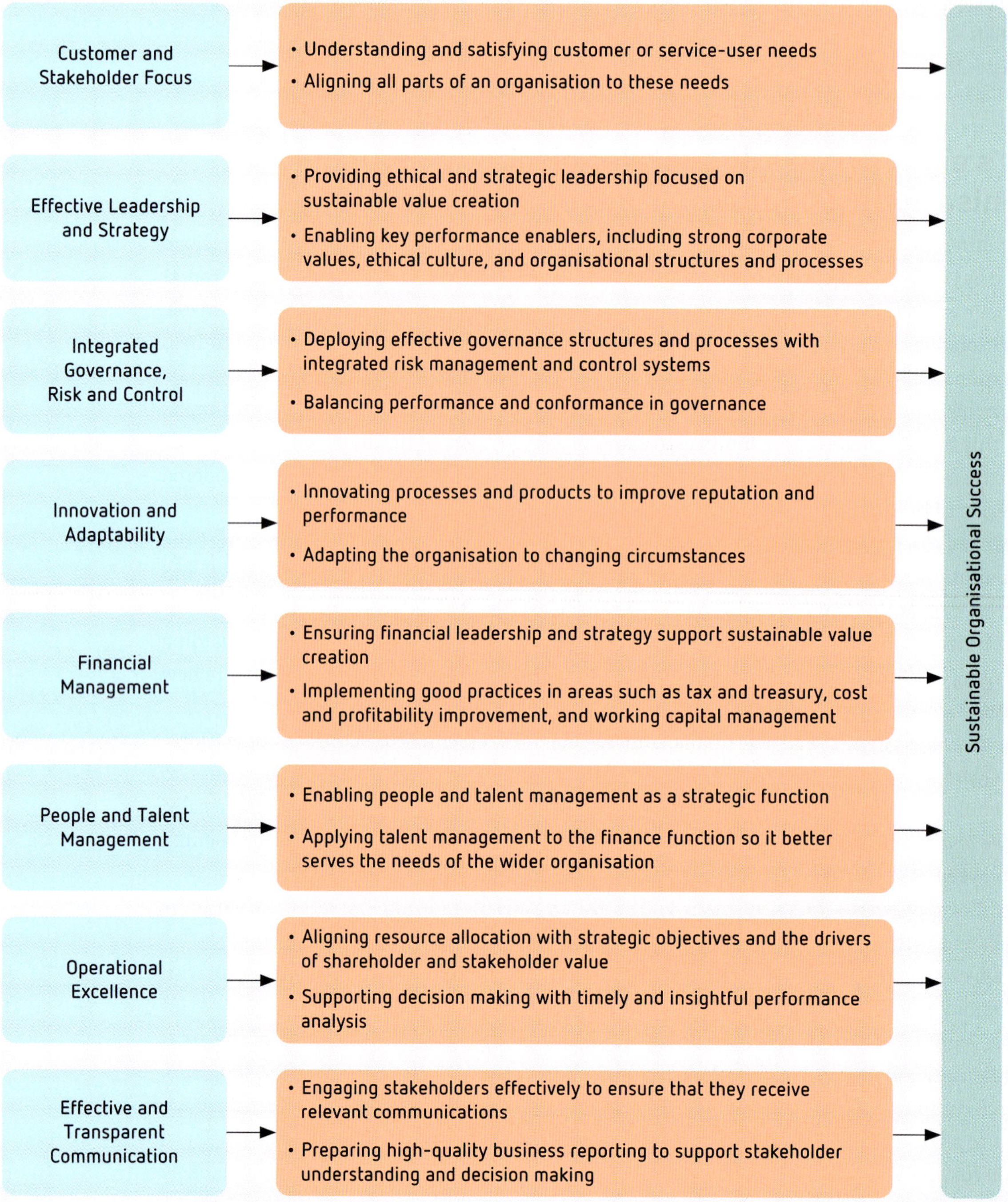

Source: International Federation of Accountants (2011), p. 14.

3.6 Learning Exercise

Instigating appropriate reward structures

In **Learning exercise 3.4** we noted that accountants have a role in encouraging and rewarding the right behaviours. Assuming that an organisation is concerned about issues associated with climate change, let's consider what mechanisms an accountant might help put in place to encourage the organisation to, for example, reduce its consumption of electricity.

An accountant and their team would first need to become familiar with the electricity consumption patterns of the organisation's property, plant and equipment. Once knowledge of the organisation's current or projected power consumption is gathered, then opportunities for electricity savings can be identified. The accountant's team might:

- cost and source alternative items of property, plant and equipment that are proven to be more energy efficient
- encourage a decision to stop producing goods or services that are highly energy intensive, and switch to the production of alternative goods or services that generate sound financial returns but consume less electricity
- devise budgets for future energy use, which can be used as targets for staff to achieve – any significant departures from these targets would be subject to investigation
- introduce an incentive scheme or bonus plan for staff who are able to significantly reduce the electricity consumption of the organisation for particular levels of production or services – once targets are set for future energy consumption, some monetary reward might be paid to these people for meeting or exceeding targeted reductions in energy use.

If a particular aspect of performance is deemed to be important to an organisation, then the achievement of that objective needs to be supported by appropriate policies and procedures inclusive of appropriate accounting processes. That is, it needs to be supported by appropriate governance mechanisms.

TABLE 3.3 Possible stakeholder perceptions of value

Stakeholder	Perceptions of what represents value	Implications for the accounting system
Shareholders	Shareholders generally value the maximisation of dividends and share price	Creates a need to measure financial performance, including the necessity to control various financial costs while attempting to maximise revenues
Lenders and creditors	Lenders and creditors will be concerned about the likelihood of repayment, and possibly that the organisations they have funded are socially and environmentally responsible. Therefore, they would value the timely repayment of funds, low risks, and being associated with socially and environmentally responsible organisations	Creates a need to provide information about current and projected profitability and cash flows, the organisation's future plans (particularly if those plans involve moving into riskier areas of operation which might put repayments at risk), and the social and environmental performance of an organisation
Employees (local)	Local employees value the timely payment of wages, a safe and healthy work environment, promotion and training opportunities, and the reputation of an organisation (people feel good about working for a reputable organisation)	Creates a need to provide an account of how safe and healthy the work environment is and how this is changing over time; an account of training for employees and how many are being retained and promoted; and an account/measure of the community's perception of an organisation
Employees (in offshore supply factories)	Offshore employees value the provision of a safe and healthy work environment, and a liveable wage	Creates a need to provide an (independent) account of the employee practices and outcomes within supply company factories

Stakeholder	Perceptions of what represents value	Implications for the accounting system
Customers	Customers value low prices, high quality, positive social and environmental impacts throughout the supply chain, and reliable after-sales service	Creates a need to provide an account of product costs and what is being done to keep these low; provide an account of the monitoring of suppliers throughout the supply chain; provide social and environmental accounts; and engage a sample of customers to assess their satisfaction with after-sales service together with actions to address any concerns
Local communities	Local communities value contributions to local activities, a safe place of work for local residents, and low social and environmental impacts	Creates a need to provide an account that addresses the key economic, social and environmental costs and benefits generated by the organisation
Suppliers	Suppliers value reliable payment and ongoing support for their products/services	Creates a need to undertake a (social) audit of suppliers' perceptions of the performance of an organisation, and provide a related account noting levels of satisfaction and key areas for improvement

3.7 Learning Exercise

The creation of value

Creating value is a core responsibility of management which should be supported by accountants. Let us consider this in the context of **Table 3.3**.

From whose perspective should we assess value?

As you can see in **Table 3.3**, different stakeholders can have different perceptions of what creates value. Which stakeholders a business appeals to will depend on which are considered to be the most important regarding the success of the organisation, as well as who the managers believe they owe responsibility to.

If a manufacturing activity effectively increases the wealth of workers and shareholders but causes environmental damage, is this creating value?

From the perspective of shareholders and workers, the increase in financial wealth might offset any concerns about the environmental damage being done, such that they see it as a net value-add. However, some shareholders and workers might be particularly concerned about the environment and they might be conflicted.

An organisation should weigh up the various positive and negative impacts of a project on different stakeholders – including the environment – to determine whether the project is overall worthwhile.

If a supermarket introduces self-service check-out machines to reduce staff numbers and wage costs, thereby increasing profits and dividends for shareholders, is this creating value?

Certainly, this is something that has been happening in supermarkets. Check-out operators have lost their jobs with the introduction of self-service machines, which has led to increased profits for supermarkets. Therefore, to many stakeholders with a financial interest in these organisations (such as shareholders or managers receiving bonuses tied to profits), this is a value-adding exercise.

However, in terms of the total value added by the organisation, we should consider the people who are now unemployed, and the social implications this has for their families as well as for the government in terms of social benefits (which are funded by taxpayers). Considering the total value being contributed by organisations is not straightforward, but it is an interesting issue to think about. It should be accepted as a component of accounting.

Make or buy?

Organisations will often be confronted with decisions about whether they should make a product themselves, or whether they should buy it from another organisation. When considering the issue of value chains, if another organisation can produce a good or service more efficiently, then it might make sense to outsource that product or service. By doing so, the organisation might also be able to utilise any spare production capacity for producing an alternative product or service that might generate better returns.

The decision to make an item or buy it (outsource it) therefore relies on an analysis of those costs and revenues that change as a result of the decision. That is, we need to focus on the relevant costs and relevant revenues, which are those that will arise in the future and differ between options.

It is common for organisations to outsource parts of their production to other organisations. For example, clothing companies headquartered in the United Kingdom, Europe, the United States, Australia, New Zealand and Canada often outsource their production to developing countries such as Indonesia, Pakistan, Thailand and Bangladesh. They do this because the costs of production in these developing countries are much lower than the costs in their own countries. However, while the incremental costs to produce particular clothing items might be lower as a result of outsourcing, care needs to be taken to ensure that the quality of the products is acceptable. Also, other non-financial issues need consideration, such as whether the treatment of employees by outside suppliers is consistent with what the organisation and its stakeholders expect, and whether the environmental performance of these outside suppliers is acceptable to the managers and other stakeholders. Many organisations have had significant damage done to their reputations, and their sales, as a result of being found to have outsourced the production of some of their goods or services to socially or environmentally irresponsible organisations. The days of successfully being able to disclaim responsibility for the social and environmental performance of key suppliers are thankfully gone. If an organisation is a significant part of your supply chain, then you must accept some responsibility for their actions.

Key concept

Outsourcing operations to irresponsible organisations can do significant damage to an organisation's sales and reputation. Responsible organisations need to be accountable for their supply chain.

To this point of the chapter, we have explained the meaning and purpose of management accounting, and we have described the phases involved in managing an organisation. In doing so, we have concentrated on the planning phase and have emphasised how sustainability and long-term considerations are paramount within the planning process. We have also explained that in managing an organisation, it is important to understand where the organisation can, or should, add value and plan accordingly to ensure this value is realised. We have discussed five primary activities that can be analysed (Porter's value chain), and we have also identified eight value drivers that can be considered within each respective activity. We have also described how value might be perceived differently by different stakeholders, and the implications these perceptions of value might have for an accounting system. Central to a lot of this discussion is a consideration of costs. The next section will offer some insights into the behaviour of costs.

LO3.6 The behaviour of costs

cost behaviour
How the cost of producing a good or service is affected by changes to the level or volume of activity

We noted earlier that one of the key components of planning is understanding the costs that will be generated by the proposed activities of an organisation, including how these costs will change, or 'behave', as a result of the level or volume of activity. Understanding **cost behaviour** means that the targets or budgets of costs can be prepared and subsequently compared with actual costs. Understanding costs is a necessary precondition for implementing initiatives to reduce certain costs, or inefficiencies, and therefore adding value at various points in the operations of an organisation.

Managers need reliable information about the costs of the goods or services they supply so that they can determine that selling prices are at least adequate to cover these costs as well as generate profits and the required cash flows. Knowledge of costs will also enable managers to determine whether it is feasible to supply particular goods or services at the prices that the market is prepared to pay. In some cases, it is possible that the price the market is prepared to pay is not greater than the costs the organisation will incur to supply the goods or services, thereby making the supply of the goods or services infeasible.

In terms of costs, various concepts such as relevant costs, variable costs, fixed costs and mixed costs are often used. We will consider these now.

Relevant costs

relevant costs
Those costs that change as a result of a particular decision

Relevant costs are those that will change as a result of a particular decision. For example, if an organisation decides to extend its hours of operation, then extra wages will need to be paid. The wage costs that fluctuate as a result of the decision are the *relevant costs*.

Relevant costs will occur in the future, and they will differ between alternative courses of action. However, what we include in the relevant costs and revenues will be influenced by factors such as the vision and mission of an organisation, its culture, stakeholders' expectations and so forth. For example, if an organisation is concerned about CO_2 emissions, then a relevant cost would be the different emissions generated by different production alternatives. (Remember, as we explained in Chapter 1, costs do not have to be measured only in financial terms.) By contrast, if an organisation is only concerned about maximising financial profits, then it might only consider the financial costs of particular decisions (although, in the long run, this would be an unwise strategy).

Variable costs

variable costs
Costs that change as a result of changing production or service volume

Variable costs are the costs that change as a result of changing production or service volume. That is, they vary as the volume of activity changes. The activity might be measured in terms of units of a product or service, machine hours, labour hours, or some other appropriate measure. While many factors might influence costs, we often simplify things by selecting that activity which seems to have the most impact on cost. Variable costs are depicted diagrammatically in Figure 3.7. As you can see, for variable costs, the cost will be zero when there is no activity.

FIGURE 3.7 Variable costs

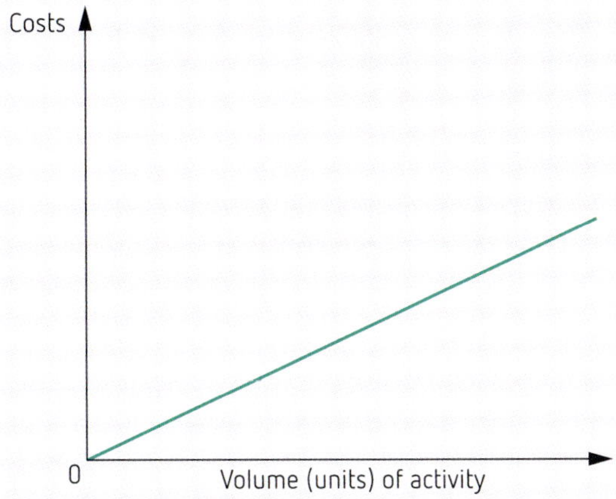

The straight line in Figure 3.7 reflects the assumption that variable costs will be the same per unit of activity regardless of the level of activity.

In terms of how we determine the variable components of costs, we often draw on past experience. If we have no such past experience, then this can be problematic. See Learning exercise 3.8 for an illustration of how to determine variable costs.

3.8 Learning Exercise

An illustration of variable cost

We will use the following scenario throughout this section as a running example for important concepts.

Lambchops is an organisation that processes wool, which is subsequently sold to manufacturers of fine suits for $1000 per bale. To process each bale of wool, the following costs and consequences are incurred or arise:

- cost of acquiring each bale of unprocessed wool (including transportation) – $450
- cost of (resources used in) processing (in practice there would be many more costs than shown here, but we are limiting them to keep this relatively straightforward):
  - labour – four hours per bale at $30 per hour
  - detergents – $10 per bale
  - water – 1000 litres per bale (at the present time, this water is extracted from a bore on the property at no financial cost – bore water is groundwater accessed by drilling a bore into underground aquifers – although there are concerns that the amount of water being taken is impacting the quality and quantity of water available to other local properties)
  - electricity – $30 per bale (50 kilowatt hours)
  - wastewater – 850 litres per bale (at the moment, this wastewater is released directly into a local waterway at no financial cost, but it is unclear what the environmental impacts are).
- costs of making sales – $40 per bale (packaging and transportation to buyer).

Let us now consider what is the variable cost associated with the production and sale of each processed bale of wool.

Financial costs

If we only consider the financial costs, then the answer is: \$450 + (4 x \$30) + \$10 + \$30 + \$40 = \$650 per bale. This means that for every additional bale of wool that is processed, the cost to Lambchops will increase by \$650.

Social and environmental implications

In practice, we also need to consider the social and environmental implications of the planned activity and how the impacts might vary as production varies. Relevant here would be the use of water, including how the amount used might impact water availability for other stakeholders living or working nearby.

Also, the impacts of wastewater on local waterways would require careful analysis, as would the types and quantities of detergents being used and whether those amounts represent an environmentally safe level of output. Some organisations would also consider the potential for reducing the amount of energy being used by the production processes, or the possibility of using energy from renewable sources.

The actual variable cost

The variable cost of \$650 shown above only relates to the variable financial costs being incurred by the organisation. It does not reflect any social and environmental factors. As such, when we subsequently consider the profit of the organisation – which is almost always reported in financial terms – then we must remember that it will not necessarily take into account some of the environmental and social impacts of the organisation.

Hence, profit is not the only thing to be considered by managers when looking at the success of an organisation, or of a planned product or service. This is something we have stressed a number of times already within this book, including earlier in this chapter when we emphasised the necessity for managers to consider sustainability in managing an organisation. A focus just on financial profits would not represent a long-term view of managing an organisation.

While we often assume that costs are linear, as in **Figure 3.7**, this might not always be the case. For example, when we are producing goods, we might be able to obtain raw materials at a fairly constant unit price. However, if we need to acquire increasing quantities of goods, and if these raw materials are relatively scarce, then the price might also increase beyond a certain level of demand. Further, earlier on in the production process we might become more efficient as we start producing more products. We might call this *economies of scale*. However, as we start trying to produce more and more output, we might find that, due to overcrowding, the overuse of machinery and so forth, production inefficiencies start to occur. Increasing sales might also lead to increased transportation charges as an organisation pursues markets that are located further away. The implication of all this is that costs per unit might be relatively low at the initial levels of production, but beyond a certain point they might start to rise as production volumes rise. We can refer to this as reaching a point where *diseconomies of scale* are occurring (see **Figure 3.8**).

While actual variable costs across different volumes of activity might not be properly represented by a straight line across all potential production levels, it is nevertheless possible

FIGURE 3.8 Changing variable costs per unit

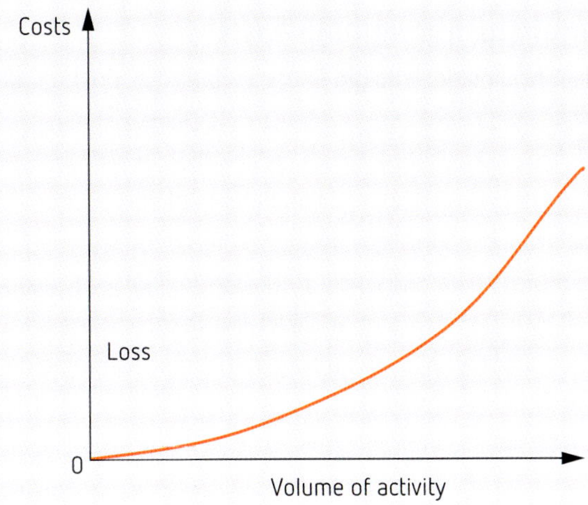

that within various ranges of operations (the relevant range – see **Learning exercise 3.12**), the total variable costs might tend to change as if on a straight line (see **Figure 3.9**). Therefore, if we are working within a particular range of activities (a relevant range), it is safe to assume that per-unit costs are constant. As noted previously, when determining whether we should generate particular information, we need to consider the costs and benefits associated with collecting that information. If it is believed that assuming costs are linear within a relevant range of activities will produce sound decisions, then it might be decided that it is not beneficial to expend further time and resources (and thus incur further costs) trying to fully understand the many points at which costs will change. See **Learning exercise 3.9** for more on this topic.

FIGURE 3.9 Variable costs can be assumed to be a straight-line function within a relevant range

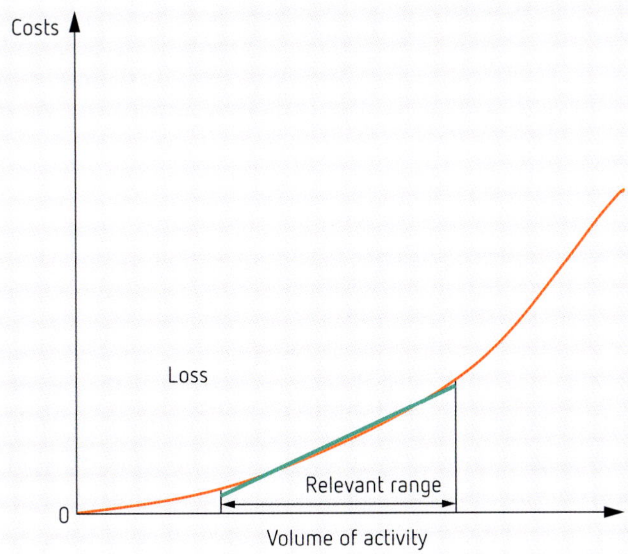

3.9 Learning Exercise

Straight-line assumptions for variable costs

Why might the assumption of constant (straight-line) variable costs not be realistic, and does this invalidate their use?

As already indicated, it is unlikely that variable costs will be exactly the same for each unit of production across all ranges of production. Early on there might be economies of scale, but as production increases, the production facilities might become more crowded, the required raw materials might become more scarce and costly, and so forth; that is, diseconomies of scale might occur. Nevertheless, for a particular range of activities, the variable costs per unit might be fairly constant, and hence the assumption of a straight line might be acceptable and allow cost-effective decisions to be made.

Fixed costs

fixed costs
Costs that do not change in a particular period as the volume of production or services changes

Fixed costs (see **Figure 3.10**) are considered to be those costs that do not change in a particular period as the volume of production or services changes. For example, rent on a factory will be the same (fixed) even where there are variations in the amount of production. Other examples include cleaning costs, insurance costs and council building rates, which will typically be fixed within a particular range of activity.

FIGURE 3.10 Fixed costs

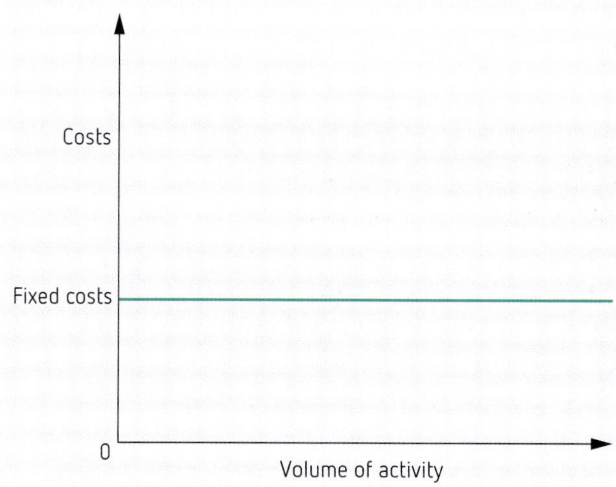

Care must be taken, however, when labelling costs as fixed, as they might be fixed only over a particular (relevant) range of activities. For example, an organisation might rent a factory at $50 000 per year. A range of production outputs could be achieved within that factory, but if production increased greatly, then an additional/different factory might sooner or later be required at additional cost. Therefore, when we identify a cost as being fixed, we mean that such costs could change but will be relatively constant, or fixed, over the short to medium term (perhaps the next year) as long as production volumes stay within a relevant range of activity.

So, effectively, costs might only be considered fixed for a particular range of activities, beyond which they will increase and then stay constant for a given range of activities, beyond which they might rise again in a step-like manner, as represented in **Figure 3.11**. For example, because of increased production, we might need to lease an additional factory which would then enable a greater amount of production. If production continues to increase, then further down the track yet another building might be required, and so forth.

For an illustration of fixed costs and how to determine total costs for a specific level of activity, see **Learning exercise 3.10** and **Learning exercise 3.11**, respectively.

FIGURE 3.11 Stepped fixed costs

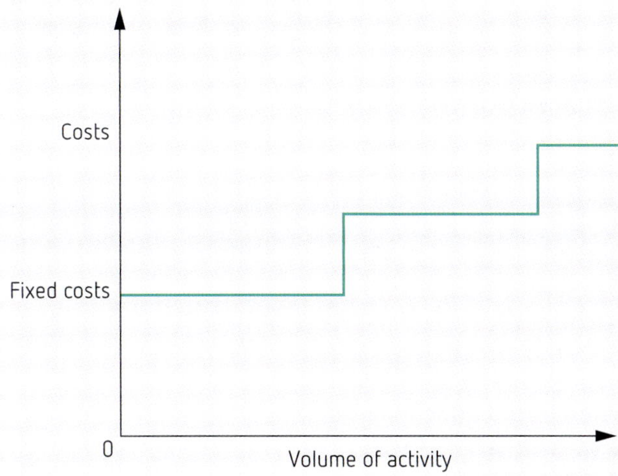

Why do I need to know about the 'behaviour' of costs?

Organisations succeed to the extent that they are able to minimise costs, and this is true whether we are talking about financial costs, social costs or environmental costs.

To minimise costs, we need to understand how costs 'behave', or change, as activities within the organisation change. Understanding that some costs fluctuate as activity levels change, while other costs remain relatively constant is important to being able to control costs. Knowing how costs are expected to behave means that we can set targets/budgets that can then be compared with actual costs, thereby enabling any variances to be identified for subsequent investigation.

3.10 Learning Exercise

An illustration of fixed costs

Following on from **Learning exercise 3.8**, apart from the variable costs already discussed, Lambchops has the following costs, all of which are expected to remain fixed for the levels of production being contemplated:

- factory rent: $60 000 per year
- administrative staff salaries: $150 000 per year

- other administrative costs: $57 500 per year
- administration-related utility costs: $30 000 per year.

What are the total fixed costs for one year?

The total fixed costs would be all of the costs listed above: $297 500.

Why are these fixed costs?

They are considered fixed costs because, for the amount of production being planned, these costs are assumed not to change within the period of analysis.

Will they be fixed forever?

They will not be fixed forever. Costs like rent and salaries will change across time. The costs are considered to be fixed for a particular period, which might be a year, and only for a particular range of activity, beyond which additional fixed costs might be incurred.

3.11 Learning Exercise

Determining the total costs for a given level of activity

Let us assume that Lambchops is expecting to produce and sell 1000 bales of processed wool.

What are the expected total financial costs?

Now that we know the variable and fixed costs, we can use a formula to calculate how the financial costs will change as production changes:

Total financial cost = Fixed costs + (variable cost per unit of output × level of output)

In Lambchops' case, this will equate to:

$$\$297\,500 + (\$650 \times 1000) = \$947\,500$$

What is the expected profit?

We know the costs that will be generated for the volume of activity, and we know the revenue, so what we are now doing is commonly referred to as *cost-volume-profit analysis*. The costs and profit for the production and sale of 1000 bales of wool are as follows:

Total revenue	1000 units × $1000		$1 000 000
Fixed costs		$297 500	
Variable costs		$650 000	$947 500
Profit			$52 500

Mixed costs

Some costs might have fixed and variable components. Such costs are referred to as semi-fixed or semi-variable costs, or **mixed costs**. For example, consider a salesperson's salary. They might be paid a fixed component, plus a bonus for each sale made. We can also consider electricity charges. Often, providers of electricity will charge a fixed-service fee for connecting a property to the power grid, plus a variable fee linked to the amount of electricity consumed. Mixed costs are depicted in Figure 3.12.

FIGURE 3.12 Mixed costs

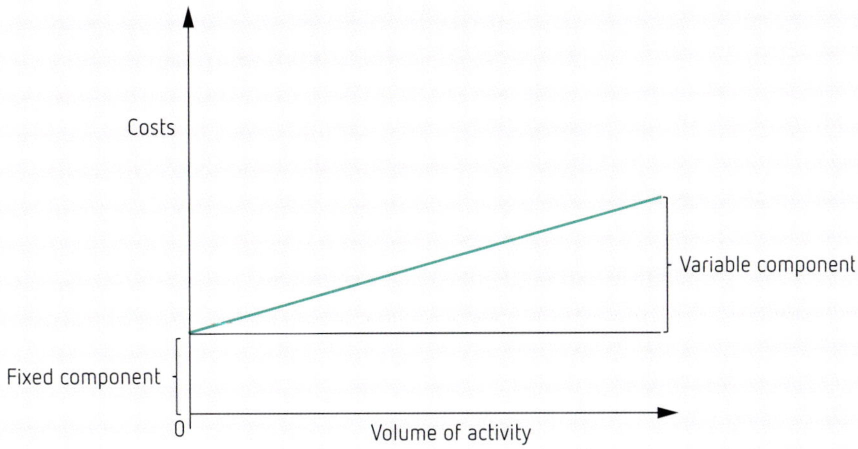

The high–low method for determining fixed and variable costs

At times, an organisation will aggregate various costs that have both a fixed and variable component. For example, an organisation might have the following data available for the production of recyclable coffee cups.

Month	Production output of recyclable coffee cups	Total production costs
April	10 000	$21 000
May	12 000	$24 000
June	8 000	$18 000
July	13 000	$25 000
August	11 000	$22 500

One relatively simple way of working out the fixed and variable components, without isolating the variable and fixed components of each and every related cost, is to use what is known as the *high–low method*. This method uses both the highest output and lowest output measures and compares the difference in total costs with the difference in output to derive the fixed and variable components.

	Production output of recyclable coffee cups	Total production costs
Highest	13 000	$25 000
Lowest	(8 000)	($18 000)
Difference	5 000	$7 000

The variable component is calculated by dividing the increase in costs by the change in volume of activity, which gives us $7000 ÷ 5000 = $1.40 per unit.

Given that an output level of 8000 gives a total cost of $18 000, then the fixed component of the costs might be estimated at $18 000 – (8000 × $1.40) = $6800. The cost function could then be represented as:

Total production costs = fixed costs + (variable cost per unit × output)

= $6800 + $1.40x

where x = the output or volume of activity

The fixed costs are the intercept of the vertical axis and the variable cost is the slope. If we expect a production output of 9000 units, then the predicted costs would be $6800 + ($1.40 × 9000) = $19 400 (see **Figure 3.13**).

FIGURE 3.13 Determination of costs using the high–low method

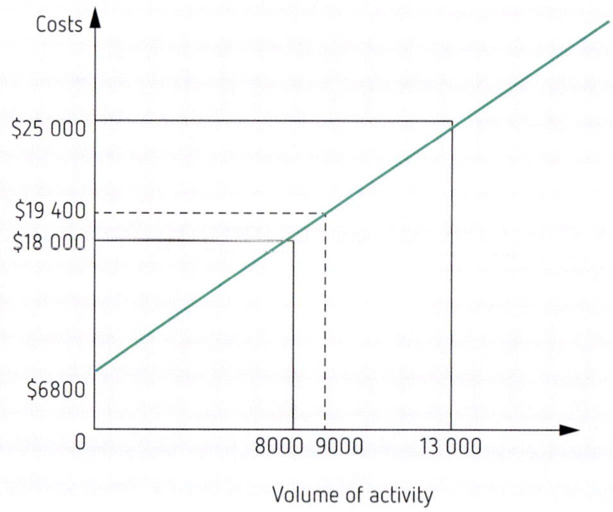

When using the high–low method, the high and low costs must fall within the relevant range which, as we know, is that range of activity in which the presumed cost behaviour holds. It will not reflect the actual costs at all levels but is a relatively straightforward (and thus low-cost) way of approximating costs. The choice of whether we want to be more accurate and technical in our approach to predicting costs will be determined by the additional costs that might be incurred in generating this information, and whether these costs are exceeded by the value (or benefit) that would be gained from having more accurate data. In practice, based on many past observations of outputs and associated costs, we could have done some form of linear or multiple regression to model cost behaviour – but again, whether we do this depends upon the associated costs versus benefits.

The other point that needs to be remembered is that, in doing this analysis by way of the high–low method, we need to be very careful in extrapolating beyond our range of observations. This might take us beyond our relevant range (see **Learning exercise 3.12** for further discussion of this concept) and therefore to a level of activity where the costs might be significantly different.

3.12 Learning Exercise

The relevant range

So what is meant by the relevant range of an activity and why is it important to know?

For the purposes of our discussion, the relevant range is the range of production output, or volume, in which our expectations regarding cost behaviour are expected to hold. That is, the range of activities in which our fixed costs are expected to stay the same in total and our variable costs per unit are expected to be constant.

This is important, as activity that goes beyond the relevant range may result in the costs being significantly different.

LO3.7 The contribution margin

In financial terms, calculation of the contribution margin of a product or service is the tool that is used to determine how much the sale of one unit of the product or service contributes to overall profit. The total **contribution margin** of a product or service is the difference between the total sales revenue and the total variable costs generated from a particular product or service; that is:

contribution margin The difference between the total variable costs and the total sales revenue generated by a particular product or service

Sales revenue – variable costs

The contribution margin per unit is the difference between the revenue per unit and the variable costs per unit; that is:

Contribution margin per unit = revenue per unit – variable cost per unit

All things being equal, items with a higher turnover would be expected to have a lower contribution margin per unit than items with a lower turnover. For example, if we were selling many thousands of pieces of fruit in our fruit shop, we could probably make a good financial return with a relatively small contribution margin per unit. However, if we were selling very expensive prestige cars, then we might only ever hope to sell a relatively small number of cars per week, but that could be acceptable if the contribution margin per unit on each car was fairly high.

See Learning exercise 3.13 for an illustration of how to determine the contribution margin per unit.

3.13 Learning Exercise

Determining the contribution margin per unit

Returning to Lambchops, and building on the answers to previous learning exercises in this chapter, we know that the sales price per processed bale of wool for Lambchops is $1000 and the variable costs per bale of wool amount to $650 per bale. Therefore, the contribution margin per unit is:

Sales revenue per unit – variable cost per unit = $1000 – $650 = $350 per unit

What this means is that for every extra bale of wool that is processed and sold by Lambchops, $350 should be added to the profits (or offset against losses).

As already indicated, an organisation will generally have a certain amount of financial costs that will be incurred regardless of the level of activity (fixed costs). There will also be costs that vary with the level of activity (variable costs). The total contribution margin (total sales revenue less total variable costs) will ideally exceed the total fixed costs; otherwise the organisation will be running at a financial loss, which is not acceptable for a business entity.

The contribution margin is something that both accountants and managers focus on. If costs are rising in a particular period, then the sales prices of an organisation's goods or services will also need to rise for the organisation to sustain its operations. At the extreme, another action managers might take if the contribution margin falls sharply is to cease supply of the good or service and perhaps invest resources into other goods or services with a higher expected contribution margin. Alternatively, if managers believe that consumers will react adversely to any product price rises (they might have done some market-related research indicating that the price point is a very sensitive factor in influencing demand), then they might focus on reducing costs per unit while keeping the sales price constant. And in doing so, managers need to be imaginative in their thinking.

One response, which is often viewed somewhat unfavourably, is to reduce the product sizes (and therefore the variable costs) while maintaining the same sales price, meaning that the contribution margin per unit will increase relative to not reducing the product size. For example, a newspaper article in the *Northern Territory News* (Rolfe, 2015, p. 8) noted that popular groceries had 'sneakily shrunk by as much as 30 per cent', but their sales price had failed to fall. The identified products included laundry liquids, chocolates, chips and deodorants, with one of the biggest reductions involving the commonly used laundry liquid OMO. The article noted that manufacturers often explain or justify product size reductions in terms of protecting the environment, sensible portion control (for foods), or saving jobs. Whether people actually believe such justifications is debatable.

Reducing the size of a product while maintaining its sales price is one way of increasing the contribution margin for each unit sold.

Source: Shutterstock.com/Keith Homan

Another newspaper article, in the *Sun Herald* (White, 2013, p. 14), noted that while pasta sauce jars, tissues and chocolate bars were all shrinking, at the same time the selling prices remained the same. Apparently, one commonly used pasta sauce brand, Dolmio, 'began to reduce its pasta sauce jar size by 75 millilitres, with parent company Mars justifying the change as a healthier option'. It was also revealed that many cafes were reducing the sizes of their coffee cups without reducing the selling prices. Cherry Ripe and other chocolate bars were also identified as reducing in size from 55 grams to 52 grams. So we can see that contribution margin per unit is something that managers take very seriously.

Using the contribution margin to determine the break-even point

break-even point
When the total financial costs equal the total financial revenues. That is, the production or service level where profit is zero

The **break-even point** occurs when the total financial costs equal the total financial revenues, resulting in the profit for a period being zero. It will generally be calculated in number of units of the product or service (we are keeping this simple by only having one product), and involves dividing the total fixed costs by the contribution margin per unit:

$$\text{Break-even point} = \frac{\text{total fixed costs}}{\text{contribution margin per unit}}$$

See **Learning exercise 3.14** and **Learning exercise 3.15** for further discussion of how to determine the break-even point and the meaning of this term, respectively.

Previously we showed how various newspaper articles provided examples of how managers consider contribution margin when making various decisions. The term 'break-even point' is

3.14 Learning Exercise

Determining the break-even point

What is the break-even point for Lambchops? This is calculated by dividing the total fixed costs by the contribution margin per unit, so $297 500 ÷ $350 = 850 bales.

To prove this, if we sell 850 bales, then:

Total revenue (850 × $1000)	$850 000
Less variable costs (850 × $650)	$552 500
Total contribution margin	$297 500
Less fixed costs	$297 500
Total profit	$0

At sales levels below the break-even point, there will be a loss. At levels above the break-even point, there will be a profit. The break-even point for Lambchops is shown in **Figure 3.14**.

FIGURE 3.14 The break-even point

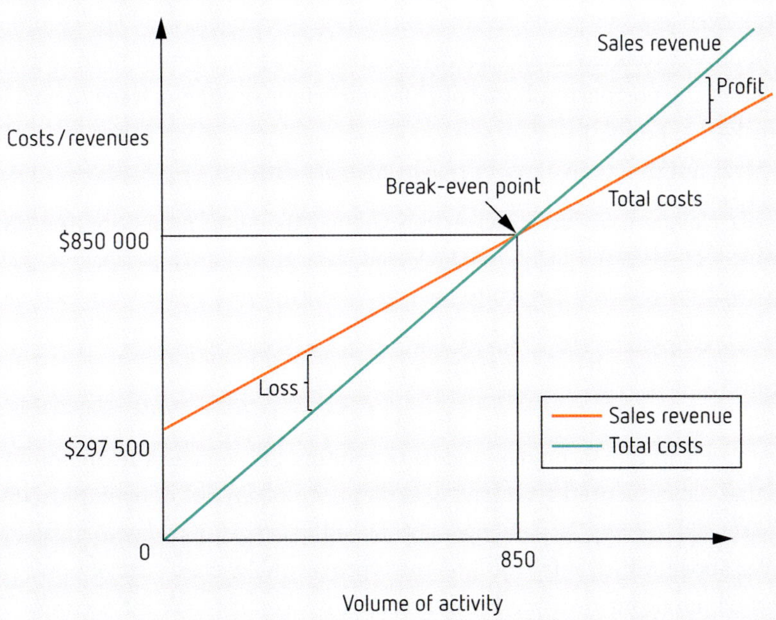

3.15 Learning Exercise

The meaning of the term 'break-even point'

What does it actually mean when we say an organisation has broken even?

It means that the organisation has made neither a profit nor a loss. That is, its total revenues equal its total costs (for our analysis, we have broken these costs up into their fixed and variable components).

Why should managers know the break-even point?

Managers need to know the break-even point as it allows them to understand what level of activity must be reached before they can start making a profit. They can then determine whether this required level of production, or service, is feasible.

Further, by knowing the break-even point, they can determine whether there is much of a margin of safety between current production and sales levels and the calculated break-even point. That is, how many sales could be lost yet the organisation remains profitable? (We focus on the margin of safety in the next section.)

a common part of business language, and we often see it in the news media. For example, an *Australian* article entitled 'New order as Emirates backs A380' (Wall, 2016, p. 28) noted that 'Airbus last year for the first time delivered A380s that reached break-even after years of losses. The company has said the program should remain at break-even this year and next, though more orders are needed to fill production technology after 2017'. In this instance, the unit of output was the A380 plane.

In another article in the *Hobart Mercury* (Flemingham, 2016, p. 62), it was noted that traffic jams were increasingly occurring throughout the city of Hobart, despite the population only being 210 000. A solution was required, with a light rail system being considered as one possibility. However, a break-even analysis suggested that six million passengers would be required annually for the light rail project to break even. The article stated that 'you would need to transport the entire population of the northern suburbs of Hobart a couple of times a week to enable the light rail to reach break-even point'.

This project was referred to in another *Hobart Mercury* article:

> The Hobart Northern Suburbs Rail Action Group, the group promoting the future development of Hobart's Light Rail, released data that shows passengers paying 39 cents per trip would be enough to raise $2.34 million in revenue each year. Based on 6 million passenger trips a year, a number estimated in government studies, the revenue would be enough to break even.
>
> Source: Smith (2016), p. 1.

In an earlier article in the Tasmanian media (Kempton, 2015, p. 13), reference was made to a ferry service that recommenced after having earlier been taken out of operation. It was noted that 'the ferry, licensed to carry 27 passengers, will need to carry 300 a day to break even'.

The examples above, which refer to different types of public transport options, allow us to also highlight the limitations of using break-even points in not-for-profit settings. The break-even analysis considers financial costs and revenues (benefits) only, not social or environmental benefits such as fewer cars on the road, people being able to live in more affordable housing and readily commute to work, increased employment from the construction and operation of public transport systems, and so forth. Nevertheless, what these real-world examples demonstrate is that considerations of the break-even point are part of planning. Determining the break-even point necessarily requires making many assumptions about costs and their behaviours, and ultimately a determination needs to be made as to whether it is actually realistic to expect the demand that is required to break even. For example, one of the newspaper articles noted how six million passengers were needed for the proposed Hobart light rail service to break even. Considering the Tasmanian capital's fairly small population, we – like the relevant managers involved – would have to question if this was realistic.

The margin of safety

Another useful measure is the **margin of safety** – something we briefly referred to in **Learning exercise 3.15** – which is the number of sales being made, or expected to be made, above the break-even point. That is, the margin of safety is determined as follows:

margin of safety
The number of sales made, or expected to be made, above the break-even point

Actual or predicted level of activity in units – break-even level of activity in units

This is referred to as the margin of safety because it calculates the number of units of a product or service that can be lost before an organisation reaches a level of activity that results in the organisation making a loss. (See **Learning exercise 3.16** for an illustration of how to determine the margin of safety.)

3.16 Learning Exercise

Determining the margin of safety

If Lambchops had a budgeted level of production of 1100 bales of wool, what would be its margin of safety?

Previously, we determined that the break-even level of production was 850 bales of wool. Therefore, the margin of safety would be 1100 – 850 = 250 bales of wool. This means that the production and sale of up to 250 bales of wool could be lost before the organisation starts to incur losses.

Operating gearing

We can link the margin of safety to the idea of *operating gearing*. High fixed costs accompanied by low variable costs are often referred to as a situation of high operating gearing. For example, let's assume that Lambchops can utilise an additional machine which will cost $100 000 to rent per period, thereby increasing fixed costs by a further $100 000. This machine will reduce variable costs to $590 per unit (down from $650 per unit), and thereby increase the contribution margin to $410 per unit (up from $350 per unit). Our new break-even point would then be determined as:

($297 500 + $100 000) ÷ 410 = 970

(rounded up to the nearest full bale)

Because the break-even point has increased from 850 bales of wool to 970 bales, this is considered to have increased the operating gearing of Lambchops, as more bales must be processed and sold before the organisation can cover its costs (that is, break even). This increases the risk to the organisation. But once we reach the break-even point, each additional bale of wool produced and sold will contribute more to profits. As a general rule, capital-intensive processes (those that rely relatively more on machinery than on people) tend to be more highly geared operationally, and therefore they are relatively riskier in times of reducing market demand.

While we have provided examples of the break-even point and margin of safety, as well as considered operating gearing, we must still remember the assumptions we have made. For example, we have assumed that costs and revenues act in a linear fashion. This will not always be the case, although the assumption might be satisfactory to the extent that we are operating within a relevant range where our costing seems to hold. We have also assumed that fixed costs will not change, but we know that, in reality, costs will not remain fixed for long periods, or they can behave in a stepped fashion. We have further assumed just one product in our various examples. The analysis would be more difficult, but certainly possible, for multiple types of products.

Generating a target financial profit

Organisations will often have a target profit in mind when performing their operations. This target profit will take into account various factors including the expectations of owners, the risks inherent in the operations, and the opportunity costs of alternative options.

opportunity costs
Benefits that could have been received but were given up because of the decision to take another course of action

For example, in terms of **opportunity costs** – the benefits that could have been received but which were given up because of the decision to take another course of action – if a person is going to devote all their time to running a new business, they need to project what earnings they might generate and compare this with the amount of salary they might have received from working for somebody else (which might have also meant less stress, more family time and so forth). So questions might have to be asked about how much income somebody expects to compensate them for the work and anxiety associated with running a business. Of course, there might be other factors that are difficult to quantify in monetary terms which motivated the decision to start a business; for example, the pride in having a business, the satisfaction of being the boss, and so forth – numbers never explain the basis of all our decisions.

The units of products or services required to be sold to generate the necessary profit is calculated by adding the desired profit to the total fixed costs and then dividing this by the contribution margin per unit. For further discussion of identifying the required level of activity for various purposes, see Learning exercise 3.17 and Learning exercise 3.18.

3.17 Learning Exercise

Determining the required level of activity to generate a given profit

If Lambchops wants to make a financial profit of $140 000, how many bales of wool will it need to process and sell, based on fixed costs of $297 500, sales price of $1000 per bale, and variable costs of $650 per bale of wool?

The answer is as follows:

(Desired profit + fixed costs) ÷ contribution margin per unit = required number of units

($140 000 + $297 500) ÷ $350 = 1250 bales

3.18 Learning Exercise

Determining the required level of activity to generate a target after-tax profit

Assume the same facts as in **Learning exercise 3.17**, except this time assume that the organisation has to pay income tax on its profits, the tax rate is 30 per cent and the organisation wants to make an after-tax profit of $140 000.

First of all, we need to convert the after-tax profit into a pre-tax profit, to ensure that the profit figure used in the subsequent calculation includes the tax component/amount. In this exercise, this equates to a pre-tax profit of $140 000 ÷ (1 – tax rate) = $140 000 ÷ 0.7 = $200 000.

We can now factor this profit figure into our calculation regarding the required level of activity:

($200 000 + $297 500) ÷ $350 = 1422 bales (rounding up to the nearest full bale)

Total revenue	1422 × $1000		$1 422 000
Fixed costs		$297 500	
Variable costs	1422 × $650	$924 300	
			$1 221 800
Profit before tax			$200 200
Tax at 30 per cent			$60 060
Profit after tax			$140 140

Note that we have a profit figure greater than $140 000 because we needed to round up to the nearest full bale of wool.

LO3.8 Consideration of non-financial variable and fixed costs

As we have already indicated, much of the analysis that we undertake – such as determining the break-even point, the number of units to be sold to generate the desired financial profit, or the margin of safety – relies on measures of variable financial costs and fixed financial costs. As we emphasised in Chapter 2, however, organisations also consume other resources and create various social and environmental impacts when undertaking their various processes.

We have already shown in this chapter how we can attribute particular variable financial costs to specific products or services. We can do the same type of analysis to reflect the use of other forms of resources, including natural resources. For example, we can determine that to produce a particular product, we need given amounts of water, raw materials, energy and so forth.

We might focus on those resources which are relatively scarce, or which potentially create the greatest environmental or social impacts. For example, if water is scarce, then we can calculate the amount of water being used per unit of product – effectively, the variable cost per unit as described in 'amount of water' rather than in monetary terms. We can also calculate the amount of energy required to produce each unit of product, particularly if the energy is coming from a source that generates relatively greater carbon emissions (for example, the energy is coming from a coal-fired power station). However, if we have an abundance of clean energy (such as from wind-powered turbines), we might not be too concerned from an environmental perspective about the amount of power being consumed.

The point stressed here is that managers should not only consider the variable financial costs of particular goods or services. They should also consider the other resources being consumed to produce particular goods or services – this consumption can also be described as a variable cost (see **Learning exercise 3.19**).

3.19 Learning Exercise

Variable use of other resources

In **Learning exercise 3.8**, we noted that Lambchops not only incurs $650 in variable financial costs to produce a bale of wool, it also consumes 1000 litres of water and 50 kilowatts of power to produce each bale. Further, processing each bale of wool also creates 850 litres of wastewater. Should managers have taken the time, and incurred the associated costs, to collect this information about water use and release, and power use?

The answer to this question is that managers should know not only the financial costs incurred in producing their goods and services, but also how the use of other resources fluctuates, or varies, with levels of activity. So yes, they should have collected the information.

It is good that the managers of Lambchops have determined that producing each bale uses 1000 litres of water. If water is scarce, then they might consider how to reduce this per-bale water consumption. Perhaps there are other more-water-efficient processing machines available, or perhaps they might consider how to recycle some of the water. What is the availability of water-recycling machines and what are the costs of running these?

In terms of the release of wastewater, the managers know that 850 litres are being released into local waterways for each bale processed. This is something that needs to be immediately addressed, unless this wastewater is somehow beneficial to the waterways (which is unlikely). Because the managers have made these measurements of wastewater release, they are better able to manage the generation of wastewater. If they do introduce water recycling, as suggested above, this would also have beneficial impacts on the amount of wastewater ultimately being released.

The managers have also determined that each bale of wool requires 50 kilowatts of power. Depending on the sources of the power (that is, whether it comes from renewable or non-renewable sources), this is something else that might need to be considered. For example, are there more-energy-efficient processing machines available, and what are the costs associated with using them?

Learning exercise 3.8 also noted that the bales of wool are packaged before sale. Another issue managers might address is the nature of this packaging, whether they can recycle it (perhaps they can institute a requirement that the packaging be returned to Lambchops), whether the amount of packaging can be reduced, and so forth.

As is the case with variable costs, fixed costs do not have to just be financial. For example, simply having a structure in a particular location could have social and environmental implications, regardless of how much it is used. In practice, the related social and environmental costs are rarely considered fixed costs. Nevertheless, as one possible example, what if we decide to build a factory in a particular area that was previously covered by trees? A fixed environmental cost might be the loss of carbon sequestration brought about by the removal of the trees. Carbon sequestration is the process of carbon capture and the long-term storage of atmospheric carbon dioxide, which assists in the mitigation of climate change. Trees are an important element in removing (sequestering) CO_2 from the atmosphere. So theoretically, a fixed cost of removing the trees for the purpose of building the factories is the lost carbon sequestration each year. It needs to be acknowledged that such fixed costs are typically not included in the sort of analysis we are doing here, but they nevertheless should not be forgotten! By building the factories where the trees once stood (and where they could stand again if the factory was removed), we are removing an ongoing environmental resource. This is a cost.

LO3.9 Maximising the return on a constraining or scarce factor

Organisations require various resources in order to produce their goods or services. Some necessary resources might be relatively scarcer than others. For example, there might be limited amounts of a particular raw material available, or a limited number of hours available from particular employees with specialised skills. There might also be a limited amount of production space available.

Where there is a constraining factor, such as the limited availability of raw materials, production capacity or skills, then an organisation will try to maximise the contribution per unit of the scarce, or constraining, factor. An illustration of this is provided in **Learning exercise 3.20**.

3.20 Learning Exercise

Consideration of a constraining factor of production

Holey Tooth Inc. makes soft drinks, ice blocks and slushies. Total fixed costs are not expected to vary between alternatives. Sales can be made for the quantities that the organisation can produce. There are 1 000 000 litres of water available per month.

	Soft drinks	Ice blocks	Slushies
Market demand	1 200 000	600 000	700 000
Sales price	\$1.50	\$1.00	\$2.00
Variable cost	\$0.40	\$0.30	\$0.50
Contribution margin per unit	\$1.10	\$0.70	\$1.50
Litres of water required per unit	0.4	0.5	1.0

What quantities of which product should Holey Tooth Inc. produce?

As you can see, each product has a positive contribution margin per unit. In the absence of any constraints on available resources, each of the products would be produced to the extent necessary to satisfy market demand. However, because there are restrictions on the amount of water available, the company needs to determine the maximum return that it can generate for the available water. The managers need to work out the contribution margin per unit of the constraining factor (water) as follows:

	Soft drinks	Ice blocks	Slushies
Contribution per litre of water	\$1.10 ÷ 0.4 = \$2.75	\$0.70 ÷ 0.5 = \$1.40	\$1.50 ÷ 1.0 = \$1.50

Since soft drinks generate the greatest contribution per litre of water, the managers should try to satisfy the full market demand for soft drinks. This will utilise 480 000 litres of the available water (1.2m × 0.4), leaving 520 000 available litres. These litres of water would then be dedicated to producing slushies, as this is the second best option, such that 520 000 slushies are produced. Because the organisation has not satisfied the full market demand for slushies, it will not consider producing the third-best option, which is ice blocks.

LO3.10 Consideration of special orders

From time to time, managers are asked whether they would be prepared to produce goods or services for special one-off orders, and to sell those goods or services at prices below what they would normally charge other customers. In considering such requests, managers need to consider whether they have sufficient excess production capacity (that is, whether they have the ability to produce the goods or services without affecting the ongoing production of goods or services to satisfy pre-existing orders) to satisfy the order, and whether the incremental revenue exceeds the incremental costs. **Learning exercise 3.21** provides an example of a special order.

3.21 Learning Exercise

Determining whether to accept a special order

Returning to the case of Lambchops, we find that the business has spare operating capacity. A buyer has asked to buy 200 bales of processed wool in a one-off transaction for the price of $800 per bale. The buyer wants the wool packed in a particular way, which will require a special-purpose packing machine that will cost $8000 to rent for the period of the order. The extra packing charge will add $40 to the cost of each bale of wool.

Should Lambchops accept this order?

In answering this question, we will consider incremental revenue and incremental costs:

Incremental revenue		
200 bales × $800 per bale =		$160 000
Incremental costs		
Variable costs ($650 + $40) × 200 bales	$138 000	
Incremental rental cost	$8 000	$146 000
Incremental profit		$14 000

In terms of the incremental revenue and the incremental costs, Lambchops should accept this special order, although there are other factors to consider which we briefly address below.

While the analysis in **Learning exercise 3.21** indicates that the special order should be accepted, other factors also require consideration. The incremental revenue exceeds the incremental costs (which can also be considered relevant costs and relevant revenues for this decision), but organisations need to price their goods or services in a way that also enables them to cover their total costs, which include their fixed costs. Pricing goods slightly above the incremental costs does not necessarily allow an organisation to cover its fixed costs if everybody is charged prices that are simply based upon the decision that the sales revenue per order must exceed the incremental costs per order.

While a special order will not change pre-existing fixed costs, if there is excess production capacity, it needs to be emphasised that, in the long run, an organisation cannot sell its goods or services at prices that do not also allow it to cover its total fixed costs. Also, organisations need to be careful that other customers do not react adversely if they are to find out that particular customers have been given special low-price deals on goods or services. That is, special orders can create some reputational damage if existing customers find out that new customers have been provided with much better deals. Ultimately, some customers might cease buying goods or services from the organisation.

LO3.11 Adding value through critical thinking and application of professional skills

We noted earlier in this chapter that accountants need to be critical thinkers. By *critical thinking*, we mean making reasoned judgements that are well considered, logical, and based on asking the right questions (developing the right problems) and collecting the appropriate supporting information. Critical thinking is a highly valued skill in itself.

In this chapter we have discussed the role of accountants in planning, monitoring and controlling organisational behaviour. We have noted that such activities need to include considerations of the long run and the short run, and sustainability-related issues, as well as the various ways in which an organisation can add value. Critical thinking is necessary to all of this.

Supporting this, data from a 2019 'Top 100 Accounting Firms survey' conducted by *The Australian Financial Review* and Chartered Accountants Australia and New Zealand, in which senior partners within accounting firms were interviewed, critical thinking and emotional intelligence were deemed to be the key competencies of successful accountants. Of the specific skill sets the profession now needs, 77 per cent said critical thinking and emotional intelligence were the most important, compared with only 36 per cent who nominated technical and sector-specific expertise. We conclude this chapter by considering the attributes of critical thinking that accountants should possess if they are going to properly satisfy the expectations of different stakeholders.

Key concept

Accountants should have certain core skills that allow them to think in an organised, knowledgeable and critical way.

Skills that accountants require

There is an expectation that accountants – particularly those that contribute relatively more value to an organisation – should have certain core skills that allow them to think in an organised, knowledgeable way, as well as communicate their ideas clearly, which in itself requires solid interpersonal skills. These are:

- intellectual skills
- technical and functional skills
- personal skills
- organisational and business management skills
- interpersonal and communication skills.

These skills are reflected in the accreditation requirements that professional accounting bodies throughout the world impose on universities' accounting educational programs. As you may or may not know, one pathway to gaining membership in a professional accounting organisation, such as CPA Australia, Chartered Accountants Australia and New Zealand (CAANZ), the Institute of Professional Accountants (IPA), the Institute of Chartered Accountants of England and Wales (ICAEW), and the American Institute of Certified Public Accountants (AICPA), is to undertake an accredited university degree in accounting and then take additional advanced units with the respective professional body. As part of their activities, professional accounting bodies will accredit the degrees being offered by universities such that they accept them as a suitable pathway towards joining their organisation.

Acknowledging that accountants require certain skills, it is interesting to note those that CPA Australia and CAANZ, for example, expect universities to instil in students before the professional accounting bodies will accredit the degrees of universities. There is an expectation that universities instil both technical and professional competencies. In relation to technical competencies, graduates are expected to be technically proficient in areas such as financial accounting and reporting, audit and assurance, business law, economics, taxation and information and communication technologies. In terms of the professional competencies CPA Australia and CAANZ want of accountants, the expectation is that university graduates will have:

Intellectual skills

Intellectual skills enable a professional accountant to evaluate data and information, apply critical thinking to solve problems, make decisions and exercise good judgement in complex organisational situations.

Interpersonal and communication skills

Interpersonal and communication skills enable a professional accountant to work with others for the common good of the organisation, receive and transmit information, form reasoned judgements and make decisions effectively.

Personal skills

Personal skills relate to the attitudes and behaviour of professional accountants. Developing these skills helps individual learning and professional development.

Ethical principles, professional values and integrity

An understanding of ethical and professional values and attitudes is an important element in the development of accounting professionals. It is expected that higher education providers will pay attention in their programs to the fundamental ethical values of integrity, objectivity and confidentiality, as well as professional competence and due care.

These expected skills/competencies are consistent with the accreditation requirements of other professional accounting bodies internationally.

International accreditation guidelines, Copyright 2015. CPA Australia Ltd, https://www.cpaaustralia.com.au/become-a-cpa/academic-institution-support/international-accreditation-guidelines

Skilful and critical accountants contribute value to an organisation. As you fulfil your education, it is essential that you acquire the sorts of skills described above if you want to differentiate yourself from others in the workplace.

STUDY TOOLS

SUMMARY

In this chapter, we have described the nature and purpose of management accounting and noted that it is predominantly unregulated, generates reports that cover a variety of time periods, covers financial and non-financial issues, and provides information about past and projected performance.

We have also provided a description of the activities undertaken by managers and stressed that accountants can, and should, contribute to all phases of management activities. We concentrated especially on the planning stage of running an organisation, emphasising the need for managers and accountants to consider the issue of sustainability, the need for long- and short-run considerations, and the need to focus on value creation. In discussing value creation, we also explored how value can be viewed in a different way by different stakeholders, and we provided insights into how different perspectives of value might be addressed by an accounting system.

We also considered the behaviour of costs, and how they can be considered as either variable or fixed costs (there can also be mixed costs). We discussed various assumptions that can be made about costs, including that variable costs per unit will remain constant and that fixed costs will remain unchanged within a relevant range of activities. We also discussed how to calculate contribution margin per unit, the break-even point, margin of safety, and how many units of a product or service need to be produced and sold to generate a desired level of profit. In doing so, we also addressed the issue of operating gearing.

We concluded the chapter by emphasising the need for accountants to be critical thinkers, and the imperative that accounting education should encourage critical thinking.

ANSWERS TO THE OPENING QUESTIONS

At the beginning of the chapter we asked the following three questions. As a result of reading this chapter, you should now be able to provide informed answers to these questions – ours are shown below.

1 What do we mean by 'cost behaviour', and why do managers need to know how costs 'behave'?
By cost behaviour, we are referring to how costs change as a result of changes in the level of activity of an organisation. Some costs change in total as activity or volume increases – these are called variable costs. Some costs remain unaltered as activity changes – these are called fixed costs. Some costs have fixed and variable components – these are called mixed costs. Managers need to know about cost behaviour so they can plan to have the necessary resources for particular levels of activity. Knowing about how costs should behave also provides managers with cost-related targets which then can be used to assess actual performance as part of the control function of managers.

2 What do we mean by 'break-even point', and how would we calculate how many units of a product or service an organisation needs to produce in order to break even?
The break-even point is the point at which the total costs incurred to produce and sell a particular good or service match the associated revenues; that is, the point at which there is neither a profit nor a loss. The break-even point is calculated by dividing total fixed costs by the contribution margin per unit. The contribution margin per unit is calculated as revenue per unit minus variable cost per unit.

3 In undertaking a break-even analysis, what assumptions are made about fixed costs and variable costs?

The assumptions we make about fixed and variable costs are that fixed costs will not change in total and the variable cost per unit will remain constant. These are assumptions, but as long as we are operating in what we refer to as the relevant range, then such assumptions are acceptable.

SELF-TEST QUIZ

Answers to this quiz appear in the Appendix of this book.

1 In relation to management accounting, which of the following statements is true?
   a Management accounting is subject to limited regulation compared to financial accounting.
   b The forms of management accounting employed within an organisation will be influenced by the organisation's mission statement.
   c The information generated through management accounting will be of interest not only to managers but also to other categories of stakeholders.
   d Some management accounting information generated within an organisation will not be disclosed publicly because of concerns that it might reduce an organisation's competitive advantage.
   e All of these choices.

The following information relates to Questions 2 to 5.

Terri Towelling is an organisation that makes one type of shirt, which it sells for $40.00 each.

The costs of Terri Towelling are:

Each shirt requires:	
Material per shirt	$10.00
Labour per shirt	$12.00
Packaging per shirt	$1.50
Electricity and other services costs per shirt	$0.50
	$24.00

Terri Towelling also has fixed costs per year of:

Rent	$45 000
Administrative staff salaries	$85 000
Other administration costs	$30 000
	$160 000

2 The contribution margin per shirt is:
   a $14 b $15 c $16 d $17 e $18

3 The break-even point is:
   a 8000 units b 9000 units c 10 000 units d 11 000 units e 12 000 units

4 The amount of sales that must be made to create a pre-tax profit of $120 000 is:
   a 16 000 b 16 500 c 17 000 d 17 500 e 18 000

5 If Terri Towelling was to produce 14 000 units, then what would be the 'margin of safety'?

a 3000 b 4000 c 5000 d 6000 e 7000

ONLINE RESOURCES

Accompanying the book is an innovative online case study that follows an organisation initially established by two friends, which grows into a large and successful company. Acquire this chapter's case study from your instructor.

CASE STUDY

Armadillo Surf Designs: Don't do anything rash

Armadillo Surf Designs (ASD) are advertising for a part-time accountant. After a successful interview, you got the job. Congratulations! The team are also excited to be launching a special edition rash vest line, but meanwhile, there has been negative media attention relating to one of ASD's competitors and this has the ASD team questioning if, and how, they should respond.

Demonstrate that an accountant can 'add value' to ASD and use your knowledge of the surfing industry to apply Porter's Value Chain to ASD. Undertake break-even analysis on the new rash vest line and consider the costs and benefits of importing surfboards. Advise if, and how, ASD should report on the origins of their surfboards.

END-OF-CHAPTER QUESTIONS

3.1 Do you agree with the statement, 'Accountants should not be involved in the management of an organisation'?

3.2 What are some of the factors that managers might have to consider when deciding whether or not to publicly disclose information that was produced within the management accounting system?

3.3 What does critical thinking mean and why should accountants be expected to be critical thinkers?

3.4 What is information overload and how might the possibility of this be reduced?

3.5 Should cost-versus-benefits considerations be applied when deciding whether or not to collect particular information?

3.6 Provide a basic list of the activities that managers undertake.

3.7 Why might the existence of well-constructed organisational plans have the effect of enabling organisations to attract the necessary funding at lower costs?

3.8 What is the role of an organisation's mission statement?

3.9 What are positive and negative screening, and how are they relevant to planning organisational activities?

3.10 Why is a focus on sustainable development considered to represent a longer-term perspective for managers?

3.11 Why might a focus on yearly profits encourage a manager to be shorter term in focus? What problems might be associated with being shorter term in focus?

3.12 Define variable costs, fixed costs and mixed costs.

3.13 What do we mean by cost behaviour and who cares about it?

3.14 Here are the costs that are incurred by Winkipop Ltd, a surfboard producer, on a monthly basis:

Factory rent per month	$20000
Insurance per month	$1000
Factory supervisor's salary per month	$5000
Cost of foam core of each surfboard	$150
Cost of fibreglass used on each surfboard	$45
Cost of resin used on each surfboard	$25
Surfboard shaper labour cost for each surfboard	$55
Surfboard sander labour cost for each surfboard	$75

You are required to identify which costs are variable and fixed, and then come up with a formula to predict what the total cost will be for a given level of production. You are then to apply the formula to calculate the total costs that would be incurred in producing 500 surfboards.

3.15 Why might fixed costs be depicted as being stepped?

3.16 With respect to costs, what do we mean by the relevant range?

3.17 Bells Bowl Ltd, which produces one type of wetsuit, uses the high–low method to predict the future costs of particular levels of production. Information about past levels of production, and the associated costs, is provided below:

Month	Production output of wetsuits	Total production costs
April	1000	$7000
May	2000	$12000
June	4000	$23000
July	3000	$18000
August	5000	$27500

You are required to provide an estimation of variable costs per unit and fixed costs using the above information. What would be the total expected costs of producing 2500 wetsuits?

3.18 What is the contribution margin and why would managers want to know it?

3.19 When might it be appropriate to outsource the production of key components to other organisations? What non-financial considerations might be relevant when considering outsourcing decisions?

3.20 What is the break-even point and why would managers want to know it?

3.21 Jan Juc Ltd produces leg ropes, and nothing else, for surfboards. The following costs are incurred in producing the leg ropes:

Rubber material per leg rope	$9
Velcro cost per leg rope	$2
Labour cost per leg rope	$3

The leg ropes sell for $34 per unit, and the following costs are also incurred:

Factory rental per month	$1000
Insurance per month	$200
Supervisor salary per month	$3000

How many leg ropes need to be produced and sold each month for Jan Juc Ltd to break even?

3.22 Using the information in Question 3.21, and assuming that Jan Juc Ltd produces and sells 300 leg ropes per month, what is the company's margin of safety? What does this number represent?

3.23 What skills should an individual possess if they are going to perform as an effective accountant in an organisation?

3.24 Should an organisation restrict its analysis of variable costs to only the financial costs that are being incurred to produce each unit of a good or service? That is, should it ignore such things as the amount of water being consumed to make each item, or the amount of energy being used per unit?

3.25 What do we mean by operating gearing? What are the implications for operating gearing if an organisation rents additional machinery to help it reduce the variable costs per unit of product?

3.26 Fishos Ltd produces blocks of surf wax which sell for $4 each. In producing the blocks of wax, the following costs are incurred:

Costs per month to rent factory space	$600
Costs per month to rent heating equipment for the wax	$400
Cost of unprocessed wax per block of wax	$ 1
Energy cost per block of wax	$0.20
Packaging cost per block of wax	$0.30

How many blocks of wax need to be sold to generate a profit of $3000 per month?

3.27 Using the information in Question 3.26, how many blocks of wax need to be sold to generate an after-tax profit of $2500, assuming a tax rate of 30 per cent?

3.28 Why do managers need to be careful in accepting a one-off special order to sell their products when the price being offered is just a few dollars above their variable costs? Should they simply reject such an order?

3.29 Torquay Point Ltd makes shoes, T-shirts and hats. Total fixed costs are not expected to vary between alternatives. Torquay Point Ltd is disconnected from the energy supply grid because of concerns about climate change. It generates its own power from solar panels that are linked to batteries which store the power. On average, the system generates 200 000 watts of power per month. The relevant information is as follows:

	Shoes	T-shirts	Hats
Market demand (units)	50 000	15 000	30 000
Sales price	$88	$45	$27
Variable cost	$27	$10	$11
Watts of power required per unit	3	2	1

What quantities of which particular product(s) should Torquay Point Ltd produce?

3.30 You have invited your friends around for dinner and prepare a simple chicken noodle soup, the ingredients being chicken, chicken stock, noodles, bok choy, bean sprouts, spring onions, soy sauce and cut chilli. Your friends love it! As you are a freelance cat trainer with flexible time commitments, the suggestion is made that you should apply to get a food licence, rent a mobile cart with cooking equipment, and sell the soup at lunchtime in the city.

a Try to identify which costs will arise, which will vary with production, and which will remain relatively fixed.

b Try to attribute a cost to the soup and determine a price per cup that would allow you to make a reasonable profit.

Your answers should not be the same as anybody else's, as you are to try and think of the types of costs that would be relevant and what they might amount to.

REFERENCES

Chartered Accountants Australia and New Zealand & Financial Review (2019). *Top 100 Accounting Firms 2019*, CAANZ, Sydney. https://ca-top100-2019.afr.com/?fbclid=IwAR32_xZWtunTZNmAfT5x9uuw3EGdt1MUbfTBBMF92vN82KRvjzI HimO_UCo)

CPA Australia (2022). Section 3: Technical and professional competency areas and learning outcomes. https://www.cpaaustralia.com.au/become-a-cpa/academic-institution-support/international-accreditation-guidelines/section-3-technical-and-professional-competency-areas-and-learning-outcomes

Flemingham, B. (2016). Changing vehicle trends challenge town planners. *Hobart Mercury*, 13 March.

Greenpeace (2022). Our core values. www.greenpeace.org/international/en/about/our-core-values

Harvard University (2022). Mission, vision and history. https://college.harvard.edu/about/mission-and-vision

International Federation of Accountants (2011). *Competent and versatile: How professional accountants in business drive sustainable success*. www.apesb.org.au/uploads/meeting/board_meeting/13112014032639_Attachment_17f_-_Competent_and_Versatile_-_How_Professional_Accountants_in_Business_Drive_Sustainable_Organizational_Success.pdf. This text is an extract from 'Competent and Versatile: How Professional Accountants in Business Drive Sustainable Success' (August 2011), and is used with permission of IFAC. Such use of IFAC's copyrighted material in no way represents an endorsement or promotion by IFAC. Any views or opinions that may be included in *An Introduction to Accounting: Accountability in Organisations and Society* 2e are solely those of Cengage Group and do not express the views and opinions of IFAC or any independent standard setting board associated with IFAC.

International Federation of Accountants (2019). Future-Fit Accountants: CFO and finance function roles for the next decade, IFAC, New York (online at www.ifac.org).

Kempton, H. (2015). Tide turns for Mersey ferry. *Hobart Mercury*, 24 October.

Porter, M. (1985). *Competitive Advantage: Creating and Sustaining Superior Performance*. New York: Free Press.

Rolfe, J. (2015). Great grocery shrink stink. *Northern Territory News*, 10 October.

Smith, M. (2016). Fare go for light rail. *Hobart Mercury*, 9 March.

Standards Australia (2003). *Good governance principles*. https://infostore.saiglobal.com/store/PreviewDoc.aspx?saleItemID=396440

Wall, R. (2016). New order as Emirates backs A380. *The Australian*, 15 April.

Walt Disney Company, The (2022). About The Walt Disney Company. www.thewaltdisneycompany.com/about

White, S. (2013). Pasta joke as products shrink. *Sun Herald*, 3 November.

World Commission on Environment and Development (1987). *Our Common Future*. Oxford: Oxford University Press.

CHAPTER 4

BUDGETING AS A MEANS OF ORGANISATIONAL PLANNING AND CONTROL

LEARNING OBJECTIVES

After completing this chapter readers should be able to:

- **LO4.1** explain what a budget is, as well as describe the context and purpose of budgeting, and the relationship between an organisation's budget and its strategic plan
- **LO4.2** identify who needs to prepare a budget
- **LO4.3** identify the various benefits associated with budgeting
- **LO4.4** explain the meaning of a 'master budget', and how the various components of this budget relate to each other
- **LO4.5** explain the meaning of a 'budget variance' and identify when to investigate such variances
- **LO4.6** understand the difference between static budgets and flexible budgets, and explain the need for flexible budgeting
- **LO4.7** explain why budgeting can be undertaken for both financial and non-financial aspects of organisational performance, and illustrate social and environmental aspects of performance that can be addressed through the process of budgeting
- **LO4.8** describe some behavioural implications of the budgetary process.

OPENING QUESTIONS

Before reading this chapter, please consider how you would answer the following questions. We will return to these questions at the end of the chapter, where we suggest some answers.

1. Is it necessary for all organisations to prepare budgets?
2. What is a master budget? Which individual budget would typically be the first one prepared within a master budget, and why?
3. Can budgets be used as a means of motivating managers, and if so, how?

Introduction

In Chapter 3, we identified that the roles of management include:

- *planning* – which we further broke down into five phases:
  - identifying the problems that need to be addressed, including how to maximise returns to owners/shareholders from a particular process while being socially and environmentally responsible
  - collecting the relevant information with which to solve the problems
  - determining alternative courses of action
  - evaluating the alternative courses of action
  - making decisions
- *implementing actions*
- *monitoring and evaluating performance against plans*
- *learning, revising and adjusting plans.*

And then going through the entire cycle yet again.

In this chapter, we explore the use of budgets and the process of budgeting. As noted in Chapter 3, compiling budgets is an important part of organisational management, particularly with regards to initially planning and understanding various organisational processes and their relationships and interdependencies. Comparing budgeted (targeted) performance with actual performance is also an important component of evaluating and controlling organisational performance.

Every organisation needs to use budgets, and there are a variety of budgets that address both financial and non-financial aspects of performance. Failure to undertake effective budgeting will likely contribute to the demise of an organisation.

LO4.1 An overview of budgeting

As noted above, and in Chapter 3, the process of budgeting is an essential component of a well-functioning organisation. Budgets are a central part of planning, monitoring and controlling an organisation. But what is a 'budget'?

What are budgets?

A budget can be defined as a detailed, quantitative plan of organisational activities for a specified time period, perhaps monthly, quarterly or yearly, and these plans can relate to both financial and non-financial aspects of performance. A budget will be developed using various sources of information, including knowledge of the organisation's mission and strategic plans, past performance, as well as expectations about changes in technology, market and community demands and expectations, government policies, available finance, and the actions of competitors.

Why are budgets prepared?

Simply stated, budgets are prepared because they are necessary for organisational survival. The budget is one of the most important means of communication within an organisation and it is essential for planning, organising and controlling activities. For example, to assess the performance of an activity, in the first instance, specific goals/objectives must be clearly established, and resources organised and allocated to allow those goals/objectives to be achieved. Various budgets will reflect the planned allocation of resources within the organisation. The budgeting process should act both to promote efficiency and to deter inefficiency and waste.

A budget essentially reflects the shorter-term goals of the organisation, but links to, and is a key part of, an organisation's longer-term strategic plan. The strategic plan – a very high-level plan that links to the organisation's mission (as discussed in Chapter 3) – usually identifies how value can be created in a way that provides the firm with an advantage over competitors in the markets in which it operates. Long-term strategic plans are typically finalised after considering the general (political, economic, social) and specific (competitors, customers, suppliers) environmental factors that might influence the organisation's operations. Strategic plans can be in place for a number of years, unlike budgets, which should be revised on an ongoing basis as new information comes to hand.

As budgets for different activities are constructed, the managers of the different activity areas of the organisation are required to communicate and plan the coordination of their respective activities. For example, the managers of marketing, purchasing and production functions need to align their activities to ensure that a product of value to the customer, or client, is provided on time, and at the quality and quantity required. The managers of the finance department must ensure that the organisation has sufficient cash to allow these activities to be undertaken (the sufficiency of cash will be reflected within the 'cash budget'). Budgets are also a way of signalling those factors that are considered important to senior management.

Budgets are an important source of feedback and control, which occurs when planned performance is compared with actual performance and variances are identified. These variances are then examined and corrective action is taken, if needed, to ensure that goals will be achieved. Comparisons of budgeted performance with actual performance, and the related feedback, also provide an account to those people held responsible for the activities about how they, and their activity area, have performed relative to targets.

To summarise, budgets are undertaken:

- as a means of operationalising the organisation's strategic plan and establishing an important element of control within the organisation
- to create a framework to understand the interconnectivity of the various activities being undertaken within the organisation
- to establish a mechanism to assist in assessing the performance of managers
- to help determine the feasibility of the organisation's plans
- to help identify possible future resource constraints
- to help ensure that an organisation will have enough cash to pay for its various commitments, as they arise

- to help ensure that enough raw materials will be on hand, when necessary, to undertake the planned activities
- to help ensure that there will be sufficient finished products to meet the expected demand
- to determine the required labour needs and associated costs
- to determine future finance needs.

Who are budgets for?

Budgets are usually provided to those people within the organisation who have responsibility (and are held to account) for the resources (for example, labour, materials, cash) used in undertaking particular activities. This might be, for example, the marketing manager (for meeting sales goals as reflected within the sales budget), the production manager (for meeting production targets as reflected in the production budget), and the purchasing manager (for purchasing the correct amount and quality of required raw materials at certain prices, as might be reflected in a direct materials budget). Each of these managers will have goals/targets for their activity area that link to the overall goals of the organisation. It is important that the goals of the individual managers are consistent with each other (which can be referred to as 'goal congruence'), so that the organisation, as a whole, can move towards satisfying its overall goals and mission.

The main audience for the budgets – those to whom the budgets are directed – are the managers within the organisation. Budgetary information would not typically be made publicly available, particularly information that relates to the costing of various processes and future plans for production, change and so forth. To release such information publicly would mean that particular stakeholders, such as competitors, could obtain it, which could be damaging to the future prospects of the organisation. Also, there could potentially be a number of reputational and legal implications for an organisation if budgetary plans were publicly released and people made decisions on the basis of those plans, only for the plans to subsequently fail to be achieved. That said, organisations will often release some aspects of their budgets that are not too sensitive, highlighting specific targets, whether they have been achieved, and if not, the initiatives in place to help them get back 'in control', and on track, to achieve targets.

How are budgets prepared?

Budgets can be prepared for any period of time depending upon the perceived needs of the managers. However, budgets that address factors that are particularly vital to the survival of an organisation tend to be produced for shorter time periods and reviewed in a very timely manner. For example, cash budgets are generally prepared for relatively short time periods – such as monthly – as organisations cannot survive without the necessary cash. Also, cash-flow problems need to be identified in advance, or if not, as quickly as possible after they arise.

The budgeting process should be formalised, with certain key people (accountants) designated responsibility for budget administration. Clear instructions should be in place. For example, many organisations will have a budget manual that indicates who is responsible for collecting particular items of information, and for checking for differences between actual performance and budgeted performance – that is, identifying variances. The information collected should, where possible, also satisfy the qualitative characteristics attributable to useful information. These were discussed in Chapter 1, where we learned that the fundamental (primary) qualitative characteristics that information should possess are relevance and reliability (or faithful representation). Where possible, the information should also satisfy the enhancing qualitative characteristics of timeliness, understandability, verifiability and comparability.

To this point in the chapter we have provided an overview of budgeting, but what types of organisations should do budgeting? The next section addresses this issue.

LO4.2 Who needs to do budgeting?

The simple answer to the question 'Who needs to do budgeting?' is that we all do – individuals and managers of organisations – at least in some form or another.

At a personal level, we need to think about where our cash might come from (salary, parents, friends, interest on deposits, dividends from shares, government payments/funding, casual work) and balance this against what we'll be paying for (food, housing, clothes, education, electricity, phone, travel, entertainment). We need to ensure that we have enough money to pay for the things we need, or want, to do. By planning (doing a budget), we might find that we need to revise our expectations, or if not, find some additional sources of finance. In short, through the process of preparing a budget we can find out a lot about our financial circumstances that we might not have otherwise known.

People often get themselves into all sorts of financial trouble because they don't take the time to prepare budgets of future payments and receipts. The need for budgeting never really disappears. As people get older, a key decision they might need to make is 'When can I retire?' Such a decision requires careful planning and the development of some budgets to see if the income in retirement will be sufficient to meet the likely expenses/payments required to satisfy particular wants and needs. Running out of money in retirement would not be fun!

The same goes for organisations, whether they be 'for-profit' or 'not-for-profit' organisations. Planning is essential for an organisation. The failure or collapse of many organisations can be attributed to poor planning – in particular the poor planning of cash flows. If an organisation does not coordinate its various activities properly, it might find itself unable to pay for the resources it requires, which can lead to its demise.

Budgeting requires an organisation's managers to take the time to understand both the organisation and the consequences of particular actions, or plans. This requires knowledge of the relationships and interdependencies between various operations and processes within the organisation. The time and costs involved in gaining this understanding are effectively an investment in the future of the organisation. Since the budgeting process requires us to link various aspects of operations in organisational planning, problems can potentially be identified in advance of them actually occurring, and solutions to such problems – such as temporary cash shortages – devised in advance as well.

For more on the need for budgeting, see **Learning exercise 4.1**.

4.1 Learning Exercise

The need for budgeting

As we have discussed, organisations need to conduct budgeting. But what level of budgeting is required for different types of organisations? Also, why is budgeting required for individuals?

Budgeting by not-for-profit organisations

Not-for-profit organisations need resources, including cash, to achieve their goals. They typically have access to limited amounts of funding, so they need to carefully manage their inflows and outflows of cash. It is therefore essential that the managers of not-for-profit organisations (as well as the managers of for-profit organisations) plan what initiatives/actions they want to address/implement and then work out the resources they need to successfully complete these initiatives. They then need to determine whether they will have access to sufficient funding to achieve what they want to achieve. This all requires careful budgeting.

Budgeting by small organisations

Smaller organisations might not do the same level of budgeting as larger organisations, or they might do it in a less sophisticated manner, but they still need to do it. At a minimum, the managers need to do budgets of the organisation's future expected cash payments and cash receipts, and determine whether:

- they will have sufficient cash to undertake what they want, and expect, to do
- they need to arrange to borrow funds to achieve their goals
- they will have to amend their expectations about what they hope to achieve.

Budgeting by individuals

Many individuals get themselves into all sorts of financial difficulty because they spend more cash than they can realistically expect to receive. This often culminates in large amounts being owed on credit cards or various types of personal loans, which in turn can incur very high rates of interest expense.

The upsurge in what has become known as *payday lending* is due to the increasing number of people who, for whatever reason, spend more cash than they receive. Payday lending is an arguably predatory practice where some organisations provide relatively small loans to individuals who desperately need funding, and these loans are expected to be repaid in a short period of time; for example, at the time the borrower receives their next salary payment. The payday lenders often charge interest rates that equate to several hundred per cent on an annualised basis. While budgeting might not prevent this from happening, it should reduce the incidence of payday lending.

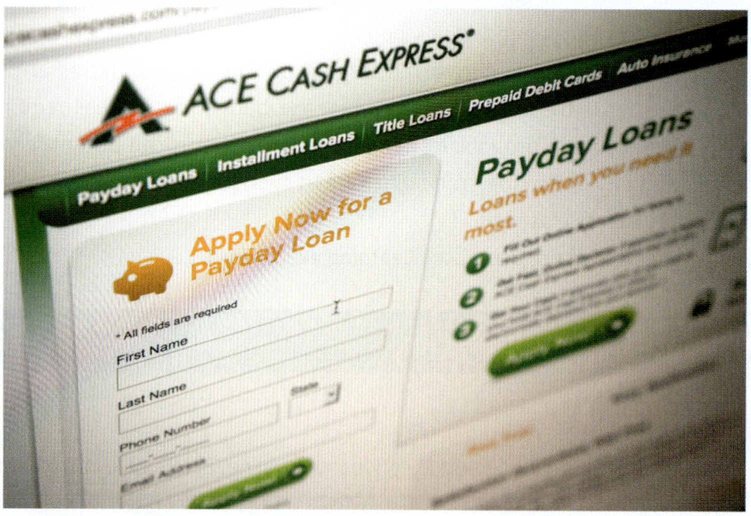

Source: Alamy Stock Photo/Richard B. Levine

Without the appropriate budgeting, there is an increased likelihood that this is where somebody might end up in their search for quick financial assistance.

LO4.3 The benefits of budgeting

From our discussion so far, it is hopefully clear that budgeting is vital to the survival of an organisation (as it is to individuals). It really should not be treated as an optional exercise. At this point, we can say that budgeting can create a variety of positive influences, as outlined in Table 4.1.

TABLE 4.1 The benefits of budgeting

Benefit	Explanation and examples
Promotes forward thinking	• The process of budgeting requires managers at various levels to plan ahead and formalise plans. • This forces managers to think about the future and to make forecasts about activity levels, associated costs, and the required support, required investments and required funding.
Provides an early warning system	• Planning ahead can highlight problems that could arise in the short term, thereby signalling the need to take action quickly. • This provides early notice of possible problems, effectively acting as an early warning system.
Facilitates the coordination of various activities	• Once you know what the levels of activity will be in one area of operations, you can then plan the activities in other related areas. • For example, if you have planned for a given volume of sales, then this in turn means you need to plan/budget for the required labour, production capacity, raw materials to acquire and so forth.
Provides a basis for evaluating future performance	• Budgets are a very important component of control. You can compare actual performance with planned performance, thereby providing a stimulus for understanding the reasons for any variances, and for implementing the necessary corrective actions if you appear to be 'out of control'. (Read more about what is meant by the term 'out of control' in Learning exercise 4.2.)
Creates benchmarks for managers throughout the organisation	• Budgeting creates a mechanism for potentially improving behaviour and motivating managers and other employees. • Budget targets can, and often are, used as a means of rewarding managers. That is, within many organisations, some form of financial bonus is directly linked to managers who achieve particular budgetary targets.

4.2 Learning Exercise

The meaning of 'out of control'

People often refer to an organisational process as being 'out of control', but what does this mean?

If a process is out of control, this means that the actual outcome is not what was planned (budgeted). For example, you might have a plan in place for producing a particular product, one that shows the organisation will use 1 kilogram of a specific type of material to make the product. Each kilogram costs the organisation $50. But when actual results are subsequently reported to managers, it's found that 1.8 kilograms of material was actually consumed for each unit of product, meaning that the material consumed cost $90 per product rather than $50 per product. This process therefore has not met the plan and can be considered out of control – it has gone off track. Some form of control now needs to be exerted in order to hopefully move the process back into control, or back on track.

Budgets act as a means of controlling future performance. When budget variances arise, this indicates that a process is out of control, necessitating some form of managerial intervention. However, a small variance between actual performance and budgeted performance (targets) is usually expected, so managers need to determine at what point a particular process is deemed to be 'out of control' and thereby requires managerial intervention. The greater the costs associated with the variance, the more likely it is that there will be such intervention.

Using budgets sensibly

While budgets can provide many benefits, and budgetary targets can be used as the basis for providing bonuses to managers, you must always be careful to ensure that managers with different responsibilities actually work together and do not just focus on their own performance – and the individual bonuses that might be linked to that performance.

For example, if a sales manager has a sales budget and receives a bonus for exceeding the targeted sales, then this manager has a private, economics-based incentive to make sales as high as possible without thinking about the consequences for the production people, or for those charged with collecting amounts owed by customers. There have been instances where sales managers who receive bonuses sell products to many customers on credit terms (meaning customers can pay later) without thinking about whether the customers actually have the capacity to pay for the goods or services. A sensible bonus system would not encourage this, but would perhaps restrict the bonuses to a range of sales that can be met with current capacity. And/or the bonus schemes might only pay the bonuses to managers *after* particular customers have actually paid the amounts due, which would encourage the sales manager to insist that sales are only made to reliable, creditworthy customers. For a discussion of bonus scheme design, see Learning exercise 4.3.

The benefits of budgeting are summarised in Figure 4.1.

4.3 Learning Exercise

Designing management bonus schemes

Many years ago, Nikita Khrushchev, the well-known politician who led the Soviet Union from 1953 to 1964, famously complained about the enormous size and weight of Russian-made chandeliers. As it turned out, managers in some Moscow factories were being rewarded with cash bonuses linked to the production of chandeliers, based on the weight of the total finished product. The result was that the chandeliers increased to a size whereby many ceilings throughout Moscow, where these chandeliers were installed, started collapsing under their weight. While this policy was an attempt to motivate managers to perform in the interests of the organisation, this was not a very thoughtful, or smart, bonus plan.

It might not have been anticipated that production managers would behave in the way they did. But common sense would suggest that using weight as a performance indicator would not be without its problems. As well as the damage and potential injuries from collapsed ceilings, and the legal and other costs relating to those collapses, there would have been wider ramifications for those in charge of delivering, installing and storing the heavy chandeliers as well.

It is essential that those managers in charge of developing bonus plans – these people might be part of a remuneration committee – carefully think about the behavioural implications of offering particular incentives to managers. As we have noted already in this book, accounting (in this case, budgeting) can create a variety of social impacts – both good and bad.

FIGURE 4.1 A summary of the benefits of budgeting

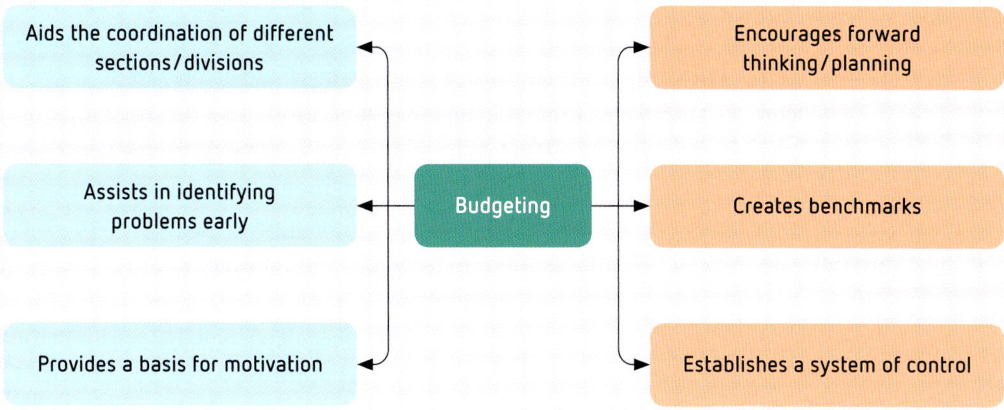

Why do I need to understand the roles that budgets have within organisations?

The role of budgets needs to be understood because they are essential for organisational survival. As is hopefully clear from the material we have just discussed, all forms of organisations should perform some form of budgeting (as should individuals and households). They are an important instrument for influencing the behaviour of managers. Budgeting is a key component of the planning process, requiring managers to develop an understanding of how the various components of an organisation work together. Budgets also provide managers with an important tool to evaluate or benchmark subsequent performance against budgeted targets. In doing so, budgets often provide targets against which managerial bonuses can be linked. Budgets enable managers to assess the feasibility of intended plans as well as highlighting the required resources necessary to achieve plans – they thereby promote forward thinking.

Therefore, moving forward in your career, it is necessary to become familiar with the budgetary process.

LO4.4 The master budget

The **master budget**, sometimes referred to as the *annual budget*, is a comprehensive set of budgets that provides coverage of an organisation's activities. To put it another way, the master budget consists of several interdependent budgets that together create a reasonably cohesive organisational plan for a specified period of time. The master budget can include:

- the **operating budgets**, which include the sales budget, the production budgets and the various cost budgets that follow (such as the direct materials budget, direct labour budget, manufacturing overhead expenses budget, and selling and administrative overhead expenses budget)

master budget
A comprehensive set of budgets that provides coverage of an organisation's activities

operating budgets
Include the sales budget, the production budgets and the various cost budgets that are impacted by these two budgets

financial budgets
Include the cash budget, budgeted income statement, and budgeted balance sheet

- the **financial budgets**, which include the cash budget, budgeted income statement (also referred to as the budgeted statement of financial performance), and budgeted balance sheet (also referred to as the budgeted statement of financial position).

A possible master budget for a manufacturing organisation is shown in Figure 4.2. The arrows represent the general sequence in which such budgets would be prepared.

As Figure 4.2 shows, for a manufacturing organisation, sales are typically the starting point in the budgeting process. The determination of target sales might be influenced by industry and market trends, general market conditions, expected promotion and advertising, pricing policies, past sales, actions of competitors, technological developments and so forth. If, at the extreme, no sales are projected, then logically there should be no production, and therefore no need for materials, labour and so forth.

As Figure 4.2 also shows, once target sales have been determined based upon the sales forecast (which needs to be realistic, and therefore not too optimistic or too pessimistic), the number of units that need to be produced to satisfy those sales can be calculated. The level of production is not normally the same as the level of sales, as stock (inventory) on hand at the beginning of the period needs to be taken into account, as does the need for sufficient stock at the end of the period.

FIGURE 4.2 A master budget for a manufacturing organisation

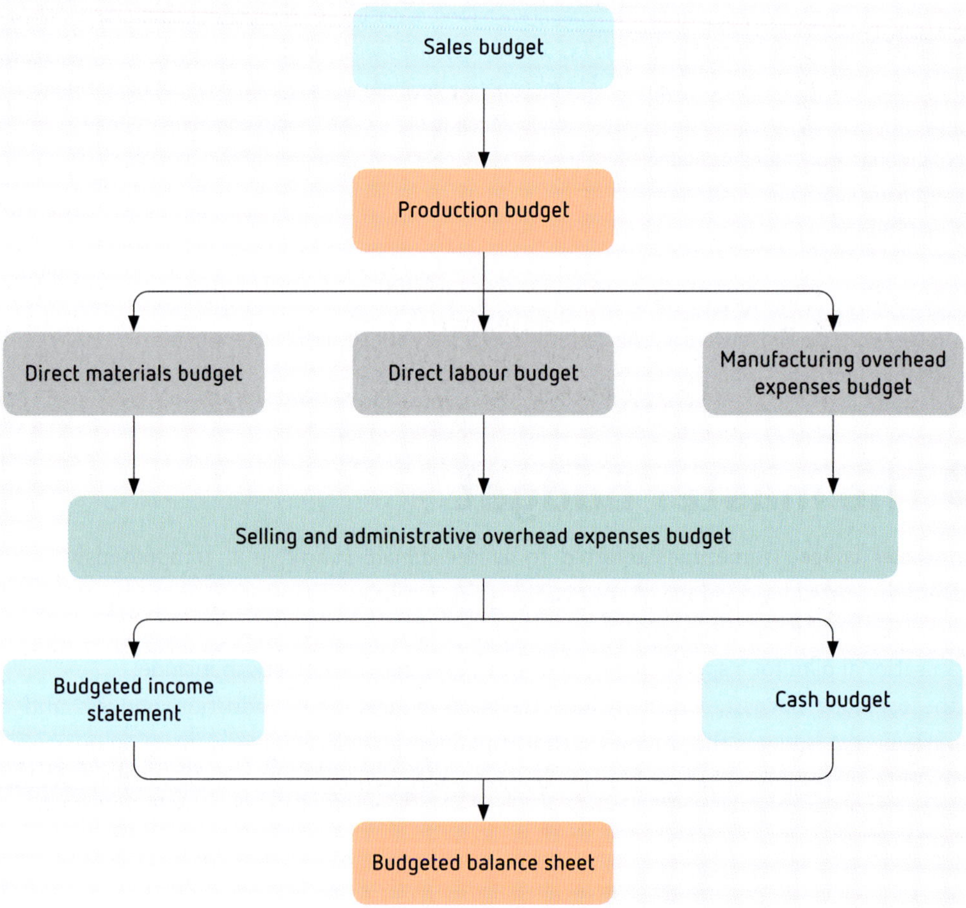

In turn, once the required units of production are known, the quantity of materials needed for production can also be determined, as well as how much labour is needed. The organisation also needs to determine what other costs need to be incurred, and we can refer to these other costs as 'overheads'. Manufacturing overheads would include those materials and services that are used in small amounts, and which might not be easily traceable to particular products or services.

overhead costs Those costs that are necessary to run an organisation, but which might not easily be directly attributed to specific activities, products, or services

Following this sequence of events, some of the other costs that might need to be incurred can be determined. Such costs might not directly relate to manufacturing (that is, to the production of goods) but are nevertheless necessary in order to run the organisation. For example, an organisation may need to advertise its products, as well as having in place people who provide overall management of the organisation, who in turn will need a building to work from, access to various workplace facilities and support, and so forth. These expenses can be addressed within the selling and administrative overhead expenses budget (although remember that an organisation can produce whatever budgets it wants, as being part of management accounting, there are no specific laws in place about how an organisation has to manage the business or what budgets it must prepare).

cash budget Contains all the expected receipts of cash, and payments of cash, that have been identified in the operating budgets that precede it

Once the operating budgets have been finalised, some budgeted financial statements can be prepared. One such statement will be the cash budget, which reflects all the expected receipts of cash, and payments of cash, that have been identified in the operating budgets that precede it.

budgeted income statement Provides an indication of the profit (or loss) that might be generated as a result of an organisation pursuing its plans

A budgeted income statement can also be prepared to provide an indication of the profit (or loss) that might be generated as a result of the plans in place. If the projected profit is not deemed sufficient, or if the plans appear likely to culminate in the creation of a loss, then this would require the managers to rethink their plans, make adjustments, and work sequentially through all the budgets yet again.

budgeted balance sheet Shows what the assets, liabilities and owners' equity of an organisation will be as a result of the organisation pursuing its plans

The last budget to be formulated is typically a budgeted balance sheet. The budgeted balance sheet shows what the assets, liabilities and owners' equity of the organisation will be as a result of the organisation pursuing its plans. We will address balance sheets, along with the meanings of 'assets', 'liabilities', and 'owners' equity', in Chapter 7, when we continue our exploration of financial accounting. Financial statements, such as balance sheets, are one of the major outputs of the financial accounting system.

The discussion above serves to reinforce the idea that a number of budgets will combine sequentially to form a master budget. In the learning exercises that follow, we will develop a master budget for a simple manufacturing organisation. Although we will be concentrating on a manufacturing organisation, it needs to be stressed that all organisations – including service organisations, not-for-profit organisations, and those that buy and sell finished goods (a trading business rather than a manufacturing business) – need budgets, as do our own households, which themselves can be considered a form of organisation. For a service organisation, for example, it might not be sales of goods but the number of customers being served that starts the process. And while there might not be a production budget for a service organisation, there is still a need for other budgets to reflect the various services to be provided, the items that need to be acquired, the labour that needs to be hired, and the various overheads that need to be incurred.

We will now consider each of the components of the master budget as reflected in Figure 4.2.

sales budget A detailed summary/plan of the estimated sales in units and associated revenues from an organisation's products, based on the sales targets, for the budgeted period

The sales budget

The sales budget provides a detailed summary/plan of the planned sales in units and associated revenues from an organisation's products for the budgeted period. It is based on the sales forecast, which involves estimating which products will be sold, in what quantities, and at what prices. Sales forecasting is a critical step in the budgeting process, and market research is often used to inform this process. The factors to consider when forecasting sales depend on the industry and nature of the organisation, but they should include:

- *internal factors*: past sales levels, new products planned, intended pricing policies, and planned advertising and promotional activities
- *external factors*: general economic trends, specific industry trends, local political and social events (and potentially global events), expected activities of competitors, and changing tastes and expectations of customers.

As we have already indicated, sales projections will in turn influence other activities within the organisation, such as the required production (to be shown in a production budget); materials (as shown in a direct materials budget); labour (as shown in the direct labour budget); production overheads (as shown in the manufacturing overhead budget); and selling and administrative overhead expenses (as shown in the selling and administrative overhead expenses budget). These activities, in turn, will influence the expected cash flows (as reflected in the cash flow budget), profits (as reflected in the budgeted income statement), and ultimately, the projected assets, liabilities and owners' equity (as reflected in the budgeted balance sheet).

If, at the extreme, there are no sales, then there will be a need to question whether there should be any subsequent activity. What would be the point? So, the projected sales volume is the starting point, and it sets targets to meet for those involved with sales; for example, the sales and advertising managers, who should be working together.

An important point that needs to be acknowledged when talking about sales is that, while we might achieve a specific amount of sales in a particular period, which would be reflected in sales revenue, this will not necessarily match the actual cash received from customers in that same period. Since some customers will not always pay cash for the goods or services (credit sales), the actual receipt of cash can eventuate some time after the sales. That is, there will be a time lag between the sale and the subsequent receipt of the cash. Nevertheless, when preparing the sales budget, we include the sales, and therefore the sales revenue, in the period in which the sale is made, and not in the later period in which the cash is ultimately received. The sales that are made now impact the production that needs to be undertaken to achieve those sales, even though the actual cash from the sales will be received from customers later on.

For more on the preparation of a sales budget, see **Learning exercise 4.4**.

4.4 Learning Exercise

Preparing a sales budget

McTavish Lifestyles produces one type of sunhat, which can be worn normally as well as out in the surf. It comes in one colour – green – and in just one size. The budgets are for the year 2025 and are broken into four quarters, with the first quarter being from 1 January to 31 March, the second quarter being from 1 April to 30 June, the third quarter being from 1 July to 30 September, and the fourth quarter being from 1 October to 31 December.

The target sales that have been determined following careful research and consideration of production capacity for 2025 by each respective quarter (Q) are:

- Q1: 10 000 units
- Q2: 11 000 units

- Q3: 12 000 units
- Q4: 12 000 units.

The selling price for each sunhat is $50, and that price will be kept constant throughout the year.

Let's consider how we could prepare the sales budget based on the sales forecast. Review the table below, which uses the following calculation:

Targeted sales × selling price per unit = budgeted sales revenue

McTavish Lifestyles sales budget for the year ending 31 December 2025

	Q1	Q2	Q3	Q4	Total
Target sales	10 000	11 000	12 000	12 000	45 000
Selling price	$50	$50	$50	$50	$50
Budgeted sales revenue	$500 000	$550 000	$600 000	$600 000	$2 250 000

To extend this, if the managers of McTavish Lifestyles were interested in additional information, the sales budget could be further broken down into geographical areas or by particular salespeople, thereby providing more direct sales targets for particular managers and/or regions.

The production budget

The **production budget** provides targets based upon the production of enough units to satisfy projected sales together with any required closing inventory, while also taking into account the inventory on hand at the start of the period. *Inventory* (or stock) is a term used to describe the total number, or value, of products an organisation holds at a particular point in time.

For an example of the preparation of a production budget, see Learning exercise 4.5.

4.5 Learning Exercise

Preparing a production budget

The managers of McTavish Lifestyles would like us to develop a production budget. According to accounting records, the beginning inventory of finished goods at the start of Q1 is 1000 sunhats, which cost $33 500 to produce in the previous year, and the inventory manager wants to increase the inventory to 2000 sunhats at the end of each quarter. Even though McTavish Lifestyles has noted that it wants to have 2000 sunhats on hand at the end of each quarter, it nevertheless also wants us to identify the issues that need to be considered when determining the appropriate level of inventory to have at any point in time.

Let's work through how to prepare a production budget for McTavish Lifestyles. First, we need to know the data in the sales budget in order to prepare the production budget. The required production starts with target (budgeted) sales, to which we add the desired/required closing inventory, and from which we subtract the beginning (opening) inventory; that is:

Target sales + required closing inventory – opening inventory = required production in units

In relation to McTavish Lifestyles' question about the appropriate level of inventory to have, it is generally accepted that having *too much* inventory raises various issues associated with the direct costs of storage, including insurance, costs of warehouse space, and so forth. There are also various other risks, such as that market tastes might change – this might be costly if a lot of inventory is on hand, as it might become obsolete.

Having *too little* inventory can also be a problem. If very little inventory is on hand, and demand increases beyond what was forecast, then the organisation will be out of stock – often referred to as a *stock-out* – and that is not good for business. In addition to the organisation missing out on potential sales, people often do not return to a business if they are unable to have their demand satisfied at a particular point in time. Another reason that a stock-out could occur is if there is a temporary problem with the production facilities and the organisation does not have enough stock to satisfy orders – again, this is not good for business. So, it is somewhat of a balancing act. The general principle in relation to inventory is *not too much but not too little*. For the purposes of this learning exercise, we will assume that a closing inventory level of 2000 units is appropriate to the circumstances.

The production budget below has been developed in terms of the required numbers to be produced.

McTavish Lifestyles production budget for the year ending 31 December 2025

	Q1	Q2	Q3	Q4	Total
Target sales in units (from sales budget)	10 000	11 000	12 000	12 000	45 000
Add: required closing inventory	2000	2000	2000	2000	2000
Subtract: opening inventory	(1000)	(2000)	(2000)	(2000)	(1000)
Required production in units	**11 000**	**11 000**	**12 000**	**12 000**	**46 000**

Note 1: The closing inventory for one quarter becomes the opening inventory for the next quarter.
Note 2: The 'Total' column represents a summary of the entire year, so the closing inventory only represents the closing inventory of quarter 4, while the opening inventory represents the opening inventory in quarter 1.

Logically, managers need to assess whether they have the production capacity to meet the production goals that have been set (which were based on sales projections). We are assuming that McTavish Lifestyles does have the required production capacity. However, had this not been the case, then some outsourcing of production in particular periods might have been necessary, or perhaps the acquisition of additional production facilities might have been seen as an option. These options would have to have been included within the budgetary plans.

No financial amounts are shown in the production budget above, only numbers of units. The financial costs of producing the required levels of production are reflected in the budgets that follow, these being a direct materials budget, a direct labour budget, and a manufacturing overhead expenses budget.

Direct materials – the focus of a direct materials budget – are those materials that can be traced fairly easily, or directly, to particular products. They are the physical resources used to manufacture a product; for example, the fibreglass used to create a surfboard is considered a direct material.

Direct labour – the focus of the direct labour budget – is the cost of the human resources, such as labourers, who work to create a product; for example, payment for the labour of a person who shapes a surfboard (surfboard shaper) would be considered direct labour. Direct labour does not include the costs of administrative managers or salespeople, as they are not directly involved in the manufacture of the product.

Manufacturing overhead expenses – the focus of the manufacturing overhead expenses budget – are the other resources used in the production process, such as cost of electricity or heating for a factory. These overheads might also include materials that are used in small amounts and are not easily traceable to particular products.

The direct materials budget

The direct materials budget follows on from the production budget, emphasising the sequential nature of budgeting that was reflected in **Figure 4.2**. As noted above, **direct materials** are those that can be fairly easily traced to the particular products being manufactured. See **Learning exercise 4.6** for how to prepare a direct materials budget.

direct materials
Materials that can be fairly easily traced to use in a product or service

4.6 Learning Exercise

Preparing a direct materials budget

Once McTavish Lifestyles has estimated its production output (as was done in **Learning exercise 4.5**), it needs to determine the quantity and costs of the material needed to manufacture the required number of sunhats identified in the production budget. Each sunhat requires half a metre of material.

The opening material inventory is 250 metres at $16 per metre, and the manager wants the materials inventory at the end of each quarter to increase to 500 metres at $16 per metre. The material cost is not expected to change for the next year.

Let's consider how to prepare a direct materials budget. Review the table below, which uses the following calculation:

(Budgeted production units × material cost per unit) + cost of targeted closing inventory – cost of opening inventory = total cost of direct material purchases for the period

McTavish Lifestyles direct materials budget for the year ending 31 December 2025

	Q1	Q2	Q3	Q4	Total
Units to be produced (from the production budget)	11 000	11 000	12 000	12 000	46 000
Material cost per hat (0.5 metres × $16)	$8	$8	$8	$8	$8
Cost of material required for production	$88 000	$88 000	$96 000	$96 000	$368 000
Add: target closing inventory of material (500 metres × $16)	$8 000	$8 000	$8 000	$8000	$8000
Total materials required	$96 000	$96 000	$104 000	$104 000	$376 000
Subtract: opening inventory of materials (250 × $16 for quarter 1)	$4 000	$8 000	$8 000	$8 000	$4 000
Total cost of direct materials purchases	**$92 000**	**$88 000**	**$96 000**	**$96 000**	**$372 000**

As with the closing inventory of finished goods, the required closing inventory of materials also needs much thought. The more inventory on hand, the greater the storage costs and the greater the risk of the stock being damaged or stolen, or becoming obsolete if production suddenly discontinues, perhaps because of declining demand for the organisation's products.

Having too little inventory also creates problems. If there are delays with material suppliers, then the company might run out of materials, which would mean that production has to stop. This would lead to lost sales and damage to the organisation's profitability and reputation. Again, the principle regarding closing materials inventory is *not too much but not too little*.

The direct labour budget

direct labour
The cost of the human resources used to create a product or service; for example, manual labour that can be directly traced to the product or service

Direct labour represents the labour that can be directly traced to being used to produce the inventory. Having prepared the preceding budgets – meaning we know how many units we are producing – we can now prepare the direct labour budget (see **Learning exercise 4.7**).

4.7 Learning Exercise

Preparing a direct labour budget

Based on the production requirements of McTavish Lifestyles, the labour hours for each sunhat are expected to be 1 hour, and the wage is $20 per hour. These costs are not expected to change during the period.

Here is how to prepare a direct labour budget for McTavish Lifestyles. Review the table below, which uses the following calculation:

Budgeted production units × labour time per unit × labour cost per hour = total direct labour cost

McTavish Lifestyles direct labour budget for the year ending 31 December 2025

	Q1	Q2	Q3	Q4	Total
Units to be produced (from the production budget)	11 000	11 000	12 000	12 000	46 000
Labour time per sunhat (in hours)	1	1	1	1	1
Total hours required	11 000	11 000	12 000	12 000	46 000
Labour cost per hour	$20	$20	$20	$20	$20
Total direct labour cost	$220 000	$220 000	$240 000	$240 000	$920 000

It should be noted that in compiling the direct labour budget, an assumption has been made that the labour force can be increased and decreased as needed to meet production needs. That is, direct labour was treated as a variable cost. This will not always be the case – in practice, a great deal of the labour used will have the nature of a fixed cost. Nevertheless, for the purposes of this learning exercise, we have treated it as a variable cost.

The manufacturing overhead expenses budget

The term overhead generally refers to costs that are necessarily incurred for running an organisation but which might not easily be directly or easily attributed to specific activities, products or services. Where only a very small amount of a resource is attributable to a particular good or service, it is often treated as an overhead. Nevertheless, overheads are still necessary for running an organisation. Many overhead costs tend to be fixed; for example, the cost of rent, insurance, administrative salaries and property taxes.

Other overheads tend to vary with the level of production and might be allocated to various products or services on the basis of some activity, such as the volume of production or amount of sales. We explained fixed and variable costs in Chapter 3 wherein we noted the following:

- *Variable costs* are the costs that change as a result of changing production or service volume. That is, they vary as the volume of activity changes. The activity might be measured in terms of units of a product or service, machine hours, labour hours, or some other appropriate measure. While many factors might influence overhead costs, we often simplify things by selecting that activity that seems to have the biggest impact on the costs.
- *Fixed costs* are generally considered to be those costs that do not change in a particular period as the volume of production or services changes. For example, the rent for a factory will be the same (fixed) even where there are variations within the amount of production. Similarly, cleaning costs, insurance costs, council building rates and so forth are typically fixed within a particular range of activity, which we refer to as the *relevant range*.

Overheads are often separated into those costs that relate specifically to manufacturing and those that relate to other general activities. For example, the rent for a factory will be treated as a **manufacturing overhead** expense, whereas the rent for an administrative building will be treated as an administrative, or general, overhead expense.

manufacturing overhead Resources beyond direct materials and direct labour used in the process of creating a product or service; for example, electricity or heating for a factory

The total overhead expenses – both manufacturing and administrative overheads – for a period, plus all the direct costs for that period, will equal all of the expenses incurred by an organisation. The direct manufacturing costs plus the manufacturing overhead expenses represent the costs that are assigned to inventory and subsequently recorded as part of costs of sales. Other overheads, such as the selling and administrative overhead expenses, are not included as part of the cost of inventory. Conventionally, only those costs that relate to the production of inventory will be included as part of the cost of inventory (or 'stock'). Inventory would be considered as an 'asset' of the organisation. When the inventory is subsequently sold, the cost of the sold inventory would be recognised as a 'cost of sales' or 'cost of goods sold'. Other expenses – such as administrative and selling costs – which are not included as part of 'inventory', would be treated as expenses at the time they are incurred.

As emphasised in Chapter 3, an organisation should determine its long-term product (selling) prices at amounts that account for both its overhead costs and direct costs, as this allows the organisation to earn a profit on a longer-term basis. However, as we also emphasised in Chapter 3, it is possible in some circumstances to ignore fixed overhead costs for the pricing of special one-time orders, where the minimum price point only has to exceed the relevant direct or variable costs (thereby providing a positive contribution margin).

See **Learning exercise 4.8** for how to prepare a manufacturing overhead expenses budget.

4.8 Learning Exercise

Preparing a manufacturing overhead expenses budget

In addition to direct labour costs and direct material costs, other costs for production and production-related departments also need to be considered when determining the cost of producing finished goods. Based on last year's information and reasonable forecasts, the managers of McTavish Lifestyles have determined the following manufacturing overhead costs:

Indirect materials (cotton, labels) per sunhat	$1.00
Electricity per sunhat	$0.80
Maintenance on machinery per sunhat	$0.20
Factory supervisor's salary per quarter	$22 500.00
Factory rent per quarter	$25 000.00
Rates and insurance for factory per quarter	$7500.00

Here is how we would prepare a manufacturing overhead expenses budget. We know that:

Variable manufacturing overhead costs + fixed manufacturing overhead costs = total manufacturing overhead expenses

McTavish Lifestyles manufacturing overhead expenses budget for the year ending 31 December 2025

	Q1	Q2	Q3	Q4	Total
Units to be produced (from the production budget)	11 000	11 000	12 000	12 000	46 000
Variable costs					
Indirect materials at $1.00 per sunhat	$11 000	$11 000	$12 000	$12 000	$46 000
Electricity at $0.80 per sunhat	$8 800	$8 800	$9 600	$9 600	$36 800
Maintenance at $0.20 per sunhat	$2 200	$2 200	$2 400	$2 400	$9 200
Fixed costs					
Factory supervisor's salary	$22 500	$22 500	$22 500	$22 500	$90 000
Factory rent	$25 000	$25 000	$25 000	$25 000	$100 000
Rates and insurance	$7500	$7500	$7500	$7500	$30 000
Total	$77 000	$77 000	$79 000	$79 000	$312 000

The selling and administrative overhead expenses budget

selling and administrative overhead expenses budget The budget for costs not associated with production that the organisation necessarily needs to incur in order to operate; for example, salaries of administrative staff

Apart from those costs – both fixed and variable – that relate to producing the goods and services of an organisation, there will be other costs that the organisation necessarily incurs in order to operate. For example, there are the salaries payable to people who are not involved in the manufacturing process but who nevertheless are important in enabling the organisation to function. Then there are the salaries payable to salespeople, and to the people who serve a general administrative function, as well as the costs associated with enabling these people to perform their duties (for example, rent and rates on administrative buildings). These costs are the subject of the **selling and administrative overhead expenses budget** (see Learning exercise 4.9).

4.9 Learning Exercise

Preparing a selling and administrative overhead expenses budget

McTavish Lifestyles expects to incur the following selling and administrative costs:

- freight out to stores and customers: $3 per sunhat sold
- advertising costs per quarter: $8000
- office salaries: $20 000 per quarter
- rent on administration building: $10 000 per quarter
- rates and insurance on administration building: $2000 per quarter.

Here is how we could prepare a selling and administrative overhead expenses budget. Please note that we are back to using the sales quantity, not the production amount, because the variable costs in this case relate to the amount sold rather than the amount produced.

McTavish Lifestyles selling and administrative overhead expenses budget for the year ending 31 December 2025

	Q1	Q2	Q3	Q4	Total
Target sales in units (from sales budget)	10 000	11 000	12 000	12 000	45 000
Variable costs					
Freight @ $3 per sold sunhat	$30 000	$33 000	$36 000	$36 000	$135 000
Fixed costs					
Advertising	$8 000	$8 000	$8 000	$8 000	$32 000
Office salaries	$20 000	$20 000	$20 000	$20 000	$80 000
Rent on admin building	$10 000	$10 000	$10 000	$10 000	$40 000
Rates and insurance	$2 000	$2 000	$2 000	$2 000	$8 000
Total	**$70 000**	**$73 000**	**$76 000**	**$76 000**	**$295 000**

Again, keep in mind that while the selling and administrative overhead expenses budget identifies the expected costs to be incurred, these costs might or might not actually be paid in the same period (a quarter, in this instance) in which they are incurred. That is, perhaps the rent was actually paid in advance, while the advertising might be paid after the related advertisements appeared. So the expenses might be recognised in a different period to the related cash flow.

Having prepared the various operating budgets (the sales budget, production budget, direct materials budget, direct labour budget, manufacturing overhead expenses budget, and selling and administrative overhead expenses budget) and as reflected in **Figure 4.2**, we would then typically prepare the financial budgets (the cash budget, budgeted income statement, and budgeted balance sheet), which are necessarily based upon the information that is provided in the operating budgets just produced.

The cash budget

The cash budget documents the planned cash receipts and planned cash payments for a particular period of time. The timing of all cash movements is important in order to identify potential cash shortages as well as unnecessary cash surpluses.

To improve the usefulness of the cash budget, it can be separated into different components. For example, it is common to subdivide cash payments, and cash receipts, into the following three components:

- *Cash flows from operating activities* – these are the budgeted cash inflows and outflows that arise as a result of an organisation undertaking the main purposes for which it has been established. In the case of McTavish Lifestyles, these receipts and payments relate to the manufacture and sale of sunhats. Ideally, net cash flows from operating activities will be positive in amount (that is, cash inflows from operations are greater than the cash outflows from operations), although in the start-up phase of a business it is not unusual for them to be negative. However, an organisation cannot sustain itself in the long run if net cash flows from operating activities are continually negative, as they provide the funding necessary for much of the investment activities of the organisation, as well as for providing payments to owners.
- *Cash flows from investing activities* – these are the predicted cash flows associated with an organisation's investment activities, which include cash flows related to the purchase or sale of property, plant and equipment, as well as investments made in other organisations.
- *Cash flows from financing activities* – these are the budgeted cash flows associated with activities such as borrowing and repaying funds from lenders such as banks, as well as predicted contributions and payments to, or withdrawals by, owners.

In calculating the projected cash balances at the end of each period, the closing cash balance of one period becomes the opening cash balance of the next period. See **Learning exercise 4.10** for how to prepare a cash budget.

4.10 Learning Exercise

Preparing a cash budget

Recognising the importance of projected cash flows, the managers of McTavish Lifestyles have asked you to prepare a cash budget. In doing so, various items of additional information are required:

- The cash balance at the beginning of January 2025 is $20 000.
- Many sales are made on credit terms. Eighty per cent of sales are collected in the quarter in which the sale is made, and the remaining 20 per cent is collected in the next quarter. The sales in the final quarter of 2024 were $450 000. This means that the closing trade debtors of $90 000 in 2024 would be collected in the first quarter of 2025. (Please note that *trade debtors* is a term used to refer to people/organisations that owe funds to an organisation, typically in relation to sales that have been made to them on credit. Another name for trade debtors is *accounts receivable*.)
- McTavish Lifestyles buys its material on credit terms. It pays its suppliers 75 per cent of the purchase price in the same quarter as the purchase, and it pays the remaining 25 per cent in the following quarter. The purchases of materials for the last quarter of 2024 amounted to $80 000. This means that the closing trade creditors of $20 000 in 2024 would be paid in the first quarter of 2025. (Please note that *trade creditors* is a term used to refer to people/organisations that are owed funds by an organisation, typically in relation to purchases that have been made by the organisation on credit terms. Another term that could be used is *accounts payable*.)
- Labour costs are paid in the quarter in which they are incurred.

- Manufacturing overhead expenses, and selling and administrative overhead expenses, are paid in the quarter in which they are incurred.
- A loan of $20 000 will be repaid in the third quarter of 2025.
- McTavish Lifestyles intends to invest in a new machine in quarter 4, at a cost of $40 000.
- The owners of McTavish Lifestyles intend to withdraw $50 000 from the business at the end of each quarter to compensate them for the investment they have made in the organisation.
- Senior management wants to maintain a minimum $12 000 in cash on hand at the end of each quarter as a buffer for any unexpected cash needs.

With the above information, we have assumed that all customers will ultimately pay the amounts they owe to McTavish Lifestyles. In practice, this is not typically the case. Some people will default on their debts, meaning that normally some bad debts can also be expected and must be recognised as part of the budgetary process. However, as noted, for this learning exercise we will assume there are no such defaults by the debtors.

While we previously prepared a sales budget, it did not provide information about how much cash will actually be received in each quarter from customers. As we have assumed that the sales are generally being made on credit terms (meaning the customer, or their credit card provider, will transfer/pay the cash at a later stage, following the sale), we need to predict when the amounts of cash will actually be received. Our assumption (provided above) is that 80 per cent of sales are collected as cash in the quarter in which they occur, and the remaining 20 per cent are collected in the next quarter. We need to construct a schedule of the expected cash receipts from customers for each quarter. In practice, this could also have been produced at the bottom of the sales budget, but we have elected to produce it as a separate schedule. Note that the quarterly budgeted sales figures from the sales budget prepared earlier are used as the basis for the schedule that follows.

Expected cash receipts from customers for McTavish Lifestyles for the year ending 31 December 2025

	Q1	Q2	Q3	Q4
Opening debtors	$90 000			
First quarter target sales: $500 000	$400 000	$100 000		
Second quarter target sales: $550 000		$440 000	$110 000	
Third quarter target sales: $600 000			$480 000	$120 000
Fourth quarter target sales: $600 000				$480 000
Cash collected from customers	**$490 000**	**$540 000**	**$590 000**	**$600 000**

Just as there will be a delay in the receipt of cash from customers, the payments made to suppliers of materials will also typically lag behind the actual purchase. This is because most suppliers give their customers a short period of time to make a payment, which is referred to as a *credit period*. This period can typically be between seven and 30 days in length, but it can also be longer. For the purposes of McTavish Lifestyles, we have assumed that it pays its suppliers 75 per cent of the purchase price in the same quarter as the purchase, and it pays the remaining 25 per cent in the following quarter.

Expected cash payments to suppliers of materials for McTavish Lifestyles for the year ending 31 December 2025

	Q1	Q2	Q3	Q4
Opening amount payable to suppliers: $20 000	$20 000			
First quarter purchases: $92 000	$69 000	$23 000		
Second quarter purchases: $88 000		$66 000	$22 000	
Third quarter purchases: $96 000			$72 000	$24 000
Fourth quarter purchases: $96 000				$72 000
Cash paid to suppliers	$89 000	$89 000	$94 000	$96 000

We are now in a position to prepare the cash budget, as follows:

McTavish Lifestyles cash budget for the year ending 31 December 2025

	Q1	Q2	Q3	Q4
Cash flows from operating activities				
Cash receipts				
From sales	$490 000	$540 000	$590 000	$600 000
Deduct payments				
Direct materials	$89 000	$89 000	$94 000	$96 000
Direct labour	$220 000	$220 000	$240 000	$240 000
Manufacturing overhead expenses	$77 000	$77 000	$79 000	$79 000
Selling and administrative overhead expenses	$70 000	$73 000	$76 000	$76 000
Total payments	$456 000	$459 000	$489 000	$491 000
Net cash flows from operating activities	**$34 000**	**$81 000**	**$101 000**	**$109 000**
Cash flows from investing activities				
Invest in new machine	–	–	–	($40 000)
Net cash flows from investing activities	**–**	**–**	**–**	**($40 000)**
Cash flows from financing activities				
Repayment of loan	–	–	($20 000)	–
Payment to owners	($50 000)	($50 000)	($50 000)	($50 000)
Net cash flows from financing activities	**($50 000)**	**($50 000)**	**($70 000)**	**($50 000)**
Net cash flows for the quarter	($16 000)	$31 000	$31 000	$19 000
Opening cash for the quarter	$20 000	$4 000	$35 000	$66 000
Expected closing balance of cash	$4 000	$35 000	$66 000	$85 000

A review of this cash budget provides a number of interesting insights. Cash flows from operating activities is positive (representing an expected net inflow of cash) in all quarters, so this appears to be a good outcome. And it does seem that the owners can withdraw $50 000 per quarter and retain a cash surplus, rather than entering a cash deficit situation; that is, where the cash balance becomes negative, meaning that the organisation might have what is typically referred to as a bank overdraft.

One issue that might need to be addressed is that the closing balance of cash is only $4000 in quarter 1, which is below the minimum balance of cash that senior management wanted to have on hand at any time, this being $12 000. As such, perhaps the owners should think about the need to either contribute some additional funds or reduce the amount they want to withdraw from the organisation in quarter 1.

You should remember that the cash budget provides a projection of what cash will be on hand *if* the operating, investing and financing activities behave as expected. Such expectations, however, are not necessarily met, so even when the cash budget indicates that there will be no cash deficits, it would nevertheless be wise for managers to make short-term financing arrangements in case the need arises – perhaps a **line of credit** with a bank. A line of credit represents an agreement negotiated with a funding provider, such as a bank, to supply an amount of cash up to a maximum level if needed, and where interest is only paid on the amount of money actually borrowed. Lines of credit are typically only extended to organisations that are deemed to be *creditworthy*, meaning they have a reputation for paying amounts that are due.

line of credit
An agreement negotiated with a fund provider, such as a bank, to supply an amount of cash up to a maximum level if needed, and where interest is only paid on the amount of money actually borrowed

Cash management

As we have emphasised, cash management is an important aspect of the overall management of an organisation, and the cash budget is a very important tool for this. Cash is central to the ongoing operations of an organisation, and it is essential that enough cash is on hand to allow the organisation to pay its debts as and when they fall due. However, you would not want to hold too much cash either, as cash itself is not a productive asset; that is, leaving cash in a simple deposit account earns an organisation very little, or no, interest revenue. If an organisation discovers it has surplus cash, then it should consider putting the cash to more productive uses, although not ones that would significantly increase the risks to the organisation.

In our illustration of McTavish Lifestyles, the budgets were compiled on a quarterly basis. While for the purpose of the above learning exercises, the cash budget was prepared on a quarterly basis, it would be wise to produce a cash budget on a monthly basis instead, to facilitate closer monitoring and control of cash.

As we have also emphasised many times, it is important for an organisation to undertake budgeting, as this effectively forces management to understand the interrelationships of the various functions, and activities, and identify when there might be cash deficiencies that need to be addressed – ideally in advance. Approaching funding providers, such as banks, well in advance of any critical need for cash will be met more positively than urgently rushing to the bank when a cash-related crisis actually occurs. If managers are able to present the image that they understand and are able to predict future funding requirements, this will give banks the impression that the managers are in control and understand their organisation. Conversely, managers who rush to the bank as crises arise look to be out of control and might find it difficult to obtain funding; or if they do, they might need to pay a higher rate of interest for the funds they require because of the perception that they are a relatively higher risk for the lenders.

Identifying and resolving cash-flow problems

If the production of a cash budget indicates that there might be future cash-flow problems, then managers can undertake a number of actions, including:

- attempting to increase sales – the role of advertising or potential changes to the product, or its pricing, might be considered
- reducing the collection time from customers – perhaps offer incentives for early payment, such as a 2 per cent discount if customers pay the amounts due within 10 days of the date of sale; alternatively, the organisation might introduce prompt follow-up emails and/or phone calls to customers as soon as the debt has been due beyond a certain number of days
- reducing stock levels – reducing the level of inventory sitting in the warehouse will free up some cash, although managers need to be careful that they do not get into a situation where they run out of stock (a 'stock-out')
- seeking external funds from different lenders at the lowest rates of interest possible, and with suitable repayment terms
- seeking internal funds – that is, seeking additional funds from the owners, or reducing the level of payments (dividend payments for a company) being made to the owners
- identifying and reducing areas of waste or inefficiency
- using credit more efficiently – for example, not paying suppliers until the latest time while being careful to retain a sound credit reputation
- potentially delaying the acquisition of new plant and equipment – although managers would need to make sure this does not undermine the future of the organisation.

The budgeted income statement

As Figure 4.2 shows, the budgeted income statement can be prepared after all the operating budgets have been prepared. The budgeted income statement provides the basis for evaluating the projected overall performance of an organisation from a financial perspective (always remember, though, that financial performance is just one aspect of the performance of an organisation – the social and environmental aspects of performance also deserve recognition!). It will deduct projected expenses from projected revenues in order to arrive at the budgeted profit.

Learning exercise 4.11 explains how to compile a budgeted income statement.

4.11 Learning Exercise

Preparing a budgeted income statement

Let's review how to prepare a budgeted income statement for McTavish Lifestyles for the year ending 31 December 2025.

In compiling the statement, we need to determine the costs of the inventory that will be sold each period – referred to as the costs of goods sold (or cost of sales). The costs of the inventory that will still be on hand at the end of each period are not considered an expense of the related sales, as the inventory has not been sold but is available for sale in the next period. Inventory on hand at the end of the accounting period is considered to be an asset, not an expense, of the period.

The costs of the inventory generally include the variable manufacturing costs plus an apportioned amount of the fixed manufacturing costs. The fixed manufacturing costs can be allocated to each item of inventory (to each sunhat, in this instance) by dividing the total fixed manufacturing costs of the period by the number of sunhats produced in that period. Costs that do not relate to the manufacturing process – such as those shown in the selling and administrative overhead expenses budget – will not be included within the cost of the inventory, but will be treated as an expense of the period in which they were incurred.

The costs of inventory can be determined as follows:

Variable manufacturing costs		
Direct materials per sunhat		$8.00
Direct labour per sunhat		$20.00
Variable manufacturing overhead expenses per sunhat		
Indirect materials	$1.00	
Electricity	$0.80	
Maintenance on machines	$0.20	$2.00
Total variable manufacturing costs per sunhat		**$30.00**
Fixed manufacturing costs		
Factory supervisor's salary	$90 000	
Factory rent	$100 000	
Rates and insurance on factory	$30 000	
	$220 000	
Divided by the number of sunhats produced (from production budget)	46 000	
Total fixed manufacturing cost per sunhat		**$4.7826**
Total fixed and variable costs per sunhat		**$34.7826**

Having calculated the cost per sunhat of $34.7826, we can now calculate the cost of sales. The cost of sales equals the cost of opening inventory (which we were previously advised was $33 500) plus the costs of production for the period, less the cost of inventory still on hand at the end of the year (closing inventory). Therefore, the projected cost of sales for the year is:

Cost of opening inventory	$33 500
Cost of production for the year: 46 000 hats @ $34.7826 per hat	$1 600 000
	$1 633 500
Less cost of closing inventory: 2000 hats @ $34.7826 per hat	$69 565
Cost of sales	**$1 563 935**

We are now in a position to prepare the budgeted income statement which will show the total revenues for the year less the total expenses for the year:

McTavish Lifestyles budgeted income statement for the year ended 31 December 2025

Sales		$2 250 000
Less cost of sales		$1 563 935
Gross profit		$686 065
Less selling and administrative expenses		
Freight to customers	$135 000	
Advertising	$32 000	
Office salaries	$80 000	
Rent on administrative building	$40 000	
Rates and insurance on administrative building	$8 000	$295 000
Profit		$391 065

Note the difference between profits and net cash flows from operating activities. Profit for the year is projected to be $391 065, but the projected net cash flows from operating activities as previously disclosed within the cash budget is projected to be $325 000 across the year ($34 000 + $81 000 + $101 000 + $109 000). The reasons why the cash flows generated from the operations of the business will be different to the profits include the following:

- Some costs will be incurred in different periods than the one in which they are paid (for example, the purchase of inventory).
- The cash flows associated with some revenue will not be received until after the actual sale. For example, the customers paid for the hats a number of days after the actual sale. By convention, we recognise sales revenue and an asset in the form of the amount receivable from the customer (the asset would be referred to as an 'account receivable' or 'trade debtor') at the point in time when the sale actually occurs and the control of the sold inventory passes to the customer, and we recognise the related cash flows when the customer subsequently pays the amount of cash that is owing).

Also note the difference between profit and the overall increase in cash between the beginning and end of the year. Profit is projected to be $391 065, but the projections anticipate that the bank balance will increase by only $65 000 for the year (closing expected cash balance of $85 000 less the opening cash balance of $20 000). The reasons why the cash flows generated from the combined operating, financing and investing activities of the business will be different to the profits include the following:

- Some of the cash payments will not be considered as expenses; for example, the drawings made by the owners will not be considered as expenses even though they reduce cash.
- Some of the cash outflows related to the purchase of inventory were included in the cost of closing inventory, which is an asset, rather than being treated as an expense.

For all of the above reasons, there will be a difference between cash flows and profits. At the extreme, a very profitable organisation might nevertheless fail because of poor cash management. At this stage, you do not need to be too concerned if you do not understand why some cash payments create expenses and others do not, as we will further address such issues when we start studying financial accounting from Chapter 7.

Once the budgeted income statement has been completed, it needs to be reviewed to determine:

- whether the projected result is what the managers of an organisation were anticipating, or whether their plans need to be amended
- if the projected profit will be sufficient given the risks involved, the amount of effort that owners might need to make, or the amount of funds that needs to be invested in the organisation
- if the projected profit is comparable with competitors in the industry. If it appears to be less than what competitors might generate for a similar level of activity, then there are some potential inefficiencies that need to be investigated and understood. Have the competitors got some advantage that the managers of the organisation do not know about?

In relation to information about competitors, keep in mind that you will not generally have access to a competitor's budget, but you might be able to access their past income statements if they are a large organisation that makes such financial information publicly available.

The budgeted balance sheet

While the final budget in the master budget is the budgeted balance sheet (refer back to Figure 4.2), we will not prepare this as we have not yet really addressed what is included within a balance sheet. We will cover this in Chapter 7. At this stage, we can simply say that the budgeted balance sheet will show the projected assets, liabilities and owners' equity of an organisation (and these terms will be explained in Chapter 7) at the end of the accounting period if the organisation operates as planned.

Why do I need to understand the fundamentals of constructing a master budget?

If you are to be a manager within an organisation – no matter what type of organisation – you will likely be involved in some role associated with the preparation of a master budget. All organisations need to prepare master budgets, so as a manager you need to know about them. By understanding the fundamentals we have just discussed, you will know and appreciate how various functions within an organisation work together, and influence each other, to ultimately create various income, expenses, profits, cash flows, assets, and liabilities. Understanding master budgets will highlight to you the interdependencies between different components or departments within an organisation and how changes in particular variables – such as changes in predicted sales or changes in predicted materials costs – will flow through to ultimately impact cash flows and profits. Budgeting is an essential component of the planning process.

LO4.5 Budget variances

Once the master budget has been prepared, it provides the necessary targets with which actual (future) performance can be compared. Differences between actual performance and budgeted performance will arise. As you know, we call these variances.

variances Differences that arise between actual performance and budgeted performance

As explained earlier, some of these variances will be controllable, whereas others might not be considered controllable. Further, some variances might be *favourable* (for example, where actual sales are above budgeted sales, or where actual expenses are below budgeted expenses) or *unfavourable* (for example, where actual sales are below targeted sales, or where certain costs exceed those that were planned for). The reasons for both favourable and unfavourable variances need to be understood. That is, even if a budget variance is favourable, the managers need to understand the reason why the variance arose – perhaps they did not fully understand how costs behave, or the actual demand within the market. If actual performance is not in accordance with budgeted, or targeted, performance, then the related processes can be deemed to be out of control. Managers then need to know why, and how, to get the process back under control.

Identifying and investigating budget variances

Variances need to be subject to critical analysis. As we discussed in Chapter 3, accountants need to be critical thinkers if they are going to add value to an organisation. The critical analysis of budget variances is crucial to the ongoing success of an organisation.

The process of identifying variances and making adjustments is depicted in Figure 4.3.

FIGURE 4.3 Identifying budget variances

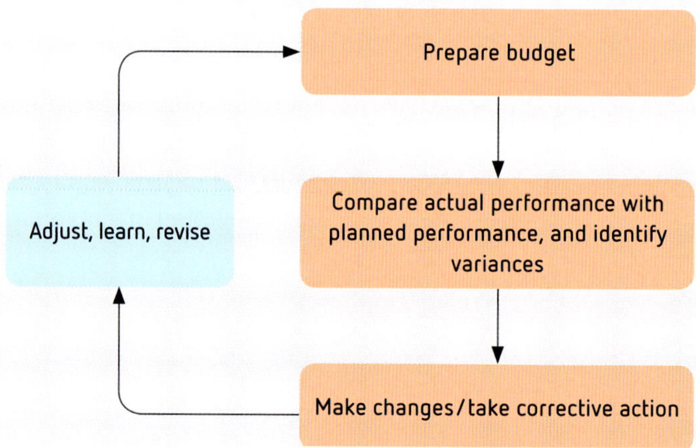

Not all variances will necessarily be investigated. As we have explained in previous chapters, the collection of information should be subjected to *cost versus benefit analysis*, and information should only be collected if the benefits of improved decision making exceed the related information costs. A variance might have occurred as a result of a one-off event that is considered unlikely to recur. For example, there might have been an industry-wide labour strike that has since been resolved, or there might have been an unexpected climatic event that caused problems for production – both events would have been beyond the control of the organisation and hence perhaps do not warrant significant attention or investigation.

Small variances might also not be investigated. In this regard, many organisations implement **materiality thresholds**; for example, they might only investigate variances that involve a difference of greater than, say, 5 per cent of the budgeted amount.

materiality threshold A variance that exceeds an agreed-upon threshold on a budgeted amount, and that an organisation would elect to investigate

Relevant range

In understanding why variances might have arisen, it is important that managers and accountants know the **relevant range** for particular cost behaviour, and are able to identify which costs are variable, and fixed, within that range. We defined the relevant range in Chapter 3 as the range of production output, or volume, in which our expectations regarding cost behaviour are expected to hold. That is, this is the range of activities in which our fixed costs are expected to stay the same (fixed) in total, and our variable costs per unit are expected to be constant.

relevant range The range of production output, or volume, in which our expectations regarding cost behaviour are expected to hold

Operating outside the relevant range might be the reason for some of the budget variances you are experiencing.

Variance control

As another general principle, when reviewing variances, and when assigning responsibility for particular variances to specific managers, it is important that a manager has some control over the variance. There is a general principle that at lower levels of management, fewer costs are controllable by lower-level managers. It is also important that variances are investigated in a timely manner. The existence of a variance is an indication that a process is out of control, and it is important that control over the process is regained as soon as possible. Therefore, reports of variances need to be quickly presented to the responsible managers.

LO4.6 Static and flexible budgets

As mentioned in Chapter 3, when making plans, it is useful to perform a 'What if?' analysis. That is, what might be the implications, for example, *if* sales do not meet targets, or *if* certain costs are slightly higher than expected, or *if* the production capacity is disrupted? 'What if?' analysis requires the use of flexible budgets. We will now discuss static budgets and flexible budgets in turn.

Static budgets

The master budget prepared in this chapter for McTavish Lifestyles can be considered a **static budget** and is not directly useful for performing a 'What if?' analysis. It was prepared based on one set of projections about sales (as per the sales budget) and these sales then drove the level of activity, and associated costs, that were reported in the other budgets that made up the respective components of the master budget. That is, only one level of activity was used for each quarter, which means the managers of the organisation would subsequently compare actual revenues and costs that were generated at different levels of activity to that used to develop the master budget. In practice, it is difficult to exactly meet projected sales. Therefore, the static budget is only appropriate for evaluating the performance of managers when the actual level of activity is very close to that used within the master budget.

static budget
A budget that does not change as certain variables, such as volume, change

As already stated, variable costs are expected to change as activity levels change. Therefore, a master budget prepared on the basis of a certain level of activity will not be very useful for assessing how managers have controlled those costs that are considered to be variable if the actual activity level – for example, the sales made – is quite different. However, the static budget can still be useful for assessing managers' performance in controlling fixed manufacturing costs and fixed selling and administrative costs, as long as the level of activity is within the bounds of that in which such costs are expected to remain fixed (the relevant range).

Since the actual level of sales influences actual levels of production, and since many costs are expected to vary as production or sales change (variable costs), then it can be somewhat misleading to compare the total costs calculated for a particular level of activity if that activity level is not met.

For example, if in quarter 2 of 2025 sales were 14 000 units for McTavish Lifestyles, and not 11 000 as projected – thereby necessitating increased production and selling activities – then it would be inappropriate to compare actual manufacturing costs, such as the total direct material or direct labour costs and variable production overheads, or the selling costs, with those that were projected for a sales level of 11 000 units. Many total costs would be higher, as we know that many costs will change in total as activity changes (although we would hope that the variable cost of production per unit does not rise but rather falls). Some of these variances will appear unfavourable. That can be misleading, but nevertheless it might still be appropriate to compare actual fixed costs with budgeted fixed costs, unless the level of activity ends up extending beyond the relevant range.

Similarly, if the sales in quarter 2 of 2025 were below target – perhaps 8000 units – then, without adjustment, many variances will appear favourable when in reality this is not the case.

So, if actual sales are different to budgeted sales, then this change in sales might be appropriate for assessing those with a responsibility for sales (for example, the sales or marketing manager). However, the other budgets prepared on the basis of the initially projected sales might no longer be very useful in assessing actual performance. That is, the original sales budget might be appropriate for assessing the performance of the sales manager, but perhaps not for assessing the other people involved in the subsequent processes.

Flexible budgets

flexible budget
A budget that does change (or flex) as certain variables, such as volume, change

With this in mind, a **flexible budget** can be prepared that adapts (or 'flexes') to changing circumstances. A flexible budget recalculates the total production costs based upon the alternative amounts of production or sales. For example, the sales level that appears in the sales budget could be adjusted, as this would all be done using a particular spreadsheet application.

Changes made in the sales budget should in turn flow through to the various budgets that come after (rely upon) the sales budget. As long as you remain within the identified relevant range, then fixed costs should not change. Of course, you need to be very clear about identifying fixed costs and variable costs, as well as knowing about the relevant range, but that should already have been determined. Flexible budgets therefore provide a more valid comparison of actual and budgeted costs when activity levels deviate from initial plans.

For an example of the use of a flexible budget, see **Learning exercise 4.12**.

4.12 Learning Exercise

Using a flexible budget

We are now required to provide a master budget, through to a cash budget, for McTavish Lifestyles under the revised assumption that sales will not increase throughout the period but will remain at 10 000 units of sales per quarter. That is, we are addressing the question of 'What if?' sales are only 10 000 units each quarter.

To develop this master budget, we will change the sales figures and then see how the projected results change throughout the master budget, as this change flows through each budget. This allows us to see what will happen if sales remain constant (the 'What if?' analysis). If set up correctly and with the use of spreadsheets, then we should only need to change the figures in the sales budget (the cells relating to target sales) – everything else should change automatically.

McTavish Lifestyles sales budget for the year ending 31 December 2025

	Q1	Q2	Q3	Q4	Total
Target sales	10 000	10 000	10 000	10 000	40 000
Selling price	$50	$50	$50	$50	$50
Total sales revenue	**$500 000**	**$500 000**	**$500 000**	**$500 000**	**$2 000 000**

Having prepared the sales budget, the revised production budget can now be prepared.

McTavish Lifestyles production budget for the year ending 31 December 2025

	Q1	Q2	Q3	Q4	Total
Target sales in units	10 000	10 000	10 000	10 000	40 000
Add: required closing inventory	2 000	2 000	2 000	2 000	2 000
Subtract: opening inventory	(1 000)	(2 000)	(2 000)	(2 000)	(1 000)
Required production in units	**11 000**	**10 000**	**10 000**	**10 000**	**41 000**

Having prepared the revised production budget, the revised direct materials budget can be prepared.

McTavish Lifestyles direct materials budget for the year ending 31 December 2025

	Q1	Q2	Q3	Q4	Total
Units to be produced	11 000	10 000	10 000	10 000	41 000
Material cost per sunhat of $8 (0.5 metres × $16)	$8	$8	$8	$8	$8
Cost of material required for production	$88 000	$80 000	$80 000	$80 000	$328 000
Target closing inventory of material (500 metres × $16)	$8 000	$8 000	$8 000	$8 000	$8 000
Total materials required	$96 000	$88 000	$88 000	$88 000	$336 000
Less opening inventory of materials (250 × $16)	$4 000	$8 000	$8 000	$8 000	$4 000
Total cost of direct materials purchases	**$92 000**	**$80 000**	**$80 000**	**$80 000**	**$332 000**

The direct labour budget also needs to be prepared.

McTavish Lifestyles direct labour budget for the year ending 31 December 2025

	Q1	Q2	Q3	Q4	Total
Units to be produced	11 000	10 000	10 000	10 000	41 000
Labour time per sunhat (in hours)	1	1	1	1	1
Total hours required	11 000	10 000	10 000	10 000	41 000
Labour cost per hour	$20	$20	$20	$20	$20
Total direct labour cost	$220 000	$200 000	$200 000	$200 000	$820 000

The revised manufacturing overhead expenses budget would then appear as follows.

McTavish Lifestyles manufacturing overhead expenses budget for the year ending 31 December 2025

	Q1	Q2	Q3	Q4	Total
Units to be produced	11 000	10 000	10 000	10 000	41 000
Variable costs					
Indirect materials at $1.00 per sunhat	$11 000	$10 000	$10 000	$10 000	$41 000
Electricity at $0.80 per sunhat	$8 800	$8 000	$8 000	$8 000	$32 800
Maintenance at $0.20 per sunhat	$2 200	$2 000	$2 000	$2 000	$8 200
Fixed costs					
Supervisor's salary	$22 500	$22 500	$22 500	$22 500	$90 000
Factory rent	$25 000	$25 000	$25 000	$25 000	$100 000
Rates and insurance	$7 500	$7 500	$7 500	$7 500	$30 000
Total	**$77 000**	**$75 000**	**$75 000**	**$75 000**	**$302 000**

The revised selling and administrative overhead expenses budget needs to be prepared.

McTavish Lifestyles selling and administrative overhead expenses budget for the year ending 31 December 2025

	Q1	Q2	Q3	Q4	Total
Target sales	10 000	10 000	10 000	10 000	40 000
Variable costs					
Freight @ $3 per sold sunhat	$30 000	$30 000	$30 000	30 000	$120 000
Fixed costs					
Advertising	$8 000	$8 000	$8 000	$8 000	$32 000
Office salaries	$20 000	$20 000	$20 000	$20 000	$80 000
Rent on administration building	$10 000	$10 000	$10 000	$10 000	$40 000
Rates and insurance	$2 000	$2 000	$2 000	$2 000	$8 000
Total	**$70 000**	**$70 000**	**$70 000**	**$70 000**	**$280 000**

Before the cash budget can be prepared, we need to prepare revised schedules of cash collections from customers, and cash payments to suppliers.

Expected cash receipts from customers for McTavish Lifestyles for the year ending 31 December 2025

	Q1	Q2	Q3	Q4
Opening debtors: $90 000	$90 000			
First quarter target sales: $500 000	$400 000	$100 000		
Second quarter target sales: $500 000		$400 000	$100 000	
Third quarter target sales: $500 000			$400 000	$100 000
Fourth quarter target sales: $500 000				$400 000
Cash collected from customers	**$490 000**	**$500 000**	**$500 000**	**$500 000**

Expected cash payments for materials for McTavish Lifestyles for the year ending 31 December 2025

	Q1	Q2	Q3	Q4
Opening amount payable to suppliers: $20 000	$20 000			
First quarter purchases: $92 000	$69 000	$23 000		
Second quarter purchases: $80 000		$60 000	$20 000	
Third quarter purchases: $80 000			$60 000	$20 000
Fourth quarter purchases: $80 000				$60 000
Cash paid to suppliers	**$89 000**	**$83 000**	**$80 000**	**$80 000**

We are now finally able to prepare our revised cash budget.

McTavish Lifestyles cash budget for the year ending 31 December 2025

	Q1	Q2	Q3	Q4
Cash flows from operating activities				
Cash receipts				
From sales	$490 000	$500 000	$500 000	$500 000
Deduct cash payments				
Direct materials	$89 000	$83 000	$80 000	$80 000
Direct labour	$220 000	$200 000	$200 000	$200 000
Manufacturing overhead expenses	$77 000	$75 000	$75 000	$75 000
Selling and administrative overhead expenses	$70 000	$70 000	$70 000	$70 000
Total	**$456 000**	**$428 000**	**$425 000**	**$425 000**
Net cash flow from operating activities	**$34 000**	**$72 000**	**$75 000**	**$75 000**
Cash flows from investing activities				
Invest in new machine	–	–	–	($40 000)
Net cash flows from investing activities	**–**	**–**	**–**	**($40 000)**
Cash flows from financing activities				
Repayment of loan	–	–	($20 000)	–
Payment to owners	$50 000	($50 000)	($50 000)	($50 000)

Net cash flows from financing activities	($50 000)	($50 000)	($70 000)	($50 000)
Net cash flows for the quarter	($16 000)	$22 000	$5 000	($15 000)
Opening cash for the quarter	$20 000	$4 000	$26 000	$31 000
Closing balance of cash	$4 000	$26 000	$31 000	$16 000

From the cash budget, it is evident that no cash deficit is still predicted, but there is not much cash on hand, so if there is a further downturn in sales, then cash flows could get tight. But apart from quarter 1, it seems that the desired cash buffer of $12 000 is on hand, so it would appear that, should sales remain constant at 10 000 sunhats per quarter, then from a cash flow perspective this should not cause too many problems. Another consideration is whether the profits generated from this level of activity are deemed satisfactory. While the 'What if?' analysis just undertaken only looked at the implications of a change in sales activity, the implications of changes in different costs could also be tested. For example, 'What if?' the price of material increases by 10 per cent, or 'What if?' labour costs increased by 15 per cent?

Having produced the required operating budgets and the cash budget, we could also now prepare the budgeted income statement and the budgeted balance sheet. However, they are not prepared in this instance.

Why do I need to understand the difference between a static master budget and a flexible master budget?

In practice, organisations will use both types of budgets. However, they have different roles that you need to understand should you be in a management role.

The static budget is useful for signalling management plans about what they expect to achieve and for providing a mechanism for understanding how the various parts of the operations link together and influence each other. However, for implementing 'what if?' analysis, flexible budgets are required.

From a flexible budget perspective, the master budgets will be set up in spreadsheets and a change in one variable – such as sales units – can be made to see what implications that has on other variables such as production units, direct materials purchases, or projected profits. That is, flexible budgets are needed for 'what if?' analysis. Analysis of variances also makes more sense using a flexible budget. For example, it would make no sense to compare wages expenses, materials costs, or variable manufacturing overheads with budgeted targets if the targets were based upon a level of activity that differed to the actual activity level.

Budgeting in 'not-for-profit' organisations

As we explained in Chapter 2, some organisations which we refer to as not-for-profit organisations are not established with the aim of generating profits. For example, organisations involved with education, religion, sports, community welfare, employee rights, environmental protection, or some government services do not have a goal of generating profits. Rather, they will have other performance goals that are largely non-financial. Nevertheless, they must also do budgets.

The budgetary process of not-for-profit organisations will be very similar to what we have described within this chapter; however, there are some key differences. Such organisations typically will not produce a 'sales budget' as the goods and services they provide might be free to targeted stakeholders. However, they will need to project what level of goods and services they expect to provide, and this will in turn influence the budgets that follow.

For example, if an organisation was established to provide emergency housing for certain vulnerable people, then the budgetary process might start with projections of people to be housed and for how many days they need to be housed, and where they will be housed. Subsequent cost budgets would be formulated to support the projected number of people to be housed for specific (budgeted) periods of time and this would then inform budgetary targets associated with respect to required funding, and so forth.

Choices would need to be made about whether predictions about available funding – perhaps through grants and estimates of donations – should drive the budgetary process or whether the forecasted needs of the stakeholders then inform the efforts and strategies to obtain funds necessary to support the predicted cash flow requirements.

LO4.7 Budgeting for non-financial aspects of performance

As emphasised at numerous points in this book, an organisation's managers will generally accept responsibilities not only in relation to financial performance, but also in relation to an organisation's social and environmental performance. Different stakeholders expect this. The master budgets considered to this point have only addressed the financial aspects of particular planned activities, which means they have only really addressed one component of organisational performance. However, concentrating solely on financial performance is a short-term and rather risky managerial perspective to embrace.

Therefore, when planning future activities, the related social and environmental impacts also warrant consideration. For example, for McTavish Lifestyles – the focus of the master budgets we prepared earlier – the production of sunhats could also have generated various wastes, consumed various amounts of energy which in turn created various emissions, some employees could have been injured as part of the production process, the transportation of the products to customers would have created various emissions, and so on. These non-financial aspects of performance are not reflected within the master budgets we just considered. However, non-financial aspects of performance, such as waste production, energy use, emissions, product quality, product safety, customer satisfaction, employee health and safety, employee satisfaction, and reputation within the community (these can be considered to represent part of the social performance of an organisation) are all commonly incorporated within targets set by organisations.

Organisations might also seek to create various positive social and/or environmental impacts, or they might seek to minimise negative social and environmental impacts, but it all ties back to what responsibilities managers believe they have – and these responsibilities might be broadly reflected within an organisation's mission statement and strategic plans.

Organisations frequently develop budgets in relation to various aspects of their projected social and environmental performance; for example, in relation to projected water use, energy use, waste generated, water released, CO_2 emissions, customer satisfaction, and employee satisfaction. Again, we emphasise that budgets do not just have to be prepared only in respect of future financial performance.

In terms of publicly disclosed targets, and how they compare with actual performance, the following disclosures made by four very different organisations can be considered, these being the world's biggest mining company BHP Ltd, the New Zealand water provider Watercare, the large US healthcare company Baxter International, and one of the world's largest carpet manufacturers, Interface Inc., which is headquartered in the United States.

The BHP Ltd 2021 Annual Report (p. 34) disclosed various targets in relation to non-financial aspects of their performance. These are reproduced as **Exhibit 4.1**. As can be seen, all the targets

EXHIBIT 4.1 Non-financial targets for BHP Ltd

Our five-year sustainability targets and FY2021 performance

	Target	FY2021 result	Year-on-year
People	Zero work-related fatalities	Workplace fatalities **0**	FY2017[1] 1 FY2018 2 FY2019[2] 1 FY2020 0 **FY2021 0**
	Year-on-year improvement of total recordable injury frequency[3] (TRIF) per million hours worked	Total recordable injury frequency decreased by **11%** compared to FY2020	FY2017[4] 4.2 FY2018[4] 4.4 FY2019[5] 4.7 FY2020 4.2 **FY2021 3.7**
	50 per cent reduction in the number of workers potentially exposed[6] to our most material exposures of diesel particulate matter, respirable silica and coal mine dust compared to our FY2017[7] baseline by FY2022	Occupational exposures **70%** reduction compared to FY2017 baseline	Adjusted FY2017 baseline 4,266 FY2018 3,032 FY2019[8] 2,192 FY2020 1,744 **FY2021[9] 1,280**
Society	Zero significant community events[10]	FY2021 **0**	FY2017 0 FY2018 0 FY2019 0 FY2020 0 **FY2021 0**
	Not less than 1 per cent of pre-tax profits[11] invested in community programs that contribute to the quality of life in the communities where we operate and support the achievement of the UN Sustainable Development Goals	Social investment spend **US$174.8m**[12]	FY2017[13] US$80.2 million FY2018 US$77.1 million FY2019[14] US$93.5 million FY2020 US$149.6 million **FY2021 US$174.8 million**
	By FY2022, implement our Indigenous Peoples Strategy across all our operated assets through the development of Regional Indigenous Peoples Plans	**Regional Indigenous People Plans** being implemented across Australia (Reconciliation Action Plan (RAP)) and North and South America	
Climate change	By FY2022, maintain operational (Scope 1 and Scope 2) greenhouse gas emissions at or below FY2017 levels[15][16] while we continue to grow our business	Greenhouse gas emissions **16.2 $MtCO_2$-e** While our annual emissions are currently higher than the FY2017 adjusted baseline, our GHG emissions forecasts suggest we are on track to meet our FY2022 target	FY2017[15] 14.6 million tonnes carbon dioxide equivalent ($MtCO_2$-e) FY2018[16] 17 $MtCO_2$-e FY2019[16] 15.9 $MtCO_2$-e FY2020[10] 15.9 $MtCO_2$-e **FY2021 16.2 $MtCO_2$-e**
Environment	Zero significant environmental events[10]	FY2021 **0**	FY2017 0 FY2018 0 FY2019 0 FY2020 0 **FY2021 0**
	Reduce FY2022 withdrawal of fresh water[17] by 15 per cent from FY2017 levels	**27%** freshwater withdrawal reduction from FY2017 baseline[18]	Adjusted FY2017 baseline[18] 156,120 ML FY2018 140,515ML FY2019 155,570ML FY2020 126,997ML **FY2021 113,444ML**
	By FY2022, improve marine and terrestrial biodiversity outcomes by developing a framework to evaluate and verify the benefits of our actions, in collaboration with others	**Progressed framework development,** including pilots and approaches to data validation in collaboration with others. On track to deliver by end of FY2022	Year-on-year progress on development of framework to evaluate and verify the benefits of our actions

(1) FY2018 and FY2019 data includes Continuing and Discontinued operations (Onshore US assets to 28 February 2019).
(2) FY2019 data includes Discontinued operations (Onshore US assets) to 28 February 2019 and Continuing operations.
(3) The sum of (fatalities + lost-time cases + restricted work cases + medical treatment cases) multiplied by 1 million/actual hours worked by our employees and contractors. Stated in units of per million hours worked. We adopt the US Government's Occupational Safety and Health Administration Guidelines for the recording and reporting of occupational injuries and illnesses.
(4) FY2017 and FY2018 TRIF data includes Continuing and Discontinued operations (Onshore US assets).
(5) FY2019 TRIF data includes Discontinued operations (Onshore US assets) to 28 February 2019 and Continuing operations.
(6) For exposures exceeding our FY2017 baseline occupational exposure limits discounting the use of personal protective equipment, where required. The baseline exposure profile (as at 30 June 2017) is derived through a combination of quantitative exposure measurements and qualitative assessments undertaken by specialist occupational hygienists consistent with best practice as defined by the American Industrial Hygiene Association.
(7) New FY2017 baseline due to the removal of 98 exposures attributed to the Onshore US assets.
(8) Data excludes Discontinued operations (Onshore US assets).
(9) As of FY2021, the Occupational Exposure Limit for Coal was reduced to 1.5 mg/m3 compared to 2.0 mg/m3 in previous years.
(10) A significant event resulting from BHP operated activities is one with an actual severity rating of four or above, based on our internal severity rating scale (tiered from one to five by increasing severity) as defined in our mandatory minimum performance requirements for risk management.
(11) Our voluntary social investment is calculated as 1 per cent of the average of the previous three years' pre-tax profit.
(12) Expenditure includes BHP's equity share for operated and non-operated joint ventures, and comprises cash, administrative costs, including costs to facilitate the operation of the BHP Foundation.
(13) FY2017 and FY2018 social investment figures includes Discontinued operations (Onshore US assets).
(14) FY2019 social investment figure includes Discontinued operations (Onshore US assets) to 31 October 2018 and Continuing operations.
(15) FY2017 will be adjusted for any material acquisitions and divestments based on GHG emissions at the time of the transaction. Carbon offsets will be used as required. FY2017 baseline is on a Continuing operations basis and has been adjusted for divestments.
(16) FY2018 GHG data includes Continuing operations and Discontinued operations (Onshore US assets). FY2019 GHG data includes Discontinued operations (Onshore US assets) to 31 October 2018 and Continuing operations and has been restated. FY2020 data has been restated.
(17) Where 'withdrawal' is defined as water withdrawn and intended for use (in accordance with 'A Practical Guide to Consistent Water Reporting', ICMM (2017)).
'Fresh water' is defined as waters other than seawater, wastewater from third parties and hypersaline groundwater. Freshwater withdrawal also excludes entrained water that would not be available for other uses. These exclusions have been made to align with the target's intent to reduce the use of freshwater sources subject to competition from other users or the environment.
(18) The FY2017 baseline data has been adjusted to account for: the materiality of the strike affecting water withdrawals at Escondida in FY2017 and improvements to water balance methodologies at WAIO, BMA and BMC and exclusion of hypersaline, wastewater, entrainment, supplies from desalination and Discontinued operations (Onshore US assets) in FY2019 and FY2020.

Source: BHP (2021), p. 34

that are disclosed have been met or are on the way to being met. What would likely be of interest to many stakeholders is how, or why, these particular targets were selected for disclosure, and whether there were other important undisclosed targets that were not met. Public disclosures about various aspects of social and environmental performance are predominantly voluntary – something that we shall explore in Chapter 6.

The Watercare annual report for 2021 (p. 38) presents various items of information about its social and environmental performance including information in relation to unplanned water supply interruptions (see Exhibit 4.2). It shows whether targets set by management were met or not. This can broadly be considered to represent part of the organisation's budgeting, where actual performance is compared with targeted performance.

For Watercare in 2020/21 one target was to ensure that there were 10 or fewer interruptions per 1000 connections during the year. This was achieved. Watercare also aims to ensure at least 95% of all unplanned water interruptions were restored within 5 hours. This was not achieved. These are both considered to be non-financial aspects of performance.

Baxter International's 2020 Corporate Responsibility Report, page 33, includes the following information (see Exhibit 4.3). Again, we can see that particular targets have been devised for managers to meet and the organisation's performance against these targets is then identified.

EXHIBIT 4.2 Watercare's use of water

Unplanned water interruptions per 1000 connections

The Auckland region covered a total of 452 093 water supply connections in 2020/21. As a measure of reliability of service, we monitor the number of times the water supply to our customers is interrupted. We aim to ensure that there are 10 or fewer interruptions per 1000 connections during the year. The result for the 2020/21 year was 8.5 for the Auckland region compared to 4.8 during 2019/2020.

Unplanned water interruptions restored within 5 hours

To minimise the impact on our customers, Watercare aims to ensure at least 95% of all unplanned water interruptions are restored within 5 hours. The result for the year was 94% for the Auckland region compared to 91% for 2019/20.

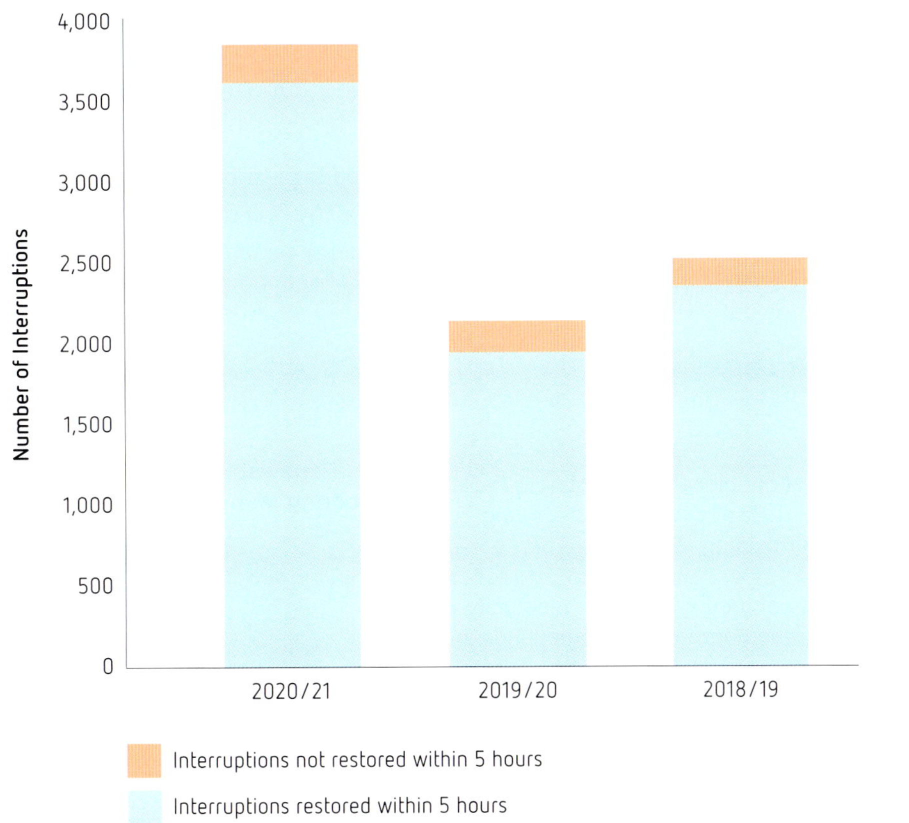

Source: Pouring our energies into tomorrow – Annual Report 2021, Watercare (2021), p. 39.

Using 2015 as a baseline, Baxter intended to:

- Pursue zero waste-to-landfill by achieving a landfill diversion rate of 95% or higher at all manufacturing locations
- Reduce total energy and water use and total waste generation by 15% indexed to revenue
- Reduce absolute GHG emissions by 10%.

We can see from **Exhibit 4.3** that while waste generation has met the target, as has GHG emissions, water use and energy use has not met the target, although the usage is tracking in the right direction.

EXHIBIT 4.3 Non-financial targets for Baxter

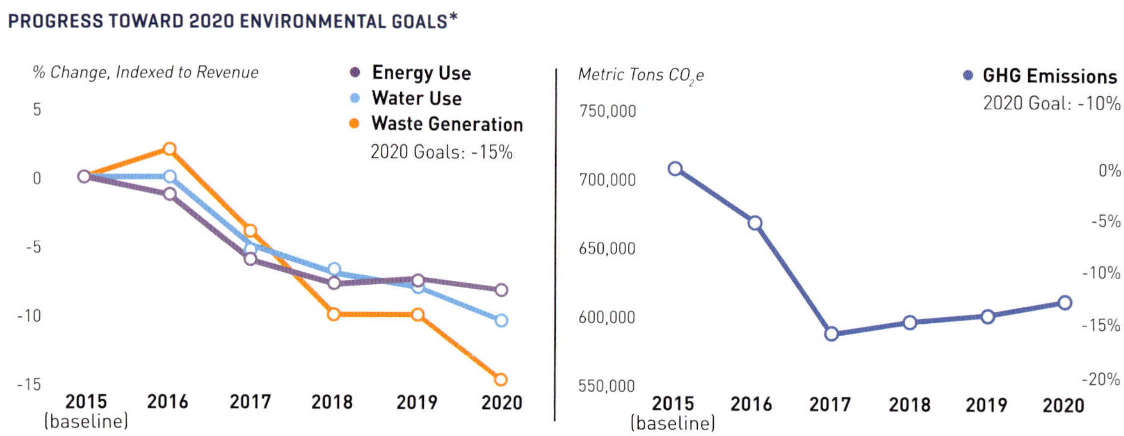

* Energy use and GHG emissions data for 2015–2019 are restated from data reported in the Baxter 2019 Corporate Responsibility Report to improve accuracy and to reflect updated GHG emission factors.

Source: Baxter International (2020 Corporate Responsibility Report), p. 33.

The US carpet manufacturer known as Interface produces various social and environmental disclosures. In its *Climate Disclosure Report: Year End 2020* (p. 3, see **Exhibit 4.4**), the organisation notes that one of its targets is that it shall source its energy requirements fully from renewable sources by 2020. At the time of reporting this has not yet been achieved.

EXHIBIT 4.4 Non-financial targets for Interface

Renewable Energy

In 2020, 75% of energy used at our global manufacturing facilities was from renewable sources – 90% at carpet manufacturing facilities and 49% at our rubber flooring facility.

Renewable energy includes use of green gas, green electricity, and our on-site solar PV arrays in Scherpenzeel, The Netherlands and Chonburi, Thailand.

Our goal is to use 100% renewable energy at all manufacturing facilities.

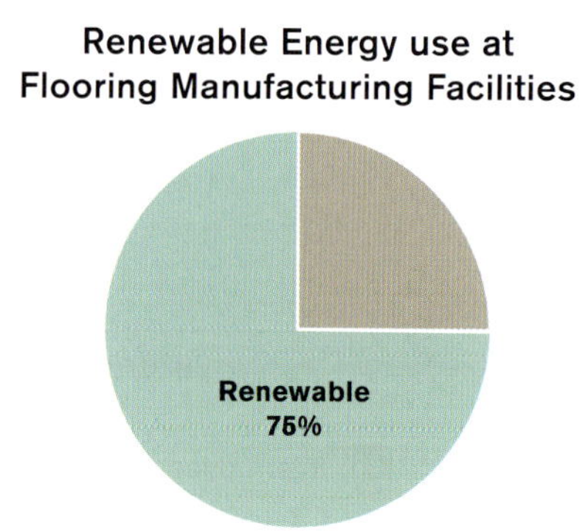

Source: Climate Disclosure Year End 2020 – An Interface Summary (2020).

Again, we need to appreciate that organisations can, and will, have various performance targets and that many of these will not just be financial; yet this is all considered to be part of the accounting process.

LO4.8 Behavioural implications of budgeting

The process of budgeting will affect almost everybody within an organisation and will generate many behavioural consequences. As should be clear by now, one of the main reasons for producing a budget is to influence the future behaviour of managers; that is, to develop targets that people then subsequently strive to achieve. However, the effectiveness of the budgetary exercise will be influenced by a number of factors including:

- Authority needs to be clearly identified, which means identifying the people in charge of developing the budget, as well as the people ultimately responsible for achieving the various budgetary targets. People should only be responsible for performance and the associated variances over which they have some control, and this includes having access to the necessary resources to meet objectives. It can be demotivating to assess people for results that they were realistically unable to influence.
- For budget targets to be accepted by those people charged with meeting the respective targets, it is generally recognised that if they are involved in developing the budget – that is, if they participate in the budgetary process (referred to as a 'participatory budgeting process') – then they are more likely to accept the goals or targets that have been set.

Participative budgeting generally encourages coordination and communication between managers, and a greater understanding and appreciation of the wider organisation. Greater participation may also lead to more accurate budget estimates, as those managers closer to the operations often have the best knowledge of the likely activity, or costs, in their respective areas. Participation also tends to generate a greater level of motivation for people to work towards the budgetary targets. In a sense, participation can cause employees to feel as though they have some personal ownership in the budget rather than feeling that the budget has been imposed upon them. However, it also needs to be appreciated that using budgetary targets as 'benchmarks' against which to subsequently assess managers' performance (comparing actual performance with budgeted targets) could potentially encourage managers to introduce '**budgetary slack**' into the budgeting process, particularly if participative budgeting is being utilised. For example, managers might purposely underestimate sales numbers, therefore making it easier to exceed sales targets, or they might purposely overestimate various expenses, thereby making it easier to generate expenses below budgetary targets.

budgetary slack
Budgetary slack can be defined as the difference between revenue, cost or other targets that have been set opportunistically, and those that would be set objectively.

- Participation in the budgetary process should also help managers understand how the budget aligns to the organisation's strategic plan and mission, thereby also contributing to the likelihood that the budget will be accepted by managers.
- Research generally indicates that budgetary-related targets should be demanding but nevertheless achievable. That is, they should not be too easy, nor should they be too hard. Budgets must be set at a level that provides challenges and which stretches the capabilities of managers, but again, this shouldn't be too difficult. If budgetary targets are not considered to be achievable, then managers might not be motivated from the start. Rather, they might simply behave as if it is all just 'too hard' and as a result they might simply 'give up'.
- Budgetary targets and related processes should be seen to have the backing of senior management, as this will likely impact the degree to which managers embrace the targets. Organisations also need to have the right culture – ideally, a supportive one.

- There should be frequent feedback on performance, so that variances are quickly addressed and managers feel they are in touch with what is going on within their respective areas of operation.
- Managers must be able to properly respond to budget variances and associated evaluations; that is, the process is not considered one-way communication. Managers need an opportunity to explain what is occurring in their responsibility areas. An inability to explain why certain things happened can also be demotivating.

To further encourage managers to meet organisational goals/budgetary targets, it is very common for managers to be paid bonuses that are linked to organisational targets. These targets can be based on various measures of financial, social and/or environmental performance. A well-functioning bonus system creates an alignment of incentives between the managers and owners of an organisation. That is, a well-developed bonus system aligns the interests of all managers in achieving outcomes that are both good for them and for the organisation as a whole. This is often referred to as a situation of '**goal congruence**'.

goal congruence
When managers share or embrace the same goals as those embraced by the organisation. Occurs within an organisation when the goals of different people coincide.

From a financial perspective, it is common to find that managers are paid bonuses tied to reported profits, sales, the return on assets, market share, or movements in share prices. From a social performance perspective, it is also common to find managers being paid bonuses that are tied to customer satisfaction, or measures of the health and safety of employees. From an environmental perspective, managers have been rewarded in terms of reducing waste, water consumption, CO_2 emissions and chemical spillages. Again, senior managers, and accountants, have to be very thoughtful (they have to be critical thinkers) when designing appropriate performance measures with which to motivate and potentially reward managers.

It is important that, whatever bonus is being offered, the manager being assessed has the ability to influence the performance measure being used. For example, while it is common for very senior managers to be rewarded with a bonus that is linked to increasing the overall share price of a company, this could be quite demotivating for lower-level managers who, realistically, are unable to influence the share price. It is also important that managers agree with how the performance indicators are being measured. For example, if 'customer satisfaction' is a measure of performance being used to assess and reward a manager, then the manager should be in a position to influence customer satisfaction, and they should actually agree with how that satisfaction is being measured.

For more on performance measures, see **Learning exercise 4.13**.

4.13 Learning Exercise

Developing appropriate performance measures

The managing director of Fizzy Drinks Company is concerned about media reports coming out of India that are critical of a division of the organisation that is operating in a rural area of that country. The company is being criticised for its use of water to make soft drinks, in particular the negative impact this is having on water availability for people in nearby villages. Apparently, water levels decline to such a level at some times of the year that some villagers are being effectively forced to buy the products of Fizzy Drinks Company just so they have something to drink in periods of low rainfall.

Some performance indicators need to be devised that can be used to motivate the local managers of Fizzy Drinks Company to be more responsive to local community concerns about water availability. Solving this issue needs careful and critical thinking – abilities we expect of both accountants and managers. If water use and community perceptions are two key issues of concern, then the performance indicators introduced need to address both of these issues.

Furthermore, at the very senior levels of management, managers might need to consider whether the organisation should actually be operating in this geographical area, or whether it should be operating in areas with greater water supply. Or, if water is more abundant in some months of the year than in others, then perhaps local managers might need to consider scheduling their production of soft drinks during those periods of greater rainfall.

Effectively, water is the constraining, or scarce, factor, and the organisation needs to consider how to maximise the contribution per unit of this constraining factor (accounting in the presence of constraining factors was considered in Chapter 3).

Alternatively, to increase water availability for local villagers, the organisation might consider the feasibility of constructing some form of dam to retain water in times of high rains (the impacts of creating a dam on downstream villages and the environment would also need to be considered).

In terms of potential performance indicators that might be used to evaluate and motivate managers to address the water scarcity problem, we could consider using the following:

- *Measures of water use*. Budgets should be established for water based on increasing the efficiency of its use. More particularly, a base level of water use for a given level of production could be established, and targets for water savings could then be developed for each budgetary period, with these targeted savings increased across time. Managers might receive a monetary bonus (which needs to be of a size likely to motivate them) that is linked to meeting or exceeding budgeted water savings. This would encourage the managers to consider all uses of water, and not only the water used to make the soft drinks but also the water used for cleaning recycled bottles, plant and machinery, and so forth, so as to identify methods to reduce water use. The possibility of water-recycling initiatives might also be addressed.
- *Measures of community acceptance*. Independent organisations might be employed by the head office of Fizzy Drinks Company to develop instruments (such as questionnaires/surveys) to assess the local community's perception of the organisation. If community acceptance of the organisation is assessed by the independent agency as improving, then this could be linked to some form of management bonus.

As we have already explained, it is important that the people being assessed are senior enough to be able to influence, and have control over, the performance indicators being used; that they participated in the target-setting process; and that they accepted the reasons for implementing the performance indicators. Also, any targets being assessed must be accepted as achievable and controllable, and managers should receive frequent feedback on how they are performing relative to the targets being set.

Another important point to be made here, linking back to the earlier chapters of this book, is that stakeholders – for example, the nearby villagers – would expect the organisation to produce an account (that is, the organisation needs to be accountable) for that area of operations for which the local villagers believe the organisation should be responsible. In this case, water use seems to be a key area of concern. Therefore, the organisation should regularly communicate with the local community about what it is doing to limit its water use and to possibly build infrastructure to support the community's ongoing access to water. Such communication, through the production of certain publicly available accounts, could act to improve the community's perceptions of the organisation. Arguably, such accountability should always be accepted by organisations operating in such areas.

The potential for negative outcomes

Just as using budgets, and assigning particular performance indicators to particular managers, can create positive behavioural outcomes, it is also possible that they can create negative behavioural outcomes. We have already considered the case of Russian chandeliers (see **Learning exercise 4.3**). In the previous discussion we also discussed the potential that managers might opportunistically introduce some form of 'budgetary slack' into the budgeting process.

A very high profile example of negative behavioural outcomes that generated huge amounts of publicity throughout the world – was the case of Volkswagen and its manipulation of emission results for some of its car models.

In summary, to achieve certain sales targets, Volkswagen cars needed to demonstrate low levels of emissions, particularly in the United States. To achieve this, software was embedded within millions of diesel cars – this has since been referred to as 'defeat device' software. When the cars were tested on a stationary platform, the software changed the way in which the cars operated such that emissions were reduced, thereby showing that the cars had extremely low emissions relative to other cars – the software triggered what was known as the 'safety mode', in which the engines ran below normal power and performance. However, when the cars were actually moving, this software was not activated and the emissions of the cars were actually very high, well beyond US emission standards.

The scandal came to light in September 2015 when the United States Environmental Protection Agency issued Volkswagen with a Notice of Violation of the *Clean Air Act* for sales made between 2009 and 2015. Following news of the scandal, the shares of Volkswagen dropped by about a third. The scandal has ultimately cost the company many billions of dollars in fines and product-recall-related costs.

In terms of Volkswagen's response, the following was reported:

> 'We've totally screwed up', said VW America boss Michael Horn, while the group's chief executive at the time, Martin Winterkorn, said his company had 'broken the trust of our customers and the public'. Mr Winterkorn resigned as a direct result of the scandal and was replaced by Matthias Mueller, the former boss of Porsche. 'My most urgent task is to win back trust for the Volkswagen Group – by leaving no stone unturned', Mr Mueller said on taking up his new post.
>
> Source: Hotten (2015).

While this is a very extreme case, it shows how a focus on certain budgetary targets – in this case sales of cars – can create very negative outcomes. That is, it can contribute to a lack of goal congruence. It also shows how the activities of managers trying to achieve certain outcomes (increasing sales) can impact the results of other managers (for example, those charged with managing the environmental performance of an organisation). Also, there would be various senior managers throughout Volkswagen who would have held shares in the organisation, or who might have received bonuses based on share price movements. They would have been impacted by the actions of those responsible for putting the 'cheating' software in the cars. Clearly, the managers did not work together as a team, and the consequence of this was that the efforts of many managers were undermined by the actions of some managers.

Whenever particular performance indicators are used (such as target sales) to reward managers, care needs to be taken to ensure that the managers are not distracted in a way that is harmful to the organisation, or to its stakeholders. That is, when setting targets, an awareness of potential behavioural impacts is necessary. Furthermore, research suggests that when budgetary targets are used to assess managers, those managers might – particularly if they participate in the budgetary process – act to create some budgetary slack in the targets, thereby making them easier to achieve. The actions of some managers at Volkswagen, however, went well beyond the potential problem of managers trying to create budgetary slack.

The practice of accounting – in this instance, the use of budgets and associated performance indicators – can potentially create many social and environmental impacts. Accounting really is very interesting, and it is very important in influencing how people behave and the impacts that behaviour might create! This again reinforces the point that has been made throughout this book, this being that 'accounting' is both a technical practice and a social practice.

Why do I need to understand the possible behavioural implications associated with the budgeting process?

One of the central purposes for compiling a budget is to provide a basis for planning that then is expected to influence relevant personnel/managers to achieve particular targets. That is, budgets are designed to influence behaviour in a way that ideally encourages all relevant people to work together towards achieving particular organisation goals. Ideally, there will be 'goal congruence' between all budgetary participants.

Given that budgets are compiled to influence behaviour then it would be expected that some aspects or attributes of budgeting will create relatively more preferred outcomes than others. A manager needs to know which attributes of budgets might create different behaviours within managerial groups, and there is a great deal of research that addresses such issues. As we have discussed, some factors that are thought to have possible behavioural implications – and which we need to understand if we become managers – include: the extent of participation in the budgetary process; the perceived level of difficulty with respect to achieving budgetary targets; senior managers' apparent support for budgetary targets; types and frequency of budgetary feedback; and the way budgetary targets are linked to payments to budgetary participants.

STUDY TOOLS

SUMMARY

In relation to budgeting, we can use our accountability model (why/to whom/what/how) to explain various facets of accounting.

In terms of *why* an organisation would undertake budgeting, it is done with the intention of encouraging managers to act in accordance with an organisation's mission and its strategic plan. While the strategic plan is a long-term plan, the budget provides guidance, and impacts behaviour, in the short term in a way that is expected to be consistent with the organisation's strategic plan and its mission. It is also useful for ensuring the organisation has adequate resources.

In terms of *to whom* the budget information is provided, it is given to managers as a means for planning and then for control. Most budgetary information will not be released externally because of the potential loss of competitive advantage. Also, the budget represents plans that may or may not be achieved. If the public was to know of all the plans, and made decisions on the basis of them, then legal and/or reputational problems might arise if budgetary targets are not subsequently met.

In terms of *what* information will be included within the budgets, they can address and create targets for both financial and non-financial aspects of performance. This chapter has emphasised that one of the most important financial budgets for any organisation is the cash budget, as all organisations need to properly control their cash. The other aspects of performance to be addressed within budgets will be influenced by the activities undertaken by an organisation, its mission, and relatedly, the responsibilities that have been accepted and embraced by managers. The contents of the budget will also be influenced by factors such as whether various managers participated in the budgetary process and therefore whether they were able to bring their insights to the process.

In terms of *how* the budget is disclosed to managers, an organisation can choose whatever way it wants to communicate the information. However, the budget-related information must be timely, reliable, and clearly indicate the relevant variances (be understandable), as well as who has responsibility for such variances.

ANSWERS TO THE OPENING QUESTIONS

At the beginning of the chapter we asked the following three questions. As a result of reading this chapter, you should now be able to provide informed answers to these questions – ours are shown below.

1 Is it necessary for all organisations to prepare budgets?

Yes, it is necessary for all organisations to prepare budgets. Budgets are a means of promoting planning and control, and putting in place short-term goals that are consistent with the longer-term strategic plans of an organisation. The preparation of cash budgets is particularly important for most organisations, as well as for most people.

2 What is a master budget? Which individual budget would typically be the first one prepared within a master budget, and why?

The master budget is a comprehensive set of budgets that provides coverage of an organisation's activities. It consists of several interdependent budgets that, when brought together as the master budget, create a reasonably cohesive organisational plan for a specified period of time. The first budget to be prepared within a master budget would be the one that relates to the activity considered to be the driver of most of the other activities. For example, in many organisations, projected sales – as reflected in a sales budget – would drive the activities that follow, such as the amount of production required (for a manufacturing organisation), or the quantity of products to be purchased (for a retail organisation), and would also feed into decisions about the resources required to facilitate the budgeted level of production or sales.

3 Can budgets be used as a means of motivating managers, and if so, how?

Budgets can be used to motivate managers. They provide managers with plans (targets) that they are expected to work towards achieving. However, as this chapter has explained, the motivation of managers will be influenced by a number of factors, including whether they have participated in the budgetary process, whether the budgetary targets are considered to be achievable, and whether they are allowed to properly explain the reasons for variances, the timeliness of variance reports, and so forth. This chapter has also indicated that the motivation of managers might be further enhanced if they were provided with monetary bonuses that were linked to budget-related targets. However, the performance indicators used in these managerial bonus schemes must be carefully considered before implementation, otherwise various dysfunctional impacts might arise (we made particular reference to Russian chandeliers and VW cars).

SELF-TEST QUIZ

Answers to this quiz appear in the Appendix of this book.

Bay of Fires Company is planning to commence a business to produce one type of boardshort. As part of its planning process, it wants you to produce a budget for the first three months of operation.

You have been provided with the following information so that you can construct a budget for the first three months (first quarter) of operations:

- The target sales for the budgetary period (first three months) are 15 000 units.
- The selling price for each boardshort is $110, and that price will be kept constant.
- There is no beginning inventory of finished goods, and the inventory manager wants to have inventory of 1000 boardshorts at the end of the first three months.
- There is no opening materials inventory, and the manager wants the materials inventory at the end of each quarter to be 400 metres at $20 per metre.
- Each boardshort requires 1 metre of material.
- The material cost of $20 per metre is not expected to change for the next year.
- The labour hours for each boardshort are expected to be 1 hour, and the wage cost is $30 per hour. These costs are not expected to change during the year.

The managers of Bay of Fires Company have determined the following manufacturing overhead costs:

Indirect materials (cotton, labels) per boardshort	$2.00
Electricity per boardshort	$0.50
Maintenance on machinery per boardshort	$0.40
Factory supervisor's salary per quarter	$40 000
Factory rent per quarter	$45 000
Rates and insurance for factory per quarter	$10 000

Bay of Fires Company expects to incur the following selling and administrative costs:

- freight out to stores and customers: $4 per boardshort sold
- advertising costs per quarter: $5000
- office salaries: $40 000 per quarter
- rent on administration building: $10 000 per quarter
- rates and insurance on administration building: $4000 per quarter

In relation to payments and receipts of cash and cash balances:

- The cash balance at the beginning of the quarter is $10 000
- Many sales are made on credit terms. Ninety per cent of sales are collected in the quarter in which the sale is made, and the remaining 10 per cent is collected in the next quarter
- There were no sales in the previous quarter
- Bay of Fires Company buys its material on credit terms. It pays its suppliers 75 per cent of the purchase price in the same quarter as the purchase, and it pays the remaining 25 per cent in the following quarter. There were no opening creditors
- Labour costs are paid in the quarter in which they are incurred
- Manufacturing overhead expenses, and selling and administrative overhead expenses, are paid in the quarter in which they are incurred
- A loan of $60 000 will be repaid in the first three months of operations
- Bay of Fires Company intends to invest in a new machine in the second month of the first quarter, at a cost of $120 000
- The owners of Bay of Fires Company intend to withdraw $100 000 from the business at the end of each quarter.

To answer the following questions you will need to construct most of the budgets that form part of a master budget.

1 How many boardshorts are projected to be produced for the first three months of operations?

a 14 000 b 15 000 c 16 000 d 17 000 e None of these choices

2 How much fabric shall be acquired in terms of both materials and purchase price?

a 16 000 metres at a total cost of $320 000 b 16 400 metres at a total cost of $328 000
c 16 800 metres at a total cost of $334 000 d 17 000 metres at a total cost of $340 000
e None of these choices

3 What will be the total required labour hours and associated labour cost?

a 14 000 hours at a total cost of $420 000 b 15 000 hours at a total cost of $450 000
c 16 000 hours at a total cost of $480 000 d 17 000 hours at a total cost of $520 000
e None of these choices

4 What will be the amount of cash to be collected from customers in the first three months of operations?

a 1 485 000 b 1 500 000 c 1 650 000
d 1 720 000 e None of these choices

5 What is the expected closing balance of cash at the end of the first three months of operations?

a $219 600 b $229 600 c $232 100
d $238 600 e None of these choices

ONLINE RESOURCES

Accompanying the book is an innovative online case study that follows an organisation initially established by two friends, which grows into a large and successful company. Acquire this chapter's case study from your instructor.

CASE STUDY

Armadillo Surf Designs: Too early to throw in the towel

A recent market and data analysis indicates that approximately 85% of Armadillo Surf Designs' (ASD) sales are from their men's lines and just 15% of sales are from their female lines. As a result, the business is launching a new beach towel range in order to broaden their appeal to the female market.

Prepare the operating budgets for the new beach towel range and consider the positive and negative impacts that may arise from the proposed reward system for manufacturing staff. Following the launch of the beach towel range, monitor favourable and unfavourable sales and cost variances and identify the potential causes of such variances.

END-OF-CHAPTER QUESTIONS

4.1 Why should an organisation prepare budgets?

4.2 Why might there be a difference between sales revenue and cash received from customers, in a given period?

4.3 What is a master budget?

4.4 Why would a sales budget typically be the first budget prepared within a master budget?

4.5 Why would the cash budget be prepared after all the operating budgets have been prepared?

4.6 If the cash budget projects a lot of cash on hand in future periods, is this actually a problem? Clearly justify your answer.

4.7 What is a budget variance, and should both favourable and unfavourable variances be investigated?

4.8 If a university is preparing a master budget, what would be the nature of the first budget prepared as part of this master budget?

4.9 If a budget creates goals or targets that are extremely hard to achieve, would this be good for motivating managers? Provide the reasoning for your answer.

4.10 What are some of the differences between the budgets prepared for a manufacturing organisation and those prepared for a retail organisation that buys and sells completed goods?

4.11 What is 'budgetary slack' and why could it exist?

4.12 If Lennox Head and Co has projected sales of 25 000 units for the year, has 1000 units in opening stock, and seeks to increase closing stock to 4000 units, how many units does it need to produce in the year?

4.13 If Crescent Head and Co starts the year with 10 000 units that cost \$85 000, produces 100 000 units during the year at a cost of \$900 000, and ends the financial year with 5000 units that cost \$45 000 to produce, then how many units did it sell and what were the costs of sales for the year?

4.14 Would we expect an organisation to make its master budget publicly available for review by interested stakeholders? Explain the reasoning used to support your answer.

4.15 In what way would comparing budgeted and actual performance assist future budgeting?

4.16 What would be the reason for saying that the longer the time frame of a budget, the more likely the various costs will be controllable?

4.17 If the managerial head of a university – who might be referred to as the vice-chancellor or president – is given a target, and an associated bonus, of increasing student numbers, what possible dysfunctional impacts might this have?

4.18 What is the difference between a static budget and a flexible budget, and why would it generally be necessary to prepare a flexible budget?

4.19 Provide an example of where a manager's fixation on achieving, or favourably exceeding, a budget target might actually have negative impacts on the organisation.

4.20 We stated that, from a social performance perspective, it is common to find managers being paid bonuses that are tied to customer satisfaction, or measures of the health and safety of employees. Identify possible ways of measuring 'customer satisfaction' or the 'health and safety of employees', then explain how these measures might be linked to managerial bonuses, and your reasoning behind why they might be linked.

4.21 Because of rising local wages and material costs, Willy Wetsuits has decided to outsource its production of wetsuits to supply factories in Dhaka, Bangladesh. What non-financial aspects of performance might Willy Wetsuits incorporate into its future budgetary processes as a result of this initiative?

4.22 It was reported that traders in the southern Indian state of Tamil Nadu would replace Coca-Cola with locally produced drinks because of concerns about how Coca-Cola was using scarce water resources, particularly during periods of low rainfall (Doshi, 2017). The article notes that while one small bottle of Coca-Cola directly uses about 1.9 litres of water, the product relies upon the growth of sugar cane, which consumes much water. If the water used to grow the sugarcane is also taken into account, then it is estimated that each bottle of cola actually takes about 400 litres of water to produce. Keeping in mind that water seems to be a constraining factor of production, suggest how the budgetary process might be used by Coca-Cola to reduce its water use, and how particular budgetary targets might be used to motivate the Indian-based managers of Coca-Cola to reduce water consumption.

4.23 Joel Parkerelli owns a large-scale surfing school – Radical Surfing School (RSS) – that operates in his friend Kelly Slateropoulos' wave pool. RSS has many students. To become a student, individuals need to sign up for membership, of which there are three levels: Gold, Silver and Bronze. Joel has come to you to help him prepare his budgets for the next 12 months, ending 31 December 2026. Based on expert marketing analysis, the number of memberships sold next year is expected to be 100 Gold, 200 Silver and 400 Bronze, and the membership fee is $8000, $4000 and $2000, respectively. Gold members have 24-hour-a-day access, including to night-surfing facilities; Silver members have daily access from 9 a.m. to 5 p.m., and Bronze members have access on weekends between 11 a.m. and 4 p.m.

RSS has hired a number of employees (10) on various salaries:

1 coaching director	$250 000 per year
3 coaches	$120 000 each per year
2 trainers	$90 000 each per year
3 administrative staff	$80 000 each per year
1 medical staff	$70 000 per year

RSS expects these operating expenses for the following 12 months:

Advertising expenses	$40 000
Insurance expense	$100 000
Surfing supplies	$50 per student per year
Rental of wave pool	$400 000 per year

You are required to prepare:

a a sales budget for the year ending 31 December 2026

b a labour budget for the year ending 31 December 2026

c a budgeted income statement for the year ending 31 December 2026.

4.24 Snacky McSnack and Co is a medium-sized and very successful manufacturer of 'healthy snack foods'. The organisation is undertaking planning for the next year and formulating budgets for its many departments, including marketing, purchasing and production. The purchasing manager, Olivia Oiarl, has found a new source of palm oil, an ingredient that is used in most of its products. Palm oil is currently sourced from an Australian organisation, Palm Plantations of Australia (www.palmplantations.com.au), a leader in the supply of sustainable palm oil. The proposed new supplier of palm oil – Cheapo de Palma – is located in South-East Asia and can supply palm oil at a price that is 50 per cent less than the current Australian supplier.

The budgeted financial profit can be substantially increased if Snacky McSnack and Co changes to the new supplier of palm oil. The budgeted purchasing and production costs can be substantially reduced, although there will be increased freight costs as the oil will be transported by road and sea. The CEO of Snacky McSnack and Co, Anna Seed, who receives a monetary bonus based on the company's profits, has decided to change to the new supplier. However, the CEO has received strong objections from the marketing manager, Lyndsey Ede, who thinks that sales of products might decline as the new palm oil is not sustainable palm oil. The marketing manager receives a monetary bonus that is based on sales revenue.

You are required to do the following:

a Provide reasons as to why the marketing manager might think sales of products will decline.

b Discuss what social and/or environmental costs or benefits might be experienced if Snacky McSnack and Co changes suppliers.

c Discuss how, or whether, these social and/or environmental costs or benefits might be accounted for in the budgets.

d Discuss whether you consider the bonus incentives that are offered to the managers at Snacky McSnack and Co beneficial to the organisation.

e What do you think the CEO will do, and why?

4.25 Farelly Shirts produces a one-size-fits-all Hawaiian shirt. You are provided with the following information in relation to the company's activities:

i The budgets are for the 2026 year and are broken into four quarters. The target sales for 2026 by each respective quarter of the year (Q) are:
- Q1 25 000 shirts
- Q2 27 000 shirts
- Q3 30 000 shirts
- Q4 30 000 shirts.

ii The selling price for each shirt is $130 and will be kept constant throughout the year.

iii The beginning inventory of shirts at the start of quarter 1 is 2500, which cost $260 000 to produce in the previous year, and the inventory manager wants to increase inventory to 5000 shirts at the end of each quarter.

iv Each shirt requires 1.25 metres of material.

v The opening material inventory is 625 metres at $40 per metre, and the manager wants materials inventory at the end of each quarter to increase to 1250 metres at $40 per metre. The material cost is not expected to change for the next year.

vi Labour hours for each shirt are expected to be 2.5 hours, while wages are $20 per hour and are not expected to increase during the period.

vii Based on last year's information and reasonable forecasts, Farelly Shirts has determined the following manufacturing overhead costs:
- indirect materials (cotton, labels) per shirt: $2.50
- electricity per shirt: $2.00
- maintenance on machinery per shirt: $0.50
- supervisor's salary per quarter: $60 000
- factory rent per quarter: $65 000
- rates and insurance per quarter: $20 000.

viii Farelly Shirts expects to incur the following selling and administrative costs:
- freight out to stores and customers: $7.00 per shirt sold
- advertising costs per quarter: $20 000
- office salaries: $40 000 per quarter
- rent on administration building: $25 000 per quarter
- rates and insurance on administration building: $5000 per quarter.

ix The cash balance at the beginning of January 2026 is $20 000.

x The sales are all made on credit terms. Ninety per cent of sales are collected in the quarter of sale and the remaining 10 per cent are collected in the next quarter. The sales in the final quarter of 2025 were $950 000.

xi The organisation buys all of its material on credit terms. It pays its suppliers 85 per cent of the purchase price in the same quarter as a purchase, and it pays the remaining 15 per cent in the following quarter. Purchases of materials for the last quarter of 2025 amounted to $200 000.

xii Labour costs are paid in the quarter in which they are incurred.

xiii Manufacturing overhead expenses, and selling and administrative overhead expenses, are paid in the quarter in which they arise.

xiv Farelly Shirts intends to use cash to invest in a new machine in quarter 3 at a cost of $100 000.

xv The owners of Farelly Shirts intend to withdraw $120 000 from the business at the end of each quarter to compensate them for the investment they have made in the organisation.

xvi Senior management wants to maintain a minimum of $25 000 in cash on hand at the end of each quarter as a buffer for any unexpected cash needs.

You are required to prepare a:

a sales budget
b production budget
c direct materials budget
d direct labour budget
e manufacturing overhead expenses budget
f selling and administrative overhead expenses budget
g cash budget, together with an evaluation of this budget
h budgeted income statement, together with an evaluation of this statement.

4.26 Think of a not-for-profit organisation that you know and then describe the various types of budgets you think they might need to use in order to manage the organisation. In doing so, you should also try to explain how each of the budgets links to, or influences, the other budgets.

REFERENCES

Baxter International (2020). *Corporate responsibility report.* https://www.baxter.com/sites/g/files/ebysai746/files/2021-07/Baxter_2020_Corporate_Responsibility_Report.pdf

Doshi, Vidhi (2017). Indian traders boycott Coca-Cola for 'straining water resources'. *The Guardian*, 2 March. www.theguardian.com/world/2017/mar/01/indian-traders-boycott-coca-cola-for-straining-water-resources

Hotten, Russell (2015). Volkswagen: The scandal explained. BBC News, 10 December. www.bbc.com/news/business-34324772

Interface (2021). Climate disclosure year end 2020. interfaceinc.scene7.com/is/content/InterfaceInc/Interface/Americas/WebsiteContentAssets/Documents/Whitepapers/Sustainability%20Climate%20Disclosure/wc_am-sustainability-climatedisclosure2020.pdf

Watercare, (2021). *Annual Report 2021.* https://watercareannualreport.co.nz/

CHAPTER 5

PERFORMANCE MEASUREMENT AND EVALUATION – FURTHER CONSIDERATIONS

LEARNING OBJECTIVES

After completing this chapter, readers should be able to:

- **LO5.1** describe the meaning of life cycle analysis and explain why managers might perform it
- **LO5.2** describe the process known as life cycle costing and explain why managers might undertake such analysis
- **LO5.3** explain material flow cost accounting and describe why managers might apply it
- **LO5.4** describe how we can use accounting techniques to reduce the quantity and financial costs of waste
- **LO5.5** describe the Balanced Scorecard approach and explain how it can be used in managing an organisation
- **LO5.6** describe the meaning of 'capital investment decisions' and explain four tools that are often used to evaluate potential capital investment projects.

OPENING QUESTION

Before reading the balance of this chapter, please consider how you would answer the following question. We will return to this question at the end of the chapter, where we suggest an answer.

The managers of an organisation are concerned that they might be generating too much waste, but their accountant tells them that there is nothing to worry about because it only costs $1000 a month for a rubbish removal contractor to take away all the waste that is generated within the organisation. Also, the managers are worried about where all the waste goes, but the accountant tells them: 'Don't worry about that. Once the contractor collects the waste from us, it is no longer our problem'.

Has the accountant provided the managers with good advice?

Introduction

This is the third chapter dealing with the broad area of management accounting. In previous chapters, a number of key areas have been addressed in terms of management accounting, specifically the following:

- The difference between management accounting and financial accounting has been explained.
- The functions that managers perform in collaboration with accountants (for example, planning future activities, implementing plans, monitoring and evaluating performance, learning, revising, and adjusting plans) have been identified.
- We have emphasised that, when planning, managers need to consider both the shorter term and the longer term, and we have highlighted the need for incorporating considerations of sustainable development into managerial planning and evaluation processes.
- The idea of 'value' and how managers should focus on creating value across their value chain has been explored, and in doing so we have explained that different stakeholders can have different perceptions of what constitutes value.
- We have explained how the 'behaviour' of costs can be analysed in terms of them being variable or fixed, and in doing so we introduced the idea of the contribution margin and break-even analysis, and we also explored how to manage an organisation in the presence of constraining factors of production.
- The process of budgeting has been introduced, and issues such as who needs to do budgeting, the benefits of budgeting, and the meaning and use of a master budget have been addressed.
- We have emphasised that budgets can be developed for both financial and non-financial aspects of performance, and we have provided insights into the potential behavioural impacts of the budgetary process, particularly when budget-related targets are being used to motivate managers through the use of related management bonus schemes.

In this chapter – the final chapter devoted to what we have labelled 'management accounting' – we will build upon what we already know, and we will consider some other approaches to performance evaluation and measurement that can be used by managers and accountants. Specifically, we will discuss the use of:

- life cycle analysis and life cycle costing
- material flow cost accounting

- the Balanced Scorecard
- tools to assist us with our capital investment decisions.

In this chapter, there is a strong emphasis on managers needing to have an in-depth understanding of their respective production and/or service processes with regard to the material flows, social and environmental life cycle impacts, and the associated cash flows. Such an understanding is necessary before managers can properly determine what aspects of performance could, or perhaps *should*, be measured and managed and perhaps what planned activities should be abandoned.

For example, if managers are concerned about the social and environmental impacts of a product or service, then arguably they should develop a full understanding of the entire life cycle of that product or service, including what happens to products at the end of their useful life. One approach here, which we briefly referred to in Chapter 2, could be life cycle analysis. Life cycle analysis is not typically undertaken in a way that measures financial costs, but rather tends to look at physical flows. Such analysis is important in allowing managers to understand various impacts that could flow from what an organisation currently does, or what it plans to do. Life cycle costing, on the other hand, attempts to attribute costs to some of the various activities, and impacts, that happen across a product's, or service's, life cycle.

Another approach to understanding how resources are used within particular processes is through a process known as material flow accounting, which focuses on recording the inputs of particular materials into a production process, and the outputs, including wastes, that come from that process.

Yet another approach to measuring overall performance is the Balanced Scorecard, which emphasises the need to develop a system of performance evaluation that explicitly considers various aspects of organisational performance – and not just those that can be measured in financial terms.

Later in this chapter, we will also identify some issues to consider when making decisions with respect to acquiring property, plant and equipment (which we will refer to as 'capital investment decisions'). Apart from emphasising the need to consider the social and environmental implications of such decisions, we will also consider a number of financially oriented tools that managers use to assess potential capital investments. Specifically, the payback period approach, the accounting rate of return, the present value model, and the internal rate of return will be discussed.

What is being emphasised here is that there is a variety of approaches available in addition to those we described within Chapters 3 and 4, which enable managers to understand, in a reasonably comprehensive or holistic way, the performance of an organisation, and, importantly, the possibilities for improvement. Organisations will not necessarily apply all these approaches (some organisations might not apply any of them). However, those managers seeking to create a competitive edge over other organisations, or seeking to operate in a socially and environmentally responsible manner, will attempt to understand the various phases of their operations, and the opportunities for adding value at these different phases. As community expectations continue to increase in relation to organisations minimising the adverse social and environmental impacts of their processes, a manager's need for greater knowledge of the various impacts and costs created by an organisation also correspondingly increases.

One last point that we will make here is that many other accounting textbooks discuss topics such as life cycle analysis, life cycle costing and material flow cost accounting in separate chapters, with titles such as 'sustainability and management accounting', 'measuring and reporting sustainability', and 'sustainable business management'. By contrast, this book sees sustainability-related issues as a core part of managing an organisation, and hence we have incorporated these issues into the main chapters addressing management accounting.

Separating or compartmentalising considerations of sustainable development away from general management functions (such as planning, monitoring and control) is arguably one of the reasons why the natural environment is becoming so degraded. We would prefer **not** to treat social and environmental issues separately.

LO5.1 Life cycle analysis

If managers do want to understand, and potentially measure and control, the important economic, social and environmental impacts created by their products and services – and in this book, we have embraced the view that all managers *should* have such an interest – *then* life cycle analysis (LCA) is one way of gaining this knowledge. LCA is exactly what the name suggests – it is the process of analysing or evaluating a product or service across its entire life, often referred to as analysing a product or service 'from the cradle to the grave'. For example, for a product, the LCA might start with the extraction of the required raw materials and end with a consideration of what happens to the product at the end of its life; that is, on disposal. Different managers will make different decisions about the extent, or range, of the life of the product that will be subject to analysis, and the types, or ranges, of impacts that they will analyse.

life cycle analysis (LCA) The process of analysing, or evaluating, a product or service across its entire life, often referred to as analysing a product or service from the cradle to the grave

Key concept

Life cycle analysis (LCA) is one important way in which managers can understand, and potentially measure and control, the significant economic, social and environmental impacts of their products and services.

Understanding the impacts of products and services

To understand the various impacts created throughout the life cycle of a product or service, research is required. Managers and accountants typically need to involve various specialists in any analysis, including people with the relevant scientific backgrounds; for example, someone to advise what the environmental implications are of the waste that is being released into waterways and buried in landfill. Such analysis might be costly, and therefore the usual costs-versus-benefits testing associated with collecting information is generally undertaken. The life cycle of a product is represented in Figure 5.1.

Once the life cycle of a product or service has been understood, managers can (with the assistance of the relevant experts) attempt to understand the various resources being consumed, and the outputs (including wastes and emissions) and impacts (including positive and negative social and environmental impacts) being generated at each phase of the life cycle.

Even though some of the organisations involved in the various life cycle phases might be unrelated to the organisation undertaking the analysis (unrelated organisations within the supply chain), LCA can, and arguably should, analyse the social and environmental impacts generated across the entire life cycle of the product or service – particularly those that are considered to be significant. Each phase of the life cycle potentially creates different impacts. For example, there could be particular economic, social and environmental impacts arising from:

- *the mining of the required raw materials* – there could be various toxic wastes created as a result of the mining, excessive use of water as part of the mining process, the destruction of important plant or animal habitats or areas of cultural significance, or the displacement of particular indigenous peoples (for some discussion of the importance of ensuring the protection of important sites of cultural significance, see **Learning exercise 5.1**)

- *the manufacture of the product* – manufacturing a product typically requires labour input, and therefore various occupational health and safety issues can arise; energy is typically required, which will likely create carbon emissions; different wastes are generated throughout the production process, which can create social and environmental impacts
- *the distribution and/or installation of the product* – there could be numerous issues to do with packaging, carbon emissions and other forms of damage by ships and vehicles, animal welfare associated with the transportation of live animals, and safety issues associated with installation
- *the use and maintenance of the product* – the use of the product might create a variety of dangers for people or the environment; and the ongoing maintenance of the product might create various social and environmental impacts
- *the ultimate disposal of the product* – various components of the product could be recycled, or will be toxic to air or water if not responsibly disposed of. In **Figure 5.1**, we show that some products might be recycled at the end of their life cycles – wholly or in part. Many organisations now strategically design their products in a way that maximises the amount of recycling that can occur, with the ultimate aim that 100 per cent of the components of the products can be recycled – something often referred to as a 'closed-loop design' – and where materials are diverted from going to landfill. In Chapter 4, we referred to the US healthcare company Baxter and identified (in **Exhibit 4.3**) how the organisation had a goal of 'zero waste to landfill'.

LCA provides managers with the information to allow them to make sustainable and responsible decisions. Once managers have this knowledge, they can then consider what improvements might be necessary, what production designs might be amended, and so forth.

FIGURE 5.1 Simple representation of the life cycle of a product

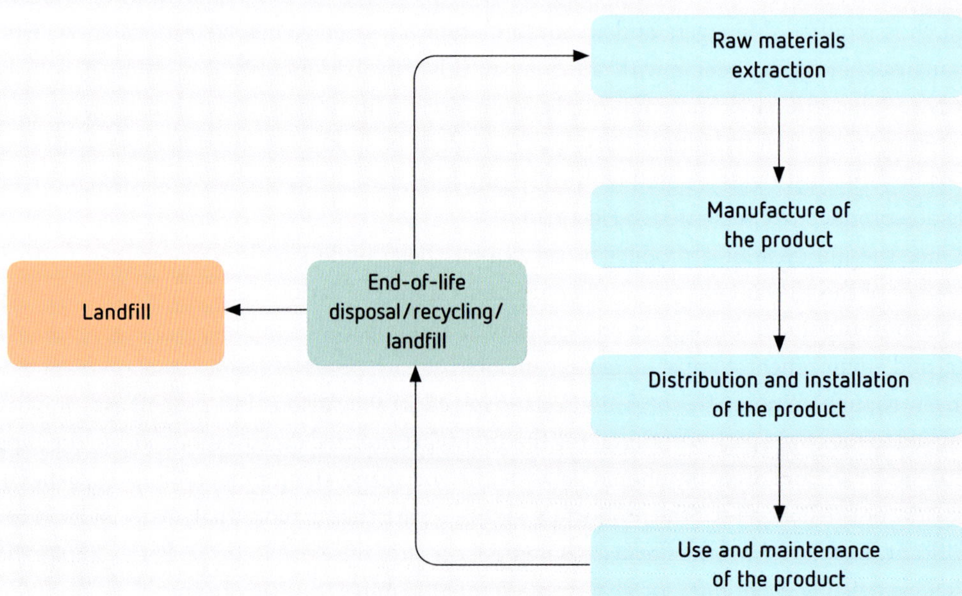

5.1 Learning Exercise

The need to consider impacts of organisational activities

In 2020 the global mining company Rio Tinto was linked to the destruction of a significant cultural site in Western Australia. The destruction received significant negative news media coverage and led to the departure of many senior staff. So, the question here is:

Should Rio Tinto have undertaken a thorough review of the intended area of mining to determine the likely impacts and implications associated with pursuing mining activities in the area?

The answer to this is an emphatic '**yes!**'. Rio Tinto should have performed a comprehensive assessment of likely impacts before progressing with its mining activities and should have embraced broader engagement with, and accountability to, affected stakeholders. In a report released in September 2021 by Rio Tinto, entitled *Communities and Social Performance Commitments Disclosure: Interim Report*, the Chief Executive of Rio Tinto stated (p. 1):

> The tragic destruction of the rock shelters in Juukan Gorge, in Western Australia, in May 2020 has had a deeply felt impact on the Puutu Kunti Kurrama and Pinikura (PKKP) people, other Traditional Owners of the lands on which we operate, Indigenous Peoples, as well as our own employees and other stakeholders in Australia and beyond. I am sorry for the pain and loss that this has created, and Rio Tinto is absolutely committed to listening, learning and showing greater care. This is a top priority.
>
> Over the past months, we have been working hard to rebuild trust and meaningful relationships with the PKKP people and other Traditional Owners. I know this will take significant time, but we are focused on improving our engagement with Indigenous Peoples and our host communities so that we can better understand their priorities and concerns, minimise our impacts, and responsibly manage Indigenous cultural heritage within our operations.
>
> We have also been working on several actions to strengthen our cultural heritage approach, processes and performance more broadly and increase transparency.
>
> Source: Communities and Social Performance Commitments Disclosure Interim Report, September (2021), riotinto.com.

As the above referenced report states, Rio Tinto has since revised how it engages with traditional owners of the lands on which they operate, and it has put in place many new governance policies to address such issues. It is clearly unacceptable for organisations to disregard such matters. Organisations must consider the various impacts that are created throughout the life cycle of their goods and services and arguably this should be done before the activities commence.

Assessing and reporting product and service impacts

Since products and services can create a multitude of social and environmental impacts, managers need to have some process at hand to objectively rank and prioritise the different impacts. They could elect to make this ranking exercise known to interested stakeholders, and they might involve various stakeholders in the ranking exercise once the data from the LCA is available. Those impacts that are most highly rated as important are then prioritised for attention and improvement.

In undertaking LCA, there is a requirement for managers to contemplate how different stakeholders view 'value creation' – other than perhaps just shareholders, who might be primarily interested in profits, or customers, who are often focused on the price and quality of the product but might not consider the social or environmental implications associated with its manufacture or disposal. As we indicated in Chapter 3, different stakeholders will have different views of 'value' creation. LCA can assist managers in determining where value can be added across the life cycles of their products and services, and this will be linked to how they rank and prioritise certain impacts for attention. The analysis should also link back to the mission and goals of the organisation, and will be useful for setting future performance targets based on notions of continuous improvement.

To the extent that managers believe they are accountable for various impacts associated with the products or services they are producing, they might also elect to make the results of their LCA publicly available – as we shall discuss later in this chapter, both the motor vehicle company Audi and the copier and camera company Ricoh do this.

As we have emphasised many times, the impacts of an organisation's operations, both good and bad, cannot all be measured in financial terms, but this does not make them unimportant, or mean that they should not be accounted for. For LCA, the use of financial measurements is not required (as we shall discuss shortly). For example, we might measure carbon emissions, water use, or wastewater release associated with production, or we might consider the implications for the environment when a product is scrapped – perhaps there will be toxic air emissions, or toxic releases to soil, which then find their way into water systems. Issues/impacts such as the loss of important animal habitats, overuse of water, contribution to global warming and so forth are often ignored by our financial accounting systems, and are often not reflected in the prices paid for goods or services. LCA can address some of this void.

Informing stakeholder decisions

From an external reporting perspective, the results of LCA will be of interest to many stakeholders, and in fact, as we have noted already, many organisations do publicly disclose information about their LCAs. By projecting a public image of accepting accountability for impacts across a product's life cycle, this becomes a sound basis for differentiating an organisation from its competitors, who might not demonstrate such a high level of accountability. Furthermore, the more informed different stakeholders (for example, consumers, investors, lenders, employees, government, the media) become about the life cycles of different products and services that are being produced by different organisations, the greater their ability to make an informed choice about whether they want to support particular organisations. As we have emphasised a number of times, knowledge provides us all with the *power* to make *more informed decisions* about the organisations we want to support.

Creating win–win scenarios

As a result of LCA, managers might be alerted to the need to find ways of reducing the use of water, energy, materials and transportation, and waste. This might not only have positive financial effects, but could also create positive social and environmental effects. This is often referred to as a win–win scenario, in which not only do the organisation and its owners win through reduced financial costs and therefore greater profits, but other stakeholders – including the environment – also win because of reduced environmental impacts.

Even if a win–win scenario cannot be demonstrated because there are no obvious financial benefits in the short run, this does not mean particular improvements should not be implemented – even though it might be somewhat harder to get the profit-seeking owners of an organisation to agree to the initiatives. Longer-term considerations of future organisational success do mean that even if a current initiative does not create a quick financial benefit for an organisation, managers should still perhaps do it as the win–win might become more apparent in future years. But again, it often comes back to the perceptions managers hold about what responsibilities they should embrace – in particular, to perceptions about *to whom* they owe a responsibility, and *for what* aspects of performance that responsibility relates to.

Encouraging eco-efficiency

One term often linked to reducing the environmental impacts associated with producing particular goods or services is *eco-efficiency*, which typically means 'doing more with less'. If we are able to produce a given quantity of units with less water, or with less raw materials, then we are being eco-efficient. However, whether we should be producing a particular good or service in the first place is a different issue to consider. For example, we might be able to produce extremely powerful cars with less materials and energy than other organisations, which is reflective of being eco-efficient, but this does not address the issue of whether any organisation should be producing such cars in the first instance. Answers to such philosophical questions are beyond the scope of this book.

Life cycle analysis of projected activities

Life cycle analysis is typically performed retrospectively in regard to production that has already occurred. But, if sufficient information is available, it can also be undertaken in relation to projected activities and as part of the planning phase of an operation. For example, if a manager is considering shifting the manufacture of their products to a different country, what are the implications? For example:

- What will be the differences in resource consumption?
- What will be the differences in social impacts; for example, are the factories there more dangerous, or are we diverting scarce water away from local communities?
- What will be the difference in environmental impacts; for example, from where does the energy come, where does the wastewater go, and what happens to other waste from the factory?
- What are the implications for transportation-related costs and impacts?

Life cycle analysis is a good basis for setting social and environmental targets for managers, and as such it can be an important complement to the budgeting processes that we discussed in Chapter 4. It also reinforces the need to incorporate issues associated with sustainable development into the planning process, something we stressed in Chapter 3.

For more discussion of the importance of conducting LCAs, see **Learning exercise 5.2**.

5.2 Learning Exercise

Why do managers need to conduct a life cycle analysis of an organisation's products?

Ideally, managers should have a detailed understanding of the various impacts that their products create – both good and bad. Also, there is arguably a moral obligation for managers to know which stakeholders (and we include the environment as a stakeholder here) might be impacted by a product or service, before they contemplate producing or selling that product or service.

It also makes good business sense for managers to know how various phases of a product or service's life cycle could potentially create adverse impacts. Being associated with adverse social and environmental outcomes may damage the reputation of an organisation, ultimately damaging its profitability. Therefore, undertaking some form of life cycle analysis is a type of risk-reduction strategy.

Which organisations usually conduct a life cycle analysis?

All managers should have knowledge of the life cycles of their goods and services, but in practice it is larger organisations that are more likely to do this type of analysis, because the volume of their activities can be linked to potentially greater impacts. They also typically have the necessary financial resources to enable them to do a life cycle analysis in a meaningful way.

Real-world examples of where life cycle analysis would have been useful

There are many instances where organisations have been linked to activities that have created adverse social and/or environmental impacts, and this has proven costly for the respective organisations. Here are a few high-profile, real-world examples:

- For many years, McDonald's was criticised for the amount of packaging and other waste being generated by its food outlets. Some customers boycotted the company's products as a result of this negative publicity. McDonald's has since undertaken a life cycle analysis and developed targets that have reduced waste and the related financial costs.
- As noted in Chapter 4, recent news articles have been highly critical of Coca-Cola for an alleged excessive use of water in places such as rural India. This has led to boycotts of its products by some groups. Life cycle analysis of the production of soft drinks in these locations would have helped highlight the levels of water use, and signalled the need to consider the impacts this use of water might have on surrounding communities.
- The mining company BHP has received much negative publicity over several decades for allowing tailings (mining wastes) to spill into rivers and other waterways, notably in Papua New Guinea, and more recently in Brazil. This has resulted in many millions of dollars in fines and other damages being awarded against the organisation. A life cycle analysis might have identified the relevant waste streams and the risks they posed to the environment and local communities.
- The destruction of culturally significant rock shelters in Juukan Gorge in Western Australia in May 2020 by the global mining company Rio Tinto created significant stress to the traditional owners of the land and to many other stakeholders. Mining companies need to do much better and to ensure that culturally significant sites are not damaged or destroyed as part of the mining process. As indicated earlier in this chapter, Rio Tinto released a report in September 2021 entitled *Communities and Social Performance Commitments Disclosure: Interim Report* (available at www.riotinto.com) which reports some of the initiatives it has introduced to help ensure this does not happen again.

Examples of life cycle analysis

LCA can potentially be carried out for any product or service. Consider the following, for example.

Life cycle of a car

Producing a car requires various raw materials, including steel, aluminium, rubber and plastics. Car production also requires energy, water and different forms of freight. Throughout its life, a car will also create various emissions, and ultimately, a car will typically be scrapped after a certain number of years and this has many social and environmental implications. Different cars, using different methods of production, and different sources and types of components, will create different impacts.

In relation to the life cycle of cars, we can consider the information provided by Audi on its website as accessed in July 2022 (www.audi.com). On the website, Audi refers to its use of LCA and also to the idea of a 'circular economy' and 'closed loops':

> **Considering the entire value chain**
>
> The full potential of the circular economy can only be exploited if the entire and very complex automotive value chain – which extends from development and material procurement to production and sales and all the way to utilization and recovery – is considered and, to a certain degree, rethought. According to Meinen: 'At Audi we want to find sustainable business models that can be implemented to the ultimate benefit of all stakeholders.' As early as 2017, for example, Audi launched an Aluminum Closed Loop in vehicle production, demonstrating just how effective a circular economy can be.
>
> With a view to bundling the ongoing activities in the company and increasing the spotlight on the topic, Audi established a project house in August 2021 with experts from all of the divisions working together to find solutions – in exchange with external partners, too.
>
> 'We cannot achieve the transformation single-handedly,' says Dennis Christian Meinen, considering the complex value chain. 'We are working hand in hand with partner companies and research organizations in the project house to take decisive steps toward a circular vehicle. The key signals are laid as early as the product design and not simply when individual parts arrive at the plant gates or even at the recycling stage.'
>
> **Keeping recycling in mind right from the outset**
>
> Who gives any thought to recycling an Audi at the first glimpse of a new one? Audi does! Aspects such as reuse and recyclability are considered as early as the development stage of a vehicle – and thus years before the first series-production vehicle leaves the plant. Statutory requirements create the framework for this planning.
>
> Each part has to be considered individually when the vehicle reaches its end of life in terms of deciding what further action to take. Initially, of course, the goal should be to reuse or repair. For instance, transmissions can be reconditioned and resold for reuse, while lithium-ion batteries from electric vehicles can start a new life as energy storage devices when they no longer meet the exacting requirements for use in a vehicle.
>
> **Using recyclates in new vehicles**
>
> Processed plastics derived from a recycling process, otherwise known as recyclates, are being used in more and more vehicles as a contribution to resource conservation. The goal is not just to reduce carbon emissions, but also to use resources efficiently.
>
> The Audi Q4 e-tron electric SUV has more than two dozen parts that contain a proportion of recycled material. The material from which these parts are manufactured comes from sources such as industrial production waste and is also used to produce components like the front-end carrier – a part that has to meet particularly high mechanical demands. What is more, a significant proportion of the headlight mounts, wheel well liners, fender covers, floor covering and the wheel spoilers is made from secondary raw materials.
>
> **Chemical recycling of plastics**
>
> Can the concept of the Aluminium Closed Loop also work with other materials and with a view to recycling vehicles? This is a challenge especially in terms of mixed plastic waste that cannot be sorted by type – but one that Audi is ready to embrace. Chemical recycling offers very promising results and can contribute to more sustainable

production. Audi is working with partner companies from research and industry on this method and successfully completed a pilot project in 2021.

The process is extremely complex, involving collecting, shredding and heating various plastics, which can also contain foreign substances and lacquers. Using pyrolysis technology – a thermochemical conversion process in which the bonds within the molecules are broken down at high temperatures – pyrolysis oil is produced at a temperature of 500 degrees Celsius, while a large proportion of the other substances settle at the bottom as solid matter. Combustion is prevented by extracting oxygen. The pyrolysis oil can then be used to produce plastic components with the same product high quality as new products. This recycled plastic can even be used for safety-relevant parts.

Smart circular systems reduce the use of resources

The chemical recycling of plastic offers enormous potential to significantly increase the number of sustainably produced automobile components. What is more, when used to produce parts, the process should help reduce CO_2 emissions in comparison with the energy recovery of plastics. The use of pyrolysis oil is a good example of how the use of resources – in this case crude oil – and the ecological footprint can be reduced while maintaining the same product quality and safety.

The 'Chemical recycling of plastics in automotive engineering' pilot project targeted the creation of smart circular systems for plastics and the establishment of this method as a complement to mechanical recycling and replacement of energy recovery. Not only was the project a success, but so too was the manner in which Audi supported and drove forward the project: with overcooperation between science and industry.

Source: 'Audi is pursuing the vision of a circular economy', AUDI AG, 17 March (2022), https://www.audi.com/en/company/sustainability/core-topics/products-and-services/circular-economy-vision.html.

What we can see here is that managers are taking LCA seriously, that they see it as a means of understanding their production processes, creating social and environmental improvements,

FIGURE 5.2 Information from the LCA undertaken by Audi

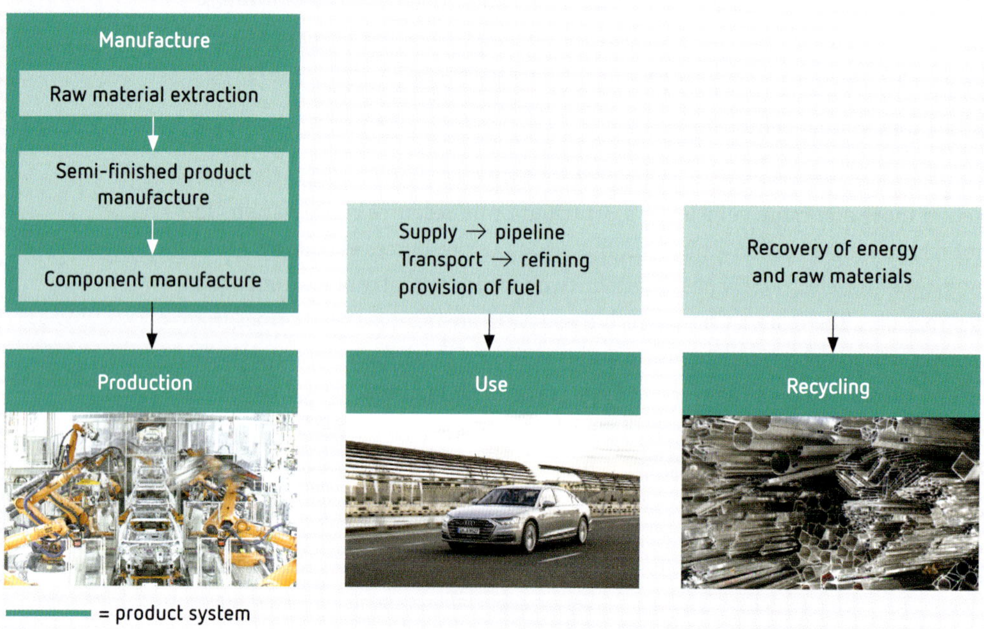

Source: Audi (2018), p. 7.

and improving financial performance. They are incorporating issues of sustainability into their planning processes – something we stressed in Chapter 3.

In undertaking LCA, managers need to be clear about the extent of the life cycle of the product that is being examined. Often, constraints are imposed because of the limitations of the available data and the costs associated with collecting the data. As Audi notes in relation to the boundaries of its own life cycle assessment (also see Figure 5.2):

> Before a life cycle assessment is compiled, its boundaries must be defined by deciding which processes should be examined. The available means, the time framework and data availability all have to be taken into account. Audi has laid down broad limits for its complete-vehicle life cycle assessments. The examination starts with the manner in which raw materials are obtained, and how individual components are manufactured. Even during the first new-model development stages, the engineering teams have to take decisions that have major effects on in-house production and the entire supply chain. Audi's experts assume for assessment purposes that vehicles will cover a distance of 200,000 kilometres. They not only take into account the emissions caused when the vehicle is being driven, but also those that occur when the fuel is produced. Recycling at the end of the vehicle's life and the use of secondary raw materials are also included in the life cycle assessment.
>
> Source: Audi (2018), p. 6.

Life cycle of a surfboard

As a further example, we can consider the work undertaken in relation to the life cycle of a surfboard. In 2008, Tobias Schultz undertook a study entitled *The surfboard cradle-to-grave* (available at http://citeseerx.ist.psu.edu/viewdoc/download?doi=10.1.1.605.1046&rep=rep1&type=pdf).

The study looked at two common types of surfboards that used two different construction processes. It was exploratory in nature but stressed that a study of this kind was vital so that the surfing community – including surfboard manufacturers, retailers and surfers – could make informed decisions that would enable them to reduce the environmental impacts of the sport. Schultz considered:

- the materials used to manufacture the surfboards, many of which were oil/petroleum-based
- the materials and energy used to maintain the boards throughout their lives
- the environmental impacts created by ongoing use of the surfboards
- their ultimate disposal.

The results suggested that during the construction phase of the life cycle, one type of surfboard, referred to as an 'epoxy construction board', generated more environmental impacts than the major alternative – the unsaturated polyester resin (UPR) boards. However, because the epoxy boards were more durable and lasted longer, the environmental impacts of both surfboards tended to be similar over time. It was noted for both types of surfboards that the manufacture of the inner core, and the resin used in that construction, created most of the environmental impacts in manufacture and hence provided a focus for managers' efforts to decrease impacts. But across the life cycle of a surfboard, the greatest environmental impacts came from the emissions created by surfers driving in search of good waves. (And as a surfer, albeit a now relatively old and slow one, the author of this book can attest to the many thousands of kilometres a surfer will drive in search of that elusive 'perfect wave'!) Therefore, many of the environmental implications associated with surfing were found to be beyond the control of surfboard manufacturers, albeit some environmental impacts could be reduced by producing more environmentally friendly surfboard cores and resins.

For an examination of the life cycle of a different item; this time a ship, see Learning exercise 5.3.

5.3 Learning Exercise

The life cycle of a ship

This learning exercise applies LCA to the life cycle of a ship, focusing particularly on what happens during the practice of ship-breaking at the end of a ship's life.

The life cycle of a ship can be broadly depicted as per Figure 5.3.

FIGURE 5.3 Simple depiction of a ship's life cycle

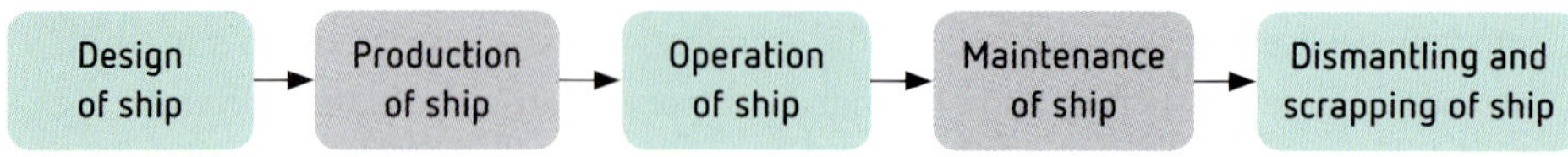

Various economic, social and environmental impacts can occur at each of the phases of a ship's life cycle; for example:

- The production of a ship requires much steel, which in turn relies on the mining of iron ore and its subsequent smelting, which requires large amounts of energy and therefore typically creates significant CO_2 emissions.
- Mining can also create various social impacts, depending on the location and type of mine involved.
- The operation of the ship will use various fuels and create various emissions and wastes that can create different forms of environmental damage.
- The dismantling of a ship can be a dangerous and polluting practice. Chemicals can be released into the sea, and beaches can be taken from local communities for the dismantling practice. Many injuries and deaths have been linked to the practice of ship-breaking.

Background to the practice of ship-breaking

In Chapter 2 we briefly referred to the practice of ship-breaking, which is when ships that have reached the end of their useful lives (which for many very large ocean-going ships is between 25 and 30 years of age) are broken up into parts that can be reused or further broken up for raw materials. Steel in particular can be converted into other products, thereby reducing the demand for iron ore as well as the energy consumption required in the production of steel.

Thousands of very large ocean-going ships are broken up annually. The great majority of this ship-breaking activity occurs in Asia, predominantly in India, Bangladesh, China and Pakistan.

Source: iStock.com/Stewart Sutton

Source: Alamy Stock Photo/Kairi Aun

The life cycle of a ship includes its ultimate scrapping

Many of these ships are sold by large Western companies to ship brokers, who arrange the dismantling of the ships. These ship brokers are typically unrelated to the original owners of the ships. Traceability back to the original owner can be made difficult by the common practice of changing the registration and name of the ship once it is sold to the brokers.

Concerns about ship-breaking

The methods employed in ship-breaking are dangerous and can create adverse environmental impacts. In many cases, the ships are simply driven at high speed onto beaches (at high tide) to become wedged in the sand, allowing the demolition to start. Many serious injuries and fatalities occur throughout the process, and various chemicals escape from the ship straight into the ocean, causing significant environmental impacts.

One of the more famous, or perhaps infamous, ship-breaking areas is Chittagong in Bangladesh. Very often, there are large numbers of partially dismantled ships on the beaches there, creating detrimental social and environmental impacts. The scale of the activity in Bangladesh is so great that the steel from the ships actually contributes about 20 per cent of the country's steel requirements each year. Another major ship-breaking area is Alang in India, where the practice has been taking place for over 30 years.

One vocal advocate for safer, more environmentally responsible practices in the ship-breaking industry is an organisation known as the Shipbreaking Platform, which is a coalition of environmental, human and labour rights organisations. Further details of the ship-breaking industry can be found on the organisation's website (**www.shipbreakingplatform.org**).

Taking this background information into account, to what extent should the managers of large shipping companies accept responsibility and accountability for the full life cycles of the ships they use?

By choosing to use particular ships in their operations, managers should take responsibility for the impacts these ships will create. As part of their planning activities, and in selecting which ships to acquire, consideration needs to be given not only to the relevant financial costs to be incurred from the acquisition, use and maintenance of the ships, but also to the impacts of alternative ships at each phase of their life cycles. Some form of prioritisation of the respective impacts needs to be undertaken, with the goal of selecting the option that is both financially viable and minimises adverse social and environmental impacts.

Why should large shipping companies undertake LCAs of the ships they are using?

It makes good business sense for managers to undertake a life cycle analysis for any major capital acquisition prior to purchase. This is an important component of planning, and as we have emphasised, planning needs to incorporate consideration of the financial, social and environmental impacts that might eventuate as a result of particular decisions. An LCA can highlight various impacts that are not only detrimental to the environment and to particular stakeholders, but also create risks for the organisation. The LCA is also a useful way of identifying where improvements can be made, and targets set so that continuous improvement might occur.

Can the LCA be used as a means of creating greater value for different stakeholders?

LCA can be used as part of the process of creating greater value for different stakeholders. For example, some stakeholders value the use of products that have lower environmental impacts, and an LCA will help facilitate areas where environmental impacts can be measured and thereafter identified for reduction.

Should shipping companies publicly disclose information about what happens to ships at the end of their life cycles?

Because of the social and environmental implications associated with ship-breaking, it does seem reasonable to argue that users of large ocean-going ships should be accountable for what happens to them at the end of their life cycle.

However, research indicates that many organisations that use large ocean-going ships provide very little or no information in relation to what happens to the ships at the end of their life cycles – but disclosure is improving across time.

In the previous edition (first edition) of this textbook we noted that the large global cruise company Carnival appeared to provide no information about what happens to its ships at the end of their lives. However, if we now look at the Carnival Corporation 2020 Sustainability Report (see **https://carnivalsustainability.com/sustainability-at-carnival**) we find various disclosures, including (p. 41):

> **Recycling Ship**
>
> At the end of a ship life cycle is the dismantle and recycle process. This is a complex process involving many components for reuse, recycling and disposal of waste materials. Carnival Corporation & PLC selected Turkey-based EGE CELIK and SIMSEKLER to recycle three of their retired cruise ships based on their track records of compliance with key national and international environmental agreements and regulations. Both recycling companies are certified by the Hong Kong Convention for the Safe and Environmentally Sound Recycling of Ships. They are also strictly required to adhere to a complex matrix of global standards set forth by the European Union (EU), International Maritime Organization (IMO), International Labour Organization (ILO) and the Basel Convention multilateral environmental agreement. In addition, the company also worked with the environmental non-profit Bellona Foundation – a lead partner in the NGO Shipbreaking Platform – and the specialized ship recycling experts Sea2Cradle to formulate an approach to dismantling and recycling the ships. The organizations also helped identify best-in-class certified maritime vessel retirement solutions worldwide that are able to reuse, reclaim and recycle retired ships in support of our commitment to a sustainable cruise industry.
>
> 'Our highest responsibility and top priorities are compliance, environmental protection, and the health, safety and well-being of our guests, the communities we visit and our crew,' said Vice Admiral William Burke USN (Ret.) Chief Maritime Officer, Carnival Corporation & PLC. 'That commitment extends to our cruise ships, starting from the moment a ship becomes part of our fleet and continuing all the way through to its retirement. In addition to limiting our vessels' impact on the environment throughout their service time in our fleet, recycling our retired ships following the European Ship Recycling Regulation ensures we are applying the highest global standards and contributing to a sustainable cruise industry.'

Source: Sustainable from Ship to Shore – 2020 Sustainability Report, Carnival Corporation (2020).

One of the world's largest users of ships, A.P. Moller – Maersk, devotes a number of pages of its 2020 *Sustainability Report* (see **www.maersk.com/en/about/sustainability/reports**) to what happens to its ships at the end of their life cycles. This indicates that the managers of this company also believe they have a responsibility and accountability for what happens to these ships when they reach the end of their lives. One extract from the A.P. Moller – Maersk 2020 *Sustainability Report* notes (p. 32):

> In 2020 we conducted an impact study at yards engaged by A.P. Moller – Maersk (Maersk) in Alang to document the outcomes. Between 2017 and 2019, in line with the Responsible Ship Recycling Standard (RSRS), nine Maersk vessels were recycled at five different Alang yards under full-time supervision with stop-work authority and a verification regime through external audits. After 3,100 training sessions, 2,000 toolbox talks and 35 Lloyd's Register audits, not a single lost time injury incident or fatality occurred. We have incentivised yards to invest in continual upgrades, which has also led to the construction of full impermeable floors in nine Maersk-approved yards and the purchase of 15 heavy-duty cranes in 11 yards that eliminate contact between vessel blocks the inter-tidal zone. There have been no major spills or incidents with hazardous materials on our projects at Maersk-engaged yards.
>
> Appointment letters and payslips, minimum wages, overtime payments, annual health checks, a 24/7 ambulance dedicated to each yard and many more such facilities are now standard practice, along with over 1200-men ILO-compliant worker dormitories built by Maersk-approved yards. For the wider Alang community and workforce, access to qualified healthcare and awareness training has led to improved health outcomes.
>
> A progressive transformation is also seen at a broader Alang industry level – approximately 80 of the total of around 120 operational yards voluntarily comply with the Hong Kong Convention, which is the only global convention on ship recycling.
>
> Source: A.P. Moller – Maersk Sustainability Report (2020), p. 32.

Should shipping companies publicly disclose the results of their LCA, if they do such analysis?

This depends on whether we believe they have an accountability to stakeholders for providing such information. While LCA is a management tool, many organisations' managers make the decision to publicly disclose such information, meaning they seem to believe they have responsibility and accountability to stakeholders for the impacts that are created across the life cycle of a product or service.

Does the sale of a ship to an unrelated ship broker remove any obligation (and responsibility, and accountability) regarding the original owner in terms of what happens when the ship is scrapped?

While the ship might no longer be the property of the original owner, it is hard to accept that they should not take some responsibility for what happens to the ship at the end of its life cycle. In reality, this is not always the case. However, stakeholders are becoming more interested in issues to do with the responsible management of products at the end of their lives, and it can be anticipated that organisations that fail to be responsible and accountable in this area of operations – as many still appear to be – will start to lose important stakeholder support.

Is the LCA really part of the accounting function?

As we have emphasised many times, accounting covers both financial and non-financial aspects of performance. It should provide information about the different resources consumed, or impacted, by an organisation's operations. LCA is part of the accounting function!

The circular economy

circular economy
An approach to production in which processes are designed to eliminate waste and pollution and in which products and related materials are designed to remain in productive use.

In part of the discussion above, we made brief reference to the '**circular economy**', which is very much linked to life cycle analysis. As we showed, the car maker Audi stated that it is attempting to move towards a production approach based upon the idea of a circular economy. A 'circular economy' exists where there is no waste, and products are either reused or recycled rather than going to landfill. In large part, this is an 'ideal', but managers should arguably strive towards developing systems which reduce waste and which encourage reuse and recycling. Unfortunately, many organisations use advertising and other practices to encourage consumers to constantly update their products without considering longer term sustainability issues. Many consumers' inclination to get the latest smartphone is an obvious example that comes to mind. A focus on the idea of a circular economy requires critical thinking and can generate both business benefits as well as social and environmental benefits. Entire industries can be established around the reuse and recycling of used products as part of a circular economy.

Key concept

The concept of 'circular economics' is a concept that is gaining momentum throughout the business (and non-business) community. In many respects it is an 'ideal', but it provides an important goal to which managers can aspire in their quest towards operating sustainably. In future years we can expect more discussion around the circular economy and 'closed loop' production.

We can contrast the circular economy with the 'linear economy'. The model of the 'linear economy' represents how many organisations ran their operations for many decades. Many organisations continue to embrace a linear approach to product design (for example, many producers of 'fast fashion'). The linear economy model is often built around single or limited use and then disposal, with products often going directly to landfill. It encourages consumption and focus on creating short term 'wants' rather than addressing actual 'needs'. For example, do we really need the very latest smartphone? **Figure 5.4** and **Figure 5.5** depict the circular economy and the linear economy.

FIGURE 5.4 A simple depiction of the circular economy

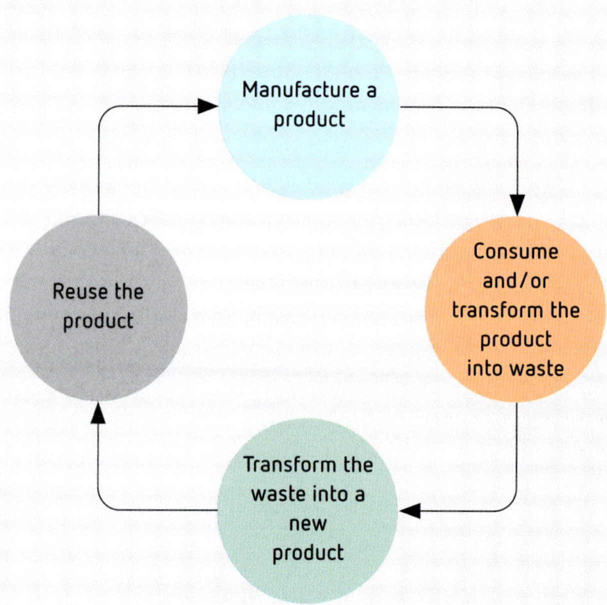

FIGURE 5.5 A simple depiction of the linear economy

The circular economy encourages innovation. For example, farm waste might then be used to create sustainable energy, or crop fertilisers. Plastic waste might go into producing some forms of furniture, carpets, or perhaps used in making roads. Thinking based around the idea of the circular economy can have many positive benefits in terms of creating employment, assisting biodiversity, and addressing climate change. Obviously, a movement towards a circular economy is just one step managers can take towards creating a more sustainable planet.

The United Nations Conference on Trade and Development, which is a permanent intergovernmental body that was established by the United Nations Global Assembly in 1963 and which is seeking to measure international progress towards meeting the UN Sustainable Development Goals (see https://unctad.org), has a whole section of its website devoted to the Circular Economy (see https://unctad.org/topic/trade-and-environment/circular-economy). It provides a diagram addressing the benefits of the circular economy (reproduced as Figure 5.6). The website (accessed July 2022) notes:

> A circular economy entails markets that give incentives to reusing products, rather than scrapping them and then extracting new resources.
>
> In such an economy, all forms of waste, such as clothes, scrap metal and obsolete electronics, are returned to the economy or used more efficiently.
>
> This can provide a way to not only protect the environment, but use natural resources more wisely, develop new sectors, create jobs and develop new capabilities .... While companies have made strides in improving their social and environmental footprints, privatizing public policy through voluntary sustainability standards and Corporate Social Responsibility (CSR) falls short from this task. In a world where most trade happens in parts and components in highly globalized value chains, promoting global resource circularity goes through international rules and cooperation, as well as individuals and consumers empowered with education.
>
> UNCTAD works on the circular economy by encouraging discussions and activities seeking to bring value out of waste streams, by encouraging discussions around collaborative economy sectors, by the examination of innovate business models and encouragement of consumer awareness and behavioural shifts. In partnership with other international organizations, UNCTAD's work on the circular economy at the national and multilateral level brings this important theme to the service of the international community.

Why do I need to know about life cycle analysis or circular economy ideals?

As a manager within an organisation, you will be confronted with growing expectations from your organisational stakeholders (such as consumers, employees, investors and lenders) to manage your organisation in a way that reduces current social and environmental impacts, and which respects the needs of future generations. Implementing life cycle analysis requires managers to understand the impacts of a product or service from cradle to grave – and such an understanding is necessary for improved practices.

FIGURE 5.6 The benefits of the circular economy according to UNCTAD

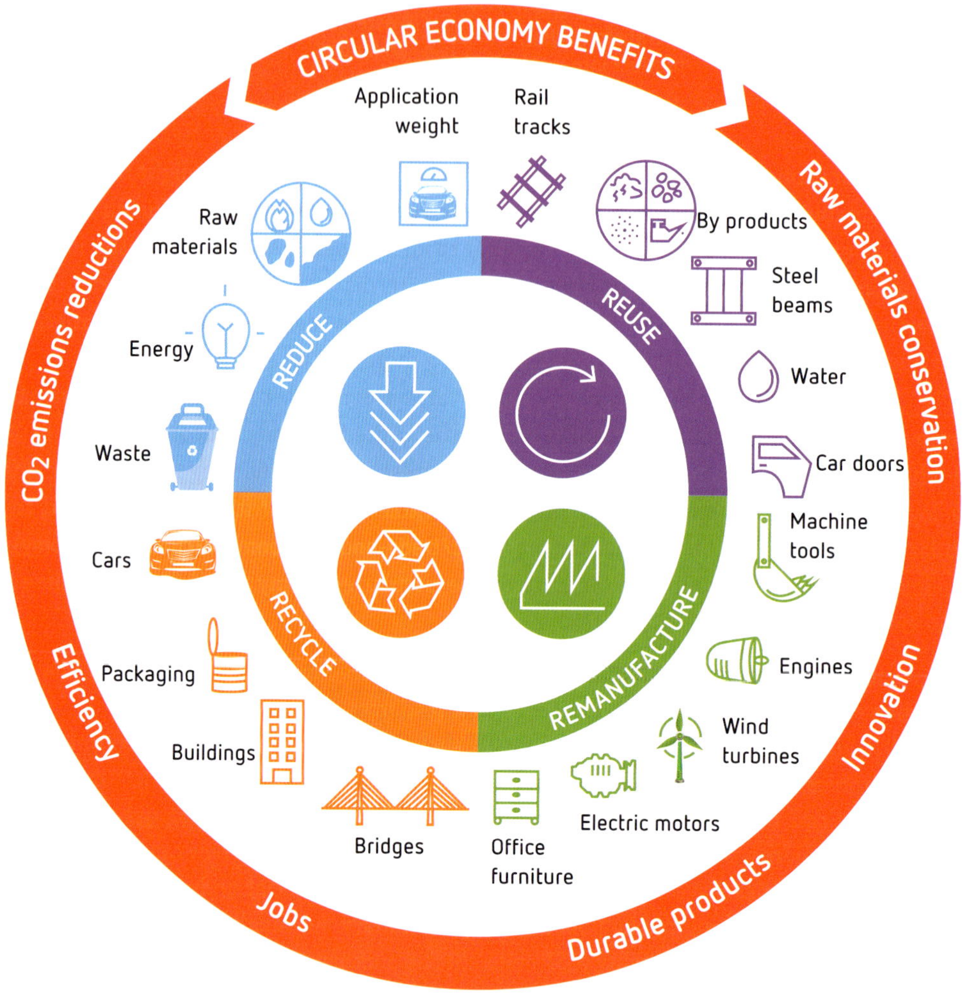

Source: UNCTAD (2022).

Linked to the practice of life cycle analysis is the concept of the circular economy. While a perfectly circular economy in which there is absolutely no waste or negative impacts on ecosystems is generally considered an impractical ideal for most organisations (at least at this point in time), embracing the concept provides a basis for ongoing improvements which will be beneficial to current and future generations, the environment and the organisation.

life cycle costing (LCC) Seeks to place a cost on the various inputs (resources used), outputs (including wastes and emissions) and the impacts created by an organisation's operations, and attribute such costs to particular activities and products

LO5.2 Life cycle costing

As we have just described, life cycle analysis does not rely upon placing a cost on particular inputs, outputs or impacts, but rather it typically provides measurements in physical terms, thereby enabling managers to make more informed decisions.

By contrast, **life cycle costing (LCC)** seeks to place a cost on the various inputs (resources used), outputs (including wastes and emissions) and the impacts created by an organisation's operations, and attribute such costs to particular activities and products. LCC is a management tool that assists an organisation to select the most cost-effective alternative from among competing alternatives, once the costs of purchasing, operating, maintaining and, ultimately, disposing of a product are taken into account.

In undertaking LCC, managers need to make decisions about what costs they intend to consider. In the early stages, when organisations are learning about how to go about doing such analysis, it may be impractical for managers to attempt to place a monetary value on many of the *externalities* associated with the activities. It may become too impractical or even too confusing to implement LCC if, at the start of the analysis, there are too many aspects being addressed.

We noted in Chapter 2 that externalities are often referred to as 'social costs'. Even though it might be difficult to attribute a monetary value to many externalities, such costs or impacts should nevertheless be identified, and, where possible, described both in qualitative terms as well as through various forms of quantitative non-monetary measurements. Information about externalities forms part of the total information upon which subsequent decisions are made. LCC, while potentially difficult to implement, has the benefit of encouraging an organisation to think beyond the current period, and beyond the range of costs that might normally be considered in choosing what activities to pursue or what assets to acquire.

A real-world example of life cycle costing

The author of this book was commissioned by the Energy Supply Association of Australia (results reported in Deegan, 2008) to undertake an investigation pertaining to the power poles used by electricity distributors. As electricity distribution uses a very large number of poles, decisions about what poles to use are very significant, particularly as different poles will create different costs.

There are many alternative construction materials for power poles; for example, timber, steel, fibreglass and concrete. Applying LCC, Deegan looked at the costs that arose over the life of a pole, noting that such costs are influenced by:

- the availability of particular materials
- the social and environmental impacts associated with producing the raw materials used in manufacturing the pole
- the strength and durability of the materials
- the current and future availability of treatments to extend the useful life of the materials and the costs (including those imposed upon the environment) associated with the treatments
- the energy used in manufacturing the pole
- transportation costs (which are influenced by such factors as the dimensions and weight of the poles)
- ongoing maintenance costs
- the recyclability or disposal value of the pole at the end of its useful life.

As Deegan (2008, p. 4) noted, while many costs associated with the life cycle of a power pole can be quantified, other costs (and benefits) are not so easily identified; for example, the impacts of energy emissions caused by production of the cement used in making concrete poles, or the impacts of methane emissions that result when old wooden poles are ultimately taken to landfill. Nevertheless, potential environmental and social impacts, even if not readily measurable in monetary terms, need to be considered when choosing between pole materials. They are a 'cost' of the poles.

Where possible, financial costs were assigned to various phases of the life cycle of the pole, which Deegan identified as the pre-purchase phase, the protective treatment phase, the installation phase, the periodic maintenance phase, and the disposal recycling phase. Where financial costs could not be easily assigned (for example, in relation to such issues as the environmental implications of treatments, greenhouse gas (GHG) emissions associated with installation and construction, impacts on local wildlife), a rating was given to the particular threats and opportunities. As Deegan stated:

> In the capital investment evaluation, a number of issues will not be costed in monetary terms. Organisations may choose to develop a ratings system to rank various threats and opportunities on the basis of their perceived importance. For example, threats may be evaluated on a five-level basis:
>
> Level 1 – Low
> Level 2 – Minor
> Level 3 – Moderate
> Level 4 – Major
> Level 5 – Extreme
>
> Opportunities could be ranked on a similar five-point basis. While it is difficult to rank threats and opportunities precisely, such a procedure will raise certain issues that might not otherwise be factored into the decision-making process.
>
> Source: Deegan (2008), p. 11.

At the end of the LCC process, managers were left with the total financial costs (that is, for those costs that could be measured in monetary terms) and a number of ratings on a scale of 1 to 5. In order to make a final decision, both the monetary and non-monetary items of information were taken into account. Again, this example illustrates how both financial, and non-financial, aspects of performance are taken into account by managers as part of their planning processes.

For a discussion of when, or whether, to conduct LCC, see **Learning exercise 5.4**.

5.4 Learning Exercise

Whether or not to apply LCC

Assume that you are a senior manager at an organisation that, as a result of an apparent increase in summertime temperatures, is about to install an air-conditioning system throughout its 10-storey corporate office building. You have been provided with the financial costs of a number of alternative systems. You need to consider whether you should make your ultimate choice on the basis of the purchase and installation costs, or whether you should also consider some form of predictive LCC of the alternatives.

Adding air conditioning would represent a major acquisition of machinery and would be referred to as a major capital expenditure decision. These air conditioners will last several years and require energy to run as well as ongoing maintenance. And ultimately, they will need to be replaced.

As a manager, you should think about the financial and other costs that will arise throughout the life of an asset when making such a major capital expenditure decision. Managers should consider such factors as:

- the up-front purchase and installation costs
- the expected life of the units

- the energy expected to be used by the units in both physical and financial terms across the life of the asset
- whether the units are expected to operate at the same level of efficiency throughout their lives
- the warranties being offered
- the reliability and reputation of the manufacturer and supplier
- the expected regular maintenance costs of the units
- the health and safety aspects of the units; for example, whether they have been associated with reports of harbouring diseases that could be released into the building
- the origin of the products in terms of where they were made, and the working conditions for the employees in the related factories
- what happens to the units at the end of their lives; for example, whether the organisation that supplied them will remove them, and if so, at what cost – and furthermore, when they remove them, the extent of the components of the air conditioner that are likely to be recycled.

From the above, we can see that there are several financial costs that need to be considered, and various non-financial issues that also need to be considered. The different non-financial issues need to be weighted in some way. The ultimate choice should certainly not be made just in terms of the up-front purchase and installation costs but should also consider various other factors.

LO5.3 Material flow cost accounting

Material flow cost accounting (MFCA) is another possible approach (or tool) for managers to use when analysing their operations. The aim of MFCA is to improve both environmental and financial performance through the more efficient use of materials (in MFCA, energy and water are classified as 'materials'), referred to earlier in this chapter as a win–win scenario. According to the International Organization for Standardization (ISO), the adoption of MFCA in an organisation occurs when:

material flow cost accounting (MFCA) Focuses on recording the inputs of particular materials into a production process, and the outputs, including wastes, that come from that process. Measurements can be made in both physical and monetary terms

> the flows and stocks of materials within an organization are traced and quantified in physical units (e.g. mass, volume) and the costs associated with those material flows are also evaluated. The resulting information can act as a motivator for organizations and managers to seek opportunities to simultaneously generate financial benefits and reduce adverse environmental impacts. MFCA is applicable to any organization that uses materials and energy, regardless of their products, services, size, structure, location, and existing management and accounting systems.
>
> MFCA can be extended to other organizations in the supply chain, both upstream and downstream, thus helping to develop an integrated approach to improving material and energy efficiency in the supply chain. This extension can be beneficial because waste generation in an organization is often driven by the nature or quality of materials provided by a supplier, or the specification of the product requested by a customer.
>
> Source: International Organization for Standardization (2011).

Reflective of the perceived importance of MFCA, the ISO has a standard specifically dedicated to MFCA, this being *ISO14051:2011 Environmental management – Material flow cost accounting: General framework* (see **www.iso.org/standard/50986.html**).

The ISO releases various guidance documents and standards on a variety of topics. According to the ISO's website:

> ISO is an independent, non-governmental international organization with a membership of 165 national standards bodies. Through its members, it brings together experts to share knowledge and develop voluntary, consensus-based, market-relevant International Standards that support innovation and provide solutions to global challenges.
>
> Source: International Organization for Standardization (2022).

Returning to MFCA, its implementation requires the development of frameworks that track and quantify the flows of materials through an organisation in both physical and monetary terms. The information generated through this analysis can then be used to identify opportunities to reduce material usage, improve the efficiency with which material and energy are used, and reduce the adverse environmental impacts and associated costs of such impacts. The process effectively maps resource inputs and related outputs, including waste.

The MFCA process

We can contrast MFCA with LCA and LCC. LCA and LCC look at resource inputs, outputs and impacts from cradle to grave. By contrast, MFCA typically restricts the analysis to the materials being used directly within the organisation and the outputs coming directly from the organisation (including wastes) and does not typically consider issues to do with what happens to a product at the end of its life cycle. MFCA also does not tend to consider impacts that cannot be measured and therefore ignores a variety of externalities. Nevertheless, if properly applied, it is a very useful management tool.

As indicated, MFCA will track aspects such as the amount of waste being generated, and the amount of energy and water being used in different processes. By tracking what is actually going into waste, managers should be better able to understand the environmental implications of the waste as they will know its components, and the relative amount of each. Furthermore, they should be able to actually determine the financial cost of the waste. We know that the greater the use of energy, the greater the financial costs, and the greater the emissions of CO_2 – which contributes to climate change if that energy is being generated by the use of fossil fuels. Tracking the use of water is also important, particularly if it is relatively scarce in the area of operations. The greater the use of water, potentially the greater amount of wastewater as well that will need to be treated, with the costs of treatment also being incurred.

MFCA works on the premise that *all* materials acquired by an organisation must either end up in products or in waste (effectively, nothing simply 'disappears'). Within MFCA, waste is often referred to as 'non-product output' or 'negative product'. Different system boundaries for MFCA can be implemented. For example, MFCA can be employed at the company level, the factory site level, the process level or the product level.

Christ and Burritt (2015) identify the main steps involved in implementing MFCA, which are reflected in Figure 5.7.

Explaining the MFCA process, Christ and Burritt (2015) provide the following comments about the different stages depicted in Figure 5.7.

> Once an appropriate system boundary has been agreed (for example, is the flow modelling just going to look at a single product, or the operations of a whole factory), it is widely accepted that the first step in implementing any MFCA experiment is to

FIGURE 5.7 The MFCA process

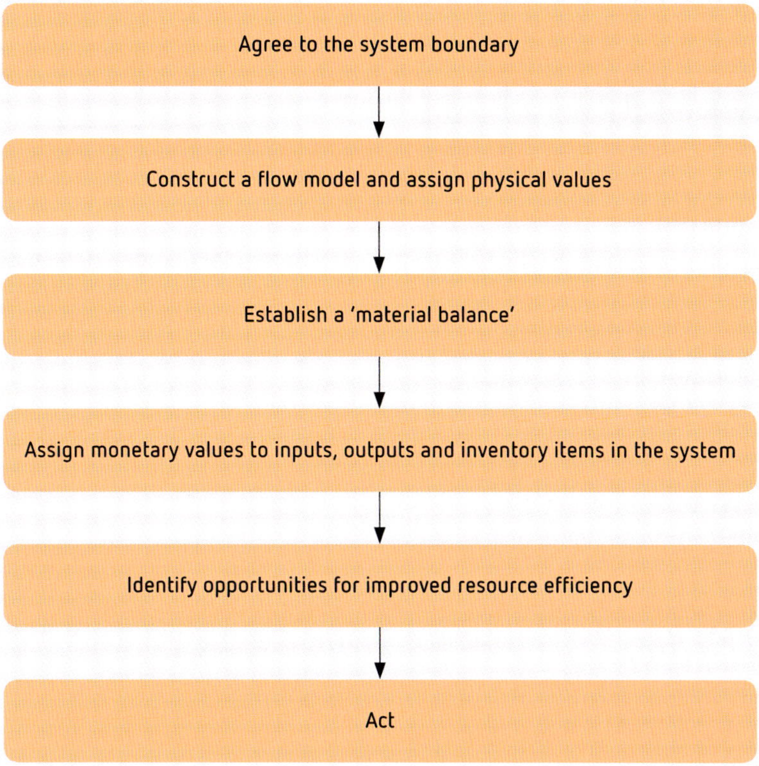

Source: Adapted from Christ and Burritt (2015), p. 1381.

develop a basic understanding of the flows of material and energy throughout the organisation. This is achieved via a visual representation commonly referred to as a 'flow model' ... Once the flow model is complete, the next step incorporates assigning values representing the amount of materials and energy that pass through or are stored within each step in the flow model ... The purpose for assigning values to the flow model is to establish a material balance, also referred to as a mass balance, input-output balance or an eco-balance (IFAC, 2005). As noted in ISO 14051 (ISO, 2011, p. 5):

Because mass and energy can neither be created nor destroyed, only transformed, the physical inputs entering a system should be equal to the physical outputs from the system, taking into account any inventory changes within the system.

Once the material balance is complete, it is necessary to assign monetary values for every input and output contained for each step in the flow model ... While the development of a mass balance flow model and the allocation of relevant costs are without doubt important steps within the MFCA process, they are not an end in themselves. Thus it is necessary for management to summarise, evaluate and interpret these results. It is also important that this data be communicated to relevant managers and staff who are likely to be familiar with the activities undertaken within individual cost/quantity centres. Once this is done, potential improvement opportunities can be identified, and appropriate action taken.

Source: Reprinted from *Journal of Cleaner Production*, 108, Christ, K., & Burritt, R., 'Material flow cost accounting: A review and agenda for future research', p. 1381, copyright 2015, with permission from Elsevier.

The benefits of MFCA

Christ and Burritt (2015, p. 1382) summarise a number of important purposes that a well-planned MFCA can fulfil, including:

- allowing areas of inefficiency to be identified and understood
- creating improved efficiency and a reduction in direct material costs
- reducing the amount of waste generated and reducing the ecological impact
- reducing other manufacturing costs (for example, waste handling, treatment and associated infrastructure costs)
- providing more accurate product costing – effectively, MFCA allows managers to more accurately determine the variable costs associated with particular products or services (we considered variable costs in detail within Chapter 3)
- providing incentives for innovation
- improving interdepartmental communication concerning resource use
- improving management control.

The need for MFCA is explored in **Learning exercise 5.5**.

5.5 Learning Exercise

The need for MFCA

You have a friend who owns a business that makes wooden furniture. Your friend's business is very successful and is generating significant profits. He is very happy with how it is going. You have looked at his business and noticed the amount of machinery, the various materials being used (for example, timber, various timber stains and varnishes, sandpapers, glues, screws, nails) and the amount of waste that seems to be collected every day by waste collectors. You suggested the use of MFCA to your friend. He laughed and said, 'Why would I change things? I am enjoying myself AND making a fortune!' Let's consider how you should respond to your friend's comment.

There is always the potential to improve performance

The reality is that your friend's attitude is quite common. Owners/managers often fail to take action and embrace new ideas because they feel that they are very successful anyway, and it would be potentially dangerous to make any change.

However, even apparently successful organisations can have inherent inefficiencies. By constructing a flow model of a few product lines, it might become apparent which lines are using more energy, creating more waste (of different types) and so forth. Being aware of this could then provide the necessary impetus for improvement, and correspondingly improved financial and environmental performance. A successful organisation could become even more successful. MFCA can form the basis for the development of targets and budgets. Managers should always be on the lookout for management tools that can help improve their organisations, whether they appear to be successful or not.

Key concept

The development of material flow model diagrams, which show the resources coming into a particular process and the outputs (including waste) coming from that process, is a very useful mechanism for managers to more fully understand the operations of an organisation, and some of the related costs, risks and opportunities.

Real-world examples of MFCA

Wool processing

The author of this book undertook an interesting case study back in 2003 in relation to the processing of wool (as reported in Deegan, 2003). Michell Wool, the largest processor of wool in Australia, commissioned Deegan to investigate opportunities for environmental performance improvements, and related financial savings.

Michell Wool buys wool of various grades and quality, and processes it so that it can then be sold to different customers that use the wool to produce various products. Lower-grade wools, in unprocessed form, tend to have relatively greater amounts of dirt, vegetable matter (for example, burrs) and water-soluble salts. A process known as 'carbonising' is used at Michell to process the lower-quality wools. Various contaminants are removed from the wool using water, detergent, acid, sodium bicarbonate, hydrogen peroxide, energy, labour and machinery. The process goes through the following stages:

1 Opening stage: separates the wool fibres, which have been tightly packed for transportation purposes.
2 Scouring stage: there are four scourers in a row – energy, water and detergent are added to clean the wool as it is scoured.
3 Acidification stage: using high temperatures, burrs and vegetable matter are turned to ash, which is then removed from the wool – energy, acid and water are used in this process.
4 Centrifuge stage: water is removed and recycled.
5 Dry baking stage: energy is used to heat the wool.
6 Crushing and dusting stage: energy is used to remove further foreign matter from the wool.
7 Neutralisation stage: acid, water, sodium bicarbonate and hydrogen peroxide are added to neutralise the wool.
8 Blending stage: the wool is blended together for wool customers.
9 Packing stage.

This process is represented in **Figure 5.8**. While this figure shows material flows (a 'flow model'), costs were also calculated (not shown here).

Apart from generating processed wool, the process also generates sludge and wool grease. The wool grease is sold to other organisations, while Michell Wool pays another organisation to take the sludge.

The case study specifically concentrated on accounting for, and potentially decreasing the use of, the following:

- *electricity* – has various environmental implications, including those related to the generation of greenhouse gas emissions
- *water* – the use and subsequent release of wastewater has obvious environmental implications
- *detergents* – necessitate removal at a wastewater treatment facility prior to release into waterways
- *transportation* – also has implications in relation to the generation of greenhouse gases.

The view taken was that if these costs were brought to the attention of management, and if they were able to find ways to reduce these costs, then prima facie, the analysis would generate positive environmental (and financial) effects. Of course, it was also likely that consideration of other costs and/or other processes would also have positive effects. But to make the project manageable, defined boundaries were set and only the above dot-points were considered.

The pre-existing practice within Michell Wool was for the electricity, water and detergent costs to be separately collected, but these costs were then simply allocated back to the processed

FIGURE 5.8 A flow model of the carbonising process

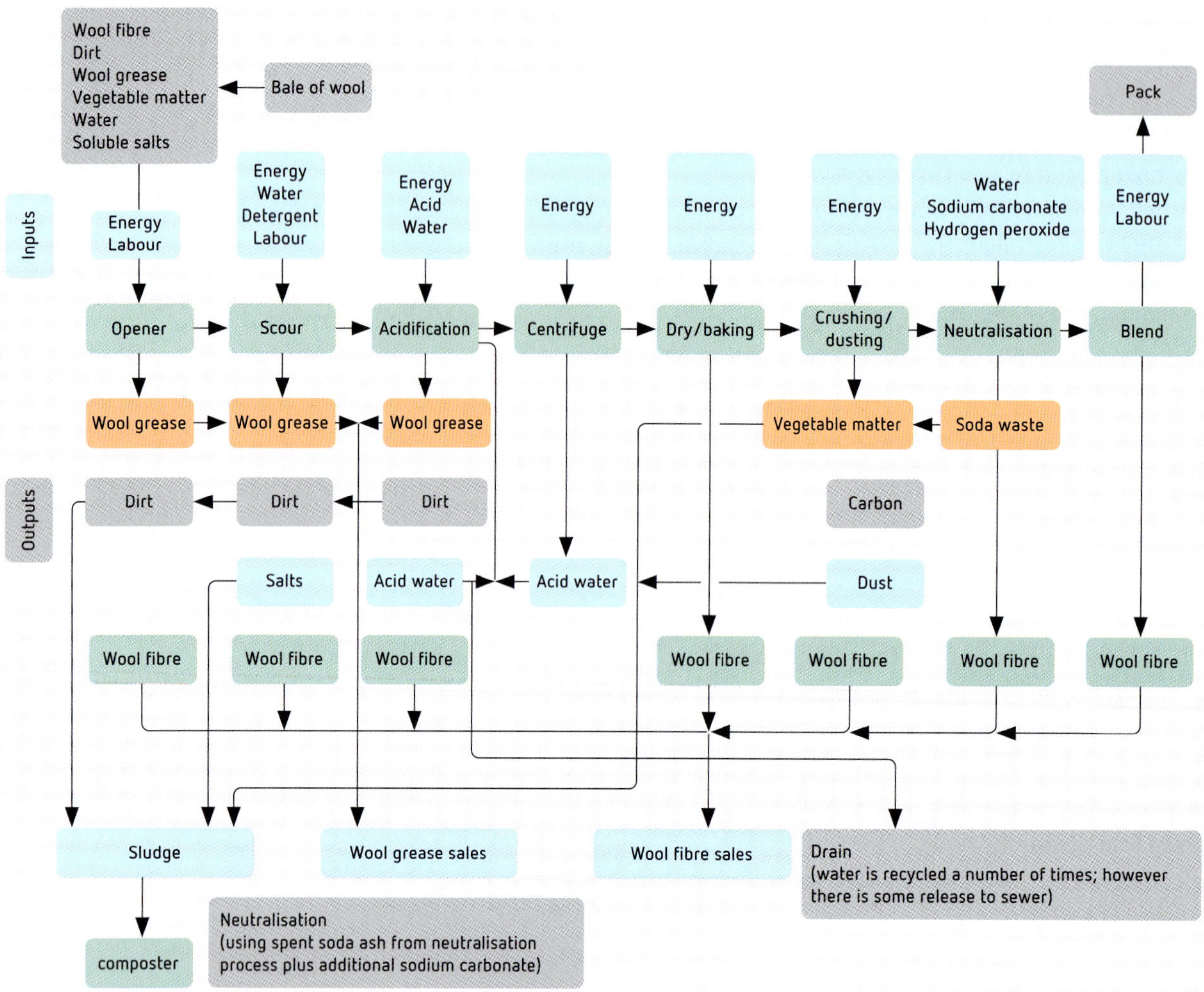

Source: Deegan (2003, p. 30).

wool on the same basis for every bale, regardless of the different quality of the wool being processed. That is, each bale of wool, regardless of the quality, was assigned the same financial costs of processing. This practice assumed that all types of wool, regardless of the associated foreign matter included therein, require the same amount of detergent, water and electricity to process. As the material flow diagram would show, this was not actually the case. Also, the dirtier low-quality wool was more expensive to transport to Michell Wool, as more of each bale contained dirt, burrs and other contaminants rather than usable wool. That is, there was less usable wool per bale.

The implication of all this was that, under the pre-existing accounting system, wherein each bale of wool was allocated the same processing costs, the 'dirty' wool inputs were being subsidised by 'clean' wool inputs, with the possibility that some wools (the particularly dirty types) which were really generating low (perhaps negative?) returns were being acquired when they ought not to be – unless, of course, the traders could acquire the wool at reduced costs that compensated for the additional processing costs. In doing the analysis, it became apparent that greater amounts of water, detergent and electricity went into processing dirtier lines of wool, yet costs were being allocated on a per bale or per kilogram of input basis.

Trials were then run, and efforts were carefully made to trace the amounts of energy, water and detergents used (materials and resource flows were studied and a flow model of actual materials use was prepared). It became apparent that significantly greater resources were used to process the lower-grade (dirtier wools), and in some cases it seemed that lower-grade wools were not actually profitable – something that had been disguised (not intentionally) under the previous accounting practices. Being more precise about how much material was used in processing the wool enabled the organisation to decide against acquiring the very-low-grade wools, and this ultimately reduced its use of materials and financial costs, and increased its profits. The wool the company did not acquire (the lower grade, dirtier wool) could be acquired by other organisations and used in applications – such as the manufacture of insulation – that did not require such extensive processing.

For interested readers, the report written in relation to Michell Wool and three other case studies was still available at the time of writing this chapter at **https://p2infohouse.org/ref/37/36463.pdf.**

Electronics manufacturing

Another example of MFCA comes from Ricoh, the global manufacturer of copiers and cameras. While the company refers to its analysis as being an 'Eco Balance' approach, this is also an example of MFCA. Ricoh also make this information publicly available, reflecting a view that the managers at Ricoh consider that they have an accountability for providing such information to interested stakeholders. According to the Ricoh website (accessed January 2022, see **www.ricoh.com/environment/management/eco.html**):

> The Ricoh Group introduced the concept of Eco Balance in fiscal 1998 to clarify the environmental impact caused by all its businesses and effectively reduce it. We have mapped out environmental action plans based upon environmental loads identified by stage under the concept of Eco Balance since fiscal 2002 and have applied the concept in the formulation of Ricoh Group Environmental Goals.
>
> Since we know that procurement of raw materials and parts is the largest contributor to greenhouse gas emissions by studying the amount at output at each stage, we have been working hard to cut down the input of resources so as to reduce the corresponding emissions. Emissions due to the use of Ricoh products are equivalent to emissions from the business sites. Taking that into consideration, we are improving energy efficiency of our products.
>
> Source: Ricoh (2022), https://www.ricoh.com/environment/management/eco.html.

From the above quote, it is apparent that the analysis undertaken by Ricoh is used in future planning and as the basis for creating various medium- and long-term goals and related targets. Hence, we can see that this sort of analysis helps to make planning and target setting – issues we discussed in Chapters 3 and 4 – more sophisticated in nature. The Ricoh Eco Balance is shown in **Figure 5.9**. Again, note that managers will use this information as a foundation to improve the future performance of the organisation. As should also be appreciated, this analysis is part of the broader accounting being undertaken by the organisation, even though it shows no financial measurements. While not reproduced here, notes are provided on the Ricoh website about how various measurements were made and the respective measurement frameworks that were adopted for the analysis.

For a discussion of the application of MFCA to a service organisation, see **Learning exercise 5.6**.

FIGURE 5.9 Flow model prepared by Ricoh

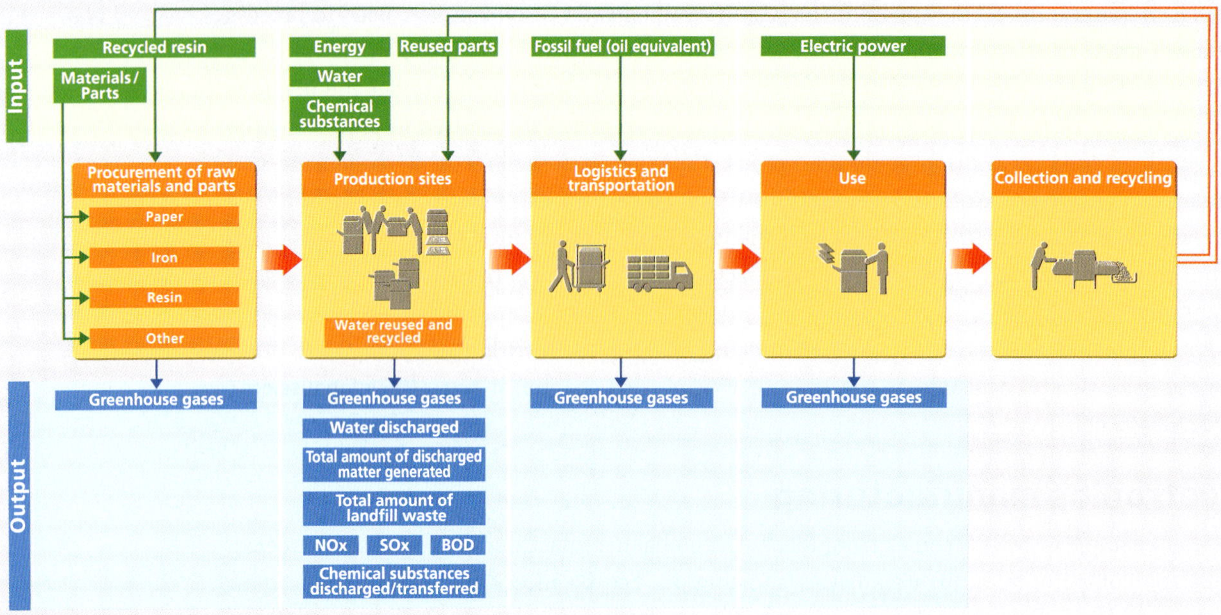

Source: Ricoh (2022), https://www.ricoh.com/environment/management/eco.html.

5.6 Learning Exercise

Applying MFCA to a service organisation

Our examples of MFCA have related its use to manufacturing organisations. Let us now consider how MFCA may be used in a service organisation such as a university.

At a university, MFCA could be undertaken at various levels. For example, universities often have a section or department that prints books. Book printing uses many inputs and creates various wastes, so some form of flow modelling is useful here to identify areas for improvement. Various schools generate different outputs; for example, engineering training might involve students designing and constructing prototypes – they could apply MFCA to consider how the construction phase could be more efficient. Many schools and departments throughout universities would benefit from some form of MFCA.

Universities use a great deal of water and electricity. MFCA can be used to see where and how this is being used, which can also highlight areas where improvements can be made. Universities also generate a great deal of waste. Some tracking of where this waste comes from, together with information about the costs of the materials going into the waste, could highlight areas for improvements and financial savings. We will specifically concentrate on the use of MFCA to reduce waste in the next section.

Other examples

Those with an interest in learning about more related MFCA case studies can refer to the following website, which documents various organisations that have used MFCA in Japan – a country in which MFCA is widely used: **www.jmac.co.jp/mfca/thinking/data/MFCA_Case_example_e.pdf**

Why do I need to know about the practice of material flow cost accounting?

We should know about MFCA as it provides useful insights into the resources being used by an organisation (and their costs), and the related outputs of the organisation, including finished goods, wastes and emissions. Performing MFCA – which requires the construction of a material flow diagram – increases the knowledge of the managers about the functioning of the organisation and highlights areas of risk and opportunity, and possibilities for cost savings.

LO5.4 A focus on waste

As we have seen, MFCA allows managers to see where waste comes from, and the amount, and costs, of materials that end up in waste. But the reality is that most organisations do not employ MFCA. Often, organisations simply recognise and report their 'waste expense' as the amount that is spent to have contractors come and remove the waste, or if waste is going to the sewer, the sewerage costs being paid. However, this ignores the actual costs of the materials that go into the waste. For example, in a manufacturing organisation, there could be various metal offcuts that go into waste, various defective products that go into waste, and so forth. These wasted items all cost money to initially acquire or make, and it is only when organisations start recognising the costs of acquired materials that are going to waste that they can start to recognise the true cost of waste. These costs should also include the handling and storage fees associated with the material before it ends up in the waste. As we have already noted, these 'additional' waste costs are frequently referred to as 'non-production output'.

According to the United Nations Division for Sustainable Development (2001):

> The largest part of all environmental costs lies in the material purchase value of non-product output and can come up to 10 to 100 times the costs of disposal, depending upon the business sector.
>
> Source: United Nations Division for Sustainable Development (2001), p. 2.

Arguably, organisations need a separate account for waste that records the costs that have been incurred in producing the waste stream – not simply the waste disposal costs. Introducing an accounting system that refines how waste is accounted for might, on its own, provide the necessary impetus for significant financial and environmental improvements. Without more complete information on waste, opportunities for waste reduction will be lost. Looking at material flows throughout an organisation allows managers to identify the locations where materials are being lost (or 'wasted') and where control needs to be exerted.

Source: Shutterstock.com/pwrmc

The true cost of waste is more than the cost of paying somebody to remove this bin.

In accounting for waste, different managers from different parts of an organisation need to collaborate. This emphasises the need for different management teams within an organisation to talk to each other. For example, if the management accountants focus primarily on the financial costs of particular products, then they might be satisfied with a particular product's performance if the product is generating a good financial margin despite the waste (which they might not know about anyway). That is, they might not have thought of trying to put a cost on waste because they may have no real idea of what is in the waste. By contrast, those managers looking after production and environmental management might know about the physical waste and the types and amounts of materials going into it, but have no idea about the financial costs of that waste. Organisations need to consider both, particularly if they are generating a relatively large amount of waste. Managers from different areas of an organisation need to 'talk'.

As Wagner (2015) states in relation to Kunert, a German textile company:

> Corporate management and management control received financial information and decided on the basis of this. Production and Environmental Management worked with physical information or indicators (number of parts produced, scrap rates, kg of waste etc.). However, in order to reach higher efficiency levels, both sides had to be considered simultaneously. As a result of the project, management was supplied with information in physical and in monetary terms, showing the entire flow of material from input to output, revealing precisely where high quantities of materials were treated, stored or lost and at what cost.
>
> Source: Wagner (2015), p. 1256.

Kunert was able to redesign its activities and reduce the waste, with the implication that there were significant reductions in materials usage, as well as financial savings.

Another example of the use of MFCA to reduce waste is provided in a report written by Kasemset, Chernsupornchai and Pala-ud (2015). They undertook their study at a textile factory in Chiang Mai, Thailand. They focused on a particular type of shirt that was being produced. According to Kasemset et al.:

> The objective of this study is to present the application of MFCA in waste reduction in a small textile factory as a case study. The case study company currently does not realize the magnitude of the amount of production waste from the production process. On a daily base, a big amount of material waste is generated and the company has to resolve this waste .... To display this waste via economical measurement using MFCA allows the company to clearly see the expense. Finally, appropriate improvement solutions are provided for the company to make the required decision based on the company's limitations.
>
> Source: Reprinted from *Journal of Cleaner Production*, 108, Kasemset, C., Chernsupornchai, J., & Pala-ud, W., 'Application of MFCA in waste reduction: case study on a small textile factory in Thailand', p. 1343, 2015, with permission from Elsevier.

Within the textile factory, costs going to the 'positive products' (completed shirts) and the 'negative products' (the waste) were determined by the researchers for each process, with the processes being identified as cutting, sewing, quality checking, dyeing, buttonhole drilling, and packing. Total costs attributed to the positive products and the negative products were 84.26 per cent and 15.74 per cent, respectively. Of the 15.74 per cent waste costs, they found that 14.73 per cent of the total waste costs were associated with wasted fabric. They then found that 80 per cent of this wasted fabric was generated in the cutting and sewing processes. Some key improvements were identified for these processes, and while waste was not totally removed, the results suggested that the cost of the negative product declined from 15.74 per cent to 11.27 per cent as a result of relatively inexpensive changes being made to the manufacturing equipment.

Because waste can be a significant cost for many organisations (and for the environment), many consulting companies offer services to clients to help them identify the amounts and costs of waste being generated. This is often referred to as a 'waste audit' and involves a physical analysis of waste composition to provide clients with a detailed understanding of what is in the waste and its potential costs to the organisation. Potential opportunities in relation to waste reduction, recycling and so forth are typically provided. Opportunities for waste reduction can also include requiring suppliers to change the shape or configuration of the materials being provided to the organisation, so that excess offcuts, excessive packaging and so forth are eliminated.

Accounting for waste is a very important aspect of accounting, but one that is often disregarded. Even a very small percentage of waste reduction per unit can add up to significant amounts when an organisation is operating on a very large scale.

For a discussion of how to account for waste in a service organisation, see **Learning exercise 5.7**.

5.7 Learning Exercise

Accounting for waste within a service organisation

Scenario: You have been appointed as a new accountant at a leading national architecture firm. You continually notice that at the end of each day, large amounts of paper are placed in the paper recycling bins. It seems that most of this paper originally came from the various printers that are located throughout the organisation. You ask the senior accountant about the cost of the wasted paper and the response is: 'We pay a contractor $3000 per month to collect the waste paper'.

Is this a useful response? What should be considered when determining the cost of the wasted paper?

This is a common response to receive, but it is not a useful response. Many organisations and their accountants consider the waste costs to simply be those costs paid to waste-removal contractors. However, as you should by now know, waste costs are typically much more than this, but they often remain hidden in other expense accounts. For example, for paper use, the costs of the waste might be included as part of the costs of office supplies, or stationery, or rental of office equipment.

Determining the costs of wasted paper is not necessarily an easy task. You need to ask yourself the following questions.

What do the financial costs of wasted paper include?

The costs of the wasted paper include:

- the cost of acquiring the paper
- the cost of storing the paper
- the cost of the printing/copying regarding the paper (energy, inks and so on)
- a proportion of the maintenance costs of the photocopier on which the printing occurred.

Can the wasted paper be reduced?

Some form of material tracking (material flow analysis) of the waste paper will show how much is simply coming from paper that was printed, when it really could have been viewed online. For example, some people print out emails when there is absolutely no need to. Indeed, many of the pages that are printed do not need to be. Once some form of financial cost is placed on the unnecessary printing that is going into waste (and a period of data collection needs to be undertaken here with associated modelling), then the magnitude of the costs associated with this waste paper can become clearer.

What other costs involved in wasted paper should be considered?

While perhaps not measured in financial terms, the greater the use of paper, the greater the potential environmental impacts; for example:

- Not all paper comes from sustainable plantations, hence there can be some significant deforestation associated with paper manufacture.
- Despite the existence of paper recyclers, much paper still ends up in landfill.
- Paper manufacture creates various environmentally damaging emissions, including nitrogen dioxide, sulphur dioxide and carbon dioxide.
- Wastewater generated from pulp and paper mills can create various environmental problems.
- Printing inks can be environmentally damaging.
- The process of recycling creates various wastes that can be environmentally damaging.

Key concept

Waste costs can be significant and once the costs of the various materials going to waste are considered, the actual cost of waste can be many times the costs incurred in having the waste taken away from the organisation. Waste is an area that deserves management attention.

LO5.5 The Balanced Scorecard

Balanced Scorecard (BSC) framework
Seeks to translate an organisation's mission and related strategies into a set of performance measures that then provide a framework for strategically managing the organisation

We will now consider yet another tool that managers can use to manage their organisation. This approach to performance management is a framework known as the **Balanced Scorecard (BSC)**, and it is very different to the management tools already discussed in this chapter – albeit that the knowledge derived from these other management tools can influence the objectives and measures that we use with the Balanced Scorecard framework.

This framework, which was initially developed many years back by Robert Kaplan and David Norton (1992), recognises that strategically, for an organisation to succeed, consideration needs to be given to a number of different performance measures that effectively link together to enable an organisation to achieve its strategic priorities. That is, the Balanced Scorecard seeks to translate an organisation's mission and related strategies into a set of performance measures that then provide a framework for strategically managing the organisation. Information pertaining to the respective performance measures is subsequently collected to assess how well the managers are achieving particular objectives.

The performance measures developed within the Balanced Scorecard framework – and which are determined after considering the organisation's missions and objectives – will represent a balanced mixture of both financial and non-financial performance measures. Because managers will be assessed (or 'scored') on the basis of a balanced mixture of performance measures, the framework was labelled the 'Balanced Scorecard'.

Many organisations use the BSC as a fundamental element of their planning, monitoring and control. The BSC framework emphasises – like much of the discussion in this book – that the use of financial indicators alone will not be sufficient to appreciate the overall performance of an organisation.

When developed by Kaplan and Norton, the BSC framework considered performance from four different but interdependent perspectives, which are outlined in the sections that follow.

The financial perspective

Central to this perspective is the question of how the organisation can create value for the main stakeholders of the organisation, whom Kaplan and Norton considered to be the owners (for example, the shareholders of a company). Kaplan and Norton specifically raise an important question for managers to answer: 'How do we look to shareholders?' That is, what view would shareholders have of the management and performance of the organisation?

Kaplan and Norton's approach assumes that owners ultimately value profitability and financial returns, and therefore Kaplan and Norton assume that the overall objective of most organisations is to maximise profits and the financial returns (dividends) going to the owners. This would not be the case for not-for profit organisations, and therefore the application of the BSC to such organisations requires some modifications of 'perspectives'. Nevertheless, the framework when modified would still be useful.

Within the BSC, the results of all the efforts of managers are ultimately judged by shareholders in terms of the profits that were earned, and in terms of what financial returns the owners (shareholders) ultimately received. Therefore, the goals of the organisation might be to create ongoing growth in sales and profits (and remember, these goals would need to be consistent with the overall mission of the organisation).

Performance measures for this perspective – and these measures are determined after we have determined the objectives for this perspective – allow us to assess our level of progress towards the objectives. The measures could include sales revenue, or the amount of income earned by owners relative to their total financial investment in the organisation (often referred to as the return on equity).

The customer perspective

Central to this perspective is the question of what existing and prospective customers expect from the organisation and what they value about the organisation. Kaplan and Norton specifically raise the following question for managers to address: 'How do customers see us?' Successful organisations focus on meeting or exceeding customers' needs and expectations rather than necessarily focusing simply upon financial measures of performance. Successful managers understand that focusing on customers is critical to achieving the financial goals of an organisation.

To satisfy performance measures established under the 'financial perspective' requires the support of customers. The overall objectives from the 'customer perspective' might be to increase customer satisfaction and the numbers of customers.

Performance measures for this perspective could include results from customer satisfaction surveys, changes in the organisation's actual share of the market, and retention and growth in customer numbers.

The internal business perspective

Central to this perspective is the question of what policies and procedures need to be in place if the organisation is to achieve its objectives in relation to the financial perspective and the customer perspective. Kaplan and Norton specifically raise the following question for managers to address: 'What must we excel at?'

Once you have established what the financial objectives are, and what the objectives are in relation to customers, then you need to ensure that the various operating policies and procedures in place are consistent with achieving such objectives. For example, to improve customer satisfaction (a possible goal within the customer perspective), you might have as a goal the improvement of the quality of, and innovation inherent within, your products and services.

To improve returns to shareholders (a possible goal within the financial perspective), you might seek to improve the efficiency of your production processes. Some performance measures for this internal business perspective might relate to the number of defective goods being returned, the amount of waste being generated, or the number of new products being developed.

The learning and growth perspective

Central to this perspective, which is also known as the *innovation and learning perspective*, is the question of how does an organisation learn and adapt in order to achieve its objectives in relation to the financial perspective and the customer perspective. Kaplan and Norton specifically raise the following question for managers: 'How can we continue to improve and add value?'

This perspective focuses upon the capabilities required within the organisation if it is expected to ultimately achieve its overall goals or objectives, which might be to maximise profits and to satisfy the expectations of those stakeholders on which it is dependent; for example, customers. These capabilities might relate to employee abilities and attitudes (employee skills, training and satisfaction). They might also be linked to the information systems in place to enable employees/managers to perform their roles.

Some objectives here might be to increase employee expertise in strategically important areas, and to increase employee workplace satisfaction. The view is that if this learning and growth perspective of performance is not properly managed, then it will be difficult for an organisation to perform well. Performance measures here might be linked to employee satisfaction surveys, the amount spent on training programs, or the number of staff with particular qualifications.

In developing the BSC, Kaplan and Norton stressed that it was important that not too many performance measures are identified for attention at any point in time. It is generally accepted that no more than three or four measures of performance should be identified for each perspective, providing up to 16 performance measures in total for managers to concentrate on based upon using the four perspectives identified by Kaplan and Norton. According to Kaplan and Norton:

> While giving senior managers information from different perspectives, the balanced scorecard minimises information overload by limiting the number of measures used. Companies rarely suffer from having too few measures. More commonly they keep adding new measures whenever an employee or a consultant makes a worthwhile suggestion. The balanced scorecard forces managers to focus on the handful of measures that are most critical.
>
> Source: Kaplan and Norton (1992), p. 72.

Summarising the BSC framework

Kaplan and Norton (1992, p. 72) provided a figure to summarise the working of their framework (see **Figure 5.10**). The managers of an organisation need to determine the goals under each

FIGURE 5.10 The Balanced Scorecard links performance measures to particular goals

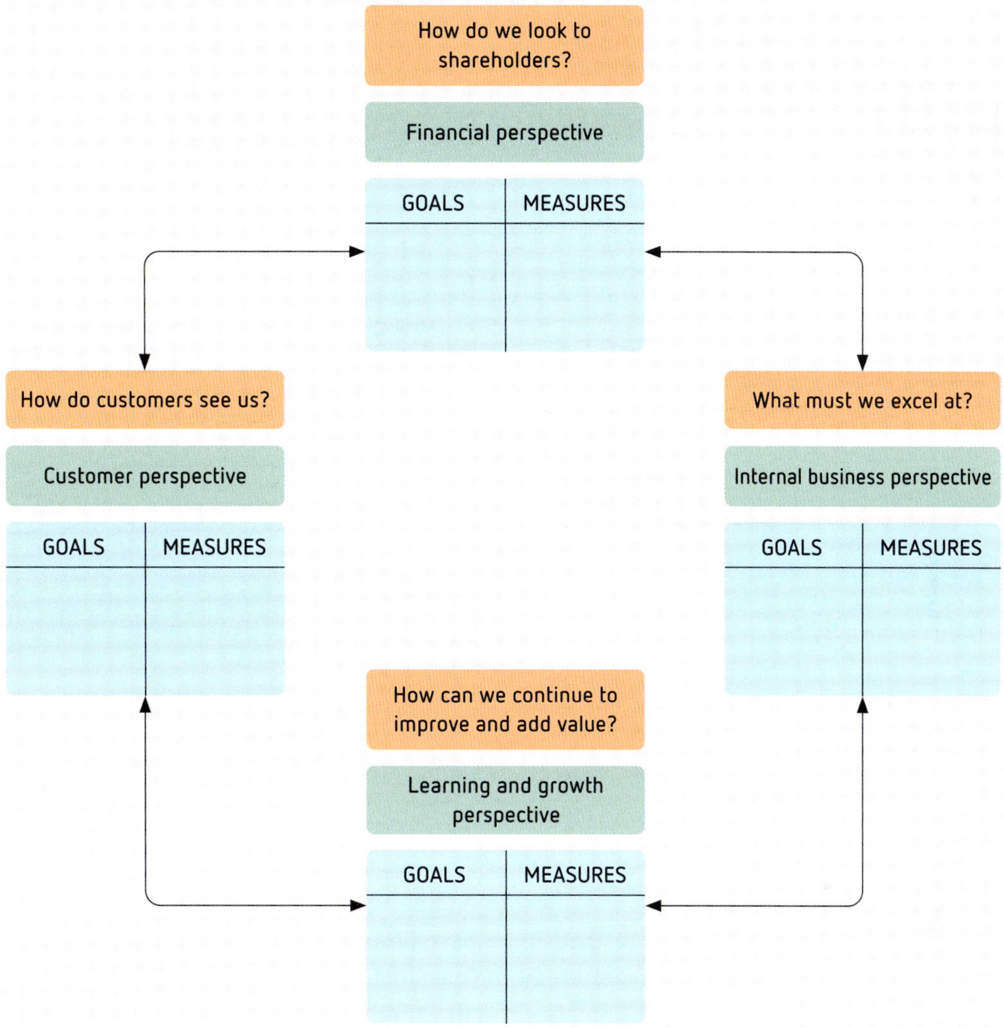

Source: Kaplan and Norton (1992), p. 72.

perspective and the respective performance measures to use to help ensure that the organisation is moving towards achieving the respective goals. We have left the goals and performance measures blank in Figure 5.10, but you might consider what you would identify as the appropriate goals, and the relevant performance measures to apply, for a particular organisation you might be interested in. Again, remember the sequencing here. The overall mission of the organisation should help us develop the goals under each perspective. Once we know the goals, we can then develop some measures to identify whether we appear to be achieving our goals.

As the discussion above has hopefully emphasised, there are various logical linkages between the various perspectives utilised within the BSC framework. For example, the policies and procedures in place to educate and train staff (part of the learning and growth perspective) will influence how things are done within the organisation (part of the internal business perspective). In turn, the way things are done within the organisation will influence the products and services provided to customers (the customer perspective), and this will in turn influence customer support and ultimately the profitability of the organisation (the financial perspective). That is, there is a causal relationship that occurs in a bottom-up direction, as reflected in Figure 5.11.

FIGURE 5.11 Causal relationship between the various performance measures used in the BSC

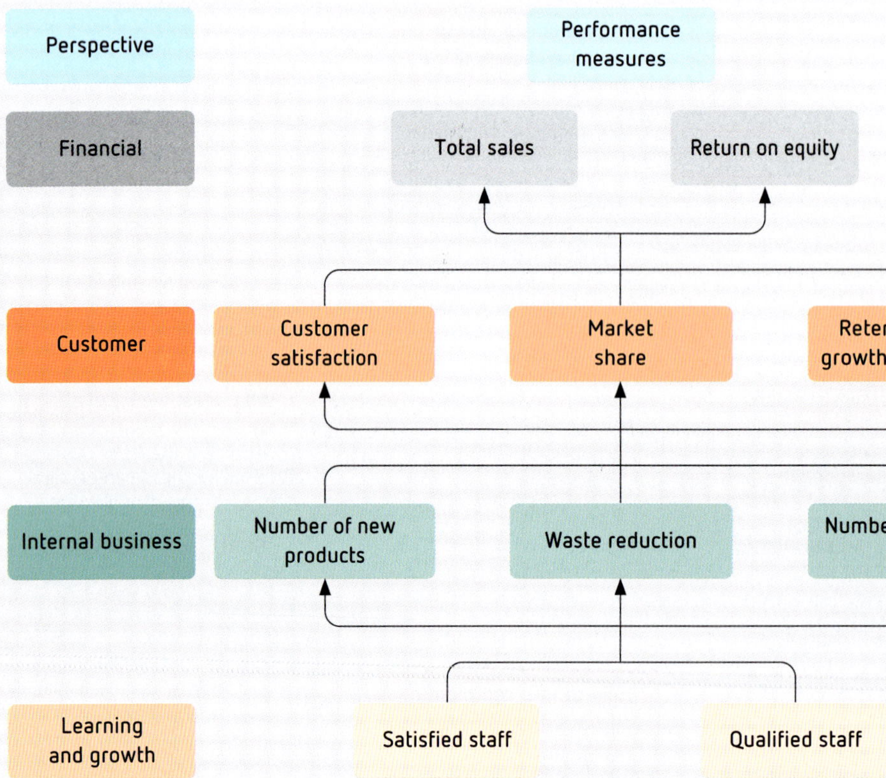

The performance measures shown in **Figure 5.11** are just an example – an organisation might choose different measures depending upon its objectives and strategy. Nevertheless, what **Figure 5.11** shows is that, if we have both satisfied staff (perhaps measured through a questionnaire administered by an independent consultant) and appropriately qualified staff (perhaps measured by the number of staff with the relevant formal qualifications), then they will more likely work towards producing new products (as measured by the number of new products available for customers within the reporting period) in an efficient manner, as reflected by less waste (perhaps measured by the amount of waste going to landfill) and by less defects (perhaps measured by the amount of products being returned to the organisation). With high-quality products being produced – due to the well-performing internal business processes – customers should be satisfied with, and supportive of, the organisation. Customer satisfaction should increase (as reflected in a customer satisfaction survey), the market share should increase (as perhaps reflected by the sales of the organisation divided by the total industry sales), and there should be a retention of existing customers together with an increase in the number of new customers. Lastly, with satisfied and increasing numbers of customers, financial performance should ultimately improve, as reflected by such measures as total sales increasing, and return on equity increasing for owners. The measures we create (10 in this case) can be used to assess and reward managers with assigned responsibilities over particular perspectives.

For more on the application of the BSC, see **Learning exercise 5.8**.

5.8 Learning Exercise

Application of the Balanced Scorecard

Scenario: Endless Summer Surfboards is a medium-sized surfboard manufacturer operating at Kaikoura on the South Island of New Zealand. It sells surfboards within New Zealand and also exports to Australia, Hawaii and Southern California. The company is owned by three well-known local surfers and employs 20 other staff. The company's reputation has been built on making high-quality, innovative surfboards that are handmade and original.

The surfboards of Endless Summer Surfboards have a reputation for incorporating the latest ideas in surf design, and are valued for being produced in a way that minimises environmental harm, and in a workplace environment in which staff health and safety is a priority.

One of the owners, Pete Way, has asked you to develop a BSC to improve the overall performance of Endless Summer Surfboards. In doing so, Pete Way has provided you with the following information:

Mission of Endless Summer Surfboards

To be the leading New Zealand surfboard manufacturer, known for the creation of innovative surfboards that are produced in a socially and environmentally responsible manner.

Some key objectives of Endless Summer as determined by its owner/managers

- *To be the leading surfboard manufacturer in New Zealand (as reflected by sales volume) within five years.*
- *To be generating a return of 15 per cent on the owners' investment in the organisation within five years.*
- *To continuously reduce the amount of waste going to landfill.*
- *To have no serious injuries or workplace-related illnesses, and to continuously improve employee satisfaction.*

What factors should be considered when developing a BSC for Endless Summer Surfboards?

You could develop your own perspectives to use in the BSC, but for the purposes of this example we will apply the four perspectives suggested by Kaplan and Norton. With this in mind, ask yourself the following question.

How do the mission and related objectives of the organisation shape the performance measures suggested under each of the four perspectives?

From the mission, we can see that financial performance is a priority, but so is social and environmental performance.

We can consider some causal relationships between potential performance measures, which are reflected in **Figure 5.12**. In devising our performance measures, we firstly consider the mission of Endless Summer Surfboards. We then come up with a number of objectives under each of the four perspectives suggested by Kaplan and Norton, as outlined in **Table 5.1**. These objectives are devised to be consistent with the mission of the organisation, which prioritises not only growth but also a high level of socially and environmentally responsible behaviour. The performance measures then identified are deemed to be consistent with the objectives. Therefore, the sequence is that the mission drives the determination of the objectives, which then drives the determination of the respective performance measures.

TABLE 5.1 Objectives and performance measures for Endless Summer Surfboards, as developed using the BSC

Objective	Performance measure
Financial perspective	
Growth in sales	Return on equity
Growth in profits	Increased sales revenue from surfboards
	Reduced average financial cost per surfboard
	Reduced energy costs
Customer perspective	
Increased customer satisfaction	Results of independent customer satisfaction survey to show improvement in satisfaction
Surfboards incorporate latest technology	Number of new designs being offered to customers increase
Surfboards create minimal social and environmental impacts	Number of new customers to increase
	Number of customer complaints reduced
Internal business processes	
Utilise latest research on design for high-performance surfboards	Number of new surfboard designs for sale to increase each year
	Results of waste audits to show reduced waste going to landfill per surfboard each year
Utilise latest research on design to reduce environmental impacts and improve health and safety of employees	Results of health and safety audits conducted by independent party to show that results are in accordance with accepted best practice
Learning and growth	
Satisfied staff	Results of independent employee satisfaction survey to show satisfaction is deemed to be in the high range
Staff have knowledge of latest innovations in design with respect to surfboard performance and waste minimisation	Increasing qualifications of staff with respect to surfboard design
	Amounts paid for training staff in relation to surfboard design and waste management to meet budgeted amount
All staff are aware of required health and safety standards to be employed for respective positions	Amounts spent training staff in relation to health and safety to meet budgeted amount

We could include more detail here about the BSC, but our intention is simply to provide you with an overview of a framework that is still used by many large organisations as part of their planning activities, as well as for monitoring and controlling actual performance. For students undertaking a major in accounting, it is likely that you will study the BSC in more depth in later subjects.

The BSC and management remuneration

Since the BSC is a key part of many organisations' planning activities, and because it sets various key performance measures that are developed with the organisations' missions and strategic priorities in mind, it is often used as a basis for paying bonuses to senior managers. For example, if we look at BHP's 2021 annual report – BHP was the world's largest global mining organisation in 2021 based on market capitalisation, which in turn is based on the total number of issued shares multiplied by their respective share price – we see that the performance measures developed within the BSC framework were used to assess senior managers/executives. These measures were used to assess employees, including the CEO (while there is no need to specifically refer to the particular regulations, within Australia it is a requirement that details of the remuneration of senior executives and managers be publicly disclosed within public companies' annual reports):

FIGURE 5.12 Causal relationship between the various performance measures adopted by Endless Summer Surfboards

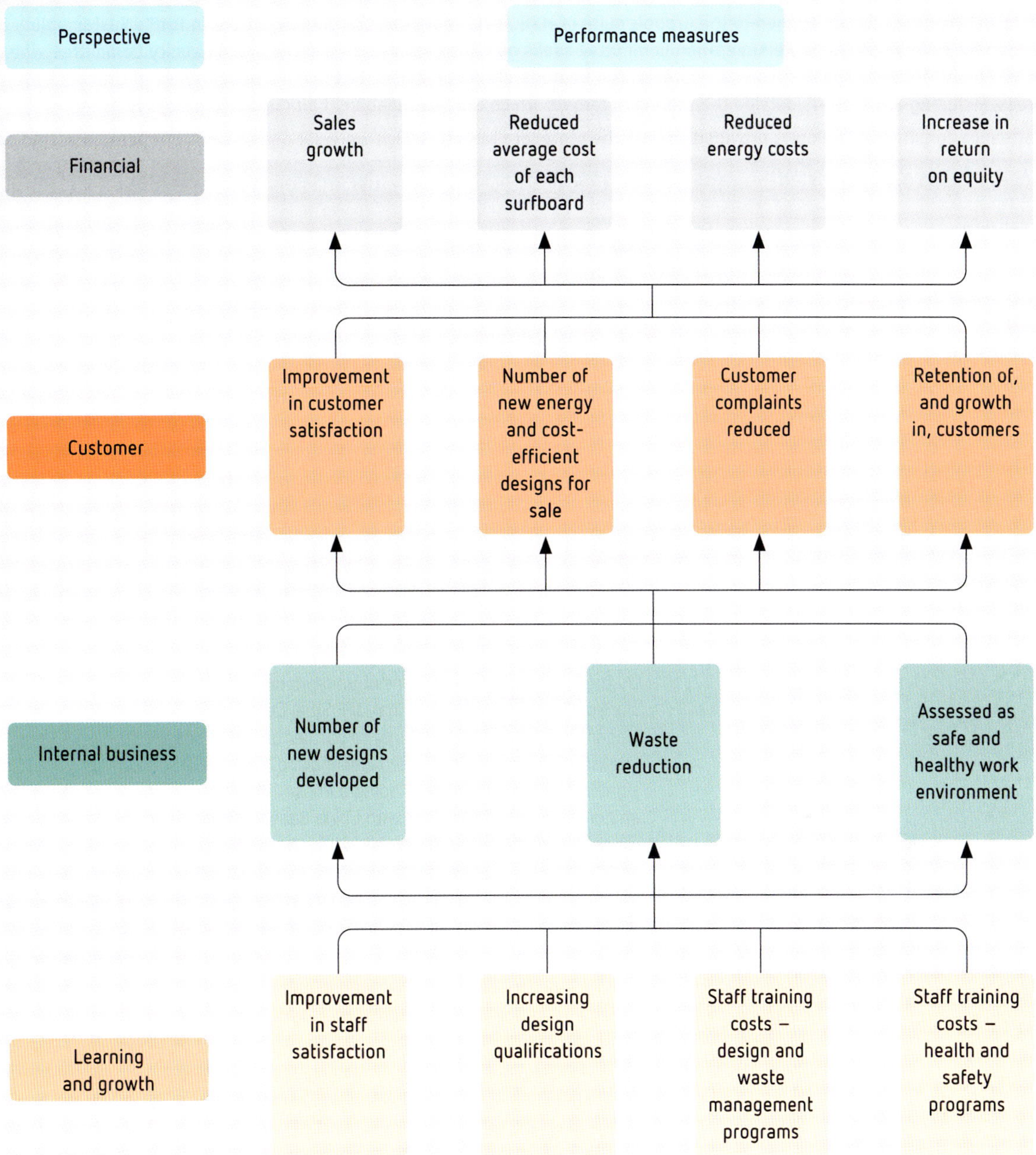

> The Committee sets a balanced scorecard of short, medium and long-term elements including HSEC, financial and individual performance measures, with targets and relative weightings at the beginning of the financial year in order to appropriately motivate the CEO to achieve outperformance that contributes to the long-term sustainability of the Group and shareholder wealth creation.
>
> Source: BHP (2021), p. 103.

While the CEO of BHP is provided with rewards linked to a number of financial and non-financial aspects of performance, specific reference is made in the 2021 annual report to the area of 'health, safety, environment and community' (HSEC; see **Exhibit 5.1**).

EXHIBIT 5.1 Extract from the *BHP Annual Report 2021* – example of the use of the BSC

HSEC

The HSEC targets for the CEO are aligned to the Group's suite of HSEC five-year public targets as set out in BHP's Sustainability Report. As it has done for several years, the Remuneration Committee seeks guidance each year from the Sustainability Committee when assessing HSEC performance against scorecard targets. The Remuneration Committee has taken a holistic view of Group performance in critical areas, including any matters outside the scorecard targets which the Sustainability Committee considers relevant.

The performance commentary below is provided against the scorecard targets, which were set on the basis of operated assets only.

HSEC measures	Scorecard targets	Performance against scorecard targets	Measure outcome
Significant events	No significant (actual level 4) health, safety (including fatalities), environment or community events during the year.	There were no fatalities or other significant HSEC events during FY2021 at operated assets. In addition, for a maximum outcome to be awarded, strong progress was required on the development and implementation of BHP's Fatality Elimination Program in all regions, and this was largely achieved for FY2021.	Close to maximum.
Climate change	Steps in place to achieve reported GHG emissions in FY2022 at FY2017 level. Decarbonisation plans developed in line with pathways to net zero and incorporated into the capital allocation plan process. Two partnerships formalised with strategic customers in the steel sector.	For FY2021, we improved on our operational GHG emissions target of 17.0Mt, with an actual result of 16.2Mt. All operated assets completed the development of decarbonisation plans which were incorporated in the capital allocation process. The new renewable power purchase agreements at Escondida and Spence, both in Chile, remain on track for first power supply in the first half of FY2022. In addition, in FY2021 we also entered into renewable power purchase agreements for Queensland Coal and Kwinana nickel refinery in Australia. During the year, memorandums of understanding were signed with China Baowu (China), JFE Steel Corporation (Japan) and HBIS Limited (China) to partner on emissions intensity reduction in integrated steelmaking. We have significantly progressed developing a Phase 1 research and development agreement with China Baowu (which we anticipate will be signed in FY2022) and significant work is also being undertaken in collaboration with our partners to convert the remaining two memorandums of understanding into executed definitive contracts.	Slightly above target.
Management of priority Tailings Storage Facilities (TSFs)	All priority TSFs are assessed based on key risk indicator data, and are either within appetite or continued operation outside appetite is approved with remediation progressing to plan.	All priority TSFs are now either within appetite based on key risk indicator data or continued operation outside appetite is approved with remediation progressing to plan. We have continued improving our key risk indicator performance with 84% of all key risk indicators for priority TSFs rated either on target or less risk being taken than target, against a target of 80%.	Slightly above target.

Source: BHP (2021), p. 109.

A review of **Exhibit 5.1** again highlights the fact that organisations appear to be accepting a responsibility, and accountability, for the social and environmental implications of their operations, and that they do incorporate social- and environment-related measures in analysis using the BSC, as well as in the incentive programs used to motivate senior managers.

For a discussion of multiple management approaches, as presented in this chapter, see **Learning exercise 5.9**.

5.9 Learning Exercise

Using multiple management approaches

Scenario: You are the senior accountant for Big Metal Mining Company. One of the company's senior managers has listened to explanations of LCA, MFCA and the Balanced Scorecard. Somebody she knows from outside the organisation has suggested that the organisation use all three management approaches, but she believes that doing all three would be wasteful and unnecessary. She has asked you to explain why anybody would think that it is a good idea to apply the LCA, MFCA and the Balanced Scorecard.

Issue: What should be considered when assessing the merits (or not) of using LCA, MFCA and the Balanced Scorecard together?

Solution: To determine if it is viable to use the LCA, MFCA, and Balanced Scorecard together, you should consider the following issues.

1 The size and resources of the organisation

To the extent that an organisation is large enough to enable it to have the resources and expertise to do it, then it should consider using all three management approaches. The three different management techniques can work together in a way that is very useful.

2 How the three different management techniques work together

LCA allows managers to understand the various phases of the life cycle of a product or service, and the associated impacts. This can highlight various risks and opportunities and, therefore, factors that warrant attention. Consideration can also be given to whether the impacts created throughout the life cycle are consistent with the organisation's mission and objectives.

Knowledge of the life cycle of a product then assists an organisation to perform its MFCA. The application of MFCA requires managers to understand the flow of materials throughout an organisation, and knowledge from LCA will help in preparing the required flow models. Therefore, although they perform different, and valuable, functions, both LCA and MFCA can usefully be used together.

The BSC allows managers to strategically develop goals under particular perspectives, together with linked measures. Knowledge gained through LCA and MFCA can highlight specific areas that need to be prioritised and addressed, and this should influence the goals and performance measures utilised with the BSC approach.

Conclusion

So, in summary, it would not be wasteful to apply all the management tools within one organisation. Many organisations throughout the world – typically larger organisations – do use all three approaches.

Why do I need to know about the balanced scorecard (BSC)?

The BSC is a frequently used management tool that links various organisational objectives to various financial and non-financial performance measures. By using the BSC, managers will be further encouraged to understand how the various activities and goals of an organisation relate to each other (and to the organisation's mission) and how achieving the various goals requires a number of well defined financial and non-financial performance measures. It encourages critical thought and is not difficult to apply.

LO5.6 Capital investment decisions

Organisations will, from time to time, make investments in assets that are going to be retained for several years, such as investments in property, plant and equipment. Generally speaking, an *investment* can be deemed to exist when we invest cash or other resources into some other resource, with the expectation of then receiving some form of future periodic gains or other appreciation in value.

capital investment decisions
An organisation's decisions about which major investments to make in respect of property, plant and equipment

The decisions about which major investments to make in respect of property, plant and equipment are often referred to as **capital investment decisions** (or capital expenditure decisions, or capital budgeting decisions), and they are made to improve the operations of an organisation. Capital investment decisions are long-term decisions by managers. In determining the acceptability of potential capital investments (for example, whether to acquire a new air-conditioning system for a factory), managers need to consider the various expected future costs and benefits associated with the investment.

Capital investments need to be carefully planned, as they often involve large expenditures and, if it is subsequently determined that a wrong decision was made, are not always easy to reverse without significant financial loss. The assets being acquired might be anticipated to be used for long periods of time, and there will always be some level of uncertainty about the future cash flows and other impacts associated with the asset. This uncertainty means there are inherently some risks involved. To remove some of this risk, careful consideration must be given to gathering the appropriate information *before* making the investment. Nevertheless, the reality is that some poor decisions will still be made from time to time. With proper planning, however, the likelihood of costly mistakes will hopefully be reduced.

Consistent with our discussion in Chapter 3, when managers make decisions – including capital investment decisions – they need to:

- identify the problem that needs to be solved – for example, what property, plant or equipment is needed, and what aspects of its performance are important to the organisation
- collect the relevant information – determine how managers will evaluate the potential acquisition (for example, which decision tool to use), and what data they will need
- determine alternative courses of action – in particular, which alternatives seem to meet the requirements of the organisation; this will require particular 'decision rules' to be established in order to guide the decision making
- evaluate (rank) the alternatives
- make a decision.

When considering the acquisition of an item of property, plant or equipment, there are many issues to consider; for example, you need to consider the initial acquisition costs. Furthermore, it needs to be determined whether the acquisition is likely to be compatible with the organisation's mission and goals – perhaps goals that have been established through the use of the BSC, as just discussed. And who will take responsibility for monitoring and evaluating the subsequent performance of any new capital investment?

The likely social and environmental impacts of the asset throughout its expected life also need to be considered in the investment decision. In this regard, some form of LCA of projected performance would be useful, as would the application of MFCA (if available data supports such analysis), in order to answer such questions as the following:

- What forms of occupational health and safety implications might flow from the acquisition of the asset?

- When operating, is this asset likely to generate waste or consume relatively high levels of materials, and how does this compare with the currently used machinery and available alternatives?
- What sorts of noise levels will the acquired assets generate and how might this impact particular stakeholders?
- How energy-efficient is the asset likely to be, and will this efficiency change as the investment gets older? What are the implications for carbon emissions?
- What will happen to the asset at the end of its life cycle? Can it be reused or recycled? Will it end up in landfill, and if so, what are the likely environmental implications?
- Will the use of the asset lead to potential clean-up or environmental remediation costs?
- Would the acquisition of this asset result in the loss of jobs for many people? For example, if a new mechanised process is acquired, will this displace workers who previously performed the work manually? Will the loss of jobs be consistent with the organisation's mission and values? What responsibility, if any, will be taken for displaced employees?
- How did the manufacturer of the equipment treat their workers and how did they ensure that workers employed across the supply chain used to manufacture the product were treated well?
- With the various impacts in mind, how would different stakeholders view the acquisition of the asset? That is, will it enhance the reputation, or image, of the organisation?

Decisions about which property, plant and machinery to acquire (and, indeed, in respect of all investments) need to consider a mixture of financial and non-financial factors. Also, while information relating to the bullet points above (referring to various social and environmental issues) might be collected and reported in qualitative or non-monetary forms, managers could consider whether the information should be quantified and potentially monetised (and the monetisation would require the use of various sorts of models which might seek to place a cost on the various externalities). Further, when considering various non-financial aspects of a potential capital investment opportunity, it might be decided that particular social and environmental performance criteria must be met before consideration is even given to financial-based assessments. In a sense, this represents a form of risk management. For example, if a machine exceeds particular noise levels, if it generates high levels of emissions, or if it is likely to be sourced from a manufacturer that potentially has modern slavery existing within its supply chain, then it might be decided that the potential investment does not fit with the organisation's mission and goals and therefore is rejected regardless of its potential financial performance and contribution. Such decision rules are reflected in **Figure 5.13**. As **Figure 5.13** also shows, one of the important final parts of the capital investment review process is the post-implementation audit which would involve managers assessing the prior decisions and the accuracy of any cash flow projections that had previously been made and used. Lessons learned can then flow through to subsequent capital investment appraisals. For readers who would like additional material on how to embed sustainability related issues within capital investment decisions, the organisation known as Accounting for Sustainability (A4S) has released a document entitled *Essential Guide to CAPEX: A practical guide to embedding sustainability into capital investment appraisal* (available at **https://www.accountingforsustainability.org/en/knowledge-hub/guides/capex.html**, accessed July 2022).

FIGURE 5.13 Depiction of a possible decision-making process associated with capital investment decisions

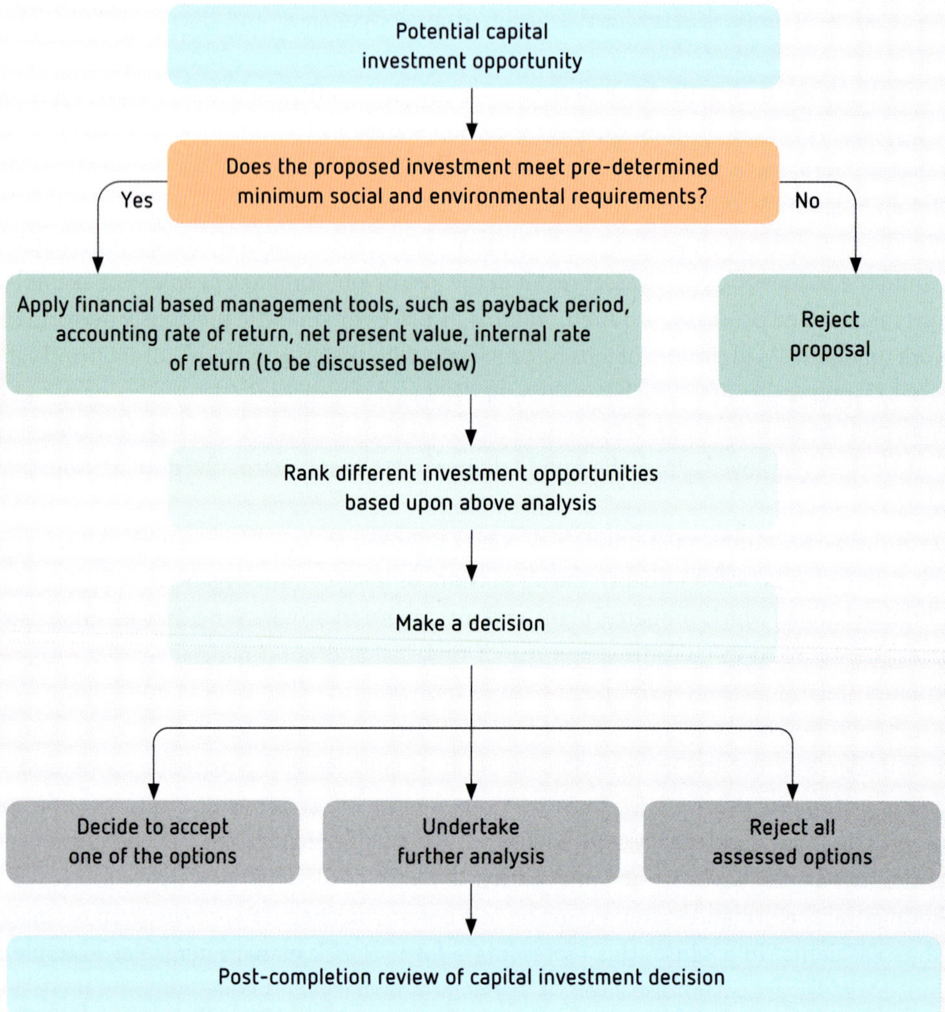

We will now consider some financial-based (monetised) management tools that are often used when appraising potential capital investments. However, keep in mind that these financial-based management tools should be used in conjunction with other non-financial and financial considerations before any potential investment is ultimately made. That is, while providing useful inputs into a decision-making process, none of the following management tools should ever be used in isolation to make a decision (as Figure 5.13 depicts).

Four financial-based management tools that can assist managers to make investment choices are (and according to CPA Australia, 2015, these are the most commonly used capital investment appraisal tools):

- the payback period
- the accounting rate of return
- the net present value
- the internal rate of return.

Keep in mind some material from previous chapters of this book. For example, remember that there are certain costs that do not alter with the level or volume of production (fixed costs), while there are other costs that change in total as activity changes (variable costs).

We will use the same information to explain each method, as outlined below.

Information for Learning exercises 5.10 to 5.13.

Goodtime Surfboards is a business that produces 1000 surfboards per year. It places its surfboards in protective packaging prior to shipping to customers. It currently pays an external party to do this packaging. Goodtime Surfboards provides the actual packaging, and the external party provides the labour to do the packaging – the packers come onsite and wrap each surfboard, at a cost of $30 per board.

A machine has become available which will do the packaging. The machine will cost $75 000, payable immediately, and is expected to last for five years, at which time it is expected to be sold for $4000, which we will refer to as its 'residual value'. Packing with the machine will use the same amount of packaging. However, the machine will generate other expenses. The operating costs of the machine are anticipated to be $5000 per year, in the form of $5 variable packing costs per surfboard (which relate to energy and machine operating costs).

Payback period

The **payback period** is an approach commonly used to assess a prospective investment. It addresses the question of how long it will take to recoup the cash that was spent on acquiring the investment. That is, how many years will it take for the sum of net cash inflows generated by the investment to equal the original cash investment? In some cases, the net cash inflows might actually relate to savings that are possible from acquiring a new machine. For instance, in the example we are going to use, if we acquire the machine, then one saving will be the $30 per surfboard we were previously paying to the packers to have the surfboards packaged.

payback period Addresses the question of how long it will take to recoup the amount that was spent on acquiring an investment

In making a decision using this management tool, managers often stipulate a maximum payback period, beyond which a project would be rejected. The general rule is that the smaller the payback period the better, particularly if the organisation is operating in a relatively risky industry. All else being equal, managers will generally select the project with the shortest payback period.

The riskier a project appears to be, then the smaller we will want the payback period to be. For example, if we are operating in an industry that is subject to rapidly changing customer expectations and technologies, and/or high levels of competition (which would make this a relatively risky industry), then we will want a relatively quick payback period, particularly if our investments cannot be redeployed to other uses. The longer it takes for an asset to generate benefits equal to its costs, the greater the chance that circumstances might change and the asset might not end up producing the intended returns. In circumstances with high levels of uncertainty, it is more important that an asset has a short payback period, so that managers can feel more confident that the asset will generate returns that are at least equal to its costs.

For a discussion of how to determine the payback period for Goodtime Surfboards, see Learning exercise 5.10.

5.10 Learning Exercise

Determining the payback period

We are required to calculate the payback period for the proposed capital investment of Goodtime Surfboards. We know that the machine will initially cost $75 000. We also know that we will not have to pay the packers $30 per surfboard, but we will need to pay $5 in variable costs for each surfboard made. This provides a net saving of $25 per surfboard. We are only considering those costs that change as a result of the investment decision – these are the 'relevant costs'.

If we sell 1000 surfboards each year, then the cash saving each year is $25 000 once we make the up-front investment of $75 000. We can use the following table to determine the payback period.

Year	Amount to 'pay back' as at the start of the year	Net cash flows for the year (represented by the savings in relevant variable costs)	Cumulative amount paid back at the end of the year	Amount still to 'pay back' at the end of the year
1	$75 000	$25 000	$25 000	$50 000
2	$50 000	$25 000	$50 000	$25 000
3	$25 000	$25 000	$75 000	$0

As we can see from the above table, when looking at the cash flows, we are looking at how the investment changes the total cash flows of the organisation. After three years, the investment will have generated net cash inflows (represented by the savings in cash outflows) that, when aggregated, equal the up-front cash investment. Therefore, the payback period is three years.

Management then needs to determine if this is acceptable. If management had stipulated a payback period of three years or less, then this project would have satisfied this requirement. Of course, there would be other criteria to be applied before a decision is made as to whether the project is ultimately accepted. Some of these other criteria will be financial in nature (as shown in the Learning exercises that follow), and as we should appreciate by now, there will be various social and environmental factors that could also be considered – for example, what will happen to the machine at the end of its life cycle, or is the machine a safe alternative for employees?

There are various advantages to using the payback period method, including that it is very easy to understand and to calculate, and it does consider risk in the sense that we will reduce the required payback period for those projects deemed to be relatively risky. However, in terms of disadvantages, the payback period method ignores the cash flows that occur after the payback period has been reached. For example, if two projects have a payback period of two years, but one of these projects has another 10 years of profitable use while the other project only has one more year of profitable use subsequent to the payback period, then both potential projects would be treated the same. Furthermore, the payback period does not consider the time value of money. That is, cash flows received in different years are all considered on the same basis without any discounting of those cash flows to be received in later years. The time value of money becomes increasingly important as we consider the value provided by capital investments over a longer time horizon.

Accounting rate of return

Another management tool for appraising potential capital investments is the **accounting rate of return method (ARR)**. This is a relatively simple measure. It is calculated by dividing the average incremental return (or profit) derived from (or traceable to) the investment (in this case the net savings) by the average investment made in the asset; that is:

accounting rate of return method (ARR)
Calculated by dividing the average incremental return (or profit) or savings derived from (or traceable to) the investment by the average investment made in the asset

$$\text{ARR} = \frac{\text{Average annual profit from the asset}}{\text{Average investment required to earn that profit}} \times 100\%$$

In calculating each period's profits (or net savings as in the case of Goodtime Surfboards), we need to acknowledge the reduction in the value of the acquired asset across time, which we shall call *depreciation*. That is, when calculating the ARR, we are including expenses that do not directly impact cash flows.

Depreciation expense per year represents the allocation of the cost of an asset (less any expected residual value) over the number of years in which benefits are expected to be derived from the asset. The total depreciation expense to be recognised across the life of the asset will be the original purchase cost less the amount we expect to receive for the investment at the end of its useful life, which we shall call the *residual value*.

depreciation expense
When calculated on a time basis, represents the allocation of the cost (or revalued amount) of an asset (less any expected residual value) over the number of periods in which benefits are expected to be derived from the asset

In relation to Goodtime Surfboards, the original cost of the investment was $75 000, the useful life of the investment is expected to be five years, and the residual value is expected to be $4000. Therefore, the total depreciation expense to be recognised across the five years amounts to $71 000, and $14 200 of this depreciation would be equally allocated to each year throughout the useful life of the investment (this is called the *straight-line method of depreciation*). We can represent the straight-line method of depreciation by the following equation:

$$\frac{\text{Acquisition cost - expected residual value}}{\text{Expected useful life of asset}} = \frac{\$75\,000 - \$4000}{5} = \$14\,200$$

When calculating the average investment – as required in the above formula for ARR – we simply add the original cost to the final residual value and divide this total amount by 2. That is, we average the value of the investment at the beginning of its life with the value of the investment at the end of its life. The average investment in the asset therefore is:

$$\text{Average investment} = \frac{\text{Acquisition cost + expected residual value}}{2}$$

In applying the ARR, there will be certain decision rules. One rule, for example, could be that the investment must at least achieve a specified target ARR, and if there are alternatives, then the project with the highest ARR would be the one selected (subject to other considerations as well – remember that these management tools should not be used in isolation). For example, perhaps the decision rule could be that a project will need to demonstrate an ARR above 15 per cent to be acceptable. Such decision rules would be decided upon by managers and will be different for different organisations, and even for different departments within organisations, or different types of investments within departments.

For a discussion of how to determine the ARR for Goodtime Surfboards, see **Learning exercise 5.11**.

5.11 Learning Exercise

Determining the accounting rate of return (ARR)

We are now required to calculate the ARR for the investment proposal of Goodtime Surfboards.

We know that the incremental savings per year amount to \$25 000. We must also consider the depreciation costs associated with using up the service potential of the asset over its useful life, which is five years. We know the asset cost \$75 000, and we expect to get \$4000 when we dispose of it in five years. We can calculate depreciation as:

$$\frac{\text{Acquisition cost} - \text{expected residual value}}{\text{Expected useful life of asset}} = \frac{\$75\,000 - \$4000}{5} = \$14\,200 \text{ per year}$$

After incorporating depreciation expense, the average incremental returns (profits) for the five years equals:

(\$25 000 – \$14 200) + (\$25 000 – \$14 200) + (\$25 000 – \$14 200) + (\$25 000 – \$14 200) + (\$25 000 – \$14 200) all divided by 5 = \$54 000 ÷ 5 = \$10 800

Other than depreciation expense, we have assumed there are no other expenses of a non-cash flow nature (such as various 'accrued' expenses). This is a simplifying assumption for the purposes of this question, but in practice, there would be many other expenses.

The average investment in the machine is:

$$\frac{\text{Acquisition cost} + \text{expected residual value}}{2} = \frac{\$75\,000 + \$4000}{2} = \$39\,500$$

therefore

$$\text{ARR} = \frac{\text{Average annual profit, or cost savings, from the asset}}{\text{Average investment required to earn that profit, or create cost savings}} \times 100\%$$

$$= \frac{\$10\,800}{\$39\,500} \times 100\%$$

$$= 27.34\ \%$$

All things being equal, the higher the ARR, the better. If the decision rule was that the ARR must be at least 15 per cent, then this capital investment would satisfy this requirement.

In terms of the advantages of the ARR method, like the payback method it is easy to understand and easy to calculate. However, also like the payback method, a disadvantage is that it ignores the time value of money, something that the net present value method – which we are about to discuss – does not ignore.

net present value method (NPV)
A method of planning for investments that considers all expected future cash flows and also considers the timing of the cash flows. A discount rate is applied to all these expected future cash flows to generate a 'net present value'

Net present value

When planning for particular investments, we consider expected future costs and benefits, not all of which can be measured in financial terms. When contemplating future financial costs and income streams, it is appropriate to discount the future cash flows back to a present value equivalent to the purchasing power of today's currency. This is where **net present value method (NPV)** considerations come into effect.

The payback period and the ARR both suffer from a major deficiency: they treat all the cash flows from different periods equivalently. That is, there is no recognition of the fact that a dollar (or any other currency denomination) received, or saved, now is worth more than one received, or saved, later. The payback period approach and the ARR simply add together all the cash flows from different periods without any discounting. However, the reality is that the present value of a dollar received today is more than the present value of a dollar received at a future date. We would all prefer to have a dollar now, rather than receiving a dollar later. A spare dollar now (or many dollars now) could be invested at some rate of interest and would grow to be more than one dollar in a year's time. It simply would not be sensible to pay out, say, \$10 000 now only to get \$10 000 back in a year's time. What you would be receiving back in the future would be worth less, and the magnitude of this difference is influenced by the interest rate being applied to the cash flows.

The interest rate applied to account for the time value of money will be influenced by:

- the preference for having cash now
- the inflation occurring
- the risks associated with the expected cash flows.

The greater our expectations regarding the risks that we will be exposed to in respect of the future cash flows associated with an investment, and the greater the rate of inflation and our desire for cash now, the greater the required rate of interest.

As an example, assume that another organisation knows that it will be able to pay us \$10 000 in a year's time, but it needs cash now. How much would we provide to the organisation now in exchange for a promise of \$10 000 in one year's time? That is, how much is \$10 000 to be received in one year's time worth now?

Logically, we know that the present value of \$10 000 in one year's time is less than the value of \$10 000 now, but to answer this we need to determine the appropriate interest rate (which we might also call the *discount rate*) to use. Given our preference for cash now, expected inflation rates, and the risk associated with loaning funds to this organisation, we might determine, for example, that the appropriate interest rate is 10 per cent. That is, for investments of this type, and with the same perceived risk, we expect to earn 10 per cent. As such, the present value (meaning the value right now) of the \$10 000 to be received in one year's time is \$9091. This can be confirmed as follows:

$$\$9091 \times (1 + \text{interest rate}) = \$9091 \times 1.10 = \$10\,000$$

This means that, for an investment of this risk, we would be indifferent between having \$9091 now, or receiving the \$10 000 in one year. They are both worth the same. The amount of \$9091 is the present value of \$10 000 in one year for this particular investment. If we had \$9091 and invested it at 10 per cent, which is our required rate of return for this type of investment, then we would have \$10 000 in one year's time.

Now, complicating this slightly, what if the agreement was that the \$10 000 was going to be paid back in two years' time, rather than in one year's time? What would be its present value now? The answer is that it would be \$8264. This can be confirmed by the following:

$$\$8264 \times 1.10 \times 1.10 = \$10\,000$$

What this means is that, at an interest rate of 10 per cent, after one year the original amount of \$8264 plus earned interest would be \$9091 (which is \$8264 × 1.10). If this full amount is then left intact for another year to earn 10 per cent, then it would ultimately become \$10 000, which is (\$9091 × 1.10).

Alternatively, we could have calculated the present value of \$10 000 to be received at the end of two years, at an interest rate of 10 per cent, as:

$$\$10\,000 \div (1.10)^2 = \$10\,000 \div 1.21 = \$8264$$

The general formula to work out the present value of a dollar to be received in the future is

$$\frac{\$1}{(1+k)^n}$$

where k is the interest rate and n is the number of years until the amount is going to be received.

Therefore, as another example, the present value of \$1 to be received in 4 years' time, discounted at 10 per cent, would equal:

$$\frac{\$1}{(1+.10)^4}$$

$$= \$0.6830$$

To apply the NPV method to evaluate potential capital investments, we need to:

- know the initial cash payment for the investment and the cash flows for each year of the investment's life
- determine the appropriate discount rate (interest rate)
- apply the discount rate to the expected cash flows to determine the present value of the expected future net cash flows from the investment.

For a discussion of how to determine the NPV for Goodtime Surfboards, see **Learning exercise 5.12**.

In terms of the advantages of the NPV method, it considers all expected future cash flows and it also considers the timing of the cash flows. In particular, it recognises that the present value of future cash flows is worth less than the same cash flows that happen sooner. However, in terms of possible disadvantages, the calculations do rely upon various estimates of cash flows as well as upon selecting the 'right' discount rate. Furthermore, the method does not actually provide us with the actual rate of return.

5.12 Learning Exercise

Determining the net present value (NPV)

We are required to calculate the NPV for the investment proposal of Goodtime Surfboards. After considering the risk of the investment, the inflation rate, and the organisation's preference for having cash now, it is determined that the appropriate discount rate is 10 per cent. For ease of calculation, we will assume that the net cash flows being generated from the investment (the savings of \$25 000 each year) occur at the end of each year. Also, we need to remember the residual value of \$4000 that we expect to receive for the machine at the end of its useful life. As the original cost of the machine, which was \$75 000, was incurred up-front, then there will be no discounting of this payment.

Year	Cash flow (undiscounted) $	Discount factor $\frac{\$1}{(1+k)^n}$	Present value of cash flows $
1	upfront payment (75 000)	1.00000	(75 000)
	25 000	0.90909	22 727
2	25 000	0.82645	20 661
3	25 000	0.75131	18 783
4	25 000	0.68301	17 075
5	25 000	0.62092	15 523
	residual amount 4 000	0.62092	2 484
Total net present value of cash savings from this initiative			$22 253

The decision rule applying the NPV method is quite simple, and would be that the NPV needs to be positive, which means that it is at least generating the required rate of return. By contrast, if the NPV is negative, then we reject it. For this capital investment, the project would be acceptable as the NPV is positive, meaning that the actual rate of return exceeds the required rate of 10 per cent.

Internal rate of return

The application of the **internal rate of return method (IRR)** relies upon using a discount rate like the net present value method. However, in this case, it requires the determination of the discount rate that would cause the present value of all the cash outflows pertaining to the investment to be equal to the present value of all the cash inflows. That is, it determines the actual discount rate which, when applied to all the cash flows associated with the project, will generate an NPV of precisely zero.

internal rate of return method (IRR)
Informs managers about what the expected rate of return on the investment is, given the predictions about future cash flows, by calculating a discount rate, which generates a net present value of zero

The IRR informs managers about what the expected rate of return on the investment is, given the predictions about future cash flows. This is then used to compare against the organisation's required rate of return for that type of investment. If the IRR is higher than the target rate – which is often referred to as the *hurdle rate* – then the project will be accepted. If there are competing projects, then the project with the highest IRR will be the one potentially selected (we also need to consider the other information derived from the other management tools).

Various spreadsheet applications can be used to determine the IRR (for example, Excel has an 'IRR function' – see the Excel online help function). It can also be calculated with many calculators. In the absence of having the appropriate calculator or spreadsheet application, determining the IRR is a matter of trial and error.

For a discussion of how to determine the IRR for Goodtime Surfboards, see **Learning exercise 5.13**.

5.13 Learning Exercise

Determining the internal rate of return (IRR)

We are now required to calculate the internal rate of return for the investment proposal of Goodtime Surfboards.

As we have already noted, although we can use some calculators to calculate IRR, we can also work out the answer by trial and error – it just takes somewhat longer.

For example, knowing that using an interest rate of 10 per cent generates a positive NPV of $22 253 (see **Learning exercise 5.12**), then we know the IRR must be considerably higher. If we use the rates of 20, 21 and 22 per cent to discount the expected future cash flows, then we will calculate the following NPVs:

Interest rate	NPV of cash flows
10%	$22573
20%	$1373
21%	–$310
22%	–$1940

Therefore, the IRR must be slightly below 21 per cent. That is, if we use a rate of about 20.8 per cent, we will get a present value of about zero. We would need to compare this rate of 20.8 per cent with the required hurdle rate that has been stipulated by managers as being expected for this type of investment. If the hurdle rate was, say, 15 per cent, then the IRR method would indicate that this project meets the hurdle requirement.

In terms of the advantages of IRR, like the NPV method, it does consider all expected future cash flows associated with the project, and the timing of when the cash flows will occur. It also identifies the actual expected interest rate on the project. However, as with all of the methods we have just discussed, it does ignore many other important issues, such as the various social and environmental impacts that might arise throughout the life of the investment. Critical thinking and critical evaluation requires a consideration of multiple factors.

For a discussion of how to use three financial-based management tools to assess a capital investment, see **Learning exercise 5.14**.

5.14 Learning Exercise

Calculation of payback period, ARR and NPV for a proposed capital investment

Scenario: Sunset Beach Company is thinking of acquiring a drink dispenser to place at the front of its shop. The machine dispenses cans of cold drinks, which will sell for $4 each.

The relevant costs are as follows:

Cost of acquiring the drink dispenser	$14400
Annual licence fees to be allowed to offer drinks	$1500
Supplier cost of each can of drink	$1.00
Expected annual electricity cost of running the drink dispenser	$1400
Fixed-price maintenance contract for the machine, per year	$2500
Expected number of sales	3000 per year
Expected life of the machine	7 years
Expected residual value at the end of its useful life	$0

Management would like the machine to:

- achieve a payback period of less than five years
- generate an accounting rate of return of at least 20 per cent
- generate a positive NPV at an interest rate of at least 10 per cent.

Task: You are required to assess this potential capital investment by using the payback, ARR and NPV methods, and make a recommendation as to whether to acquire the drink dispenser.

Solution: To answer these questions, you need to determine the following.

1 The payback period

We can calculate the annual net cash flows as follows (we have assumed that the income and expenses remain the same each year, and that the costs and cash flows occur in the same period):

Income			
Soft-drink sales	3000 × $4		$12000
Variable costs			
Cans of drink	3000 × $1	$3000	
Fixed costs			
Annual licence fees	$1500		
Annual electricity costs	$1400		
Annual maintenance contract	$2500	$5400	$8400
Net annual cash flows			$3600

Year	Amount to 'pay back' as at the start of the year	Net cash flows for the year (represented by the savings in variable costs)	Cumulative amount paid back at the end of the year	Amount still to 'pay back' at the end of the year
1	$14400	$3600	$3600	$10800
2	$10800	$3600	$7200	$7200
3	$7200	$3600	$10800	$3600
4	$3600	$3600	$14400	$0

The payback period of this investment is therefore four years. This satisfies the decision rule provided by management, which was that the payback period be less than five years.

2 The accounting rate of return

We know the incremental cash flows that are expected to arise following the investment in the new drink dispenser. Because the machine is only expected to last seven years, we must also consider the amount by which the machine has fallen in value throughout each year. That is, we must also consider the depreciation costs associated with using up the asset over its useful life, which is seven years. We know the asset cost $14 400 and we expect it not to have any residual value in seven years' time. We can calculate the annual depreciation expense as:

$$\frac{\text{Acquisition cost} - \text{expected residual value}}{\text{Expected useful life of asset}} = \frac{\$14\,400 - \$0}{7} = \$2057 \text{ per year}$$

The average incremental returns (profits) for the seven years equals:

($3600 – $2057) + ($3600 – $2057) + ($3600 – $2057) + ($3600 – $2057) + ($3600 – $2057) + ($3600 – $2057) + ($3600 – $2057) all divided by 7 = $1543

The average investment in the machine is:

$$\frac{\text{Acquisition cost} + \text{expected residual value}}{2} = \frac{\$14\,400 + \$0}{2} = \$7200$$

$$\text{Therefore, the ARR} = \frac{\text{Average annual profit from the asset}}{\text{Average investment required to earn that profit}} \times 100\%$$

$$= \frac{\$1543}{\$\,7200} \times 100\%$$

$$= 21.43 \text{ per cent}$$

All things being equal, the higher the ARR, the better. An ARR of 21.43 per cent would generally be considered a good rate. It satisfies the decision rule stipulated by the management of Sunset Beach Company, which was that the rate must exceed 20 per cent.

3 The NPV method

We will use the following table to work out the net present value of the capital investment. Management has said that they want to apply an interest rate of 10 per cent to this type of investment.

Year	Cash flow (undiscounted) $	Discount factor $\frac{\$1}{(1+k)^n}$	Present value of cash flows $
1	(14 400)	1.00000	(14 400)
	3600	0.90909	3273
2	3600	0.82645	2975
3	3600	0.75131	2705
4	3600	0.68301	2459
5	3600	0.62092	2235
6	3600	0.56447	2032
7	3600	0.51315	1847
Total net present value of cost savings from this initiative			$3126

Using an interest rate of 10 per cent, the present value of the cash flows is positive. This therefore meets the decision rule set by the managers of Sunset Beach Company.

4 Overall decision to purchase, or not

In terms of the three tools we have just applied, this proposal satisfies all the requirements stipulated by the managers of Sunset Beach Company. However, prior to accepting the project, consideration should be also given to other factors. Does the proposed investment perform in a way that is consistent with the organisation's mission and goals? Are there any other opportunities that would provide better returns and that might be pursued if this investment is not made? Also, are there any environmental or social implications throughout the life cycle of the investment that are inconsistent with the responsibilities that the managers accept (such factors might have already been considered before the financial calculations were performed)? In the absence of any negative information in these respects, the managers of the Sunset Beach Company should probably pursue this investment opportunity.

Why do I need to know about the various judgements that need to be made as part of capital investment decisions?

Capital investment decisions are very important to an organisation. They can involve the expenditure of large amounts of funds and can 'lock an organisation into' a particular operating process for many years into the future. Therefore, managers need to 'get it right' and they need tools to consider the various financial and non-financial costs and benefits that will be generated by the potential investment. There is a lot at stake in such decisions, and many associated risks and opportunities that require careful consideration before the commitment to a particular capital investment.

STUDY TOOLS

SUMMARY

In this chapter, we have considered a number of different tools that managers might use as part of their planning, monitoring and controlling of activities. The coverage across this, and the previous two chapters, has by no means been exhaustive. Rather, it should have given you an insight into some of the management tools that are available to organisations. Nevertheless, by reading these three chapters dedicated to management accounting, you should now have a solid understanding of the types of issues that need to be considered by managers in performing their functions, and how accounting can help them do their job successfully.

We commenced the chapter with a discussion of life cycle analysis. LCA is a very useful tool that allows managers to understand the different phases in the life of a product or service. We argued that if managers decide to, for example, acquire particular assets (one of our examples was a ship), then they should know about, and take responsibility for, the various economic, social and environmental implications generated by the asset from the cradle to the grave. Ideally, they should know about the likely life cycle impacts before they acquire particular assets, and this knowledge should be used in the planning stages. As we learned, some organisations also make the results of their LCA publicly available; however, many do not. Managers that accept that they have a responsibility to be accountable for the life cycle impacts of their products tend to make their assessments publicly available. Linked to the practice of LCA is the concept of the circular economy. We briefly discussed how managers' consideration of the concept of the circular economy is useful to them in identifying opportunities to reduce the environmental impacts of their goods and services by encouraging them to consider ways of reusing or recycling their products once the initial useful life is over.

Our attention then moved to the related area of life cycle costing. We learned that some organisations practise LCC and attempt to place a cost on various activities, or impacts, that occur throughout the life cycle of a product or service. We learned that managers need to not only consider the costs involved in acquiring an asset, but also the costs associated with the construction, maintenance and ultimate disposal of the asset. We learned that not all costs across the life cycle of a product or service can easily be measured in financial terms, but that does not mean that the costs (or impacts) are not important. In such cases, we might use some ranking scheme to rank the severity, or risks, associated with potential impacts. Ultimately, decisions about particular products or services might be made on the basis of the joint consideration of both financial and non-financial factors.

The chapter then considered material flow cost accounting, and we learned that it is a very useful tool for informing managers about how much material is going into products, as well as how much material is going into non-product outputs (waste). We used the example of Michell Wool to show that once we become more informed about how much material (including energy and water) is actually going into particular products, and how much waste is being generated, we can make improvements that create financial and environmental benefits. We identified the steps that need to be taken in MFCA. In particular, we noted that one of the important steps is to construct a flow model that assigns physical values to the material being used within a particular product or process. We also explained that some organisations elect to make the results of their material flow modelling publicly available (one example we provided was that of Ricoh). A key point in our discussion was explaining how the 'waste cost' of many organisations is often unknown or greatly understated. We explained how MFCA can be used as a means to more accurately account for waste costs, and to provide the basis for reducing the waste being created by organisations.

Our attention then moved to the Balanced Scorecard. We described how the BSC is used within organisations to develop goals and associated performance measures. As with the other management tools described in this chapter, the BSC is an important tool for planning, monitoring and controlling the activities of an organisation. We learned that the BSC has a number of perspectives (we used the Kaplan and Norton approach in this chapter, so we identified four perspectives), which will each have a number of related goals, which in turn will have a number of related performance measures that are identified. In developing the goals and performance measures with the BSC, managers will consider important aspects of performance identified within LCA, LCC and MFCA (if these techniques are being used), and those that are prioritised as being significant will likely be addressed within the goal-setting phase of developing the BSC.

In concluding the chapter, we discussed capital investment decisions. In effect, some of the previous material in the chapter (LCA, LCC and MFCA) is relevant in making capital investment decisions. However, we introduced four additional considerations of a financial nature that could be taken into account when making a capital investment decision. The management tools we discussed were the payback period, the accounting rate of return, the net present value method, and the internal rate of return. We emphasised that, ultimately, the decision as to what capital investment decisions are made will be based upon a mixture of financial and non-financial considerations.

ANSWERS TO THE OPENING QUESTIONS

At the beginning of the chapter we asked the following question. As a result of reading this chapter, you should now be able to provide an informed answer to this question – ours is shown below.

The managers of an organisation are concerned that they might be generating too much waste, but their accountant tells them that there is nothing to worry about because it only costs $1000 a month for a rubbish removal contractor to take away all the waste that is generated within the organisation. Also, the managers are worried about where all the waste goes, but the accountant tells them: 'Don't worry about that. Once the contractor collects the waste from us, it is no longer our problem'. Has the accountant provided the managers with good advice?

No, the accountant has not provided good accounting advice. As this chapter has demonstrated, the real cost of waste can be significantly greater than the amount that is paid to have the waste removed. For example, the waste could include various materials that were acquired at a cost by the organisation, as well as costs that could be attributed to storing and processing the materials that ended up in waste. Many studies have shown that the actual cost of waste can be many times what is paid to have the waste removed. It is often recommended that organisations do some form of material tracking to see exactly what ends up in waste, in terms of both the quantities of particular materials and the financial costs of these wasted materials. There are also potential social and environmental impacts associated with the initial production of the materials that are being wasted. Some form of material flow analysis, with associated costing (as done with material flow cost accounting), is recommended. Another activity that could be worthwhile is to employ a specialist to do a waste audit. In terms of the claim that the organisation has no responsibility for what happens to the waste, or where it goes, we would argue that is a very poor attitude to take. As we have argued in this chapter, if we decide to produce particular products, then we must accept some level of responsibility, and accountability, for the social and environmental impacts of that product throughout its life cycle – including what happens to the waste that is generated by the production activities. Organisations that do not properly consider their waste streams are exposing themselves to various risks, including risks of a legal nature as well as risks that different stakeholders will potentially discontinue their support for the organisation.

SELF-TEST QUIZ

Answers to this quiz appear in the Appendix of this book.

The Torquay Milkbar is considering putting a surfing simulator ride in its shop. Customers who use the surfing simulator will pay $4 per ride. The relevant costs are as follows:

Cost of acquiring the surfing simulator	$75 000
Annual insurance costs for the machine	$4000
Expected annual electricity cost of running the machine	$3000
Fixed-price maintenance contract for the machine, per year	$6000
Expected number of rides on the machine	9500 per year
Expected life of the machine	5 years
Expected residual value at the end of its useful life	$1000
Required interest rate	10 per cent

1 The payback period of this proposed investment is:
   a 2 years   b 3 years   c 4 years
   d 5 years   e 6 years
2 The accounting rate of return of this proposed investment is:
   a 20.44%   b 24.56%   c 26.84%
   d 28.34%   e 30.00%
3 The net present value of this proposed investment is approximately:
   a $18 457   b $19 322
   c $19 854   d $20 390
   e None of these choices
4 The internal rate of return of this proposed investment is:
   a approximately 10%   b approximately 15%
   c approximately 20%   d approximately 25%
   e None of these choices
5 In making a decision about the possible capital investment, what non-financial factors should you consider?
   a Whether installing the machine will create unwelcome noise or other negative implications for local residents.
   b The safety of the machine for users.
   c Who manufactured the machine and what their reputation is with respect to how they treat their workers.
   d The energy to be used by the machine.
   e All of these choices.

ONLINE RESOURCES

Accompanying the book is an innovative online case study that follows an organisation initially established by two friends, which grows into a large and successful company. Acquire this chapter's case study from your instructor.

CASE STUDY

Armadillo Surf Designs: A balancing act

Archer, Maddie and Dillon are keen to better understand the overall performance of Armadillo Surf Designs (ASD) and are also looking for ways to both reduce costs and to boost sales. They are considering increasing the automation of their manufacturing operations in order to lower labour costs and are also considering participating in a fundraising campaign that will promote their brand and may therefore increase their sales.

Prepare a balanced scorecard for ASD to assist the Directors to better understand the overall performance of the business. Carry out various types of analysis in order to assist the Directors to decide whether to undertake the proposed activities related to automation and promotion.

END-OF-CHAPTER QUESTIONS

5.1 What is a life cycle analysis, and should accountants be aware of such analysis?

5.2 Do you think that managers should understand the life cycle of a product or service before deciding to participate in the production or sale of that product or service?

5.3 Should an organisation publicly disclose details of any life cycle analysis that it has performed?

5.4 Why do you think managers might decide to publicly disclose information about any life cycle analysis they have undertaken?

5.5 In recent times, there has been much discussion about the treatment of animals when they are exported overseas (often referred to as 'live exports'). For example, there have been recent media stories about large numbers of sheep dying on ships, often because of extreme heat stress (while very confronting, information on this can be found at https://secure.animalsaustralia.org/take_action/live-export-shipboard-cruelty/). Do you think that farmers should be responsible, or accountable, for what happens to the animals once they are sold?

5.6 What does 'eco-efficiency' mean?

5.7 Should managers be responsible for what happens to their products at the end of their life cycles? Why?

5.8 What does a 'circular economy' represent and is it the role of managers to work towards the goal of implementing processes that are consistent with a circular economy?

5.9 If a shipping company acquires a new ship that is expected to last 30 years, should it:

- **a** at the end of the ship's life, disclose actual details of what happened to the ship
- **b** before the end of the ship's life cycle, disclose its intentions/plans with respect to what it will do with ships once they are no longer being used?

5.10 What is 'life cycle costing'? Does life cycle costing place a cost on all the impacts created by a product throughout its life cycle?

5.11 If you were thinking of buying a fleet of new trucks, what factors do you think you should consider when making the choice as to which trucks to acquire?

5.12 What is material flow cost accounting and how can its use help an organisation?

5.13 Material flow cost accounting typically uses a flow model. What is this?

5.14 How can material flow cost accounting help the financial performance of an organisation?

5.15 How can the use of material flow cost accounting help the environment?

5.16 If an organisation decides to invest in new machinery to increase its profits, but this new machinery will replace many people and therefore make them redundant, does the organisation have any responsibility, and accountability, for the employees that will lose their jobs?

5.17 You are a newly appointed accountant and have been asked to place a cost on the amount of wasted paper coming from the organisation. How might you do this?

5.18 What is the purpose of the Balanced Scorecard?

5.19 What is a 'perspective' as used within the Balanced Scorecard?

5.20 How do we determine 'goals' and 'measures' when applying the Balanced Scorecard?

5.21 Should managers use the Balanced Scorecard framework at the same time as they use life cycle analysis and material flow cost accounting?

5.22 What is a capital investment decision?

5.23 What factors might you consider when making a capital investment decision?

5.24 Do you agree or disagree with the following statement, and why. 'When making a capital investment decision, various factors of a social and environmental nature should only be considered to the extent that such factors can be quantified in monetary terms'.

5.25 Assume that you are in charge of the decision to acquire a new fleet of delivery trucks for your organisation. What non-financial factors, if any, would you consider as part of this decision?

5.26 Explain how the payback period is calculated.

5.27 What are some of the strengths and limitations of using the payback period to evaluate capital investment projects?

5.28 Explain how the accounting rate of return is calculated.

5.29 What are some of the strengths and limitations of using the accounting rate of return to evaluate capital investment projects?

5.30 Is the following statement true or false? Explain why. 'The lower the discount rate, the greater the present value of projected cash flows'.

5.31 Explain what the decision rule is when applying the net present value method.

5.32 How is the internal rate of return calculated?

5.33 Why might it be important to undertake a post-completion review (audit) of a capital investment decision?

5.34 Brighton Fish and Chip Shop is considering putting an old-style pinball machine in its shop. Customers who use the pinball machine will pay $2 per game.

The relevant costs are as follows:

Cost of acquiring the pinball machine	$11500
Annual insurance costs for the machine	$1000
Expected annual electricity cost of running the pinball machine	$1600
Fixed-price maintenance contract for the pinball machine, per year	$2400
Expected number of games to be played on the machine	4500 per year
Expected life of the machine	5 years
Expected residual value at the end of its useful life	$500

You are required to assess this potential capital investment by using the:

a payback method

b accounting rate of return method

c net present value method

d internal rate of return method.

You are also required to make a recommendation as to whether to acquire the pinball machine. Management would like the machine to:

- achieve a payback period of less than five years;
- generate an accounting rate of return of at least 20 per cent
- generate a positive net present value at an interest rate of 12 per cent.

5.35 The Big Apple Farming Company is considering replacing fruit pickers with a fruit-picking machine. Each year, the company spends $80 000 on fruit pickers. These pickers will no longer be required if the fruit-picking machine is acquired.

The relevant costs are as follows:

Cost of acquiring the fruit-picking machine	$200 000
Annual insurance costs for the fruit-picking machine	$10 000
Annual registration cost for the fruit-picking machine	$3000
Expected annual fuel cost of running the fruit-picking machine	$6000
Fixed price maintenance contract for the fruit-picking machine, per year	$4000
Expected life of the fruit-picking machine	8 years
Expected residual value at the end of the machine's useful life	$10 000

You are required to assess this potential capital investment by using the:

a payback method
b accounting rate of return method
c net present value method
d internal rate of return method.

You are also required to make a recommendation as to whether to acquire the fruit-picking machine. Management would like the machine to:

- achieve a payback period of less than six years
- generate an accounting rate of return of at least 18 per cent
- generate a positive net present value at an interest rate of 10 per cent.

5.36 Assume that you are a senior manager within the Eastern Plains Zoo – a zoo located in a regional area. The mission of the zoo is 'to become known as one of the leading zoos in the world, one which focuses on animal welfare and helping the preservation of endangered and rare species of animals'.

Some key objectives of the zoo have been identified as:

- within five years, to be the most popular zoo in the country in terms of visitor numbers
- to be self-sufficient financially and not require funding support from government
- to be known as a leading research centre with respect to protecting rare and endangered species of animals.

You are required to develop a Balanced Scorecard to improve the overall performance of Eastern Plains Zoo. In doing so, you will use the four perspectives suggested by Kaplan and Norton, and you will identify the goals and measures within each perspective.

REFERENCES

A.P. Moller – Maersk A/S (2020). *Sustainability report 2020.* www.maersk.com/en/about/sustainability/reports

Audi (2018). *Life cycle assessment: Audi looks one step ahead.* https://www.audi.com/content/dam/gbp2/company/sustainability/downloads/documents-and-policies/umweltbilanzen/en/Audi_A6_LCA_English.pdf

Audi (2020). *Audi is pursuing the vision of a circular economy.* https://www.audi.com/en/company/sustainability/core-topics/products-and-services/circular-economy-vision.html

BHP (2017). *BHP annual report 2017.* https://www.bhp.com/-/media/documents/investors/annual-reports/2017/bhpannualreport2017.pdf

BHP (2018). *BHP annual report 2018.* https://www.bhp.com/-/media/documents/investors/annual-reports/2018/bhpannualreport2018.pdf

BHP (2021). *BHP annual report 2021.* https://www.bhp.com/investors/annual-reporting/annual-report-2021

Christ, K., & Burritt, R. (2015). Material flow cost accounting: A review and agenda for future research. *Journal of Cleaner Production*, 108, pp. 1378–89.

CPA Australia (2015). *Sustainability and capital investment case studies.* CPA Australia, Melbourne.

Deegan, C. (2003). *Environmental Management Accounting: An Introduction and Case Studies for Australia.* Sydney: Institute of Chartered Accountants in Australia. http://infohouse.p2ric.org/ref/37/36456.pdf

Deegan. C. (2008). Environmental costing in capital investment decisions: Electricity distributors and the choice of power poles. *Australian Accounting Review,* 18(44), pp. 2–15.

International Federation of Accountants (2005). https://www.ifac.org/.

International Organization for Standardization (2011). ISO 14051:2011 Environmental management – Material flow cost accounting: General framework. www.iso.org/standard/50986.html

International Organization for Standardization (2018). All about ISO. www.iso.org/about-us.html

Kaplan, R. S., & Norton, D. P. (1992). The Balanced Scorecard – Measures that Drive Performance. *Harvard Business Review,* (January-February 1992), p. 72.

Kasemset, C., Chernsupornchai, J., & Pala-ud, W. (2015). Application of MFCA in waste reduction: case study on a small textile factory in Thailand. *Journal of Cleaner Production,* 108, pp. 1342–51.

Ricoh (2022). Sustainable environmental management indicators: Eco Balance. www.ricoh.com/environment/management/eco.html

Rio Tinto (2021). *Communities and social performance commitments disclosure: Interim report,* September. https://www.riotinto.com/sustainability

United Nations Conference on Trade and Development (UNCTAD) (2022). Sustainable Development Goals, https://unctad.org/topic/trade-and-environment/circular-economy. From 'Circular Economy', by UNCTAD, © 2022 United Nations. Reprinted with the permission of the United Nations. The content of this publication has not been approved by the United Nations and does not reflect the views of the United Nations or its officials or Member States.

United Nations Division for Sustainable Development (2001). *Environmental Management Accounting: Procedures and Principles.* New York: United Nations.

Wagner, B. (2015). A report on the origins of Material Flow Cost Accounting (MFCA) research activities. *Journal of Cleaner Production,* 108, pp. 1255–61.

MODULE 3

ACCOUNTABILITY FOR SOCIAL AND ENVIRONMENTAL PERFORMANCE

CHAPTER 6

The external reporting of social and environmental performance information

CHAPTER 6

THE EXTERNAL REPORTING OF SOCIAL AND ENVIRONMENTAL PERFORMANCE INFORMATION

LEARNING OBJECTIVES

After completing this chapter, readers should be able to:

- **LO6.1** identify some of the reasons why an organisation will report social and environmental information; the stakeholders to whom the information could, or should, be directed; the types of social and environmental information that could be disclosed; and common reporting frameworks that can be applied
- **LO6.2** explain the meaning of 'corporate social responsibility' and 'corporate social responsibility reporting', as well as the meaning of 'sustainability reporting'
- **LO6.3** understand how the practice of corporate social responsibility reporting has grown across the years, and be aware of evidence that shows that it is now a mainstream activity for larger organisations
- **LO6.4** explain, in some detail, the requirements of specific sustainability reporting frameworks, and in doing so, describe some of the qualitative characteristics that social and environmental performance information is expected to possess
- **LO6.5** explain the difference between a reporting framework and a measurement framework, and identify when you might require a measurement framework
- **LO6.6** explain the meaning of 'climate change' and 'modern slavery' and describe some approaches that organisations can embrace to report information about both their climate change-related activities and the risks that modern slavery exists within their supply chains
- **LO6.7** explain the meaning of, and reasons for, the existence of 'counter accounts'
- **LO6.8** offer reasons why third-party independent reviews of corporate social responsibility reports are often undertaken.

OPENING QUESTIONS

Before reading this chapter, please consider how you would answer the following four questions. We will return to these questions at the end of the chapter, where we suggest some answers.

Organisations, particularly larger organisations, often produce some form of corporate social responsibility report. In this regard:

1. What does 'corporate social responsibility' mean?
2. What is 'corporate social responsibility reporting'?
3. What are some of the reasons why an organisation might produce a corporate social responsibility report?
4. Are frameworks available that can guide the preparation of a corporate social responsibility report, and if so, what are some of them?

Introduction

In the previous chapters of this book, particularly within Chapters 1 and 2, we considered various issues to do with:

- the role of accountants and accounting
- the meaning of accountability
- the relationship between accounting and organisational responsibilities, and accountabilities.

We also emphasised that accounting is both a technical and a social practice. In Chapters 3 to 5, we focused on accounting for internal decision making, which we referred to as 'management accounting'. We noted that the types, and focus, of the accounts that managers might use to plan, monitor, and control and demonstrate accountability with respect to their organisational activities (the management accounts) will be influenced by the perceptions that managers hold with respect to why they are reporting (the '*Why report?*' question) and about the stakeholders to whom they believe they have a responsibility (the '*To whom to report?*' question). We also learned that the focus of management accounting is influenced by what aspects of performance managers accept responsibility for (the '*For what?*' question).

The focus in the remaining chapters of this book now shifts to explicitly considering **external reporting**; that is, the provision of information to stakeholders that are external to the organisation. In this chapter – Chapter 6 – we will consider some approaches and frameworks that managers might use to publicly disclose social and environmental (and sustainability-related) information. In Chapters 7 to 11, we will consider the external reporting of financial information about the organisation. And in Chapter 12, we will consider some commonly used tools for analysing publicly available reports prepared by organisations.

external reporting
The provision of reports and information to stakeholders that are external to an organisation

Organisations create a variety of social and environmental impacts. Different stakeholders have different expectations about how accountable managers *should* be for the social and environmental impacts that the managers' decisions ultimately create – and managers' decisions will have many social and environmental impacts (both directly, and indirectly). Across time, there has been an increase in society's expectations concerning organisational social and environmental performance, particularly in respect to issues such as organisational contributions to climate change, use of water, waste generation, and the treatment of workers throughout supply chains inclusive of issues to do with the potential existence of modern slavery. As a result of these heightened expectations, the incidence of organisations producing publicly available reports addressing various aspects of their social and environmental performance has also increased in recent times. This has in turn led to an increase in the number of social and environmental reporting and measurement frameworks that have been developed by different organisations throughout the world.

As Business for Social Responsibility (BSR, 2020, p. 4) states:

> Externally, disclosure expectations are increasing. Sustainability reporting helps companies meet disclosure requirements – whether regulatory, insurance-related, or customer-specific – and improve relationships with stakeholders who expect, or would like to review, the company's sustainability data. Reporting provides critical information for stakeholders to evaluate performance and make decisions (e.g. whether to invest). Reporting also helps companies enhance their reputation and perceived trustworthiness. Finally, investors are increasingly calling for companies to make their sustainability risks and opportunities transparent in a standardized way. Not only does sustainability reporting aim to meet these expectations, it underlines the prospect of lower cost of capital tied to sustainability performance.
>
> Internally, sustainability reporting can clarify and improve a company's performance on sustainability issues. Reporting helps crystallize strategic priorities, demonstrate how these priorities are embedded in business priorities, and pinpoint areas where change, continuous improvement, or innovation is needed to set strategies, meet goals, or align with peers. Disclosure against reporting frameworks' requirements demands identifying key sustainability risks and opportunities, which helps to increase awareness and management of vulnerabilities. Reporting can alert companies to emerging issues or trends, allowing for early management of risks and improved performance on opportunities. Finally, highlighting strong sustainability programs attracts new purpose-driven talent, improves retention, and increases employee motivation.
>
> Source: Five Steps to Good Sustainability Reporting, BSR (2020), p. 4.

Identifying and reporting the significant social and environmental impacts of an organisation is both an interesting and vital role for accountants. It is also sometimes controversial activity, as identifying and prioritising the social and environmental impacts for which an organisation should be accountable involves a great deal of professional judgement. As you will learn, social and environmental reporting is both an important and exciting area of 'accounting'.

LO6.1 Social and environmental accountability

In introducing the topic of social and environmental reporting, it is useful to place this form of reporting in context by again applying the accountability model we introduced back in Chapter 1 (see **Figure 1.3**). That is, the familiar why, who, what and how questions will now be considered. As we remember, answers to the 'why report?' question then informs our response about 'to whom to report?', which then informs our response to 'what to report?' and then ultimately the question 'where to report?'

Why report social and environmental information?

Legally required

The public disclosure of information about various facets of an organisation's social and environmental performance is, in most countries, predominantly a voluntary exercise. However, countries often have legislative requirements that social and/or environmental performance-related information be disclosed to government, including in relation to:

- occupational health and safety (for example, accidents and injuries)
- workplace equality indicators, including information about workplace composition, flexible working arrangements (for example, within Australia, the Workplace Gender Equality Act requires various disclosures by larger organisations – see **https://www.wgea.gov.au/about**)
- the risks that modern slavery are present within supply chains (which are addressed in various countries by way of national Modern Slavery Acts)
- carbon emissions (for example, within Australia, the National Greenhouse and Energy Reporting Act (NGER) requires heavily emitting organisations to make disclosures to the government (see **http://www.cleanenergyregulator.gov.au/NGER**)
- the release of particular dangerous chemicals (for example, within Australia the National Pollutant Inventory requires organisations that have emitted or released an amount above a certain threshold of any of 93 substances to report the emissions or releases annually to government (see **http://www.npi.gov.au**).

The above information will often be published and made publicly available on government-backed websites, but the actual choice by an organisation itself to produce standalone social and environmental reports – or, as they might also be referred to, 'sustainability reports', or 'corporate social responsibility reports' – or to make particular social and environmental website disclosures, is often entirely voluntary (see **Learning exercise 6.1**). This can be contrasted to financial reporting, which, as we explained in earlier chapters, is very regulated, particularly for larger organisations. Such financial reporting regulations mandate the disclosure of various items of information pertaining to financial performance.

6.1 Learning Exercise

Potential reasons for the relatively lower regulation of social and environmental reporting

As has been discussed, financial reporting, which is of particular relevance to investors and others (such as creditors) with a financial interest in an organisation, is heavily regulated, particularly for larger organisations. By contrast, the reporting of information about the social and environmental impacts of an organisation, which potentially affects many more stakeholders, including future generations, is relatively unregulated.

The issue we shall consider now is what might be some of the factors that have led to this disparity between the extent of regulation applied to financial reporting as opposed to social and environmental reporting. There is not one single answer to this, but the following factors offer some potential explanation.

One reason has to do with history. That is, the history of financial reporting is much longer than that of social and environmental reporting, and hence it has had more time to become regulated. A further possible, and related, reason is that community concerns about social and environmental performance, and the belief that business organisations have many social and environmental responsibilities for which they should be accountable, are a relatively recent phenomenon. Therefore, government might need more time to determine what disclosures to include within the law. A report by the international accounting firm KPMG – which we will refer to later in this chapter – identifies the fact that, throughout the world, governments and securities exchanges are on the verge of introducing greater legislative requirements for the disclosure of information about organisations' social and environmental performance. However, what is also interesting is that there is evidence that when governments introduce initiatives to increase the social and environmental disclosure requirements for business entities, many such entities directly oppose this and lobby government to leave social and environmental largely unregulated (for evidence of this, see Deegan and Shelly, 2014).

Another possible reason for the relative disparity in disclosure regulation is the difference in the power of the stakeholders demanding the information. Those stakeholders with an interest in financial reporting include investors. Investors tend to have relatively more wealth than other stakeholders, and this wealth can give them the power to effectively coerce managers and government regulators to put in place mechanisms to provide the information they want. Traditionally, investors have wanted information about the financial performance of the organisations in which they have invested, as this will influence the value of the investment and the dividends investors are likely to receive, which will impact their wealth.

We could provide more discussion here, but as a reader, you should consider for yourself whether you think organisations, particularly larger ones, should be required by law to be more accountable for their social and environmental impacts, particularly in relation to such issues as their contribution to climate change, their use of water, the generation of waste, and the treatment of employees throughout their supply chains.

Organisations listed on securities exchanges throughout the world are also often required to disclose – as part of the listing requirements – whether they are exposed to any significant economic, environmental or social risks and to provide information about how they are managing such risks (for example, *Recommendation 7.4 of the Australian Securities Exchange's Corporate Governance Principles and Recommendations* requires such disclosure). Further, in larger organisations' annual reports, there will generally be a document referred to as an 'Operating and Financial Review' (OFR) which is required by many nations' corporations legislation (an OFR will typically report information that shareholders would reasonably require to assess an entity's operations, financial position, and business strategies and prospects for future financial years). It would be expected that an OFR will provide clear information about the risks, and opportunities, that climate change poses for the organisation.

In response to stakeholder expectations

Within the broader social system, it is generally (though not universally) accepted that managers *do* have a responsibility (and associated accountability) for their organisations' social and environmental impacts. The failure of an organisation to report information about certain important aspects of its social and environmental performance could, from the perspective of various stakeholders, undermine the acceptability, or legitimacy, of the organisation.

As we emphasised throughout Chapters 3 to 5, for internal management purposes, managers need to have information available about various aspects of their organisation's social and environmental performance in order to properly *manage* the operations of the organisation. That is, apart from requiring various types of information about financial performance, managers might also need information about the organisation's use of water, energy, raw materials, the waste they generate, the treatment of employees throughout supply chains, the training of employees, and so forth.

Various stakeholders external to the organisation will also expect to receive information about the social and environmental performance of an organisation. This might impact various decisions the external stakeholders make, such as whether they will invest in the organisation, buy its products, work for it, or lobby the government to take actions against the organisation. For example, some organisations might only buy products from suppliers that demonstrate compliance with particular social and/or environmental performance expectations or standards.

Therefore, in terms of *why* an organisation might externally report social and environmental performance information, it might be because various stakeholders external to the organisation expect to have such information, and managers feel a responsibility, and accountability, to provide it. In a sense, the reporting could also be part of a process of managing various stakeholders. By providing this information, managers might expect to influence (manage) the support they receive from particular stakeholder groups.

In response to heightened new media attention

Research also shows that the decision to disclose particular social and environmental information often comes in the wake of critical news media attention, particularly after significant events or crises. For example, Deegan, Rankin and Tobin (2002) undertook a study of the social and environmental disclosures made by the world's largest mining company, BHP, over a 15-year period. They were able to provide evidence of a positive correlation between negative media attention aimed at certain social and environmental issues associated with the company, and the volume of disclosures being made by BHP in relation to those issues. The negative media attention was seen as being an indicator of society's concerns about the respective issues being reported upon, based on the assumption that high levels of media attention tend to influence community expectations in relation to an issue (and this positive relationship between community expectations or concerns about an issue and the news media coverage of that respective issue is explained through a theory known as Media Agenda Setting Theory).

As another example of how reporting has been shown to vary as community expectations or concerns change, and within the context of companies that source their products from developing countries, Islam and Deegan (2010) undertook a review of the social and environmental disclosure practices of two leading multinational sportswear and clothing companies: Nike and Hennes & Mauritz. The researchers found a direct relationship between the extent of global news media coverage, of a critical nature, being attributed to particular social issues relating to the industry, and the extent of social disclosures being made by the two companies. The authors demonstrated that, once the news media started producing stories that exposed poor working conditions and the use of child labour in developing countries, the multinational companies appeared to subsequently respond by voluntarily making various disclosures pertaining to initiatives that were being undertaken to ensure that the respective company did not source their products from factories that had abusive or unsafe working conditions, or use child labour. This was consistent with the view that the news media influenced the expectations of Western consumers, thereby causing legitimacy or reputational problems for the companies (numerous other studies have also demonstrated this linkage), and the companies used disclosure as a strategy to respond to the negative media publicity.

Islam and Deegan (2010) also provided evidence that, prior to the time at which the news media started running stories about the labour conditions in developing countries (the media attention devoted to these issues appeared to significantly increase in the mid-1990s), there was a general absence of related social disclosures being made by the large multinational companies. This was despite the fact that evidence suggested that poor working conditions and the use of child labour existed in developing countries (those from which the organisations were sourcing their garments) for many years prior to the newspapers' coverage of the issues. The authors speculated that, had the Western news media not run stories exposing the working conditions in developing countries, the multinational companies would not have embraced initiatives to improve working conditions, nor would they have provided disclosures about the initiatives being undertaken in relation to working conditions.

Similar findings to those described above have been demonstrated across many other industries. Therefore, in considering the issue of *why* organisations might voluntarily elect to disclose social and environmental information (the first step of our four-step accountability model), we need to be aware of such evidence. It is not appropriate to simply believe that managers are making particular disclosures because they think they have a responsibility to make the disclosures. Healthy scepticism is always warranted. If some managers are shown to be making disclosures of a *reactionary* nature – for example, in reaction to negative news stories being circulated about their operations, or those of other members of their industry – then such disclosures would seem to be more about managing stakeholders than about demonstrating proper levels of accountability. If organisations want to demonstrate high levels of accountability, they will not wait until something goes wrong, or some crisis arises, before they start making disclosures.

For more discussion of corporate disclosure in the wake of media attention, see **Learning exercise 6.2**.

6.2 Learning Exercise

Corporate disclosure reactions to media attention

Evidence shows that organisational social and environmental reporting is often a response to negative media attention. Such evidence supports the view that managers will publicly disclose information as a means of strategically managing different stakeholders, including winning stakeholder support. Let us briefly consider whether this should be of concern to us.

Some accounting researchers argue that the voluntary disclosure of social and environmental information enables managers to react to particular crises as they arise, and to project an image of corporate concern and responsibility, while at the same time enabling them to carry on operating in a 'business as usual' manner. To many accounting researchers, this is a matter of concern, as they believe that real changes in the operating practices of organisations are necessary. This is because current business practices are creating long-term adverse social and environmental impacts.

There is also evidence that shows that the greater the perceived threat to an organisation's legitimacy (or reputation), the greater the likelihood that managers will respond with public disclosures primarily aimed at restoring this legitimacy, which we might refer to as 'legitimising disclosures'. Deegan, Rankin and Tobin (2002) note some concern in respect of such managerial responses:

> Legitimising disclosures are linked to corporate survival. In jurisdictions where there are limited regulatory requirements to provide social and environmental information, management appear to provide information when coerced into doing so. Conversely, where there is limited concern, there will be limited disclosures. The evidence suggests that higher levels of disclosure will only occur when community concerns are aroused, or alternatively, until such time that specific regulation is introduced to eliminate managements' disclosure discretion. However, if corporate legitimising activities are successful, then perhaps public pressure for government to introduce disclosure legislation will be low and managers will be able to retain control of their social and environmental reporting practices.
>
> Source: Deegan, Rankin and Tobin (2002)

The ideal situation would be that managers make social and environmental disclosures because it is the *right thing* to do, and because stakeholders have a right to know about particular aspects of an organisation's operations. Not all managers will be opportunistic with their disclosures, but whether they should be left with so much discretion in terms of what they disclose is debatable.

Other reasons for social and environmental disclosures

A publication by the global accounting organisation Ernst and Young (which trades as EY) identified some other reasons *why* organisations might disclose social and environmental information, including the desire to mitigate risk:

> The process of reporting compels businesses to look at their value chains and disclose material information. Collecting and analysing that data can help to identify risks, as well as the potential for improving efficiency and finding new markets. This can have a significant impact on overall performance, as well as investors' perceptions and access to capital.
>
> Source: EY (2014), p. 6.

EY identified further reasons why an organisation might make social and environmental accounts publicly available, including the possibility of obtaining a competitive advantage, to identify potential areas of cost savings, and as a means of attracting and retaining quality staff.

Chapter 1 also suggested a number of reasons why managers might voluntarily report this information, including:

- to counter any moves by government to introduce disclosure regulations that could be onerous
- because powerful stakeholders want the information
- because there is a perception by managers that the disclosures will ultimately assist the financial performance of the organisation.

For further discussion of why an organisation might choose to publicly disclose social and environmental information, see **Learning exercise 6.3**.

6.3 Learning Exercise

Decisions about whether to produce and publicly disclose social and environmental information

Having read the material provided so far within this chapter, consider the following questions:

- What are some reasons why a manager might choose to produce and publicly disclose social and environmental information – or conversely, to not make such disclosures?
- What types of information might a company choose to disclose, and why?

  In answering these questions, there are several factors to consider.

Impact on stakeholders

Aspects of a company's social and environmental performance can have great impacts upon stakeholders – present and future.

There are some key social and environmental aspects of performance that most people would agree managers should always address, and be accountable for, such as ensuring safe and healthy workplaces for employees, that the goods and services being provided are not detrimental to consumers' health, that any toxic waste being released is minimised, and so forth. However, there are many examples of situations where organisations have not accepted any responsibility or accountability for social and environmental impacts linked to their operations. For example, while some large shipping companies provide details of what happens to their ships at the end of their life cycles, together with information about the health and safety standards and performance of the organisations involved in salvaging material from the ships, many such companies provide no such detail.

The reasons behind producing accounts that provide information about various aspects of social and environmental performance, or not, are multifaceted. Two areas of consideration that might have a significant effect on these decisions are potential reputational impact and likely financial impact.

Impact on reputation

There is a growing trend for companies to behave as good global citizens. While one aspect of this may be ethical leadership, another is undoubtedly the creation of reputational benefits and to prevent reputational damage. Hurting stakeholders such as employees or local communities, as well as those stakeholders who work across supply chains, does not play well publicly. There is also a growing movement towards ethical spending and investing, which in turn promotes public scrutiny of the accountability of companies.

Impact on the financial bottom line

It is often argued that, by providing information that projects a positive picture of an organisation's social and environmental performance, greater support will be generated from various stakeholders (including customers), and this increase in support will inevitably improve organisational profitability.

What should be disclosed?

Determining what should be disclosed can involve a great deal of judgement. As such, the reports released by an organisation should provide information about how and why management has decided to provide information about some aspects of its social and environmental performance. This will help readers of the report understand the reasons behind the information being disclosed.

There are many reasons why an organisation might report social and environmental information. Since the choice by managers to produce this information is often voluntary, we again emphasise that it is important that we consider *why* managers have decided to report, as the answer to this question could impact whether users of this information *should* be relying upon it when making decisions. That is, it will impact whether we believe the information being disclosed is *reliable*.

Why do I need to know about the potential reasons or motivations that might be driving an organisation to disclose particular social and environmental information?

This is important because it allows us to understand the context of the disclosures. If, for example, we believe that the managers of an organisation are disclosing information simply to improve the image and profitability of their organisation (perhaps in reaction to negative news media articles), we might be less inclined to believe such disclosures.

The benefits of social and environmental reporting

The most prominent organisation in the world in terms of providing guidance pertaining to social and environmental (and sustainability) reporting is the Global Reporting Initiative (GRI; www.globalreporting.org). It also identifies various reasons why an organisation should undertake this reporting (see Exhibit 6.1), although it refers to them as the benefits of reporting. As should be expected, there will be some overlap between the discussion above and the contents of Exhibit 6.1. Having now considered the issue of *why* managers might be reporting particular social and environmental information, and the implications our assessment of this question might have on the level of reliance we are prepared to place upon the information within these reports, the next issue we can consider is '*To whom to report?*' social and environmental information.

EXHIBIT 6.1 The benefits of reporting sustainability-related information, as identified by the GRI

INTERNAL BENEFITS

Internal benefits for companies and organisations can include:

- Increased understanding of risks and opportunities
- Emphasising the link between financial and non-financial performance
- Influencing long-term management strategy and policy, and business plans
- Streamlining processes, reducing costs and improving efficiency
- Benchmarking and assessing sustainability performance with respect to laws, norms, codes, performance standards, and voluntary initiatives
- Avoiding being implicated in publicised environmental, social and governance failures
- Comparing performance internally, and between organisations and sectors

EXTERNAL BENEFITS

External benefits of sustainability reporting can include:

- Mitigating – or reversing – negative environmental, social and governance impacts
- Improving reputation and brand loyalty
- Enabling external stakeholders to understand the organisation's true value, and tangible and intangible assets
- Demonstrating how the organisation influences, and is influenced by, expectations about sustainable development

Source: Global Reporting Initiative (2018a).

To whom to report social and environmental information?

There are many different stakeholders who might have an interest in an organisation's social and environmental performance: managers, investors, employees, employee unions, customers, suppliers, government, the media, social and environmental groups, local communities, and so on. As emphasised previously, managers need to make judgements about *to whom* they owe a responsibility/accountability (this is often referred to as a 'stakeholder mapping exercise') and whether it includes both those stakeholders who can impact the organisation (those with power over the organisation), and those stakeholders who are impacted by the organisation but who are not directly able to influence it (that is, those without obvious power). In Chapter 1 we defined a stakeholder as any group or individual who can affect, or is affected by, the achievement of the organisation's objectives.

Across time, there has been a general increase in the demand by different stakeholder groups for social and environmental information, particularly in relation to issues such as climate change, water use, waste disposal, recycling, and the treatment of employees and other workers within supply chains. Therefore, the group of stakeholders to whom organisations are reporting has broadened across time (see **Learning exercise 6.4**).

6.4 Learning Exercise

Identifying stakeholders

Assume that you are the general manager of a large cruise ship company and you are considering whether the groups identified below (passengers, investors, environmental groups and workers) are stakeholders of your organisation. By extension, you also need to consider if you would provide these respective groups with social and/or environmental performance information, and why.

Passengers

Passengers are stakeholders because the organisation is dependent upon them, as customers, for financial resources. The operations of the organisation also have an impact on the passengers, which may relate to various aspects of health and safety. Therefore, passengers will impact the organisation and, in turn, be impacted by the organisation, which is consistent with the definition of stakeholders provided elsewhere in this book. The passengers might demand information to assess whether the services being offered by the organisation are of a nature that protects their health and safety, and fulfils their expectations in terms of the quality of service offered. Passengers might select a cruise ship company on the basis of various aspects of environmental, health and safety performance and related policies.

Investors

Investors are stakeholders. The organisation's operations are dependent on (impacted by) the support of investors, and the wealth of investors will be impacted by the operations of the organisation. Apart from wanting information about the financial performance of the organisation, investors also frequently want information about an organisation's social and environmental performance, as this can impact organisational profitability and risk. Furthermore, some investors are simply not prepared to invest in organisations with a poor record of social and environmental performance.

Environmental groups

Environmental groups are collectively a stakeholder. They represent and act in the interests of the environment, and in so doing are 'the voice' for various flora and fauna as well as future generations. Environmental groups, through their various lobbying activities, can influence the operations of an organisation. They would be interested in information about a variety of social and environmental impacts of a cruise ship company, including the generation and discharge of waste, the effects on reefs of the movement of vessels, policies for sourcing the raw materials used on the ships, and policies for recycling ships at the end of their life cycles.

Workers

There are various workers who gain employment from cruise ships. For example, there are the people who operate the ships and there are those who provide services to passengers. These people receive a salary from the company and therefore are stakeholders, as their wealth and livelihood is directly influenced/impacted by the company. The success of the organisation is also impacted by the actions of the workers. Such workers could want a variety of social and environmental information. They might be particularly interested in aspects of the organisation's health and safety-related performance and policies. Workers employed to break up a ship at the end of its life cycle are also stakeholders of the organisation because the shipping company has the ability to determine where and how the ship recycling activities are undertaken, and this will impact workers' health and safety. They are stakeholders even though they might not be directly employed by the company. It is known that many workers are injured or killed in ship-breaking activities, as these activities are often undertaken in developing countries where health and safety standards are relatively poor. While the ship-breaking workers might not directly demand information, various interest groups who work on their behalf (and who might be considered surrogates for the workers) might seek information from the company about how the managers are trying to ensure a safe working environment for those people performing the ship-breaking. Such information might include details about what monitoring is being undertaken by the company, and information about accidents that have occurred and the initiatives being introduced to reduce the incidence of these.

What social and environmental information should be reported?

Applying our 'accountability model', once we have determined 'to whom' we are reporting, we can then determine 'what to report'. This will involve some form of engagement with the identified stakeholders.

Since organisations can have a multitude of social and environmental impacts, not all of which can be meaningfully reported, some prioritisation needs to occur in identifying, measuring, managing and reporting specific aspects of an organisation's social and environmental performance. Given the predominantly voluntary nature of social and environmental reporting at the organisational level, much of the information that is reported will be influenced by the responsibilities and accountabilities that are accepted by managers. It will also be impacted by the demands of stakeholders, and how the different stakeholders' demands for information are prioritised by managers. Stakeholder engagement exercises (meetings with different stakeholder groups) will identify the information that stakeholders need or expect.

For example, if an organisation operates in an environment in which water is scarce, it could be particularly relevant to report information about water use and water-saving initiatives (this would be considered environmental information). Furthermore, because of stakeholder concerns about climate change, an energy-intensive organisation might elect to disclose information about its carbon emissions, and about any plans to reduce such emissions (this would also be considered environmental information). As another example, because of concerns about the treatment of employees throughout supply chains, managers of organisations that outsource aspects of their production might provide information derived from independent factory audits about the safety of the buildings, the health and safety policies in place within supply factories, and about the use of child labour (this would be considered social information).

To more fully understand the context of particular organisational disclosures it is important that the readers of reports, including sustainability reports, understand why managers have decided to report particular information and not report other information. This is particularly the case for sustainability-related information where managers have a great deal of choice about what social and environmental impacts they publicly disclose within their reports. That is, it is useful for readers to understand why managers thought that particular information would be relevant, or material to, the readers of the report. High quality sustainability reports typically include a section towards the commencement of the report that discloses information about the 'materiality determination process' (the process that led managers to decide that particular information was material to readers of the reports, and therefore warranted disclosure). The information would typically disclose which stakeholder groups were engaged to determine their information demands; how the stakeholders were engaged; what aspects of social and environmental performance were considered as important to the respective stakeholders; how the organisation then prioritised the information demands of the various stakeholder groups; and where within the report are the information demands of different stakeholders addressed. The materiality determination process also typically involves a review of various types of news media.

Key concept

The materiality determination process (also referred to by other titles such as 'materiality assessment process') is an important process that organisations undertake to determine what particular items of information to publicly report. It involves various forms of engagement with stakeholders and a prioritisation of particular stakeholders' information demands. Reporting information about the materiality determination process helps to provide context about the information being reported.

Since organisations do have a choice as to what aspects of their social and environmental performance they report, it is important that the reports being released clearly explain the reason why an organisation has elected to make some disclosures in preference to others. That is, why is particular information perceived by managers as being potentially material to stakeholders? (See **Learning exercise 6.5**.) Knowledge of this will help to place the disclosures within the appropriate context. According to the Global Reporting Initiative (GRI 1, 2021c, Glossary), something is a 'material topic', and therefore warranting disclosure if it is part of the 'topics that represent the organization's most significant impacts on the economy, environment, and people, including impacts on their human rights'.

In this respect, it is worthwhile considering the following note provided in the ANZ Bank 2021 ESG Supplement (2021, p. 6) which refers to the bank's 'materiality assessment' process. This note will likely help report readers understand why particular information was disclosed by the bank. It is therefore arguably a very useful inclusion within the bank's report.

> Through our annual materiality assessment we engage with internal and external stakeholders to inform our identification of environment, social and governance (ESG) risks and opportunities. We seek to identify those issues with the most potential to impact our ability to operate successfully and create value for our shareholders and other stakeholders.
>
> We use the results to inform our strategy, public ESG targets and external reporting.
>
> This year we obtained stakeholder views on a broad range of ESG issues.
>
> External views were sought from institutional investors, retail shareholders, consumer advocates, financial counsellors, customers and analysts. One-on-one interviews were conducted with the external stakeholders by an independent consultant.
>
> Overall, climate change emerged as the highest priority issue, with stakeholders noting both the social and environmental impacts and the influence the bank can have in terms of deploying capital to finance the transition to a net zero carbon economy.
>
> Fairness and ethical conduct continued to be seen as critical to everything we do and key to our social license to operate. Financial wellbeing was viewed as 'core business' and our efforts in this area can improve customer experience and positively impact the broader community. Finally, innovation and technology were seen as essential to supporting customer experience in today's digital world.
>
> External stakeholders also highlighted biodiversity and human rights as issues of rising significance. Internal stakeholders highlighted cyber security and data protection and housing.
>
> These insights were presented to our executive Ethics and Responsible Business Committee and Board Ethics, Environment, Social and Governance Committee and helped to inform the development of our public ESG targets.
>
> Source: ANZ Bank (2021), 2021 ESG Supplement: Shaping a world where people and communities thrive, p. 6.

6.5 Learning Exercise

Determining the materiality of information

What does it mean if it is said that information is material?

If information is material, this basically means that the information is important to (material to) the individual or group that is making a decision. That is, information is material if its presence or absence is likely to influence the decisions being made by readers of that information; for example, whether an investor invests in an organisation, or a consumer purchases goods or services from an organisation, or an employee decides to work for a particular organisation.

If something is deemed to be material, then what implication does this have for disclosure?

If information is considered to be material, then the general principle is that, subject to various considerations – the costs of collecting and disclosing the information, the implications for the organisation's ability to compete, the reliability of the information, other available information – an organisation should publicly disclose the information notwithstanding that there might be no regulatory requirement to do so.

The influence of stakeholders

Different stakeholders tend to identify, and rate as important, different aspects of social and environmental performance. They might therefore tend to develop different assessments of the performance of an organisation. This raises the possibility that the reports issued by organisations – particularly larger organisations – could incorporate the views of different stakeholders (such as those of managers, employee representatives, environmental groups and consumer groups) rather than simply presenting just the managers' views of how the organisation has performed.

We will return to this suggestion later in this chapter when we consider monologic and dialogic accounting, but at this point, it needs to be understood that managers' views of how well, or otherwise, their organisation is operating with respect to its social and environmental performance will not necessarily be shared by all stakeholders. Indeed, some stakeholders, such as particular social and environmental groups, often challenge managers' assertions about performance and devise their own set of accounts about an organisation's operations. These accounts, which are referred to as 'counter accounts' or 'shadow accounts', can provide a very different assessment of how an organisation has performed. We will consider counter accounts in more depth later in this chapter.

How should social and environmental information be reported?

As already noted, the reporting of social and environmental performance-related information by an organisation within its own reports is largely voluntary and therefore there is great variation in the reporting practices applied by those organisations that elect to publicly report. There are a number of reporting frameworks available for use (most notably the GRI Standards, which we will discuss in this chapter), and the reported information is typically made available on organisational websites. However, there are hundreds of alternative frameworks that have been developed internationally, with some having more support or credibility than others. Also, there will be some organisations that elect to develop their own approach to reporting, rather than applying the available frameworks:

> The GRI has identified 180 initiatives from 45 different countries and regions relating to sustainability reporting, and the Climate Disclosure Standards Board (CDSB) has to date identified 383 provisions that directly or indirectly affect the way in which companies prepare sustainability disclosures. In the broadest view, the Global Initiative for Sustainability Ratings (GISR) has uncovered over 1500 indicators addressing almost 600 issues ... The difficulty is that this can result in great variability in the quality, quantity, timeliness and relevance of information disclosed, which can be the cause of considerable confusion to reporters.
>
> Source: EY (2014), p. 13.

As the above EY quote emphasises, the existence of a large number of alternative reporting guidelines potentially makes it even more difficult to compare or benchmark the performance of one organisation against another. Later in this chapter, we will discuss in more depth some of the more commonly used guidelines.

The medium for reporting is often a standalone social and environmental report, and such reports have various titles. **Table 6.1** identifies a number of large organisations that produce such reports. The disclosures can also be made by way of various website approaches, where different web pages are devoted to different aspects of performance. Many organisations are also now including social and environmental performance information within their annual report, alongside all their information about financial performance and financial position. Later in this chapter, we will show just how extensive the practice of social and environmental reporting actually is.

TABLE 6.1 Examples of companies that produce social and environmental reports

Company	Industry sector	Name of report and related Internet address
ANZ	Banking	*ANZ 2021 ESG Supplement* https://www.anz.com.au/content/dam/anzcom/shareholder/2021-esg-supplement.pdf
Royal Dutch Shell	Global energy	*Sustainability report 2021* https://reports.shell.com/sustainability-report/2021/_assets/downloads/shell-sustainability-report-2021.pdf
Westpac	Banking	*Sustainability Supplement 2021* https://www.westpac.com.au/content/dam/public/wbc/documents/pdf/aw/ic/2021_Sustainability_Supplement.pdf
Apple	Electronics	*Environmental progress report 2022* https://www.apple.com/. Search for 'environment'.
Adidas	Sportswear	*Adidas Green Company Performance Analysis 2020* https://www.adidas-group.com/media/filer_public/f8/10/f8105750-28cb-4a13-9e2c-7031785b2c92/adidas_gcr_2020_en.pdf
Audi	Automobile manufacturing	*Audi report 2021: Combined annual and sustainability report* https://www.audi-mediacenter.com/en/publications/corporate/audi-report-2021-combined-annual-and-sustainability-report-1139

You may wish to review the websites of the organisations above and see the sorts of social and environmental information they have disclosed. You will find that different organisations tend to focus on different aspects of their social and environmental performance.

LO6.2 Corporate social responsibility reporting

corporate social responsibility (CSR) The responsibilities an organisation accepts to various stakeholders and the environment over and above their legal obligations

We often hear the terms **corporate social responsibility (CSR)** and *corporate social responsibility reporting*. What we have discussed so far in this chapter could also be referred to as corporate social responsibility reporting – and please note that, even though the word 'corporate' appears here, the way the term is used is not restricted to organisations of a corporate form, such that an organisation that is not a company can still be considered to be undertaking corporate social responsibility reporting.

Defining corporate social responsibility

The term 'corporate social responsibility' has no fixed meaning but generally refers to the responsibilities an organisation accepts over and above the requirements of the law, and the way in which it focuses its attention on the wellbeing of various stakeholders, and the environment.

Because different people have different perspectives about the social responsibilities of an organisation, it is probably not surprising that there is no single accepted definition of CSR. As the Australian Corporations and Markets Advisory Committee notes:

> The term 'CSR' does not have a precise or fixed meaning. Some descriptions focus on corporate compliance, with the spirit as well as the letter of applicable laws regulating corporate conduct. Other definitions refer to a business approach by which an enterprise takes into account the impacts of its activities on interest groups (often referred to as stakeholders) including, but extending beyond, shareholders, and balances longer-term societal impacts against shorter-term financial gains. These societal effects, going beyond the goods and services provided by companies and their returns to shareholders, are typically subdivided into environmental, social and economic impacts.
>
> Source: Australian Corporations and Markets Advisory Committee (2006), p. 13.

The quote above emphasises that definitions of CSR typically extend the responsibilities of corporations beyond their shareholders alone, and include activities over and above those relating to the usual provision of goods and services. However, whether business organisations, which are owned by shareholders in the case of companies, can realistically be expected to balance the needs of other stakeholders – many of them without any financial power or influence – with the fundamental quest of maximising the wealth of shareholders is a question that will generate different responses from different people.

While many people believe that both organisations and markets have a responsibility to make choices that benefit society and the environment, there are others who believe that the fundamental quest of business organisations is to maximise profits and shareholder value (for example, consider the views of the famous economist Milton Friedman, as discussed in Chapter 1). There are many interesting opinions and debates in the broad area of CSR. However, the philosophy underpinning this book is that organisations create social and environmental impacts that go beyond their economic impacts, and these can enhance or diminish the collective good or wider societal progress. This requires acceptance by managers of broader accountabilities.

While there is a multitude of definitions for CSR, one generally accepted definition, which is consistent with the perspective adopted by this book, is provided by the Commission of European Communities, which states that CSR is

> a concept whereby companies integrate social and environmental concerns in their business operations and in their interaction with their stakeholders on a voluntary basis. Being socially responsible means not only fulfilling legal expectations, but also going beyond compliance and investing more into human capital, the environment and the relations with stakeholders.
>
> Source: Commission of European Communities (2001), p. 6.

Another definition consistent with this is provided by the World Business Council for Sustainable Development, which defines CSR as

> the continuing commitment by business to contribute to economic development while improving the quality of life of the workforce and their families as well as of the community and society at large.
>
> Source: World Business Council for Sustainable Development (2006).

As already addressed earlier in this chapter, ideally, an organisation should clearly inform its stakeholders about the extent/breadth of its accepted responsibilities. That is, organisations should be clear about the aspects of social and environmental performance they are prioritising, and why. CSR reporting should then provide information about how an organisation has addressed, and performed in relation to, its social responsibilities.

Social reporting and environmental reporting are components of CSR reporting. We will consider these in a little more depth now.

YouTube resource

In a YouTube video (**www.youtube.com/watch?v=Z5KZhm19EO0**), Alex Edmans, Professor of Finance at the London Business School, discusses the long-term impacts of social responsibility, and challenges the idea that caring for society and the environment comes at the expense of profit. Indeed, he argues that better social and environmental performance can have positive implications for profit.

Please watch the video, appreciating that this is just one view of CSR. Please also consider whether you agree with what Professor Edmans is saying.

Social reporting

We provided a brief overview of social reporting in Chapter 2. As we noted, social reporting provides information about an organisation's impacts upon particular people and societies. Social reports might provide information about an organisation's:

- training of employees
- diversity and equal opportunity policies as they relate to employees
- health and safety aspects of products
- support of community projects
- treatment of employees within the supply chain
- actions taken to respect indigenous cultures and values
- customer privacy policies
- compliance with occupational health and safety requirements
- compliance with various social codes of conduct.

Information about all the items in the above list can be considered to be generated by an accounting system, despite the potential absence of measurements being made in financial terms.

Environmental reporting

We provided a brief overview of environmental reporting in Chapter 2. As we noted, environmental reporting provides information about an organisation's impacts upon living and non-living natural systems, including land, air, water and ecosystems. Environmental reporting addresses issues associated with:

- materials used
- effluent and waste generated
- energy consumed
- emissions (including CO_2) generated
- water consumed
- impacts of transportation
- environmental assessments of suppliers
- wastewater generated and impacts of this wastewater
- impacts (positive and negative) on biodiversity
- compliance with environmental regulations.

Sustainability reporting

Sustainability reporting, another term used in relation to CSR reporting, is obviously linked to the idea of sustainable development. The sustainability reporting practices of organisations should ideally provide insights into how they are performing in relation to the goal of sustainable development. As noted in Chapter 3, sustainable development is generally accepted as: 'Development that meets the needs of the present world without compromising the ability of future generations to meet their own needs' (World Commission on Environment and Development, 1987).

Many organisations now make public statements about how sustainability is a core focus of their operations. For example, BHP 2021 Annual Report (2021, p. 3) states that:

> We view our management of sustainability as core to our efforts to generate social value including:
>
> - putting the health and safety of our people first
> - being environmentally responsible
> - respecting human rights
> - supporting the communities where we operate.
>
> We recognise sustainability is integral to the work we do at BHP. We believe it leads to higher performance by making us more productive and safe.

Of course, whether we believe such public declarations is a matter of personal judgement and is influenced by the managers' past performance, and reputation, with respect to their efforts to be sustainable. Our acceptance of such statements also depends on whether we believe that business organisations can truly put sustainability ahead of the shorter-term quests to maximise profitability and the wealth of shareholders.

There is much variation in the nature of sustainability reporting, and again it needs to be appreciated that (arguably wrongly) the term 'sustainability reporting' is often used interchangeably with other terms, such as 'CSR reporting'. According to the GRI:

> A sustainability report is a report published by a company or organization about the economic, environmental and social impacts caused by its everyday activities. A sustainability report also presents the organization's values and governance model, and demonstrates the link between its strategy and its commitment to a sustainable global economy.
>
> Sustainability reporting can help organizations to measure, understand and communicate their economic, environmental, social and governance performance, and then set goals, and manage change more effectively. A sustainability report is the

> key platform for communicating sustainability performance and impacts – whether positive or negative.
>
> Sustainability reporting can be considered as synonymous with other terms for non-financial reporting; triple bottom line reporting, corporate social responsibility (CSR) reporting, and more. It is also an intrinsic element of integrated reporting; a more recent development that combines the analysis of financial and non-financial performance.
>
> Source: Global Reporting Initiative (2018b).

To be a 'true' sustainability report, it could reasonably be expected that a report must actually address the concept of sustainable development, and how the organisation's activities and initiatives are helping the planet move towards a sustainable existence and sustainable future. However, in practice, organisations typically fall short of this expectation. They often provide a selection of economic, social and environmental indicators/measures that do not necessarily link or sit well together, nor do managers typically put their performance in a context that clearly shows how they have helped society move towards the goal of sustainable development.

Also, addressing sustainability at the individual organisational level is problematic. Sustainable development is really a big concept that involves the consideration of larger environments and societal requirements, something that is beyond the confines of any single organisation. The quest for sustainable development requires the coordinated actions of all organisations, governments and communities.

Regardless of these concerns about the appropriateness, or otherwise, of single organisations producing sustainability reports, an increasing number of organisations now report against the 17 Sustainable Development Goals (SDGs) of the United Nations Development Program (UNDP; see **www.undp.org/content/undp/en/home/sustainable-development-goals.html**). These are shown in **Figure 6.1**.

FIGURE 6.1 The United Nations Sustainable Development Goals

Source: From Sustainable Development Goals, by United Nations, © 2015 United Nations. Reprinted with the permission of the United Nations. The content of this publication has not been approved by the United Nations and does not reflect the views of the United Nations or its officials or Member States.

The SDGs have been developed by the UNDP to provide guidelines and targets for countries to adopt in accordance with their own priorities and the social and environmental challenges of the world at large. Each SDG is supported by various components of documentation and guidance. The view taken by the UNDP is that achieving the SDGs requires a partnership of governments, the private sector, civil society and citizens in order that we leave a better planet for future generations to enjoy. As an example of an organisation that publicly refers to the SDGs, the ANZ Bank states:

> We are committed to the United Nations Sustainable Development Goals (SDGs) and believe that business has an important role to play in their achievement. Our 2022 ESG targets support 12 of the 17 SDGs.
>
> In 2019 we became a founding signatory to the UN Principles for Responsible Banking. Under the Principles we are required to set at least two targets that address our most significant (potential) positive and negative impacts, aligned with the SDGs and the Paris Climate Agreement. We have reported our progress towards implementing the Principles using the Reporting and Self-assessment Index, available on pages 66–74.
>
> Source: ANZ Bank (2021), 2021 ESG Supplement: Shaping a world where people and communities thrive, p. 4.

Why do I need to know about the nature of the UN SDGs?

The UN SDGs are gaining a great deal of publicity and traction worldwide and are influencing the operational and reporting policies of larger organisations globally. Therefore, it is important that we understand their role and the reason for their creation.

LO6.3 The incidence of CSR reporting

If we were to look at evidence of past practices of social and environmental reporting, we would find that prior to the 1990s, there was very little social and environmental reporting activity going on (some organisations were doing it, but they were in the minority). This perhaps reflected a lower awareness in society then of, and concern for, the impacts of organisations on the environment, or the perception that organisations did not really have extensive social and environmental responsibilities, or need to be accountable for such responsibilities.

In the early 1990s, however, reporting practices started to change, and in many countries, organisations – particularly larger ones operating in environmentally sensitive industries – started producing various types of information about aspects of their environmental performance. Interestingly, this increase in reporting seemed to occur at the same time as the community membership numbers of many environmental groups around the world also greatly increased (Deegan and Gordon, 1996, provide evidence of this association), which was reflective of people becoming more concerned about the deteriorating state of the environment (see **Learning exercise 6.6**).

6.6 Learning Exercise

The link between community concern for the environment and corporate reporting

In an early research project that explored the incidence of social and environmental reporting, Deegan and Gordon (1996) noted how an increase in organisations producing social and environmental information seemed to coincide with increases in the total membership numbers of environmental groups. Could this relationship just be a coincidence?

The evidence

There is much evidence that the reporting practices of organisations are responsive to stakeholders' and community expectations. Therefore, a change in stakeholder expectations could be expected to have an effect on organisational reporting practices. Growing membership numbers of environmental groups can be seen as reflective of growing community concern about the environment. This environmental concern is likely to be associated with a growing interest in how different organisations' activities are impacting the environment, and how accountable they are being for this impact.

Therefore, if what is being reported by organisations is typically related to stakeholders' expectations of organisations' responsibilities, then increasing community concern for the environment would be expected to be matched (perhaps with some short time lag) with the information being produced about corporate environmental performance. This would suggest that the connection between an increase in social and environmental reporting and increased membership of environmental groups is more than just a coincidence.

An issue here, however, is that if such a relationship exists, then what if no-one cared about the environment? Would this mean that companies would not monitor, control and report various aspects of their environmental performance? Perhaps.

Following the increase in environmental reporting, the mid to late 1990s then saw an expansion in the amount of social disclosures, with many organisations starting to produce separate social reports as well. In subsequent years, the practice evolved to a situation where organisations started to produce reports that combined various aspects of their social and environmental performance. Ultimately, we have now moved to a situation where many organisations produce reports that include a range of economic, social and environmental information, and these are often now referred to as 'sustainability reports'. Indeed, the practice is now becoming quite *mainstream* in nature (although there is also an emerging trend towards providing financial, social, and environmental information in single 'integrated reports').

One organisation that performs a regular survey of CSR reporting is the large global accounting firm KPMG. The results of a recent survey were released in 2020 (KPMG, 2020). KPMG used two broad samples for its research. It surveyed the reporting practices of a global sample of 5200 companies, which was made up of the top 100 companies from 52 different countries (referred to as the N100 companies). It also surveyed the reporting practices of the world's largest companies by revenue based on the Fortune 500 ranking of companies (referred to as the G250 companies).

KPMG (2020) reports that 96 per cent of G250 companies and 80 per cent of N100 companies publicly report about sustainability. The leading reporting countries are Japan, Mexico, Malaysia, India, United States, Sweden, Spain, France, South Africa, United Kingdom, Taiwan, Australia, Canada and Germany, with reporting rates for the N100 companies in these countries ranging from 92 per cent to 100 per cent. For the minority of large companies that do not report sustainability-related information, KPMG warns:

> The small minority of companies not yet reporting will find themselves seriously out of step with global norms. This misalignment with accepted global practice in itself poses risks to non-reporting companies, but the leaders of these companies should also be

> aware that sustainability reporting cannot easily be solved overnight with a quick fix. Reporting methodologies and approaches are complex and dynamic, requiring deep professional knowledge and expertise and must be backed up with robust sustainability strategies and risk management processes. So, the advice to any company that has yet to start the sustainability reporting journey is to take it seriously and begin now. The laggards will soon be left behind.
>
> Source: KPMG (2020). The time has come: The KPMG survey of corporate responsibility reporting 2020, p. 7.

Other findings within the KPMG 2020 survey reveal the following:

- Some industries have higher rates of reporting than others. For example, at the higher end of reporting, 84 per cent of N100 companies in the technology, media and telecommunications sectors embrace sustainability reporting, as do 84 per cent of N100 companies in the mining sector.
- The assurance of sustainability-related information by independent third parties – something we will discuss later in this chapter – has increased in recent years. Seventy-one per cent of G250 companies now have their sustainability information assured by independent third parties, while 51 per cent of N100 companies have their sustainability-related information assured. Against this trend, KPMG (2020, p. 23) report that only one third of Chinese G250 companies currently invest in the assurance of their publicly available sustainability information. A favourable opinion from an independent assurer/auditor helps to increase the credibility of the information being reported.
- In terms of the most commonly used reporting framework, it was the GRI Standards that were most commonly used. Seventy-three per cent of the G250 companies and 67 per cent of the N100 companies use the GRI standards as the basis of their reporting.
- Many of the companies – 72 per cent of G250 companies and 69 per cent of N100 companies – link their CSR activities to the UN Sustainable Development Goals, which we discussed earlier in this chapter. In this regard KPMG (2020, p. 44) states:

> The 17 SDGs were introduced by the UN as a blueprint to achieve a better and more sustainable future for all by addressing global challenges including poverty, inequality, climate change, environmental degradation, peace and justice. Many companies have since adopted the SDGs as a guide for their sustainability programs.

However, KPMG (2020) note that reporting on the UN SDGs tends to focus almost exclusively on the positive contributions companies make towards achieving the SDGs, and the reporting tends to lack transparency in relation to negative impacts relative to the SDGs. KPMG (2020, p. 48) notes:

> Balanced SDG reporting is important to show that a company is aware of how it contributes to global problems as well as how it helps to solve them. Disclosing both positive and negative impacts on the SDGs provides enhanced transparency and can therefore help to build trust between the company and its stakeholders.
>
> Companies that turn a blind eye to their negative impacts and focus their reporting only on the positive, risk losing credibility and public trust.
>
> They also open themselves to accusations of 'SDG washing', the practice of using the SDGs as a platform to create positive PR for themselves rather than as a framework to deliver genuine change. Similarly, if companies are serious about helping to deliver the SDGs, then they need to set clear SDG-related performance goals and report on progress against them.

Also, KPMG found that while some of the 17 SDGs were widely reported, some were seldom reported upon by most organisations.

- In relation to targets pertaining to climate change, the majority of G250 companies (76 per cent) disclose targets to cut their carbon emissions; 65 per cent of N100 companies also disclose these targets. In this regard, KPMG (2020, p. 41) notes:

  > Any leading company that does not yet report carbon targets is now clearly out of step with global good practice.

  We will discuss the important issue of climate change in more depth later in this chapter.
- Apart from producing information about carbon and other GHG emissions, information about the business risks of climate change is also described as useful. In this regard, the number of companies that acknowledge the risk of climate change has increased significantly since the earlier 2017 survey by KPMG. Forty-three per cent of N100 companies (up from 28 per cent in 2017) and 56 per cent of G250 companies (up from 48 per cent in 2017) acknowledge this risk in their reports. In discussing this increase, KPMG (2020, p. 36) notes:

  > This growth is in large part due to the work of the Task Force on Climate-related Financial Disclosures (TCFD) in raising corporate and regulator awareness of climate change as a financial risk, and in developing recommendations for disclosure of climate-related risk. The work of the Task Force has resulted in increasing investor scrutiny of corporate disclosures on the topic and growing momentum towards mandatory climate risk disclosure in many jurisdictions around the world.

- KPMG (2020) reports that 18 per cent of N100 companies and 37 per cent of G250 companies report in line with the recommendation of the Task Force on Climate-related Financial Disclosures. These recommendations were launched in 2017 with the purpose of improving corporate reporting on climate-related risks and to enable financial stakeholders (investors, lenders and insurers) to factor climate-related risks into their decisions. We will consider the recommendations of the TCFD in more depth later in this chapter.
- KPMG (2020) also referred to the need for improved reporting relating to 'biodiversity risk'. All of us, including businesses, are reliant upon biodiversity. Biodiversity is a term that often creates confusion. 'Bio' means life, while 'diversity' means variability. Properly functioning ecosystems rely upon a great diversity of plant and animal life. No organism or animal exists in isolation and a healthy ecosystem requires a multitude of species. There is a great deal of interconnectedness and relationships between different species, much of which is not understood. However, it is accepted that the long-term survival of the planet relies upon maintaining biodiversity. There has even been some speculation that the degradation of biodiversity enabled COVID-19 to jump from nature to humans – though there is not definitive proof. At a narrower level, biodiversity is also a fundamental requirement for business survival. As KPMG (2020, p. 28) states:

  > Businesses rely on nature and ecosystem services to provide critical inputs for production processes, to treat and dissipate waste, and to maintain soil, air and water quality. It is, therefore, critical for companies to understand and disclose the risks that biodiversity loss poses to their businesses, as well as the impact their businesses have on biodiversity.

  KPMG (2020) report that only about a quarter of N100 and G250 companies that are deemed to be at high or medium risk from biodiversity loss report information about the risks that biodiversity losses pose to the business. KPMG point to this area as being an area of reporting that requires rapid improvement. KPMG (2020) note a number of sectors that are at high risk from biodiversity loss, and these include construction and building materials, leisure and hotels, food and drug retailers and mining. For readers with an interest in biodiversity risks and losses you can refer to the following publications for further information:

- WWF (2020), Living Planet Report 2020, https://livingplanet.panda.org/en-us
- United Nations (2020) The Global Biodiversity Outlook, https://www.unep.org/resources/report/global-biodiversity-outlook-5-gbo-5

  The Task Force on Nature-related Financial Disclosures (TNFD) was launched in 2021 and this is expected to generate specific guidance in relation to biodiversity reporting.

Key concept

Biodiversity is not only important for the proper functioning of ecosystems globally, and therefore for the health of all living species on the planet, but biodiversity is also important for business organisations. Biodiversity loss creates various risks for organisations (such as supply chain risks), with some sectors more immediately threatened than others.

The KPMG report also highlights that, internationally, governments and securities exchanges are looking at increasing the regulation of CSR-related disclosures, and this will have obvious implications for increasing the amount of disclosures being made. Therefore, the evidence is clear. This focus of reporting is here to stay, and therefore accountants and managers need to be very well aware of it!

LO6.4 CSR and sustainability reporting frameworks

Having discussed the meaning of CSR/sustainability reporting, and having established that it is a widespread practice globally, we will now return to the issues associated with '*What to report?*' and '*How to report?*' In doing so, we will discuss a number of reporting frameworks that organisations might elect to use. There is a vast number – indeed hundreds – of reporting frameworks available, so we can only consider a limited number of them – specifically, some of the higher-profile frameworks being used. The first reporting framework we will look at is that of the GRI.

The Global Reporting Initiative

Globally, the most commonly used framework for CSR/sustainability reporting is that of the Global Reporting Initiative (GRI), an organisation we have already referred to numerous times in this chapter. This is affirmed by the results of the KPMG survey, as just discussed.

The GRI commenced operations in 1997. According to its website (www.globalreporting.org, accessed February 2022):

> GRI (Global Reporting Initiative) is the independent, international organization that helps businesses and other organizations take responsibility for their impacts by providing them with the global common language to communicate those impacts. We provide the world's most widely used standards for sustainability reporting – the GRI standards.

> The GRI secretariat is headquartered in Amsterdam, the Netherlands, and we have a network of seven regional hubs ensuring we can support organizations and stakeholders worldwide.
>
> Source: About GRI (2022), https://www.globalreporting.org/about-gri/. Accessed April 2022.

GRI standards and reporting principles

GRI has been releasing new/revised guidance for about 25 years. In 2016, the GRI transitioned from producing what it referred to as 'guidelines' to developing 'standards' – which it refers to as the 'GRI Standards'. **Figure 6.2** summarises the history of the GRI.

FIGURE 6.2 The history of the GRI Standards

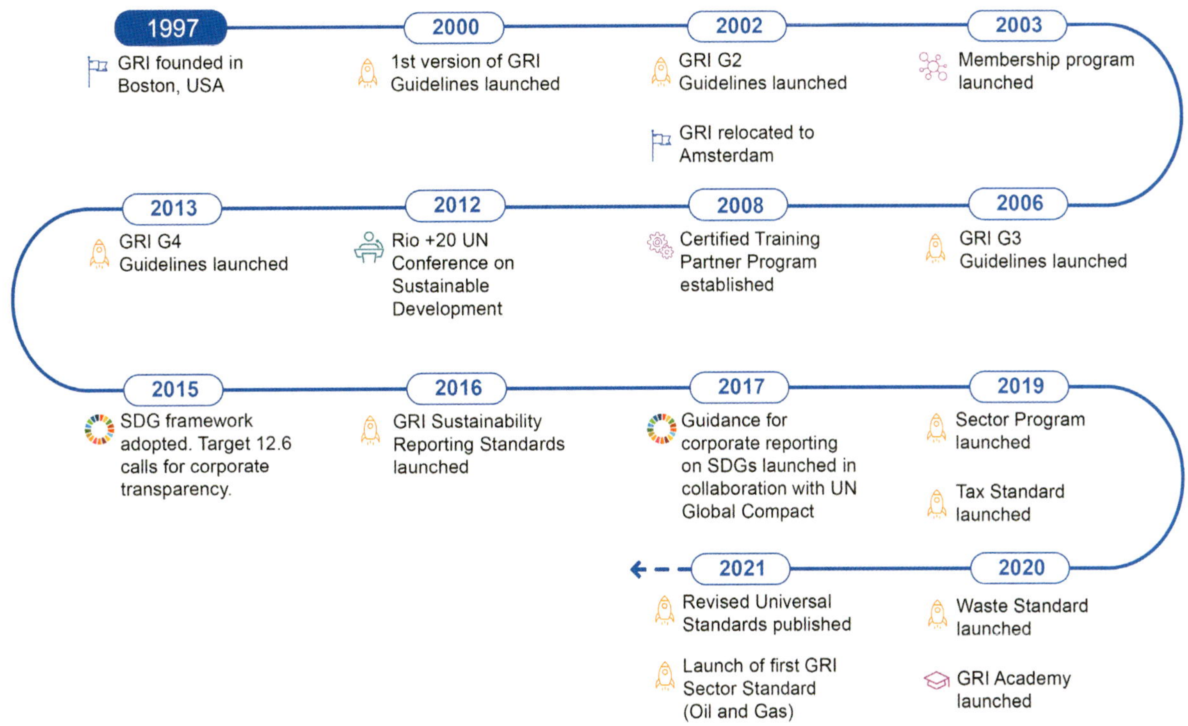

Source: GRI (2022). GRI continuously works at maintaining the GRI standards up to date and therefore it is important for users of the Standards to check the latest information on our website, https://www.globalreporting.org.

The GRI Standards are a modular system of interconnected standards that are released as three different types of Standards, these being:

- Universal Standards
- Sector Standards
- Topic Standards.

We shall explain these three different types of standards shortly. Reflecting the evolving nature of the GRI Standards, the current Universal Standards (referred to as GRI 1, GRI 2 and GRI 3) replaced the former Universal Standards (GRI 101, GRI 102 and GRI 103) in 2021 (with the new Universal Standards being effective from 1 January 2023), and the first Sector Standard (for the oil and gas sector) was also released in 2021 with various Sector Standards for other sectors expected to follow in the near term.

The GRI Standards identify 'disclosures' that reporting entities will make. The disclosures include both 'requirements' and 'recommendations'. The 'requirements' list the information that organisation must report in order to comply with the Standards, whereas the 'recommendations' encourage certain disclosures.

GRI stakeholders

In terms of the potential users of the GRI Standards, GRI (2022, p. 2) states:

> Any organization, large or small, public or private, from any sector or location, can use the GRI Standards. Reporters, stakeholders, and other information users draw on the Standards.
>
> Reporters within an organization use the Standards to report on the organization's impacts in a credible way that is comparable over time and in relation to other organizations. The Standards also help stakeholders and other information users understand what is expected from an organization to report on and use the information published by organizations in various ways.
>
> The organization can use the disclosed information to assess its policies and strategies or to guide decision-making, such as setting goals and targets. Stakeholders can also use this information. For example, investors can use the reported information to assess how an organization integrates sustainable development into its strategy to identify financial risks and evaluate its long-term success. The information provided can also help other information users, such as analysts and policymakers in benchmarking and forming policy, and academics in their research.
>
> Source: GRI (2022), p. 2.

GRI 3 (2021c, p. 9) provides further insights into which stakeholders should be addressed as part of the reporting process:

> The organization should identify who its stakeholders are across its activities and business relationships and engage with them to help identify its impacts.
>
> The organization should draw a full list of individuals and groups whose interests are affected or could be affected by the organization's activities. Common categories of stakeholders for organizations are business partners, civil society organizations, consumers, customers, employees and other workers, governments, local communities, non-governmental organizations, shareholders and other investors, suppliers, trade unions, and vulnerable groups. The organization can further distinguish between individuals and groups whose human rights are affected or could be affected, and individuals and groups with other interests.
>
> When identifying its stakeholders, the organization should ensure it identifies any individuals or groups it does not have a direct relationship with (e.g., workers in the supply chain or local communities that live at a distance from the organization's operations) and those who are unable to articulate their views (e.g., future generations) but whose interests are affected or could be affected by the organization's activities.
>
> Different lists of stakeholders can be drawn per activity, project, product or service, or other classification that is relevant for the organization.

As we can see from the above quotation, the GRI Standards are intended to be of relevance to a broad cross-section of 'stakeholders'. This can be contrasted to financial reporting – we shall explore in Chapters 7 to 11 – which identifies investors, potential investors, lenders and other creditors as the target audience of general purpose financial reports (that is, standard setters – such as the International Accounting Standards Board which develops financial reporting guidance – have a much more restricted perspective of 'stakeholders' relative to that of the GRI). In relation to 'stakeholders', GRI 1 (2021a, p. 10) also states:

> Stakeholders are individuals or groups that have interests that are affected or could be affected by an organization's activities. Common categories of stakeholders for organizations are business partners, civil society organizations, consumers, customers, employees and other workers, governments, local communities, non-governmental organizations, shareholders and other investors, suppliers, trade unions, and vulnerable groups ... Stakeholder interests can be negatively or positively affected by the organization's activities. Due diligence focuses on identifying stakeholder interests that are or could be negatively affected by the organization's activities.
>
> Stakeholders may not always have a direct relationship with the organization. For example, the workers in the organization's supply chain can also be its stakeholders, or there can be individuals or groups living at a distance from the organization's operations who can be affected or potentially affected by these operations. ... Engaging with stakeholders helps the organization identify and manage its negative and positive impacts. Not all stakeholders will be affected by all activities of the organization. The organization should identify the stakeholders whose interests have to be taken into account in connection with a specific activity (i.e., 'relevant stakeholders'). Where it is impossible to engage with all relevant stakeholders directly, the organization can engage with credible stakeholder representatives or proxy organizations (e.g., non-governmental organizations, trade unions).

Key concept

The stakeholders of the organisation (and we explained the meaning of 'stakeholders' in Chapter 1) will include individuals, groups or other living beings that do not necessarily have a direct relationship with the organisation. There is an expectation that an organisation has an obligation, or accountability, to report about significant impacts on stakeholders even in the absence of any direct relationship with them.

The position embraced within the GRI Standards is that managers need to create processes which enable their organisation to be accountable for significant impacts (which then are considered as 'material topics') imposed upon the organisation's stakeholders particularly from the perspective of 'sustainable development'. GRI 1 (2021a, p. 4) states:

> Through their activities and business relationships, organizations can have an effect on the economy, environment, and people, and in turn make negative or positive contributions to sustainable development. Sustainable development refers to 'development which meets the needs of the present without compromising the ability of future generations to meet their own needs'. The objective of sustainability reporting using the GRI Sustainability Reporting Standards (GRI Standards) is to provide transparency on how an organization contributes or aims to contribute to sustainable development.
>
> The GRI Standards enable an organization to publicly disclose its most significant impacts on the economy, environment, and people, including impacts on their human rights and how the organization manages these impacts. This enhances transparency on the organization's impacts and increases organizational accountability.

GRI reporting principles

The GRI standards identify a number of reporting principles that organisations should embrace, together with the disclosures that organisations are expected to make. In terms of the format of the disclosures, GRI 1 (2021a, p. 7) notes:

> The organization can publish or make information accessible in a range of formats (e.g., electronic, paper-based) across one or more locations (e.g., a standalone sustainability report, web pages, an annual report). The terms 'report' and 'reported information' in the GRI Standards both refer to information reported across all locations.
>
> The GRI content index provides an overview of the organization's reported information and shows the location where information users can find it. The content index also shows which GRI Standards and disclosures the organization has used.
>
> If the organization intends to publish a standalone sustainability report, it does not need to repeat information that it has already reported publicly elsewhere, such as on web pages or in its annual report. In such a case, the organization can report a required disclosure by providing a reference in the GRI content index as to where this information can be found (e.g., by providing a link to the web page or citing the page in the annual report where the information has been published).

The GRI standards are generally accepted by many people (but not *all* people) as representing current best practice for sustainability reporting. They are structured as a set of interrelated standards. An overview of the GRI standards is presented in **Exhibit 6.2**.

Referring to **Exhibit 6.2**, we can see that the Universal Standard *GRI 1: Foundation 2021* is the starting point for using the full set of GRI standards. That is, GRI 1 is the first Standard that organisations should consult to understand how to report using the GRI Standards. GRI 1 includes the 'reporting principles' that need to be adopted by reporters in relation to report content and quality, and which are fundamental to good-quality reporting. GRI 1 also identifies some 'key concepts' that lay the foundation for sustainability reporting. These key concepts are:

- impact
- material topics
- due process
- stakeholder.

The above four key concepts are explained by GRI as follows.

An 'impact' is defined in the Glossary to GRI 1 as an:

> effect the organization has or could have on the economy, environment, and people, including on their human rights, which in turn can indicate its contribution (negative or positive) to sustainable development.

The general principle is that an organisation should understand its impacts and thereafter report on impacts that are judged as significant.

'Material topics' are defined in the Glossary to GRI 1 as:

> topics that represent the organization's most significant impacts on the economy, environment, and people, including impacts on their human rights.

EXHIBIT 6.2 The structure of the GRI standards framework

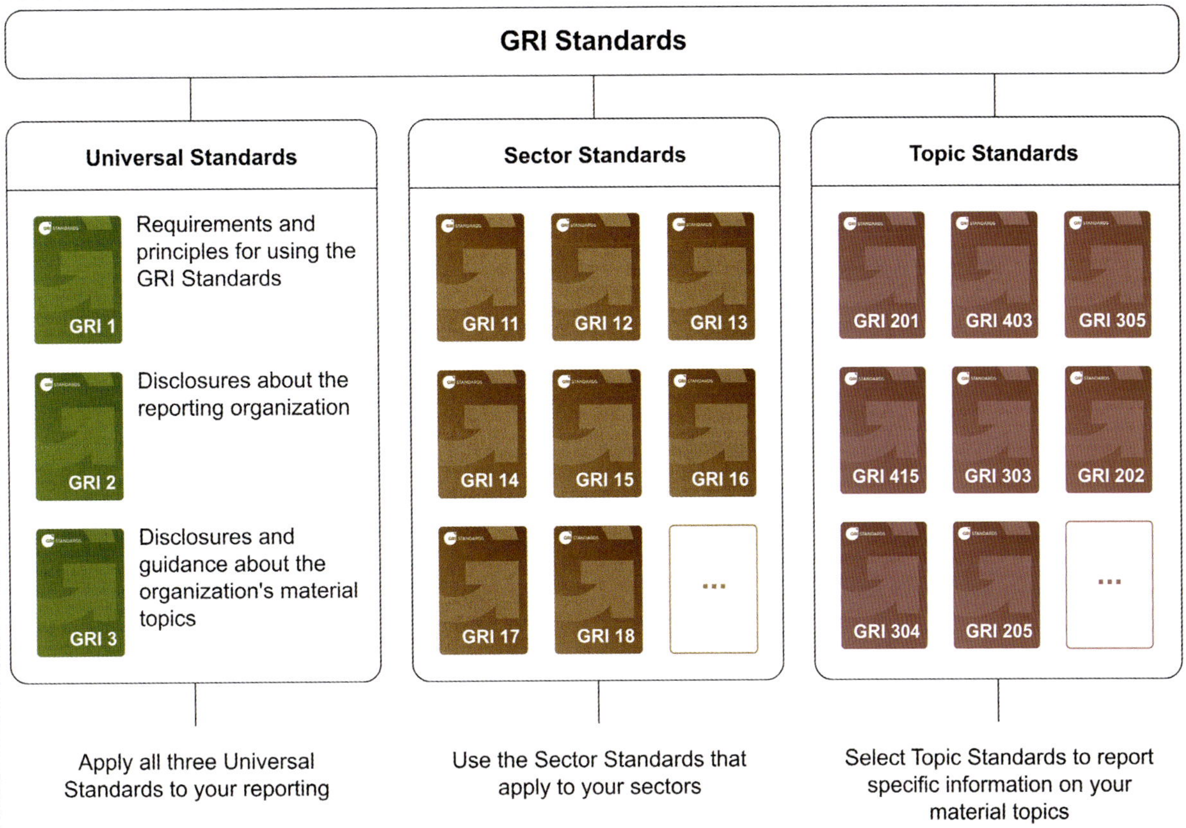

Source: Global Reporting Initiative (GRI 1, 2021), p. 3.

GRI 1 notes that the organisation needs to be accountable for its 'material impacts'. GRI 1 (2021a, p. 8) notes:

> When using the GRI Standards, the organization prioritizes reporting on those topics that represent its most significant impacts on the economy, environment, and people, including impacts on their human rights. In the GRI Standards, these are the organization's material topics.

'Due diligence' is defined in the Glossary to GRI 1 as the:

> process to identify, prevent, mitigate, and account for how the organization addresses its actual and potential negative impacts.

GRI 1 requires reporting organisations to report information about the due diligence processes that have been implemented.

The fourth 'key concept' identified within GRI 1 (as indicated above) is 'stakeholder'. We have already discussed how the GRI Standards address 'stakeholders'.

Apart from the key concepts that we have just discussed, the reporting organisation is required to apply the reporting principles referred to in GRI 1 if it is to claim that its sustainability report has been prepared in accordance with the GRI Standards. The reporting principles are:

- Accuracy
- Balance

- Clarity
- Comparability
- Completeness
- Sustainability context
- Timeliness
- Verifiability.

Exhibit 6.3 provides additional explanation of the qualitative characteristics that are expected to be satisfied if information is going to prove useful to its readers.

EXHIBIT 6.3 An overview of the GRI reporting principles

1 Accuracy	The organisation shall report information that is correct and sufficiently detailed to allow an assessment of the organisation's impacts.
2 Balance	The organisation shall report information in an unbiased way and provide a fair representation of the organisation's negative and positive impacts.
3 Clarity	The organisation shall present information in a way that is accessible and understandable.
4 Comparability	The organisation shall select, compile, and report information consistently to enable an analysis of changes in the organisation's impacts over time and an analysis of these impacts relative to those of other organisations.
5 Completeness	The organisation shall provide sufficient information to enable an assessment of the organisation's impacts during the reporting period.
6 Sustainability context	The organisation shall report information about its impacts in the wider context of sustainable development.
7 Timeliness	The organisation shall report information on a regular schedule and make it available in time for information users to make decisions.
8 Verifiability	The organisation shall gather, record, compile, and analyse information in such a way that the information can be examined to establish its quality.

Source: Global Reporting Initiative (GRI 1, 2021a).

If we look at the attributes above (or qualitative characteristics) that sustainability-related information should have, we will see that these are similar to the attributes we identified in Chapter 1 as being relevant to all accounting information, whether it be financial, social or environmental in nature.

For a discussion of consideration of the views of stakeholders, see Learning exercise 6.7.

6.7 Learning Exercise

Identifying and considering the views of stakeholders

Consider the following statement from GRI 101:

> When making decisions about the content of its report, the organization is to consider the reasonable expectations and interests of stakeholders. This includes those who are unable to articulate their views and whose concerns are presented by proxies (for example, NGOs acting on their collective behalf); and those with whom the organization cannot be in constant or obvious dialogue. The organization is expected to identify a process for taking such views into account when determining whether a topic is material.
>
> Source: GRI 101: FOUNDATION 2016, Global Reporting Initiative, 2018, p. 8.

What is the role of a proxy stakeholder?

Many organisational stakeholders who might be greatly impacted by the operations of an organisation do not have the ability to voice their expectations, or interests, regardless of how valid or important these concerns might be. They therefore rely upon others to do so for them, and we might refer to these other people or groups as 'proxies' or 'surrogate stakeholders'.

Some examples of proxy stakeholders and the impacts they can have on organisations

- *Environmental groups* – These groups voice the concerns of many people in the community who might not otherwise be able to be heard. They also act on behalf of threatened and endangered species, as well as future generations of people. Organisations would be wise to have ongoing communications with environmental groups.
- *Animal welfare groups* – These groups speak on behalf of various animals, which again are unable to have a voice. In working on behalf of animals, these groups can make information known about cruel and inhumane practices that are perhaps unknown to stakeholders. For example, currently, many animal protection organisations are publicising information about particular countries' treatment of the animals used in the production of various items of clothing, and associated accessories, and this has caused a number of large clothing companies to change their practices. Many such companies now directly engage with animal welfare groups as an important part of managing their business.
- *Consumer groups* – These groups speak on behalf of individual consumers who, again, individually might not have much power over an organisation. Large consumer groups have been able to create various changes in company operations and reporting practices. It is sensible for managers to work with these groups, as they are able to bring valuable expertise, as well as valuable insights from the community.
- *Labour groups* – These groups speak on behalf of individual workers who might be employed directly by an organisation, or are employed throughout supply chains. Many times, these groups will provide insights into organisations that were previously unknown to managers. For example, various labour groups are known to gain access to factories in developing countries and then publicise information about the working conditions there.

Since these proxy, or surrogate, stakeholder groups can impact an organisation's operations, it makes sense that managers should try to work with them (rather than ignore them), and that they should try to understand, and if possible produce, some of the information the groups expect to receive. Because business organisations are part of the broader society, it is imperative that they are responsive to the expectations of society. The groups identified above are able to provide insights into what certain parts of society expect.

A review of **Exhibit 6.2** shows that, once we have considered GRI 1, we then need to consider GRI 2 and GRI 3. We will not cover these two standards in depth (for interested readers, these two standards are also freely accessible on the GRI website), but briefly:

- *GRI 2: General Disclosures* requires organisations to report information about their reporting practices; activities and workers; governance; strategy, policies, and practices; and stakeholder engagement. This information gives insight into the profile and scale of organisations and provides a context for understanding their impacts. The Standard is structured as follows:
  - Section 1 contains five disclosures, which provide information about the organisation, its sustainability reporting practices, and the entities included in its sustainability reporting.

  - Section 2 contains three disclosures, which provide information about the organisation's activities, employees, and other workers.
  - Section 3 contains 13 disclosures, which provide information about the organisation's governance structure, composition, roles, and remuneration.
  - Section 4 contains seven disclosures, which provide information about the organisation's sustainable development strategy and its policies and practices for responsible business conduct.
  - Section 5 contains two disclosures, which provide information about the organisation's stakeholder engagement practices and how it engages in collective bargaining with employees.
- *GRI 3: Material Topics 2021* provides step-by-step guidance for organisations with respect to how to determine material topics. It also explains how the Sector Standards are used in this process. 'Material topics' are topics that represent an organisation's most significant impacts on the economy, environment, and people, including impacts on their human rights. GRI 3 requires organisations to report information about their process for determining material topics (which we refer to as the 'materiality determination process' – something that we discussed earlier within this chapter), their list of material topics, and how they manage each of their material topics. The Standard is structured as follows:
  - Section 1 provides step-by-step guidance on how to determine material topics.
  - Section 2 contains three disclosures, which provide information about the organisation's process of determining material topics, its list of material topics, and how it manages each topic.

GRI 3 (2021c, p. 7) provides a useful diagrammatic overview of how to determine 'material impacts'. It is reproduced as Figure 6.3.

FIGURE 6.3 Process to determine material impacts

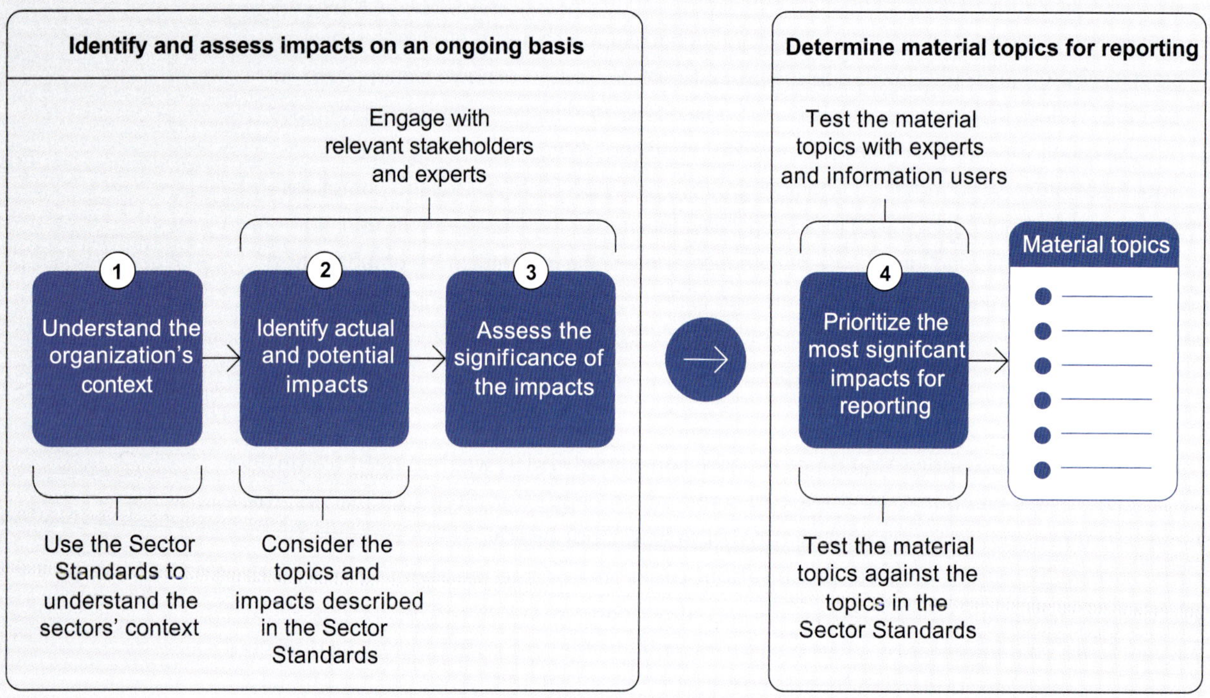

Source: GRI 3 (2021c), p. 7.

In discussing how an organisation reports information about how it determined its material impacts, GR1 3 (2021c, p. 7) notes:

> The organization should document its process of determining material topics. This includes documenting the approach taken, decisions, assumptions, and subjective judgments made, sources analyzed, and evidence gathered.

GRI 3 identifies a number of other disclosure requirements, including:

Disclosure 3-1 Process to determine material topics

The organization shall:

a. describe the process it has followed to determine its material topics, including:
  i. how it has identified actual and potential, negative and positive impacts on the economy, environment, and people, including impacts on their human rights, across its activities and business relationships;
  ii. how it has prioritized the impacts for reporting based on their significance;

b. specify the stakeholders and experts whose views have informed the process of determining its material topics.

Disclosure 3-2 List of material topics

The organization shall:

a. list its material topics;

b. report changes to the list of material topics compared to the previous reporting period.

Disclosure 3-3 Management of material topics

For each material topic reported under Disclosure 3-2, the organization shall:

a. describe the actual and potential, negative and positive impacts on the economy, environment, and people, including impacts on their human rights;

b. report whether the organization is involved with the negative impacts through its activities or as a result of its business relationships, and describe the activities or business relationships;

c. describe its policies or commitments regarding the material topic;

d. describe actions taken to manage the topic and related impacts, including:
  i. actions to prevent or mitigate potential negative impacts;
  ii. actions to address actual negative impacts, including actions to provide for or cooperate in their remediation;
  iii. actions to manage actual and potential positive impacts;

e. report the following information about tracking the effectiveness of the actions taken:
  i. processes used to track the effectiveness of the actions;
  ii. goals, targets, and indicators used to evaluate progress;
  iii. the effectiveness of the actions, including progress toward the goals and targets;
  iv. lessons learned and how these have been incorporated into the organization's operational policies and procedures;

f. describe how engagement with stakeholders has informed the actions taken (3-3-d) and how it has informed whether the actions have been effective (3-3-e).

The concept of 'materiality' referred to above is very important. As we have indicated elsewhere in this chapter, information is considered to be material if it is likely to impact the decisions that stakeholders make about an organisation. Determining whether particular items of information might be important to stakeholders requires an organisation to engage with stakeholders to determine what information they would prefer the organisation to disclose. As we have already noted, this process is often referred to as a 'materiality determination process' (see Learning exercise 6.8).

6.8 Learning Exercise

The importance of disclosing information about the materiality determination process

Information about the materiality determination process outlines the processes that the managers of an organisation establish to determine which items of information are considered important enough to disclose, and conversely, to explain why other information is excluded from reports.

What are the benefits to report readers of knowing about the materiality determination process?

Where the disclosure of information is predominantly voluntary – as is the case with much social and environmental information – then it would be reasonable for readers to question the logic, or merit, of why particular information was, or was not, disclosed. If managers are able to provide a clear, overall rationale for why particular information was deemed important enough to disclose, then even though readers might not agree with the materiality determination processes that the managers have employed, the disclosure about the processes should enable readers to better understand the context for why some information is reported and other information is not, and this should increase the understandability of the report.

Reporting with the Sector Standards

The GRI Sector Program – commenced in 2021 – is expected to ultimately develop standards for 40 sectors, starting with those that have the highest impact. The Sector Standards are designed to help identify a sector's most significant impacts and reflect stakeholder expectations for sustainability reporting. They describe the sustainability context for a specific sector, outline organisations' likely material topics based on the sector's most significant impacts, and list the disclosures that are likely to be relevant for the sector to report on. Oil and gas, coal, agriculture, aquaculture, and fishing were the first sectors prioritised under the Sector Program based on their significant environmental, social and economic impacts.

The first Sector Standard – *GRI 11: Oil and Gas Sector 2021* – was released in 2021 with an effective date of 1 January 2023. It identifies likely material topics for organisations in the oil and gas sector, and the required disclosures. GRI 11 (2021d, p. 13) identifies the likely material topics for the oil and gas sector. Each topic describes the sector's most significant impacts related to the topic and lists disclosures that are considered relevant for reporting on by oil and gas organisations. Likely 'material topics' for organisations within the oil and gas sector are identified in GRI 11 as:

1. GHG emissions
2. Climate adaptation, resilience, and transition
3. Air emissions
4. Biodiversity
5. Waste
6. Water and effluents
7. Closure and rehabilitation
8. Asset integrity and critical incident management
9. Occupational health and safety
10. Employment practices

11. Non-discrimination and equal opportunity
12. Forced labour and modern slavery
13. Freedom of association and collective bargaining
14. Economic impacts
15. Local communities
16. Land and resource rights
17. Rights of indigenous peoples
18. Conflict and security
19. Anti-competitive behaviour
20. Anti-corruption
21. Payments to governments
22. Public policy.

Sector Standards for Coal (GRI 12) and Agriculture, Aquaculture, and Fishing (GRI 13) were released in 2022.

In this book, we have not really differentiated between economic and financial performance. We can see here that the GRI standards refer to economic performance as a major category, rather than financial performance. Many people do treat the terms as being the same, but technically, they are not the same. When we talk about financial performance, we might be talking about such things as organisational profits, cash flows, returns on assets, sales revenue and so forth. How these are measured is typically on the basis of specific rules that are incorporated into such places as financial reporting standards (we will discuss financial reporting standards in subsequent chapters), and the financial measures tend to be historical in nature – that is, they reflect past financial performance rather than future financial performance.

By contrast, when we talk about economic performance – which is a focus of the GRI – we might be talking about the influence an organisation has had, and might have in the future, on communities and other organisations that are external to the organisation, through such mechanisms as tax payments, financial contributions or support to local communities, employment of workers and the associated payments of salaries, payments of dividends, and so forth. Measures of economic performance can be seen as potentially identifying the impacts certain expenditures, or payments, have on different stakeholders. The GRI identifies a number of economic components of performance that should be reported, including details of the various recipients of payments made by an organisation; financial assistance received from the government; payments made to different government bodies; and payments made to local suppliers.

The difference between financial and economic performance will not be pursued further here. However, it should be appreciated that some people do believe there is a difference between economic performance, which can be measured using various frameworks, and financial performance, which is typically measured using financial accounting standards issued by such bodies as the International Accounting Standards Board and the International Public Sector Accounting Standards Board.

Table 6.2, Table 6.3 and Table 6.4 summarise the topic-specific disclosures within the GRI standards, and the respective disclosures of economic, social or environmental information required by them. The standards to be applied by an organisation will be determined by whether the managers believe that the respective topics are material in the context of the organisation's operations. Review these tables and consider whether you believe the various items of information would be relevant to you if you wanted to assess the performance of an organisation.

TABLE 6.2 Topic-specific standards: GRI 200 – economic

GRI standards	Topic-specific disclosures
GRI 201 – Economic performance	Disclosure 201-1: Direct economic value generated and distributed
	Disclosure 201-2: Financial implications and other risks and opportunities due to climate change
	Disclosure 201-3: Defined benefit plan obligations and other retirement plans
	Disclosure 201-4: Financial assistance received from government
GRI 202 – Market presence	Disclosure 202-1: Ratios of standard entry-level wage by gender compared with local minimum wage
	Disclosure 202-2: Proportion of senior management hired from the local community
GRI 203 – Indirect economic impacts	Disclosure 203-1: Infrastructure investments and services supported
	Disclosure 203-2: Significant indirect economic impacts
GRI 204 – Procurement practices	Disclosure 204-1: Proportion of spending on local suppliers
GRI 205 – Anti-corruption	Disclosure 205-1: Operations assessed for risks related to corruption
	Disclosure 205-2: Communication and training about anti-corruption policies and procedures
	Disclosure 205-3: Confirmed incidents of corruption and actions taken
GRI 206 – Anti-competitive behaviour	Disclosure 206-1: Legal actions for anti-competitive behaviour, anti-trust and monopoly practices
GRI 207 - Tax (introduced in 2019)	Disclosure 207-1: Approach to tax
	Disclosure 207-2: Tax governance, control, and risk management
	Disclosure 207-3: Stakeholder engagement and management of concerns related to tax

Source: https://www.globalreporting.org/how-to-use-the-gri-standards/gri-standards-english-language/

TABLE 6.3 Topic-specific standards: GRI 300 – environment

GRI standards	Topic-specific disclosures
GRI 301 – Materials	Disclosure 301-1: Materials used by weight or volume
	Disclosure 301-2: Recycled input materials used
	Disclosure 301-3: Reclaimed products and their packaging materials
GRI 302 – Energy	Disclosure 302-1: Energy consumption within the organisation
	Disclosure 302-2: Energy consumption outside of the organisation
	Disclosure 302-3: Energy intensity
	Disclosure 302-4: Reduction of energy consumption
	Disclosure 302-5: Reduction in energy requirements of products and services
GRI 303 – Water	Disclosure 303-1: Interactions with water as a shared resource
	Disclosure 303-2: Management of water discharge-related impacts
	Disclosure 303-3: Water withdrawal
GRI 304 – Biodiversity	Disclosure 304-1: Operational sites owned, leased, managed in, or adjacent to, protected areas and areas of high biodiversity value outside protected areas
	Disclosure 304-2: Significant impacts of activities, products and services on biodiversity
	Disclosure 304-3: Habitats protected or restored
	Disclosure 304-4: IUCN Red List species and national conservation list species with habitats in areas affected by operations

GRI standards	Topic-specific disclosures
GRI 305 – Emissions	Disclosure 305-1: Direct (Scope 1) GHG emissions
	Disclosure 305-2: Energy indirect (Scope 2) GHG emissions
	Disclosure 305-3: Other indirect (Scope 3) GHG emissions
	Disclosure 305-4: GHG emissions intensity
	Disclosure 305-5: Reduction of GHG emissions
	Disclosure 305-6: Emissions of ozone-depleting substances
	Disclosure 305-7: Nitrogen oxides (NOX), sulfur oxides (SOX) and other significant air emissions
GRI 306 – Effluents and wastes	Disclosure 306-1: Water discharge by quality and destination
	Disclosure 306-2: Waste by type and disposal method
	Disclosure 306-3: Significant spills
	Disclosure 306-4: Transport of hazardous waste
	Disclosure 306-5: Water bodies affected by water discharges and/or run-off
GRI 307 – Environmental compliance	Disclosure 307-1: Non-compliance with environmental laws and regulations
GRI 308 – Supplier environmental assessment	Disclosure 308-1: New suppliers that were screened using environmental criteria
	Disclosure 308-2: Negative environmental impacts in the supply chain and actions taken

Source: https://www.globalreporting.org/how-to-use-the-gri-standards/gri-standards-english-language/

TABLE 6.4 Topic-specific standards: GRI 400 – social

GRI standards	Topic-specific disclosures
GRI 401 – Employment	Disclosure 401-1: New employee hires and employee turnover
	Disclosure 401-2: Benefits provided to full-time employees that are not provided to temporary or part-time employees
	Disclosure 401-3: Parental leave
GRI 402 – Labour/management relations	Disclosure 402-1: Minimum notice periods regarding operational changes
GRI 403 – Occupational health and safety	Disclosure 403-1: Occupational health and safety management system
	Disclosure 403-2: Hazard identification, risk assessment, and incident investigation
	Disclosure 403-3: Occupational health services
	Disclosure 403-4: Worker participation, consultation, and communication on occupational health and safety
GRI 404 – Training and education	Disclosure 404-1: Average hours of training per year per employee
	Disclosure 404-2: Programs for upgrading employee skills and transition assistance programs
	Disclosure 404-3: Percentage of employees receiving regular performance and career development reviews
GRI 405 – Diversity and equal opportunity	Disclosure 405-1: Diversity of governance bodies and employees
	Disclosure 405-2: Ratio of basic salary and remuneration of women to men
GRI 406 – Non-discrimination	Disclosure 406-1: Incidents of discrimination and corrective actions taken
GRI 407 – Freedom of association and collective bargaining	Disclosure 407-1: Operations and suppliers in which the right to freedom of association and collective bargaining may be at risk
GRI 408 – Child labour	Disclosure 408-1: Operations and suppliers at significant risk for incidents of child labour
GRI 409 – Forced or compulsory labour	Disclosure 409-1: Operations and suppliers at significant risk for incidents of forced or compulsory labour
GRI 410 – Security practices	Disclosure 410-1: Security personnel trained in human rights policies or procedures
GRI 411 – Rights of indigenous people	Disclosure 411-1: Incidents of violations involving rights of indigenous peoples

GRI standards	Topic-specific disclosures
GRI 412 – Human rights assessment	Disclosure 412-1: Operations that have been subject to human rights reviews or impact assessments
	Disclosure 412-2: Employee training on human rights policies or procedures
	Disclosure 412-3: Significant investment agreements and contracts that include human rights clauses or that underwent human rights screening
GRI 413 – Local communities	Disclosure 413-1: Operations with local community engagement, impact assessments and development programs
	Disclosure 413-2: Operations with significant actual and potential negative impacts on local communities
GRI 414 – Supplier social assessment	Disclosure 414-1: New suppliers that were screened using social criteria
	Disclosure 414-2: Negative social impacts in the supply chain and actions taken
GRI 415 – Public policy	Disclosure 415-1: Political contributions
GRI 416 – Customer health and safety	Disclosure 416-1: Service categories
	Disclosure 416-2: Incidents of non-compliance concerning the health and safety impacts of products and services
GRI 417 – Marketing and labelling	Disclosure 417-1: Requirements for product and service information and labelling
	Disclosure 417-2: Incidents of non-compliance concerning product and service information and labelling
	Disclosure 417-3: Incidents of non-compliance concerning marketing communications
GRI 418 – Customer privacy	Disclosure 418-1: Substantiated complaints concerning breaches of customer privacy and loss of customer data
GRI 419 – Socioeconomic compliance	Disclosure 419-1: Non-compliance with laws and regulations in the social and economic area

Source: https://www.globalreporting.org/how-to-use-the-gri-standards/gri-standards-english-language/

Having discussed the various requirements across the suite of GRI Standards we can now summarise the steps reporting entities will take if they are seeking to be reporting in accordance with the GRI standards. GRI 1 (2021a, p. 11) identifies the steps as being:

- Requirement 1: Apply the reporting principles
- Requirement 2: Report the disclosures in GRI 2: General Disclosures 2021
- Requirement 3: Determine material topics
- Requirement 4: Report the disclosures in GRI 3: Material Topics 2021
- Requirement 5: Report disclosures from the GRI Topic Standards for each material topic
- Requirement 6: Provide reasons for omission for disclosures and requirements that the organization cannot comply with
- Requirement 7: Publish a GRI content index
- Requirement 8: Provide a statement of use
- Requirement 9: Notify GRI

If the organisation does not comply with all of the nine requirements, it cannot claim that it has prepared the reported information in accordance with the GRI Standards.

GRI (2022, p. 5) also provides a diagrammatic summary of the above steps. This is shown in Figure 6.4.

Selective reporting of GRI data

While it is generally agreed that the GRI Standards have brought about improvements to CSR/sustainability reporting, it must be acknowledged that, with the standards not being mandatory, many organisations are selective about which indicators they choose to use in their reporting, often selecting those which project the best impression of the organisation. Nevertheless, such companies might still indicate that they are using the GRI Standards, thereby potentially gaining the legitimacy associated with using the guidelines. This possibility is supported by Boiral (2013), who reviewed the sustainability reports of 23 mining and energy companies that were identified as being highly compliant with the GRI requirements. Boiral utilised various sources of publicly available information about the social and environmental performance of the companies and then compared this with the information produced in the 'GRI-compliant sustainability reports'. His results showed that 90 per cent of the significant adverse events identified from alternative publicly available sources were either not discussed at all in the sustainability reports, or were discussed in a fairly biased manner. The reports were also found to be very biased in terms of providing information about positive achievements and in terms of prioritising 'self-praise'. Hence, we really need to be careful in assuming that, just because a reporting guideline exists and is *apparently* being applied by an organisation, the reports themselves are credible reflections of actual performance. This is where some level of third-party (independent) assurance, or auditing, of the reports can be useful, something that we discuss more fully later in this chapter.

FIGURE 6.4 Reporting using the GRI Standards

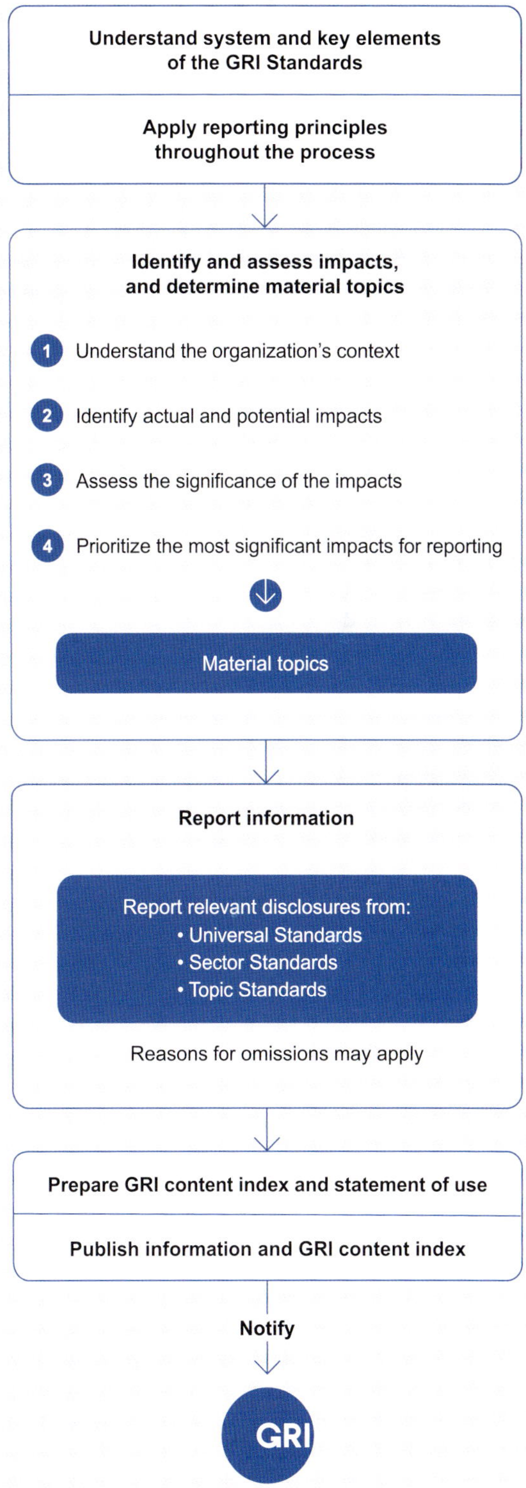

Why do I need to know about the role of the GRI Standards?

In the area of sustainability reporting (and social and environmental reporting) the Standards developed by the GRI represent the most widely used sustainability reporting standards worldwide. Given that GRI Standards are so widely used it is arguably important that we understand the nature of the standards and their desired purpose

The International Integrated Reporting Framework

Another framework for corporate reporting – and for CSR reporting – that is attracting a great deal of attention is *integrated reporting*, a term that is becoming widely used within business.

Most larger organisations produce an annual report that includes a number of financial statements and associated note disclosures, as required by financial accounting standards, corporations law and securities exchange listing requirements. The same organisations also often release a quite separate CSR or sustainability report. However, there is usually little or no link between the separate reports (and they are often prepared by quite different people), and this has led to calls for a form of reporting – integrated reporting – in which various types of information necessary for assessing and evaluating a company's performance are reported in a comprehensive fashion within an integrated report.

An organisation known as the International Integrated Reporting Council (IIRC) released its first International Integrated Reporting Framework, also referred to as The International <IR> Framework, in December 2013. This was then revised and reissued in January 2021. In June 2021, the Framework was subsequently placed in the control of an organisation known as the Value Reporting Foundation, before ultimately being transferred to the control of the International Sustainability Standards Board (ISSB) in June 2022. We will discuss the ISSB shortly. The Framework is a principles-based framework, rather than one that stipulates lists of required disclosures, so it is quite different to the GRI standards previously discussed. As stated in the Framework document (IIRC, 2021, p. 5):

> The International <IR> Framework (the Framework) takes a principles-based approach. The intent is to strike an appropriate balance between flexibility and prescription that recognizes the wide variation in individual circumstances of different organizations, while enabling a sufficient degree of comparability across organizations to meet relevant information needs. It does not prescribe specific key performance indicators, measurement methods, or the disclosure of individual matters, but does include a small number of requirements that are to be applied before an integrated report can be said to be in accordance with the <IR> Framework.
>
> Source: International Integrated Reporting Committee (2021), p. 5.

The Framework provides 'guiding principles' and 'content elements' that are to be used to govern the overall content of an integrated report, and to explain the fundamental concepts that underpin the report. These principles and elements are reproduced in **Exhibit 6.4**. Reading through them, you will probably agree that they seem to be logical and, if applied properly, would assist an organisation to produce reports that are relatively more useful to external stakeholders (relative to reports that are prepared without following such principles). You should also be able to see that there is some degree of overlap between these guiding principles and the principles for defining report quality included within the GRI standards, as previously discussed. This should not be unexpected, as such principles are generally relevant to any information that an organisation produces for the use of different stakeholders, whether it relates to social, environmental or financial performance.

A more in-depth review of the Framework reveals a number of other interesting (and some concerning) aspects of the guidelines, some of which are discussed below. In our review of the Framework, we will apply some of the knowledge we have already gained in this book to evaluate whether the Framework appears to be one that can assist stakeholders to assess how managers of an organisation have acted in respect of the responsibilities they should have embraced. And we will particularly be interested in assessing whether the Framework will realistically assist us in evaluating an organisation's accountability with respect to its social and environmental performance.

EXHIBIT 6.4 Guiding principles and content elements

GUIDING PRINCIPLES

The following Guiding Principles underpin the preparation of an integrated report, informing the content of the report and how information is presented:

- **Strategic focus and future orientation**: An integrated report should provide insight into the organisation's strategy, and how it relates to the organisation's ability to create value in the short, medium and long term, and to its use of and effects on the capitals.
- **Connectivity of information**: An integrated report should show a holistic picture of the combination, interrelatedness and dependencies between the factors that affect the organisation's ability to create value over time.
- **Stakeholder relationships**: An integrated report should provide insight into the nature and quality of the organisation's relationships with its key stakeholders, including how and to what extent the organisation understands, takes into account and responds to their legitimate needs and interests.
- **Materiality**: An integrated report should disclose information about matters that substantively affect the organisation's ability to create value over the short, medium and long term.
- **Conciseness**: An integrated report should be concise.
- **Reliability and completeness**: An integrated report should include all material matters, both positive and negative, in a balanced way and without material error.
- **Consistency and comparability**: The information in an integrated report should be presented: (a) on a basis that is consistent over time; and (b) in a way that enables comparison with other organisations to the extent it is material to the organisation's own ability to create value over time.

CONTENT ELEMENTS

An integrated report includes eight Content Elements that are fundamentally linked to each other and are not mutually exclusive:

- **Organisational overview and external environment:** What does the organisation do and what are the circumstances under which it operates?
- **Governance:** How does the organisation's governance structure support its ability to create value in the short, medium and long term?
- **Business model:** What is the organisation's business model?
- **Risks and opportunities:** What are the specific risks and opportunities that affect the organisation's ability to create value over the short, medium and long term, and how is the organisation dealing with them?
- **Strategy and resource allocation:** Where does the organisation want to go and how does it intend to get there?
- **Performance:** To what extent has the organisation achieved its strategic objectives for the period and what are its outcomes in terms of effects on the capitals?
- **Outlook:** What challenges and uncertainties is the organisation likely to encounter in pursuing its strategy, and what are the potential implications for its business model and future performance?
- **Basis of presentation:** How does the organisation determine what matters to include in the integrated report and how are such matters quantified or evaluated?

Source: International Integrated Reporting Committee (2021), pp. 25–36.

Value creation versus accountability

Accountability itself is referred to at the start of the Framework. Specifically, it is stated (IIRC, 2021, p. 2) that:

> <IR> aims to enhance accountability and stewardship for the broad base of capital (financial, manufactured, intellectual, human, social and relationship, and natural) and promote understanding of their independencies.
>
> Source: International Integrated Reporting Committee (2021), p. 2.

Unfortunately, accountability is not really explored in a useful way within the Framework. Paragraph 3.14 does note that an integrated report enhances transparency and accountability which are essential to building 'trust and resilience', while paragraph 3.15 states:

> Accountability is closely associated with the concept of stewardship and the responsibility of an organization to care for, or use responsibly, the capitals that

> its activities and outputs affect. When the capitals are owned by the organization, a stewardship responsibility is imposed on management and those charged with governance via their legal responsibilities to the organization.

It would have been useful for the Framework to more fully explore the stakeholders to whom an organisation is responsible for and for what aspects of performance it is accountable.

As emphasised throughout this book, accountability is a central and logical component of accounting, and hence any reporting framework needs to be clear about accountability in terms of *why* an organisation should report, *to whom* the organisation should report, *what* it shall report, and *how* it should report.

According to the Framework document, integrated reporting is defined (IIRC, 2021, p. 53) as follows:

> A process founded on integrated thinking that results in a periodic integrated report by an organization about value creation, preservation or erosion over time and related communications regarding aspects of value creation, preservation, or erosion.
>
> Source: International Integrated Reporting Committee (2021), p. 53.

The above definition is interesting. The focus of this framework – which is gaining much attention in the international business community, hence why we are discussing it in so much depth here – is on value creation, preservation or erosion rather than on accountability. This will be of concern to the many people who had hoped that the emphasis of integrated reporting will be to increase the transparency of organisations in regards to a broad group of interested stakeholders, many of whom are not directly interested in value creation. This is not to say that a focus on value creation is wrong. Rather, perhaps the goal of demonstrating a high level of accountability should also be strongly prioritised. We explored value creation in Chapter 3, where we stressed that successful organisations tend to be those that are relatively better at creating value throughout the various processes they undertake. Managers need to concentrate on value creation – and the Framework does stress this.

Materiality

The IIRC also emphasises the centrality of materiality to the reporting process. This is important, as assessments of materiality/significance are central to any reporting framework – something that we have already stressed earlier in this chapter, and in other chapters of this book. That is, it needs to be made very clear why an organisation elects to report certain information, but not report other information. In terms of the guiding principle of materiality, we know from **Exhibit 6.4** that it states that: 'An integrated report should disclose information about matters that substantively affect the organization's ability to create value over the short, medium and long term' (International Integrated Reporting Committee, 2021, p. 7).

The Framework document further states (paragraph 3.20, p. 30):

> To be most effective, the materiality determination process is integrated into the organization's management processes and includes regular engagement with providers of financial capital and others to ensure the integrated report meets its primary purpose as noted in paragraph 1.7.
>
> Source: International Integrated Reporting Committee (2021), p. 30.

This provides a very narrow view of materiality, and therefore, if applied by managers, it could greatly impede the accountability that organisations might demonstrate. When we then review the Framework to see the perspective adopted with respect to the 'primary purpose' of an integrated report, we find: 'The primary purpose of an integrated report is to explain to providers of financial capital how an organization creates, preserves or erodes value over time' (IIRC, 2021, paragraph 1.7, p. 11).

To many people, the restricted definition of the perceived users of integrated reports is extremely disappointing. This perspective in which shareholders and debt providers are seen as the focal stakeholders of an organisation is often referred to as the 'shareholder primacy perspective'. They are elevated to being the most important stakeholders. This acts to limit the usefulness of a reporting framework to provide accountability to a broader group of stakeholders beyond shareholders. What perhaps needs to be accepted is that an organisation – which operates within society, and effectively with the permission to operate being given by that society – has a responsibility, and therefore an accountability, to a broad group of stakeholders and not just to those parties that provide financial capital. Nevertheless, the restricted view of accountability apparently embraced within the Framework does reflect the views of many people in business (but not all people!). Furthermore, the way in which materiality is described in the Framework tends – perhaps expectedly – to emphasise the risks and opportunities for the reporting organisation, and how it can mitigate or capitalise on those risks and opportunities. If materiality was considered from a broader sustainability perspective (one of the focuses of this chapter), then perhaps more consideration would be explicitly given to an organisation's impacts on the 'outside world'.

The capitals

A particularly interesting aspect of the Framework is that it makes reference to 'capitals', in particular to six different capitals. The Framework (IIRC, 2021, p. 6) notes that:

> An integrated report aims to provide insight about the resources and relationships used and affected by an organization – these are collectively referred to as 'the capitals' in this Framework. It also seeks to explain how the organization interacts with the external environment and the capitals to create, preserve and erode value over the short, medium and long term.
>
> The capitals are stocks of value that are increased, decreased or transformed through the activities and outputs of the organization. They are categorized in the <IR> as financial, manufactured, intellectual, human, social and relationship, and natural capital, although organizations preparing an integrated report are not required to adopt this categorization or to structure their report along the lines of the capitals.
>
> Source: International Integrated Reporting Committee (2021), p. 6.

Therefore, for the purposes of the Framework, the value being created by an organisation resides in capitals. As we explained in Chapter 3, organisations tend to focus on different aspects of value that they seek to add, and therefore different organisations might find a need to consider using capitals other than those described in the Framework. The Framework states (IIRC, 2021, p. 18):

> 2.10 All organizations depend on various forms of capital for their success. In this Framework, the capitals comprise financial, manufactured, intellectual, human, social and relationship, and natural, although as discussed in paragraphs 2.17–2.19, organizations preparing an integrated report are not required to adopt this categorization ...

> 2.12 The overall stock of capitals is not fixed over time. There is a constant flow between and within the capitals as they are increased, decreased or transformed. For example, when an organization improves its human capital through employee training, the related training costs reduce its financial capital. The effect is that financial capital has been transformed into human capital. Although this example is simple and presented only from the organization's perspective, it demonstrates the continuous interaction and transformation between the capitals, albeit with varying rates and outcomes.
>
> Source: International Integrated Reporting Committee (2021), p. 18.

In relation to changes in capital, it is further stated in the Framework (IIRC, 2021, p. 18):

> Although organizations aim to create value overall, this can involve the erosion of value stored in some capitals, resulting in a net decrease to the overall stock of capitals (i.e. value is eroded).
>
> Source: International Integrated Reporting Committee (2021), p. 18.

Figure 6.5 reproduces the value creation process depicted within the framework.

Natural capital (the environment) is defined in the Framework (IIRC, 2021, p. 19) as:

> All renewable and non-renewable environmental resources and processes that provide goods or services that support the past, current or future prosperity of an organization. It includes:
>
> - air, water, land, minerals and forests
> - biodiversity and eco-system health.
>
> Source: International Integrated Reporting Committee (2021), p. 19.

FIGURE 6.5 The process through which value is created, preserved, or eroded as depicted in the <IR> Framework (IIRC, 2021, p. 22)

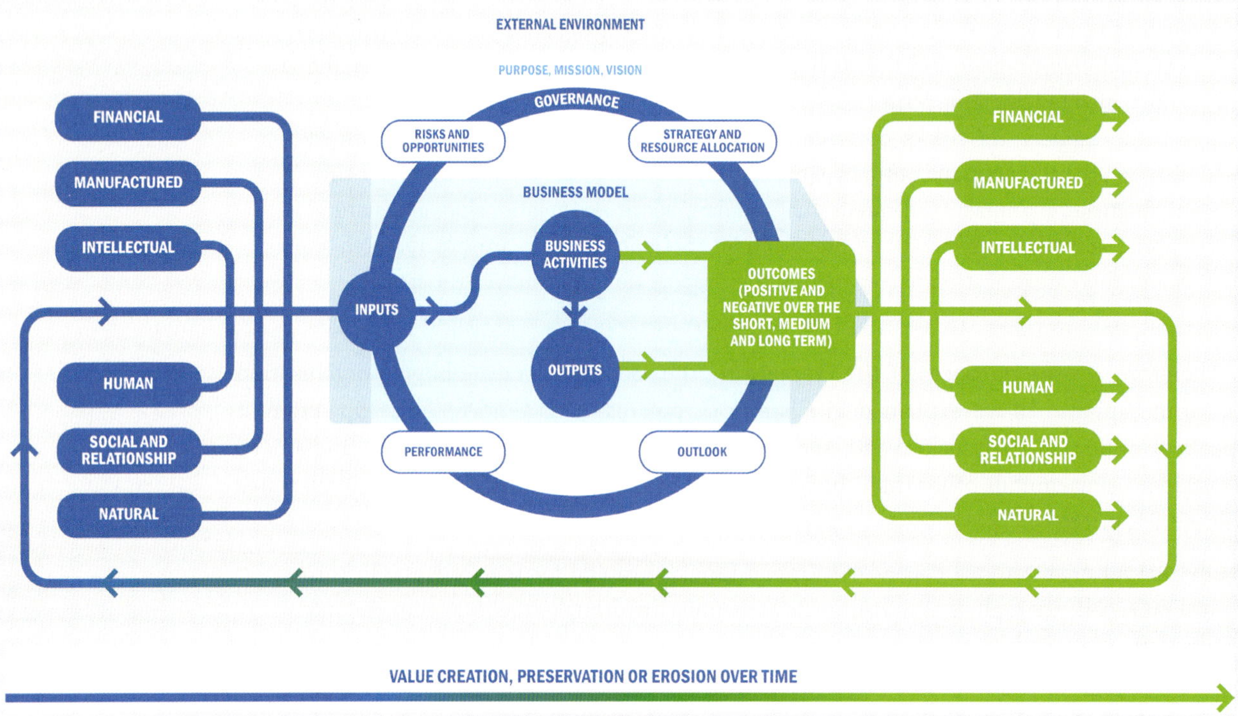

Source: International Integrated Reporting Committee (2021)

Again, there are some broader philosophical issues to consider. As we can see from the above definition of 'natural capital', the environment seems to be considered on the basis of how it supports 'the past, current or future prosperity of an organization'. We might question whether the environment should be considered in such an organisation-centric manner. Is this not one of the very reasons that the planet has the environmental and social problems that it currently has? Referring to the environment as part of 'capital' also seems to promote a view that it can be 'drawn down' to support growth in other capitals. Again, this view that the environment can justifiably be utilised and degraded in exchange for economic gains is a major contributory factor to our current global problems. In relation to the various trade-offs, the Framework (IIRC, 2021, p. 51) states:

> It is important, however, that an integrated report disclose the interdependencies that are considered in determining its reporting boundary, and the important trade-offs that influence value creation over time, including trade-offs:
>
> - Between capitals or between components of a capital (e.g., creating employment through an activity that negatively affects the environment)
> - Over time (e.g., choosing one course of action when another course would result in superior capital increment but not until a later period)
> - Between capitals owned by the organisation and those owned by others or not at all.

However, it is again emphasised that many people would argue that, when it comes to the environment, there should be no 'trade-off'.

Some shortfalls and some strengths of the International <IR> Framework

We could provide further comment on the International <IR> Framework, but suffice to say that it was a disappointment to many people, particularly those who initially hoped that integrated reporting would provide improvements in the social and environmental accountability being demonstrated by organisations, particularly larger business organisations. It is not at all clear that the Framework provides much hope in terms of extending the accountability of organisations in regards to the various non-financial aspects of their operations. By discussing this framework in the manner we have, it should demonstrate to you that people have dissenting views about the worth of different reporting frameworks. As 'thinking people', we should critically challenge things we do not agree with – but hopefully do so in a way that is constructive. Obviously, the author of this book, who has a great deal of experience in the area, is not a supporter of this framework. Challenging such frameworks – if we see problems – is a way for us to try to move forward the accountability of organisations.

However, while a number of negative aspects of the Framework have been identified, we should also – for balance – acknowledge some of the positive aspects (just as we previously noted that the principles were logical and helpful). These include that the Framework (IIRC, 2021, p. 3):

- specifically encourages 'integrated thinking' which is defined in the Framework as 'the active consideration by an organization of the relationships between its various operating and functional units and the capitals that the organisation uses or affects'. Integrated thinking leads to integrated decision making and actions that consider the creation of value over the short, medium and long term.
- requires consideration of connectivity/interdependencies within an organisation. As we explained in Chapter 5, when we consider how different operations/activities within an

organisation influence one another, this can lead to important changes and cost savings. For example, we might even terminate some products/processes that otherwise looked profitable in isolation.

- requires explicit consideration of the context within which the organisation operates. This is important as information can lack relevance if not enough information is provided about the environment within which an organisation operates.
- requires explicit commentary on why particular items are reported – that is why they are material – which arguably helps the credibility of reports.
- requires explanation of how the reporting boundary has been identified.
- requires explicit consideration of the social, environmental and economic challenges/risks confronting the organisation. Again, at a general level, this makes sense.
- encourages information to be disclosed about how remuneration and incentives are linked to value creation in the short, medium and long term, including how they are linked to the organisation's use of, and effects on, the capitals. Knowing how managers are remunerated in terms of various assigned KPIs is important as it provides insights into what aspects of performance are actually prioritised within an organization, despite corporate rhetoric.
- encourages use of diagrams of inputs, business activities, and outputs, all of which can assist in increasing people's understanding of what is being reported.
- requires answers to 'Where does the organisation want to go and how does it intend to get there?' Such 'road maps' are a valuable addition to reporting.
- requires the identification of significant frameworks and methods used to quantify or evaluate material matters included within the report. Again, this is important for placing the reported information within proper context.
- emphasises there is no set time dimension for reporting.
- requires the organisation to note how its governance structure supports the organisation's ability to create value in the short, medium and long term. While details of the governance structure should extend beyond just their role in creating value, the view that more information about governance is required also has merit.

A report by the Association of Chartered Certified Accountants titled *Insights into integrated reporting: Challenges and best practice responses* (www.accaglobal.com/, search for 'insights into ir') provides some good examples of innovative reporting, including the use of interesting diagrams. In terms of the future of the International <IR> Framework, as we noted earlier, the Framework was transferred to the control of the ISSB in June 2022. The Framework will be reviewed by the ISSB and ultimately is expected to be part of a conceptual framework for connecting financial and sustainability-related disclosures.

The International Sustainability Standards Board

In late 2021 the Trustees of the IFRS Foundation – which oversees the International Accounting Standards Board (that develops the requirements for general purpose financial reporting which we shall explore in Chapters 7 to 11) – announced the creation of the International Sustainability Standards Board (ISSB); see https://www.ifrs.org/groups/international-sustainability-standards-board/. The ISSB is to release two *IFRS Sustainability Disclosure Standards* in 2023 that focus on providing sustainability-related financial disclosures for capital markets, including disclosures that address the financial implications associated with climate change. For the purposes of the

Standards, sustainability-related financial disclosures are disclosures about sustainability-related risks and opportunities that are deemed to be useful to users of general purpose financial reports when they seek to assess an entity's 'enterprise value', including information about its governance, strategy and risk management, and related metrics and targets. In terms of the Standards:

- IFRS S1 *General Requirements for Disclosure of Sustainability-related Financial Information* requires companies to disclose information about all their significant sustainability-related risks and opportunities
- IFRS S2 *Climate-related Disclosures* focuses on climate-related risks and opportunities. It incorporates the recommendations of the Task Force on Climate-Related Financial Disclosures (TCFD) – to be discussed shortly – and includes metrics tailored to industry classifications derived from the industry-based Sustainability Accounting Standards Board (SASB) Standards (also to be discussed shortly).

The requirement will be that the sustainability-related financial disclosures will be published at the same time as the reporting entity's financial statements. The objective of IFRS S1 is to require an entity to disclose information about its significant sustainability-related risks and opportunities that is useful to the primary users of general purpose financial reporting (that are identified as investors, potential investors, lenders and other creditors) when they assess 'enterprise value' and when they decide whether to provide resources to the entity. Within IFRS S1, 'enterprise value' is defined as the total value of the entity and is the sum of the value of the entity's equity (market capitalisation) and the value of the entity's net debt.

The sustainability-related financial information would be linked to an organisation's governance, strategy, risk management, and the metrics and targets it uses to measure, monitor, and manage significant sustainability-related risks and opportunities. In relation to governance, the requirement is that the information disclosed should be sufficient to enable investors to understand the governance processes, controls and procedures used by the organisation to monitor and manage significant sustainability-related risks and opportunities throughout its supply chains. Risks would encompass both physical risks and transition risks.

IFRS S2 *Climate-related Disclosures* has a more restricted objective (relative to S1) and has been developed to require an entity to disclose information about its exposure to significant climate-related risks and opportunities that will potentially impact entities' financial position, financial performance and cash flows for the current reporting period, and the anticipated financial effects over the short, medium, and long term. The climate related risks to be considered will include both physical risks and transition risks – risks we will discuss shortly when we discuss the requirements issued by the TCFD. Among other things, IFRS S2 also requires reporting entities to disclose their greenhouse gas emissions and there would be a requirement that the emissions would be calculated using a measurement framework known as the *GHG Protocol* – something that is also to be discussed shortly. In terms of the mandatory nature of the Standards, it would be up to national regulators to determine whether the Standards should be mandatory for certain forms of reporting entities.

What is clear is that the ISSB Standards are quite restricted in the stakeholders whose information needs they are designed to address (limited to financial stakeholders), and in terms of their focus being restricted to financial measurements. The application of the materiality concept as used in general purpose financial reporting means that no disclosures would be made if it was assessed that the risks – physical or transitional – could not be linked to some form of financial measurement. Therefore, while arguably important to financial stakeholders, these Standards really do not encourage greater organisational accountability in relation to various social and environmental impacts which cannot be measured in ways other than financial.

The Sustainability Accounting Standards Board

Another organisation that attracted attention in respect of providing guidance for CSR/sustainability reporting was the Sustainability Accounting Standards Board (SASB). The SASB is a US non-profit organisation that was established in 2011. As with the IIRC, the standards of the SASB were transferred to the control of the ISSB in June 2022.

The SASB standards will provide the starting point for the ISSB's industry-specific standards and are expected to be used until such time as the ISSB produces industry-specific requirements. Therefore, it is worthwhile discussing them here, even though the SASB no longer operates in its own right. The standards have been developed primarily with investors in mind, to assist them to understand those sustainability-related risks and opportunities confronting organisations, and which are likely to ultimately impact an organisation's financial performance.

The SASB standards were developed on the basis that different industries are exposed to different social and environmental risks and opportunities, and so specific disclosure guidance for different industries was needed. The SASB arranged industries into a classification system, which it referred to as its Sustainable Industry Classification System, or SICS, based on the similarity of companies' sustainability challenges and opportunities. The SASB then identified those sustainability topics that it believed are particularly relevant to investors in those companies within each respective SICS industry code. Seventy-nine industries were identified, each seen as belonging within one of 11 sectors:

- Health care
- Financials
- Technology & communications
- Non-renewable resources
- Transportation
- Services
- Resource transformation
- Consumption I
- Consumption II
- Renewable resources & alternative energy
- Infrastructure.

Within the Transportations sector, for example, sustainability accounting standards were developed for the following industries:

- automobiles
- auto parts
- car rental and leasing
- airlines
- air freight and logistics
- marine transportation
- cruise lines
- rail transportation
- road transportation.

Exhibit 6.5 and **Exhibit 6.6** reproduce tables that appear in the Automobiles Sustainability Accounting Standard and the Airlines Sustainability Accounting Standard, respectively. The accounting standards provide further written advice on each of the 'accounting metrics' identified within the tables.

EXHIBIT 6.5 Extract from the SASB Automobiles Sustainability Accounting Standard

Topic	Accounting metric	Category	Unit of measure	Code
Product safety	Percentage of vehicle models rated by NCAP programs with an overall 5-star safety rating, by region	Quantitative	Percentage (%)	TR-AU-250a.1
	Number of safety-related defect complaints, percentage investigated	Quantitative	Number, percentage (%)	TR-AU-250a.2
	Number of vehicles recalled	Quantitative	Number	TR-AU-250a.3
Labor practices	Percentage of active workforce covered under collective bargaining agreements	Quantitative	Percentage (%)	TR-AU-310a.1
	(1) Number of work stoppages and (2) total days idle	Quantitative	Number, Days idle	TR-AU-310a.2
Fuel economy and use-phase emissions	Sales-weighted average passenger fleet fuel economy, by region	Quantitative	Mpg, L/km, gCO_2/km, km/L	TR-AU-410a.1
	Number of (1) zero emission vehicles (ZEV), (2) hybrid vehicles, and (3) plug-in hybrid vehicles sold	Quantitative	Number	TR-AU-410a.2
	Discussion of strategy for managing fleet fuel economy and emissions risks and opportunities	Discussion and analysis	n/a	TR-AU-410a.3
Materials sourcing	Description of the management of risks associated with the use of critical materials	Discussion and analysis	n/a	TR-AU-440a.1
Materials efficiency and recycling	Total amount of waste from manufacturing, percentage recycled	Quantitative	Metric tons (t), percentage (%)	TR-AU-440b.1
	Weight of end-of-life material recovered, percentage recycled	Quantitative	Metric tons(t), percentage (%)	TR-AU-440b.2
	Average recyclability of vehicles sold	Quantitative	Percentage (%) by sales-weighted metric tons(t)	TR-AU-440b.3

Source: Sustainability Accounting Standards Board, Automobiles (2018a).

Review **Exhibit 6.5** and **Exhibit 6.6** and consider whether you agree that the respective accounting metrics provide information that would likely be of interest to investors who have interests in the companies operating in the automobile and airline industries. Furthermore, you could also consider whether you believe the information would be of interest to stakeholders other than investors (and perhaps, why it would be of interest).

Again, unlike the GRI standards that we discussed earlier in this chapter, and which are designed to provide guidance to a wide variety of stakeholders, the SASB standards were designed with investors' needs in mind – they focus on issues that are considered likely to ultimately create risks and opportunities that could impact financial performance. The management of the respective companies is ultimately responsible for determining which information is material. Hence, as is often the case with accounting disclosures, managers need to determine whether the information is likely to impact decisions being made by the users of those reports. If it is considered likely, then disclosures should be made. The SASB acknowledged that establishing what is material in relation to information that is fundamentally non-financial can be a rather complex task.

As noted, going forward, the standards developed by the SASB are expected to form the foundation of the industry-specific standards to be developed by the ISSB.

EXHIBIT 6.6 Extract from the SASB Airlines Sustainability Accounting Standard

Topic	Accounting metric	Category	Unit of measure	Code
Greenhouse gas emissions	Gross global Scope1 emissions	Quantitative	Metric tons (t) CO_2-e	TR-AL-110a.1
	Discussion of long-term and short-term strategy or plan to manage Scope 1 emissions, emissions reduction targets, and an analysis of performance against those targets	Discussion and analysis	n/a	TR-AL-110a.2
	(1) Total fuel consumed, (2) percentage alternative, (3) percentage sustainable	Quantitative	Giga joules (GJ), Percentage (%)	TR-AL-110a.3
Labor practices	Percentage of active workforce covered under collective bargaining agreements	Quantitative	Percentage (%)	TR-AL-310a.1
	(1) Number of work stoppages and (2) total days idle	Quantitative	Number, days idle	TR-AL-310a.2
Competitive behavior	Total amount of monetary losses as a result of legal proceedings associated with anti-competitive behaviour regulations	Quantitative	Reporting currency	TR-AL-520a.1
Accident and safety management	Description of implementation and outcomes of a Safety Management System	Discussion and Analysis	n/a	TR-AL-540a.1
	Number of aviation accidents	Quantitative	Number	TR-AL-540a.2
	Number of governmental enforcement actions of aviation safety regulations	Quantitative	Number	TR-AL-540a.3

Source: Sustainability Accounting Standards Board, Airlines (2018b).

The Task Force on Climate-Related Financial Disclosures

The Task Force on Climate-Related Financial Disclosures (TCFD) developed the *CEO guide to climate-related financial disclosures* (available at **www.wbcsd.org/Overview/Resources/General/CEO-Guide-to-climate-related-financial-disclosures**). The TCFD was established by the Financial Stability Board, an international body that monitors and makes recommendations about the global financial system:

> In April 2015, at the request of G20 Finance Ministers and Central Bank Governors, the Financial Stability Board (FSB) convened representatives of the private and public sector to review how the financial sector could take account of climate-related issues.
>
> The conclusion was that financial markets need better, more comparable and complete information about climate change.
>
> In response, the FSB established the Task Force on Climate-related Financial Disclosures (TCFD) in December 2015.
>
> The TCFD encourages companies with annual revenue exceeding US$1 billion or equivalent to disclose against all recommendations and to conduct robust analyses to assess the resilience of their strategies against a range of climate-related scenarios.
>
> Generally, disclosures are to be made in companies' public annual financial filings. The TCFD believes that climate-related issues are, or could be, material for many organizations and that its recommendations are therefore useful in complying with existing disclosure obligations.
>
> Source: Task Force on Climate-related Financial Disclosures (2017), p. 6.

EXHIBIT 6.7 Recommended disclosures pertaining to the risks and opportunities associated with climate change

Governance	Strategy	Risk Management	Metrics and Targets
Disclose the organisation's governance around climate-related risks and opportunities.	Disclose the actual and potential impacts of climate-related risks and opportunities on the organisation's businesses, strategy, and financial planning where such information is material.	Disclose how the organisation identifies, assesses, and manages climate-related risks.	Disclose the metrics and targets used to assess and manage relevant climate-related risks and opportunities where such information is material.
Recommended Disclosures	Recommended Disclosures	Recommended Disclosures	Recommended Disclosures
a) Describe the board's oversight of climate-related risks and opportunities.	a) Describe the climate-related risks and opportunities the organisation has identified over the short, medium, and long term.	a) Describe the organisation's processes for identifying and assessing climate-related risks.	a) Disclose the metrics used by the organisation to assess climate-related risks and opportunities in line with its strategy and risk management process.
b) Describe management's role in assessing and managing climate-related risks and opportunities.	b) Describe the impact of climate-related risks and opportunities on the organisation's businesses, strategy, and financial planning.	b) Describe the organisation's processes for managing climate-related risks.	b) Disclose Scope 1, Scope 2, and, if appropriate, Scope 3 greenhouse gas (GHG) emissions, and the related risks.
	c) Describe the resilience of the organisation's strategy, taking into consideration different climate-related scenarios, including a 2°C or lower scenario.	c) Describe how processes for identifying, assessing, and managing climate-related risks are integrated into the organisation's overall risk management.	c) Describe the targets used by the organisation to manage climate-related risks and opportunities and performance against targets.

Source: Final Report: Recommendations of the Task Force on Climate-related Financial Disclosures (June 2017)

We will return to the important issue of climate change later in this chapter, but it is becoming increasingly obvious that there is an expectation that organisations are accountable for their actions in alleviating, or contributing to, climate change. They are also increasingly being held accountable for providing information about the risks and opportunities climate change creates for their organisation.

Exhibit 6.7 reproduces a table from the TCFD *Recommendations* (p. 7) that summarises the recommendations and supporting recommended disclosures. Again, review these disclosures and consider whether you agree that they would be useful for you in assessing the climate change-related risks that an organisation might be exposed to. These disclosures are commonly made within an organisation's annual report (which includes all the financial statements), and also often in separate sustainability reports. Many organisations are also releasing separate statements that they refer to as Climate Change Positions Standards (or a similar title) which specifically addresses various risks and opportunities associated with climate change.

The TCFD Guide also provides guidance on how organisations can identify climate risks and opportunities. Climate risk and opportunities are classified into two distinct categories by the TCFD:

- *Transition impacts* which reflect the risks and opportunities associated with changes in the economy, including growth impacts, sector re-weighting and other macroeconomic factors.
- *Physical impacts* which reflect changes in the physical climate (for example, altered rainfall amounts, intensities, and timings) that may impact future business activities.

Exhibit 6.8 and **Exhibit 6.9** show the TCFD guidance relating to identifying climate risks and opportunities respectively.

When the ISSB developed IFRS S2 Climate-related Disclosures (previously discussed) it incorporated the recommendations of the TCFD. For further discussion of the reporting of risks and opportunities in relation to climate change, see **Learning exercise 6.9**.

EXHIBIT 6.8 TCFD guidance regarding identifying climate risks

Climate-related risks		
Transition risk	**Policy and legal**	**Technology**
	Increased pricing of GHG emissions Enhanced emissions reporting obligations Mandates on, and regulation of, existing products and services Exposure to litigation	Substitution of existing products and services with lower emissions options Unsuccessful investment in new technologies Costs to transition to lower emissions technology
	Market	**Reputation**
	Changing customer behaviour Uncertainty in market signals Increased cost of raw materials	Shifts in consumer preferences Stigmatisation of sector Increased stakeholder concern or negative stakeholder feedback
Physical risk	**Acute**	**Chronic**
	Increases severity of extreme weather events such as cyclones and floods	Changes in precipitation patterns and extreme variability in weather patterns Rising temperatures Rising sea levels

Source: TCFD (2017), p. 12.

EXHIBIT 6.9 TCFD guidance regarding identifying climate opportunities

Climate-related opportunities		
Resource efficiency	**Energy source**	**Products and services**
Use of more efficient modes of transport Use of more efficient production and distribution processes Use of recycling Move to more efficient buildings Reduced water usage and consumption	Use of lower emission sources of energy Use of supportive policy incentives Use of new technologies Participation in carbon markets Shift toward decentralised energy generation	Development and/or expansion of low emission goods and services Development of climate adaptation and insurance risk solutions Development of new products or services through R&D and innovation Ability to diversify business activities Shift in consumer preferences
Markets	**Resilience**	
Access to new markets Use of public-sector incentives Access to new assets and locations needing insurance coverage	Participation in renewable energy programs and adoption of energy efficient measures Resource substitutes/diversification	

Source: TCFD (2017), p. 13.

6.9 Learning Exercise

Reporting the risks and opportunities of climate change

The managers of an organisation are considering whether it is important for the organisation to publicly disclose information about the risks and opportunities associated with climate change. So let us consider some factors that might be considered in addressing this issue.

Our first point to consider is that governments, industry bodies, consumers and investors are increasingly reacting to the issue of climate change. Such stakeholder groups often have policies in place that cause them to support organisations that are addressing the problems of climate change (and conversely, not to support organisations that are ignoring these issues). The application of such policies can only be expected to increase across time as the impacts of climate change become more pronounced. Therefore, it seems important for organisations to be clear about how they are addressing climate change if they want to receive the support of different stakeholders.

Different industries, depending upon the carbon intensity of the products they produce or acquire, or the locations in which they operate, will be affected differently – in some industries, the impacts of changing legislation to deal with climate change, and changing community expectations, will be significant. To understand the likely future of organisations, it is important that we know about the risks and opportunities climate change poses to an organisation. How, or whether, management is acknowledging and responding to these will be important in assessing the likely future prospects of an organisation. It is therefore an important aspect of reporting.

The United Nations Global Compact

The Global Compact is an initiative of the United Nations (see www.unglobalcompact.org). This initiative represents a network of UN agencies, governments, and business, labour and non-government bodies that have put in place plans to encourage organisations to voluntarily adopt 10 principles in the areas of human rights, labour, the environment and anti-corruption. The 10 principles were developed from the Universal Declaration of Human Rights, the International Labour Organization (ILO) Declaration on Fundamental Principles and Rights at Work, the Rio Declaration on Environment and Development, and the UN Convention against Corruption. As of 2022, there were over 19 000 participants from over 180 countries that publish, in either their annual report or sustainability report, descriptions of the actions they are undertaking to support the 10 principles, which are as follows:

Human Rights

Principle 1: Businesses should support and respect the protection of internationally proclaimed human rights; and

Principle 2: make sure that they are not complicit in human rights abuses.

Labour

Principle 3: Businesses should uphold the freedom of association and the effective recognition of the right to collective bargaining;

Principle 4: the elimination of all forms of forced and compulsory labour;

Principle 5: the effective abolition of child labour; and

Principle 6: the elimination of discrimination in respect of employment and occupation.

Environment

Principle 7: Businesses should support a precautionary approach to environmental challenges;

Principle 8: undertake initiatives to promote greater environmental responsibility; and

Principle 9: encourage the development and diffusion of environmentally friendly technologies.

Anti-Corruption

Principle 10: Businesses should work against corruption in all its forms, including extortion and bribery.

Source: United Nations Global Compact (2018).

Earlier in this chapter, in the section titled 'Sustainability reporting', we discussed the Sustainable Development Goals developed by the United Nations Environmental Program (as you might recall, there were 17 goals). For those readers seeking to further understand the relationship between the above 10 principles and the 17 SDGs, you can refer to a United Nations White Paper titled *The UN Global Compact ten principles and the Sustainable Development Goals: Connecting, Crucially*, which is available at **www.unglobalcompact.org/docs/about_the_gc/White_Paper_Principles_SDGs.pdf**

Other frameworks

We could discuss many more reporting guidance documents here. Some reporting frameworks have been developed for narrow aspects of social and environmental performance. For example, the use of water is one specific aspect of sustainability, and one organisation, the Water Accounting Standards Board (WASB) – an Australian Government-funded body – is an international leader in the area of accounting for water. The water accounting framework of the WASB (available at **http://www.bom.gov.au/water/standards/wasb/awas.shtml**) currently comprises three major documents:

- Water Accounting Conceptual Framework
- Water Accounting Standard 1
- Water Accounting Standard 2.

Interestingly, for water accounts to satisfy the requirement of being useful to readers, the WASB makes reference to required qualitative characteristics, specifically relevance, faithful representation, comparability, verifiability, timeliness and understandability. These qualitative characteristics for water-related information seem to be very similar to, or indeed the same as, the qualitative characteristics that we have seen for other reporting frameworks. Again, we see that there are certain attributes that various types of information should possess if it is to be useful. When we turn our attention to financial reporting (in the following chapters), you will see that the same qualitative characteristics are also presented within financial reporting frameworks.

In this section on reporting frameworks, we have hopefully shown that there is much guidance out there for organisations seeking to report. Furthermore, many industries have developed their own industry-specific disclosure guidance – for example, industry-specific guidelines have been developed by the mining industry, the property development industry, the electricity industry, the fishing industry and the timber industry. Also, many social, environmental and consumer (NGO) groups have developed reporting standards with which they expect organisations to comply, including proposed guidelines for the gambling industry, the clothing industry, organisations that source products that use animal-based products, and organisations that make or source products that use palm oil. Apart from embracing particular reporting frameworks, many reporting organisations also develop their own innovative approaches to reporting.

LO6.5 CSR and sustainability-related measurement frameworks

While reporting frameworks such as those discussed above can assist managers to determine what types of information to report, you might require further guidance in terms of how to quantify particular disclosures that are required to be in numerical form.

For example, various environmental reporting guidelines suggest that we should disclose our greenhouse gas emissions, or perhaps our usage of water. The reporting guidelines do not necessarily tell us how to measure these aspects of performance. Therefore, we might need to also look at different measurement frameworks. Below, we will consider one framework we might use to measure greenhouse gas emissions. However, please understand that there are many measurement frameworks available that cover a multitude of different social and environmental aspects of performance.

The Greenhouse Gas Protocol

According to the website of the Greenhouse Gas Protocol (GHG Protocol; **www.ghgprotocol.org/corporate-standard**):

> The GHG Protocol Corporate Accounting and Reporting Standard provides requirements and guidance for companies and other organizations preparing a corporate-level GHG emissions inventory. The standard covers the accounting and reporting of seven greenhouse gases covered by the Kyoto Protocol – carbon dioxide (CO_2), methane (CH_4), nitrous oxide (N_2O), hydrofluorocarbons (HFCs), perfluorocarbons (PFCs), sulphur hexafluoride (SF_6) and nitrogen trifluoride (NF_3).
>
> Source: Greenhouse Gas Protocol (2022).

The GHG Protocol is one of the most widely used international accounting tools for quantifying greenhouse gas emissions.

Pursuant to the GHG Protocol, emissions can be divided into three categories: Scope 1, Scope 2 and Scope 3:

- *Scope 1* – those emissions directly occurring from sources that are owned or controlled by an institution, including:
  - combustion of fossil fuels
  - mobile combustion of fossil fuels in vehicles owned/controlled by the organisation
  - fugitive emissions.

Fugitive emissions, referred to above, result from the intentional or unintentional release of greenhouse gases (for example, the leakage of hydrofluorocarbons from refrigeration and air-conditioning equipment).

- *Scope 2* – emissions generated in the production of electricity consumed by an organisation, where that electricity is generated outside the organisation's measurement boundary (that is, the electricity is generated by a different entity, namely an electricity generator).
- *Scope 3* – all the other indirect emissions that are a consequence of the activities of an organisation, but occur from sources not owned or controlled by the organisation, such as:
  - commuting
  - air travel for work-related activities
  - waste disposal
  - embodied emissions from the extraction, production and transportation of purchased goods
  - outsourced activities

- contractor-owned vehicles
- line loss from electricity transmission and distribution.

The requirement to report information about different 'scopes' reflects the fact that some emissions (Scope 1) are considered easier to monitor and control than others. Different countries have different requirements in relation to reporting GHG emissions. In Australia, for example, entities and corporate groups that meet certain reporting thresholds (that is, large emitters) must report their Scope 1 and Scope 2 emissions under the Australian *National Greenhouse and Energy Reporting Act (NGER)*, and the GHG Protocol is considered an appropriate framework to measure these emissions.

For a consideration of the difference between reporting and measurement frameworks, see **Learning exercise 6.10**.

6.10 Learning Exercise

Difference between a reporting framework and a measurement framework

What is the difference between a reporting framework and a measurement framework?

In answering this question, we can note that, basically, a reporting framework provides guidance in terms of what items of information should be reported, what types of organisations should be doing the reporting, when should the information be reported, and perhaps in what format should the information be reported. The reporting frameworks might also address issues such as the objectives of reporting, the qualitative characteristics that the information should possess, the expected or intended users of the information, and the expected expertise of the users of the information.

A measurement framework typically provides guidance about how particular aspects of performance, or how particular resources or obligations, shall be measured. For example, while particular reporting frameworks such as the GRI standards suggest that GHG emissions should be reported, measurement frameworks such as the GHG Protocol inform us as to how those measurements are to be made.

LO6.6 Corporate responsibilities: The cause of climate change

As is clear to us all, a specific issue of great relevance to current and future generations – and all our various ecosystems and the inhabitants thereof – is climate change. Due to its central importance to all of us, and the role of business organisations in contributing to it (and potentially providing solutions to it), it is worthwhile spending some time considering it. Many people believe that climate change is the most serious of all the problems confronting the planet. The activities of business organisations are a major contributor to climate change. Arguably, managers and accountants should therefore understand the science of climate change.

In terms of its meaning, and according to the Australian Academy of Science (see **www.science.org.au**), climate change is a change in the pattern of weather, and related changes in oceans, land surfaces and ice sheets, occurring over time scales of decades or longer. The issue of climate change can best be explained in terms of what is known as the greenhouse effect. Natural gases in the Earth's atmosphere allow infra-red radiation from the Sun to enter the Earth's atmosphere, thereby warming the surface of the Earth. Our atmosphere stops a proportion of this heat from leaving (otherwise the whole world would freeze); however, a certain percentage of heat (about a third) is reflected away from the Earth by the atmosphere, by clouds, and by the surface of the Earth. It is necessary that some of this heat does leave, otherwise the planet would overheat.

One greenhouse gas is carbon dioxide, and like a number of other gases, it plays an important role in moderating the Earth's temperature. Carbon dioxide is generated by animals and humans, the burning of biomass, the burning of oil and other fossil fuels, through oil and gas production, and so on. Human actions are increasing the concentration of greenhouse gases, including carbon dioxide. As these concentrations of greenhouse gases increase, less heat can be reflected from the planet (that is, more heat becomes 'trapped'), and generally speaking, temperatures rise. The greenhouse effect is diagrammatically represented in **Figure 6.6**.

FIGURE 6.6 A diagrammatic representation of the greenhouse effect

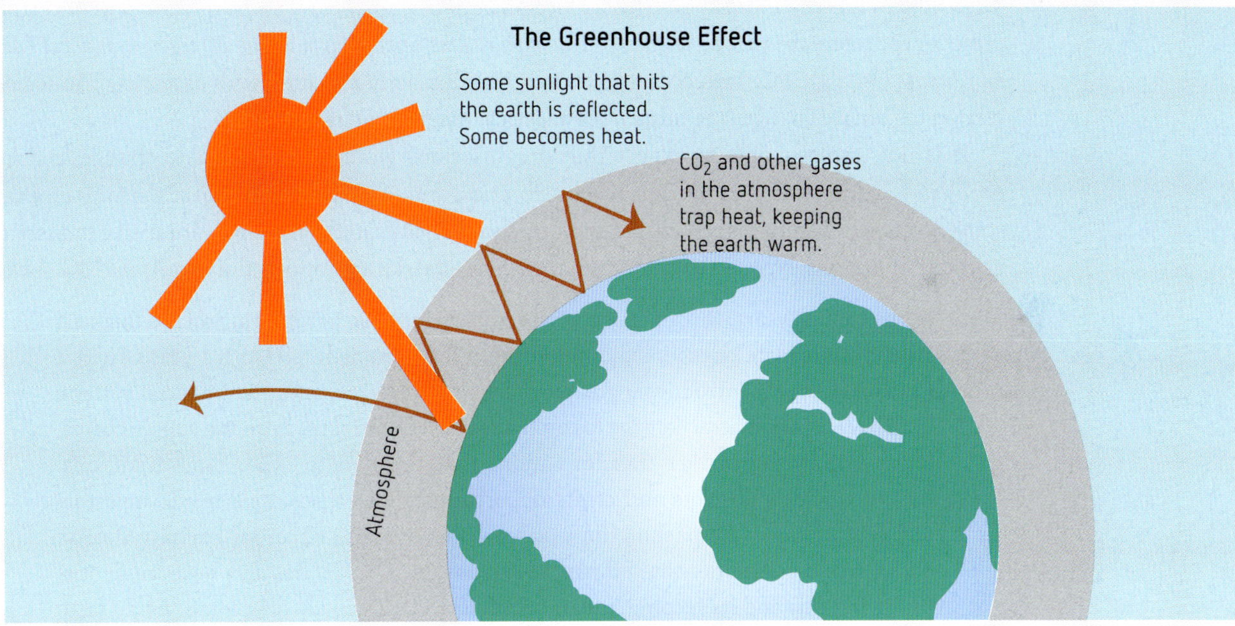

Source: Gilles, Shakes (2018).

The Australian Academy of Science has produced a fairly easy-to-understand overview of climate change called *The science of climate change: Questions and answers*, which is freely available at **www.science.org.au/files/userfiles/learning/documents/climate-change-r.pdf**. According to this report:

> If society continues to rely on fossil fuels to the extent that it is currently doing, then carbon dioxide (CO_2) concentrations in the atmosphere are expected to double from pre-industrial values by about 2050, and triple by about 2100. This 'high emissions' pathway for CO_2, coupled with rises in the other greenhouse gases, would be expected to result in a global average warming of around 4.5°C by 2100, but possibly as low as 3°C or as high as 6°C.
>
> Source: Australian Academy of Science (2015), p. 16.

This report emphasises that the expected temperature rises will have dramatic economic, environmental and social impacts, and that it is absolutely crucial that we address the issue now (indeed, we should have done a great deal more already). It is particularly important that the managers of business organisations throughout the world address the issue.

YouTube resources

The following two YouTube videos provide interesting explanations of climate change, and you might like to view them:

www.youtube.com/watch?v=Sv7OHfpIRfU

www.youtube.com/watch?v=ifrHogDujXw

Climate change is expected to impact everyone, and from an organisational point of view, some organisations will be impacted more than others. Those organisations relying on carbon-intensive production processes are expected to be greatly impacted, as will other organisations that are operating in areas that are particularly susceptible to weather and temperature changes, and associated changes in water availability and sea levels. Organisations involved in electricity generation, resource extraction (particularly resources such as coal) and manufacturing are likely to be impacted most by climate change, and by local and global initiatives to address it. For people interested in reading more about the science of climate change, and some of the very concerning projections, reference can be made to the *Sixth Assessment Report of the Intergovernmental Panel on Climate Change (IPCC)* which is the United Nations body assigned with assessing the science related to climate change (see **https://www.ipcc.ch/assessment-report/ar6/**).

It is not unreasonable to expect that organisations would accept climate change as a key problem to address as part of their responsibilities, and we would also expect them to embrace some accountability in this regard, particularly those organisations in carbon-intensive industries, or those industries exposed to climate change-related risks and opportunities. As KPMG states:

> In the coming years, we can expect to see a sharp increase in reporting on the financial risks from climate change, building on the rates demonstrated in this year's survey. Climate change is introducing greater risk and uncertainty into the financial system, both by causing physical damage to companies' assets, infrastructure and supply chains, and by catalyzing market transformations that threaten to make some traditional business models obsolete and create opportunities for others. As a result, investors and central banks are pushing for greater disclosure. The Financial Stability Board's Task Force on Climate-related Financial Disclosures (TCFD) has also been influential in driving this and its recommendations of July 2017 will likely become the de facto framework for reporting of this kind in coming years.
>
> Source: KPMG (2017), p. 36.

KPMG also emphasises that organisations should not only disclose information about their actual emissions of GHGs, but they should also disclose information about the risks and opportunities climate change creates for them:

> Climate-related risk disclosure is very different from reporting carbon emissions or environmental impacts. It's about turning the telescope around, understanding the impact of a changing climate on the company and asking searching questions. Does the company need to move its operations? Is its supply chain vulnerable to weather events? Will it be able to take out insurance in future? Should it change its business model entirely?
>
> This change in reporting approach will also require a change in roles and responsibilities. Traditionally, thinking about climate change has been the function of

corporate responsibility or sustainability teams, but now the responsibility needs to sit with the executive who has the best understanding of a company's financial risks and opportunities – namely the Chief Financial Officer.

For companies that have just begun the process of reporting on climate-related financial risks, or have not yet started at all, a qualitative approach is a good foundation and the TCFD's guidelines are helpful here. Companies should bring together the main stakeholders from around the business to look at the potential financial risks and opportunities presented by climate change, and then carry out qualitative scenario analysis. For example, if you are a brewing corporation, what would happen if you ran out of water in critical production locations or if the costs of water rise dramatically? If you're an oil company, will you still have a market for your products in 10 or 20 years' time? After that, companies can start building sophisticated models that properly project the full gamut of financial risks and opportunities associated with climate change, eventually integrating these models into their decision making and adapting the business strategy accordingly.

Source: KPMG (2017), p. 36.

Some of the risks and opportunities that climate change creates for organisations have been identified by the Task Force on Climate-related Financial Disclosures (see Table 6.5).

TABLE 6.5 Risks and opportunities for business from climate change

Risks	Opportunities
• Increased costs associated with generating GHG emissions • Regulated restrictions to be enforced in relation to existing products and services • Increasing possibility of litigation against the organisation • Changing customer behaviour • Increased costs of some materials • Damage created by increased severity of weather events, including those related to rising sea levels and rising temperatures • Changing supplies of necessary resources, such as water • Costs incurred in transition to lower emission practices	• Encourage recycling • More energy-efficient plant and equipment to be used • More efficient transportation options • Reduced water and energy consumption • Government incentives for cleaner technologies • Use of carbon markets • Development of low-emission goods and services • Increased returns by being reactive to changing consumer demands • Resource substitution/diversification.

Source: Adapted from Task Force on Climate-related Financial Disclosures (2017).

One organisation that has some very useful and interesting resource materials available in relation to climate change is the Climate Reality Project (see www.climaterealityproject.org/truth), which is linked to the famous advocate for addressing climate change, Al Gore. Exhibit 6.10 comes from the website of this organisation. It identifies some of the costs that will arise as a result of the massive amounts of carbon that are being generated by human activities, thereby emphasising how crucial it is that all people take some responsibility for this – as managers, as consumers, as product and service users.

The website of the Climate Reality Project also provides information about global surface temperatures, which are reported as having gradually increased since about 1970, and global sea temperatures, which are reported as having increased since 1950. The website also indicates that 16 out of the 17 hottest years on record have occurred since 2001.

Earlier in this chapter, we discussed various reporting frameworks that included disclosure requirements pertaining to climate change, including:

- the Global Reporting Initiative standards (particularly GRI 302 on energy, and GRI 305 on emissions)
- the International Sustainability Standards Board

EXHIBIT 6.10 The implications ('costs') from continuing to rely upon carbon

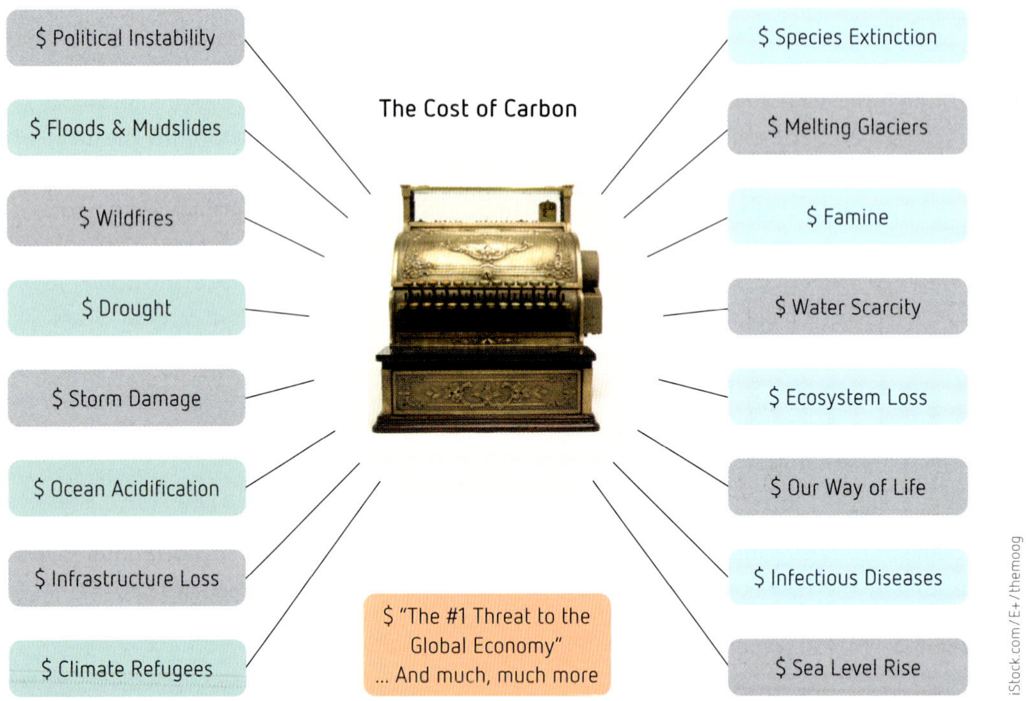

Source: The Climate Reality Project (2022).

- the Task Force on Climate-related Financial Disclosures
- the Sustainable Development Goals.

We also discussed measurement frameworks, of which the Greenhouse Gas Protocol has specific relevance. One other related initiative we can now briefly consider is the Carbon Disclosure Project.

The Carbon Disclosure Project

The Carbon Disclosure Project (CDP) – see (**www.cdp.net**) – was formed in 2000. The CDP has offices throughout the world and focuses on the implications of climate change for shareholder value and commercial operations. The CDP seeks information on the business risks and opportunities presented by climate change and greenhouse gas emissions for the world's largest companies. It publishes emissions data for thousands of the world's largest corporations, which are thought to account for over a third of the world's anthropogenic emissions (the word 'anthropogenic' can be used to refer to any changes in nature that are caused by people). According to the project's website (accessed February 2022):

> We want to see a thriving economy that works for people and planet in the long term. We focus investors, companies, cities and governments on building a sustainable economy by measuring and acting on their environmental impact. We must act urgently to prevent dangerous climate change and environmental damage. That starts by being aware of our impact so that investors, companies, cities and governments can make the right choices now. CDP runs the global environmental disclosure system. Each year CDP supports thousands of companies, cities, states and regions to measure and manage their risks and opportunities on climate change, water security and deforestation. We do so at the request of their investors, purchasers and city stakeholders.
>
> Source: Carbon Disclosure Project (2022).

The view of the CDP is that carbon emissions and climate change represent significant business risks, and therefore, an organisation's policies and performance in relation to climate change should be factored into investment decisions. Furthermore, the CDP has the view that information about greenhouse gas emissions is useful to investors, corporations and regulators in making informed decisions that take into account corporate risk from future government legislation, possible future lawsuits, and shifts in consumers' perceptions towards heavy emitters. Organisations wishing to publicly report their greenhouse gas emissions and climate change strategies can do so through the CDP, and interested parties can do searches on the CDP website by company name. The CDP is also now collecting information about organisations' use of water, and the use of forestry-related resources.

Why do I need to know about climate change and understand some of the ways in which organisations can report information about their performance and initiatives in relation to climate change?

As future business leaders, it is essential that we understand the global crisis represented by climate change. It is important that we comprehend the necessity for all people and organisations – including those we will work for – to address climate change and to develop policies to reduce or ideally eliminate their carbon-related emissions. Because of the responsibility that all organisations have with respect to climate change, managers need to understand the various frameworks that are available to demonstrate their accountability with respect to climate change.

LO6.6 Corporate responsibilities: The reduction of modern slavery

Another very important area of organisational social responsibility relates to modern slavery. 'Modern slavery' refers to the use of human trafficking or forced labour that amounts to slavery, or slavery-like practices. It directly links to United Nations Sustainable Development Goal 8. According to the International Labour Organization (ILO) Forced Labour Convention, 1930 (No. 29), 'forced or compulsory labour' is all work or service that is exacted from any person under the threat of a penalty and for which the person has not offered himself or herself voluntarily.

As an example, many Australian organisations source materials and products from the Asia-Pacific region, which is accepted as a high-risk area in terms of the use of forced labour and human trafficking. Indeed, estimates by the ILO suggest there are at least 12 million victims of forced labour in the Asia-Pacific region.

According to International Labour Organization (ILO, 2017), in 2017:

- 40 million people worldwide were victims of modern slavery, with 25 million being in forced labour and 15 million in forced marriage
- women and girls accounted for 71 per cent of modern slavery victims
- one in four victims of modern slavery were children
- modern slavery occurs in every region of the world
- 4 million people were in state-imposed forced labour.

The ILO also estimates that US$150 billion in illegal profits are generated annually through the use of 'modern slaves'.

Apart from the immoral nature of such activity, there are many risks (which we might refer to as 'reputational risks') to an organisation if it is found to be associated with forced labour.

For example, we can consider the vast amount of negative publicity the leading surf company Rip Curl received back in 2016. In one related newspaper article entitled 'Surf clothing label Rip Curl using "slave labour" to manufacture clothes in North Korea' (by Nick McKenzie and Richard Baker, *Sydney Morning Herald*, 20 February 2016), it was noted:

> In a major embarrassment that raises serious questions about Rip Curl's garment sourcing practices, a Fairfax Media investigation can reveal that workers at the Taedonggang Clothing Factory near the North Korean capital Pyongyang were contracted to make some of Rip Curl's 2015 winter range of clothing. Workers in North Korea are routinely exploited. North Korean defectors have told investigators from NGOs, including Human Rights Watch, that employees are forced to work long hours with minimal or sometimes no pay. Workers who do not obey orders are imprisoned in work camps. After Fairfax Media sent Rip Curl photos of its garments being made in North Korea, the company's chief financial officer Tony Roberts released a statement that said the firm 'takes its social compliance obligations seriously'. 'We were aware of this issue, which related to our Winter 2015 Mountain-wear range, but only became aware of it after the production was complete and had been shipped to our retail customers.'

Such publicity would have been extremely detrimental to the organisation's reputation (which is effectively based on a healthy sporting image) and this would likely have had an impact on its profitability. That is, consumers and the market would have potentially punished the company for its apparent link to forced labour – which is the rationale for why the Australian Government (and other governments internationally, including the United Kingdom and Californian government) have introduced a Modern Slavery Act. The *Modern Slavery Act 2018* (the Act) was introduced within Australia in 2018 and aims, through corporate disclosures, to necessarily create awareness within organisations about where they are sourcing their goods from, and how employees in those supply chains are being treated (thereby hopefully averting situations like that in which Rip Curl got embroiled), as well as informing consumers and the public more widely about an organisation's sourcing policies.

Within Australia, the Act applies to larger organisations, specifically those with annual consolidated revenue of $100 million or more. Such reporting applies to both 'for-profit' organisations and 'not-for-profit' organisations. Therefore, it applies to business organisations as well as to universities, churches and charities. Organisations that do not meet the $100 million threshold can still voluntarily elect to report in compliance with the Act – and many do.

The Act within Australia requires organisations to report annually – by way of a 'Modern Slavery Statement' – on the steps organisations are taking, across their supply chains, to address and monitor the risk that modern slavery is present within their supply chains. Specifically, paragraph Section 16 of the Act requires:

> This Part requires modern slavery statements to be given annually to the Minister, describing the risks of modern slavery in the operations and supply chains of reporting entities and entities owned or controlled by those entities.
>
> The statements must also include information about actions taken to address those risks.
>
> **Mandatory criteria for modern slavery statements**
>
> (1) A modern slavery statement must, in relation to each reporting entity covered by the statement:

(a) identify the reporting entity; and
(b) describe the structure, operations and supply chains of the reporting entity; and
(c) describe the risks of modern slavery practices in the operations and supply chains of the reporting entity, and any entities that the reporting entity owns or controls; and
(d) describe the actions taken by the reporting entity and any entity that the reporting entity owns or controls, to assess and address those risks, including due diligence and remediation processes; and
(e) describe how the reporting entity assesses the effectiveness of such actions; and
(f) describe the process of consultation with:
  (i) any entities that the reporting entity owns or controls; and
  (ii) in the case of a reporting entity covered by a statement under section 14 – the entity giving the statement; and
(g) include any other information that the reporting entity, or the entity giving the statement, considers relevant.

Example: For paragraph (d), actions taken by an entity may include the development of policies and processes to address modern slavery risks, and providing training for staff about modern slavery.

Source: *Modern Slavery Act 2018, No. 153, 2018*. Based on content from the Federal Register of Legislation at 20 April 2022. For the latest information on Australian Government law please go to https://www.legislation.gov.au.

The 'modern slavery statement' must be signed off by a nominated person in the peak governing body of the entity (such as the Board of Directors), thereby ensuring that the information is directly brought to the attention of the most senior people within an organisation. The Act does not apply any penalties to organisations for information uncovered and disclosed as a result of the audits of their supply chains. As already noted, the intention is to leave it to 'the market' and consumers to punish perceived poor behaviour. However, this relies upon key assumptions that:

- consumers actually want to be aware of such information
- they will then act negatively towards organisations that are associated with modern slavery.

That is, the intended impacts of the Act rely on concerns managers have about their 'reputational risk' – wherein reputational risk can be considered to relate to the potential of negative publicity, or negative public perceptions, to create adverse impacts on a company's reputation, thereby affecting its revenue streams, and therefore its profitability. The further assumption here is that managers, being concerned about their reputational risk, will take actions to ensure that elements of modern slavery are not in existence within their supply chains and this ultimately will lead to a reduced incidence of modern slavery throughout the world.

Because Australia imports many products from high-risk areas, the central tenet of the Australian Government's initiative is that the buying power of Australian organisations is sufficiently large that it can be utilised to create positive social change. However, it is not always obvious that this 'reputational risk' exists for all organisations. That is, it is not at all clear that all organisations are subject to the same levels of reputational risk, and some organisations are likely to be more reliant on their reputation and image than others. For example, throughout 2019 there were many newspaper and television stories about Australian casinos allegedly being linked to organised crime (with some of the associated people being linked to forced labour) and money laundering, but there was no clear impact on their profitability.

All modern slavery statements are to be submitted to a government-backed repository, meaning that the publicly available reports shall all be accessible at one place.

According to CPA Australia (2019, p. 12), some of the consequences of the new modern slavery laws would include:

- managers revising their governance policies and developing revised policies and action plans, including updating or initiating supplier codes of conduct
- implementing systematic reviews of human rights issues in procurement processes, tender processes and contractual terms (including supplier pre-qualification processes)
- establishing targets and key performance indicators, internal awareness raising and training in the firm and with key or high-risk suppliers.

The Act does not actually define 'supply chains' and it has effectively been left to organisations to self-define their 'supply chain'. Research reported by CPA (2019) reveals that the majority of firms appear to be interpreting it very narrowly to mean suppliers with which they have a 'direct payment relationship' (which we referred to as Tier 1 suppliers in Chapter 2). It is hoped that this interpretation will broaden over time, but nevertheless it does require self-analysis by organisations in terms of what they consider to be their 'supply chain'.

The effectiveness of Modern Slavery Acts relies upon firms organising or commissioning appropriate auditing and monitoring processes throughout supply chains. For example, organisations will need to arrange audits within suppliers' factories throughout various developing countries and to report the results of such audits. However, legislators and others need to be aware of the available evidence, which casts significant doubt over the robustness or objectivity of such audits, before, perhaps naively, simply believing the information being produced by apparently independent third-party auditors/assurance providers. In an in-depth investigation of compliance audits undertaken of the supply chains of multinational corporations (MNCs) in the context of the Bangladesh garments industry, Islam, Deegan and Gray (2018, p. 214) report:

> What seems to have emerged is a complex interplay of motives, assumptions and influences. The actual conduct of a social compliance audit is predominantly a requirement instituted by the MNC as a pre-condition of the supply contract. There is very little evidence that, all things being equal, the MNCs exert much in the way of resources or effort to assess the reliability of these audits which appear to have a symbolic role and allow the MNC to continue to make claims that appear to play well with western consumers ... Consequently, the audits are generally of a cursory nature and we found little evidence that they make much constructive impact on the lives of workers and communities. Such accountability as is owed to the relatively powerless workers and communities remains largely undischarged ... Thus, a social compliance audit becomes a ritualistic practice that supports MNCs' maintenance of legitimacy to the wider community rather than creating real accountability.

Hence, as with all reported information, we must always be careful not to necessarily be naive and believe everything we read. We must consider the reputation of the parties involved in gathering and reporting the information, as well as the potential motivations for introducing an element of bias into the reported information.

Interested readers who want to refer to the Australian Government Repository for Modern Slavery Statements might wish to refer to **https://modernslaveryregister.gov.au**.

A final point to make in relation to modern slavery is that certain industries globally have set up networks of different organisations to work (and buy) together as a group to improve their ability and power to address modern slavery within their supply chains. For example, within the Australian context is the Australian University Procurement Network (AUPN) (and remember, the Modern Slavery Act within Australia applies to both 'for profit' and 'not for profit' entities). The AUPN represents 39 Australian and New Zealand organisations from the university sector.

According to their website (https://www.hes.edu.au/australian-universities-procurement-network, accessed July 2022):

> The AUPN is leading a sector collaboration to support member universities to meet the challenge of human rights transparency and risk management in their supply chains and contribute to the fulfillment of Modern Slavery Act 2018 (Cth) reporting requirements. By working together, we hope to minimise the duplication of activities and associated costs across individual universities, including risk assessment, implementation of systems and remediation. We also hope that leveraging our aggregated buying power will improve our capacity to identify and action any modern slavery risks, and drive more effective changes through our supply chains.
>
> Source: 'The Australian Universities Procurement Network', HES (2022). https://www.hes.edu.au/australian-universities-procurement-network.

Key concept

Modern slavery – which can include forced or involuntary labour, debt bonded labour, labour coerced through threat, human trafficking, traditional slavery, domestic servitude and child labour – can potentially exist throughout most organisations' supply chains. Managers need to take every effort to ensure that they contract with, and therefore support, organisations throughout their supply chains that actively work to eliminate modern slavery. Managers are responsible and accountable for addressing the risks that modern slavery could exist within their supply chains.

LO6.7 Counter (shadow) accounts

All forms of accounting typically involve an element of judgement by those making the disclosures, and this is even more so when the form of reporting is largely unregulated, as is the case with much social and environmental/sustainability reporting. Therefore, the managers of an organisation might – through their disclosures – provide a particular perspective of their organisation's performance (potentially a partisan perspective), but such perspectives of performance might not be shared by other stakeholder groups. There realistically could be an element of bias to the reporting being undertaken.

Apart from managers, stakeholder groups with an interest in an organisation, which may include particular employee groups, consumer groups or environmental groups, might have access to particular information about that organisation and be able to provide 'alternative accounts' about how an organisation has performed. That is, they might produce accounts or reports that challenge, or contest, the accounts released by the managers. These accounts, produced by stakeholders other than managers, are often referred to as **counter accounts** or *shadow accounts*. These accounts are often developed from different philosophical and political standpoints and can contradict the accounts prepared by managers.

counter accounts Also called shadow accounts, and usually produced by stakeholders outside an organisation, these accounts often challenge, or contest, the accounts released by an organisation's managers

Counter accounts incorporated within organisational reporting

Typically, these counter accounts, if prepared, are released independently by the respective stakeholder group. However, there is some argument that when organisations prepare their CSR/sustainability reports, and particularly where there are contested perspectives about performance (that is, where different stakeholders do not share the same view as management about how well the organisation is performing), then the alternative views held by other stakeholders should arguably also be included within the reports being released by the organisation. For example, if an organisation produces social information relating to how it has advanced the interests of its employees, possibly through implementing various educational or training initiatives, or by introducing policies that assist in the employment of people with disabilities, it might also be useful to provide the views of particular labour union officials about whether they also believe that the organisation has been successful in promoting the interests of employees.

As we have discussed already in this chapter, various sustainability reporting frameworks encourage or require engagement with various stakeholder groups so that the organisation can understand the different and potentially conflicting views of different stakeholder groups. Therefore managers should be aware of the potentially 'counter' views held by stakeholders.

dialogic accounting
Where there is typically more than one 'logic' that could be employed to assess organisational performance, and these different logics (based on different perspectives about what aspects of performance are important, or otherwise) could be used to develop different accounts

Brown (2009) provides an insightful discussion of this possibility, referring to the concept of **dialogic accounting** and focusing on the sustainability area for illustrative purposes. By dialogic accounting, Brown is referring to a situation in which there is typically more than one 'logic' that could be employed to assess organisational performance, and these different logics (based on different perspectives about what aspects of performance are important, or otherwise) could be used to develop different accounts. Producing dialogic accounts encourages debate and enhances possibilities for revisions in how managers manage the organisation. Brown's perspective of dialogic accounting is consistent with what we have referred to as the production of counter accounts.

monologic accounting
Reflects the accounting traditions currently in place, wherein only the managers' perspective of performance is reported

Brown provides an interesting comparison of dialogic accounting with **monologic accounting** – monologic accounts represent only one view or logic, this being that of the managers. As she explains, monologic accounting reflects the accounting traditions currently in place, wherein only the managers' perspective of performance is reported to external stakeholders. This is the traditional approach to reporting to which we are accustomed. However, according to Brown, the non-reporting of other stakeholders' perspectives inevitably provides bias in situations where there are conceivably alternative viewpoints.

According to Brown (2009, p. 317), dialogic accounting, in recognising the existence of different views of organisational performance, allows for a situation where different and sometimes conflicting views are allowed to coexist. Pursuant to this view, corporate reporting could become a vehicle to foster democratic interaction. The aim of dialogic accounting is not necessarily to replace one dominant form of accounting with another, but rather to foster the development and use of more multidimensional accounting and accountability systems, capable of engaging a variety of perspectives and facilitating wide-ranging discussion and debate about organisational matters. This is a very interesting suggestion, one that runs counter to the views often proffered by many accounting practitioners and researchers, wherein there is presumed to be only one view of the world that can be captured by managers and objectively reflected within accounting reports. As Brown states:

> Given the essentially contestable nature of sustainability, new accountings should not be aimed at producing incontrovertible accounts. Societal worth should be judged not in terms of the expert production of the 'right answer' but in the facilitation and broadening of debate ... Accountants need to develop systems that prevent premature closure and which infuse debate and dialogue, facilitating genuine and informed citizen participation in decision making processes ... A framework of a dialogical approach would: recognise ideological assumptions; avoid monetary reductionism; be open about the objective and contestable nature of calculations; enable accessibility of non-experts;

ensure effective participatory processes; be attentive to power relations; and recognise the transformative potential of dialogic accounting.

Source: Brown (2009), p. 318.

According to Brown, a form of accounting that embraces a dialogic approach will have considerable transformative potential in areas such as sustainable development. Again, the views embodied by Brown (2009) would seem to be of great value in informing debate to extend corporate accountability, and to project different views about corporate performance and success. However, despite its merits, it is probably unlikely that the current monologic practices, which tend to dominate reporting practices, will be displaced any time soon by dialogic approaches.

For more on the inclusion of alternative views in organisational reporting, see Learning exercise 6.11.

6.11 Learning Exercise

Including alternative views in corporate reports

Let us consider the suggestion from Brown (2009) that the alternative views held by different stakeholders should also be included within the reports being released by an organisation. What are some factors that should be considered in determining whether to include different stakeholders' perceptions within organisational reports?

Would the introduction of counter accounts within corporate reports be useful to the readers of the reports?

The introduction of counter accounts would potentially be useful to readers of organisational reports. Traditional practice is that organisational reports only reflect the managers' views of performance. This could include an element of bias – either intentionally or unintentionally introduced. Because there are different perspectives that can be taken of social and environmental performance, it can be useful to know about other stakeholders' views, but we would also need to determine how reliable those views are and whether they are intentionally biased.

Could the introduction of dialogic accounting increase the possibility that organisational practices will change?

The argument is that reporting different stakeholders' views of performance can stimulate debate about whether managers might be seeing or prioritising aspects of performance differently than others see or prioritise them. This could lead to further analysis, which in turn could lead to changing the way the organisation conducts its operations and how performance is reported. It could also lead to the discovery of new opportunities, or reveal potential risks that need to be addressed. Furthermore, if managers know that a counter (dialogic) account will be published alongside their account, they might be more proactive in reporting negative information in order to pre-empt the counter account. Knowing that they will need to report this information, they may then be more proactive in actually addressing the issues associated with such negative information in order to avoid their occurrence in the first place.

Is such an approach likely to be implemented by managers?

It is unusual for the reports released by organisations to include the opinions of other stakeholders, other than perhaps auditors/assurance providers. It is not certain that this will change in the future, despite the potential benefits.

Separate counter accounts

Apart from the possibility that alternative views, or counter accounts, might be included within the reports compiled by managers, another approach that is sometimes adopted is for particular interest/stakeholder groups to separately present their own counter accounts about specific organisations' operations.

As one very notable example – one that has attracted a lot of publicity throughout the world – the environmental group known as Friends of the Earth has, on a number of occasions, produced a counter account about the large oil company Shell, in which it has sought to highlight various negative aspects of the company's performance. They titled their report *The other Shell report* in direct reference to the title given by Shell to their own CSR report, which was *The Shell report*.

This counter accounting is also a form of accounting, but it is undertaken by stakeholders other than managers and uses information that may, or may not be, available to managers. Whether we would rely upon the contents of these counter accounts is a matter of opinion, and tied to our views about the reputation, philosophical perspectives and motivations of the stakeholder group preparing the report. Friends of the Earth have not prepared *The other Shell report* for a number of years; nevertheless, the 2004 report is still available at **https://www.foei.org/resources/publications/publications-by-subject/resisting-mining-oil-gas-publications/behind-the-shine-the-other-shell-report**. In the foreword to the report, it is stated that:

> Friends of the Earth is privileged to present this third alternative Shell Corporate Social Responsibility (CSR) report on behalf of several of the many communities that live on Shell's 'fence lines' – next to Shell's refineries, depots and pipelines. *Lessons Not Learned – The Other Shell Report 2004* builds on reports of the past two years – *Failing the Challenge* (2002) and *Behind the Shine* (2003) – which chronicled Shell's impacts around the world. It gives updates of Shell's woeful performance over the past year, documenting a consistent story of the company pushing forward with business as usual, disregarding the rights of its stakeholders.
>
> Source: Friends of the Earth (2004), p. 2.

Friends of the Earth has also produced counter accounts pertaining to the activities of the global mining company BHP.

Another well-known example of counter accounts being issued about a company relates to the large chocolate company Hershey. In 2010, Hershey released its first CSR report, in which it outlined various successes it had had in relation to the broad area of sustainability. However, shortly after this, a group of social and environmental NGOs and activists released their own account (counter account) of Hershey's performance, wherein they detailed various human rights abuses they claimed were associated with the company in relation to the production and sourcing of cocoa. Counter accounts have also been prepared in relation to a number of other companies.

So, in concluding this short section on counter accounts, we can hopefully appreciate the possibility that there can be different perspectives about an organisation's performance depending upon the values, expectations, evidence and accounting methods being employed by those producing the accounts. In reality, the actual social and environmental (or sustainability-related) performance of an organisation might best be represented by a position that is somewhere in-between what the managers report (which research evidence seems to suggest will often present an overly favourable view of an organisation's operations) and what the respective interest groups report. This section has also emphasised that there can be various alternative sources of information about an organisation's performance available to society, all of which might have differing levels of reliability.

Key concept

Organisations can create many different types of social and environmental impacts and in doing so can potentially impact many different stakeholders. There can be various (sometimes conflicting) perspectives held by different stakeholders about how 'well' an organisation is performing. Managers will have a particular view about what are the significant impacts, and to whom these impacts relate. Such views will likely not be shared by all stakeholders with an interest in the organisation.

LO6.8 Independent review of CSR reports

In the above section, we considered the potential reliability of alternative sources of information. Reliability is an important qualitative characteristic that useful information possesses – we have seen it identified in various reporting frameworks as a fundamentally required qualitative characteristic. The reliability of the information published by an organisation – whether financial, social or environmental – is typically accepted as being higher when the information is reviewed by a qualified and independent third party, and the results of the review (the 'opinion' of the auditor or assurance provider) are included within the body of the report being released by the organisation.

As indicated in the previous section on counter accounts, managers will provide a particular view on their performance. There could potentially be a number of alternative views, and the different views could suffer from biases. A third-party review can act to provide interested stakeholders with an expert's opinion about whether an organisation's report has been properly prepared, and whether actual performance is consistent with what managers purport it to be. As we have emphasised a number of times throughout this book, we always need to be careful not to believe everything that we read, particularly when the accounts are being prepared by managers. That is, our message remains that we always need to apply a healthy dose of scepticism when reviewing different accounts of organisational performance.

As a general principle, if reports are prepared by management, then there can be incentives, at times, for managers to be less than objective when preparing those reports. In this regard, we can refer to the idea of 'creative accounting', wherein managers might use various accounting techniques and the selective disclosure of some information in preference to other information, to (creatively) project the best, or most favourable, picture of an organisation.

An independent review of a report, if conducted by an auditor or assurance provider that is considered to be an expert in the area, will tend to add credibility and therefore value to the report. Because an independent review can act to increase stakeholder support for an organisation, it is actually in the organisation's interest to pay for the third-party review. However, if the independent review was performed by individuals who have no clear expertise in the area, then any potential increase in the credibility of the information in the report being assured would be questionable.

Therefore, with the above brief discussion in mind, something to consider when reviewing any reports produced by an organisation is not only the reputation of those managers associated with preparing the report, but also who, if anybody, reviewed/audited the reports prior to them being publicly released, and what was the expert's opinion of the information included within the report.

Unlike financial reporting, for social and environmental reporting there is generally no specific regulation pertaining to how assurance activities should be undertaken, or how the assurance report should be prepared. When reviewing an external audit/assurance report, there are a few questions we should consider in determining whether we should rely upon the independent third-party opinion, including:

- What is the purpose of the third-party review? For example, was it to check conformity with particular reporting or performance standards? Was it for the whole report or part thereof?
- Who is the intended audience of the assurance report?
- Against what standards was the audit/assurance undertaken, and what form of testing/risk assessment was undertaken by the assurance provider?
- Who did the audit? What is their reputation? What are their relevant qualifications?
- Did it provide a clear and unambiguous opinion about the report, and what is the nature of the opinion?

If the opinion provided within an assurance report is that the reports being reviewed were poorly prepared, perhaps breaching particular standards and guidelines, then we might actually be wasting our time reviewing the reports. Arguably, one of the first components of a CSR report that should be reviewed, if one is available, is the assurance report.

An example of an independent third-party review/audit, specifically the independent assurance report prepared by Ernst and Young (EY) in relation to the sustainability data disclosures in BHP's 2021 annual report (BHP did formerly produce a standalone sustainability report but in 2021 incorporated sustainability data within the annual report together with all its information about financial position and performance), is shown in **Exhibit 6.11**. To the best of your ability, review the report in **Exhibit 6.11** and consider whether its inclusion within BHP's 2021 annual report would influence the credibility you would attribute to the BHP disclosures.

For more on third-party assurance reports, see **Learning exercise 6.12**.

6.12 Learning Exercise

Third-party assurance reports

The inclusion of third-party assurance reports, when prepared by auditors/assurance providers with expertise and a good reputation in the area, and which give an opinion that the accounts are properly stated, act to increase the confidence we have in the contents of the report.

However, as the evidence in KPMG (2020) shows, not all CSR/sustainability reports do include assurance reports. So, if a sustainability report has been prepared by the managers of an organisation, and it is not accompanied by a third-party assurance report, should we be inclined to trust the contents of the report?

To answer this question, we can argue that, when determining the reliability of a sustainability report unaccompanied by a third-party review, we should consider past evidence. If evidence suggests that the managers have, in the past, reported in a professional and objective manner, then we may be inclined to have confidence in the contents of a report even in the absence of a third-party review. However, if the managers are unknown to us, or have a history of poor or biased reporting, then we would be inclined not to rely upon the information if it is unaccompanied by third-party assurance.

EXHIBIT 6.11 An example of a third-party assurance report

1.13.16 Independent Assurance Report to the Management and Directors of BHP Group Limited and BHP Group Plc (BHP)

EY
Building a better working world

What we assured

Ernst & Young (EY) was engaged by BHP to provide limited assurance over certain sustainability data and disclosures in BHP's Annual Report for the year ended 30 June 2021 ('FY21 Annual Report') and online, in accordance with the noted criteria, as defined in the following table:

What we assured (Limited Assurance Subject Matter)	What we assured it against (Criteria)
BHP's qualitative disclosures in sections 1.12 and 1.13 of the FY21 Annual Report	– Management's own publicly disclosed criteria
BHP's Sustainability policies and standards as disclosed in the ICMM tab in BHP's ESG Standards and Databook www.bhp.com/FY21ESGStandardsDatabook.	– International Council on Mining and Metals (ICMM) Mining Principles and relevant Performance Expectations (PE) (2020) and mandatory Position Statements (Subject Matter 1)
BHP's identification and reporting of its material sustainability risks and opportunities described within the FY21 Annual Report and online at bhp.com/materialityassessment	– ICMM Subject Matter 2 – Global Reporting Initiative (GRI) Principles for defining report content
BHP's implementation of systems and approaches to manage its material sustainability risks and opportunities	– ICMM Subject Matter 3
BHP's reported performance of its material sustainability risks and opportunities in sections 1.12, 1.13, and 4.8 of the FY21 Annual Report	– ICMM Subject Matter 4 – Management's own publicly disclosed criteria including GRI Topic Specific Standards and Sustainability Accounting Standards Board (SASB) Mining and Metals Standard
BHP's prioritisation process for the selection of assets for PE validation reported online at bhp.com/sustainabilitystandards	– ICMM Subject Matter 5
Water stewardship reporting, at an asset level, in the FY21 Annual Report and supporting disclosures included online at bhp.com/water	– ICMM guidance and minimum disclosure Standards: A Practical Guide to Consistent Water Reporting

In addition, we were engaged by BHP to provide reasonable assurance over the following information in accordance with the noted criteria:

What we assured (Reasonable Assurance Subject Matter)	What we assured it against (Criteria)
Scope 1 and 2 Greenhouse Gas emissions as reported in section 1.13.7 and 4.8.5 of the FY21 Annual Report	– World Resource Institute/World Business Council for Sustainable Development (WRI/WBCSD) Greenhouse Gas Protocol – BHP's Basis of Preparation

Our Conclusions

- **Limited Assurance**
  Based on the procedures we have performed and the evidence we have obtained, nothing has come to our attention that suggests that BHP's sustainability data and disclosures and asset level water stewardship disclosures reported in sections 1.12, 1.13 and 4.8 of the FY21 Annual Report have not been prepared, in all material respects, in accordance with the Criteria defined above.
- **Reasonable Assurance**
  In our opinion, the Scope 1 and 2 greenhouse gas emissions, as reported in section 1.13.7 and 4.8.5 of the FY21 Annual Report are prepared, in all material respects, in accordance with the Criteria defined above.

Emphasis of Matter

We draw attention to section 4.8.6 in the FY21 Annual Report and online at bhp.com/water, in which BHP discloses performance metrics as it relates to water withdrawals, consumption and discharges. The collation of water storage data during FY21 has identified uncertainty in the water models currently used at BHP's Coal Assets (BMA, BMC and NSW Energy Coal). As a result, the disclosed water performance data for the Coal Assets is subject to estimation uncertainty but is based on the best information available at the time of reporting. Our conclusion is not modified in respect of this matter.

Key responsibilities

EY's responsibility and independence

Our responsibility was to express limited and reasonable assurance conclusions on the noted subject matter as defined in the 'what we assured' column in the tables above (Subject Matter).

We were also responsible for maintaining our independence and confirm that we have met the requirements of the APES 110 *Code of Ethics for Professional Accountants* (including Independence Standards) and have the required competencies and experience to conduct this assurance engagement.

BHP's responsibility

BHP's management was responsible for selecting the Criteria and preparing and fairly presenting information presented and referenced in the FY21 Annual Report in accordance with that Criteria. This responsibility includes establishing and maintaining internal controls, adequate records and making estimates that are reasonable in the circumstances.

Our approach to conducting the Review

We conducted our procedures in accordance with the *International Federation of Accountants' International Standard for Assurance Engagements Other Than Audits or Reviews of Historical Financial Information* (ISAE 3000), the *Standard for Assurance on Greenhouse Gas Statements* (ISAE 3410) and the terms of reference for this engagement as agreed with BHP on 27 January 2021.

We adapted our approach to undertaking our review procedures in response to the COVID-19 travel restrictions and social distancing requirements. We visited one BHP site in person with the remaining 'site visits' undertaken virtually by phone and video-conference. The performance of the year end corporate review procedures at head office was also required to be conducted remotely and was supported through the use of collaboration platforms for discussions and delivery of requested evidence.

The procedures we performed were based on our professional judgement and included, but were not limited to:

- Interviewing select corporate and site personnel to understand the reporting process at group, business, asset and site level, including management's processes to identify BHP's material issues
- Reviewing BHP policies and management standards to determine alignment with the ICMM's 10 Sustainable Development principles and position statements
- Checking the FY21 Annual Report to understand how BHP's identified material risks and opportunities are reflected within the qualitative disclosures
- Evaluating whether the information disclosed in the FY21 Annual Report and related disclosures is consistent with our understanding of sustainability management and performance at BHP
- Evaluating the suitability and application of the Criteria and that the Criteria have been applied appropriately to the Subject Matter
- Conducting a mix of virtual and in-person site procedures at eight BHP locations to evidence site level data collection and reporting to Group as well as to identify completeness of reported water and emission sources
- Undertaking analytical procedures of the quantitative disclosures in the FY21 Annual Report and related online disclosures
- Reviewing data, information or explanation about the sustainability performance data and statements included in the FY21 Annual Report and related online disclosures
- Reviewing other information within the FY21 Annual Report for consistency and alignment with our assurance subject matter
- On a judgemental sample basis, re-performing calculations to check accuracy of claims in the FY21 Annual Report
- Checking the water balance for each asset and judgementally selecting a sample of water streams for further testing
- On a sample basis, based on our professional judgement, agreeing claims to source information to check accuracy and completeness of claims, which included invoices, incident reports, meter calibration records, and meter data
- For our reasonable assurance of Greenhouse Gas emissions, selecting key items and representative sampling, based on statistical audit sampling tables and agreeing to source information to check accuracy and completeness of performance data, which included invoices, metre calibration records and metre data.

We believe that the evidence obtained is sufficient and appropriate to provide a basis for our reasonable and limited assurance conclusions

Other Matters

We have not performed assurance procedures in respect of any information relating to prior reporting periods, including those presented in the FY21 Annual Report, other than sustainability data and disclosures relating to BHP's Annual Report for the year ended 30 June 2020. Our report does not extend to any disclosures or assertions made by BHP relating to case studies and future performance plans and/or strategies disclosed in the FY21 Annual Report. While we considered the effectiveness of management's internal controls when determining the nature and extent of our procedures, our assurance engagement was not designed to provide assurance on internal controls. Our procedures did not include testing controls or performing procedures relating to checking aggregation or calculation of data within IT systems.

Limited and Reasonable Assurance

Procedures performed in a limited assurance engagement vary in nature and timing from, and are less in extent than for, a reasonable assurance engagement. Consequently, the level of assurance obtained in a limited assurance engagement is substantially lower than the assurance that would have been obtained had a reasonable assurance engagement been performed. While our procedures performed for our reasonable assurance engagement are of a higher level of assurance, due to the use of sampling techniques, it is not a guarantee that it will always detect material misstatements.

Use of our Assurance Statement

We disclaim any assumption of responsibility for any reliance on this assurance report to any persons other than management and the directors of BHP, or for any purpose other than that for which it was prepared.

Ernst & Young

Ernst & Young
Melbourne, Australia
2 September 2021

Mathew Nelson
Partner

Source: BHP (2021), p. 52.

STUDY TOOLS

SUMMARY

In this chapter, we have explored a number of issues relating to corporate social responsibility reporting. We defined CSR reporting and provided insights into the meaning of sustainability reporting.

We were able to show that corporate social responsibility reporting is a rapidly growing area of reporting, and that larger organisations are increasingly likely to produce these reports. We identified various reasons *why* organisations might elect to report social and environmental information, and we also identified various stakeholders *who* will have an interest in such information. Furthermore, we described *what* types of social and environmental disclosures might be made, and *how* that information might be disclosed.

In addressing the issues associated with what information to produce, and how to produce it, we referred to a number of reporting frameworks as well as discussing the need for measurement frameworks. We identified the Global Reporting Initiative's Sustainability Reporting Standards as being the most commonly used reporting framework, and we also identified a number of other high-profile reporting frameworks. What we also demonstrated was that the various frameworks tend to identify the same qualitative characteristics that information is expected to possess if it is to be useful, including relevance, reliability, comparability, timeliness, consistency and verifiability.

We identified climate change as being a necessary focus of corporate social responsibility reporting. We also discussed the types of disclosures that organisations should ideally make in relation to climate change, including the need to clearly report the risks and opportunities associated with it. We also discussed the need for organisations to be accountable with respect to the efforts they are undertaking to minimise that modern slavery exists within their supply chains.

We discussed the idea of counter accounts and noted how different interest groups might generate a different account of an organisation's performance. We emphasised that accounts prepared by different stakeholders (such as managers and interest groups) can be subject to some bias. We concluded the chapter with a discussion of third-party reviews of social and environmental information, and we noted how such reviews can act to increase the confidence users have in the information being reported.

One thing we emphasised in the chapter is that report readers should not be naive and necessarily believe everything managers tell them. Care is always needed. What should be apparent from reading this chapter is that, when reviewing the corporate social responsibility reports released by organisations (and much of the information is reported on a voluntary basis), there are certain important issues to consider before you make judgements about how reliant you should be on the reported information. The issues to consider include:

- Why did management prepare the report? Is the information being disclosed as a means of trying to manage particular stakeholder groups? (Perhaps there has been a recent crisis that has attracted adverse media attention and the organisation is now trying to win back community support.) More preferably, is the information being disclosed because managers believe they have a responsibility, and an accountability, to provide information to stakeholders that are potentially impacted by the organisation's operations? Answers to such questions about the managers' motivations for reporting will have implications for how much faith can be placed in the information being reported.
- What is the reputation of the managers preparing the reports? If the managers have a reputation for providing high-quality, objective accounts of their performance, then we might be more likely to rely upon the information.

- Why has management decided to disclose particular social and environmental information and not disclose other information? The report should be clear about the reasoning for different disclosures being made in preference to others, which we referred to as the materiality determination process. Failure to do so will undermine the relevance we can attribute to particular information.
- Related to the above point, has the context of the organisation's operations been properly explained so as to provide some rationale for particular information being disclosed? For example, where is the organisation located, in what industry does the organisation operate, and what are the significant social and environmental aspects of the location and industry? As just two examples, is the organisation operating within an area of important biodiversity? If so, is the report clear about the particular risks that the organisation creates by being there, and how these risks are being managed? A good report should explain such aspects. As a further example, is the organisation operating within an area that is close to, or above, important water catchments or water tables? If it is near important aquifers, then the report should be clear about what efforts are being made to ensure that important water sources are not contaminated.
- Which reporting frameworks have been used to report the information, and are they the appropriate frameworks to be applied? For example, if the organisation has used the GRI framework, has it used the framework objectively, or has it decided only to disclose those items within the framework that project a favourable image of the organisation?
- Was the report subject to audit, or assurance, by an independent third party? If the audit or assurance report has been prepared by an audit/assurance firm that is known to have sound expertise and a good reputation, and if it provides an opinion that the information is correctly stated, then this will act to increase the confidence we have in the information being reported.

Social and environmental reporting has shown much growth since the 1990s, becoming a mainstream activity, particularly for larger organisations. Therefore, in our professional careers, we can expect to be exposed to this important focus of reporting. The reporting covered within this chapter is here to stay, and therefore accountants and managers need to be very well aware of it!

ANSWERS TO THE OPENING QUESTIONS

At the beginning of the chapter we asked the following four questions. As a result of reading this chapter, you should now be able to provide informed answers to these questions – ours are shown below.

1 What does 'corporate social responsibility' mean?

One commonly accepted definition of corporate social responsibility was provided by the Commission of European Communities, which describes CSR as:

> a concept whereby companies integrate social and environmental concerns in their business operations and in their interaction with their stakeholders on a voluntary basis. Being socially responsible means not only fulfilling legal expectations, but also going beyond compliance and investing more into human capital, the environment and the relations with stakeholders.
>
> Source: Commission of European Communities (2001), p. 6.

2 What is 'corporate social responsibility reporting'?

Corporate social responsibility reporting is reporting that provides evidence of how an organisation has addressed, and performed against, the social responsibilities it has identified itself as accepting. An organisation should be clear about what it identifies as its corporate social responsibilities.

3 What are some of the reasons why an organisation might produce a corporate social responsibility report?

There are many possible reasons why an organisation might produce a corporate social responsibility report, and these will not be mutually exclusive, meaning that there can be a mixture of reasons why managers might produce a report. These reasons include the following:

- because managers believe they have a responsibility to provide an account of their social and environmental performance to various stakeholders
- as a means of managing particular stakeholder groups
- because powerful stakeholders want or expect the information
- as a response to particular environmental or social crises
- as a means of assisting the identification of significant social and environmental risks and opportunities
- for competitive advantage
- to assist the financial performance of the organisation
- as a means of attracting and retaining quality staff
- to counter any moves by government to introduce more onerous social and environmental reporting requirements.

4 Are frameworks available that can guide the preparation of a corporate social responsibility report, and if so, what are some of them?

There are various reporting frameworks that can be used, including the Global Reporting Initiative's Sustainability Reporting Standards and the <IR> Framework.

SELF-TEST QUIZ

Answers to this quiz appear in the Appendix of this book.

1 What are some potential reasons that managers might elect to publicly disclose social and environmental information?

a As a response to negative news media attention

b Because they believe they have a responsibility to be accountable for various aspects of their social and environmental performance

c Because particular stakeholders demand it

d Because such disclosures might help create a positive reputation for the organisation and also help the financial performance of an organisation

e All of these choices

2 In this chapter we discussed the 'materiality determination process'. Which of the following is true in relation to this process?

- a The materiality determination process relates to the processes undertaken by organisations to guide them to determine what information they will disclose to stakeholders.
- b Not all organisations disclose information about their materiality determination process.
- c Information about the materiality determination process will help readers of reports understand why managers reported particular information.
- d The materiality determination process requires organisations to actively engage with stakeholders.
- e All of these choices.

3 Which of the following is not true in relation to climate change?

- a It is not managers' responsibility to explicitly consider climate change when planning organisational activities.
- b Many organisations are producing separate climate change reports, often referred to as climate change statements.
- c The performance of managers in some organisations is assessed in terms of performance indicators linked to climate change.
- d Stakeholders, including investors, are known to want information about the risks and opportunities that climate change poses to an organisation.
- e Climate change is one of the biggest problems confronting the planet.

4 Which of the following is true in relation to 'counter accounts'?

- a Counter accounts are also referred to as shadow or dialogic accounts.
- b Counter accounts represent the views of stakeholders other than management.
- c The production of counter accounts can help stimulate useful debate.
- d Counter accounts are produced to reflect the fact that different stakeholders will often have a different perspective of organisational performance to that of management.
- e All of these choices.

5 Which of the following is true in relation to independent third-party reviews of sustainability-related information?

- a All companies have their sustainability-related information assured by independent third parties.
- b The credibility of sustainability-related information is not enhanced as a result of an independent third-party review.
- c Managers will always be objective and therefore it is a waste of resources to employ the services of an assurance provider.
- d In most countries, more than 50 per cent of the top 100 companies now have their sustainability-related information subject to an independent review.
- e None of these choices.

ONLINE RESOURCES

Accompanying the book is an innovative online case study that follows an organisation initially established by two friends, which grows into a large and successful company. Acquire this chapter's case study from your instructor.

CASE STUDY

Armadillo Surf Designs: The moment of truth

Maddie, Archer and Dillon are considering what information they might provide to the public regarding the operations and performance of Armadillo Surf Designs (ASD). While ASD has performed well in some areas, there have been some instances of poor social and environmental performance.

You will discuss the factors that may motivate an organisation to report on social and environmental performance, as well as the potential benefits for ASD from reporting this information. You will identify items of information that ASD may report, the stakeholders who would be interested in this information, and the relevant GRI topic-specific disclosure, if applicable. You will also reflect on how your own system of values might influence the decisions you make in relation to the voluntary reporting of negative information.

END-OF-CHAPTER QUESTIONS

6.1 What does 'accountability' mean?

6.2 Explain the meaning of 'environmental reporting', and provide some examples of what information might be reported by way of environmental reporting.

6.3 Explain the meaning of 'social reporting', and provide some examples of what information might be reported by way of social reporting.

6.4 Provide some reasons why an organisation might report social and environmental information.

6.5 What is 'corporate social responsibility' and what is 'corporate social responsibility reporting'?

6.6 Will we all agree on what the social responsibilities of a particular organisation are? Why?

6.7 What is 'integrated reporting', and is it a good idea? Why?

6.8 What are some potential benefits for an organisation that might arise from releasing a CSR report?

6.9 Do you think that an increase in news media attention directed towards a particular social or environmental issue associated with an organisation will influence the reporting practices of that organisation? Why?

6.10 Should managers only produce a CSR report if doing so is expected to be beneficial to the shareholders (owners) of the organisation?

6.11 Identify three CSR/sustainability reporting frameworks. Which framework seems to be the one most commonly used by reporting entities?

6.12 Why do you think that, since the 1990s, there has been a significant increase in the proportion of organisations producing CSR reports?

6.13 The GRI Standards identify some reporting principles that should be followed in order to generate a quality report. What are they?

6.14 The GRI standards identify reporting principles for defining report content and reporting quality. What are they?

6.15 Does an organisation have an accountability to stakeholders that it does not directly interact with but who are affected indirectly by the organisation?

6.16 Do managers have a responsibility for reducing their organisation's contribution to climate change?

6.17 Is there a measurement framework available for measuring greenhouse gas emissions, and if so, what is it?

6.18 What are some of the risks and opportunities that climate change poses for business organisations? Should such risks and opportunities be disclosed by an organisation? Why?

6.19 Would you expect an organisation to publicly make climate change-related disclosures? Why?

6.20 What is modern slavery?

6.21 Do organisations have a responsibility for trying to eliminate modern slavery within their supply chains? Why?

6.22 Do you think that managers have an accountability for explaining what they are doing to address the risks that modern slavery exists within their supply chains? Why?

6.23 What are the UN Sustainable Development Goals (SDGs), and should managers of organisations pay any attention to them?

6.24 Should managers publicly disclose information about if, and how, their organisation is addressing the UN SDGS?

6.25 Why might an independent assurance report add value to a CSR report?

6.26 What is a counter account, and do you think it would be a good idea for the views of different stakeholders to be included in a sustainability report issued by a business organisation? Why?

6.27 How do managers determine whether particular information should be disclosed in a CSR report?

6.28 The evidence seems to indicate that organisations often change their reporting behaviour following major social or environmental crises. Why would they do this, and is this something that should concern us?

6.29 This chapter identified some potential limitations of the <IR> Framework. What are some of these limitations?

6.30 Organisations create a multitude of social and environmental impacts on various stakeholders. Realistically, not all impacts can be reported. A good CSR report will describe the processes an organisation undertook to determine what information will be reported and what will not be reported. This can be referred to as the materiality determination process. Why should an organisation clearly describe this process, and why would this description be useful for report readers?

6.31 Assume that you are the manager of a large organisation that has never produced a CSR report. It has been decided that the organisation will produce its first report and you have been placed in charge of outlining the steps that need to be undertaken to do so. In this regard, what are some initial factors that need to be considered in determining what aspects of social and environmental performance will be addressed within the CSR report?

6.32 In a document released by the global accounting firm EY, it was stated that:

European Commissioner Michel Barnier said, 'We can't afford to return to business as usual. We need to eliminate the short-termism that has dominated the corporate sector for too long'. He continued: 'Most importantly, the way these commitments are met should be made public and transparent. Transparency is part of the solution, not the problem. That's why non-financial reporting is such an important issue … it serves the interests of investors, shareholders, employees and society at large'.

Source: EY (2014), p. 18.

Evaluate the above statement.

6.33 KPMG warns that:

The small minority of companies not yet reporting will find themselves seriously out of step with global norms. This misalignment with accepted global practice in itself poses risks to non-reporting companies, but the leaders of these companies should also be aware that sustainability reporting cannot easily be solved overnight with a quick fix. Reporting methodologies and approaches are complex and dynamic, requiring deep professional knowledge and expertise and must be backed up with robust sustainability strategies and risk management processes. So, the advice to any company that has yet to start the sustainability reporting journey is to take it seriously and begin now. The laggards will soon be left behind.

Source: KPMG (2020), p. 9.

Why might ignoring sustainability impact upon an organisation's ability to remain in business in the long term?

6.34 Identify a large organisation that you know and are interested in, and provide some details of what social and environmental reporting information they are reporting, and how they are reporting it. For example, are they stating that they are applying any particular reporting frameworks or guidelines?

REFERENCES

ANZ Bank (2021). *2021 ESG Supplement: Shaping a world where people and communities thrive,* https://www.anz.com.au/content/dam/anzcom/shareholder/2021-esg-supplement.pdf

Association of Chartered Certified Accountants (2017). *Insights into integrated reporting: Challenges and best practice responses.* London: ACCA. www.accaglobal.com/an/en/technical-activities/technical-resources-search/2017/april/insights-into-integrated-reporting.html

ASX (2019). *Australian Securities Exchange's Corporate Governance Principles and Recommendations,* 4th edition, ASX, Sydney.

Australian Academy of Science (2015). *The science of climate change: Questions and answers.* www.science.org.au/files/userfiles/learning/documents/climate-change-r.pdf

Australian Corporations and Markets Advisory Committee (2006). *The Social Responsibility of Corporations.* Canberra: Australian Government.

BHP (2021). *Annual report 2021: The future is clear,* https://www.bhp.com/-/media/documents/investors/annual-reports/2021/210914_bhpannualreport2021.pdf?sc_lang=en&hash=15F0B58BC27ADFA860F0BE29B61E199D

Boiral, O. (2013). Sustainability reports as simulacra? A counter-account of A and A+ GRI reports. *Accounting, Auditing and Accountability Journal,* 26(7), pp. 1036–71.

Brown, J. (2009). Democracy, sustainability and dialogic accounting technologies: Taking pluralism seriously. *Critical Perspectives on Accounting,* 20, pp. 313–42.

Business for Social Responsibility (2020). *Five Steps to Good Sustainability Reporting: A Practical Guide for Companies.* www.bsr.org

Carbon Disclosure Project (2022). About us. www.cdp.net/en/info/about-us

Commission of European Communities (2001). Promoting a European Framework for corporate social responsibility. Green paper. Brussels: Commission of European Communities.

Commonwealth Bank (2017). *Corporate responsibility report 2017.* www.commbank.com.au/content/dam/commbank/about-us/shareholders/pdfs/corporate-responsibility/2017/2017-corporate-responsibility-report.pdf

Climate Reality Project, The (2022). www.climaterealityproject.org/truth

CPA Australia (2019). *Regulating transparency and disclosure on modern slavery in global supply chains: A conversation starter or a tick-box exercise?* CPA Australia, Melbourne.

Deegan, C., & Gordon, B. (1996). A study of the environmental disclosure policies of Australian corporations. *Accounting and Business Research*, 26(3), pp. 187–99.

Deegan, C., Rankin, M., & Tobin, J. (2002). An examination of the corporate social and environmental disclosures of BHP from 1983–1997: A test of legitimacy theory. *Accounting, Auditing & Accountability Journal*, 15(3), pp. 312–43.

Deegan, C., & Shelly, M. (2014). Corporate social responsibilities: Alternative perspectives about the need to regulate. *Journal of Business Ethics*, 121(4), pp. 499–526.

EY (2014). *Sustainability reporting: The time is now.* www.ey.com/Publication/vwLUAssets/EY_Sustainability_reporting_-_the_time_is_now/$FILE/EY-Sustainability-reporting-the-time-is-now.pdf

Friends of the Earth (2004). *Lessons not learned: The other Shell report.* https://friendsoftheearth.uk/sites/default/files/downloads/lessons_not_learned.pdf

Gilles, Shakes (2018). What is the greenhouse effect? *The Talking Democrat.* www.thetalkingdemocrat.com/2018/03/what-is-the-green-house-effect/

Global Reporting Initiative (2016). GRI 101: Foundation 2016. www.globalreporting.org/standards/media/1036/gri-101-foundation-2016.pdf

Global Reporting Initiative (2018a). Benefits of reporting. www.globalreporting.org/information/sustainability-reporting/Pages/reporting-benefits.aspx

Global Reporting Initiative (2018b). About sustainability reporting. www.globalreporting.org/information/sustainability-reporting/Pages/default.aspx

Global Reporting Initiative (2021a). Universal Standard – GRI 1: Foundation 2021. GRI, Amsterdam.

Global Reporting Initiative (2021b). Universal Standard – GRI 2: General Disclosures 2021. GRI, Amsterdam.

Global Reporting Initiative (2021c). Universal Standard – GRI 3: Material Topics 2021. GRI, Amsterdam.

Global Reporting Initiative (2021d). Sector Standard – GRI 11: Oil and Gas Sector 2021. GRI, Amsterdam.

Global Reporting Initiative (2022). A Short Introduction to the GRI Standards. https://www.globalreporting.org/media/wtaf14tw/a-short-introduction-to-the-gri-standards.pdf. GRI continuously works at maintaining the GRI standards up to date and therefore it is important for users of the Standards to check the latest information on our website, https://www.globalreporting.org.

Greenhouse Gas Protocol (2022). Corporate standard. https://ghgprotocol.org/corporate-standard

International Integrated Reporting Council (2021). The International <IR> Framework, January 2021. IIRC.

International Labour Organization (2017). Global estimates of modern slavery: Forced labour and forced marriage. ILO, Geneva.

Islam, M. A., & Deegan, C. (2010). Media pressures and corporate disclosure of social responsibility performance information: A study of two global clothing and sports retail companies. *Accounting and Business Research*, 40(2), pp. 131–48.

Islam, M. A., Deegan, C. & Gray, R. (2018). Social compliance audits and multinational corporation supply chain: evidence from a study of the rituals of social audits. *Accounting and Business Research*, 48(2), pp. 190–224.

KPMG (2017). The road ahead: The KPMG survey of corporate responsibility reporting 2017. https://assets.kpmg/content/dam/kpmg/xx/pdf/2017/10/kpmg-survey-of-corporate-responsibility-reporting-2017.pdf

KPMG (2020). The time has come: The KPMG survey of corporate responsibility reporting 2020. https://assets.kpmg/content/dam/kpmg/xx/pdf/2020/11/the-time-has-come.pdf

Sustainability Accounting Standards Board (2018a). *Automobiles: Sustainability accounting standard.* www.sasb.org/wp-content/uploads/2018/11/Automobiles_Standard_2018.pdf

Sustainability Accounting Standards Board (2018b). *Airlines: Sustainability accounting standard.* www.sasb.org/wp-content/uploads/2018/11/Airlines_Standard_2018.pdf

Task Force on Climate-related Financial Disclosures (TCFD) (2017). *CEO guide to climate-related financial disclosures.* World Business Council for Sustainable Development https://docs.wbcsd.org/2017/12/CEO_Guide_to_climate-related_financial_disclosure.pdf

United Nations Global Compact, The (2018). The ten principles of the UN Global Compact. www.unglobalcompact.org/what-is-gc/mission/principles

US Securities and Exchange Commission (2002). Commission statement about management's discussion and analysis of financial condition and results of operations. www.sec.gov/rules/other/33-8056.htm

US Securities and Exchange Commission (2008). Topic 9: Management's discussion and analysis of financial position and results of operations (MD&A). www.sec.gov/corpfin/cf-manual/topic-9

World Business Council for Sustainable Development (2006). Corporate social responsibility (CSR). http://old.wbcsd.org/work-program/business-role/previous-work/corporate-social-responsibility.aspx

World Commission on Environment and Development (1987). *Our Common Future (the Brundtland Report)*. Oxford University Press. www.un-documents.net/our-common-future.pdf

MODULE 4

ACCOUNTABILITY FOR FINANCIAL PERFORMANCE

CHAPTER 7

AN INTRODUCTION TO FINANCIAL ACCOUNTING

LEARNING OBJECTIVES

After completing this chapter, readers should be able to:

- **LO7.1** apply our accountability model to provide some insight into *why* organisations produce financial statements, and *who* might be considered the main readers of those financial statements. You will also be able to use our accountability model to explain *what* financial disclosures might be made, and *how* the information will be presented
- **LO7.2** explain how the separation of ownership and management of an organisation will in turn influence the need for financial statements
- **LO7.3** explain the objective of financial reporting
- **LO7.4** explain that financial statements typically provide information that is historical in nature, thereby reflecting the results of past transactions and events
- **LO7.5** describe some generally accepted accounting principles that are to be applied when performing financial accounting
- **LO7.6** identify some of the sources of regulation of financial reporting
- **LO7.7** explain the purpose of a conceptual framework for financial reporting
- **LO7.8** identify and explain the qualitative characteristics that useful financial accounting information is expected to possess
- **LO7.9** identify the five elements of financial accounting, and provide their respective definitions
- **LO7.10** understand the concept of 'profit' from a financial accounting perspective
- **LO7.11** explain the role of the 'accounting equation', understand the impact of business transactions on the accounting equation, and be able to summarise business transactions within a worksheet using this equation
- **LO7.12** prepare some relatively simple financial statements.

OPENING QUESTIONS

Before reading this chapter, please consider how you would answer the following three questions. We will return to these questions at the end of the chapter, where we suggest some answers.

1 What are the five elements of financial accounting?
2 Which elements of financial accounting are reported in the balance sheet, and which elements of financial accounting are reported in the income statement?
3 How is the balance of owners' equity determined, and what causes the balance of owners' equity to change during an accounting period?

Introduction

In this chapter, and the four chapters that follow, we will concentrate on the topic of 'financial accounting'. The practice of financial accounting involves the preparation and presentation of financial information for a variety of users, for the purposes of providing information about the financial performance and financial position of an organisation. This information might be used by financial statement readers to make decisions about where they will allocate their resources, and provide them with an indication of how well an organisation has been performing from a financial perspective. Financial accounting information is used by people within an organisation (for example, the managers), as well as by a variety of stakeholders that are external to an organisation.

The outputs of the financial accounting system are often referred to in various societal contexts. For example, we often read or hear about the 'profits' (or 'losses') of particular organisations. Indeed, when some of the larger organisations in our society (such as the large banks) disclose information about their profits for a particular year, this often makes headlines in various news media. Such profits are in turn often referred to as being 'good' or 'poor', and therefore financial accounting measures such as profits are often used within society as a measure of the *success* or *failure* of an organisation. Further, the reported profits of an organisation are often used by different groups to support particular arguments about an organisation. For example, labour unions might refer to the large reported profits of an organisation as justification for arguing that employees should be paid higher salaries. Alternatively, consumer groups might refer to large profits as a basis for arguing that an organisation can afford to drop the prices it is charging its customers for its goods or services. If profits are high, managers might also refer to the reported profits as a basis for arguing that the organisation is being well managed.

Because of the way in which financial accounting numbers are used throughout society, and because they do provide a basis for us to determine whether an organisation is being well managed from a financial perspective, and whether it is financially sound, then it is very important that we do have some knowledge of the financial accounting process. By reading this chapter, and the chapters that follow, you will have a greater understanding of how measures such as an organisation's 'profits', 'liabilities' and 'assets' are calculated.

LO7.1 Applying the accountability model to financial accounting

Returning to the general accountability model that we have used throughout this book, recall that it consists of four basic questions, these being '*Why report?*', '*To whom to report?*', '*What to report?*' and '*How to report?*'. Please refer back to **Figure 1.3** for a diagrammatic depiction of our four-step accountability model. We will consider each of these questions in turn as they relate to financial accounting.

Why disclose financial accounting information?

The most obvious answer here is that an extensive amount of regulation requires the disclosure of financial information about an organisation, in particular about larger organisations. Governments throughout the world typically require larger organisations to prepare what are often referred to as 'general purpose financial statements', which are financial statements prepared in compliance with the many accounting standards – which are also referred to as financial reporting standards – that currently exist. Governments impose this regulation so that those stakeholders with a financial interest in an organisation (such as shareholders, creditors and lenders) are more likely to receive reliable information about financial performance, and are therefore more able to adopt strategies that safeguard their financial interests – for example, if an organisation is not performing well financially, then one strategy that investors might adopt is to sell their investments in the organisation and move their funds to alternative investments. Further, governments typically want people to have confidence in capital markets, as this will support economic growth. Regulating the financial disclosures that larger organisations are required to make helps to promote investors' confidence in capital markets. Nevertheless, even without regulation, investors and other stakeholders with a financial interest in an organisation would still demand financial statements. Investors (owners) would demand financial statements that allow them to assess how well their funds are being used in terms of their investment aims (which might be high capital growth and the receipt of dividends), thereby effectively reducing the risks of the investment.

Receiving financial reports reduces the risks of those stakeholders with a financial interest in, or claim on, an organisation because the information provides a means of monitoring, on a periodic basis, the financial performance and position of the organisation, thereby assisting the stakeholders to assess, on an ongoing basis, the security of their financial interests in the organisation.

Financial accounting is also important for managers as it provides information that is useful for managing an organisation. Hence, it is again stressed that even in the absence of regulation we would still expect financial statements to be prepared, albeit they might be prepared in a multitude of ways. Indeed, history shows that financial statements were voluntarily prepared long before regulation required them – although in the absence of regulation, there was much variation in the reporting practices adopted by different organisations, thereby making comparisons (and therefore 'benchmarking') between organisations difficult.

Importantly, in the absence of producing externally available financial statements, organisations would find it very difficult to attract funds. Most of us would be reluctant to invest in an organisation, or loan funds to an organisation, if that organisation was not prepared to provide us with periodic reports on its financial position and financial performance. For example, a lender would want to know that the organisation to which it has loaned funds is in a financial position that enables it to ultimately repay the funds that have been borrowed.

To increase the perceived reliability of the information contained within financial statements, such statements are also generally accompanied by an audit report from a qualified, independent third party. The audit report provides an opinion about the information being presented, and in particular, whether it has been prepared in accordance with the accounting standards that have been issued by the accounting standard-setter with jurisdiction in that country. While typically required by regulation (particularly for larger organisations), financial statements were subjected to independent audits for many years prior to the introduction of legislation requiring them to be audited. The basis of this demand for auditing is that if we allow managers, and their appointed accountants, to prepare reports about their own financial performance, then at times the managers will possibly have incentives to manipulate those reports. This possibility of manipulation potentially reduces the perceived reliability we associate with financial statements. Therefore, to increase the perceived reliability of financial statements, the statements are subject to an audit by an independent third party.

Key concept

Stakeholders with a financial interest (or stake) in an organisation need information to assess the ongoing performance or risks associated with that investment. Even in the absence of regulation we would expect managers to provide information about financial performance and financial position, else managers will find it difficult or costly to attract funds.

To whom are the financial disclosures directed?

The primary audience of financial accounting information is generally considered to be current and potential investors, lenders and other creditors. Managers also use the information generated by the financial accounting system. Many other stakeholders also have an interest in the financial position, financial performance and cash flows of an organisation.

Employees, and their representatives such as labour unions, might also have an interest in knowing about an organisation's financial performance – to determine not only whether the organisation can continue to pay current salaries, but also whether it could, or *should*, pay higher salaries. Customers might also have an interest in the financial performance of an organisation; for example, if the organisation is earning large profits, then this might justify calls for price decreases for its goods or services. There are many other ways in which financial accounting assists the decisions made by different stakeholders.

What types of disclosures are made?

As we know, the types of disclosures to be made will be influenced by the expectations of the stakeholders to whom the information is being directed. Accounting standard-setters, such as the International Accounting Standards Board, do much research – often in conjunction with university-based accounting researchers – to determine what types of information the main users of financial reports (who are assumed to be investors, potential investors, lenders and other creditors) want, or need. Once an accounting standard-setter determines that particular information is justifiably needed by financial statement users, then the standard-setter will tend to initiate actions leading to the introduction of regulations in respect of that information.

Requirements for particular financial accounting disclosures will be incorporated within the accounting standards (which we shall also label as 'financial reporting standards') released by the standard-setters, and different financial accounting disclosure requirements might also be included within a country's securities exchange and corporations law requirements. We will consider some of these requirements throughout this and the following chapters.

How are disclosures made?

The format of the disclosures, and the medium for disclosures, also tend to be regulated (with respect to the general purpose financial statements being issued by larger organisations). For example, there are accounting standards that stipulate how to define, recognise, measure and disclose various transactions and events. Accounting standards also provide guidance about what types of financial statements will be prepared, and what information will be disclosed within the respective financial statements.

LO7.2 The separation of ownership from management, and the resulting need for regulation

Many people, as well as organisations, have large amounts of their wealth invested in organisations, yet they often have nothing to do with an organisation's ongoing management. For example, the shareholders of a large company typically have nothing to do with the management of the organisation, and they rely upon (or perhaps trust) managers to protect, and hopefully grow, the value of their investments. For example, we might have invested a great deal of our personal wealth in a company that is listed on a securities exchange. In doing so, we have become an owner (shareholder) of that company. However, we have no direct role in managing that company.

Apart from investors, there are also many individuals and organisations – which we might refer to as lenders and other creditors – who might be owed large amounts of money by organisations. For example, perhaps they sold merchandise or equipment to the organisation and the organisation has agreed to pay them at some future time. Or perhaps they have loaned the organisation money for which they are receiving interest income.

For some larger organisations, investors might have invested, in total, many millions or even billions of dollars. These same organisations might also owe millions, or even billions, of dollars to lenders and creditors. For example, the financial statements of the large electronics company Apple Inc. (which makes the iPhone and iPad you might be using) show that the total amount of liabilities at 25 September 2021 was $287 912 000 000, whilst the total amount of the shareholders' financial interests in the organisation (the owners' equity in the organisation) was $63 090 000 000.

To help assess the risk related to their investments, or the amounts due, stakeholders (for example, existing and potential investors, lenders and other creditors) will need, amongst other things, information about the ongoing financial performance and financial position of an organisation, and this is one of the central roles of financial accounting. For larger organisations, where there is a separation of ownership and management (or control) (see **Learning exercise 7.1**), and where there are large amounts of funds invested by shareholders (owners) and owed to lenders and creditors, a system is needed to ensure that the relevant people and organisations receive information about the security of their investments or loans. Because large organisations generate and disseminate so much wealth, governments throughout the world typically require financial statements to be produced on a regular basis – for example, yearly or half-yearly – and the regulations require that the financial statements be prepared and presented in accordance with particular rules or standards.

7.1 Learning Exercise

The separation of ownership and management

As discussed in Chapter 2, the separation of the ownership and management of a company means that those parties that own the company (the shareholders) often have little or nothing to do with the management of the company. The owners of the company are thus dependent upon receiving financial statements from the company in order to inform them as to how the managers have used the shareholders' funds.

What interest do owners have in the financial performance of a company?

Even if the owners of an organisation have nothing to do with its management, they will nevertheless have an interest in knowing about the financial performance and financial position of the organisation (and hopefully they will also have an interest in the social and environmental performance of an organisation, something that we have stressed throughout this book). The owners need financial information to enable them to evaluate whether their investment is secure and being properly managed, or whether it might be appropriate to withdraw those funds and invest elsewhere. Knowing about the financial performance also provides insight into whether dividend payments to owners will, or should, be made.

What implications does this separation of ownership and management have for the financial accounting practices being used by an organisation?

Where there is a separation of ownership and management, there will be an expectation that the managers of the organisation, in conjunction with their accountants, periodically prepare financial statements for the owners. If the organisation is large and has many owners, the expectation is that these financial statements and supporting notes cannot be expected to meet all the *specific* information needs of each individual owner, but they should nevertheless aim to *generally* meet most of the financial information needs of the owners.

Governments have traditionally embraced the view that organisations – particularly larger corporations – must demonstrate a high level of accountability in relation to their financial performance and financial position. Because of this perspective, minimum levels of disclosure have been legislated. That is, the managers of larger organisations cannot simply disclose what financial information they would prefer to disclose. We can contrast this with what we learned in Chapter 6, this being that disclosures of social and environmental performance are relatively unregulated (which in itself seems strange given that organisations arguably should be required to demonstrate a high level of responsibility, and accountability, for their significant social and environmental impacts).

For smaller organisations, which typically have less separation of ownership and management, there tends to be less financial reporting regulation (see **Learning exercise 7.2**). The reason for this is that there is a general view that those people with a financial stake in smaller organisations are expected to be able to access the information they want in order to monitor the financial position, and financial performance, of these organisations. They have relatively more *power* to demand the information they want or need and hence do not rely upon general purpose financial reports which are produced on a periodic basis.

7.2 Learning Exercise

The regulation of financial accounting

As discussed, the regulatory requirements in relation to how an organisation performs its financial accounting differ depending upon the size of the organisation. Consider the following two organisations:

Organisation A is a large public company with many thousands of shareholders.

Organisation B is a small printing company that has two owners and employs five people.

Which organisation would be expected to be subject to regulations in relation to how it performs its financial accounting, and why?

Organisation A

This organisation would be subject to regulation in relation to its financial accounting. As it is a large organisation, it would have many stakeholders who might have a significant financial interest in the organisation, but who would not have the necessary *power* to individually demand the financial information they need. Regulation effectively forces managers to make general purpose financial information available to such stakeholders.

Organisation B

This organisation would be subject to minimal regulatory requirements in relation to financial reporting, as it would be expected that those individuals with a significant financial interest in the organisation would be able to access the specific financial information they need or want. That is, they would be expected to have the necessary *power* (or influence) to obtain the particular information they require. Therefore, there would be relatively little need to regulate the financial reporting practices of Organisation B.

With the financial interests of investors, lenders and other creditors in mind, financial accounting is highly regulated with respect to the procedures to be used to generate general purpose financial statements. This can be contrasted to management accounting, which, as we noted in chapters 3 to 5, is quite unregulated because those people managing the business (the managers) are best able to determine what information (management accounting information) they need, or want, in order to manage the organisation.

The regulation of financial reporting helps to ensure that current financial statements are prepared in a way that is comparable with an organisation's previous financial statements, as well as with those of other organisations. Regulation should also restrict the ability of managers to manipulate the information they present to different stakeholders about the financial performance, and financial position, of an organisation. That is, regulation tends to restrict the choices the managers and financial accountants within an organisation have available to them with respect to when they might recognise, measure and present particular financial accounting information (see **Learning exercise 7.3**).

7.3 Learning Exercise

Regulation restricts the accounting methods available to an organisation

Scenario: As part of its business, Sandon Point Ltd – a large public company – has acquired some inventory (which we might also call *stock*) that it has purchased with the intention of selling at a profit. Specifically, it has bought 1 million sunhats for a cost of $10 each, which it believes it can sell for $25 each. Thus, these hats cost $10 million in total, but the amount of cash that they are expected to generate for the business when sold is $25 million.

Issue: What factors should be considered when determining how the value of these hats should be measured and reported?

Solution: Determining how inventory should be measured is dependent upon regulatory requirements. It is important to understand the implications of these requirements and why they are in place.

inventory
Represents assets held for sale in the ordinary course of business. Would also include materials or supplies to be consumed within the organisation's production processes, or in the process of providing services

To measure inventory at cost or market value? What are the regulatory requirements?

If a balance sheet was prepared straight after these hats were acquired (as we will show later in this chapter, and discuss in more depth in Chapter 9, a balance sheet shows the assets, liabilities and owners' equity of an organisation at a particular point in time), should we measure and report the hats at their cost of $10 million or their market value of $25 million?

Because inventory (stock) can be a very significant asset in many organisations, accounting regulators have for many years had a rule in place that requires inventory to be recorded at cost in a situation where the organisation believes the inventory can be sold for more than cost. Even though the managers of Sandon Point Ltd think they can generate $25 million for the hats, they are not allowed to present inventory at a value of $25 million. They would be required to measure inventory at $10 million. This is what the specific accounting standard requires (at the international level, the relevant accounting standard is IAS 2: Inventories, although for the purposes of this book you are not expected to remember the numbers of particular accounting standards). Again, please remember that accounting standards are typically only required to be adhered to by larger organisations, such that the management, and accountants, of smaller organisations might elect to measure inventory in a different manner for the purposes of disclosure within their financial reports.

Why do these regulations exist?

If managers were left with a choice as to how they could measure inventory, then some managers might choose 'cost', whilst others might choose 'market value'. This could create confusion, particularly if we are trying to compare the inventory balances of different organisations. Also, without regulation, managers within a single organisation might choose different approaches in different years, which would make it hard to compare the information provided in current financial statements with previous periods' financial statements.

What are the advantages and disadvantages of regulation?

As we will see in subsequent chapters, there are many financial reporting standards in place that relate to different types of assets (as well as to different types of liabilities, income and expenses) and that require specific measurement practices to be employed for the respective classes of assets. Regulation leads to some form of *standardisation* in financial accounting practice. This is often considered to be an advantage of regulation, but there are some people who believe that when you impose a regulation requiring all organisations to produce financial statements using the same accounting methods, it effectively creates a 'one size fits all' outcome. Hence, this stops managers from using accounting methods that they might actually believe better reflect the circumstances of their organisation, thereby introducing an element of inefficiency into financial reporting. We will not pursue this issue further here other than to note that whilst it is generally agreed that there are many advantages to having the high levels of regulation of financial reporting that we have, there are nevertheless many people who argue that financial reporting is too heavily regulated, and that this does not enable managers to exercise discretion in selecting alternative methods that might actually be more appropriate for their unique circumstances.

LO7.3 What is the objective of financial reporting?

The Conceptual Framework for Financial Reporting issued by the International Accounting Standards Board (and which we will hereafter simply refer to as the Conceptual Framework), which underwent a major revision in 2018, provides an internationally used framework for financial reporting (we consider the Conceptual Framework in more depth later in this chapter). In respect of the objective of financial reporting, the Conceptual Framework (paragraph 1.2) states:

> The objective of general purpose financial reporting is to provide financial information about the reporting entity that is useful to existing and potential investors, lenders and other creditors in making decisions relating to providing resources to the entity.
>
> Source: International Accounting Standards Board (2022a).

Given this objective, there is a perception that if financial reporting is undertaken properly, then it will enhance the 'decision usefulness' of the information being generated. That is, the reporting practices employed should provide information that is useful for making decisions – in particular, 'decisions about providing resources to the entity'.

As we have already stressed, for smaller organisations there are relatively fewer financial accounting regulations that are required to be followed. Smaller organisations still need to produce reports required by the taxation office (and the taxation office will impose particular measurement rules that an organisation must use when calculating its taxable profits) and other government regulators, but how they produce financial reports for other possible users (such as for shareholders and lenders) will be a choice the managers and accountants of the smaller organisations make. As we have already noted, this is justified on the basis that for smaller organisations there will be very few people with a significant financial interest in the organisation who do not have the power to access the necessary information to enable them to assess how well the organisation is being managed, or how secure their financial interest is. That is, people with a significant financial interest in smaller organisations will typically have the necessary information available to them for making the decisions they want to make, and they would not need regulation to direct the managers of an organisation to make this information available.

However, and as we have emphasised, as organisations get larger, and as the separation between ownership and management increases, and as the financial resources under the control of the management of the organisation increase, the regulation of financial reporting necessarily increases. The regulation increases because there will be many people whose only access to information will involve the general purpose financial statements being prepared by an organisation, and they will need to rely on this information to make their decisions, given they will not have access to other information within the organisation.

In the above discussion, we have made reference to 'general purpose financial statements'. We can say that the practice of financial accounting leads to the generation of what are known as either general purpose financial statements or special purpose financial statements. Let us now consider these two broad categories of financial statements in greater detail.

General purpose financial statements (GPFSs)

General purpose financial statements (GPFSs) include, for example, the balance sheet, income statement, statement of cash flows, and statement of changes in equity, each of which will be discussed later in greater detail. These general purpose financial statements comply with accounting standards and are intended to meet the information needs common to users of financial information who are unable to command the preparation of financial statements tailored to suit their own specific information needs. For example, the financial statements prepared by large companies listed on securities exchanges would be GPFSs. GPFSs are required to comply with accounting standards.

general purpose financial statements (GPFSs) Financial statements that comply with accounting standards and are intended for users of financial information who are unable to command the preparation of statements tailored to their specific information needs

For large public companies, there will be many thousands of people and organisations who have a financial interest in an organisation and who rely upon GPFSs as a source of information about the organisation. These different stakeholders – which might number in the many thousands – would be expected to have some differences in the types of information they need, and not all their individual information needs can realistically be met. However, it is expected that the financial statements and supporting notes being released by larger organisations, and which are subject to much regulation, will *generally* meet the information needs of such stakeholders. Hence, such financial statements are referred to as 'general purpose financial statements'. The expectation would be that the GPFSs satisfy the objective of financial reporting, as noted above.

Special purpose financial statements (SPFSs)

Special purpose financial statements (SPFSs) is the term used to describe the financial statements designed to meet the needs of a specific group of stakeholders, or to satisfy a specific purpose. For example, a bank might have the necessary *power* to demand a particular financial statement from a lender. SPFSs do not need to comply with accounting standards, and by referring to the financial statements as SPFSs, this actually signals that they do not comply with the accounting standards and other disclosure requirements typically required of larger organisations. Therefore, smaller organisations, with a relatively low level of separation of owners and managers, will generally issue SPFSs, and these do not need to comply with accounting standards.

special purpose financial statements (SPFSs) Financial statements designed to meet the needs of a specific group of stakeholders or to satisfy a specific purpose. Would not necessarily comply with accounting standards

We summarise the requirements for producing GPFSs in Figure 7.1.

FIGURE 7.1 The requirement to produce general purpose financial statements

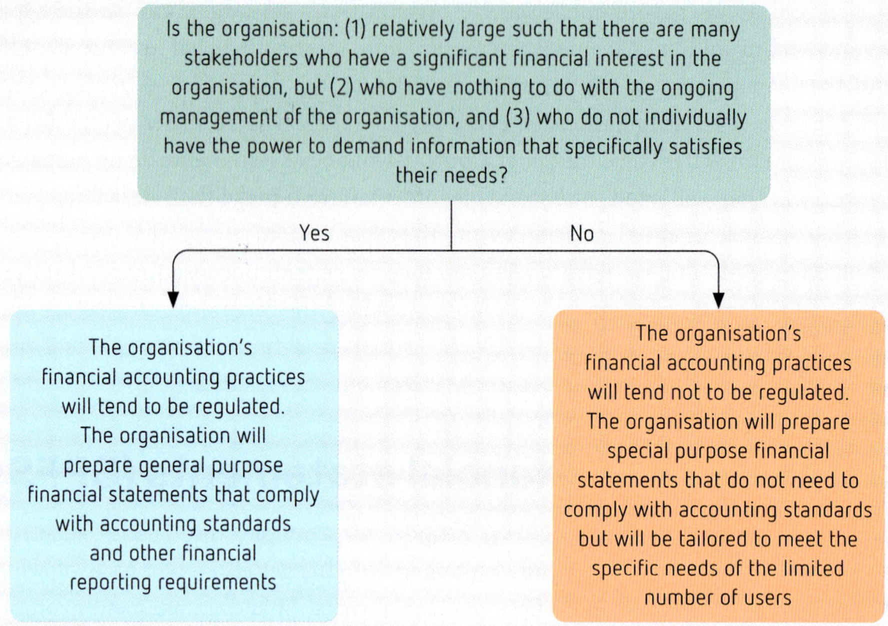

Why do I need to know about the meaning of general purpose financial statements and special purpose financial statements?

They are quite different types of financial statements. If we are told that a report is a general purpose financial statement then that signals that the financial statements are prepared in accordance with accounting standards and other required reporting regulations and that the financial statements have been prepared to generally satisfy a diverse group of stakeholders who generally have nothing to do with the management of the organisation. They are 'general purpose' documents. By contrast, if we are told that a report is a special purpose financial statement then that signals that the report has been prepared for a specific purpose and likely for a specific stakeholder (for example, a particular bank), and that the reports do not comply with accounting standards or any other disclosure regulation.

LO7.4 The historical nature of financial reports

For external reporting purposes, financial reporting tends to be historical in nature. That is, it provides the results for a past time period – for example, financial accounting provides information about:

- the profits or losses for the preceding year, which appear within the income statement (or as it is also known, the statement of profit or loss, or the statement of financial performance)
- the cash flows for the preceding year that appear within the statement of cash flows
- the assets, liabilities and owners' equity of the organisation as at a recently past date (the reporting date) and that appear within the balance sheet (or as it is also known, the statement of financial position).

We will explore each of these financial statements (the income statement, statement of cash flows, and the balance sheet) throughout this and the following chapters. Financial statements are also often accompanied by many pages of supporting notes (for large companies, these supporting notes can extend well beyond 100 pages).

Being historical in nature means that financial statements provide an indication of how management has used the funds provided to the organisation, and this is often considered to represent a **stewardship function**. Stewardship refers to the responsibilities accepted by managers for safeguarding the use of an organisation's funds in a way that best protects the interests of those stakeholders who advanced the funds.

stewardship function The responsibilities accepted by managers for safeguarding the use of an organisation's resources

Even though financial accounting generates information about past results (performance), this might also provide an indication of future performance. However, and somewhat obviously, just because an organisation has a history of reporting profits does not mean it will always be profitable.

Key concept

A basic purpose of financial accounting is to assist the managers of an organisation to perform their stewardship function and to be accountable to a group of stakeholders for how they have used the funds that have been entrusted to them.

LO7.5 Key financial accounting principles and terms

When preparing financial statements – and specifically GPFSs – there are some generally accepted accounting principles that govern the way in which financial accounting information is recorded and subsequently reported. These principles have been developed over many years and are generally accepted by accountants as representing appropriate practice. Apart from these accounting principles that guide how we record and report financial accounting information, there are also some qualitative characteristics that financial accounting information should possess if it is to be useful to the readers of financial statements. We will consider these qualitative characteristics later in this chapter.

Entity concept

Pursuant to the **entity concept**, the accountant is only to recognise transactions and events that affect the financial performance and/or position of the reporting organisation. The organisation is considered as being separate from the owners and other entities such that the personal transactions of the owners are to be kept separate from those of the organisation. For financial accounting purposes, an organisation is considered to be a separate entity and has its own identity, regardless of whether it is a sole trader, partnership or company. Impacts upon other organisations are ignored unless the event also impacts the resources, or financial obligations, of the reporting organisation. As we explained in Chapter 2, the 'reporting boundary' for financial reporting is restricted relative to other forms of reporting – such as various types of social and environmental reporting, which can have a broader reporting boundary. (See **Learning exercise 7.4** for more on the topic of the entity concept.)

entity concept Principle that requires that the transactions of an organisation be kept separate from the personal transactions of the owners of the organisation, and which considers the organisation to be separate to, or distinct from, other entities

7.4 Learning Exercise

Application of the entity concept

Applying the entity concept, consider the following transactions and determine which ones would be recognised within the financial accounts of an organisation.

The owner, who is a sole trader, contributes personal cash for use in the business

This transaction would be recognised within the financial accounts as it impacts the resources controlled by an organisation. Specifically, the cash controlled by the organisation would increase and the owner's equity in the business would also increase to reflect the investment the owner has made in the business.

The business uses the cash to buy some inventory (stock), which it hopes to sell for a profit

This transaction would be recognised within the financial accounts as it reflects a change in the types of resources being controlled by the organisation. Cash would decrease and inventory would increase.

The business pays management fees by way of a cash payment

This transaction would be recognised within the accounts as it impacts the resources controlled by the organisation. The cash controlled by the organisation would decrease and an expense of the organisation would be recognised.

The owner uses his own cash to purchase a new car for one of his children

This transaction would not be recognised. This is a transaction undertaken by the owner that has nothing to do with the business – it is deemed to be outside of the reporting entity and does not impact the resources or financial obligations of the organisation. It is therefore ignored for financial accounting purposes.

Accounting period convention

Whilst the life of an organisation might be indefinite, an accountant nevertheless determines the financial performance of the organisation for smaller periods of time – for example, for six or 12 months, or some other arbitrary period of time. This period of time is referred to as the **accounting period**. It can also be referred to as the *reporting period*.

accounting period
The timespan over which managers elect to report the transactions or events that affect the organisation. It is an established period of time in which accounting functions are performed, and where the results of transactions are aggregated, and analysed.

Breaking up the life of an organisation into smaller periods of time is necessary in order to be able to devise indicators for how well, or otherwise, the organisation is performing (one indicator might be the profits for the period). It would not make sense to wait until the organisation ceases to operate, which might, for example, be 50 years after it started, before we work out the total returns/profits that have been generated by the organisation.

While it is understandable that we need to create separate accounting periods, separating the life of a business into relatively short periods of time can create a variety of potentially dysfunctional effects, as will be discussed in the following chapters. Briefly, the problem is that, by being required to calculate profits for smaller periods of time (such as a year), managers might undertake activities that are aimed at maximising profits in the short run, but which might not be in the interests of the organisation's long-term objectives.

For example, if an organisation is close to making a loss (meaning its expenses are greater than its income) for a particular accounting period (perhaps 12 months), and if it has a choice about whether to undertake some necessary ongoing maintenance of its equipment near the end of the accounting period (which would create an expense), then it might elect not to because the maintenance expense could ultimately cause the organisation to report a loss for the period. Managers typically prefer not to report 'losses'. So, as a result of focusing on profits for 12 months, the managers might defer the necessary maintenance, thereby improving short-term profitability, but in the long run perhaps damaging the organisation's equipment, thereby impacting a future period's profits. Deferring the necessary maintenance might also create various adverse social effects given that the equipment might not be as safe to use as it should be. Thus, the way in which we divide the life of an organisation (which might be many decades or more) into relatively short time periods can encourage managers to focus on the short term rather than the long term. This can be further compounded if managers are paid bonuses that are linked to each year's profits – something that is actually very common.

Key concept

Dividing the life of an organisation into short time periods can encourage managers to focus on the short term rather than the long term.

Monetary unit convention

The practice of financial accounting typically only recognises transactions or events if a related monetary value can be assigned to those transactions or events. The measurement unit to be used is generally the currency of the country in which the organisation is operating. The requirement, or convention, that only those transactions or events that can be measured in financial terms shall be recognised for financial accounting purposes also creates some dysfunctional effects that we will consider elsewhere in this book. However, as an example, many social and environmental impacts created by an organisation cannot easily be measured in monetary terms, and therefore the related 'costs' do not get recognised in the financial statements. The implication is that they often then get ignored (and not managed) such that a profitable company might also be one that creates many unrecognised, and therefore unreported, social and environmental impacts.

For example, if an organisation releases many thousands of tonnes of CO_2 into the atmosphere (which, as we learned in Chapter 6, contributes to climate change) but is not required to pay any related taxes (such as carbon taxes), or any fines, then it is generally considered too hard, or even inappropriate within financial accounting, to place a monetary cost on the emissions. The result is that the failure to be able to measure the emissions (and the resulting contribution to climate change) in monetary

Source: Shutterstock.com/TTstudio

If emissions aren't taxed, they are generally not reported in financial accounting, and the (environmental) cost is often overlooked.

terms means that the related costs do not appear in the organisation's financial statements. This means that the emissions will often simply be ignored – particularly if the organisation is one that focuses primarily on financial performance, rather than also trying to manage social and environmental performance.

Going concern assumption

going concern
An assumption that an organisation will be able to continue to operate in the normal way for the foreseeable future

An organisation that is a **going concern** is one that is considered likely to continue operating into the foreseeable future, and without the likelihood of encountering any problems that could result in the organisation being wound up/discontinued. Unless there is evidence to the contrary, the financial accountant typically assumes that an organisation (the accounting entity) will continue operating into the foreseeable future. This has various implications for how assets, liabilities, income and expenses are measured.

For example, an organisation might have acquired, or had constructed, some very specialised equipment at a cost of, say, $2 million. Due to its specialised nature, the equipment might not be easily sold to other organisations, and it will only create value by being used by the one particular organisation that controls it. The specialised equipment has value to the extent that the organisation can use it over future years; that is, it has value to the extent that the organisation remains a going concern. However, if the organisation is not a going concern, perhaps meaning that it is likely to cease operations very soon, then perhaps the specialised equipment has very little value to any other organisation, other than as scrap. So, if we no longer assume that an organisation is a going concern, then we will need to measure equipment at scrap value, or liquidation value, and not at cost.

liquidation values
The amounts that an organisation would expect to receive from a quick sale of its assets

The general principle is that if it is considered that an organisation is not a going concern (for example, the organisation does not appear able to pay its debts as and when they fall due, and therefore is likely to be wound up), then financial statements have to be prepared on another basis – for example, on the basis of **liquidation values**. Liquidation values represent the amounts that an organisation would expect to receive from a quick sale of its assets. As the Conceptual Framework (paragraph 3.9) states:

> Financial statements are normally prepared on the assumption that the reporting entity is a going concern and will continue in operation for the foreseeable future. Hence, it is assumed that the entity has neither the intention nor the need to enter liquidation or to cease trading. If such an intention or need exists, the financial statements may have to be prepared on a different basis. If so, the financial statements describe the basis used.
>
> Source: International Accounting Standards Board (2022a).

For more on the application of the going concern assumption, see **Learning exercise 7.5**.

Key concept

A going concern is an organisation that is considered likely to continue operating into the foreseeable future. Unless advised otherwise, we can assume that financial statements are prepared on the basis that an organisation is considered to be a going concern.

7.5 Learning Exercise

Application of the going concern assumption

Scenario: Company A has acquired some custom-made machinery at a cost of $2 500 000. The machinery has the capacity to be used for the next 15 years and can produce products that, in total, will generate income well in excess of the cost of the machine. If the machinery was required to be sold (instead of being used within the organisation), it would only be sold for $10 000, which is its scrap value, as no other organisations can use such machinery.

Issue: Is it appropriate to record the machinery at cost if it becomes apparent that the organisation is unlikely to be able to pay its debts as and when they fall due, and therefore is likely to cease operations in the near future?

Solution: In this instance, Company A no longer appears to be a going concern. That is, it does not appear that this organisation will continue operating into the foreseeable future. The implication of this is that the assets should be measured at the amounts that the organisation would expect to receive from the sale of the assets in the short run. Therefore, it is no longer appropriate to record the machinery at its cost. Instead, the machinery should be measured at the amount that would be expected from a quick sale, which in this case would be $10 000.

Accrual basis of accounting

Financial accounting reports are generally prepared on what is known as an **accrual basis**. This means, for example, that income is recognised when it is earned (which is not necessarily when the related cash is ultimately received), and expenses are recognised as the expense is incurred or consumed (which is not necessarily at the same time as the related cash payment is made). Accrual accounting can be contrasted with cash accounting, which is undertaken on a *cash basis*, whereby transactions and events are only recorded if they affect cash (that is, if they result in a cash inflow or cash outflow). The difference between accrual accounting and cash accounting will become clearer as we proceed through the following chapters. In the absence of evidence to the contrary, we can assume that financial reports have been prepared on an accrual basis.

accrual basis
Under the accrual basis of accounting, income is recognised as it is earned, not necessarily when the related money is actually received, and expenses are recognised when they are incurred which is not necessarily when they are paid

For examples of the difference between accrual and cash accounting, see Learning exercise 7.6.

7.6 Learning Exercise

Some examples of the difference between accrual accounting and cash accounting

Let us consider the following transactions and how they might be accounted for under both a cash basis of accounting and an accrual basis of accounting.

1 An organisation provides consulting services in exchange for a customer's promise to pay in two weeks.

2 An organisation has employed some people for three days to work on a special project, but they have not yet been paid.

Cash basis of accounting

Under the cash basis of accounting, the organisation would not recognise either transaction as there has been no movement of cash. This means that although the organisation has effectively earned some income, and incurred some expenses (which together will impact profits under an accrual basis of accounting), because no cash has been received or paid, the recognition of transactions would be deferred until such time as the related cash flows occur.

Accrual basis of accounting

Under the accrual basis of accounting, which is an approach to financial accounting generally used by most organisations, both transactions would be recognised as they occur. In relation to the consulting services, the income would be recognised when the service is provided to the customer, and the claim to cash (which would represent an accounts receivable) would be considered an asset of the organisation.

The wages payable in respect of the special project would be recognised as an expense when the employees provide the service, and the amount owing to the workers would be considered as a liability of the organisation until such time that the workers are paid.

Key concept

Accrual accounting is adopted by most organisations and means that income is recognised when it is earned, and expenses are recognised when they are incurred. This can be quite different to when the related cash flows ultimately occur.

Why do I need to know about the various financial accounting principles and conventions?

As we have just learned, there are a number of principles that financial accountants apply when producing general purpose financial statements, including the entity concept, accounting period convention, monetary unit convention, going concern assumption, and accrual accounting. If we want to understand what the financial accounting numbers represent, and given the numbers are generated by applying these principles, then it makes sense that we need to understand what these principles represent.

LO7.6 Sources of accounting standards

We have mentioned accounting standards/financial reporting standards a number of times already in this chapter. Simply stated, an accounting standard is a technical pronouncement that sets out the required accounting procedures for particular types of transactions and events, and therefore affects the preparation, and presentation, of an organisation's financial statements. As you already appreciate, accounting standards are generally required to be followed by larger organisations.

There are two major accounting standard-setters in the world: the International Accounting Standards Board (IASB), and the US Financial Accounting Standards Board (FASB).

IASB standards

Once upon a time, many countries throughout the world developed their own accounting standards, and some still have their own financial accounting standard-setting bodies. However, since the mid-2000s, the majority of countries throughout the world have used the accounting standards developed by the IASB, an organisation located in London. For example, within Australia, the Australian Accounting Standards Board (AASB) uses the accounting standards released by the IASB, but it rebadges and then releases them as the accounting standards of the AASB. Like many other national accounting standard-setters, the AASB has also developed and released a limited number of additional accounting standards (that is, in addition to those that come from the IASB), where there is a belief that specific guidance is currently needed but the particular issue is not being addressed by the IASB. However, in a country like Australia, the large majority of accounting standards being used for financial reporting purposes were developed by the IASB.

The IASB refers to its standards as the International Financial Reporting Standards (IFRS). According to the website of the IASB (accessed July 2022):

> Our mission is to develop IFRS Standards that bring transparency, accountability and efficiency to financial markets around the world. Our work serves the public interest by fostering trust, growth and long-term financial stability in the global economy.
>
> IFRS Standards bring transparency by enhancing the international comparability and quality of financial information, enabling investors and other market participants to make informed economic decisions.
>
> IFRS Standards strengthen accountability by reducing the information gap between the providers of capital and the people to whom they have entrusted their money. Our Standards provide information needed to hold management to account. As a source of globally comparable information, IFRS Standards are also of vital importance to regulators around the world.
>
> IFRS Standards contribute to economic efficiency by helping investors to identify opportunities and risks across the world, thus improving capital allocation. Use of a single, trusted accounting language lowers the cost of capital and reduces international reporting costs for businesses.
>
> IFRS Accounting Standards are currently required in more than 140 jurisdictions and permitted in many more.
>
> Source: International Accounting Standards Board (2022b).

Countries that use IFRS are identified at **www.ifrs.org/use-around-the-world/use-of-ifrs-standards-by-jurisdiction**. These countries include Australia, Brazil, China, Denmark, Egypt, Fiji, France, Germany, India, Indonesia, Japan, Malaysia, New Zealand, the Philippines, Russia, Singapore, South Africa, Sweden, Thailand, the United Kingdom and Vietnam. The accounting standards cover a variety of issues, and the number of standards on issue has grown significantly across the years. That is, general purpose financial reporting has become increasingly regulated. For a list of the various accounting standards issued by the IASB, visit the organisation's website (**www.ifrs.org/issued-standards/list-of-standards**).

You might also like to refer to a short video on the role of the IASB (**www.ifrs.org/about-us**).

FASB standards

The other major accounting standard-setter in the world is the FASB. For a number of years, it did seem that the United States would also adopt IFRS, but this has not happened – the US still uses its own financial reporting standards, which are developed by the FASB. These accounting standards are very similar to those of the IASB. Whilst US organisations are required to use the accounting standards developed by the FASB, foreign companies operating within the US, and listed on the US Securities Exchange, are permitted to use IFRS within the country.

The enforcement of accounting standards

One interesting point to note is that accounting standard-setters such as the IASB have no direct legal power to enforce their accounting standards. Rather, it is up to the governments in each country to enforce compliance through that nation's corporations legislation. For example, local accounting standard-setters typically adopt the accounting standards issued by the IASB (they might also develop some local accounting standards), and then the respective national government, through its own corporations legislation, will require that certain types of organisations (for example, large companies) must comply with the accounting standards or else suffer some sanctions. Organisations that are listed on securities exchanges, such as large public companies, will also need to comply with the disclosure requirements of the respective securities exchange on which they are listed.

It is often argued that because different countries adopt IFRS (that is, the same accounting standards), this will lead to global consistency in financial reporting. However, this is a naive perspective, albeit one that is embraced by the IASB. There will be global uniformity in accounting practices only when governments, and financial statement auditors, ensure that claims that the IFRS are being properly applied can actually be checked, and enforced. The reality is that many governments throughout the world do very little to ensure that accounting standards are properly applied by the organisations within their countries, the result being that the financial statements in many countries are not really complying with the IFRS, despite the respective governments' claims. Therefore, we need to appreciate that we have to be careful in assuming that all countries that say their organisations are using IFRS are actually doing so. As Ball states:

> Does anyone seriously believe that implementation will be of an equal standard in all the countries that have announced adoption of IFRS in one way or another? The list of adopters ranges from countries with developed accounting and auditing professions and developed capital markets (such as Australia) to countries without a similarly developed institutional background (such as Armenia, Costa Rica, Ecuador, Egypt, Kenya, Kuwait, Nepal, Tobago and Ukraine). Even within the EU, will implementation of IFRS be at an equal standard in all countries? The list includes Austria, Belgium, Cyprus, Czech Republic, Denmark, Germany, Estonia, Greece, Spain, France, Ireland, Italy, Latvia, Lithuania, Luxembourg, Hungary, Malta, Netherlands, Poland, Portugal, Slovenia, Slovakia, Finland, Sweden and the UK. It is well known that uniform EU economic rules in general are not implemented evenly, with some countries being notorious standouts. What makes financial reporting rules different? ...
>
> Substantial international differences in financial reporting quality are inevitable, and my major concerns are that investors will be misled into believing that there is more uniformity in practice than actually is the case and that, even to sophisticated investors, international differences in reporting quality now will be hidden under the rug of seemingly uniform standards.
>
> Source: Ball (2006), p. 16.

In subsequent research undertaken by Ball (Ball, 2016), his concerns had not diminished. Ball (2016) raises further issues associated with the ongoing international differences in reporting within countries claiming to adopt IFRS. He notes:

> One potential effect is dilution of the IFRS brand name. Another is that a uniform IFRS label discards information about reporting quality differences.

Ball (2016) also raises other concerns relating to having a centralised accounting standards setting body. One concern is the possible implications for reducing innovation in reporting. As he states (p. 556):

> Competition among alternative economic systems, including financial reporting systems, is conducive to healthy innovation. History is replete with examples of one system learning from the institutional structure of a competing system, the most famous example in accounting being the near worldwide adoption of the Italian method of double entry bookkeeping .... In my view, adopting uniform worldwide standards invites risky centralisation and reduced innovation.

Therefore, whilst financial accounting might appear to be subject to regulation, this ultimately – and somewhat obviously – depends upon the extent to which the application of the regulation is actually monitored, and enforced, within a particular country.

Why do I need to know about the regulation of financial accounting?

If we have an interest in the practice of financial accounting then it makes sense that we should have understanding about if, and how, that practice is regulated.

LO7.7 The role of the Conceptual Framework for Financial Reporting

We have already briefly referred to the Conceptual Framework for Financial Reporting. It sets out the concepts that underlie the preparation and presentation of GPFSs. Effectively, it provides the basic structure for financial reporting.

Organisations operating within countries that use IFRS (the accounting standards issued by the IASB) are also required to apply the Conceptual Framework for Financial Reporting developed by the IASB. The Conceptual Framework provides the underlying framework for general purpose financial reporting without going into specific details about how particular assets, liabilities, income or expenses will be measured and presented. That is, it provides 'high-level' guidance. Specific details about how to account for particular types of assets, liabilities, income or expenses tend to be incorporated within financial reporting standards.

For example, if we want to know how to account for inventory we go to the accounting standard on inventories (IAS 2: Inventories); if we want to know how to account for the liabilities and assets associated with leases, we go to the accounting standard on leases (IFRS 16: Leases); if we want to know how to account for shares acquired in other organisations, we go to the accounting standard on financial instruments (IFRS 9: Financial Instruments); and if we want to know how to account for payments made to employees, then we go to the accounting standard on employee benefits (IAS 19: Employee Benefits). We could give many more such examples, but the point is that there are many accounting standards that deal with specific types of transactions and events. By contrast, the Conceptual Framework provides guidance that has general applicability to general purpose financial reporting.

A central goal in developing a conceptual framework is to establish consensus on key issues such as:

- the *scope* and *objective* of financial reporting
- the *qualitative characteristics* that all financial information should possess
- what the *elements* of financial reporting are, including consensus on the characteristics, and recognition criteria for assets, liabilities, income, expenses and equity.

The Conceptual Framework also serves a number of other purposes, including the following:

- It acts as a frame of reference when the IASB (and other accounting standard-setters) develops new accounting standards and other reporting guidance.
- It is a useful reference for account preparers and auditors when there is no specific accounting standard that addresses a particular issue.
- It is useful to financial statement users when trying to understand and interpret the financial reports they are reviewing.

A useful introduction to conceptual frameworks is provided here: **https://www.youtube.com/watch?v=v56_VJkjAX4**

LO7.8 Qualitative characteristics of financial accounting information

We previously described some generally accepted accounting principles that financial accountants are expected to adopt when preparing financial statements, these being the entity concept, the accounting period convention, the monetary unit convention, the going concern assumption, and accrual accounting. Apart from these generally accepted accounting principles, and with the goal of satisfying the objective of general purpose financial reporting (which, as we know, is identified within the Conceptual Framework as providing useful information to those stakeholders considering providing resources to an entity), the Conceptual Framework identifies a number of qualitative characteristics that financial information should possess.

You will see that these qualitative characteristics (discussed below) are very similar to other qualitative characteristics identified by other reporting frameworks that we have already covered within this book, such as those developed by the Global Reporting Initiative, the Task Force on Climate-related Financial Disclosures, the International Sustainability Standards Board, and the Water Accounting Standards Board (all discussed in Chapter 6).

The qualitative characteristics of financial information are classified as being either 'fundamental' or 'enhancing'. Fundamental qualitative characteristics are deemed to be the most important, while enhancing qualitative characteristics are assumed to be likely to enhance the usefulness of information that is both relevant and faithfully represented. The qualitative characteristics will now be considered in more depth.

Fundamental qualitative characteristics

Relevance

The first of two fundamental qualitative characteristics of financial reporting as identified within the Conceptual Framework is *relevance*. Under the Conceptual Framework, information is regarded as relevant if it is considered capable of influencing the decisions of users of the financial statements. Specifically, the Conceptual Framework (paragraph 2.6) states:

> Relevant financial information is capable of making a difference in the decisions made by users. Information may be capable of making a difference in a decision even if some users choose not to take advantage of it or are already aware of it from other sources.
>
> Source: International Accounting Standards Board (2022a).

Relevant information is also expected to have predictive value and/or confirmatory value. That is, it should have some use for predicting future events (such as the profit of the next period) and/or for confirming past events (for example, establishing last year's profits, and whether the profits were as previously expected). If information is considered to be relevant, then the implication is that it should be reported (subject to the information providing a faithful representation of the underlying transaction or event – see below).

Faithful representation

The other primary qualitative characteristic, as identified in the Conceptual Framework, is **faithful representation** (a similar term used in other reporting frameworks is *reliability*). The view taken by accounting standard-setters is that, to be useful, information needs to not only represent the relevant phenomena, but to do so faithfully. According to the Conceptual Framework (paragraph 2.13):

faithful representation Information is faithfully represented when it is complete, neutral, and free from error; the characteristic of faithful representation is similar to the concept of reliability

> To be a perfectly faithful representation, a depiction would have three characteristics. It would be complete, neutral and free from error. Of course, perfection is seldom, if ever, achievable. The Board's objective is to maximise those qualities to the extent possible.
>
> Source: International Accounting Standards Board (2022a).

Ideally, financial information should be both relevant and representationally faithful (**Learning exercise 7.7**). However, it is possible for information to faithfully represent an underlying transaction or event (and remember, the term 'faithfully represent' is very similar to the idea of 'reliability') but not be very relevant, or the other way around. Such information would, in this case, not be deemed to be 'useful', as it is expected that useful information would have both characteristics. As the Conceptual Framework states:

> Information must be both relevant and provide a faithfull representation of what it purports to represent if it is to be useful. Neither a faithful representation of an irrelevant phenomenon nor an unfaithful representation of a relevant phenomenon helps users make good decisions.
>
> Source: International Accounting Standards Board (2022a).

7.7 Learning Exercise

A consideration of potentially relevant and representationally faithful information

Assume you are the chief accountant for Surf Coast Company, which is listed on a securities exchange and has over $500 million in assets. Consider the following three items of information and determine whether they should be separately disclosed within the company's financial statements. In doing so, you should consider both the *relevance* of the information as well as issues to do with the *faithful representation* of the financial information.

Information item 1

The company purchased $70 million of inventory (many luxury cars) which it intended to sell to customers at a good profit. However, the company's large storage facility has just been flooded and the managers of Surf Coast Company are not sure whether the cars are permanently damaged or not, nor do they really know the extent of the damage. They are hoping that they will still be able to sell the cars for at least their purchase price of $70 million. They are going to attribute a value of $70 million to the cars within the financial statements.

Information item 2

The company acquired a new printer for $3000. The price is clearly shown on the related purchase invoice, which has been paid.

Information item 3

The company has some land that has a current fair value of $65 million. This fair value was very recently determined by two separate, reputable and independent property valuers.

Solution

We will consider each of these items in turn. In relation to item 1, clearly this inventory of luxury cars cost the organisation a lot of money, and it is important to the company, and to its stakeholders, that these cars can still be sold for at least their cost. Therefore, given the magnitude of the amount involved, the realisable value of these cars after the flood would be very relevant to readers of the financial statements. However, the amount of $70 million might not provide a faithful representation of the cars' actual value, as the managers of the company really do not know the extent of damage. Therefore, it would *not* be appropriate for the company to report a value of $70 million for the cars. Whilst the test of relevance has been satisfied, the amount being disclosed is potentially not reliable and does not appear to pass the test of being representationally faithful. Some further investigation needs to be undertaken so that a reliable value can be attributed to the cars. It would not be appropriate to let the readers of the financial statements make decisions based on information that is considered relevant but which is not representationally faithful.

In relation to item 2 (the printer), it really would not matter whether details of this asset are separately disclosed or not. The company has $500 million of assets, so interested readers of the financial statements really do not need to know about the existence of a $3000 printer. It simply is not relevant. Therefore, although the amount attributed to the asset might be reliable and faithfully represent the underlying transaction, because the information is not very relevant, separate disclosure is *not* required.

In relation to item 3 (the land), given the magnitude of the amount attributed to the land, readers of the financial statements do need to know about this asset. That is, land worth $65 million is very relevant in the context of this organisation. Because two qualified valuers have independently determined the same valuation, then $65 million would also seem to faithfully represent the current fair value. Therefore, the amount attributed to the asset meets the tests of relevance and representational faithfulness and should be separately disclosed.

So the lessons here are that if information is likely to be both relevant and representationally faithful, then it should be disclosed because it is likely to influence the decisions of those people reading the information. Some professional judgement is required in assessing whether the information satisfies these fundamental qualitative characteristics.

If information is not considered to be relevant, then it need not be disclosed, regardless of whether or not it is representationally faithful. If information is relevant but is not considered to be representationally faithful, then it potentially could be misleading and should not be disclosed (unless action is taken to help ensure it is faithfully represented).

Enhancing qualitative characteristics

Apart from the above two fundamental qualitative characteristics of relevance and faithful representation, which are deemed to be the most important qualitative characteristics, there are also four enhancing qualitative characteristics referred to within the Conceptual Framework. The perspective taken is that the usefulness of financial accounting information that satisfies the primary qualitative characteristics of relevance and representational faithfulness will be further *enhanced* if the information is also able to satisfy the characteristics of comparability, verifiability, timeliness and understandability.

As the Conceptual Framework states:

> Comparability, verifiability, timeliness and understandability are qualitative characteristics that enhance the usefulness of information that both is relevant and provides a faithful representation of what it purports to represent.
>
> Source: International Accounting Standards Board (2022a).

We will now consider each of these four enhancing characteristics.

Comparability

In relation to the enhancing qualitative characteristic of *comparability*, to facilitate the comparison of the financial statements of different entities (and that of the financial statements of a single entity over time), methods of measurement and disclosure should be consistent but can be changed if no longer relevant to an entity's circumstances.

Verifiability

In relation to the enhancing qualitative characteristic of *verifiability*, the Conceptual Framework (paragraph 2.30) states:

> Verifiability helps assure users that information faithfully represents the economic phenomena it purports to represent. Verifiability means that different knowledgeable and independent observers could reach consensus, although not necessarily complete agreement, that a particular depiction is a faithful representation. Quantified information need not be a single point estimate to be verifiable. A range of possible amounts and the related probabilities can also be verified.
>
> Source: International Accounting Standards Board (2022a).

Timeliness

If the collection of information spans too long a period, it can become no longer relevant. The more *timely* (or up-to-date) that financial information is, the more useful it will be. As the Conceptual Framework (paragraph 2.33) states:

> Timeliness means having information available to decision-makers in time to be capable of influencing their decisions. Generally, the older the information is the less useful it is. However, some information may continue to be timely long after the end of a reporting period because, for example, some users may need to identify and assess trends.
>
> Source: International Accounting Standards Board (2022a).

Understandability

The fourth and final enhancing qualitative characteristic is *understandability*, the view being that for information to be useful, it needs to be understandable to the users. In the Conceptual Framework, information is considered understandable if it is likely to be understood by users with some business and accounting knowledge. Issues of understandability require judgements to be made about the capabilities of financial statement users.

Why do I need to know about qualitative characteristics that useful financial accounting should possess?

If we find ourselves in a role that requires us to prepare financial information about an organisation, then we should always keep in mind the qualitative characteristics – both fundamental and enhancing – that information should possess. We should attempt to maximise the extent to which these qualitative characteristics have been applied to the information we are producing. As readers of financial reports – particularly general purpose financial reports – it is also useful for us to be aware of the factors (including the qualitative characteristics) that did, or should have, influenced the preparers of the financial information we are reading.

Overview of the qualitative characteristics

The qualitative characteristics of general purpose financial reporting are summarised in **Figure 7.2**. What this figure seeks to demonstrate is that the fundamental qualitative characteristics are the first characteristics that typically need to be considered. Once those characteristics have been established as potentially existing for particular information, then the relevance and/or faithful representation of financial information can be further enhanced by considering issues associated with comparability, verifiability, timeliness and understandability. Efforts to increase the comparability, verifiability, timeliness and understandability of the financial information

FIGURE 7.2 An overview of the qualitative characteristics of useful financial information

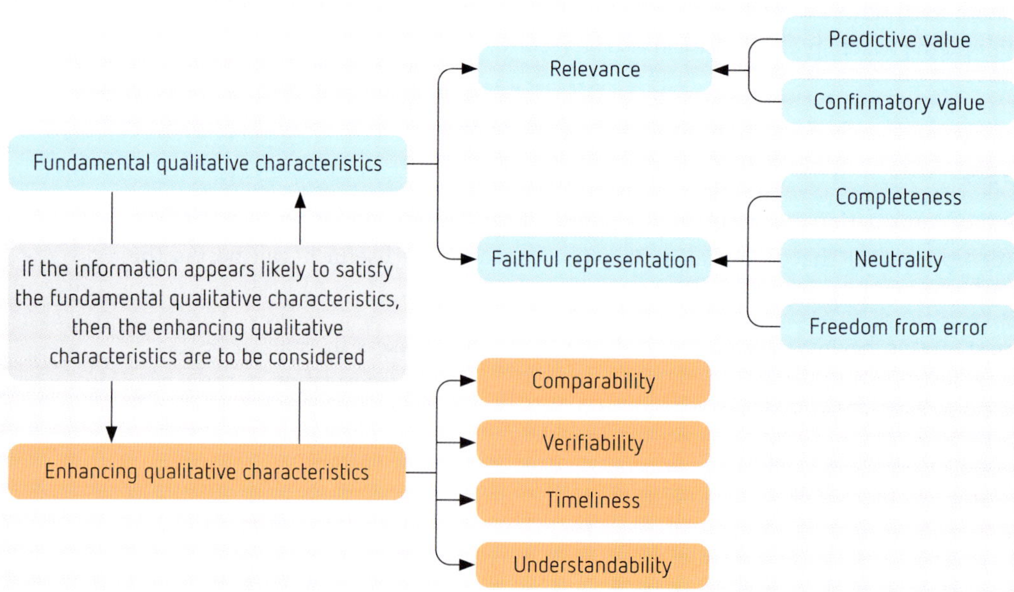

can also effectively 'feed back' to improve the relevance and representational faithfulness of the information (as represented in the figure by the broken arrow pointing from 'enhancing qualitative characteristics' back to 'fundamental qualitative characteristics').

Costs versus benefits

An issue that we have noted elsewhere in this book is consideration of the costs and benefits associated with producing particular accounting information. These same arguments apply to financial accounting information. Collecting and reporting some information of a potentially relevant and representationally faithful nature can be costly, so we also need to consider the potential costs and benefits associated with producing the information. The benefits associated with the disclosure should exceed the costs of making that information available. Cost–benefit decisions tend to limit the amount of information an organisation will provide, although it is really not an easy exercise to place a cost or a benefit on information. As the Conceptual Framework (paragraph 2.39) states:

> Cost is a pervasive constraint on the information that can be provided by financial reporting. Reporting financial information imposes costs, and it is important that those costs are justified by the benefits of reporting that information.
>
> Source: International Accounting Standards Board (2022a).

Having identified some qualitative characteristics that useful financial accounting information should possess, we will now turn our attention to the elements of financial reporting.

LO7.9 The elements of financial accounting

By convention, financial accounting consists of five basic elements. The financial effects of the transactions and events associated with an entity are recorded (recognised) where they impact at least one of these five basic elements. Conversely, if a transaction or event does not impact one of the five elements of financial accounting, then for financial accounting purposes it will be ignored.

According to the Conceptual Framework, the five elements of financial reporting are:

- assets
- liabilities
- equity
- income
- expenses.

It is again emphasised that if a transaction or event does not impact on one of the above elements, then it is not recognised within the financial statements.

The elements that appear within the balance sheet – and which relate to an organisation's financial position – are assets, liabilities and equity. The elements that appear within the income statement – and which relate to an organisation's financial performance – are income and expenses. These elements, and their role, are represented in Figure 7.3.

To undertake financial accounting, we, perhaps obviously, have to understand what the above elements actually are. That is, we need clear definitions so we can, for example, determine whether amounts we have spent have created something that might be referred to as an 'asset', or alternatively, can be considered an 'expense'. The definitions of these elements – and these definitions are crucial to the practice of financial accounting – are provided within the Conceptual Framework.

FIGURE 7.3 The elements of financial accounting

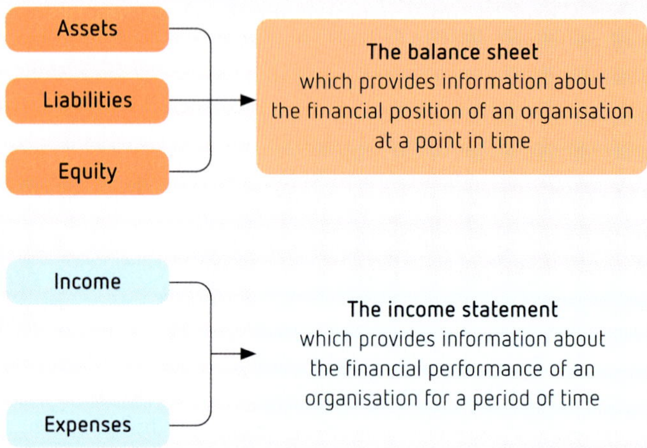

Assets

According to the Conceptual Framework (paragraph 4.3), an *asset* is defined as:

> a present economic resource controlled by the entity as a result of past events.
>
> Source: International Accounting Standards Board (2022a).

The above definition of an asset refers to an 'economic resource', which is defined in the Conceptual Framework as 'a right that has the potential to produce economic benefits'. Rights can take many forms, including rights to receive cash; rights to receive goods or services; or rights over physical objects, such as property, plant and equipment or inventories (where the right to use the property, plant, equipment or inventories might have been established as a result of buying or leasing the item).

Components of the definition of an asset

There are three separate components to the above definition of assets that we need to consider. All three requirements must exist if we are to consider that a particular transaction or event has created an asset. The components are as follows:

1. An asset is an economic resource *controlled* by the entity.
2. An asset exists as a result of *past events*.
3. The right has the potential to produce economic benefits.

Let us now consider each of these components separately.

Control

An asset does not necessarily have to be owned for it to be recognised as an asset of an organisation. Rather, it needs to be *controlled*, meaning that leased assets are often shown as 'assets'. Further, the definition does not require the asset to be a physical asset. For example, the legal right to produce a book or an album of music (and this legal right can be considered an intangible asset) can be an asset, despite the fact that this right does not have a physical presence like, for example, a truck.

Control relates to the capacity of a reporting entity to benefit from an asset, and to deny or regulate the access of others to that benefit. Hence, it is important to realise that control and not legal ownership is required before an asset can be shown within the body of an entity's balance sheet (the balance sheet is also known as the statement of financial position).

Because only controlled resources can be recognised by an organisation for financial reporting purposes, this means that although some resources might be necessary and important to the functioning of an organisation, if they are not controlled by the organisation then they shall not be recognised within the balance sheet. For example, an organisation might require local roads or waterways to transport its products – they are important resources. However, because they are not controlled by the organisation, then they are not assets of the organisation and hence will not be recognised within the financial statements.

Taking this further, this means that if a resource such as local waterways is damaged (for example, perhaps the organisation using the local waterways accidentally releases thousands of litres of oil into the water, thereby severely damaging that environment), because the waterways are not recognised in the financial accounts as an asset, then their damage is also not recognised as an expense unless some fines are imposed or unless actions are taken by the organisation to clean the waterway. As we explained in earlier chapters, organisations can create many negative social and environmental impacts (which we referred to as externalities). As a financial cost is often not assigned to such costs, they are ignored by financial accounting and therefore are not reflected in the financial accountant's profit measures. We must always keep in mind what aspects of performance are incorporated within the performance indicator known as 'profits', as well as those aspects of performance that are not recognised when measuring profits.

Past events

This part of the definition of assets requires that the control of the asset currently exists and is not subject to a future event. Therefore, if an organisation agrees to purchase some equipment in the future, it is not currently an asset of the organisation.

Future economic benefits

For something to be considered an asset, there must also be an expectation (and therefore a judgement made) that future economic benefits will potentially flow from the item. In the absence of potential to generate economic benefits an asset shall not be recognised, and any related expenditure would be treated as an expense. As an example, cash is an asset owing to the benefits that can flow to an organisation as a result of the purchasing power cash generates. A machine is also an asset to the extent that economic benefits are anticipated to flow from using it.

There is not a requirement that an item must have a value in exchange (that is, that it can be sold, perhaps for cash) before it should be recognised as an asset. The economic benefits may result from its ongoing use (often referred to as *value-in-use*) within the organisation. For example, although a particular machine might not easily be able to be sold to any other organisation, to the extent that it allows the organisation to manufacture products that will subsequently be sold (thereby creating future economic benefits), it is an asset.

For a discussion of how to determine if an item is an asset, see **Learning exercise 7.8**.

7.8 Learning Exercise

Determining whether an item is an asset

As we have discussed, there are three separate components to the definition of assets, these being 'control', 'past events' and 'potential to produce economic benefits'. Consider these necessary components of the definition in determining which of the following are (or are not) assets of an organisation:

1. cash
2. a factory building
3. some unused housing near an abandoned and remote mine site, where there is no demand for such buildings
4. machinery
5. inventory
6. debtors (accounts receivable)
7. shares held in another organisation
8. employees
9. the managing director who is very valuable to an organisation
10. the underground water supply that flows under the organisation, and from which the organisation extracts water
11. the river the organisation uses to transport its goods to market.

Solution: The above items can be split into those that should be considered assets of the organisation and those that should not.

Assets

1. The *cash* would be an asset because it can be used to acquire other items that would be expected to generate future economic benefits. It could also be deposited into an account that generates interest income.
2. The *factory building* would be an asset as it would be expected to be an integral component of the organisation and would contribute to the organisation's capacity to generate future economic benefits – such as producing goods that can later be sold.
3. *Machinery* would be an asset of the organisation to the extent that it is associated with generating future economic benefits.
4. *Inventory* would be an asset of the business to the extent that there is an expectation that it will be sold in the future, thereby generating future economic benefits.
5. *Debtors*, or accounts receivable as they are also known, represent amounts due from the customers of the organisation. This claim to cash would represent an asset because of the economic benefits that will flow from the use of that cash.
6. *Shares held in another organisation* would be considered an asset as there would be an expectation, or potential, that this investment would generate economic returns from dividends, and/or from any ultimate sale of those shares.

Not assets

1. The *abandoned housing* initially would have been recorded as an asset given the buildings were a necessary part of the business, and therefore associated with generating economic benefits. However, the fact that they are no longer used in the business, and that they perhaps cannot be sold, means that there is no clear potential economic benefits associated with owning them. Therefore, the buildings no longer satisfy the definition of an asset as they have minimal potential to generate future economic benefits. As such, there would be a need to remove these buildings from the assets of the organisation, the consequence being that an associated expense would be recognised.
2. The *employees* of an organisation would be a valuable resource of the organisation. However, it is generally accepted that employees cannot be considered to be 'controlled'. Hence, they would not be recorded as assets.
3. The *managing director* would be very important to the organisation. However, as with the employees, the managing director cannot be considered to be controlled and hence would not be reported in the financial statements as an asset.
4. The *underground water* might be a very important resource for the organisation, but to the extent that the organisation does not control the use of the water, then this water source would not be recorded as an asset of the organisation.
5. The *river* also would be an important resource for the organisation. However, if the organisation cannot control the use of the river – which would mean being able to regulate how other people might use it – then it is not recorded as an asset of the organisation.

Classifying assets

We now know the definition of an asset. Another issue to consider is how to present assets in the financial statements we prepare. There are accounting standards that prescribe how to present the financial statements, and what will be disclosed within those financial statements. Remember, smaller organisations do not typically have to comply with these requirements as they do not have investors or creditors who rely upon GPFSs to monitor their financial interests in the organisation.

Current and non-current assets

When preparing a balance sheet, assets (and liabilities) will generally be disclosed as either current or non-current. This is the most common practice. However, an alternative presentation format is to disclose the assets (and liabilities) in order of liquidity if it is considered that this form of presentation provides information that is more relevant and reliable. This is more common for financial institutions. **Liquidity** is a measure of how quickly assets can be converted into cash, or how quickly liabilities need to be settled. Cash is the most liquid of assets, whilst property, plant and equipment are considered not to be highly liquid.

liquidity
Measure of how quickly assets can be converted into cash, or how quickly liabilities need to be settled

If assets are disclosed on a current/non-current basis – and this is the most common approach – then those assets that are considered to be held for the short term are the ones that are deemed to be **current assets**. Such assets would include cash and all those other assets that are expected to be converted into cash, or consumed, within the next 12 months, or within the organisation's normal operating cycle. More specifically, the accounting standard that addresses the presentation of financial statements (which at the international level is IAS 1: Presentation of Financial Statements) (paragraph 66) says:

current assets
An asset that can reasonably be expected to be sold, consumed, or otherwise exhausted within a year, or within the normal operating cycle of an organisation (whichever period is longer)

> An entity shall classify an asset as current when:
>
> a it expects to realise the asset, or intends to sell or consume it, in its normal operating cycle;
>
> b it holds the asset primarily for the purpose of trading;
>
> c it expects to realise the asset within twelve months after the reporting period; or
>
> d the asset is cash or a cash equivalent unless the asset is restricted from being exchanged or used to settle a liability for at least twelve months after the reporting period.
>
> An entity shall classify all other assets as non-current.
>
> Source: International Accounting Standards Board (2022c).

normal operating cycle
The average period of time between the initial acquisition of particular assets for processing or use, and the time at which cash is ultimately realised in relation to disposing of those assets

The above requirements make reference to the **normal operating cycle**, which is the average period of time between the initial acquisition of particular assets for processing, and the time at which cash is ultimately realised in relation to disposing of those assets. Current assets are typically those assets that are used in the day-to-day activities of a business and include cash, short-term money market deposits, inventory (stock) and accounts receivable (trade debtors).

As we will learn in a subsequent chapter, many of the sales made by business organisations are not for cash, but rather for a subsequent receipt of cash. Because we are generally required to use accrual accounting, we still recognise the sales income, and the claim to cash (the accounts receivable), at the time of sale. Most accounts receivable will be current assets, but in those rare cases where goods or services are sold and the amount is due to be paid beyond 12 months of the reporting date, then such accounts receivable would be disclosed as non-current assets.

Non-current assets are those that do not meet the definition of current assets. They tend to be held for the long run and for generating wealth. For example, property, plant and equipment would be considered non-current assets. They are not typically held for the purposes of resale. Non-current assets can be considered tangible or intangible in nature.

Tangible and intangible assets

Tangible assets are those assets that have a physical substance – for example, property, plant and equipment. A great proportion of the non-current assets held by an organisation are classified as property, plant and equipment. These are tangible assets that:

1 are held for use in the production of, or supply of, goods or services, for rental to others, or for administrative purposes
2 are expected to be used during more than one period.

Property, plant and equipment includes land, buildings, various types of machinery, and furniture. As we will learn in later chapters, non-current assets are initially recorded at cost, but because they typically will not last forever, and will decline in productive capacity as time goes on (except perhaps for land), some depreciation will be recognised as an expense and the reported net value of the non-current asset will be reduced. As subsequent chapters will also explain, property, plant and equipment will sometimes be revalued to fair value.

By contrast, intangible assets are those assets that, while potentially providing future economic benefits, have no physical substance. These include, for example, copyrights, patents, trademarks, purchased goodwill, software and licences. Accounting standards require that intangible assets be disclosed in the balance sheet separately to other assets.

For more on the classification of assets as current or non-current, see **Learning exercise 7.9**.

Tangible assets have physical substance, like aircraft or aviation machinery. Intangible assets provide economic benefits without having a physical substance, like the patents for the aircraft.

7.9 Learning Exercise

Classifying assets as current or non-current

Why is it useful to financial statement readers that assets be disclosed separately according to whether they are current or non-current?

Solution

Current assets include those assets that are currently in the form of cash, or that are likely to be consumed or converted into cash, generally within the next 12 months. This provides users with knowledge of an organisation's ability to pay amounts due within the next 12 months. The current assets are often compared with the current liabilities of an organisation to provide an indication of whether the organisation can pay those debts that are due in the near term; for example, within the next 12 months. All things being equal, it is generally inadvisable for the current liabilities of an organisation to exceed the current assets.

The total value of non-current assets provides an indication of an organisation's investment in productive assets. These are the assets that will generate economic benefits in the long run.

As an example of how assets might be presented, **Exhibit 7.1** shows the assets that appeared in the balance sheet of Qantas Airways as at 30 June 2021. These amounts are reported in millions of dollars such that the total assets of Qantas as at 30 June 2021 amount to approximately $18 billion.

EXHIBIT 7.1 Assets shown in the balance sheet of Qantas as at 30 June 2021

	2021 $M	2020 $M
CURRENT ASSETS		
Cash and cash equivalents	2 221	3 520
Receivables	579	520
Lease receivables	5	2
Other financial assets	176	216

	2021 $M	2020 $M
Inventories	279	306
Assets classified as held for sale	1	58
Income tax receivable	-	137
Other	169	193
Total current assets	3430	4952
NON-CURRENT ASSETS		
Receivables	54	101
Lease receivables	47	23
Other financial assets	185	139
Investments accounted for under the equity method	57	59
Property, plant and equipment	10787	11726
Right of use assets	1109	1440
Intangible assets	849	1050
Deferred tax assets	675	167
Other	687	369
Total non-current assets	14450	15074
Total assets	17880	20026

Source: Qantas (2021), p. 68.

Liabilities

Liabilities represent the financial claims against the organisation held by individuals, and organisations, other than by the owners of the organisation, whose investments in the organisation would not create liabilities. Liabilities arise from activities such as borrowing funds, or through acquiring inventory on credit, or incurring other expenses without yet paying for them. Within the Conceptual Framework, a *liability* is defined (paragraph 4.26) as:

> a present obligation of the entity to transfer an economic resource as a result of past events.
>
> Source: International Accounting Standards Board (2022a).

The above definition of liability refers to an 'obligation'. An obligation is defined in the Conceptual Framework as 'a duty or responsibility that the entity has no practical ability to avoid'. That is, the obligation would be expected to be satisfied at some time in the future.

Components of a liability

From the above definition of a liability we can see that – as with assets – there are three separate components to this definition:

1. A liability represents a *present obligation* of the entity.
2. It arises from *past events*.
3. It ultimately results in an *outflow from the entity of economic resources embodying economic benefits*.

Let us consider each of these three components separately.

Present obligation

For a liability to be recognised and reported within the financial statements, the obligation must currently be in existence and therefore not be contingent upon future events. A liability exists when, at a given point in time, an organisation effectively has no reasonable alternative other than to settle the obligation at a future date.

Past events

The event that creates the obligation must have occurred. For example, if an organisation has placed an order for some inventory, but the inventory has not actually been placed in the control of the organisation, then an obligation to pay for the inventory will typically not be recognised.

Outflow from the entity of resources embodying economic benefits

For a liability to be recognised, the organisation must expect to ultimately transfer something that has financial value. That is, it has to give up something that constitutes economic benefits. This outflow of economic benefits does not have to only be in the form of cash. For example, if an organisation has an obligation to transfer some other asset, other than cash, in order to settle an obligation, then that obligation would still constitute a liability.

For more on classifying items as liabilities, see **Learning exercise 7.10**.

7.10 Learning Exercise

Classifying items as liabilities

As we have discussed, there are three separate components to a liability. That is:

1 There must be a present obligation.
2 The obligation must have arisen because of a past event.
3 The obligation is expected to culminate in an outflow of economic benefits.

Consider these necessary components of a liability and then determine which of the following items are (or are not) liabilities:

1 bank overdraft
2 loan from bank
3 rent payable
4 wages payable
5 creditors (accounts payable)
6 obligation to clean up contaminated land
7 an organisation has guaranteed the debts of another organisation
8 an organisation has spilled tonnes of oil into the sea.

Solution

The first six of the above items would constitute liabilities, as in all of these cases there is a present obligation to transfer economic benefits in the future as a result of a past transaction or event. Number 7 would not be a liability, and number 8 might be a liability (we need to have more information). More specifically:

1 A *bank overdraft* exists when a bank has agreed to provide a line of credit to an organisation when its bank account becomes overdrawn. It essentially allows an organisation to withdraw more funds than the organisation currently has on deposit with the bank. This creates an obligation to repay these funds to the bank, and this would be a liability.

2 A *loan from the bank* creates an obligation to transfer economic benefits to the bank in the future, and is a liability.

3 *Rent payable* would be an obligation – the organisation has to pay for the rent expenses it has incurred but not yet paid. The obligation relates to a required future payment and is a liability.

4 *Wages payable* would represent an obligation to pay for services already performed by employees, which are not yet paid for. It is a liability.

5 *Creditors* represent those organisations to whom amounts are due, often in relation to the acquisition of inventory that was bought on credit terms. This is an obligation that arises as a result of a past transaction and is a liability.

6 In respect of *contaminated land*, to the extent that an organisation has a legal obligation to clean up the site, or has made a public commitment to clean up the site, then the amount estimated to be paid in the future will be a liability.

7 In respect of the *guaranteed debt*, organisations often guarantee the debts of other organisations, particularly if these other organisations are related to the organisation providing the guarantee. The act of guaranteeing the debts of another organisation does not create a liability. A liability requires that there be a present obligation to transfer economic benefits. However, the organisation guaranteeing the debts of the other organisation will only have an obligation if the other organisation actually defaults on paying its debts. That is, it is dependent (contingent) upon some future event. At that future point in time, if the other organisation defaults, then the organisation would recognise a liability.

8 The act of *spilling tonnes of oil* into the sea will not necessarily create a liability. A liability will arise only if the organisation is legally obliged to address the environmental damage (perhaps through government action taken against the organisation), or if it has made a public commitment to take action to try to fix up the damage done to the environment. If the obligation is recognised, then an associated expense would also be recorded. However, if the organisation is not required by law to fix up the damage, and if it has no intention of accepting any responsibility, then no liability (and no related expense) would be recognised within the financial accounts. This would be despite the environmental damage that has been created.

Classifying liabilities

As was also the case with assets, another issue to consider is how we present these liabilities in the financial statements that we prepare. Again, the relevant accounting standard (IAS 1: Presentation of Financial Statements) provides guidance, which we shall now discuss.

Current and non-current liabilities

current liabilities Obligations that are due to be settled within one year of the reporting date, or within the normal operating cycle of an organisation (whichever period is longer)

The classification rules here are similar to those for current assets. **Current liabilities** are those obligations that will be settled in the near term; for example, within the next 12 months.

According to the accounting standard pertaining to the presentation of financial statements (IAS 1, paragraph 69), an entity shall classify a liability as 'current' when:

a it expects to settle the liability in its normal operating cycle;

b it holds the liability primarily for the purposes of trading;

c the liability is due to be settled within twelve months after the end of the reporting period; or

d it does not have the right at the end of the reporting period to defer settlement of the liability for at least twelve months after the reporting period.

An entity shall classify all other liabilities as non-current.

Source: International Accounting Standards Board (2022c).

Current liabilities would include such obligations as accounts payable (which might relate to the acquisition of stock), loans repayable within 12 months, or revenue received in advance of actually providing the related goods or services.

Differentiating between current and non-current liabilities can provide useful information about those obligations that need to be settled (paid) relatively soon. These obligations can then also be compared with the current assets to provide some indication of whether an organisation appears to be currently able to meet its upcoming financial obligations.

Provisions

A **provision** is an estimated liability for which there is greater uncertainty regarding the amount, or timing, of the amount than there might be for other liabilities. For example, a bank loan would not be considered a provision as the amount that needs to be paid is known, and no estimation is needed. However, the defining characteristic of a provision is that the timing of the payment, and perhaps the amount of the payment, are not known with absolute certainty. Therefore, a provision can be defined as a liability of uncertain timing and/or amount.

provision
Liability for which there is greater uncertainty regarding the amount or timing of the obligation relative to other liabilities

One example here could be a provision for remediating (or cleaning up) a contaminated site. An organisation might be given an order by the government to clean up some environmental contamination of a site. It might not know exactly how much it will cost, or how long it will take, but it should be able to come up with a reasonable approximation which would then be recorded and reported within the financial statements as a provision (which is a liability), in this case perhaps described as a 'Provision for site remediation'.

Other provisions might relate, for example, to obligations associated with product warranties. For example, when an organisation sells its products to customers, it might accept an obligation to repair, or replace, any faulty or defective products. This offer will create a liability, as the organisation, through offering customers a warranty, has created an obligation that will result in the outflow of economic benefits in the future. This is a liability, albeit there will be some uncertainty as to how much will actually be paid in the future to satisfy various warranty claims.

Provisions can be disclosed as current or non-current liabilities depending upon the timing of when they are expected to be paid/settled.

For more on the presentation of liabilities, see **Learning exercise 7.11**.

7.11 Learning Exercise

The presentation of liabilities

The financial statements of organisations contain information that is useful to owners and other interested stakeholders. Consider why a stakeholder might find the following aspects of an organisation's financial statements useful:

- the differentiation between current and non-current liabilities
- the separate disclosure of provisions from other liabilities.

Solutions

Differentiation between current and non-current liabilities

Current liabilities are those liabilities that are due to be paid within the next 12 months or within the normal operating cycle (whichever is the longer). It is important to know whether an organisation can pay its debts as and when they fall due. In this regard, as we have previously noted, it is useful to compare the current liabilities – those that need to be paid within the next 12 months or within the normal operating cycle – with the current assets of the organisation. If the current liabilities exceed the current assets, this can be an issue of concern and might point to the need for the organisation to arrange additional funds, either from lenders or investors.

Separate disclosure of provisions

As we have explained, provisions are liabilities that have some level of uncertainty associated with them in terms of the final amounts to be paid, and/or the timing of the payment. For example, an organisation might record a provision for cleaning up some contaminated land, and whilst it might be able to reasonably estimate the future cost, it cannot be absolutely certain about how much the final cost will be. By identifying something as a provision, this indicates to the financial statement readers that the amount is an estimate, and the final amount to be paid might be somewhat more or less than the reported amount.

Contingent liabilities

contingent liability
A potential liability that will ultimately arise only if a specific transaction or event happens in the future. Also refers to present obligations that arise from past events for which the probability of the outflow of economic benefits, or the amount of the obligation, cannot be determined with sufficient reliability.

A **contingent liability** is a potential liability that will ultimately arise only if something specific happens in the future to turn it into a present liability. That is, there is no existing obligation, and there will only be a liability if a specific future event occurs. Therefore, contingent liabilities do not appear in the financial statements (balance sheet) because they relate to obligations that might arise if something else happens in the future. As we learned earlier, there are three conditions that must be met to meet the definition of a liability and therefore to permit the recognition of a liability. These conditions were that there is a (i) present obligation, which (ii) arises from past events, and (iii) which will result in the outflow of economic resources. A contingent liability does not meet these conditions. Examples of contingent liabilities include:

- guarantees of the debts of other organisations, which, as we explained earlier, will only create an actual obligation if the organisation that has been supported with the guarantee is subsequently unable to pay its debts
- potential obligations associated with future legal cases (for example, an organisation has been sued by a customer because of an injury caused by one of the organisation's products), whereby a liability will only be recognised at the time a court makes a ruling against the organisation that specific amounts must be paid.

The notes that accompany an organisation's financial statements will include details of the contingent liabilities known to exist.

For more on the disclosure of information about contingent liabilities, see **Learning exercise 7.12**.

7.12 Learning Exercise

The disclosure of information about contingent liabilities

Scenario: Organisation A has guaranteed the debts of Organisation B.

Issue: Should this liability be disclosed in the balance sheet of Organisation A?

Solution: Organisation A will only have a liability for the debts of Organisation B if Organisation B defaults on its debts at a future date. That is, there is no present obligation (one of the key requirements for something to be recognised as a liability) because the company has not defaulted on paying its debts, which makes this a contingent liability for Organisation A. That is, it is a possible future liability that will only become a liability if a future event occurs. As we have discussed, contingent liabilities are not disclosed within the balance sheet. Thus, this should not be disclosed as a liability in the balance sheet of Organisation A.

As we have stressed, contingent liabilities shall not be recorded in the financial statements and therefore will not appear as a liability in the balance sheet. This is because they do not satisfy the requirements necessary to be recognised as a liability. Nevertheless, there is a generally accepted requirement that contingent liabilities be disclosed in the notes that accompany the financial statements. The reason for this is that it is important that the readers of the financial statements know of current arrangements, or events, that could *potentially* lead to significant obligations being recognised in future periods. It is argued that it would be misleading not to tell financial stakeholders about events that the managers are currently aware of and that might happen in the future, and which might result in significant outflows of resources away from the organisation.

Presentation of liabilities

As an example of how liabilities might be presented, **Exhibit 7.2** shows the liabilities that appeared in the balance sheet of Qantas Airways as at 30 June 2021. If you look at the current liabilities of Qantas, you will see they are $7595 million. This is more than double the current assets of $3430 million that were shown in **Exhibit 7.1**. This would necessitate some level of investigation as this would normally be an issue of concern.

However, when we look at the current liabilities of Qantas, we see that nearly half of them relate to 'revenue received in advance', which in the case of Qantas will mostly relate to payments made by people who have booked flights but have not yet flown (technically meaning that the organisation might be expected to repay the amounts paid if they could no longer provide flights). As such, there would not be an expectation that most of these amounts would need to be repaid to customers, and hence our initial concern would be allayed.

EXHIBIT 7.2 Liabilities shown in the balance sheet of Qantas as at 30 June 2021

	2021 $M	2020 $M
CURRENT LIABILITIES		
Payables	1813	2351
Revenue received in advance	3277	2784
Interest-bearing liabilities	969	868
Lease liabilities	383	524
Other financial liabilities	17	238

	2021 $M	2020 $M
Provisions	1136	1539
Total current liabilities	7595	8304
NON-CURRENT LIABILITIES		
Payables	44	99
Revenue received in advance	2154	2256
Interest-bearing liabilities	5861	5825
Lease liabilities	1016	1318
Other financial liabilities	5	47
Provisions	689	651
Total non-current liabilities	9769	10196
Total liabilities	17364	18500

Source: Qantas (2021), p. 68.

The definitions of assets and liabilities are fundamental because the definitions of the other three elements of financial accounting – equity, income and expenses – flow directly from them, as we shall see (remember, in total, there are five elements of financial accounting).

Owners' equity

According to the Conceptual Framework (paragraph 4.63), *equity* is defined as:

> the residual interest in the assets of the entity after deducting all its liabilities.
>
> Source: International Accounting Standards Board (2022a).

owners' equity Also referred to as net worth or net assets, it is the total value of an organisation's assets minus the total value of its liabilities

Note that the Conceptual Framework uses the term 'equity' rather than 'owners' equity'. We will use the terms interchangeably. **Owners' equity** can sometimes be described as net worth; that is, it is the total amount recorded for assets, less the total amount recorded for liabilities. In the form of a mathematical formula, we can say:

Owners' equity = assets – liabilities

We can see that the definition of equity is therefore directly dependent on the definition of assets and liabilities, as it is simply the difference between the two. That is, if certain transactions and events lead to the recognition of assets, and others to the recognition of liabilities, then the balance of owners' equity directly follows as being the difference between the two. As we can see from **Figure 7.3** provided earlier, equity appears in the balance sheet.

For a discussion of how to determine the balance of equity, see **Learning exercise 7.13**.

7.13 Learning Exercise

Determining the balance of equity

Scenario: In 2024, Lenny started an organisation called Lenny's Longboards. As at 30 June 2024, Lenny's Longboards has the following assets and liabilities:

ASSETS	
Current assets	
Cash	\$1 500
Stock of surfboards	\$12 500
Non-current assets	
Machinery	\$25 000
Land and buildings	\$161 000
	\$200 000
LIABILITIES	
Current liabilities	
Amounts owing to suppliers	\$4 000
Non-current liabilities	
Amount owing to bank relating to bank loan	\$51 000
	\$55 000

Issue: What is the value of Lenny's Longboards owners' equity, and what does this represent?
Solution: We can use the formula:

Owners' equity = assets – liabilities

The owners' equity is therefore \$200 000 – \$55 000, which equals \$145 000. This \$145 000 represents the owners' (in this case Lenny's) share, or equity, in assets of the business. The balance of \$55 000 is attributable to the suppliers, and to the bank. That is, of the total assets of \$200 000, lenders and creditors have a total claim against the assets of \$55 000 and the residual claim, or owners' equity in the organisation is \$145 000.

Another way in which we can represent the accounting equation is:

Assets = liabilities + owners' equity

In this case, \$200 000 = \$55 000 + \$145 000, which means that the organisation has \$200 000 of assets against which the suppliers and the bank have a claim of \$55 000, leaving the owners with equity in the organisation of \$145 000.

Types of equity accounts

The total value of owners' equity will comprise different components:

1 capital contributions from owners – in the case of a company, this would be referred to as 'share capital'
2 retained earnings – the accumulated profits of current, and past, accounting periods, less any dividends paid in these periods
3 reserves – various reserves will be created across time (we will consider some possible types of reserves in subsequent chapters).

If you refer back to **Exhibit 7.1** and **Exhibit 7.2**, you will see that the total assets of Qantas as at 30 June 2021 were \$17 880 million, whilst the total liabilities were \$17 364 million.

Therefore, using our formula of OE = A – L, the total equity of Qantas as at 30 June 2021 should be \$17 880 million less \$17 364 million, which is \$516 million. This is confirmed by looking at the equity section of the 2021 balance sheet of Qantas, which is reproduced in **Exhibit 7.3** below.

EXHIBIT 7.3 Owners' equity as presented in the balance sheet of Qantas as at 30 June 2021

	2021 $M	2020 $M
EQUITY		
Issued capital	3186	3104
Treasury shares	(18)	(51)
Reserves	432	(173)
Accumulated losses	(3087)	(1357)
Equity attributable to the members of Qantas	513	1523
Non-controlling interests	3	3
Total equity	516	1526

Source: Qantas (2021), p. 68.

Another financial statement that larger organisations are required to prepare is a statement of changes in equity. This simply provides a reconciliation of total equity at the beginning of the period with total equity at the end of the accounting period. The statement of changes in equity shows the extent to which various equity accounts have changed, and why. An example of this financial statement will be shown later in this chapter, and will be covered in greater detail within Chapter 10.

For a discussion of the differences between liability and equity, see **Learning exercise 7.14**.

7.14 Learning Exercise

Some differences between liabilities and equity

Having defined and discussed liabilities and equity, let us now try to identify some differences between the two. These include the following:

1 Liabilities include amounts due to lenders and creditors, whereas equity represents the owners' financial interest in an organisation.

2 There is typically a legal obligation to pay lenders and creditors. By contrast, an organisation does not have an obligation to transfer to owners the amount of equity that is attributed to them.

3 Periodic payments made to lenders (apart from the payment of the principal of the loan amount) are referred to as an 'interest expense', and being an expense, this reduces profits. Periodic payments made to owners are referred to as distributions (or dividends in the case of companies) – these distributions are not expenses and do not impact profits. Rather, distributions (dividends) paid to owners are distributions of the profits.

4 If an organisation collapses/dissolves, then lenders and creditors must be paid first and owners will only receive funds if there are any funds left after the obligations to lenders and creditors (liabilities) have been taken care of.

5 Owners will typically only receive a distribution (dividend payment) if there are profits, and even when there are profits, the managers do not typically have to pay a dividend. Managers might retain funds for future expansion, rather than pay dividends. By contrast, agreed amounts must be paid to lenders and creditors regardless of whether the organisation is generating a profit.

Having now discussed the three elements that represent the financial position of the organisation (that is, assets, liabilities and equity, which are shown within a balance sheet), we will now shift our attention to the remaining two elements of accounting that relate to financial performance: income and expenses. It needs to be noted that income is measured for a period of time, which could be a month or perhaps a year. The same can be said for expenses. This can be contrasted with assets, liabilities and equity, which represent values as at a point in time.

> **Key concept**
>
> Equity, or 'owners' equity', represents the owners' share of the assets of the organisation, and is the difference between total assets and total liabilities (which also means that equity equals 'net assets').

Income

The fourth element of financial accounting that we will now consider is *income*. Within the Conceptual Framework (paragraph 4.68), income is defined as follows:

> Income is increases in assets, or decreases in liabilities, that result in increases in equity, other than those relating to contributions from holders of equity claims.
>
> Source: International Accounting Standards Board (2022a).

The above definition of income refers to 'equity claims'. These are claims against the organisation that do not meet the definition of a liability. These would be claims held by the owners of the organisation.

In the definition of income provided above, there are therefore two essential characteristics of income:

1 an increase in assets or a reduction in liabilities
2 an increase in equity, other than as a result of a contribution from holders of equity claims (owners).

Income can therefore be considered to relate to transactions or events that cause an increase in the net assets of the reporting entity, other than increases in net assets that arise as a result of owner contributions. That is, contributions from owners does not constitute income. *Net assets* is the balance of assets less liabilities, which we know is equity. Therefore, if a transaction or event increases equity, and the transaction or event does not involve owners contributing equity (capital), then, generally speaking, the transaction or event represents income (see Learning exercise 7.15).

7.15 Learning Exercise

Classifying transactions as income

Discuss whether the following transactions would be considered income (or not), and why (or why not):

1 contribution of cash by an owner
2 sale of inventory to a customer for $1000, and the customer will pay in two weeks' time
3 sale of inventory to a customer for $1000 cash

4 a loan of $10 000 from a bank
5 interest from a bank on cash deposits.

Solution

As we now know, there are two essential characteristics of income: an increase in assets or a reduction in liabilities, and an increase in equity (other than as a result of a contribution from owners). Therefore:

1 *The contribution of cash by the owner* would be a contribution that acts to increase owners' equity but would not be income.
2 *The sale of inventory to a customer, with the customer to pay in two weeks*, would be income, which we might refer to as sales revenue. Because we generally use the accrual basis of accounting (one of the principles of financial accounting that we discussed earlier in this chapter), we would recognise the income, even though we have not received the cash. What we would recognise is the claim to cash, which would be an increase in an asset that is referred to as an accounts receivable (or a debtor). Therefore, this transaction results in the assets increasing, but liabilities are unchanged. Using our formula of OE = A – L, we can see that equity has increased, and as the increase was not the result of a contribution from the owners, then this sale would be considered income.
3 *The sale of inventory to a customer, paid in cash*, would be income. As noted previously, it does not matter whether we have received cash, or a claim to cash. In either case, income would be recognised. Therefore, in this instance, sales revenue – which is income – would be recognised.
4 *A loan of cash from the bank* is not income. It represents an increase in liabilities. Therefore, for this transaction we would have an increase in assets (perhaps cash) and an increase in liabilities (perhaps referred to as a bank loan). Since our assets and liabilities have both increased by the same amount, there has not been an increase in equity (OE = A – L), and as such, the loan of cash from the bank is not considered income.
5 *Interest from a bank on cash deposits* would be income, and would be referred to as interest income. There would be an increase in assets that results in an increase in equity.

Expenses

The fifth and final element of financial accounting is *expenses*. Within the Conceptual Framework (paragraph 4.67), expenses are defined as follows:

> Expenses are decreases in assets, or increases in liabilities, that result in decreases in equity, other than those relating to distributions to holders of equity claims.
>
> Source: International Accounting Standards Board (2022a).

There are therefore two essential characteristics of expenses:

1 a decrease in assets, or an increase in liabilities
2 a decrease in equity, other than as a result of distributions to owners.

Therefore, unless we understand what the assets and liabilities are, we will not be able to understand what an expense is. As we noted earlier, the definitions of equity, income and expenses are all based on the definitions given to assets and liabilities. Expenses may be considered to be transactions or events that cause reductions in the net assets or equity of the reporting entity, other than those caused by distributions to the owners (which can also be referred to as dividends).

For example, let us consider rent expense. If rent is paid in cash, then the expense – the rent expense – will also be associated with a decrease in cash, which is an asset. If, by contrast, the rent expense has been incurred but not yet paid, then the rent expense will be associated with an increase in liabilities; specifically, rental expenses payable. Again, when recognising expenses, we see that it does not matter whether the amount has been paid or not. If the expense has been *incurred* and needs to be paid at some future date, then it must be recognised, even if it has not been paid.

Let us consider another example. Assume that flood waters have ruined some stock (inventory) of an organisation. The flood damage would be recognised as an expense, and there would be a reduction in the assets of the organisation in the form of the reduction in inventory.

As we can see above, an expense will arise when we use up, or possibly damage, the assets of an organisation. As we know, one of the defining characteristics of assets is control. But what if we damage an important resource that we do not control? Would that be an expense? The answer is that, to the extent that no liabilities or fines are imposed for the damage, then no expenses will be recognised by the organisation. As an example, if an organisation pollutes the environment, but it incurs no fines for doing so, and has no intention of fixing any damage, then no expenses will be recognised because the environment is not controlled by the organisation. We will return to this issue in subsequent chapters.

For further discussion of the identification of expenses, see **Learning exercise 7.16**.

7.16 Learning Exercise

Identification of expenses

Determine whether, and why, the following items would, or would not, be considered expenses:

1 distribution of cash to an owner by way of a dividend payment of $2000
2 purchase of inventory from a supplier for cash
3 repayment of a loan of $10 000 from a bank
4 interest paid to a bank on a bank loan
5 payment of wages
6 theft of inventory
7 spillage of tonnes of oil into the river that flows past an organisation's factory
8 emissions from an organisation's factory of hundreds of tonnes of CO_2 into the atmosphere.

Solution

As we have discussed, there are two essential characteristics of expenses: a decrease in assets or an increase in liabilities, and a decrease in equity (other than as a result of a withdrawal from owners, such as dividends). Therefore:

1 *Distribution of cash to an owner* would not be an expense. It is a distribution of profits to the owner, which has the effect of decreasing equity and assets (cash decreases).
2 *Purchase of inventory from a supplier* is not an expense. The transaction involves the substitution of one asset (inventory) for another (cash), and would not cause a change in liabilities or equity.
3 *Repayment of a loan* is a repayment of a liability and is not an expense. This would represent a reduction in an asset (cash) and a reduction in a liability (bank loan). There is therefore no change in equity.

4 *Interest paid on a bank loan* would represent an expense (interest expense), and the payment would also decrease cash (an asset).

5 *Payment of wages* would represent an expense (wages expense), which would also be associated with a decrease in assets (cash).

6 *Theft of inventory* would be an expense, which would also be associated with a decrease in an asset (inventory).

7 *Spillage of tonnes of oil into a river* – the actual loss of oil would be an expense, as this oil would have been recorded as an asset of the organisation. At issue here, however, is whether any cost associated with the environmental damage is an expense. If the organisation has a legal obligation to clean up the environment, or has made a public commitment to do so, then an expense and an associated liability would be recognised for the future clean-up costs. But if no obligation has been accepted to fix up the environment, then no expense for the clean-up would be recognised by the organisation.

8 *The emitting of hundreds of tonnes of CO_2 into the atmosphere* is similar to the above point. If the managers are not fined for the emissions, or if there are no associated taxes (for example, carbon taxes), then no expenses will be recognised despite the negative impacts these emissions might have on the environment. This is a point we emphasise regularly in this book – that the profit reported in the financial statements measures financial performance using the various rules that relate to financial accounting, but it does not necessarily provide a good indication of social or environmental performance. Indeed, a very profitable organisation from a financial accounting perspective could be causing significant social and environmental harm.

Why do I need to know the definitions of the five elements of financial accounting?

In the practice of financial accounting, it is just the five elements of accounting (assets, liabilities, equity, income and expenses) that are considered to be influenced by recognised transactions and events. Further, it is only these five elements of financial accounting that therefore appear within the suite of financial statements released by an organisation. As a result, it is essential that we understand what these elements mean, else we really will not understand what the financial statements represent.

LO7.10 What is profit?

Profit is the difference between income and expenses and is reported in an income statement (or, as it is also called, a statement of profit or loss, or a statement of financial performance). The aggregated profits (or losses) of the current years and all previous years, less the distribution of profits to owners (dividends), are recorded in the balance sheet within an account known as *retained earnings* (also referred to as *retained profits*).

Exhibit 7.4 represents the income statement for Qantas Airways for the year ending 30 June 2021. At this stage of your accounting education, you are not expected to understand the meaning of everything within this income statement. This income statement shows a number of interesting things including how COVID-19 caused a reduction in passenger revenue in 2021 relative to 2020.

EXHIBIT 7.4 Income statement of Qantas for the year ending 30 June 2021

	2021 $M	2020 $M
REVENUE AND OTHER INCOME		
Net passenger revenue	3766	12183
Net freight revenue	1316	1045
Other revenue and income	852	1029
Revenue and other income	5934	14257
EXPENSES		
Manpower and staff related	1970	3646
Aircraft operating variable	1555	3520
Fuel	835	2895
Depreciation and amortisation	1929	2045
Share of net loss of investments accounted for under the equity method	129	53
Impairment of assets and related costs	270	1456
De-designation of fuel and foreign exchange hedges	(33)	571
Redundancies and related costs	297	565
Net gain on disposal of assets	(26)	(7)
Other	1058	1950
	7984	16694
Statutory loss before income tax expense and net finance costs	(2050)	(2437)
Finance income	20	33
Finance costs	(321)	(304)
Net finance costs	(301)	(271)
Statutory loss before income tax expense	**(2351)**	**(2708)**
Income tax benefit	623	744
Statutory loss for the year	(1728)	(1964)

Source: Qantas (2021), p. 66.

We have already defined each of the elements of financial accounting. A summary of these definitions is provided below in **Table 7.1**. (For discussions of how transactions impact equity and other elements of financial accounting, see **Learning exercise 7.17** and **Learning exercise 7.18** respectively.)

TABLE 7.1 Summary of the elements of financial accounting

Element	Definition	Reported within
Asset	A present economic resource controlled by the entity as a result of past events	The balance sheet (also known as the statement of financial position)
Liability	A present obligation of the entity to transfer an economic resource as a result of past events	The balance sheet
Equity	The residual interest in the assets of the entity after deducting all of its liabilities	The balance sheet
Income	Increases in assets, or decreases of liabilities, that result in increases in equity, other than those relating to contributions from holders of equity claims	The income statement (also known as the statement of profit or loss)
Expense	Decreases in assets, or increases in liabilities, that result in decreases in equity, other than those relating to distributions to holders of equity claims	The income statement

7.17 Learning Exercise

Transactions that impact equity

Why, and how, would the following items impact equity?

1 capital contributions
2 distribution of funds to owners
3 income
4 expenses.

Solution

Recall that equity is the residual interest in the assets of an entity after deducting its liabilities. Thus, the listed items can be classified as follows:

Those that increase equity:

1 *Capital contributions* increase equity. For example, if an owner contributes $100 000 cash to an organisation, then assets will increase by $100 000, but liabilities (which represent the claims against the organisation that are held by parties who are not owners) will be unchanged. Given that equity = assets – liabilities, then equity must increase by $100 000.
2 *Income* increases equity. For example, if an organisation provides services to a customer in exchange for $15 000 cash, then assets will increase by $15 000, but liabilities will be unchanged. Given that equity = assets – liabilities, then equity must increase by $15 000.

Those that decrease equity:

3 *Distributions of funds to owners* (for example, dividends) decrease equity. For example, if an owner is paid dividends of $5000, then assets will decrease by $5000 but liabilities will be unchanged. Given that equity = assets – liabilities, then equity must decrease by $5000.
4 *Expenses* decrease equity. For example, if an organisation employs somebody to provide a service for which they pay wages of $3000 in cash, then assets will decrease by $3000 and liabilities will be unchanged. Given that equity = assets – liabilities, then equity must decrease by $3000.

7.18 Learning Exercise

Determining which elements of financial accounting are impacted by particular transactions and events

As you have seen, it is essential that financial accountants are able to identify which elements of financial accounting are affected by the various transactions and events associated with an organisation. Consider the following transactions of a business and identify which of the five elements of financial accounting are affected by the respective transaction:

1 The business pays $500, in cash, for wages.
2 The business acquires a new car for $40 000 with a bank loan.
3 The business hires a new employee.
4 The business pays a cash dividend to owners of $10 000.
5 The business receives an electricity bill for $800 that remains unpaid.
6 The business receives $3000 cash for services performed for a customer.

Solution

As we now know, the elements of financial accounting are assets, liabilities, equity, income and expenses. The transactions above impact the following elements of financial accounting:

1. *The business pays $500, in cash, for wages* – This will increase expenses (wages expense) and decrease assets (cash).
2. *The business acquires a new car for $40 000 with a bank loan* – This will increase assets (motor vehicle) and increase liabilities (bank loan).
3. *The business hires a new employee* – This will not directly impact any of the elements of financial accounting. However, once the employee starts working, then an expense will need to be recognised (and if the wages are paid with cash, a reduction in an asset will also be recognised).
4. *The business pays a cash dividend to owners of $10 000* – This will decrease equity (dividend) and decrease assets (cash).
5. *A business' unpaid electricity bill of $800* – This will increase liabilities (electricity payable) and increase expenses (electricity expense).
6. *Receipt of $3000 cash from a customer* – This will increase income (services income) and increase assets (cash).

Now that we have defined the elements of financial accounting, we need to:

- determine when to actually recognise the transactions or events; that is, we need to determine *when* to make adjustments to the respective financial accounts that comprise the assets, liabilities, income, expenses and equity of an organisation
- determine how to financially measure the respective transactions or events so that we know how much to put in the accounts
- determine what to disclose and how to present the respective elements of accounting within the financial statements.

That is, once we understand the definitions of the elements of financial accounting, the next step we need to take is to determine when we should recognise the related amount within our financial accounts. We need some sort of guidance, which we shall refer to as 'recognition criteria'. For example, whilst we might believe that an asset has been created, or income has been earned, we need to have a rule to determine when the assets, and income, should be placed within (recognised within) the financial statements. The Conceptual Framework, and various accounting standards, provide guidance here, and we will cover this in the following chapters.

Once we understand the definitions of the elements of accounting (and therefore understand whether we should treat something as an asset, an expense, or as a liability or income), and once we know when we should *recognise* it (the point we referred to above), the next step we need to take is to *measure* the related amount. That is, we need to be able to measure the amount that should be recorded within the accounts. We need some measurement rules, and these appear in various financial accounting standards. Some of the many measurement rules that exist within financial accounting will be discussed in the following chapters.

A subsequent step is then to determine whether particular types of transactions should be disclosed, and if so, where and how the related information shall be presented. For example, if we are required to disclose certain types of assets (such as intangible assets), issues to consider would include whether we should present them as current or non-current, and what details in respect of those assets must be disclosed. We summarise these steps in Figure 7.4. Across the following chapters we will consider some of these steps. In this chapter, however, we will continue to focus primarily on the first step, which involves definitions of the elements of financial accounting.

FIGURE 7.4 A summary of some of the steps undertaken within the accounting process

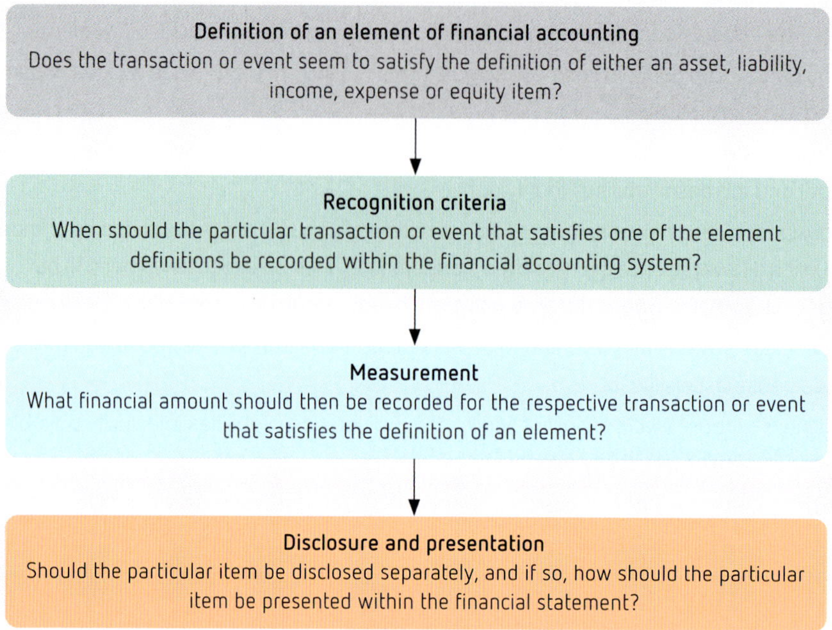

LO7.11 The accounting equation

The practice of financial accounting relies upon the use of the *accounting equation*. We can start with the simple representation of the accounting equation that we used earlier:

$$\text{Owners' equity (OE)} = \text{assets (A)} - \text{liabilities (L)}$$

Rearranging this, the accounting equation can be represented as:

$$\text{Assets (A)} = \text{liabilities (L)} + \text{owners' equity (OE)}$$

Let us consider this equation. What it is telling us is that when an organisation has assets, particular stakeholders – either owners or external creditors – will have a claim against those assets. The total of assets will balance the total of liabilities and owners' equity. This, as we already know, will be reflected within the balance sheet.

For example, let's assume that an organisation commences operations by having the owner contribute $500 000 in cash. This would impact our accounting equation as follows:

$$A = L + OE$$

$$\$500\,000 = \$0 + \$500\,000$$

At this point, as there are no liabilities (debt), the owner has a claim (which can be referred to as an equity claim) on all the assets of the organisation (the accounting entity).

If the organisation then acquires a factory for $1 000 000 by way of a bank loan for the full amount, the equation becomes:

$$A = L + OE$$

$$\$1\,500\,000 = \$1\,000\,000 + \$500\,000$$

The total assets now have a value of $1 500 000, of which the bank has a claim against the assets of $1 000 000, and the owners' equity (share) of the assets is the residual, which is $500 000. Remember that equity is defined as the residual interest in the assets of the entity after deducting all of its liabilities. What this effectively means is that if the organisation suddenly ceased operations, the bank would make a claim for payment of $1 000 000, and if the factory could be sold for $1 000 000, then the owners would receive the residual amount of $500 000 which corresponds to 'equity'.

For further discussion of the accounting equation, including its application, see **Learning exercises 7.19**, **7.20** and **7.21**.

7.19 Learning Exercise

Application of the accounting equation

In December 2023, Pam Burridge resigns from her job as a marketing manager of a multinational company. She then commences her own wholesale clothing business (sole trader), known as Pammy Surfco. The business commences on 1 January 2024. The transactions for the month of January 2024 undertaken by Pammy Surfco are listed below.

We will analyse each of the following transactions using the basic accounting equation of A = L + OE. We will also calculate the total assets, liabilities and equity after each transaction.

1 On 1 January 2024, Pam commences the business by contributing $50 000 cash and a motor vehicle worth $30 000. The business now has cash (asset) of $50 000, a vehicle (asset) worth $30 000, and equity (residual interest of assets less liabilities) of $80 000.

2 On 4 January 2024, the business acquires a warehouse at a cost of $400 000 by way of a bank loan that is repayable in two years. The business now has another asset (warehouse) valued at $400 000, and a new liability (bank loan) of $400 000. There is no change to equity.

3 On 8 January 2024, the business acquires some inventory (stock), on credit, for $50 000 payable in 20 days' time. The business now has another asset (inventory) valued at $50 000 and a new liability (accounts payable) of $50 000. There is no change to equity.

4 On 15 January 2024, the business sells half of the inventory to customers, on credit terms, for $60 000. The amount is to be paid by the customers within 14 days. There are four parts to this transaction to consider. The business now has decreased its inventory (asset) by $25 000 and received another asset (accounts receivable) of $60 000, and made a profit of $35 000 (increase in owners' equity). The profit is the difference between the income from the sale of $60 000 and the cost of goods sold of $25 000.

5 On 21 January 2024, the business pays wages of $1 000. The business has reduced its cash (asset) by $1 000, as well as reducing its profit (owners' equity) by $1 000.

6 On 28 January 2024, the business receives the amount of $60 000 due from debtors. The business has received cash of $60 000, which increases cash (asset) by $60 000, and as the accounts receivables (debtors) have paid their debt and these funds are no longer owing to the business, the asset (accounts receivable) is decreased by $60 000.

7 On 29 January 2024 the business pays the amount owing to creditors. The business has reduced its cash (asset) by $50 000 and decreased its liability (accounts payable) by $50 000.

8 On 30 January 2024, Pam withdraws $2000 for private purposes. The cash (asset) has decreased by $2000 as the owner has received a distribution of $2000, which also reduces the value of the owners' equity in the business.

To show the changes to the elements of financial accounting, we can use the following table. Note that after each transaction, A = L + OE.

Date	Assets	=	Liabilities	+	Owners' equity
1 January	Increase cash by $50 000 Increase motor vehicle by $30 000		No effect		Increase owners' claim by $80 000
	Total assets $80 000	=	**Total liabilities $0**	+	**Total OE $80 000**
4 January	Increase building by $400 000		Increase bank claim by $400 000		No change
	Total assets $480 000	=	**Total liabilities $400 000**	+	**Total OE $80 000**
8 January	Increase inventory by $50 000		Increase accounts payable by $50 000		No change
	Total assets $530 000	=	**Total liabilities $450 000**	+	**Total OE $80 000**
15 January	Increase accounts receivable by $60 000 Decrease inventory by $25 000		No change		Increase profit by $35 000
	Total assets $565 000	=	**Total liabilities $450 000**	+	**Total OE $115 000**
21 January	Decrease cash by $1000		No change		Decrease profit by $1000
	Total assets $564 000	=	**Total liabilities $450 000**	+	**Total OE $114 000**
28 January	Increase cash by $60 000 Decrease accounts receivable by $60 000		No change		No change
	Total assets $564 000	=	**Total liabilities $450 000**	+	**Total OE $114 000**
29 January	Decrease cash by $50 000		Decrease accounts payable by $50 000		No change
	Total assets of $514 000	=	**Total liabilities $400 000**	+	**Total OE $114 000**
30 January	Decrease cash by $2000		No change		Decrease equity by $2000
	Total assets $512 000	=	**Total liabilities $400 000**	+	**Total OE $112 000**

Therefore, from the analysis above, the accounting equation at the end of January 2024 would appear as follows:

Assets = liabilities + owners' equity

$512 000 = $400 000 + $112 000

It balances! Indeed, it must balance or otherwise we have made a mistake.

7.20 Learning Exercise

The accounting equation

1 If we record all the transactions of a period and the total assets do not equal the sum of liabilities and owners' equity, have we made a mistake?

2 If we record all the transactions of a period and the total assets equal the sum of liabilities and owners' equity, have we made a mistake?

Solution

1. If we have recorded transactions and we find that the total of assets does not equal the totals of both liabilities and equity, then we have made a mistake. The value of total assets must be matched by the sum of the claims held by the owners (the equity claims) and the claims held by lenders and other creditors (liabilities).
2. If we have recorded all the transactions and the total of assets does equal the combined total of liabilities and equity, then this does not necessarily mean we have correctly recorded all transactions. Perhaps we have neglected to record an entire transaction, or perhaps we have made compensating errors that just happen to 'balance out'. So the principle to be learned here is that, although our accounting equation might balance after we have recorded the transactions, and whilst this is comforting, this does not *absolutely* mean that we have not made some errors.

The double-entry effect of transactions

What we can see in the preceding analysis is that if a particular asset is affected – say increased – then there needs to be a corresponding decrease in another asset, and/or a corresponding increase in liabilities or equity. Otherwise, the equation will not balance! It should always balance, and if it does not, you have made a mistake.

7.21 Learning Exercise

Application of the accounting equation

Scenario: An organisation has borrowed some money from a bank.

Issue: If a particular liability increases – for example, by increasing the debt owed to a bank – then what other effects could there be on the accounting equation?

Solution: Given that we expect the accounting equation of A = L + OE to balance, then if we borrowed some money, thereby increasing liabilities, the other possible effects could be:

1. *A decrease in another liability.* For example, the borrowings might be used to pay another liability. This would mean that one liability increased (bank loan) and another liability decreased, and we would have a balanced accounting equation.
2. *An increase in an asset.* For example, the borrowings might be placed in the cash at bank account. This would mean that a liability (bank loan) increased and an asset increased (cash at bank), and we would have a balanced accounting equation.
3. *A decrease in owners' equity.* Whilst it would be a poor business practice, the borrowings might be distributed to the owners. This would mean that a liability (bank loan) increased and equity decreased (as a result of the drawings), and we would have a balanced accounting equation.

Expanding our accounting equation to incorporate specific changes in equity

Our original accounting equation took the form:

$$A = L + OE$$

Owners' equity will be *increased* by profits – which arises when income exceeds expenses (I – E), as well as by contributions from owners (C). By contrast, owners' equity will be *decreased* by distributions made to owners (D). That is, changes in owners' equity equals:

$$\text{Profits} + C - D$$

Given profits is the difference between income and expenses, that is:

$$\text{Profits} = I - E$$

then the above equation of *Profits + C – D* which represents the changes in equity can become:

$$(I - E) + C - D$$

Substituting this equation into the original accounting equation (above) gives us:

$$A = L + OE$$

$$A = L + [(I - E) + C - D]$$

Rearranging this equation (by adding E and D to both sides) gives us our new equation, which we can say is our expanded accounting equation:

$$A + E + D = L + I + C$$

We can say that the left-hand side of the equation represents the *application of funds*, and the right-hand side represents the *sources of the funds*. That is, the sources of funds – the right-hand side of the equation above – coming into the organisation will be income, owners' contributions or borrowings (liabilities). Once the funds are in the organisation, they can be used (applied) to acquire assets, pay expenses, or pay for distributions to owners (dividends). The sources of funds will equal the application of funds. That is, all funds that come into an organisation logically will go somewhere.

For further discussion of applying the expanded accounting equation, see **Learning exercise 7.22** and **Learning exercise 7.23**. Later in this chapter, **Learning exercise 7.25** similarly illustrates the use of the expanded accounting equation.

Why do I need to know the accounting equation?

The accounting equation represents a cornerstone of financial accounting. That is, the entire financial accounting system (including the conventional use of debits and credits) is fundamentally built on the accounting equation.

7.22 Learning Exercise

Applying the expanded accounting equation

Analyse the following transactions using our expanded accounting equation of A + E + D = L + I + C:

1. An owner contributes a car to their business worth $20 000.
2. The business performs services for an organisation for a fee of $1500 cash.
3. The business acquires merchandise (inventory, or stock) for $600 on credit terms.
4. The business pays a creditor $300.
5. The business buys some machinery for $2000 cash.

6 The business pays rental expense of $500 with cash.

7 The owner withdraws $100 for personal expenses.

You are also to provide the totals for A, E, D, L, I and C after all these transactions have been accounted for.

Solution

1 The source of the funds is the owner's contribution, and the application of those funds is the increase in the assets of $20 000.

A	+	E	+	D	=	L	+	I	+	C
$20 000										$20 000

2 The funds received from performing the services go into assets in the form of cash (the application of the funds), and the source of the funds was income.

A	+	E	+	D	=	L	+	I	+	C
$1500								$1500		

3 The source of the funds here is the credit provided by the supplier, and these funds have been used to acquire assets (inventory).

A	+	E	+	D	=	L	+	I	+	C
$600						$600				

4 The source of the funds is the cash at bank (asset) which now decreases, and the application of the funds is the payment of the creditor meaning liabilities also decreases.

A	+	E	+	D	=	L	+	I	+	C
($300)						($300)				

5 The source of the funds is the cash at bank (asset), and the application of the funds is the acquisition of the machinery (asset). Here we can see that one asset increases and another asset decreases.

A	+	E	+	D	=	L	+	I	+	C
$2000										
($2000)										

6 The source of the funds is the cash at bank (asset), which has decreased, and the application of the funds is the payment of expenses (rental expense).

A	+	E	+	D	=	L	+	I	+	C
($500)		$500								

7 The source of the funds is the cash at bank (asset), and the application of the funds is the payment to the owner (which could be treated as a dividend).

A	+	E	+	D	=	L	+	I	+	C
($100)				$100						

The totals of the five different elements at the end of January, following all of the above transactions, are:

A	+	E	+	D	=	L	+	I	+	C
$21 200		$500		$100		$300		$1500		$20 000

As we can see, the accounting equation balances – as it should!

Financial accountants depict any increase in the left-hand side of the expanded accounting equation – that is, the increases in A, E and D – as *debit* entries, whereas any increase in the right-hand side of the expanded accounting equation, being L + I + C, is depicted as *credit* entries. Conversely, any decrease in the left-hand side is a *credit*, and any decrease in the right-hand side is a *debit*. The rule applied is that total debits must always equal total credits, otherwise an error has been made. We will not talk further about debits and credits in this chapter. They are discussed within Chapter 8.

7.23 Learning Exercise

A further application of the expanded accounting equation

We will use the same transactions used earlier in **Learning exercise 7.19** for Pammy Surfco. However, this time you are to record the transactions using our expanded accounting equation.

1 On 1 January 2024, Pam commences the business by contributing cash of $50 000 and a motor vehicle worth $30 000.

2 On 4 January 2024, the business acquires a warehouse at a cost of $400 000 by way of a bank loan repayable in two years.

3 On 8 January 2024, the business acquires some inventory (stock), on credit, for $50 000 payable in 20 days' time.

4 On 15 January 2024, the business sells half of the inventory to customers, on credit terms, for $60 000. The amount is to be paid by the customers within 14 days.

5 On 21 January 2024, the business pays wages of $1000.

6 On 28 January 2024, the business receives the amount due from debtors (accounts receivable).

7 On 29 January 2024, the business pays the amount owing to creditors.

8 On 30 January 2024, Pam withdraws $2000 for private purposes.

Solution

We can summarise the effects of each transaction on assets, expenses, drawings, liabilities, income and contributions in the table below. After each transaction, we must ensure that the equation balances, otherwise we have made a mistake. Note that the numbers are in thousands of dollars.

Date	A	+	E	+	D	=	L	+	I	+	C
1/1	80										80
4/1	400						400				
8/1	50						50				
15/1	60								60		
	(25)		25								
21/1	(1)		1								
28/1	60										
	(60)										
29/1	(50)						(50)				
30/1	(2)				2						
Total	512	+	26	+	2	=	400	+	60	+	80

Again, it balances! As we know, if it did not balance, then we would have made a mistake.

The need for separate accounts

From **Learning exercise 7.23**, we know what the aggregated totals are for each of the elements of A, E, D, L, I and C, *but* this is of limited use. It is not very useful to know that we have a total amount of assets of, say, $512 000. What types of assets are they? Are they the types that can easily be sold for cash? Are they current or non-current assets? Are they tangible or intangible assets? Are they owned or leased?

We need to set up separate accounts for each item of information we would like to know about. For example, we might have a separate account for each of the assets 'cash at bank', 'motor vehicle', 'warehouse', 'inventory', 'accounts receivable' and so forth.

An organisation will typically have a 'chart of accounts' that identifies the various accounts being used; that is, the various asset, liability, income, expense and equity accounts. In a subsequent chapter, we will provide an illustration of a chart of accounts.

For a discussion of the impacts of transactions on separate accounts, see **Learning exercise 7.24**.

7.24 Learning Exercise

Recording the impact of transactions on individual accounts

Referring back to the transactions of Pammy Surfco (used in **Learning exercise 7.19** and **Learning exercise 7.23**), we will now do an analysis of changes in individual financial accounts.

1. On 1 January 2024, Pam commences the business by contributing cash of $50 000 and a motor vehicle worth $30 000.
2. On 4 January 2024, the business acquires a warehouse at a cost of $400 000 by way of a bank loan repayable in two years.
3. On 8 January 2024, the business acquires some inventory (stock), on credit, for $50 000 payable in 20 days' time.
4. On 15 January 2024, the business sells half of the inventory to customers, on credit terms, for $60 000. The amount is to be paid by the customers within 14 days.
5. On 21 January 2024, the business pays wages of $1000.
6. On 28 January 2024, the business receives the amount due from debtors.
7. On 29 January 2024, the business pays the amount owing to creditors.
8. On 30 January 2024, Pam withdraws $2000 for private purposes, and this is considered to represent a distribution of profits.

Solution

Note that the numbers in the table below are in thousands of dollars.

Date	Cash	Inventory	Accounts receivable	Motor vehicle	Warehouse	Cost of goods sold	Wages	Distributions	Accounts payable	Bank loan	Sales	Contributions
1/1	50			30								80
4/1					400					400		
8/1		50							50			
15/1		(25)	60			25					60	
21/1	(1)						1					
28/1	60		(60)									
29/1	(50)								(50)			
30/1	(2)							2				
Total	57	25	0	30	400	25	1	2	0	400	60	80

Assets + Expenses + Distributions – Liabilities + Income + Contributions

$512 000 + $26 000 + $2000 = $400 000 + $60 000 + $80 000

Now that we have all this information about the account balances at the end of the accounting period, we are in a position to produce some financial statements. As we know, assets, liabilities and equity are reported in the balance sheet, whilst income and expenses are reported in the income statement.

LO7.12 Preparing simple financial statements

Following the preceding transactions, let us now compile some financial statements. The first financial statement we shall present is the balance sheet. The balance sheet presents information about the financial position of the organisation, and provides information about the assets, liabilities and equity of the organisation. The equity to be recorded within the balance sheet will be the opening balance of equity plus the income and contributions of the reporting period, less the expenses and distributions of the reporting period. That is, for Pammy Surfco:

Owners' equity at the end of the accounting period = owners' equity at the beginning of the period + income – expenses + contributions – distributions

As this is the first month of the organisation's operation, the opening owners' equity is therefore zero, meaning owners' equity at the end of the accounting period is:

\$0 + \$60 000 – \$26 000 + \$80 000 – \$2000 = \$112 000

BALANCE SHEET OF PAMMY SURFCO
as at 31 January 2024

	$
Current assets	
Cash at bank	57 000
Inventory	25 000
Non-current assets	
Motor vehicle	30 000
Warehouse	400 000
Total assets	**512 000**
Non-current liabilities	
Bank loan	400 000
Total liabilities	**400 000**
Net assets	**112 000**
Owners' equity	
Retained earnings*	32 000
Capital contributions	80 000
Total Owners' equity	112 000

* Profits that are left in the business and not distributed are called *retained earnings*. In this case, it is the \$34 000 profit less the \$2000 drawings.

The above balance sheet is of the form A – L = OE. Balance sheets can also be presented in the form A = L + OE.

We will now present the income statement of Pammy Surfco for the month ending 31 January 2024. As we know, the income statement shows income and expenses, and the difference between the two will be profits. If this difference is negative, however – that is, income is less than expenses – then there will be a loss. Using the numbers provided in Learning exercise 7.24, the income statement appears as follows:

INCOME STATEMENT FOR PAMMY SURFCO
for the month ending 31 January 2024

	$
Income	
Sales revenue	60 000
Expenses	
Cost of goods sold	(25 000)
Wages	(1000)
Profit	34 000

Another financial statement that will typically be presented is the statement of cash flows. This financial statement will be covered in more depth in Chapter 11, but at this stage, all you need to know is that the statement of cash flows provides a reconciliation of opening and closing cash (cash is an asset that appears in the balance sheet). The cash flows (cash inflows and cash outflows) of an organisation are typically classified as being from operating activities, financing activities and investing activities, where:

- cash flows from *operating activities* relate to the provision of goods and services, and other activities related to the normal operations of the organisation
- cash flows from *investing activities* relate to the acquisition and disposal of non-current assets (including property, plant and equipment, and other productive assets) and other investments
- cash flows from *financing activities* relate to contributions from, and distributions to, owners, and borrowings from, and repayments to, lenders.

However, we again stress that we shall cover the statement of cash flows more fully in Chapter 11.

STATEMENT OF CASH FLOWS FOR PAMMY SURFCO
for the month ending 31 January 2024

	$	$
Cash flows from operating activities		
Receipts from customers	60 000	
Payments to suppliers	(50 000)	
Payments to employees	(1000)	9000
Cash flows from financing activities		
Capital contribution from owner	50 000	
Drawing by owner	(2000)	48 000
Net increase in cash		57 000
Opening cash		0
Closing cash		57 000

A fourth financial statement that is typically presented in general purpose financial statements is the statement of changes in equity. This financial statement will be covered in more depth in Chapter 10, but at this stage, all you need to know is that the statement of changes in equity provides a reconciliation of opening and closing equity as it appears within the balance sheet.

STATEMENT OF CHANGES IN EQUITY FOR PAMMY SURFCO for the month ending 31 January 2024			
	Capital contribution $	Retained earnings $	Total equity $
Balance at 1/1/20	0	0	0
Capital contributed	80 000		80 000
Drawings by owners		(2 000)	(2 000)
Profit for the month		34 000	34 000
	80 000	32 000	112 000

7.25 Learning Exercise

Another illustration of the use of the expanded accounting equation

Scenario: On 1 October 2024, Tommy Carroll commenced his own business – Tom's Printing. Over the next month, Tom recorded the following transactions:

- On 1 October 2024, to commence the business, Tommy contributes $5000 cash, and 20 printers which are worth $4000 in total.
- On 2 October 2024, Tom's Printing borrows $40 000 cash from a bank, to be repaid in four years.
- On 6 October 2024, Tom's Printing purchases office supplies for $2000 on credit terms.
- On 15 October 2024, Tom's Printing pays insurance expenses of $3000.
- On 18 October 2024, Tom uses his personal credit card to purchase a mobile phone worth $1000 for personal use.
- On 21 October 2024, Tom's Printing receives cash of $9000 for printing services performed.
- On 27 October 2024, Tom's Printing pays $2000 owing to creditors.
- On 28 October 2024, Tom's Printing pays office rent of $2000.
- On 30 October 2024, Tommy withdraws $1000 from his business to purchase a computer for personal use.

Task: You are required to prepare some financial statements for Tom's Printing, specifically:

- a balance sheet as at 31 October 2024
- an income statement for the month ending 31 October 2024
- a statement of cash flows for the month ending 31 October 2024
- a statement of changes in equity for the month ending 31 October 2024.

Solution: The following table summarises the above transactions (in thousands of dollars).

Date	Cash	Office equipment	Office supplies	Insurance expense	Rent expense	Distributions	Accounts payable	Bank loan	Printing revenue	Contributions
1/10	5	4								9
2/10	40							40		
6/10			2				2			
15/10	(3)			3						
21/10	9								9	
27/10	(2)						(2)			
28/10	(2)				2					
30/10	(1)					1				
Total	46	4	2	3	2	1	0	40	9	9

Assets	+	Expenses	+	Distributions	=	Liabilities	+	Income	+	Contributions
$52 000	+	$5000	+	$1000	=	$40 000	+	$9000	+	$9000

This can also be represented as:

$$\text{Assets} = \text{liabilities} + \text{owners' equity}$$

$$\$52\,000 = \$40\,000 + \$12\,000$$

Please pay particular attention to how owners' equity was calculated!

You should note from the above analysis that for financial accounting purposes, we have ignored the transaction that occurred on 18 October. This is because the transaction did not affect any of the financial accounts of the organisation. That is, the transaction was outside of the accounting entity; it was of a private nature.

Following the recording of the transactions, we can now compile some financial statements, as follows.

BALANCE SHEET FOR TOM'S PRINTING as at 31 October 2024	
	$
Current assets	
Cash at bank	46 000
Office supplies	2 000
Non-current assets	
Office equipment	4 000
Total assets	**52 000**
Non-current liabilities	
Bank loan	40 000
Total liabilities	**40 000**
Net assets	**12 000**
Owners' equity	
Retained earnings	3 000*
Contributions	9 000
	12 000

*Retained earnings equals the profits of $4000 less the distribution of $1000.

INCOME STATEMENT FOR TOM'S PRINTING for the month ending 31 October 2024	
	$
Income	
Printing revenue	9 000
Expenses	
Insurance	(3 000)
Rent	(2 000)
Profit	**4 000**

STATEMENT OF CASH FLOWS FOR TOM'S PRINTING for the month ending 31 October 2024		
	$	$
Cash flows from operating activities		
Receipts from customers	9000	
Payments to suppliers	(2000)	
Payments to others	(5000)	2000
Cash flows from financing activities		
Capital contribution from owner	5000	
Proceeds of loan	40000	
Drawings by owner	(1000)	44000
Net increase in cash		46000
Opening cash		0
Closing cash		**46000**

STATEMENT OF CHANGES IN EQUITY FOR TOM'S PRINTING for the month ending 31 October 2024			
	Capital contributions $	Retained earnings $	Total equity $
Balance at 1/10/2024	0	0	0
Capital contributed	9000		9000
Distributions		(1000)	(1000)
Profit for the month		4000	4000
Balance at 31/10/2024	9000	3000	12000

STUDY TOOLS

SUMMARY

This chapter is the first in this book dedicated to financial accounting. In this chapter we learned that:

- financial accounting provides information about the financial position, and financial performance, of an organisation for a past period of time
- the objective of financial accounting is primarily linked to providing information to existing and potential investors, lenders and other creditors in order to assist them in making decisions about providing resources to an organisation (although we also acknowledged that other stakeholders will have an interest in financial accounting information). Managers will also use financial accounting information although they will have access to information beyond that reported within general purpose financial reports.
- financial accounting can generate either special purpose financial statements or general purpose financial statements, and that larger organisations are relatively more likely to prepare GPFSs, with those statements being produced to comply with various financial accounting regulations

- there are various principles of financial accounting that need to be applied when undertaking the practice of financial accounting, such as the entity concept, the accounting period convention, the monetary unit assumption, the going concern principle, and the accrual basis of accounting
- there are fundamental qualitative characteristics that useful financial accounting information should possess (these being relevance and representational faithfulness), as well as enhancing qualitative characteristics (these being comparability, verifiability, timeliness and understandability)
- financial accounting relies on the identification of five elements – assets, liabilities, equity, income and expenses – and we learned the definition of each of these elements. In doing so, we became aware of the fact that not all of the resources used by an organisation are recognised as assets, which in turn means that some costs created by an organisation ultimately do not get recognised as expenses of the organisation
- the elements of financial accounting known as assets, liabilities and equity appear in a balance sheet, whereas income and expenses appear in an income statement
- assets and liabilities can be further subdivided into current and non-current components
- the accounting equation can be used as the basis for recording a series of transactions for organisations, which ultimately culminated in us preparing some financial statements for organisations.

The subsequent chapters on financial accounting will expand on the knowledge that we have gained from reading this chapter.

ANSWERS TO THE OPENING QUESTIONS

At the beginning of the chapter we asked the following three questions. As a result of reading this chapter, you should now be able to provide informed answers to these questions – ours are shown below.

1 What are the five elements of financial accounting?

The five elements of financial accounting are assets, liabilities, income, expenses and equity.

2 Which elements of financial accounting are reported in the balance sheet, and which elements are reported in the income statement?

Assets, liabilities and equity are reported in the balance sheet, and income and expenses are reported in the income statement.

3 How is the balance of owners' equity determined, and what causes the balance of owners' equity to change during an accounting period?

The balance of owners' equity is calculated by subtracting the liabilities of an organisation from its assets. The balance of owners' equity will change during an accounting period in the following way:

- it will increase as a result of income being earned during the accounting period, and as a result of contributions from the owners
- it will decrease as a result of expenses being incurred during the accounting period, and as a result of drawings made by the owners during the accounting period.

SELF-TEST QUIZ

Answers to this quiz appear in the Appendix of this book.

1 In relation to the qualitative characteristics expected of useful financial accounting information, useful financial accounting information should be:

a relevant
b representationally faithful
c understandable
d verifiable
e All of these choices

2 Which of the following is false in relation to 'assets'?

a An asset is an 'economic resource' controlled by the entity.
b An asset must be legally owned by the entity.
c For the purposes of defining an asset, an 'economic resource' is defined as 'a right that has the potential to produce economic benefits'.
d The 'rights' associated with an asset shall have the potential to produce economic benefits.
e An asset exists as a result of past events.

3 The expanded accounting equation is:

a A + L + E = I + C + D
b A + C + E = I + L + D
c A + L + D = I + C + E
d A + E + D = I + C + L
e A + L + I = E + C + D

4 Sandy Bay Company starts the reporting period with equity of $150 000. During the reporting period the organisation earns income of $780 000, incurs expenses of $270 000, pays dividends to owners of $100 000, and the owners contribute equity of $60 000. What is the equity at the end of the reporting period?

a $670 000
b $620 000
c $580 000
d $610 000
e None of these choices

5 The following transactions relate to Salamanca Limited for the month of October. Salamanca Limited commenced operations on 1 October.

i. On 1 October the owner contributed cash of $30 000 and a car worth $35 000
ii. On 5 October the organisation acquired inventory at a cost of $40 000 with the amount payable within two weeks
iii. On October 10 the organisation sold half of the inventory for $55 000 cash
iv. On October 15 the organisation paid salaries expense of $12 000
v. On October 19 the organisation paid the amount due to creditors for the inventory purchased on 5 October
vi. On October 25 the organisation paid the owners $3000 cash in dividends

Which of the following is true in relation to the total balances at the end of October?

a Total assets will be $80 000 and total income will be $55 000
b Total assets will be $85 000 and profits will be $43 000
c Total assets will be $85 000 and equity will be $85 000
d Total assets will be $105 000 and profits will be $23 000
e None of these choices

ONLINE RESOURCES

Accompanying the book is an innovative online case study that follows an organisation initially established by two friends, which grows into a large and successful company. Acquire this chapter's case study from your instructor.

CASE STUDY

Armadillo Surf Designs: Help wanted

You have been promoted to the position of manager of the accounting and finance department at Armadillo Surf Designs (ASD). Well done! Now that ASD is a listed company, you have asked that an additional accountant be employed to help you with the financial reporting obligations. However, Maddie isn't convinced that an additional accountant is required. In addition, some IT issues have impacted your accounting software, and some transactions and events are missing from the system.

You will explain to Maddie that ASD's reporting requirements are now different as a publicly listed company compared with when ASD first started as a partnership. Before you commence finalising the annual financial statements, you will consider the impact of each of the missing transactions and events on the financial statements.

END-OF-CHAPTER QUESTIONS

7.1 What are the elements of financial accounting?

7.2 Define each of the elements of financial accounting.

7.3 What is a balance sheet?

7.4 What is an income statement?

7.5 If the assets of an organisation are $1.5 million, and the liabilities are $1.1 million, what is the value of equity of the organisation?

7.6 Which financial statement do assets and liabilities appear within?

7.7 Are all the resources used by an organisation included within the assets reported by it?

7.8 What does it mean to say that an organisation is a going concern? What are the implications for financial accounting if it is decided that an organisation is not a going concern?

7.9 What is the purpose of a conceptual framework for financial reporting?

7.10 Explain the implications that the 'entity principle' has for determining what transactions and events are recorded for financial accounting purposes.

7.11 What does it mean if we say that particular financial accounting information is considered 'relevant'?

7.12 If an organisation does not control a resource, then should that resource appear within the organisation's financial statements?

7.13 What is a current liability and a current asset?

7.14 If an organisation has an opening balance of owners' equity of $125 000, income of $670 000, expenses of $325 000, contributions during the accounting period of $35 000, and distributions during the accounting period of $12 000, what is the value of owners' equity at the end of the reporting period?

7.15 Why might we compare the current assets of an organisation with its current liabilities?

7.16 What is a contingent liability, and will a contingent liability appear within a balance sheet?

7.17 Why would a partnership, or sole trader, be expected to have fewer financial reporting requirements than a large public company?

7.18 Should all relevant information be disclosed to interested stakeholders?

7.19 What is a general purpose financial statement, and which organisations generate such statements?

7.20 According to the Conceptual Framework for Financial Reporting, what is the objective of general purpose financial reporting?

7.21 What are the fundamental qualitative characteristics of useful financial accounting information, and why are they considered 'fundamental'?

7.22 What are the enhancing qualitative characteristics of useful financial accounting information, and why are they considered 'enhancing'?

7.23 If information is not considered relevant and representationally faithful, what implications does this have for the disclosure of that information?

7.24 Would damage to a business owner's private residence be recognised as an expense of the business? Why or why not?

7.25 Why is it that the regulation of financial accounting is directed relatively more towards larger organisations?

7.26 What is an accounting period?

7.27 Are there any potentially dysfunctional impacts that might arise as a result of dividing the life of an organisation up into relatively short accounting periods?

7.28 What does it mean to say that an organisation is using the accrual basis of accounting?

7.29 Do all of the costs incurred or generated by an organisation get included within the income statement?

7.30 Applying the definition of expenses, would large amounts of CO_2 emissions by an organisation be considered an expense of an organisation?

7.31 If an organisation elected not to invest in a profitable venture, would these 'lost' earnings (or opportunity costs) be shown within the income statement?

7.32 Analyse the following transactions of a reporting period using the expanded accounting equation of A + E + D = L + I + C:

- **a** An owner contributes $15 000 in cash to commence a business.
- **b** The business purchases office equipment for $6000 cash.
- **c** The business performs services for an organisation for a fee of $3000, which is paid by the customer in cash.
- **d** The business acquires merchandise (or inventory, or stock) for $1000 on credit terms.
- **e** The business pays a creditor $500.
- **f** The business receives an electricity invoice for $600 that remains unpaid.
- **g** The business pays rent expense of $700 with cash.
- **h** The owner withdraws $50 cash for personal expenses.

You are also to provide the total of A, E, D, L, I and C after all these transactions have been accounted for.

7.33 Analyse the following transactions of a reporting period using the expanded accounting equation of A + E + D = L + I + C:

- **a** An owner contributes $20 000 in cash to commence a business.
- **b** The business purchases a motor vehicle for $10 000 using cash.
- **c** The business performs services for an organisation for a fee of $12 000, for which the cash is to be received one week later.
- **d** The business acquires merchandise (inventory or stock) for $700 on credit terms.
- **e** The business pays a creditor $700.
- **f** The business receives $12 000 from a debtor (accounts receivable).
- **g** The business receives an electricity invoice for $800 that remains unpaid.
- **h** The business pays rent expense of $900 with cash.
- **i** The owner withdraws merchandise that cost $100 for personal use.
- **j** The owner uses her own cash to acquire some new gym equipment for her home.

You are also to provide the total of A, E, D, L, I and C after all these transactions have been accounted for.

7.34 On 1 October 2024, Shane Horan commenced his own business, Shane's Painting. During the following month, Shane's Painting had the following transactions:

- **a** On 1 October 2024, to commence the business, Shane contributes $10 000 cash.
- **b** On 2 October 2024, Shane's Painting acquires office equipment for $6000 using cash.
- **c** On 2 October 2024, Shane's Painting borrows $30 000 from a bank, to be repaid in two years.
- **d** On 6 October 2024, Shane's Painting purchases painting supplies for $5000 on credit terms. These supplies are to be used for upcoming jobs.
- **e** On 15 October 2024, Shane's Painting pays insurance expenses of $2000.
- **f** On 21 October 2024, Shane's Painting receives a cash payment of $10 000 for painting services performed that week. In performing these services, $3000 in painting supplies (acquired on 6 October) were used.
- **g** On 27 October 2024, Shane's Painting pays $5000 that was owed to creditors.
- **h** On 28 October 2024, Shane's Painting pays office rent of $2000.
- **i** On 29 October 2024, Shane's Painting pays interest expenses of $550.
- **j** On 30 October 2024, Shane withdraws $1000 from his business to purchase a computer for personal use.

You are required to prepare a balance sheet as at 31 October 2024, and an income statement for the month ending 31 October 2024, for Shane's Painting.

7.35 On 1 October 2024, Layne Beachley commences her own business, Beachley Decorations. During the following month, Beachley Decorations undertakes the following transactions:

- **a** On 1 October 2024, to commence the business, Layne contributes $15 000 cash and a motor vehicle worth $15 000.
- **b** On 2 October 2024, Beachley Decorations acquires office equipment for $8000 cash.
- **c** On 4 October 2024, Beachley Decorations borrows $25 000 from a bank, to be repaid in nine months.
- **d** On 6 October 2024, Beachley Decorations purchases decorating supplies for $3000 cash. These supplies are to be used on future jobs.
- **e** On 7 October 2024, Beachley Decorations purchases decorating supplies for $4000 on credit terms. These supplies are to be used on future jobs.

- **f** On 15 October 2024, Beachley Decorations pays insurance expenses of $3000.
- **g** On 22 October 2024, Beachley Decorations receives a cash payment of $12 000 for decorating services performed in the preceding week. The supplies that were acquired on 6 October were fully used in performing the service.
- **h** On 28 October 2024, Beachley Decorations pays $4000 owing to creditors.
- **i** On 29 October 2024, Beachley Decorations pays office rent of $2500.
- **j** On 29 October 2024, Beachley Decorations pays electricity expenses of $700.
- **k** On 30 October 2024, Layne withdraws $1000 from the business to purchase a new surfboard for personal use.

You are required to prepare a balance sheet as at 31 October, and an income statement for the month ending 31 October 2024 for Beachley Decorations.

REFERENCES

Ball, R. (2006). International financial reporting standards: Pros and cons for investors. *Accounting and Business Research*, International Accounting Policy Forum, pp. 5–27.

Ball, R. (2016). IFRS – 10 years later. *Accounting and Business Research*, 46(5), pp. 545–571. Available at SSRN: https://ssrn.com/abstract=2745245 or http://dx.doi.org/10.2139/ssrn.2745245.

International Accounting Standards Board (2022a). *Conceptual Framework for Financial Reporting.* https://www.ifrs.org/issued-standards/list-of-standards/conceptual-framework.html/content/dam/ifrs/publications/html

International Accounting Standards Board (2022b). About us. https://www.ifrs.org/about-us/who-we-are/

International Accounting Standards Board (2022c), IAS 1: Presentation of Financial Statements. www.ifrs.org/issued-standards/list-of-standards/ias-1-presentation-of-financial-statements.html/content/dam/ifrs/publications/#standard

Qantas (2021) *Qantas annual report 2021.* https://investor.qantas.com/FormBuilder/_Resource/_module/doLLG5ufYkCyEPjF1tpgyw/file/annual-reports/2021-Annual-Report.pdf

CHAPTER

8

RECORDING TRANSACTIONS IN JOURNALS AND LEDGERS – MORE DETAIL ON THE FINANCIAL ACCOUNTING PROCESS

LEARNING OBJECTIVES

After completing this chapter readers should be able to:

- **LO8.1** explain the meaning and role of source documents as used within a financial accounting information system
- **LO8.2** describe the function of the journal, the meaning of debits and credits, and record transactions within a journal by assigning debits and credits to different types of transactions
- **LO8.3** explain the meaning of a 'ledger account', and transfer data from the journal to the respective ledger accounts
- **LO8.4** explain the purpose of compiling a trial balance
- **LO8.5** explain why we need to prepare adjusting journal entries at the end of the accounting period
- **LO8.6** explain why we are required to prepare closing entries at the end of the accounting period
- **LO8.7** understand the role of specialised journals and subsidiary ledgers
- **LO8.8** through the use of a comprehensive example of the financial accounting system, generate some financial statements.

OPENING QUESTIONS

Before reading this chapter, please consider how you would answer the following four questions. We will return to these questions at the end of the chapter, where we suggest some answers.

1. Within financial accounting, what is the role of the 'journal'?
2. What is a 'debit' and what is a 'credit'?
3. What is a 'trial balance'?
4. What are 'closing entries', and why do we need to do them?

Introduction

The previous chapter of this book was the first chapter dedicated to financial accounting. In that chapter, a number of important issues were considered, including:

- the meaning and objective of financial accounting
- the meaning and role of general purpose financial statements (GPFSs) and special purpose financial statements (SPFSs)
- some of the key principles to be applied when performing financial accounting
- the fundamental and enhancing qualitative characteristics that useful financial accounting information should possess
- definitions of the elements of financial accounting.

We also introduced the accounting equation in its simple form (A = L + OE) and in its expanded form (A + E + D = L + I + C). We then used the accounting equation, in conjunction with some worksheets that incorporated various additions and subtractions to accounts, to analyse the transactions of some organisations. Recall that from a financial accounting perspective, transactions affect assets, liabilities and/or owners' equity. We then used the aggregated information from these worksheets to prepare some financial statements.

Chapter 7 provided you with a very broad overview, and understanding, of how financial statements such as the balance sheet and the statement of profit or loss come into existence (the statement of profit or loss is also often referred to as an income statement, and we use the terms interchangeably in this book). However, Chapter 7 did not provide detail on how transactions are actually recorded and processed within 'real-life' financial accounting information systems. The way in which we accounted for the transactions in Chapter 7, by utilising a worksheet with various additions and subtractions, would be inefficient for larger numbers of transactions – albeit the use of worksheets was useful for describing the basics of financial statement preparation. Therefore, in this chapter, we will be introducing an approach that reflects what actually occurs in the 'real world'.

In the real world, most of what we are going to demonstrate in this chapter is done by computerised accounting packages such as MYOB, Xero and QuickBooks. What these packages do 'internally' is effectively what we are going to describe in this chapter – it is just hidden from view when it is done by a computer. That is, in this chapter we will be focusing on a manual accounting system in which we have to perform all the steps, but the principles of how we are doing this do not change if a computerised system is used. However, the computer will do most of the work for us – and much quicker than we could do it manually.

Having covered some of the important foundations of financial accounting in Chapter 7, in this chapter we will now further explore the accounting process by discussing and explaining:

- the role of source documents
- the use of journals
- the use of debits and credits
- the role of ledger accounts
- the role of the trial balance
- the need to prepare adjusting journal entries and closing journal entries at the end of the accounting period.

We will provide quite a bit of detail in this chapter. If you are going to major in accounting, you will need to understand this detail at some stage of your accounting education. The issues we cover in this chapter will be covered in even more detail in the future subjects you undertake as part of your accounting program.

For the non-accountant, this information is also very important. The processes we are going to describe form the foundation of many of the financial statements that you will see from time to time (such as balance sheets and statements of profit or loss), so it is worth knowing more about the processes leading to the preparation of these important financial statements. The reality is that financial statements – rightly or wrongly – play a very big role in the functioning of society, and influence where large amounts of financial resources are channelled. Furthermore, many financial documents use accounting terminology such as 'debits' and 'credits' (for example, some bank statements still use the terminology on accounts sent to customers, and various accounting software packages also often provide information in the form of debits and credits), so some knowledge of debits and credits will be useful.

LO8.1 The role of source documents

As detailed in Chapter 7, for a transaction or event to be recorded within a financial accounting system, it needs to be measurable in financial terms, and it needs to impact at least one of the five elements of accounting:

- assets
- liabilities
- income
- expenses
- equity.

Obviously, financial statements do not simply generate themselves. Financial statements – such as the balance sheet (or, as it is also known, the statement of financial position), income statement (or statement of profit or loss, or statement of financial performance), statement of cash flows, and statement of changes in equity – are the result of the application of the financial accounting process. The process of generating financial statements starts with analysing *source documents* and determining which accounts are impacted by the respective transactions or events to which the source documents relate.

A source document provides evidence of, or verifies the existence of, a transaction or event that influences one or more of the five elements of financial accounting. Source documents are the source of original financial accounting data. For example, an electricity bill and a sales invoice are both source documents and provide evidence – perhaps for the first time – that the assets of an organisation, or its liabilities, have changed, which might also have consequences for the owners' equity of the organisation.

More specifically, an electricity bill provides information about an expense (the electricity expense, which will decrease owners' equity) and a liability (electricity expenses payable, which needs to be recognised by the organisation as a liability). As another example, when an organisation makes a sale to a customer on credit terms, a sales invoice will be provided to the customer, and a copy will be retained by the organisation. The retained copy becomes a source document that provides evidence of the sale (it is sales revenue, which is part of the element 'income', which increases owners' equity) and the creation of an account receivable (which increases assets). If a cash sale is made to a customer, then a sales receipt will be given to the customer and a record of the sale – possibly recorded internally in a cash register – is retained by the organisation. This would also be a source document. The important point to learn here is that, for transactions to be recorded within the financial accounting system, an organisation *must* have a source document. A review of the source document initiates the recognition of the transaction or event within the financial accounting system.

In accordance with the entity principle that we learned about in Chapter 7, we only record transactions that affect the organisation (the accounting entity). Therefore, the source document must relate to the organisation. For example, if the source document related to the acquisition of furniture for personal use by an owner, using the owner's personal cash, then that source document is not of relevance to the organisation and would be ignored.

Some examples of relevant source documents are provided in **Table 8.1**. As can be seen, source documents can take a variety of forms. There are many other types of source documents in addition to those shown in **Table 8.1**.

TABLE 8.1 Examples of source documents

Transaction or event	Source document	*Accounts that would be affected (remember the equations A = L + OE and A + E + D = L + I + C*
Cash contribution from owner	Cash receipt slip	• Cash at bank (asset) increased • Contributions (equity) increased
Purchase of inventory on credit	Purchase invoice from supplier	• Inventory (asset) increased • Creditors (liability) increased
Sales of inventory on credit terms to a customer	Sales invoice generated by the organisation (a copy is retained by the organisation)	• Sales income (income) increased • Debtors (asset) increased • Cost of sales (expense) increased • Inventory (asset) decreased
Payment made to the supplier of inventory for inventory previously acquired on credit	Payment authorisation / cheque butt	• Cash (asset) decreased • Creditors (liability) decreased
Receipt of cash from accounts receivable / debtor	Notification of direct deposit from bank / cash deposit slip	• Cash (asset) increased • Debtors (asset) decreased
Purchase of machinery for cash	Purchase invoice from seller	• Machinery (asset) increased • Cash (asset) decreased

The source document – such as a sales invoice, or a purchase invoice – provides the raw data necessary for information to be entered into the accounting system. Again, the accountant needs to determine from the source document whether particular accounts have been impacted, and if so, by how much.

Key concept

A source document provides the information that is entered into the financial accounting system. All transactions and events require a source document before the transaction or event shall be recognised.

Up to this point, we have not recorded anything within the accounting system – we have simply collected and reviewed source documents that might have been prepared externally, or internally. The next step is to record the information from the source document in the financial accounting system – specifically in the journal, which will be covered next.

LO8.2 Recording transactions within the journal

The journal is the first point of entry for transactions/events into the financial accounting system. This is why the **journal** is often referred to as the book of prime (or original) entry. It is the first place we record the financial effects of a transaction, or event, appearing on a source document.

journal
In accounting, the journal is the first place in which the effects of transactions or events – typically evidenced on a source document – are entered into the accounting system. The journal will record the date of the transaction or event, the accounts to be adjusted and the associated amounts of debits and credits

In recording the effects of a transaction or event evidenced by a source document, we need to identify which accounts are affected. That is, rather than using a worksheet, as we did in Chapter 7, where all transactions are recorded, added and subtracted, we use *accounts*. There will be an individual account that records increases and decreases in a specific type of asset, liability, income, expense, or equity item.

As an example, assets might be broken down into the individual accounts of cash, accounts receivable, inventory, office furniture and so forth. To determine what accounts are being used by an organisation – different organisations will use different accounts – reference can be made to the organisation's chart of accounts. The **chart of accounts** provides a list of the accounts, typically giving an account number and account name for each one, with these classified under the respective element of accounting to which they belong. An example of a possible chart of accounts of an organisation that is a sole trader is provided in Exhibit 8.1.

chart of accounts
The chart of accounts provides a complete listing of every account in the general ledger of an organisation, often broken down into subcategories

EXHIBIT 8.1 An example of a chart of accounts

Chart of accounts for Wayne Lynch Painting Services		
	Account number	Account name
Assets (100–150)	100	Cash at bank
	105	Accounts receivable
	108	Paint and brushes supplies
	110	Prepaid rent
	120	Office equipment
	125	Painting equipment
	130	Motor vehicles
	140	Land
Liabilities (151–199)	155	Accounts payable
	165	Wages payable
	170	Bank loan

Chart of accounts for Wayne Lynch Painting Services		
	Account number	**Account name**
Equity (200–250)	201	W. Lynch, capital account
	230	Drawings
	240	Profit or loss summary
Income (251–299)	251	Painting income
	260	Interest income
Expenses (300–350)	310	Wages expense
	315	Cost of painting supplies used
	320	Rent expense
	340	Interest expense
	350	Electricity expense

As you can see from **Exhibit 8.1**, each of the five elements of accounting are broken up into smaller components that we call accounts. To the extent that these accounts are in a ledger (which is where all the accounts identified in the chart of accounts are located), they are called **ledger accounts**. Therefore, our first two steps in the financial accounting process so far are:

ledger accounts
A ledger account contains a record of transactions. It is a separate record or account that is assigned to a specific type of asset, liability, equity item, revenue, or expense type. The various ledger accounts being used will be shown in the chart of accounts

1. review the source document to determine if it refers to a transaction or event that affects the assets, liabilities, income, expenses, or equity of an organisation, and if it does,
2. record the transaction or event in the journal (this process is discussed below).

Financial accounting systems will differ from one organisation to another, with different organisations using different accounts (and therefore having different charts of accounts). The reasons for this include differences in:

- the nature of the organisation
- the ownership structure
- the types of transactions the organisation is involved in
- the mission, objectives and goals of the organisation (which influences what information is considered relevant)
- the number of transactions that occur
- managerial perspectives on organisational responsibilities and accountabilities (which links to the mission, objectives and goals)
- the information demands and expectations of stakeholders.

There is a degree of flexibility in choosing the names of the respective accounts. For example, some organisations might have an account called 'inventory', whereas other organisations might instead have an account called 'stock' or 'merchandise', with these three terms effectively meaning the same thing. There is no requirement, or standard, that specific names must be used for all ledger accounts. Further, the numbering system should be such that it allows additional accounts to be added in the future, as required. Organisations can choose the account numbers that they would prefer to use.

general journal
A journal that can generally be used to record all the transactions and events that affect the accounts of an organisation

The journal used in **Learning exercise 8.1** is the form of the journal we will use throughout this chapter. We refer to this as a **general journal** because it can be used for all transactions that enter the accounting system. That is, it has a 'general' application.

8.1 Learning Exercise

An example of the use of a journal

Scenario: As an example of the use of a journal, consider the following transactions, the details of which have been extracted from specific source documents:

- An owner – W. Lynch – contributes $10 000 to an organisation on 1 January 2025.
- The organisation acquires paint and brushes for $1000 on credit from Paintworks on 2 January 2025.

Task: You are to record these transactions in the journal.

Solution: The journal entries would appear as follows. We will explain these entries in more detail shortly.

General Journal — Page 1

Date	Account name	Account number	Debit $	Credit $
1 Jan 2025	Cash at bank	100	10 000	
	W. Lynch, Capital Account	201		10 000
	Owner contributed $10 000			
2 Jan 2025	Paint and brushes supplies	108	1 000	
	Accounts payable	155		1 000
	The business acquired painting equipment with cash			

Each general journal entry will include the date of the transaction, the accounts to be adjusted, and the associated debits and credits, which we will explain shortly. Some transactions might include multiple debits or credits, but it is essential that the total credits and total debits balance within each transaction (as we shall also learn shortly). A journal entry is made for each transaction when using the general journal. Each journal entry is also often followed by a brief description of the transaction, which we call a **narration**.

The journal is the first point within the accounting process at which we use debits and credits. Having not discussed debits and credits previously, and as the journal is the first place in which they are used, we will now explain these terms.

Why do I need to know about all the steps that occur in order to produce financial statements given that there is accounting software that will do most of this for me?

It is true that once we enter the details of particular transactions and events into a particular accounting software package then a lot of the work will be done automatically within the 'black box' and therefore will be out of sight. However, to more fully comprehend what the different financial statements represent and how particular transactions and events influence the various 'accounts', we believe it makes sense to describe what happens within the inner workings of the accounting software. Nevertheless, you do need to appreciate that a lot of the rather tedious and time-consuming work that we will document and explain in the following pages would not be done manually (although it was done manually for many centuries up until about the early 1980s). However, we stress that unless you understand how the original recognition of a transaction and event is entered, adjusted, aggregated with other transactions and events, and so on, then it would be very difficult to fully comprehend what the final product – the financial statements – actually represent. For example, if we did not provide a detailed description of the financial accounting process, then you might not understand that when we recognise unpaid expenses at the end of the financial period, we also concurrently make adjustments to certain liability accounts. Also, as another example, when we recognise depreciation expense at the end of the reporting period, we also concurrently recognise a reduction in assets through certain contra accounts. This would not be obvious if we were simply using accounting software.

Use of debits and credits within the journal

As we learned in Chapter 7, the accounting equation can be simply presented as

Asset = liabilities + owners' equity

or

A = L + OE

What the above formula shows is that an organisation will have a total amount of financially measurable and controlled resources that are expected to provide future economic benefits (assets) against which stakeholders – lenders and creditors (liabilities), and owners (equity) – will have a claim.

For example, if an organisation has \$100 000 in assets and it has borrowed nothing, then effectively all the assets belong to the owners and no creditors or lenders have a claim against the assets; that is:

A = L + OE

\$100 000 = \$0 + \$100 000

If another \$50 000 in assets were acquired by way of a loan from a bank, then assets would increase to \$150 000 and the owners' share (or owners' equity) of the assets would remain as \$100 000. The liabilities (in this case represented by the bank loan) would represent a claim against the assets of \$50 000; that is:

A	=	L	+	OE
\$100 000	=	\$0	+	\$100 000
+ \$50 000	=	+ \$50 000	+	______
\$150 000		\$50 000		\$100 000

Every time assets change in total, this means there will also be a change in either the owners' equity or the liabilities (with liabilities representing the claims against the assets by stakeholders who are not owners). The equation A = L + OE *must* always balance.

The accounting equation, and the view that it must always balance, are not new. In fact, this idea was first introduced over 600 years ago with one of the most famous explications of 'double-entry accounting' provided by a Franciscan monk named Luca Pacioli, who is often referred to as the 'father of accounting'. Pacioli documents double-entry accounting in his 1494 book published in Venice, *Summa de Arithmetica, Geometria, Proportioni et Proportionalita*. That book described debits and credits, meaning that the terminology has been around for over 600 years and can be traced back to what is known as the Renaissance period. Modern-day accountants therefore have a noble history to be proud of!

Returning to the basic accounting equation A = L + OE, and the requirement that it *must* always balance, the only way that an asset may increase is if it is matched by either:

- a decrease in another asset (for example, where a motor vehicle is purchased for cash)
- an increase in liabilities (for example, where a motor vehicle is purchased by way of a bank loan); or
- an increase in owners' equity (for example, where a motor vehicle is contributed to a business by an owner).

Simply put, there is no way to create or increase an asset without, at the same time, reducing another asset, incurring a liability, or increasing owners' equity. If one attempts to do so, the accounting equation will not balance, and that would not make sense. Recall from Chapter 7 that if the accounting equation does not balance, then this means that you have made a mistake.

Rather than saying that assets, equity and liabilities increase or decrease, accountants use two words – these being **debits** and **credits**. It is not clear why these particular words were chosen, but whatever the reason, these are the words that accountants have continued to use and we are effectively stuck with them – and have been for hundreds of years. The terms are part of the 'language' of financial accounting.

So, rather than simply saying that assets will increase, the accountant will say that there is a need to 'debit assets'. Conversely, when assets decrease, we say that we 'credit assets'. The other 'golden rule' of financial accounting is that *debits must equal credits*. If there is a debit entry, then there must be a credit entry, and the total debits must equal the total credits. As already mentioned, this system of accounting is frequently referred to as **double-entry accounting**. When preparing journal entries, if the total debits do not equal the total credits, then you have made a mistake.

debit
In double entry accounting, debits (and credits) are entries made in accounts to record changes in value resulting from the transactions and events that relate to an organisation. A debit is an accounting entry that results in either an increase in assets, expenses, or distributions, or a decrease in liabilities, income or contributions. In financial accounting, debits are balanced by credits

credit
In double entry accounting, credits (and debits) are entries made in accounts to record changes in value resulting from the transactions and events that relate to an organisation. A credit is an accounting entry that results in either an increase in liabilities, income, or contributions, or a decrease in assets, expenses or distributions. In financial accounting, credits are balanced by debits

double-entry accounting
A system for recording transactions and events where each recorded transaction and event creates one or more debit and credit entries, and where the total debits recorded must equal the total credits recorded

Key concept

In the double-entry accounting system, *debits must equal credits*. If there is a debit entry, then there must be a credit entry, and the total debits must equal the total credits.

It is called double-entry accounting because every time there is an entry for an account – for example, a debit entry – then there must be a corresponding credit entry for the same amount to another account (or perhaps more than one account). For example, if we were to buy some land for $1 000 000 on 1 January 2025 by using cash of $400 000 and a bank loan of $600 000, then we would have a debit entry of $1 000 000 for land, a credit entry to cash at bank for $400 000, and a credit entry to bank loan for $600 000. The total debits of $1 000 000 would equal the total credits of $1 000 000! When assets increase then that requires a debit entry, whereas when assets decrease, a credit entry is required. When liabilities increase then that is a credit entry. The journal entry would be:

Date	Account name	Debit $	Credit $
1 Jan 2025	Land	1 000 000	
	Cash at bank		400 000
	Bank loan		600 000
	Acquiring land with cash and a bank loan		

When we create ledger accounts – which we will discuss next – there will be a column for debit entries and there will be a column for credit entries for each account. The balance of the ledger account will be the difference between the total debits and total credits. If the total debits within a ledger account are greater than the total credits in that account, then the ledger account will have a *debit balance*. Conversely, if the total credits within a ledger account are greater than the total debits in that account, then it will have a *credit balance*. However, the total of all the individual ledger accounts with a debit balance must equal the total of all the individual accounts with a credit balance.

Another convention is that debits appear on the left-hand side of the respective ledger account and credits appear on the right-hand side. There is no obvious reason for this other than this is traditionally what has already been done – it's simply a long held convention.

Referring back to our basic accounting equation of A = L + OE, and remembering the requirement that debits must equal credits, an increase in assets represents debit entries, and an increase in liabilities and owners' equity represents credits. That is, an increase in the left-hand side of the equation (which we call debits) must be matched by an increase in the right-hand side of the equation (which we call credits). Conversely, a decrease in an asset would represent a credit, and a decrease in liabilities and owners' equity would be a debit. We can summarise this either in the form of a formula (see below) or by way of a table (see **Table 8.2**):

Assets = liabilities + owners' equity

↑ Debit ↑ Credit

↓ Credit ↓ Debit

TABLE 8.2 The rules relating to the use of debits and credits

Broad accounts (A, L, OE)	Increased by	Decreased by
Assets	Debit	Credit
Liabilities	Credit	Debit
Owners' equity	Credit	Debit

By convention, debits and credits are often abbreviated to 'Dr' and 'Cr', respectively. Some readers will question how 'debit' can be abbreviated to Dr when there is actually no 'r' in debit. There is no consensus on why the 'r' appears. As we mentioned earlier in this chapter, the origin of double-entry accounting – as we apply it – can be traced back over 600 years to Europe when Latin was commonly used. Debit (Dr) and credit (Cr) come from the Latin words *debere* and *credere*, respectively – so that's possibly why we use 'Dr' as an abbreviation. Another reason that has been suggested for why we use 'Dr' is that it stands for 'debit record', and Cr stands for 'credit record'. Hence, there are at least two possible reasons why debit is often abbreviated to 'Dr', and credit is often abbreviated to 'Cr'.

For further discussion of the application of rules for debits and credits, see **Learning exercise 8.2**.

8.2 Learning Exercise

Applying the rules of debits and credits

Using the rules in Table 8.2, we will refer to the transactions below and then describe the accounts affected, and whether the required change in the account would be made using a *debit entry* or a *credit entry*. Remember for every debit amount there must be corresponding credits. The transactions are as follows:

- The organisation uses cash to purchase inventory.
- The organisation purchases a building using a bank loan.
- The organisation pays its rent expense using cash.
- The owner withdraws cash from the business for personal use.
- The organisation performs services for a customer, and receives cash.

  We work through the solution in the table below.

Details of transaction	Accounts affected (remember, A = L + OE)	Is it a debit or credit entry?
Organisation uses cash to purchase inventory	Inventory (asset) increases	Debit
	Cash at bank (asset) decreases	Credit
Organisation purchases a building using a bank loan	Building (asset) increases	Debit
	Bank loan (liability) increases	Credit
Organisation pays its rent expense using cash	Rent expense – expenses increase, meaning equity decreases	Debit
	Cash at bank (asset) decreases	Credit
The owner withdraws cash from the business for personal use	Drawings (equity) – drawings increase, meaning equity decreases	Debit
	Cash at bank (asset) decreases	Credit
Organisation performs services for a customer and receives cash	Cash at bank (asset) increases	Debit
	Service income increases, meaning equity increases	Credit

We already know that the initial recognition of an accounting transaction within the financial accounting information system occurs within the journal. This is where we initially identify the debit and credit entries. These are then posted to the ledger account, which has a column for debit entries and a column for credit entries.

8.3 Learning Exercise

Preparing journal entries

Scenario: The following two transactions occur:

- On 1 January 2025, an organisation borrows $100 000 in cash by way of a bank loan.
- On 2 January 2025, the organisation acquires a motor vehicle for $45 000 using cash.

Task: What would be the journal entries, and what would be the balance of cash at bank, after these two transactions have been processed?

Solution: Assuming that we have separate accounts (as noted in the chart of accounts, and we will assume that the same ledger account numbers are used as shown in **Exhibit 8.1**) for:

- cash at bank
- bank loan, and
- motor vehicle,

then the journal entries would be:

Date	Account name	Account number	Debit $	Credit $
1 Jan 2025	Cash at bank	100	100 000	
	Bank loan	170		100 000
	Organisation has borrowed cash from the bank			

In terms of our basic accounting equation of A = L + OE, following the above transaction, assets increase (the debit entry) and liabilities also increase (the credit entry). The equation balances.

Date	Account name	Account number	Debit $	Credit $
2 Jan 2025	Motor vehicle	130	45 000	
	Cash at bank	100		45 000
	Organisation has purchased a motor vehicle for cash			

In terms of our basic accounting equation of A = L + OE, following the above transaction, one asset increases (the debit entry for motor vehicle) and another asset decreases (the credit entry for cash at bank). The equation balances.

After the above two transactions, and if we assume the opening balance of cash at bank was zero, the asset cash at bank would have a balance of $55 000 debit. This is because we initially *debited* the cash at bank account with $100 000 on 1 January, and then on 2 January we *credited* the cash at bank account with $45 000. The balance of the ledger account is the difference between the total debits and the total credits (which in this case is $55 000), and because the total of the debits exceeded the total of the credits, then the account has a debit balance. Assets would be expected to have debit balances.

Please note: By looking at the above journal entries – and please remember that these journal entries are made in a separate place called the journal – you will notice a number of things:

- The date is noted in the journal with respect to when the transaction occurred.
- The credit entry is indented relative to the debit entry – this is simply convention.
- The ledger accounts affected by the transaction are identified. These accounts will be listed within the chart of accounts.
- The debit entry goes in the left-hand column and the credit entry goes in the right-hand column. Again, there is no clear reason for this – it has simply always been like this; similarly, the requirement that the debit entry is noted before the credit entry.
- Under each transaction, there is a brief description which is called a narration.

Returning to our basic accounting equation of A = L + OE, we learned in Chapter 7 that owners' equity will increase as a result of profits – that is, it will increase through income and reduce through expenses. We also learned that owners' equity will increase through contributions from owners, and decrease through distributions to (drawings by) owners. That is, a change in owners' equity for a period will equal:

$$\text{Change in OE} = \text{income} - \text{expenses} + \text{contributions} - \text{distributions}$$

The balance of owners' equity at a point in time will be the aggregate of all prior profits (or losses) plus all prior contributions, less all prior distributions. As we learned above, an increase in owners' equity is called a credit entry. Therefore, contributions from owners and income earned (which increase owners' equity) will both be credits. A decrease in owners' equity (brought about by expenses and distributions) is created by a debit entry.

Given that:

$$\text{OE end of period} = \text{OE beginning of period} + I - E + C - D$$

then assuming that it is the first period of operations and opening OE is zero,

$$A = L + (I - E + C - D)$$

which reorganised becomes:

$$A + E + D = L + I + C$$

Any increase in the left-hand side of the above equation is called a debit. These effectively represent *applications* (or uses) of funds. That is, funds can be used, or applied, to acquire assets (A), and to pay for expenses (E), or pay for distributions (D) to owners.

Conversely, any increase in the right-hand side of the above equation is a credit, and effectively, these all represent *sources* of funds. That is, the funds of the organisation can come from three sources – from borrowings (L), from income generated by the organisation (I), or from contributions made by the owners (C). Again, any increase in these sources of funds is called a credit. *All* applications of funds must have a related source of those funds. Debits (application of funds) must equal credits (sources of funds).

The reverse can also be said. If the left-hand side of the expanded accounting equation (A + E + D) decreases, then that is recorded as a credit, and if the right-hand side (L + I + C) decreases, then this is recorded as a debit. This is summarised diagrammatically below and in Table 8.3.

$$\underbrace{A + E + D}_{} = \underbrace{L + I + C}_{}$$

A + E + D	L + I + C
↑ = Debit	↑ = Credit
↓ = Credit	↓ = Debit

Key concept

Acquiring assets (A), incurring expenses (E), and making distributions to owners (D) are the ways in which an organisation can use its funds. These are applications of funds. When these elements increase, they are debits with debits reflecting the application of funds.

An increase in liabilities (L), the earning of income (I), and the receipt of contributions from owners (C) are the ways in which an organisation receives funds. They are sources of funds. When these elements increase, they are credits with credits reflecting the sourcing of funds.

TABLE 8.3 The expanded accounting equation and the related debits and credits

Expanded accounting equation	Increased by	Decreased by
Assets	Debit	Credit
Expenses	Debit	Credit
Drawings	Debit	Credit
Liabilities	Credit	Debit
Income	Credit	Debit
Contributions	Credit	Debit

It needs to be noted that the terms debit and credit do not mean *increase* or *decrease*. For example, while a debit entry will increase assets, it is a credit entry which also increases liabilities. Also, debit or credit does not mean *good* or *bad*, despite how the terms are often used in conversation.

For a discussion of 'normal' account balances and entering transactions in the ledger journal, see **Learning exercise 8.4** and **Learning exercise 8.5**, respectively.

8.4 Learning Exercise

The 'normal' balances of particular accounts

Let us consider what the 'normal' balances of the following ledger accounts might be. That is, would they normally be expected to have a debit or a credit balance?

- Inventory
- Wages expense
- Building
- Bank loan
- Sales revenue
- Capital account.

Since assets will be increased by debit entries, and because assets will not really be decreased below a zero balance, we would expect them to have a debit balance. Similarly, liabilities are increased from zero by way of credit entries, therefore we would expect liabilities to have a credit balance. See the table below for further clarification.

Account	Element to which it belongs	Normal balance
Inventory	Asset	Debit
Wages expense	Expense	Debit
Building	Asset	Debit
Bank loan	Liability	Credit
Sales revenue	Income	Credit
Capital account	Equity	Credit

8.5 Learning Exercise

Entering a number of transactions in the general journal

Scenario: Wayne Lynch Painting Services – a sole trader – commenced operations on 1 January 2025. It had the following transactions in January 2025. The details of these transactions were extracted from relevant source documents. We will also use these transactions in several of the Learning exercises that follow.

Date	Description	Amount
1 Jan	Cash contribution from owner Wayne	$10 000
2 Jan	Acquired paint and brushes on credit from Paintworks	$1000
2 Jan	Purchased ladder for cash	$300
5 Jan	Invoiced customer – J. Smith – for painting services. These services consumed paint and brushes which were acquired on 2 January and cost $450.	$2600
7 Jan	Paid wages	$700
8 Jan	Received cash from debtor – J. Smith	$2600
10 Jan	Acquired paint for cash	$300
12 Jan	Purchased paint mixer for cash	$750
14 Jan	Paid creditor – Paintworks	$1000
16 Jan	Received cash for one day of painting. This service consumed paint and brushes which cost $200.	$800
21 Jan	Paid wages	$700
22 Jan	Invoiced customer – B. Brown – for painting services. These services consumed paint and brushes which cost $400.	$3000
23 Jan	Acquired paint and brushes on credit from Paintworks	$900
24 Jan	Received cash from debtor – B. Brown	$3000
25 Jan	Invoiced customer – W. White – for painting services. These services consumed paint and brushes which cost $450.	$2750
27 Jan	Wayne withdrew cash for personal use	$2000

Task: Applying debits and credits, we are required to record the above transactions in a general journal. In doing so, we will use the chart of accounts provided earlier in this chapter (see **Exhibit 8.1**).

Solution: Each of the above journal entries will be entered into the journal in chronological (date) order. Each transaction will record the accounts affected, and whether these accounts are debited or credited. Within each transaction recorded in the journal (that is, within each journal entry), the debits must equal the credits. Each transaction will also be accompanied by a brief description known as a narration.

General journal Page 1

Date	Account name	Account number	Debit $	Credit $
1 Jan 2025	Cash at bank	100	10 000	
	W. Lynch capital account	201		10 000
	Owner contributed $10 000			
2 Jan 2025	Paint and brushes supplies	108	1000	
	Accounts payable	155		1000
	Acquired paint and brushes on credit from Paintworks			
2 Jan 2025	Painting equipment	125	300	
	Cash at bank	100		300
	Acquired painting equipment with cash			
5 Jan 2025	Accounts receivable	105	2600	
	Painting income	251		2600
	Performed painting services on credit terms (J. Smith)			
	Cost of painting supplies used	315	450	
	Paint and brushes supplies	108		450
	Cost of materials used to provide service			
7 Jan 2025	Wages expense	310	700	
	Cash at bank	100		700
	Paid wages with cash			
8 Jan 2025	Cash at bank	100	2600	
	Accounts receivable	105		2600
	Received amount due from customer J. Smith			
10 Jan 2025	Paint and brushes supplies	108	300	
	Cash at bank	100		300
	Acquired paint for cash			
12 Jan 2025	Painting equipment	125	750	
	Cash at bank	100		750
	Acquired painting equipment with cash			
14 Jan 2025	Accounts payable	155	1000	
	Cash at bank	100		1000
	Paid accounts payable – Paintworks			

General journal Page 2

Date	Account name	Account number	Debit $	Credit $
16 Jan 2025	Cash at bank	100	800	
	Painting income	251		800
	Performed painting services for cash			
	Cost of painting supplies used	315	200	
	Paint and brushes supplies	108		200
	Cost of materials used to provide service			
21 Jan 2025	Wages expense	310	700	
	Cash at bank	100		700
	Paid wages expense with cash			
22 Jan 2025	Accounts receivable	105	3000	
	Painting income	251		3000
	Performed painting services on credit terms for B. Brown			
	Cost of painting supplies used	315	400	
	Paint and brushes supplies	108		400
	Cost of materials used to provide service			
23 Jan 2025	Paint and brushes supplies	108	900	
	Accounts payable	155		900
	Acquired paint and brushes on credit from Paintworks			
24 Jan 2025	Cash at bank	100	3000	
	Accounts receivable	105		3000
	Received amount due from customer B. Brown			
25 Jan 2025	Accounts receivable	105	2750	
	Painting income	251		2750
	Performed painting services on credit terms for W. White			
	Cost of painting supplies used	315	450	
	Paint and brushes supplies	108		450
	Cost of materials used to provide service			
27 Jan 2025	Drawings	230	2000	
	Cash at bank	100		2000
	Owner withdrew cash			

Note that, as the journal entries above refer to a sole trader, we have used just one capital account for the owner, Wayne Lynch. This is common practice. This capital account will ultimately accumulate the contributions made by the owner, the profits generated by the operations, and the drawings of the sole trader.

In the journal entries provided above, you will also note that there is a column for the respective ledger account number (which would also be reflected within the chart of accounts). In practice, these account numbers are generally inserted at the same time the respective amounts are transferred to the relevant ledger account – a process we will consider next.

Another thing to notice in the above journal entries is that each time we provided the painting service, we recognised, as an expense, the amount of paint supplies used to provide the service, and we also reduced this amount from our supplies of paint and brushes (see the journal entries for 5, 16, 22 and 25 January).

Why do I need to know about debits and credits?

Unless you are going to be employed in an accounting function, then you probably do not need to know about them. We can read and interpret financial statements, such as a balance sheet and an income statement, without knowing the background about debits and credits. But if we are working in a financial accounting role, and as financial statements are prepared on the basis of the double-entry accounting system (which applies debits and credits), then we do need to know about them.

LO8.3 Posting entries from the journal to the ledger

posted
The effects of a transaction are deemed to be 'posted' when the amount recorded within the journal for that transaction or event is transferred to the respective account in the ledger

The entries in the general journal, which we have just described, will be **posted** to the respective ledger accounts that have been identified in the general journal. An example of a ledger account is provided in **Exhibit 8.2**. When transactions are posted from the journal to the ledger account, the debit entries in the journal go to the debit column (the left-hand column) in the respective account, and the credit entries in the journal go to the credit column (the right-hand column) of the account. These accounts reside within the ledger and are therefore typically referred to as ledger accounts.

The journal could include hundreds, or thousands, of journal entries that reflect a variety of transactions. If a manager needs information about a particular aspect of performance, such as sales, then such information could not be easily obtained directly from the journal. Rather, it is best to have a specific account in the ledger (the ledger account) that records information only about sales.

The ledger is comprised of many accounts and these are identified within the chart of accounts. Every account identified in the chart of accounts has its own account in the ledger. The ledger accounts are where all the transactions relating to that particular account are accumulated to provide a balance for that particular account. Every type of asset, liability, equity, expense and income, which the organisation seeks to separately collect and report information about will have a separate ledger account in which all transactions that impact that specific ledger account (and remember, these transactions are initially recorded within a journal before they are 'posted' to the ledger) are recorded. In a manual accounting system, which is typically not used these days, the ledger accounts can be in an individual book, or on separate cards, that would be referred to as the ledger.

EXHIBIT 8.2 A ledger account for Cash at bank

100 Cash at bank

Date	Detail	Journal page no.	Debit amount $	Date	Detail	Journal ref.	Credit amount $
1 Jan 2025	Wayne Lynch, capital account	1	10 000	2 Jan 2025	Painting equipment	1	300
8 Jan 2025	Accounts receivable	1	2600	7 Jan 2025	Wages expense	1	700
16 Jan 2025	Painting income	2	800	10 Jan 2025	Paint and brushes supplies	1	300
24 Jan 2025	Accounts receivable	2	3000	12 Jan 2025	Painting equipment	1	750
				14 Jan 2025	Accounts payable	1	1000
				21 Jan 2025	Wages expense	2	700
				27 Jan 2025	Drawings	2	2000

The number of separate accounts created within the ledger depends upon the perceived usefulness of having that level of information. There needs to be a balance between having too many ledger accounts and having too few. For example, it would likely be ineffective to have a separate ledger account for every chair owned within an organisation, but information could be aggregated into a single account that accounted for all chairs, or further condensed into an account for all office furniture. As with all information, the costs and benefits of collecting and reporting information need to be considered when determining the number of ledger accounts to create.

As an example of a ledger account, we can again consider **Exhibit 8.2**, which provides a ledger account for 'Cash at bank'. You will see that, for each transaction that has been posted to the ledger account, the other ledger account affected by each respective transaction is also identified. For example, for the entry on 1 January 2025, we can see that the cash at bank account increases (and therefore was debited) because the owner made a capital contribution of $10 000. For the entry on 2 January, we can see that cash at bank decreased because painting equipment costing $300 was acquired with cash. By identifying the other account affected by each transaction, it makes it easier when looking at the ledger account to understand why the account has changed throughout the accounting period.

Because the entries in the ledger account are recorded in chronological order, they provide a history of the movements in the account. The ledger account can have debit and credit entries where, as we have already stated, the left-hand side is for debits and the right-hand side is for credits (and again, the reason for this convention is unclear – it has simply just been like this for hundreds of years).

The ledger accounts will have a balance, which will either be a debit or a credit. In the ledger account shown above, the balance would be $10 650 debit (meaning there is cash in the bank – an asset), and this represents the total of the debit column ($16 400) less the total of the credit column ($5750).

For more on the effects of transactions on ledger accounts, and the posting of journal entries to these accounts, see **Learning exercise 8.6** and **Learning exercise 8.7**, respectively.

8.6 Learning Exercise

Transaction effects on ledger accounts

For the following transactions, and assuming that the organisation uses a similar chart of accounts as provided in **Exhibit 8.1**, we are required to determine:

- the likely ledger accounts affected by the financial transaction
- whether the ledger accounts are part of equity, assets or liabilities
- whether the respective ledger account is increased or decreased
- which ledger accounts will be debited, and which ledger accounts will be credited.

The transactions are as follows:

1. An owner contributes $100 000 in cash to the business.
2. The business uses cash to acquire a motor vehicle for $35 000.
3. The business buys some inventory (stock) on credit for $20 000.
4. The business sells all of its inventory for $50 000 cash.
5. The business purchases some land for $150 000 by way of a bank loan.

Solution

Remember our simple accounting equation A = L + OE, and also remember that:

$$A = L + OE$$

A: ↑ Dr, ↓ Cr   L + OE: ↑ Cr, ↓ Dr

Transaction number and details	Ledger accounts affected	Part of owners' equity, assets or liabilities?	Is owners' equity, assets, or liabilities increased or decreased?	Is the ledger account to be debited or credited?
1 An owner contributes $100 000 in cash to the business	Cash at bank Capital account	Asset Owners' equity	Increased Increased	Debited Credited
2 The business uses cash to acquire a motor vehicle for $35 000	Motor vehicles Cash at bank	Asset Asset	Increased Decreased	Debited Credited
3 The business buys some inventory (stock) on credit for $20 000	Inventory Accounts payable	Asset Liability	Increased Increased	Debited Credited
4 The business sells all of its inventory for $50 000 cash	Cash Sales income Cost of sales Inventory	Asset Owners' equity Owners' equity Asset	Increased Increased Decreased Decreased	Debited Credited Debited Credited
5 The business purchases some land for $150 000 by way of a bank loan	Land Bank loan	Asset Liability	Increased Increased	Debited Credited

8.7 Learning Exercise

Posting journal entries to the ledger accounts

Returning to the journal entries recorded for Wayne Lynch Painting Services in **Learning exercise 8.5**, we are now required to post the journal entries to the respective ledger accounts.

As you know, 'posting' means transferring the effects of each transaction in the journal to the respective account in the ledger – the journal entries in the debit column of the journal shall be transferred to the debit (left-hand) side of the respective ledger account, and the journal entries in the credit column of the journal shall be transferred to the credit (right-hand) side of the respective ledger account.

In a computerised accounting system, these postings are done automatically, thereby saving the accountant much time.

100 Cash at bank

Date	Detail	Jnl ref.	Debit amount $	Date	Detail	Jnl ref.	Credit amount $
1 Jan 2025	W. Lynch, capital account	1	10 000	2 Jan 2025	Painting equipment	1	300
8 Jan 2025	Accounts receivable	1	2 600	7 Jan 2025	Wages expense	1	700
16 Jan 2025	Painting income	2	800	10 Jan 2025	Paint and brushes supplies	1	300
24 Jan 2025	Accounts receivable	2	3 000	12 Jan 2025	Painting equipment	1	750
				14 Jan 2025	Accounts payable	1	1 000
				21 Jan 2025	Wages expense	2	700
				27 Jan 2025	Drawings	2	2 000

105 Accounts receivable

Date	Detail	Jnl ref.	Debit amount $	Date	Detail	Jnl ref.	Credit amount $
5 Jan 2025	Painting income	1	2 600	8 Jan 2025	Cash at bank	1	2 600
22 Jan 2025	Painting income	2	3 000	24 Jan 2025	Cash at bank	2	3 000
25 Jan 2025	Painting income	2	2 750				

108 Paint and brushes supplies

Date	Detail	Jnl ref.	Debit amount $	Date	Detail	Jnl ref.	Credit amount $
2 Jan 2025	Accounts payable	1	1000	5 Jan 2025	Cost of painting supplies used	1	450
10 Jan 2025	Cash at bank	1	300	16 Jan 2025	Cost of painting supplies used	2	200
23 Jan 2025	Accounts payable	2	900	22 Jan 2025	Cost of painting supplies used	2	400
				25 Jan 2025	Cost of painting supplies used	2	450

125 Painting equipment

Date	Detail	Jnl ref.	Debit amount $	Date	Detail	Jnl ref.	Credit amount $
2 Jan 2025	Cash at bank	1	300				
12 Jan 2025	Cash at bank	1	750				

155 Accounts payable

Date	Detail	Jnl ref.	Debit amount $	Date	Detail	Jnl ref.	Credit amount $
14 Jan 2025	Cash at bank	1	1000	2 Jan 2025	Paint and brushes supplies	1	1000
				23 Jan 2025	Paint and brushes supplies	2	900

201 Wayne Lynch, capital account

Date	Detail	Jnl ref.	Debit amount $	Date	Detail	Jnl ref.	Credit amount $
				1 Jan 2025	Cash at bank	1	10000

230 Drawings

Date	Detail	Jnl ref.	Debit amount $	Date	Detail	Jnl ref.	Credit amount $
27 Jan 2025	Cash at bank	2	2000				

251 Painting income

Date	Detail	Jnl ref.	Debit amount $	Date	Detail	Jnl ref.	Credit amount $
				5 Jan 2025	Accounts receivable	1	2600
				16 Jan 2025	Cash at bank	2	800
				22 Jan 2025	Accounts receivable	2	3000
				25 Jan 2025	Accounts receivable	2	2750

310 Wages expense

Date	Detail	Jnl ref.	Debit amount $	Date	Detail	Jnl ref.	Credit amount $
7 Jan 2025	Cash at bank	1	700				
21 Jan 2025	Cash at bank	2	700				

315 Cost of painting supplies used

Date	Detail	Jnl ref.	Debit amount $	Date	Detail	Jnl ref.	Credit amount $
5 Jan 2025	Paint and brushes supplies	1	450				
16 Jan 2025	Paint and brushes supplies	2	200				
22 Jan 2025	Paint and brushes supplies	2	400				
25 Jan 2025	Paint and brushes supplies	2	450				

You will note that the ledger accounts used in **Learning exercise 8.7** each have a column titled **journal reference** ('Jnl ref.'). This signifies where the journal entry came from – in this instance, the entries came from page 1 or 2 of the journal. Providing this reference allows us to cross-check back to the journal in terms of determining whether there is an error. This is often referred to as creating an *audit trail*.

Key concept

Providing a journal reference in the ledger allows us to cross-reference and back-check information, to prevent errors and create an audit trail.

The steps we have taken so far in this chapter are summarised in **Figure 8.1**, although there are still more steps to come in the financial accounting process.

The next step in the financial accounting process will be to prepare a trial balance, which we will now discuss.

FIGURE 8.1 Where we are up to now in the financial accounting process

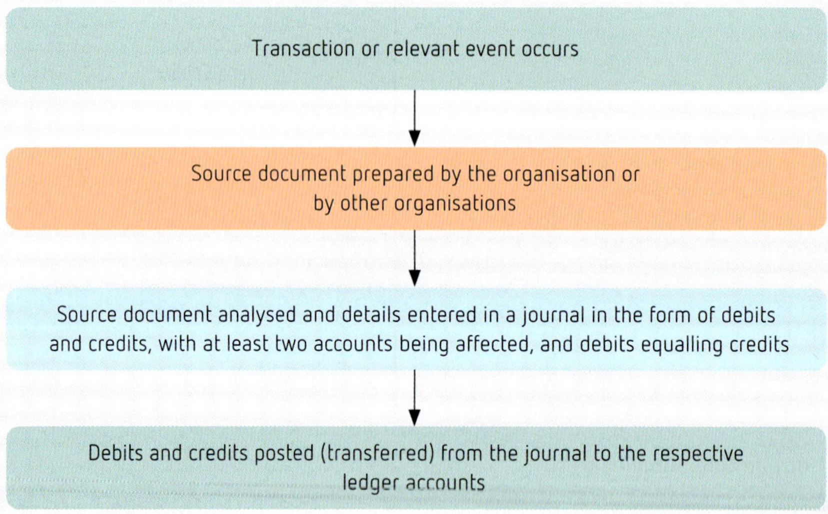

LO8.4 Preparing a trial balance

Once we have posted all of the journal entries to the respective ledger accounts, we can then determine the 'balance' of each ledger account at the end of the accounting period, and note these balances in a trial balance. The **trial balance** represents a listing of the ledger accounts, and their balances, at the end of an accounting period.

trial balance
A listing of the ledger accounts, and their balances, at the end of an accounting period. The total of all the accounts with debit balances in the trial balance must equal the total of all accounts with credit balances (otherwise a mistake has occurred)

The trial balance allows for a level of checking. It provides no new information – just a summary of the ledger account balances. If every journal entry is made with equal debits and credits (as it should be), then the total of all the ledger accounts with debit balances will equal the total of all the ledger accounts with credit balances. The trial balance allows us to test whether the debit balances equal the credit balances before we proceed towards preparing the financial statements. If our trial balance shows that these amounts do not balance, then we have made a mistake. This mistake would need to be identified and corrected.

To prepare a trial balance, we need to know the balance of each ledger account:

- We add all the debit entries for each ledger account.
- We add all the credit entries for each ledger account.
- The balance of the ledger account will be the difference between the two columns.
- This is done for each account in the ledger.
- A common practice is to add an amount on the side with the lesser total to make the columns balance (equal), and this will be referred to as the 'closing balance'.
- This same amount is then written as the 'opening balance' as at the beginning of the next reporting period. For example, if we look at **Exhibit 8.3** – the cash at bank ledger account

for Wayne Lynch Painting Services – we can see that, following a series of transactions, the organisation had $10 650 in cash at the end of the accounting period. This means it has $10 650 in cash at the start of the next accounting period.

EXHIBIT 8.3 Determining the balance of a ledger account

100 Cash at bank

Date	Detail	Jnl ref.	Debit amount $	Date	Detail	Jnl ref.	Credit amount $
1 Jan 2025	W. Lynch, capital account	1	10 000	2 Jan	Painting equipment	1	300
8 Jan 2025	Accounts receivable	1	2 600	7 Jan	Wages expense	1	700
16 Jan 2025	Painting income	2	800	10 Jan	Paint and brushes supplies	1	300
24 Jan 2025	Accounts receivable	2	3 000	12 Jan	Painting equipment	1	750
				14 Jan	Accounts payable	1	1 000
				21 Jan	Wages expense	2	700
				27 Jan	Drawings	2	2 000
					Closing balance		10 650
			16 400				16 400
1 Feb 2025	Opening balance		10 650				

We would need to determine the balance of each ledger account in the same way as we did above for cash at bank.

As we have already noted, asset accounts normally have a debit balance, meaning that the total value of the debits to specific asset ledger accounts should exceed the total value of the credits. Conversely, liability accounts normally have a credit balance, with the credit entries exceeding the debit balances.

Knowing what the 'normal' balances should be allows us to identify potential errors from the trial balance. For example, if the trial balance indicates the asset 'Office furniture' has a credit balance, then that does not really make sense and would require further investigation to determine what might have potentially caused an error. In the same way, expenses should have a debit balance and income items should have a credit balance. If this is not the case, then some investigation is warranted.

For more detail on compiling a trial balance, see Learning exercise 8.8.

8.8 Learning Exercise

Compiling a trial balance

Continuing our example, using the information in the ledger accounts of Wayne Lynch Painting Services as determined from Learning exercise 8.7, we are now required to produce a trial balance. Assuming there are no further adjustments to be made to the income and expenses of the organisation, we are also then required to produce a statement of profit or loss for the month ending 31 January 2025.

Worked solution

To work out the totals of each ledger account, we need to calculate closing balances for each account, as we did in **Exhibit 8.3**. That step is not reproduced here.

Trial balance of Wayne Lynch Painting Services as at 31 January 2025

Account number	Account name	Debits $	Credits $
100	Cash at bank	10650	
105	Accounts receivable	2750	
108	Paint and brushes supplies	700	
125	Painting equipment	1050	
155	Accounts payable		900
201	W. Lynch capital account		10000
230	Drawings	2000	
251	Painting income		9150
310	Wages expense	1400	
315	Cost of paint supplies used	1500	
Totals		**20050**	**20050**

From the above trial balance, we can see that the total debit balance of $20050 equals the total credit balance of $20050. If this was not the case, then there would be an error (or errors) that would need to be located before proceeding. However, just because it does balance does not absolutely mean there will not be an error. For example, we might have forgotten to post an entire journal entry (that is, both the debits and the credits) to the respective ledger accounts, or perhaps we have made some compensating errors in our postings. That said, in this Learning exercise there are no errors and the trial balance is correct. Assuming that no further adjustments are required to any ledger accounts, we can compile the statement of profit or loss.

Statement of profit or loss for Wayne Lynch Painting Services for the month ending 31 January 2025

	$
Income	
Painting income	9150
Expenses	
Cost of paint supplies used	(1500)
Wages expense	(1400)
Profit	6250

Again, we can summarise where we are up to in terms of the entire financial accounting process – see Figure 8.2 (and yes, there are still more steps to come).

FIGURE 8.2 Where we are up to now in the financial accounting process

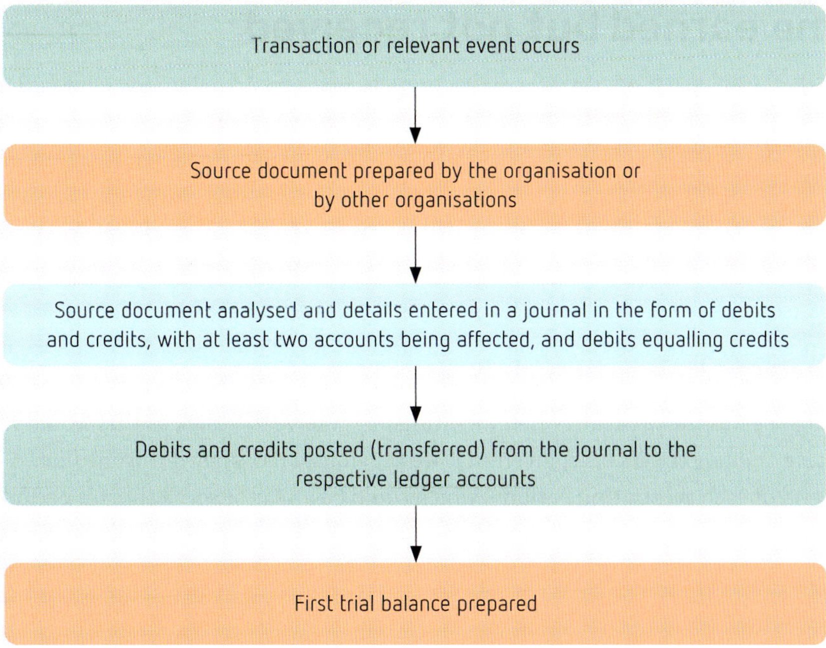

LO8.5 Adjusting journal entries

As we learned in Chapter 7, financial accounting is typically undertaken on an accrual basis rather than on a cash basis. Because we use the accrual basis of accounting, there will often be a number of adjustments the accountant will need to make at the end of the accounting period. Remember that the accounting period could be a month, six months or a year. As we also learned, under the accrual basis of accounting, we recognise expenses when they are incurred (which does not necessarily occur at the same time as the expenses are paid which could be some time later), and we recognise income when it is earned (which is not necessarily at the same time as the related cash amounts are actually received which could be some time later).

Recognising expenses before they are paid means that, at the same time as we recognise the unpaid expense (which decreases equity), we also recognise the associated obligation (liability) relating to the required future payment (thereby increasing liabilities). Conversely, recognising income before the associated cash has been received means that, at the same time as we recognise the income (and income increases equity), we also recognise an associated claim to the related cash (which increases assets in the form of an increase in accounts receivable).

Some of the adjustments the accountant might be required to make at the end of the accounting period will relate to:

- income earned but not received
- expenses incurred but not yet paid

- income received in advance
- prepayments
- depreciation.

We will now consider each of these in turn.

Income earned but not received

Organisations often perform services or sell goods prior to actually receiving cash from the customer. Rather, they do so in exchange for a claim to cash – which is an asset, and which we might refer to as a receivable (or a debtor).

In **Learning exercise 8.5**, we recognised such income (and assets) when we produced journal entries to record painting services performed on credit terms, rather than for cash. That is, the fact we did not receive the cash directly after performing the services does not mean we do not record the income. If we have an enforceable right to collect the cash at a future point in time (an asset), then we can recognise the income in advance of receiving the cash. When we eventually receive the cash, we will substitute one asset (cash) for another asset (the account receivable). We do not recognise income yet again when we ultimately receive the cash, as that would represent a case of *double counting* the income, given that we previously recognised this income.

At the end of each accounting period – which could be a year or some shorter period of time – the accountant must consider whether there are any amounts that have been earned by the organisation but that have not yet been recorded within the financial accounting system (that is, the transactions have not yet been recorded within the journal). If there is some income that has been earned but not yet recorded, then the accountant should recognise the amount through initiating the relevant journal entry. These journal entries act to increase assets (often in the form of an increase in some type of receivable) and increase equity (in the form of an increase in some type of income).

Earlier in this chapter, we noted that for a journal entry to be made, there is a requirement that some form of source document exists. In the case of income earned but not received, the relevant source document might need to be prepared internally and be properly approved. For example, if a painting business was doing some painting of a customer's house, but has only completed 60 per cent of the job and has not yet invoiced the customer (perhaps there is an agreement that the painting needs to be finished before an invoice is sent), then some form of internal documentation noting the amount of revenue earned (but not received) needs to be prepared and properly authorised, and this in itself can act as the necessary source document. As an internally developed source document, it might be referred to as a *memorandum*, and it would provide details such as the date of the transaction, a description of the transaction or event, and the financial amounts involved.

In terms of our simple accounting equation of A = L + OE, the increase in the asset (in the form of a recognition of a receivable or other asset) on the left-hand side of the equation would be balanced by an increase in owners' equity (OE) on the right-hand side of the equation (in the form of a recognition of some form of income, which increases equity).

For more discussion of recording income earned but not yet received, see **Learning exercise 8.9**.

8.9 Learning Exercise

Recording income earned but not yet received

Scenario: On 31 January 2025, which is the last day of the accounting period, the accountant of XYZ Company determined that the organisation has earned \$15 000 in interest income on a long-term deposit it has with a bank. The deposit and all accumulated interest will be paid to XYZ Company at the end of the deposit period, which is in another six months.

Task: You are required to provide the 31 January adjusting journal entry for XYZ Company to account for this income earned but not yet received.

Solution: In this case, using our simple accounting equation A = L + OE, we can see that assets will increase by \$15 000 (and that this will be recognised by increasing the asset that might be known as 'Long-term bank deposit', rather than increasing a receivable), and that income will also increase by \$15 000 (and that this will be recognised by increasing 'Interest revenue' by \$15 000). As we know, owners' equity increases through income and contributions, and reduces by way of expenses and distributions (or drawings). We will assume that the numbers for the ledger accounts titled long-term bank deposit and interest revenue are 160 and 260, respectively.

We should also hopefully remember that increases in assets are debits and increases in owners' equity are credits (see **Table 8.2**). Therefore, the adjusting journal entry on 31 January would be as follows:

Date	Account name	Account number	Debit \$	Credit \$
31 Jan 2025	Long-term bank deposit	160	15 000	
	Interest revenue	260		15 000
	To recognise interest earned on long-term bank deposit			

Again, remember that transactions firstly need to be recorded within the journal before they can subsequently be posted to the ledger.

Expenses incurred but not yet paid

Organisations often incur expenses prior to making the related payment. They might receive the services, or the goods, in exchange for a promise to pay the cash – which is a liability, and which we might refer to as a payable (or a creditor).

At the end of each accounting period, the accountant must consider whether there are any expenses that have been incurred by the organisation but which have not yet been recorded within the financial accounting system (that is, within the journal). If these are ignored, then both expenses and liabilities will be understated, and the resulting financial statements could be misleading, and not faithfully represent the organisation's financial performance and financial position for that accounting period.

If there are some expenses that have been incurred but not recorded, then the accountant should recognise the amount through initiating the relevant journal entry. These journal entries would act to increase expenses and increase liabilities.

In terms of our simple accounting equation A = L + OE, the increase in the liability (in the form of a recognition of some form of payable) on the right-hand side of the equation would be balanced, or matched, by a decrease in owners' equity also on the right-hand side of the equation (in the form of a recognition of some form of expense).

For more on recording income incurred but not yet paid, see **Learning exercise 8.10**.

8.10 Learning Exercise

Recording expenses incurred but not yet paid

Scenario: On 31 January 2025, which is the last day of the accounting period, the accountant determined that XYZ Company incurred some expenses for which it has not yet paid:

- Wages of $4000 have been earned by employees of XYZ Company up until 31 January that are due to be paid on 2 February, which is in the next accounting period.
- Electricity expenses of $1000 have been incurred by XYZ Company up to 31 January, but have not yet been paid.

Task: You are required to provide the 31 January adjusting journal entries for XYZ Company to account for these expenses incurred but not yet paid.

Solution: We can use our expanded accounting equation to show the overall effects of the above transactions:

	A	+	E	+	D	=	L	+	I	+	C
Wages	–		$4000		–	=	$4000		–		–
Electricity	–		$1000		–	=	$1000		–		–

In this case, we can see that on the right-hand side of the accounting equation, liabilities will increase in total by $5000 (and this will be acknowledged by recognising a liability perhaps called 'Wages payable' of $4000 and another liability perhaps called 'Electricity payable' of $1000). This increase in the right-hand side of the equation (in liabilities) will be matched by an increase of the same magnitude in expenses on the left-hand side of the equation (and this will be recognised by increasing 'Wages expense' by $4000 and 'Electricity expense' by $1000). As we know, owners' equity increases through income and contributions, and reduces by way of expenses and distributions (drawings). Therefore, owners' equity will decrease as a result of the wages expense and electricity expense.

We will assume that the numbers for the ledger accounts entitled wages expense, electricity expense, wages payable and electricity payable are 320, 330, 150 and 170, respectively.

We know that decreases in owners' equity are debits and increases in liabilities are credits (see **Table 8.2**). Therefore, the adjusting journal entry on 31 January would be as follows:

Date	Account name	Account number	Debit $	Credit $
31 Jan 2025	Wages expense	320	4000	
	Electricity expense	330	1000	
	Wages payable	150		4000
	Electricity payable	170		1000
	To recognise expenses incurred during the accounting period but not yet paid			

Alternatively, there could be just one liability in the ledger account entitled 'Accrued expenses'. Again, the accountant needs to make a choice about the number and variety of ledger accounts being used, and identified, within the chart of accounts.

Income received in advance

Organisations often receive a payment for services in advance of performing the required service. For example, an insurance company will typically charge (or invoice) its clients for insurance to be provided for the next 12 months. When insurance companies initially receive this amount, the correct financial accounting treatment for the insurance company is to treat the amount received as a liability, referred to as something like 'Insurance revenue received in advance'. It is a liability because the organisation has a present obligation arising from past transactions to provide economic benefits (in this case, insurance services) to another organisation. However, as time passes, the insurance company will earn this income as it provides the insurance services, and the liability will decrease as the related income is earned. Once all contracted services have been performed, the liability will no longer exist.

Using our example of an insurance company, let us assume that the company has a financial year (accounting period) ending 30 June 2025, and that it produces financial statements on an annual basis. Let us also assume that on 1 January 2025, the insurance company receives an amount of $12 000 from a customer for an insurance contract for the next 12 months' insurance services. On that date, the insurance company has not actually earned any of this amount, and it has an obligation to provide the services for the next 12 months, or return the money to the customer.

We will assume that the numbers for the ledger accounts entitled cash at bank, interest revenue received in advance, and interest revenue are 100, 180 and 250, respectively.

The journal entry on the date of receiving the $12 000 would be as follows.

Date	Account name	Account number	Debit $	Credit $
1 Jan 2025	Cash at bank	100	12 000	
	Insurance revenue received in advance	180		12 000
	To recognise a liability in relation to revenue received in advance of providing the service			

The above journal entry increases an asset (cash at bank) and increases a liability (insurance revenue received in advance), hence our accounting equation A = L + OE would balance, as expected.

After six months, the adjusting journal entry to record the fact that half of this amount has now been earned by the insurance company would be as follows.

Date	Account name	Account number	Debit $	Credit $
30 June 2025	Insurance revenue received in advance	180	6000	
	Insurance revenue	250		6000
	To recognise insurance revenue that has been earned			

The above journal entry decreases a liability (insurance revenue received in advance) and increases income (insurance revenue, which increases equity) and hence our accounting equation A = L + OE would again balance, as expected. Effectively, half of the amount received on 1 January 2025 has now been earned.

Looking at a real-life example, the 2021 consolidated balance sheet for the large company QBE Insurance shows that, as at 31 December 2021, the organisation had US$8.637 billion of insurance revenue received in advance, which it referred to as a liability called 'unearned premium'. In explaining the meaning of the 'unearned premium', note 2.5 to QBE's 2021 annual report states:

> The unearned premium liability is that portion of gross written premium that QBE has not yet earned in profit or loss as it represents insurance coverage to be provided by QBE after the balance date.
>
> Source: QBE Insurance Group (2021), p. 101.

As another real-life example of income (or revenue) received in advance, we can refer to the 2021 balance sheet of Qantas, the global airline company (we also referred to this in Chapter 7). In its balance sheet, Qantas discloses a total of $431 billion (of which some is a current liability and some is a non-current liability) for 'revenue received in advance', which would mostly relate to payments made by people who have booked flights but have not yet flown (technically meaning that the organisation might be expected to repay the amounts paid if they could no longer provide the flights).

Source: Shutterstock.com/tratong

In cases where people have paid a company up-front for a good or service yet to be delivered, like an aeroplane flight they haven't taken yet, this would show on the company's balance sheet as revenue received in advance.

As a general rule, at the end of each accounting period, the accountant must consider whether there are any amounts that have been received by the organisation but which have not yet been earned.

For a further discussion of recording revenue received in advance, see **Learning exercise 8.11**.

8.11 Learning Exercise

Recording revenue received in advance

Scenario: Ocholupo Mowing Services has a 12-month reporting period ending on 30 June 2025. On 31 March 2025, the organisation receives $6000 from a customer for gardening services to be provided over the next six months, ending 30 September 2025.

Task: You are required to provide the accounting journal entries that should be made on:

- 31 March 2025
- 30 June 2025 (the adjusting entry).

Solution: We can use our expanded accounting equation to show the overall effects of the above transactions.

	A	+	E	+	D	=	L	+	I	+	C
31 March	$6000		–		–	=	$6000		–		–
30 June	–		–		–	=	($3000)		$3000		–

When the amount was received on 31 March, this represented revenue received in advance, and it would represent a liability to provide future services. In this case, and using our accounting equation, we can see that on the left-hand side of the equation, assets will increase by $6000 (cash at bank will increase by $6000). This increase in the left-hand side of the equation for assets will be matched by an increase in liabilities on the right-hand side of the equation in the form of an increase in liabilities related to the unearned income of $6000.

We will assume that the numbers for the ledger accounts entitled cash at bank, gardening revenue received in advance, and gardening revenue are 100, 170 and 260, respectively.

Therefore, the journal entry on 31 March would be as follows:

Date	Account name	Account number	Debit $	Credit $
31 March 2025	Cash at bank	100	6000	
	Gardening revenue received in advance	170		6000
	To recognise a liability in relation to gardening revenue received in advance of providing the service			

Across time, as the gardening services are provided, the $6000 will be earned by Ocholupo Mowing Services and the liability will decrease. As at 30 June, three months (or half) of the total amount of $6000 has been earned. That is, $3000 has been earned. In this case, and again using our accounting equation (see above), the left-hand side of the equation will not change. However, as the income is earned, there will be a reduction in the liability. This reduction in the liability of $3000 will be matched by an increase in income (which increases owners' equity) of $3000, representing the gardening income that has now been earned.

Therefore, the adjusting journal entry on 30 June would be:

Date	Account name	Account number	Debit $	Credit $
30 June 2025	Gardening revenue received in advance	170	3000	
	Gardening revenue	260		3000
	Recognition of gardening revenue earned			

At the start of the next accounting period, there would still be a liability of $3000 in relation to the gardening revenue received in advance.

Prepayments

It is also common for organisations to pay for services in advance of receiving them. For example, an organisation might pay to rent a factory upfront for the following six months. This payment is for a future economic benefit and would represent an asset called a *prepayment*. It is an asset because the organisation has a right to receive a future economic benefit, in this case the use of a building for the next six months, as a result of making the payment. As we know from Chapter 7, one of the defining characteristics of an 'asset' is that the related right must have the potential to produce economic benefits (it must also be controlled as a result of a past transaction or event). At the end of the accounting period, an adjusting journal entry would need to be made to account for the amount of the prepayment that has been consumed, or used up, by the organisation. This would be an expense.

For example, assume that Slater Company has a financial year ending on 31 December 2025. It pays $30 000 for six months' rent in advance on 1 November 2025.

We will assume that the numbers for the ledger accounts entitled cash at bank, prepaid rent, and rent expense are 100, 150 and 320, respectively.

On 1 November, the accounting journal entry would be as follows:

Date	Account name	Account number	Debit $	Credit $
1 Nov 2025	Prepaid rent	150	30 000	
	Cash at bank	100		30 000
	Organisation has paid 6 months' rent in advance			

The above journal entry would have the effect of increasing one asset (prepaid rent), and decreasing another (cash at bank). In terms of our simple accounting equation of A = L + OE, the increase on the left-hand side (to assets in the form of the prepayment) would be matched by a decrease also on the left-hand side of the equation (in the asset, cash at bank). That is, one asset is replaced by another asset.

At the end of the accounting period (which we can also refer to as the *reporting date*), which in this case is 31 December, the organisation needs to consider how much of the asset has been used up, or consumed, since it was acquired and therefore needs to be 'expensed'. Two months, or one-third has been used, and therefore the adjusting journal entry would be as follows:

Date	Account name	Account number	Debit $	Credit $
31 Dec 2025	Rent expense	320	10 000	
	Prepaid rent	150		10 000
	Organisation has incurred rent expense of $10 000			

The above journal entry would have the effect of increasing an expense (rent expense), thereby decreasing equity. It would also decrease an asset (prepaid rent). In terms of our simple accounting equation of A = L + OE, the decrease on the left-hand side (to assets in the form of the prepayment) would be matched by a decrease on the right-hand side of the equation (in the form of the expense which decreases owners' equity).

For more on recording and adjusting prepayments, see **Learning exercise 8.12**.

8.12 Learning Exercise

Recording and adjusting prepayments

Scenario: Steadman Consulting Services has a 12-month reporting period ending on 30 June 2025. On 31 March 2025, the organisation pays $12 000 in advance for insurance coverage for the following 12 months.

Task: You are required to provide the accounting journal entries that should be made by Steadman Consulting on:

- 31 March 2025
- 30 June 2025 – the adjusting journal entry.

Solution: We can use our expanded accounting equation to show the overall effects of the above transactions:

	A	+	E	+	D	=	L	+	I	+	C
31 March	$12 000 ($12 000)		–		–	=	–		–		–
30 June	($3 000)		$3 000		–	=	–		–		–

When the amount was paid on 31 March, this represented a prepayment which is an asset, and it would represent a right to receive future services for 12 months that have economic value. In this case, and using our accounting equation, we can see that on 31 March 2025, the left-hand side of the equation will increase through an increase in assets of $12 000 (prepayments will increase by $12 000). This increase in the left-hand side of the equation for assets will be matched by a decrease in assets – also on the left-hand side – in the form of a decrease in another asset, cash at bank, of $12 000.

We will assume that the numbers for the ledger accounts entitled cash at bank, prepaid insurance, and insurance expense are 100, 160 and 310, respectively.

Therefore, the journal entry on 31 March would be as follows:

Date	Account name	Account number	Debit $	Credit $
31 March 2025	Prepaid insurance	160	12 000	
	Cash at bank	100		12 000
	Prepayment of insurance for 12 months			

Across time, as the insurance services are consumed, the $12 000 will be expensed and the asset (prepayment) will decrease. As at 30 June, three months (or one-quarter) of the total amount of $12 000 has been used up. That is, $3000 needs to be expensed. In this case, and again using our accounting equation above, the left-hand side of the equation will decrease as the asset (prepayment) decreases by $3000. This reduction in the asset of $3000 will be matched by an increase in expenses of $3000, representing the insurance expenses that have been incurred (and we know expenses decrease owners' equity).

Therefore, the adjusting journal entry on 30 June would be as follows:

Date	Account name	Account number	Debit $	Credit $
30 June 2025	Insurance expense	310	3 000	
	Prepaid insurance	160		3 000
	To recognise insurance expense for the accounting period			

After the above adjusting journal entry, the organisation would still have an asset, prepaid insurance, with a balance of $9000. In the next accounting period, this prepaid insurance would be used up and a journal entry would need to be made to recognise the insurance expense, and the reduction of the asset, prepaid insurance.

Depreciation

depreciation
The systematic periodic allocation of the cost, or fair value, of a non-current asset over the accounting periods expected to benefit from the use of the asset. The amount calculated is referred to as a depreciation expense

Most non-current assets do not last forever. For example, when we acquire a building or an item of machinery, there is an expectation that it will have a limited useful life. With this in mind, we typically 'depreciate' an asset. **Depreciation** itself can be considered to represent the allocation of the cost of an asset (or its revalued amount if asset revaluations are being used – we will consider asset revaluations in Chapter 9), over the periods in which the economic benefits generated by the asset are expected to be derived.

We will cover depreciation more fully in Chapter 9. However, at this point we will simply acknowledge that at the end of the accounting period, we need to recognise – through an appropriate adjusting journal entry – that the service potential of property, plant and equipment will usually decline throughout the accounting period. This decline is recognised as an expense, which is called 'depreciation expense'.

For example, if at the beginning of the accounting period we acquired an item of machinery at a cost of $1 000 000, and we believed that it would last for 10 years, after which time it would have no value, then we need to allocate the total cost of the machine to each of the next 10 years. That is, we would depreciate the value of the machine by $100 000 each year and this would be treated as depreciation expense. We can summarise the effects of the acquisition, and depreciation, of the machine by using our accounting equation:

	A	+	E	+	D	=	L	+	I	+	C
At the beginning of the year	$1 000 000 ($1 000 000)		–		–	=	–		–		–
At the end of the year	($100 000)		$100 000		–	=	–		–		–

That is, at the beginning of the year, when we acquire the machinery, we are substituting one asset, machinery, for another asset, cash. At the end of the year, we will reduce the value of the machinery by $100 000 and recognise the expense – the depreciation expense – associated with this decline in value.

When details of the machine are disclosed by the organisation, it will typically be done as follows:

Machinery, at cost	$1 000 000	
Less: accumulated depreciation	($100 000)	$900 000

The accumulated depreciation account would represent what is known as a *contra asset*. A contra asset account is an account that is *offset* against another account, and it would have its own separate ledger account. The reason for having a contra account is that it might be useful to know what the original cost of the machine was, and what the accumulated depreciation of the machine is at any given point in time.

For more on recording depreciation expense, see **Learning exercise 8.13**.

8.13 Learning Exercise

Recording depreciation expense

Scenario: M. Potter & Co acquire a truck on 1 January 2025 for $130 000. It is expected to have a useful life of 10 years, after which time it will have no economic value. It is expected to provide the same economic benefits in each year of its use. The organisation has a 12-month reporting period ending on 31 December 2025.

Task: You are required to provide the accounting journal entries to recognise the acquisition of the truck and the recognition of depreciation expense (the adjusting entry) on 31 December 2025.

We will assume that the numbers for the ledger accounts entitled cash at bank, trucks, depreciation expense, and accumulated depreciation are 110, 170, 330 and 175, respectively.

Solution: When M. Potter & Co acquire the truck on 1 January 2025, the journal entry would be as follows:

Date	Account name	Account number	Debit $	Credit $
1 Jan 2025	Trucks	170	130 000	
	Cash at bank	110		130 000
	Acquisition of a truck for cash			

In the above journal entry, one asset is being replaced by another asset. That is, the right-hand side of the simple accounting equation A = L + OE is not affected. The reduction in cash would represent the source of funds (the credit entry), and the acquisition of the truck would represent the application of funds (the debit entry).

The depreciation expense for the year will, in this case, be determined by dividing the cost of the asset over its expected useful life, which will be $13 000 a year.

Using our simple accounting equation of A = L + OE, we will reduce assets by $13 000 and we will decrease owners' equity by $13 000 (owners' equity will decrease because we will recognise depreciation expense).

When recognising depreciation expense, we typically do not credit (decrease) the specific asset directly. Rather, as we have just noted, we use what is known as a contra asset account – an account that is offset against the relevant asset account. Again, we will address accounting for depreciation more fully in Chapter 9.

Therefore, the journal entry on 31 December 2025 would be as follows:

Date	Account name	Account number	Debit $	Credit $
31 Dec 2025	Depreciation expense	330	13 000	
	Accumulated depreciation	175		13 000
	To recognise depreciation expense for the year			

As the name suggests, accumulated depreciation is an account used to accumulate the total depreciation recognised to date in relation to that asset. In the balance sheet, the related disclosure would be as follows:

Trucks, at cost	$130 000	
Less: accumulated depreciation	($13 000)	$117 000

Our discussion of adjusting journal entries (which has included a discussion of the adjustments necessary for income earned but not received, expenses incurred but not yet paid, income received in advance, prepayments, and depreciation) is not fully comprehensive and certainly does not address every type of adjustment that needs to be made at the end of an accounting period. As this is an introduction to the general area of adjusting journal entries, we really do not need to go into more depth. Nevertheless, our discussion highlights the need for the accountant to consider a number of issues at the end of the reporting period, and accordingly, make the necessary adjusting journal entries before financial statements are prepared.

Our discussion of adjusting entries emphasises how the use of accrual accounting requires us to recognise income when it is earned and not simply when the cash is received, and to recognise expenses when they are incurred, not simply wait until the related cash is paid. We have learned that when we recognise revenue in advance of receiving the related cash, we recognise a related asset. We have also learned that when we recognise expenses in advance of paying the related cash, we recognise a related liability.

Failure to undertake the types of adjusting we have just discussed will result in financial statements being released that could potentially be quite misleading. They would not be reliable and therefore would not satisfy one of the fundamental qualitative characteristics expected of useful financial accounting information, this being faithful representation.

Once we have completed the adjusting journal entries at the end of the accounting period, this leads us to the preparation of a second trial balance, which we might refer to as the 'post-adjusting journal entries trial balance'. This trial balance will provide us with a further opportunity to check whether the ledger accounts seem to have the normal balance expected (for example, assets are expected to have a debit balance), and to check whether total credits are equal to total debits. If your first trial balance balances but your second trial balance does not, this means that you have made a mistake when processing your adjusting entries. The adjusted trial balance also indicates which income and expense accounts need to be 'closed off' – something that we will do in the next section of this chapter.

We will again summarise where we are up to in terms of the entire financial accounting process – see **Figure 8.3** (and yes, there are still more steps to come).

FIGURE 8.3 Where we are up to now in the financial accounting process

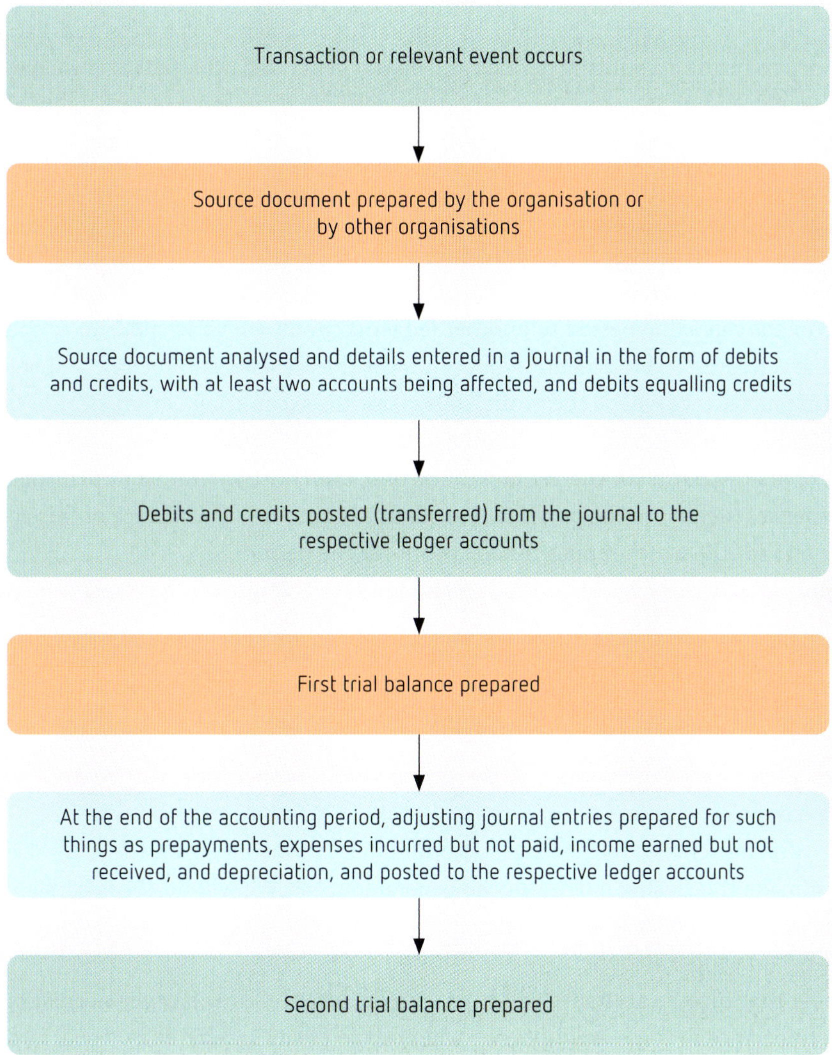

Why do I need to know about adjusting journal entries?

If you work in a financial accounting function there will typically always be a need to adjust the financial accounts at the end of the period to take into account issues and adjustments associated with depreciation, prepayments, income received in advance of performing services, expenses incurred but not paid, and income earned but not received. A failure to make the required adjustments would undermine the representational faithfulness of the financial statements.

LO8.6 Closing entries

As new accounting periods (reporting periods) commence, we would expect the balance of all the various revenue and expense accounts to subsequently begin the new accounting period with a zero balance. This is necessary so that we can record the expenses and income for that period of time, and so that income and those expenses are not mixed in with the expenses and income of previous accounting periods. By contrast, the balance of assets and liabilities will carry forward to future accounting periods and do not get closed off – that is, if we have an asset or liability at the end of an accounting period, we will also have an asset or liability at the start of the next accounting period. For example, if we have cash or buildings at the close of business on 31 December, and if that is the end of the accounting period, then at the start of the next day (the new accounting period), we would still have the cash and the buildings.

Returning to income and expenses, in an effort to create a zero balance in expenses and income accounts in preparation for the next accounting period, we need to transfer the balances at the end of the reporting period to another ledger account, which we refer to as the 'profit or loss summary account'. This account will then have all expenses and income transferred to it, meaning that its balance will be the profit, or loss, for the accounting period.

For example, if the total of all the income accounts for the period is $350 000, and the total of all the expense accounts for the period is $280 000, then once we transfer the income (credits) and the expenses (debits) to the profit or loss summary account, the balance of this account will be a credit of $70 000, which represents the profit for the period.

Ultimately, the balance of the profit or loss summary account will be transferred to another equity account, perhaps owner's capital in the case of a sole trader. For a company, the balance of the profit and loss summary account would be transferred to 'retained earnings'. For companies, there is a general legal requirement that accumulated profits (or losses) be kept separate from the capital contributions of shareholders (which would be shown in an account called 'share capital') as well as kept separate from various other reserve accounts that form part of the shareholders' equity of a company.

As we know, any entries to the ledger accounts must first come from the journal. Therefore, we need to make the closing entries in the general journal. We will do these at the end of the accounting period to create a zero balance in all expense and income accounts, as well as the distributions (drawings) account.

We know that income accounts will have a credit balance. This is their normal balance. To create a zero balance in these accounts, we will need to create a debit entry equal in amount to the credit balance of the income account. The credit entry will be to the profit or loss summary account. For example, if we have sales income of $290 000 for the accounting period ending 31 December 2025 (and this would be a credit balance), then our entry to close off the sales income account would be as follows (assuming the same ledger account numbers shown in **Exhibit 8.1** are also used by this business):

Date	Account name	Account number	Debit $	Credit $
31 Dec 2025	Sales income	250	290 000	
	Profit or loss summary	240		290 000
	To close off sales income at the end of the accounting period to profit or loss summary			

After the above closing journal entry, the debit and credit columns of the sales income ledger account will be the same, meaning that the account will have a zero balance.

We also know that expense accounts will have a debit balance. To create a zero balance in these accounts, we therefore will need to create a credit entry equal in amount to the debit balance of the income account. The debit entry will be to the profit or loss summary account. Therefore, for example, if we have wages expense of $100 000, cost of sales of $60 000, and electricity expenses of $10 000 for the accounting period (these would all have debit balances), then our entry to close off the respective expenses would be as follows:

Date	Account name	Account number	Debit $	Credit $
31 Dec 2025	Profit or loss summary	240	170 000	
	Wages expense	310		100 000
	Cost of sales	315		60 000
	Electricity expense	350		10 000
	To close off expenses at the end of the accounting period to profit or loss summary			

Note that for the above journal entry, we used a 'compound entry' wherein we combined the closing off of a number of expenses in one journal entry. This is common practice.

If the above income and expense accounts were the only income and expenses for the accounting period, then our profit or loss summary account would have a credit balance of $120 000, and this would represent the profit for the accounting period. The profit or loss summary account is then closed off to an owners' equity account. In the case of a sole trader, it would be closed off to the owner's capital account. The third closing entry would therefore be as follows, for the information we have already used above:

Date	Account name	Account number	Debit $	Credit $
31 Dec 2025	Profit or loss summary	240	120 000	
	J. Smith, capital account	201		120 000
	To close off the profit or loss summary account to the capital account			

During the accounting period, the owner might have also withdrawn assets from the business for personal use. Because it is usual for information to be produced to show how much was withdrawn by owners within an accounting period, drawings are also closed off at the end of the accounting period.

We know that drawings will have a debit balance. To create a zero balance in this account, we therefore will need to create a credit entry equal in amount to the debit balance of the drawings account. For a sole trader, the debit entry will be to the capital account. Therefore, for example, if we have drawings of $25 000 for the accounting period (this would be a debit balance), then our fourth closing entry to close off drawings would be as follows:

Date	Account name	Account number	Debit $	Credit $
31 Dec 2025	J. Smith, capital account	201	25 000	
	Drawings	230		25 000
	To close off drawings to the capital account			

Ultimately, after the closing entries are performed, only non-zero balances in accounts that relate to assets, liabilities and equity will be left. This then leads to the preparation of a third trial balance, which might be referred to as the 'post-closing entry trial balance'. This trial balance will provide a further opportunity to check whether the ledger accounts seem to have the normal balance, and also to check whether total credits are equal to total debits. These remaining accounts with a non-zero balance will now be shown in the balance sheet.

For more on the preparation of closing journal entries, see **Learning exercise 8.14**.

8.14 Learning Exercise

Preparation of closing journal entries

Scenario: Using the information from **Learning exercises 8.5**, **8.7** and **8.8**, we have the following trial balance for Wayne Lynch Painting Services for the month ending 31 January 2025. This is the trial balance before closing entries have been made.

We have assumed that no adjusting journal entries are required. That is, for Wayne Lynch Painting Services we have assumed that no adjustments are necessary for any income earned but not received, expenses incurred but not yet paid, income received in advance, prepayments, and depreciation. Had these adjustments been necessary (as they generally would be), then adjusting journal entries would have been made before any closing journal entries were made.

Trial balance of Wayne Lynch Painting Services as at 31 January 2025

Account number	Account name	Debits $	Credits $
100	Cash	10 650	
105	Accounts receivable	2 750	
108	Paint and brushes supplies	700	

Trial balance of Wayne Lynch Painting Services as at 31 January 2025			
Account number	Account name	Debits $	Credits $
125	Painting equipment	1050	
155	Accounts payable		900
201	W. Lynch capital account		10000
230	Drawings	2000	
251	Painting income		9150
310	Wages expense	1400	
315	Cost of paint supplies used	1500	
Totals		20050	20050

Task: You are required to prepare:

- the closing journal entries for Wayne Lynch Painting Services
- the post-closing entry trial balance for Wayne Lynch Painting Services as at 31 January 2025
- the balance sheet of Wayne Lynch Painting Services as at 31 January 2025.

Solution:

Closing journal entries for Wayne Lynch Painting Services				
Date	Account name	Account number	Debit $	Credit $
31 Jan	Painting income	251	9150	
	Profit or loss summary	240		9150
	To close off painting income to profit or loss summary			
31 Jan	Profit or loss summary	240	2900	
	Cost of paint supplies used	315		1500
	Wages expense	310		1400
	To close off expenses to profit or loss summary			
31 Jan	Profit or loss summary	240	6250	

Closing journal entries for Wayne Lynch Painting Services				
Date	**Account name**	**Account number**	**Debit $**	**Credit $**
	W. Lynch capital account	201		6250
	To transfer the balance of profit or loss summary to the capital account			
31 Jan	W. Lynch capital account	201	2000	
	Drawings	230		2000
	To transfer the balance of drawings to the capital account			

The above journal entries would then be posted to the respective ledger accounts, and the balances determined. We have not reproduced that step here; however, the balances that would then be recorded in a third trial balance, the post-closing entry trial balance, are shown below. After the closing entries have been posted to the ledger, we will just be left with asset, liability and equity accounts.

Post-closing entry trial balance of Wayne Lynch Painting Services as at 31 January 2025			
Account number	**Account name**	**Debits $**	**Credits $**
100	Cash	10650	
105	Accounts receivable	2750	
108	Paint and brushes supplies	700	
125	Painting equipment	1050	
155	Accounts payable		900
201	Wayne Lynch, capital account		14250
Totals		15150	15150

We should know by now that the accounts shown in the above post-closing entry trial balance are from the elements of financial accounting that appear within a balance sheet (or as it is also called, the statement of financial position). The balance sheet we have prepared below is of the form A – L = OE. This is a common presentation format.

Balance sheet of Wayne Lynch Painting Services as at 31 January 2025	
	$
Current assets	
Cash	10 650
Accounts receivable	2 750
Paint and brushes supplies	700
	14 100
Non-current assets	
Painting equipment	1 050
Total assets	**15 150**
Current liabilities	
Accounts payable	900
Net assets	**14 250**
Owners' equity	
W. Lynch, capital account	**14 250**

An overview of which accounts get closed off at the end of the accounting period is provided in Figure 8.4. As the figure shows, the income, expense and drawings (or distributions) accounts are ultimately closed off to the owners' equity account. For a sole trader, this equity account might just be referred to as the 'capital account'.

FIGURE 8.4 An overview of the procedure to close off accounts at the end of the accounting period

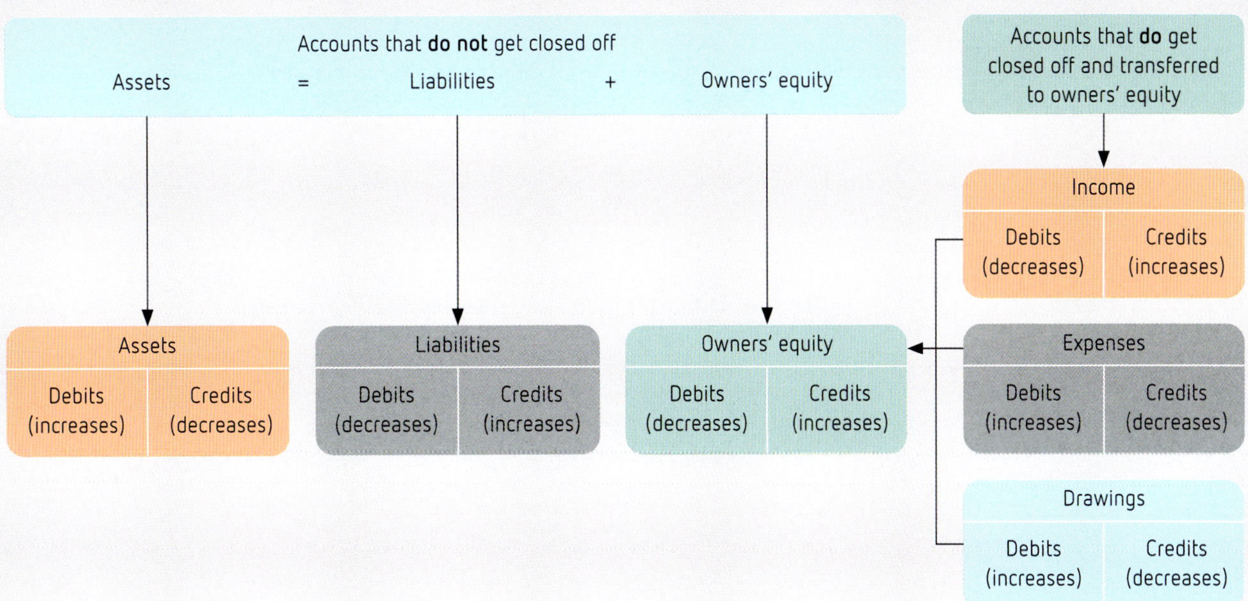

We have now covered a number of steps in this chapter. These are summarised in **Figure 8.5**. We have added two important last steps to this figure, these being to evaluate the financial statements that have ultimately been produced by our financial accounting information system, and to plan for the future. It would be relatively pointless to do all this work and generate financial statements such as a statement of profit or loss, and a balance sheet, if these statements were not then reviewed to assess the financial performance, and financial position, of the organisation. Once assessments have been made of the financial performance and financial position, and how these compare with previously constructed plans and budgets, this information would then be

FIGURE 8.5 The steps in the financial accounting puzzle

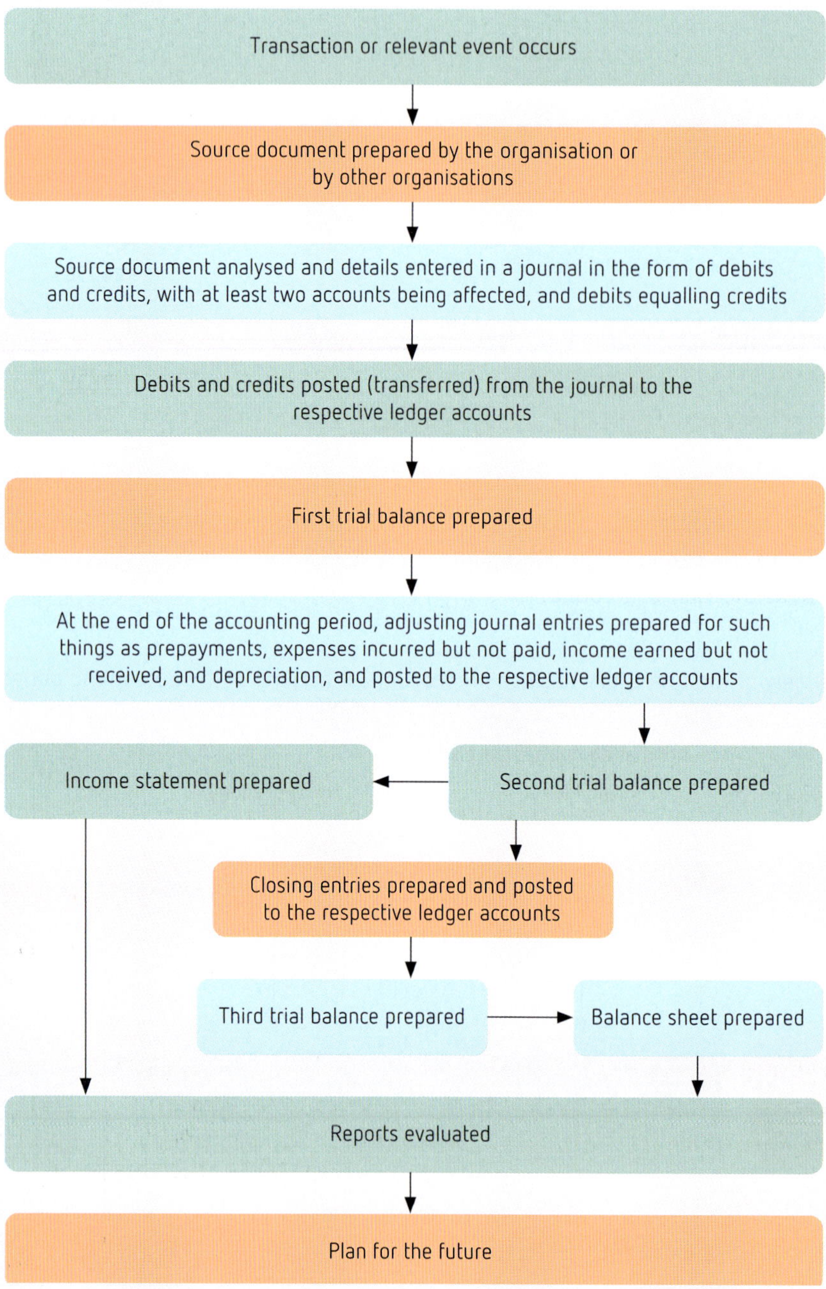

used to plan, or revise, future strategies and actions. Of course, the financial statements will also be of relevance to many other stakeholders not directly involved with the management of the organisation.

We have spent a good deal of time discussing closing entries. Modern-day computerised accounting systems will actually perform the closing off process at the click of a button, provided the system has been set up correctly. Nevertheless, it is important that you understand the processes that are taking place within such a system.

Key concept

At the very commencement of each new reporting period (accounting period), all expenses, income and distribution accounts in the ledger should have a zero balance so that the various expense, income and distribution accounts will only include the transactions and events that have happened in the new reporting period. This is the role of closing entries.

LO8.7 Real-world refinements to the accounting information system

Multiple journals

In the learning exercises provided in this chapter, we have only used one journal to record all our transactions. Whilst we have not been using this terminology, this journal is often referred to as the *general journal*. It is worth noting that organisations often use several different types of journals to record transactions. However, even with multiple journals, a transaction or event would only be recorded in the one journal (that is, the same transaction or event would not be recorded in multiple journals).

In an organisation, there could be several journals, with each one capturing transactions of a particular nature. For example, rather than recording all the cash payments throughout the general journal, it is common to record all cash payments in one journal, which would be known as the cash payments journal. Such a journal would record *all* cash payments and would have separate columns for routine types of payments. A specific person might be in charge of looking after this journal. Similarly, there will often be other journals, often referred to as *special journals*, such as the following:

- cash receipts journal – records details of *all* cash receipts
- sales journal – records details of *all* sales made on credit terms
- purchases journal – records information about *all* purchases of inventory on credit terms.

Again, in large organisations, different people tend to look after each of these journals. As with the general journal, the details in these special journals will ultimately be posted to the ledger, just as we post entries from the general journal to the ledger.

Even when an organisation does have special journals, such as the four briefly described above, there will still need to be a general journal, so that transactions or adjustments – such as period end adjusting entries, and closing entries – that do not belong in any of the special journals, can be entered into the financial accounting information system.

Therefore, in the 'real world' you might hear about different types of journals, but they all basically serve the same function: to ultimately record the financial effects of particular transactions and events, and to provide numbers that are then posted to the relevant ledger accounts.

Subsidiary ledgers

subsidiary ledger
A subsidiary ledger is a group of similar accounts whose combined balances equal the balance in a specific general ledger account. A subsidiary ledger captures individual details that might be required for management purposes, e.g. records of inventory, accounts receivable, and accounts payable

Another refinement we can briefly consider is the use of **subsidiary ledgers**. In this chapter we have used ledger accounts for various types of assets, liabilities, and income, expense and equity items, and the total number of ledger accounts is reflected within the chart of accounts. However, for particular items, such as inventory, accounts receivable, and accounts payable, we logically need more information than simply a total balance. For example, we might find that the total accounts receivable (or 'debtors') of an organisation is $1 500 000. Whilst that is useful to know, for management purposes we need more information, such as:

- Who are the individual debtors?
- How much does each of them owe the organisation?
- How long have they owed the money to the organisation?

We need individual details so we know who to follow up for payment. With this in mind, organisations will have subsidiary ledgers that provide further detail about individual debtors. Each debtor will have its own individual sub-account located within the subsidiary ledger. For example, whilst the ledger account for accounts receivable might show a balance of $1 500 000, the subsidiary ledgers will provide a breakdown of this total amount. It might show the following balances:

Debtor	Amount owing
Jack Black	$80 000
Sirius Black	$120 000
Corbin Blue	$60 000
Jackie Brown	$140 000
Simon Cream	$160 000
Frank Green	$140 000
Zane Grey	$45 000
Elvis Paisley	$55 000
Alicia Pink	$275 000
Alvin Purple	$225 000
Betty White	$110 000
Patrick White	$90 000
	$1 500 000

Each of the above debtors would have a separate subsidiary ledger account that shows the respective increases and decreases in the amount owed by the respective debtor. We would then know who to follow up for payment. Therefore, for our purposes, we just need to understand that whilst there might be a single ledger account for accounts receivable that perhaps has a total balance of $1 500 000, there will be further details of this total balance kept elsewhere in the accounting system, and the total of the individual debtor accounts would be expected to equal the balance of the ledger account for accounts receivable.

The other point to be made here is that when there are transactions that impact the ledger account called accounts receivable, there will not only be an adjustment to the overall ledger account (as a result of our normal posting process), there will also be adjustments made to the specific details of the debtor as recorded in the subsidiary ledger.

Just as we need a further breakdown of accounts receivable, individual accounts would also be kept for all the individuals/organisations to whom the organisation owes money (the creditors or accounts payable), and the totals of these individual sub-accounts would equal the balance for accounts payable as shown in the ledger.

Similarly, we would also be expected to have individual sub-accounts (subsidiary ledger accounts) for each type of inventory item, and the total financial amounts attributed to each type of inventory should reconcile back to the total for inventory as recorded in the ledger.

Source : iStock.com/onurdongel

Organisations must keep subsidiary ledgers with information about individual debtors, so that they can follow up payment with each person as necessary.

LO8.8 A comprehensive example of recording transactions

We will conclude the chapter with a comprehensive example that includes the use of journals, ledgers, trial balances and closing entries, and which requires the preparation of both a statement of profit or loss (or 'income statement'), and a balance sheet.

Hardman Prestige Vehicles is a sole trader that sells prestige motor vehicles. It commences business on 1 January 2025. Below, you are provided with Hardman Prestige Vehicles' chart of accounts, as well its transactions for the month of January 2025.

You are to prepare a statement of profit or loss for Hardman Prestige Vehicles for the month of January 2025, as well as a balance sheet as at 31 January 2025.

Chart of accounts for Hardman Prestige Vehicles		
	Account number	**Account name**
Assets (100–150)	100	Cash at bank
	110	Accounts receivable
	120	Motor vehicle inventory
	125	Prepaid rent
	130	Office equipment
	135	Maintenance equipment
	140	Buildings
	145	Land
Liabilities (151–199)	155	Accounts payable
	165	Wages payable
	170	Bank loan

>>>

Chart of accounts for Hardman Prestige Vehicles		
	Account number	**Account name**
Equity (200–250)	201	D. Hardman, capital account
	230	Drawings
	240	Profit or loss summary
Income (251–299)	251	Sales income
	260	Interest income
Expenses (300–350)	310	Cost of sales
	320	Wages expense
	330	Rent expense
	335	Electricity expense
	340	Interest expense

The transactions for the month of January were as follows:

Date	Description	Amount
1 Jan	Cash contribution from Damian Hardman as owner	$550 000
1 Jan	Acquired motor vehicles for inventory on credit from Shady Wholesalers	$400 000
1 Jan	Purchased maintenance equipment for cash	$110 000
3 Jan	Borrowed cash from Loan Shark Bank	$135 000
5 Jan	Sold car on credit to Terry Day. The cost of this car to the business was $60 000	$105 000
6 Jan	Paid wages	$7700
8 Jan	Received cash from debtor – Terry Day	$105 000
11 Jan	Acquired motor vehicle for inventory for cash	$30 000
14 Jan	Purchased machine to adjust car odometers, for cash	$5700
14 Jan	Paid creditor – Shady Wholesalers	$400 000
16 Jan	Received cash for one car. The car cost the business $25 000	$65 000
21 Jan	Paid wages	$3700
22 Jan	Invoiced customer – Peter Drouyn – for the sale of a motor vehicle. The car cost the business $45 000	$65 000
23 Jan	Acquired cars on credit terms from Shonky Sam Motors	$100 000
23 Jan	Paid electricity expense	$700
24 Jan	Received cash from debtor – Peter Drouyn	$65 000
25 Jan	Invoiced customer – Cheyne Horan – for the sale of a motor vehicle. The car cost the business $45 000	$70 000
29 Jan	Paid interest to Loan Shark Bank	$12 000
31 Jan	Damian Hardman withdrew cash for personal use	$50 000

Solution

Our first step is to record the details of the individual transactions (as determined by reviewing source documents) into the general journal. This is done as follows – we will assume that these journal entries take up the first two pages of the general journal. We are not using special journals (such as a cash payments journal or a sales journal) here even though it would be common for them to be used in 'real life':

General journal Page 1

Date	Account name	Account number	Debit $	Credit $
1 Jan 2025	Cash at bank	100	550 000	
	D. Hardman, capital account	201		550 000
	Owner contributed $550 000			
1 Jan 2025	Motor vehicle inventory	120	400 000	
	Accounts payable	155		400 000
	Acquired motor vehicles on credit from Shady Wholesalers			
1 Jan 2025	Maintenance equipment	135	110 000	
	Cash at bank	100		110 000
	Acquired maintenance equipment with cash			
3 Jan 2025	Cash at bank	100	135 000	
	Bank loan	170		135 000
	Bank loan taken out			
5 Jan 2025	Accounts receivable	110	105 000	
	Sales income	251		105 000
	Sold motor vehicle on credit terms to T. Day			
	Cost of sales	310	60 000	
	Motor vehicle inventory	120		60 000
	Cost of sold motor vehicle			
6 Jan 2025	Wages expense	320	7700	
	Cash at bank	100		7700
	Paid wages with cash			
8 Jan 2025	Cash at bank	100	105 000	
	Accounts receivable	110		105 000
	Received amount due from customer T. Day			
11 Jan 2025	Motor vehicle inventory	120	30 000	
	Cash at bank	100		30 000
	Acquired motor vehicle for inventory for cash			

Date	Account name	Account number	Debit $	Credit $
14 Jan 2025	Maintenance equipment	135	5700	
	Cash at bank	100		5700
	Acquired maintenance equipment with cash			
14 Jan 2025	Accounts payable	155	400000	
	Cash at bank	100		400000
	Paid accounts payable – Shady Wholesalers			

General journal **Page 2**

Date	Account name	Account number	Debit $	Credit $
16 Jan 2025	Cash at bank	100	65000	
	Sales income	251		65000
	Sold motor vehicle for cash			
	Cost of sales	310	25000	
	Motor vehicle inventory	120		25000
	Cost of motor vehicle sold			
21 Jan 2025	Wages expense	320	3700	
	Cash at bank	100		3700
	Paid wages with cash			
22 Jan 2025	Accounts receivable	110	65000	
	Sales income	251		65000
	Sold motor vehicle on credit terms to P. Drouyn			
	Cost of sales	310	45000	
	Motor vehicle inventory	120		45000
	Cost of sold motor vehicle			
23 Jan 2025	Motor vehicle inventory	120	100000	
	Accounts payable	155		100000
	Acquired motor vehicles for inventory on credit from Shonky Sam Motors			
23 Jan 2025	Electricity expense	335	700	
	Cash at bank	100		700
	Paid electricity expense			
24 Jan 2025	Cash at bank	100	65000	
	Accounts receivable	110		65000
	Received amount due from customer P. Drouyn			
25 Jan 2025	Accounts receivable	110	70000	
	Sales income	251		70000
	Motor vehicle sold on credit terms to C. Horan			

Date	Account name	Account number	Debit $	Credit $
25 Jan 2025	Cost of sales	310	45 000	
	Motor vehicle inventory	120		45 000
	Cost of motor vehicle sold			
29 Jan 2025	Interest expense	340	12 000	
	Cash at bank	100		12 000
	Interest expense paid			
31 Jan 2025	Drawings	230	50 000	
	Cash at bank	100		50 000
	Owner withdrew cash			

Once we have entered the details of the various transactions into the journal, our next task is to post each journal transaction to the respective ledger accounts. Doing this manually is quite time-consuming. In a computerised accounting system, all these postings will be done automatically by the computer. Once the above journal entries are transferred to the ledger accounts, those accounts will appear as follows:

100 Cash at bank

Date	Detail	Jnl ref.	Debit amount $	Date	Detail	Jnl ref.	Credit amount $
1 Jan 2025	D. Hardman, capital account	1	550 000	1 Jan 2025	Maintenance equipment	1	110 000
3 Jan 2025	Bank loan	1	135 000	6 Jan 2025	Wages expense	1	7700
8 Jan 2025	Accounts receivable	1	105 000	11 Jan 2025	Motor vehicle inventory	1	30 000
16 Jan 2025	Sales income	2	65 000	14 Jan 2025	Maintenance equipment	1	5700
24 Jan 2025	Accounts receivable	2	65 000	14 Jan 2025	Accounts payable	1	400 000
				21 Jan 2025	Wages expense	2	3700
				23 Jan 2025	Electricity expense	2	700
				29 Jan 2025	Interest expense	2	12 000
				31 Jan 2025	Drawings	2	50 000

110 Accounts receivable

Date	Detail	Jnl ref.	Debit amount $	Date	Detail	Jnl ref.	Credit amount $
5 Jan 2025	Sales income	1	105 000	8 Jan 2025	Cash at bank	1	105 000
22 Jan 2025	Sales income	2	65 000	24 Jan 2025	Cash at bank	2	65 000
25 Jan 2025	Sales income	2	70 000				

120 Motor vehicle inventory

Date	Detail	Jnl ref.	Debit amount $	Date	Detail	Jnl ref.	Credit amount $
1 Jan 2025	Accounts payable	1	400 000	5 Jan 2025	Cost of sales	1	60 000
11 J÷an 2025	Cash at bank	1	30 000	16 Jan 2025	Cost of sales	2	25 000
23 Jan 2025	Accounts payable	2	100 000	22 Jan 2025	Cost of sales	2	45 000
				25 Jan 2025	Cost of sales	2	45 000

135 Maintenance equipment

Date	Detail	Jnl ref.	Debit amount $	Date	Detail	Jnl ref.	Credit amount $
1 Jan 2025	Cash at bank	1	110 000				
14 Jan 2025	Cash at bank	1	5700				

155 Accounts payable

Date	Detail	Jnl ref.	Debit amount $	Date	Detail	Jnl ref.	Credit amount $
14 Jan 2025	Cash at bank	1	400 000	1 Jan 2025	Motor vehicle inventory	1	400 000
				23 Jan 2025	Motor vehicle inventory	2	100 000

170 Bank loan

Date	Detail	Jnl ref.	Debit amount $	Date	Detail	Jnl ref.	Credit amount $
				3 Jan 2025	Cash at bank	1	135 000

201 D. Hardman, capital account

Date	Detail	Jnl ref.	Debit amount $	Date	Detail	Jnl ref.	Credit amount $
				1 Jan 2025	Cash at bank	1	550 000

230 Drawings

Date	Detail	Jnl ref.	Debit amount $	Date	Detail	Jnl ref.	Credit amount $
31 Jan 2025	Cash at bank	2	50 000				

251 Sales income

Date	Detail	Jnl ref.	Debit amount $	Date	Detail	Jnl ref.	Credit amount $
				5 Jan 2025	Accounts receivable	1	105 000
				16 Jan 2025	Cash at bank	2	65 000
				22 Jan 2025	Accounts receivable	2	65 000
				25 Jan 2025	Accounts receivable	2	70 000

310 Cost of sales

Date	Detail	Jnl ref.	Debit amount $	Date	Detail	Jnl ref.	Credit amount $
5 Jan 2025	Motor vehicle inventory	1	60 000				
16 Jan 2025	Motor vehicle inventory	2	25 000				
22 Jan 2025	Motor vehicle inventory	2	45 000				
25 Jan 2025	Motor vehicle inventory	2	45 000				

320 Wages expense

Date	Detail	Jnl ref.	Debit amount $	Date	Detail	Jnl ref.	Credit amount $
6 Jan 2025	Cash at bank	1	7700				
21 Jan 2025	Cash at bank	2	3700				

335 Electricity expense

Date	Detail	Jnl ref.	Debit amount $	Date	Detail	Jnl ref.	Credit amount $
23 Jan 2025	Cash at bank	2	700				

340 Interest expense

Date	Detail	Jnl ref.	Debit amount $	Date	Detail	Jnl ref.	Credit amount $
29 Jan 2025	Cash at bank	2	12 000				

Once we have posted the journal entries, we need to determine the balance of each ledger account. We have not shown that step here, but it needs to be done in the same manner as shown in **Exhibit 8.3**. Once we have the balance of each ledger account, we can then prepare a trial balance, as shown below. As you know, the total of all accounts with debit balances must equal the total of all accounts with credit balances.

Trial balance for Hardman Prestige Vehicles as at 31 January 2025

Account number	Account name	Debits $	Credits $
100	Cash at bank	300 200	
110	Accounts receivable	70 000	
120	Motor vehicle inventory	355 000	
135	Maintenance equipment	115 700	
155	Accounts payable		100 000
170	Bank loan		135 000
201	D. Hardman, capital account		550 000
230	Drawings	50 000	
251	Sales income		305 000
310	Cost of sales	175 000	
320	Wages expense	11 400	
335	Electricity expense	700	
340	Interest expense	12 000	
Totals		**1 090 000**	**1 090 000**

Once we have prepared the above trial balance, we are then in a position to prepare the statement of profit or loss for the organisation. We have assumed that there are no end-of-accounting-period adjusting entries required for such things as income earned but not received, expenses incurred but not yet paid, income received in advance, prepayments, and depreciation.

Profit or loss statement for Hardman Prestige Vehicles for the month ending 31 January 2025

	$
Income	
Sales income	305 000
Expenses	
Cost of sales	(175 000)
Electricity expense	(700)
Interest expense	(12 000)
Wages	(11 400)
Profit	**105 900**

We need to prepare our closing journal entries so that we can transfer income, expenses and drawings to the capital account of Damian Hardman. Preparing and posting the closing entries to the respective ledger accounts will also ensure that the balances of all the expense, income and drawings accounts will be zero at the commencement of the next accounting period. The closing journal entries would be as follows:

General journal **Page 3**

Date	Account name	Account number	Debit $	Credit $
31 Jan 2025	Sales income	251	305 000	
	Profit or loss summary	240		305 000
	To close off sales income to profit or loss summary			
31 Jan 2025	Profit or loss summary	240	199 100	
	Cost of sales	310		175 000
	Wages expense	320		11 400
	Electricity expense	335		700
	Interest expense	340		12 000
	To close off expenses to profit or loss summary			

Date	Account name	Account number	Debit $	Credit $
31 Jan 2025	Profit or loss summary	240	105 900	
	D. Hardman, capital account	201		105 900
	To transfer the balance of profit or loss summary to the capital account			
31 Jan 2025	D. Hardman, capital account	201	50 000	
	Drawings	230		50 000
	To transfer the balance of drawings to the capital account			

We would then post the above closing journal entries to the respective ledger account and the account balances would be calculated – we have not shown that step here, but it needs to be done. Once the closing entries have been posted to the ledger accounts, we are left with the following trial balance, which will only include asset, liability and equity accounts.

The post-closing entry trial balance of Hardman Prestige Vehicles as at 31 January 2025

Account number	Account name	Debits $	Credits $
100	Cash at bank	300 200	
110	Accounts receivable	70 000	
120	Motor vehicle inventory	355 000	
135	Maintenance equipment	115 700	
155	Accounts payable		100 000
170	Bank loan		135 000
201	D. Hardman, capital account		605 900
Totals		840 900	840 900

Having performed all of these steps, we are now in a position to finally produce the balance sheet. As you can see, the following balance sheet is in the form of A – L = OE.

Balance sheet of Hardman Prestige Vehicles as at 31 January 2025	
	$
Current assets	
Cash at bank	300 200
Accounts receivable	70 000
Motor vehicle inventory	355 000
	725 200
Non-current assets	
Maintenance equipment	115 700
	$
Total assets	840 900
Current liabilities	
Accounts payable	100 000
Non-current liabilities	
Bank loan	135 000
Total liabilities	235 000
Net assets	605 900
Represented by:	
Owners' equity	
D. Hardman, capital account	605 900

STUDY TOOLS

SUMMARY

In this chapter we have provided an overview of how a financial accounting information system works. We know that the financial accounting system records transactions that can be measured in financial terms, and which affect at least one of the elements of financial accounting (assets, liabilities, income, expense or equity) as they relate to the organisation in question.

We learned that the starting point in the process is when the accountant reviews source documents to determine if any of the accounts of the organisation – as reflected in the chart of accounts – is affected by a transaction or event. Once the source document is reviewed and the particular affected accounts identified, the effects of that transaction are recorded within the journal. In doing so, the accountant makes use of debits and credits. We learned the rules in relation to debits and credits.

Once the transactions are entered in the journal, the next step is to transfer the entries in the journal to the respective ledger accounts and to determine the balance of each of these accounts. Once these postings have occurred and the balances have been determined, the accountant will typically produce a first trial balance.

The next step would be to prepare some adjusting journal entries at the end of the accounting period. These adjusting journal entries would relate to such things as: income earned but not received, expenses incurred but not yet paid, income received in advance, prepayments, and depreciation. These adjusting journal entries would then be posted to the respective ledger accounts.

We would then prepare a second trial balance, which would form the basis for preparing a statement of profit or loss for the accounting period. Following this, the accountant would prepare some closing entries that would have the effect of transferring all income and expense accounts to an owners' equity account, such as a capital account. The drawings account would also be closed to the capital account. The closing entries would also mean that the balances of all the income, expense and drawings accounts would be zero in preparation for the next accounting period.

A third trial balance would then be prepared from which a balance sheet can be prepared. Other financial statements, such as a statement of cash flows or a statement of changes in equity, might also be prepared at this time. The various financial statements would then be reviewed by various stakeholders and decisions made on the basis of the reported information. These financial statements help managers monitor and evaluate the performance of an organisation from a financial perspective, as well as help them learn, revise and adjust plans for future operations. Other stakeholders would also be interested in the financial position, and financial performance, of the organisation.

ANSWERS TO THE OPENING QUESTIONS

At the beginning of the chapter we asked the following four questions. As a result of reading this chapter, you should now be able to provide informed answers to these questions – ours are shown below.

1 Within financial accounting, what is the role of the 'journal'?

The journal, also known as 'the book of prime entry', is the first point within a financial accounting information system at which information is entered. The information is extracted from 'source documents'. Information in the journal is then posted to the relevant ledger account. By entering the information in the journal, this process converts the details of the transactions into debits and credits and allows us to check that each transaction balances before posting it to the ledger. It also creates an audit trail as it provides a narration for the transaction, which is something that the ledger accounts do not do.

2 What is a 'debit' and what is a 'credit'?

Debits and credits are part of the language of financial accounting. They signify an increase or decrease in the respective elements of accounting. As we learned in this chapter, if assets or expenses are to be increased, then the respective ledger account relating to these elements of accounting are to be *debited*. If assets or expenses are to be decreased, then they are to be *credited*. For liabilities, income and equity accounts, any increase thereof is performed by way of a credit entry. If these elements of accounting are to be decreased, then a debit entry would be required. Debits and credits are part of what has become known as 'double-entry accounting', and there is a requirement that total debits must equal total credits. If this is not the case, then an error has occurred. The use of debits and credits, and the rule that debits must equal credits, allows us to ensure that the accounting equation – upon which the practice of financial accounting is based – remains in balance. In essence, debits represent the application of funds while credits represent the sources of funds.

3 What is a 'trial balance'?

A trial balance is a list of all the ledger accounts being used together with details of the debit or credit balance of the respective ledger accounts. The total of all the ledger accounts with a debit balance should equal the total balance of all the ledger accounts with a credit balance, otherwise an error has occurred.

4 What are 'closing entries', and why do we need to do them?

'Closing entries' are journal entries that we prepare at the end of the accounting period and which serve the purpose of transferring all expense, income and drawing accounts to an owners' equity account – such as a 'capital account'. The other purpose served by closing entries is that they cause the balance of income, expenses and drawings accounts to be zero at the very end of the reporting period in preparation for the next accounting period.

SELF-TEST QUIZ

Answers to this quiz appear in the Appendix of this book.

1 Which of the following is false?
   - a The normal balance of inventory is a debit balance.
   - b The normal balance of distributions/dividends is a debit balance.
   - c The normal balance of sales revenue is a credit balance.
   - d The normal balance of property, plant and equipment is a debit balance.
   - e The normal balance of bank loan is a debit balance.

2 Which of the following is true?
   - a Transactions and events shall first be recorded in a journal before the amounts are subsequently transferred to the respective ledger accounts.
   - b The trial balance provides the balances of the respective ledger accounts.
   - c In the trial balance, the total of all the accounts with a debit balance must equal the total of all the ledger accounts with a credit balance.
   - d Adjusting journal entries need to be made within the journal and posted to the respective ledger accounts before the profit or loss of the reporting period can be determined.
   - e All of these choices.

3 If an organisation was to acquire $10 000 in inventory with an agreement to pay the supplier in 10 days, then there would be:
   - a no journal entry until such time as the cash has been paid.
   - b a debit to inventory (an asset) and a credit to accounts payable (a liability).
   - c a credit to inventory (an asset) and a debit to accounts payable (a liability).
   - d no accounting entry until such time as the inventory has been sold.
   - e None of these choices.

4 Assume that an organisation has a reporting period that ends on 31 December. If that organisation paid for 12 months insurance in advance on 1 October for $120 000 and it treated that payment as creating an asset (prepaid insurance), then what would be the adjusting journal entry on 31 December?
   a Debit insurance expense of $90 000, and credit prepaid insurance (an asset) of $90 000
   b Debit insurance expense of $30 000, and credit prepaid insurance (an asset) of $30 000
   c Debit prepaid insurance (an asset) of $90 000, and credit prepaid insurance of $90 000
   d Debit prepaid insurance (an asset) of $30 000, and credit prepaid insurance of $30 000
   e None of these choices.

5 If an organisation ends a reporting period with total sales revenue of $820 000 and expenses which were: wages expense $200 000, cost of sales $210 000 and rental expenses of $50 000, then the closing journal entries would include:
   a A debit to Profit or Loss Summary of $820 000 and a debit to Sales Revenue of $820 000;
   A debit to Profit or Loss Summary of $460 000 and a credit to Wages Expense of $200 000, a credit to Cost of Sales of $210 000 and a credit to Rental Expenses of $50 000.
   b A debit to Profit or Loss Summary of $820 000 and a debit to Sales Revenue of $820 000;
   A credit to Profit or Loss Summary of $460 000 and a debit to Wages Expense of $200 000, a debit to Cost of Sales of $210 000 and a debit to Rental Expenses of $50 000.
   c A debit to Sales Revenue of $820 000 and a credit to Profit or Loss Summary of $820 000;
   A debit to Profit or Loss Summary of $460 000 and a credit to Wages Expense of $200 000, a credit to Cost of Sales of $210 000 and a credit to Rental Expenses of $50 000.
   d A credit to Profit or Loss Summary of $820 000 and a debit to Sales Revenue of $820 000;
   A debit to Profit or Loss Summary of $460 000 and a debit to Wages Expense of $200 000, a credit to Cost of Sales of $210 000 and a credit to Rental Expenses of $50 000.
   e None of these choices.

ONLINE RESOURCES

Accompanying the book is an innovative online case study that follows an organisation initially established by two friends, which grows into a large and successful company. Acquire this chapter's case study from your instructor.

CASE STUDY

Armadillo Surf Designs: For the record

The team of accountants at Armadillo Surf Designs (ASD) are busy trying to finalise the financial accounts for the last financial year. As the manager of the accounting and finance department, you need to ensure that all necessary transactions have been correctly recorded. You are particularly concerned about the work that has been carried out by Hamish, as he is not yet fully qualified and is quite inexperienced.

You will review the journal entries prepared by Hamish and prepare new journal entries to account for missing transactions. You will also consider the need for adjusting journal entries and will prepare these if required. In addition, you will calculate and record depreciation expense.

END-OF-CHAPTER QUESTIONS

8.1 What is a source document, and what role does it play within a financial accounting information system?

8.2 What source documents would you expect to see in relation to the following transactions?
- **a** sale of inventory
- **b** purchase of inventory
- **c** acquisition of machinery.

8.3 What is a ledger account?

8.4 What do we mean when we refer to the practice of double-entry accounting?

8.5 Is double-entry accounting a new approach to accounting?

8.6 What is an accounting period?

8.7 What is the role of the journal?

8.8 What do we mean when we say we are posting a transaction from the journal to the ledger?

8.9 What is the ledger?

8.10 What is the role of the trial balance?

8.11 What is a chart of accounts?

8.12 What is:
- **a** a prepayment
- **b** revenue received in advance
- **c** revenue earned but not received?

8.13 What is an adjusting journal entry and why do we do one?

8.14 What are closing journal entries, which accounts do they relate to, and why do we do them?

8.15 What do we mean when we say that we are determining the 'balance' of an account?

8.16 Identify the different steps that need to be taken in the financial accounting information system in order to generate financial statements.

8.17 Debits are good and credits are bad. Is this right?

8.18 What is a debit entry and when do we do one?

8.19 What is a credit entry and when do we do one?

8.20 Why should the total of the debit entries equal the total of the credit entries?

8.21 What is the normal balance (that is, debit or credit) for each of the following:
- **a** inventory
- **b** accounts receivable
- **c** furniture
- **d** accounts payable
- **e** bank loan
- **f** electricity expense
- **g** sales income
- **h** capital.

8.22 For each of the following ledger accounts, indicate what the normal balance would be, and the impact that a debit and credit entry would have on the account.

Account	What is the normal balance? (debit or credit)	Would a debit entry increase or decrease the account?	Would a credit entry increase or decrease the account?
Inventory			
Accounts payable			
Sales income			
Furniture			
Accounts receivable			
Wages expense			

8.23 Provide journal entries for the following transactions:

a paid wages of $10 000 with cash on 5 January 2025

b purchased $150 000 of inventory from a supplier on credit terms on 10 January 2025

c purchased some office furniture for $50 000 with cash on 12 January 2025

d paid amount owing of $150 000 to a supplier of inventory on 17 January 2025.

8.24 Provide journal entries for the following transactions:

a A sole trader, Robert August, contributes $100 000 cash and $140 000 in inventory to the business on 1 July 2025.

b On 4 July 2025, the business sells inventory to a customer on credit terms for the amount of $200 000. The inventory has cost the organisation $120 000.

c The organisation pays $20 000 for 12 months' insurance in advance on 9 July 2025.

d The organisation receives $200 000 cash from the customer on 10 July 2025 (relating to the previous sale that was made on credit terms).

8.25 In respect of the following information, you are required to provide the adjusting journal entries that would be made at the end of the accounting period, which is 31 December 2025:

a On 1 October 2025, the organisation prepays rent for the next 12 months for a total amount of $60 000.

b On 1 September 2025, the organisation receives $30 000 for computer support services it will provide to a customer for the next six months.

8.26 You are provided with the following trial balance as at 31 December 2025, which is the end of the 12-month accounting period. This trial balance was produced prior to adjusting journal entries. You are to prepare the adjusting journal entries for the following transactions, and then provide the adjusted trial balance.

Trial balance for Bob Mac Services
as at 31 December 2025

Account number	Account name	Debits $	Credits $
100	Cash	100 000	
105	Accounts receivable	40 000	
110	Prepaid rent	30 000	
125	Computer equipment	20 000	

140	Accounts payable		30 000
145	Service income received in advance		60 000
160	Bank loan		25 000
201	Bob Mac, capital account		25 000
210	Drawings	10 000	
240	Service income		200 000
300	Wages expense	100 000	
320	Advertising expense	15 000	
325	Rent expense	20 000	
330	Electricity expense	2 000	
340	Interest expense	3 000	
Totals		**340 000**	**340 000**

Information required for the adjusting journal entries:

a The prepaid rent of $30 000 was paid on 1 September 2025 and is for the next 12 months.

b The service income received in advance of $60 000 was received on 1 November 2025 and is for six months of future services to be provided to a customer.

c Wages of $3000 are incurred (but not yet recorded) by the organisation at 31 December and will be paid on 2 January 2026.

8.27 You are provided with the following trial balance and are required to provide closing journal entries to close off the income, expenses and drawings accounts at the end of the accounting period.

Trial balance for Mac Coy Consulting as at 31 January 2025

Account number	Account name	Debits $	Credits $
102	Cash	35 000	
105	Accounts receivable	55 000	
110	Office supplies inventory	15 000	
120	Office equipment	30 000	
145	Accounts payable		50 000
160	Bank loan		25 000
201	Mac Coy, capital account		25 000
210	Drawings	5 000	
240	Consulting income		205 000
300	Wages expense	90 000	
310	Advertising expense	25 000	
320	Rent expense	40 000	
330	Electricity expense	5 000	
340	Interest expense	5 000	
Totals		**305 000**	**305 000**

8.28 Richard Keith is a musician and works as a sole trader operating under the name of Musical Pipeline. He commences the business on 1 January 2025.

You are provided with Musical Pipeline's chart of accounts, as well its transactions for the month of January. You are to prepare a statement of profit or loss for Musical Pipeline for the month of January 2025, as well as a balance sheet as at 31 January 2025. In doing so, you will need to:

- provide the required journal entries to record the transactions
- post the required journal entries to the respective ledger accounts
- prepare the relevant trial balances
- prepare the required closing entries.

There are no adjusting journal entries required for the end of the accounting period.

Chart of accounts for Musical Pipeline

	Account number	Account name
Assets	100	Cash at bank
	110	Accounts receivable
	125	Musical instruments
	130	Musical instrument maintenance equipment
	135	Van – motor vehicle
Liabilities	160	Accounts payable
	165	Wages payable
	170	Bank loan
Equity	201	R. Keith, capital account
	210	Drawings
	220	Profit or loss summary
Income	250	Performance income
	260	Interest income
Expenses	310	Travelling expenses
	320	Wages expense
	330	Musical instrument repairs
	340	Motor vehicle repairs
	350	Advertising expenses
	360	Interest expense

Date	Description	Amount
1 Jan 2025	Cash contribution from Richard Keith as owner	$100 000
1 Jan 2025	Acquired van with cash, for carrying musical instruments and musicians to performances	$45 000
1 Jan 2025	Purchased musical instrument maintenance equipment for cash	$9 000
3 Jan 2025	Borrowed cash from Musicians' Bank	$25 000
5 Jan 2025	Performed musical services for cash	$15 000

>>>

5 Jan 2025	Paid wages with cash to support crew	$1000
8 Jan 2025	Paid travelling expenses with cash	$600
11 Jan 2025	Paid for repairs to van (motor vehicle) with cash	$1900
14 Jan 2025	Purchased new guitar (musical instrument) with cash	$3000
14 Jan 2025	Performed musical services for The Playroom on credit terms	$10000
14 Jan 2025	Paid wages with cash to support crew	$1200
21 Jan 2025	Incurred advertising expenses, which are to be paid within 30 days	$5500
22 Jan 2025	Performed musical services for the Bondi Lifesaver Club on credit terms	$15000
22 Jan 2025	Paid wages with cash to support crew	$2000
22 Jan 2025	Acquired new guitar for cash	$13000
22 Jan 2025	Paid travelling expenses with cash	$500
24 Jan 2025	Received cash from debtor – The Playroom	$10000
25 Jan 2025	Performed musical services for Selina's Hotel on credit terms	$10000
25 Jan 2025	Paid wages with cash to support crew	$1500
25 Jan 2025	Paid travelling expenses with cash	$900
28 Jan 2025	Paid interest to Musicians' Bank	$1000
31 Jan 2025	R. Keith withdrew cash for personal use	$15000

8.29 Layne Beachley works as a sole trader and provides surfing lessons throughout the world. She commences her business, known as Surf to the Beach, on 1 January 2025.

You are provided with Surf to the Beach's chart of accounts, as well its transactions for the month of January. You are to prepare a statement of profit or loss for Surf to the Beach for the month of January 2025, as well as a balance sheet as at 31 January 2025. In doing so, you will need to:

- provide the required journal entries to record the transactions
- post the required journal entries to the respective ledger accounts
- prepare the relevant trial balances
- prepare the required closing entries.

There are no adjusting journal entries required for the end of the accounting period.

Chart of accounts for Surf to the Beach

	Account number	Account name
Assets	100	Cash at bank
	110	Accounts receivable
	120	Surfing equipment for hire
	130	Surfboard repair equipment
	140	Van – motor vehicle

>>>

Liabilities	150	Accounts payable
	160	Wages payable
	170	Bank loan
Equity	201	L. Beachley, capital account
	210	Drawings
	220	Profit or loss summary
Income	230	Income from surf lessons
	240	Interest income
Expenses	300	Travelling expenses
	310	Wages expense
	320	Surfboard repairs
	330	Motor vehicle repairs
	340	Advertising expenses
	350	Interest expense

Date	Description	Amount
1 Jan 2025	Cash contribution from Layne Beachley as owner	$70 000
1 Jan 2025	Acquired VW Kombi van (motor vehicle) with cash, for carrying surfboards and wetsuits	$45 000
1 Jan 2025	Purchased 20 surfboards with cash, to use in surf lessons	$11 000
1 Jan 2025	Purchased 40 wetsuits with cash, to use in surf lessons	$7 500
1 Jan 2025	Purchased some equipment with cash, for making surfboard repairs	$2 500
3 Jan 2025	Borrowed cash from Reef Bank	$15 000
5 Jan 2025	Provided surfing lessons to a corporate group known as Important CEOs on credit terms	$6 000
5 Jan 2025	Paid wages to surf instructors with cash	$800
8 Jan 2025	Paid travelling expenses with cash	$500
11 Jan 2025	Paid for repairs to VW Kombi Van (motor vehicle) with cash	$2 900
12 Jan 2025	Important CEOs paid the amount due	$6 000
14 Jan 2025	Purchased new surfboards with cash	$4 000
14 Jan 2025	Provided surfing lessons to Torquay Pensioners Club for cash	$8 000
14 Jan 2025	Paid wages to surf instructors with cash	$800
21 Jan 2025	Incurred advertising expenses, which are to be paid within 30 days	$6 000

Date	Description	Amount
22 Jan 2025	Provided surfing lessons to members of Geelong Bowls Club on credit terms	$10 000
22 Jan 2025	Paid wages to surf instructors with cash	$800
22 Jan 2025	Acquired new wetsuits for cash	$3 000
22 Jan 2025	Paid travelling expenses with cash	$600
24 Jan 2025	Received cash from debtor – Geelong Bowls Club	$10 000
25 Jan 2025	Provided surfing lessons to Cronulla Football Club on credit terms	$12 000
25 Jan 2025	Paid wages to surf instructors with cash	$1 000
25 Jan 2025	Paid travelling expenses with cash	$900
28 Jan 2025	Paid interest to Reef Bank	$600
31 Jan 2025	Layne Beachley withdrew cash for personal use	$10 000

REFERENCE

QBE Insurance Group (2021). *2021 Annual Report*. www.qbe.com/investor-relations/reports-presentations

CHAPTER 9

THE BALANCE SHEET

LEARNING OBJECTIVES

After completing this chapter, readers should be able to:

- LO9.1 understand the role of the balance sheet, and describe the steps that need to be undertaken within an accounting information system in order to prepare a balance sheet
- LO9.2 define assets, liabilities and equity, and explain why it is possible for an item to meet the definition of one of the elements of financial accounting but nevertheless not be recognised within the financial statements
- LO9.3 explain the criteria that need to be satisfied before an organisation recognises assets
- LO9.4 explain how an accountant measures various classes of assets
- LO9.5 describe the meaning of 'recoverable amount', and understand why we need to determine the recoverable amount of assets
- LO9.6 explain how assets should be presented within a balance sheet
- LO9.7 describe the criteria that need to be satisfied before an organisation recognises liabilities
- LO9.8 understand how to measure liabilities
- LO9.9 explain how liabilities should be presented within a balance sheet
- LO9.10 explain how to recognise and measure equity
- LO9.11 explain how equity should be presented within a balance sheet
- LO9.12 understand the extent to which the contents of the balance sheet are shaped by professional judgements, and explain some of the potential limitations of the information included within balance sheets.

OPENING QUESTIONS

Before reading this chapter, please consider how you would answer the following four questions. We will return to these questions at the end of the chapter, where we suggest some answers.

1. What are the recognition criteria applied to the elements of financial accounting?
2. Is it a requirement that all classes of assets be measured on the same basis?
3. If liabilities are to be paid beyond the next 12 months, are they to be measured at their present value?
4. How do we determine the 'recoverable amount' of an asset, and when do we recognise 'impairment losses' in relation to assets?

Introduction

This chapter focuses on the balance sheet. As will be explained, the balance sheet is a very important document for understanding the financial position of an organisation, and therefore for understanding some of the financial risks associated with an organisation. The balance sheet is a valuable document in terms of helping stakeholders answer a series of important questions about an organisation, some of which will relate to the risks associated with the organisation, the sources of funding used by it, the ability of the organisation to pay its debts, the efficiency of its management, and so forth.

This chapter explains that the balance sheet reports information about the assets, liabilities and equity of an organisation, and that for an asset, liability or equity item to appear within the balance sheet, accountants first need to ensure that the item meets the definition of the respective element of financial accounting. Following this, accountants then need to determine that the item satisfies the criteria necessary for recognition. This can, at times, require a great deal of professional judgement. We will then learn that, once an accountant has decided that it is appropriate to recognise an item in the balance sheet, reference must be made to the respective measurement approaches to be used for the asset or liability in question. Finally, once a measurement has been ascribed to a particular asset or liability, decisions need to be made about what information to disclose and how to present that information to financial statement readers.

In this chapter, we will learn that different classes of assets are measured in a variety of ways, and that different classes of liabilities are also measured in different ways. The chapter emphasises the degree to which professional judgement is used in financial accounting, and how this judgement ultimately impacts what is reported within the balance sheet. As we shall stress, it would be very unlikely that different teams of accountants would actually end up with the same balance sheet if the different teams were asked to prepare a balance sheet for an organisation using identical information about the organisation's transactions and events.

Corporate balance sheets are identified as being very important documents within society, but it should also be stressed that we need to take great care when reading a balance sheet. Balance sheets often fail to report many valuable resources of an organisation, or can attribute a value to resources that is significantly less than their fair value. The potential impacts of 'creative accounting' on balance sheets are also highlighted within this chapter.

Key concept

The balance sheet is a very important document for enabling stakeholders to make judgements about the financial position of an organisation, and the related financial risks of the organisation, inclusive of the risks associated with its ability to pay its debts as and when they fall due.

LO9.1 Overview of the balance sheet

balance sheet
A financial statement that provides information about the financial position of an organisation. It provides information about an organisation's assets, liabilities and equity as at a certain point in time

In this chapter, our focus will be on one financial statement – the **balance sheet**, or as it is also called, the *statement of financial position*.

The balance sheet provides information about the financial position of an organisation as at a particular point in time. This means that it provides information about the monetary values assigned to the assets held by the organisation, together with information about the monetary values assigned to the liabilities of the organisation, as well as to the owners' equity.

As you know, owners' equity is calculated by subtracting the total liabilities of an organisation from the total assets of the organisation (that is, owners' equity = assets – liabilities). The liabilities and owners' equity represent the claims against the total assets of an organisation, with the liabilities representing the 'external' claims against the assets, and the owners' equity representing the 'internal' (or ownership) claims against the assets.

Because the information within the balance sheet is presented as at a point in time (often referred to as the balance date, the reporting date, or the end of the reporting period), it effectively provides a snapshot of the assets, liabilities and equity in place at this time. If this snapshot was taken at a different point in time, then the assets and liabilities of an organisation might be quite different, particularly if an organisation operates in an industry that is seasonal, or cyclical, in nature. Therefore, a balance sheet prepared several months earlier might no longer provide a reasonable reflection of the financial position of an organisation, and could suffer from a lack of relevance.

The balance sheet will be prepared annually, but it can be prepared more regularly. It is also common practice for the balance sheet to have at least two columns of data – one for the current accounting period and one for the previous accounting period, thereby providing comparative data.

Source: Shutterstock.com/oticki

Source: Getty Images Plus/E+/georgeclerk

It is important to keep in mind that the balance sheet provides a snapshot of the value of a business' assets at a single point in time and may not reflect the value of the organisation's assets at all times, especially in seasonal industries.

For larger organisations, the preparation of the balance sheet will be influenced by a number of factors, including:

- the application of accounting principles (as we noted in Chapter 7, these principles include the entity concept, the accounting period convention, the monetary unit convention, the going concern assumption, and the convention of accrual accounting)
- efforts taken to ensure that the financial information being presented satisfies the qualitative characteristics that useful financial information is expected to possess (which, as we know, include the fundamental qualitative characteristics of relevance and representational faithfulness, as well as the enhancing qualitative characteristics of comparability, verifiability, timeliness and understandability)
- efforts to comply with the requirements embodied within accounting standards.

The structure of the balance sheet (statement of financial position) is directly linked to the basic accounting equation of assets = liabilities + owners' equity. For example, large organisations, such as public companies, typically prepare their balance sheets in the format of asset – liabilities = owners' equity, which is a rearrangement of the basic accounting equation, and which emphasises that owners' equity is the residual interest in an organisation held by its owners. Many organisations also prepare their balance sheets in the format of assets = liabilities + owners' equity.

Exhibit 9.1 shows how large companies typically present their balance sheets, wherein the net assets (assets minus liabilities) are shown to be equal to total equity. Again, we should remember that the balance sheet is a direct representation of the accounting equation.

EXHIBIT 9.1 Typical presentation format of a balance sheet as used by large companies

Balance sheet of Typical Big Company as at 31 December 2026		
	2026 ($ million)	2025 ($ million)
Current assets		
Cash and cash equivalents	100	110
Receivables	110	90
Inventories	330	290
Other	20	30
Total current assets	**560**	**520**
Non-current assets		
Property, plant and equipment	1040	980
Intangible assets	380	320
Other	20	30
Total non-current assets	**1440**	**1330**
Total assets	**2000**	**1850**
Current liabilities		
Accounts payable	70	80
Income tax payable	90	100
Provisions	40	30
Other	10	20
Total current liabilities	**210**	**230**

>>>

	2026 ($ million)	2025 ($ million)
Non-current liabilities		
Loans	410	450
Provisions	80	70
Other	10	20
Total non-current liabilities	**500**	**540**
Total liabilities	**710**	**770**
Net assets	1290	**1080**
Equity		
Share capital	950	950
Other reserves	50	40
Retained earnings	290	90
Total equity	**1290**	**1080**

Why prepare a balance sheet?

In terms of *why* a balance sheet would be prepared, for larger organisations there are generally legal requirements (often incorporated in a country's corporations law) for balance sheets to be prepared so that different stakeholders, in particular shareholders, lenders and other creditors, who do not have access to special purpose financial reports, are able to know the value and types of assets controlled by an organisation, and its liabilities.

For smaller organisations, where there is no legal requirement to prepare a balance sheet, it is still common to find that balance sheets are prepared, because they are useful documents for managers and other stakeholders. Further, smaller organisations will also often need to borrow money from banks, or lease various types of assets, and such activities may require an organisation to produce a balance sheet – in order to be able to obtain a loan, or to lease assets. Also, in many countries, small businesses are required to disclose information about their assets and liabilities in their annual tax returns.

Knowing about the types, and amounts, of different assets and liabilities is important for a variety of reasons, as per the following sections.

To determine the ability to pay debts

Particularly important here would be the information in the balance sheet about the available cash of an organisation, as well as other resources that might be converted into cash in a relatively short time (such as accounts receivable, and short-term money market deposits). The total of cash, together with those assets that can be relatively quickly converted into cash, can then be compared with the liabilities that need to be paid relatively quickly (such as accounts payable, bank overdrafts, and short-term loans). If the balance sheet shows that the total monetary amount of the short-term liabilities exceeds the total monetary amount of the short-term assets, then this could signal that the organisation might have difficulty meeting the financial obligations that need to be paid in the coming months. This would suggest that there is some risk that the entity will not be able to pay its debts as and when they fall due, and at the extreme, this could lead to the collapse of the organisation. For example, if we look at the balance sheet of Typical Big Company (provided earlier) we can see that it has $220 million in assets that are cash, or likely to be converted to cash in the short term (the receivables). If we assume that the income tax payable will not be payable for some months, then the amount it needs to pay in the short term appears to be $70 million (the accounts payable). On the basis of the information in the balance sheet, the organisation does not appear to have any short-term liquidity problems.

To determine the ability of an organisation to change the nature of its operations

If the balance sheet shows that a significant proportion of an organisation's total assets are invested in property, plant and equipment, then this would indicate that the organisation could have difficulty moving into other areas of operations, particularly if that property, plant and equipment is highly specialised in nature and therefore not easily sold. Many non-current assets are not easily converted into cash – their value comes from their 'value-in-use', rather than through their sale.

To assist in determining the value of an organisation

All things being equal, the greater the monetary amount assigned to an organisation's assets, and the less the monetary amount assigned to the liabilities, the greater the value of an organisation. However, some care needs to be taken regarding this, as many valuable resources of an organisation are recorded at cost (not necessarily at their current fair value). For example, the inventories of Typical Big Company are reported in the balance sheet at an amount of $330 million. This would represent the cost of the inventories to the organisation. The actual amount that might be realised from the sale of these inventories might be considerably more. Also, many valuable resources of an organisation are not recognised in the balance sheet – as we shall learn later in this chapter.

To determine the sources of funding used by the organisation

The funding used by an organisation to acquire its assets, and to maintain its operations, can come either from external sources (liabilities) or internal sources (from owners). The balance sheet provides information about the sources of funding. It is useful for readers of financial statements to be able to understand how the organisation has financed its operations, and its asset acquisitions. For example, looking at the balance sheet of Typical Big Company we see that the total liabilities are $710 million whereas the total equity is $1290 million. That is, approximately 65 per cent of the assets are funded by the owners and 35 per cent funded from external sources (liabilities). Generally speaking, this would not be considered to be very risky.

The greater the relative reliance an organisation has on external sources of funds (liabilities), then the greater the financial risk this imposes upon an organisation. If an organisation sources its funds from external sources, such as through loans, then it will have legally enforceable commitments to pay both the interest and the loan principal, regardless of how profitable the organisation is, and regardless of its actual cash flows. This might create problems in the future, particularly if profits and cash flows show great variation and are low in some periods, and potentially not sufficient to meet the necessary debt repayment and interest obligations.

If, by contrast, funds are sourced from owners' contributions, then there is no legal obligation to make payments in the future. Therefore, in difficult times, an organisation might simply elect not to make dividend payments to owners.

It is generally recommended that organisations that operate in industries with relatively higher volatility in profits, and relatively higher volatility of cash flows, should rely relatively less upon external sources of funding (debt) and more upon equity capital (an internal source of funds).

To help determine the efficiency of management

The information provided within the balance sheet can be used in conjunction with information provided from other sources. For example, the relationship between profits (as reported in the statement of profit or loss) and total assets (as reported within the balance sheet) can be considered to determine how efficiently an organisation is being operated. We will return to financial statement analysis, which in part will focus on determining the efficiency with which assets have been used, in the final chapter of this book.

Whilst the balance sheet can fulfil many purposes, including those identified above, it will typically be only one page in length. However, it will be supported by many pages of additional information (sometimes over 100 pages worth), known as the *notes to the financial statements*. These notes are numbered, and the relevant note numbers will appear on the balance sheet to refer users to this additional information. These notes will, among other things, provide additional information about particular amounts shown in the balance sheet, including information about the accounting policies used in calculating the various monetary amounts attributed to the assets and liabilities.

An overview of some of the steps necessary to generate a financial statement

In Chapter 7, we noted the need for specific and clear definitions for each element of financial accounting (assets, liabilities, equity, income and expenses). As we learned, for a transaction to be considered to belong to a particular element of financial accounting, it needs to comply with one of the definitions of the five elements of financial accounting as provided within the Conceptual Framework for Financial Reporting.

Once the definition of the respective element of financial accounting has been satisfied, such as an asset, the next step is to determine when we should recognise that element in the financial accounting information system – that is, for example, on what date (if any) particular assets should be placed within our financial accounts. Knowing what an 'asset' is in terms of the definition of the term (as well as the other elements of financial accounting), and knowing when to recognise it, we will then need to determine the monetary amount that we should assign to it. That is, we will need to know how to measure it. Once we know how to *define*, *recognise* and *measure* an element of financial accounting, we then need to know what information we should *disclose* in respect of the item, and how that information should be *presented* within the financial statements. This sequence of events was diagrammatically depicted in Chapter 7 and is reproduced in Figure 9.1.

Given that we have already addressed, in depth, the respective definitions of the elements of financial accounting in Chapter 7, in this chapter we will primarily concentrate on the issues of recognition, measurement, and disclosure and presentation as they relate to assets, liabilities and equity – and therefore, as they relate to the balance sheet. In Chapter 10, we will consider these issues with respect to income and expenses, and therefore as they relate to the statement of profit or loss.

FIGURE 9.1 A summary of some of the steps undertaken within the financial accounting process

Definition of an element of financial accounting
Does the transaction or event seem to satisfy the definition of either an asset, liability, income, expense or equity item?

↓

Recognition criteria
When should the particular transaction or event that satisfies one of the element definitions be recorded within the financial accounting system?

↓

Measurement
What financial amount should be recorded for the respective transaction or event that satisfies the definition of an element?

↓

Disclosure and presentation
Should the particular item be disclosed separately, and if so, how should the particular item be presented within the financial statement?

Why do I need to know about the respective steps involved in generating financial statements?

As students of accounting, we should know about the various steps that need to be taken to generate financial statements. Financial statements produced by large organisations are used by potentially thousands of stakeholders and are important documents in terms of influencing the flow of resources throughout the economy. So we should know about them. Also, knowing about the respective steps helps us to understand the functions that financial accountants undertake, and to understand the nature of the professional judgements required at each step of the financial accounting process. This allows us to more fully understand the context of the financial numbers we might be reviewing. Further, each step of the process involves a number of unique but interdependent decisions which are easier to understand if we consider each step in turn.

LO9.2 The definitions of assets, liabilities and equity

As we learned in Chapter 7, the Conceptual Framework for Financial Reporting released by the International Accounting Standards Board (IASB), defines an asset (paragraph 4.3) as:

> a present economic resource controlled by the entity as a result of past events.
>
> Source: International Accounting Standards Board (2022a).

As we stressed in Chapter 7, and as the above definition indicates, if a resource is not 'controlled' by the organisation (and control relates to the capacity of a reporting entity to benefit from a resource and to have the ability to deny or regulate the access of others to that resource), then that resource should not be considered to be an 'asset' of the organisation. This means that the non-controlled resource shall not be recorded in the balance sheet. For example, valuable resources necessary to an organisation, such as air, waterways, labour forces and so on are not controlled, and therefore shall not be recognised as 'assets' for financial accounting purposes. As we shall discuss further in Chapter 10, the consequence of this is that, given such resources are not recognised as 'assets' by the organisation, then any diminution in their value shall also not be recognised as an 'expense' (we must recognise a resource as an 'asset' before any subsequent reduction in its value can be considered as an 'expense'). This in turn means that reported 'profits' (which is the difference between 'income' and 'expenses') will fail to reflect many social and environmental costs – but again, this is an issue we shall return to in Chapter 10.

Key concept

'Assets' as reported in the balance sheet shall exclude resources that are not 'controlled' by the organisation. This means any reductions in the value of such non-controlled resources, which might be attributed to the organisation's actions, will not be recognised as 'expenses' for financial reporting purposes (unless, perhaps fines or other related taxes have been imposed).

For an 'asset' to be recognised, the definition also requires that there must already have been an event – a 'past event' – that has occurred which has given the organisation control of the resource. That is, the control of the resource is not dependent upon some future event.

The above definition of an asset also refers to an 'economic resource', which is defined in the Conceptual Framework as 'a *right* that has the potential to produce *economic benefits*'.

Two key terms have been highlighted above, these being 'rights' and 'economic benefits'. Rights can take many forms, including rights to receive cash, rights to receive goods or services, and rights over physical objects, such as property, plant and equipment or inventories (where the right to use the property, plant, equipment or inventories might have been established as a result of buying or leasing the item).

There is also a requirement that an asset has the potential to generate economic benefits for an organisation. These economic benefits might take a variety of forms. As the Conceptual Framework (paragraph 4.16) states:

> An economic resource could produce economic benefits for an entity by entitling or enabling it to do, for example, one or more of the following:
>
> (a) receive contractual cash flows or another economic resource;
> (b) exchange economic resources with another party on favourable terms;
> (c) produce cash inflows or avoid cash outflows by, for example:
>   (i) using the economic resource either individually or in combination with other economic resources to produce goods or provide services;
>   (ii) using the economic resource to enhance the value of other economic resources; or
>   (iii) leasing the economic resource to another party;
> (d) receive cash or other economic resources by selling the economic resource; or
> (e) extinguish liabilities by transferring the economic resource.
>
> Source: International Accounting Standards Board (2022a).

Therefore, if an organisation has control of a factory (and therefore has a right to use the factory), and that factory will generate products that can be sold, then the factory is an asset. If an organisation has control of land that can be used to grow crops for sale, then the land is also an asset as it has the potential to produce economic benefits (in this case, crops that can be sold for cash).

Following from our discussion above, we should now understand that there are three separate and important components to the definition of 'assets' that we need to remember. All three requirements must exist if we are to consider that a particular transaction or event has created an asset. If these components are not satisfied, the transaction or event did not create an asset. Directly related to the definition of an asset, these components are as follows:

- An asset is a resource *controlled* by an entity.
- This control arises as a result of *past events*.
- The resource has the potential to produce economic benefits.

Financial accountants are required to make sure the above components, or attributes, are present before they recognise an asset for financial reporting purposes.

Turning our attention to liabilities, within the Conceptual Framework, a liability is defined (paragraph 4.26) as:

> a present obligation of the entity to transfer an economic resource as a result of past events.
>
> Source: International Accounting Standards Board (2022a).

The above definition of liability refers to an 'obligation', which is defined in the Conceptual Framework as 'a duty or responsibility that the entity has no practical ability to avoid'. That is, the obligation would be expected to be satisfied at some time in the future.

As with assets, there are also three separate components to this definition of liabilities:

- A liability represents a *present obligation* of an entity.
- It arises from *past events*.
- It results in an *outflow from the entity of resources embodying economic benefits*.

The third element that appears within the balance sheet is owners' equity. According to the Conceptual Framework (paragraph 4.63):

> Equity is the residual interest in the assets of the entity after deducting all its liabilities.
>
> Source: International Accounting Standards Board (2022a).

Whilst the above points were addressed in Chapter 7, in that chapter we did not consider the issue of recognition in any significant depth. We address this important issue now, before we then consider the subsequent steps summarised in Figure 9.1, these being the *measurement* and *disclosure and presentation* phases. We will address assets first, before turning our attention to liabilities, and then lastly to equity.

LO9.3 Recognising assets

In Figure 9.1 we identified recognition as the second step to consider, following that of definition. But what does recognition mean from a financial accounting perspective? According to the Conceptual Framework for Financial Reporting (paragraph 5.1):

> Recognition is the process of capturing for inclusion in the statement of financial position (balance sheet), or the statement of financial performance (income statement), an item that meets the definition of one of the elements of financial statements – an

> asset, liability, equity, income or expenses. Recognition involves depicting the item in one of those statements – either alone or in aggregation with other items – in words and by a monetary amount, and including that amount in one or more totals in that statement. The amount at which an asset, a liability or equity is recognised in the statement of financial position is referred to as its 'carrying amount'.
>
> Source: International Accounting Standards Board (2022a).

Therefore, and simply stated, a transaction or event is considered as having been 'recognised' if it is included within a financial statement, either individually or aggregated with other items presented in that financial statement. Whatever amount is shown in the statement of financial position (balance sheet) for a particular account, this amount is referred to as its 'carrying amount'. For example, if the balance sheet shows that an organisation controls land measured at \$1 500 000, then the carrying amount of that land is \$1 500 000.

The Conceptual Framework provides general recognition criteria for all of the five elements of financial accounting: assets, liabilities, income, expenses and equity. It states (paragraph 5.6):

> Only items that meet the definition of an asset, a liability or equity are recognised in the statement of financial position. Similarly, only items that meet the definition of income and expenses are recognised in the statement of financial performance. However, not all items that meet the definition of one of those elements are recognised.
>
> Source: International Accounting Standards Board (2022a).

Therefore, and consistent with **Figure 9.1**, the first step in the recognition of a particular item in the financial statements (and therefore in our financial accounting system) is determining that the item meets the definition of an element of accounting. However, as the above quote indicates, further criteria (other than meeting the definition of an element of financial accounting) are required to be satisfied before an item is recognised for financial accounting purposes. That is, it is not sufficient for recognition purposes that an item satisfies the definition of a particular element of financial accounting. More is required.

The Conceptual Framework specifically requires that accountants must consider the fundamental qualitative characteristics of relevance and faithful representation (which were discussed in depth in Chapter 7) when deciding if an item should be recognised within the financial statements. Specifically, the Conceptual Framework states (paragraph 5.7):

> An asset or liability is recognised only if recognition of that asset or liability and any resulting income, expenses or changes in equity provides users of financial statements with information that is useful; that is, with:
>
> a *relevant information* about the asset or liability, and about any resulting income, expenses or changes in equity; and
>
> b a *faithful representation* of the asset or liability and any resulting income, expenses, or changes in equity.
>
> Source: International Accounting Standards Board (2022a).

As we know from Chapter 7, relevance and faithful representation are the two fundamental qualitative characteristics that useful financial accounting information is expected to possess. As we also learned in Chapter 7, relevant financial information is information that is capable of making a difference to the decisions made by users, whereas for faithful representation to be provided, the financial information should ideally be complete, neutral and free from error.

Information must both be relevant and provide a faithful representation of what it purports to represent, if it is to be useful. Therefore, it seems logical that the Conceptual Framework stipulates that decisions about recognising assets and liabilities in the balance sheet require the accountant to make a judgement about whether the disclosure of the respective asset or liability will ultimately provide information that is relevant and representationally faithful – and therefore *useful* to the users of the financial statements. If this conclusion cannot be reached, then the information about the respective asset and liability should not be included within the balance sheet.

Because the accountants' decision to recognise a particular transaction or event for financial statement purposes is directly linked to considerations of relevance and faithful representation, much professional judgement is therefore required in terms of when, or if, to recognise an asset, liability, equity, income or expense. The Conceptual Framework, however, provides some general guidance in relation to linking recognition to relevance and faithful representation, which we now consider.

Relevance

In relation to the qualitative characteristic of relevance, the Conceptual Framework (paragraph 5.12) states:

> Information about assets, liabilities, equity, income and expenses is relevant to users of financial statements. However, recognition of a particular asset or liability and any resulting income, expenses or changes in equity may not always provide relevant information. That may be the case if, for example:
> (a) it is *uncertain* whether an asset or liability exists; or
> (b) an asset or liability exists, but the *probability* of an inflow or outflow of economic benefits is low.
>
> Source: International Accounting Standards Board (2022a).

From the above, we can see that if there is sufficient uncertainty about whether a particular right exists – and remember that assets are considered to represent rights (for example, rights to use a particular machine, where those rights might have been obtained as a result of purchasing the machine) that have the potential to produce economic benefits – then an asset should *not* be recognised. As the Conceptual Framework (paragraph 4.13) states:

> For example, an entity and another party might dispute whether the entity has a right to receive an economic resource from that other party. Until that existence uncertainty is resolved – for example, by a court ruling – it is uncertain whether the entity has a right and, consequently, whether an asset exists.
>
> Source: International Accounting Standards Board (2022a).

Therefore, in recognising an asset, a judgement needs to be made about the extent of any possible **existence uncertainty**, which is defined in the Conceptual Framework as 'uncertainty about whether an asset or liability exists'. For example, if an organisation has some farming land, but considerable doubt has been raised about whether it has proper legal title over that land, then it might be appropriate (prudent) not to recognise the land within the financial statements until such time as there is clarity about who is permitted to occupy the land.

existence uncertainty
Uncertainty about whether an asset or liability exists

In determining whether information is relevant to the users of financial statements, we can see from the quote provided above that there is also a requirement to consider the *probability* associated with any expected future inflow or outflow of economic benefits. In this regard, the Conceptual Framework (paragraph 5.17(b)) states:

> If there is only a low probability that the asset or liability will result in an inflow or outflow of economic benefits, users of financial statements might not regard the recognition of the asset and income, or the liability and expenses, as providing relevant information.
>
> Source: International Accounting Standards Board (2022a).

For example, an organisation might have an item of machinery that it no longer uses and it is very unsure whether any other organisation would buy it. In this case, it might be deemed that there is a low probability associated with future inflows of economic benefits, and so information about the asset might not be relevant to financial statement users and should not be disclosed within the balance sheet.

Therefore, in considering whether the disclosure of information about an asset would be relevant, two factors for managers and their accountants to consider are:

- *existence uncertainty*
- the *probability associated with the expected inflow of economic benefits*.

Faithful representation

In relation to the other fundamental qualitative characteristic of 'faithful representation' that requires consideration when determining whether or not to recognise an asset, or another element of financial accounting, the Conceptual Framework (paragraph 5.18) states:

> Recognition of a particular asset or liability is appropriate if it provides not only relevant information, but also a faithful representation of that asset or liability and of any resulting income, expenses or changes in equity. Whether a faithful representation can be provided may be affected by the level of measurement uncertainty associated with the asset or liability, or by other factors.
>
> Source: International Accounting Standards Board (2022a).

As you know, for an asset or liability to be recognised within the financial statements, it must be measured in monetary terms. We need to attribute a financial amount to an item before that item can be included within a financial statement. Many of the measures attributed to assets are based upon estimates, meaning that, inherently, the attributing of amounts regarding some assets (and other elements of financial accounting) is often done with some level of uncertainty. Some level of uncertainty is acceptable. However, if the different measures that could be attributed to an asset (or other element of financial accounting) are all considered to have a high level of **measurement uncertainty**, then the asset should not be recognised within the financial statements. Measurement uncertainty is defined in the Appendix to the Conceptual Framework as:

measurement uncertainty
Uncertainty that arises when monetary amounts in financial reports cannot be observed directly and must instead be estimated

> uncertainty that arises when monetary amounts in financial reports cannot be observed directly and must instead be estimated.
>
> Source: International Accounting Standards Board (2022a).

In relation to the issue of measurement uncertainty referred to in the above quote, the Conceptual Framework (paragraph 5.20) further states:

> In some cases, the level of uncertainty involved in estimating a measure of an asset or liability may be so high that it may be questionable whether the estimate would provide a sufficiently faithful representation of that asset or liability and of any resulting income, expenses or changes in equity.
>
> Source: International Accounting Standards Board (2022a).

As an example of measurement uncertainty, an organisation might have some machinery that it no longer uses and it is very unsure about how much it can now sell the machinery for. This would be an instance of measurement uncertainty. If the level of measurement uncertainty is high, then this might indicate that a faithful representation of the value of the machinery cannot be provided to the users of the financial statements, and the assets shall not be recognised within the balance sheet.

With the above discussion of relevance and faithful representation in mind, we now know that existence uncertainty, probability of expected inflows or outflows of economic benefits, and measurement uncertainty, are among the key factors to consider before an accountant should recognise an asset, liability, income, expense or equity item within the financial statements.

Key concept

Probability, measurability and existence uncertainty are key factors to consider before we recognise an asset, liability, income, expense or equity item within the financial accounts.

As already emphasised, factors relating to existence uncertainty, probability and measurement uncertainty can require a great deal of professional judgement, and as such, different accountants might make different judgements in respect of whether particular items should be included within the financial statements. Any differences in judgements made by accountants would, in turn, ultimately result in different financial statements being prepared, and different profits being reported. The point being made here is that, because we require accountants to make various judgements about such factors as the expected probabilities associated with expected flows of economic benefits, the level of uncertainty associated with the measurement of the expected future economic benefits, and whether rights associated with the future economic benefits are clearly in existence, then this necessarily introduces a degree of professional judgement into the accounting process.

Conceivably, different accountants will make different judgements. This means that if different accountants were to be provided with the same information, they may process the information differently and therefore produce different financial statements. Indeed, if different teams of accountants were given details of all the transactions and events that an organisation was involved with throughout a particular accounting period, and each team was asked to separately prepare financial statements for that organisation, then it would be quite improbable that they would generate identical financial statements. As we have emphasised many times, the preparation of financial statements requires a great deal of professional judgement, and this has direct implications for what appears within the financial statements.

If an asset is recognised within the financial statements at one point in time, it might need to be removed from the financial statements at a future time. For example, accountants might initially make a professional judgement that an item satisfies the criteria necessary to be recognised within the financial statements. However, at a subsequent point in time, additional information might come to light, or new conditions might arise, that create significant uncertainty about factors such as:

- the expected probabilities associated with expected flows of economic benefits
- the level of uncertainty associated with the measurement of the associated economic benefits.

If the uncertainties become sufficiently high, then the asset should be removed from the balance sheet, and this would be referred to as the *derecognition* of the asset. Derecognition is defined in the Conceptual Framework as 'the removal of all or part of a recognised asset or liability from an entity's statement of financial position'. Derecognition will create an expense which we might refer to as an 'impairment loss'.

Learning exercise 9.1 discusses the decision to recognise an asset.

9.1 Learning Exercise

The decision to recognise an asset (or not)

Big Books Company has acquired the rights to publish a book written by Arthur Orfa. The company paid $750 000 to Arthur for these publishing rights, which could be considered to be an intangible asset. An intangible asset is a non-monetary asset without physical substance. Intangible assets, as a class, are generally disclosed separately within the balance sheet.

The accountants of Big Books Company initially recognised the asset in the company's balance sheet. However, because of subsequent poor reviews of the book by various well-known critics, the managers of Big Books Company now have a high degree of uncertainty about whether many sales of the book will occur, and if they do occur, about the price that people will actually be prepared to pay to purchase the book. The managers, however, are confident that they do have the proper legal rights to the book.

The managers of Big Books Company have sought our advice about whether they can continue to recognise the publishing rights as an asset in their balance sheet. They also want to know the implications for the financial statements if a professional judgement is made that they should no longer recognise the asset.

Should the asset be recognised?

As you know, the first thing to consider is the requirement within the Conceptual Framework that only items that meet the definition of an asset, liability or equity are recognised in the balance sheet.

If we consider the publishing rights, and the definition of an asset, then it would seem that the publishing rights do satisfy the definition of an asset; specifically:

- An asset is a resource *controlled* by the entity. The organisation does seem to be able to control the use of the book publishing rights, so this condition is satisfied.
- An asset exists as a result of *past events*. Big Books Company has already acquired the book publishing rights, so this condition is therefore satisfied.
- An asset exists where the organisation has a right that has the potential to produce *economic benefits* for the entity. The expectation is that some books will be sold, and therefore economic benefits will be generated, so this condition appears to be met.

Therefore, the publishing rights do seem to satisfy the definition of an asset. As we know, however, not all items that meet the definition of one of the elements of financial accounting are to be recognised within the financial statements. To recognise an asset, accountants need to make the judgement that the disclosure of the asset will provide information that is both relevant and representationally faithful.

As we have already discussed, two factors to consider in determining whether the disclosure of information about an asset would be relevant to financial statement users are:

- existence uncertainty
- probability associated with the expected inflow of economic benefits.

Big Books Company seems to have a clear legal right to use the publication rights, so there appears to be little or no existence uncertainty. Big Books Company, however, has a high degree of uncertainty pertaining to the probability associated with the expected inflow of economic benefits. Therefore, the information about the publishing rights might not be very relevant or useful to the users of the financial statements.

In relation to the issue of faithful representation, one factor that we have already identified is measurement uncertainty. The higher the level of measurement uncertainty, the less able are accountants to provide a measurement that faithfully represents the value of the asset. In this case, there does seem to be significant uncertainty in relation to the monetary amounts that will be generated from the book.

As a result of the high level of measurement uncertainty (which undermines the faithful representation of the asset, and therefore the usefulness of the information), and the uncertainties pertaining to the probability associated with the expected inflow of economic benefits (which undermines the relevance of information about an asset and therefore the usefulness of the information), it would appear inappropriate to recognise the book rights as an asset in the balance sheet of Big Books Company.

What are the implications if the asset can no longer be recognised in the balance sheet?

We can use our expanded accounting equation to answer this question. When the publishing rights were initially acquired, the organisation exchanged cash (an asset) for the rights (also an asset). Therefore, one asset increased and another decreased. The other elements of financial accounting would not have changed. Using our expanded accounting equation:

A	+	E	+	D	=	L	+	I	+	C
$750 000		–		–		–		–		–
($750 000)										

However, as it has subsequently been determined through professional judgement that the asset does not meet the criteria associated with relevance and faithful representation (see above), the asset should be removed from the balance sheet. This is referred to as derecognition. To remove the asset, an expense will be recognised. This recognition of an expense at the same time as the derecognition of the asset enables the accounting equation to remain in balance. This expense can be referred to as an 'impairment loss'. In terms of our accounting equation, the recognition of this impairment loss, and the derecognition of the asset, can be represented as follows:

A	+	E	+	D	=	L	+	I	+	C
($750 000)		$750 000		–		–		–		–

Learning exercise 9.2 further considers how the recognition of an item in the financial statements relies upon professional judgement.

9.2 Learning Exercise

The role of professional judgement in financial accounting

Scenario: The whitegoods company WG & Co uses an external firm of accountants known as Barry Balance & Co to prepare its financial statements. When the general manager of WG & Co, Betty White, was asked why she selected the accountants from Barry Balance & Co to prepare the financial statements, she responded with the following answer: 'It doesn't really matter which accounting firm I selected. They all do the same thing, and apply the same rules, so ultimately the financial statements prepared by one accounting firm will be exactly the same as the financial statements that would be prepared by any another accounting firm'.

Issue: Is Betty White correct? If she is not right, then what implications does this have for the financial statements, and the degree to which stakeholders should rely upon them?

Solution: Betty is incorrect. It is highly unlikely that different teams of accountants would generate identical financial statements. The way in which the transactions of an organisation are interpreted and recorded by accountants often depends on the professional judgements made by those accountants. Not all accountants will make the same judgements.

What judgements might contribute to a difference in the financial statements?

In creating financial statements, judgements need to be made that will influence reported assets, liabilities, income and expenses, and therefore the equity of the organisation. There are many instances throughout the accounting process where accountants need to determine whether income has been earned, or expenses incurred, and whether the related flows of economic benefits associated with an asset or liability will actually eventuate. There are also various obligations that an organisation has which require much judgement to be made in terms of the obligations' measurement. So it is unlikely that the different teams will make identical judgements for all transactions and events.

For example, whilst WG & Co might have accepted an obligation to repair any defective goods it sold during an accounting period, determining the amount that will need to be paid to repair the defects will not be precisely ascertainable and will require some judgement. There might also be differences in expectations about the collectability of accounts receivable, the useful life of non-current assets that need to be depreciated, or about whether particular items of inventory can be sold above their cost. Different professional judgements will have implications for how assets are valued, and for the income and expenses to be recognised.

So with all these judgements, should the financial statements be relied on?

For larger organisations, independent financial statement auditors will be appointed who, among other things, will provide an opinion about whether the judgements made by the managers and accountants appear reasonable, and whether the financial statements appear to provide a fair representation of the organisation's financial performance and financial position. Because many judgements need to be made by managers and their accountants, it is wise (particularly if there is a separation of the ownership and management of the organisation) to have a competent independent third party audit the financial statements and provide an opinion on their reliability before they are issued to external stakeholders. Many smaller organisations also have their financial statements audited by qualified, independent financial statement auditors. Effectively, financial statement auditors act as *arbiters* in deciding whether financial statements are properly prepared, and should therefore be relied upon.

Learning exercise 9.3 and Learning exercise 9.4 provide further illustrations of the types of judgements accountants need to make when determining whether or not to recognise assets within financial statements. The judgements of accountants are made on the basis of the available evidence. It is very important that we appreciate the extent to which professional judgement influences the financial statements being prepared by organisations.

9.3 Learning Exercise

Considerations of probability and measurability

Scenario: Anderson Mining owns a mine site located in a remote desert location, complete with housing for mining families, which it used to refer to as its mining town. But the company decided to abandon the mine one year ago, and all employees who used to live in the mining town have left and the town is now deserted. There is no other town nearby, and there appears to be no interest from anybody in terms of buying the mining town from Anderson Mining. It also appears very unlikely that there will be any interest in the property in the future.

Task: You are required to advise the company how it should account for the mine within its financial statements. Currently, the mining town is shown in the financial statements as an asset, with a carrying amount of $10 million.

Solution: At issue here is the fact that there appears to be a very low probability that any future inflows of economic benefit will be generated by the asset. Therefore, the judgement should be made that the disclosure of the asset in the financial statements would not provide relevant information. There would also be a high level of uncertainty associated with measuring any potential future flows of economic benefits associated with the asset. Therefore, it would be very difficult to provide a faithful representation of the value of the asset.

In this instance, then, and on the basis of the available evidence, the mining town should *not* appear as an asset in the balance sheet, and therefore needs to be removed (derecognised) from the balance sheet. The amount that is removed from the balance sheet will be shown as an expense, which would be referred to as an asset impairment loss.

A point to be emphasised here is that assets, such as property, plant and equipment that are owned or controlled by an organisation, will not always be shown as assets in the balance sheet despite the fact that they have the *potential capacity* to generate future economic benefits.

9.4 Learning Exercise

A further consideration of probability and measurability

Scenario: Organisations will often spend large amounts of money on advertising, the purpose of which is to hopefully generate future sales. The managing director of a large beer brewing company has recently authorised the expenditure of $7 250 000 on an advertising campaign to promote its new type of beer, specifically its new Fruity Pale Ale. The managing director has asked you whether this advertising expenditure can be shown as an asset in the financial statements. She understands that financial accountants typically treat amounts spent on advertising as an expense, rather than as an asset. However, she wants to depart from this practice. She wants the amount spent on beer advertising to be shown as an asset.

Issue: Can advertising expenditure be recognised as an asset?

Solution: Advertising will be undertaken with the expectation of increasing the sales of an organisation's goods or services. That is, it is undertaken with the expectation of generating future flows of economic benefits.

However, because there will be uncertainties about whether the advertising directly influences sales, and about the value of this influence, then it is generally accepted by accountants that the measurement of the future economic benefits relating to advertising are too uncertain and difficult to measure. As such, given the high levels of measurement uncertainty, it is accepted within financial accounting that payments for advertising campaigns that have been completed should be treated as an expense, and not as an asset.

The above discussion of 'relevance' and 'faithful representation' means that any assumption that a particular type of object, or right, will always be an asset is incorrect. For example, whilst machinery owned by an organisation would normally be associated with future economic benefits – and therefore would usually be considered an asset – circumstances might arise where it would no longer qualify as an asset because it has become obsolete, or unusable, and has no scrap value.

So, in summarising where we are up to so far in this chapter, we know that for an item to be included within the balance sheet as an asset:

- it must satisfy the definition of an asset (meaning it must be *controlled* by the entity as a result of a *past transaction* or event, and it must have the potential to *generate future economic benefits*)
- information about the asset must be capable of being considered *relevant* and *representationally faithful*.

Why do I need to know about the recognition criteria for assets and liabilities?

If we are likely to become financial accountants, or if we are going to be readers of financial statements, we really should understand the various professional judgements that must be made before the accountant decides to recognise a transaction or event for financial accounting purposes. We also need to understand how these judgements in turn influence reported profits. For example, if the accountant decides that particular expenditure does not meet the recognition criteria necessary for asset definition (linked to considerations of relevance and representational faithfulness), then the related expenditure will be treated as an expense rather than an asset. This then has implications for reducing reported profits. Also, if the accountant, for example, makes a professional judgement not to recognise a particular liability, meaning it will be left off the balance sheet, then this might mean that related expenses are not recognised either, and this also has implications for reported profits.

As an example, let us assume that some local residents have taken some legal action against a company in which they are claiming that the organisation polluted a local waterway causing great damage. If the financial accountant makes a judgement that it is highly unlikely that the residents' action will be successful (thereby meaning that the information is not relevant from a financial reporting perspective), then no liability and no expense would be recognised. However, if by contrast, the accountant (or a different accountant) decided that it is likely that the residents would be successful in their action (thereby making the information relevant), and if the accountant also believed that she could determine a reliable estimate of the likely amount to be payable (meaning the information would also be representationally faithful) then both an expense and a related liability would be recognised, and the reported profits of the organisation would fall. A difference in judgement about whether to recognise the event has a direct implication for reported profits.

We summarise the conditions necessary for the recognition of assets in Figure 9.2. It needs to be understood that all four of the initial steps identified in Figure 9.2 must be met before an asset is recognised. That is, if one of the requirements is missing, then the item should not be considered an asset and therefore should not appear within the balance sheet. It should also be emphasised that an asset does not have to have a physical form. An asset might have no physical form but still be recognised. Such assets would be intangible assets, and would include such items as copyrights, goodwill, patents and brand names. We will consider intangible assets in more depth later in this chapter.

LO9.4 Measuring assets

We have so far discussed the definition of assets and the rules pertaining to when we should recognise an asset (recognition criteria). If all these requirements are satisfied, then the item can be shown as an asset in the financial statements; that is, it can be recognised. The next issue we need to address is what financial amount we should assign to the asset. That is, how should we measure assets? By 'measure', we mean attributing a financial amount to the asset that will be included within the financial statements.

To recognise an asset, a decision needs to be made that a useful measurement of the future flow of economic benefits can be provided to the users of the financial statements. However, we need to determine which measurement basis is the most appropriate to fulfil the role of providing useful financial information.

Some measurement bases might be based on historical costs, whilst others might be based on current values. Current values might be determined on the basis of fair value (which would be the price that would currently be received for the sale of an asset in a market-based transaction between knowledgeable, independent parties), or perhaps on the basis of *value-in-use* (which would measure the asset based on the present value of the expected future net cash flows to be generated from using the asset). The Conceptual Framework (paragraph 6.45) states:

> The information provided by a measurement basis must be useful to users of financial statements. To achieve this, the information must be relevant and it must faithfully represent what it purports to represent. In addition, the information provided should be, as far as possible, comparable, verifiable, timely and understandable.
>
> Source: International Accounting Standards Board (2022a).

Whilst it might seem logical that all assets of all types will be measured in the same way (perhaps at cost, or at their fair value), this is not the case. Assets (and liabilities) are measured in a variety of ways depending upon the type, or class, of the assets in question. We can use a multitude of measurement approaches, and the approach we do use will depend on what type of asset we are accounting for. For example, the international financial reporting standards (IFRS) issued by the IASB require that:

- inventory is measured at the lower of cost and net realisable value
- non-current assets such as property, plant and equipment can be measured at historical cost less accumulated depreciation, or they can be measured at fair value
- leased assets are measured at the present value of the future expected lease payments
- other assets, such as financial assets (for example, shares in other companies), are measured at fair value.

These different measurement rules are contained in the different accounting standards issued by accounting standard setters such as the IASB and the US Financial Accounting Standards

FIGURE 9.2 Conditions to be satisfied before an asset can be recognised for financial accounting purposes

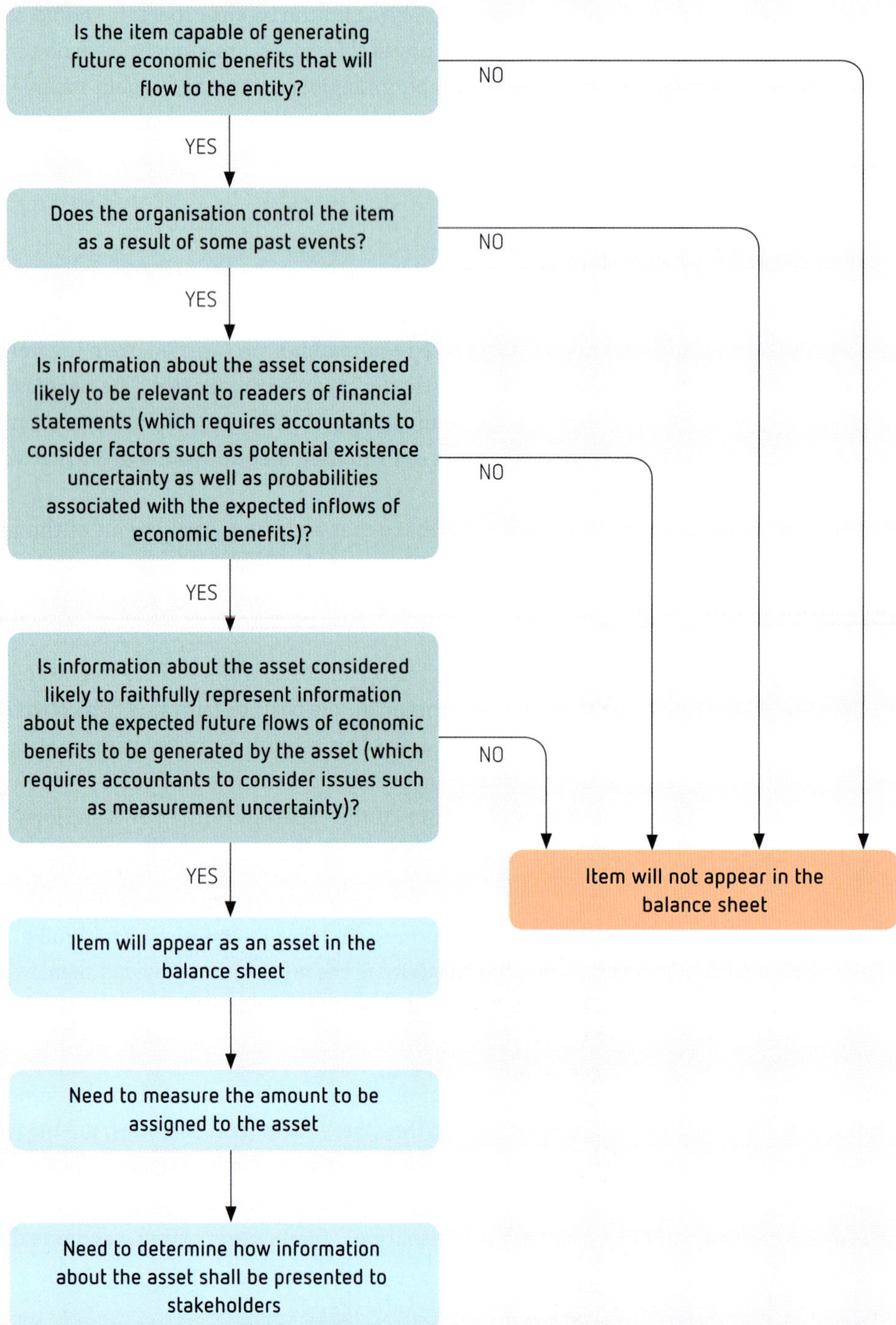

Board. For example, there are specific accounting standards (also referred to as financial reporting standards) issued by the IASB, with specific measurement rules, for different categories of assets, such as the following (the respective IASB accounting standard is shown in brackets):

- Inventories (IAS 2: Inventories)
- Property, plant and equipment (IAS 16: Property, Plant and Equipment)

- Leased assets (IFRS 16: Leases)
- Financial assets (IFRS 9: Financial Instruments)
- Investment properties (IAS 40: Investment Property)
- Intangible assets (IAS 38: Intangible Assets)
- Agricultural assets (IAS 41: Agriculture).

The multiplicity of measurement principles currently in use has resulted in financial accountants using what is often referred to as a 'mixed attribute accounting model'. Because we measure different classes of assets in different ways, this also creates what we might refer to as an 'additivity problem' (see **Learning exercise 9.5**). Since we are adding up the amounts attributed to different classes of assets, and because different classes of assets are measured in different ways, then what the total balance of all assets represents – after the various classes are added together – is actually far from clear. Some assets might be measured at cost, some might be measured at fair value, some might be measured at present value, and others might be measured at their net selling price. This means that the total monetary amount of all assets when added together is neither cost, fair value nor present value, but rather is simply an aggregated number. We must be careful when interpreting the amount shown as 'total assets'. This is why it is important that people who read and make judgements based upon the contents of financial statements actually have knowledge of the requirement of various financial reporting standards, including the requirements pertaining to measurement.

Key concept

Not all classes of assets are measured on the same basis. This has implications for understanding what the total monetary amount attributed to 'Total Assets' in the balance sheet actually represents.

9.5 Learning Exercise

An illustration of the additivity problem

Scenario: Bombo Co has only three classes of assets: inventory, machinery and land. Bombo Co measures its assets in accordance with the requirements of accounting standards. The amounts attributed to each class of assets, and the basis of measurement, are as follows:

Class of asset	Measurement basis required/allowed by accounting standards	Amount
Inventory	Lower of cost and net realisable value	$160 000
Machinery	Cost less accumulated depreciation	$440 000
Land	Fair value	$900 000
Total assets		$1 500 000

Issue: What does the amount of total assets represent?

Solution: Because the different classes of assets are measured in different ways, the amount calculated for total assets is simply the sum of the amounts calculated for different classes of assets. That is, it is an aggregated number and not a reflection of the total costs of all the recognised assets, or the fair value of the assets, controlled by an organisation.

As an example of the disclosure of assets as they appear on the face of a balance sheet, refer to **Exhibit 9.2**, which represents the assets component of the balance sheet of the global mining company BHP as at 30 June 2021. As you can see, there are different classes of assets. We will discuss the measurement requirements relating to some of these classes of assets in the following pages; specifically, we will discuss how to measure:

- cash
- accounts receivable
- inventories
- prepayments (which in the case of BHP would be included in 'Other current assets')
- property, plant and equipment
- marketable securities (which in the case of BHP would be included in 'Other financial assets')
- intangible assets
- leased assets (which in the case of BHP would be included in 'Property, plant and equipment').

EXHIBIT 9.2 Extract of the assets section from the balance sheet of BHP as at 30 June 2021

	2021 US$ million	2020 US$ million
ASSETS		
Current assets		
Cash and cash equivalents	15 246	13 426
Trade and other receivables	6 059	3 364
Other financial assets	230	84
Inventories	4 426	4 101
Assets held for sale	324	–
Current tax assets	279	366
Other	129	130
Total current assets	**26 693**	**21 471**
Non-current assets		
Trade and other receivables	337	267
Other financial assets	1 610	2 522
Inventories	1 358	1 221
Property, plant and equipment	73 813	72 362
Intangible assets	1 437	1 574
Investments accounted for using the equity method	1 742	2 585
Deferred tax assets	1 912	3 688
Other	25	43
Total non-current assets	**82 234**	**84 262**
Total assets	**108 927**	**105 733**

Source: BHP (2021), p. 131.

Cash

Cash is the easiest asset to measure. It is measured at *face value*, which is the value shown on the face of the currency. The amount of cash that an entity controls is usually quite easy to determine from the bank records that are reconciled back to an organisation's accounting records. Cash should generally not constitute a significant proportion of the total assets of an organisation, as it generates minimal returns relative to other types of assets that are more productive.

Accounts receivable

Accounts receivable, which are also commonly referred to as *debtors*, represent the amounts owed to an organisation. Accounts receivable typically arise as a result of an organisation selling goods, or services, to customers on credit terms (rather than for cash). Accounts receivable are recognised in the financial accounts because organisations typically apply the accrual basis of accounting, which means that income is recognised when it is earned, not deferred until such time that the cash is ultimately received.

As an example, if an organisation provides services to a customer on credit terms, then income will be recognised (which increases owners' equity) and the claim to cash will also be recognised (as an account receivable, which is an asset). That is, in terms of our accounting equation, assets will increase and income (and equity) will increase. For accounts receivable that are expected to be received in the next 12 months, the common practice is to measure the asset at face value, less an allowance for doubtful debts (which will be covered shortly).

Providing goods and services to customers on credit terms – that is, providing goods and services to a customer in exchange for a promise by the customer to pay the amount due at a future date – is common. However, organisations need to be careful when selling goods and services on credit. They need to ensure, as best they can, that customers who are granted credit are creditworthy – that they will actually be able to, or be prepared to, make the future payment. Organisations should have clear policies for extending credit to customers, and these policies should be adhered to at all times.

Even with sound credit-granting policies in place, it would be unrealistic to believe that all debtors will ultimately pay an organisation the amounts that are due. That is, even with sound credit policies in place, it should be anticipated that some approved debtors will unfortunately not pay. It is therefore normal practice to recognise, within the financial accounts, that a certain percentage will ultimately not pay. Failure to acknowledge this would effectively result in an overstatement of assets, and an overstatement of profits.

Allowance for doubtful debts

If an organisation has \$10 million in outstanding accounts receivable (debtors), which in aggregate includes the amounts owed by hundreds of different debtors, then it is unlikely that all these debtors will ultimately pay. Perhaps past experience indicates that 5 per cent of debtors typically will not pay. Therefore, it might be more realistic to disclose that the organisation expects to receive \$9 500 000, which is the actual amount receivable by the organisation, less an amount that is considered to be 'doubtful', which in this case is 5 per cent of the full amount. The 5 per cent that is considered doubtful is typically referred to as an **allowance for doubtful debts**. When determining the value of an asset, an organisation is allowing for the fact that not all debtors will ultimately pay. The amount owing by debtors could be disclosed in the financial statements as follows:

allowance for doubtful debts
An allowance to account for the fact that not all debtors will ultimately pay, designed to be offset against the accounts receivable balance. It is an example of a 'contra account'

Accounts receivable	\$10 000 000
Less: allowance for doubtful debts	(\$500 000)
Net accounts receivable	\$9 500 000

contra account
Any account designed to be offset against another account

Alternatively, the net amount only might be disclosed on the face of the balance sheet, whilst the details about the allowance for doubtful debts might be disclosed in the notes to the financial statements. The allowance for doubtful debts is an example of a **contra account**, which is an account that is offset against another account (accumulated depreciation – which we shall discuss shortly – is another example of a contra account). When the balance of the allowance for doubtful debts is subtracted from the balance of accounts receivable, the result represents the net realisable value of the accounts receivable. That is, it represents how much of the accounts receivable we realistically expect to receive.

To create the allowance for doubtful debts (which effectively decreases total assets), we also recognise an associated expense, which we refer to as a doubtful debts expense. In terms of our expanded accounting equation of A + E + D = L + I + C, when we recognise the allowance for doubtful debts, we reduce assets (by creating a contra asset account, which reduces assets) and we also increase expenses (by recognising a doubtful debts expense, which reduces owners' equity).

The allowance for doubtful debts represents management's, and the accountant's, best estimate of the amount of the accounts receivable that will not ultimately be received from customers. Therefore, professional judgement is involved. Because it is an estimation based on past experience, it will not necessarily reflect the actual amounts that will subsequently be collected. What is actually collected in the future accounting period could differ significantly from expectations – only time will tell (this is a particular example of where the value of an asset is based upon professional judgement, which necessarily involves a degree of measurement uncertainty). If actual collections from accounts receivable significantly differ from expectations, then management should adjust its estimation techniques in order to bring the allowance for doubtful debts more into alignment with actual results, making the allowance for doubtful debts more relevant and representationally faithful.

There are various ways of estimating the allowance for doubtful debts, including:

- *using an aged debtors analysis*, in which debtors are categorised on the basis of the age of their debt, which is the amount of time their debt has been outstanding. For example, the amounts owing to an organisation might be placed into categories such as 1–30 days, 31–60 days, 61–90 days, and more than 90 days. Different percentages of collectability might be applied to the different periods of outstanding debt. For example, for those debts that have been outstanding for less than 30 days, it might be assumed that 2 per cent of the debtors might not pay. By contrast, it might be assumed that for debts that have been outstanding for over 90 days, 20 per cent of these debtors will not pay. The assumption here is that the longer an amount has been outstanding (owing), the less likely it is that it will ultimately be received. (Also see **Learning exercise 9.6**.)
- *using a simple percentage*. Some organisations simply assume, based on past experience, that for every amount of credit sales, a certain percentage of debtors will not pay (for example, 5 per cent of the amounts outstanding at a point in time will not be collectable), and they calculate the allowance for doubtful debts on the basis of the percentage
- *classifying each debtor into a particular risk category and then assigning a probability for the debt not being collected to each risk category*. The allowance for doubtful debts would be calculated by multiplying the total of debtors in each risk category by the respective probability.

Because managers, and accountants, use their judgement to determine the amount to assign to the allowance for doubtful debts, it is always possible that the amount assigned might be manipulated so as to create a preferred financial result. We always need to be aware of such possibilities. *Creative accounting* does exist, and it would be naive to believe otherwise.

For example, if managers prefer to show higher profits (or lower losses) in a particular accounting period, then they might decide to reduce the allowance for doubtful debts. This would increase both profits and assets, and would be an instance of creative accounting.

As you should appreciate, many judgements are made as part of the financial accounting process, thereby providing numerous instances where accountants, and their managers, can be 'creative'. If the financial accounts are being audited by an independent third party. Then hopefully the auditors will be able to identify instances of creative accounting, and subsequently note them within their audit report. An opinion by auditors that the financial statements are not properly prepared thereby alerts financial statement readers to the need to be cautious before relying on the contents of the financial statements. However, not all instances of creative accounting can realistically be identified by auditors, as they do not check each and every transaction undertaken, and recorded, by an organisation. Also, creative accounting, if performed 'well' by managers, is done with the intended aim of *not* being detected.

9.6 Learning Exercise

Accounting for doubtful debts using an aged debtors' analysis

Scenario: Kiama Company has $7 700 000 in accounts receivable as at 31 December 2025. On the basis of past experience, the managers and accountants have determined the amount of debt that will not be collectable. The age of the various amounts owing, and estimates of their 'uncollectability', are as follows:

Period of time debt has been outstanding	Amount owing	Percentage of the debt that is not expected to be collected
1–30 days	$5 000 000	2%
31–60 days	$2 000 000	5%
61–90 days	$500 000	10%
More than 90 days	$200 000	20%
	$7 700 000	

Issue: You are required to calculate the required amount for the allowance for doubtful debts.

Solution: Using the above information, we can calculate the allowance for doubtful debts as follows:

	1–30 days	31–60 days	61–90 days	More than 90 days	Total
Amount owing	$5 000 000	$2 000 000	$500 000	$200 000	$7 700 000
Percentage not expected to be collected	2%	5%	10%	20%	
Doubtful debt amount	$100 000	$100 000	$50 000	$40 000	$290 000

The total amount of doubtful debts therefore would be $290 000. The information about accounts receivable would be disclosed in the financial statements as follows:

Accounts receivable	$7 700 000
Less: allowance for doubtful debts	($290 000)
Net accounts receivable	$7 410 000

Accounting for amounts to be received in more than 12 months

The above discussion relates to debtors that have been extended credit on the basis that they will pay the amounts due in a relatively short period of time. Where debts are due in less than 12 months' time, the normal practice is not to discount the amount owing to its present value.

By contrast, where accounts receivable are expected to be received in more than 12 months' time, then some discounting is required to bring the amount owing back to its present value. As you would know, the present value of a unit of currency held now, such as a dollar, is worth more than the same amount received at a future date. The extent of the difference in value will depend upon the interest (or discount) rate being applied, and this rate will be influenced by factors such as the risks associated with the cash flows, current inflation rates, and preferences for having, and using, the cash now.

For example, an organisation might decide to sell some inventory to another organisation for $10 million. The contract of sale might allow the purchaser to pay the amount due in three years. If the normal expected earnings rate of the organisation is, say, 5 per cent, then the normal financial accounting practice would be to report the sale, and the account receivable, at the present value of the $10 million discounted at 5 per cent, which would be calculated as $10 000 000 ÷ $(1.05)^3$, which equals $10 000 000 ÷ 1.157625, which is $8 638 376. So the present value of receiving $10 000 000 in three years' time is $8 638 376, meaning that the managers would be indifferent between receiving $8 638 376 now or receiving $10 000 000 in three years' time. That is, if an organisation expects to earn 5 per cent per year, then $8 638 376 would become $10 000 000 in three years' time ($8 638 376 × 1.05 × 1.05 × 1.05 = $10 000 000).

An amount of $8 638 376 would be recognised for the accounts receivable, and for the sales income, at the time of sale.

Inventory

Moving our attention now to a different class of assets, *inventory* (also known as *stock* or merchandise) can be a significant asset for many organisations. It includes assets:

- held for sale in the ordinary course of business
- in the process of production for sale
- in the form of materials or supplies to be consumed in the production process, or in the rendering of services.

Determining whether a particular type of asset is inventory will be influenced by the type of organisation in question. For example, a motor vehicle would be a non-current asset in most organisations (part of property, plant and equipment); however, for a motor vehicle dealer it would be part of inventory.

Inventory can also be further subdivided into work in progress (WIP) and finished goods. WIP represents those assets that are being produced for sale but are not yet finished, perhaps requiring further work or processing. For example, partly completed clothes would be WIP for a clothing manufacturer, and a partly completed building would be WIP for a construction organisation.

There is a general requirement within accounting standards (specifically within IAS 2: Inventory) that inventory shall be measured at 'the lower of cost and net realisable value'. That is, the *lower* value is required to be selected from the two values that are determined:

1. cost
2. net realisable value.

In explaining this requirement, we obviously need to understand the meaning of both 'cost' and 'net realisable value'. These terms are both defined within accounting standards.

Cost of inventory

The 'cost' of inventory includes those costs associated with bringing the inventories to their present location and condition. Such costs include:

- costs of purchase
- costs of conversion
- other costs incurred in bringing the inventory to its current condition and location.

Costs of purchase include the purchase price, import duties and other taxes together with the required transportation and handling costs necessary to move the inventory to the location of sale.

Costs of conversion relate to the costs necessary to complete the inventory, and include direct labour and other costs allocated to activities such as labelling and packaging.

Other costs might include the costs of modifications necessary to meet the needs of specific customers.

Once we calculate cost, we then need to compare it with net realisable value, given the requirements in accounting standards that inventory is to be measured at the lower of cost and net realisable value.

For more on determining the cost of inventory, see **Learning exercise 9.7**.

9.7 Learning Exercise

Determining the cost of inventory

Scenario: Sandon Corp sells high-performance stand-up paddleboards. The following costs were incurred in relation to 50 boards that were recently acquired:

Amount paid to the supplier of the boards	$20 000
Import duties	$2 000
Transportation costs to point of sale	$2 500
Costs of modifying boards prior to sale	$3 000
Advertising costs	$3 500
Costs of transporting boards to customers	$1 000

Issue: You are to determine the cost of the inventory of stand-up paddleboards.

Solution: The cost of inventory is required to include those costs associated with bringing the inventories to their location of sale, and to bringing them to the condition they are in at the point of sale. Such costs do not include other costs such as advertising, or costs associated with transportation away from the point of sale (only transportation costs to the point of sale are included within 'cost'). Therefore, the cost of the asset known as 'inventory' is as follows:

Amount paid to the supplier of the boards	$20 000
Import duties	$2 000
Transportation costs to point of sale	$2 500
Costs of modifying boards prior to sale	$3 000
	$27 500

Net realisable value of inventory

Net realisable value is the estimated proceeds of sale less the estimated costs of completion and costs to sell. For example, if an organisation believes it can sell an item of inventory for $700 after it incurs additional manufacturing costs of $50 and advertising costs of $40, then the net realisable value of that inventory would be $610. So, effectively, if the net realisable value of inventory falls below its cost, then accounting standards require inventory to be written down to the value that it could be expected to be sold for, less the incremental costs associated with creating the sale.

The other point to be made is that inventory could be worth many times the amount that is reported within the balance sheet. For example, inventory might have cost $100 000 but might be saleable for $600 000. Accounting standards require the *lower* number to be reported – in this case, $100 000. Therefore, just because the balance sheet attributes a particular monetary value to inventory (for example, $100 000), it could nevertheless be worth much more than this amount (for example, $600 000).

Determining net realisable value is yet another area where professional judgement is required, and therefore is another area where the potential for creative accounting exists. The calculation of net realisable value relies upon judgements about the current demand for the inventory that is held (which impacts sales prices), as well as judgements about the expected costs to complete and sell the inventory. Depending upon the circumstances, managers might make financial accounting 'judgements' that generate the desired financial results rather than involving objective calculations. Again, the practice of financial accounting requires many professional judgements to be made, and it would be naive to believe that these judgements will always be made objectively, free from any form of bias. We are not trying to suggest here, or elsewhere, that every set of financial statements has been manipulated. Our expectation is that the overwhelming majority of financial statements are not creatively manipulated. However, we need to be open to the possibility that some might be.

For more on applying the measurement principle of lower of cost and net realisable value, see Learning exercise 9.8.

9.8 Learning Exercise

Applying the measurement principle of lower of cost and net realisable value

Extending the information in **Learning exercise 9.7**, it is determined that the best that Sandon Corp could realistically do with its inventory is to sell the stand-up paddleboards for $30 000 to a buyer in Geelong. However, this requires that the boards be slightly modified yet again at a further cost of $2500, and that Sandon Corp pays to transport the boards to Geelong at a cost of $1500 before they can be sold.

Issue: What amount should be reported in the balance sheet for the inventory of Sandon Corp?

Solution: Once the cost of inventory has been determined, it then needs to be compared with the net realisable value of that inventory. For balance sheet purposes, the lower amount should be reported, consistent with the requirement stipulated within financial reporting standards that inventory be valued at the lower of cost and net realisable value.

Therefore, we need to determine both the cost of the inventory and the net realisable value, and then use the lower amount.

Learning exercise 9.7 revealed the cost of inventory to be $27 500. The net realisable value is the estimated proceeds of sale, less the estimated costs of completion and costs to sell. This would be $30 000 – $2500 – $1500, which equals $26 000. As this is lower than the cost of $27 500, the inventory will be reported in the balance sheet at $26 000, which is the lower of cost and net realisable value.

If the inventory was originally recognised as an asset at the amount of $27 500 (its cost), then its value would need to be reduced to $26 000, and this writedown would be referred to as an 'inventory writedown expense', or something similar. In terms of our equation of A + E + D = L + I + C, there would be a reduction in assets (inventory) of $1500, and an increase in expenses (inventory writedown expense) of $1500.

Prepayments

The next class of assets that we will consider is **prepayments**. We learned in previous chapters that financial accounting is typically undertaken using the accrual basis of accounting. According to the accrual concept, expenses should be recognised in the period in which they are incurred, rather than the period in which they are paid. And income should be recognised in the period in which the income is earned, not simply in the period in which the related cash is received. The timing of the related cash flow is not directly relevant.

prepayment
An amount paid to another organisation for goods or services prior to the goods or service being received or consumed

It is common to pay certain expenses in advance (that is, to prepay them). For example, rent, insurance and various service contracts are often paid in advance of receiving the related services. As part of a rental agreement, an organisation might be required to pay 12 months' rent in advance for a factory building. At the time of initial payment, none of this economic benefit (this being the right to use the factory) has been used, meaning that there is no actual expense. Rather, there is a right to use the building for the next 12 months. This right is controlled by the entity as a result of the past event (making the payment), and the right is expected to generate future economic benefits. The benefits would have limited measurement uncertainty, and the probabilities associated with the future flow of economic benefits would not be considered low. Therefore, it would generally be appropriate to recognise an asset at the time of the payment, which we would call a 'prepayment'. Specifically, in this instance, we might refer to the asset as 'prepaid rent'. (See **Learning exercise 9.9** for another example of a prepayment that would be recorded in the financial statements.)

amortisation
The process of apportioning the value of an asset to different accounting periods

At the end of the accounting period, we need to then apportion the value of the asset (prepayment) between the value that now has been used up, and the value that remains. This process of apportioning the value of an asset, like a prepayment, to different accounting periods is often referred to as **amortisation**.

9.9 Learning Exercise

Example of a prepayment that would appear in the financial statements

Scenario: On 1 April 2025, Mack Tavish Ltd pays $120 000 cash for 12 months' rent in advance for a factory. The 12-month accounting period for this business ends on 30 June 2025.

Issue: What is the amount that would be shown as a prepayment (prepaid rent) at 30 June 2025, and why is prepaid rent an asset?

Solution: On 1 April 2025, a prepayment, perhaps labelled 'prepaid rent' – which is an asset – would be recognised, and another asset, cash at bank, would be reduced by $120 000. One asset would increase and one would decrease, and our accounting equation of A + E + D = L + I + C would continue to balance.

On 30 June 2025, which is three months later and which is the reporting date, 3/12 of this asset would have been used up. We would recognise rent expense of $30 000 (which reduces owners' equity), and we would reduce the asset prepaid rent by $30 000. The $30 000 is calculated as $120 000 x 3/12. We would be left with a balance of $90 000 in the asset prepaid rent as at 30 June 2025, and this represents the right to use the factory for the next nine months from 30 June 2025.

Prepaid rent is an asset because the organisation has a right to use the factory for the following period, and this right to use the factory has the potential to generate future economic benefits for the organisation.

Property, plant and equipment

The balance sheets of large organisations typically show a total amount that is attributed to the broad category of 'property, plant and equipment'. This category includes such items as land, buildings, office equipment, production machinery and motor vehicles. Property, plant and equipment are tangible items (that is, they have physical substance) that:

- are held for use in the production or supply of goods or services, for rental to others, or for administrative purposes
- are expected to be used during more than one accounting period.

The amounts attributed to property, plant and equipment can be significant. For example, if we refer back to the extract from the balance sheet of BHP as at 30 June 2021 (see **Exhibit 9.2**), we see that property, plant and equipment makes up 68 per cent of the value of all assets recognised by the organisation, this amount for property, plant and equipment being US$73 813 million.

Whilst a total monetary amount will be attributed to property, plant and equipment on the face of the balance sheet, the accompanying notes to the financial statements will provide greater details about the types of property, plant and equipment controlled by the organisation. The notes to the financial statements will also provide information about the accounting policies used to account for property, plant and equipment.

Property, plant and equipment is initially recorded at cost, which effectively includes all the costs necessarily incurred to acquire the asset, and to bring it to the initial location of use, and in the condition necessary for use (see **Learning exercise 9.10**). 'Cost' would therefore include:

- the asset's purchase price, including import duties and non-refundable purchase taxes, after deducting trade discounts and rebates
- any costs directly attributable to bringing the asset to the location and condition necessary for it to be capable of operating in the manner intended by management, including installation and assembly costs, as well as those costs associated with initially testing the performance of the asset prior to it being placed into use.

9.10 Learning Exercise

Determining the cost of an item of property, plant and equipment

Scenario: A computer network costs $400 000 to initially acquire (including import taxes of $15 000), plus $5000 to transport the equipment to its place of use, plus an additional $75 000 paid to computer consultants to make the equipment suitable for use.

Issue: What is the cost that should be attributed to this asset?

Solution: The acquisition cost of this asset would be the aggregate amount of the expenditure for the computer – in this case, $480 000. This total amount, to be recognised in the financial accounts as an asset, and which represents the necessary costs to get the computer to its place of use, and in a condition suitable for use ($400 000 + $5000 + $75 000), would subsequently be depreciated over the future periods in which the benefits are expected to be derived.

Acquisition of property, plant and equipment other than with cash

Whilst determining cost is relatively easy if the costs are paid for with cash, what if property, plant and equipment is acquired not with cash but by exchanging non-cash assets for the item of property, plant and equipment? The general principle is that if an item of property, plant and equipment is acquired in exchange for non-cash assets, then the cost of the acquired item is the fair value of the assets being exchanged. 'Fair value' is the amount for which an asset could be exchanged in an orderly transaction on a given date between knowledgeable and willing parties that are not related to each other (that is, they are independent and at 'arm's length').

For example, if an organisation acquired some machinery in exchange for some land it owns, and that land has a carrying amount of $200 000 (the **carrying amount** being the amount at which the asset is shown within the financial accounts), and a fair value of $280 000, then the acquired machinery would be treated as having a cost of $280 000 in the financial accounts of the acquiring company.

carrying amount
The amount at which an asset, liability, or equity item is shown within the financial accounts

For more on determining cost when an item of property, plant and equipment is acquired other than with cash, see **Learning exercise 9.11**.

9.11 Learning Exercise

Determining the cost of an item of property, plant and equipment acquired with non-cash consideration

Scenario: Westerly Windana Corporation acquires some land in exchange for the following:

- cash of $250 000
- a vintage truck with a cost of $120 000 but a fair value of $220 000
- legal and professional fees associated with the transfer of the land: $12 000.

Issue: What is the cost of the land to Westerly Windana Corporation?

Solution: The cost of the land is the fair value of the assets exchanged for the land, not their carrying amount in the financial accounts. Therefore, the cost of the land that would be recognised in the accounts of Westerly Windana Corporation would be $482 000, calculated as follows:

Cash	$250 000
Vintage truck, at fair value	$220 000
Professional fees paid in relation to the acquisition	$12 000
Cost of land	**$482 000**

The use of cost or fair value

Although organisations will initially recognise their property, plant and equipment at cost, in many countries, accounting standards subsequently provide the managers of organisations with a choice between measuring an asset at cost or at fair value (and remember, smaller organisations do not have to follow accounting standards and can effectively measure their assets on the basis they believe is most appropriate to their needs).

For example, the accounting standard released by the IASB pertaining to property, plant and equipment (IAS 16: Property, Plant and Equipment) allows property, plant and equipment to be measured at either cost or fair value. Further, whilst it is a requirement within the accounting standard that all property, plant and equipment of a certain class must be measured on the same basis (cost or fair value), different classes of property, plant and equipment can be valued using either cost or fair value as the basis of the valuation.

The above paragraph makes reference to a 'class of property, plant and equipment'. Within accounting standards, a class of property, plant and equipment is considered to be a grouping of assets of a similar nature and use in an organisation's operations. Examples of separate classes might include land, machinery, ships, aircraft, motor vehicles, furniture and fixtures, and office equipment.

Regardless of whether cost or fair value is the chosen basis of measurement for different classes of property, plant and equipment, the actual choice of measurement basis should be linked to the fundamental qualitative characteristics that useful financial information should possess – relevance and representational faithfulness.

Reporting assets at their cost might be considered a reliable depiction of value, as cost can be relatively easily ascertained and proven if necessary. Therefore, cost would generally rate highly in terms of the fundamental qualitative characteristic of representational faithfulness.

However, cost might suffer from problems of relevance. For example, an organisation might be able to reliably report that it paid $2 million for some land and buildings back in 1980, but this is not terribly relevant, particularly if property prices have surged. Of more relevance would be a current valuation of its fair value. For example, the land and buildings might currently be worth $100 million, thereby making the cost measurement of $2 million rather irrelevant. The determination of the asset's fair value will be based on judgement and therefore will not be as representationally faithful as saying the cost was $2 million, but the current valuation would be a lot more relevant. There is typically a trade-off between relevance and representational faithfulness, and accountants need to make a choice with both factors in mind and with the ultimate goal that the reported information will be useful to the readers of the financial statements.

If the cost model is chosen, then an item of property, plant and equipment will have a carrying amount that will be its cost, less any accumulated depreciation, and less any accumulated impairment losses. We will address accumulated depreciation and accumulated impairment losses shortly.

If the revaluation model is used, then an item of property, plant and equipment will be measured at its fair value at the date of revaluation, less any subsequent accumulated depreciation, and subsequent accumulated impairment losses.

We can use the basic accounting equation of A = L + OE to explain the impacts on the financial statements when we revalue assets upwards to their fair value. Assets will increase, and owners' equity will increase. Liabilities will not change.

While upward revaluations of property, plant and equipment to fair value are permitted in many countries – notably those countries that have adopted accounting standards issued by the IASB (therefore, for example, revaluations of property, plant and equipment to fair value are permitted within Australia) – the accounting standard-setter in the US, which is the Financial Accounting Standards Board (FASB), does not permit US organisations to revalue their property, plant and equipment upwardly to fair value. It is interesting that one major financial accounting standard-setter thinks that the use of asset revaluations are appropriate, whereas the other major financial accounting standard-setter does not. However, the US accounting standards do require impairment losses to be recognised if the value of the asset drops below the carrying amount of the asset. We will consider impairment losses shortly.

For a discussion of measuring property, plant and equipment at cost or fair value, see **Learning exercise 9.12**.

9.12 Learning Exercise

Measuring property, plant and equipment at cost or fair value

Scenario: Lopez Corporation, a large New Zealand company, has the following classes of property, plant and equipment, with the following costs and fair values:

	Cost	Fair value
Land	$650 000	$2 000 000
Buildings	$500 000	$700 000
Artworks	$250 000	$900 000
Vintage motor vehicles	$270 000	$750 000
Machinery	$330 000	$350 000
	$2 000 000	$4 700 000

The managers of Lopez Corporation have made the decision that land, buildings and artworks are to be measured at fair value, whereas vintage motor vehicles and machinery are to be measured at cost.

Issue: You are required to answer the following:

- Can the managers of Lopez Corporation make the choice to measure some classes of property, plant and equipment using the cost model, whilst also measuring other classes using the fair value model?
- What total amount would be shown in the balance sheet for property, plant and equipment?
- What does this total amount actually represent?
- Will future depreciation expenses be affected following a revaluation?

Solution: Consider the following.

Cost model or fair value model?

Managers and accountants in countries that use the financial reporting standards issued by the IASB can make the choice to measure some classes of property, plant and equipment at cost, and other classes of property, plant and equipment at fair value (this can be contrasted to organisations within the US, which does not permit upward asset revaluations). As Lopez Corporation is a New Zealand-based company, and as New Zealand uses the accounting standards of the IASB, the company is permitted to use asset revaluations.

The balance sheet amount for property, plant and equipment

The amount that would be shown within the balance sheet, given the measurement choices made by the managers of Lopez Corporation, would be as follows:

Land, at fair value	$2 000 000
Buildings, at fair value	$700 000
Artworks, at fair value	$900 000
Vintage motor vehicles, at cost	$270 000
Machinery, at cost	$330 000
	$4 200 000

What does the total amount represent?

The total amount calculated above of $4 200 000 does not represent the fair value of the total property, plant and equipment (which is $4 700 000), nor does it represent the cost (which is $2 000 000). It is simply a mixed measure that can be confusing for people who do not understand that the total balance is calculated on a mixed method basis.

Effect of revaluation on future depreciation expenses

When upward revaluations occur, this will act to increase depreciation expense, as depreciation – which we shall discuss in more depth below – will then be calculated based upon the higher revalued amount. The fact that upward revaluations of property, plant and equipment to fair value can lead to higher depreciation expenses (and therefore lower profits) can potentially act to discourage some managers from electing to measure property, plant and equipment at fair value. This reluctance will be further increased if they are paid bonuses which are linked to reported profits.

Enabling managers to have a choice between using cost and fair value gives an organisation further ability to generate financial statements that depict a preferred picture. For example, if managers wish to show higher assets, and the fair value of a class of assets is higher than its carrying amount, then they might choose to undertake asset revaluations.

Such measurement choices mean that care needs to be taken when comparing the financial performance, and financial position, of different organisations that are potentially using different bases for measuring their property, plant and equipment.

For example, some organisations might have a policy of measuring their property, plant and equipment at cost. This will lead them to show relatively lower amounts for their assets in the balance sheet than would otherwise be the case. Further, by not revaluing their assets upwardly to fair value, the depreciation expenses would be lower relative to similar organisations that make the choice to use fair values. This is because depreciation will be calculated on the basis of the lower cost.

As an example, Exhibit 9.3 provides an extract from the notes to the financial statements of BHP for the year ending 30 June 2021. As we can see, BHP has made the decision not to perform revaluations of its property, plant and equipment. Therefore, we need to be careful when comparing the financial position, and financial performance, of BHP with other mining and resources organisations that do perform asset revaluations.

EXHIBIT 9.3 An accounting policy note pertaining to the measurement of property, plant and equipment – from the annual report of BHP for the year ending 30 June 2021

Property, plant and equipment is recorded at cost less accumulated depreciation and impairment charges. Cost is the fair value of consideration given to acquire the asset at the time of its acquisition or construction and includes the direct costs of bringing the asset to the location and the condition necessary for operation and the estimated future costs of closure and rehabilitation of the facility.

Source: BHP (2021), p. 152.

Depreciation

Non-current assets – both tangible and intangible – have useful lives that might be either finite or indefinite. If an asset is considered to have a 'finite useful life', this means that the asset is expected to have a useful life of a particular number of accounting periods (or perhaps the life of the asset might be limited to producing a particular number of units of output). An asset would be considered to have an indefinite life if, at a given point in time, there appears to be no foreseeable limit to the useful life of the asset. For most items of property, plant and equipment, there is an expectation that the useful life – and related economic benefits – is finite (other than perhaps land) and therefore will require some depreciation expense to be recognised within the financial accounts.

In the above paragraph, we refer to the 'useful life' of an asset. It needs to be understood that this does not always mean how long the asset will last. Rather, the useful life is the period of time during which the organisation expects to obtain an economic benefit from the asset before it elects to dispose of or sell the asset. The asset might still be working at the end of its useful life, but it might not be operating in a way that efficiently provides the necessary economic benefits to the organisation.

As an example of depreciation expense, if a machine is purchased, then it is typically known that it will not last forever. Across time it will start to physically deteriorate, as well as become technically obsolete as more efficient machinery becomes available. The accountant will tend to allocate the initial cost of the machine across those accounting periods expected to benefit from the use of the machine, which is called its useful life.

For example, if an organisation acquires a machine at a cost of $120 000 and believes it can be used for five years before being scrapped, and if the amount the organisation expects to receive for the machine as scrap in five years is $10 000 (we can call this its *residual value*), then we know that the value of the machine will be reducing by $110 000 (the original cost less the residual value) over the useful life of the machine. If we believe that the pattern of economic benefits to be derived from the asset is fairly constant over its useful life, then we would allocate this amount of $110 000 equally over the five years. The resulting annual depreciation of $22 000 would be treated as an expense of each accounting period, which we call depreciation expense.

depreciation
The systematic periodic allocation of the cost, or fair value, of a non-current asset over the periods expected to benefit from the use of the asset. The amount calculated is referred to as a depreciation expense

Depreciation expenses are recognised because we generally prepare financial statements on an accrual basis, which means expenses are recorded when they are incurred. When an item of property, plant and equipment is initially acquired, it represents an asset, as it effectively provides a source of future economic benefits. No expense is recorded at the time the item is acquired. However, as the service potential of the asset declines over time, the related depreciation expense will be recognised. As an allocation of cost, depreciation expense is an example of an expense that does not involve a cash flow. The actual cash flow arose some time earlier, when the asset was acquired.

Therefore, from an accountant's perspective, depreciation expense is the allocation of the cost of an asset (or its revalued amount) over the accounting periods in which the economic benefits are expected to be generated by the asset. Depreciation does not represent a valuation process; that is, depreciation expense does not represent the decrease in the market value, or fair value, of an asset.

In calculating depreciation expense, we must make three broad judgements about the following:

- *The depreciable base*. This is the total amount to be depreciated and often is simply the cost of the item less its expected residual value (the residual value being the amount expected to be received on disposal of the asset at the end of its useful life).
- *The asset's useful life*. This is based on professional judgement and is influenced by considerations of the expected usage of the asset, expected wear and tear on the asset, maintenance programs expected to be in place, likelihood of the asset becoming technically or commercially obsolete as alternative technologies become available, and any legal or similar restrictions placed upon the use of the asset.
- *The appropriate method of cost apportionment of the asset*. The managers and accountant need to make judgements about the pattern of benefits to be generated by the asset. If the pattern of benefits is expected to be fairly uniform, with the economic benefits being equally shared across different accounting periods, then an approach that allocates the depreciable amount equally to each future accounting period would seem appropriate. We would call this the 'straight-line method' of depreciation. By contrast, if we believe that the economic benefits from the asset are consumed relatively more in the earlier accounting periods, then we would use a method that recognises higher depreciation expenses in the earlier years, such as the 'diminishing balance method' of depreciation (to be discussed shortly). As another alternative, if the asset's productive capacity is limited to a given level of output, then we might use the 'units-of-production method'.

We will now learn how to apply different approaches to calculating depreciation in **Learning exercises 9.13**, **9.14** and **9.15**.

9.13 Learning Exercise

Applying the straight-line method of depreciation

Scenario: Waimea Ltd paid $40 000 for an item of machinery at the beginning of the year. The estimated useful life for this machinery is three years, with an expected $4000 residual value. The depreciable base is therefore $36 000, which represents the cost of $40 000 minus the expected residual value of $4000, which is the amount of money the organisation expects to receive when the machinery's useful life is over (the $4000 could be the value of useable parts left in the machine at the end of its useful life).

Once we know the depreciable base ($36 000) and the useful life of the asset (three years), we then need to determine the appropriate method of cost apportionment. If Waimea Ltd believes that the asset will generate uniform benefits across its useful life, then use of the straight-line method of depreciation for this machinery would be appropriate.

Issue: With this information in mind, how much depreciation expense would be recognised in the income statement for each of the next three reporting periods? What disclosures would be made in respect of the measurement of the machine after two years of depreciation?

Solution: Using the straight-line method of depreciation, the depreciation is calculated as:

(Cost – expected residual value) ÷ Expected life of the asset

The annual depreciation expense will therefore be:

($40 000 – 4000) ÷ 3 years = $12 000

	Year 1	Year 2	Year 3
Carrying amount at start of year	$40 000	$28 000	$16 000
Annual depreciation expense	($12 000)	($12 000)	($12 000)
Carrying amount at end of year	$28 000	$16 000	$4000

In terms of how the asset would be presented in the financial statements after two years' depreciation, the disclosure would be as follows:

Machinery, at cost	$40 000
Less: accumulated depreciation	($24 000)
	$16 000

The accumulated depreciation account would be considered a contra account (like the allowance for doubtful debts that we considered earlier in this chapter) and it is offset against the cost of the asset. It accumulates the current and previous years' depreciation.

Calculating depreciation is yet another area where a great deal of professional judgement is required, thereby raising the possibility of creative accounting. For example, judgements need to be made about the expected residual value of an asset, the expected useful life of the asset, and the pattern of benefits to be generated by the asset. Whilst the overwhelming majority of accountants will make these judgements objectively, from time to time accountants – perhaps with the 'encouragement' of managers – might select depreciation approaches that generate the financial position and/or financial performance preferred by management.

9.14 Learning Exercise

Applying the diminishing balance method of depreciation

Scenario: We will use the same information as in **Learning exercise 9.13**, except this time we will make the assumption that the pattern of economic benefits being generated by the machinery is such that more benefits are being generated in the earlier years. Given this, we will use a method of cost apportionment that recognises more depreciation in the earlier years. One such method is known as the diminishing balance method of depreciation.

Issue: What would the depreciation expense be for each of the next three years using the diminishing balance method of depreciation?

Solution: Using the diminishing balance method of depreciation, the percentage to be applied to the opening carrying amount of the asset is determined by using the following formula:

percentage = 1 – the nth root of (residual value ÷ cost)

where n = the life of the asset, which in this case is 3,

and where the residual value ÷ cost = \$4000 ÷ \$40 000, which equals 0.1

$$= 1.0 - \sqrt[3]{0.1}$$

$$= 1.0 - 0.4642$$

$$= 0.5358$$

Year	Annual depreciation calculation	Depreciation expense
1	0.5358 × (\$40 000)	= \$21 432
2	0.5358 × (\$40 000 – \$21 432)	= \$9 949
3	0.5358 × (\$40 000 – \$21 432 – \$9 949)	= \$4 619
		\$36 000

Again, the use of the diminishing-balance approach would be appropriate where the economic benefits expected to be derived from the asset will be greater in the earlier years of the asset's life than in the latter years.

9.15 Learning Exercise

Applying the units of production method of depreciation

Scenario: We will again use the same information as in **Learning exercise 9.13**, except that this time we will make the assumption that machinery is expected to only produce 10 000 units in total. That is, the ability of the machinery to generate economic benefits is tied to the number of units to be produced by the asset and not to some other measure, such as time.

Given this information, we shall use a method of depreciation known as the units of production method of depreciation. To use this method, we need to know the production level in each year. We will assume that the units of production will be as follows:

Year	Units of production
1	3500
2	4000
3	2500
	10000

Issue: What would the depreciation expense be for each of the three years using the units of production method of depreciation?

Solution: If the machine cost $40 000 and has an expected residual value of $4000, then we will allocate the *depreciable base* of $36 000 to each unit of production. That is, $36 000 ÷ 10 000, which equals $3.60 depreciation expense per unit of production.

Year	Annual depreciation calculation	Depreciation expense
Year 1	3500 × $3.60	= $12 600
Year 2	4000 × $3.60	= $14 400
Year 3	2500 × $3.60	= $9000
		$36 000

One other point to be made in relation to depreciation is that the depreciation methods used for financial accounting purposes (and which would be consistent with the requirements embodied within accounting standards) will not always be consistent with the methods used when calculating profits for taxation purposes. Tax rules for depreciation, which will vary across countries, can be different to financial accounting rules for depreciation.

Maintenance, repairs and improvements

Following the acquisition of an item of property, plant and equipment, additional expenditure will generally be incurred. These costs can range from ordinary repairs and maintenance to significant upgrades, additions and improvements. The major problem in this area is the decision about whether or not to capitalise these payments (that is, treat the expenditures as increasing the value of assets) or treat them as expenses. Secondly, if the expenditures *are* capitalised rather than expensed, we also need to determine the number of periods over which the expenditure should be depreciated.

A general approach adopted within financial accounting is to capitalise expenditures that increase the likely future economic benefits expected to be generated by an asset relative to its original state, but expense those subsequent expenditures that simply maintain a given level of services.

Therefore, we will capitalise those expenditures that extend the life of the asset, or increase its capacity or efficiency. Because payments made on repairs and maintenance only maintain an asset's life or current condition, then such payments will be treated as expenses. For example, replacing a roof on an existing factory with comparable material is a repair expense, whilst upgrading the roof by using longer-lasting roof cladding is likely to increase the building's useful life and would be considered as a capital expenditure. Capitalised expenditures need to be depreciated over the future accounting periods expected to benefit from the expenditure.

Marketable securities

Organisations often use some of their available funds to acquire investments that generate financial returns. For example, an organisation might acquire shares in other companies for the purpose of generating dividend income, and for capital appreciation (in relation to shares, if the fair value of the shares increases, this is often referred to as *capital appreciation*).

The general practice – which is in accordance with the financial reporting standards issued by the IASB (in particular, in accordance with IFRS 9 *Financial Instruments*) – is to measure such investments at their fair value, with this amount being updated at the end of each accounting period. Increases in fair value are treated as income of the accounting period in which the change in fair value occurs, whilst decreases in fair values are treated as expenses of an accounting period. Any dividends received during the accounting period are treated as income.

9.16 Learning Exercise

Accounting for equity investments in other organisations

Scenario: Southside Company, which has an accounting period of 12 months ending on 30 June 2026, acquires shares in a listed public company named ABC Ltd for $460 000 on 1 July 2025.

During the financial year to 30 June 2026, ABC Ltd pays cash dividends of $20 000 to Southside Company. By 30 June 2026, the fair value of the shares held in ABC Ltd has increased to $550 000.

Issue: You are required to determine the amount Southside Company should disclose in the balance sheet for this investment. You are also required to determine the income to be recognised in the year to 30 June 2026 in relation to the investment.

Solution: For marketable securities, the general requirement within financial reporting standards is that they should be measured at their fair value, and that any changes in fair value that occur within the accounting period are included within profit or loss for that period. Therefore, at 30 June 2026, the investment in ABC Ltd would be measured at $550 000. The increase that occurred in the accounting period of $90 000 would be treated as income. Therefore, in terms of the basic accounting equation of A + E + D = L + I + C, we would have an increase in both assets and income of $90 000.

The dividends received from ABC Ltd of $20 000 would also be shown as income in the accounts of Southside Company. This means that the total investment income for the year would be $110 000.

Intangible assets

Intangible assets can be defined as non-monetary assets without a physical substance. In terms of this definition, 'monetary assets' would include cash, bank deposits, accounts receivable, and government bonds. Intangible assets include copyrights, patents, brand names, publishing titles, franchise agreements, goodwill, and research and development. A significant amount of a firm's value can be linked to its intangible assets. Accounting standards, which as we know apply to larger organisations, require intangible assets to be disclosed separately from other assets.

Within accounting standards, there are quite strict requirements about the intangible assets that are allowed to be recognised in the financial statements. Generally speaking, only externally acquired (purchased) intangible assets can be recognised for balance sheet purposes. Those intangible assets that have been developed internally, and therefore not purchased from external sources, are not permitted by accounting standards to be recognised and shown in the balance sheet. The implication of this is that many valuable intangible assets do not ever appear on the balance sheets we see, thereby significantly undermining the potential usefulness, and relevance, of the balance sheet.

The requirement that internally generated intangible assets generally be excluded from being recognised in the balance sheet as assets (the only exception to this rule pertaining to the 'development' component of research and development expenditure) represents a departure from the 'normal' asset recognition requirements embodied within the Conceptual Framework, which are linked to issues associated with the expected probabilities of future economic flows of benefits, and any measurement and existence uncertainties associated with those benefits.

Given the requirement that internally developed intangible assets – those that are developed within the organisation, rather than being acquired at cost from an external party – are not to be shown as assets in a balance sheet, users of financial statements will not know about many intangible assets controlled by an organisation, and which might have significant value. As noted above, this tends to undermine the usefulness of financial statements, particularly given that it is becoming accepted that increasingly across time, intangible assets contribute greatly to the value of organisations.

As an example, if an organisation like Coca-Cola develops its soft-drink formula internally and patents that formula (a patent is said to exist when a government authority, or other conferring organisation, provides an organisation with a right, typically for a set period of time, to exclusively make, use or sell a particular invention), then despite the fact that the soft-drink formula might be worth many billions of dollars, no value can be recognised within the financial statements because it was internally developed. However, should another organisation come along and buy the rights to control the use of that formula from Coca-Cola, then that other organisation can recognise the asset, and the cost paid, for the rights even though Coca-Cola could not. This does appear somewhat illogical, but these are the rules of financial accounting as they apply to larger organisations that are required to follow financial reporting standards. (For another example of the recognition and measurement of intangible assets, see **Learning exercise 9.17**.)

9.17 Learning Exercise

The recognition and measurement of intangible assets

Scenario: Sunset Ltd has the following intangible assets under its control:

Type of intangible asset	Cost of acquiring, or developing, the intangible asset	Was the intangible asset internally developed or purchased from another organisation?
Publishing title	$250 000	Internally developed
Copyright	$450 000	Internally developed
Brand name	$500 000	Purchased from another organisation
Franchise agreement	$200 000	Purchased from another organisation
	$1 400 000	

Issue: Which of these intangible assets can be recognised within the financial accounts and therefore included within the balance sheet, and what would be the total amount shown for intangible assets?
Solution: Sunset Ltd, being a public company, is required to comply with accounting standards. Therefore, the only intangible assets that are permitted to be recognised will be the intangible assets that were purchased from an external party, these being the brand name and the franchise agreement. The total amount to be shown in the balance sheet for intangible assets would therefore be $700 000. The other valuable intangible assets would not be shown within the balance sheet. Further, the costs involved in developing these unrecognised intangible assets are required to be treated as expenses, and therefore reduce reported profits in the year in which they are developed. So not only does this non-recognition of valuable intangible assets impact the usefulness of the balance sheet, it also impacts reported profits.

It should be noted that the rules embodied within accounting standards take precedence over the guidance provided in the Conceptual Framework. That is, if there is a conflict between the two, the accounting standard must be followed. Whilst we could logically think that the rules within accounting standards will always be consistent with the Conceptual Framework, this is not always the case. As the accounting standard pertaining to intangible assets requires that internally developed intangible assets shall not be recognised, accountants therefore need to comply with this requirement.

In our previous discussion of property, plant and equipment, we noted that following the initial acquisition (which should be recorded at cost), property, plant and equipment can be measured by using either the cost model or the fair value model. However, the requirements for revaluing intangible assets are much stricter.

For those intangible assets that are permitted to be recognised in the financial accounts – and we now understand that this typically only includes those intangible assets that have been purchased from outside the organisation – they can only subsequently be revalued if there is an 'active market' for such assets.

According to accounting standards, an *active market* exists where the assets being traded are homogeneous (that is, the assets are all effectively the same), willing buyers and sellers can normally be found, and prices are publicly available. Because active markets do not exist for most intangible assets (as they are typically unique in some way), then most intangible assets shall not be revalued following initial acquisition. This further acts to reduce the monetary amount that can be associated with intangible assets, and to reduce the potential relevance of the information being presented within balance sheets.

Therefore, based on the information you have just read about intangible assets, you should be aware of why the balance sheet is not very useful for demonstrating accountability as it pertains to intangible assets. Many intangible assets are excluded from recognition. For those relatively few intangible assets that can be recognised, they can typically only be recorded at cost, which might be significantly below their fair value.

Many people believe that the way in which accounting standards require intangible assets to be accounted for is far too conservative and restrictive, and thereby undermines the ability of financial statements to provide sound information about the financial position, and performance, of an organisation. Perhaps the accounting standards pertaining to intangible assets will be amended at some future date so that more relevant information about intangible assets can be provided to the readers of financial statements.

Accounting for goodwill

Goodwill is a specific type of intangible asset. Because it is an intangible asset that is in many balance sheets, we will specifically address it now.

Goodwill arises when one organisation acquires another organisation, or a part thereof, and such goodwill would be considered to be externally acquired, or purchased, goodwill. Other than being purchased, goodwill can also be developed across time within an organisation, and this would be referred to as internally developed goodwill. Goodwill represents the future economic benefits that are generated as a result of such factors as efficient management, reliable suppliers, an existing and loyal customer base, and so forth. Consistent with the treatment of other intangible assets, accounting standards only allow purchased goodwill to be recognised within the financial accounts. Accounting standards do not permit the recognition in the financial statements of internally generated goodwill. This is because accounting standard-setters believe that purchased goodwill can be measured more objectively, and on the basis of the amount paid, whereas there are too many uncertainties when it comes to placing a value on internally generated goodwill (thereby undermining representational faithfulness).

goodwill
An intangible asset that represents the future economic benefits that are expected to be generated as a result of factors such as efficient management, reliable suppliers, existing customer base, and so forth. Goodwill is generally recognised when one organisation acquires another organisation, or part thereof, and is measured as the excess of the fair value of the purchase price over the fair value of the identifiable net assets of the organisation acquired. Goodwill can also be internally developed; however accounting standards prohibit the recognition of internally developed goodwill

Since accounting standards prohibit the recognition of internally developed goodwill, this means that a potentially very valuable asset will not be shown in the balance sheet of the organisation that develops the goodwill. However, as soon as another organisation acquires that business, they will be able to show that goodwill in the balance sheet. Again, as with other intangible assets, this represents a departure from the general 'recognition criteria' included within the Conceptual Framework. But as we now know, accounting standards take precedence over the Conceptual Framework; that is, if there are some differences in requirements between accounting standards (and there are specific accounting standards relating to goodwill and other intangible assets) and the Conceptual Framework, then it is the requirements of the accounting standards that must be followed. Whilst purchased goodwill can be recognised within the financial accounts, it is not permitted to be subsequently revalued.

Purchased goodwill is measured as the difference between the fair value of the purchase consideration paid, and the fair value of the net assets acquired (other than the goodwill). As we know, net assets represent assets minus liabilities.

When goodwill has been recognised within the financial accounts, there is also a requirement within the accounting standards that the purchased goodwill be reviewed at the end of each accounting period to determine whether the value has been impaired – and if it has been, the organisation is required to recognise a related impairment loss.

For more on the determination of goodwill, see **Learning exercise 9.18**.

9.18 Learning Exercise

Determination of goodwill

Scenario: On 1 January 2026, Farrelly Surf Company purchases Great Times Surfboards for the following consideration:

Cash:		\$200 000
Land:	Carrying amount	\$400 000
	Fair value	\$800 000

The balance sheet of Great Times Surfboards, at the date of acquisition, shows assets of $1 500 000 and liabilities of $750 000.

All the assets of Great Times Surfboards are fairly valued, except some land that has a carrying amount of $100 000 but a fair value of $300 000.

Issue: What is the value of the purchased goodwill?

Solution: In this case, goodwill will represent the difference between the fair value of the purchase consideration paid, and the fair value of the identifiable net assets acquired:

Fair value of purchase consideration paid		
Cash	$200 000	
Land, at fair value	$800 000	$1 000 000
Less: Fair value of net assets acquired		
Carrying amount of assets	$1 500 000	
Excess of fair value of land over the carrying amount	$200 000	
Fair value of assets acquired	$1 700 000	
Less liabilities	($750 000)	($950 000)
Goodwill		$50 000

Leased assets

Many organisations lease some of their assets rather than buying them. For some large organisations, these leases can involve many billions of dollars of leased assets and related lease liabilities. A *lease* is an agreement conveying the right from a lessor (typically the legal owner) to a lessee to use an asset – typically property, plant and equipment – for a stated period of time in return for a series of lease payments.

If we lease an item of property, plant and equipment – rather than owning it – should we recognise it as an 'asset'? The answer is 'Yes'. Remember our definition of assets, which relies upon control rather than legal ownership. If an organisation were, for example, to enter an agreement to lease some farming land, for say five years, then this right to use the land would be controlled, and it has the potential to generate future economic benefits. It is therefore an asset.

When we sign the leasing contract, then, we are also accepting an obligation (a liability) to make future lease payments for the duration of the lease. Therefore, in terms of our basic accounting equation of A = L + OE, when we enter into a lease, we will increase both assets and liabilities. But how do we determine the monetary amount to recognise?

The answer is that leased assets (and the lease liability) are required by accounting standards to be measured at the present value of the lease payments if the leasing period is greater than 12 months. **Learning exercise 9.19** provides an example of how we measure leased assets. An important point for us to again remember, therefore, is that not all assets that are recognised in the balance sheet are owned by an organisation. Rather, the assets are controlled, and this control can come either through legal ownership or through the acquisition of rights to use the asset that have been conferred by way of a lease agreement.

9.19 Learning Exercise

Recognition and measurement of leased assets

Scenario: Nimbin Co-op leased some farming land to grow some crops. The lease agreement requires the following:

- initial up-front payment made at the beginning of the financial year: \$40 000
- four subsequent lease payments of \$60 000 per year, to be made at the beginning of each of the next four subsequent financial years (that is, the first of these subsequent payments is to be made in one year's time)
- life of the lease: five years
- interest rate: 5 per cent, which also represents Nimbin's usual borrowing rate.

Issue: You are required to determine the financial amount to be attributed to the leased asset, and lease liability, at the start of the lease period.

Solution: When determining this answer, consider the following.

What's the asset and what's the liability?

By entering the lease contract, Nimbin Co-op has acquired the right to use the farming land for the next five years, and across this five years it would expect to generate future economic benefits associated with the crops it will produce and sell. Therefore, it has acquired an asset, which we shall recognise, and which we might refer to as 'leased land', and this asset will have a life of five years.

By entering the lease contract, Nimbin Co-op has also established an obligation to make cash payments for the duration of the lease. This represents a liability. Therefore, we know we need to recognise both a leased asset and a lease liability.

The next step is to determine the measurement of this leased asset and the lease liability.

How do we determine the measurement of the leased asset and leased liability?

For leases with a life beyond 12 months, the required practice is to recognise the leased asset (often referred to as a 'right-of-use asset') and the lease liability at the present value of the lease payments. Therefore, we need to determine the present value of the payments Nimbin Co-op is required to make pursuant to the lease agreement.

To determine the present value, we discount the future payments at a specific interest rate (also referred to as a *discount rate*). In this instance, we will discount the payments at Nimbin Co-op's usual borrowing rate, which we are told is 5 per cent. We can use a financial calculator, or we can use a table that provides us with present values.

Nimbin Co-op's lease agreement requires an up-front payment of \$40 000. As this is paid now, rather than in the future, then it will not be discounted. However, the stream of four future payments of \$60 000 per year, starting at the end of year 1, do need to be discounted to their present value.

The present value of a stream of \$1 a year to be paid at the beginning of each of the next four years is \$3.5460. This number would be available from present value tables, or on a financial calculator. It equals:

$$\frac{1.0}{(1.05)^1} + \frac{1.0}{(1.05)^2} + \frac{1.0}{(1.05)^3} + \frac{1.0}{(1.05)^4}$$

Therefore, the present value of the required lease payments is:

Up-front lease payment (with cash)	$40 000
Four lease payments each to be made at the beginning of each year: $60 000 × 3.5460	$212 760
Total present value of lease payments	$252 760

Therefore, at the commencement of the lease, Nimbin Co-op will recognise a leased asset, which is often disclosed as a 'right-of-use asset', of $252 760, a lease liability of $212 760 (representing the present value of the future lease payments to be made for the leased asset), and a reduction in cash at bank (an asset) of $40 000, which was the amount of the up-front payment of cash. Using our accounting equation:

A	+	E	+	D	=	L	+	I	+	C
$252 760 ($40 000)		–		–	=	$212 760		–		–

The amount recognised for the right-of-use asset at the commencement of the lease, being $252 760, would then be depreciated over the life of the asset – which in this case is five years.

Summary of asset measurement rules

We have now discussed how to measure various classes of assets – of course, there are many other classes of assets we have not discussed, but the measurement of these other assets may be covered in further accounting education you might undertake. As a result of this discussion, we now know that there are several ways in which assets are measured. The measurement rule we use will depend upon the type of asset under consideration. Many people who have not studied accounting would be unaware that assets are actually measured in a variety of ways, and therefore they really would not understand what the amount attributed to 'total assets' actually represents. It can be a confusing number.

The measurement bases for the different classes of assets discussed so far are summarised in Table 9.1.

TABLE 9.1 Measurement rules for different classes of assets

Asset	Measurement rule
Cash	Face value
Accounts receivable	Face value, less an allowance for doubtful debts
Inventory	Lower of cost and net realisable value
Prepayments	Amortised cost (valued at cost, which is then reduced as the asset is used)
Property, plant and equipment	At cost or fair value, less accumulated depreciation expenses and accumulated impairment losses
Marketable securities	Fair value
Intangible assets	Generally, only externally acquired intangible assets can be recognised, meaning that many valuable intangible assets shall not be shown within the balance sheet. For those acquired intangible assets that can be recognised, recognition is generally at cost, given the restrictions on revaluations
Leased assets	For leases of more than 12 months' duration, measured at the present value of the expected lease payments

We again return to the question of what does the total financial amount of all assets appearing in the balance sheet actually represent? Does it make sense to add together amounts that have been measured in different ways, including cost, fair value and present value? Possibly not, but that's what occurs in practice and we should be aware of this. It is what we referred to earlier as the additivity problem. We also know that the monetary amount assigned to total assets does not include the values of many valuable resources controlled by an organisation, such as internally developed intangible assets.

This discussion highlights the dangers involved when people who are not trained in financial accounting try to use financial statements to inform the various decisions they make (for example, whether to invest in an organisation, whether to sell shares held in the organisation, whether to loan funds to the organisation, or whether to provide goods on credit to the organisation).

People unskilled in accounting might believe that the amount shown for total assets represents the current value (fair value) of all the assets owned by an organisation, and which could ultimately be sold. But as we are now learning, this is simply not the case. The balance sheet includes assets that are not owned (for example, leased assets will be included), and the balance sheet will include various classes of assets that are measured at cost, even though their fair value might be significantly higher. The balance sheet will also exclude many valuable assets, such as internally developed intangible assets. So in reality, it is probably safer to stay away from financial statements unless you actually understand the rules governing their preparation. A trained accountant will know that assets are measured in a variety of ways, and that total assets simply represent the summation of different classes of assets that have been measured in a variety of ways. Hopefully our discussion about asset measurement has highlighted to you how careful you need to be when interpreting the meaning of this aggregated amount. Do you think that many investors who read financial statements are actually aware of this?

Why do I need to know about the existence of different asset measurement rules?

Within the balance sheet, which is an extremely important document for assessing the financial position and associated risks of an organisation, one of the key disclosures is 'Total Assets'. Unless we understand the different asset measurement rules which ultimately culminate in this total for assets, then we will be unable to comprehend what this total actually represents. Nor would we be able to comprehend what 'Total Equity' represents (given equity is the difference between assets and liabilities). As a result, in the absence of such knowledge, the balance sheet could be quite misleading to us.

LO9.5 The recoverable amount of an asset

To this point in our discussion of the measurement of assets, we have discussed the use of different approaches to measurement, the most common of which is either the cost approach or the fair value approach. One last requirement we should refer to is the requirement that no asset should ever be reported in the financial statements at more than its **recoverable amount**. That is, the carrying amount of an asset, which is the net amount shown in the financial accounts for the asset, must be equal to or less than the asset's expected recoverable amount. This is consistent with the general principle that assets should *never* be overstated.

recoverable amount
The higher of an asset's fair value less costs of disposal (sometimes called net selling price), and its value in use

The above paragraph makes reference to the net amount shown for an asset. By this, we mean the amount shown for the asset less the various contra accounts that might be associated with the account. For example, if we had accounts receivable of $500 000 and an associated allowance for doubtful debts of $25 000, then the net amount (or carrying amount) would be $475 000. Similarly, if we have some machinery with a cost of $600 000 and accumulated depreciation (also a contra account) of $60 000, then the net amount (carrying amount) reported for machinery would be $540 000.

The recoverable amount of an asset refers to the monetary value that is expected to be generated by the asset. It represents the value that the organisation expects to be able to *recover* from the asset as a result of selling the asset, or through the ongoing use of the asset. Consistent with this, within accounting standards, the recoverable amount of an asset is defined as the higher of an asset's fair value less costs of disposal (sometimes called net selling price), and its value in use.

The 'value in use' of an asset refers to the net cash flows that an asset is expected to generate throughout its remaining useful life, and it is measured as the net present value of the expected future cash flows, or other economic benefits, that an asset generates for a specific organisation under a specific use.

impairment loss
An expense that is recognised when the recoverable amount is less than the carrying amount of an asset

The recoverable amount of the asset, which is the higher of the fair value of the asset less costs of disposal, and its value in use, is to be compared with the carrying amount of the asset, and if the recoverable amount is less than the carrying amount of the asset, then an **impairment loss** must be recognised. This is a general requirement for all assets. The recognition of an impairment loss has the effect of reducing the carrying amount of the asset and increasing the expenses of the organisation (thereby reducing owners' equity).

Impairment losses should not be confused with depreciation. As we learned earlier in this chapter, depreciation is an allocation of the cost, or revalued amount, of an asset over its useful life, and is not a valuation process. Even if an asset has been depreciated, it is possible that a subsequent impairment loss will still need to be recognised if the depreciated amount is still higher than the expected recoverable amount of the asset. If an impairment loss has been recognised, then future depreciation will be based upon the revised carrying amount of the asset.

For more on the recognition of impairment losses, see **Learning exercise 9.20**.

9.20 Learning Exercise

Determining whether an impairment loss needs to be recognised

Scenario: Pipeline Inc owns a machine that has a carrying amount of $155 000. This is comprised of its original cost of $180 000 less accumulated depreciation of $25 000.

The machine can either be sold or retained for use. If it is sold, it would achieve a sale price of $75 000 and there would also be associated sale costs of $7000 to make the sale. By contrast, if it is held to be used, then it is anticipated that it would generate net cash flows of $40 000 per year for the next four years, after which time it would have zero residual value. The appropriate interest rate, which in this case represents the rate of return that would typically be expected for this type of asset, is 6 per cent.

Issue: Should an impairment loss be recognised, and if so, what amount would be recognised for the loss, and how would the machine be disclosed within the financial statements?

Solution: Consider the following.

When should an impairment loss be recognised?

As you know, an impairment loss needs to be recognised if the recoverable amount of the asset is less than its carrying amount.

What's the recoverable amount?

The recoverable amount is determined as the *higher* of the asset's net selling price and its value in use. In this case, the net selling price is $75 000 less $7000, which is $68 000.

To determine the value in use, we need to determine the present value of the expected cash flows to be generated from using the asset. The present value of an annuity of $1 for four years discounted at 6 per cent is $3.4651, which equals:

$$\frac{1.0}{(1.06)^1} + \frac{1.0}{(1.06)^2} + \frac{1.0}{(1.06)^3} + \frac{1.0}{(1.06)^4}$$

For simplicity, we will assume that all the cash flows occur at the end of the year. The present value of the future cash flows therefore is $40 000 × 3.4651, which equals $138 604. This is deemed to be the asset's value in use.

The recoverable amount is determined as the higher of the net sales price (which is $68 000) and the value in use (which is $138 604). Therefore, the recoverable amount is $138 604.

Is the recoverable amount less than the carrying amount?

The recoverable amount of $138 604 is less than the carrying amount of $155 000. Therefore, we need to recognise an impairment loss.

What amount should be shown as the impairment loss?

We need to recognise an impairment loss of:

Carrying amount of machine	$155 000
Recoverable amount of the machine	$138 604
Impairment loss	**$16 396**

How should the machine be disclosed in the financial statements?

Following the recognition of the impairment loss, the machine would be disclosed within the financial statements as follows:

Machine, at cost	$180 000
Less: accumulated depreciation expenses	($25 000)
Less: accumulated impairment losses	($16 396)
Carrying amount of machine	$138 604

The accumulated impairment loss would be considered a contra account (in the same way that an allowance for doubtful debts and accumulated depreciation were considered to be contra accounts).

This means that following the recognition of an impairment loss, the assets will decrease (given that the balance of the contra account – accumulated impairment losses – will increase), and total expenses will increase as a result of the recognition of an impairment loss (meaning equity, which is A – L, will decrease). That is:

A	+	E	+	D	=	L	+	I	+	C
($16 396)		$16 396		–	=	–		–		–

The point to be made here is that, even though we measure assets using particular required measurement bases, at the end of each accounting period, we also need to ensure that the carrying amount of the asset does not exceed its recoverable amount. Again, the general rule is that the carrying amount of an asset – the amount attributed to it in the financial statements – should *never* exceed the asset's recoverable amount. In all those cases where the carrying amount of an asset does exceed its recoverable amount, an impairment loss must be recognised. This principle applies to all classes of assets.

Key concept

Recoverable amount is the higher of an asset's fair value less costs of disposal, and its value in use. For financial reporting purposes, the general principle is that no asset should be measured at an amount in excess of its recoverable amount.

To this point we have discussed the definition, recognition and measurement of assets. The next issue to discuss is the presentation of information about assets to the users of the financial statements.

LO9.6 Presenting assets in the balance sheet

As noted earlier in this chapter, the balance sheet is often presented in the form A – L = OE, although it is also sometimes presented in the form of A = L + OE. A balance sheet will be prepared at least once a year, but it can be prepared more often if required.

As we learned in Chapter 7, for balance sheet purposes, assets are generally subdivided into current and non-current assets, where current assets are those assets that are expected to be sold, consumed or otherwise used to create income within one year of the date of the balance sheet, or within the normal operating cycle of the business.

Current assets are typically separated from other assets because an organisation generally relies on its current assets to fund ongoing operations, and hence knowledge of the currently available resources is important. Examples of the current assets that appear on a typical balance sheet include:

- cash
- accounts receivable
- inventory
- prepaid expenses
- investments expected to be sold.

Current assets are more likely to be used to generate cash in the short run, and hence they provide some indication of future cash flows.

By classifying some assets as 'current', we are therefore able to identify which assets we are able to sell or liquidate more easily. This helps us to assess some aspects of the financial risk of an organisation, particularly when we compare the current assets with the current liabilities.

Since a balance sheet is prepared on the basis that it can be presented on just one page, the information is necessarily highly aggregated. As such, we will usually just be provided with aggregate figures for different classes of assets (refer back to **Exhibit 9.2** for BHP). If we want more information in respect of particular classes of assets, then we will need to look through the notes that accompany the financial statements. These notes will provide us with information about the accounting policies used to account for that class of asset, as well as information about the financial amounts attributed to different components of that class of assets.

For example, if we look at the balance sheet of BHP as at 30 June 2021 (see **Exhibit 9.2**), we will see that under current assets there is an amount attributed to inventory of US$4426 million, and that under non-current assets there is a further amount of US$1358 million attributed to inventory. However, apart from these totals, the balance sheet provides no further detail about inventory. To learn more, we need to refer to the various notes that accompany the balance sheet. In the case of BHP, if we look through the notes (see **Exhibit 9.4**), we will find information that might be of interest to us.

It is interesting that within the inventory note provided by BHP, the company specifically acknowledges the role that judgements and related estimates have on financial reporting. This is something that we have emphasised throughout this chapter.

Similarly, if we look at the balance sheet of BHP (see **Exhibit 9.2**), we find that within the non-current assets, there are intangible assets with a total monetary amount of US$1437 million. As was the case with inventories, if we want to know more about these intangible assets, then we need to refer to the notes that accompany the financial statements. In BHP's case, the notes disclosure is reproduced in **Exhibit 9.5**.

EXHIBIT 9.4 Disclosures about inventories as they appear in the annual report of BHP for the year ending 30 June 2021

Note 9: Inventories

	2021 US$M	2020 US$M	Definitions
Raw materials and consumables	**1904**	1787	Spares, consumables and other supplies yet to be utilised in the production process or in the rendering of services.
Work in progress	**3046**	2814	Commodities currently in the production process that require further processing by the Group to a saleable form.
Finished goods	**834**	711	Commodities held-for-sale and not requiring further processing by the Group.
Total (1)	**5784**	5322	
Comprising:			Inventories classified as non-current are not expected to be utilised or sold within 12 months after the reporting date.
Current	**4426**	4101	
Non-current	**1358**	1221	

(1) Inventory write-downs of US$58 million were recognised during the year (2020: US$37 million; 2019: US$16 million). Inventory write-downs of US$27 million made in previous periods were reversed during the year (2020: US$13 million; 2019: US$21 million).

Recognition and measurement

Regardless of the type of inventory and its stage in the production process, inventories are valued at the lower of cost and net realisable value. Cost is determined primarily on the basis of average costs. For processed inventories, cost is derived on an absorption costing basis. Cost comprises costs of purchasing raw materials and costs of production, including attributable mining and manufacturing overheads taking into consideration normal operating capacity.

Minerals inventory quantities are assessed primarily through surveys and assays, while petroleum inventory quantities are derived through flow rate or tank volume measurement and the composition is derived via sample analysis.

Key estimates

Accounting for inventory involves the use of judgements and estimates, particularly related to the measurement and valuation of inventory on hand within the production process. Key estimates, including expected metal recoveries and work in progress volumes, are calculated by engineers using available industry, engineering and scientific data. Estimates used are periodically reassessed by the Group taking into account technical analysis and historical performance. Changes in estimates are adjusted for on a prospective basis.

Source: BHP (2021), p. 151.

EXHIBIT 9.5 Disclosures about intangible assets as they appear in the annual report of BHP for the year ending 30 June 2021

Note 12: Intangible assets

	2021			2020		
	Goodwill US$M	Other intangibles US$M	Total US$M	Goodwill US$M	Other intangibles US$M	Total US$M
Net book value						
At the beginning of the financial year	**1 197**	**377**	**1 574**	247	428	675
Impact of change in accounting policies [(1)]	**–**	**–**	**–**	950	–	950
At the beginning of the financial year (restated)	**1 197**	**377**	**1 574**	1 197	428	1 625
Additions	**–**	**23**	**23**	–	98	98
Amortisation for the year	**–**	**(93)**	**(93)**	–	(118)	(118)
Impairments for the year [(2)]	**–**	**(52)**	**(52)**	–	–	–
Transferred and other movements	**–**	**(15)**	**(15)**	–	(31)	(31)
At the end of the financial year	1 197	240	1 437	1 197	377	1 574
– Cost	**1 197**	**1 506**	**2 703**	1 197	1 580	2 777
– Accumulated amortisation and impairments	**–**	**(1 266)**	**(1 266)**	–	(1 203)	(1 203)

(1) Intangible assets has been restated to reflect changes to the Group's accounting policy following a decision by the IFRS Interpretations Committee on IAS 12 'Income Taxes', resulting in the retrospective recognition of US$950 million of Goodwill at Olympic Dam. Refer to note 39 'New and amended accounting standards and interpretations and changes to accounting policies' for further information.

(2) Refer to note 13 'Impairment of non-current assets' for information on impairments.

Recognition and measurement

Goodwill

Where the fair value of the consideration paid for a business acquisition exceeds the fair value of the identifiable assets, liabilities and contingent liabilities acquired, the difference is treated as goodwill. Where consideration is less than the fair value of acquired net assets, the difference is recognised immediately in the income statement. Goodwill is not amortised and is measured at cost less any impairment losses.

Other intangibles

The Group capitalises amounts paid for the acquisition of identifiable intangible assets, such as software, licences and initial payments for the acquisition of mineral lease assets, where it is considered that they will contribute to future periods through revenue generation or reductions in cost. These assets, classified as finite life intangible assets, are carried in the balance sheet at the fair value of consideration paid less accumulated amortisation and impairment charges. Intangible assets with finite useful lives are amortised on a straight-line basis over their useful lives. The estimated useful lives are generally no greater than eight years.

Initial payments for the acquisition of intangible mineral lease assets are capitalised and amortised over the term of the permit. A regular review is undertaken of each area of interest to determine the appropriateness of continuing to carry forward costs in relation to that area. Capitalised costs are only carried forward to the extent that they are expected to be recovered through the successful exploitation of the area of interest or alternatively by its sale. To the extent that capitalised expenditure is no longer expected to be recovered, it is charged to the income statement.

Key judgements and estimates

Determining the recoverable amount of intangible assets may require significant management judgement. If a judgement is made that recovery of previously capitalised intangible mineral lease assets is unlikely, the relevant amount will be written off to the income statement. This requires management to make certain estimates and assumptions as to future events and circumstances, in particular whether an economically viable extraction operation can be established.

Where indicators of impairment exist for intangible assets, in the absence of quoted market prices, estimates are made regarding the present value of future post-tax cash flows. These estimates require significant management judgement and are subject to risk and uncertainty that may be beyond the control of the Group; hence, there is a possibility that changes in circumstances will materially alter projections, which may impact the recoverable amount of assets at each reporting date. The estimates are made from the perspective of a market participant and include prices, future production volumes, operating costs, tax attributes and discount rates.

Source: BHP (2021), p. 154.

Notice should again be taken of the discussion of key judgements and estimates, this time as reflected in **Exhibit 9.5**. As we have emphasised many times, the professional judgements made by managers and their accountants directly influence the financial statements that are ultimately presented to stakeholders. This is a fact that is unknown by many non-accountants. Indeed, the amount of judgement within financial accounting has led many people to refer to financial accounting as being more like an art than a science!

There are often over 100 pages of supporting notes to the financial statements providing additional details about other amounts presented on the balance sheet, and on the income statement. The 2021 Annual Report of BHP also provides a great deal of information about its efforts to address issues associated with sustainable development – something we discussed within Chapter 6.

Having now discussed issues associated with the definition, recognition, measurement and presentation of information about assets, we will now turn our attention to liabilities. Earlier in the chapter we addressed the definition of liabilities, so we will start our discussion here with a consideration of the recognition criteria for liabilities, before turning our attention to the measurement and disclosure of liabilities.

LO9.7 Recognising liabilities

The recognition criteria for liabilities are consistent with those for assets. As with assets, for a liability to be recognised in the financial statements, the item needs to meet the definition of a liability, which is:

> a present obligation of the entity to transfer an economic resource as a result of past events.
>
> Source: International Accounting Standards Board (2022a).

As we also know, an 'obligation' (as referred to in the above definition) is defined in the Conceptual Framework as 'a duty or responsibility that the entity has no practical ability to avoid'. That is, the obligation would be expected to be satisfied by the organisation at some time in the future.

Many liabilities recognised by organisations are legally enforceable. However, for a liability to be recognised, it is not necessary that the obligation be legally enforceable. What is required is that the organisation 'has no practical ability to avoid' transferring resources in the future.

When determining whether or not to recognise a liability, the intentions or actions of management need to be considered. Of relevance here is whether the entity has any realistic alternative to making the future sacrifice of economic benefits. If the situation implies that there is no discretion, then a liability would be recognised regardless of whether or not it is legally required to be paid. In cases where the managers of an organisation retain discretion to avoid making any future sacrifice of economic benefits, a liability does not exist and would not be recognised.

For example, the managers of an organisation might decide that they will offer to repair a defect recently discovered in some of their products, even though the nature of the defect is such that the purchasers of the product would not expect the organisation to do so. Until such time that the managers make public that offer, or commit in some other way to making the repairs, there is no present obligation, and no liability would need to be recognised.

Referring back to the definition of a liability, there are three important components, specifically:

- a liability represents a *present obligation* of the entity
- it arises from *past events*
- it results in an *outflow from the entity of resources embodying economic benefits*.

Apart from satisfying the definition of a liability, the recognition of a liability is – just like assets – directly linked to professional judgements about whether the information to be disclosed is 'relevant' and 'faithfully represents' the underlying obligation.

Relevance

As we already know, and consistent with our discussion pertaining to the recognition of assets, two important factors are:

- existence uncertainty
- assessments about the probabilities of an outflow of economic benefits.

For a liability to be recognised, it needs to be reasonably apparent that an obligation exists. This will be based on the available facts. If there is clearly little option to avoid making a future transfer of economic benefits to another party, then the level of existence uncertainty might be considered low, and the recognition of a liability would, subject to other criteria, be expected. Conversely, if the level of existence uncertainty is high, then it might be inappropriate to recognise the liability in the financial statements.

As an example of a situation where there might be a high level of existence uncertainty, we could consider the situation wherein an organisation has been told it is being taken to court for some alleged wrongdoing. Before the court case is held, it might be very uncertain that an obligation exists, and therefore it might be inappropriate to recognise a liability. As the Conceptual Framework notes:

> In some cases, it is uncertain whether an obligation exists. For example, if another party is seeking compensation for an entity's alleged act of wrongdoing, it might be uncertain whether the act occurred, whether the entity committed it or how the law applies. Until that existence uncertainty is resolved – for example, by a court ruling – it is uncertain whether the entity has an obligation to the party seeking compensation and, consequently, whether a liability exists.
>
> Source: International Accounting Standards Board (2022a).

In relation to considerations regarding the perceived probability of future outflows of economic benefits, the greater the uncertainties in terms of predicting the likelihood of any future cash flows occurring, the less relevant would be the recognition of a liability. For example, if an organisation has broken a particular law in terms of how it should be operating its business, but the managers are unable to determine the probability associated with whether they will have to pay a penalty, then no liability for the non-compliance would be recognised.

Faithful representation

As we know, another factor to consider when determining whether to recognise an asset, or liability, is measurement uncertainty. If there is a high level of uncertainty with regards to the amount of future cash outflows likely to occur in relation to a particular liability – meaning that a faithful representation of the liability is potentially not possible – then it might be inappropriate to recognise the liability in the financial statements. Using the example provided in the above paragraph, if the organisation knows that it will be prosecuted for failure to comply with particular laws, but managers are unable to reasonably determine the magnitude of the future fine, then because of the high level of measurement uncertainty, no liability would be recognised.

Therefore, various factors associated with both the probability of an outflow of economic benefits, and measurement uncertainty, require consideration when determining whether to recognise a liability – as they also do with the other elements of accounting.

Since the recognition of liabilities relies upon professional judgements about the probability and measurability of expected future cash flows, then, as with the other elements of financial accounting, some managers and their accountants might use potential difficulties, or uncertainties, associated with assessing probabilities, and reliable measurements as an 'excuse' not to recognise liabilities. Because professional judgement is involved, it can at times be difficult for other people to determine whether any failure to recognise liabilities is actually justified or not.

Within Australia, Ji and Deegan (2011) investigated actual instances where managers and their accountants might have opportunistically relied on apparent difficulties in determining reliable measurements of liabilities as a justification for not recognising liabilities. Through an analysis of various sources of information, Ji and Deegan identified a number of significant and severely environmentally contaminated sites that were controlled by Australian companies, and for which the respective organisations were under a clear legal obligation to remove the contamination and remediate the land. In many cases, the expected costs associated with cleaning and remediating the sites were tens or hundreds of millions of dollars. Once companies had been identified as having significant legal obligations (liabilities) to clean and remediate contaminated sites, Ji and Deegan then reviewed the respective companies' financial statements to see whether the liabilities were actually recognised within the balance sheet. Overwhelmingly, the authors found that the companies failed to recognise the liabilities in the balance sheet, with the companies noting that they did not do so mainly because they felt that they were unable to determine a reliable measurement for the future payments.

Ji and Deegan were of the opinion that the companies were potentially using the claims about measurement uncertainty as an excuse not to recognise the liabilities, and the authors questioned the credibility of the claims and arguments that the companies could not reasonably calculate a fairly reliable measure of the costs associated with fixing up the contaminated land. There is a general belief that managers, when given a choice, prefer not to disclose liabilities in the financial statements, as the greater the reported liabilities, the greater the perceived financial risk that is often associated with the organisation.

The results of the analysis in Ji and Deegan were very similar to the results of research into Canadian and US mining companies reported some years earlier by Repetto (2004), thereby indicating that, internationally, some managers and their accountants potentially use issues associated with measurement uncertainty and low probabilities of outflows of economic benefits as factors to justify the non-recognition of liabilities. In related research, McGregor et al. (2021) reviewed a sample of Australian companies listed on the Australian Securities Exchange (ASX) to see how particular companies were accounting for obligations they had to clean up sites that were known to be significantly contaminated with asbestos. In general, there was found to be a lack of recognition and disclosure in relation to the known obligations – results consistent with Ji and Deegan (2011) discussed above.

So the point of this discussion is that we need to be careful when relying on balance sheets, as it is always possible that certain liabilities have been omitted that arguably should have been recognised. The authors referred to above believed that they had justification for questioning why certain liabilities were not being recognised within the financial statements.

Whilst most managers and accountants would not opportunistically use the recognition criteria associated with relevance and faithful representation as a justification for not recognising liabilities within a balance sheet, we must nevertheless understand that when professional judgements need to be made using such criteria, then it is always possible that the judgement criteria will be used in a way that allows an organisation to present a more favourable picture of its financial position, and financial performance, than perhaps should be the case. This is an important point that we have now stressed a number of times.

Contingent liabilities

Liabilities that are not recognised because of perceived low probabilities assigned to future outflows of economic benefits, or because of perceived measurement uncertainties, might nevertheless warrant some form of disclosure within the notes to the financial statements. This is because knowledge of the 'potential' liabilities could be relevant to the users of the financial statements when they are making decisions about how to allocate their resources.

For example, an entity might, at the end of the accounting period (the reporting date), be subject to legal action that might ultimately cause a large outflow of economic benefits from the organisation, but it is not clear at the reporting date whether the legal action will be successful or not. That is, there is doubt about the associated probability of payment. There might also be some doubt about how much the organisation will need to pay to settle the legal action (thereby creating measurement uncertainty). In either case, a *contingent liability* would be considered to exist.

The managers of some organisations might also decide to guarantee the debts of another organisation. This can be quite common, particularly if the other organisations are somehow related. To enable an organisation to borrow funds, another organisation that is seen as successful, and stable, might agree to guarantee repayment of the debt in the event of the other organisation defaulting. Lending funds to the other organisation would therefore not be considered as being so risky in the presence of the guarantee, meaning that the organisation borrowing the funds should be able to attract the funds at a lower interest rate. In this case, the organisation that guarantees the debt would be liable *only* if the other party defaults on paying. That is, the existence of a liability would be contingent upon a future event (the other company failing) and so would be considered a contingent liability that warrants disclosure in the notes to the financial statements.

A contingent liability can therefore be defined as an obligation that is payable contingent upon a future event, or an obligation that has a low probability of culminating in an outflow of economic benefits from an organisation, and/or is currently not measurable with sufficient reliability.

Therefore, the general principle is that a liability does not meet the definition and recognition criteria necessary to be recognised as a liability if it:

- has a high level of measurement uncertainty
- has a low probability of culminating in an outflow of economic benefits; or
- is contingent upon the occurrence of a future event.

However, to the extent that the liability – if it occurs – would potentially be of significant monetary value, then some form of disclosure should be made within the notes to the financial statements. In effect, this provides a warning to the readers of the financial statements about the possibility (not probability) of a future significant payment being required and how much that payment could potentially be.

Our description of a contingent liability is consistent with how this term is defined within accounting standards. The relevant accounting standard (IAS 37: Provisions, Contingent Liabilities and Contingent Assets) states:

> A contingent liability is:
>
> (a) a possible obligation that arises from past events and whose existence will be confirmed only by the occurrence or non-occurrence of one or more uncertain future events not wholly within the control of the entity; or
>
> (b) a present obligation that arises from past events but is not recognised because:
>
> (i) it is not probable that an outflow of resources embodying economic benefits will be required to settle the obligation; or
>
> (ii) the amount of the obligation cannot be measured with sufficient reliability.
>
> Source: International Accounting Standards Board (2022b).

Pursuant to the relevant accounting standard (IAS 37 Provisions, Contingent Liabilities and Contingent Assets), when a contingent liability is disclosed within the notes to the financial statements, the contingent liability note should disclose the nature of the contingent liability and, where practicable:

a an estimate of its financial effect
b an indication of the uncertainties relating to the amount or timing of any outflow
c the possibility of any related reimbursement.

Financial statement readers should be diligent and know to look through the notes to the financial statements to see if there are some reported contingent liabilities. Again, they will not be recorded within the balance sheet, but knowledge of their existence could influence judgements being made about the organisation in question.

For an example of a real-world contingent liability note, refer to **Exhibit 9.6**, which reproduces the contingent liability note from the 2021 financial statements of BHP. For more on accounting for a contingent liability, see **Learning exercise 9.21**.

EXHIBIT 9.6 Disclosures about contingent liabilities as they appear in the annual report of BHP for the year ending 30 June 2021

Note 34: Contingent liabilities

	2021 US$M	2020 US$M
Associates and joint ventures [1]	1532	1314
Subsidiaries and joint operations [1]	1615	1534
Total	3147	2848

(1) There are a number of matters, for which it is not possible at this time to provide a range of possible outcomes or a reliable estimate of potential future exposures, and for which no amounts have been included in the table above.

A contingent liability is a possible obligation arising from past events and whose existence will be confirmed only by occurrence or non-occurrence of one or more uncertain future events not wholly within the control of the Group. A contingent liability may also be a present obligation arising from past events but is not recognised on the basis that an outflow of economic resources to settle the obligation is not viewed as probable, or the amount of the obligation cannot be reliably measured.

When the Group has a present obligation, an outflow of economic resources is assessed as probable and the Group can reliably measure the obligation, a provision is recognised.

The Group has entered into various counter-indemnities of bank and performance guarantees related to its own future performance, which are in the normal course of business. The likelihood of these guarantees being called upon is considered remote.

The Group presently has tax matters, litigation and other claims, for which the timing of resolution and potential economic outflow are uncertain. Obligations assessed as having probable future economic outflows capable of reliable measurement are provided at reporting date and matters assessed as having possible future economic outflows capable of reliable measurement are included in the total amount of contingent liabilities above. Individually significant matters, including narrative on potential future exposures incapable of reliable measurement, are disclosed below, to the extent that disclosure does not prejudice the Group.

Uncertain tax and royalty matters	The Group is subject to a range of taxes and royalties across many jurisdictions, the application of which is uncertain in some regards. Changes in tax law, changes in interpretation of tax law, periodic challenges and disagreements with tax authorities, and legal proceedings result in uncertainty of the outcome of the application of taxes and royalties to our business. Areas of uncertainty at reporting date include the application of taxes and royalties to the Group's cross-border operations and transactions. To the extent uncertain tax and royalty matters give rise to a contingent liability, an estimate of the potential liability is included within the table above, where it is capable of reliable measurement.
Samarco contingent liabilities	The table above includes contingent liabilities related to the Group's equity accounting investment in Samarco to the extent they are capable of reliable measurement. Details of contingent liabilities related to Samarco are disclosed in note 4 'Significant events – Samarco dam failure'.
Demerger of South32	As part of the demerger of South32 Limited (South32) in May 2015, certain indemnities were agreed under the Separation Deed. Subject to certain exceptions, BHP Billiton Limited indemnifies South32 against claims and liabilities relating to the Group Businesses and former Group Businesses prior to the demerger and South32 indemnifies the Group against all claims and liabilities relating to the South32 Businesses and former South32 Businesses. No material claims have been made pursuant to the Separation Deed as at 30 June 2021.

Source: BHP (2021), p. 184.

9.21 Learning Exercise

Accounting for a contingent liability

Scenario: At the start of the current accounting period, and in an effort to assist another organisation to attract funding at a lower interest rate, Mac Incorporated guaranteed a bank loan of Coy Company, meaning that should Coy Company default on paying the loan, then Mac Incorporated would have the obligation to make the payment. At the time Mac Incorporated guaranteed the loan, Coy Company was in a strong financial position, and this has been maintained. The loan is for $10 million, and is financially significant.

Issue: Should Mac Incorporated recognise a liability in relation to the loan guarantee? What disclosures should Mac Incorporated make in respect of the guarantee?

Solution: When answering these questions, consider the following.

What is the likelihood of an outflow of economic benefits?

On the basis of the information provided, it is currently very unlikely that any outflow of economic benefits from Mac Incorporated will occur as a result of the guarantee. Therefore, no liability will be recognised within the financial statements.

What disclosures should be made in relation to the guarantee?

However, details of the guarantee should be provided with the notes to the financial statements in the form of a contingent liability note. It is a contingent liability because the recognition of the liability is contingent on (dependent on) a future event – in this case, Coy Company being unable to pay its debts. The contingent liability note should disclose the nature of the contingent liability and, where practicable, an estimate of its financial effect, an indication of the uncertainties relating to the amount or timing of any outflow, and the possibility of any related reimbursement.

Key concept

A contingent liability exists when a possible obligation has arisen which is dependent upon a future event, or where there is a present obligation that is judged to have a low probability of leading to an outflow of resources, or which cannot be measured reliably. Contingent liabilities are not recognised for balance sheet purposes, but material contingent liabilities should be disclosed within the notes accompanying the financial statements. Readers of financial reports should make sure they are aware of the organisation's contingent liabilities.

LO9.8 Measuring liabilities

We will now return our attention to those liabilities that satisfy the required recognition criteria and which will therefore be included within the balance sheet. If it is determined that a liability should be recognised, meaning it meets the definition and satisfies the recognition criteria tied to considerations of relevance and representational faithfulness, then the next step (as with assets) is to determine how to measure the liability. Some liabilities will be measured at face value, whilst others will be measured at expected value, or present value. As with assets, this is called a *mixed measurement* approach.

There are different classes of liabilities, and we will discuss the measurement requirements relating to some of them in the following pages. Specifically, we will discuss how to measure:

- bank overdrafts
- accounts payable
- provisions
- corporate bonds
- lease liabilities.

Bank overdrafts

A **bank overdraft** is a line of credit designed to cover short-term cash flow shortfalls, and it occurs when money is withdrawn from a bank account and the available balance goes below zero. A bank overdraft will typically attract an interest expense. A bank overdraft is a current liability and will be measured at its face value – that is, at the actual amount by which the account has been overdrawn (the amount owing).

bank overdraft
A line of credit designed to cover short-term cash flow shortfalls that occurs when money is withdrawn from a bank account and the available balance goes below zero

Accounts payable

Accounts payable is a term that is often used to describe the amounts that are owed to suppliers of goods and services when purchases of those supplies and services are made on credit terms. Organisations will acquire goods on credit because it is often easier to do so than paying in cash. Also, by delaying payment for goods and services, this effectively provides short-term finance for the organisation, as the suppliers of the goods and services are, in a sense, providing the organisation with a short-term loan. Since such obligations are normally due for payment within 30 days or less, they will typically be presented as a current liability, and will be measured at their face value without discounting to present value. The general principle is that liabilities payable within 12 months are not discounted to their present value, but rather, are reported at their face value.

accounts payable
Used to describe the amounts that are owed to suppliers of goods and services when purchases of those supplies and services are made on credit terms

Provisions

As we explained in Chapter 7, the term *provision* is used in relation to liabilities that are subject to some uncertainty about the timing and/or amount of the future expenditure; for example, a provision for warranty repairs, employee benefits, or site rehabilitation. They relate to payments that the organisation is obliged to make in the future, but for which the actual amount, whilst reasonably measurable, cannot be measured with absolute precision.

The amount to be recognised for these forms of liabilities will be the best estimate of the expenditure required to settle the obligation. Where a provision is expected to be settled beyond 12 months, then there is a requirement that it will be discounted to its present value. The interest rate to be used will take into account the time value of money, and the risks specific to the particular liability.

For more on the calculation of a provision, see **Learning exercise 9.22**.

9.22 Learning Exercise

Calculation of a provision

Scenario: On 30 June 2026, Huge Power Company completes the construction of its electricity generating plant. In doing so, a great deal of forest has been removed and the character of the land has been greatly altered. The facility is expected to have an economic life of 25 years, after which time it will be closed. To gain approval from government to operate the site for 25 years, the managers of the company have agreed to a legal obligation that the site on which the electricity generating plant exists will be restored to its former character in 25 years' time. As at 30 June 2026, the best estimate of the costs to be incurred in 25 years to rehabilitate and restore the land is \$50 000 000.

Issue: You are required to determine the amount that should be recognised for the provision as at 30 June 2026. Given the risks associated with the project, and factors associated with inflation and so forth, it is determined that the appropriate interest rate to apply is 8 per cent. The present value of \$1 to be received in 25 years, discounted at 8 per cent, is \$0.1460.

Solution: Since the obligation associated with the provision is to be paid in more than 12 months' time, the provision is to be measured at the present value of the obligation. In this instance, the total amount that needs to be recognised in the financial accounts, and disclosed within the balance sheet, is \$50 000 000 × 0.1460 = \$7 300 000.

Corporate bonds

corporate bonds
Represent a form of borrowing (loan) undertaken by an organisation wherein there is documentation that identifies when the related borrowing (principal) must be repaid to the bondholders, what amount of interest shall be paid and when that interest must be paid

Larger organisations will, from time to time, issue **corporate bonds**, meaning that the organisation borrows funds (a loan) – often through a direct offer to the public (if it is a public company that is permitted by law to make such an offer to borrow funds). The borrowing organisation is then obliged to pay the bondholder interest on a periodic basis, and also to repay the principal at a later date, often referred to as the *maturity date*.

Corporate bonds that are due for repayment beyond 12 months will be measured at their present value, with the interest rate being the rate that the market expects to receive on such securities. Again, the general principle within financial accounting is that liabilities due to be paid beyond 12 months will be measured at their present value. This is consistent with our discussion of lease liabilities earlier in this chapter.

Lease liabilities

Earlier in the chapter we discussed how to measure a leased asset. When we recognise a leased asset we also need to recognise a related lease liability. The lessee – the organisation leasing the asset from another organisation – shall measure the lease liability at the present value of the lease liabilities that must be paid in the future. The interest rate to use in calculating the present value is the interest rate implicit in the lease agreement if that can be determined; otherwise the lessee shall use its normal borrowing rate.

Why do I need to know how different types of liabilities are measured?

Simply stated, to understand the numbers in the balance sheet we need to understand the measurement rules that generated them. The general principle we need to remember is that liabilities payable within 12 months will typically be measured at their face value whereas liabilities due beyond 12 months will be measured at their present value. This necessarily requires us to understand the meaning of 'present value'.

LO9.9 Presenting liabilities in the balance sheet

As with assets, for balance sheet purposes, liabilities are generally subdivided into current and non-current liabilities (although they can also be disclosed in order of liquidity, as discussed within Chapter 7).

Current liabilities are the liabilities of an organisation that are to be settled within 12 months, or within the normal operating cycle of a given organisation, whichever period is longer. Examples of current liabilities on a typical balance sheet include:

- bank overdraft
- accounts payable
- accrued expenses
- revenue received in advance
- dividends payable
- short-term loans.

Non-current liabilities typically include:

- loans of more than 12 months
- provisions where the expected settlement is more than 12 months away
- corporate bonds of more than 12 months
- lease liabilities of more than 12 months.

Knowing which liabilities might have to be paid within one year, or in the normal operating cycle of an organisation, is important to lenders, financial analysts, owners, and the managers of the organisation, particularly when compared with current assets. If the current liabilities exceed the current assets, this could be indicative of the possibility that an organisation will have difficulty paying its debts as and when they fall due.

The disclosure of information about an organisation's liabilities will also indicate the extent to which the organisation is funded by long-term borrowings. As we discussed earlier in this chapter, where a relatively high proportion of the funding of an organisation comes from loans (an external source of funding), this creates financial risks, as interest must be paid regularly and the principal must be paid too, regardless of what level of profits are being generated by the organisation. Managers need to find the appropriate balance between long-term finance and equity capital.

As you know, the balance sheet is typically only one page in length. Further details of the respective classes of liabilities can be found in the notes to the financial statements, together with details of the accounting policies used to account for the various classes of liabilities.

Having discussed assets and liabilities we will now turn our attention to equity.

LO9.10 Recognising and measuring equity

equity The residual interest in the assets of the entity after deducting its liabilities

As you know, **equity** is defined as the residual interest in the assets of the entity after deducting its liabilities. That is, equity = assets – liabilities. As a residual interest, then in the event of an organisation being wound up, all liabilities must be met before any distribution can be made to owners.

Defining equity as a residual interest is based on the perspective that equity cannot be defined independently of the other elements comprising the balance sheet, these being assets and liabilities. Therefore, assets and liabilities must be clearly defined – as they are within the Conceptual Framework – before a definition of equity can be made operational.

Given that equity is the residual interest in the assets of an entity, and given that the amount assigned to equity will equal the excess of the amounts assigned to assets over the amounts assigned to liabilities, the criteria for the recognition of assets and liabilities effectively provide the criteria for the recognition of equity. There is therefore no need for separate recognition criteria or measurement rules for equity. For example, if assets have been measured at $12 500 000 and liabilities at $10 000 000, then the measure of equity would simply be the difference between the two, which in this case would be $2 500 000.

LO9.11 Presenting equity in the balance sheet

The presentation of equity in the balance sheet will vary between different types of organisations. A sole trader might simply have a single capital account that would include the contributions made by the owner, plus the accumulated profits of the business, less the drawings made by the owner.

For a large company, the equity disclosures would be different. For example, the owners' equity section of a company will typically include:

- share capital
- retained earnings
- reserves.

Share capital

share capital The capital contributed by the owners (the shareholders) to the company in exchange for receiving shares in the company

Share capital represents the capital contributed by the owners (the shareholders) to the company in exchange for receiving shares in the company. For companies that are listed on securities exchanges, these shares might then be sold by some investors to other investors. When shares are then traded in the marketplace by one investor to another, this does not directly impact the company, as the company is not directly involved in this trading and the capital of the company does not change. This is because when shares are sold amongst investors, no money goes to the company, and no related monetary transactions are recorded by the company.

Retained earnings

Retained earnings in a company represent the sum of current and past profits and losses, less payments of dividends to shareholders, and less any transfers made from retained earnings to reserves. The balance of retained earnings therefore represents undistributed profits. Because dividends usually must be paid from retained earnings, the balance reported in retained earnings is often seen as a signal to readers of the financial statements as to the amounts potentially available to be paid as dividends in the future.

If managers are contemplating the need to 'lock in' funds – perhaps they want to expand into different operations and would like to retain funds rather than pay dividends – then a common practice is to transfer amounts from retained earnings (thereby decreasing one owners' equity account) to some reserve, which might be referred to as a *general reserve* (thereby increasing another owners' equity account).

retained earnings
The sum of current and past profits and losses, less payments of dividends to owners (shareholders), and less any transfers made from retained earnings to reserves. It is a component of equity

Reserves

Reserves, which are a component of equity, can take on a variety of types. One example is an asset revaluation reserve (also referred to as a revaluation surplus account). An asset revaluation reserve is created at the time non-current assets are upwardly revalued. That is, when we increase the non-current asset account as a result of a revaluation to its current fair value, we then increase an equity account called the asset revaluation reserve. Another example is a general reserve – as we noted above, general reserves are often created as a result of transferring amounts from retained earnings.

For a discussion of how to determine the balance of retained earnings and other equity accounts, see **Learning exercise 9.23**.

reserves
A reserve is a component of equity and is disclosed within the balance sheet. There can be many types of reserves, and a reserve can be created in a variety of ways, including as a result of a transfer from retained earnings or as a result of a revaluation on a non-current asset

9.23 Learning Exercise

Determining the balance of retained earnings and other equity accounts

Scenario: Anglesea Corp starts business on 1 July 2025, as a result of owners contributing $1 million in exchange for shares in the company. Its financial year ends on 30 June each year. The table below contains the results achieved, the dividends paid to owners, and the transfers from retained earnings made to reserves for the years 2026–2029.

Year ending	Profit or loss for the year	Dividend paid	Transfers to reserves
30 June 2026	Loss of $50 000	–	–
30 June 2027	Profit of $70 000	$10 000	–
30 June 2028	Profit of $140 000	$40 000	$50 000 to general reserve
30 June 2029	Profit of $50 000	$20 000	–

Issue: What is the balance of the respective equity accounts as at 30 June 2029?

Solution: Movements in the retained earnings account are as follows:

Year	Opening balance	Profit or (loss)	Dividends paid	Transfer to reserve	Closing balance
2026	0	(50 000)	–	–	(50 000)
2027	(50 000)	70 000	(10 000)	–	10 000
2028	10 000	140 000	(40 000)	(50 000)	60 000
2029	60 000	50 000	(20 000)	–	90 000

Therefore, the balance of the equity accounts at 30 June 2029 would be as follows:

Paid up capital (contributed on 1 July 2025)	$1 000 000
Retained earnings (see the calculation above)	$90 000
General reserve (transferred from retained earnings)	$50 000
	$1 140 000

One issue that often causes confusion for non-accountants is how an organisation can report in its balance sheet that it has various reserves, as well as retained earnings, but potentially have little or no cash. **Learning exercise 9.24** addresses this issue.

9.24 Learning Exercise

Does a reserve represent cash?

Scenario: Fairhaven Inc. has the following equity accounts as at 30 June 2025:

Paid up capital	$4 000 000
Retained earnings	$2 500 000
General reserve	$1 500 000
Total equity	$8 000 000

Issue: Does this mean that there is cash available to pay dividends to shareholders, or to make a bonus payment to employees for their hard work?

Solution: No, it does not mean this. To know whether there is cash available, we simply need to look at the account 'cash at bank'. The above accounts are equity accounts, not asset accounts.

Whilst accountants will understand that the existence of retained earnings and various reserves does not necessarily mean there is any available cash, non-accountants often do not understand this. For example, when we say that we are transferring an amount from retained earnings to a general reserve, we actually are not touching the cash at bank account. There is no movement of cash. Indeed, the organisation might have no cash. Rather, we will be increasing one equity account (general reserve) and decreasing another equity account (retained earnings), and our accounting equation will remain in balance.

As we have emphasised many times in this book, financial statements can create a great deal of confusion for people who are not trained in financial accounting. The general rule should be that if somebody does not have an understanding of financial accounting, then they should not mistakenly believe they can understand the contents of financial statements.

LO9.12 Further reflections on the balance sheet

As indicated many times throughout this chapter, accountants necessarily make many judgements about what might or might not happen in the future; for example, in relation to the following:

- Accounts receivable – many judgements need to be made in relation to the ultimate collectability of amounts owing by debtors, and this influences the allowance for doubtful debts and the doubtful debts expense.
- Inventory – many judgements need to be made about net realisable value, and such judgements will influence the carrying amount of inventory and any potential inventory writedown expenses.
- Property, plant and equipment – many judgements need to be made about assets' useful lives, residual values, patterns of use, recoverable amounts and fair values. All such judgements will influence reported assets as well as expenses such as depreciation expense and impairment losses.
- Liability provisions – many judgements need to be made about the amount of the ultimate payment, the timing of the payment, and the appropriate interest rate to apply. These judgements will impact both reported liabilities and expenses.

Different judgements will potentially create significant differences in the reported assets, liabilities, income, expenses and, therefore, equity. This creates potential problems when comparing the financial positions and financial performances of different organisations. Some differences in reported results might be due to different judgements being made by different teams of accountants.

Differences in reported results might also be due to different accounting methods being applied – for example, different organisations might measure their property, plant and equipment at fair value, whilst others measure their property, plant and equipment at cost. Therefore, readers of financial statements should carefully review the accounting policy notes that accompany the financial statements, as these can explain some of the reasons why one organisation's financial statements might be different to those of another organisation.

Even if we do not become accountants, we will nevertheless be exposed to balance sheets in our work, or by way of the news media. The language of accounting is everywhere! We should now be able to understand that reported total assets – a fairly central number for financial accounting purposes – does not represent the fair value of all the assets, or the cost, or replacement value of them. Rather, it is the sum of various different measurement bases applied to different classes of assets. Therefore, total assets is a number that needs to be reviewed/used with much care.

As you should also now appreciate, total assets as it appears in an organisation's balance sheet does not include many valuable assets. For example, most internally generated intangible assets – which might have great value – are not recognised within financial accounting (accounting standards prohibit their recognition), and hence do not appear on the balance sheet. Also, many other key resources of an organisation – such as its labour force, key intellectual capital, valuable customer and supplier networks, and so forth – are also not recognised within the balance sheet. This is because such resources are not controlled.

Therefore, the total resources of an organisation and its reported total assets (as determined by the financial accountants) can be quite different. Nevertheless, the accounting standard-setters must believe that the balance sheet provides information that satisfies the objective of financial reporting, which is to provide financial information about the reporting entity that is *useful* to existing and potential investors, lenders and other creditors in making decisions about providing resources to the entity.

As this chapter has also indicated, there is evidence that some managers, and their accountants, might opportunistically use arguments that they are unable to reliably measure a liability, or are unable to determine the probability associated with flows of economic benefits, so as to justify not recognising a liability.

What is being stressed is that we all need to be careful about how we use financial accounting reports, such as balance sheets. If we do not understand the rules of financial accounting (including knowledge of what assets do not appear, and the mixed measurement requirements for different categories of assets), the balance sheet can actually be a rather misleading, and perhaps dangerous, document to deal with!

For example, and as we have already noted, uninformed users of financial statements might incorrectly believe that total assets reflects the current fair value of all assets held by an organisation. You should reflect on how you would have previously interpreted the meaning of total assets before reading this chapter.

A last point we will make is that the financial statements are not the only source of information about an organisation. There are various government registers that include information about an organisation, and the news media is also often a useful place to find out information about larger organisations. Securities exchanges also provide various forms of information about organisations with securities listed on them.

For a concluding consideration of the value of an organisation, see **Learning exercise 9.25**.

Key concept

Many valuable resources that are relied upon by an organisation do not appear within the balance sheet.

9.25 Learning Exercise

A consideration of the value of an organisation

Scenario: You own 10 000 shares in Tea Tree Bay Company. The balance sheet shows that the total assets of the company are $250 million and the total liabilities are $100 million, meaning that the net assets (or equity) amount to $150 million. Ten million shares have been issued by the company, meaning that the net assets per share (often referred to as net asset backing per share) is $15 per share. This is calculated by dividing the net assets of $150 million by the number of shares, which is 10 million.

Dodgy Dealings Corporation is seeking to acquire a controlling interest in Tea Tree Bay Company and has offered all shareholders $30 per share. You think this is a great price as it is twice the calculated net assets per share.

Issue: What should you consider when evaluating this apparently generous offer?

Solution: In evaluating the Dodgy Dealings Corporation's offer, you should consider the following.

What other information is required?

Before deciding to accept the offer, more information is required. As a result of reading this chapter, you know that many valuable assets are not recognised within the balance sheet (in particular, many intangible assets will not be recognised), and many assets will be measured at cost which might be considerably lower than their fair value. Therefore, the financial value of the assets controlled by an organisation might be considerably more than the amount recognised within the balance sheet.

What are the liabilities of the organisation?

We would also want to carefully investigate the liabilities of an organisation. It is possible that liabilities might have not been recognised because managers made certain judgements about measurability and probability that other teams of accountants might disagree with.

Is the information in the balance sheet sufficient to make a decision?

It would be very unwise to accept the offer being made without gathering further information. The information included within balance sheets should be used with great care. Balance sheets can provide very useful information about the financial position of an organisation, but such information can and should be supplemented with information from other sources.

STUDY TOOLS

SUMMARY

This chapter has focused on the balance sheet and the elements of financial accounting that are reported on within the balance sheet, these being assets, liabilities and equity. We discussed the role of the balance sheet, and the typical format of a balance sheet.

We discussed the recognition criteria to be applied when recognising assets and liabilities, these criteria being linked to considerations of *relevance* and *faithful representation*. In relation to relevance, we learned that factors to consider before recognising an asset or liability include *existence uncertainty* and the *probabilities associated with the expected inflow or outflow of economic benefits*. In relation to faithful representation, we learned that accountants need to consider the extent of *measurement uncertainty* before they recognise an asset or liability within the balance sheet.

We stressed that the recognition criteria rely upon professional judgement and we noted the possibility that, from time to time, some managers and their accountants might opportunistically use the recognition criteria to produce financial statements that project a more favourable picture of an organisation's financial position and financial performance than would otherwise be the case.

We noted that different classes of assets will be measured using different measurement rules, and we referred to the problems this might create when trying to understand what total assets actually represent. We discussed the difference between tangible and intangible assets, and we explained the reason why many valuable intangible assets do not appear within balance sheets. We also explained that many of the assets that appear within balance sheets might be leased rather than owned. The various issues associated with the depreciation and revaluation of assets were also discussed, as was the general requirement that no assets should be shown in the financial statements at an amount that exceeds their recoverable amount.

We also explained the meaning of *contingent liabilities*, and the need for note disclosures to be made about them.

In relation to the measurement of liabilities, we learned that the measurement of liabilities due to be paid beyond 12 months should be done at their present value.

We concluded the chapter by emphasising the role of professional judgement in accounting, and we also emphasised the care that must be taken when reviewing balance sheets.

ANSWERS TO THE OPENING QUESTIONS

At the beginning of the chapter we asked the following four questions. As a result of reading this chapter, you should now be able to provide informed answers to these questions – ours are shown below.

1 What are the recognition criteria applied to the elements of financial accounting?

An item that meets the definition of an element of financial accounting should be recognised if the recognition of that asset or liability, and any resulting income, expenses or changes in equity, provides users of financial statements with useful information; that is:

a relevant information about the asset or liability, and any resulting income, expenses or changes in equity

b information that provides a faithful representation of the asset or liability, and any resulting income expenses, or changes in equity.

In determining relevance, factors such as existence uncertainty and the probabilities associated with the expected inflows or outflows of economic benefits need to be considered. When considering faithful representation, one factor to consider is measurement uncertainty.

2 Is it a requirement that all classes of assets be measured on the same basis?

No. As this chapter explains, different measurement rules will be applied to different classes of assets. For example, inventory is to be measured at the lower of cost and net realisable value, whereas property, plant and equipment can be measured at either cost or fair value. This means we have to be careful when considering the meaning of total assets.

3 If liabilities are to be paid beyond the next 12 months, are they to be measured at their present value?

Yes. Liabilities that are due for payment beyond 12 months are to be measured at their present value. Liabilities due for payment in 12 months or less can be measured at their face value.

4 How do we determine the 'recoverable amount' of an asset, and when do we recognise 'impairment losses' in relation to assets?

The recoverable amount of an asset is the higher of an asset's net selling price and its value in use. Value in use is measured based on the present value of the net cash flows expected to be generated by an asset. Net selling price is the current fair value of the asset less the costs of disposal. We recognise an impairment loss when the 'carrying amount' of an asset exceeds its 'recoverable amount'.

SELF-TEST QUIZ

Answers to this quiz appear in the Appendix of this book.

1 Why would an organisation prepare a balance sheet?

a For larger organisations, there is requirement within accounting standards to do so.

b It helps various stakeholders determine the ability of the organisation to pay its debts as and when they fall due.

c It helps various stakeholders understand the ability of an organisation to shift from its current operations to others.

d It helps various stakeholders determine what the sources of funds were that enabled the organisation to have the assets it has under its control at reporting date.

e All of these choices.

2 Which of the following is true about the balance sheet? The balance sheet:

a shows the fair value of all the assets held by the organisation at reporting date.

b reports an amount for total equity that corresponds to how much cash the organisation has under its control.

c provides a measure of the fair value of the inventory held by the organisation.

d shows a total for 'Total Assets' which was likely determined by applying a number of different measurement approaches for different classes of assets.

e All of these choices.

3 Which of the following is true about the assets reported in the balance sheet?

a Inventory as reported in the balance sheet is measured at the lower of cost and net realisable value.

b Property, plant and equipment can be measured at cost or at fair value, although it must be measured consistently within a particular class of assets.

c Financial assets, such as an organisation's investment in shares in listed companies, shall generally be measured at fair value.

d Investments in long-term government bonds shall be measured at the present value of the expected future cash flows associated with the bonds.

e All of these choices.

4 Which of the following steps must be satisfied before an asset can be recognised for financial accounting purposes?

a It must be determined that the resource is capable of generating future economic benefits that will flow to the organisation.

b It must be determined that the organisation has control over the resource as a result of a past transaction or event.

c It must be determined that information about the resource is considered likely to be relevant to the readers of the financial statements.

d It must be determined that information about the resource is likely to faithfully represent information about the expected future flows of economic benefits to be generated by the resource.

e All of these choices.

5 Inventory was acquired by an organisation at a total cost of $150 000, which includes $10 000 in import taxes and freight costs to the point of sale. It is expected that the inventory can be sold for $200 000 less associated advertising costs of $5000 and less other selling costs of $8000. At what amount should the inventory be measured for financial reporting purposes?

a $140 000
b $150 000
c $187 000
d $200 000
e None of these choices.

ONLINE RESOURCES

Accompanying the book is an innovative online case study that follows an organisation initially established by two friends, which grows into a large and successful company. Acquire this chapter's case study from your instructor.

CASE STUDY

Armadillo Surf Designs: To Kombi or not to Kombi, that is the question

In order to reduce courier costs, Armadillo Surf Designs (ASD) is purchasing its own delivery van in order to undertake local deliveries itself. The directors are considering two different options. The first is a brand-new delivery van, and the second is a vintage Kombi van which is considered iconic within the surfing community.

You will assist Archer, Maddie and Dillon to review the assets of ASD and provide the directors with relevant information to assist them to make a decision regarding the purchase of the delivery van. You will also identify potential contingent liabilities, and help Maddie to better understand the differences between retained earnings and the available cash in the business.

END-OF-CHAPTER QUESTIONS

9.1 What is the role of the balance sheet?

9.2 What does 'recognition' mean from a financial accounting perspective?

9.3 When should an asset be recognised for financial accounting purposes?

9.4 What type of account is 'retained earnings', and how is the balance of retained earnings determined?

9.5 Provide some examples of resources that would be of value to an organisation, but which would not appear in the financial accounts.

9.6 What factors require consideration in determining whether a faithful representation of an asset can be provided to the readers of the financial statements?

9.7 What are some of the measurement rules used for different classes of assets?

9.8 Because we measure different classes of assets in different ways, this creates what we might refer to as an 'additivity problem'. Briefly explain the nature of this problem.

9.9 What is depreciation expense?

9.10 When determining depreciation expense, we need to make judgements about three broad factors. What are these factors?

9.11 This chapter identified three methods that can be used to calculate depreciation expense. What are these methods, and when should they be used?

9.12 Inventory is to be measured at the 'lower of cost and net realisable value'. What does this mean?

9.13 What does an 'allowance for doubtful debts' represent, and how should it be disclosed?

9.14 Why could 'total assets' be a potentially misleading number for readers of financial statements who are not trained in financial accounting?

9.15 If the accountant uses fair value to measure assets, will this tend to have positive effects on both the relevance and faithful representation of the information being disclosed?

9.16 Property, plant and equipment are initially to be recorded at cost. What should this 'cost' include?

9.17 Evaluate the following statement: 'To determine the value of the organisation, we should look at the balance sheet'.

9.18 Should leased assets be shown within the balance sheet, and if so, how should they be measured?

9.19 An organisation owns an item of machinery that it acquired three years earlier for $700 000. The machinery has not been used for a year and it appears unlikely that the machinery will again be used within the organisation. Is the machinery an asset? Should the machinery be recognised within the financial statements?

9.20 If an accountant considers that the probability of an inflow of economic benefits from a particular resource controlled by an organisation is low, then how should the accountant treat any related expenditure made in respect of that resource?

9.21 From a financial accounting perspective, what does 'fair value' mean?

9.22 What is the 'recoverable amount', and why might an accountant need to understand what the recoverable amount of certain assets is?

9.23 When should an organisation recognise an impairment loss?

9.24 Would an impairment loss need to be recognised if an organisation already has a policy for depreciating its non-current assets?

9.25 What is a contingent liability, and when would one exist?

9.26 What disclosures should be made with respect to contingent liabilities?

9.27 Many senior executives of large organisations have no training in accounting. Should the senior executives of an organisation understand financial accounting?

9.28 If different teams of accountants were given details of all the transactions that an organisation was involved with in a particular accounting period, and each team was asked to separately prepare financial statements for that organisation, why would it be improbable that they would each generate identical financial statements?

9.29 In relation to the measurement of property, plant and equipment:

a Can the managers of an organisation make the choice to measure some classes of property, plant and equipment using the cost model whilst also measuring other classes using the fair value model?

b If some classes of property, plant and equipment are measured at cost and some at fair value, then what does the total of all property, plant and equipment actually represent?

c Will future depreciation expenses be affected following a revaluation?

9.30 Why might managers and their accountants revalue their property, plant and equipment to fair value?

9.31 How should accountants treat payments made for repairs and maintenance of property, plant and equipment?

9.32 What is a 'provision', when should it be recognised, and how should it be measured?

9.33 Is there a difference between how the liability for an account payable due in less than 12 months is measured, compared with how a long-term liability is measured?

9.34 Do we need recognition criteria and measurement rules for equity? Why or why not?

9.35 What is goodwill and how is it measured?

9.36 Can all of the goodwill of an organisation be recognised within the balance sheet?

9.37 If the retained earnings of an organisation are $2 000 000, and if a general reserve – which is part of equity – has a balance of $1 000 000, then the organisation must have at least $3 000 000 in cash. Is this statement correct?

9.38 Coogee Corp's balance sheet, as at 30 June 2026, shows total assets of $22 500 000 and total liabilities of $13 500 000. Does this mean that if all the assets of Coogee Corp were sold on 30 June 2026, and all the liabilities were paid on that date, then $9 000 000 would be available for payment to the owners? Explain your answer.

9.39 Dion Company purchases Nat Co for the following consideration:

Cash		$400 000
Land	Carrying amount:	$500 000
	Fair value:	$1 100 000

The Balance Sheet of Nat Co, at the date of acquisition, shows assets of $1 800 000 and liabilities of $850 000.

All the assets of Nat Co are fairly valued, except some land which has a carrying amount of $250 000 but has a fair value of $350 000. Nat Co has no contingent liabilities.

What is the value of goodwill acquired by Dion Company? Can this goodwill be shown in the balance sheet and, if it increases in value in future years, can it then be revalued?

9.40 Bombo Plc has $12 300 000 in accounts receivable as at the end of the reporting period. On the basis of past experience, the managers and accountants have determined the amount of debt that will not be collectable for particular periods for which the amounts have been owing to the organisation. The age of the various amounts owing, and estimates of their 'uncollectability', are as follows:

Period of time debt has been outstanding	Amount owing	Percentage of the debt that will not be collected
1–30 days	$8 000 000	1%
31–60 days	$3 000 000	3%
61–90 days	$900 000	10%
More than 90 days	$400 000	25%
	$12 300 000	

You are required to calculate the estimated amount for the allowance for doubtful debts.

9.41 Kembla Inc sells kite-boards. The following costs were incurred in relation to 100 boards that were recently acquired:

Amount paid to the supplier of the boards	$55 000
Import taxes duties	$5 000
Transportation costs to point of sale	$2 500
Costs of modifying kites prior to sale	$4 000
Advertising costs	$2 500
Sales commissions expected to be paid to salespeople who will sell the boards	$3 000
Costs of transporting boards to customers after a sale has been made	$1 000

You are to determine the cost of the inventory of kite-boards.

9.42 Drouyn Corporation acquires some machinery in exchange for the following:
- cash of $100 000
- some land with a cost of $220 000 but a fair value of $400 000
- legal and professional fees associated with the acquisition of the machinery: $1000.

What is the cost of the machinery to Drouyn Corp?

9.43 Angourie Corp has inventory on hand that cost $290 000. Investigations indicate that the best alternative for the company with respect to the inventory is to sell it to Crescent Ltd for $300 000.

Crescent Ltd requires that the inventory be modified at Angourie Corp's cost of $20 000. Crescent Ltd also requires Angourie Corp to deliver the products to its location as part of the sale agreement. These transportation costs will be $5000.

What amount should be reported in the balance sheet for the inventory of Angourie Corp?

9.44 If somebody was to say that the practice of financial accounting is more like *art* than *science*, what would they be implying?

REFERENCES

BHP (2021). *Annual report 2021*. https://www.bhp.com/-/media/documents/investors/annual-reports/2021/210914_bhpannualreport2021.pdf?sc_lang=en&hash=15F0B58BC27ADFA860F0BE29B61E199

International Accounting Standards Board (2022a). *Conceptual Framework for Financial Reporting*. https://www.ifrs.org/issued-standards/list-of-standards/conceptual-framework.html/content/dam/ifrs/publications/html

International Accounting Standards Board (2022b). IAS 37: Provisions, Contingent Liabilities and Contingent Assets. www.ifrs.org/issued-standards/list-of-standards/ias-37-provisions-contingent-liabilities-and-contingent-assets/

Ji, S., & Deegan, C. (2011). Accounting for contaminated sites: How transparent are Australian companies? *Australian Accounting Review*, 21(2), pp. 131–53.

McGregor, W., Potter, B, Soderstrom, N., Stevenson, K. (2021). Asbestos Contamination: Governance and Financial Reporting Issues in the Public, Private and Not-for-profit Sectors. *Australian Accounting Review*, 31(4), pp. 307–320.

Repetto, R. (2004). *Silence Is Golden, Leaden, and Copper: Disclosure of Material Environmental Information in the Hard Rock Mining Industry*. New Haven, CT: Yale School of Forestry & Environmental Studies.

CHAPTER 10

THE INCOME STATEMENT AND THE STATEMENT OF CHANGES IN EQUITY

LEARNING OBJECTIVES

After completing this chapter, readers should be able to:

- LO10.1 explain the role of the income statement
- LO10.2 explain that the numbers presented within an income statement are often used within the contractual arrangements negotiated between an organisation and different stakeholders
- LO10.3 clearly define income and expenses, and be aware that a focus on an accounting period's income and expenses can potentially encourage managers to focus upon short-term performance rather than longer-term performance
- LO10.4 explain when, and how, income and expenses should be recognised
- LO10.5 explain how income and expenses, and therefore 'profits', are measured
- LO10.6 understand that accounting rules will change over time, thereby potentially making the comparison of the current year's profits with past years' profits problematic
- LO10.7 describe how income and expenses are disclosed within an income statement and understand the difference between profit or loss, and total comprehensive income
- LO10.8 explain the role of the statement of changes in equity
- LO10.9 provide an opinion about whether profit, as determined by a financial accountant, is a good measure of an organisation's overall performance.

OPENING QUESTIONS

Before reading this chapter, please consider how you would answer the following five questions. We will return to these questions at the end of the chapter, where we suggest some answers.

1 If we sell an item of inventory to another organisation in exchange for an asset that is not in the form of cash, how do we measure the amount of income to be recognised?

2 Does 'control' of an asset have to pass to a customer before the related income from the transaction is recognised?

3 What is an 'inventory cost-flow assumption' and why do we need it?

4 Do the accounting rules embodied within accounting standards change across time? If they do, then what implications does this have for comparing the profits of one accounting period with the profits of another accounting period?

5 Is a profitable company necessarily a 'good company'?

Introduction

Organisational profits are generally considered an important indicator of how well an organisation is performing from a financial perspective. Unprofitable organisations will ultimately collapse if they fail to become profitable, and such collapse can have many adverse consequences throughout society. Focusing on projected and actual profit is an important component of the planning and control functions performed by management. Organisational profit also represents a performance measure that can attract a great deal of attention from various stakeholders throughout the community.

The news media, for example, often pay a great deal of attention to the reported profits of organisations, particularly our larger organisations. Whilst shareholders, and those owed money by an organisation (lenders and creditors), will typically be happy when an organisation reports higher profits, what we will show within this chapter is that other stakeholders within the community will, at times, see high reported profits as a signal that the organisation is somehow exploiting particular stakeholders, such as the employees, consumers, local communities or 'the environment'. Therefore, the amount of profit reported by an organisation creates various 'signals' for the community about how an organisation is performing, and can evoke different forms of reactions – both positive and negative – from community members.

Accounting numbers, such as profits, are used in many contractual arrangements that organisations negotiate with various stakeholders, such as lenders of funds, and with senior managers. Therefore, because various payments will be contractually linked to reported profits, there can be real financial (and social) consequences for particular stakeholders depending on the profits being reported.

The need to improve or maximise profits is also often used as a justification by management to reduce various expenses, and to change the nature of certain operations. However, this focus on profits and the reduction of expenses can, at times, cause various negative social and environmental impacts that do not get captured within the financial accounting system.

The point being made here is that information about organisational profits (and, therefore, about income and expenses) is used within organisations, and throughout society, in a variety of ways – ways that cause a variety of impacts. Therefore, it is very important that we understand how income and expenses are recognised and measured, how income statements are prepared and presented, and so forth, together with insights into the potential limitations inherent within the information provided in income statements. This chapter provides these important insights.

LO10.1 Overview of the income statement

In the last chapter, our focus was on one financial statement: the balance sheet. In this chapter, our main focus is the income statement, or, as it is also called, the statement of financial performance, or the statement of profit or loss. We will also discuss a third financial statement – the statement of changes in equity – towards the end of this chapter. In the next chapter, we will explore another commonly presented financial statement: the statement of cash flows. Together, chapters 9, 10 and 11 cover the four main financial statements that are prepared and presented by larger organisations.

As we learned in the last chapter, and in Chapter 7, assets, liabilities and equity are presented in the balance sheet. The income statement provides information about the income and expenses (and therefore, the 'profits', where profit equals income minus expenses) of an organisation for a period of time, which might be for a year, or for a shorter period of time. It does this by applying generally accepted accounting principles and, for larger organisations, by applying the many rules embodied within the numerous financial reporting standards that have been released.

The balance sheet and the income statement are both important reports, and one is not a substitute for, or more important than, the other. The income statement provides an indicator about how the wealth of an organisation (as measured in financial accounting terms) has changed during a period of time – known as the accounting period, or the reporting period – as a result of the operations of the organisation. This change in wealth is also reflected by changes that have occurred to the balance sheet during the accounting period.

Presentation of the income statement

The income statement can be presented in a variety of ways, but however it is presented, it will show the income less the expenses of an organisation for a period of time, thereby showing the profit or loss of the organisation. It is important that the title of the income statement clearly indicates the length of the accounting period to which it relates (also referred to as the reporting period). To evaluate the profit, the period of time must be clearly known. For example, a profit of $500 000 might be reasonable for a year, but the same result for a period of six months might be excellent.

One possible format of presentation of the income statement is provided in **Exhibit 10.1**, which arranges the expenses of the organisation by way of their 'function'. Consistent with the convention used elsewhere in this book, the numbers in brackets represent negative numbers. When an income statement is presented by function, cost of sales will be separately disclosed, and other expenses will be grouped together into their respective functions. For example, they will be grouped into those costs that relate to the distribution function, the administrative function, the finance function, and 'other' costs. We will consider other possible formats of presentation later in this chapter.

EXHIBIT 10.1 Possible presentation format of an income statement, with expenses arranged by function

Income statement for Collaroy Company for the year ending 30 June 2026		
	2026 $000	2025 $000
Sales revenue	3450	2900
Cost of sales	(1400)	(1200)
Gross profit	**2050**	**1700**
Other income	250	200
Distribution expenses	(400)	(350)
Administrative expenses	(500)	(450)
Finance expenses	(400)	(500)
Other expenses	(100)	(90)
Profit before tax	**900**	**510**
Tax	(300)	(210)
Profit for the year	**600**	**300**

The accountability model and the income statement

In providing our overview of the income statement, we can again use the accountability model we introduced in Chapter 1, which identified four key issues:

- why report?
- to whom to report?
- what to report?
- how to report?

Why report using the income statement?

The managers of an organisation might provide information about the financial performance of their organisation because they believe that they have an accountability to certain stakeholders in respect of the organisation's financial performance, or because they are under a legal obligation to report. For larger organisations particularly, it is a legal requirement to produce an income statement. Therefore, for managers of larger organisations, there is effectively no option – an income statement must be prepared, and presented. Larger companies – which must comply with accounting standards – are required to report information about their profit or loss every 12 months, and in some jurisdictions, there is a legal requirement for larger organisations to report every six months (in some other jurisdictions, there is even a requirement to report on profits on a quarterly basis, meaning every three months). However, even in the absence of legislative requirements, we would expect all profit-seeking organisations to produce income statements. An income statement can be produced for any time period required by management.

Both internal and external users demand information about an organisation's financial performance. From an internal perspective, managers will use information about income and expenses and profits in order to evaluate whether organisational achievements are consistent with prior plans and related budgets. The income statement therefore provides a mechanism for feedback about performance that can then be compared with the projected income statement that was generated as part of the budgeting process (we considered budgets in Chapter 4), thereby providing the basis for corrective action, if needed. This forms part of the planning and control cycle discussed in Chapter 3. Apart from comparing the profits with budgeted targets, comparisons can be made with the performance of other organisations in a similar line of business.

The managers of organisations might also have negotiated a number of contractual agreements that use financial accounting numbers within the contracts. For example, when an organisation borrows funds from lenders, such as banks, the managers often agree that the organisation's profits will stay above a certain agreed level, otherwise the organisation is deemed to be in technical default of the contractual agreement. If this occurs, then the lender could potentially insist on immediate repayment of the borrowed funds. Such a directive from a lender might demand that immediate repayment be made before the resources of the organisation fall lower, which would otherwise undermine the ability of the organisation to repay the funds to that lender.

Managers of organisations also often receive management bonuses that are linked to reported profits. Hence, the existence of contractual arrangements that use accounting numbers, such as profits, further means that the timing of the recognition of income, or expenses, will also be an important factor to managers of a reporting entity.

From an external stakeholder perspective, investors will want information about profits, and information about how those profits were derived, in order to determine, for example, likely future dividend payments (dividends are typically only paid out of accumulated profits, as shown within 'retained earnings'), and the ability of the organisation to continue operating and growing, thereby leading to growth in the value of the shares held by investors. Lenders and other creditors will want to know whether an organisation is likely to be able to repay amounts due, and this will influence whether credit is granted to the organisation in the first instance. If an organisation is not generating profits, then its ability to repay debts, and dividends, will tend to be questioned.

Employees and labour unions will also demand information about profits, as they might be interested in knowing whether it appears that an organisation is likely to be able to keep paying wages, and also if the organisation has the apparent capacity to pay higher wages to employees. Local communities, and other interest groups, will also want to know the level of profits being generated by an organisation, as this will provide an indication of whether – on the basis of the organisation's apparent financial capacity to assist – it appears that the organisation is doing enough for community-level projects, as well as being supportive of various social and environmental initiatives. It will also provide an indication of whether the organisation will be able to provide ongoing job opportunities for local workers.

Source: AAP Image/Joe Castro

Income statements can be important to different people for different reasons. Shareholders may welcome high profits, but labour unions and employees may see things differently if they believe they are being underpaid while a company generates huge profits that ultimately benefit shareholders.

Reporting profits, particularly high profits, might be welcomed by many stakeholders, including investors. However, consistent with our discussion above, high reported profits can also be used by some members of society as a basis, or 'excuse', for justifying calls for a reduction in the prices of an organisation's goods or services. As an Australian example, a newspaper article (Benns, 2017) made reference to the 'whopping profits' produced by the large national energy distributor Origin Energy, and how such profits were generated – in the opinion of a member of the Australia Institute (a think tank that researches a range of economic, social and environmental issues) – at the expense of 'long-suffering consumers', who were described as being 'ripped off' by the organisation. The argument in the article was that the organisation only needed to generate a 'reasonable return' and not the 'massive profit' that it reported. The large profit was used in the article as the basis for arguing that the company should reduce the energy charges imposed on customers to a level that enables the organisation to generate a lower but 'reasonable level' of profit. There are many instances in the news media where different stakeholder groups use high reported profits as a means of justifying calls for better deals for workers, customers, and the community.

Financial accounting profits, therefore, is a number that can be used in various forms of debate throughout society, which might or might not be in the best interests of the organisation.

Key concept

The contents of the income statement will be of interest to a diverse range of stakeholders.

Why do I need to know that a diverse group of stakeholders have an interest in the reported profits of an organisation?

By knowing this we are better able to understand the social role that financial accounting numbers can play. A diverse group of stakeholders do have an interest in the financial performance of an organisation because it provides a signal of how the organisation can, or should, address some of their concerns. For example, unions may want information about profits to justify claims for wages increases, customers might use high profits as a justification to demand a decrease in the prices of the organisation's products, investors might want information about profits to determine whether to invest further in the organisation, and so forth. It is important that we understand that, particularly for larger organisations, reported 'profits' can generate various reactions from stakeholders – some positive and some negative. This further emphasises to us that accounting is both a technical and a social practice.

To whom should the income statement be provided?

There are many different stakeholders who might have an interest in an organisation's profitability – investors, potential investors, investment advisers, creditors, lenders, potential lenders, employees, potential employees, employee unions, customers, government, news media, local communities, and so on. The larger an organisation, the greater its potential financial, economic and social impacts across society, and therefore the greater the likely number of stakeholders who are potentially impacted by the organisation, and who have an interest in its financial performance.

The corporations law in most countries recognises the possibility of these potential impacts, and makes it mandatory for larger organisations to publicly disclose information about their financial performance. Accounting profit is a number that influences many actions and decisions throughout society, again emphasising the point that we have stressed multiple times throughout this book: accounting is both a technical and a social practice. Society's members *do* react to accounting-based numbers such as profits (again, consider the newspaper article referred to above and the way in which profits were used as means to justify a claim that customers were paying too much for particular services).

For smaller organisations that are not compelled by law to make details of their financial performance publicly available, managers need to consider to whom they owe an accountability for their financial performance. The owners of an organisation would expect to receive information about financial performance, as would the major lenders of debt funds (who might also make the periodic receipt of information about financial performance a mandatory requirement of the loan). Employees would also expect to be provided with some information (perhaps not all the details) about the financial performance of an organisation, given that their ongoing employment relies upon the continued financial viability of the organisation. There could be many other stakeholders with an interest in the financial performance of a smaller organisation. However, so that competitors do not find out about specific aspects of the financial performance of an organisation (for example, information about the profitability of particular product lines), the release of financial performance information is typically restricted to some extent by the managers.

What should be reported on the income statement?

Organisations will report various income and expense items (together with comparatives for prior periods). What is reported will depend upon the information needs of managers (which is linked back to organisational goals and related strategies), as well as the information needs, and rights to information, of different stakeholders.

For larger organisations, accounting standards (which we have also been referring to as financial reporting standards) specifically require the disclosure of information about certain income and expenses, some of which we will discuss shortly. For smaller organisations, which are not required to follow accounting standards, we expect a degree of variation in how they report the information about income and expenses. The formats of the disclosure, and the items to be disclosed will also be influenced by the demands of those stakeholders who are closely linked to the organisation, such as the owner/managers and the organisation's major providers of finance (such as banks).

Managers' perspectives about what aspects of financial performance they have accountability for will also influence what financial performance-related information they disclose. For example, if managers believe they have a responsibility for financially supporting local sporting clubs, then they might also believe they have an accountability to make public information about the amount of monetary support provided to such clubs.

How should the income statement be presented?

For larger organisations, the information will generally be prepared in accordance with accounting standards and will be presented within an annual report, which will also include a balance sheet, a statement of cash flows, a statement of changes in equity, and supporting notes. For smaller organisations, managers can choose how best to disclose the information to stakeholders in order to provide the stakeholders with information that is relevant to the various decisions they make, as well as satisfying the qualitative characteristic of faithful representation.

As with the balance sheet (as discussed in the previous chapter), the income statement will typically be only one page in length. However, for larger organisations, it will be supported by many pages of additional information (as we have previously noted, sometimes over 100 pages of additional information will accompany the financial statements), which we refer to as the notes to the financial statements. These notes will, amongst other things, provide additional information about particular amounts shown in the income statement, including information about the accounting policies used to calculate the various monetary amounts attributed to different income and expense items.

The income statement and the news media

Rightly or wrongly, profit is the aspect of corporate performance that seems to draw the most stakeholder attention. The profits or losses of our larger companies make 'big news', being projected as some form of objective measure of organisational performance. The news stories, almost without exception, make no reference to the actual accounting methods being used, or the accounting policies adopted by the respective organisations. Profit is therefore projected as some form of objective reality.

However, as we know, profit is directly influenced by professional judgement, and by the choices of accounting methods and policies made by managers and their accountants, such that, even if different teams of accountants were provided with the same information, they would produce financial statements that could show very different measures of profits. Also, reported profits of different organisations will typically be compared directly within news media stories without any form of adjustments, despite the fact that different accounting policies might be used by the different organisations.

The news media rarely reports stories about the total assets of an organisation, or about the social or environmental performance of an organisation (unless some social or environmental catastrophe occurs). Corporate profits really do tend to be *the focus* of much community attention. In **Learning exercise 10.1**, we explore the reasons why the news media pay so much attention to corporate profits.

Key concept

Reported profits is a number that many stakeholders, including the news media, focus upon. Reported profits are often used by different stakeholder groups to justify particular actions being taken against an organisation.

10.1 Learning Exercise

Media attention to corporate profits

So why do the reported profits of our largest companies attract so much media publicity?

Whenever our largest companies disclose their annual profits, mention of them is typically made in the print and online news media, radio, and on television. The community, and the authors of the news pieces, obviously see reported profits as an important aspect of performance, one that is perceived as providing some form of truth about the results of managers' strategies and choices. However, as we know, measures of assets, liabilities, income and expenses are influenced by many judgements about such issues as existence uncertainty, measurement uncertainty and probability, as well as by the different accounting policy choices made by managers and their accountants.

Reported profits are seen as important, as they in turn provide an indication of an organisation's ability to pay dividends and wages; to grow, thereby generating further jobs growth and investment; to support community projects; to pay taxes; and so forth. Many individuals' livelihood and prosperity are linked to corporate financial performance. If an organisation is generating losses, this might be seen as an indicator that the organisation will need to cut back its workforce, pay less taxes to the government, or reduce the amount of goods and services it is acquiring from local suppliers.

Whilst financial performance is important, it is only one aspect of performance. It is a shame that the media do not pay as much, if not more, attention to the social and environmental performance of organisations. If they did, then perhaps the planet would not be in the poor state that it is in. Do you agree?

LO10.2 The use of accounting numbers in contractual arrangements negotiated by an organisation

As we know, when organisations need funding for particular activities, they often go to banks or other financial institutions (which we can refer to as lending bodies). These funds, which will be recognised as liabilities and create an external claim against the assets of an organisation, will need to be repaid at a later date, and require interest expenses to be paid throughout the term of the loan.

Organisations often include financial accounting numbers in the various contractual agreements that they negotiate with stakeholders. For example, when borrowing funds from lenders (such as banks and other financial institutions), the managers of an organisation will often contractually agree to clauses (often referred to a *debt covenants*) that require:

- the company to maintain certain levels of profits; for example, there might be an agreement that profits must exceed total interest expenses by, say, four times those interest expenses (often referred to as an *interest coverage clause*);
- debt levels to be kept below a certain level of total assets; for example, that total debt not become more than 50 per cent of total assets (or some other measure of assets)
- the company to maintain total equity above a specific monetary amount.

The reason why managers agree to such restrictive clauses within lending agreements – which, as we now know, are referred to as debt covenants – is that agreeing to these requirements tends to reduce the financial risks to the lenders, and therefore enables the organisations (the borrowers) to attract funds from those lenders at lower costs (lower interest rates) than might otherwise be possible.

If the borrowing organisation fails to comply with the agreed contractual requirements (the debt covenants), then this is referred to as the organisation being in *technical default* of the lending agreement. If this occurs, it can provide the lender (the bank or other financial institution) with the right to seize assets, including cash, from the organisation in order to pay for the amount that was borrowed. By establishing the restrictive debt covenant, the lending body is able to take this action potentially before the borrowing organisation actually collapses, thereby increasing the likelihood that the lending body will be repaid.

To further reduce the risks of the organisation that is lending funds to the organisation, that loan provider will insist that the financial accounting numbers being used for contractual purposes be audited by an independent auditor (otherwise, the managers might manipulate the accounting numbers so as to avoid being in technical default of the contractual agreement). Where financial accounting numbers are used in debt contracts, this gives managers further reasons to focus on the financial performance of their organisation – and therefore on profits – so as to avoid breaching the requirements of particular debt covenants. This might increase their motivation to manipulate these numbers, thereby providing further justification for having the financial statements audited before they are released to interested stakeholders.

As we have explained elsewhere, it is also common for organisations to include accounting numbers in the management bonus plans negotiated with managers.

Why do I need to know that profit-related numbers are used in many contractual arrangements that have been negotiated with stakeholders?

To understand the context of reported numbers – such as profits – we need to know how they are then used throughout society. We know that profit-related numbers are used in borrowing agreements, in management bonus plans, in various government funding agreements and so forth. The reported profits of an organisation therefore can influence the operations and viability of an organisation as a result of these profit-related contractual arrangements. Knowing this in turn provides further explanation for why managers care so much about the 'profit' they report, and also why they might have incentives, at times, to be 'creative' with their accounting.

LO10.3 Definitions of income and expenses

The income statement or as it is also called, the statement of profit or loss, provides details of the income and expenses of an organisation, and therefore the profit of the organisation. So income and expenses require clear definitions. As we learned in Chapter 7:

> Income is increases in assets, or decreases in liabilities, that result in increases in equity, other than those relating to contributions from holders of equity claims.
>
> Source: International Accounting Standards Board (2022a).

To understand the meaning of 'income', we therefore need to understand the meanings of 'assets' and 'liabilities', which we have discussed in previous chapters. Given that the definition of income is directly related to assets and liabilities, the measurement of income will *also* therefore be directly influenced by how assets and liabilities are measured. A change in how assets and liabilities are measured will change the amount of income and expenses being recognised, and therefore will create changes in reported profits.

Expenses are defined in the Conceptual Framework as follows:

> Expenses are decreases in assets, or increases in liabilities, that result in decreases in equity, other than those relating to distributions to holders of equity claims.
>
> Source: International Accounting Standards Board (2022a).

Again, and as with income, to understand the meaning of 'expenses', we need to understand the meaning of 'assets' and 'liabilities'.

Applying the above definition of expenses to the activities of a little corner shop, when that shop sells some of its stock to a customer, the associated expense is the reduction in the asset brought about by removing the inventory item from the assets of the shop (thereby reducing the total assets of the shop).

As we can see from the definition provided above, to qualify as income or expenses, the changes in assets or liabilities must have the effect of changing equity; that is:

$$OE_{\text{end of period}} = OE_{\text{beginning of period}} + (\text{income} - \text{expenses}) + \text{contributions} - \text{distributions}$$

Therefore, transactions such as the purchase of assets or the issuance of debt are not considered income because they do not result in an increase in equity. Purchasing assets with cash simply involves substituting one asset for another, whereas borrowing cash increases both assets (cash), and liabilities, with no direct effect on equity.

The Conceptual Framework for Financial Reporting does not include profit (or loss) as one of the elements of financial accounting. As we know, the five elements are assets, liabilities, income, expenses and equity. Profit is simply the difference between income and expenses, both of which are defined, and hence there is no need for separate recognition criteria for profits.

Potential focus on short-term performance

Income, expenses and profit are calculated for a period of time, and therefore – unlike the balance sheet – the income statement does not present a snapshot as at a particular point in time. It provides information about performance for a period of time.

Because profit is calculated for a relatively short period of time (commonly 12 months or six months), this provides some encouragement for managers to focus on short-term performance rather than long-term performance. This is not always in the longer-term interests of the owners of an organisation, and can potentially create some dysfunctional behaviour. But given the way in which the news media and other stakeholders focus on reported profits, it is potentially understandable.

As we have emphasised, the news media often give much publicity to profits – particularly those of our larger corporations – and they highlight instances where profits have fallen or are lower than expectations. Indeed, the share market often reacts negatively if an organisation reports a profit that is lower than that anticipated by the market. The negative share market reaction will be in the form of a drop in the share price of the company. The short-term focus of managers will be further exacerbated if those managers are paid bonuses that are linked to short-term measures of performance, such as accounting profit.

One industry that in recent times has been subject to much criticism globally for its short-term focus on profits has been the banking industry. In Australia, for example, there was recently a large-scale inquiry into the banking industry. The Royal Commission into Misconduct in the Banking, Superannuation and Financial Services Industry was established in 2017 and it released its final report in 2019 (see https://financialservices.royalcommission.gov.au). In that report, it was specifically noted that 'the pursuit of profit at the expense of basic standards of honesty' was apparent across the industry. The report also noted that profits were, at times, prioritised above compliance with laws, and above the consideration of customer rights.

Profits – an accounting measure – are therefore widely seen as a key indicator of the success or failure of an organisation. However, as we stressed in the earlier parts of this book, not all organisations have the generation of profits as their key mission or objective.

Key concept

When managers are required to report profits for a period of time – such as a year – that can motivate them to adopt short-term strategies that maximise profit for that period of time, but which might not be in the longer-term interests of their organisation.

Focus of not-for-profit organisations

Not-for-profit organisations, such as environmental groups, labour unions, animal welfare associations and some educational organisations, might be more concerned with objectives other than profits, such as fulfilling particular social and/or environmental needs. Their focus might be more on ensuring that they have sufficient sources of funds than on trying to maximise any measure of profits, or another measure of financial performance. That is, not-for-profit organisations have different responsibilities. They are not normally expected to generate profits but instead provide much-needed services. Therefore, as their responsibilities are different, their accountabilities, including their financial accountabilities, should also be different. They would nevertheless be expected to be accountable for various aspects of their financial performance, including inflows of financial support, expenses being incurred, and the overall cash flows of the organisation.

Also, we need to appreciate that even in the case of profit-seeking organisations, there are many important aspects of performance that are not financial. That is, we must always remember that financial performance measures, such as profits, are not comprehensive measures of organisational performance. Social and environmental aspects of performance *should* also be relevant. We will return to this point later in this chapter.

For a discussion of the role of accounting standards and principles regarding providers of public services, see Learning exercise 10.2.

10.2 Learning Exercise

The use of accounting standards and generally accepted financial accounting principles in organisations that provide public services

Government organisations, such as museums, art galleries and hospitals, often produce financial statements using accrual accounting, and which are in compliance with accounting standards. In doing so, they provide information about their financial performance and financial position. Let us consider if this focus on financial performance is appropriate, or if it could take away attention from the main functions they are trying to achieve.

Many people argue that it is inappropriate to require some organisations, particularly those that provide a community service, to produce reports that identify and highlight financial profits. Museums, art galleries and hospitals are in existence to satisfy important social requirements, and whether they produce various levels of profits should not, ideally, be a central concern. Arguably, they should use their financial resources wisely, and in a way that maximises the positive community benefits they generate. So therefore, even though it is questionable whether they should be calculating profit, it would seem appropriate for such organisations to provide some accounts of how they have used the funds they have received, and the level of efficiency with which the funds have been used.

Over recent decades, many government-owned organisations have been required to embrace financial accounting systems that calculate measures such as profits. Previously, government departments typically accounted for their operations on a cash basis, with very limited use of accrual accounting, and limited attention to profitability. However, throughout the world, greater focus is being placed on the profitability of government departments, and like large businesses, they are now required to follow many accounting standards.

Supporters of this approach argue that it forces managers to be more *accountable* for their organisation's, or department's, financial performance. However, others argue that it is highly inappropriate for institutions such as government-controlled employment agencies, hospitals, museums, art galleries and national parks to be judged on their ability to generate profits – in fact, focusing on accounting profits potentially distracts them from pursuing the proper goals of their organisations: the provision of necessary social services. It might also encourage the managers to have a short-term focus, when the community really needs them to have a longer-term focus. As one example, it is often argued that the large number of homeless people on city streets is due to the fact that organisations such as hospitals are increasingly being judged on the basis of their financial performance. This encourages the hospitals to limit the help provided to many people, including those with mental-health problems, many of whom will fail to cope with real-world problems and pressures, and who ultimately end up back on the streets. In the longer run, this is probably shifting costs – both financial and social costs – to other organisations, and other stakeholders within the community.

There continues to be much debate in the accounting literature about the appropriateness, or otherwise, of requiring organisations that fulfil important roles in society to produce financial statements that comply with accounting standards that were designed primarily for organisations that have the generation of profits as their main focus.

Key concept

Not-for-profit organisations should not normally be evaluated in terms of 'profits'. They tend to have different responsibilities and accountabilities other than generating a profit.

The subdivision of income into revenues and gains

Some organisations further subdivide income into two broad categories: revenues and gains. Traditionally, the term **revenue** has been used to refer to the main areas in which an organisation generates its income – for example, sales revenue or consulting revenue. That is, revenue is seen as arising from the 'ordinary activities' of an organisation.

revenue
Income that is derived in the course of the ordinary activities of an organisation

Gains, on the other hand, represent other items that meet the definition of income and may, or may not, arise in the course of the ordinary activities of an entity. When gains are recognised in the income statement, they are usually displayed separately because knowledge of them is useful for the purpose of making economic decisions.

gains
Income sourced from areas that may or may not relate to an organisation's main activities

The differentiation between revenues and gains is based on some degree of professional judgement, and it is very possible that something that is deemed a gain by one accountant might be deemed revenue by another. The classification of an item as revenue or a gain will not affect the total of profit or loss, as they are both included within income. So, at this point, we just need to appreciate that some organisations will divide their income into two components: revenues and gains. In this text we tend to use the terms 'income' and 'revenue' interchangeably, particularly when the income in question comes from the ordinary activities of an organisation. When income is generated as a result of selling goods and services to customers, then we often call this 'revenue' (although, as just indicated, we could also call it 'income').

LO10.4 Recognising income and expenses

As you know, financial statements are typically prepared on an accrual basis. Indeed, larger organisations are required by accounting standards to use the accrual basis of accounting. This means that income is recognised when it is earned, and expenses are recognised when the expense is incurred. This can be quite different to when the related cash flows occur.

By contrast, many smaller organisations prepare their financial statements on a cash basis, meaning that they recognise expenses when they are actually paid, and recognise income when the related cash is actually received, not beforehand. Calculating profits on a cash basis tends to provide a poor account of the financial performance of an organisation, but it is easier to do, and this can be attractive to smaller organisations. **Learning exercise 10.3** emphasises the difference between profits and cash flows.

10.3 Learning Exercise

A simple illustration of the difference between profits and cash flows

As you would appreciate, the receipt of cash and the related provision of a good or service by an organisation to its customers might not match. Similarly, the payment of cash and the incurring of expenses might not match. There are also many transactions that affect cash but which do not impact income or expenses – for example, the acquisition of property, plant and equipment with cash, cash contributions and distributions from/to owners, and the repayment of debt, all impact cash but will not impact income or expenses.

Scenario: Jerry Lopez starts Lightning Bolt Inc on 1 January 2025 by contributing $200 000 in cash. During the year, the following transactions and events occur:

- Total sales of $1 million are made on credit terms to customers (these sales are recognised as income, even though no cash is received at the point of sale).
- By the end of the year, debtors have paid $900 000 of the amount due. The rest of the customers are expected to make their payments in the next month, so no allowance for doubtful debts has been created due to a very stringent credit-granting policy (this cash received from debtors is not income when the cash is received, as we recognised the income when the sale was made earlier).
- To enable the sales to be made, inventory that cost the company $600 000 is sold to the customers. At the end of the year, $50 000 is still owing to suppliers for the inventory purchased (this means that only $550 000 has been paid to the creditors).
- Plant and equipment with a cost of $150 000 is acquired with cash on 1 January 2025. It is expected to have a useful life of 10 years and to have no residual value. (The acquisition of the plant and equipment is not a cost. Rather, we recognise some depreciation expense, which in this case would be $15 000 per year using the straight-line method of depreciation.)
- Some land is acquired with cash for $290 000 on 23 December 2025 as a site for a future factory. (This transaction does not affect profits. It is an exchange of one asset – cash – for another asset – land.)
- Lightning Bolt pays salaries of $100 000 during the year and has $20 000 wages payable at the end of the year (the total salaries expense therefore is $120 000).

Issue: You are required to calculate Lightning Bolt Inc's profit for the year to 31 December 2025, and the closing cash balance on 31 December 2025. You are also to provide a statement of cash flows for the year ending 31 December 2025 (we provided examples of simple statements of cash flows in Chapter 7).

Solution

Income statement for Lightning Bolt Inc for the year ending 31 December 2025	
Sales	$1 000 000
Less: cost of sales	($600 000)
Gross profit	**$400 000**
Salaries	($120 000)
Depreciation	($15 000)
Profit	**$265 000**

To calculate the closing cash balance, we can use the following table:

Opening cash	$0
Cash from customers	$900 000
Salary payments	($100 000)
Payments to creditors for inventory	($550 000)
Purchase of plant and equipment	($150 000)
Purchase of land	($290 000)
Contribution from owner	$200 000
Cash as at 31 December 2025	**$10 000**

From the above table, we can now prepare the statement of cash flows.

Statement of cash flows for Lightning Bolt Inc for the year ending 31 December 2025		
Cash flows from operating activities		
Cash from customers	$900 000	
Salary payments	($100 000)	
Payments to creditors for inventory	($550 000)	$250 000
Cash flows from investment activities		
Purchase of plant and equipment	($150 000)	
Purchase of land	($290 000)	($440 000)
Cash flows from financing activities		
Contribution from Jerry Lopez		$200 000
Cash flows for the year		**$10 000**
Opening cash as at 1 January 2025		$0
Cash as at 31 December 2025		**$10 000**

As you can see here, the profit of a business can be quite different to the net cash flows that are generated. In this case, the company generated sound profits of $265 000 but it has very little cash (only $10 000). It would therefore be in potential trouble if an unexpected cost arose that needed to be paid for immediately. To survive, it might need to borrow funds, or ask for additional equity contributions from the owner. There are many instances where profitable organisations have collapsed because of poor cash management. In this example, the organisation might have been well advised to defer the acquisition of the land, or it could have considered leasing the property, plant and equipment, or taking out a loan to fund the purchase of its non-current assets.

As we learned in Chapter 9, whether an item is recognised within the financial statements depends on whether the information about the item is judged to be relevant and representationally faithful. We have also learned that the recognition of income and expenses is directly related to whether there has been a change in assets and/or liabilities during the accounting period. As the Conceptual Framework states:

> (a) the recognition of income occurs at the same time as:
> (i) the initial recognition of an asset, or an increase in the carrying amount of an asset; or
> (ii) the derecognition of a liability, or a decrease in the carrying amount of a liability.
>
> (b) the recognition of expenses occurs at the same time as:
> (i) the initial recognition of a liability, or an increase in the carrying amount of a liability; or
> (ii) the derecognition of an asset, or a decrease in the carrying amount of an asset.

Source: International Accounting Standards Board (2022a).

As we also emphasised in Chapter 9, the recognition of assets and liabilities (which in turn impacts the recognition of income and expenses, and therefore profits) relies on judgements about:

- the probabilities associated with expected flows of economic benefits
- the level of uncertainty associated with measurement of the associated economic benefits (which is referred to as measurement uncertainty).

For example, if the probability of an expected inflow of economic benefits is judged to be very low, or if there is a high degree of measurement uncertainty about the value of certain economic benefits to be received, then an increase in assets should not be recognised, with the consequence that income will not be recognised.

Decisions about probability and measurability can be rather subjective at times, and different accountants frequently make different judgements (so again, they will not all record the same profits, assets and/or liabilities). As we have emphasised numerous times, these judgements might not always be made on a purely objective basis – occasionally, some managers and their accountants will let self-interest influence their choice of accounting policies and methods. That is, they might employ 'creative accounting'.

Where managers and their accountants make particular judgements in order to generate the desired financial results, this is often referred to as *earnings management*. It is done so as to influence the perceptions some stakeholders might have about an organisation, or to impact certain outcomes that are linked to financial accounting numbers. (For a broader discussion of why managers care when income is recognised, see **Learning exercise 10.4**.)

10.4 Learning Exercise

The decision as to when to recognise income

Let us consider why managers, especially those who work within large organisations, might care when income is recognised.

Obviously, whether and how income is recognised will in turn impact profits. From an objective perspective, managers should be concerned that income is recognised when it has actually been earned (and when there have been related changes in assets and/or liabilities).

In terms of why managers might care about when income is recognised, there are many reasons, including the following:

- The news media pay a lot of attention to the profits of larger organisations. Many stakeholders have an interest in these profits and, rightly or wrongly, interpret them as a key measure of the 'success' of an organisation. Therefore, because of the attention managers believe profit attracts, they might prefer to disclose higher profits. The higher profits might indicate that managers have been performing their duties well. However, as we have already noted, high profits can be used by some stakeholders as an excuse to argue that the organisation is making excessive profits, and that it should decrease the prices it charges for its goods or services, and/or increase the payments it makes to its employees.
- It is common for managers to receive bonus payments that are linked to profits. For example, the managers might receive a fixed salary plus a bonus that comprises a specified percentage of profit. Because managers would prefer to receive a bonus now rather than later (the present

value of a dollar received now is greater than the present value of a dollar received later), then managers who have been offered an accounting-based (profit-based) bonus will typically prefer that income (and profits) be recognised earlier than later. However, if the managers believe they will not reach the target level of profits required for a bonus to be paid, they might prefer to defer the recognition of income until the following year, so as to help reach next year's target and enable a bonus to be paid.

- Organisations that borrow funds often sign debt contracts that include clauses (debt covenants) that are linked to financial accounting numbers. As we know, managers agree to these contracts because it allows their organisation to attract debt funds at a lower cost, as it provides safeguards to lenders. For example, the debt contract might have a requirement that profits must be maintained at a certain level (for example, a specific multiple of total interest costs) – thereby providing a margin of safety that the debt-holders will receive the required interest payments – or that a certain level of profit is earned before dividends can be paid to owners. If organisations are close to breaching these contractual requirements, then managers will potentially be motivated to recognise income as early as possible so as to ensure compliance with the restrictive covenants.

We could give many more reasons as to why managers might care about when income and expenses are recognised, but the point to again be made is that profit is a number that attracts much attention, and it is used within many agreements that an organisation is party to. It is a measure of performance that is of interest to many stakeholders. Therefore, the *timing* of the recognition of income is an issue that managers do care about.

As you know from the previous chapters on financial accounting, the application of accrual accounting will – amongst other things – lead to the recognition of various assets and liabilities, such as:

- an asset – accounts receivable – where income is recognised prior to the receipt of the related cash flow (for example, when inventory is sold on credit terms)
- a liability – income received in advance – where cash is received before the related income is earned (for example, where payment for a service is received before the service is provided)
- an asset – prepaid expenses – where the cash is paid before the related expense is incurred (for example, where rent for the next year has been paid in advance)
- a liability – accrued expenses – where the expense is incurred before the related cash is paid (for example, where wages expense has been incurred but the employees have not yet been paid).

Table 10.1 considers the potential timing difference between the delivery of a service to customers and receipt of the related cash. If the timing coincides, then no liability or receivable (an asset) will be recognised. However, if the timing does not coincide, then either an asset (accounts receivable) or a liability (revenue received in advance) will be recognised. Make sure you understand each of the cells of **Table 10.1**.

TABLE 10.1 Differences in timing between the receipt of cash and the earning of income

	The organisation has received the cash (thereby increasing the cash at bank account)	The organisation has not received the cash
The organisation has performed the related service and has issued an invoice to the customer	If the organisation receives the cash at the same time as providing the service, then it will recognise the income and the receipt of cash • Cash at bank (asset) increases • Income increases (equity increases)	Recognise the income and recognise an asset, perhaps called an account receivable • Accounts receivable (asset) increases • Income increases (equity increases)
The organisation has not performed the related service	Do not recognise the income. Instead, recognise the increase in cash, and recognise a liability: revenue received in advance • Cash at bank (asset) increases • Revenue received in advance (liability) increases	Nothing to recognise

Table 10.2 considers the potential timing difference between the receipt of a service from another organisation and payment of the related cash to the other organisation. If the timing coincides, no liability or prepayment (an asset) will be recognised. However, if the timing does not coincide, then either an asset (a prepaid expense) or a liability (accounts payable) will be recognised. Again, make sure you understand each of the cells within Table 10.2.

TABLE 10.2 Differences in timing between the payment of cash and the incurring of an expense

	The organisation has paid the cash	The organisation has not paid the cash
The organisation has received the related service and the related invoice	If the organisation pays the cash at the same time as receiving the service, it will recognise the expense and recognise the reduction in cash • Expense increases (equity decreases) • Cash at bank (asset) decreases	Recognise the expense and recognise a liability: 'accounts payable' • Expense increases (equity decreases) • Accounts payable (liability) increases
The organisation has not received the related service	Do not recognise the expense. Instead, recognise an asset, 'prepaid expense', and recognise the reduction in cash • Prepaid expense (asset) increases • Cash at bank (asset) decreases	Nothing to recognise

In Learning exercises 10.5, 10.6, 10.7 and 10.8, we consider the different timing differences that can occur within financial accounting with respect to the recognition of income and expenses.

10.5 Learning Exercise

Income earned but not received

Scenario: On 28 June 2025, Torquay Surf School provides surfing lessons to a group of aged pensioners for which it has already issued an invoice for payment. The fee is $1000, but as at the end of the financial year, which is 30 June 2025, it has not been paid by the group of pensioners.
Issue: You have been asked to establish:

- what accounts would be affected by recognising this income
- if the accounts receivable is an asset.

Solution: When determining the solution, consider the following.

What accounts will be affected?

Recognition of the income of $1000 would increase income (and therefore equity), and increase assets. Specifically, we would increase an account called 'surfing fees revenue' (or something similar), and we would increase 'accounts receivable'.

Is the accounts receivable an asset?

The 'accounts receivable' is an asset because it represents a *right* to receive future economic benefits (remember our definition of assets: a present economic resource controlled by the entity as a result of past events). These future economic benefits will arise as a result of the subsequent receipt of the cash, which can in turn be used as necessary within the organisation to create other economic benefits.

10.6 Learning Exercise

Income received in advance of performing the service

Scenario: On 1 March 2025, the Torquay Surf School also receives a $20 000 tuition fee for the coming surfing semester (the surfing semester will be from 1 April to 31 July).
Issue: What should be considered when determining how to recognise the income and expenses?
Solution: When determining how to recognise the income and expenses, consider the following.

How should the transaction initially be recorded within the financial accounting information system?

Under the accrual accounting system, the tuition fee revenue should not be recognised as income by the school when the cash is received in March, since the school has not yet provided the surfing lessons. It would be under an obligation to return the funds, unless the lessons were actually provided.

Therefore, on 1 March we would increase cash at bank (which is an asset) and increase revenue received in advance (a liability). In terms of our simple accounting equation, and applying it just to this transaction:

	A	=	L	+	OE
1 March	20 000	=	20 000	+	0

How much income should be recognised in the year ending 30 June 2025?

The amount that was paid was for four months' tuition from 1 April to 31 July. Therefore, 75 per cent of this income can be assumed to have been earned up to 30 June 2025, and as at 30 June 2025 the organisation has an obligation to provide only one more month's tuition. We would therefore decrease the liability 'revenue received in advance' by \$15 000 (\$20 000 × 3/4), and recognise this \$15 000 as income (thereby increasing equity).

	A	=	L	+	OE
1 March	20 000	=	20 000	+	–
30 June	–	=	(15 000)	+	15 000

Is there any liability existing at 30 June 2025?

The liability – 'revenue received in advance' – existing at 30 June 2025 would be \$5000 (which is \$20 000 – \$15 000), and this represents one month of surfing lessons that still need to be provided by the Torquay Surf School.

Why is 'revenue received in advance' a liability?

The 'revenue received in advance' is a liability because the organisation is under an obligation to provide future services, and it has not actually earned all the income associated with the up-front payment. If Torquay Surf School did not provide the remaining lessons, it would be under an obligation to repay the cash for those lessons that have not been provided.

10.7 Learning Exercise

Expense incurred but not paid

Scenario: Torquay Surf School Ltd has a five-day working week, and a total wages bill of \$2500 per week. The wages are paid in arrears (that is, they are paid after the service is provided by the employees) on Friday each week. The end of the financial period (the date on which we need to prepare financial reports) is 30 June, which is a Thursday.

Issue: What amount of accrued wages needs to be recognised at the end of the accounting period, and how should it be recognised?

Solution: When determining the answers to these questions, consider the following.

What amount of accrued wages needs to be recognised on 30 June, and what accounts will be affected?

At the end of each accounting period, managers and their accountants must think about whether there are any expenses that have been incurred but have not yet been paid. In this instance, there are four days of wages that have been incurred but have not yet been paid. This means there is \$2000 (which is \$2 500 × 4/5) in expenses (\$500 per day), and liabilities, that have to be recognised on 30 June 2025.

How will the transactions affect the accounting equation?

The recognition of the expense has the effect of reducing equity. In terms of our simple accounting equation, and applying it just to this transaction:

	A	=	L	+	OE
June	–	=	2000	+	(2000)

Why are expenses incurred, but not paid, a liability?

The expenses incurred but not paid in this instance amount to $2000. It is considered to be a liability because at the end of the accounting period, which is 30 June, the organisation has an obligation to pay its employees $2000 for the four days of work that have been performed, but which have not yet been paid for.

10.8 Learning Exercise

Payment made for expense yet to be incurred

Scenario: Torquay Surf School prepays $3600 for 12 months of property insurance on 1 January 2025.

Issue: What amount of prepaid insurance needs to be recognised at the end of the accounting period, and what accounts will be impacted?

Solution: When answering these questions, consider the following.

Accounts to be affected

Under accrual accounting, the surf school should increase prepaid insurance (asset) and decrease cash at bank (asset) on 1 January 2025. The accounting equation is affected as follows:

	A	=	L	+	OE
1 January	3600	=	–	+	–
	(3600)	=	–	+	–

At the end of the reporting period, which is 30 June, the school should increase Insurance Expense by $1800 (6/12 × $3600 = $1800) to recognise the insurance that has been used, which decreases equity, and should also decrease the asset, 'Prepaid Insurance'. The accounting equation is affected as follows:

	A	=	L	+	OE
1 January	3600	=	–	+	–
	(3600)	=	–	+	–
30 June	(1800)	=	–	+	(1800)

The balance of prepaid insurance (asset) in the balance sheet as at 30 June 2025, after the above adjustment, will be $1800. This represents the six months of insurance that have been paid for the period 1 July 2025 to 31 December 2025, and which have not yet been used.

Why are prepaid expenses an asset?

The prepayment is considered an asset as it provides the organisation with a right to a future economic benefit – in this instance, future insurance coverage.

In our discussion of property, plant and equipment in Chapter 9, we discussed depreciation expenses. Depreciation represents an expense that is recognised in a period that differs from when the underlying asset was acquired (and therefore when the related cash flow occurred). Therefore, depreciation expense is an expense that does not directly involve a cash flow. If accrual accounting was not applied, then depreciation expense would not be recognised.

At the end of each accounting period, managers and accountants need to take the time to carefully consider which expenses have been incurred, and which items of income have been earned, but have not yet been recognised within the financial accounting information system. Failure to do so might result in a misleading account being provided about an organisation's income, expenses, profits, assets and liabilities (and therefore equity). Failure to recognise various accruals would mean that the financial reports would potentially not provide a representationally faithful depiction of the organisation's financial performance. As we learned in Chapter 7, the two fundamental qualitative characteristics that useful financial information shall possess are relevance and representational faithfulness.

Income recognition and the requirement that control of the good or service has passed to the customer

As you know, when recognising assets and liabilities, and related income and expenses, professional judgement needs to be made about factors such as:

- the probabilities associated with expected flows of economic benefits
- the level of uncertainty associated with the measurement of the associated economic benefits (referred to as measurement uncertainty).

If probabilities of expected flows of economic benefits are assessed as very low, or where there is a high level of measurement uncertainty then the asset or liability, and the related income or expense, should not be recognised. We will now consider an additional consideration relating to 'control'.

Revenue recognition in relation to contracts with customers is also dependent on the requirement that the entity has transferred control of the underlying asset (such as inventory) to the customer – this is a specific requirement of IFRS 15: Revenue from Contracts with Customers (IFRS stands for International Financial Reporting Standard and represents a standard released by the IASB). That is, transfer of control of the related asset is a central requirement in the recognition of revenue under our accounting standards. Control of an asset refers to the ability to direct the use of, and obtain substantially all of the remaining benefits from, the asset, including the ability to prevent other organisations or people from directing the use of, and obtaining the benefits from, an asset.

Therefore, if control of the underlying asset (the item of inventory) has not been transferred to a customer, it is generally accepted that the related income should not be recognised. For services, it is generally accepted that control of the service passes to the customer when the service is performed. **Learning exercise 10.9** considers this issue.

10.9 Learning Exercise

Recognition of income depends upon the passing of control of the underlying asset to the customer

Scenario: Richards Company sells portable spa baths. It has received a deposit from a buyer for a spa bath, but the bath is still at the factory of Richards Company.

Issue: Should Richards Company recognise income in relation to the sale of the spa bath?

Solution: When answering this question, consider the following.

Has the control of the asset passed to the customer?

The general principle is that the sales revenue (income) should not be recognised until such time that the control of the asset has actually passed to the customer. In this case, the customer is not in control of the asset, and therefore no income should be recognised.

How should Richards Company recognise the deposit in relation to the sale of the spa?

Until such time that the customer takes control of the spa bath, the deposit should be recognised as a liability by Richards Company. That is, the cash deposit has resulted in an increase in cash at bank (an asset), and an increase in a liability (perhaps labelled 'customer deposit').

Long-term construction contracts

Depending on the nature of the activities of the reporting entity, income in relation to particular goods or services might be recognised at a point in time (such as the point of sale), or it might be recognised over a period of time. For example, in relation to a long-term construction contract, such as the construction of a large building or ship that might take years to complete, income might be recognised 'over a period of time', which covers a number of accounting periods (rather than at a 'point in time'). However, as noted above, the transfer of control is a required precondition before income is recognised at a point in time, or over a period of time.

Therefore, where performance obligations are satisfied over an extended period of time, rather than at a point in time, income can be recognised to the extent that the reporting entity's performance creates or enhances an asset (for example, work in progress in the form of a building) that the customer controls while the asset is being created or enhanced, or the organisation's performance creates an asset with no alternative use and the organisation has an enforceable right to payment for performance completed to date.

For more on the recognition of income, see **Learning exercise 10.10**.

10.10 Learning Exercise

Recognition of income

Keeping in mind what you have just learned, and that the transfer of control is a required precondition before income is recognised at a point in time, or over a period of time, then should the following transactions and events be recognised as income?

1 An organisation receives $2000 cash in advance for a service to be delivered in the next reporting period.

2 An organisation receives $3000 cash for services provided in the previous reporting period.
3 A construction company has completed 30 per cent of a building that it is constructing for a specific customer.

Solutions

- **$2000 cash in advance for a service to be delivered in next reporting period:** No. The service has not been provided, so when the cash is received, a liability should be recognised, and an increase in cash should also be recognised.
- **$3000 received cash for services provided in the previous reporting period:** No. The income should have been recognised in the previous accounting period, in which the services were provided. At that point in time, an asset (accounts receivable) would have been recognised, and the service fee revenue would have been recognised. When the related cash is subsequently received, then we would increase cash at bank (an asset) and decrease accounts receivable (an asset).
- **30 per cent completion of a building for a specific customer:** The accounting standards allow the construction company to recognise revenue if progress on the construction and the costs and revenue associated with the project can be reliably determined, and if the customer is in control of the building whilst the construction is being undertaken. In those instances where the customer does not have control of the asset, the accounting standards do allow income to be recognised throughout the project (on the basis of how much of the project has been completed) if the building has no alternative use, and the organisation has an enforceable right to payment for work already performed.

In **Learning exercise 10.11**, we consider in more depth how to recognise the income from a long-term construction contract.

10.11 Learning Exercise

Recognition of income from a long-term construction contract

Scenario: Noosa Co has agreed to build a large factory for Tea Tree Bay Ltd. The total contract price is $30 million and the project will take three years to complete. The completion of the factory, which could be used for various purposes, can be broken up into eight phases, and on completion of each phase, the following amounts will be due to be paid to Noosa Co by Tea Tree Bay Ltd:

Phase	Amount due at completion of phase
Development of approved plans	$400 000
Levelling and clearing of construction site	$2 750 000
Completion of building foundations	$6 500 000
Completion of walls	$6 500 000
Completion of roof	$4 550 000
Completion of fit-out of building	$7 500 000
Painting of building	$850 000
Landscaping around building	$950 000
Total contract revenue	**$30 000 000**

Issues: Should Noosa Co recognise revenue before the construction is completed?

Solution: If the stage of completion can be reliably determined, the related expenses can be reliably determined, and if Tea Tree Bay Ltd has control of the asset whilst it is being constructed by Noosa Co, then income can be recognised at the completion of each phase of the construction. That is, revenue can be recognised throughout the construction contract. The amount to be recognised as revenue is the amount that is due at the completion of each stage.

Long-term service contracts

Whilst most services will be performed in a relatively short time period, some services might be provided for a number of years. For example, an organisation might agree to provide services in relation to the installation of a new computer system for an entire university. This task might take several years. If the contracted services can be broken down into a number of discrete components, then we can account for the service income in the same way that we accounted for the long-term construction project above. That is, if the service contract involves several different components, each of which is of value and use to the customer, and the completion of each separate component can be identified, then the related revenue can be recognised when each component of the overall service agreement is completed.

Other services might be of a continuous and repetitive nature. For example, an organisation might provide photocopier maintenance services to customers. In such instances, it is typically assumed that the services are being provided uniformly over the contract period, and therefore the income can be recognised evenly across the contractual period.

In those situations where it is not possible to break down the rendering of a service into smaller components, the income will not be recognised until the service has been completed. For example, if an accountant has agreed to produce the financial statements for a client, then the service would not be considered to have been completed until those financial statements are prepared, and no income would be recognised until the service is complete.

Revenue recognition policy notes

Because organisations make various choices in relation to revenue and expense recognition, asset and liability measurement, and so forth, there is a general requirement that the financial statements be accompanied by notes that explain significant accounting policies. Before we compare the financial position and financial performance of different organisations, it is important to understand whether the different organisations are using the same accounting policies.

Exhibit 10.2 and **Exhibit 10.3** illustrate the revenue recognition policy provided within the notes to the financial statements of two large companies. By reading these policy notes, you will see the sorts of disclosures large organisations make with respect to how they recognise income.

EXHIBIT 10.2 The revenue recognition and measurement policy as provided within the notes to the financial statements that appear in the 2021 annual report of BHP Ltd

Recognition and measurement

The Group generates revenue from the production and sale of commodities. Revenue is recognised when or as control of the promised goods or services passes to the customer. In most instances, control passes when the goods are delivered to a destination specified by the customer, typically on board the customer's appointed vessel. Revenue from the provision of services is recognised over time, but does not represent a significant proportion of total revenue and is aggregated with the respective asset and product revenue for disclosure purposes. The amount of revenue recognised reflects the consideration to which the Group expects to be entitled in exchange for the goods or services.

Where the Group's sales are provisionally priced, the final price depends on future index prices. The amount of revenue initially recognised is based on the relevant forward market price. Adjustments between the provisional and final price are accounted for under IFRS 9/AASB 9 'Financial Instruments' (IFRS 9) and separately recorded as other revenue. The period between provisional pricing and final invoicing is typically between 60 and 120 days. Revenue from concentrate is net of treatment costs and refining charges.

Revenue from the sale of significant by-products is included within revenue. Where a by-product is not significant, revenue is credited against costs.

The Group applies the practical expedient to not adjust the expected consideration for the effects of the time value of money if the period between the delivery and when the customer pays for the promised good or service is one year or less.

Source: BHP (2021), p. 139.

EXHIBIT 10.3 The revenue recognition and measurement policy as provided within the notes to the financial statements that appear in the 2021 annual report of Qantas

(D) REVENUE RECOGNITION

i. Passenger and Freight Revenue

i. **Net Passenger and Net Freight Revenue** Net passenger revenue primarily arises within the Qantas Domestic, Qantas International and Jetstar Group segments. Net freight revenue primarily arises within the Qantas International segment except where belly space is utilised in Qantas Domestic and the Jetstar Group.

Passenger, freight revenue, capacity hire and air charter revenue are recognised when the travel or service is provided. Revenue recognised on travel is net of sales discounts, passenger and freight interline/IATA commission and the Goods and Services Tax. Net freight revenue includes amounts the Group receives as operating lease income in relation to freighters leased to customers.

At the time of expected travel, revenue is also recognised in respect of tickets that are not expected to be used. Unused tickets are recognised as revenue using estimates based on the terms and conditions of the ticket, experience, historical and expected future trends. The Group generally does not recognise revenue in respect of unredeemed travel credits due to the extended redemption conditions and typically, the ability for the passenger to request a refund.

Passenger travel and freight services are generally paid for in advance of travel and are deferred on the balance sheet as revenue received in advance. Travel credits are classified as revenue received in advance where they are available for future flights or in certain circumstances for refund, if requested. Where customers have made refund claims these are classified as payables, where the balance of refunds is material in aggregate.

Where the passenger is also a Qantas Frequent Flyer member and earns Qantas Points on travel, the allocation of revenue is on a proportional basis using relative stand-alone selling prices and the consideration allocated to Qantas Points is deferred as unrecognised redemption revenue.

Consideration received in relation to certain ancillary services regarding passenger travel such as credit card fees and change fees are not considered to be distinct from the passenger flight. Revenue relating to these ancillary services is deferred until uplift to align with the related passenger travel. These amounts are included within net passenger revenue.

Passenger recoveries (including fuel surcharge on passenger tickets) are included in net passenger revenue. Freight fuel surcharge is included in net freight revenue.

Source: Qantas (2021), p. 122.

Summary of income and expense recognition

We have prepared two diagrams that help to summarise some of our discussion. **Figure 10.1** addresses whether income and expenses should be recognised, and **Figure 10.2** addresses the point in time at which income should be recognised. If the income is being derived from the sale of goods to a customer, then an additional criterion that needs to be added to **Figure 10.1** is that control of the goods must have been passed to the customer.

FIGURE 10.1 The recognition of income and expenses

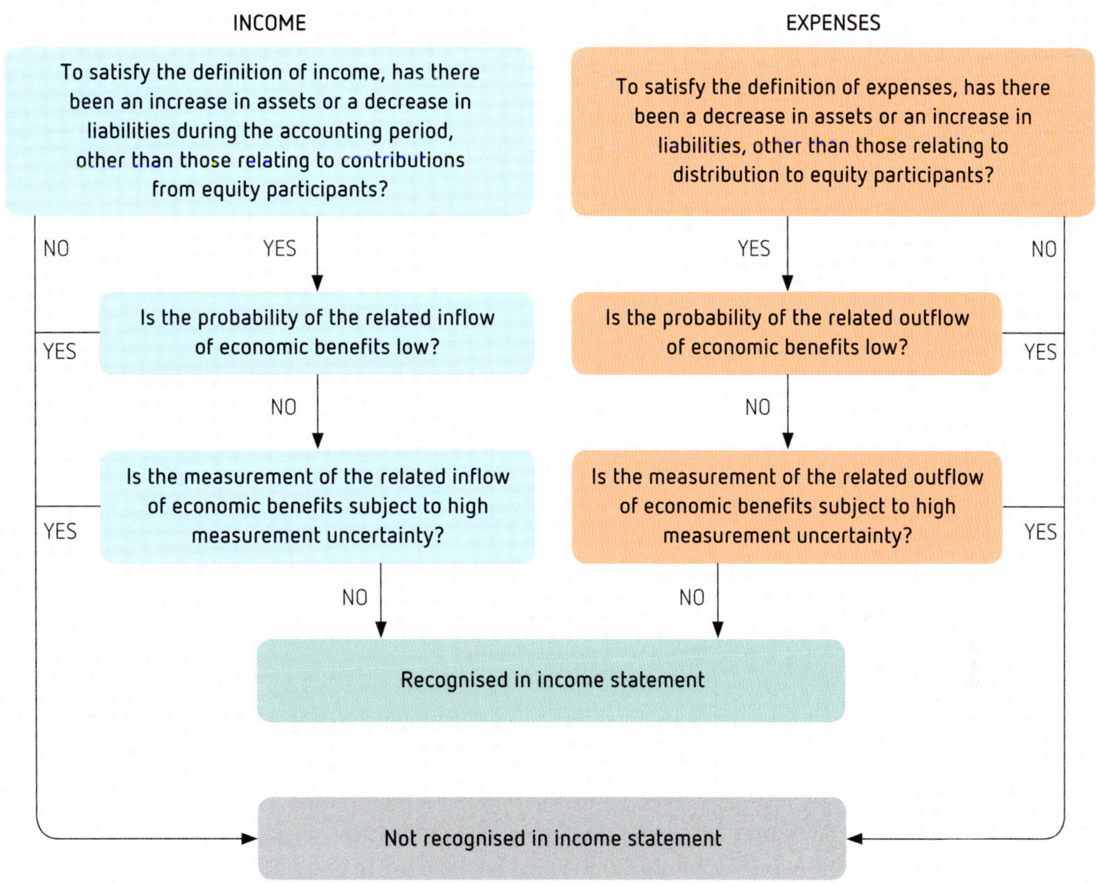

Figure 10.2, which is adapted from Coombes and Martin (1982), identifies possible points in the acquisition–production–marketing cycle at which income could be recognised by a manufacturing organisation, starting from the point at which an idea is devised, and progressing through to the point at which cash is collected from the sale of products. For a retailing organisation, points 3 to 7 would not be relevant. From what we have already discussed in this chapter, when recognising income, we need to consider:

- whether the probability associated with the expected flow of economic benefits is low, in which case income would not be recognised
- whether the expected flow of economic benefits can only be measured with a high degree of measurement uncertainty, in which case the income would not be recognised
- if it involves a customer, whether control of the underlying good or service has been transferred to the customer. If control has not passed, then typically the income shall not be recognised.

FIGURE 10.2 Possible points in the recognition of income and expenses

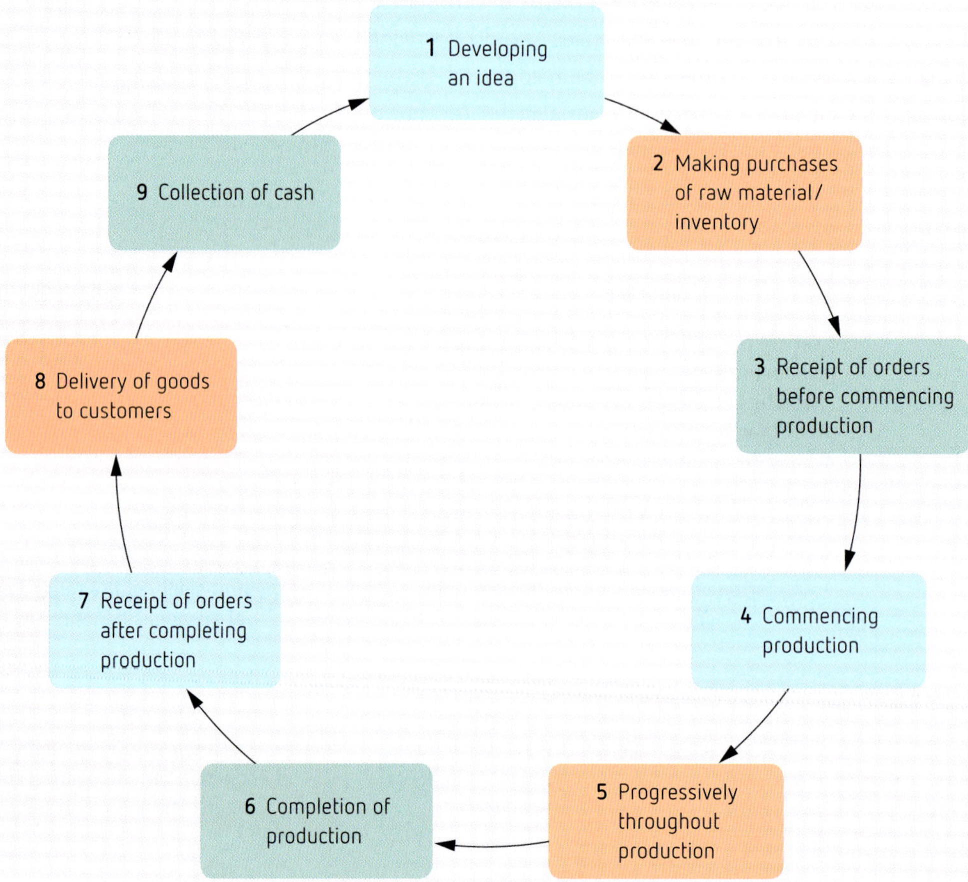

Adapted from Coombes and Martin (1982).

For most sales of goods, it would be point 8 at which control has passed, and at which the flow of economic benefits would be of sufficient probability and measurable with reasonable accuracy. Therefore, income would typically be recognised at this point with a corresponding increase in the asset 'accounts receivable'. However, if there is great uncertainty about the collectability of the debt, then income recognition could be deferred to point 9.

To recognise income at points 1–4 would be considered too early in the revenue recognition cycle because of the many uncertainties involved in determining whether there will be future flows of economic benefits to the organisation. For long-term construction contracts, income could be recognised progressively throughout the project (point 5), as long as the customer is in control of the asset being constructed (such as a building or ship), and the extent of the project's completion and the associated income and expenses can be reliably measured, or if the organisation has created an asset with no alternative use and the organisation has an enforceable right to payment for the work completed to date.

For more on the point in time at which revenue should be recognised, see **Learning exercise 10.12**.

10.12 Learning Exercise

The point in time when revenue should be recognised

Scenario: An airline company requires its customers to pay their airfares before they travel. In some cases, the payments for the airfares will be made many months before they travel.

How should the airline company treat the receipt of the cash from the customers, and when should it recognise the revenue?

Solution: When determining how the company should treat the receipt of cash, and when it should recognise the revenue, consider the following.

When does the airline perform the service?

At the time when the airline company receives the cash, thereby increasing the asset 'cash at bank', it has not performed the service. It therefore has an obligation to the customer to either perform the service or refund the money. A liability is recognised.

How should the airline recognise the money (before the service is performed)?

When the cash is initially received, the airline company recognises an increase in cash at bank (an asset) and an increase in the liability revenue received in advance.

When should the airline recognise the revenue as income?

When the customer travels, the revenue would be considered to have been earned, at which point the airline company will recognise the income and reduce the liability. This is consistent with the way in which Qantas accounts for its revenue (see **Exhibit 10.3**), with the revenue from passengers being recognised when they are 'uplifted', and the initial cash received from customers likely being recorded as 'revenue received in advance', which is a liability.

Why do I need to know about the different income and expense recognition rules?

Profit is a measure that attracts a lot of attention from different stakeholders. To understand what 'profit' actually represents, we need to understand the rules governing when income and expenses shall be recognised. If we do not understand these rules, then we really do not understand what 'profit' represents.

LO10.5 Measuring income and expenses

As we have already noted, how we measure assets and liabilities directly impacts reported profits; for example:

- If we revalue our property, plant and equipment upwards to fair value, this will increase depreciation expense which will therefore decrease profits (depreciation expense is based on the carrying amount of the asset – if the carrying amount is increased, then so is depreciation expense, which then has consequential effects on profits).
- If we measure liability provisions – such as provisions for warranty or for site remediation – at their present value, then this means there will be less expense (and less liabilities) than if we had measured them at their undiscounted value.

We could come up with many more such examples, but the point to be made is that choosing between different measurement bases for assets and liabilities will in turn impact the measurement of income and expenses, and will therefore also impact profits (see **Learning exercise 10.13**).

10.13 Learning Exercise

An example of how a change in the way assets are measured will lead to a change in profits

Scenario: On 1 January 2024, Ship Sterns Company acquires some machinery at a cost of $100 000. The machinery has an expected useful life of 10 years and no expected residual value at the end of its useful life. The asset is expected to generate economic benefits uniformly throughout its useful life. The company has a policy of recording its property, plant and equipment at cost.

On 1 January 2027, the company decides to change its accounting policies and to measure its machinery at fair value, rather than at cost. The fair value of the machinery is believed to be $90 000 on 1 January 2027.

Ship Sterns Company has a 12-month accounting period that ends on 31 December.

Issue: Will this change in the way the machinery is measured have any impact on profits?

Solution: When assessing this issue, consider the impact this change in measurement will have on depreciation expense.

What is its depreciation expense when the asset is measured at cost?

Up until 31 December 2026, the asset has been used for three years. Since the asset is expected to have a useful life of 10 years, have no residual value, and generate uniform economic benefits throughout its life, then yearly depreciation expense using the straight-line method of depreciation would be $10 000 per year, calculated as $100 000 ÷ 10 (we discussed different approaches to depreciation in Chapter 9). The accumulated depreciation after three years – which is a contra asset (as we learned in Chapter 9) – would have a balance of $30 000.

How much will the depreciation expense be when the asset is measured at fair value?

If an asset is revalued to fair value, then the depreciation is required to then be based upon the revalued amount. Once the asset is revalued to its fair value on 1 January 2027, and with seven years' life of the asset remaining, the new depreciation will be $12 857 per year, calculated by dividing the new fair value by the remaining useful life, which equates to $90 000 ÷ 7. This is an increase in the yearly depreciation expense of $2857.

How does this affect the profits?

This change in the accounting policy used for measuring machinery will impact profits. Depreciation expense will be based on the cost, or the revalued amount, of the asset. If the amount attributed to a depreciable asset is increased because the asset is now measured at fair value and not cost, then depreciation expense will also increase.

Therefore, we can see here that changing the way in which we measure machinery will impact profits. In this instance, it will decrease profits.

Key concept

Choices made with respect to how to measure assets and liabilities will have direct consequences for the measurement of income and expenses, and therefore for reported profits.

Measuring income when the receipt of cash has been deferred beyond 12 months

If the transaction price is not expected to be paid to an organisation by a customer for more than a year, then the price shall be discounted to its present value in order to recognise the time value of money. That is, the general requirement within financial accounting is that if the payment to be received for goods and services is to be deferred beyond 12 months, then the income to be recognised will be discounted to its present value. **Learning exercise 10.14** provides an example of a transaction with an interest component.

10.14 Learning Exercise

Receipt of a deferred payment for the provision of services

Scenario: In July 2025, Cornish Surfboards, an organisation involved in the surfing industry, provides two weeks of surfboard-making lessons to a group of senior executives from a Chinese organisation named Cino Surfing. They are interested in the business opportunities surfing creates. They have negotiated to defer the payments to periods of one and two years in the future. The lessons conclude on 15 July 2025. The agreement requires Cino Surfing to make two deferred payments of $50 000 each to Cornish Surfboards on 15 July 2026 and 15 July 2027. Cornish Surfboards typically provides credit arrangements to such customers at a rate of 10 per cent.
Issue: How much income should Cornish Surfboards recognise on 15 July 2025 in relation to the surfboard-making lessons?
Solution: When determining the answer to this question, consider the following:

Has Cornish Surfboards performed the required services?

Yes. On 15 July 2025, Cornish Surfboards has performed services, for which it has a claim to cash.

How should it recognise the income?

On 15 July 2025, the organisation should recognise the income to the extent it believes that there is not a low probability that there will be an inflow of economic benefits, and that there is limited measurement uncertainty in relation to the economic benefits.

The general principle is that if the amount will be received in more than 12 months, then the amount to be recognised will be the present value of the expected future cash flows.

What is the present value of the income Cornish Surfboards should recognise?

We need to work out the present value (PV) of the income to be received. Using a discount rate of 10 per cent, this can be calculated as follows:

PV of amount to be received on 15 July 2026: $50 000 × 0.9091	=	$45 455
PV of amount to be received on 15 July 2027: $50 000 × 0.8264	=	$41 320
Income to be recognised on 15 July 2025	=	$86 775

The above numbers used to calculate present values would be available in present value tables. They can also be calculated as follows:

$$\text{The present value of \$1 to be received in n periods time} = \frac{1}{(1+i)^n}$$

where i = rate of interest.

For an interest rate of 10% $1 to be received in one year and two years can be calculated respectively as:

$$\frac{\$1}{1.1} = \$0.9091$$

$$\frac{\$1}{(1.1)^2} = \$0.8264$$

So what income should Cornish Surfboards recognise?

On 15 July 2025, Cornish Surfboards would therefore recognise income of $86 775 (thereby increasing equity) as well as recognising an account receivable (asset) of $86 775. In terms of the expanded accounting equation:

A	+	E	+	D	=	L	+	I	+	C
$86 775		–		–		–		$86 775		–

The difference between the cash that will be received in the future accounting periods ($100 000 in total) and the revenue initially recognised ($86 775) will be recognised as interest income in the accounting periods in which the cash is received.

Measuring income when the asset being received is not cash

There is a general principle that organisations are to measure income at the fair value of the assets they receive for providing goods and services. If the consideration received for the sale of goods or services is cash, then it is obviously easier to measure the fair value of the consideration relative to the situation where the consideration is of a non-cash form (see **Learning exercise 10.15**). For example, a customer might pay for a good or service by transferring some land to an organisation, rather than paying cash. Where non-cash consideration is received, it will be measured at the fair value of what is being received.

10.15 Learning Exercise

Provision of services for a payment that is not in the form of cash

Scenario: Ocean Grove Ltd provides consulting services to Lonsdale Ltd. Rather than being paid in cash, it is agreed that Lonsdale Ltd will transfer some equipment to Ocean Grove Ltd.

The equipment is recorded in Lonsdale Ltd's financial accounts at a cost of $100 000 and with accumulated depreciation of $30 000. The fair value of the machinery is assessed as being $80 000.
Issue: How much revenue should Ocean Grove Ltd recognise, and what accounts would be affected by the transaction?
Solution: When considering the answer to this question, it is important to note that it is the fair value of the payment that is relevant, not the carrying amount of the equipment as recorded in Lonsdale Ltd's accounts (that carrying amount would be $70 000). Thus, the revenue recognised by Ocean Grove Ltd would be $80 000. The equipment account (an asset) of Ocean Grove Ltd would increase by $80 000 and its consulting revenue account (which will increase equity) would also increase by $80 000. In terms of our expanded accounting equation:

A	+	E	+	D	=	L	+	I	+	C
$80 000		–		–		–		$80 000		–

In the previous chapter, and in our discussion of assets, we discussed how to measure depreciation expense, impairment expenses, and doubtful debts expense. We will not repeat that discussion here, albeit to say that these expenses appear on the income statement. In Chapter 9 we also discussed inventory, specifically how to determine the cost of inventory for balance sheet purposes. However, we did not go into detail about how to calculate the cost of sales (the cost of the inventory sold) for income statement purposes, so we will cover this below. It will also be evident that there are a number of choices to be made in determining how cost of sales is measured. We will also briefly discuss another common expense: income tax expense.

Measuring the cost of sales

In Chapter 9, we discussed how to determine the cost of inventory together with the general rule for inventory measurement – this rule being that inventory should be measured at the lower of cost and net realisable value. We will not cover that again here. Rather, we will discuss how to calculate the cost of inventory sold, which is often just referred to as **cost of sales** or *cost of goods sold*. We will use the terms interchangeably. For retailers and manufacturers, the cost of sales can be one of the most significant expenses incurred. As we shall see, there are some choices to be made in how cost of sales is measured.

cost of sales
The expense calculated to account for the cost of inventory sold

Organisations often sell items that are very similar; they can be hard to differentiate. They also tend to buy or produce the inventory at different times during an accounting period, and the costs of this inventory will typically fluctuate. For example, let us assume that a sporting goods retailer, with a financial year ending on 30 June 2026, sells 10 tennis balls to a customer on 30 June 2026 for a total price of $120. We will assume these are the only tennis balls sold for the year. The retailer only sells one type of tennis ball, and it has 100 identical tennis balls in stock prior to the sale, which were acquired on the following dates and at the following costs:

Date acquired	Number of tennis balls acquired	Cost per tennis ball
15 December 2025	15	$6
20 January 2026	35	$7
30 June 2026	50	$8
	100	

Because the tennis balls are all identical – they cannot be differentiated – it might not be possible to determine which batch of purchases the tennis balls being sold came from. Therefore, some assumption must be made about which tennis balls were sold. For example, were they from the tennis balls acquired on 15 December (which would mean they cost \$6 each), or were they from the batch acquired on a different date at a different cost? If the managers, and their accountants, assume that the first inventory items that come into the organisation are the first ones to be sold, then the cost allocated to the sale would be \$60, which is 10 × \$6. Hence, the point we are making here is that it is often necessary to make inventory cost-flow assumptions. We will describe some of the different cost-flow assumptions accountants might make below.

When organisations sell inventory, they also have a choice in determining whether they will recognise the cost of the sale, and the reduction in inventory, each time an inventory item is sold (which would be referred to as a 'perpetual inventory system'), or, by contrast, whether they will wait until the end of the accounting period to determine the total costs of sales, and the amount of inventory being held (which would be referred to as a 'periodic' or 'physical inventory system'). We will also discuss the difference between the periodic inventory system and the perpetual inventory system below.

Inventory cost-flow assumptions

As we learned in Chapter 9 when we discussed the asset inventory, the cost of inventory includes those costs associated with bringing the inventories to their present location, and in the condition necessary for sale. These include:

- costs of purchase
- costs of conversion
- other costs incurred in bringing the inventory to its current condition and location.

The costs of the individual inventory items manufactured, or acquired, during an accounting period typically fluctuate. If the items being sold are very different in nature and appearance, then it might be possible to determine the specific cost of each item sold. However, if the items being sold are very similar or identical, then managers and their accountants might not be able to, or want to, go to the effort to identify the specific cost of each individual item sold. Doing so might be considered inefficient. As a result, certain cost-flow assumptions will be made in order to allocate a cost to each sale.

So, rather than attempting to identify sold items specifically, together with their specific costs, a cost-flow assumption is frequently made and consistently applied in determining the cost of goods sold, and the cost of closing inventory. Thus, the actual physical flow of goods, and the flow of goods according to the cost-flow assumption, might be different. Nevertheless, this is common accounting practice.

In selecting a cost-flow method, management should exercise judgement to ensure that the inventory cost-flow assumption chosen provides the most practical accounting reflection of the real movements in inventory. In accordance with the accounting standard IAS 2: Inventories, the costs of inventories will be assigned to particular items of inventory through one or more of the following methods:

- specific identification – this method assigns specific costs to identified units of inventory
- weighted-average cost – this method assigns weighted-average costs, arrived at by means of a continuous calculation, a periodic calculation, or a moving periodic calculation
- first-in, first-out (FIFO) – this method assigns costs on the assumption that the inventory being sold is the inventory that was first purchased or produced, and the inventory on hand at the end of the accounting period is the last purchased or produced.

Again, the method of accounting chosen should be appropriate to the circumstances (that is, there should be some level of correspondence between the cost-flow assumption and the actual physical flow of inventory), and the accounting method should be applied consistently from one accounting period to the next.

Specific-identification method

Under the **specific-identification method** of inventory valuation, the seller determines which item is sold, and the cost of that specific item is included within cost of sales. The ending inventory is calculated at the cost of the specific individual items on hand at the end of the year. Items with a significant dollar value, such as motor vehicles, are frequently accounted for by the specific-identification method, particularly when the items being sold are fewer in number and have a unique characteristic, such as a unique product or identification number that makes identification and record-keeping relatively easy.

specific-identification method
A method of inventory valuation where the seller determines which item is sold, and the cost of that specific item to be included within cost of sales. Usually applied to items of inventory that have some form of unique attribute

For example, the cars sold by a car dealership might each have their own specific identifiable characteristics, such as model, colour, chassis number and engine number. A separate record is kept for each car that details the related costs. Given that the car dealership only sells a relatively limited number of cars, individual record-keeping is not considered too onerous or costly. When a car is sold, the cost of that car is specifically identified, and recognised as the cost of the sale.

For goods that are ordinarily interchangeable because they appear to be the same, or are not produced and segregated for specific projects, the accounting standard requires that the costs be assigned to cost of sales using the weighted-average cost or the FIFO method.

Weighted-average-cost approach

Under the **weighted-average-cost approach**, an average cost is determined based on the cost of beginning inventory, and the costs of the items purchased, or manufactured, since the beginning of the accounting period. The various costs of the individual units are weighted by the number of units at a particular purchase price. The units in ending inventory and units sold are costed at this average cost. The weighted-average-cost method is appropriate where the goods are homogeneous in nature and the turnover of items is high.

weighted-average-cost approach
An approach to inventory valuation where the cost of each item is determined from the weighted average of the cost of similar items at the beginning of a period, and the cost of similar items purchased or produced during the period

Returning to the example provided earlier with the tennis balls, the use of the weighted-average approach would lead to a cost of sale on the tennis balls of $73.50, calculated as follows:

Date of purchase	Number purchased	Cost per unit	
15 December 2025	15	$6	$90
20 January 2026	35	$7	$245
30 June 2026	50	$8	$400
	100		$735
Divided by			100 units
Weighted average cost per unit			**$7.35**

The cost of the 10 tennis balls sold would be $73.50 (10 × $7.35), and the value of closing inventory of 90 balls would be 90 × $7.35, which equals $661.50.

First-in, first-out cost-flow method

Under the **first-in, first-out cost-flow method (FIFO)** of inventory valuation, any goods existing in opening inventory, and the earliest purchases of inventory, are assumed to be the first goods sold. This would seem to reflect the pattern of selling behaviour in most entities. Inventory held

first-in, first-out cost-flow method (FIFO)
A method of inventory valuation where any goods existing in opening inventory, and the earliest purchases of inventory, are assumed to be the first goods sold

at the end of the accounting period is assumed to be made up of the more recent purchases, or the more recently manufactured items, and therefore represents a more-current value of the inventory for the balance sheet.

While FIFO is commonly used throughout the world, it is often criticised because it tends to match old or outdated inventory costs with current sales prices, and by doing so tends to result in inflated profits relative to what would be recorded if up-to-date costs were used to determine cost of goods sold (assuming that inventory prices increase over time, rather than decrease). However, the use of FIFO does mean that the closing inventory balance as shown in the balance sheet is more reflective of current costs.

Using our previous example of the tennis balls, the cost of sale of 10 tennis balls would be $60, as that was the cost of the earliest acquired inventory on hand ($6 × 10) at the time the tennis balls were sold. Again, under this accounting method, the first item of inventory 'in' is assumed to be the first item of inventory 'out'.

From this brief illustration, we can see that the choice of cost-flow assumption will have an effect on cost of sales expense, and therefore on profits. The cost of sale using weighted-average cost was $73.50, whilst the cost using FIFO was $60. Therefore, this is yet another example of where the choice of accounting method by managers, and their accountants, will impact accounting profits, again demonstrating that we need to be careful when comparing the profits of different organisations, particularly if those different organisations use different accounting methods.

Last-in, first-out cost-flow method

last-in, first-out cost-flow method (LIFO)
A method of inventory valuation where the most recent items purchased, or manufactured, are assumed to be the first items sold

The **last-in, first-out cost-flow method (LIFO)** of inventory valuation is not permitted by organisations that use the accounting standards issued by the IASB. However, it is discussed here for the sake of completeness.

Under the LIFO cost-flow method, the most recent items purchased, or manufactured, are assumed to be the first items sold. Therefore, closing inventory is assumed to be composed of the oldest goods acquired or manufactured. This could result in inventory reported in the balance sheet being valued at costs that were paid or incurred some years before. The cost of sales contains relatively current costs, thus arguably creating a better match of the current costs with current revenues. In a period of rising prices, LIFO adopters would show lower profits and lower closing inventory than FIFO adopters. Returning to our tennis ball example, the cost of sales using LIFO would be $80, compared with $60 when using FIFO.

Interestingly, LIFO can be used in the United States for financial reporting purposes. As mentioned previously in this book, the US has its own financial reporting standards setter – this being the FASB. If LIFO is used within the US, it can also be used for the purposes of calculating the entity's taxation liability. In a period of rising prices, adopting LIFO effectively results in higher cost of goods sold, lower profits and, consequently, lower taxes.

The perpetual and periodic systems of inventory management

The determination of cost of sales (for inclusion in the income statement) and closing inventory (for inclusion in the balance sheet) under each of the cost-flow assumptions further depends on the method used to record movements in the inventory; that is, whether the periodic inventory system or the perpetual inventory system is used.

We can use either the perpetual or periodic inventory method to work out the number of units of inventory on hand. So, in determining cost of goods sold (necessary for calculating profit or loss) and the value of closing inventory (for the balance sheet), we not only need to consider what cost-flow assumptions have been made (for example, FIFO, specific-identification, or the weighted-average method), we also need to determine whether the perpetual system or periodic system is being employed to determine the actual number of units of inventory on hand.

Under the **periodic inventory system** (which is also often referred to as the *physical inventory system*), inventory is counted periodically (for example, at year end) and then a cost is assigned to that closing inventory. Each time an item of inventory is sold, the sale is recognised in the financial accounts (meaning sales revenue increases, which increases equity, and either cash or accounts receivable increases, which increases assets). However, when the periodic inventory system is used, the cost of sales is not recognised each time a sale is made, and the inventory account (asset) is also not reduced when the sale is made. The adjustment to the inventory account is deferred until the end of the accounting period.

periodic inventory system
An inventory management system also referred to as a physical inventory system, where the amount of inventory on hand, and the cost of goods sold for the period, is determined at the end of the accounting period

Therefore, if the periodic inventory system is used, then throughout the accounting period, no adjustments are made to the inventory account each time an inventory item is sold. This means that the inventory account will not inform managers of the value and number of units of inventory on hand at any point of time during the accounting period. Instead, we need to do a stocktake (a physical count of the entire inventory on hand) at the end of the year (or some other time) to ascertain what inventory is on hand, and then at that point we can update our inventory account balance (which will appear in the balance sheet) and we can also work out an aggregated cost of sales. This cost of sales would be determined at the end of the accounting period as follows:

Opening inventory (as reflected by the balance in the last balance sheet)	\$100 000
Plus cost of purchases / cost of manufacturing in the current accounting period	\$800 000
Inventory available for sale	\$900 000
Less cost of closing inventory (amount of stock is determined by way of a stocktake undertaken at the end of the accounting period)	(\$200 000)
Equals cost of sales	\$700 000

By contrast, under the **perpetual inventory system** (also known as the *continuous inventory system*), a running 'up-to-date' total is kept of the units on hand (and possibly their value) by recording all increases and decreases in inventory as they occur. That is, the inventory account is constantly kept up-to-date, so that every time an acquisition or sale of inventory occurs, adjustments are made to the inventory account and also to the cost of sales account (if a sale occurs), and the total of inventory items is known. Under the perpetual inventory system, cost of sales is determined each time there is a sale, rather than waiting until a stocktake is done at the end of the accounting period. At any point in time, managers know how much stock should be on hand, and this can be important to a business.

perpetual inventory system
An inventory management system where every time an acquisition or sale of inventory occurs, adjustments are made to the inventory account and also to the cost of goods sold account. At any time, managers will know how much stock should be on hand

Given the technology currently available, including various scanning devices that can update inventory records as inventory movements occur (most items have barcodes), most organisations now tend to use a perpetual inventory system. However, there are still some organisations, particularly smaller ones, that use a periodic inventory system (see **Learning exercise 10.16** for an example of a periodic inventory system in use), but the application of this approach has become less frequent.

10.16 Learning Exercise

An illustration of different inventory cost flow assumptions

Scenario: Fanning Company uses the periodic inventory system and sells one type of beach hat. It has the following inventory transactions for the financial year ending 30 June 2026:

Opening inventory at 1 July 2025	1000 units @ $10	$10 000
Purchases on 1 September 2025	2000 units @ $12	$24 000
Purchases on 15 January 2026	4000 units @ $14	$56 000
Purchases on 10 June 2026	6000 units @ $15	$90 000
Total	13 000 units	$180 000

During the year, Fanning Company sells 9000 units and therefore should have 4000 units on hand at year end. Fanning Company uses the periodic system to record inventory.

Task: Compute the cost of sales and value of ending inventory under the following cost-flow methods:

1 first-in, first-out (FIFO)
2 weighted average
3 last-in, first-out (LIFO).

Solution

FIFO

Sales of 9000 units occurred. The cost of sales comprises the beginning inventory of 1000 units and the next 8000 units purchased. That is, the first items of inventory that came in were assumed to be the first ones that went out – first in, first out. The ending inventory comprises the last 4000 units purchased.

Cost of sales = (1000 @ $10) + (2000 @ $12) + (4000 @ $14) + (2000 @ $15) = $120 000

Ending inventory (for the balance sheet) = (4000 @ $15) = $60 000

Weighted-average cost

The cost of sales and ending inventory are costed at the weighted-average price of beginning inventory and purchases.

Weighted-average cost = $180 000 ÷ 13 000 units = $13.8462 per unit

Cost of sales = 9000 @ $13.8462 = $124 615

Ending inventory (for the balance sheet) = 4000 @ $13.8462 = $55 385

LIFO

The cost of sales comprises the last 9000 units purchased. The ending inventory of 4000 units is assumed to comprise the beginning inventory of 1000 units, 2000 units purchased on 1 September 2025, and 1000 units purchased on 15 January 2026.

Cost of sales = (6000 @ $15) + (3000 @ $14) = $132 000

Ending inventory (for the balance sheet) = (1000 @ $10) + (2000 @ $12) + (1000 @ $14) = $48 000

Learning exercise 10.17 uses the perpetual inventory system rather than the periodic inventory system. As we have noted, if the perpetual inventory system is used, then each time an item of inventory is sold, the inventory account is updated and the related cost of sales is recognised. Contrast this with what we just did in **Learning exercise 10.16** wherein the periodic inventory system was used. A separate record is kept for each type of inventory, and when the perpetual inventory system is used this record clearly shows the dates on which inventory increases, and the dates on which it decreases, thereby continuously providing up-to-date information about the inventory on hand. As already noted, most organisations use the perpetual inventory system.

10.17 Learning Exercise

An illustration of the use of the FIFO cost-flow assumptions in conjunction with the perpetual inventory system

Scenario: Snapper Rocks Inc commences manufacturing and selling one-size-fits-all rash-shirts for surfing in 2025. Whilst each shirt is identical, the unit cost of manufacturing them has fluctuated due to rising material costs. Snapper Rocks Inc adopts a FIFO cost-flow assumption and employs a perpetual inventory system. Details of the manufacturing costs are as follows.

Date completed	Number completed	Unit manufacturing costs $
5 July 2025	1000	14.00
30 August 2025	2000	15.00
15 January 2026	2250	16.00
11 March 2026	3000	18.00
15 June 2026	2000	20.00
	10250	

Details of sales are as follows:

Date of sale	Number sold	Unit sales price $
15 July 2025	800	30.00
1 September 2025	2100	30.00
20 January 2026	2300	30.00
28 March 2026	2800	32.00
25 June 2026	1500	32.00
	9500	

Issue: What is the cost of sales for the financial year ended 30 June 2026, and what is the value of inventory for balance sheet purposes as at 30 June 2026?

Solution: Because the inventory items (which are rash-shirts) are identical, we cannot precisely determine the cost of each specific item sold. For example, is the firm selling items in January that were in fact produced in July, August or January? Typically, we would not know and we need to make a cost-flow assumption. In this exercise, we assume that the first rash-shirts produced are the first ones sold; that is, we have adopted the FIFO cost-flow assumption. With this assumption, cost of goods sold would be $159 000, determined as follows:

Date	Manufactured	Sold	Balance
5 July	1000 @ $14 = $14 000		1000 @ $14
15 July		800 @ $14 = $11 200	200 @ $14
30 August	2000 @ $15 = $30 000		200 @ $14
			2000 @ $15
1 September		200 @ $14 = $2800	100 @ $15
		1900 @ $15 = $28 500	
15 January	2250 @ 16 = $36 000		100 @ $15
			2250 @ $16
20 January		100@$15 = $1500	
		2200 @ $16 = $35 200	50 @ $16
11 March	3000 @18.00 = $54 000		50 @ $16
			3000 @ $18
28 March		50@ $16 = $800	
		2750 @$18 = $49 500	250 @ $18
15 June	2000 @ 20 = $40 000		250 @ $18
			2000 @ $20
25 June		250 @$18 = $4500	
		1250 @20 = $25 000	750 @ $20
	10 250 $174 000	9500 $159 000	

Looking at the above table and considering the sales transaction on 1 September, we had 2200 items on hand at the time with 200 units costing $14 and 2000 units costing $15. If we then sell 2100 units then we assume that we sell all the earlier items first (200 @ $14) before the balance of the sale (1900 units) is taken from the 2000 produced for $15.

Closing inventory, which would be reported in the balance sheet, would therefore be valued at $15 000 (which is 750 × $20). It represents the difference between what was manufactured ($174 000) and what was sold ($159 000).

The selection of a particular inventory cost-flow assumption creates a different cost of goods sold, and different balances of closing inventory for use within the balance sheet. In times of rising prices, LIFO will generate the highest cost of goods sold and the lowest closing inventory, whereas FIFO will generate the lowest cost of goods sold and the highest closing inventory. Weighted-average cost will generate results in between those generated by LIFO and FIFO.

The periodic system was used for the calculations in **Learning exercise 10.16**. The implication of this is that calculations of cost of goods sold are done periodically; for example, at the end of the financial period, rather than each time a sale is made. Contrast these calculations with those shown in **Learning exercise 10.17**, where the perpetual inventory system is used, and cost of goods sold and inventory balances are updated each time a sale occurs. As you can see from this example, if the perpetual system is used, the balance of inventory on hand is kept up-to-date.

In considering the use of the perpetual inventory system versus the periodic inventory system, a number of advantages of the perpetual system become apparent:

- Managers will have more up-to-date information about inventory during the accounting period, thereby enabling more-informed decisions to be made.
- The speed with which inventory is being sold can be determined, and slow-moving and fast-moving products can be identified. Further purchases of the slow-moving stock might be decreased, whereas purchases of the fast-moving stock might be increased. Understanding demand can also enable more-informed pricing decisions.
- The reordering of inventory can be done more efficiently. For example, reorder points might be linked to times when the level of stock reaches a predetermined minimum number of units. This can help reduce instances of stockouts, and therefore reduce the amount of lost sales. Reordering can be automated.
- Interim reports about income and expenses can be undertaken without the need to perform a stocktake.
- Stock losses can be determined. Because the organisation knows how much inventory *should* be on hand, when a stocktake is undertaken and a discrepancy is identified, this can point to the loss of stock, perhaps as a result of theft, thereby triggering the need to implement improved stock controls.

Before concluding our discussion of the differences between the periodic and perpetual inventory system, we will further consider the role of an end-of-period stocktake using the perpetual and periodic methods of accounting for inventory.

Under the perpetual system, we constantly update our records of inventory as sales, purchases and returns are made. The role of the stocktake in this case would be to determine whether what is on hand actually corresponds with what our accounting records indicate. A difference might indicate, for example, that a theft has occurred. The stocktake might also reveal obsolete or damaged inventory.

By contrast, where a periodic system is used, the stocktake is needed to tell us how much inventory is on hand, as under this system we do not update inventory each time an inventory movement occurs. Therefore, any discrepancies in stock – from theft, for example – cannot be identified and accounted for.

Exhibit 10.4 reproduces the accounting policy note pertaining to inventories as presented in the notes to the financial statements of the large Australian retailer Myer. As you can see, Myer uses the weighted-average-cost method.

EXHIBIT 10.4 Accounting policy note pertaining to inventory, as reported in the 2021 annual report of Myer Ltd

Accounting policy

Inventories are valued at the lower of cost and net realisable value. Cost is determined using the weighted average cost method, after deducting any purchase settlement discount and including logistics expenses incurred in bringing the inventories to their present location and condition.

Volume-related supplier rebates and supplier promotional rebates are recognised as a reduction in the cost of inventory and are recorded as a reduction of cost of goods sold when the inventory is sold.

Critical accounting estimates and judgements - recoverable amount of inventory

Management has assessed the value of inventory that is likely to be sold below cost using past experience and judgement on the likely sell through rates of various items of inventory, and booked a provision for this amount. To the extent that these judgements and assumptions prove incorrect, the Group may be exposed to potential additional inventory write-downs in future periods.

Source: Myer (2021), p. 62.

Why do I need to know about the different inventory cost flow assumptions?

Cost of goods sold (an expense which impacts profits), and the value of inventory (an asset reported in the balance sheet) will both be impacted by the inventory cost flow assumption made. Therefore, to be able to interpret 'profits' and 'inventory' – particularly for organisations that are involved in selling inventory (as opposed to service organisations, for example) – we need to understand the financial implications associated with managers selecting one inventory cost flow assumption instead of another.

Income tax expense

Income tax expense (tax expense) will appear as an expense in the income statement, and it will typically be a significant expense. We will not devote much space here to discussing tax expense. This is because it is a complicated area, and a full discussion would be beyond the ambit of this book. Students doing further studies in accounting will consider this issue more fully in subsequent subjects. However, at this point it is important to emphasise that the taxes imposed by taxation authorities in different countries will typically be levied on the basis of each country's taxation legislation, and on what they might refer to as taxable profit (which is the profit calculated using local taxation legislation), not on the basis of the accounting profits shown in the financial statements.

Different countries have different tax rules, will assess various items of income differently, and will treat various expenses differently. For example, certain expenditures that we refer to as creating assets in financial accounting might be considered as deductible expenses for tax purposes. Also, certain cash inflows that we, as financial accountants, consider to be liabilities – for example, revenue received in advance – might be taxed as received in cash by a country's taxation authority. Lastly, certain items that we consider as expenses might not be considered as expense deductions by some countries' taxation authorities. For example, in many countries, the impairment of certain intangible assets, such as goodwill impairment, is an expense for financial accounting purposes but is not a deductible expense for taxation purposes.

Therefore, the profit that we calculate using accounting standards – which are uniform internationally, particularly for those countries using the accounting standards issued by the IASB – will not necessarily be the same as the profit – 'taxable profit' – that an organisation generates from the perspective of the local taxation authority. Taxation rules tend to be different in every country, so the same sets of transactions and events will generate different taxable profits in different countries.

Therefore, to determine how much taxation is payable in a certain country, we cannot simply multiply the financial accounting profit (which amongst other things will be determined by applying accounting standards) by a country's taxation rates. The difference between 'accounting profit' and 'taxable profit' can, at times, be very significant, such that in some instances, a company that reports high profits from a financial reporting perspective might actually generate no taxable profit when applying the rules within a country's taxation legislation (and vice versa).

LO10.6 Accounting rules change over time

As you should now appreciate as a result of reading up to this point in the book, professional judgement – including judgements about such things as: the useful lives of assets; the probability that amounts owing to the organisation will ultimately be received; or, the likelihood that certain obligations will become payable – will influence the assets, liabilities, income and expenses (and therefore, the profits and equity) reported by an organisation. The accounting policy choices we make, such as whether to use FIFO or the weighted-average-cost method for inventory, or the cost model or the fair value model for property, plant and equipment, will also impact profits and assets. Apart from professional judgement, and the choices amongst allowable accounting policies, the issuance of new accounting standards can also significantly impact the profit that is calculated and presented within the income statement.

It is very common for new accounting standards to be issued. The International Accounting Standards Board (IASB) – which issues the accounting standards/financial reporting standards that are used within many countries throughout the world (the other major accounting standard-setter being, as we know, the US Financial Accounting Standards Board, or FASB, which issues accounting standards for US organisations) – commonly has years when it thoroughly revises some existing accounting standards and issues new accounting standards. These new and revised accounting standards will often change how particular assets and/or liabilities are required to be measured, and this in turn will impact how income and expenses are required to be measured by larger organisations (smaller organisations such as sole traders, partnerships and private companies are not required to apply accounting standards, and therefore a change in accounting standards has no impact upon their reporting).

For example, the IASB released a new accounting standard known as IFRS 16: Leases, which provides guidance on how leased assets, lease liabilities and lease-related expenses are to be recognised and measured (we discussed leased assets and lease liabilities in Chapter 9). This accounting standard, which was to be applied by large organisations from 1 January 2019, created significant changes in how organisations account for their leases. For larger organisations, with many leases, this new accounting standard had significant impacts on reported profits, reported assets and reported liabilities.

As another example, the IASB also issued IFRS 15: Revenue from Contracts with Customers, which was effective from 1 January 2018. This created a number of changes in the timing and measurement of income to be recognised from contracts with customers, and also caused significant changes to the reported profits of many organisations.

As another example of how profits can be affected by changes in the rules governing the measurement of assets, we can consider another accounting standard issued some time earlier by the IASB, this being IAS 41: Agriculture (IAS stands for International Accounting Standards and was the prefix that was given to accounting standards issued by the IASB prior to it changing the prefix for recently released accounting standards to IFRS). IAS 41 addresses how we account for biological assets, which are defined as living animals or plants. The accounting standard requires that biological assets, such as forestry assets or livestock, are to be measured on the basis of their fair value, with any increase in fair value recognised as income. This represents a significant change from previous practice whereby many organisations measured their agricultural assets on the basis of historical cost, with income not being recognised until the assets were actually sold. For some organisations with relatively high investments in biological assets, the impacts on profits were significant when the accounting standard was issued.

As a final example of how a change in accounting standards can impact reported profits, we can refer to IAS 38: Intangible Assets. In many countries throughout the world, internally generated intangibles (we discussed these in Chapter 9) were traditionally recognised within the balance sheet. However, when countries adopted the accounting standards of the IASB (many countries' governments decided to do this in the mid-2000s), the larger organisations within those countries had to comply with IAS 38, and this required that the expenditure on internally generated intangible assets be treated as an expense rather than as an asset. Again, this change brought about by the changed financial reporting rules had significant impacts on many organisations' financial performance and financial position.

We could give many more examples here of the impacts on financial statements when new accounting standards are issued. Such accounting changes will continue to happen as accounting standard-setters embrace new views on how different transactions and events should be accounted for from a financial accounting perspective.

Therefore, what we need to appreciate and understand is that the rules of financial accounting are not static. Rather, they regularly change, and this means that the profit or loss that we might have calculated for a specific series of transactions and events using the 'old' rules could actually be significantly different to the profit we would now calculate using the 'new' rules. That is, for exactly the same set of transactions and events, the rules adopted within the accounting standards we have at one point of time will generate different results to those results that would be generated using the accounting standards in place at a different time. As a result, this means that it is very problematic to compare current period reported profits with previous year profits. Using a sporting analogy, the rules of the game will typically have changed, and therefore the 'scoring system' that we use to generate information about financial performance can be quite different.

This very real fact, that accounting measurement rules regularly change across time, is often ignored by people who nevertheless compare current year financial performance with previous years' financial performance (it is common to see this done in the news media, thereby bringing into question the actual financial accounting knowledge of those people writing the articles). Without thinking, people undertaking this form of analysis are often comparing profits that could have been calculated using different rules – this is simply illogical, but it happens regularly. A logical approach would be to understand what changes have occurred in accounting rules and then try, as best as possible, to make adjustments to prior profits so as to make them logically comparable with current profits.

Throughout our lives, we will probably be exposed to situations where we see corporate profits being compared across several years; for example, as in Figure 10.3. Using information such as that which appears in Figure 10.3, some people – including some 'so-called' financial experts – will look for trends, and in this case, they might suggest that on the basis of movements in profit, it is likely that the future profits of this organisation will continue falling. But such trend analysis is extremely naive because unadjusted profits are being used from different periods wherein the accounting rules were potentially quite different. In Figure 10.3, the apparent downturns in profits might actually be due to changing accounting standards that were profit-decreasing, rather than by changes in the organisation's actual actions. Again, the theme we are trying to highlight is that we need to understand financial accounting rules, and changes therein, before we try to understand the contents of financial accounting statements. If we do not understand the rules, then we need to be very careful when relying upon financial statements to inform the various decisions we are contemplating making.

FIGURE 10.3 Trend analysis of the reported profits of a single organisation

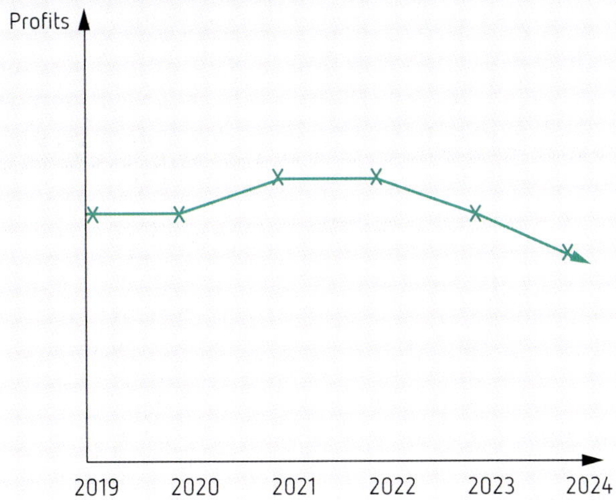

Therefore, if you find yourself in a situation where somebody is comparing current period profits with past profits, and particularly if the number of years being compared are numerous, then you should ask how they are controlling for possible changes in accounting standards, and wait for the presenter's response. This could then create an 'interesting' discussion (or perhaps an extended period of silence).

LO10.7 Presenting income and expenses in the income statement

Larger organisations – such as public companies – that are required to comply with accounting standards, have a choice about how they present their income statements. They can present their income statements in a way that classifies their expenses based on:

- the *function of the expenses*
- the *nature of the expenses.*

If an organisation presents its expenses based on the function-of-expenses approach, which we referred to earlier in this chapter, then expenses will be classified according to their function. Those costs relating to the cost of sales will be separately disclosed, as will the costs of distribution or administrative activities (and other functions that can logically be derived by adding different expenses together). This approach to disclosure can provide more-relevant information to users than the classification of expenses by nature (discussed below), but allocating costs to functions may require arbitrary allocations and involve considerable judgement. An example of a classification using the function-of-expense approach follows:

Example of an income statement presented using the function-of-expenses approach

Income statement of Southside Company for the year ending 31 December 2026	
Revenue	$500 000
Cost of sales	($250 000)
Gross profit	$250 000
Other income	$50 000
Distribution costs	($90 000)
Administrative expenses	($70 000)
Other expenses	($10 000)
Profit before tax	**$130 000**
Taxation expense	($50 000)
Profit	**$80 000**

In the above classification of expenses based on the function of the expenses, a separate amount for gross profit is disclosed. Gross profit is the difference between sales revenue and cost of sales. We have already addressed both of these items, so you'll remember that:

- Sales revenue will be recognised when the probability of the inflow of economic benefits is not considered low, there is limited measurement uncertainty, and control of the item has passed to the customer.
- Cost of sales will include the cost of inventory sold (we have discussed what will be included in this cost) and will be affected by the choices of inventory cost-flow assumption, and whether the organisation uses the periodic or perpetual inventory system. The costs of inventory can include manufacturing costs, raw material expenses, direct labour expenses, and other directly attributable expenses.

gross profit
The difference between sales revenue and cost of sales

Gross profit – being the difference between sales revenue and cost of sales – is a number that attracts great attention from managers and other stakeholders. It is an important measure because it indicates the efficiency of management in using labour, material and other supplies in the production or retail process. Since further expenses will be deducted from gross profits, an organisation will not generate profits if gross profits are not sufficiently large. Should gross profit be negative, a loss will almost be a certainty.

Gross profit is a number that is of relevance to retailers and manufacturing organisations, but it is not a useful measure for organisations that are more service-oriented (such as, for example, architects, lawyers, accountants and hotels), as the revenue being generated is based more on the use of labour and professional expertise than on the sale of physical products. As a result, and related to the idea of 'relevance', we can see that the type of product or service being produced/provided by an organisation will impact the form in which the income statement will be presented.

For those organisations to which a gross profit amount is relevant (for example, manufacturers and retailers), a lower than expected gross profit needs to be investigated to determine whether sales prices might need to be increased, and/or production costs (or costs of inventory purchases) need attention in order to be lowered. Perhaps better staff training or more efficient production techniques are required, or more attention needs to be directed towards acquiring materials that are of lower cost (but not of lower quality).

With any analysis of gross profit, it needs to be kept in mind that what is an acceptable gross profit will be impacted by industry considerations, as well as considerations pertaining to the current economic climate. Also, some organisations might elect to reduce their gross profit by lowering their prices (therefore reducing sales revenue) in order to attract new customers, but an organisation cannot maintain operations in the longer run with low gross profits.

Having discussed the approach where expenses are classified by function, the other option for larger organisations that are required to comply with accounting standards is for expenses to be classified according to their nature. If this is done, the organisation will aggregate expenses according to their nature (for example, depreciation, purchases of materials, transport costs, employee benefits and advertising costs) and will not reallocate them among functions within the entity. This method is relatively simple to apply because no allocations of expenses to functional classifications are necessary. An example of an income statement presented using the nature of expenses approach is as follows:

Example of an income statement presented using the nature of expenses approach

Income statement of Northside Company for the year ending 31 December 2026	
Revenue	$650 000
Other income	$50 000
	$700 000
Advertising expenses	($90 000)
Depreciation expenses	($40 000)
Employee salaries	($200 000)
Interest expenses	($45 000)
Office supplies consumed	($35 000)
Rent	($50 000)
Other expenses	($15 000)
Profit before tax	**$225 000**
Taxation expense	($100 000)
Profit	**$125 000**

Smaller organisations that do not have to comply with accounting standards (such as sole traders, partnerships, and smaller private companies) can elect to present their income statement in the format that is most useful/relevant to their respective stakeholders. Smaller organisations might tend to show more details about specific expenses, whereas larger organisations tend to aggregate many of their expenses.

Smaller organisations that are not required to follow accounting standards often subdivide their income statement in two sections, one of which might be the 'operating section' and the other being the 'other items section'. The operating section includes those items of income and expenses that relate to the primary operating activities of the organisation, whilst the other items section includes those items of income and expenses that do not relate directly to the primary operations of the organisation, such as interest expense and interest revenue. By presenting an income statement in this format (see below), more attention can be directed to those items on income and expense that relate to the ordinary operations of an organisation.

Income statement for Kirra Company for the year ending 31 December 2026		
Sales revenue		$2 500 000
Cost of sales		$1 300 000
Gross profit		$1 200 000
Operating expenses		
Selling and distribution expenses	$20 000	
Advertising expenses	$50 000	
Sales staff salaries	$230 000	
Other expenses of sales staff	$50 000	($350 000)
General and administrative expenses		
Office staff salaries	$90 000	
Office rent	$60 000	
Office supplies consumed	$40 000	
Other office expenses	$10 000	($200 000)
Operating profit		$650 000
Other items of income and expense		
Interest income		$25 000
Interest expense		($35 000)
Profit before tax		**$640 000**
Taxation expense		($200 000)
Profit		**$440 000**

As already noted, smaller organisations often produce income statements that have more detail than those organisations that are required to comply with accounting standards. In part, this is because the financial statements of smaller organisations are directed more towards the managers, who might also be the owners, rather than towards external stakeholders. For smaller organisations that are not required by law to make their financial statements publicly available, there will generally be efforts made to keep the information in the income statements confidential so that competitors cannot learn about the profitability of the organisation. These smaller organisations will, however, often make their income statements available to organisations such as banks, as this might be a necessary requirement associated with attracting and keeping a loan.

So, in summary, managers have some choice in how they present the income statement. They need to choose the format that is more likely to provide 'relevant information' – one of the fundamental qualitative characteristics that useful financial information possesses.

Disclosing exceptional or unusual items

From time to time, there will be items of income and expense that are unusual, or out of character, compared with what would normally be expected from the ordinary, ongoing operations of an organisation. For example, an organisation might have unexpectedly incurred:

- unusual and unexpected writedowns of inventory
- unexpected and significant losses on the disposal of property, plant and equipment

- large costs as a result of losing a legal case brought against it by a customer
- major losses as a result of significant and unexpected changes in foreign currency exchange rates.

To the extent that such costs are unusual, and have had a significant impact on the financial performance of an organisation, good financial reporting practice would see the accountant separately identifying the impacts of these unusual items, either on the face of the income statement or in the notes accompanying the statement. Specifically, disclosure should be made of the nature, and the amount, of the related income and/or expense associated with the unusual events (the events themselves might not be unusual, but the magnitude of the associated amounts might be). This disclosure requirement relies upon professional judgement concerning the financial significance of the item (that is, its *materiality*) and whether it is 'unusual', or different in magnitude, to what would reasonably be expected.

Since financial statements are used, in part, to help us predict what might happen in the future, it is important for us to know whether the financial performance of a particular accounting period has been impacted by unusual events, or transactions, which are not expected to occur again in the future. In predicting future performance, we might be more interested in those items of income and expense that are expected to recur.

As an example of disclosures that might be made in the notes to the financial statements, refer to **Exhibit 10.5**, which shows disclosures made in the annual report of the global mining company BHP about what have been termed exceptional items.

EXHIBIT 10.5 Disclosure of 'exceptional Items' as provided in the notes to the 2021 annual report of BHP

Exceptional items are those gains or losses where their nature, including the expected frequency of the events giving rise to them, and impact, is considered material to the Financial Statements. Such items included within the Group's profit from Continuing operations for the year are detailed below.

Year ended 30 June 2021	Gross US$M	Tax US$M	Net US$M
Exceptional items by category			
Samarco dam failure	(1 087)	(71)	(1 158)
COVID-19 related costs	(546)	146	(400)
Impairment of Energy coal assets	(1 523)	(651)	(2 174)
Impairment of Potash assets	(1 314)	(751)	(2 065)
Total	(4 470)	(1 327)	(5 797)
Attributable to non-controlling interests	(34)	10	(24)
Attributable to BHP shareholders	(4 436)	(1 337)	(5 773)

Source: BHP (2021), p. 140.

Profit or loss derived from discontinued operations

A discontinued operation is a component of an entity that either has been disposed of or is classified as 'held for sale'. It could represent a separate major line of business or geographical area of operations.

In trying to predict what future profits will be, it would make little sense to consider past results that relate to discontinued operations. Therefore, for larger organisations that are required to comply with accounting standards, there is a requirement that they segregate, within the income statement, those items of profit or loss that come from continuing operations, and those that come from discontinuing operations. Focusing on the income and expenses associated with continuing operations provides a better indication of what might be expected in the future.

Other comprehensive income

Some accounting standards specifically exclude some items from being included within profits or losses despite the fact they might seem to fit the definition of income. As we know, income is defined as:

> increases in assets, or decreases in liabilities, that result in increases in equity, other than those relating to contributions from holders of equity claims.
>
> Source: International Accounting Standards Board (2022a).

As an example, when we revalue an item of property, plant and equipment upwardly (because the fair value has increased), this increases assets and equity, and is not a contribution from owners. Hence it fits the definition of 'income'. However, for larger organisations, the accounting standard pertaining to property, plant and equipment has a requirement that increases in fair value will not be included in profits (as income) but rather will be identified as being part of 'other comprehensive income' and included in equity (specifically in a reserve account referred to as an 'asset revaluation reserve' or 'revaluation surplus account').

Therefore, whilst the revaluation increase should not be included in income – and therefore as part of accounting profits – it should be included within a measure of financial performance known as **other comprehensive income**, which is defined in the IASB accounting standards as follows:

other comprehensive income
Other comprehensive income comprises items of income and expense that are not recognised in profit or loss as required or permitted by other Accounting Standards

> Other comprehensive income comprises items of income and expense that are not recognised in profit or loss as required or permitted by other Accounting Standards.
>
> Source: International Accounting Standards Board (2022b).

'Other comprehensive income' – which is required to be disclosed by larger organisations that must comply with accounting standards – includes all changes in equity that have occurred during the accounting period that have not already been incorporated within 'profit' or 'loss', and which do not represent contributions by owners, or distributions to them. As examples of some accounting standards that require particular gains or losses to be included in other comprehensive income, rather than profit and loss, we can consider:

- the gains generated through asset revaluations – IAS 16: Property, Plant and Equipment specifically states:

  > If an asset's carrying amount is increased as a result of a revaluation, the increase shall be recognised in other comprehensive income and accumulated in equity under the heading of revaluation surplus.
  >
  > Source: International Accounting Standards Board (2022c).

- foreign exchange differences associated with translating the financial statements of an organisation's foreign operations – IAS 21: The Effects of Changes in Foreign Exchange Rates specifically states:

> In the financial statements that include the foreign operation and the reporting entity (e.g. consolidated financial statements when the foreign operation is a subsidiary), such exchange differences shall be recognised initially in other comprehensive income and reclassified from equity to profit or loss on disposal of the net investment.
>
> Source: International Accounting Standards Board (2022d).

- gains or losses on a hedging instrument in a cash flow hedge – IAS 39: Financial Instruments: Recognition and Measurement specifically states:

> If a cash flow hedge meets the conditions in paragraph 88 during the period, it shall be accounted for as follows: (a) the portion of the gain or loss on the hedging instrument that is determined to be an effective hedge (see paragraph 88) shall be recognised in other comprehensive income.
>
> Source: International Accounting Standards Board (2022e).

Whilst there is *not* an expectation at this stage of your accounting education that you will understand the specific requirements above, the reason for providing these points is to emphasise that not all financial gains and losses will necessarily be included in profits or losses. Specific accounting standards will prohibit certain gains and losses from being included in profit or loss. Therefore, some gains and losses must be transferred to a reserve account and be included within 'other comprehensive income'.

So just be aware that we have a measure called 'profits', and another measure called 'other comprehensive income', of which the total of the two is referred to as **total comprehensive income**.

total comprehensive income
The total of profit or loss, and other comprehensive income

Statement of comprehensive income

Organisations that are required to comply with accounting standards must present details of the profit or loss of the organisation for a period of time, as well as information about 'other comprehensive income' for that period. In presenting this information, organisations have a choice. They can either:

- produce a single statement that includes details of profit and loss, and other comprehensive income; or
- prepare a separate income statement, and a separate statement of comprehensive income that adds the other comprehensive income to accounting profit (from the income statement) to then produce a total amount known as *total comprehensive income*.

Generally, the gains and losses that are recorded as part of 'other comprehensive income' are outcomes that do not relate to the ordinary activities of an organisation. Therefore, stakeholders (including the news media) tend to focus more on the profit or loss of an organisation as reported within the income statement, rather than on the total comprehensive income as reported within the statement of comprehensive income.

Exhibit 10.6 and **Exhibit 10.7** together provide an example of where an organisation – in this instance, BHP – provides a separate income statement and a separate statement of comprehensive income. Produced within the 2021 annual report of BHP, both statements are accompanied by many supporting notes.

EXHIBIT 10.6 An example of where the income statement is presented separately to the statement of comprehensive income

Consolidated income statement for BHP for the year ended 30 June 2021				
	Notes	2021 US$M	2020 US$M	2019 US$M
Continuing operations				
Revenue	2	60 817	42 931	44 288
Other income	5	510	777	393
Expenses excluding net finance costs	5	(34 500)	(28 775)	(28 022)
Loss from equity accounted investments, related impairments and expenses	31	(921)	(512)	(546)
Profit from operations		25 906	14 421	16 113
Financial expenses		(1378)	(1 262)	(1510)
Financial income		73	351	446
Net finance costs	22	(1305)	(911)	(1064)
Profit before taxation		24 601	13 510	15 049
Income tax expense		(10 921)	(4 708)	(5 335)
Royalty-related taxation (net of income tax benefit)		(229)	(66)	194)
Total taxation expense	6	(11 150)	(4774)	(5 529)
Profit/(loss) after taxation from continuing operations		13 451	8 736	9 520
Discontinued operations				
Loss after taxation from discontinued operations	29	-	-	(335)
Profit/(loss) after taxation from continuing and discontinued operations		13 451	8 736	9 185

Source: BHP (2021), p. 130.

EXHIBIT 10.7 An example of a statement of comprehensive income

Consolidated statement of comprehensive income for BHP for the year ended 30 June 2021			
	2021 US$M	2020 US$M	2019 US$M
Profit after taxation from Continuing and Discontinued operations	13 451	8 736	9 185
Other comprehensive income			
Items that may be reclassified subsequently to the income statement:			
Hedges:			
Gains/(losses) taken to equity	863	(315)	(327)
(Gains)/losses transferred to the income statement	(837)	297	299
Exchange fluctuations on translation of foreign operations taken to equity	5	1	1
Exchange fluctuations on translation of foreign operations transferred to income statement	–	–	(6)

Consolidated statement of comprehensive income for BHP for the year ended 30 June 2021			
	2021 US$M	2020 US$M	2019 US$M
Tax recognised within other comprehensive income	(8)	24	8
Total items that may be reclassified subsequently to the income statement	23	(12)	(25)
Items that will not be reclassified to the income statement:			
Re-measurement gains/(losses) on pension and medical schemes	58	(81)	(20)
Equity investments held at fair value	(2)	(2)	1
Tax recognised within other comprehensive income	(20)	26	19
Total items that will not be reclassified to the income statement	36	(57)	-
Total other comprehensive (loss)/income	59	(69)	(25)
Total comprehensive income	13 510	8 667	9 160

Source: BHP (2021), p. 130.

When looking at the income statement of BHP (**Exhibit 10.6**), you will notice that it is produced in a manner that does not provide great detail of the expenses incurred. However, the income statement refers us to notes to the financial statements that provide greater detail. For example, if we want to know more about what comprises 'Other income' or the 'Expenses' that are shown in the BHP income statement, then we need to look at note 5, which is reproduced in **Exhibit 10.8**. This note shows that the expenses have been classified in accordance with the 'nature of expenses' format we discussed earlier in this chapter, rather than the 'function of expenses' format. When you look at the financial statements of any large organisation, you will find that the financial statements refer to many notes that support them.

EXHIBIT 10.8 Details of the expenses and 'other income' impacting profit or loss, as detailed in the notes to the 2021 annual report of BHP

Note 5 – Expenses and other income			
	2021 US$M	2020 US$M	2019 US$M
Employee benefits expense:			
Wages, salaries and redundancies	4 399	3706	3683
Employee share awards	124	129	138
Social security costs	3	2	4
Pension and other post-retirement obligations	316	283	292
Less employee benefits expense classified as exploration and evaluation expenditure	(119)	(65)	(85)
Changes in inventories of finished goods and work in progress	(334)	(326)	496
Raw materials and consumables used	4940	5 509	4 591
Freight and transportation	2037	1981	2 378
External services	5260	4404	4745
Third-party commodity purchases	2 230	1139	1 069
Net foreign exchange (gains)/losses	310	(603)	(147)

Note 5 – Expenses and other income	2021 US$M	2020 US$M	2019 US$M
Fair value change on derivatives(1)	145	422	8
Government royalties paid and payable	3 217	2 362	2 538
Exploration and evaluation expenditure incurred and expensed in the current period	430	517	516
Depreciation and amortisation expense	6 824	6 112	5 829
Net impairments:			
Property, plant and equipment	2 583	494	250
Goodwill and other intangible assets	52	-	14
All other operating expenses	2 083	2 709	1 703
Total expenses	34 500	28 775	28 022
Insurance recoveries(2)	(46)	(489)	(57)
Other income(3)	(464)	(288)	(336)
Total other income	(510)	(277)	(393)

(1) Fair value change on derivatives is principally related to commodity price contracts, foreign exchange contracts and embedded derivatives used in the ordinary course of business as well as derivatives used as part of the funding of dividends.

(2) Insurance recoveries is principally related to claims received from Samarco dam failure. Refer to note 4 'Significant events – Samarco dam failure' for further information.

(3) Other income is generally income earned from transactions outside the course of the Group's ordinary activities and may include certain management fees from non-controlling interests and joint arrangements, dividend income, royalties, commission income and gains or losses on divestment of subsidiaries or operations.

Source: BHP (2021), p. 146.

Key concept

For larger organisations that are required to apply financial reporting standards, not all gains and losses go to profit or loss. Some gains and losses are required to be assigned to 'other comprehensive income'.

You will also notice that within the income statement, 'revenue' and 'other income' are separated in a manner consistent with what we discussed earlier in this chapter – that is, 'revenue' is the term that relates to the income from the normal operating activities of an organisation. However, rather than calling other income 'gains', BHP refers to 'other income'. Note 5 to BHP's financial statements (see **Exhibit 10.8**) describes what BHP means by the term 'other income'.

Again, the approach generally taken by larger organisations is to separate the income that comes from the ordinary operations (revenue) from that income which does not come from the ordinary operations. Consistent with our earlier discussion, you will also notice within the income statement of BHP that it separately discloses any profit or loss associated with 'discontinued operations' (presented towards the bottom of the income statement). As we indicated earlier within this chapter, if certain aspects of an organisation's operations have been discontinued, then it is useful for the readers of the financial statements for the results associated with the discontinued operations to be separated from the results of the aspects of the organisation's operations that are considered to be continuing.

When looking at BHP's statement of comprehensive income (**Exhibit 10.7**), there is not an expectation that you understand all its contents. You just need to appreciate that where a statement of comprehensive income is presented separately, then the profit or loss from the income statement is the starting point at which other gains and losses that are recorded directly in equity accounts (reserves), and not through profit or loss, are added to give a broader measure of financial performance known as total comprehensive income.

You will also have noticed that the statements have 'Consolidated' in their title. This is because the financial statements are not for a single company but have been produced by 'consolidating' (or combining, with various adjustments and eliminations) the financial statements of the parent company with those of all the organisations that it controls (which are referred to as subsidiaries). That is, the consolidated financial statements are for a group of organisations; we discussed consolidated financial statements in Chapter 2. In some cases, some large public companies control over 100 other organisations (which will be called their 'subsidiaries'), all of which would have their financial statements consolidated (combined) to produce the consolidated financial statements.

Lastly, in the preceding exhibits, you will have noticed that BHP has provided three years of comparative numbers. Whilst it is usual for organisations to just provide numbers for the current and preceding year, some organisations do produce another year of comparative figures.

Why do I need to know about the difference between 'profit or loss' and 'other comprehensive income'?

When larger organisations – such as large public companies – report their financial performance, they will report an amount for 'profit or loss' and a separate amount for 'other comprehensive income'. When these two amounts are added together, this gives 'total comprehensive income' – see **Exhibit 10.7**.

Because large organisations will report these two amounts (and the total), it is helpful for us to have some degree of understanding about what the numbers represent. As we have noted, some accounting standards specifically note that certain gains and losses must not be included in profits or losses, whereas other gains or losses must be included within 'other comprehensive income'. For example, if an organisation revalues its property, plant and equipment upwards, then accounting standards specifically note that this increment above cost shall be treated as a gain that must be included with 'other comprehensive income' and not within profits. The reasons why some gains and losses are permitted to be included within profit or loss, and others are not, is a little bit too complicated for us to understand at this stage of accounting education. Nevertheless, the point to be made is that if you want to know what the total gains and losses of an organisation have been from a financial perspective, then you should look at 'total comprehensive income' rather than profit or loss.

LO10.8 The statement of changes in equity

Organisations that are required to comply with accounting standards, such as public companies, must produce a statement of changes in equity for the accounting period. Those other organisations that are not required to follow accounting standards can also choose to do so voluntarily.

As we know, equity is the residual interest in the assets of the entity after deducting its liabilities. For a sole trader, the financial statements might only show one equity account, which might be referred to as the capital account.

In other organisations, total equity might be comprised of a number of accounts. For a company, equity might be made up of a number of components; for example:

- share capital
- retained earnings
- reserves.

statement of changes in equity
Provides a reconciliation of opening and closing equity and details of the various equity accounts that are impacted by the period's total comprehensive income

The role of the **statement of changes in equity** is to provide a reconciliation of opening and closing equity, and also to provide details of the various equity accounts that are impacted by the period's total comprehensive income. It therefore shows why/how the equity accounts presented within the balance sheets have changed from one accounting period to the next. It also provides information about the effects of transactions with owners in their capacity as owners (distributions to, and capital contributions from, owners).

In Chapter 7, we provided an example of a simple statement of changes in equity for an organisation that only had two equity accounts, these being retained earnings and share capital. This is reproduced below in **Exhibit 10.9**.

Key concept

The statement of changes in equity provides a reconciliation of opening and closing equity, and details of the various equity accounts that are impacted on by the period's total comprehensive income. It shows why and how the equity accounts presented within the balance sheets have changed from one accounting period to the next.

EXHIBIT 10.9 Example of a simple statement of changes in equity

Statement of changes in equity for Lenny's Longboards for the month ending 31 January 2024

	Capital contribution $	Retained earnings $	Total equity $
Balance at 1/1/24	0	0	0
Capital contributed	80 000		80 000
Drawings by owners		(2 000)	(2 000)
Profit for the month		34 000	34 000
Balance at 31/1/24	80 000	32 000	112 000

As an example of a statement of changes in equity for a larger organisation, we can consider the statement of changes in equity of the international airline company Qantas. If we look at the balance sheet of Qantas for the year ending 30 June 2021, we find that equity amounts for 2021 and 2020 are as follows:

	2021 $m	2020 $m
Issued capital	3 186	3 104
Treasury shares	(18)	(51)
Reserves	432	(173)
Accumulated losses	(3 087)	(1357)
Equity attributable to the members of Qantas	**513**	**1 523**
Non-controlling interests	3	3
Total equity	**516**	**1 526**

Source: Qantas (2021), pp. 69–70.

The statement of changes in equity for Qantas, as reproduced in **Exhibit 10.10**, then provides details about why the equity balance of Qantas moved from $1526 million in 2020 to $516 million in 2021. A thorough understanding of the detail in this statement of changes in equity is beyond the scope of understanding required at this stage of your accounting education.

EXHIBIT 10.10 An example of a statement of changes in equity, as prepared by a large organisation

Qantas consolidated statement of changes in equity for the year ended 30 June 2021									
30 June 2021 $M	Issued Capital	Treasury Shares	Employee Compensation Reserve	Hedge Reserve	Foreign Currency Translation Reserve	Other(1) Reserves	Accumulated Losses	Non-controlling Interests	Total Equity
Balance as at 1 July 2020	3104	(51)	54	(147)	4	(84)	(1 357)	3	1 526
TOTAL COMPREHENSIVE (LOSS)/INCOME FOR THE YEAR									
Statutory loss for the year	–	–	–	–	–	–	(1 728)	–	(1 728)
Other comprehensive income/(loss)									
Effective portion of changes in fair value of cash flow hedges, net of tax	–	–	–	201	–	–	–	–	201
Transfer of effective hedging losses from hedge reserve to the Consolidated Income Statement, net of tax	–	–	–	49	–	–	–	–	49
De-designation of fuel and foreign exchange hedges to the Consolidated Income Statement, net of tax				15					15
Recognition of effective cash flow hedges on capitalised assets, net of tax	–	–	–	4	–	–	–	–	4
Net changes in hedge reserve for time value of options, net of tax	–	–	–	42	–	–	–	–	42
Foreign currency translation of controlled entities	–	–	–	–	10	–	–	–	10
Foreign currency translation of investments accounted for under the equity method	–	–	–	–	12	–	–	–	12

30 June 2021 $M	Issued Capital	Treasury Shares	Employee Compensation Reserve	Hedge Reserve	Foreign Currency Translation Reserve	Other(1) Reserves	Accumulated Losses	Non-controlling Interests	Total Equity
Share of other comprehensive income of investments accounted for under the equity method	–	–	–	12	–	–	–	–	12
Defined benefit actuarial gains, net of tax						251			251
Fair value gains on investments, net of tax						29			29
Total other comprehensive income for the year	–	–	–	323	22	280	–	–	625
Total comprehensive (loss)/income for the year	–	–	–	323	22	280	(1 728)	–	(1 103)
TRANSACTIONS WITH OWNERS RECORDED DIRECTLY IN EQUITY									
Contributions by and distributions to owners									
Capital raising, net of tax	82	–	–	–	–	–	(6)	–	76
Share-based payments	–	–	19	–	–	–	–	–	19
Shares vested and transferred to employees/shares unvested and lapsed	–	33	(39)	–	–	–	4	–	(2)
Total contributions by and distributions to owners	82	33	(20)	–	–	–	(2)	–	93
Total transactions with owners	82	33	(20)	–	–	–	(2)	–	93
Balance as at 30 June 2021	3 186	(18)	34	176	26	196	(3 087)	3	516

(1) Other Reserves includes the Defined Benefit Reserve and the Fair Value Reserve.

Source: Qantas (2021), p. 69.

Why do I need to know about the role of the statement of changes in equity?

There are four main financial statements (the balance sheet, the income statement, the statement of cash flows, and the statement of changes in equity), of which the statement of changes in equity is one. It provides a reconciliation of opening and closing equity and shows how and why the components of equity have changed. It also provides information that might not be readily available within other financial statements, such as transactions with owners in their capacity as owners, and adjustments to retained earnings as a result of the correction of prior period errors. Knowing the intended role of the statement of changes in equity, and the information it reports that is not available elsewhere, highlights the useful nature of the statement.

LO10.9 Is profit a 'good' measure of an organisation's performance?

A central role of financial accounting is to calculate and report the profit or loss of an organisation (as well as identifying items of 'other comprehensive income'). As we are aware from media reports, profits and losses often appear to be used as an indicator of the 'success' or 'failure' of an organisation. However, there are many gains, and costs, that relate to an organisation's activities that do not appear within financial statements, and are not incorporated in the measurement we refer to as profits, or total comprehensive income.

The increases in the financial value of many assets do not appear in the financial statements. As we learned in Chapter 9, accounting standards provide organisations with a choice between using 'cost' or 'fair value' to measure their property, plant and equipment. If the cost model is used, then any gains in fair value will not be recognised and therefore the gains in fair value will not be included within other comprehensive income. We also know from Chapter 9 that intangible assets that have been generated internally (that is, have not been acquired from another party) are prohibited – by virtue of rules incorporated within financial reporting standards – from being recognised within the financial accounts, despite the value they might create for an organisation. Further, there is a general prohibition on the revaluation of intangible assets (unless an 'active market' exists for them, and this is uncommon for intangible assets). Therefore, the gains in the value of intangible assets will also be ignored within financial accounting.

However, whilst gains, such as those mentioned above, might be of relevance to many users of financial statements, arguably of more concern to many people is the manner in which financial accounting treats the social and environmental impacts, or costs, created by organisations. Generally speaking, financial accounting ignores most of the social and environmental impacts caused by organisations, despite the potential severity of some of these impacts.

In Chapter 7 we learned that one of the key financial accounting principles is the 'entity concept' (also referred to as the 'entity assumption'). The 'entity concept' is a cornerstone of financial accounting and it requires the accountant to treat an organisation as an entity distinct from its owners, other organisations and other stakeholders. Consistent with what we have done in this book, the entity assumption or concept is typically taught to students of financial accounting at the introductory stages. According to this concept, an organisation is treated as an accounting unit that is quite distinct and separate from the owners and other organisations, and the accountant must define the organisation's area of interest in such a way as to limit the events and transactions to be included in the financial statements. The organisation and the many external stakeholders of that organisation are treated as very separate accounting entities. The entity assumption allows the accountant to measure the financial performance and position of each entity, independent of all other entities. According to the entity assumption, if a transaction or event does not directly affect the financial resources or obligations of the entity (the organisation that we are preparing the financial statements for), then the transaction or event is to be ignored for financial reporting purposes. This means that the externalities caused by reporting entities will typically be ignored, and that performance measures (such as 'profits') are incomplete from a broader societal (as opposed to a 'discrete entity') perspective. We can relate the entity principle to the profits that might be reported by a tobacco manufacturer. It is generally accepted that cigarettes cause many health problems, yet externalities that relate to the products of a reporting entity are ignored for financial reporting purposes. That is, reported profits are not affected by such externalities. In a similar vein, we can consider the operations of casinos. They are often very 'profitable'; however, such profit measures ignore the social costs gambling causes in the community, and how the actions of gambling providers in supplying gambling opportunities contribute to such social costs. Arguably, any moves towards accounting for sustainability would require a modification to, or a move away from, the entity assumption. A further factor that reduces the potential for financial accounting to recognise various social and environmental costs is the way we define the elements of financial accounting.

As you know, from a financial accounting perspective, expenses are defined as:

> decreases in assets, or increases in liabilities, that result in decreases in equity, other than those relating to distributions to holders of equity claims.
>
> Source: International Accounting Standards Board (2022a).

To understand the meaning of 'expenses', we need to understand the meanings of 'assets' and 'liabilities'. From a financial accounting perspective, we know that assets are defined as:

> a present economic resource controlled by the entity as a result of past events.
>
> Source: International Accounting Standards Board (2022a).

The establishment of 'control' is therefore central to the recognition of an asset. If a resource is not controlled by the organisation (for example, air, oceans and waterways, and an organisation's workforce are not controlled), then that resource is excluded from asset recognition, and therefore will not appear within the balance sheet. If the resource is not recognised as an asset, then any decrease in value, or damage or harm done to that resource, will not be recognised as an expense of the organisation. That is, any diminution in the non-controlled resource's value or quality, such as pollution's adverse effect on air quality, will not be recognised as an expense of the organisation because it was never initially recognised as an asset of the organisation.

Let us consider some examples of some negative social and environmental impacts an organisation's activities might create, but which (unfortunately) will be ignored by financial accounting practices.

In recent years, many companies in the clothing industry have been criticised for acquiring their products from factories in developing countries where the work environment is unhealthy and unsafe for workers. In developing countries like Bangladesh, many hundreds of people involved in manufacturing clothing for international companies have died as a result of building collapses and factory fires, which in turn have been blamed on poor health and safety policies being utilised within the factories. It is generally believed that large multinational companies buy their products from developing countries because they can obtain reasonable quality products at very low prices. These low prices mean the cost of sales of the multinational companies is low, and reported profits are higher than might otherwise be the case if they were to source the products from suppliers that have excellent – and often relatively costly to implement – health and safety practices in place. But how does the death and injury of many workers associated with the production impact 'profits'? The answer is that the death and injury of workers does not impact reported profits. As we know, our simple accounting equation is A = L + OE. Because the dead and injured workers are not 'assets' from a financial accounting perspective (they are not controlled), then reported assets will not be decreased. Consequently, to balance our accounting equation – which is another cornerstone of financial accounting – equity also cannot be decreased, otherwise our accounting equation will not balance, and to financial accountants this would clearly not make sense (but of course, how we – as financial accountants – could ignore such costs associated with the death and injury of workers might not make sense to non-accountants).

Organisations also often decide to reduce their expenses by replacing people within their workforce with some form of modern automated technology. This tends to increase accounting profits, because the related machinery and technology is cheaper to run than the salaries and wages that might otherwise have been paid to the employees. But how are the 'social costs' relating to the sacked workers accounted for? Simply stated, these social costs are also ignored by financial accounting. The ignored costs include the hardship created for employees and their families, particularly for those employees who are unable to find new jobs. Obviously, such costs are extremely difficult to measure, but it is nevertheless the case that they are completely overlooked by financial accounting.

An argument can be made that the news media are often complicit in lauding profitable organisations without considering the consequences of the organisations' actions that led to the profits.

The news media often seem to praise the efforts of corporate managers who reduce wages expense without having any regard for the hardship that such sackings or redundancies might create for the employees and their families. For example, an article in the *Australian Financial Review* (Eyers & de Kretser, 2022) reported that the large Australian bank, Westpac, initiated a 20 per cent reduction in head office positions to keep 'costs under control'. It was noted that more than 1100 jobs had been cut in the previous three months, with around the same number to go in the following three months. It was noted in the article that as a result, profits rose by about $1.58 billion in the three months ended 31 December, apparently 'beating expectations because of stronger revenue and faster cost-cutting'.

At issue is whether we should really say that 'cost cutting' has occurred when so many people will potentially become unemployed? This is an instance where expenses, as defined by financial accounting, will indeed fall, but unrecorded 'social costs' will climb. In a similar way, an article in *The Age* newspaper (Hatch, 2022) noted that the international airline Qantas will be able to report a profit while flying emptier planes than its rivals because of an 'aggressive pandemic cost-cutting drive', which financial analysts were reported as saying would help shield Qantas from its competitors. The number of passengers Qantas would need in order to be profitable was reduced 'thanks to its cost-cutting efforts, which included laying off almost one-third of its workforce'. Again, this ignores potential 'social costs'.

As another example of where the discussion of costs seems to totally ignore social costs, we can refer to a newspaper article in *The Australian* (Grieve, 2021) in which it was reported that some bank staff would potentially be made redundant as a result of the large Australian bank – the Commonwealth Bank of Australia – outsourcing some of its service roles to India. Within the article, the national secretary of the Finance Sector Union was quoted as saying 'it is disappointing for our members that despite the CBA making $8.65 billion in profits, the bank's management is still prepared to slash jobs and risk customer service standards in pursuit of more profits'. This quote again emphasises the point that the social costs associated with 'slashing jobs' are not recognised within reported profits. 'Expenses' as defined by the financial accountant excludes, or ignores, such costs. As a last example (and there are many more examples we could have used), a newspaper article in *The Age* newspaper (Dankert, 2019) reported that 'National Australia Bank's incoming boss Ross McEwan has signalled plans to ramp up a massive transformation program that includes thousands of job cuts, which the troubled bank hopes will return it to success' (Source: Dankert, S., (2019), 'New NAB boss to ramp up cost-cutting', *The Age*, July 20). As we can see here, the newspaper article equates the slashing of thousands of jobs with 'cost-cutting' and 'success'.

Again, the fixation on financial expenses, and profits, tends to motivate managerial actions that are not always in the interests of all members of society, and this reinforces the claim that we have made many times throughout this book that accounting is a practice that impacts many people throughout society, thereby making accounting a social practice. As you can see, positive improvement in financial accounting profits often seems to be given more priority than the impacts on workers, and their families. Perhaps it would be better if the news media had an interest in broader aspects of organisational performance, other than just profits. This would be consistent with a more 'caring' society.

In the discussion above, we referred to casinos. Casinos often report very high profits. However, for problem gamblers (those who can be defined as people who have difficulty limiting the amount of money and time they spend gambling, and whose gambling activities create adverse consequences for themselves, others and/or the community), the 'services' supplied by casinos can create much hardship and loss. How are the social problems created for the many problem gamblers recognised by casinos within their financial accounting systems? (See **Learning exercise 10.18**.) The answer is that they are not recognised as, again, given the way we define assets and expenses, the 'social costs' associated with problem gambling, which create various social impacts, simply do not fit into the definition of expenses within the system of financial accounting we use.

10.18 Learning Exercise

Recognising the social costs of gambling

Gambling is a source of enjoyment for some people, but it is a source of misery for others. Gambling is known to have destroyed the lives of many people, who are often referred to as problem gamblers, as well as badly impacting the family and friends of these problem gamblers.

Why are the social costs of gambling not recognised as an expense in the financial accounts of casinos?

The social costs of gambling can be immense. However, these costs do not appear as an expense of a casino because there is no decrease in the value of any asset controlled by the organisation, and there is no increase in any liabilities of the organisation. The failure to account for such costs is also consistent with the entity principle we discussed in Chapter 7, which is a key convention of financial accounting. The entity principle effectively requires that an organisation be treated as an entity that is separate to its owners and the communities in which it operates.

Where do these costs appear?

These social costs of gambling do not appear in the financial statements of casinos. However, indirectly, these costs impact the financial performance of other entities. For example, organisations that provide services to problem gamblers, and organisations that find housing for those people who become homeless, have their services used by problem gamblers, and this creates expenses for them. Government support, in terms of various social services, is also affected by problem gambling. Therefore, whilst the 'services' provided by casinos, and which impact problem gamblers, cause social problems that are not recognised in the financial accounts of the casinos, the gambling services create expenses for many other organisations that have to care for the affected problem gamblers. That is, the services provided by casinos generate various externalities that are imposed on various stakeholders within the community.

Is a profitable casino a 'good' organisation?

This is a matter of opinion. Some people believe that if an organisation is operating in accordance with the law and generates profits, then it is a good organisation. However, for those people who are opposed to gambling, or who see the devastation caused by problem gambling, then no casino – whether it is profitable or not – can be seen as a good organisation.

As another example, if an entity pollutes the ocean water in its local environs, thereby killing all local sea creatures and coastal vegetation, there will be no direct impact on reported profits, unless fines or other related cash flows are incurred. No externalities – which can be defined as impacts that an entity has on parties external to an organisation, where such external parties did not agree or take part in the action causing, or the decisions leading to, the cost or benefit – will be recognised, and the reported assets and profits of the organisation will not be affected. The performance of such an organisation could, depending upon the financial transactions undertaken, be portrayed as being very successful if profit is our focus – which it appears to be to many people.

Source: AAP Image / Joe Castro

When companies retrench large numbers of their workforce and replace them with mechanised processes, this often reduces reported expenses and improves profits, but the reported profits fail to reflect the social costs that result from the termination of many people's employment.

As a last example, what about all those plastic water bottles that wash up on our beaches and cause so many environmental problems? Do the profits of those companies selling the bottled drinking water reflect the social and environmental costs that the ongoing, inappropriate disposal of their products creates? Again, the answer is 'No'.

We could give many more such examples. The point being made is that the operations of organisations create many externalities (we also discussed externalities in Chapter 2), yet these externalities typically go unrecognised within our financial accounts. Nevertheless, stakeholders such as the news media continue to focus on profits, seeming to commend profitable companies and to condemn loss-making companies for being 'failures'.

Source: Shutterstock.com/Shemyakina Tatiana

When the organisations that sell bottled water report their financial results, such results fail to reflect the costs often generated by the impacts their products have on the environment.

Whilst the above discussion has focused on social and environmental costs, financial accounting also tends to ignore the social and environmental 'benefits' that might be created by an organisation. For example, if an organisation spends resources to support local community initiatives (for example, supporting educational initiatives, or finding accommodation for homeless people, or caring for lost animals), such expenditure is typically treated as an expense (with an adverse impact on profits), even though the expenditure generates important social and/or environmental benefits. Because the expenditures on these initiatives are treated as expenses (and this is because, for financial reporting purposes, the expenditure does not create an 'asset' and therefore must be treated as an 'expense'), this tends to discourage managers from undertaking such initiatives, which might otherwise create some positive social and environmental impacts and be good for the reputation of the organisation.

Another problem inherent in financial reporting is its focus on the short term. As we would appreciate, the focus of the news media is typically on the annual, or perhaps at times on the half-yearly and quarterly, financial results of an entity. As accountants, we do tend to emphasise short-term (annual) performance through our practices of dividing the life of the organisation up into somewhat artificial periods of time. Managers are also often rewarded in terms of measures of performance such as annual profits. This can have the effect of discouraging us from making long-term investments in new technologies (including those that will provide longer-term social and environmental benefits).

Therefore, we perhaps should question our approaches to profit measurement that make certain income and expenses visible but disregard many others, and which potentially signals great success (high profits) at the same time as many adverse social and environmental impacts are being created. Many people believe that it is the obsession of managers, investors, media commentators and other stakeholders with maximising 'profits' (as calculated by the financial accountant applying financial reporting standards) that has contributed greatly to the many social and environmental problems confronting the world. Perhaps if we did not apply financial accounting rules in the way we do, then the planet would be in better shape. What do you think? Can we realistically argue that financial accounting is somewhat complicit in creating many of the social and environmental problems we regularly hear about?

We will conclude this chapter by emphasising the point that a profitable company therefore is not always necessarily a 'good' company. The issues associated with recognising the social and environmental implications of an entity's operations are the subject of ongoing debate, but at this stage it is important to recognise that financial performance indicators, such as profits and losses and total comprehensive income, are not comprehensive indicators of the overall 'performance' of an organisation. For a comprehensive view of an organisation's performance, financial measures such as profitability should be supplemented with other types of performance-based information, perhaps tied to the social and environmental performance of the entity – something that we have emphasised throughout this book, and something we specifically focused upon in Chapter 6.

Key concept

The reported 'profits' of an organisation do not incorporate many of the social and environmental costs (and benefits) generated by an organisation because of reasons such as the way we define the elements of financial accounting (with the reliance upon 'control') and because of the way financial accountants are taught to apply the 'entity concept'.

Why do I need to know that measures such as 'profit or loss' or 'total comprehensive income' do not represent a holistic measure of organisational performance?

Arguably, it is just as important to understand what 'profits or losses' include as it is to understand what they do not include.

The view of the author of this book is that it is far too simplistic to believe that a 'profitable company' is a 'good company', or that a profitable organisation is an organisation that is *always* performing to the benefit of a broad cross-section of stakeholders. 'Profits' as reported through the application of financial reporting rules and principles simply represents a number that is calculated by applying, with various assumptions, particular rules and principles. Such rules and principles tend to ignore many social and environmental impacts, in large part because of the way in which the elements of financial accounting are defined. As such, it is important that apart from simply reviewing the financial reports of an organisation, we should also carefully review the social and environmental reports of the organisation (which we addressed in Chapter 6) before we decide whether, or not, to support a particular organisation.

STUDY TOOLS

SUMMARY

This chapter has focused on describing the role and the contents of the income statement. The income statement is used by a variety of stakeholders and for a variety of purposes. The profit or loss reported in the income statement is a measure of performance that draws a great deal of attention, particularly the profits of our larger organisations. The reported profits of an organisation are also often used within various contractual arrangements to which an organisation is a party, including debt contracts negotiated with lenders, and management bonus plans negotiated with managers.

We learned that profit is calculated for a period of time, and as a result it requires managers to make many judgements about what items of income and expenses should be allocated to particular accounting periods. We also learned that the income statement can be presented in different formats, and that the impacts on profits from unusual events, and from discontinuing operations, should be separately disclosed in order to increase the relevance of the information being presented.

We discussed the various stages at which income can be recognised, and we learned that in those situations in which an organisation sells goods to customers, the related revenue will be recognised when the related goods are in the *control* of the customer and the related flow of economic benefits are considered not to be of low probability, as well as measurable with reasonable accuracy. We explored the very real differences between cash flows and profits. We also stressed that the measurement of income and expenses is impacted by the asset and liability measurement approaches adopted by an organisation.

A specific cost that we explored within the chapter was the cost of sales. In doing so, we showed that the cost of sales is influenced by the inventory cost-flow assumptions made, as well as by whether the perpetual or periodic inventory system is used.

We have emphasised that the accounting rules incorporated within accounting standards change over time, such that the rules for determining profit or loss for larger organisations can be quite different across time. This needs to be considered by people who attempt to compare the profits of recent years with the profits from years gone by.

The chapter introduced the concept of 'other comprehensive income', which refers to those items of income and expense that are recognised as gains or losses, but which are not permitted to be included within 'profit or loss'. Within the statement of comprehensive income, other comprehensive income is added to the profit or loss of the accounting period to provide a measure of performance known as 'total comprehensive income'.

The statement of changes in equity was explored, and its role in providing a reconciliation of opening and closing equity was identified. We concluded the chapter by emphasising that reported profits or losses typically fail to reflect many social and environmental impacts, or costs, and benefits created by organisations. This was described as a fundamental limitation of financial accounting, and can be traced back to how we define the elements of financial accounting, and by how we apply core accounting principles such as the entity principle within financial accounting.

Even though this chapter has emphasised some important limitations inherent within the practice of financial accounting – particularly in the way it fails to account for many social and environmental impacts, as well as the way financial accounting fails to acknowledge many controlled resources such as internally developed intangible assets – it is nevertheless important for people who are in business to understand how financial accounting is undertaken. We can be critical of the rules of financial accounting, but the reality is that financial accounting does generate much information that is used in many different ways, so it is important for us to understand the rules of financial accounting, even if we think they are flawed in some respects. The final chapter of this book (Chapter 12) will look in more detail at how to analyse such reports and to draw meaningful conclusions therefrom.

ANSWERS TO THE OPENING QUESTIONS

At the beginning of the chapter we asked the following five questions. As a result of reading this chapter, you should now be able to provide informed answers to these questions – ours are shown below.

1 If we sell an item of inventory to another organisation in exchange for an asset that is not in the form of cash, how do we measure the amount of income to be recognised?
  If an organisation sells some inventory to another organisation, then the amount of revenue to be recognised will be measured at the 'fair value' of the consideration that has been received.

2 Does 'control' of an asset have to pass to a customer before the related income from the transaction is recognised?
  Yes. The general requirement is that control of an asset being sold must have transferred to a customer before the related income is recognised.

3 What is an 'inventory cost-flow assumption' and why do we need it?

An inventory cost-flow assumption is an assumption made about which item of inventory is being sold, so that the cost of the sold item can be determined. Inventory cost-flow assumptions include first-in, first-out (FIFO) and weighted-average cost. We generally need to use these assumptions because for similar or identical units it is difficult, if not impossible, to specifically identify which item of inventory was actually sold.

4 Do the accounting rules embodied within accounting standards change across time? If they do, then what implications does this have for comparing the profits of one accounting period with the profits of another accounting period?

Accounting standards do change across time, meaning that across time the rules used to measure assets and liabilities change, and this means profits will be affected. As the rules of financial accounting can change, this can often make it inappropriate to compare the profits from one accounting period with the profits calculated in another period, unless some form of adjustment is made.

5 Is a profitable company necessarily a 'good company'?

This is a matter of opinion. Profits are determined on the basis of financial accounting rules and principles, and these rules and principles tend to ignore many of the social and environmental impacts created by an organisation. Therefore, it is possible that an organisation that reports high levels of profits might actually be creating significant social and environmental harm. So we need to be careful before we simply accept that a profitable organisation is a 'good organisation'. Our judgement really depends on our perspectives on organisational responsibilities and whether the profitable companies have accepted a responsibility, and an accountability, for those aspects of performance that we think are important. This is obviously quite subjective.

SELF-TEST QUIZ

Answers to this quiz appear in the Appendix of this book.

1 Which of the following statements is false in relation to the recognition of income?

a If the income relates to the provision of services to a customer, and the customer has already paid the cash, then the income can be recognised when the cash is received even if the service has not been provided.

b To recognise income, the transaction must satisfy the definition of income which requires that there has been an increase in assets or a decrease in liabilities which does not represent a contribution from the owners of the organisation.

c The probability of the ultimate inflow of economic benefits related to the income should not be assessed as low.

d There should not be a high level of measurement uncertainty related to the associated inflow of economic benefits.

e If the income relates to the sale of inventory, then the customer must have control of the inventory before the organisation shall recognise income.

2 In relation to the presentation of information about income and expenses, which of the following statements is true?

a Larger companies will disclose 'profit or loss' and 'other comprehensive income' separately.

b 'Other comprehensive income' will include those items of income and expense that are not permitted to be recognised in 'profit or loss' due to rules within particular financial reporting standards.

c Significant or material 'exceptional' or 'unusual' items of income and expense should be separately disclosed within the income statement/statement of comprehensive income.

d Profits or losses relating to 'discontinued operations' should be separately disclosed.

e All of these choices.

3 Bay of Fires Ltd has sold inventory to a customer for $30 000 on credit terms. The inventory cost Bay of Fires $20 000 to produce. The customer's order for the inventory was placed on 1 February, the inventory was transferred to the customer on 15 February, and the customer paid the amount due in cash on 28 February. Which of the following statements is false?

a When the cash is received on 28 February, no income should be recognised but there should be a reduction in accounts receivable on that date.

b The income recognition should be deferred until 28 February.

c The sales revenue of $30 000 should be recognised on 15 February.

d An account receivable of $30 000 should be recognised on 15 February.

e Cost of goods sold of $20 000 should be recognised on 15 February.

4 An organisation has a reporting date ending on 30 June, which is a Friday. Its employees work five days per week, Monday to Friday, and the weekly wages expense is $20 000. Employees are paid each Thursday for work performed for the preceding week until the close of business on the Thursday. Which of the following statements is false?

a On 30 June, a liability for unpaid wages (accrued wages expense) should be recognised for the amount of $8000.

b On 30 June, an expense of $4000 should be recognised for the unpaid wages.

c On 30 June, a liability of $4000 should be recognised for the unpaid wages.

d When the payment of $20 000 is subsequently made on Thursday 6 July an expense of $16 000 for wages expense should be recognised.

e When the payment of $20 000 is subsequently made on Thursday 6 July the liability for unpaid wages should be reduced to zero.

5 Measures such as 'profits' are often criticised because 'profit' fails to recognise many social and environmental impacts. In this regard, which of the following statements is true?

a The recognition of an 'expense' requires a decrease in the assets of an organisation, or an increase in the liabilities of the organisation which does not represent a distribution to owners.

b For a resource to be considered an 'asset', the resource needs to be controlled.

c If the resource is not controlled (for example, the 'environment' or the employees), then any negative impact on it/reduction in its value will not be recognised as an 'expense'.

d The application of the entity concept also contributes to the failure to recognise many social and environmental impacts given that other organisations, people or the environment are considered to be outside the entity for which the financial statements are being prepared.

e All of these choices.

ONLINE RESOURCES

Accompanying the book is an innovative online case study that follows an organisation initially established by two friends, which grows into a large and successful company. Acquire this chapter's case study from your instructor.

CASE STUDY

Armadillo Surf Designs: Keeping watch on profitability

Armadillo Surf Designs (ASD) is implementing further cost-cutting strategies across the business in an effort to improve operating efficiencies. In addition to cutting back on costs, ASD is also implementing strategies to increase its revenues. As part of this strategy, the company is expanding its product offering and is now selling waterproof sports watches. The watches are proving very popular – ASD has reordered the watches a number of times in order to keep up with the high number of sales.

You will assist the directors to understand how professional judgement may have impacted on ASD's reported profitability. You will also determine the cost of sales and ending inventory amounts for the new sports watches, and assist Archer to better understand changes in ASD's equity.

END-OF-CHAPTER QUESTIONS

10.1 Would you expect all organisations to produce an income statement?

10.2 Should the following accounts appear in the income statement or in the balance sheet?

- **a** income receivable
- **b** income received in advance
- **c** depreciation expense
- **d** accumulated depreciation
- **e** contributions from owners
- **f** prepaid salary expenses
- **g** salary expenses.

10.3 What is 'other comprehensive income', and what is the difference between 'profits' and 'total comprehensive income'?

10.4 A corner shop sells some stock to customers for cash, and sells some stock to other customers who have two weeks to pay. Should the sales revenue from these two different types of sales be treated differently?

10.5 Why might we want to know about an organisation's accounting policies?

10.6 When do the following occur?

- **a** the recognition of a prepayment
- **b** the recognition of an accrued expense
- **c** the recognition of an account receivable.

10.7 For what purposes would managers use the information that is included within an income statement?

10.8 If the owner of a business withdraws some inventory for personal use, is this an expense of the business?

10.9 Why should we disclose profits from continuing operations separately from profits from discontinued operations?

10.10 When would an airline company recognise the revenue from passengers?

10.11 When we say we can disclose expenses by 'function' or by 'nature', what does this mean? What would cause us to choose one presentation format in preference to the other?

10.12 Which of the following, if any, would be recognised as income, and why?

a receipt of cash from an accounts receivable

b receipt of some inventory from a supplier

c receipt of some office furniture from a customer in exchange for some inventory that is sold by the organisation to the customer.

10.13 Identify five reasons why external stakeholders will want to know about the profitability of an organisation.

10.14 Is taxable profit and accounting profit the same thing?

10.15 If an item of expense or income is potentially quite significant but cannot be measured reliably, what should the accountant do?

10.16 Winkipop Ltd provides consulting services to Rincon Ltd. Rather than being paid in cash, it is agreed that Rincon Ltd will transfer some equipment to Winkipop Ltd. The equipment is recorded in Rincon Ltd's accounts at a cost of $90 000 and with accumulated depreciation of $40 000. The fair value of the machinery is assessed at $80 000. How much income should be recognised by Winkipop Ltd, and what accounts will be affected by the transaction from Winkipop Ltd's perspective?

10.17 What is an inventory cost-flow assumption and why is it necessary?

10.18 In a time of rising prices, which inventory cost-flow assumption would generate the lowest profit?

10.19 What is the difference between a perpetual inventory system and a periodic inventory system?

10.20 If an organisation is constructing a building for a customer, and that construction will take three years to complete, does the organisation have to wait until the building is completed before it recognises any related income?

10.21 Which financial statement is more important: the income statement or the balance sheet?

10.22 Why is income often broken down into 'revenues' and 'gains'?

10.23 Is profit influenced by the way in which we measure assets and liabilities? Why?

10.24 If we revalue our property, plant and equipment, will this have any impact on future profits? Why?

10.25 What is the purpose of a statement of changes in equity?

10.26 When a large organisation reports its yearly profit, could this create social impacts? Why?

10.27 Do financial accounting rules change across time, and if so, what implications does this have for comparing current profits with past profits?

10.28 Is it appropriate to compare one company's profit with the profit of a similar company in the same industry, to determine which company is performing better?

10.29 What is a 'debt covenant' and how might this rely on the contents of an income statement?

10.30 A retailer of boats receives an order from a customer. When should the retailer recognise the revenue? Is it:

a at the time when the order is made?

b at the time when the boat is received by the customer?

c at the time when the customer makes the cash payment?

10.31 Is the tax to be paid to a country's taxation office calculated by multiplying financial accounting profit (as determined by the application of financial reporting standards) by the local tax rate?

10.32 Do you think the stakeholders associated with not-for-profit organisations see 'profit' as an important measure of performance? Why?

10.33 A person who claims to be an expert in financial reporting and investing is running a seminar in which she identifies companies that she believes are likely to increase their profits and share value. As part of her presentation, she provides a chart that shows how the reported profits of a company have changed over the last 10 years, and on the basis of this chart she predicts what future profits will be. Would you rely on the recommendations of this person? Why?

10.34 Is accounting profit a *good measure* of organisational performance? Why?

10.35 Give some examples of some social and environmental 'costs' that are ignored by financial accounting. Does it really matter that they are ignored?

10.36 Is it ridiculous to argue that the way in which we have performed financial accounting for many years, and the way in which we define and recognise the elements of financial accounting, have contributed to the many social and environmental problems that confront the world? Why or why not?

10.37 How might the contents of an income statement be used in the contractual arrangements an organisation negotiates with its managers or with the providers of debt capital?

10.38 What type of dysfunctional behaviour might managers practise if they focus their attention on maximising a given year's profit?

10.39 What is 'earnings management' and why might managers do this?

10.40 Critically evaluate the following statement that was reported within *The Age* newspaper (Dankert, 2019):

> *National Australia Bank's incoming boss Ross McEwan has signalled plans to ramp up a massive transformation program that includes thousands of job cuts, which the troubled bank hopes will return it to success.*

10.41 Farrelly Ltd sells one type of surfboard and has the following inventory transactions for the year ending 30 June 2026:

Opening inventory at 1 July 2025	500 units @ $250	$125 000
Purchases on 1 August 2025	1000 units @ $260	$260 000
Purchases on 15 February 2026	500 units @ $290	$145 000
Purchases on 20 June 2026	900 units @ $300	$270 000
Total	2900 units	$800 000

During the year, Farrelly Ltd sells 2500 surfboards. The company uses the periodic system to manage inventory.

You are required to calculate the cost of sales, and ending inventory values, using the following cost-flow methods:

a first-in, first-out (FIFO)
b weighted average
c last-in, first-out (LIFO).

10.42 Greenmount Inc commences selling one type of beach umbrella in 2025. Whilst each umbrella is identical, the unit costs of manufacturing them has fluctuated due to rising material and labour costs. Greenmount Inc employs a perpetual inventory system. Details of the manufacturing costs are as follows:

Date completed	Number completed	Unit manufacturing costs $
8 July 2025	250	50.00
4 September 2025	500	55.00
19 January 2026	565	60.00
15 March 2026	750	62.00
19 June 2026	500	65.00
	2565	

Details of sales are as follows:

Date of sale	Number sold	Unit sales price $
19 July 2025	200	90.00
6 September 2025	525	90.00
24 January 2026	575	90.00
3 April 2026	700	95.00
29 June 2026	375	100.00
	2375	

What is the cost of sales for the year ended 30 June 2026, and what is the value of inventory for balance sheet purposes as at 30 June 2026 assuming that Greenmount Inc uses:

a FIFO
b weighted average cost?

REFERENCES

Benns, M. (2017). Rip-offs the origin of profits, *Daily Telegraph*, August 17.

BHP (2021). *Annual report 2021: The future is clear.* https://www.bhp.com/-/media/documents/investors/annual-reports/2021/210914_bhpannualreport2021.pdf?sc_lang=en&hash=15F0B58BC27ADFA860F0BE29B61E199D

Coombes, R. J., & Martin, C. (1982). *The Definition and Recognition of Revenue under Historical Cost Accounting,* Accounting Theory Monograph 3. Melbourne: Australian Accounting Research Foundation.

Dankert, S. (2019). 'New NAB boss to ramp up cost-cutting'. *The Age*, July 20.

Eyers, J., & de Kretser, (2022). Shake up at top and head office cuts at Westpac. *Australian Financial Review,* February 4, 2022, p. 15.

Grieve, C. (2021). 'CBA to send 100 technology and compliance roles to India'. *The Age*, August 16, p. 24.

Hatch, P. (2022). 'Qantas set for half-empty profit'. *The Age*, January 28, p. 28.

International Accounting Standards Board (2022a). *Conceptual Framework for Financial Reporting.* www.ifrs.org/issued-standards/list-of-standards/conceptual-framework

International Accounting Standards Board (2022b). IAS 1: Presentation of financial statements. https://www.ifrs.org/issued-standards/list-of-standards/ias-1-presentation-of-financial-statements/

International Accounting Standards Board (2022c). IAS 16: Property, Plant and Equipment. www.ifrs.org/issued-standards/list-of-standards/ias-16-property-plant-and-equipment/

International Accounting Standards Board (2022d). IAS 21: The Effects of Changes in Foreign Exchange Rates. www.ifrs.org/issued-standards/list-of-standards/ias-21-the-effects-of-changes-in-foreign-exchange-rates/

International Accounting Standards Board (2022e). IAS 39: Financial Instruments: Recognition and Measurement. www.ifrs.org/issued-standards/list-of-standards/ias-39-financial-instruments-recognition-and-measurement/

Myer (2021). *Annual report 2021*. https://investor.myer.com.au/FormBuilder/_Resource/_module/dGngnzELxUikQxL5gb1cgA/file/Myer_Annual_Report_2021

Qantas (2021). *Qantas annual report 2021*. https://investor.qantas.com/FormBuilder/_Resource/_module/doLLG5ufYkCyEPj-F1tpgyw/ file/annual-reports/2021-Annual-Report.pdf

CHAPTER 11

THE STATEMENT OF CASH FLOWS, AND CASH CONTROLS

LEARNING OBJECTIVES

After completing this chapter, readers should be able to:

- **LO11.1** explain the role of the statement of cash flows, and how it differs from the other financial statements prepared by an organisation
- **LO11.2** understand the meaning of 'cash' and 'cash equivalents' as applied within the context of preparing a statement of cash flows
- **LO11.3** explain some of the reasons why there will be a difference between the cash flows and profits of an organisation
- **LO11.4** understand why the statement of cash flows is less prone to managerial manipulation than the balance sheet and the income statement
- **LO11.5** describe how a statement of cash flows should be presented, and explain the meaning of cash flows from operating activities, investing activities and financing activities
- **LO11.6** prepare a statement of cash flows
- **LO11.7** understand that cash is an asset that is vulnerable to theft and other forms of misappropriation, and describe some internal controls that should be in place within an organisation to protect cash.

OPENING QUESTIONS

Before reading this chapter, please consider how you would answer the following three questions. We will return to these questions at the end of the chapter, where we suggest some answers.

1 Accounting standards require that a statement of cash flows be prepared that reports information about flows of cash and cash equivalents. What is a cash equivalent?

2 The statement of cash flows classifies the cash flows for an accounting period into three broad categories. What are these categories?

3 Identify four reasons why the profits of an organisation for a period of time might potentially be higher than the cash flows the organisation has generated from its operating activities for that same period of time.

Introduction

An important point that we have stressed a number of times throughout this book is that the management and control of cash, and related cash flows, is vital to the survival and success of any organisation, whether it is a profit-seeking organisation, a not-for-profit organisation, a small organisation, a large organisation, or otherwise. In discussing *cash flows*, we are referring to movements in cash that are created as a result of transactions with people, or organisations, that are external to an organisation.

An organisation that poorly manages its cash flows will inevitably encounter problems. It therefore is understandable that different stakeholders – both internal and external to an organisation – will have an interest in learning about the cash flows of an organisation for a period of time, as well as the trends in cash flows across recent accounting periods. That is, information about cash flows is considered *relevant* to the decision-making processes of various stakeholders. As we know from previous chapters, *relevance* is a fundamental qualitative characteristic that financial accounting information is expected to possess, and it is reasonable to expect that information about past cash flows would likely make a difference to the decisions being made by the users of the financial statements. The ability of managers to manage and control cash flows is vital to the success of an organisation. Therefore, managers of all organisations should feel some responsibility, and accountability, to provide information about cash flows to those stakeholders who have a right to know about such information.

In Chapter 4 we discussed the practice of budgeting, and in doing so we talked about the budgeted statement of cash flows. We emphasised the importance to managers of all organisations of producing a projected cash flow statement so that managers can anticipate potential problems relating to cash before they actually arise, and plan and adjust accordingly. The statement of cash flows that we are exploring within this chapter provides a historical, or past, perspective of cash flows. That is, in this chapter we are concentrating on the statement of cash flows that is prepared for a past period of time (the past accounting period), and for actual past transactions, as opposed to cash flow projections for a future period of time. The statement of cash flows is a very important financial statement.

LO11.1 Overview of the statement of cash flows

statement of cash flows
Reports information about movements in cash and cash equivalents for the accounting period, and in doing so, provides a reconciliation of the opening and closing balances of cash and cash equivalents as reported within the balance sheet

The **statement of cash flows** provides a very useful complement to the other financial statements produced by organisations, these other financial statements typically being the balance sheet, the income statement (and the statement of comprehensive income, for organisations required to comply with accounting standards), and the statement of changes in equity.

As you have already learned in this book, the balance sheet reports information about assets, liabilities and owners' equity as at a certain date (this date being the end of the accounting period). The balance sheet therefore will, amongst other things, show the opening and closing balances of cash (because comparative information from the prior accounting period is also normally provided within the balance sheet, thereby providing data for the current and prior accounting periods). However, the balance sheet will not show what caused the movements in cash during the accounting period. That is, the balance sheet will not present information to answer questions about where the cash came from, and where the cash went, throughout the accounting period.

As you have also learned in this book, the income statement reports information about income and expenses, and therefore about the profit or loss that has been generated for a period of time as a result of adopting the process of *accrual accounting*. The income and expenses will be recognised within an accounting period, regardless of whether the related cash flows have occurred.

The statement of changes in equity provides a reconciliation of opening and closing equity, as well as details of the various equity accounts that have been impacted as a result of that period's operations. It also provides information about the effects of transactions with owners in their capacity as owners (that is, it provides information about distributions to owners and capital contributions from owners).

The statement of cash flows, on the other hand, reports information about movements in cash (as well as in cash equivalents, as we will explain shortly) for the accounting period, and in doing so, it provides a reconciliation of the opening and closing balances of cash (and cash equivalents) as reported within the balance sheet. The statement of cash flows will report the sources, and uses, of cash in terms of the *net cash flows* that have been generated from:

- operating activities
- investing activities, and
- financing activities.

Net cash flows, as referred to above, are the differences between cash inflows and cash outflows, and they can be either positive or negative. The information provided within the statement of cash flows is not directly available by simply looking at the balance sheet or at the income statement.

In terms of the benefits of providing a statement of cash flows, the accounting standard on statements of cash flows provides some interesting insights. At the international level, the relevant accounting standard issued by the International Accounting Standards Board (IASB) is IAS 7: Statement of Cash Flows. The insights from the accounting standard include the following:

> A statement of cash flows, when used in conjunction with the rest of the financial statements, provides information that enables users to evaluate the changes in net assets of an entity, its financial structure (including its liquidity and solvency) and its ability to affect the amounts and timing of cash flows in order to adapt to changing

> circumstances and opportunities. Cash flow information is useful in assessing the ability of the entity to generate cash and cash equivalents and enables users to develop models to assess and compare the present value of the future cash flows of different entities. It also enhances the comparability of the reporting of operating performance by different entities because it eliminates the effects of using different accounting treatments for the same transactions and events.
>
> Historical cash flow information is often used as an indicator of the amount, timing and certainty of future cash flows. It is also useful in checking the accuracy of past assessments of future cash flows and in examining the relationship between profitability and net cash flow and the impact of changing prices.
>
> Source: International Accounting Standards Board (2022).

The information provided in a statement of cash flows is therefore important in assisting various stakeholders to assess the ability of an organisation to pay its debts; acquire property, plant and equipment; pay dividends; and borrow funds. It provides insights into questions relating to how much cash was generated from an organisation's operating activities, and what the net cash flows were with respect to its investing and financing activities. Ultimately it is cash – not profits – that is actually used to pay for the various resources acquired by an organisation.

The relationship between cash flows and profits and losses

As you would now understand from reading the material provided in the other chapters of this book, profits and losses are typically determined by the use of accrual accounting, and there are frequently significant differences between cash flows and either profits or losses. The exception to this relates to some small or 'simple' organisations that prepare their financial accounts on a cash basis. For example, in relation to their financial performance, some smaller clubs, such as local sporting clubs, will simply prepare a statement of cash receipts and cash payments, not an income statement, because measures such as profits are probably not relevant to the members of the club, given the purpose for which the club was established.

Profitable firms can, and do, fail because of poor cash management, not necessarily because their products and services are not popular with customers. Organisations can fail if they have an inability to make the cash payments that they are obliged to pay at a specific point in time. For example, using accrual accounting, an organisation might have generated some sales on extended credit terms (for instance, the sales proceeds might not be receivable for two months). Such sales would be recognised as income within the current period despite the fact that cash might not be received until a subsequent accounting period. The same organisation might incur wage expenses that need to be paid weekly, or fortnightly, as well as other expenses (such as those relating to the sale of inventory, rent expenses, electricity expenses, and so on) that might need to be paid within 30 days. Given that the cash collection relating to the sales has been deferred until the debtors pay, the organisation might not have sufficient cash to meet its expenses when they fall due for payment. It might therefore face a **liquidity crisis**, even though its reported profit, which is determined on an accrual basis, appears to be sound.

liquidity crisis
A lack of positive cash flows within an organisation to meet obligations that need to be paid in the short run

A liquidity crisis is characterised by a lack of positive cash flows within an organisation, and a situation where an organisation does not have sufficient liquid assets – typically considered to be cash or assets that can be quickly converted into cash – to meet obligations that need to be paid in the short run. If a liquidity crisis is not quickly resolved, it can lead to the demise of an organisation.

The accountability model and the statement of cash flows

In providing our overview of the statement of cash flows, we will again use our accountability model (see Figure 1.3), which identifies four key issues: why report, to whom to report, what to report, and how to report.

Why report using the statement of cash flows?

In answering the question of *why* an organisation should prepare and report a statement of cash flows, we can answer that the managers and accountants of an organisation might generate information about the cash flows of their organisation because they believe that knowledge of cash flows is important to the various stakeholders who expect managers to carefully manage the use of an organisation's cash. Managers have a responsibility, and associated accountability, to use cash wisely and to report information about cash flows. For many organisations, particularly larger ones, it is a legal requirement to produce a statement of cash flows.

Both internal and external users will demand information about an organisation's cash flows. From an internal perspective, managers will use information about actual cash flows to evaluate whether the cash flows are consistent with prior plans and the related budgets, and whether the reported cash flows signal any potential future problems in respect of the ability of the organisation to pay debts as, and when, they fall due.

External users, such as providers of loans, might also insist on periodically receiving a statement of cash flows as part of their lending agreement with an organisation. Ultimately, lenders expect to be repaid with cash, and the statement of cash flows helps determine whether any future repayments are potentially in jeopardy.

From an external stakeholder perspective, investors will want information about the sources and uses of cash during an accounting period, and whether the way cash has been used will create risks for investors in terms of potential changes in the value of the organisation and in its propensity to pay future cash dividends. If an organisation is not generating positive cash flows from its operating activities, and this deficiency has been occurring across a number of periods, then the future ability of the organisation to repay debts, and dividends, will tend to be questioned. This would have a negative impact on the value of the organisation. As another example, employees and creditors will be interested in information about an organisation's cash, and cash flows, as this will indicate whether the organisation may have difficulty in paying the amounts due to them, now or in the future.

To whom should the statement of cash flows be addressed?

In terms of the question of *to whom* the statement of cash flows is relevant, you can understand that there are many different stakeholders who might have an interest in an organisation's cash flows. Indeed, most stakeholders who are interested in financial performance relating to profits will also have an interest in an organisation's cash flows. Informed people will know that profit is calculated on an accrual basis, and that whilst knowledge of profits or losses is useful in assessing financial performance, additional information is also required about the underlying cash flows of an organisation.

As already noted, larger organisations that are required to comply with accounting standards are compelled to produce a statement of cash flows that complies with the requirements of the accounting standard pertaining to such statements. For smaller organisations that are not compelled by law to make details of their past cash flows publicly available, managers will nevertheless prepare statements of cash flows. However, they tend to restrict the number of stakeholders who will receive the information. Managers of smaller organisations do not want their competitors to receive information about their cash flows, as this could place them at a competitive disadvantage.

What should be reported on the statement of cash flows?

In terms of *what* to report, the detail of what is reported, and how it is reported, will depend on the information needs of managers (which will be linked back to organisational goals and related strategies), as well as the information needs, and rights to information, of different stakeholders. For larger organisations, accounting standards specifically require the disclosure of information about certain cash flows, which in turn must be categorised as cash flows from operating activities, cash flows from investing activities, or cash flows from financing activities.

For smaller organisations, those that are not required to follow accounting standards, we would expect a degree of variation in how they report the information about cash flows. The format of the disclosure, the items to be disclosed and the level of aggregation will all be influenced by the demands of those stakeholders who are closely linked to the organisation, such as the owners and the major providers of finance (such as banks).

How should the statement of cash flows be presented?

For an example of *how* a large organisation that is required to comply with accounting standards would present a statement of cash flows, refer to **Exhibit 11.1**, which is the statement of cash flows produced by the large international airline Qantas, as presented in its 2021 annual report.

EXHIBIT 11.1 An example of a statement of cash flows
Qantas consolidated cash flow statement for the year ended 30 July 2021

	Notes	2021 $M	2020 $M
CASH FLOWS FROM OPERATING ACTIVITIES			
Cash receipts from customers		7507	14460
Cash payments to suppliers and employees (excluding cash payments to employees for redundancies and related costs and discretionary payments to non-executive employees) and refunds to customers from receipts in prior periods		(6726)	(12870)
Cash payments to employees for redundancies and related costs		(926)	(58)
Discretionary bonus payments to non-executive employees		–	(6)
Interest received		15	29
Interest paid (interest-bearing liabilities)		(183)	(146)

	Notes	2021 $M	2020 $M
Interest paid (lease liabilities)	16(C)	(73)	(82)
Dividends received from investments accounted for under the equity method		–	15
Australian income taxes paid	9(D)	–	(255)
Foreign income taxes paid	9(D)	–	(4)
Net cash (outflow)/Inflow from operating activities	29	(386)	1083
CASH FLOWS FROM INVESTING ACTIVITIES			
Payments for property, plant and equipment and intangible assets		(747)	(1549)
Interest paid and capitalised on qualifying assets	8	(21)	(48)
Payments for investments held at fair value		–	(22)
Proceeds from disposal of property, plant and equipment		94	50
Payments for investments accounted for under the equity method		(48)	(2)
Net cash (outflow) from investing activities		(722)	(1571)
CASH FLOWS FROM FINANCING ACTIVITIES			
Payments for share buy-back		–	(443)
Proceeds from share-issuance, net of costs		58	1342
Payments for treasury shares		–	(5)
Proceeds from interest-bearing liabilities, net of costs	21(D)	937	2155
Repayments of interest-bearing liabilities	21(D)	(759)	(625)
Repayments of lease liabilities	16(C)	(420)	(367)
Proceeds from finance leases		3	–
Dividends paid to shareholders	10(A)	–	(204)
Net cash (outflow)/Inflow from financing activities		(181)	1853
Net (decrease)/Increase in cash and cash equivalents held		(1289)	1365
Cash and cash equivalents at the beginning of the year		3520	2157
Effects of exchange rate changes on cash and cash equivalents		(10)	(2)
Cash and cash equivalents at the end of the year	21(A)	2221	3520

Source: Qantas (2021), p. 71.

cash
Money in the form of notes or coins that are either in the physical possession of an organisation or have been deposited in an at-call account with a bank. Would also generally include cheques received by an organisation and in the organisation's possession

cash equivalents
Short-term, highly liquid investments that are readily convertible to known amounts of cash, and which are subject to an insignificant risk of changes in value

LO11.2 Understanding cash, and cash equivalents

For many smaller organisations that produce a statement of cash flows, the statement might simply provide information about movements in the amounts of cash held within the organisation's bank account, as reflected by the financial account 'cash at bank'. However, for larger organisations, the statement of cash flows provides information about movements in cash as well as movements in cash equivalents (refer back to Exhibit 11.1, which refers to both cash and cash equivalents).

The accounting standard issued by the IASB that specifically relates to the statement of cash flows (IAS 7) notes within the initial 'Objectives' section of the standard that:

> Information about the cash flows of an entity is useful in providing users of financial statements with a basis to assess the ability of the entity to generate cash and cash

> equivalents and the needs of the entity to utilise those cash flows. The economic decisions that are taken by users require an evaluation of the ability of an entity to generate cash and cash equivalents and the timing and certainty of their generation. The objective of this Standard is to require the provision of information about the historical changes in cash and cash equivalents of an entity by means of a statement of cash flows which classifies cash flows during the period from operating, investing and financing activities.
>
> Source: International Accounting Standards Board (2022).

The accounting standard requires the statement of cash flows prepared by larger organisations to report movements in both 'cash' and 'cash equivalents'. We therefore need to understand what constitutes these cash equivalents. The accounting standard (paragraph 6) defines 'cash equivalents' as:

> short-term, highly liquid investments that are readily convertible to known amounts of cash and that are subject to an insignificant risk of change in value.
>
> Source: International Accounting Standards Board (2022).

Hence, for larger organisations, which are required to comply with accounting standards, the statement of cash flows actually provides a reconciliation of opening and closing cash and cash equivalents, where 'cash and cash equivalents' as represented in the statement might actually relate to the total value of a number of different accounts shown in the balance sheet, rather than a single account such as cash at bank. These accounts may also include bank overdrafts and short-term money market deposits. The short-term deposits might not be convertible to cash for a period of time. To the extent that the time to conversion to cash is not greater than 90 days, then they would be considered 'cash equivalents'. As IAS 7 (paragraph 7) states:

> Cash equivalents are held for the purpose of meeting short-term cash commitments rather than for investment or other purposes. For an investment to qualify as a cash equivalent it must be readily convertible to a known amount of cash and be subject to an insignificant risk of changes in value. Therefore, an investment normally qualifies as a cash equivalent only when it has a maturity of, say, three months or less from the date of acquisition.
>
> Source: International Accounting Standards Board (2022).

With this in mind, and to reduce the potential confusion of readers of the financial statements, the accounting standard requires that the amount of cash and cash equivalents as at the end of the financial year, as presented in the statement of cash flows, be reconciled – by way of a note to the financial statements – to the related items in the balance sheet. As we can see in **Exhibit 11.1**, the total of cash and cash equivalents at the end of the most recent accounting period for Qantas was $2 221 000 000. **Exhibit 11.2** tells us what accounts make up this total balance. As we can see for Qantas, the statement of cash flows provides an explanation of the movements throughout the accounting period in three types of asset accounts:

- cash
- cash at call (which represents cash that will be available for use after a short period of time, perhaps after a day or two)
- short-term money market securities and term deposits (which would be converted into cash in three months or less).

The accounting standard also requires the disclosure of the policy adopted by an organisation for determining which items are classified as 'cash' and 'cash equivalents' in the statement of cash flows. Explicit disclosure of this policy would help users to understand the organisation's statement of cash flows. Refer to the final part of **Exhibit 11.2** to see the Qantas policy for defining cash and cash equivalents.

EXHIBIT 11.2 Reconciliation of the cash and cash equivalents balance of Qantas Ltd (as shown in the statement of cash flows) to the respective balance sheet account balances

Note 21: Cash and cash equivalents

	2021 $M	2020 $M
Cash balances	143	249
Cash at call	327	733
Short-term money market securities and term deposits	1751	2538
Total cash and cash equivalents	2221	3520

Cash and cash equivalents comprise cash at bank and on hand, cash at call and short-term money market securities and term deposits that are readily convertible to a known amount of cash and are subject to an insignificant risk of change in value. Short-term money market securities of $250 million (2020: $76 million) held by the Qantas Group are pledged as collateral under the terms of certain operational financing facilities when underlying unsecured limits are exceeded. The collateral cannot be sold or repledged in the absence of default by the Qantas Group.

Source: Qantas (2021), p. 92.

As cash equivalents are required to be highly liquid, financial accounts such as accounts receivable or accounts payable, any borrowings subject to a term facility, and equity securities (such as shares in other companies), would be excluded from the definition of cash equivalents.

See **Learning exercise 11.1** for more on determining cash equivalents.

11.1 Learning Exercise

Determining the items that would be considered cash equivalents

Let us consider which of the following would be considered 'cash equivalents':

1 inventory
2 one-month money-market deposit offering a fixed rate of return of 3 per cent
3 accounts receivable
4 deposit with a bank, which is repayable to the company as soon as the company notifies the bank.

Solution

As we now know, a cash equivalent is a short-term, highly liquid investment that is readily convertible into a known amount of cash, and that is subject to an insignificant risk of change in value. Therefore:

1 *Inventory*: this does not satisfy the definition of a cash equivalent as the inventory is not readily convertible into cash (it needs to be sold and then the amount owing by a debtor needs to be paid), and there would be a risk that the value of inventory would change.
2 *One-month money-market deposit offering a fixed rate of return*: This does satisfy the definition of a cash equivalent because the organisation would know how much it will receive in cash, and there would be a limited chance of non-payment. Also, the time period fits within the 90-day rule identified in the accounting standard, which requires that cash equivalents must have a period to maturity of no more than 90 days.

3 *Accounts receivable*: This would not be a cash equivalent as there is always a chance that the debtor might not pay cash, or that the debtor might pay the cash at a time that is beyond what was expected, or the debtor might only pay part of the amount outstanding.

4 *Bank deposit repayable to the company*: This satisfies the definition of a cash equivalent because the managers of the organisation would know how much the organisation will receive in cash, and there would be a limited chance of non-payment.

LO11.3 The difference between cash flows and accounting profits

As you know, using accrual accounting, income and expenses are recognised when an underlying transaction or event occurs, which is not necessarily when the related cash flow occurs. Also, cash flows can occur when there is no impact on profits – for example, when an organisation acquires property, plant and equipment (which would increase property, plant and equipment, and reduce cash), or when an organisation receives or repays a loan (which would impact loans, which are a liability, and also cash, which is an asset).

Let us compare the cash flows from the operating activities of Qantas with its profits or losses. As we can see from **Exhibit 11.1**, the cash flows from operating activities – which relate to the principal revenue-producing activities of the organisation – for the year ending 30 June 2021 are negative \$386 million – representing net cash outflows. By comparison, the loss of Qantas for the year ending 30 June 2021 was \$1728 million, which is a much higher negative result. Profit or loss will be impacted by a number of expenses that do not involve cash flows. For example, Qantas has depreciation, amortisation and impairment expenses of \$2199 million in 2021, which reduced profits/increased losses but did not involve a cash flow, hence explaining, in part, why the loss reported by Qantas was much larger than the net cash outflow from operating activities.

There are many reasons why cash flows from operating activities and the profit or loss reported for the year can be different. We discuss and explain some of these reasons below.

Key concept

There can be a significant difference between the cash flows that an organisation generates from its operating activities in a given accounting period and the profit or loss it reports for that same period.

Why do I need to know that there can be significant differences between the cash flows that an organisation generates, and its reported profits or losses?

For-profit organisations are expected to generate profits, and generally speaking, the bigger the profit, the better. However, just because an organisation has generated profits does not mean it will survive. Survival depends upon a number of factors and one very important factor is cash flows. Many profitable organisations have failed because of poor management of cash flows. Therefore, we need to understand the reasons for the difference between cash flows and profits, and we need to ensure that an organisation manages both properly.

Changes in accounts receivable

It is possible that sales have been made during an accounting period (thereby increasing profits), but that a lesser amount of cash has been received than these total sales. An increase in the balance of accounts receivable between the start and end of the accounting period represents a lesser amount of cash actually being received from customers during the accounting period relative to the total sales for the period. Conversely, a decrease in the balance of accounts receivable between the start and end of the accounting period represents a greater amount of cash received from customers compared to sales. In saying this, we are assuming that the decrease in accounts receivable was due to cash being received from customers, rather than being the result of bad or doubtful debts, a discount being allowed to accounts receivable, or sales returns.

For more on determining the amount of cash received from customers, see **Learning exercise 11.2**.

11.2 Learning Exercise

Determining the amount of cash received from customers

Scenario: The sales of an organisation within an accounting period were \$100 000, opening accounts receivable was \$25 000, and closing accounts receivable was \$35 000. There were no doubtful debts expenses for the period. All sales were made on credit terms, meaning there were no cash sales.

Issue: How much cash was actually received from customers within the accounting period?

Solution: As there were no doubtful debt expenses for the period, or any discounts provided to debtors, the closing accounts receivable balance, which represents the amount owed by customers of the organisation, is changed as follows:

Accounts receivable at the beginning of the period	\$25 000
Plus sales during the period	\$100 000
	\$125 000
Less cash received from customers	(\$X)
Equals accounts receivable at the end of the period	\$35 000

'X' is clearly the missing number above, and it is the number that will be reported in the statement of cash flows. This can be calculated as \$90 000. In order to determine the cash received from customers, we could also use the following equation:

Cash received from customers = sales + opening balance of accounts receivable – closing balance of accounts receivable

= \$100 000 + \$25 000 – \$35 000 = \$90 000

Because the balance of accounts receivable increased during the accounting period, this means that the organisation is owed more money from customers at the end of the accounting period compared with the amount owed at the beginning of the accounting period. The more money that the company is owed from customers at the end of the accounting period, the less money it must have received from customers during the accounting period. Therefore, if the accounts receivable balance increases during the accounting period, this means that the cash received from customers was less than the sales made in that accounting period.

Changes in accounts payable and inventory

If we seek to determine how much cash was paid to suppliers of inventory (see **Learning exercise 11.3**), then we need to consider one income statement account (cost of goods sold) and two balance sheet accounts (inventory, and accounts payable).

11.3 Learning Exercise

Determining the cash paid to suppliers of inventory

Scenario: Tamarama Company sells skateboards. The following information was derived from its balance sheet and income statement:

- The company started the accounting period with inventory of $100 000, and it ended the accounting period with inventory of $120 000.
- It uses the first-in, first-out (FIFO) inventory cost-flow assumption (Chapter 10 explains this cost flow assumption).
- It started the accounting period with accounts payable of $50 000, and ended the accounting period with accounts payable of $45 000.
- Cost of goods sold for the accounting period was $320 000.

All purchases of inventory are made on credit terms, and the company uses the perpetual system of inventory management (see Chapter 10), meaning that cost of goods sold is recognised each time a sale is made. There were no inventory losses during the accounting period.

For this organisation, it is assumed that the accounts payable account only includes amounts payable to suppliers of inventory.

Issue: You are required to determine how much cash was paid to the suppliers of inventory.

Solution: In working out how much was paid to the suppliers of inventory, determine the following:

How much inventory was acquired during the period?

If the organisation sold $320 000 worth of inventory throughout the entire accounting period, then that inventory had to come from somewhere. Either it was purchased or the company already had it in stock. We are told that the organisation started the accounting period with $100 000 in stock. If we assume that this stock was sold first (the FIFO method was used), then if we subtract this amount of $100 000 from the $320 000, we know that $220 000 of the stock that was sold must have been purchased during the accounting period. In addition, if we know that there was another $120 000 of stock remaining at the end of the period, then this also must have come from somewhere. Since we have assumed that all of our opening stock has already been sold, this $120 000 stock must have also been purchased during the period, and so we need to add this to the $220 000 purchases that we have already determined. This gives us total purchases during the period of $340 000.

That is:

Purchases = cost of goods sold + closing balance of inventory – opening balance of inventory

= $320 000 + $120 000 – $100 000

= $340 000

Having determined this, we can therefore determine what was paid to suppliers.

How much was paid to suppliers?

If the accounts payable balance at the beginning of the accounting period was $50 000, purchases amounted to $340 000, and the closing balance of accounts payable was $45 000, then payments to suppliers throughout the accounting period must have been $345 000; that is:

Cash payments to suppliers = opening balance of accounts payable – closing balance of accounts payable + purchases of inventory

= $50 000 – $45 000 + $340 000

= $345 000

Changes in accrued expenses

accrued expenses
A liability that represents expenses that have been incurred but not yet paid by the organisation

Accrued expenses are those expenses that have been incurred but not yet paid. They represent liabilities. As we know, many expenses are recognised in advance of them being paid. The amount paid in relation to an accrued expense will equal the opening balance of the accrued expense liability, plus the expense that has been recognised in the accounting period, less the closing balance of the accrued expense liability. The greater the closing balance of the accrued expense liability, the less cash that has actually been paid in relation to the expense that is being accrued.

For more on this topic, see **Learning exercise 11.4**.

11.4 Learning Exercise

Determining the cash paid in relation to expenses that have been accrued

Scenario: Bronte Corp started the accounting period with the liability 'accrued wages' of $75 000. Wages expense for the year was $980 000, and the closing balance of accrued wages was $50 000.

Issue: How much cash was paid to employees?

Solution: The opening balance of accrued wages was $75 000. This relates to expenses that were incurred in the last accounting period but had not been paid. This $75 000 would have been paid in the current accounting period. In addition, there was $980 000 of wages expenses in the current period; however, this includes $50 000 of expenses that have been incurred but will not be paid until the next accounting (reporting) period. Therefore, to calculate the actual amount of wages paid, we start with the $75 000 paid, to which we add the $980 000 of wages expense for the current accounting period, and then we subtract the $50 000 which will not be paid until the next period; that is:

Cash payments to employees = opening balance of accrued salary expenses + salary expense incurred during the accounting period – closing balance of accrued salary expenses

= $75 000 + $980 000 – $50 000

= $1 005 000

As you can see, the greater the closing balance of the accrued expense (and therefore the greater the liability), the less the actual cash payments made to the employees.

Changes in prepaid expenses (prepayments)

As we have learned in other chapters, when an expense is **prepaid**, it is treated as an asset and not as an expense. It is an asset because the payment generates a future right to a particular service that is expected to economically benefit the organisation. The cash flow occurs prior to the expense being recognised. As time goes by, the prepayment will be recognised within the financial accounts as an expense, and the asset (the prepayment) will decrease. We referred to this as a process of amortising the prepayment.

prepaid expense
An asset that represents a payment made prior to the associated expense being incurred and, therefore, prior to the service being consumed by the organisation. Also known as a prepayment

For more on determining the amount of cash paid in relation to prepayments, see Learning exercise 11.5.

11.5 Learning Exercise

Determining the cash paid in relation to prepayments

Scenario: Clovelly Ltd pays for its insurance in advance of receiving the insurance service. It started the accounting period with prepaid insurance of $5000. The insurance expense for the year was $110 000 and the closing balance of prepaid insurance was $12 000.

Issue: How much cash was actually paid for insurance in the accounting period?

Solution: If Clovelly Ltd started the year with prepaid insurance of $5000, recognised insurance expenses of $110 000 for the accounting period, and ended the accounting period with prepaid insurance of $12 000, then $117 000 must have been paid in relation to insurance; that is:

Cash payment for insurance = closing balance of prepaid insurance + insurance expense recognised during the accounting period – opening balance of prepaid insurance

= $12 000 + $110 000 – $5000

= $117 000

Changes in revenue received in advance

Revenue received in advance represents a liability for cash payments received by an organisation for services that have not yet been provided to the customer, and therefore have not yet been earned. It is a liability because the organisation would generally be under an obligation to return the funds to the customer until such time that the organisation provides the related service. The greater the increase in this liability, the more cash that has been received but not yet earned.

revenue received in advance
A liability for cash payments received by an organisation for services that have not yet been provided to the customer, and therefore have not yet been earned

For more on this topic, see Learning exercise 11.6.

11.6 Learning Exercise

Determining cash received from customers when revenue received is initially treated as a liability

Scenario: Gordons Bay Inc is an airline company. It started the accounting period with revenue received in advance of $65 000, and ended the accounting period with revenue received in advance of $90 000. Passenger revenue recognised as income during the accounting period was $1 200 000.

Issue: How much cash was received from the customers of Gordons Bay Inc within the accounting period?

Solution: Given that the revenue recognised during the accounting period was \$1 200 000, and that the balance of revenue received in advance increased by \$25 000 during the accounting period, then \$1 225 000 cash must have been received from the airline passengers; that is:

Cash received from customers where cash received is initially recorded as a liability = closing balance of revenue received in advance + revenue recognised during the accounting period – opening balance of revenue received in advance

= \$90 000 + \$1 200 000 – \$65 000

= \$1 225 000

Changes in provisions

In Chapters 7 and 9, we defined a provision as a liability that is recognised in the financial accounts, but which has some degree of uncertainty with respect to the timing, and amount, of the expected future payment. Therefore, if something is reported in the balance sheet as a 'provision' then this indicates that it is an estimate of an amount that is expected to be paid in relation to the type of expense to which the provision relates. For example, a 'Provision for warranty repairs' would represent management's best estimate of how much the organisation will have to spend in the future to repair, under warranty, goods that have already been sold to customers.

If a liability for a future payment is recognised, there will be an increase in the related expense, and an increase in the liability. At the time when the expense is recognised, there are no cash flows and there will be an increase in liabilities, and an increase in expenses (and therefore a decrease in equity). The cash flows will occur in the future when the obligation is paid (settled).

The more a liability provision increases within an accounting period, the less the actual cash that was paid in relation to the underlying expense to which the provision relates. Conversely, the more a liability provision decreases within an accounting period, the more the actual cash that was paid in relation to the underlying expense to which the provision relates.

For more on determining the amount of cash paid in relation to a provision account, see Learning exercise 11.7.

11.7 Learning Exercise

Determining the cash payments made in relation to a provision account

Scenario: Coogee Company sells wetsuits, which it guarantees for 12 months after the date of sale. In each accounting period, it recognises the likely future expenses that will be incurred to repair faulty wetsuits. That is, the company recognises an expense for future warranty repairs at the time of sale based upon estimates of how many wetsuits are likely to be repaired, together with estimates of the average future repair cost. Repairs are performed by another organisation unrelated to Coogee Company.

Coogee Company commenced the accounting period with a provision for warranty repairs (a liability) of $15 000. During the accounting period, it recognised warranty expenses of $105 000 and had a closing provision for warranty repairs of $10 000.

Issue: How much cash was paid in relation to warranty repairs?

Solution:

Cash payments for warranty repairs = opening balance of provision for warranty repairs + warranty repairs expense recognised during the accounting period – closing balance of provision for warranty repairs

= $15 000 + $105 000 – $10 000

= $110 000

Depreciation and impairment losses

Depreciation and impairment expenses are recognised in relation to non-current assets that are controlled by an organisation. As we explained in Chapter 9, when depreciation is recognised, we recognise depreciation expense (which decreases profits and therefore equity) as well as an increase in accumulated depreciation (which is a contra asset that is offset against the respective class of property, plant and equipment). Depreciation expense does not involve a cash flow. The actual cash flow might have occurred in a previous accounting period when the item was initially acquired.

As we also explained in Chapter 9, an impairment loss is recognised when the carrying amount of an asset exceeds its recoverable amount. As is the case with depreciation expense, the recognition of an impairment loss does not involve a cash flow, as the related non-current asset typically would have been acquired in a prior accounting period. When an impairment loss is recognised, an expense will be recognised (which decreases equity) and a contra asset – accumulated impairment losses – will be recognised (which decreases assets).

In concluding this section, we note that as accountants, or students of accounting, we understand the difference between cash flows – which are shown within the statement of cash flows – and profits, which are reported within the income statement. However, it may reasonably be assumed that this difference will not be clearly understood by all users of financial statements; albeit if particular financial statement readers do not understand such differences, then arguably they should not be reading, and potentially relying on, the information contained within the financial statements.

Given the potential confusion that might arise as a result of the differences between cash flows and profits, organisations often provide a note to the financial statements that reconciles the cash flows from operating activities to the profit or loss for the period (or vice versa). As an example of this kind of reconciliation, consider **Exhibit 11.3**, which provides the reconciliation of Qantas Ltd's profits or loss to its cash flows from operating activities for the year ended 30 June 2021.

EXHIBIT 11.3 Reconciliation of profit or loss for the year to cash flows from operating activities as provided by Qantas Ltd in its 2021 annual report

Note 29: Reconciliation of statutory loss for the year to net cash from operating activities

		$M	
	Notes	2021	2020
Statutory loss for the year		(1728)	(1964)
Adjusted for:			
Depreciation and amortisation	5	1929	2045
Impairment of assets and related costs	25(C)	270	1456
Hedging-related activities		(64)	419
Share of net loss on investments accounted for under the equity method	14	129	53
Share-based payments	26	19	28
Amortisation of deferred financing fees and lease benefits		15	15
Net gain on disposal of assets	6	(26)	(7)
Discount rate changes impact on provisions	7	(4)	7
Other items		51	(49)
Dividends received from investments accounted for under the equity method	14	–	15
Changes in other items:			
Receivables		(14)	531
Inventories		19	(24)
Other assets		58	112
Payables		(416)	(196)
Revenue received in advance		402	(955)
Provisions		(403)	608
Deferred tax assets/liabilities and tax payable/receivable		(623)	(1011)
Net cash (outflow)/inflow from operating activities		(386)	1083

Source: Qantas (2021), p. 109.

When reviewing **Exhibit 11.3**, see if you can understand why certain amounts are added whilst other amounts are subtracted, when reconciling profit or loss to cash flows from operating activities. However, there is no expectation that you will understand the nature of *all* the reconciling items in **Exhibit 11.3**. As we explained earlier in this chapter, profit will generally be lower (or losses higher) than net cash flows from operating activities because of expenses, such as depreciation and impairment expenses, which do not involve an actual cash flow. As we can see in **Exhibit 11.3**, the 2021 loss for Qantas – as reported within its Income Statement was $1.728 billion, but its net cash outflow from operating activities was $386 million.

LO11.4 The reduced risk of managerial manipulation

As you know, when an accountant determines the income and expenses (and therefore the profit) for an accounting period, many professional judgements necessarily need to be made. Judgements have to be made about when to recognise income, and the collectability of accounts receivable, and about the useful life of a non-current asset, its residual value, and the pattern of benefits to be derived from the asset when calculating depreciation expense. Many other examples could also be provided where professional judgement is required when determining income and expenses, but the point being made is that it is necessary, when accrual accounting is used, to make many judgements about when income is earned and when expenses are incurred. Sometimes, these judgements might be made in a way that is not objective, and a level of bias might be introduced into the financial accounts. That is, there might be some creative accounting.

By contrast, there is less ability to manipulate data reported within a statement of cash flows, as the balance of opening and closing cash and cash equivalents can be verified by reference to particular external records prepared by a third party, such as bank statements generated by a bank. Therefore, it is commonly argued that the data reported in a statement of cash flows is likely to be more reliable than profit-related data.

The view that the statement of cash flows is a financial statement that is harder for managers to manipulate is one that has been promoted within the news media. For example, an article in Australia's *Daily Telegraph* (Koch and Koch, 2014) stresses that profit is an 'accounting figure' that is relatively easy to 'push' in a particular direction so as to generate a reported result that best suits the interests of management. The authors emphasise the importance to investors of the statement of cash flows because it is more difficult to 'mask with financial trickery' relative to the balance sheet and income statement. The authors of the newspaper article also note that if an organisation's cash flows have decreased, but profit has risen, there could be grounds for being suspicious that some form of creative accounting has been used, and it could therefore be worth 'digging a little deeper' to determine whether profit has actually been manipulated by managers.

In another article, in *The Age*, Bell (2013) argues that the statement of cash flows should be the first financial statement that readers should look at. Bell also notes that the statement of cash flows is the financial statement that is the 'hardest for management to manipulate'.

Whilst the material provided above suggests that the statement of cash flows is less likely to be manipulated than other financial statements, any suggestion that any form of financial statement – be it a statement of cash flows or any other statement – is *never* likely to be subject to some form of creative accounting, or another error or manipulation, is quite naive.

The opening and closing balances of cash and cash equivalents as provided in the statement of cash flows should reconcile directly with particular amounts shown within the balance sheet, and with amounts that can be externally verified; for example, to an independently prepared bank statement (we will discuss bank reconciliations later in this chapter). The reported sources of movements within cash and cash equivalents throughout the period are the amounts that are perhaps more easily manipulated.

One highly publicised case of an inappropriately prepared statement of cash flows involved the large international law firm Slater and Gordon. Whilst this firm is often employed to investigate and take action against other organisations for inappropriate behaviour, it was found that an organisation directly related to Slater and Gordon was under government investigation as a result of being associated with the reporting of a questionable statement of cash flows.

Some of Slater and Gordon's British operations were undertaken through an organisation known as Quindell. An article in *The Australian Financial Review* (Thompson, 2015) reports that the law firm acknowledged that within the statement of cash flows released by Quindell, the cash receipts were overstated and this occurred in conjunction with an overstatement of cash payments. This allegedly allowed the organisation to project a view that it was more efficient at converting the amounts owed by customers into cash than was actually the case. The article notes that if managers manipulate cash receipts, then they would also need to manipulate certain cash payments, otherwise the final balance of cash appearing in the statement of cash flows could not be confirmed (by auditors) back to the independently prepared bank statements that are prepared by banks. The article notes that it is very unusual to find an 'accidental mis-statement in cash receipts from customers' that by coincidence seems to be matched exactly by the same 'mis-statement in the cash payments'.

Therefore, although the statement of cash flows is developed in a way that is less influenced by professional judgement (relative to accrual accounting), we always need to have a level of *healthy scepticism* when using the information provided to us by managers of an organisation. The appointment of external auditors, whose role is to provide an opinion about the reliability of the information contained within the financial statements, should provide the financial statements readers with greater confidence that the financial statements have been properly prepared. By law, larger organisations, such as public companies, are required to have their financial statements audited by an independent external auditor prior to those financial statements being released to shareholders and other interested stakeholders.

Key concept

Because there is less professional judgement involved, it is less likely that reported cash flows will have been subjected to 'creative accounting' compared to reported profits.

LO11.5 Presenting the statement of cash flows

As we have already mentioned, the accounting standard IAS 7: Statement of Cash Flows requires that, for those organisations that are required to follow accounting standards, cash flows should be separately classified into those relating to:

- operating activities
- investing activities
- financing activities.

We will now discuss each of these three classifications of cash flows.

Operating activities

Operating activities are defined in the accounting standard IAS 7: Statement of Cash Flows as:

> the principal revenue-producing activities of the entity and other activities that are not investing and financing activities.
>
> Source: International Accounting Standards Board (2022).

Operating activities would be activities that relate to the provision of goods and services, and other activities that cannot be classified as either investing or financing activities. Cash flows relating to operating activities would include those relating to acquiring and selling the goods and services of an organisation, as well as the cash flows associated with supporting these activities, such as rental costs, administrative costs, salary costs and interest costs.

Effectively, the amount reported for the cash flows from operating activities provides an insight into the ability of an organisation to generate cash flows from its ordinary day-to-day activities. Such information is important as, in the long run, an organisation cannot rely on the cash flows from financing activities and investing activities to support its operations. Significant changes in the cash flows from operating activities should be thoroughly investigated, as these cash flows are of vital importance to a business.

As already discussed, cash inflows from operating activities typically will be higher than the reported profits (or the cash outflows from operating activities will be lower than reported losses) because of expenses such as depreciation and impairments losses that reduce profits but which do not involve a cash flow. As we indicated earlier, if we look at the cash flow from the operating activities of Qantas, which was a net cash outflow of $386 million, we see that this is considerably different (lower) than its reported loss of $1728 million for the same period of time.

Organisations that sell goods will purchase inventory and subsequently have to make the cash payment for that inventory as well as possible costs – perhaps payments to employees – in relation to the conversion of this inventory. They will then sell this inventory, often on credit terms, and then wait to receive the cash from the sale. These activities are all considered to relate to cash flows from operating activities. There can often be a significant time lag between acquiring the inventory from suppliers and receiving the cash from customers from the sale of the inventory.

Organisations will typically seek to minimise the time between when they need to make the payment to suppliers for the inventory and when they receive the cash from the subsequent sale of that inventory. This time period is often referred to as an organisation's *operating cycle*, which the accounting standard IAS 1: Presentation of Financial Statements defines as 'the time between the acquisition of assets for processing and their realisation in cash or cash equivalents'. The shorter the organisation's operating cycle, the less the reliance on other funds, such as borrowings, and therefore the less the related interest expenses of the organisation. Organisations need controls to ensure that the operating cycle is kept as short as possible given the nature of the goods and services. Organisations that manufacture products typically will have a longer operating cycle than organisations that acquire and then sell finished goods (that is, retailers).

The operating cycle of a retailing organisation is diagrammatically depicted in Figure 11.1.

FIGURE 11.1 Simple depiction of the operating cycles of a retailing organisation that sells goods on credit terms

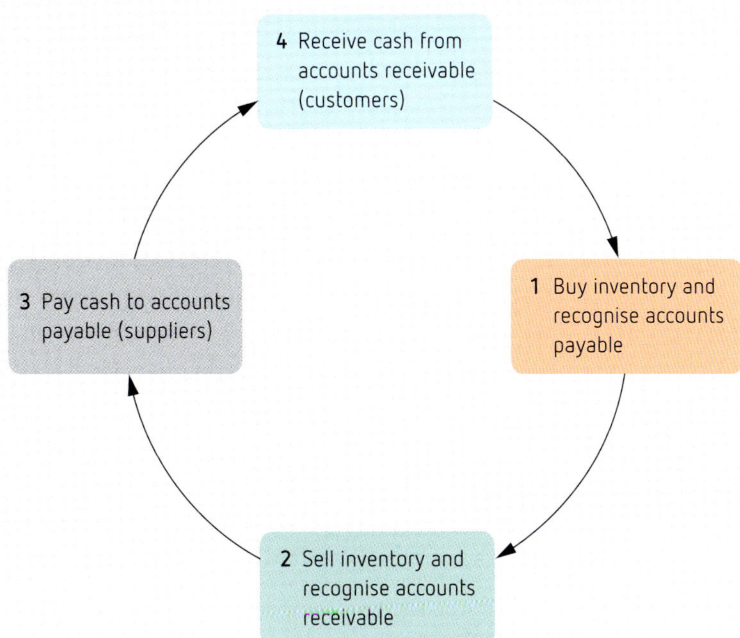

Ideally, an organisation wants to delay paying suppliers for as long as possible, and to receive cash from customers as quickly as possible. In terms of Figure 11.1, managers want to minimise the length of the time period between when they pay cash to the suppliers (point 3) and when they receive cash from customers (point 4). Ideally, the timing would match, or even better, the receipt from the customer would come before the supplier needs to be paid, but this is often not possible. In organising the payment of suppliers, care must be taken not to damage the organisation's reputation. Suppliers might not want to trade with an organisation that is known to unreasonably defer paying its debts.

In terms of delaying payments, some strategies would be to use credit when it is made available by suppliers and not paying suppliers more quickly than is expected, or perhaps – particularly for smaller organisations – using credit cards for acquisitions, thereby receiving a period of time before the related cash payments are due. Another strategy would be to not acquire more inventory than is necessary (whilst being careful not to run out of stock, as this can also cause reputational damage for an organisation).

In terms of receiving amounts due from customers as quickly as possible, an organisation must ensure that it sends out invoices quickly after the service has been performed or the goods have been delivered, and it must routinely follow up slow payments by sending reminders to customers. Managers might also consider offering customers a discount for early payment.

Investing activities

Investing activities are defined in accounting standard IAS 7 (paragraph 6) as:

> the acquisition and disposal of long-term assets and other investments not included in cash equivalents.
>
> Source: International Accounting Standards Board (2022).

Therefore, cash flows from investing activities include those relating to buying and selling property, plant and equipment; investments made in other organisations (which generates dividend income), and loans made to other organisations (which generates interest income). It should be noted that when interest revenue is earned on loans to other organisations, or when dividends are received from investments in other organisations, these cash flows are often reported as part of the operating activities of an organisation, and not as part of investing activities.

If a business has been expanding the scale of its operations, then the additional investment in non-current assets should be clearly reflected within the statement of cash flows, and the cash flows reported from investing activities would likely be negative. If we look at the statement of cash flows of Qantas (see Exhibit 11.1), we see that the cash flows from investing activities were negative, and a lot of this was created by acquisitions of additional non-current assets. What is also of interest is that the net cash outflows from investing activities were much lower in 2021 relative to 2020. This would be expected given the problems being created by the COVID-19 pandemic in 2021.

Financing activities

Financing activities are defined in the accounting standard IAS 7 (paragraph 6) as:

> activities that result in changes in the size and composition of the contributed equity and borrowings of the entity.
>
> Source: International Accounting Standards Board (2022).

Cash flows relating to financing activities therefore include cash flows associated with investors contributing equity capital to an organisation, and the related dividends paid by the organisation to shareholders, as well as those cash flows associated with borrowing and repaying funds obtained from external parties. Reviewing the statement of cash flows of Qantas, we can see that a lot of the cash inflows associated with financing activities related to receipts from issuing interest-bearing liabilities while the cash outflows associated with financing activities related to repaying other interest-bearing liabilities as well as paying liabilities associated with lease arrangements. Of interest is that unlike previous periods, there is no payment of dividends to shareholders in 2021. This would seem appropriate given the losses that were incurred in 2021 and the poor cash flows in 2021. This would have been one of the only years in recent times when Qantas did not pay dividends to owners.

Once the various cash flows have been determined, closing balances of cash and cash equivalents will typically be presented in the following way (we have just inserted some numbers here for illustrative purposes):

Net cash flows from operating activities	\$900 000
Plus (or minus) net cash flows from investing activities	(\$300 000)
Plus (or minus) net cash flows from financing activities	(\$400 000)
Net increase (decrease) in cash and cash equivalents during the financial period	\$200 000
Plus opening cash and cash equivalents	\$100 000
Closing cash and cash equivalents	**\$300 000**

Having discussed the different classifications of cash flows, a few additional comments can be made. In the start-up phase of a business, positive cash flows from financing activities are likely, as are negative cash flows from both investing and operating activities. Beyond a certain period of time, however, it would be hoped that the majority of cash flows would be generated through the operating activities of the business, as an entity cannot rely indefinitely on finance from external sources to survive. Ideally, cash flows from operating activities will generate sufficient cash flows to enable the expansion of the organisation. As has already been indicated, the cash flows from operating activities for Qantas were negative in 2021 – that is, there were net cash outflows. This would normally be of great concern to stakeholders. However, given COVID-19 effectively brought air travel to a stop in 2021, the result would have been expected. However, to survive in the long run, Qantas will need to return to positive cash inflows from operating activities in the near future – which it likely will.

An important point to make here is that positive cash flows – where cash inflows exceed cash outflows – are not always necessarily a good sign. For example, cash flows from investing activities could be positive because the organisation has sold some of its vital plant and equipment, perhaps to meet debts that were overdue. However, whilst this might create positive cash flows in the current period, selling some of the important plant and equipment of the organisation might be detrimental to future cash flows from operations.

Positive cash flows aren't always a good sign; for example, if a company has to sell vital equipment to meet overdue debts.

Source: iStock/Getty Images Plus/drewhadley

We can diagrammatically depict some of the different types of cash flows that relate to the three classifications of activities we have identified – see Figure 11.2.

FIGURE 11.2 Examples of cash flows that are typically included in the three classifications of cash flows

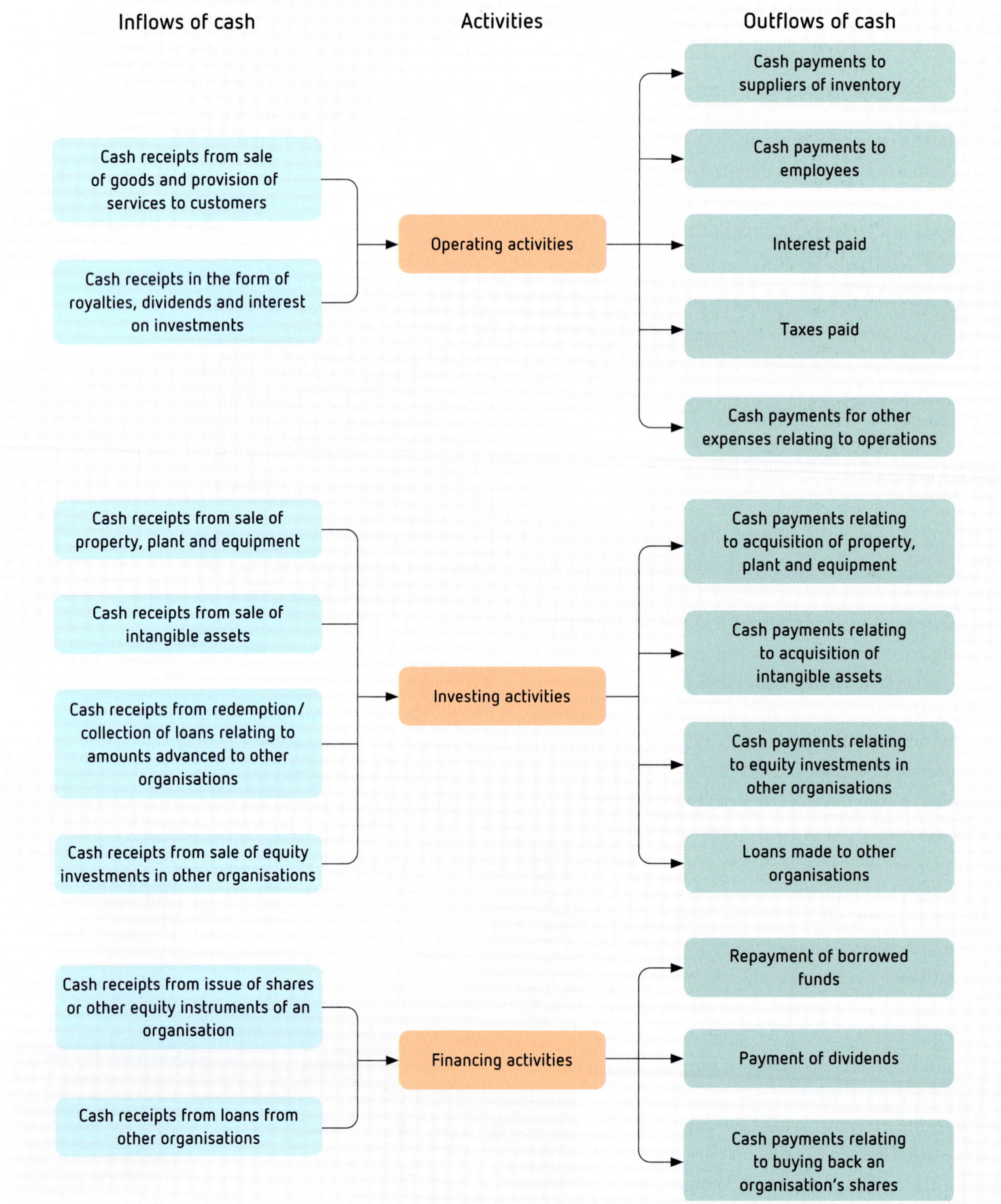

Supporting information for the statement of cash flows

The accounting standard relating to the presentation of the statement of cash flows requires that the statement of cash flows be accompanied by some additional supporting information, some of which is discussed below.

Non-cash financing and investing activities

The statement of cash flows reports the effects of those transactions that involve cash or cash equivalents. There can be numerous transactions that are part of the investing and financing activities of an organisation that do not directly involve cash or cash equivalents. For example, an organisation might purchase certain non-current assets by issuing additional equity or by way of a bank loan. It might also convert certain liabilities to equity, or certain non-cash assets to other non-cash assets (for example, it might swap some land for some buildings).

The accounting standard relating to the statements of cash flow requires that information about transactions and events that do not result in cash flows during the accounting period, but which affect assets and liabilities that have been recognised within the financial accounts, are to be disclosed in the notes to the financial statements when the transactions and other events:

- involve parties external to the organisation
- relate to the financing or investing activities of the entity.

Disclosure of financing facilities

Apart from disclosing additional information about non-cash financing and investing activities, the accounting standard suggests that the financial statements (by way of a note) should disclose information about the external financing arrangements of the entity, as at the end of the financial year. The reason for disclosing this information in the notes to the financial statements is to provide further information to the reader about what additional cash funding is available should the need for such funding arise. This information could allay the concerns of some readers, particularly if the statement of cash flows seems to be indicating potential cash flow difficulties in the future.

As an example of the type of note disclosure that could be made about available financing facilities, Exhibit 11.4 provides a note from the 2021 annual report of BHP Ltd.

EXHIBIT 11.4 Note relating to the finance facilities available to BHP Ltd

Standby arrangements and unused credit facilities
The Group's committed revolving credit facility operates as a back-stop to the Group's uncommitted commercial paper program. The combined amount drawn under the facility or as commercial paper will not exceed US$5.5 billion. As at 30 June 2021, US$ nil commercial paper was drawn (2020: US$ nil). During the year, the Group completed a one-year extension to the facility which is now due to mature on 10 October 2025. A commitment fee is payable on the undrawn balance and an interest rate comprising an interbank rate plus a margin applies to any drawn balance. The agreed margins are typical for a credit facility extended to a company with the Group's credit rating.

Source: BHP (2021), p. 165

Why do I need to know about the reporting requirements for larger organisations in respect of past cash flows?

The statement of cash flows provides detailed information about the cash inflows and outflows for a period of time separated into operating, investing, and financing activities. The accounting standard also requires additional disclosures in the notes to the financial statements about non-cash financing and investing activities as well as about available financing facilities.

Knowing about these requirements means that we will know to look within the financial report (annual report) to find this information. In the absence of knowing that there are such disclosure requirements we might not go looking for such information, meaning that we would potentially be missing some very useful (relevant) financial information about the organisation.

LO11.6 Preparing the statement of cash flows

We can prepare a statement of cash flows by referring directly to the cash payments and cash receipts of an organisation as typically recorded within its cash payments journal and cash receipts journal.

An alternative way to prepare a statement of cash flows is to use the information provided within the income statement and the balance sheet (together with some additional information). By reconciling the movements in the accounts shown within the balance sheet, we can work out the related cash flows – if any – in particular accounts and then transfer this information to the statement of cash flows. This is the way we did it in the earlier section of this chapter entitled 'The difference between cash flows and accounting profits' (see LO11.3).

To highlight the differences between cash flows and the results that are generated using accrual accounting, we will use the information within the balance sheet and income statement to prepare a statement of cash flows (see **Learning exercise 11.8**).

11.8 Learning Exercise

Preparation of a statement of cash flows

Scenario: The income statement and balance sheet of Bondi Company are shown below:

Income statement for Bondi Company for the year ended 30 June 2026				
	2026 $000		2025 $000	
Income				
Sales		1200		1100
Expenses				
Cost of goods sold	400		320	
Depreciation – buildings	50		50	
Depreciation – plant and equipment	80		50	

	2026 $000		2025 $000	
Electricity and rates	50		40	
Income tax expense	100		80	
Interest expense	20		15	
Rental expenses	120		100	
Salaries	260	(1080)	210	(865)
Profit		120		235

Balance sheet of Bondi Company as at 30 June 2026

	2026 $000	2025 $000
Current assets		
Cash	210	170
Accounts receivable	300	250
Inventory	240	200
	750	620
Non-current assets		
Land	400	300
Buildings	600	600
Accumulated depreciation – buildings	(150)	(100)
Plant and equipment	500	350
Accumulated depreciation – plant and equipment	(130)	(50)
	1220	1100
Total assets	**1970**	**1720**
Current liabilities		
Accounts payable	210	150
Accrued salary expenses	10	15
Accrued rental expenses	5	10
Income tax payable	100	80
	325	255
Non-current liabilities		
Long-term loans	160	100
Total liabilities	**485**	**355**
Net assets	**1485**	**1365**
Shareholders' funds		
Share capital	1000	1000
Retained earnings	485	365
Total shareholders' funds	**1485**	**1365**

Additional information:

- All sales are made on credit terms (meaning there have been no cash sales).
- Salaries and rental expenses are all accrued prior to payment.
- Electricity and rates and interest expenses are all paid as incurred.
- The accounts payable account is used only for the purchase of inventory.

- The organisation uses the perpetual inventory system (see Chapter 10) to account for its inventory, meaning that cost of goods sold is recognised each time an item of inventory is sold.
- There were no inventory write-downs. The FIFO cost flow assumption is used for inventories.
- There were no sales of property, plant and equipment, and there were no non-cash-related acquisitions of property, plant and equipment. There were also no impairments to, or revaluation of, assets.
- There was no repayment of loans during the year.

Issue: Prepare a statement of cash flows for Bondi Company for the year ended 30 June 2026, together with a note reconciling profit to net cash provided from operating activities.

Solution: To prepare a statement of cash flows, together with a note reconciling profit to cash flows from operating activities, we will firstly consider the cash flows from operating activities. We will then consider the cash flows from investment activities, and then the cash flows from financing activities, before ultimately preparing the statement of cash flows for the company.

Cash flows from operating activities

In this example, some expenses (electricity and rates and interest) are accounted for on a cash basis, meaning that they are paid in cash as incurred. Therefore, as the expense is recognised at the same time as the cash flow, these amounts can be moved directly from the income statement to the statement of cash flows.

However, calculations need to be made for those items of income and expense that are recognised on an accrual basis. We now consider these.

Receipts from customers

If accounts receivable decreases across the accounting period, then we can assume that more cash was collected from debtors in that accounting period than the amount of credit sales generated in that accounting period. Conversely, if the closing balance of accounts receivable is greater than the opening balance of accounts receivable, then less cash was received during the accounting period than there were credit sales in that accounting period. We can determine the cash flows from customers as:

Cash received from customers = sales + opening balance of accounts receivable – closing balance of accounts receivable

= \$1200 000 + \$250 000 – \$300 000

= \$1150 000

Purchases of inventory

When we calculated the cash flows from customers, we considered one account from the income statement (sales) and one account from the balance sheet (accounts receivable). By contrast, when we calculate cash flows pertaining to payments made to suppliers, we need to consider one income statement account (cost of goods sold) and two balance sheet accounts (inventory and accounts payable).

We are told that Bondi Company commences the period with \$200 000 of inventory. After using \$400 000 of inventory (cost of goods sold), it has a closing inventory balance of \$240 000. Given that there are no inventory write-offs, this means that \$440 000 of inventory must have been purchased; that is:

Purchases = cost of goods sold + closing balance of inventory – opening balance of inventory

= \$400 000 + \$240 000 – \$200 000

= \$440 000

Given that accounts payable has an opening balance of $150 000, purchases have now been calculated as $440 000 (see above), and the closing balance of accounts payable is $210 000, then $380 000 must have been paid in cash to the suppliers; that is:

Cash payments to suppliers = opening balance of accounts payable – closing balance of accounts payable + purchases of inventory

= $150 000 – $210 000 + $440 000

= $380 000

Accrued expenses (relating to salary and rental expenses)

In this example, salary and rental expenses are accrued prior to payment.

If the opening balance of accrued salary expenses is $15 000, salary expenses total $260 000, and the closing balance of accrued salary expenses is $10 000, then $265 000 must have been paid; that is:

Cash payments to employees = opening balance of accrued salary expenses + salary expenses incurred during the period – closing balance of accrued salary expenses

= $15 000 + $260 000 – $10 000

= $265 000

If the opening balance of accrued rental expenses is $10 000, rental expenses total $120 000, and the closing balance of accrued rental expenses is $5000, then $125 000 must have been paid; that is:

Cash payments for rent = opening balance of accrued rental expenses + rental expenses incurred during the period – closing balance of accrued rental expenses

= $10 000 + $120 000 – $5000

= $125 000

Taxation expenses

If the opening balance of income tax payable is $80 000, the closing balance of income tax payable is $100 000, and the income tax expense is $100 000, then $80 000 must have been paid; that is:

Cash payments for taxation = opening balance of income tax payable – closing balance of income tax payable + income tax expense

= $80 000 – $100 000 + $100 000

= $80 000

We can now calculate the total cash flows from operating activities as follows:

Total cash flows from operating activities	
	$000
Receipts from customers	1150
Payments to suppliers	(380)
Payments for accrued salary expenses	(265)
Payments for accrued rental expenses	(125)
Interest payments	(20)

	$000
Electricity and rates	(50)
Taxation payments	(80)
	230

Cash flows from investing activities

Land

As there were no sales of non-current assets and there were no non-cash acquisitions of property, plant and equipment (for example, no acquisitions were made as a result of the swapping of some non-current assets for others, or in exchange for the issuance of shares in the company), then all increases in property, plant and equipment must be due to cash acquisitions. As land increased by $100 000, this land must have been acquired during the period, that is:

Cash acquisition of land = closing balance of land – opening balance of land

= $400 000 – $300 000

= $100 000

Plant and equipment

As plant and equipment increases by $150 000, this amount of plant and equipment must have been acquired during the period; that is:

Cash acquisition of plant and equipment = closing balance of plant and equipment – opening balance of plant and equipment

= $500 000 – $350 000

= $150 000

We can now calculate the total cash flows from investing activities as follows:

Total cash flows from investing activities	
	$000
Payment for land	(100)
Payment for plant and equipment	(150)
	(250)

Cash flows from financing activities

The only cash flow from financing relates to $60 000 from long-term loans. The long-term loan increased from $100 000 to $160 000.

Having reconciled the movements in all the balance sheet accounts, we can now feel comfortable that we have identified all cash flows.

Total cash flows for the period	
	$000
Opening cash balance	**170**
Cash flows from operating activities	230
Cash flows from investing activities	(250)
Cash flows from financing activities	60
Closing cash balance	**210**

Statement of cash flows

We are now able to present a statement of cash flows for Bondi Company.

Statement of cash flows for Bondi Company for the year ended 30 June 2026	
	$000
Cash flows from operating activities	
Receipts from customers	1150
Payments to suppliers of inventory	(380)
Payment to employees	(265)
Payment for rental expenses	(125)
Payment for electricity and rates	(50)
Interest paid	(20)
Income taxes paid	(80)
Net cash provided from operating activities (1)	230
Cash flows from investing activities	
Payment for property, plant and equipment	(250)
Net cash provided from investing activities	(250)
Cash flows from financing activities	
Proceeds from borrowings	60
Net cash provided from financing activities	60
Net increase in cash held	40
Cash at the beginning of the financial year	170
Cash at the end of the financial year	210

We will now provide a reconciliation of profit to cash flows from operating activities. Remember, profit is determined on an accrual basis, whereas cash flows from operating activities is determined on a cash basis. As we can see below, cash flows from operating activities were higher than profit after tax (almost double), with most of this difference being due to depreciation expense, which is an expense that does not involve a cash flow (that is, depreciation is an example of a non-cash flow expense).

Note 1. Reconciliation of profit to net cash provided from operating activities	
	$000
Profit after tax	120
Depreciation expenses	130
Increase in income taxes payable	20
Increase in accounts receivable	(50)
Increase in inventories	(40)
Increase in accounts payable	60
Decrease in accrued expenses (salaries and rental expenses)	(10)
Net cash provided from operating activities	230

LO11.7 Cash controls

Cash is one of the most vulnerable assets of an organisation, and it is the asset subject to the highest level of theft. It is an asset that does not have individual characteristics that are recorded by organisations, thereby making the identification of stolen money difficult. Cash is also extremely easy to transport and dispose of, unlike many other assets controlled by an organisation.

internal controls
Policies or procedures implemented by an organisation with the aim of ensuring that an organisation operates: effectively and efficiently; in conformance with the organisation's mission and objectives; in compliance with relevant laws and regulations; and, that the organisation's systems of accounting enable relevant and representationally faithful reports to be prepared for the use of internal and external stakeholders

segregation of duties
A control that seeks to ensure that those people who have access to particular assets, such as cash, are not the same people who account for the movements in the asset. A full segregation of duties would ensure that different individuals would initiate a transaction, approve the transaction, record the transaction and have access to the asset to which the transaction relates

An organisation should have various **internal controls** for cash, some of which we will discuss below. Many of these controls rely upon a separation of duties (also referred to as a **segregation of duties**) between those people who have access to the actual cash and those people who account for movements in the cash. As a general principle, and if the organisation is sufficiently large enough, an individual should never be able to initiate a transaction, approve the transaction, record the transaction, and have access to the asset to which the transaction relates.

Internal controls should be clearly documented to avoid confusion, made clearly known to employees, and, in a larger organisation, somebody (perhaps an internal auditor who is an employee of the organisation) should be appointed to periodically check that the required internal controls are actually being followed and not circumvented. External auditors are also sometimes employed to provide an independent review of the effectiveness of internal controls.

Internal controls include those policies and procedures an organisation has in place to help ensure that:

- operations are conducted efficiently
- operations are conducted in accordance with the objectives, policies and plans of the organisation
- assets are safeguarded
- errors, fraud and theft are minimised
- the accounting data being produced are relevant and faithfully represent the underlying transactions and events (it is free of error and the impacts of fraud) and ultimately will enable the preparation of timely management and financial accounting information.

The extent of the controls that are put in place will be subject to the usual considerations of both the costs associated with implementing the control and the related benefits associated with having the control in place. A well-designed system of internal controls is considered to be part of an organisation's overall corporate governance system.

We will now discuss some internal controls pertaining to cash receipts, and cash payments, that organisations should implement to safeguard cash.

Key concept

Cash is one of the assets most likely to be misappropriated. As such, it is essential that all organisations have well-functioning internal controls designed to minimise the likelihood of cash theft.

Cash receipts

While the use of cash is declining rapidly within society, we can still expect some transactions to be made in cash. Also, regardless of whether transactions with customers and suppliers are made on non-cash (credit) terms, or by way of credit cards or direct bank transfers, organisations will still have cash deposits with banks that need to be safeguarded. This necessitates the implementation of appropriate cash controls.

In relation to cash receipts, the internal controls to be implemented could include the following:

- Cash registers should be used for cash receipts from customers. This is what we – as customers – typically expect. Each cash sale should generate a uniquely numbered cash receipt that is given to the customer. The cash register should also include an internal record of each sale that represents the first point at which the sales and cash receipts data are entered into the financial accounting information system. Customers expect to receive a cash receipt, so this helps the maintenance of this control. To further encourage this expectation, there could be a sign indicating to customers that they will receive a cash receipt for each cash purchase.

Only designated people should be permitted to use the cash register.

- When an employee completes their duties each day, somebody else should be appointed to ensure that the total recorded cash receipts equal the amount actually in the cash register. Any discrepancies should immediately be reported to the designated manager.
- When amounts are received from accounts receivable, the person responsible for opening the mail (which is not that common any more given the ability to transfer funds electronically) should not be responsible for accounting for accounts receivable. This is a separation of duties. If the person responsible for opening the mail also has access to the accounts receivable accounts, then they would be able to take the payment themselves and perhaps write the debtor off as a bad debt, thereby potentially eliminating any follow-up action to see why the debtor has not paid. In the absence of follow-up action, there would be no investigation of where the payment had gone.
- All cash receipts should be deposited daily and not kept on the premises overnight. This reduces the cash onsite and also provides an independent record created by the bank of cash being received.
- Customers should be encouraged to use electronic funds transfers (EFT) to transfer amounts owing to the organisation, rather than sending cheques or cash. Cheques and cash are more vulnerable to theft.

Source: Alamy Stock Photo/Phil Wills

Cash is one of the most vulnerable assets of a business, subject to the highest level of theft. Keeping receipts of cash transactions, tallying recorded receipts versus actual cash in the register, and removing cash from the business premises overnight are all common and sensible cash-control methods.

Cash payments

In relation to cash payments, whether by direct bank transfers, cheques, or cash (payments of cash should be quite rare and should be discouraged), internal controls could include the following:

- All payments should be properly authorised and linked to documentation. For example, prior to making a payment to a supplier, an approved purchase order plus evidence that the goods or services were actually delivered (for example, a delivery docket) needs to be evidenced.
- Paid invoices should be stamped with 'PAID' to ensure that they are not paid twice.
- Payments should not be made directly from cash takings (from cash registers).
- Where possible, employees should be paid directly into their bank account.
- Regular bank reconciliations should be conducted by somebody who has no access to cash, and no responsibility for recording cash receipts or payments, to ensure that what the managers of an organisation think they have in cash actually reconciles with what the bank records indicate.

A number of the controls above will work to the extent that there is a segregation of duties. Whilst a proper segregation of duties is recommended in relation to the control of all types of assets – including cash – it does need to be acknowledged that acts of collusion can circumvent well-designed controls. Collusion occurs when two or more people work together to beat internal controls. The possibility of collusion needs to be considered at all times, and actions should be periodically taken by managers to check for the possibility that collusion is taking place. Where automated payment transactions have been set up for particular suppliers, such arrangements should be regularly reviewed to ensure proper authorisation.

Bank reconciliations

bank reconciliation
A reconciliation of an organisation's records of cash with the records held by the bank. It identifies the cause of any discrepancies

A very important internal control for cash that we briefly referred to above is the bank reconciliation. A **bank reconciliation** allows a comparison of an organisation's records of cash with the records held by the bank. There will be timing differences such that what the bank reports is in the customer's bank account will rarely agree with the amount that the organisation reports within its own financial accounts. Timing differences will occur for a number of reasons, including:

- direct deposits that are made to the bank that then need to be recognised by the organisation
- deposits that have been made with the bank by the organisation, but which have not yet been recorded in the bank's records (we refer to these as 'deposits not yet recognised by the bank')
- automated payments initiated by the bank that are yet to be recognised by the organisation
- cheques that have been written by the organisation (and therefore recognised within the organisation's financial accounts) but have not yet been banked by the payee/receiver of the cheque, meaning that the amount has not come out of the organisation's bank account – they are commonly termed 'unpresented cheques' as they have not been presented for payment at the payee's bank
- interest expenses and bank fees imposed by the bank, which have not yet been recognised by the organisation
- interest earned on the bank deposit, which has yet to be recognised by the organisation
- deposits of cheques that the bank has subsequently dishonoured because of insufficient funds in the bank account of the payer.

Differences between the balance of cash as reported on the bank statement and as recorded by an organisation in its ledger accounts (for example, in the cash at bank account) might also be due to either party making an error.

Performing a bank reconciliation involves comparing the organisation's cash at bank account as recorded within the organisation's ledger with the balance of the customer's bank balance as shown on the statement produced by the bank, which we refer to as the 'bank statement'. The person performing the bank reconciliation will need to check that the details of all payments and receipts of cash, as recorded by the organisation, are matched by movements that are shown in the bank statement produced by the bank. Discrepancies will be the reason why the balance of cash at bank as reported within the bank statement does not match the balance of cash at bank as recognised by the organisation. Where the reconciliation highlights transactions that were previously unknown by the company (for example, some direct deposits made to the bank, some interest charges and bank fees, and some dishonoured cheques), this will require the organisation to subsequently recognise the information within its financial accounts.

In Chapter 8, a brief mention was made of cash payments journals and cash receipts journals. Once an organisation becomes large enough, it is common for different people to be in charge of recording cash payments and cash receipts. The cash payments will be recorded within a *cash payments journal* that will show details of the date, amount and nature of each transaction (for example, payment for wages, inventory, rent, electricity, and cash distributions to owners). Similarly, cash receipts will be recorded within a *cash receipts journal* that shows details of the date, amount and nature of each transaction (for example, the receipt of cash from cash sales, accounts receivable and owners' contributions, and dividends payments from other organisations).

Exhibit 11.5 provides an example of how a bank reconciliation might be presented. The bank reconciliation is provided for internal use and, as an important component of management controls, would not be released to external stakeholders.

EXHIBIT 11.5 Possible form of a bank reconciliation statement

Cash balance as per the bank statement prepared by the bank	xx
Add:	
Deposits not yet recognised by the bank	xx
Direct payments of expenses initiated by the bank	xx
Interest expenses charged by the bank	xx
Bank fees charged by the bank	xx
Deduct:	
Unpresented cheques	(xx)
Amounts deposited directly to the bank by another organisation	(xx)
Cash balance as per organisation's cash at bank account	**(xx)**

Learning exercise 11.9 provides an insight into how bank reconciliations have traditionally been prepared. However, with internet banking, EFTPOS, direct debits, PayPal, and an increasingly cashless society, the use of bank deposits and cheques has decreased and the timing of transactions recognised in the accounting system and the bank have become increasingly synchronised. Most accounting software will now connect directly to your bank to import your bank transaction information and assist you to perform a bank reconciliation. Nevertheless, the bank reconciliation remains a necessary component of a sound system of internal controls.

11.9 Learning Exercise

Preparation of a bank reconciliation

Scenario: Diamond Head Company commences operations on 1 January 2026. Details of the cash payments and cash receipts of the company as recorded in its cash payments journal and cash receipts journal for its first month of operations are provided below. With total cash receipts of $29 450 and total cash payments of $9900 being recognised by the company, this means that the company has a cash at bank balance of $19 550 as recorded within its financial accounts.

While any cash held with the bank would be considered an asset by the company (and by convention, assets have debit balances), from the bank's perspective, the amount deposited by the company would be considered a liability of the bank because the bank has an obligation to make a payment to the company on demand for an amount equal to the balance reported on the bank statement.

From the perspective of the bank, it has an obligation (or liability) to pay back the funds to the company as and when required, and because liabilities by convention have a credit balance, then the bank statement will show a credit balance when customers have cash deposits with the bank. Further, when we look at a bank statement prepared by a bank, we will see that any cash going into a customer's bank account appears in the credit column of the statement (to reflect the bank's perspective of the liability to the customer now increasing). The amounts in the debit column represent amounts leaving the customer's account as payments, which from the bank's perspective is a reduction in their liability to the customer.

Issue: As a means of controlling the use and security of cash, you are required to reconcile the balance of cash, as recorded by the company in the cash at bank account (which we now know is $19 550), with the balance of cash as reported on the bank statement prepared independently by the bank, which is provided below. The bank statement shows a balance of $17 930, which is $1620 less than the balance of cash at bank as recorded within the company's own financial accounts.

Cash receipts journal

Date	Details	Amount $	Accounts receivable $	Cash sales $	Other accounts $	Amount banked $
1 Jan	Owner contribution	10 000			10 000	10 000✓
3 Jan	Cash sales	1200		1200		1200✓
5 Jan	Debtor – M. Jones	1400	1400			
	Cash sales	1000		1000		2400✓
10 Jan	Cash sales	2350		2350		2350✓
14 Jan	Debtor – P. Smit	3100	3100			
	Cash sales	2900		2900		6000✓
20 Jan	Cash sales	3250		3250		3250✓
25 Jan	Cash sales	1450		1450		1450✓
31 Jan	Debtor – B. Brown	2000	2000			
	Cash sales	800		800		2800
		29 450	6500	12 950	10 000	29 450

Cash payments journal

Date	Cheque number	Details	Accounts payable $	Salaries $	Rent $	Other amount $	Total payment $
2 Jan	#001	Rent			1000		1000✓
7 Jan	#002	Salaries		1200			1200✓
10 Jan	#003	Act pay – Whiteco	1800				1800✓
14 Jan	#004	Salaries		1200			1200✓
20 Jan	#005	Dividend to owners				1100	1100✓
22 Jan	#006	Act pay – Blackco	1400				1400✓
22 Jan	#007	Salaries		1200			1200✓
31 Jan	#008	Rent			1000		1000
			3200	3600	2000	1100	9900

Bank statement Surfside branch Diamond Head Company		Account number 0076969 Statement period 1 Jan 2026 – 31 Jan 2026		Statement 1 Closing balance 17 930 CR
Date	**Transaction**	**Debit**	**Credit**	**Balance**
01 Jan	Cash deposit		$10 000.00✓	$10 000 CR
04 Jan	Cash deposit		$1200.00✓	$11 200 CR
05 Jan	Cheque #001	$1000.00✓		$10 200 CR
05 Jan	Cash deposit		$2400.00✓	$12 600 CR
05 Jan	Direct deposit – Sale to J. Jones		$1100.00	$13 700 CR
07 Jan	Cheque #002	$1200.00✓		$12 500 CR
11 Jan	Cash deposit		$2350.00✓	$14 850 CR
13 Jan	Cheque #003	$1800.00✓		$13 050 CR
14 Jan	Cash deposit		$6000.00✓	$19 050 CR
14 Jan	Cheque #004	$1200.00✓		$17 850 CR
20 Jan	Cheque #005	$1100.00✓		$16 750 CR
20 Jan	Direct debit 0001 Oceanic Bank insurance policy	$900.00		$15 850 CR
20 Jan	Cash deposit		$3250.00✓	$19 100 CR
22 Jan	Cheque #007	$1200.00✓		$17 900 CR
25 Jan	Cash deposit		$1450.00✓	$19 350 CR
25 Jan	Cheque #006	$1400.00✓		$17 950 CR
30 Jan	Bank fee	$20.00		$17 930 CR

Solution: When preparing a bank reconciliation, do the following.

First, identify those transactions that appear in both the company's records and in the bank statement

When deposits are made with the bank, there can be a delay in the timing with which the bank records the deposit. If deposits are made with the bank late in the day, then the deposit might not appear in the bank statement until a later day.

When cheques are sent to people or organisations, there will be a delay between when the cheque is recorded by the organisation (the details and amount of the cheque will be recorded by the organisation at the time the cheque is written) and when the cheque is presented to the bank by the recipient, and reported on the bank statement. This delay can be many days. If the cheque fails to be presented to the bank for weeks, then action should be taken by the organisation to determine why the recipient of the cheque has failed to bank it – perhaps they did not receive it.

In this Learning exercise, we have already ticked those items that appear in both sets of records. Those items that are not ticked represent the reasons why the balance of the cash at bank account in the company accounts does not match the balance shown by the bank within the bank statement prepared by the bank.

Second, identify the details of the 'unticked' items that therefore do not appear in both sets of records

- Reviewing the cash receipts journal, we find that the amount recorded on 31 January of $2800 in total has not yet been recognised by the bank. It therefore is a reconciling item as the company already knows about it, but it is not reflected in the bank statement. This can be referred to as a 'deposit not yet recognised by the bank'.

- Reviewing the cash payments journal, we find that cheque number #008 for $1000 has not yet been recognised by the bank, as the recipient probably has not yet taken it to the bank. This is a reconciling item as the company already knows about it, but it is not reflected in the bank statement. These are commonly referred to as 'unpresented cheques'.
- When we look at the bank statement, we can see three items without a tick, meaning they have not been recognised by the company within the company's own records. These items are:
  - a direct deposit made to the bank by a customer on 5 January for $1100
  - a payment of an insurance expense initiated directly by the bank on 20 January for $900
  - fees imposed by the bank of $20 on 30 January.

These three items represent 'new' information for the company. The details and amounts of these payments need subsequently to be entered into the company's financial accounts.

While the three items above are now added to the company's financial accounts to update them, items that the bank is not aware of cannot be added to the bank statement. Instead, a bank reconciliation statement is prepared where the starting point is the cash balance from the bank statement. This, in effect, is providing an updated figure of what the balance of the bank statement would have been if the bank was aware of the 'deposit not yet recognised by the bank' and the 'unpresented cheques' on the day the bank statement was issued.

Third, prepare the bank reconciliation

Having now determined the reasons why the balance of the company's cash at bank balance does not agree with the bank statement prepared by the bank, we can prepare the bank reconciliation:

Diamond Head Company Bank reconciliation as at 31 January 2026	
Cash balance as per bank statement prepared by the bank	**$17 930**
Add:	
Deposits not yet recognised by the bank	$2 800
Direct payments of expenses initiated by the bank (Insurance)	$900
Bank fees charged by the bank	$20
Deduct:	
Unpresented cheque (#008)	($1000)
Amounts deposited directly by a customer to the bank (J. Jones)	($1100)
Cash balance as per organisation's cash at bank account	**($19 550)**

Notice that the final balance in the bank reconciliation statement is the cash balance that should now reconcile with cash at bank according to the organisation's accounts. That is, both sets of records have now been reconciled. Because the bank statement has been reconciled to the cash at bank account, the managers of the organisation can be confident that there are no outstanding movements in cash that they are not aware of and which might have involved theft. A bank reconciliation should be prepared regularly, perhaps weekly or monthly.

Petty cash funds

Apart from bank accounts, organisations often also have a **petty cash fund** for very small payments that require cash. Petty cash – a small amount of cash typically kept in a locked box, perhaps amounting to $100 to $200 – might be used to pay for somebody's bus or taxi fare for work purposes, or to pay for a cake for an employee's birthday, or for a coffee for a visitor to the organisation. It is not efficient to use cheques or make electronic transfers of cash for such small amounts.

petty cash fund
A small amount of cash an organisation will typically keep on site, for very small incidental cash payments

The petty cash will be kept in a secure place and the balance (which as we indicated might be as low as $100 or $200) will be replenished periodically as the cash is used. What typically happens is that people will use their own cash or credit card to make a payment and will obtain a receipt for the related payment, which they will then seek to claim back from the organisation. Clear guidelines should be available in terms of what expenses can be claimed from petty cash.

A designated person is in charge of the petty cash fund. They might record a 'petty cash docket' that is signed by the claimant and the 'petty cash officer', and this docket and the related invoice are stapled and retained within the petty cash box at the time the cash is given to the claimant. The total of the cash in the petty cash box and all the receipts should, at any point in time, equal the total of the petty cash fund. At a particular point in time – perhaps the end of the week – another designated person reviews the receipts and dockets, and if the payments have been made in accordance with company policy, then an amount of cash equal to the total of all the receipts is put into the petty cash box to take it back up to its designated balance (often referred to as the petty cash *float*).

Expenses are recognised by an organisation in respect of the various payments that have been made from the fund. The amount of cash in the fund is considered to be an asset of the organisation and included within cash.

Because the amount of petty cash is typically very low, the internal controls associated with petty cash do not need to be too sophisticated given that it would be hard to justify the costs of sophisticated controls on a cost-versus-benefits basis.

Why do I need to know about cash controls?

Of all the assets organisations have, cash is the one most likely to be subject to theft, Therefore, if we are managing a business, we need to be aware of, and understand, how the chance of cash theft can be minimised. We therefore need to have an awareness of policies and procedures that can be put in place to minimise the likelihood that cash will be stolen.

STUDY TOOLS

SUMMARY

In this chapter we have explored the role of an important financial statement: the statement of cash flows. We emphasised that there are many stakeholders who have an interest in an organisation's cash flows, and we also made reference to the view held by many people that the data contained within a statement of cash flows tend to be influenced less by professional judgement than other financial statements. Therefore, it is less likely to be subjected to some form of managerial-related manipulation.

We noted a number of reasons why there can be significant differences between cash flows and profits, with profits being calculated by way of accrual accounting. It was stressed that profitable organisations can fail if they do not carefully plan, monitor and control their cash flows.

We learned that, for larger organisations, the statement of cash flows provides information about the sources and use of cash and 'cash equivalents'. We also learned that cash flows are classified into those that relate to operating activities, investing activities and financing activities. In discussing the cash flows from operating activities, we also discussed the 'operating cycle' of business organisations, and the need to try to shorten the period of time between when suppliers of goods and services need to be paid and when customers pay amounts due to an organisation.

We demonstrated how to use the income statement and balance sheet, in conjunction with some additional information, to produce a statement of cash flows. In doing so, we also identified some supporting notes that can accompany the statement of cash flows, including a note that reconciles profits to cash flows from operating activities, and notes about non-cash financing and investing activities, and the available financing facilities.

At the end of the chapter, we moved our focus to cash controls. We stressed that cash is an asset that is vulnerable to misappropriation, and we identified a number of internal controls that an organisation might put in place to safeguard, and properly account for, cash. It was noted that effective controls typically rely on a segregation of duties that fulfil the general principle that a single person should not be involved in more than one of the following activities: initiating a transaction, approving a transaction, recording a transaction, and having access to the underlying asset (in this case, cash). One control that we explored in depth was the preparation of a bank reconciliation statement, something that needs to be performed regularly by somebody who has no role in handling cash, recording cash payments, or recording cash receipts.

ANSWERS TO THE OPENING QUESTIONS

At the beginning of the chapter we asked the following three questions. As a result of reading this chapter, you should now be able to provide informed answers to these questions – ours are shown below.

1 Accounting standards require that a statement of cash flows reports information about flows of cash and cash equivalents. What is a cash equivalent?

Cash equivalents are defined in accounting standard IAS 7: Statement of Cash Flows as 'short-term, highly liquid investments that are readily convertible to known amounts of cash and that are subject to an insignificant risk of change in value'. Cash equivalents include short-term money market deposits and bank bills to the extent that the time to conversion to cash is not greater than 90 days.

2 The statement of cash flows classifies the cash flows for an accounting period into three broad categories. What are these categories?

For those organisations that are required to comply with accounting standards, cash flows should be divided into those that relate to:

a operating activities

b investing activities

c financing activities.

Even for those organisations not required to comply with accounting standards, there would be an expectation that this classification scheme would also provide very useful information for the users of the reports.

3 Identify four reasons why the profits of an organisation for a period of time might potentially be higher than the cash flows the organisation has generated from its operating activities for that same period of time.

Reasons why the *profits* of an organisation might be higher than the organisation's *cash flows from operating activities* include the following:

a Sales have been made on credit terms and the cash has yet to be received (or more directly, the closing balance of accounts receivable is greater than the opening balance).

b The balance of accrued expenses has decreased during the accounting period, meaning that some of the cash outflows relate to paying obligations for expenses that were recognised in a previous period.

c There has been an increase in prepaid expenses during the accounting period. Cash payments in relation to prepayments will not negatively impact profits (prepayments are assets), but they do involve a cash outflow.

d The closing balance of a provision is less than the opening balance of the provision, meaning that the cash flow in relation to the related expense was greater than the amount of the related expense that was recognised within the accounting period.

SELF-TEST QUIZ

Answers to this quiz appear in the Appendix of this book.

1 According to the accounting standard for statements of cash flows, specific disclosures should be made with respect to the cash flows for a period of time. In this regard, which of the following statements is false?

- **a** The statement of cash flows should separately disclose information about cash flows from operating activities.
- **b** The statement of cash flows should separately disclose information about cash flows from construction activities.
- **c** The statement of cash flows should separately disclose information about cash flows from investing activities.
- **d** The statement of cash flows should separately disclose information about cash flows from financing activities.
- **e** The notes to the statement of cash flows should provide information about non-cash financing and investment activities, as well as about available financing facilities.

2 Which of the following would not be considered to represent a cash flow from operating activities?

- **a** Cash payments to employees
- **b** Cash payments to suppliers of inventory
- **c** Cash receipts from sale of goods and services to customers
- **d** Taxes paid
- **e** Payment of dividends

3 Waimea Bay started the accounting period with the liability 'accrued wages' of $70 000. Wages expense for the year was $920 000, and the closing balance of accrued wages was $40 000. How much cash was paid to employees in the accounting period?

a $920 000 b $940 000 c $950 000 d $970 000 e None of these choices

4 Sunset Beach Inc. is a gardening service company. It started the accounting period with revenue received in advance of $85 000 and ended the accounting period with revenue received in advance of $100 000. Service revenue recognised during the accounting period was $920 000. All payments are received in advance, so there are no doubtful debts. How much cash was received from the customers of Sunset Beach Inc in the accounting period?

a $925 000 b $935 000 c $945 000 d $955 000 e None of these choices

5 Pipeline Company sells helmets for surfing. The following information was extracted from its balance sheet and income statement:

- It started the accounting period with inventory of $105 000 and ended the accounting period with inventory of $125 000.
- It started the accounting period with accounts payable of $40 000 and ended the accounting period with accounts payable of $45 000.
- Cost of goods sold for the accounting period was $385 000.
- All purchases are made on credit terms, and the company uses the perpetual system of inventory management and adopts the first-in, first-out (FIFO) inventory cost flow assumption. There were no inventory losses during the accounting period.
- The accounts payable account only includes amounts payable to suppliers of inventory.

How much cash was paid to the suppliers of inventory?

a $370 000 b $380 000 c $390 000

d $400 000 e None of these choices

ONLINE RESOURCES

Accompanying the book is an innovative online case study that follows an organisation initially established by two friends, which grows into a large and successful company. Acquire this chapter's case study from your instructor.

CASE STUDY

Armadillo Surf Designs: Cash is down but something's up

Armadillo Surf Designs (ASD) recently hosted a beach clean-up event and seems to have sold less items of merchandise than expected. In addition to being concerned about the reduced sales at the event, Dillon has some broader cash-flow concerns. He has asked you to meet with him to discuss the cash flow of the business.

You will explain to Dillon how ASD might improve its cash flow from operations, and advise whether the bank balance can go down when the business is generating a profit. You will also prepare a cash flow statement and use this to discuss ASD's cash flow. You will describe the bank reconciliation process and also discuss the risk of theft associated with the recent beach clean-up day.

END-OF-CHAPTER QUESTIONS

11.1 What is the role of the statement of cash flows?

11.2 The statement of cash flows reports information about cash and cash equivalents. What is a 'cash equivalent'?

11.3 The statement of cash flows classifies cash flows into three broad categories. What are these categories?

11.4 Is it possible that a profitable organisation can fail because of an inability to pay debts? Why?

11.5 Which of the following would be considered a cash equivalent?

a accounts receivable
b accounts payable
c a money market deposit that earns a fixed 4 per cent rate of return and is repayable on demand
d shares in a listed company
e a fixed-term bank deposit of two months.

11.6 Why is a reconciliation of the profit for a year to the cash flows from operating activities often provided within the notes that accompany an organisation's financial statements?

11.7 Why is it often considered that the statement of cash flows is more difficult for managers and their accountants to manipulate in comparison to information that is reported in the income statement and the balance sheet?

11.8 What is an organisation's operating cycle, and why is knowledge of it relevant to managers?

11.9 In relation to internal controls, what do we mean by a 'segregation of duties'?

11.10 Identify four controls we might implement in relation to safeguarding the cash of an organisation.

11.11 The sales for an organisation within an accounting period were $340 000, opening accounts receivable was $40 000, and closing accounts receivable was $15 000. There were no doubtful debts expenses for the period. All sales are made on credit terms, meaning there were no cash sales. How much cash was actually received from customers within the accounting period?

11.12 Sunshine Beach Company sells skimboards. The following information was derived from its balance sheet and income statement:

- It started the accounting period with inventory of $75 000 and ended the accounting period with inventory of $60 000.
- It started the accounting period with accounts payable of $20 000 and ended the accounting period with accounts payable of $25 000.
- Cost of goods sold for the accounting period was $275 000.

All purchases are made on credit terms, and the company uses the perpetual system of inventory management and adopts the first-in, first-out (FIFO) inventory cost flow assumption. There were no inventory losses during the accounting period.

The accounts payable account only includes amounts payable to suppliers of inventory.

You are required to determine how much cash was paid to the suppliers of inventory.

11.13 Alexandria Bay started the accounting period with the liability accrued wages of $50 000. Wages expense for the year was $780 000 and the closing balance of accrued wages was $65 000. How much cash was paid to employees?

11.14 Granite Bay Ltd started the accounting period with prepaid rent of $12 000. The rent expense for the year was $145 000, and the closing balance of prepaid rent was $8000. How much was actually paid for rent in the accounting period?

11.15 Tea Tree Bay Inc is a photocopier service company. It started the accounting period with revenue received in advance of $35 000 and ended the accounting period with revenue received in advance of $45 000. Service revenue recognised during the accounting period was $670 000. All payments are received in advance, so there are no doubtful debts. How much cash was received from the customers of Tea Tree Bay Inc?

11.16 Boiling Pot Company sells surfboards that are imported from China and which the company guarantees for 12 months after a sale. Each accounting period, it recognises the likely expenses that will be incurred to repair faulty surfboards. Repairs are performed by another organisation unrelated to Boiling Pot Company.

Boiling Pot Company commenced the accounting period with a provision for warranty repairs of $24 000. During the accounting period it recognised warranty expenses of $225 000 and had a closing provision for warranty repairs of $52 000. How much cash was paid in relation to warranty repairs?

11.17 How is depreciation expense reported within the statement of cash flows?

11.18 Organisations often provide information in the notes to their financial statements about financing facilities they have available to them. Why might stakeholders want such information?

11.19 Classify the following cash flows as relating to operating activities, investing activities or financing activities:

- **a** cash paid to suppliers of inventory
- **b** cash paid to employees
- **c** repayment of a loan
- **d** payment for shares in another company
- **e** dividends received from an investment in another company
- **f** income tax paid
- **g** proceeds from sale of machinery
- **h** acquisition of a new factory.

11.20 The income statement and balance sheet of Margaret River Company are shown below:

Income statement for Margaret River Company
for the year ended 30 June 2026

	2026 $000		2025 $000	
Income				
Sales		8 400		7700
Expenses				
Cost of goods sold	2 800		2 240	
Depreciation – buildings	350		350	
Depreciation – plant and equipment	560		350	
Electricity and rates	350		280	
Income tax	700		560	
Interest expense	140		105	
Rental expenses	840		700	
Salaries	1820	7 560	1470	6 055
Profit		840		1645

Balance sheet for Margaret River Company
as at 30 June 2026

	2026 $000	2025 $000
Current assets		
Cash	1470	1190
Accounts receivable	2100	1750
Inventory	1680	1400
	5250	4340
Non-current assets		
Land	2800	2100
Buildings	4200	4200
Accumulated depreciation – buildings	(1050)	(700)
Plant and equipment	3500	2450
Accumulated depreciation – plant and equipment	(910)	(350)
	8540	7700
Total assets	**13790**	**12040**
Current liabilities		
Accounts payable	1470	1050
Accrued expenses	105	175
Income tax payable	700	560
	2275	1785
Non-current liabilities		
Long-term loans	1120	700
Total liabilities	**3395**	**2485**
Net assets	**10395**	**9555**
Shareholders' funds		
Share capital	7000	7000
Retained earnings	3395	2555
Total shareholders' funds	**10395**	**9555**

Additional information

- All sales are made on credit terms (meaning there have been no cash sales).
- Salaries and rental expenses are accrued prior to payment.
- Electricity and rates and interest expenses are paid as incurred.
- The accounts payable account is used only for the purchase of inventory.
- The organisation uses the perpetual inventory system (see Chapter 10) to account for its inventory, meaning that cost of goods sold is recognised each time an item of inventory is sold. The FIFO cost flow assumption is applied.
- There were no sales of land, buildings, or plant and equipment, and there were no non-cash-related acquisitions of land, buildings, plant and equipment.
- There were no impairments to, or revaluations of, assets.

You are required to prepare a statement of cash flows for Margaret River Company for the year ended 30 June 2026, together with a note reconciling profit to cash flows from operating activities.

11.21 Snapper Rocks Company commences operations on 1 January 2026. Details of the cash payments and cash receipts of the company as recorded within its cash payments journal and cash receipts journal for its first month of operations are provided below. With total cash receipts of $26 650 and total cash payments of $20 700 being recognised by the company, this means that the company has a recorded cash at bank balance of $5950.

You are required to reconcile the balance of cash, as recorded by the company, with the balance of cash as reported on the bank statement produced by the bank, which is provided below.

Cash receipts journal

Date	Details	Amount $	Accounts receivable $	Cash sales $	Other accounts $	Amount banked $
1 Jan	Owner contribution	8 000			8 000	8 000
4 Jan	Cash sales	3 200		3 200		3 200
5 Jan	Debtor – P. Break	2 400	2 400			2 400
14 Jan	Cash sales	7 000		7 000		7 000
20 Jan	Cash sales	2 250		2 250		2 250
24 Jan	Cash sales	1 000		1 000		1 000
31 Jan	Debtor – O. S. Wind	2 800	2 800			2 800
		26 650	5 200	13 450	8 000	26 650

Cash payments journal

Date	Cheque number	Details	Accounts payable $	Salaries $	Rent $	Other amount $	Total payment $
1 Jan	#001	Rent for the month			10 000		10 000
7 Jan	#002	Salaries		2 400			2 400
10 Jan	#003	Act pay – F. Chop	1 300				1 300
19 Jan	#004	Drawings				1 500	1 500
22 Jan	#005	Act pay – L. Board	1 500				1 500
22 Jan	#006	Salaries		2 000			2 000
31 Jan	#007	Act pay – L. Rope	2 000				2 000
			4 800	4 400	10 000	1 500	20 700

Bank statement Gold Coast Bank Beachside branch Snapper Rocks Company	Account number 004567 Statement period 1 Jan 2026 – 31 Jan 2026	Statement 1 Closing balance 5 900 CR

Date	Transaction	Debit	Credit	Balance
01 Jan	Cash deposit		$8000.00	$8000 CR
05 Jan	Cash deposit		$3200.00	$11200 CR
05 Jan	Cheque #001	$10000.00		$1200 CR
05 Jan	Cash deposit		$2400.00	$3600 CR
06 Jan	Direct deposit – Sale to W. Suit		$2000.00	$5600 CR
07 Jan	Cheque #002	$2400.00		$3200 CR
13 Jan	Cheque #003	$1300.00		$1900 CR
14 Jan	Cash deposit		$7000.00	$8900 CR
19 Jan	Cheque #004	$1500.00		$7400 CR
19 Jan	Direct debit 0001 Solar Power Electricity Company	$1200.00		$6200 CR
20 Jan	Cash deposit		$2250.00	$8450 CR
22 Jan	Cheque #006	$2000.00		$6450 CR
24 Jan	Cash deposit		$1000.00	$7450 CR
25 Jan	Cheque #005	$1500.00		$5950 CR
30 Jan	Bank fee	$50.00		$5900 CR

REFERENCES

Bell, N. (2013). Insight comes from 30 minutes clocking value via a study of company reports. *The Age*, 14 August.

International Accounting Standards Board (2022). IAS 7: Statement of Cash Flows. www.ifrs.org/issued-standards/list-of-standards/ias-7-statement-of-cash-flows

Koch, D., & Koch, L. (2014). How to avoid the slide. *Daily Telegraph*, 25 August.

Thompson, S. (2015). More to come: Warning for Slater and Gordon. *Australian Financial Review*, 30 June.

MODULE 5

TOOLS FOR REVIEWING AN ORGANISATION'S PUBLICLY AVAILABLE REPORTS

CHAPTER 12
The analysis of organisations' external reports

CHAPTER 12

THE ANALYSIS OF ORGANISATIONS' EXTERNAL REPORTS

LEARNING OBJECTIVES

After completing this chapter, readers should be able to:

- **LO12.1** explain the meaning and role of 'financial statement analysis', and have some insight into *who* should perform financial statement analysis and *why* they might do it
- **LO12.2** describe different approaches to undertaking financial statement analysis
- **LO12.3** understand the usefulness of accounting ratios in financial statement analysis, and calculate and interpret various types of accounting ratios relevant to evaluating organisational profitability, efficiency, financial stability and liquidity, as well as those ratios that provide insights into how an organisation is perceived by participants in the share market
- **LO12.4** describe some of the important information that appears in the notes to the financial statements, and explain why the information is important to the process of financial statement analysis
- **LO12.5** explain why it is useful, when undertaking financial statement analysis, to know about the accounting-based contracts that an organisation has negotiated with different stakeholders
- **LO12.6** understand that the total assets reported by organisations within their balance sheets needs to be interpreted with caution as many key resources of an organisation are either excluded from the balance sheet, or are measured at amounts that are well below their fair value or recoverable amount
- **LO12.7** describe some of the key factors to consider when assessing the *quality* of the social and environmental disclosures being made by an organisation, and explain why judgements about the quality of the information will influence the perceived usefulness of the information being produced
- **LO12.8** describe the roles of, and the need for, independent audits/assurance of the social, environmental and financial information produced by managers of an organisation.

OPENING QUESTIONS

Before reading this chapter, please consider how you would answer the following seven questions. We will return to these questions at the end of the chapter, where we suggest some answers.

1. What is financial statement analysis?
2. What are financial accounting ratios?
3. Accounting ratios can be separated into five broad categories. What are these categories?
4. In determining the liquidity of an organisation (which refers to its ability to pay its debts as and when they fall due), which financial accounting ratios are particularly relevant?
5. When performing financial statements analysis, should we also carefully review the notes accompanying those financial statements?
6. When reviewing an organisation's social and environmental accounts, is it important to be aware of the social and environmental context of an organisation? Why?
7. If you were asked to assess the 'quality' of an organisation's social and environmental disclosures, what are four criteria that you might apply?

Introduction

Central to the material presented within this book is the view that stakeholders have expectations about how the managers of an organisation *should* conduct the operations of that organisation. Different stakeholders will prioritise alternative aspects of performance, and therefore will tend to concentrate on different types of 'accounts' being presented by the managers of an organisation. Stakeholders will have different views about the responsibilities and accountabilities that an organisation should demonstrate. A stakeholder's analysis of the accounts presented by an organisation will provide the stakeholder with insights into whether the organisation is performing in accordance with their expectations. This will in turn impact the decisions stakeholders make with regards to if, and how, they will deal with an organisation.

For stakeholders that are primarily interested in financial performance, their focus might tend to be primarily on analysing the contents of the financial statements, and the supporting notes. By contrast, those stakeholders who are focused upon particular aspects of an organisation's social and environmental performance will tend to concentrate more on the social and environmental reports being produced by it. For example, for those stakeholders particularly concerned about climate change, they will tend to focus on the environmental disclosures made by an organisation, and in particular on those accounts provided about any climate change-related emissions and related initiatives employed by the company to further reduce their emissions (we discussed some of these accounts in Chapter 6). Many stakeholders will be interested in both the financial performance *and* the social and environmental performance of an organisation.

The usefulness of the various reports that are publicly released by an organisation – be they financial, social or environmental in nature – is influenced by a number of factors, and we will explore some of these in this chapter. In doing so, we will identify some 'tools' that can be used as part of the analysis, and particular factors to consider to enhance the usefulness of the information being presented by an organisation.

We will start by focusing on the analysis of financial statements, and the notes that accompany the financial statements. We will then move our focus to analysing the social and environmental accounts/reports released by an organisation.

LO12.1 The role of financial statement analysis

financial statement analysis
The process of reviewing and evaluating an organisation's financial statements and supporting notes in an endeavour to form a judgement about an organisation's financial performance and financial stability, and its likely future prospects

Financial statement analysis is the process of reviewing and evaluating an organisation's financial statements, including the income statement, balance sheet, statement of cash flows, and statement of changes in equity, as well as any supporting notes. The goal of such analysis is to develop an understanding of the organisation's financial performance and stability, and its likely future prospects. This may enable more-effective decisions to be made about the organisation.

Who performs financial statement analysis?

The first issue to consider when discussing financial statement analysis is *who* would (or perhaps 'should') perform financial statement analysis. The obvious answer to this is any person, or organisation, that has an interest or stake in the financial performance and financial position of an organisation. There can be many stakeholders – both within and outside an organisation – with such an interest.

As we have stressed within this book, information about an organisation's financial performance, and financial position, is produced through the application of various financial accounting principles and rules. Many of these rules will be incorporated within accounting standards that are amended from time to time as standard-setters – such as the members of the International Accounting Standards Board (IASB) – decide to change the principles, or rules, of general purpose financial reporting.

Many of the rules used to recognise and measure the financial performance and financial position of an organisation will not necessarily match what non-accountants (people without accounting training) might expect – something we stressed in our chapters on financial accounting. For example, accounting standards require different measurement approaches to be applied to different types of assets and liabilities, and they also prohibit the recognition of some very valuable resources, such as internally generated intangible assets. People without training in financial accounting would not necessarily expect or understand this. Also, many financial accounting requirements, as incorporated within the multitude of financial accounting standards on issue, can be very complicated and well beyond the expertise of people without a formal education in financial accounting.

Therefore, in considering who *should* undertake financial statement analysis, the view embraced within this book is that an informed analysis of financial statements really requires that the person undertaking it has a sound knowledge of financial accounting in terms of the current rules and conventions of financial accounting. It should also be remembered that accounting standards frequently change, thereby requiring financial accountants to undertake continuing education in financial accounting. The changing nature of accounting standards also needs to be taken into consideration when undertaking financial statement analysis that is extended over several periods of time to identify trends, or to make comparisons with prior periods.

Financial analysts are a specific group of stakeholders who undertake financial statement analysis. They collect various items of financial data from a variety of sources, including information about general market trends, expectations of growth and inflation, industry-specific growth data, and the performance and financial position of particular companies, in order to make investment recommendations to their clients or employers. Financial analysts often work for large companies, superannuation funds, investment banks, and stockbroking firms. As part of their information-collection activities, financial analysts are particularly interested in the financial statements being issued by different companies, particularly where such companies are the focus of potential investment advice to be provided to others (perhaps in terms of suggestions to buy or sell investments in the company).

Why undertake financial statement analysis?

Having discussed *who* would, or perhaps who *should*, perform financial statement analysis, the next issue to consider is *why* would somebody perform financial statement analysis. There could be various reasons for undertaking financial statement analysis. Perhaps the people who do so might be:

- thinking of investing in an organisation
- advising others about whether to invest (or divest)
- thinking about working for the organisation or loaning money to it
- selling goods on credit to the organisation.

For these various purposes, they might want to know:

- how efficiently the managers of the organisation are using the resources under its control
- how profitable the organisation is relative to other organisations
- the ability of the organisation to pay its debts as and when they fall due.

Financial statement analysis can provide important insights into such issues.

Financial accounting numbers are also used in many agreements between an organisation and different stakeholders, meaning that the reported numbers can impact these stakeholders, thereby creating a multitude of social impacts; for example:

- Shareholders might only receive dividends if the organisation generates profits beyond a certain level.
- The bonuses paid to managers might be linked to accounting profits (meaning that lower profits lead to lower or no bonuses).
- Lenders might have negotiated restrictions – such as the maximum level of debt allowed relative to assets – with a borrowing organisation, meaning that should the organisation breach the debt covenant, then the lenders might have the power to insist on immediate repayment of those funds loaned to the organisation (which in turn might have implications for the ability of the organisation to continue operations).

Employees will also have an interest in the reported profits, and financial position, of an organisation, as they will want to know about the security of their future employment.

Therefore, many stakeholders will be interested in undertaking some form of financial statement analysis. Their own wealth and livelihoods can be influenced by the numbers presented within the financial statements. Having established that many stakeholders will have an interest in the contents of an organisation's financial statements, and that some financial accounting expertise should be held prior to doing such analysis, the next step is to consider how to perform financial statement analysis.

LO12.2 An overview of how financial statement analysis can be performed

Financial statement analysis can be undertaken in a variety of ways, as outlined in Table 12.1.

TABLE 12.1 Methods of financial statement analysis

Method	Explanation
Simple comparison	A *simple comparison* of this year's amount (perhaps of a particular expense or revenue item) with the previous year's amount might be undertaken. This can be referred to as a form of *horizontal analysis*. However, we need to ensure there is nothing fundamentally different about the organisation from one year to the next, or that the accounting policies being applied have not changed since last year, and in a way that might hamper a meaningful comparison. Whilst potentially useful, a downside in just comparing two years of performance is that important trends in performance that have been occurring across a number of years might be ignored.
Ratio analysis	When *ratio analysis* is applied, particular amounts within the financial statements are compared with other amounts within the financial statements, which can be referred to as a form of *vertical analysis*. For example, profits (as reported within the income statement) might be compared with (or divided by) total assets (from the balance sheet) to give some indication of how efficiently managers are using an organisation's assets to create profits. Ratio analysis can be used to evaluate various aspects of an organisation; for example, its profitability, efficiency, liquidity or solvency. We will consider the use of accounting ratios within financial statement analysis shortly.
Trend analysis	*Trend analysis* occurs when we can look at various financial indicators – perhaps accounting ratios – over a number of accounting periods to see if there is an apparent pattern of improvement or deterioration. Trend analysis is relatively simple to do and can provide some useful insights.
Comparison with benchmarks	Different performance measures, which might be encapsulated in various ratios, might be compared with those of other organisations, or to industry averages, in order to determine or 'benchmark' how the organisation is performing relative to other organisations. However, as we stressed in earlier chapters, we need to be careful when comparing the financial accounting numbers generated by different organisations. Different organisations in different industries are subject to different risks, and therefore simply comparing their profitability might not be appropriate. Also, we must consider size. For example, is it sensible to compare the financial performance of large national or international supermarket chains with that of a corner store? Geographical location is also important as, for example, different countries can pose different risks and different costs of operation, thereby making comparisons problematic. Different organisations might also use different accounting policies, therefore making comparisons of financial accounting numbers problematic. Apart from comparing performance with that of other organisations, actual performance can also be compared with budgeted, or targeted, performance. However, most external stakeholders undertaking financial statement analysis will not have access to the budgets being used within the organisation (as we discussed in earlier chapters of this book, budgets are part of management accounting, and management accounts are typically not made publicly available).

Horizontal and vertical analysis

In **Table 12.1**, we refer to both **horizontal analysis** and **vertical analysis**. **Figure 12.1** provides an example of the difference between the two. Horizontal analysis occurs when we are comparing account balances over time – for example, comparing the sales of one year with those of the next – whereas vertical analysis occurs when we compare one item of the financial statements to another item in the financial statements within a particular year of operations; for example, comparing the profit of the organisation with the sales of the organisation (which can be referred to as the *profit ratio*).

horizontal analysis Comparing account balances over time

vertical analysis Comparing one item of the financial statements to another within a particular accounting period

FIGURE 12.1 The difference between vertical analysis and horizontal analysis

Income statement for Bondi Company
for the year ended 30 June 2026

	2026 $000		2025 $000	
Income				
Sales		1200		1100
Expenses				
Cost of goods sold	400		320	
Depreciation – buildings	50		50	
Depreciation – plant and equipment	80		50	
Electricity and rates	50		40	
Interest expense	20		15	
Rental expenses	120		100	
Salaries	260	980	210	785
Profit before tax		220		315
Income tax		100		80
Profit		120		235

Vertical analysis

Horizontal analysis

Additional information

The valuable information residing within the notes and other documentation accompanying the financial statements also requires consideration as part of the process of analysing financial statements; for example:

- Is there an *independent auditor's report*? Large organisations will typically be required by law to include an audit report with their annual financial statements as presented within the organisation's annual report. We are particularly interested in the opinion the auditor provides within the auditor's report with respect to the financial statements. In light of the auditor's opinion, we can consider whether the financial statements should be relied on. For example, if the auditor's report provides an opinion that the financial statements do not comply with accounting standards, and/or have been prepared on some other basis that brings into question the reliability of the financial information, then we might decide that it is not appropriate to perform any form of analysis on the contents of the financial statements as the information is inherently unreliable to start with, thereby meaning that the results of any analysis will also be questionable.

- What *financial accounting policies* are being used by the organisation? With respect to how some transactions and events are accounted for, managers and their accountants do – in certain circumstances – have a choice as to which accounting policy to apply. These choices can impact reported financial performance, and reported financial position. For example, whether managers decide to measure property, plant and equipment at cost or at fair value will have direct implications for reported assets, depreciation expenses, and profits on sale of the assets. Therefore, to better understand an organisation's reported financial performance and position, and to place it in context, it is necessary for the person undertaking the analysis to carefully read the accounting policy notes provided by the organisation and which accompany the financial statements (we should appreciate that people without a knowledge of financial accounting will have a limited likelihood of understanding the contents of much of the accounting policy notes).
- Are there any *significant events* that have occurred since the end of the reporting period that are not reflected within the financial statements, but which are of potential relevance to the decisions being made by stakeholders in relation to an organisation? As will be covered later in this chapter, organisations that are required to comply with accounting standards (which are typically larger organisations) are expected to describe, within the notes to the financial statements, details of significant events that have occurred since the end of the reporting period, but before the financial statements were authorised for issue to external stakeholders.
- Are there some potentially significant *contingent liabilities* that might undermine the ongoing operations of an organisation? As indicated elsewhere in this book, contingent liabilities are not recognised within the financial statements because the future sacrifice of economic benefits is not deemed to be very likely, cannot be measured in a way that faithfully represents the underlying transaction or event, or is dependent on the happening of a future event. Nevertheless, details of significant or 'material' contingent liabilities are to be reported in the notes to the financial statements, and people undertaking an analysis of the financial statements should make sure they are aware of the contingent liabilities of an organisation.
- How are an organisation's managers and senior executives being *rewarded for the work they perform*? To understand the aspects of performance that are being prioritised within an organisation, it is useful to know what performance indicators are being used to assess the performance of managers and senior executives, and as a basis of paying them bonuses. The notes to the financial statements often provide information about the nature of the bonuses paid to the key personnel within an organisation. They also often provide information about the debt covenants that managers have negotiated with lenders. Such information is also relevant when assessing the financial position of an organisation.

We will consider the above information in more depth later in this chapter (see the upcoming section 'Important information also resides in the notes to the financial statements'). However, we will now consider financial statement analysis undertaken through the application of financial accounting ratios.

Key concept

Apart from the useful information which resides within the financial statements, there is also much useful information to be found within the notes that accompany the financial statements.

LO12.3 Using accounting ratios

Much financial statement analysis is undertaken through the use of *ratios*. Ratio analysis can be considered a form of vertical analysis, wherein one number from a financial statement can be compared with another number from the financial statements of the same year. Ratio analysis is also often combined with horizontal analysis, wherein ratios are compared over time to determine trends. It can also be combined with benchmarking, where ratios are compared between organisations or against industry averages – for example, comparisons of different organisations' gross profit ratio.

A ratio is a relationship between two quantities, normally expressed as one divided by the other – for example, a debt to equity ratio is calculated by dividing total reported liabilities by total reported equity (which is shareholders' funds in the case of a company), and this ratio is then considered to provide insights into how an organisation is financed, as well as the financial risks of the organisation.

Accounting ratios can help put particular financial accounting numbers into context. For example, if we just look at reported profits in isolation, then we really cannot tell how efficient an organisation is. If an organisation generated a profit of $200 000, that might appear to be impressive, particularly if the total assets of the organisation were $1 million, but it would not be impressive if the total assets were $100 million. Knowing the total assets helps to put the reported profit into context.

Source: Dreamstime.com/Steve Lovegrove

Source: Shutterstock.com/Alena Varchenko

Accounting ratios are more useful than simply reporting a profit figure in isolation, because ratios allow us to better grasp the scale of growth and put the reported profit into context.

We can calculate a variety of accounting ratios, which are often classified into the following categories:

- profitability ratios
- operating efficiency ratios
- financial gearing (or stability) ratios
- liquidity ratios
- investment-based ratios.

Profitability ratios

Profitability ratios provide an insight into the ability of an organisation to generate a profit. Therefore, this category of accounting ratios is appropriate in respect of organisations that are established to generate profits, but it might not be relevant for evaluating the performance of not-for-profit entities, such as charities, sporting clubs and other community-based organisations.

profitability ratios
A measure of an organisation's ability to generate a profit

Profitability ratios compare particular measures of profits with other amounts reported within the financial statements, such as sales, total assets and owners' equity. Such ratios include return on assets, return on owners' equity, profit margin and gross profit margin.

Return on assets

One way to analyse the profitability of an organisation is to compare its profit with the amount that has been invested in the assets within the organisation. Instead of using the amount reported for total assets at the end of the last accounting period, an average of total assets is used in this ratio (which is calculated by adding together the opening total assets and the closing total assets and dividing this total by two). Using an average of the organisation's investment in assets eliminates the bias that could arise if total assets increased significantly towards the end of the accounting period thereby causing the assets held at the end of the reporting period to be unrepresentative of the assets held throughout the reporting period. However, even calculations based upon averages can be problematic, as the values at these two points in time do not necessarily reflect the changes that have occurred to assets throughout the accounting period.

The return on assets, which can be presented in the form of a percentage, can therefore be calculated as:

$$\frac{\text{Profit}}{\text{Average total assets}} \times 100 = \begin{array}{l}\text{A measure of profit calculated as a}\\ \text{percentage of average total assets}\end{array}$$

The return on assets provides an indication of how much profit is being generated for every dollar of assets controlled by the organisation. A higher return on assets represents a relatively more efficient use of the organisation's assets. However, whilst this is a ratio that is often used by many analysts, care must be taken in undertaking such analysis. For example, we should be careful when comparing such measures across different organisations, as they will each have different risk profiles (depending upon the type of industry that organisations are operating within, their financial structure, their country of operation, and so forth), and all things being equal, the greater the perceived risk, the higher the expected rate of return (to compensate for the higher risk).

We also know that many assets of an organisation are not recognised within the financial statements and therefore are not included within total assets, as recorded within the balance sheet. For example, as we noted in Chapter 9, many valuable intangible assets controlled by an organisation are not recognised if they have been internally generated, rather than being purchased from an external party. Therefore, if one organisation purchased its intangible assets, but another organisation generated them internally across time, then the reported total assets of the first organisation would be higher. This will have implications for the calculation of the return on assets ratio – more specifically, the return on assets of the organisation that purchased the intangible assets, and therefore recognised them within the balance sheet, would be lower.

Further, as we have already discussed, some organisations might report their non-current assets at cost (using the cost model), whilst another, comparable organisation might report their non-current assets at fair value (using the revaluation model), which typically will be higher. This would mean that the return on assets of the revaluing organisation could be biased downwards. Therefore, different organisations might have different accounting policies, making financial performance comparisons problematic.

Also, the age of the assets influences the amount reported for total assets. Assets measured at cost and which were acquired many years ago tend to be lower in cost and have higher accumulated depreciation. This will have the effect of improving the return on assets (unless the assets are both old *and* inefficient) relative to organisations with newer assets.

We also need to emphasise that, across time, accounting policies will change (for example, an organisation might switch from the cost model to the revaluation model). Accounting standards will also change across time, and this can change which assets we recognise, and how we measure different classes of assets. Therefore, as we have explained before, comparing financial accounting results across multiple accounting periods for one organisation can also be misleading, as, for example, the way we might measure assets can change from one year to the next.

The point being made here is that, although we have only considered one accounting ratio in depth so far, the general rule when considering any financial accounting ratio is that we need to be careful to understand the context of the accounting numbers that are being used, in terms of such issues as:

- the accounting policies used by the organisation in question (and how the policies might be different to other organisations' policies, which is relevant if we are comparing the ratios with those of other organisations)
- the assets that are not included within the analysis (such as many intangible assets that are internally developed)
- whether there have been recent changes in the accounting policies applied by the organisation (which has implications for comparing recent period ratios with previous ratios that might have been calculated using accounting recognition and measurement rules that are different, thereby potentially undermining the comparison).

Key concept

When undertaking financial statement analysis, we need to be mindful of the accounting policies that have been applied. The choice of different accounting policies (such as the choice to measure property, plant and equipment at 'fair value' rather than at 'cost') can potentially impact many accounting ratios.

Adjusted measures of return on assets

The ratio just discussed (return on assets), whilst widely used, does not take into account the sources of funding. As we know:

- Assets equals liabilities plus owners' equity, meaning that all assets are either funded by external funds (liabilities) or by way of internal funds (owners' equity).
- Considering the sources of funding is important, as they have different implications for the financial statements of an organisation.
- For equity funding (for example, where a company's finances have come from shareholders acquiring shares in the company), owners are paid dividends, which are not an expense (dividends are a distribution of profits) and therefore do not reduce profits.
- For debt funding, lenders are paid interest, which is an expense, and therefore *does* reduce profits.

By adding back interest expense to profits, we are removing the effects on profits associated with where the funds are sourced from, and therefore the efficiency of asset use might be better assessed once we have removed differences in profits that are simply due to differences in how the funds of the organisation were sourced. The adjusted ratio therefore becomes:

$$\frac{\text{Profit + interest expenses}}{\text{Average total assets}} \times 100 = \text{An adjusted measure of profit calculated as a percentage of average total assets}$$

Some analysts also add back taxation expenses so as to remove the effects of different tax regimes and other arrangements. This revised measure of profit is known as *earnings before interest and taxes (EBIT)*, which is sometimes also referred to as *operating income*. It provides an indication of how an organisation has generated profits from its operations alone, without considering interest expenses and taxes. This further adjustment leads us to the following ratio:

$$\frac{\text{Profit + interest expenses + tax expense}}{\text{Average total assets}} \times 100 = \text{EBIT as a percentage of average total assets}$$

Return on owners' equity

The return on owners' equity provides an indicator of how effectively an organisation has used owners' capital to generate profits. The return on owners' equity provides a measure of the profit being generated – which ultimately might benefit the owners in the form of dividends, or an increase in the value of their shares – for each dollar of equity the owners have within the organisation. This measure provides a basis of comparison for investors with other investment opportunities.

The rate of return calculated for a business organisation should hopefully be higher than low-risk returns, such as returns on bank deposits. There is no absolute 'right' percentage that needs to be achieved, but there is a need to compare the calculated ratio with benchmarks, such as:

- the return on equity calculated for the organisation in previous periods
- the budgeted (targeted) return on equity
- the return on equity for similar organisations
- the return on equity expected from different forms of investment.

Generally, the larger the return on equity, the better it is, and an improving trend across time is preferred. The return on owners' equity can be calculated as:

$$\frac{\text{Profit}}{\text{Average owners' equity}} \times 100 = \text{Percentage of average owners' equity being earned in profits}$$

As you can see, and like the last ratios discussed, this ratio takes information from both the income statement (profit) and the balance sheet (total assets). Average owners' equity can simply be calculated as opening owners' equity plus closing owners' equity, with the total being divided by 2 (this assumes that changes that occurred from the opening balance to the closing balance occurred evenly throughout the accounting period). For a company, owners' equity is represented by 'shareholders' funds' and will include the total of paid-up capital, retained earnings, and the various reserves that might exist.

Profit ratio

The profit ratio is calculated as:

$$\frac{\text{Profit}}{\text{Sales revenue}} \times 100 = \text{The amount of profit generated as a percentage of sales}$$

This ratio – also sometimes known as *return on sales* – provides an indication of the extent to which each dollar of sales contributes to profits. A measure of, say, 18 per cent means that for every dollar of sales, the organisation generated a profit of 18 cents. The ratio can be compared with similar organisations, previous periods, and budgets, to determine whether the costs being incurred, relative to sales, are higher or lower, thereby providing an indication of cost efficiency/control and changes therein.

Gross profit ratio

The relationship between an organisation's sales revenue and the associated cost of sales is crucial to its success. If the costs of making a sale (which include the inventory purchase costs inclusive of all inventory conversion costs and other costs necessary to bring the inventory to the place of sale) starts to increase disproportionately to the sales price, this can have negative implications for the ongoing survival of an organisation. Effectively, the gross profits from trading provide the necessary operating funds to pay for all the other expenses of the organisation. The gross profit ratio – which indicates the gross profit earned in cents per dollar of sales – can be calculated as:

$$\frac{\text{Sales revenue} - \text{cost of goods sold}}{\text{Sales revenue}} \times 100 = \text{Percentage of sales revenue that is represented by gross profit}$$

The gross profit ratio provides an insight into an organisation's pricing strategy (its 'mark-ups'), which can be compared with those of similar organisations in similar industries. Organisations with a higher turnover of stock (inventory) will generally be able to survive on the basis of relatively lower gross profit margins.

For more on the calculation of profitability ratios, see **Learning exercise 12.1**.

12.1 Learning Exercise

Calculation of various profitability ratios

Scenario: The income statement and balance sheet of Bondi Company (as also used within Chapter 11, with slight modifications) are shown below:

Income statement for Bondi Company for the year ended 30 June 2026

	2026 $000		2025 $000	
Income				
Sales		1200		1100
Expenses				
Cost of goods sold	400		320	
Depreciation – buildings	50		50	
Depreciation – plant and equipment	80		50	
Electricity and rates	50		40	
Interest expense	20		15	
Rental expenses	120		100	
Salaries	260	(980)	210	(785)
Profit before tax		220		315
Tax		(100)		(80)
Profit		120		235

Balance sheet for Bondi Company as at 30 June 2026	2026 $000	2025 $000
Current assets		
Cash	180	170
Accounts receivable	300	250
Inventory	240	200
	720	620
Non-current assets		
Land	400	300
Buildings	600	600
Accumulated depreciation – buildings	(150)	(100)
Plant and equipment	500	350
Accumulated depreciation – plant and equipment	(130)	(50)
	1220	1100
Total assets	1940	1720
Current liabilities		
Accounts payable	210	150
Accrued expenses	15	25
Income tax payable	100	80
	325	255
Non-current liabilities		
Long-term loans	160	100
Total liabilities	485	355
Net assets	1455	1365
Owners' equity (Shareholders' funds)		
Share capital	1000	1000
Retained earnings	455	365
Total shareholders' funds	1455	1365

Issue: You are required to calculate the following ratios for 2026 and then give your opinion as to whether the organisation is performing well.

Ratios to calculate:

- return on assets
- adjusted return on assets based on EBIT
- return on owners' equity
- profit ratio
- gross profit ratio.

Solution: Before you can give a considered opinion regarding Bondi Company's performance, you will need to work out the ratios.

The ratios

The worked solutions, using the appropriate formulas, are laid out in the following table to help you step though the process.

Ratio	Formula	Calculated amount $000
Return on assets	$\frac{\text{Profit}}{\text{Average total assets}} \times 100$	$= \frac{120}{1830} \times 100 = 6.56\%$
Adjusted measure of return on assets	$\frac{\text{Profit + interest expenses + taxes}}{\text{Average total assets}} \times 100$	$= \frac{120 + 20 + 100}{1830} \times 100 = 13.11\%$
Return on owners' equity	$\frac{\text{Profit}}{\text{Average owners' equity}} \times 100$	$= \frac{120}{1410} \times 100 = 8.51\%$
Profit ratio	$\frac{\text{Profit}}{\text{Sales revenue}} \times 100$	$= \frac{120}{1200} \times 100 = 10\%$
Gross profit ratio	$\frac{\text{Sales revenue − cost of goods sold}}{\text{Sales revenue}} \times 100$	$= \frac{1200 - 400}{1200} \times 100 = 66.67\%$

Now that you have determined the ratios, you need to consider what other information is required to make a determination of Bondi Company's performance. Consider the following.

The riskiness of the organisation

To determine whether the organisation is performing well, we need to have additional information about the riskiness of the organisation – the greater the risk of an organisation, the higher the returns investors will expect to receive to compensate them for that higher risk.

The risk of an organisation will be influenced by factors such as the types of products being sold and whether they seem vulnerable to changing community tastes; the amount of reliance on debt; the availability of skilled employees; the availability of the necessary raw materials; the social, political, environmental and economic environment; how competitive the industry is; and so forth.

The returns of the competitors

The returns being generated by competitors are also relevant, as is the return on low-risk investments, such as bank deposits. For example, if we could simply put money in the bank and receive a return of 4 per cent, then we would expect to receive a return higher than this from our investment in this organisation.

Pulling it all together

Simply looking at the numbers that we have calculated above, we would probably consider that the organisation is operating satisfactorily. A return on assets of 6.5 per cent is not fantastic, but it is reasonable to the extent that the organisation is not operating in a highly risky industry or place. The other ratios also appear acceptable, but it is very important that the numbers are compared with those of competitors, prior periods and budgeted targets.

Why do I need to know about profitability ratios?

Profitability ratios provide important insights into an organisation's ability to generate profits. 'For-profit' organisations need to generate profits to survive, and these ratios provide insights into the efficiency with which managers are generating profits. These ratios can then be benchmarked with previous periods and with other organisations to provide an indication of the relative efficiency of managers.

Operating efficiency ratios

operating efficiency ratios
Provide a measure of how efficiently an organisation's managers are managing the organisation's assets and liabilities

Operating efficiency ratios provide insight into how efficiently an organisation's managers are managing its assets and liabilities. Such ratios include inventory turnover, debtors' turnover, and operating cash flow margin.

Inventory turnover

Inventory turnover indicates how many times within an accounting period an organisation has turned over (or sold) its inventory, and therefore provides insights into how efficiently managers are managing and controlling their inventory. The greater the number of times inventory is turned over in an accounting period, the more efficiently managers are managing their stock. Inventory turnover can be calculated as:

$$\frac{\text{Cost of goods sold}}{\text{Average inventory}} = \begin{array}{l}\text{Number of times inventory is turned}\\ \text{over in the accounting period}\end{array}$$

For example, if the cost of goods sold for an accounting period was \$900 000 and the average inventory (which is opening and closing inventory added together and then divided by 2) was \$50 000, then this means inventory was turned over 18 times in the accounting period. If the accounting period is a year, then that means that, on average, the average amount of inventory is sold every 20.3 days (which is 365 days divided by the inventory turnover of 18).

Greater levels of inventory turnover act to reduce the total time involved in the operating cycle of an organisation (something we discussed in Chapter 11), which in turn can act to reduce the organisation's reliance on outside debt (and therefore the need to pay additional interest expenses). As we learned in Chapter 11, the operating cycle of an organisation represents the amount of time between initially acquiring inventory and ultimately receiving the cash from selling that inventory to customers. Any efforts to sell inventory to customers more quickly increases inventory turnover and therefore acts to reduce the length of the operating cycle. When evaluating inventory turnover by way of an accounting ratio – such as the inventory turnover ratio – various factors should be considered, including:

- the types of products being sold
- the inventory turnover in previous periods
- the targeted or budgeted results.

Common sense needs to be applied in interpreting the inventory turnover. We would, for example, expect a shop selling fresh fruit and vegetables to turn over its inventory much more often than an organisation selling luxury motor vehicles. That is, inventory turnover rates are different across different industries.

A lower inventory turnover is a potential sign of inefficiency and also exposes the organisation to various risks, such as increased risk of inventory spoilage, theft of inventory and inventory obsolescence. One reason for a low inventory turnover ratio might be that too much inventory is being held in stock, which increases various inventory storage-related costs (such as store-room rental, insurance costs, inventory obsolescence and so forth).

Source: Shutterstock.com/Anton Glavas

Source: iStock/Getty Images Plus/torque

High or low turnover depends on the context of the business in question: we would expect a much higher inventory turnover at a greengrocer than at a luxury car dealership.

Debtors' (accounts receivable) turnover

This ratio is very similar to the inventory turnover ratio just discussed. However, rather than determining the turnover of inventory, debtors' turnover provides an indication of the number of times during the period that debtors 'turn over' – the number of times debtors pay, on average, the amounts due to the organisation. The greater the number of times debtors are turned over in a particular accounting period, the more efficiently debtors are being managed by the organisation, with accounts receivable not being left outstanding for relatively long periods. Debtors' turnover can be calculated as:

$$\frac{\text{Credit sales}}{\text{Average accounts receivable}} = \text{Number of times debtors turn over in the accounting period}$$

When an organisation sells inventory to customers on credit terms, it then needs to collect the amounts due from debtors so as to complete the operating cycle. The higher the number of times debtors are turned over, the less the amount of cash remaining with (owed by) debtors, and the lower the number of days within the organisation's operating cycle. Therefore, increasing both the inventory turnover and the debtors' turnover will have the effect of reducing the number of days in the organisation's operating cycle.

Debtors' turnover provides an indication of the effectiveness of credit-granting policies and debtor follow-ups. The longer the amounts owed to the organisation stay with the debtors, the lower the probability of payment, and the greater the potential liquidity problems.

The average collection period (365 ÷ debtors' turnover) provides a measure of how many days it takes to collect cash from debtors. For example, if the debtors' turnover is calculated as 14 times per year, then this means that the amounts owed by debtors, on average, are collected every 26 days. Some reference should be made to the terms of the credit arrangements provided to debtors (customers). If the usual terms are 30 days, then we would hope for an average debtors' turnover of at least 12 times.

Operating cash flow margin

The operating cash flow margin provides a measure of the amount of cash generated from each dollar of sales. The measure tells us what amount of cash flow in cents is generated, on average, from each dollar of sales. In Chapter 11, we explained that one important component of total cash flows is 'cash flows from operating activities' (the other cash flows within the statement of cash flows are classified into cash flows from investing activities and cash flows from financing activities). The operating cash flow margin is calculated as:

$$\frac{\text{Cash flows from operating activities}}{\text{Sales revenue}} = \text{Cash flow in cents per dollar of sales}$$

The higher the cash flows from operating activities, the better. Changes in this measure from period to period need to monitored, and apparent differences in comparison to similar organisations need to be investigated to identify the existence of potential inefficiencies that can be addressed.

For more on the calculation of operating efficiency ratios, see Learning exercise 12.2.

12.2 Learning Exercise

Calculation of various operating efficiency ratios

Scenario: The income statement and balance sheet of Bondi Company were provided in Learning exercise 12.1. We now also provide the statement of cash flows for Bondi Company.

Statement of cash flows for Bondi Company for the year ended 30 June 2026	
	$000
Cash flows from operating activities	
Receipts from customers	1150
Payments to suppliers of goods and services	(380)
Payment to employees	(265)
Payment for rental expenses	(125)
Payment for electricity and rates	(50)
Interest paid	(20)
Income taxes paid	(80)
Net cash provided from operating activities	230
Cash flows from investing activities	
Payment for property, plant and equipment	(250)
Net cash provided from investing activities	(250)
Cash flows from financing activities	
Proceeds from borrowings	60
Dividends paid	(30)
Net cash provided from financing activities	30
Net increase in cash held	10
Cash at the beginning of the financial year	170
Cash at the end of the financial year	180

We will assume that all sales are made on credit terms.

Issue: You are required to calculate the following ratios and form an opinion on whether the organisation is performing efficiently.

Ratios to calculate:

- inventory turnover
- debtors' turnover
- operating cash flow margin.

Solution: Before you can form a considered opinion regarding Bondi Company's performance efficiency, you will need to work out the ratios.

The ratios

The worked solutions, using the appropriate formulas, are laid out in the following table to help you step though the process.

Ratio	Formula	Calculated amount $000
Inventory turnover	$\frac{\text{Cost of goods sold}}{\text{Average inventory}}$ = number of times	$= \frac{400}{220} =$ 1.818 times
Debtors' turnover	$\frac{\text{Credit sales}}{\text{Average accounts receivable}}$ = number of times	$= \frac{1200}{275} =$ 4.36 times
Operating cash flow margin	$\frac{\text{Cash flows from operating activities}}{\text{Sales revenue}}$	$= \frac{230}{1200} =$ 19.17 cents per dollar of sales

Now that you have determined the ratios, you need to consider what information is required to make a determination of Bondi Company's efficiency of performance. Consider the following.

Inventory

Looking at the above ratios, it would probably be reasonable to argue that managers are not being efficient with respect to managing either inventory or debtors, and this in turn has implications for the operating cash flow margin. Of course, we need more information about the industry the organisation is operating within, and the performance of competitors, as well as information about the performance of the organisation in previous periods. However, unless the organisation is selling inventory that reasonably only turns over a few times a year (perhaps the construction of customised boats or other large objects), the inventory turnover of less than 2 is very poor.

Debtors

The debtors' turnover is also very poor and exposes the organisation to various risks associated with non-payment. A debtors' turnover of 4.36 means that, on average, debtors are only paying the amounts due to the organisation every 84 days (calculated as 365 divided by 4.36), and in most industries this would not be acceptable.

The poor debtors' turnover and the poor inventory turnover in turn have negative implications for the length of the organisation's operating cycle. The longer the operating cycle, the greater the reliance of the organisation on external sources of funding – such as borrowed funds that incur interest expenses.

The operating cash flow margin

The cash flows from operating activities also seem quite low at just over 19 cents per dollar of sales, and this, in part, is linked to the poor inventory turnover and poor debtors' turnover. However, there is a need to compare this amount with those of competitors, prior period performance and budgeted performance.

Pulling it together

Looking at the information we now have in relation to Bondi Company, it would be reasonable to assess Bondi Company's operating efficiency as relatively poor. Further action would be needed in terms of understanding what is behind this apparent underlying inefficiency, and what, if anything, can be done to make the organisation more efficient.

Why do I need to know about operating efficiency ratios?

Operating efficiency ratios provide insights into how efficiently the organisation is operating in terms of selling inventory and then collecting amounts due from customers. While a firm might be profitable, an analysis of these ratios might signal that relative to another organisation, or previous reporting periods, improvements in efficiency should be made which can further enhance the profitability of an organisation.

Financial gearing (or stability) ratios

financial gearing (or stability) ratios
Provides a measure of how an organisation has been funded, and some indication of financial stability or risk

Financial gearing (or stability) ratios provide an insight into how an organisation is being funded (by owners or through debt) and therefore provides some indication of the financial risk, or stability, of the organisation. Accounting ratios within this category include the debt to assets ratio and the debt to equity ratio.

Organisations can receive their funding from internal sources (owners) or external sources (lenders and other creditors). *Gearing* represents a measure of the extent to which an organisation is funded by external sources of finance. The relative use of debt to equity is often referred to as the *capital structure* of an organisation.

The relative reliance upon debt to equity also impacts profits, and therefore a number of the ratios we have already considered within this chapter. For example, if an organisation borrows funds to finance its acquisition of assets, then it will have to pay interest expenses, and this will reduce profits. By contrast, if the organisation receives the same level of funding from owners (shareholders), then the payments made to these owners is not an expense, given that dividends (distributions) paid to shareholders (owners) are considered to be a distribution of profits and not an expense. Whenever funds are borrowed to acquire assets, the expectation should be that the rate of return on those acquired assets will exceed the costs of borrowing those funds used to acquire the assets.

A highly geared organisation would be considered an organisation that is funded relatively more from debt finance as opposed to equity finance; that is, where a relatively high proportion of the assets controlled by the organisation have been financed through liabilities. Highly geared organisations are considered to have relatively higher financial risk. This is because liabilities need to be repaid regardless of the cash flows, or the profitability, of the organisation. By contrast, funds that come from owners do not have to be repaid, and dividends will only be paid to owners if the managers of the organisation believe that the organisation can afford to do so.

However, whilst there are some risks associated with attracting higher levels of debt, the issuance of additional shares will sometimes not be favoured by pre-existing shareholders. For example, if the managers of an organisation decide to attract additional funds from new shareholders, rather than by borrowing additional debt funds, then this will lead to a dilution in the relative ownership of those shareholders who held shares in the company prior to the issue of the additional shares. This might not be favoured by those shareholders who want to maintain their percentage ownership of an organisation. When the number of shares outstanding increases, each pre-existing shareholder owns a smaller, or diluted, percentage of the company, thereby potentially making each share less valuable.

Changes in financial gearing ratios will provide an indication of the changing risk profile of an organisation. We consider several financial gearing (or stability) ratios below.

Debt to assets ratio

The debt to assets ratio is a measure of the extent to which an organisation's assets have been funded by lenders/creditors. All things being equal, the greater the percentage, the greater the risk of an organisation, given that debt needs to be repaid and attracts interest expenses that also have to be paid (as opposed to organisations that are funded primarily by equity). The debt to assets ratio can be calculated as:

$$\frac{\text{Total liabilities}}{\text{Total assets}} \times 100 = \begin{array}{l}\text{The amount of liabilities represented}\\ \text{as a percentage of total assets}\end{array}$$

If the debt to assets ratio is above 50 per cent, this indicates that the organisation's acquisitions of assets have, on average, been financed more from external sources (liabilities) than from internal sources (owners' equity).

Different organisations/industries have different abilities to support debt. For example, organisations with high variability in earnings and related cash flows could have greater trouble servicing debt in some accounting periods. Therefore, it would be 'safer' for such organisations to rely relatively more upon equity finance than debt finance.

As with all such analysis, we need to consider how financial accounting policy choices can influence the measurement of assets and liabilities, and also that total assets do tend to understate the actual resources that are controlled by the organisation.

Ratios like the debt to assets ratio are often used in debt contracts to reduce the risks of lenders. For example, there could be a stipulation within a contract negotiated between the managers of an organisation and the providers of finance (the lenders) that the debt to assets ratio will not exceed a certain percentage, such as 60 per cent. Should the balance sheet subsequently show that this agreement has been breached by the organisation (perhaps because debt has risen), then the lender can often insist on immediate repayment of the funds, thereby safeguarding the assets of the lending organisation, but potentially leading to the collapse of the organisation that borrowed the funds.

When providers of finance to the organisation (the lenders) demand immediate repayment of funds because of a breach of a debt covenant, this acts to reduce the risks of the lenders because, if the funds were left longer with the organisation, it is possible that conditions within the organisation will worsen further and less funds might subsequently be available to repay the debt to the lender. Having the debt covenants in place allows the lender to access funds earlier, potentially before the organisation ultimately collapses.

The debt to assets ratio does not differentiate between debt that is current (requiring payment within 12 months) and non-current debt. If a great deal of the debt is current, this creates additional risks for the organisation.

Debt to equity ratio

This is another way of measuring the capital structure of an organisation and providing insights into the risks relating to how the organisation has been financed. The debt to equity ratio provides an indication of how much the liabilities are per dollar of equity, and therefore provides another indicator of the extent to which an organisation is dependent on debt financing.

$$\frac{\text{Total liabilities}}{\text{Total owners' equity}} \times 100 = \text{The amount of liabilities represented as a percentage of owners' equity}$$

If the debt to equity ratio is in excess of 100 per cent, this indicates that the organisation is more reliant on funding from its lenders than from its owners. Consistent with what we have already said, all things being equal, the greater the relative reliance on debt financing, the riskier the organisation. As we know, this is because, for debt, there are legal requirements for payments in terms of both principal and interest. For equity, there is generally no legal requirement to pay dividends. Dividends will be paid to owners when the managers consider that there are sufficient funds available to do so.

For more on the calculation of gearing/stability ratios, see **Learning exercise 12.3**.

12.3 Learning Exercise

Calculation of various gearing (or stability) ratios

Scenario: We will again consider Bondi Company, which we know from **Learning exercise 12.1** has total assets of $1 940 000, total liabilities of $485 000, and total owners' equity therefore of $1 455 000.

Issue: You have been asked to calculate the following ratios and comment on the apparent riskiness of the organisation.

Ratios to calculate:

- debt to assets
- debt to equity.

Solution: Before you can form a considered opinion regarding Bondi Company's financial risk, you will need to work out the ratios.

The ratios

The worked solutions, using the appropriate formulas, are laid out in the following table to help you step though the process.

Ratio	Formula	Calculated amount $000
Debt to assets	$\frac{\text{Total liabilities}}{\text{Total assets}} \times 100$	$\frac{485}{1940} \times 100 = 25.00\%$
Debt to equity	$\frac{\text{Total liabilities}}{\text{Total owners' equity}} \times 100$	$\frac{485}{1455} \times 100 = 33.33\%$

Interpreting the information

On the basis of the above ratios, we would argue that the organisation is not overly reliant on debt sources. For example, total debt is only 25 per cent of total assets and 33 per cent of total owners' equity. Therefore, a large proportion of the organisation's funds have come from owners in the form of issuing shares and from profits that have been retained within the business (retained earnings) and which could have been used to acquire assets for the company. Therefore, from a 'capital structure' perspective, the organisation does not appear to be subject to high levels of financial risk.

Why do I need to know about gearing ratios?

The financial gearing of an organisation (the total debt relative to total assets or equity) provides an indication of the risk of an organisation. All things being equal, the greater the debt relative to assets or equity, the greater the financial risk of the organisation. For organisations that have a high variability in earnings, it can be particularly risky to have high levels of gearing. Also, various gearing ratios are often used within contractual arrangements negotiated with lenders. Hence, the measures calculated for these ratios can have direct implications for the survival of the organisation. So, we should be aware of these ratios.

Liquidity ratios

liquidity ratios Measures that provide an indicator of the ability of an organisation to pay its debts, as and when they become due

Liquidity ratios provide insights into the ability of an organisation to pay its debts as, and when, they fall due. Accounting ratios within this category include the current ratio, the quick ratio, interest coverage ratio, and cash flows from operating activities to current liabilities.

Liquidity analysis generally focuses on the ability of an organisation to pay those debts which are due for payment in 12 months or less. These include various payments that cannot be forestalled, such as payments to employees and to the suppliers of inventory. Poor management of inventory (reflected in ratios such as the inventory turnover ratio) and debtors (reflected in ratios such as the debtors' turnover ratio) will contribute towards poor liquidity. This emphasises the interconnected nature of many of the ratios we are considering.

Current ratio

To assess whether an organisation will be able to pay its debts as and when they fall due, it is common to compare current assets with current liabilities by way of the current ratio. As you know, generally speaking, current assets are those assets that are expected to be used up or turned into cash within the next 12 months, whereas current liabilities are those obligations due for payment within the next 12 months. The current ratio is calculated as:

$$\frac{\text{Current assets}}{\text{Current liabilities}} = \text{Measure of current assets represented as a multiple of current liabilities}$$

There is a very general rule that the current ratio should not fall below 1. If the ratio is above 1, then the general conclusion often made is that the organisation will be able to meet the debts that are payable within the next 12 months. The lower this number gets, the greater the assumed difficulty an organisation will have in meeting its short-term liabilities. A current ratio of, say, 1.2 would indicate that the organisation has $1.20 of current assets for every $1 of current liabilities.

Whilst a current ratio below 1.0 might be considered to represent 'bad news', a high number might indicate inefficiencies, with too much of the organisation's funds being held in cash, accounts receivable and inventory, all of which can create their own risks and costs. Deposits in cash typically generate low returns relative to other options (including paying off debt which might be attracting interest expenses). Therefore, it is not a good idea to have too much wealth simply residing in cash.

Having too much invested in inventory can also have negative implications in terms of higher storage costs, insurance costs, potential inventory damage, obsolescence and theft. The greater the amount residing in debtors, the greater the potential bad and doubtful debts that might subsequently arise. Therefore, there is a need to balance the relationship between current assets and current liabilities such that the ratio is neither too small nor too large.

Because it is vital for an organisation to be able to pay its debts as and when they fall due, a comparison of current liabilities and current assets should be regularly undertaken by managers, certainly not just once a year when the annual financial statements are prepared for external stakeholders.

Quick ratio

The quick ratio (or as it is also called, the 'acid-test ratio') is also used to assess the ability of an organisation to pay its debts as, and when, they are due for payment. Whilst the current ratio focuses on the liquidity of the organisation over the next 12 months, the quick ratio focuses more on its immediate liquidity.

This measure typically excludes inventory and prepayments from the current assets balance because inventory can take several months to be converted into cash (for example, the inventory needs to be sold and then further time needs to pass before customers/debtors pay the amount due), and prepayments typically cannot be refunded in cash, or if they can be, it might take several months to organise any refund. That is, neither inventory or prepayments can be 'quickly' converted into cash.

The quick ratio also often excludes bank overdrafts from the measure of current liabilities used within the denominator of the ratio because banks often allow the overdraft to stay in place indefinitely, even though in principle it could be demanded at short notice. A bank overdraft exists when more cash is drawn from an organisation's bank account than was deposited. Organisations often negotiate an *overdraft facility* with a bank wherein the bank does allow the account to be overdrawn up to a certain pre-specified overdraft limit. When a bank account goes into overdraft, the bank will charge the organisation interest expenses.

The quick ratio can be calculated as:

$$\frac{\text{Current assets} - \text{inventory} - \text{prepayments}}{\text{Current liabilities} - \text{bank overdraft}} = \text{The adjusted measure of current assets as a multiple of the adjusted measure of current liabilities}$$

A number below 1.0 for the quick ratio can indicate potentially high financial risk.

Interest coverage ratio

The interest coverage ratio (also known as the 'times interest earned ratio') provides an indication of an organisation's ability to service its debt-paying requirements by comparing the earnings (or profits) before interest and taxes with total interest costs. It is calculated as:

$$\frac{\text{Earnings before interest and taxes}}{\text{Interest costs}} = \text{Number of times interest is covered by EBIT}$$

The interest coverage ratio provides an indication of the ease with which an organisation can meet its interest expense obligations. For example, if the interest coverage ratio is calculated to be 10, this would mean that for every dollar of interest expense, the organisation earns $10 in profits (before interest and taxes). The greater the number, the easier the ability of the organisation to meet its interest payment obligations. A number below 1.0 would represent a financially unsustainable situation and reflect high financial risk. A number slightly above 1.0 can also be problematic since organisations need to pay tax obligations, plus, generally, there are also principal repayments required on loans as well. Organisations can potentially be wound up if they are unable to pay their interest expense commitments.

All things being equal, the greater the number of times an organisation can cover its interest-payment requirements, the better. Interest coverage clauses are often included within borrowing agreements wherein a minimum number of times is stipulated within the negotiated debt contract. For example, a negotiated debt covenant might require that an organisation's interest coverage ratio be maintained at a minimum of at least five times.

Cash flows from operating activities to current liabilities

This measure provides an indication of the ability of an organisation to meet its financial obligations from its operating activities, rather than relying on cash flows from financing or investing activities. Because this measure uses actual cash flows rather than profits (and therefore is potentially subject to less manipulation or 'creative accounting'), many analysts prefer this to other ratios as a measure to indicate the ability of an organisation to meet the debts payable within the next 12 months. The cash flow from operating activities to current liabilities can be calculated as:

$$\frac{\text{Cash flows from operating activities}}{\text{Current liabilities}} = \text{Number of times current liabilities is covered by cash flows from operating activities}$$

Generally, the higher this ratio is, the better it is. As an indicator, if the average time required for the payment of current liabilities is 30 days, then 12 times per year would seem to be a sensible point at which to start in determining an acceptable number of times that cash flows from operating activities cover current liabilities.

For more on the calculation of liquidity ratios, see Learning exercise 12.4.

12.4 Learning Exercise

Calculation of various liquidity ratios

Scenario: We return once again to the case of Bondi Company as used in the previous learning exercises. Bondi Company has current assets of $720 000, current liabilities of $325 000, inventory of $240 000, no prepayments, no bank overdraft, profits of $120 000, interest expenses of $20 000, and tax expense of $100 000.

Issue: You are required to calculate the following ratios and make an assessment of the liquidity of Bondi Company.

Ratios to calculate:

- current ratio
- quick ratio

- interest coverage ratio
- cash flows from operating activities to current liabilities ratio.

Solution: Before you can make an assessment of the liquidity of Bondi Company, you will need to work out the ratios.

The ratios

The worked solutions, using the appropriate formulas, are laid out in the following table to help you step through the process.

Ratio	Formula	Calculated amount $000
Current	$\frac{\text{Current assets}}{\text{Current liabilities}}$	$\frac{720}{325} = 2.22$ times
Quick	$\frac{\text{Current assets} - \text{inventory} - \text{prepayments}}{\text{Current liabilities} - \text{bank overdraft}}$	$\frac{720-240-0}{325-0} = 1.48$ times
Interest coverage	$\frac{\text{Earnings before interest and taxes}}{\text{Interest costs}}$	$\frac{120 + 20 + 100}{20} = 12$ times
Cash flows from operating activities to current liabilities	$\frac{\text{Cash flows from operating activities}}{\text{Current liabilities}}$	$\frac{230}{325} = 0.71$ times

Interpreting the information

If we refer to the current ratio, quick ratio and interest coverage ratio, then the general conclusion to be reached is that the organisation does not have any significant liquidity problems, and therefore would be likely to be able to pay its debts as and when they fall due.

However, the cash flows from operating activities to current liabilities do seem quite low and require attention. This low measure is also consistent with our earlier results that showed that both inventory turnover and debtors' turnover was very low. If the inventory turnover and debtors' turnover could be improved, this would also have positive implications for the cash flows from operating activities to current liabilities ratio.

Why do I need to know about liquidity ratios?

Liquidity ratios provide insights into an organisation's ability to pay its debts as and when they fall due. Failure to pay debts when due can lead to the failure of an organisation. Therefore, these ratios are of great importance to analysts.

Investment-based ratios

Investment-based ratios provide an insight into the dividend returns being generated by an organisation, as well as how the share market values, or perceives, an organisation. Ratios within this category include dividends per share, dividend yield, earnings per share, and the price earnings ratio.

investment-based ratios Measures that provide insights into how the share market values and/or perceives, an organisation

These ratios are applicable to companies that are established to generate profits, and some of these measures also are more relevant to companies that are listed on a securities exchange wherein the market price of shares can be readily determined.

Dividends per share

This ratio is calculated as:

$$\frac{\text{Total dividends announced during the accounting period}}{\text{Weighted average number of shares on issue from the company}} = \text{Dividend per share for an accounting period}$$

This ratio informs us about the cash returns to investors for each share that is held in the company. We need to remember that not all of the profits and related cash flows of a company will be used to pay dividends to shareholders. Managers can elect to retain some of the funds within the company to enable future expansion, rather than pay them out as dividends. Organisations in the growth stages of their life will often pay relatively small amounts of dividends. Therefore, low amounts of dividend payments are not necessarily a bad thing.

Funds that are retained within the organisation belong to the shareholders (the owners) and therefore should help to increase the value of the shares. Apart from dividends, the total returns earned by an investor will also include the increases in the market value of the organisation's shares within the accounting period (often referred to as a *capital gain*).

The dividend per share is calculated on the basis of the weighted average number of shares on issue. This can sometimes be a complicated number to calculate. It is determined by taking into account the number of days a certain quantity of shares was on issue, and weighting this number of shares by this number of days. For example, if at the beginning of the financial year, which we will assume is 1 July, a company had 500 000 shares on issue, and if it then issued another 100 000 shares on 1 April, then the weighted average number of shares would be calculated as follows:

Period	Proportion of year	×	Number of shares outstanding	=	Weighted average
1 July – 31 March	274 ÷ 365		500 000		375 342
1 April – 30 June	91 ÷ 365		600 000		149 589
					524 931

Dividend yield

The dividend yield represents the ratio of the dividends per share (as calculated above), divided by the market price of the company's share. It is calculated as:

$$\frac{\text{Dividend per share}}{\text{Market price per share}} \times 100 = \text{A measure of the amount of dividends paid per share as a percentage of the current market price of each share}$$

Therefore, if the market price of a share in a company was $20 and the company was paying annual dividends of $0.50 per share, that would represent a dividend yield of 2.5 per cent (calculated as 0.5 divided by 20 × 100). Such a yield would be compared with other available investment opportunities. Different taxation treatments associated with dividend receipts compared with other sources of income can also be factored into this analysis.

Earnings per share

Earnings per share is calculated by comparing the accounting profit generated by a company with the number of shares that have been issued. Companies with shares listed on a securities exchange will often disclose this calculation within their annual report, typically at the bottom of the income statement. In basic terms, earnings per share is calculated as:

$$\frac{\text{Profit}}{\text{Weighted average number of shares on issue from the company}} = \text{Earnings per share}$$

Earnings per share is a number that is widely used by investment analysts and is seen as an important indicator of the performance of an organisation over time. It also provides an indicator of possible future dividend payments. Comparing the earnings per share of one company with those of another is not appropriate as different companies divide their share capital into different numbers of shares that were issued at different amounts per share.

Price earnings ratio

The price earnings ratio compares the market price of a company's shares with its earnings per share. The market price of a company's shares will be influenced by many factors, including assessments of the financial performance and financial position of the organisation (and hopefully also considerations of the organisation's social and environmental performance) undertaken by investors and their advisers using information sourced from such places as the financial statements of the organisation. This analysis might be undertaken by way of using many of the accounting ratios discussed in this chapter.

If a share is trading at $20 and the earnings per share (which as we know is calculated as profit divided by the average number of shares on issue for the period) is $2, then the price earnings ratio is 10 (calculated as 20 divided by 2), meaning that investors are prepared to pay a price for the organisation's shares that is 10 times its profits per share. Effectively, the number calculated for the price earnings ratio represents how many dollars must be invested for each dollar of earnings. The price earnings ratio can be calculated as:

$$\frac{\text{Market price per share}}{\text{Earnings per share}} = \begin{array}{l}\text{Number of multiples of EPS that investors} \\ \text{will pay for a share in a company}\end{array}$$

For listed companies, a price earnings ratio in the range of 20–25 is quite common. The price earnings ratio provides an indication of how many times earnings the share market is prepared to pay for a share. A higher number relative to similar organisations indicates greater market acceptance of the organisation. The market might believe that the organisation with the higher price earnings ratio has relatively lower risk and/or it has good growth prospects – so a higher number seems to be a good thing. A low price earnings ratio might indicate that investors believe that the organisation is relatively risky, or that its earnings are expected to fall in the future. However, a low price earnings ratio is also consistent with the possibility that the price of an organisation's shares is currently undervalued and represents a potentially good investment opportunity – however, care would need to be taken before immediately accepting this as an explanation for a low price earnings ratio.

The industry to which an organisation belongs will impact the price earnings ratio, and therefore it can be inappropriate to compare the price earnings ratios of companies in different industries.

Price earnings ratios can sometimes get very high, to the point that they seem to defy explanation and are potentially indicative of an 'overheated market', and that a market adjustment (at the extreme, a market 'crash') is imminent. For example, prior to the global financial crisis of 2009, many leading companies' price earnings ratios had climbed to above 40. Within months, many of these had dropped to around 20, and massive losses were incurred by many investors.

For more on the calculation of investment-based ratios, see **Learning exercise 12.5**.

12.5 Learning Exercise

Calculation of investment-based ratios

Scenario: Let's return once more to the Bondi Company, as examined in the last few learning exercises. As we know from the financial statements provided earlier in this chapter, the profits of the company were $120 000, and the company announced dividends during the accounting period amounting to a total of $30 000.

Additionally, the share capital of the company is comprised of 500 000 shares that were issued for $2 each. The number of shares has not changed throughout the accounting period. The current market price of each share is $2.45.

Issue: You are required to calculate the following ratios, and to provide some comment on what you think the ratios indicate:

- dividends per share
- dividend yield
- earnings per share
- price earnings ratio.

Solution: Before you can make an assessment of the ratios, you will need to work them out.

The ratios

The worked solutions, using the appropriate formulas, are laid out in the following table to help you step though the process.

Ratio	Formula	Calculated amount $000
Dividends per share	$\frac{\text{Total dividends announced during the accounting period}}{\text{Weighted average number of shares on issue from the company}}$	$= \frac{\$30\,000}{500\,000}$ = $0.06 per share

Ratio	Formula	Calculated amount $000
Dividend yield	$\frac{\text{Dividend per share}}{\text{Market price per share}} \times 100$	$= \frac{\$0.06}{\$2.45} \times 100$ $= 2.45\%$
Earnings per share	$\frac{\text{Profit}}{\text{Weighted average number of shares on issue from the company}}$	$= \frac{\$120\,000}{500\,000}$ $= \$0.24$
Price earnings ratio	$\frac{\text{Market price per share}}{\text{Earnings per share}}$	$= \frac{\$2.45}{\$0.24}$ $= 10.21$ times

Interpreting the ratios

The dividends per share, and the dividend yield, seem very low. Comparison needs to be made with the dividend yields available on other investments, as well as the returns on low-risk investments, including the returns on bank deposits.

The future prospects of the organisation need to be considered. If the managers of Bondi Company have proposed paying smaller dividends because they have decided to retain funds for expansions, and for good investment opportunities within the organisation, then shareholders might be satisfied with the low dividend payments as long as there is an expectation that returns will increase in the future. We also need to remember that the total returns made by investors will include any increase in the market values of the shares throughout the accounting period which are not reflected within these ratios.

When reviewing earnings per share, we need to consider trends in this ratio. This number on its own does not mean much. For example, if Bondi had 1 million shares at $1 each, rather than 500 000 shares at $2 (which is the same share capital in total), then the earnings per share would only be $0.12. Earnings per share takes on greater relevance, however, when it is used to compute the price earnings ratio. A price earnings ratio of 10.21 is relatively low. This ratio should be compared with those of other organisations, and if the ratios of the other organisations are significantly higher, then this might reflect the fact that the share market is not viewing the company favourably. Perhaps there is a belief that future profits will fall, or that the organisation is relatively risky. The other possibility is that the share price might be undervalued – but as we have stressed before, care would need to be taken before reaching this conclusion.

Having considered all five categories of ratios independently, it is also important to then review them together to provide more-comprehensive insights into how the organisation is performing and how financially stable it appears. If we consider all the ratios together for Bondi Company, it does appear that the organisation is not subject to any significant financial risks. Its profitability might be acceptable to many stakeholders, but there are some apparent problems with the efficiency with which the organisation is being operated. These concerns about efficiency might be one of the reasons for the low price earnings ratio.

Why do I need to know about investment-based ratios?

Investment-based ratios provide insights into the returns being provided to investors as well as providing insights into the value investors attribute to an organisation. These ratios provide an indicator of the earnings that investors have earned, and perhaps may expect to earn in the future (although they ignore capital gains). Therefore, they are relevant to investment decisions. The ratios also provide an insight into how investors perceive the organisation relative to other organisations. This would be relevant to the managers of an organisation, particularly if they are considering raising additional equity funds.

LO12.4 Important information also resides in the notes to the financial statements

Moving our attention away from the financial statements themselves, as already noted earlier within this chapter and other chapters of this book, we can also find some very important information in the notes that accompany the financial statements. So, as well as reviewing the financial statements as part of our analysis, we also should spend time carefully reading through the accompanying notes. The financial reporting standards issued by standard-setters such as the IASB and FASB not only provide requirements about such issues as to when to recognise transactions and events and how to measure and report assets and liabilities, they also typically require additional information to be disclosed within the notes that accompany the financial statements.

The notes that accompany financial statements can sometimes make up 50–100 pages of an annual report. Within these notes, many important issues are addressed. You should think of a large public company that you know and then go to their website and download their most recent annual report. Have a look at the financial statements and then look at the many pages of notes that provide additional information about the numbers that appear within the financial statements. Also, the notes will provide some information that does not directly relate to the numbers in the financial statements but is nevertheless very important to understanding the financial performance and position of the organisation. We will consider four topics that are commonly addressed within the notes to the financial statements, although please remember there will be many other items of important information in the notes as well. These four topics are:

- the accounting policies
- significant events occurring after the end of the reporting period
- contingent liabilities
- how senior managers/executives are being paid – what types of incentives are provided to employees.

Accounting policies

Accounting policies are the specific principles, bases, conventions, rules and practices applied by an organisation when preparing and presenting financial statements. Whilst often very difficult to understand (even for experienced accountants), the first notes that generally accompany financial statements are the 'accounting policy notes'. In this regard, IAS 1: Presentation of Financial Statements requires that:

> An entity shall disclose its significant accounting policies comprising:
>
> a The measurement basis (or bases) used in preparing the financial statements; and
>
> b The other accounting policies used that are relevant to an understanding of the financial statements.
>
> Source: International Accounting Standards Board (2022).

In providing a rationale for the required disclosure of an organisation's accounting policies, the accounting standard IAS 1 further explains:

> It is important for an entity to inform users of the measurement basis or bases used in the financial statements (for example, historical cost, current cost, net realisable value, fair value or recoverable amount) because the basis on which an entity prepares the financial statements significantly affects users' analysis. When an entity uses more than one measurement basis in the financial statements, for example when particular classes of assets are revalued, it is sufficient to provide an indication of the categories of assets and liabilities to which each measurement basis is applied.
>
> In deciding whether a particular accounting policy should be disclosed, management considers whether disclosure would assist users in understanding how transactions, other events and conditions are reflected in reported financial performance and financial position. Each entity considers the nature of its operations and the policies that the users of its financial statements would expect to be disclosed for that type of entity. Disclosure of particular accounting policies is especially useful to users when those policies are selected from alternatives allowed in Accounting Standards.
>
> Source: International Accounting Standards Board (2022).

As there can be a choice between alternative measurement bases for some assets and liabilities, it is important to ensure that if two or more organisations are being compared, they should ideally be applying the same policies, or else the comparison can be misleading.

Organisations will also change accounting policies over time. Often, this might be because new accounting standards have been released, or because managers and their accountants believe that previously used accounting methods no longer provide 'relevant' information about the financial performance, and financial position, of the organisation. Again, interested stakeholders should be familiar with the accounting policies being used by an organisation to generate its financial statements prior to reviewing those financial statements.

Calculations like 'profits', 'total assets', 'total liabilities' and so forth only really make sense if we understand the rules (policies) that have been used to generate the numbers – rules that can frequently change. So there is a need to be careful when comparing accounting numbers (and therefore the ratios that have been calculated from those numbers) across time, as there is a very real chance that the underlying rules for calculating those numbers have changed. It would actually be very misleading to compare a profitability measure from this year – such as return on assets – with the same measure calculated 10 years ago for the same organisation, as the rules for measuring various assets, liabilities, income and expenses would have changed in that time, thereby potentially making comparisons somewhat meaningless.

This brings into question much of the (naive) financial statement analysis that can often be seen, which charts aspects of financial position or financial performance over an extended and sometimes lengthy period of analysis to identify possible trends. As we highlighted within Chapters 9 and 10, people that do such analysis often really do not understand financial accounting, particularly the fact that the recognition and measurement rules for various expenses, revenues, assets and liabilities often change across time as new and revised financial reporting standards are released.

As an example of an accounting policy for measuring assets, we can consider an accounting policy note about property, plant and equipment that appears within the notes to the 2021 financial statements of BHP:

> **Property, plant and equipment**
>
> Property, plant and equipment is recorded at cost less accumulated depreciation and impairment charges. Cost is the fair value of consideration given to acquire the asset at the time of its acquisition or construction and includes the direct costs of bringing the asset to the location and the condition necessary for operation and the estimated future costs of closure and rehabilitation of the facility.
>
> Source: BHP (2021), p. 152.

As we can see, BHP does not measure its property, plant and equipment at fair value (which is an option it has available). Rather, it has elected to use cost as the basis for measurement. This means in general that, relative to organisations that measure their property, plant and equipment at fair value, BHP's depreciation costs would be lower, and profit on the sale of property, plant and equipment would be higher. That is, reported profit would be higher than had fair value been used to measure property, plant and equipment.

Ratios such as 'return on assets' might also look relatively stronger, as the asset base (the denominator) would be lower. Therefore, you can hopefully see that it would be problematic to compare BHP's performance with that of another organisation that measured its property, plant and equipment at fair value.

So again, we need to make sure that, if we are comparing organisations when doing financial statement analysis, the organisations are using the same accounting policies in respect of important measurement decisions. Otherwise, we might need to make some adjustments to our analysis. Hence, reviewing accounting policies is an important first step in financial statement analysis – even though many analysts seem to ignore it.

Why do I need to know about the accounting policies applied by an organisation?

The accounting policies applied by an organisation will have direct implications for the assets, liabilities, equity, income and expenses that are reported by an organisation. A change of accounting policies can have direct implications for the financial statements. Therefore, to more fully understand the context of the numbers being reported, knowledge of the accounting policies being applied to generate those numbers is essential.

Significant events occurring after the end of the reporting period

As you learned in other chapters of this book, the balance sheet is prepared as at a certain point in time and represents a snapshot of the assets, liabilities and equity of an organisation as at that point in time. By contrast, the income statement, statement of cash flows, and statement of changes in equity are prepared for a period of time (perhaps 12 months or less).

Once an organisation reaches the end of the accounting period (reporting period), some time is needed to prepare and check the financial statements and supporting notes before they are released to interested stakeholders. If, for example, the end of the accounting period (also known as the *reporting date*) is 30 June, then time is needed to prepare the financial statements, supporting notes need to be completed, auditors need time to do their audit, reports need to be formatted, and so forth. The result is that the annual report (which includes the financial statements, notes to the financial statements, and some other reports such as the auditor's report which relates to the reporting period ending on 30 June (which is common within Australia)) is typically released in September, which is up to three months after the reporting period has ended.

For example, BHP and Qantas both have a financial year that ends on 30 June. Their 2021 annual reports were issued to shareholders and external stakeholders on 2 September 2021 and 17 September 2021, respectively. This date coincides with when the auditor's report was signed by the auditors, and the directors' report and directors' declaration were signed by the directors. It is at this point that the annual report is *authorised for issue* to shareholders and other interested stakeholders.

Whilst the financial statements reflect the transactions and events that occurred up to the reporting date (for example, 30 June), many important things can happen in the period between the end of the reporting period and the date of release of the financial statements to the stakeholders. This can be diagrammatically represented as in **Figure 12.2**.

FIGURE 12.2 Events occurring after the end of reporting period

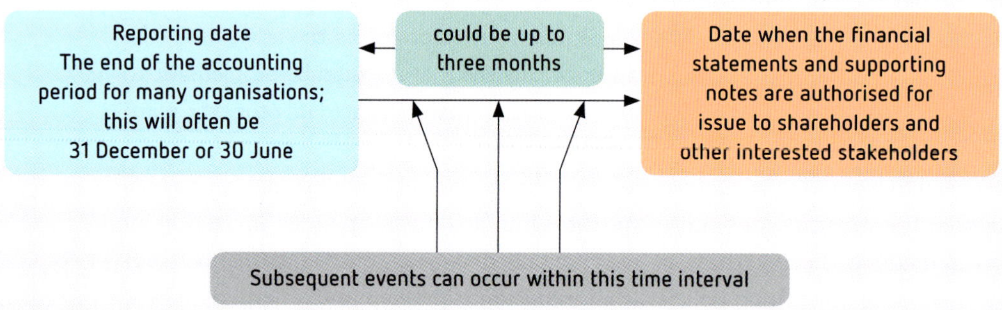

Significant events that could occur in the time period between the end of the accounting period and the date on which the financial statements are authorised for issue to shareholders, and other interested stakeholders, include such things as losses of major customers or major markets, major changes in foreign exchange rates that will impact the future profitability of the organisation, a significant change in the capital structure or operating structure of the organisation, uninsured losses of significant property, plant and equipment, and so forth.

These transactions and events will not be recognised within the financial statements to the extent that they are outside the accounting period, as this would breach the *accounting period convention* (which we discussed in Chapter 7). With this in mind, there is a requirement in the accounting standards that states that, in respect of significant events that occur after the end of the reporting period (and therefore are likely to impact the *future* financial performance and financial position of the organisation), but before the financial statements have been authorised for issue, the organisation will disclose in the notes to the financial statements:

1. the nature of the event
2. an estimate of its financial effect, or a statement that such an estimate cannot be made.

Therefore, when reviewing financial statements, you should always remember to look through the notes to the statements for information about such events, as they might create impacts material to future financial performance and financial position. As an example of a note disclosure referring to significant events that have occurred since the end of the reporting period, consider **Exhibit 12.1**, which provides the related information from the annual report of BHP for the year ending 30 June 2021.

EXHIBIT 12.1 An example of a note referring to events that have occurred since the end of the reporting period – from the 2021 annual report of BHP

Note 35 Subsequent events

On 27 July 2021, the Group entered into a definitive Support Agreement with Noront Resources (Noront) to make an all-cash takeover offer for Noront.

On 17 August 2021, the Group announced a major growth investment of US$5.7 billion (C$7.5 billion) in the Jansen Stage 1 potash project, which is aligned with its strategy of growing its exposure to future facing commodities in world class assets.

On 17 August 2021, the Group announced the proposed merger of our Petroleum assets with Woodside. On completion of the proposed transaction, BHP's oil and gas business would merge with Woodside, and Woodside would issue new shares to be distributed to BHP shareholders, at which time it is expected that Woodside would be owned 52 per cent and 48 per cent by existing Woodside and BHP shareholders, respectively. The merger, which has a proposed effective date of 1 July 2021, is subject to confirmatory due diligence, negotiation and execution of full form transaction documents, and satisfaction of conditions precedent including shareholder, regulatory and other approvals. The Group continues to assess the full financial reporting impacts of the proposed merger. However, the preliminary terms of the merger did not provide an indicator of impairment for our Petroleum assets at 30 June 2021. The merger is expected to be completed during the first half of CY2022, at which time, we would derecognise the carrying value of our Petroleum assets, which at 30 June 2021 included, but was not limited to, property plant and equipment and closure and rehabilitation provisions of approximately US$11.9 billion and US$3.9 billion, respectively.

On 17 August 2021, the Group announced its intention to realise simplification and enhanced strategic flexibility benefits through unifying its corporate structure under its existing Australian parent company.

Other than the matters outlined above, no matters or circumstances have arisen since the end of the financial year that have significantly affected, or may significantly affect, the operations, results of operations or state of affairs of the Group in subsequent accounting periods.

Source: BHP (2021), p. 185.

For more on the disclosure of information about significant events that occur after the end of the reporting period, see **Learning exercise 12.6**.

12.6 Learning Exercise

Disclosure of information about significant events that occur after the end of the reporting period

Scenario: Twin Fin Ltd has a financial year that ends on 31 December 2026. The expectation is that the financial statements and supporting material will not be authorised by the directors for issue to shareholders and other stakeholders until mid-March 2027.

On 24 January 2027, Twin Fin Ltd's operations in Patagonia are suspended because the Patagonian Government is trying to encourage more local production. This suspension is expected to last at least two years. In 2026, the operations in Patagonia represent about 20 per cent of Twin Fin Ltd's total sales, and whilst the company will remain viable, the event will significantly impact future profitability.

Issue: For financial accounting purposes, how should Twin Fin Ltd account for this event?

Solution: Because this event occurred outside of the accounting period, no adjustments will be made to the financial statements being prepared for the accounting period ending 31 December 2026. However, because of the significance of the event, the notes to the financial statements should disclose information about the nature of the event and the expected impact it will have on future profitability.

In the absence of such a note, analysts might otherwise wrongly believe that the profitability of 2026 will be repeated, or possibly improved upon, in 2027.

Why do I need to know about the disclosure requirements pertaining to significant events that occur after the end of the reporting period?

As we know, the financial statements take many weeks to complete before they are released to stakeholders. Many events can occur between the time that the financial reporting period ends, and when the financial reports are completed and authorised for issue to shareholders.

These subsequent events will not be reflected within the current financial statements themselves, but nevertheless might have significant implications for the next reporting period's financial performance and position. That is, the information could be very relevant to the users of the financial statements. Therefore, we need to know to look through the notes to the financial statements to find this information.

Contingent liabilities

As we know from Chapter 9, a contingent liability is an obligation that is payable contingent upon a future event, or an obligation that is possible though perhaps not probable (in terms of resource outflows), or is not measurable with sufficient reliability.

As we also know from Chapter 9, contingent liabilities are not recognised within the financial statements and hence will not be reflected within our ratio analysis. Rather, we need to look at the notes accompanying the financial statements to find details of potentially significant or material contingent liabilities. Organisations are required to disclose information about the nature of the contingent liability and, where practicable, provide:

1. an estimate of its financial effect
2. an indication of the uncertainties relating to the amount or timing of any outflow
3. the possibility of any related reimbursement.

Therefore, as part of our financial statement analysis, we should review the notes to the financial statements to see if there are any significant contingent liabilities. At the extreme, contingent liabilities can potentially threaten the ongoing existence of an organisation – so it is very important to be aware of them. We need to factor the potential risks associated with contingent liabilities into our analysis and subsequent decision making.

A consideration of contingent liabilities is often undertaken on a worst case scenario basis. For example, the reported contingent liabilities might include:

- a guarantee that has been given by an organisation to pay an amount that has been borrowed by a related organisation if that related organisation defaults on paying the debt
- a liability that could arise in relation to existing legal action taken by a customer because of injuries allegedly caused to the customer by goods sold by the organisation, and which the customer claims were both faulty and dangerous
- an order by the local environmental protection authority to clean up a site that was contaminated by the organisation.

Whilst unlikely to occur, some analysts might factor in what would happen if all of these events actually occurred, and how that would then impact the future viability of the organisation. Whilst not all analysts will perform such worst case scenario testing, it is important that contingent liabilities – if they exist – are considered as part of the financial statement analysis. Each contingent liability acts to increase the risk exposure of the organisation.

As an example of a contingent liability note, refer back to **Exhibit 9.6**.

Why do I need to know about the disclosure requirements pertaining to contingent liabilities?

Contingent liabilities are not reported within the balance sheet, but they can potentially have very significant implications for the continued operations of the organisation. Therefore, to more fully understand the financial position of an organisation, it is essential that we look beyond the financial statements and to the notes to the financial statements to find the note relating to contingent liabilities.

Remuneration policies

Organisations – particularly larger organisations – often include several pages of information in their annual reports about how senior managers and other key personnel are paid and otherwise remunerated. This is a corporations law requirement within many countries.

Managers in organisations typically receive bonuses (referred to commonly as 'performance-based rewards' or 'at risk rewards'). That is, it is virtually never the case that senior managers simply receive just a fixed salary.

Bonuses can be linked to various performance indicators. Some performance indicators might involve financial accounting numbers. For example, a senior manager might receive a bonus that is a specific percentage of profits, return on assets, or sales revenue. This is very common. When bonuses are linked to the financial results of one accounting period, these are often referred to as 'short-term' bonuses, as they are just based on 12 months' performance.

Managers and other key personnel are also often provided with longer-term bonuses. For example, they might be provided with a bonus linked to changes in the organisation's share prices over a period of multiple years. They might be given a bonus linked to the improvement in share price over the next five years, which would encourage them to put in place initiatives that provide improvements in the longer-run performance of the organisation. A mixture of fixed-salary and shorter-term and longer-term bonuses is commonly provided to senior managers in many organisations.

Management bonuses could also be linked to various measures of social and environmental performance. For example, senior managers might receive a bonus if there are no instances of non-compliance with environmental laws, no spillages of toxic chemicals, if reductions in the emission of greenhouse gases reach predetermined targets, or if there are no instances of workplace injuries.

The central idea behind offering bonuses, such as those discussed above, is that they motivate managers to strive to achieve certain performance-related objectives, the assumption being that managers prefer higher pay, and without offering such incentives, managers might not work quite as hard to achieve particular performance targets.

Disclosures about the form of bonuses being offered by an organisation to its managers inform the reader/analyst about certain priorities of the organisation, and what types of performance the organisation appears particularly intent on improving. This information can also potentially help the reader/analyst identify risks and inconsistencies in the actions and rhetoric of an organisation.

For example, if an organisation has publicly promoted the view that environmental sustainability is as important to the organisation as being profitable (we often read or hear of managers within organisations making public claims that they would never put profits before principles), but we find, within the notes to the financial statements, that the remuneration/

bonus plans only link managerial rewards to measures of financial performance (and not to any form of social and environmental performance), then we would rightly question the statements being made by the organisation about their concern for society and the environment, and we might question whether the organisation is actually operating in a socially responsible manner. There would appear to be a decoupling of the 'public face' of the organisation, in which it promotes an appearance of social and environmental responsibility, from their actual behaviour within the organisation, and that would be a reason for concern.

If an organisation is rewarding its managers in terms of profits and nothing else, then this might also motivate managers to be short term in focus, which creates various risks for the organisation and therefore for its stakeholders.

It should now be clear why knowledge of management remuneration plans and the associated bonuses are relevant to the process of financial statement analysis. It provides further insights into the direction being taken by the organisation. For large companies with shares listed on a securities exchange, it is common to find many pages within an annual report devoted to providing information about how senior executives and other key personnel are paid, with much detail about what incentives are provided to them, and whether these incentives/bonuses are considered to be shorter-term or longer-term in nature.

Why do I need to know about the remuneration policies used to reward managers?

The reality is that one of the best ways to motivate managers to achieve particular objectives or targets is to link their financial rewards to these objectives or targets. By looking at the way the organisation uses various key performance indicators to reward their managers we are better able to understand the true priorities of the organisation, rather than simply relying upon the statements, or rhetoric, coming from the organisation. A disparity between the public statements made by an organisation (for example, that certain aspects of performance are important to the organisation) and the elements of performance that it actually relies upon to reward its managers might indicate to us that we need to be careful relying upon many of the claims being made by managers. Also, if an organisation fails to incorporate, for example, aspects of social and environmental performance within the bonus plans negotiated with managers, then this could arguably signal that the organisation is rather risky as it is failing to put in place mechanisms to motivate managers to attend to important aspects of performance.

LO12.5 Information about accounting-based contractual agreements

Ideally, when undertaking financial statement analysis (or perhaps beforehand), an interested stakeholder should try to be aware of the accounting-based contracts the organisation has entered into – we already partially discussed this when talking about bonus plans.

The reason for suggesting this is because the existence of certain contracts between an organisation and other stakeholders, which rely upon reported financial accounting numbers, can potentially motivate the managers of an organisation to manipulate those particular numbers in order to create favourable contractual outcomes for the organisation and/or for themselves. Some financial accounting numbers might be more susceptible to manipulation than others because of their use within particular contractual arrangements; for example:

- When borrowing funds, managers of organisations will often agree to various accounting-based debt covenants so as to reduce the perceived risks of the lenders, and therefore reduce the cost of obtaining the funding from those lenders. For instance, there might be negotiated debt-to-asset restrictions, or minimum interest coverage requirements, that an organisation has negotiated and must comply with, or else be considered to be in technical default of the borrowing agreement.
- Managers might be rewarded in terms of the reported financial accounting numbers. For instance, they might receive bonuses based upon reported profits, reported sales or return on assets.

Having accounting-based contracts such as those briefly discussed above can at times provide incentives for managers to use accounting methods that are income-increasing or asset-increasing. For example, research shows that where an organisation is close to breaching an agreed debt covenant, such that the debts to asset ratio must not exceed 60 per cent, then managers often will inflate the value of assets beyond their real value to loosen the restriction. Research has also shown that managers who receive a bonus that is linked to accounting profits will, in conjunction with their accountants, be relatively more likely to select accounting methods that inflate profits, and therefore the size of their own bonus.

Therefore, we should factor consideration of various accounting-based contracts into our analysis if the information about the existence of accounting-based contractual arrangements is publicly available.

Also, because an organisation can potentially be wound up if it defaults on its accounting-based lending agreements, knowledge of such agreements is useful in assessing the future of the organisation. For example, if we know that an organisation has negotiated an agreement that its debt to assets ratio must be kept at or below 60 per cent, and if the latest balance sheet shows that the ratio is 59 per cent, then we might be concerned that if more debt is taken on in the next financial period (or if reported assets decline), then the negotiated requirement will be breached and the organisation might be required to pay back significant amounts of funding, which could lead to its demise.

Auditors should certainly make efforts to be aware of the accounting-based contracts in place (see **Learning exercise 12.7**), as this will provide a possible indication of when management might have been motivated to manipulate the financial accounting numbers that the auditors are auditing – for example, the possibility of manipulation might be higher in those situations where the organisation appears to be close to breaching the debt covenants.

Research evidence does actually indicate that organisations that are close to breaching accounting-based debt contracts are indeed more likely to opportunistically adopt:

- accounting methods that are asset increasing, and
- accounting methods that are income increasing.

Action that is taken to generate financial statements that are more favourable to management is often referred to as 'creative accounting' – something that we have discussed previously within this book. The point to be made here is that, because of the way in which accounting numbers are used within society and in various contractual arrangements, we need to accept that they will not always be prepared objectively; that is, they might not always be 'representationally faithful'. To assume otherwise is – as we have emphasised many times – naive. It is always sensible to have an element of healthy scepticism when reviewing the reports prepared by managers.

12.7 Learning Exercise

Importance of knowing about the accounting-based contracts that an organisation has negotiated

Scenario: Kirra Company is an organisation that produces sailboards for sale within Australia as well as for export to various other countries. The organisation has negotiated a number of accounting-based contracts including the following:

- The senior managers of Kirra Company receive a bonus that is 2 per cent of reported profits. They also receive a bonus linked to reported sales. Other than these bonuses, they receive a fixed salary as well.
- The company borrowed $50 million from Burleigh Bank for a period of five years. To reduce the risk to Burleigh Bank, and to enable the company to pay a lower rate of interest, the company's managers contractually agreed to restrict the company's total debts to no more than 50 per cent of total reported assets. If the company breaches this agreement, then Burleigh Bank is entitled to demand immediate repayment of the total amount loaned to the company.

Issue: Would knowledge of these accounting-based contractual arrangements be of relevance to a financial statement analyst and an auditor of the company's financial statements? Why?

Solution: Knowledge of these accounting-based contractual arrangements would be of relevance to somebody undertaking financial statement analysis, as well as to the auditors. When determining the importance of this information, consider the following.

Bonus plans

Information about the bonus plans negotiated with managers signifies those aspects of performance that seem to be prioritised by the organisation. It also provides a warning that there could be some incentive for managers to manipulate the sales revenue and the profits of the organisation so as to receive a greater bonus. This should be taken into consideration by both analysts and auditors. The absence of any bonuses linked to social and environmental performance could also signal that the organisation prioritises financial performance well above social and environmental performance. In the long run, this might not be in the interests of the owners of the organisation, or society in general and it may act to increase the risks of the organisation.

Accounting-based debt covenants

It is also useful for analysts and auditors to know about the accounting-based debt covenants that have been negotiated between the organisation and its lenders. If the organisation is close to breaching this debt covenant, then it is possible that managers might have an incentive to make accounting policy choices that inflate assets or reduce liabilities, thereby easing the threat of the debt covenant being breached. Hence, if an organisation is close to breaching these covenants, an auditor might increase the amount of audit testing done in relation to these numbers so as to be more confident that the numbers have not been manipulated. From a financial analyst's perspective, the higher the debt to asset ratio gets, the greater the financial risks associated with investing in the organisation.

Why do I need to know about the accounting-based debt contracts that the organisation has negotiated?

The survival of an organisation can be jeopardised if it fails to comply with accounting-based debt contracts. For example, to attract funds, an organisation might agree to keep its debt to assets ratio below a certain percentage. If that percentage is exceeded, then the organisation would be in 'technical default' which could mean that the organisation will need to immediately repay the borrowed funds. This could have implications for the survival of the organisation. Also, as an organisation approaches a point at which they are close to breaching accounting-based debt contracts, we should be aware that this may encourage managers to opportunistically use accounting methods that increase reported assets and/or increase reported profits through various forms of 'creative accounting'. As such, we should ideally know about the various accounting-based contractual arrangements that the organisation has negotiated as it will help us more fully understand the consequences that might arise when particular financial accounting numbers are reported.

LO12.6 Further reflections on assets

As we emphasised in Chapter 9, reported total assets – a fairly central number for financial accounting purposes (and which equals the total of liabilities and equity) – does not represent the fair value of all the assets, or the cost or replacement value of them. Instead, it is a mixture of different measurement approaches applied to certain assets that are permitted to be recognised by an organisation. Therefore, the number 'total assets' needs to be reviewed/used with much care.

As we should also appreciate, total assets as it appears within the balance sheet does not include many valuable assets. For example, most internally generated intangible assets – which might have great value – are not recognised within financial accounting (because accounting standards prohibit their recognition) and hence do not appear on the balance sheet. Financial statement analysts need to factor this into the analysis.

Also, many other key resources of the organisation – such as its labour force, key intellectual capital, valuable customer and supplier networks, and so forth – are not reported on the balance sheet. Therefore, the total resources of the organisation, and its reported total assets – as determined by the financial accountants – can be quite different.

So we need to be careful with how we use financial accounting statements such as balance sheets when undertaking financial statement analysis – many valuable resources are not there, or if they are there, they might be reported at a historical cost that is quite different to their fair value. Therefore, we often need to supplement our financial statement analysis with other information, such as information about valuable resources controlled by the organisation that are significant to future performance, but which do not appear within the financial statements. Financial statements, somewhat obviously, are just one source of information about an organisation and its operating environment – a source that, while useful, does have several limitations.

The discussion in this chapter has so far focused on analysing reports that provide information about the financial performance and position of an organisation. We will now turn our attention to analysing external reports that address important issues in relation to the social and environmental performance of organisations. As we know, for an organisation to survive in the longer run, it is becoming accepted that it must consider not only its financial performance but must also demonstrate *responsibility* and *accountability* in relation to its social and environmental performance.

LO12.7 Analysing social and environmental (sustainability) reports

As you would, or should, appreciate by now, the practice of financial reporting is highly regulated, particularly as it relates to medium-sized and larger organisations. Financial reporting requirements are included with accounting standards, corporations law, and securities exchange criteria – and these requirements are extensive.

By contrast, and as explained in Chapter 6, the preparation of publicly available social and environmental (also called sustainability, or corporate social responsibility or CSR) reports is predominantly unregulated. That is, although larger organisations are required to report various types of social and environmental information to government (for example, about emissions of greenhouse gases, releases of particular toxic chemicals, or information about workplace injuries), and some of these disclosures will then be publicly reported on government websites, the decision by managers for their organisation to publicly report sustainability-related information is predominantly voluntary. This means that managers have many choices about to whom to disclose social and environmental performance information, what information to disclose, how to disclose it, and where to disclose it. This all leads to much variability in social and environmental reporting practice. As such, and given the voluntary nature of the reporting, when reviewing a sustainability report, it is important to try to understand:

- why management has prepared the report (that is, what is the motivation for reporting)
- why they have decided to disclose the particular social and environmental information that they have disclosed, whilst electing to not disclose other information
- to which stakeholders the disclosures seem to be directed.

There is a multitude of social and environmental impacts that could potentially be reported by managers, so it is important to a social and environmental report user/analyst that they be given sufficient information to enable them to understand why particular information has been selected by managers for disclosure.

It is also useful to be informed by managers about why particular reporting and measurement frameworks were selected from the various options available to management. For example, if the organisation has used the Global Reporting Initiative's sustainability reporting framework (which was discussed in depth in Chapter 6), then an explanation should be provided about why that framework was considered by managers to be the most appropriate framework. A reader of the report should also consider whether the reporting framework appears to have been used objectively, or if it appears that managers have decided only to disclose those items within the framework that project a favourable image of the organisation.

Again, it needs to be remembered that such considerations are not generally relevant when reviewing financial disclosures, as most of the disclosures within financial statements are mandated. That is, the management of larger organisations does not have a great deal of choice in respect of many aspects of financial disclosure, although they do have some choice in how they measure particular assets and liabilities. However, they have much choice in respect of social and environmental disclosures.

Sustainability-related information can be reported in various documents/reports. For example, sustainability-related information might be reported in separate sustainability/CSR reports. However, many organisations are now choosing to disclose much of their sustainability-related information in their annual reports, along with the financial statements and supporting notes (meaning that for these organisations, their annual reports can be up to 300 pages in length).

Therefore, there is a mixture of media being used to report sustainability-related information. When analysing a sustainability report, a corporate social responsibility report, or the sustainability-related disclosures included within the annual report, it is also important for the reader/analyst to understand the context of the organisation. For example, information about the locations of the organisation's operations, the key social and environmental characteristics or attributes of these locations, the key stakeholders in those environments, the significant social and environmental impacts created by the organisation, and so forth, are all relevant in trying to understand why an organisation is voluntarily reporting particular social and environmental performance information.

Once we have some background information – or context – regarding the organisation, and the social and environmental risks and opportunities associated with its operations, then we are in a better position to determine whether the report addresses our information needs. In many instances, we might need to look beyond the organisation's reports and review other publicly available information as well. Such information might come from news reports, government reports (for example, governments may collect and make publicly available certain information about organisations' emissions and non-compliance with environmental laws), and reports of various non-government organisations (such as reports released by various environmental groups, or groups established to safeguard the health and safety of workers).

Why has the sustainability-related information been reported?

As we have already stressed, because the public disclosure of various aspects of an organisation's social and environmental performance is predominantly voluntary, it makes sense for a reader/analyst of organisational social and environmental reports to reflect on why the managers of the organisation have decided to report the information.

Due to the predominantly voluntary nature of social and environmental reporting, many accounting researchers have explored the question of *why* managers elect to voluntarily report social and environmental performance information. We addressed this issue in depth in Chapter 6, but in summary, a lot of the research has shown that organisational social and environmental disclosure has tended to:

- highlight the positive aspects of an organisation's social and environmental performance whilst downplaying the negative aspects
- be particularly responsive to 'legitimacy threatening' events; for example, when an organisation is linked to a particular social or environmental crisis/catastrophe, it has been common to find firms responding by making disclosures that highlight positive aspects of their performance as well as the introduction of governance policies that will address such crises in the future
- be used as a means of managing powerful stakeholders whilst neglecting the information needs of less powerful stakeholders. For example, if an organisation is particularly dependent on certain customers, then managers will typically ensure that the organisation is reporting the information such stakeholders want/need. By contrast, research has shown that if there is no interest from powerful stakeholders in respect of particular aspects of an organisation's social and environmental performance, then managers of that organisation are less likely to produce an account of that performance. That is, research has shown that, without pressure being exerted by powerful stakeholders, managers are less likely to be accountable for their actions.

The evidence clearly seems to show that we all need to be careful when reviewing/analysing such voluntarily prepared reports. We also need to place each report within the context of the events occurring around that point in time, and also within the context of changing stakeholder expectations.

The evidence to date suggests that much social and environmental disclosure appears to be motivated by profitability and the survival considerations of managers, rather than being reflective of management accepting accountability for their social and environmental performance. Hence, we must not be naive and necessarily believe/trust everything we read!

Key concept

The motivations driving managers to voluntarily disclose particular information should be considered before relying upon that information.

The organisational context

As already emphasised, to understand whether an organisation is performing well from a social or environmental perspective, we need to know something about the environment in which it is operating. That is, we need to be able to understand the social and environmental context of an organisation before we can give meaning to the social and environmental performance information being disclosed.

Therefore, well-prepared social and environmental information will be clear about the context of the organisation. Interested stakeholders must also undertake their own research to understand organisational context and associated risks. For example, management should be very clear within their social and environmental disclosures about the following issues.

Business and market environment

To understand the pressures being exerted on the organisation, as well as related risks and opportunities, the report should be clear about the business and market environments within which the organisation operates, and recent changes in such environments.

Is the organisation operating within an area of important biodiversity?

Biodiversity refers to the different plants, animals and micro-organisms that exist within a particular area. If an organisation is operating in an area of important biodiversity, then managers need to be even more responsible and accountable when it comes to not releasing substances, or causing damage, that could impact that area. Report readers/analysts should be given information about the particular risks that the organisation creates by being there, and how these risks are being monitored and managed. This is not only important from an accountability perspective, but with rising concern within the community about the environment, any organisation that creates significant impacts in important areas of biodiversity can expect to suffer financially as various stakeholders elect to cease transacting with the organisation.

Is the organisation operating within an area that is close to, or above, important water sources?

As we have emphasised, managers should be clear about where their operations are located and what risks the organisation creates to the environment by operating there. If operations are near important aquifers, then a reader/reviewer of a report should want to know what efforts are being made to ensure that important water sources are not being contaminated.

Organisations often provide information about their water use, and water-saving measures, without contextualising this. So why is the information disclosed? If the organisation is operating in very high rainfall areas, is this information really relevant? By contrast, if the organisation is operating in low water supply environments, then it might be very important (consider the case of Coca-Cola as described in Chapter 4, wherein the company was expected to be very accountable for its water use given the low water supplies available to villagers in areas where Coca-Cola was producing its soft drinks). Again, as a reader of a report, we need to be able to understand the context regarding measures such as water usage. Managers need to be clear about why they are, or are not, providing information about water consumption. Similar comments could also be made about other scarce resources that are being consumed by an organisation.

Is the organisation operating in an industry with many unskilled or 'low power' employees?

It is often the case that unskilled workers work in environments that are dangerous to their health and safety. For example, in many developing countries, goods can be produced at low costs because of the absence of many health and safety controls. So again, we need to know about context. If an organisation is relying on the use of unskilled labour, is the health and safety of workers being properly attended to and being accounted for by managers? If not, why not? An important issue to address would be the risks that modern slavery exists within the supply chains of the organisation, and what is being done to reduce those risks (we discussed modern slavery in Chapter 6). An absence of disclosure indicates a lack of accountability for people in the supply chain. Poor accountability can lead to high levels of criticism of an organisation – and potentially large-scale consumer boycotts, with direct implications for profitability.

Is the organisation operating within a carbon-intensive industry?

As described in Chapter 6, climate change is a major risk confronting both the planet and business organisations. Organisations with high carbon emissions arguably should be accountable for this; however, if emissions are very small, we might question the relative importance of the disclosure (again, because organisations have many social and environmental impacts, some prioritisation of these impacts is necessary). Further, with various initiatives being implemented around the world, carbon-intensive manufacturers will be at higher risk in terms of being a 'going concern' – so for larger carbon-intensive operations, we particularly need to know what they are doing to address the issue.

Is the organisation operating in a dangerous industry?

Some industries – for example, mining and construction – are more dangerous than others. For organisations involved in these industries, it might be particularly important to note the relevant governance practices as they pertain to health and safety. An absence of relevant disclosures might indicate that an organisation does not accept a responsibility, and associated accountability, for ensuring safe work practices.

Does the organisation source animal-based products?

Different countries have different standards for animal welfare. If we know that an organisation is sourcing animal products from different countries, and if we are concerned about the welfare of animals, then we should review the report to see what information, if any, is provided in relation to protecting the welfare of animals. Failure to be accountable for the proper treatment of animals, whilst simply being morally wrong, also exposes the organisation to many associated financial risks.

Many more comments and examples could be given about identifying the context of an organisation, but what is important is that a report prepared by an organisation should be very clear about why particular information has been voluntarily disclosed in preference to other information. That is, within the report, managers need to be very clear about why the information that is being disclosed is considered to be relevant to stakeholders in enabling them to assess the organisation's performance.

A summary of some issues to consider when evaluating the 'quality' of a social and environmental report

The author of this book was, for over 10 years, a member of the judging committee of a leading national sustainability reporting award. There were some specific criteria – judging criteria – that he applied when making judgements about the quality of different organisations' sustainability/CSR reports. These criteria – some of which are shown below – would also be useful to other stakeholders when analysing and evaluating the quality of the information contained within an organisation's report. If positive answers cannot be provided to many of the following questions, then the reader of an organisation's social and environmental report would be justified in deciding not to rely on the information provided within it.

Good quality sustainability reporting is important for a number of reasons. Good quality sustainability-related information – which would satisfy the qualitative characteristics of useful information that we discussed in Chapter 1 (for example, useful information shall be relevant, reliable, comparable, verifiable, understandable and timely) – enables informed decision-making by stakeholders. That is, quality information provides 'power' to stakeholders to enable them to make informed decisions about whether to support an organisation, or not. Ideally, it will be the organisations that have embraced the sustainability agenda that are supported, while those organisations acting less responsibly will receive less support – but again, stakeholders need good quality information to make such decisions. Many different classes of stakeholders will have an interest in sustainability-related information. In the previous sections of this chapter, we considered tools that stakeholders, particularly investors and financial analysts, might use to assess financial reporting information. Investors and analysts will also have an interest in sustainability-related information as poor social and environmental performance will expose an organisation to various risks, many of which will translate into negative implications for financial performance. As we have emphasised at various points in this book, the 'success' of an organisation needs to be evaluated from both a financial and a sustainability-related perspective.

Apart from satisfying the information needs of external stakeholders, good quality information also allows for better management internally of social and environmental impacts, and this provides benefits for all stakeholders. From a 'business benefits' perspective, good quality sustainability reporting also enables organisations to enhance their reputation and perceived trustworthiness. Good quality reporting also helps organisations to identify strategic priorities, to demonstrate how these strategic priorities have been incorporated within organisational plans, and to highlight areas where change or improvement is needed.

Some criteria used to assess the quality of a sustainability report – and therefore the amount of reliance that can be placed on the sustainability-related information – would include the following:

1 Is the report clear about context? We have dealt with this issue in some depth above, so hopefully the importance of explaining organisational context is now clear. Without clear context, many items of social and environmental performance information can be relatively meaningless. (See **Learning exercise 12.8**.)
2 Does the report provide information about the social and environmental impacts we believe *should* be addressed by the organisation? That is, does the report provide us with information to enable us to assess whether the organisation has acted responsibly in terms of what we consider to be the responsibilities of an organisation in that particular industry? Further, is the report clear about how managers identified the major social and environmental impacts?
3 How are the key stakeholders of the organisation identified, and which stakeholders were consulted in the development of the report? Further, were stakeholders consulted when the key social and environmental impacts of the organisation, and the related information to be disclosed, were determined or identified? That is, does the report provide clear information about the 'materiality determination process' (which we discussed within Chapter 6)?
4 Is the report clear about how the concept of sustainability is interpreted by the organisation, and how it is incorporated within the overall organisation strategies? What is the organisation's 'sustainability vision' (which would represent the relationship between the core activities of the organisation and 'sustainability')? How is sustainability incorporated within organisational strategies?
5 Is the report clear about the risks and opportunities, and 'tensions', that sustainability creates for, and within, the organisation? Is it clear about how the risks and opportunities are identified and what actions are in place to mitigate the risks and maximise the opportunities?
6 While Criterion 5 above addresses sustainability-related risks and opportunities generally, is clear information specifically provided about what has been done to identify the risks that modern slavery exists across the organisation's supply chains (modern slavery was discussed in Chapter 6) and what has been done to reduce these risks?
7 Does the organisation specifically provide information about the risks and opportunities that climate change poses to the organisation (we addressed climate change in Chapter 6), together with a clear description of actions take to reduce these risks and maximise these opportunities?
8 Is the target audience of the report clearly identified within the report? The report should show signs of being tailored to meet the information needs of identified stakeholders and should be clear about how the choice of particular measurement or reporting frameworks links to these identified audiences. For example, if investors are identified as the key audience of the report, then this would explain why an organisation might elect to adopt the reporting guidelines developed by the ISSB or the TCFD (see Chapter 6) as both of these frameworks have been developed principally to meet the information needs of investors.
9 Is the report clear about how stakeholder engagement impacted the organisation's sustainability-related strategies?

10 Is the report clear about the reporting boundaries employed. For example, is the report clear about what segments of the organisation, or sites, are being reported upon?

11 Because loss of biodiversity is a critical problem (see Chapter 6) that warrants immediate attention by us all, does the report address the actions the organisation is taking to preserve 'at risk' areas of biodiversity?

12 Does the reported information demonstrate that managers have an awareness and understanding of the breadth and nature of the social and environmental impacts across the entire life cycle of the organisation's goods and services? As we indicated in chapters 2 and 6, it is arguably the responsibility of managers to know about the significant social and environmental impacts created by a product or service throughout its life cycle. Diagrammatic representations of the life cycle of the organisation's goods and services should be considered.

13 Why are particular reporting and measurement frameworks used, and are they appropriate and credible? That is, is the use of particular frameworks justified? Further, are the frameworks used in a comprehensive way, or are just aspects of the frameworks applied?

14 Does the report include an index – perhaps at the back of the report – linking the disclosures within the report to particular reporting standards? For example, the disclosure requirements of the GRI and ISSB (as discussed within Chapter 6) both suggest the use of an index which cross-references particular disclosures within a report with the specific requirements of the respective reporting standard.

15 Is the information being reported by the organisation balanced (or 'representationally faithful') in nature (that is, free from apparent bias)? Does it provide both favourable and unfavourable information about an organisation's social and environmental performance? A report that only provides positive information should be viewed with a greater level of scepticism.

16 Further, whilst unusual, do the reports incorporate the views of different stakeholders about the performance of the organisation, or is only management's view provided? As we have discussed elsewhere, there can be different perspectives about the nature of an organisation's social and environmental performance.

17 Is the media used for reporting the sustainability-related information tailored to meet the needs of the identified stakeholders? For example, are different languages used, are reports available in braille, and so forth?

18 How, if at all, is the incentivisation of employees linked to particular aspects of social and environmental performance or to the sustainability strategy of the organisation? Readers should be able to understand the linkage between remuneration and sustainability-related performance. As we stressed earlier in this chapter, if an organisation claims to have a central focus on social and environmental performance, but all of the bonuses paid to key personnel are linked to financial performance measures, then we would rightly question the real commitment of the organisation to society and the environment.

19 Does the report provide clear information about the organisation's vision and mission, important organisational policies/governance practices applied to manage social and environmental impacts, and how these policies are communicated and applied across the organisation? For example, is information disclosed about procurement policies or capital investment policies? Is information provided about whether, for example, the environmental manager reports directly to the board of directors, or who on the board of directors has responsibility for aspects of social and environmental performance?

20 Does the report include important social and environmental targets, and performance against past targets, together with information about implications and actions linked to not meeting targets?

21 Is the report clear about what has been learned from 'failures' and where and how improvements will be made?

22 Does the report provide benchmarks against which performance can be evaluated – perhaps benchmarks based upon 'leading edge' organisations within the same industry?

23 Does the report provide website links to more detailed information about social and environmental performance, perhaps on a site-based approach or to information provided to other organisations, such as climate related information provided to the Carbon Disclosure Project (see Chapter 6)?

24 Does the report provide clear information about compliance/non-compliance with social and environmental legislation, and information about remedial actions taken in the event of non-compliance with legislation?

25 Is the report clear about the level of independent external assurance (auditing) that has been applied to the information being reported by the organisation? Is the audit/assurance report provided to stakeholders clear about the assurance and reporting frameworks applied? What was the level of investigation undertaken – for example, did it involve site visits, and where? Is the audit/assurance report clear about any concerns the auditor/assurance provider had with respect to the information being reported by the organisation?

26 How does the information in the social and environmental report rate in terms of 'readability' and 'understandability', or does the information prepared by the organisation appear to assume some higher level of social and environmental knowledge than would reasonably be expected of most stakeholders?

27 Is the information provided in a timely manner, and does it come from all organisational sites or just some?

28 Does the report provide linkage to feedback mechanisms for interested or concerned stakeholders?

29 Is there a glossary provided within the report in which key terms are clearly defined?

How we answer the above questions will impact the perceived quality that we individually attribute to the information being produced by managers. Not all stakeholders will necessarily think that all of the above questions are important. Our own individual perceptions of the required responsibilities of an organisation will impact the accountability we expect to be embraced by the managers of that organisation. If we were trying to score the 'quality' of a sustainability report using the criteria provided above, we might decide to equally weight each item in our list, or perhaps we would weight some items more highly than others.

Why do I need to know about some criteria that can be used to assess the quality of a sustainability report?

If I am ever involved in preparing sustainability-related disclosures, then I should try to make sure that the information is considered to be of high quality. Good quality sustainability-related information enables an organisation to manage its operations more responsibly and will tend to increase stakeholder support for the organisation.

As users of sustainability-related information, we should consider whether the information is of reasonable quality before we use it as part of our decision-making processes. As such, we should apply some criteria to assess the quality of the report before we place too much reliance on the information included within the respective report.

12.8 Learning Exercise

The importance of placing context around social and environmental disclosures

Scenario: Point Danger Co is an Australian company that imports fabrics from Pakistan, Bangladesh and India, and then uses this fabric to locally produce a range of T-shirts. The managers of Point Danger Co decide in 2026 to release their first publicly accessible social and environmental report. Within the report, disclosures are made about:

- water usage for each of the last three years
- electricity usage for the last two years
- compliance with environmental laws
- health and safety policies for employees, together with details of injuries
- training provided to employees.

Disclosures are also made about various other aspects of the social and environmental performance of the organisation.

Issue: You are required to give an opinion about whether the disclosure of the above information would be useful to somebody analysing an organisation's social and environmental report. How useful would this information be?

Solution: All of the above information would have some use, but generally speaking, a lack of information about organisational context can act to undermine the usefulness of the information. Let us look at the disclosures one at a time.

Water usage

All things being equal, it is appropriate for the organisation to try to control and minimise water usage. However, to enhance the relevance of the information to the reader of the report, the reader needs to be informed about whether the organisation is operating in an area with low, medium or high levels of water availability. Some benchmarking against other comparable organisations with respect to their water use would be useful.

Electricity usage

Information about electricity usage is important, but it would be more useful if we were provided with information about the source of the electricity. If the electricity is sourced from abundant reserves of renewable energy (for example, wind power generated onsite), then our interest in energy savings will arguably be less than if the energy is being sourced from highly polluting coal-fired power stations. Some benchmarking against other comparable organisations with respect to their energy usage would be useful.

Compliance with environmental laws

Knowledge of compliance with environmental laws is generally important to users of social and environmental reports. In many countries, it is now a mandated reporting requirement. However, because all the fabrics are being imported, we need to know more about the environmental performance across the supply chain, not just locally. For example, while we might have information about water usage and energy usage, it would be useful to know about the environmental policies of our suppliers (and their suppliers).

Health, safety, injuries, and employee training

Information about the health and safety and training of employees is also important. However, considering the context of this organisation, we would also hope that the organisation provides insights into how employees across the supply chain are treated and protected, and that the pay received for work is fair. Of particular relevance is any information about the risks that modern slavery is present across the supply chain.

LO12.8 Independent auditing of information in reports

The final issue we will now discuss is the independent (third party) reviewing/auditing of external reports. This discussion applies to all reports prepared by managers – financial reports and also social and environmental reports.

We have said many times throughout this book that we need to be careful not to believe everything we read, particularly when the information is being prepared voluntarily by managers. A theme that we have embraced is that we all need to have a healthy dose of scepticism when reading reports prepared by managers.

As a general principle, if reports are prepared by management, then there will perhaps be incentives, at times, for managers to be less than objective. Remember the idea of 'creative accounting' discussed earlier, whereby managers might use various accounting techniques to project the best picture of an organisation. Creative accounting can be applied to social, environmental and financial accounting information.

An independent expert review of a report – whether it is financial, social or environmental in focus – will tend to add credibility and 'value' to a report. Since an external audit acts to reduce the risks of external stakeholders when assessing such things as whether to invest in the organisation, loan funds to the organisation, sell on credit to the organisation, or acquire goods or services from the organisation (for example, we do not want to acquire goods and services that are associated with poor social and environmental practices/inputs) it is actually in the organisation's interest to pay for the third-party review. It adds value.

As has already been indicated, large organisations will typically be required by law to include an audit report with their annual financial statements, as presented within the organisation's annual report. The opinion provided by the auditor should influence our judgement about whether we should rely on the contents of the financial statements being released by an organisation. If the auditor provides an opinion that the financial information has *not* been compiled in accordance with accounting standards and other generally accepted accounting principles, then we might be unwise to use the information in any analysis we are doing of the organisation.

By contrast, managers are not typically required by law to have their social and environmental reports subjected to an independent third-party review. Nevertheless, many organisations – particularly larger organisations – do have their social and environmental reports audited. As explained in Chapter 6, one organisation that performs a regular survey of social and environmental reporting is the large global accounting firm KPMG. In 2020, it surveyed the reporting practices of a global sample of 5200 companies, which was made up of the top 100 companies from 52 different countries (referred to as the N100 companies). It also surveyed the reporting practices of the world's largest companies by revenue based on the Fortune 500 ranking of companies (referred to as G250 companies). KPMG (2020) report that 71 per cent of

G250 companies had their CSR reports assured (audited) by independent third parties, whilst 51 per cent of N100 companies had their CSR reports assured. Therefore, it is becoming an expectation that social and environmental reports also be subjected to an independent review/audit before they are publicly released to various stakeholders.

So something to consider when reviewing the reports produced by organisations is:

- who prepared the financial reports or the social and environmental reports (typically managers, but for some reports it might also be a public relations organisation)
- who subsequently reviewed/audited them, and what was their opinion?

When reviewing an external audit or assurance report, there are a few issues that we should consider before deciding whether we might rely on the independent third-party opinion, including the following:

- What was the purpose of the third-party review? For example, was it to check conformity with particular standards? Was it for the whole report or part thereof?
- Who is the intended audience of the audit or assurance report?
- Against what standards was the audit work undertaken, and what form of testing/risk assessment was undertaken?
- Who conducted the audit? What is their reputation? What are their relevant qualifications? If the independent review was performed by individuals who have no clear expertise, its value would be questionable.
- Does it provide a clear and unambiguous opinion about the report prepared by managers?

If the opinion provided by the auditor/assurance provider is that a report is poorly prepared – perhaps in breach of particular reporting standards and guidelines – then we might actually be wasting our time reviewing such a report prepared by managers.

Concluding comments

We have now concluded the final chapter of this book. We hope that you have enjoyed reading this book, and that various prior beliefs you held about accounting have been challenged. Hopefully, your understanding of accounting has evolved significantly. You should now understand that 'accounts' can take many forms and can address various aspects of organisational activities, and that organisational responsibility, organisational accountability, and accounting are all closely linked.

Hopefully, you also now appreciate that accounting seems to be *everywhere*, and that the practice of accounting can – perhaps surprisingly – be extremely interesting and thought-provoking, something you might not have thought possible before reading this book. We all make choices about what to consume, what resources to use when producing items, where to work, which organisations to support, where to invest, and so forth. Information is central to many of these decisions – accounting information provides us with the knowledge and *power* to make informed decisions.

Accountants generate much of the information that is used by various stakeholders to make important decisions about how or if they will interact with an organisation. Such decisions ultimately can be linked to various social and environmental impacts. As such, accountants, as providers of information, are indeed very powerful people! Indeed, accountants are arguably among the most powerful people in all of society. For those of you who go on to practise accounting, please use this power wisely and responsibly. Good luck!

STUDY TOOLS

SUMMARY

In this chapter, we explored various issues to do with the analysis and interpretation of externally available organisational reports. We emphasised that the information that external stakeholders demand and use will be influenced by the stakeholders' perceptions of the responsibilities that they believe managers within organisations should embrace.

In relation to financial statement analysis, we stressed that people performing the analysis should have some expertise in financial accounting, as otherwise they could be misled by the analysis. We noted that financial statement analysis can be done in a variety of ways, which can involve different forms of horizontal and vertical analysis. We noted that the use of financial ratios was a common approach to financial statement analysis, and we showed that these ratios can be classified as those that relate to organisational profitability, efficiency, stability (or gearing), and liquidity, as well as those that provide insights into how the share market perceives an organisation to be operating.

We stressed that, apart from looking at the financial statements, those people performing financial statement analysis should spend some time carefully reviewing the notes that accompany the statements. In this regard, we discussed the importance of reviewing those notes to the financial statements that address accounting policies, significant events occurring after the end of the reporting period, contingent liabilities, and the reward structures (bonuses) offered to senior personnel within an organisation.

We also noted that, when performing financial statement analysis, it would be useful for the analyst to have some knowledge of the various accounting-based contracts that the managers within an organisation have negotiated. When particular financial accounting numbers are used within particular contractual arrangements, and where cash flows will thereafter be influenced by those accounting numbers, then those numbers can become relatively more vulnerable to manipulation. Our discussion also stressed that there are many assets and resources that do not appear within the financial statements but which nevertheless have real value to the organisation, and therefore should be acknowledged as part of the process of evaluating the financial performance and position of the organisation.

This chapter also addressed a number of issues associated with the analysis of social and environmental reports. We again stressed that the contents of such reports are often voluntarily produced, and therefore it is wise for a reader/analyst of the reports to consider what might be motivating managers to produce the information, and whether these likely motivations might undermine the reliability that we might attribute to the reports. We noted the importance of understanding an organisation's social, environmental, economic and political context when evaluating the relevance of particular social and environmental disclosures. We also identified a number of reporting criteria that can be considered when assessing the quality of social and environmental disclosures. The reason for doing this was that if the disclosures are considered to be of higher quality, then we will be more justified in relying on them when performing our analysis of the social and/or environmental performance of an organisation.

We concluded the chapter by discussing the role of independent audits of the reports prepared by managers. We noted that the reliability of the information prepared by managers and their accountants will be enhanced if it has been subjected to an independent review by appropriately qualified experts.

ANSWERS TO THE OPENING QUESTIONS

At the beginning of the chapter we asked the following seven questions. As a result of reading this chapter, you should now be able to provide informed answers to these questions – ours are shown below.

1 **What is financial statement analysis?**

'Financial statement analysis' can be defined as the process of reviewing and evaluating an organisation's financial statements (which would include the income statement, balance sheet, statement of cash flows, and statement of changes in equity) and supporting notes in an endeavour to develop an understanding and appreciation of the organisation's financial performance and financial stability, and its likely future prospects, thereby enabling more-effective decisions to be made with respect to that organisation.

2 **What are financial accounting ratios?**

Financial accounting ratios incorporate a form of vertical analysis, wherein one number from a financial statement can be compared with another number from the financial statements of the same year. A financial accounting ratio represents a relationship between two quantities, normally expressed as one divided by the other – for example, a debt to equity ratio is calculated by dividing total reported liabilities by total reported equity.

3 **Accounting ratios can be separated into five broad categories. What are these categories?**

Financial accounting ratios are often divided into profitability ratios, operating efficiency ratios, financial gearing (or stability) ratios, liquidity ratios, and investment-based ratios. They enable different aspects of an organisation's financial performance and/or financial position to be investigated.

4 **In determining the liquidity of an organisation (which refers to its ability to pay its debts as, and when they fall due), which financial accounting ratios are particularly relevant?**

In exploring the liquidity of an organisation, it is common for analysts of financial statements to consider the current ratio, the quick ratio, the interest coverage ratio, and the ratio of cash flows from operating activities to current liabilities.

5 **When performing financial statements analysis, should we also carefully review the notes accompanying those financial statements?**

Yes, we should. The notes that accompany the financial statements provide a great deal of important information that can help to both place the numbers appearing in the financial statements into context (for example, information will be provided about how assets are measured) and provide data that are not found within the financial statements; for example, information about contingent liabilities, or about significant events occurring between the end of the reporting period and the point in time when the financial statements are authorised for issue to shareholders, and other interested stakeholders.

6 **When reviewing an organisation's social and environmental accounts, is it important to be aware of the social and environmental context of an organisation? Why?**

It is very important to be aware of the social and environmental context of an organisation. We need to know about the attributes of the particular societies and environments in which the organisation is operating in order to give proper meaning to the disclosures being made. Some environments are more vulnerable in particular respects than others. For example, if an organisation is operating in an important area of biodiversity, then information about its actual emissions, and its policies to control emissions, might be particularly important. If water is scarce in particular areas, then information about water use, and water use policies, might have particular relevance.

7 **If you were asked to assess the 'quality' of an organisation's social and environmental disclosures, what are four criteria that you might apply?**

Factors to consider in assessing whether a report is of higher quality could include the following:

- Does the report provide clear information about the social and environmental context within which the organisation is operating?
- Does the organisation provide information about the various impacts of its products or services across their life cycles?
- Is the report clear about what reporting frameworks have been used, and why?
- Is the report clear about what 'sustainability' means from the perspective of the managers of the organisation, and the risks and opportunities that an increased community focus on sustainability creates for the organisation?

SELF-TEST QUIZ

Answers to this quiz appear in the Appendix of this book.

The following balance sheet will be used for Questions 1 to 4.

Balance sheet for Coogee Company
as at 30 June 2026

	2026 $000	2025 $000
Current assets		
Cash	800	600
Accounts receivable	1050	400
Inventory	150	300
	2000	1300
Non-current assets		
Land	3000	2000
Buildings	2500	2500
Accumulated depreciation – buildings	(500)	(400)
Plant and equipment	1900	1600
Accumulated depreciation – plant and equipment	(300)	(200)
	6600	5500
Total assets	8600	6800
Current liabilities		
Accounts payable	400	300
Accrued expenses	140	200
Income tax payable	460	300
	1000	800

	2026 $000	2025 $000
Non-current liabilities		
Long-term loans	4000	4000
Total liabilities	5000	4800
Net assets	3600	2000
Owners' equity (Shareholders' funds)		
Share capital	1800	1800
Retained earnings	1800	200
Total shareholders' funds	3600	2000

1 What is the debt to assets ratio?

a 55% b 58% c 65% d 70% e 72%

2 What is the current ratio?

a 1.5 times b 2 times c 2.5 times d 3 times e 3.5 times

3 What is the quick ratio?

a 1.6 b 1.8 c 1.85 d 1.9 e 2.0

4 On the basis of the three ratios just calculated, would the organisation be considered to be of high risk of not being able to pay its debts as and when they fall due?

a Yes b No

5 If you were assessing the quality of the sustainability-related information being produced by an organisation, which of the following would be important?

a The sustainability-related information being provided is clear about the social and environmental context within which the organisation is operating.

b The sustainability-related information addresses the types of social and environmental impacts that you believe are likely to be created by such an organisation.

c The sustainability-related information provides information about the sustainability-related performance indicators used to provide bonuses to the managers.

d The sustainability-related information provides information about the risks and opportunities that climate change poses for the organisation.

e All of these choices.

ONLINE RESOURCES

Accompanying the book is an innovative online case study that follows an organisation initially established by two friends, which grows into a large and successful company. Acquire this chapter's case study from your instructor.

CASE STUDY

Armadillo Surf Designs: Branching out

Armadillo Surf Designs (ASD) is keen to invest in a company that has established itself in the female surfing market. It is considering an investment in one such company, named Sea Salt Surf Ltd. Archer, Maddie and Dillon have requested a meeting with you to discuss this potential investment.

You will prepare a report on the profitability and efficiency of Sea Salt Surf Ltd and will consider the debt covenants and change in the accounting policy undertaken by this company. You will also analyse the sustainability report of Sea Salt Surf Ltd and will assist the directors to better understand whether the value of a company will or will not be equal to its net assets.

END-OF-CHAPTER QUESTIONS

12.1 What is financial statement analysis and what is its role?

12.2 What are some general ways in which we can perform financial statement analysis?

12.3 Who would, or should, perform financial statement analysis?

12.4 What is horizontal analysis and what is vertical analysis as they pertain to financial statement analysis?

12.5 Should we read the auditor's report before or after performing financial statement analysis?

12.6 Of what relevance to financial statement analysis is knowledge of the accounting policies being used by an organisation?

12.7 What is a financial accounting ratio?

12.8 You are comparing the financial position and financial performance of two similar organisations. One organisation measures its non-current assets at fair value, while the other organisation uses cost. What implications does this have for your financial statement analysis?

12.9 Why might a large number calculated for the current ratio not necessarily represent good news?

12.10 What would a high price earnings ratio indicate?

12.11 What financial accounting ratio would be useful in assessing the ability of an organisation to pay its debts over the next 2–3 months?

12.12 Why can it be argued that an organisation that is financed relatively more from debt funds (external sources) is riskier than an organisation that is relatively more highly funded by equity capital?

12.13 What is a 'significant event that occurs after the end of the reporting period', and why should a financial statement analyst want to know about such an event?

12.14 Should financial statement analysis include a consideration of the contingent liabilities of an organisation? Why?

12.15 Why would senior managers of an organisation be provided with performance-related bonuses, and what implications does the existence of such bonuses have for people who undertake financial statement analysis?

12.16 Could the existence of particular accounting-based bonus plans provide an incentive for managers to manipulate accounting numbers? Why, and is the possibility of such manipulation of relevance to financial statement analysts?

12.17 Why would an organisation's managers agree to the inclusion of an accounting-based debt covenant within a debt contract negotiated with lenders?

12.18 Organisations that borrow funds often negotiate debt covenants that use financial accounting numbers. Would the existence of accounting-based debt covenants be of relevance to financial statement analysts, or to the auditors of the financial statements?

12.19 When analysing the social and environmental disclosures made by an organisation, why is it important to understand the organisational context of the disclosures?

12.20 When reviewing a social and environmental report produced by an organisation, why is it important to consider the possible factors motivating managers to produce this report?

12.21 Accounting researchers have undertaken a great deal of research on the motivations driving managers to produce publicly available social and environmental performance information. Is this research relevant to people reviewing corporate social responsibility disclosures?

12.22 Identify five issues you would consider to be important in evaluating the quality of social and environmental disclosures. Why would it be important to make an assessment of the 'quality' of the information contained in a social and environmental report?

12.23 As a reader of organisational social and environmental reports, would you expect an organisation that imports goods from a developing country to provide information about the social and environmental performance of key suppliers within its supply chain? Would a failure to provide such information undermine your perceptions of the quality of the report?

12.24 If an organisation makes a public claim that caring for the environment and communities in which it operates is a fundamental aspect of its operations, but you find that senior managers receive performance-based bonuses that are solely linked to the organisation's financial performance, would this be a matter that would concern you? Why?

12.25 If you were analysing the sustainability-related information produced by an organisation, why could it be particularly important to you that the organisation discloses information about:

i the risks that modern slavery is present within its supply chains, and what is being done to reduce those risks?

ii the risks and opportunities that climate change poses to the organisation and what the organisation is doing to reduce those risks and to respond to the opportunities?

The following information is required for end-of-chapter questions 12.26–12.30.

Income statement for Maroubra Company
for the year ended 30 June 2026

	2026 $000		2025 $000	
Income				
Sales		4000		3100
Expenses				
Cost of goods sold	1100		950	
Depreciation – buildings	40		40	
Depreciation – plant and equipment	50		50	
Electricity and rates	30		25	
Interest expense	50		45	
Rental expenses	70		60	
Salaries	300	(1640)	250	(1420)
Profit before tax		2360		1680
Tax		(700)		(500)
Profit		**1660**		**1180**

Balance sheet for Maroubra Company
as at 30 June 2026

	2026 $000	2025 $000
Current assets		
Cash	400	280
Accounts receivable	450	400
Inventory	310	320
	1160	1000
Non-current assets		
Land	2900	2900
Buildings	2300	2300
Accumulated depreciation – buildings	(200)	(160)
Plant and equipment	1900	1900
Accumulated depreciation – plant and equipment	(150)	(100)
	6750	6840
Total assets	**7910**	**7840**

	2026 $000	2025 $000
Current liabilities		
Accounts payable	200	500
Accrued expenses	40	200
Income tax payable	700	500
	940	1200
Non-current liabilities		
Long-term loans	3400	3540
Total liabilities	**4340**	**4740**
Net assets	**3570**	**3100**
Owners' equity (Shareholders' funds)		
Share capital	3000	3000
Retained earnings	570	100
Total shareholders' funds	**3570**	**3100**

Statement of cash flows for Maroubra Company
for the year ended 30 June 2026

	$000
Cash flows from operating activities	
Receipts from customers	3950
Payments to suppliers of goods and services, inclusive of labour	(1950)
Interest paid	(50)
Income taxes paid	(500)
Net cash provided from operating activities	**1450**
Cash flows from investing activities	
Payment for property, plant and equipment	0
Cash flows from financing activities	
Repayment of borrowings	(140)
Dividends paid	(1190)
Net cash provided from financing activities	**(1330)**
Net increase in cash held	**120**
Cash at the beginning of the financial year	280
Cash at the end of the financial year	400

Other information:

- *All sales of Maroubra Company are made on credit terms.*
- *The share capital of Maroubra Company is comprised of 1500000 shares of $2 each and has not changed throughout the year.*
- *The latest market price of the company's shares is $31.20.*

12.26 You are required to calculate the following ratios for Maroubra Company for the year ended 30 June 2026:
- return on assets
- adjusted return on assets based upon earnings before interest and taxes (EBIT)
- return on owners' equity
- profit ratio
- gross profit ratio.

You are also required to give an opinion about whether the organisation is performing well.

12.27 You are required to calculate the following ratios for Maroubra Company for the year ended 30 June 2026:
- inventory turnover
- debtors' turnover
- operating cash flow margin.

You are also required to give an opinion on whether the organisation is performing efficiently.

12.28 You are required to calculate the following ratios for Maroubra Company for the year ended 30 June 2026:
- debt to assets ratio
- debt to equity ratio.

You are also required to comment on the apparent 'riskiness' of the organisation.

12.29 You are required to calculate the following ratios for Maroubra Company for the year ended 30 June 2026:
- current ratio
- quick ratio
- interest coverage ratio
- cash flows from operating activities to current liabilities ratio.

You are also required to make an assessment of the liquidity of the organisation.

12.30 You are required to calculate the following ratios for Maroubra Company for the year ended 30 June 2026:
- dividends per share
- dividend yield
- earnings per share
- price earnings ratio.

You are also required to provide some comments about what you think the ratios indicate.

REFERENCES

BHP (2021). *Annual report 2021: The future is clear.* https://www.bhp.com/-/media/documents/investors/annual-reports/2021/210914_bhpannualreport2021.pdf?sc_lang=en&hash=15F0B58BC27ADFA860F0BE29B61E199D

International Accounting Standards Board (2022). IAS 1: Presentation of Financial Statements. www.ifrs.org/issued-standards/list-of-standards/ias-1-presentation-of-financial-statements

KPMG (2020). *The time has come: The KPMG survey of corporate responsibility reporting 2020.* https://assets.kpmg/content/dam/kpmg/xx/pdf/2020/11/the-time-has-come.pdf

Qantas (2021). *Annual Report 2021.* https://investor.qantas.com/FormBuilder/_Resource/_module/doLLG5ufYkCyEPjF1tpgyw/file/annual-reports/2021-Annual-Report.pdf

Appendix: Answers to self-text quizzes

CHAPTER 1

1 d

As the chapter explains, the sequence of the four-step accountability model is: why report?; to whom to report?; what to report?; How to report? It is very important that you understand the logic behind this sequence.

2 b

As the chapter explains, for any information to be useful it needs to be both relevant and reliable. These are considered as the two most important, or fundamental qualitative characteristics of useful information. To further increase the relevance and reliability of information, there are certain enhancing qualitative characteristics (comparability, verifiability understandability, and timeliness).

3 b

To enhance the relevance and reliability of information, accountants should strive to make sure the information being produced is comparable, verifiable, understandable, and timely.

4 e

As the chapter explains, all of these answers are correct.

5 b

All of these answers are correct as options a, c, d, and e can all be considered to be examples of the stakeholders of an organisation. However, in terms of a definition, answer b is the best. The definition emphasises that stakeholders can be perceived as those individuals or groups with power to impact an organisation, as well as those groups or individuals who are likely without power but will be impacted by the organisation.

CHAPTER 2

1 e

How far an organisation's managers extend the reporting boundary will be influenced by judgements by the managers in respect of to whom they believe they owe a responsibility, and for what aspects of performance they are responsible. Managers will typically report much information voluntarily – that is, they will go beyond their legal requirements. The broader the accepted responsibilities, the broader the reporting boundary. Typically, larger organisations have broader reporting boundaries because larger organisations tend to have greater numbers of stakeholders and more significant social and environmental impacts.

2 a

The use of many resources, particularly those that are freely available, are often ignored for accounting and reporting purposes. Because of the way 'assets' are defined – with the reliance on 'control' – many resources used by an organisation are not recognised such that their use is not recognised as an 'expense' by the organisation and not reflected in reported profits. Organisations that produce sustainability reports will often provide information about their use of non-controlled resources and will often refer to these are 'costs' created by the organisation even though they might not attempt to place a financial cost on such costs. For example, a 'cost' of particular operations might include the related carbon emissions, water usage, or damage to particular areas of important biodiversity.

3 e

Larger organisations are required by law to produce financial statements. They also often voluntarily produce social and environmental performance information, including information about recycling initiatives employed, and what happens to their goods at the end of their useful life. Because not-for-profit organisations have different responsibilities to for-profit organisations, the accounts they generate will tend to be different and will tend to have a greater focus on the social and/or environmental outcomes related to their organisation's mission and objectives.

4 e

As the chapter indicates, partnerships include all of the attributes listed within the question.

5 e

Larger organisations often report information about various aspects of their financial, social and environmental performance, including all those items listed within the question.

CHAPTER 3

1 e

All these answers are true. Management accounting is not regulated like financial accounting and the types of management accounting undertaken will be related to an organisation's mission. For example, if the mission required that the organisation produce goods and services for minimal environmental impact, then the management accounts would include various measures relating to the environment (perhaps water use, greenhouse gas emissions, wastes). Many stakeholders would have an interest in the information that managers are using to manage the organisation however the organisation would typically not release all of its information because of various competitive and legal concerns.

2 c

The contribution margin per unit is equal to
the sales price per unit – variable cost per unit
= $40 – $24 = 16.

3 c

The break-even point is the point where the fixed costs are matched by the total contribution generated by the shirts. That is, the break-even point occurs when the profit is $0.
Break-even point = total fixed costs ÷ contribution margin per unit
= $160 000 ÷ $16 = 10 000 units.

4 d

The number of units needed to be sold to generate a specific profit equals:
(desired profit + total fixed costs) ÷ contribution margin per unit
= ($120 000 + $160 000) ÷ $16
= 17 500 units.

5 b

The margin of safety is the amount of sales expected to be made above the break-even point, and it represents the number of units of sales that could be lost before the organisation makes a loss.
Margin of safety = expected sales – break even number of sales
= 14 000 units – 10 000 units = 4000 units.

CHAPTER 4

1 c

The amount of boardshorts to be produced in the first three months is 16,000 units. To determine this, we needed to compile a sales budget and then a production budget as follows.

Bay of Fires Company Sales Budget for first three months of operations	
	Q1
Target sales	15 000
Selling price	$110
Budgeted sales revenue	$1 650 000

Bay of Fires Company Production Budget for first three months of operations	
	Q1
Target sales in units (from sales budget)	15 000
Add: required closing inventory	1000
Subtract: opening inventory	0
Required production in units	**16 000**

2 b

The amount of fabric to be acquired will be determined by compiling a direct materials budget. The amount required in the first three months is 16 400 metres at a total cost of $328 000.

Bay of Fires Company Direct Materials Budget for first three months of operations	
	Q1
Units to be produced (from the production budget)	16 000
Material cost per boardshort (1.0 metre × $20)	$20
Cost of material required for production	$320 000
Add: target closing inventory of material (400 metres × $20)	$8 000
Total materials required	$328 000
Subtract: opening inventory of materials	$0
Total cost of direct materials purchases	**$328 000**

3 c

To determine the total required labour hours and associated labour cost we need to prepare a direct labour budget. It shows that 16 000 hours are needed at a total cost of $480 000.

Bay of Fires Company Direct Labour Budget for first three months of operations	
	Q1
Units to be produced (from the production budget)	16 000
Labour time per sunhat (in hours)	1
Total hours required	16 000
Labour cost per hour	$30
Total direct labour cost	$480 000

4 a

To determine the amount of cash to be collected from customers in the first three months of operations we need to use information from the Sales Budget and then work out the expected cash receipts based on predictions of the time debtors take to pay amounts due. We are told that the expectation is that debtors will pay 90% of the amount due in the three months of the sales, with the balance being paid in the following quarter. Therefore, $1 485 000 will be collected from customers in the first quarter of operations.

Expected cash receipts from customers for Bay of Fires Company for first three months of operations		
	Q1	Q2
Opening debtors	$0	
First quarter target sales: $1650 000 x 90%	$1485 000	$165 000
Cash collected from customers	**$1485 000**	**$165 000**

5 a

To determine the expected closing balance of cash at the end of the first three months of operation we need to produce a cash budget. However, before we can do this, we also need to compile the manufacturing overhead budget and the selling and administrative overhead expense budget as these both impact cashflows. This highlights how the various budgets link together within a master budget. We find that the closing cash balance after three months of operations will be $219 600.

Bay of Fires Company Cash Budget for first three months of operations	
	Q1
Cash flows from operating activities	
Cash receipts	
From sales (90% collected in quarter of sale)	$1485 000
Deduct payments	
Direct materials (75% paid of $328 000)	$246 000
Direct labour (we are told that it is paid as incurred)	$480 000
Manufacturing overhead expenses (we are told that it is paid as incurred)	$141 400
Selling and administrative overhead expenses (we are told that it is paid as incurred)	$119 000
Total payments	$986 400
Net cash flows from operating activities	**$498 600**
Cash flows from investing activities	
Invest in new machine	(120 000)
Net cash flows from investing activities	**(120 000)**
Cash flows from financing activities	
Repayment of loan	(60 000)
Payment to owners	($100 000)
Net cash flows from financing activities	**($160 000)**
Net cash flows for the quarter	**$218 600**
Opening cash for the quarter	**$10 000**
Expected closing balance of cash	**$219 600**

While not required for this question, there would also be an expectation that a budgeted income statement and a budgeted balance sheet would also be compiled. Management would need to assess whether the projected profit would be sufficient for the efforts undertaken, and the risks incurred. They would also need to determine whether the closing balance of cash of $219 600 is excessive and whether the cash should be diverted to more productive uses.

CHAPTER 5

1 b

We have assumed that the income and expenses remain the same each year and that the expenses and cashflows occur in the same period:

Income

Expected rides:	9500 x $4	$38 000
Fixed costs		
Annual insurance costs	$4000	
Annual electricity costs	$3000	
Annual maintenance contract	$6000	$13 000
Net annual cash flows		$25 000

Year	Amount to 'pay back' as at the start of the year (the residual of $1000 is expected to be received in year 5)	Net cash flows for the year	Cumulative amount paid back at the end of the year	Amount still to 'pay back' at the end of the year
1	75 000	25 000	25 000	50 000
2	50 000	25 000	50 000	25 000
3	25 000	25 000	75 000	0

The payback period of this potential investment is therefore 3 years.

2 c

We know the asset cost $75 000 and we expect it to have a residual value of $1000 in five years' time. We can calculate annual depreciation expense as

(Acquisition cost-expected residual value)/(expected useful life of asset) = ($75 000 – $1000)/5 = $14 800 per year.

The average incremental returns (profits) for the 5 years equals:

($25 000 – $14 800) + ($25 000 – $14 800) + ($25 000 – $14 800) + ($25 000 – $14 800) + ($25 000 – $14 800) + all divided by 5 = $10 200

The average investment in the machine is:

(Acquisition cost + expected residual value)/2 = ($75 000+$1000)/2 = $38 000

Therefore, the ARR = (Average annual profit from the asset)/(Average investment required to earn that profit) x 100%

= $10 200/$38 000 x 100%

= 26.84 per cent

3 d

Management has said that they want to apply an interest rate of 10 per cent to this type of investment.

Year	Cash flow (undiscounted) $	Discount factor $\frac{1}{(1+k)^n}$	Present value of cash flows $
I	(75 000)	1.00000	(75 000)
	25 000	0.90909	22 727.25
2	25 000	0.82645	20 661.25
3	25 000	0.75131	18 782.75

>>>

Year	Cash flow (undiscounted) $	Discount factor $\frac{1}{(1+k)^n}$	Present value of cash flows $
4	25 000	0.68301	17 075.25
5	26 000	0.62092	16 143.92
Total NPV			20 390.42

4 c

We need to find the rate of interest (which we depict as 'k') that makes the PV of the net cash flows equal to zero. That is, in this case:

$[25\,000 \div (1 + k)] + [25{,}000 \div (1 + k)^2] + [25\,000 \div (1 + k)^3] + [25\,000 \div (1 + k)^4] + [25\,000 \div (1 + k)^5] + [1{,}000 \div (1 + k)^5] - 75\,000 = 0$

Through trial and error we can find that the discount rate is approximately 20 per cent.

5 e

There would be various non-monetary factors to consider when making a capital investment decision, many of which might be social or environmental in nature. All of the listed factors should be considered.

CHAPTER 6

1 e

Managers will have a mixture of reasons why they might disclose social and environmental information. All of the reasons listed are possible in certain situations.

2 e

All of the reasons shown are correct. The materiality determination process is a very important process in determining what information to report. It involves engagement with various stakeholders and should ideally be disclosed within a corporate report to thereafter enable readers to understand why particular disclosures were made.

3 a

The position taken in this text is that managers do have a responsibility to reduce their organisation's contribution to climate change.

4 e

All of the answers are correct. The production of counter accounts is useful to stimulate debate amongst different stakeholders by reflecting the fact that there is more than one way of reporting and assessing organisational performance.

5 d

The results of KPMG (2020), as reported within this chapter, indicate that more than 50 per cent of the largest 100 companies from 53 countries have their sustainability-related information reviewed by independent third parties. Such audits/assurance work help to raise the credibility of the reported information as there is always the chance that the information reported by managers is biased, either intentionally or unintentionally.

CHAPTER 7

1 e

All of the answers are correct. Relevance and representation faithfulness are fundamental qualitative characteristics, and understandability and verifiability are enhancing qualitative characteristics.

2 b

All of the answers are correct except for b). An asset does not have to be legally owned for it to be recognised for financial reporting purposes. Rather, it must be 'controlled'. This means that leased assets, for example, will be eligible for asset recognition.

3 d

The expanded accounting equation is A + E + D = I + C + L. The left-hand side represents the application of funds whereas the right-hand side represents the sources of funds.

4 b

The equity at the end of the reporting period will equal:
Opening equity + Income – Expenses + Contributions – Drawings =
150 0000 + $780 000 – $270 000 + $60 000 – $100 000 = $620 000

5 c

We can use the following table to determine the answer. Remember Equity = Assets – Liabilities. As there were no closing liabilities, assets will equal equity.

Date	A	+	E	+	D	=	L	+	I	+	C
1/10	$65 000										65 000
5/10	$40 000						$40 000				
10/10	$55 000		$20 000						$55 000		
	($20 000)										
15/10	($12 000)		$12 000								
19/19	($40 000)						(40 000)				
25/10	($3 000)				$3 000						
	$85 000		$32 000		$3 000		–		$55 000		$65 000

CHAPTER 8

1 e

A bank loan is a liability, and liabilities are expected to have a credit balance. Increases in liabilities are credit entries.

2 e

All of the answers are true.

3 b

In this case an asset increases, and a liability increases. When assets increase this creates a debit entry, and when liabilities increase this is a credit entry.

4 b

When the insurance was paid, this created an asset of $120 000 which can be called 'Prepaid Insurance'. This would have a debit balance. At the same time there would have been a credit to Cash at Bank of $120 000.

After 3 months, a quarter of this prepaid asset – which amounts to $30 000 – would have been consumed. This amount consumed would be referred to as Insurance Expense. To reduce the asset, Prepaid Insurance, we will credit it by $30 000 and we will recognise – by way of a debit entry – $30 000 in Insurance Expenses.

5 c

At the end of the accounting period, we need to close all income and expense accounts. We do this by transferring the amounts to another account called Profit or Loss Summary. Income accounts will need to be debited to close them, and expense accounts will need to be credited to close them.

CHAPTER 9

1 e

These are all reasons why an organisation would prepare a balance sheet.

2 d

The balance sheet provides information about assets, liabilities, and equity items. Different classes of assets and liabilities will be measured in different ways, such as at cost, face value, fair value or present value. Not all assets will be measured at fair value. For example, inventory shall be measured at the lower of cost and net realisable value. Equity, which equals A – L, does not provide a measure of 'cash'. The separate asset 'Cash at Bank' reports what cash is controlled by the organisation.

3 e

All of these answers are correct. Different classes of assets have their own measurement rules.

4 e

All of these answers are correct as all of these steps must be satisfied before an asset shall be recognised.

5 b

Inventory shall be measured at the lower of cost and net realisable value. This is a requirement embodied within financial reporting standards.

In this case 'cost' is $150 000. Cost includes all those costs necessary to get the inventory to its condition at, and position of, sale. Therefore 'cost' includes import taxes and freight in costs.

The net realisable value equals the expected sale price less all the additional costs necessary to complete the sale. In this case the amount expected to be received from the sale less the advertising and other selling costs is $187 000.

Cost of $150 000 is lower than the net realisable value of $187 000. Therefore, inventory shall be reported at the amount of $150 000.

CHAPTER 10

1 a

All of the answers are true, other than a). Option a) is false because income should not be recognised until it has been earned, which requires that services actually be performed by the organisation for the customer.

2 e

All of the statements are true.

3 b

All of the statements are true other than b). Income should be recognised when the goods are transferred to the control of the customer – which is on 15 February – even if the customer has not yet paid (as long as it is expected that the customer will ultimately pay).

4 a

$20 000 is paid for a week's work. This is $4000 per day. Employees were paid for service performed until Thursday, which was 29 June. There is a further one day of work performed in the reporting period to 30 June which has not been paid. Therefore, an expense and an associated liability of $4000 needs to be recognised at the end of the reporting period. When the wages are subsequently paid, part of this relates to the accrued wages from the previous period, with the balance representing an expense.

5 e

All of the statements are true. Both the entity concept and the way we define expenses and assets – with the reliance upon 'control' – means that many social and environmental impacts are not recognised for financial reporting purposes.

CHAPTER 11

1 b

As the Chapter indicates, apart from option b), the Accounting Standard pertaining to the statement of cash flows (IAS 7: Statement of Cash Flows) requires disclosure of all the options listed, apart from option b).

2 e

All of the options would be considered to be cash flows from operating activities, other than option e) which would be considered to represent a cash flow from financing activities.

3 c

Cash payments in relation to an accrued expense = opening balance of accrued expense + related expense incurred during the accounting period – closing balance of accrued expense

= \$70 000 + \$920 000 – \$40 000 = \$950 000

4 b

Cash received from customers where cash received is initially recorded as a liability = Closing balance of Revenue Received in Advance + revenue recognised during the accounting period – opening balance of Revenue Received in Advance

= \$100 000 + \$920 000 – \$85 000 = \$935 000

5 d

Purchases = cost of goods sold + closing balance of inventory – opening balance of inventory

= \$385 000 + \$125 000 – \$105 000 = \$405 000

Cash payments to suppliers = opening balance of accounts payable – closing balance of accounts payable + purchases

= \$40 000 – \$45 000 + \$405 000 = \$400 000.

CHAPTER 12

1 b

The debt to assets ratio is total liabilities ÷ total assets x 100 = 5000 ÷ 8600 x 100 = 58%. This would not generally be a number that would cause concern, although we would like to know what accounting-based debt contract have been negotiated with lenders and how close this calculated amount is to the negotiated percentage.

2 b

The current ratio is current assets ÷ current liabilities = 2000 ÷ 1000 = 2. This would not generally be a number that would cause concern as it is well above 1.0.

3 c

The quick ratio is (current assets – inventory – prepayments) ÷ (current liabilities – bank overdraft) = (2000 – 150 – 0) ÷ (1000 – 0) = 1.85. This would not generally be a number that would cause concern as it is well above 1.0. A number less than one would be a concern.

4 b

On the basis of the answers to Questions 1 to 3, Coogee Company does not appear to be at risk of not being able to pay its debts as and when they fall due. Of course, it would be wise to supplement the balance sheet data with other information, such as any information about potential contingent liabilities or significant events occurring after the end of the reporting period.

5 e

All of these items of information should be reported by the organisation. The chapter lists 29 reporting criteria that should arguably be addressed in good quality sustainability-related disclosures.

Glossary

accountability
The duty to provide an account of those actions for which an organisation is deemed to be responsible. The accounts can take a variety of forms and would be provided to those stakeholders most affected by the activities of the organisation.

accounting entity concept
The principle within financial accounting that an organisation should have its own dedicated accounting records separate from those of its owners or other people involved in its operations.

accounting period
The timespan over which managers elect to report the transactions or events that affect the organisation. It is an established period of time in which accounting functions are performed, and where the results of transactions are aggregated, and analysed.

accounting rate of return method (ARR)
Calculated by dividing the average incremental return (or profit) or savings derived from (or traceable to) the investment by the average investment made in the asset.

accounts
Records detailing an organisation's performance in relation to a specific aspect of performance.

accounts payable
Used to describe the amounts that are owed to suppliers of goods and services when purchases of those supplies and services are made on credit terms.

accrual basis
Under the accrual basis of accounting, income is recognised as it is earned, not necessarily when the related money is actually received, and expenses are recognised when they are incurred, which is not necessarily when they are paid.

accrued expenses
A liability that represents expenses that have been incurred but not yet paid by the organisation.

allowance for doubtful debts
An allowance to account for the fact that not all debtors will ultimately pay, designed to be offset against the accounts receivable balance. It is an example of a 'contra account'.

amortisation
The process of apportioning the value of an asset to different accounting periods.

asset
A present economic resource controlled by the entity as a result of past events.

balance sheet
A financial statement that provides information about the financial position of an organisation. It provides information about an organisation's assets, liabilities and equity as at a certain point in time.

Balanced Scorecard (BSC) framework
Seeks to translate an organisation's mission and related strategies into a set of performance measures that then provide a framework for strategically managing the organisation.

bank overdraft
A line of credit designed to cover short-term cash flow shortfalls that occurs when money is withdrawn from a bank account and the available balance goes below zero.

bank reconciliation
A reconciliation of an organisation's records of cash with the records held by the bank. It identifies the cause of any discrepancies.

break-even point
When the total financial costs equal the total financial revenues. That is, the production or service level where profit is zero.

budgetary slack
Budgetary slack can be defined as the difference between revenue, cost or other targets that have been set opportunistically, and those that would be set objectively.

budgeted balance sheet
Shows what the assets, liabilities and owners' equity of an organisation will be as a result of the organisation pursuing its plans.

budgeted income statement
Provides an indication of the profit (or loss) that might be generated as a result of an organisation pursuing its plans.

capital investment decisions
An organisation's decisions about which major investments to make in respect of property, plant and equipment.

carrying amount
The amount at which an asset, liability, or equity item is shown within the financial accounts.

cash
Money in the form of notes or coins that are either in the physical possession of an organisation or have been deposited in an at-call account with a bank. Would also generally include cheques received by an organisation and in the organisation's possession.

cash budget
Contains all the expected receipts of cash, and payments of cash, that have been identified in the operating budgets that precede it.

cash equivalents
Short-term, highly liquid investments that are readily convertible to known amounts of cash, and which are subject to an insignificant risk of changes in value.

chart of accounts
The chart of accounts provides a complete listing of every account in the general ledger of an organisation, often broken down into subcategories.

circular economy
An approach to production in which processes are designed to eliminate waste and pollution and in which products and related materials are designed to remain in productive use.

company
An organisation that has a separate legal personality from that of its owners, meaning they are not personally responsible for its debts.

comparable
Information is comparable if it is selected, compiled and measured in a similar way so that reports from different periods (and different organisations) can be compared.

contingent liability
A potential liability that will ultimately arise only if a specific transaction or event happens in the future. Also refers to present obligations that arise from past events for which the probability of the outflow of economic benefits, or the amount of the obligation, cannot be determined with sufficient reliability.

contra account
Any account designed to be offset against another account.

contribution margin
The difference between the total variable costs and the total sales revenue generated by a particular product or service.

corporate bonds
Represent a form of borrowing (loan) undertaken by an organisation wherein there is documentation that identifies when the related borrowing (principal) must be repaid to the bondholders, what amount of interest shall be paid and when that interest must be paid.

corporate social responsibility (CSR)
The responsibilities an organisation accepts to various stakeholders and the environment over and above their legal obligations.

cost behaviour
How the cost of producing a good or service is affected by changes to the level or volume of activity.

cost of sales
The expense calculated to account for the cost of inventory sold.

costs
A measure, either expressed in financial or non-financial terms, of the value of resources consumed or impacted as a result of the operations of an organisation. Can include both 'private costs' and 'social and environmental costs' ('external costs').

counter accounts
Also called shadow accounts, and usually produced by stakeholders outside an organisation; these accounts often challenge, or contest, the accounts released by an organisation's managers.

credit
In double entry accounting, credits (and debits) are entries made in accounts to record changes in value resulting from the transactions and events that relate to an organisation. A credit is an accounting entry that results in either an increase in liabilities, income, or contributions, or a decrease in assets, expenses or distributions. In financial accounting, credits are balanced by debits.

creditors
External parties to whom an organisation (or individual) owes a debt, often in relation to goods or services provided to the organisation on credit terms.

current assets
An asset that can reasonably be expected to be sold, consumed, or otherwise exhausted within a year, or within the normal operating cycle of an organisation (whichever period is longer).

current liabilities
Obligations that are due to be settled within one year of the reporting date, or within the normal operating cycle of an organisation (whichever period is longer).

debit
In double entry accounting, debits (and credits) are entries made in accounts to record changes in value resulting from

the transactions and events that relate to an organisation. A debit is an accounting entry that results in either an increase in assets, expenses, or distributions, or a decrease in liabilities, income or contributions. In financial accounting, debits are balanced by credits.

depreciation
The systematic periodic allocation of the cost, or fair value, of a non-current asset over the periods expected to benefit from the use of the asset. The amount calculated is referred to as a depreciation expense.

depreciation expense
When calculated on a time basis, represents the allocation of the cost (or revalued amount) of an asset (less any expected residual value) over the number of periods in which benefits are expected to be derived from the asset.

dialogic accounting
Where there is typically more than one 'logic' that could be employed to assess organisational performance, and these different logics (based on different perspectives about what aspects of performance are important, or otherwise) could be used to develop different accounts.

direct labour
The cost of the human resources used to create a product or service; for example manual labour that can be directly traced to the product or service.

direct materials
Materials that can be fairly easily traced to use in a product or service.

dividends
Distributions of profits made to owners (shareholders) of a company.

double-entry accounting
A system for recording transactions and events where each recorded transaction and event creates one or more debit and credit entries, and where the total debits recorded must equal the total credits recorded.

entity concept
Principle that requires that the transactions of an organisation be kept separate from the personal transactions of the owners of the organisation, and which considers the organisation to be separate to, or distinct from, other entities.

environmental accounting
The identification, measurement, recording and communication of information about an organisation's impact on living and non-living natural systems (including land, air, water and ecosystems).

environmental performance
The impacts – positive and negative – that an organisation has on the physical and natural environments in which it operates.

equity
The residual interest in the assets of the entity after deducting its liabilities.

existence uncertainty
Uncertainty about whether an asset or liability exists.

external accounts
Information about an organisation's position and performance intended for use by people outside the organisation, such as shareholders, NGOs, customers, local communities, news media and regulators.

external reporting
The provision of reports and information to stakeholders that are external to an organisation.

externallties
Impacts that an entity has on parties external to the organisation, where such parties are not the buyers or sellers of the goods or services, or did not agree to, or take part in, the activities causing the externality.

faithful representation
Information is faithfully represented when it is complete, neutral, and free from error; the characteristic of faithful representation is similar to the concept of reliability.

financial accounting
The identification, measurement, recording and communication of information about the financial performance and financial position of an organisation for external users.

financial budgets
Include the cash budget, budgeted income statement, and budgeted balance sheet.

financial gearing (or stability) ratios
Provides a measure of how an organisation has been funded, and some indication of financial stability or risk.

financial performance
A measure or assessment of an organisation's performance measured in financial terms, perhaps through the application of financial accounting standards.

financial statement analysis
The process of reviewing and evaluating an organisation's financial statements and supporting notes in an endeavour to form a judgement about an organisation's financial performance and financial stability, and its likely future prospects.

first-in, first-out cost-flow method (FIFO)
A method of inventory valuation where any goods existing in opening inventory, and the earliest purchases of inventory, are assumed to be the first goods sold.

fixed costs
Costs that do not change in a particular period as the volume of production or services changes.

flexible budget
A budget that does change (or flex) as certain variables, such as volume, change.

gains
Income sourced from areas that may or may not relate to an organisation's main activities.

general journal
A journal that can generally be used to record all the transactions and events that affect the accounts of an organisation.

general purpose financial statements (GPFSs)
Financial statements that comply with accounting standards and are intended for users of financial information who are unable to command the preparation of statements tailored to their specific information needs.

goal congruence
When managers share or embrace the same goals as those embraced by the organisation. Occurs within an organisation when the goals of different people coincide.

going concern
An assumption that an organisation will be able to continue to operate in the normal way for the foreseeable future.

goodwill
An intangible asset that represents the future economic benefits that are expected to be generated as a result of factors such as efficient management, reliable suppliers, existing customer base, and so forth. Goodwill is generally recognised when one organisation acquires another organisation, or part thereof, and is measured as the excess of the fair value of the purchase price over the fair value of the identifiable net assets of the organisation acquired. Goodwill can also be internally developed; however accounting standards prohibit the recognition of internally developed goodwill.

gross profit
The difference between sales revenue and cost of sales.

horizontal analysis
Comparing account balances over time.

impairment loss
An expense that is recognised when the recoverable amount is less than the carrying amount of an asset.

informed decision
A decision based on reliable and relevant information.

internal accounts
Information about an organisation's position and performance intended for use by people within the organisation, such as managers.

internal controls
Policies or procedures implemented by an organisation with the aim of ensuring that an organisation operates: effectively and efficiently; in conformance with the organisation's mission and objectives; in compliance with relevant laws and regulations; and, that the organisation's systems of accounting enable relevant and representationally faithful reports to be prepared for the use of internal and external stakeholders.

internal rate of return method (IRR)
Informs managers about what the expected rate of return on the investment is, given the predictions about future cash flows, by calculating a discount rate which generates a net present value of zero.

inventory
Represents assets held for sale in the ordinary course of business. Would also include materials or supplies to be consumed within the organisation's production processes, or in the process of providing services.

investment-based ratios
Measures that provide insights into how the share market values and/or perceives, an organisation.

journal
In accounting, the journal is the first place in which the effects of transactions or events – typically evidenced on a source document – are entered into the accounting system. The journal will record the date of the transaction or event, the accounts to be adjusted and the associated amounts of debits and credits.

journal reference
A number assigned to signify where a journal entry came from, often a page number from a journal.

last-in, first-out cost-flow method (LIFO)
A method of inventory valuation where the most recent items purchased, or manufactured, are assumed to be the first items sold.

ledger accounts
A ledger account contains a record of transactions. It is a separate record or account that is assigned to a specific type of asset, liability, equity item, revenue, or expense type. The various ledger accounts being used will be shown in the chart of accounts.

liabilities
A present obligation of the entity to transfer an economic resource as a result of past events.

life cycle analysis (LCA)
The process of analysing, or evaluating, a product or service across its entire life, often referred to as analysing a product or service from the cradle to the grave.

life cycle costing (LCC)
Seeks to place a cost on the various inputs (resources used), outputs (including wastes and emissions) and the impacts created by an organisation's operations, and attribute such costs to particular activities and products.

limited liability
An ownership arrangement for companies whereby each owner pays a set amount for a number of shares in a company and has no responsibility for the company's debts beyond the cost of their shares.

line of credit
An agreement negotiated with a fund provider, such as a bank, to supply an amount of cash up to a maximum level if needed, and where interest is only paid on the amount of money actually borrowed.

liquidation values
The amounts that an organisation would expect to receive from a quick sale of its assets.

liquidity
Measure of how quickly assets can be converted into cash, or how quickly liabilities need to be settled.

liquidity crisis
A lack of positive cash flows within an organisation to meet obligations that need to be paid in the short run.

liquidity ratios
Measures that provide an indicator of the ability of an organisation to pay its debts, as and when they become due.

management accounting
The process of generating financial and non-financial information to be used by managers for planning, monitoring and controlling an organisation.

manufacturing overhead
Resources beyond direct materials and direct labour used in the process of creating a product or service; for example, electricity or heating for a factory.

margin of safety
The number of sales made, or expected to be made, above the break-even point.

master budget
A comprehensive set of budgets that provides coverage of an organisation's activities.

material flow cost accounting (MFCA)
Focuses on recording the inputs of particular materials into a production process, and the outputs, including wastes, that come from that process. Measurements can be made in both physical and monetary terms.

materiality threshold
A variance that exceeds an agreed-upon threshold on a budgeted amount, and that an organisation would elect to investigate.

measurement uncertainty
Uncertainty that arises when monetary amounts in financial reports cannot be observed directly and must instead be estimated.

mixed cost
A single cost that has part-fixed and part-variable components.

monologic accounting
Reflects the accounting traditions currently in place, wherein only the managers' perspective of performance is reported.

mutual agency
The idea that each partner becomes responsible for the actions undertaken by other partners, just as they would be if they had made particular decisions themselves.

narration
A brief description of a transaction recorded as part of the journal entry.

negative screening
A strict rule that certain activities or products shall not be supported or acquired because of concerns about their risks or impacts on particular parts of society, or on the environment.

net present value method (NPV)
A method of planning for investments that considers all expected future cash flows and also considers the timing of the cash flows. A discount rate is applied to all these expected future cash flows to generate a 'net present value'.

normal operating cycle
The average period of time between the initial acquisition of particular assets for processing or use, and the time at which cash is ultimately realised in relation to disposing of those assets.

operating budgets
Include the sales budget, the production budgets and the various cost budgets that are impacted by these two budgets.

operating efficiency ratios
Provide a measure of how efficiently an organisation's managers are managing the organisation's assets and liabilities.

opportunity costs
Benefits that could have been received but were given up because of the decision to take another course of action.

organisational objectives
An organisation's primary aims.

other comprehensive income
Other comprehensive income comprises items of income and expense that are not recognised in profit or loss as required or permitted by other Accounting Standards.

overhead costs
Those costs that are necessary to run an organisation, but which might not easily be directly attributed to specific activities, products, or services.

owners' equity
Also referred to as net worth or net assets, it is the total value of an organisation's assets minus the total value of its liabilities.

partnership
When two or more people establish an organisation for a common purpose, sharing its control and management, and being jointly responsible for all of its debts.

payback period
Addresses the question of how long it will take to recoup the amount that was spent on acquiring an investment.

performance
The results, impacts, or accomplishments associated with completing a particular task or group of tasks.

periodic inventory system
An inventory management system also referred to as a physical inventory system, where the amount of inventory on hand, and the cost of goods sold for the period, is determined at the end of the accounting period.

perpetual inventory system
An inventory management system where every time an acquisition or sale of inventory occurs, adjustments are made to the inventory account and also to the cost of goods sold account. At any time, managers will know how much stock should be on hand.

petty cash fund
A small amount of cash an organisation will typically keep on site, for very small incidental cash payments.

positive screening
An organisational requirement that prior to their acceptance, support or acquisition, particular products or services shall have specific attributes, such as utilising processes that satisfy particular environmental or social standards.

posted
The effects of a transaction are deemed to be 'posted' when the amount recorded within the journal for that transaction or event is transferred to the respective account in the ledger.

prepaid expense
An asset that represents a payment made prior to the associated expense being incurred and, therefore, prior to the service being consumed by the organisation. Also known as a prepayment.

prepayment
An amount paid to another organisation for goods or services prior to the goods or service being received or consumed.

production budget
Provides production targets in units based upon the production of enough units to satisfy targeted sales and any required closing inventory.

profit
The difference between the total income and total expenses of an organisation for a specified period of time.

profitability ratios
A measure of an organisation's ability to generate a profit.

provision
Liability for which there is greater uncertainty regarding the amount or timing of the obligation relative to other liabilities.

recoverable amount
The higher of an asset's fair value less costs of disposal (sometimes called net selling price), and its value in use.

relevant
In terms of information, information is relevant if it is capable of making a difference to the decisions made by the recipients of that information.

relevant costs
Those costs that change as a result of a particular decision.

relevant range
The range of production output, or volume, in which our expectations regarding cost behaviour are expected to hold.

reliable
In terms of information, information is reliable if it is free from error, complete, and free from bias.

reporting boundary
A reflection of how far the responsibilities of the organisation have been extended both in terms of to which stakeholders it owes an accountability, and for what aspects of performance it should be accountable.

reporting framework
A standardised format for presenting accounting information.

reserves
A reserve is a component of equity and is disclosed within the balance sheet. There can be many types of reserves, and a reserve can be created in a variety of ways, including as a result of a transfer from retained earnings or as a result of a revaluation on a non-current asset.

resource
Something that has value in the sense that it allows an organisation to undertake an activity so as to enable it to achieve a desired outcome.

retained earnings
The sum of current and past profits and losses, less payments of dividends to owners (shareholders), and less any transfers made from retained earnings to reserves. It is a component of equity.

revenue
Income that is derived in the course of the ordinary activities of an organisation.

revenue received in advance
A liability for cash payments received by an organisation for services that have not yet been provided to the customer, and therefore have not yet been earned.

sales budget
A detailed summary/plan of the estimated sales in units and associated revenues from an organisation's products, based on the sales targets, for the budgeted period.

securities exchange
A specialised financial marketplace for the buying and selling of securities such as shares and bonds, which has specific rules for how share-trading organisations must maintain and report information.

segregation of duties
A control that seeks to ensure that those people who have access to particular assets, such as cash, are not the same people who account for the movements in the asset. A full segregation of duties would ensure that different individuals would initiate a transaction, approve the transaction, record the transaction and have access to the asset to which the transaction relates.

selling and administrative overhead expenses budget
The budget for costs not associated with production that the organisation necessarily needs to incur in order to operate; for example, salaries of administrative staff.

share capital
The capital contributed by the owners (the shareholders) to the company in exchange for receiving shares in the company.

social accounting
The identification, measurement, recording and communication of information about an organisation's impact on particular societies, or stakeholders.

social performance
The impacts – both positive and negative – that an organisation's activities have on its stakeholders, including employees, customers and the wider community.

sole trader
An organisation where one individual controls and manages a business, and is responsible for all of its debts.

special purpose financial statements (SPFSs)
Financial statements designed to meet the needs of a specific group of stakeholders or to satisfy a specific purpose. Would not necessarily comply with accounting standards.

specific-identification method
A method of inventory valuation where the seller determines which item is sold, and the cost of that specific item to be included within cost of sales. Usually applied to items of inventory that have some form of unique attribute.

stakeholder
Any group or individual who can affect, or is affected by, the achievement of an organisation's objectives.

statement of cash flows
Reports information about movements in cash and cash equivalents for the accounting period, and in doing so, provides a reconciliation of the opening and closing balances of cash and cash equivalents as reported within the balance sheet.

statement of changes in equity
Provides a reconciliation of opening and closing equity and details of the various equity accounts that are impacted by the period's total comprehensive income.

static budget
A budget that does not change as certain variables, such as volume, change.

stewardship function
The responsibilities accepted by managers for safeguarding the use of an organisation's resources.

subsidiary
An organisation that is controlled by another organisation.

subsidiary ledger
A subsidiary ledger is a group of similar accounts whose combined balances equal the balance in a specific general ledger account. A subsidiary ledger captures individual details that might be required for management purposes, e.g. records of inventory, accounts receivable, and accounts payable.

supply chain
The network between an organisation and its suppliers and customers, as necessary to produce and distribute a specific good or service.

sustainability reporting
A form of reporting, both financial and non-financial, that takes into account an organisation's impacts on the communities and environments in which it operates, and which provides insights into how the organisation's operations are consistent with the idea of sustainable development.

timeliness
Information should be provided to stakeholders in quick enough time to be able to influence their decisions. Generally, the older the information is the less useful it is.

total comprehensive income
The total of profit or loss, and other comprehensive income.

trial balance
A listing of the ledger accounts, and their balances, at the end of an accounting period. The total of all the accounts with debit balances in the trial balance must equal the total of all accounts with credit balances (otherwise a mistake has occurred).

understandable
In terms of information, presented so that its meaning, and the basis of its compilation, are clear to the user.

unlimited liability
Liability that extends beyond the assets of an organisation. In the case of a sole trader, if a business fails then the sole trader's personal assets may have to be used to repay debts.

value chain analysis
Reviewing each step required to create a product or service, and identifying ways of increasing the efficiency of each part of the value chain.

variable costs
Costs that change as a result of changing production or service volume.

variances
Differences that arise between actual performance and budgeted performance.

verifiable
Information is verifiable if different people who are knowledgeable and independent could reach agreement that it reliably depicts a particular item, phenomenon or event.

vertical analysis
Comparing one item of the financial statements to another within a particular accounting period.

weighted-average-cost approach
An approach to inventory valuation where the cost of each item is determined from the weighted average of the cost of similar items at the beginning of a period, and the cost of similar items purchased or produced during the period

Index

H

I

P

S

X

Z